Because convergence is such an important issue, we provide a discussion of international accounting standards at the end of each chapter called **IFRS Insights**. This feature will help you understand the changes that are taking place in the financial reporting area as we move to one set of international standards. Each IFRS Insights, as shown here, consists of four sections.

An **introduction** typically lists the international accounting pronouncements related to the chapter topic.

IFRS Insights

The basic accounting and reporting issues related to recognition and measurement of receivables, such as the use of allowance accounts, how to record discounts, use of the allowance method to account for bad debts, and factoring, are similar for both IFRS and GAAP. *IAS 1* ("Presentation of Financial Statements") is the only standard that discusses issues specifically related to cash. *IFRS 7* ("Financial Instruments: Disclosure")

RELEVANT FACTS

- The accounting and reporting related to cash is essentially the same under both IFRS and GAAP. In addition, the definition used for cash equivalents is the same. One difference is that, in general, IFRS classifies bank overdrafts as cash.

Relevant Facts explain similarities and differences of GAAP and IFRS.

About the Numbers generally discusses and provides examples of IFRS applications (in many cases, using real international companies).

ABOUT THE NUMBERS

Impairment Evaluation Process

IFRS provides detailed guidelines to assess whether receivables should be considered uncollectible (often referred to as *impaired*). GAAP does not identify a specific approach. Under IFRS, companies assess their receivables for impairment each reporting period and start the impairment assessment by considering whether objective

ON THE HORIZON

The question of recording fair values for financial instruments will continue to be an important issue to resolve as the Boards work toward convergence. Both the IASB and the FASB have indicated that they believe that financial statements would be more transparent and understandable if companies recorded and reported all financial instruments at fair value. That said, in *IFRS 9*, which was issued in 2009, the IASB

On the Horizon discusses convergence progress and plans related to the accounting topics presented in the chapter.

IFRS Insights also includes *IFRS Self-Test Questions*, as well as *IFRS Concepts and Application*, so students can test their understanding of the material. An *International Financial Reporting Problem*, based on Marks and Spencer plc, offers students an opportunity to analyze IFRS-based financial statements.

Having a basic understanding of international accounting is becoming ever more important as the profession moves toward convergence of GAAP and international standards. Thus, in addition to the **IFRS Insights** pages discussed above, we continue to include marginal **International Perspectives**, marked with the icon shown here, which we updated throughout to reflect changes in international accounting. These notes describe or compare IFRS as well as accounting practices in other countries with GAAP. This feature helps you to understand that other countries sometimes use different recognition and measurement principles to report financial information.

OTHER INTERNATIONAL COVERAGE

INTERNATIONAL PERSPECTIVE

www.wileyplus.com

ALL THE HELP, **RESOURCES**, AND PERSONAL **SUPPORT** YOU AND YOUR STUDENTS NEED!

www.wileyplus.com/resources

2-Minute Tutorials and all of the resources you & your students need to get started.

Student support from an experienced student user.

Collaborate with your colleagues, find a mentor, attend virtual and live events, and view resources.
www.WhereFacultyConnect.com

Pre-loaded, ready-to-use assignments and presentations. Created by subject matter experts.

Technical Support 24/7 FAQs, online chat, and phone support.
www.wileyplus.com/support

Your *WileyPLUS* Account Manager. Personal training and implementation support.

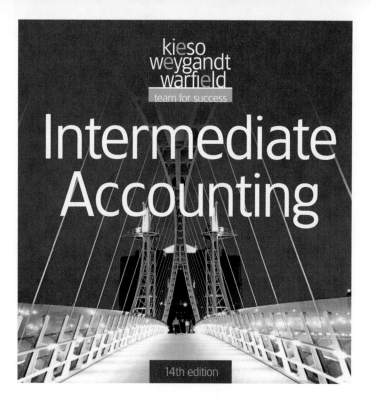

kieso
weygandt
warfield
team for success

Intermediate Accounting

14th edition

Volume 2: Chapters 15–24

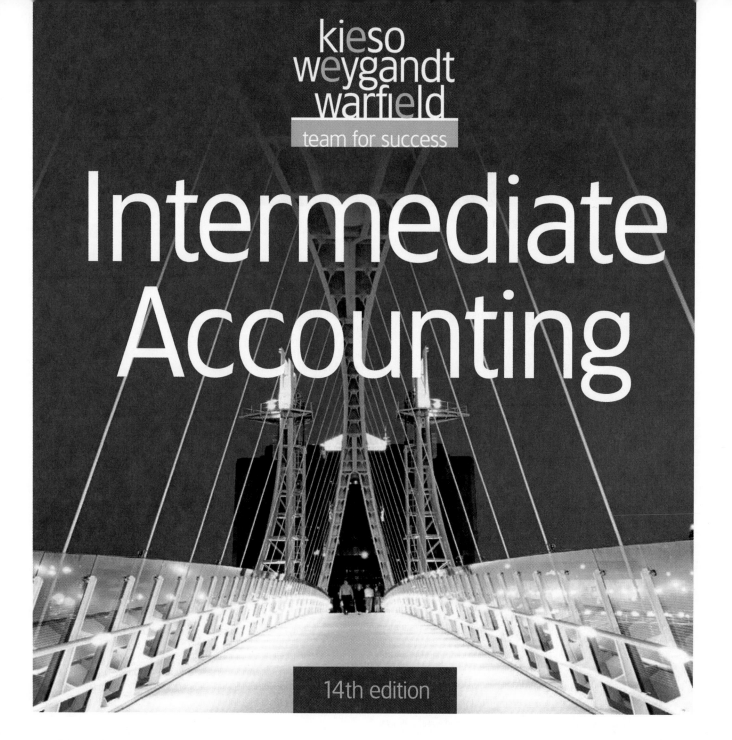

kieso
weygandt
warfield
team for success

Intermediate Accounting

14th edition

Volume 2: Chapters 15–24

WILEY

John Wiley & Sons, Inc.

Donald E. Kieso PhD, CPA
Northern Illinois University
DeKalb, Illinois

Jerry J. Weygandt PhD, CPA
University of Wisconsin—Madison
Madison, Wisconsin

Terry D. Warfield, PhD
University of Wisconsin—Madison
Madison, Wisconsin

Dedicated to
our wives, **Donna, Enid, and Mary,**
for their love,
support, and encouragement

Vice President & Publisher	George Hoffman
Associate Publisher	Christopher DeJohn
Senior Acquisitions Editor	Michael McDonald
Project Editor	Brian Kamins
Development Editor	Terry Ann Tatro
Production Manager	Dorothy Sinclair
Project Editor	Yana Mermel
Senior Production Editor	Trish McFadden
Associate Director of Marketing	Amy Scholz
Marketing Manager	Karolina Zarychta Honsa
Executive Media Editor	Allie K. Morris
Media Editor	Greg Chaput
Senior Designer	Jim O'Shea
Production Management Services	Ingrao Associates
Creative Director	Harry Nolan
Senior Photo Editor	Mary Ann Price
Senior Editorial Assistant	Jackie Kepping
Cover Photo	Jon Arnold Images/SuperStock, Inc.
Chapter Opener Photo	Paul Fawcett/iStockphoto
Cover Credit	© Gerald Hoberman/Photolibrary

This book was set in Palatino by Aptara®, Inc. and printed and bound by Courier Kendallville.
The cover was printed by Courier Kendallville.

This book is printed on acid-free paper. ∞

To order books or for customer service, please call 1-800-CALL WILEY (225-5945).

Material from the Uniform CPA Examinations and Unofficial Answers, copyright © 1965, 1966, 1967, 1968, 1969, 1970, 1971, 1972, 1973, 1974, 1975, 1976, 1977, 1978, 1979, 1980, 1981, 1982, 1983, 1984, 1985, 1986, 1987, 1988, 1990, 1991, 1992, and 1993 by the American Institute of Certified Public Accountants, Inc., is adapted with permission.

This book contains quotations from *Accounting Research Bulletins, Accounting Principles Board Opinions, Accounting Principles Board Statements, Accounting Interpretations,* and *Accounting Terminology Bulletins,* copyright © 1953, 1956, 1966, 1968, 1969, 1970, 1971, 1972, 1973, 1974, 1975, 1976, 1977, 1978, 1979, 1980, 1981, 1982 by the American Institute of Certified Public Accountants, Inc., 1211 Avenue of the Americas, New York, NY 10036.

This book contains citations from various FASB pronouncements. Copyright © by Financial Accounting Standards Board, 401 Merritt 7, P.O. Box 5116, Norwalk, CT 06856 U.S.A. Reprinted with permission. Copies of complete documents are available from Financial Accounting Standards Board.

Material from the Certificate in Management Accounting Examinations, copyright © 1975, 1976, 1977, 1978, 1979, 1980, 1981, 1982, 1983, 1984, 1985, 1986, 1987, 1988, 1989, 1990, 1991, 1992, and 1993 by the Institute of Certified Management Accountants, 10 Paragon Drive, Montvale, NJ 07645, is adapted with permission.

Material from the Certified Internal Auditor Examinations, copyright © May 1984, November 1984, May 1986 by The Institute of Internal Auditors, 249 Maitland Ave., Altemonte Springs, FL 32701, is adapted with permission.

The financial statements and accompanying notes reprinted from the 2009 Annual Report of Procter & Gamble Company are courtesy of P&G, copyright © 2009, all rights reserved.

ISBN-13 978-0-470-58729-4

Printed in the United States of America

10 9 8 7 6 5 4 3 2 1

Author Commitment

Don **Kieso**

Donald E. Kieso, PhD, CPA, received his bachelor's degree from Aurora University and his doctorate in accounting from the University of Illinois. He has served as chairman of the Department of Accountancy and is currently the KPMG Emeritus Professor of Accountancy at Northern Illinois University. He has public accounting experience with Price Waterhouse & Co. (San Francisco and Chicago) and Arthur Andersen & Co. (Chicago) and research experience with the Research Division of the American Institute of Certified Public Accountants (New York). He has done post-doctorate work as a Visiting Scholar at the University of California at Berkeley and is a recipient of NIU's Teaching Excellence Award and four Golden Apple Teaching Awards. Professor Kieso is the author of other accounting and business books and is a member of the American Accounting Association, the American Institute of Certified Public Accountants, and the Illinois CPA Society. He has served as a member of the Board of Directors of the Illinois CPA Society, then AACSB's Accounting Accreditation Committees, the State of Illinois Comptroller's Commission, as Secretary-Treasurer of the Federation of Schools of Accountancy, and as Secretary-Treasurer of the American Accounting Association. Professor Kieso is currently serving on the Board of Trustees and Executive Committee of Aurora University, as a member of the Board of Directors of Kishwaukee Community Hospital, and as Treasurer and Director of Valley West Community Hospital. From 1989 to 1993, he served as a charter member of the national Accounting Education Change Commission. He is the recipient of the Outstanding Accounting Educator Award from the Illinois CPA Society, the FSA's Joseph A. Silvoso Award of Merit, the NIU Foundation's Humanitarian Award for Service to Higher Education, a Distinguished Service Award from the Illinois CPA Society, and in 2003 an honorary doctorate from Aurora University.

Jerry **Weygandt**

Jerry J. Weygandt, PhD, CPA, is Arthur Andersen Alumni Emeritus Professor of Accounting at the University of Wisconsin—Madison. He holds a Ph.D. in accounting from the University of Illinois. Articles by Professor Weygandt have appeared in the *Accounting Review, Journal of Accounting Research, Accounting Horizons, Journal of Accountancy,* and other academic and professional journals. These articles have examined such financial reporting issues as accounting for price-level adjustments, pensions, convertible securities, stock option contracts, and interim reports. Professor Weygandt is author of other accounting and financial reporting books and is a member of the American Accounting Association, the American Institute of Certified Public Accountants, and the Wisconsin Society of Certified Public Accountants. He has served on numerous committees of the American Accounting Association and as a member of the editorial board of the Accounting Review; he also has served as President and Secretary-Treasurer of the American Accounting Association. In addition, he has been actively involved with the American Institute of Certified Public Accountants and has been a member of the Accounting Standards Executive Committee (AcSEC) of that organization. He has served on the FASB task force that examined the reporting issues related to accounting for income taxes and served as a trustee of the Financial Accounting Foundation. Professor Weygandt has received the Chancellor's Award for Excellence in Teaching and the Beta Gamma Sigma Dean's Teaching Award. He is on the board of directors of M & I Bank of Southern Wisconsin. He is the recipient of the Wisconsin Institute of CPA's Outstanding Educator's Award and the Lifetime Achievement Award. In 2001, he received the American Accounting Association's Outstanding Educator Award.

Terry **Warfield**

Terry D. Warfield, PhD, is the Robert and Monica Beyer Professor of Accounting at the University of Wisconsin—Madison. He received a B.S. and M.B.A. from Indiana University and a Ph.D. in accounting from the University of Iowa. Professor Warfield's area of expertise is financial reporting, and prior to his academic career, he worked for five years in the banking industry. He served as the Academic Accounting Fellow in the Office of the Chief Accountant at the U.S. Securities and Exchange Commission in Washington, D.C. from 1995–1996. Professor Warfield's primary research interests concern financial accounting standards and disclosure policies. He has published scholarly articles in *The Accounting Review, Journal of Accounting and Economics, Research in Accounting Regulation,* and *Accounting Horizons,* and he has served on the editorial boards of *The Accounting Review, Accounting Horizons,* and *Issues in Accounting Education.* He has served as president of the Financial Accounting and Reporting Section, the Financial Accounting Standards Committee of the American Accounting Association (Chair 1995–1996), and on the AAA-FASB Research Conference Committee. He also served on the Financial Accounting Standards Advisory Council of the Financial Accounting Standards Board. Professor Warfield has received teaching awards at both the University of Iowa and the University of Wisconsin, and he was named to the Teaching Academy at the University of Wisconsin in 1995. Professor Warfield has developed and published several case studies based on his research for use in accounting classes. These cases have been selected for the AICPA Professor-Practitioner Case Development Program and have been published in *Issues in Accounting Education.*

for Students

WileyPLUS

WileyPLUS is an innovative, research-based, online environment for effective teaching and learning.

What do STUDENTS receive with *WileyPLUS*?

WileyPLUS increases confidence through an innovative **design** that allows greater **engagement**, which leads to improved learning **outcomes**.

Design

The *WileyPLUS* design integrates relevant resources, including the entire digital textbook, in an easy-to-navigate framework that helps students study more effectively and ensures student engagement. Innovative features, such as calendars and visual progress tracking, as well as a variety of self-evaluation tools, are all designed to improve time-management and increase student confidence.

Engagement

WileyPLUS organizes the textbook content into smaller, more man-ageable learning units with demonstrable study objectives and out-comes. Related media, examples, and sample practice items are integrated within each section to reinforce the study objectives. Throughout each study session, students can assess progress and gain immediate feedback on strengths and weaknesses in order to ensure they are spending their time most effectively.

Outcomes

Throughout each study session, students can assess their progress and gain immediate feedback. *WileyPLUS* provides precise reporting of strengths and weaknesses, as well as individualized quizzes, so that students are confident they are spending their time on the right things. With *WileyPLUS*, students always know the exact outcome of their efforts.

With increased confidence, motivation is sustained so students stay on task longer, leading to success.

www.wileyplus.com

Explorer

What do INSTRUCTORS receive with *WileyPLUS*?
Support and Insight into Student Progress

WileyPLUS provides reliable, customizable resources that reinforce course goals inside and outside of the classroom, as well as visibility into individual student progress. Pre-created materials and activities help instructors optimize their time.

For class preparation and classroom use:
- Lecture Notes
- PowerPoint Slides
- Tutorials

For assignments and testing:
- Gradable Reading Assignment Questions (embedded with online text)
- Question Assignments: all end-of-chapter problems coded algorithmically with hints, links to text

For course planning: *WileyPLUS* comes with a pre-created **Course Plan** designed by a subject matter expert uniquely for this course. Simple drag-and-drop tools make it easy to assign the course plan as-is or modify it to reflect your course syllabus.

For progress monitoring: *WileyPLUS* provides instant access to reports on trends in class performance, student use of course materials, and progress toward learning objectives, helping inform decisions and drive classroom discussions.

Experience *WileyPLUS* for effective teaching and learning at **www.wileyplus.com**.

Powered by proven technology and built on a foundation of cognitive research, *WileyPLUS* has enriched the education of millions of students, in numerous countries around the world.

The Wiley Faculty Network

The Place Where Faculty Connect ...

The Wiley Faculty Network is a global community of faculty connected by a passion for teaching and a drive to learn and share. Connect with the Wiley Faculty Network to collaborate with your colleagues, find a mentor, attend virtual and live events, and view a wealth of resources all designed to help you grow as an educator. Embrace the art of teaching—great things happen where faculty connect!

Discover innovative ideas and gain knowledge you can use.

- Training
- Virtual Guest Lectures
- Live Events

Explore your resources and development opportunities.

- Teaching Resources
- Archived Guest Lectures
- Recorded Presentations
- Professional Development Modules

Connect with colleagues— your greatest resource.

- Find a Mentor
- Interest Groups
- Blog

Find out more at
www.WHEREFACULTYCONNECT.com

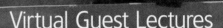

Virtual Guest Lectures
Connect with recognized leaders across disciplines and collaborate with your peers on timely topics and discipline specific issues, many of which offer CPE credit.

Live and Virtual Events
These invitation-only, discipline-specific events are organized through a close partnership between the WFN, Wiley, and the academic community near the event location.

Technology Training
Discover a wealth of topic- and technology-specific training presented by subject matter experts, authors, and faculty where and when you need it.

Teaching Resources
Propel your teaching and student learning to the next level with quality peer-reviewed case studies, testimonials, classroom tools, and checklists.

Connect with Colleagues
Achieve goals and tackle challenges more easily by enlisting the help of your peers. Connecting with colleagues through the WFN can help you improve your teaching experience.

From the Authors

Accounting is the most employable, sought-after major for 2012, according to entry-level job site **CollegeGrad.com**. One reason for this interest is found in the statement by former Secretary of the Treasury and Economic Advisor to the President, Lawrence Summers. He noted that the single-most important innovation shaping our capital markets was the idea of generally accepted accounting principles (GAAP). We agree with Mr. Summers. Relevant and reliable financial information is a necessity for viable capital markets. Without it, our markets would be chaotic, and our standard of living would decrease.

This textbook is the market leader in providing the tools needed to understand what GAAP is and how it is applied in practice. Mastery of this material will be invaluable to you in whatever field you select.

Through many editions, this textbook has continued to reflect the constant changes taking place in the GAAP environment. This edition continues this tradition, which has become even more significant as the financial reporting environment is exploding with major change. Here are three areas of major importance that are now incorporated extensively into this edition of the text.

Convergence of U.S. GAAP and IFRS

As mentioned above, the most important innovation shaping our capital markets was the idea of U.S. GAAP. It might be said that it would be even better if we had one common set of accounting rules for the whole world, which will make it easier for international investors to compare the financial results of companies from different countries. That is happening quickly as U.S. GAAP and international accounting standards are quickly converging toward **International Financial Reporting Standards (IFRS)**, to be used by all companies. And you have the chance to be on the ground floor as we develop for you the similarities and differences in the two systems that ultimately will be one.

A Fair Value Movement

The FASB believes that fair value information is more relevant to users than historical cost. As a result, there is more information that is being reported on this basis, and even more will occur in the future. The financial press is full of articles discussing how financial institutions must fair value their assets, which has led to massive losses during the recent credit crisis. In addition, additional insight into the reliability related to fair values is being addressed and disclosed to help investors make important capital allocation decisions. As a result, we devote a considerable amount of material that discusses and illustrates fair value concepts in this edition.

> "If this book helps teachers instill in their students an appreciation for the challenges, worth, and limitations of financial reporting, if it encourages students to evaluate critically and understand financial accounting concepts and practice, and if it prepares students for advanced study, professional examinations, and the successful and ethical pursuit of their careers in accounting or business in a global economy, then we will have attained our objectives."

A New Way of Looking at Generally Accepted Principles (GAAP)

Learning GAAP used to be a daunting task, as it is comprised of many standards that vary in form, completeness, and structure. Fortunately, the profession has recently developed the Financial Accounting Standards Board Codification (often referred to as the Codification). This Codification provides in one place all the GAAP related to a given topic. This textbook is the first to incorporate this Codification—it will make learning GAAP easier and more interesting!

Intermediate Accounting Works

Intermediate Accounting is the market-leading textbook in providing the tools needed to understand what GAAP is and how it is applied in practice. With this Fourteenth Edition, we strive to continue to provide the material needed to understand this subject area. The book is comprehensive and up-to-date, and provides the instructor with flexibility in the topics to cover. We also include proven pedagogical tools, designed to help students learn more effectively and to answer the changing needs of this course. Page xviii describes all of the learning tools of the textbook in detail.

We are excited about *Intermediate Accounting*, Fourteenth Edition. We believe it meets an important objective of providing useful information to educators and students interested in learning about both GAAP and IFRS. Suggestions and comments from users of this book will be appreciated. Please feel free to e-mail any one of us at *AccountingAuthors@yahoo.com*.

Donald E. Kieso
DeKalb, Illinois

Jerry J. Weygandt
Madison, Wisconsin

Terry D. Warfield
Madison, Wisconsin

WHAT'S NEW?

The Fourteenth Edition expands our emphasis on student learning and improves upon a teaching and learning package that instructors and students have rated the highest in customer satisfaction. Based on extensive reviews, focus groups, and interactions with other intermediate accounting instructors and students, we have developed a number of new pedagogical features and content changes, designed both to help students learn more effectively and to answer the changing needs of the course.

Major Content Revisions

In response to the changing environment, we have significantly revised several chapters.

Chapter 2   Conceptual Framework for Financial Reporting
- Chapter rewritten to reflect latest IASB/FASB work: reliability replaced with faithful representation, fundamental qualities differ, and secondary qualities are now enhancing qualities (and now contain some of the previous primary qualities); the framework now just includes the cost constraint (previously cost-benefit and materiality, materiality now a company-specific aspect of relevance).
- Constraints rewritten per above and prudence/conservatism is discussed as in conflict with the quality of neutrality; as a result, text discussion eliminated, but added a footnote explaining this position.
- Updated discussion of fair value, in light of recent FASB developments. Updated fair value discussions, including discussion of the fair value option, in Chapters 7, 14, and 17.

Chapter 3   The Accounting Information System
- Reduced the number of account titles throughout chapter for simplification.
- Completely new approach to illustrating transaction analysis; each illustration includes Basic Analysis, Equation Analysis, Debit-Credit Analysis, Journal Entry, and Posting sections.

Chapter 5   Balance Sheet and Statement of Cash Flows
- Moved Statement of Cash Flows material before Additional Information section, for improved discussion flow.

Chapter 7   Cash and Receivables
- Reconfigured chapter headings, so chapter now broken into four major sections (cash, accounts receivable, notes receivable, and special issues) instead of just two, for improved readability.
- Rewrote sections on direct write-off and allowance methods, for more current discussion of this material.

Chapter 18   Revenue Recognition
- Updated Current Environment section, with more recent developments in FASB revenue recognition guidelines.
- Revised and updated Revenue Recognition at Point of Sale (e.g., buyback, returns, and bill and hold) section to include new illustrations that demonstrate revenue recognition problems and solutions, as well as discussion on principal-agent relationships and multiple-deliverable arrangements (including an expanded discussion on consignments).

Chapter 23   Statement of Cash Flows
- Revised and updated Section 2: Special Problems in Statement Presentation, to discuss adjustments to net income (depreciation and amortization, losses and gains, stock options, postretirement benefit cost, extraordinary items).

Updated International Financial Reporting Standards (IFRS) Content

As we continue to strive to reflect the constant changes in the accounting environment, we have added new material on International Financial Reporting Standards (IFRS). A new end-of-chapter section, **IFRS Insights**, includes an overview section (Relevant Facts), differences between GAAP and IFRS (About the Numbers), IFRS/GAAP convergence efforts (On the Horizon), and IFRS Self-Test Questions and IFRS Concepts and Application. An international financial reporting problem is also included, based on Marks and Spencer plc (a leading U.K. department store) financial statements, as well as a research case addressing the IFRS literature for each chapter.

Enhanced Homework Material

In each chapter, we have updated Questions, Brief Exercises, Problems, and Concepts for Analysis. In addition, in the Using Your Judgment section, we now offer a new review exercise in each chapter, entitled *Accounting, Analysis, and Principles,* to help students evaluate and analyze information from the chapter. Students review the accounting introduced in the chapter ("Accounting"), consider how the information provided by the accounting is useful to investors and creditors ("Analysis"), and reflect on how the accounting is related to accounting principles and concepts ("Principles"). Such exercises, reinforced with end-of-chapter homework activities, give students the practice they will need to build decision-making skills using the accounting concepts and procedures they are learning. Finally, we have updated the *Professional Simulation* and included it in the textbook.

Chart of Accounts

It is important to always try to eliminate unnecessary barriers to student understanding. Sometimes, the accounting course can seem unnecessarily complicated to students because so many account titles are used. In order to reduce possible confusion, and to keep students focused on those concepts that really matter, in this edition of the textbook we undertook to reduce the number of account titles used. In some chapters, we were able to cut the number of accounts used by more than half.

ENHANCED FEATURES OF THE 14TH EDITION

This edition was also subject to an overall, comprehensive revision to ensure that it is technically accurate, relevant, and up-to-date. We have continued and enhanced many of the features of the 13th Edition of *Intermediate Accounting*, including the following.

Codification

The Codification was introduced in the 13th Edition—the first textbook to do so. The genesis for the Codification is explained in Chapter 1, with all previous references to the FASB literature with references to the Codification throughout the textbook. The complete citations and correspondence to prior FASB literature are presented in the FASB Codification section at the end of the chapter. Each chapter has Codification exercises and a research case (similar to the FARS Cases in the pre-codification editions of *Intermediate Accounting*).

Underlying Concepts

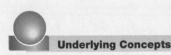

These marginal notes relate topics covered within each chapter back to the conceptual principles introduced in the beginning of the textbook. This continual reinforcement of the essential concepts and principles illustrates how the concepts are applied in practice and helps students understand the *why*, as well as the *how*.

Updated Supplements

All supplements are updated, including newly designed PowerPoint presentations with more review questions, and over 500 new Test bank questions.

Real-World Emphasis

One of the goals of the intermediate accounting course is to orient students to the application of accounting principles and techniques in practice. Accordingly, we have continued our practice of using numerous examples from real companies throughout the textbook. The names of these real companies are highlighted in red. Illustrations and exhibits marked by the icon shown here in the margin are excerpts from actual financial statements of real firms.

What do the numbers mean?

At the start of each chapter, we have updated and introduced new chapter-opening vignettes to provide an even better real-world context that helps motivate student interest in the chapter topic. Also, throughout the chapters, the "What Do the Numbers Mean?" boxed inserts also provide real-world extensions of the material presented in the textbook. In addition, Appendix 5B contains the 2009 annual report of The Procter & Gamble Company (P&G). The book's companion website contains the 2009 annual reports of The Coca-Cola Company and of PepsiCo, Inc. Problems in the *Using Your Judgment* section involve study of the P&G annual report or comparison of the annual reports of The Coca-Cola Company and PepsiCo. Also, links to many real-company financial reports appear in the company database at the *Gateway to the Profession*.

Currency and Accuracy

Accounting continually changes as its environment changes; an up-to-date book is therefore a necessity. As in past editions, we have strived to make this edition the most up-to-date and accurate textbook available. For the 14th Edition, we added an additional round of accuracy checking.

International Coverage

INTERNATIONAL PERSPECTIVE

As discussed above, having a basic understanding of international accounting is becoming ever more important as the profession moves toward convergence of GAAP and international standards. Thus, in addition to the **IFRS Insights** discussed earlier, we continue to include marginal *International Perspectives*, marked with the icon shown here, which we updated throughout to reflect changes in international accounting. These notes describe or compare IFRS and international accounting practices with GAAP. This feature helps students understand that other countries sometimes use different recognition and measurement principles to report financial information.

Streamlined Presentation

We also have continued our efforts to keep the topic coverage of *Intermediate Accounting* in line with the way instructors are *currently* teaching the course. Accordingly, we have moved some optional topics into chapter-end appendices, and we have omitted altogether some topics that formerly were covered in appendices. Details are listed in the specific content changes on pages xii–xiii. We have continued efforts to maintain the readability of the textbook, following the thorough editorial review of the 13th Edition.

Additional Exercises

Our study of the intermediate accounting course indicates the importance of the end-of-chapter Exercises for teaching and practicing important accounting concepts. In the 14th Edition, therefore, we have prepared an additional set of exercises, available at the book's companion website. (Solutions are available at the instructor's portion of the website.) Also, in the 14th Edition, a new Review and Analysis exercise at the book's companion website gives an additional opportunity for students to review the accounting techniques and analysis behind each chapter topic.

Using Your Judgment Section

We have revised and updated the *Using Your Judgment* section at the end of each chapter. Elements included in this section include the following.

- A Financial Reporting Problem, featuring The Procter & Gamble Company.
- A Comparative Analysis Case, featuring The Coca-Cola Company and PepsiCo, Inc., that asks students to compare and contrast the financial reporting for these two companies.
- A Financial Statement Analysis Case that asks students to use the information in published accounting reports to conduct financial analysis.
- A review exercise in each chapter entitled *Accounting, Analysis, and Principles*. As discussed above, this integrated exercise helps students evaluate and analyze information from the chapter.
- A *Professional Research: FASB Codification* case that gives students practice conducting authoritative research using the FASB Codification research system.
- A full presentation of *Professional Simulations*, newly revised for this edition, that model the new computerized CPA exam.

The *Using Your Judgment* assignments are designed to help develop students' critical thinking, analytical, and research skills.

Content Changes by Chapter

Chapter 1 Financial Accounting and Accounting Standards
- Moved "The Challenges Facing Financial Accounting" to later in the chapter, for improved discussion.
- Rewrote "Objective of Financial Reporting" per new conceptual framework guidelines.
- New WDNM box on fair value accounting.

Chapter 2 Conceptual Framework for Financial Reporting
- "Conceptual Framework" rewritten to reflect latest IASB/FASB work: the framework now just includes the cost constraint (previously cost-benefit and materiality, materiality now a company-specific aspect of relevance), reliability replaced with faithful representation, fundamental qualities differ, and secondary qualities are now enhancing qualities (and now contain some of the previous primary qualities).
- Constraints rewritten per above—also, prudence/conservatism now considered to conflict with quality of neutrality, so text discussion eliminated, but added a footnote explaining this position.

Chapter 3 The Accounting Information System
- Reduced the number of account titles throughout chapter, for simplification.
- Completely new approach to illustrating transaction analysis; each illustration includes Basic Analysis, Equation Analysis, Debit-Credit Analysis, Journal Entry, and Posting sections.

Chapter 4 Income Statement and Related Information
- New opening story, "Watch Out for Pro Forma," about the use of pro forma reporting practices and effects and the SEC's response (issuing Regulation G).
- New WDNM boxes: "Four: The Loneliest Number," about managing earnings and the quadrophobia effect, and "Different Income Concepts," about the performance metrics analysts use/create from a company's income statement.

Chapter 5 Balance Sheet and Statement of Cash Flows
- New opening story, "Hey, It Doesn't Balance," about FASB/IASB discussion paper on possible new format of balance sheet (statement of financial position).
- Moved Statement of Cash Flows material before Additional Information section, for improved discussion flow.
- Appendix 5B updated for 2009 P&G annual report information.

Chapter 7 Cash and Receivables
- Completely rewritten opening story on Nortel.
- Reconfigured chapter headings, so chapter now broken into 4 major sections (cash, accounts receivable, notes receivable, and special issues) instead of just 2, for improved readability.

- New WDNM box, "Deep Pockets," about cash hoarding.
- Rewrote sections on direct write-off and allowance methods, for more current discussion of this material.
- New section on Fair Value Option under Special Issues.
- New detailed footnote on FASB new rules on when a transfer of receivables is recorded as a sale.
- Completed revised WDNM box, "Return to Lender," about debt securities.
- Updated discussion of presentation of receivables.
- Deleted WDNM box in Appendix 7A on consequences of bouncing a check.
- Deleted Background section in Appendix 7B (Impairment of Receivables), as dated.

Chapter 8 Valuation of Inventories: A Cost-Basis Approach
- Rewrote much of the opening story, to incorporate recent information about auto industry slowdown and government bailouts.
- Updated WDNM box on Wal-Mart, to include recent information about how it's cutting its supply chain cost.
- New International Perspective, to provide latest IFRS views on inventory methods.
- New WDNM box, on possibility and economic consequences of repealing LIFO as acceptable method under GAAP.

Chapter 9 Inventories: Additional Valuation Issues
- Updated opening story, for most recent information about retailers' restocking process, its advantages, and its potential pitfalls.
- In Lower-of-Cost-or-Market section, now use cost-of-goods-sold and loss methods, instead of direct/indirect methods.
- Updated use of real company data throughout chapter.

Chapter 10 Acquisition and Disposition of Property, Plant, and Equipment
- Updated Financial Statement Analysis Case for Johnson & Johnson.
- New Professional Simulation exercise.

Chapter 11 Depreciation, Impairments, and Depletion
- New opening story, "Here Come the Write-Offs," about affects (impairment losses) of the 2008 credit crisis.
- New International Perspective on component depreciation and depletion.

Chapter 12 Intangible Assets
- New opening story, "Are We There Yet?" about gap between government economic measures and those same measures adjusted for intangible investments.
- New WDNM box, "Impairment Risk," about how goodwill impairments spiked in 2007 and 2008, coinciding with stock market downturn.
- Revised chart on R&D expenditures, to include rationale for specific accounting treatment.

Chapter 13 Current Liabilities and Contingencies

- Updated opening story, "Now You See It, Now You Don't," to provide more of an international perspective of disclosure requirements of contingent liabilities.
- New *International Perspectives* on classification of long-term debt, the IFRS use of the term *provisions,* and how IFRS companies report noncurrent liabilities before current liabilities.

Chapter 14 Long-Term Liabilities

- New opening story, "Bonds versus Notes," about recent trend of companies borrowing more from bond investors than banks; previous opening story now a new WDNM box.
- New section, Fair Value Option, which discusses both measurement and controversy.
- Updated WDNM boxes, "All About Bonds," to replace current discussion with one on 2 different companies, Wal-Mart and Alcoa, and "How's My Rating?" to incorporate more recent downward trend of S&P ratings.
- New *International Perspectives* on IFRS required use of effective-interest method, how bond issue costs must reduce the carrying amount of the bond, and troubled-debt restructurings.

Chapter 15 Stockholders' Equity

- Updated Reacquisition of Shares section, to discuss recent buyback developments/trend.
- New WDNM boxes, "Not So Good Anymore," about decreased share repurchase activity, and "Dividends Up, Dividends Down," about the recent sharp decrease in companies paying dividends.

Chapter 16 Dilutive Securities and Earnings per Share

- Updated opening story, "Kicking the Habit," about recent trend of companies issuing restricted stock versus stock options.
- New *International Perspectives* on IFRS share-based compensation and employee stock-purchase plans.

Chapter 17 Investments

- New opening story, "What to Do?" about how recent write-down of mortgage-backed securities has led to discussion on how to value financial instruments (e.g., amortized cost, fair value).
- New *International Perspectives* on IFRS classification of debt investments, IFRS valuation of debt investments, and valuation of equity method investments.
- Updated WDNM boxes, "What Is Fair Value?" to include current debate on use of mathematical models as basis for valuations, and "Risky Business" to discuss use of credit default swaps to facilitate sales of mortgage-backed securities.
- New WDNM box, "Who's in Control Here?" about the companies Molson Coors and Lenovo Group.
- New discussion on FASB/IASB proposal to simplify comprehensive income reporting and the recent amendment to variable-interest entities consolidation rules.

Chapter 18 Revenue Recognition

- Updated Current Environment section, with more recent developments in FASB/IASB revenue recognition policies and guidelines.
- Revised and updated Revenue Recognition at Point of Sale (e.g., buyback, returns, and bill and hold) section, to include new illustrations that demonstrate revenue recognition problems and solutions, as well as discussion on principal-agent relationships and multiple-deliverable arrangements (including an expanded discussion on consignments).

Chapter 19 Accounting for Income Taxes

- New opening story, "How Much Is Enough?" about Citigroup's handling of its deferred tax assets.
- New WDNM box, "Global Tax Rates," about how personal and corporate tax rates vary among countries.

Chapter 20 Accounting for Pensions and Postretirement Benefits

- Updated to reflect all recent data on pensions and postretirement benefits.

Chapter 21 Accounting for Leases

- Updated WDNM box, "Are You Liable?" for international impact on new lease-accounting rule.
- New discussion and illustration of expense front-loading of operating leases if brought on-balance-sheet.

Chapter 22 Accounting Change and Error Analysis

- Updated opening story and charts about types and numbers of recent accounting changes.
- New WDNM box, "Guard the Financial Statements!" about how restatements sometimes occur because of financial fraud.

Chapter 23 Statement of Cash Flows

- Updated opening story, "Show Me the Money!" to discuss how investors analyze companies' free cash flow.
- Revised and updated Section 2: Special Problems in Statement Presentation, to discuss adjustments to net income (depreciation and amortization, losses and gains, stock options, postretirement benefit cost, extraordinary items).

Chapter 24 Full Disclosure in Financial Reporting

- New company note disclosures from more recent annual reports, for example, Xerox, Johnson & Johnson, Tootsie Roll Industries, Best Buy Co., PepsiCo, and Home Depot.
- New discussion/illustrations in Fraudulent Financial Reporting section.
- New WDNM box, "Disclosure Overload" about six important areas still to be converged between GAAP and IFRS.
- Deleted Appendix 24B, as international coverage now discussed throughout textbook.

Teaching and Learning Supplementary Material

For Instructors

Active-Teaching Aids

In addition to the support instructors receive from *WileyPLUS* and the Wiley Faculty Network, we offer the following useful supplements.

Book's Companion Website.   On this website, *www.wiley.com/college/kieso*, instructors will find electronic versions of the Solutions Manual, Test Bank, Instructor's Manual, Computerized Test Bank, and other resources.

Instructor's Resource CD.   The Instructor's Resource CD (IRCD) contains an electronic version of all instructor supplements. The IRCD gives instructors the flexibility to access and prepare instructional materials based on their individual needs.

Solutions Manual, Vols. 1 and 2.   The Solutions Manual contains detailed solutions to all questions, brief exercises, exercises, and problems in the textbook as well as suggested answers to the questions and cases. The estimated time to complete exercises, problems, and cases is provided.

Solution Transparencies, Vols. 1 and 2.   The solution transparencies feature detailed solutions to brief exercises, exercises, problems, and "Using Your Judgment" activities. Transparencies can be easily ordered from the book's companion website.

Instructor's Manual, Vols. 1 and 2.   Included in each chapter are lecture outlines with teaching tips, chapter reviews, illustrations, and review quizzes.

Teaching Transparencies.   The teaching transparencies are 4-color acetate images of the illustrations found in the Instructor's Manual. Transparencies can be easily ordered from the book's companion website.

Test Bank and Algorithmic Computerized Test Bank.   The test bank and algorithmic computerized test bank allow instructors to tailor examinations according to study objectives and learning outcomes, including AACSB, AICPA, and IMA professional standards. Achievement tests, comprehensive examinations, and a final exam are included.

PowerPoint™.   The new PowerPoint™ presentations contain a combination of key concepts, images, and problems from the textbook.

WebCT and Desire2Learn.   WebCT or Desire2Learn offer an integrated set of course management tools that enable instructors to easily design, develop, and manage Web-based and Web-enhanced courses.

Solutions to Rockford Practice Set and Excel Workbook Templates.   Available for download from the book's companion website.

For Students

Active-Learning Aids

Book's Companion Website.   On this website, students will find:

- A *B Set of Additional Exercises*
- *Self-Study Tests and Additional Self-Tests*
- A complete *Glossary* of all the key terms used in the text
- A new *Review and Analysis Exercise, with Solution*
- *Financial statements* for The Procter & Gamble Company, The Coca-Cola Company, PepsiCo, and Marks and Spencer plc

Student Study Guide, Vols. 1 and 2.   Each chapter of the Study Guide contains a chapter review, chapter outline, and a glossary of key terms. Demonstration problems, multiple-choice, true/false, matching, and other exercises are included.

Problem-Solving Survival Guide, Vols. 1 and 2. This study guide contains exercises and problems that help students develop their intermediate accounting problem-solving skills. Explanations assist in the approach, set-up, and completion of accounting problems. Tips alert students to common pitfalls and misconceptions.

Working Papers, Vols. 1 and 2.   The working papers are printed templates that can help students correctly format their textbook accounting solutions. Working paper templates are available for all end-of-chapter brief exercises, exercises, problems, and cases.

Excel Working Papers.   The *Excel Working Papers* are Excel templates that students can use to correctly format their textbook accounting solutions.

Excel Primer: Using Excel in Accounting.   The online Excel primer and accompanying Excel templates allow students to complete select end-of-chapter exercises and problems identified by a spreadsheet icon in the margin of the textbook.

Rockford Corporation: An Accounting Practice Set.   This practice set helps students review the accounting cycle and the preparation of financial statements.

Rockford Corporation: An Accounting Practice Set (General Ledger Software Version).   The computerized Rockford practice set is a general ledger software version of the printed practice set.

Gateway to the Profession

The *Gateway to the Profession* resources include the following content.

Professional Resources

Consistent with expanding beyond technical accounting knowledge, the *Gateway to the Profession* materials emphasize certain skills necessary to become a successful accountant or financial manager. The following materials will help students develop needed professional skills.

Financial Statement Analysis Primer.   An online primer on financial statement analysis is provided, along with related assignment material. This primer can also be used in conjunction with the database of annual reports of real companies.

Database of Real Companies.   Links to more than 20 annual reports of well-known companies, including three international companies, are provided. Assignment material provides some examples of different types of analysis that students can perform.

Writing Handbook.   A handbook on professional communications gives students a framework for writing professional materials. This handbook discusses issues such as the top-10 writing problems, strategies for rewriting, how to do revisions, and tips on clarity. This handbook has been class-tested and is effective in helping students enhance their writing skills.

Working in Teams.   Recent evaluations of accounting education have identified the need to develop more skills in group problem solving. The *Gateway to the Profession* materials include a second primer dealing with the role that work-groups play in organizations. Information is included on what makes a successful group, how you can participate effectively in the group, and do's and don'ts of group formation.

Ethics in Accounting.   The Professional Toolkit contains expanded materials on the role of ethics in the profession, including references to speeches and articles on ethics in accounting, codes of ethics for major professional bodies, and examples and additional case studies on ethics.

Chapter-Level Resources

Also included at the *Gateway to the Profession* are features that help students process and understand the course materials. They are:

Interactive Tutorials.   To help students better understand some of the more difficult topics in intermediate accounting, we have developed a number of interactive tutorials that provide expanded discussion and explanation in a visual and narrative context. Topics addressed are the accounting cycle; inventory methods, including dollar-value LIFO; depreciation and impairment of long-lived assets; and interest capitalization.

These tutorials are for the benefit of the student and should require no use of class time on the part of instructors.

Expanded Discussions.   The Expanded Discussion section provides additional topics not covered in-depth in the textbook, thereby offering the flexibility to enrich or expand the course.

Spreadsheet Tools.   Present value templates are provided. These templates can be used to solve time value of money problems.

Additional Internet Links.   A number of useful links related to financial analysis are provided to expand expertise in analyzing real-world reporting.

Acknowledgments

Intermediate Accounting has benefited greatly from the input of focus group participants, manuscript reviewers, those who have sent comments by letter or e-mail, ancillary authors, and proofers. We greatly appreciate the constructive suggestions and innovative ideas of reviewers and the creativity and accuracy of the ancillary authors and checkers.

Fourteenth Edition

Noel Addy
Mississippi State University

Richard Alltizer
University of Central Oklahoma

Paul Bahnson
Boise State University

James Bannister
University of Hartford

Ira Bates
Florida A&M University

Mitra Bathai
Kennesaw State College

Kimberly Brickler
Lindenwood University

Alisa Brink
Virginia Commonwealth University

Helen Brubeck
San Jose State University

Mary Ellen Carter
Boston College

Judson Caskey
University of California, Los Angeles

Bruce Caster
Valdosta State University

Jeff Casterella
Colorado State University

Nancy Christie
Virginia Tech University

Katie Cordova
University of Arizona

Araya Debassay
University of Delaware

Laura Delaune
Louisiana State University

Terry Elliott
Morehead State University

Ed Etter
Eastern Michigan University

Diana Franz
University of Toledo

Lisa Gillespie
Loyola University Chicago

Jodi Gissel
Marquette University

James Gong
University of Illinois at Urbana Chamapaign

Jeff Gramlich
University of Southern Maine

Pamela Graybeal
University of Central Florida

Abo-El-Yazeed Habib
Minnesota State University—Mankato

Penny Hanes
Mercyhurst College

Chuck Harter
Georgia Southern University

John Hassell
IUPUI

Jerry Haugland
Chadron State College

Wendy Heltzer
DePaul University

Kathy Horton
College of DuPage

Marianne James
California State University, Los Angeles

I. Richard Johnson
Utah State University

Mary Keener
University of Tampa

Nathan Kessar
Brooklyn College

Ching-Lih Jan
California State University, Hayward

Steve Lim
Texas Christian University

Tony Lopez
California State University, Fullerton

Hung Yuan Lu
California State University, Fullerton

Ming Lu
Santa Monica College

Stephanie Mason
Hunter College/CUNY

Florence McGovern
Bergen Community College

Paul McKillop
Salve Regina University

David Medved
Thomas Edison State College

Barbara Merino
University of North Texas

Louella Moore
Arkansas State University

Mary Ellen Morris
University of Massachusetts

Derek Oler
Texas Tech University

Sy Pearlman
California State University, Long Beach

Byron Pike
Minnesota State University—Mankato

Catherine Plante
University of New Hampshire

Kevin Poirier
Johnson & Wales University

Pete Poznanski
Cleveland State University

Karl Putnan
University of Texas at El Paso

Krishnamurthy K. Raman
University of North Texas

SD Ray
Arkansas State University

Terry Reilly
Albright College

Jay Rich
Illinois State University

Mark Riley
Northern Illinois University

William Riter
Cornerstone University

Robert Rutledge
Texas State University

Ken Ryack
Northern Kentucky University

Mary Ryan
Bergen Community College

August Saibeni
Consumnes River College

Monica Salomon
University of West Florida

Carol Springer Sargent
Georgia State University

Lewis Shaw
Suffolk University

George Smith
Newman University

Nancy Snow
University of Toledo

Vic Stanton
University of California, Berkeley

Sarah Stanwick
Auburn University

Gina Sturgill
Franklin University

David Sulzen
Ferrum College

Mohsen Nasser Tavakolian
San Francisco State University

Dan Teed
Troy University

Katheren Terrell
University of Central Oklahoma

xx

Brenda Thalacker
Chippewa Valley Technical College

Leslie Turner
Palm Beach Atlantic University

Isabel Wang
Michigan State University

Jeannie Welsh
La Salle University

Wendy Wilson
Southern Methodist University

Suzanne Wright
Penn State University

Yan Xiong
California State University, Sacramento

Yifeng Zhang
State University of New York at Albany

Prior Edition Reviewers

Diana Adcox
University of North Florida

Noel Addy
Mississippi State University

Roberta Allen
Texas Tech University

James Bannister
University of Hartford

Charles Baril
James Madison University

Kathleen Buaer
Midwestern State University

Janice Bell
California State University at Northridge

Larry Bergin
Winona State University

Lynn Bible
University of Nevada, Reno

John C. Borke
University of Wisconsin—Platteville

Tiffany Bortz
University of Texas, Dallas

Lisa Bostick
University of Tampa

Greg Brookins
Santa Monica College

Phillip Buchanan
George Mason University

Tom Buchman
University of Colorado, Boulder

Suzanne M. Busch
California State University—Hayward

Eric Carlsen
Kean College of New Jersey

Tom Carment
Northeastern State University

Tommy Carnes
Western Carolina University

Jeff Custarella
Colorado State University

Robert Cluskey
Tennessee State University

Edwin Cohen
DePaul University

Gene Comiskey
Georgia Tech University

W. Terry Dancer
Arkansas State University

Laura Delaune
Louisiana State University

Lynda Dennis
University of Central Florida

Lee Dexter
Moorhead State University

Judith Doing
University of Arizona

Joanne Duke
San Francisco State University

Richard Dumont
Teikyo Post University

William Dwyer
DeSales University

Claire Eckstein
CUNY—Baruch

Dean S. Eiteman
Indiana University—Pennsylvania

Bob Eskew
Purdue University

Larry R. Falcetto
Emporia State University

Dave Farber
University of Missouri

Richard Fern
Eastern Kentucky University

Richard Fleischman
John Carroll University

Stephen L. Fogg
Temple University

William Foster
New Mexico State University

Clyde Galbraith
West Chester University

Marshall Geiger
University of Richmond

Susan Gill
Washington State University

Harold Goedde
State University of New York at Oneonta

Ellen Goldberg
Northern Virginia Community College

Marty Gosman
Quinnipiac College

Lynford E. Graham
Rutgers University

Donald J. Griffin
Cayuga Community College

Konrad Gunderson
Missouri Western University

Marcia I. Halvorsen
University of Cincinnati

Garry Heesacker
Central Washington University

Kenneth Henry
Florida International University

Julia Higgs
Florida Atlantic University

Wayne M. Higley
Buena Vista University

Judy Hora
University of San Diego

Geoffrey Horlick
St. Francis College

Kathy Hsu
University of Louisiana, Lafayette

Allen Hunt
Southern Illinois University

Marilyn Hunt
University of Central Florida

M. Zarar Iqbal
California Polytechnic State University—San Luis Obispo

Daniel Ivancevich
University of North Carolina at Wilmington

Susan Ivancevich
University of North Carolina at Wilmington

Cynthia Jeffrey
Iowa State University

Scott Jeris
San Francisco State University

James Johnston
Louisiana Tech University

Jeff Jones
University of Texas—San Antonio

Mary Jo Jones
Eastern University

Art Joy
University of South Florida

Celina Jozci
University of South Florida

Ben Ke
Penn State University

Douglas W. Kieso
Aurora University

Paul D. Kimmel
University of Wisconsin—Milwaukee

Martha King
Emporia State University

Florence Kirk
State University of New York at Oswego

Mark Kohlbeck
Florida Atlantic University

Lisa Koonce
University of Texas at Austin

Barbara Kren
University of Wisconsin—Milwaukee

Steve Lafave
Augsburg College

Ellen Landgraf
Loyola University, Chicago

Tom Largay
Thomas College

David B. Law
Youngstown State University

Henry LeClerc
Suffolk Community College—Selden Campus

Patsy Lee
University of Texas—Arlington

Lydia Leporte
Tidewater Community College

Timothy Lindquist
University of Northern Iowa

Ellen Lippman
University of Portland

Barbara Lippincott
University of Tampa

Gary Luoma
University of Southern California

Matt Magilke
University of Utah

Daphne Main
University of New Orleans

Mostafa Maksy
Northeastern Illinois University

Danny Matthews
Midwestern State University

Noel McKeon
Florida Community College

Robert J. Matthews
New Jersey City University

Alan Mayer-Sommer
Georgetown University

Robert Milbrath
University of Houston

James Miller
Gannon University

John Mills
University of Nevada—Reno

Joan Monnin-Callahan
University of Cincinnati

Michael Motes
University of Maryland
University College

Mohamed E. Moustafa
California State University—Long Beach

R.D. Nair
University of Wisconsin—Madison

Ed Nathan
University of Houston

Siva Nathan
Georgia State University

Kermit Natho
Georgia State University

Joseph Nicassio
Westmoreland County Community College

Hugo Nurnberg
CUNY—Baruch

Ann O'Brien
University of Wisconsin—Madison

Anne Oppegard
Augustana College, SD

Patricia Parker
Columbus State Community College

Richard Parker
Olivet College

Obeau S. Persons
Rider University

Ray Pfeiffer
Texas Christian University

Alee Phillips
University of Kansas

Marlene Plumlee
University of Utah

Wing Poon
Montclair State University

Jay Price
Utah State University

Robert Rambo
University of New Orleans

Debbie Rankin
Lincoln University

MaryAnn Reynolds
Western Washington University

Vernon Richardson
University of Arkansas

Richard Riley
West Virginia University

Jeffrey D. Ritter
St. Norbert College

Paul (Jep) Robertson
Henderson State University

Steven Rock
University of Colorado

Larry Roman
Cuyahoga Community College

John Rossi
Moravian College

Bob Rouse
College of Charleston

Tim Ryan
Southern Illinois University

Victoria Rymer
University of Maryland

James Sander
Butler University

John Sander
University of Southern Maine

George Sanders
Western Washington University

Howard Shapiro
Eastern Washington University

Douglas Sharp
Wichita State University

Tim Shea
Foley and Lardner

Jerry Siebel
University of South Florida

Phil Siegel
Florida Atlantic University

John R. Simon
Northern Illinois University

Keith Smith
George Washington University

Pam Smith
Northern Illinois University

Douglas Smith
Samford University

Billy S. Soo
Boston College

Karen Squires
University of Tampa

Carlton D. Stolle
Texas A&M University

William Stout
University of Louisville

Pamela Stuerke
Case Western Reserve University

Ron Stunda
Birmingham Southern College

Eric Sussman
University of California, Los Angeles

Diane L. Tanner
University of North Florida

Gary Taylor
University of Alabama

Gary Testa
Brooklyn College

Lynn Thomas
Kansas State University

Paula B. Thomas
Middle Tennessee State University

Tom Tierney
University of Wisconsin—Madison

Elizabeth Venuti
Hofstra University

James D. Waddington, Jr.
Hawaii Pacific University

Dick Wasson
Southwestern College

Frank F. Weinberg
Golden Gate University

David Weiner
University of San Francisco

Jeannie Welsh
LaSalle University

Shari H. Wescott
Houston Baptist University

Michael Willenborg
University of Connecticut

William H. Wilson
Oregon Health University

Kenneth Wooling
Hampton University

Joni Young
University of New Mexico

Paul Zarowin
New York University

Steve Zeff
Rice University

Special thanks to Kurt Pany, Arizona State University, for his input on auditor disclosure issues, and to Stephen A. Zeff, Rice University, for his comments on international accounting.
In addition, we thank the following colleagues who contributed to several of the unique features of this edition.

xxii

Gateway to the Profession and Codification Cases

Jack Cathey
University of North Carolina—Charlotte

Michelle Ephraim
Worcester Polytechnic Institute

Erik Frederickson
Madison, Wisconsin

Jason Hart
Deloitte LLP, Milwaukee

Frank Heflin
Florida State University

Mike Katte
SC Johnson, Racine, WI

Kelly Krieg
E & Y, Milwaukee

Jeremy Kunicki
Walgreens

Courtney Meier
Deloitte LLP, Milwaukee

Andrew Prewitt
KPMG, Chicago

Jeff Seymour
KPMG, Minneapolis

Matt Sullivan
Deloitte LLP, Milwaukee

Matt Tutaj
Deloitte LLP, Chicago

Jen Vaughn
PricewaterhouseCoopers, Chicago

Erin Viel
PricewaterhouseCoopers, Milwaukee

"Working in Teams" Material

Edward Wertheim
Northeastern University

Ancillary Authors, Contributors, Proofers, and Accuracy Checkers

LuAnn Bean
Florida Institute of Technology

Mary Ann Benson
John C. Borke
University of Wisconsin—Platteville

Jack Cathey
University of North Carolina—Charlotte

Jim Emig
Villanova University

Larry Falcetto
Emporia State University

Coby Harmon
University of California, Santa Barbara

Marilyn F. Hunt

Douglas W. Kieso
Aurora University

Mark Kohlbeck
Florida Atlantic University

Maureen Mascha
Marquette University

Barbara Muller
Arizona State University

Jill Misuraca
Middlesex Community College

Yvonne Phang
Borough of Manhattan Community College

John Plouffe
California State Polytechnic University—Pomona

Rex A. Schildhouse
University of Phoenix—San Diego

Lynn Stallworth
Appalachian State University

Sheila Viel
University of Wisconsin—Milwaukee

Dick D. Wasson
Southwestern College, San Diego University

WileyPLUS Developers and Reviewers

Carole Brandt–Fink
Laura McNally
Melanie Yon

Advisory Board

We gratefully acknowledge the following members of the Intermediate Accounting Advisory Board for their advice and assistance with this edition.

Steve Balsam
Temple University

Jack Cathey
University of North Carolina—Charlotte

Uday Chandra
State University of New York at Albany

Ruben Davila
University of Southern California

Doug deVidal
University of Texas—Austin

Dan Givoly
Pennsylvinia State University

Leslie Hodder
University of Indiana—Bloomington

Celina Jozsi
University of South Florida

Jocelyn Kauffunger
University of Pittsburgh

Adam Koch
University of Virginia

Roger Martin
University of Virginia

Linda Nichols
Texas Tech University

Sy Pearlman
California State University—Long Beach

Mark Riley
Northern Illinois University

Pam Smith
Northern Illinois University

Practicing Accountants and Business Executives

From the fields of corporate and public accounting, we owe thanks to the following practitioners for their technical advice and for consenting to interviews.

Mike Crooch
FASB (retired)

Tracy Golden
Deloitte LLP

John Gribble
PricewaterhouseCoopers (retired)

Darien Griffin
S.C. Johnson & Son

Michael Lehman
Sun Microsystems, Inc.

Tom Linsmeier
FASB

Michele Lippert
Evoke.com

Sue McGrath
Vision Capital Management

David Miniken
Sweeney Conrad

Robert Sack
University of Virginia

Clare Schulte
Deloitte LLP

Willie Sutton
Mutual Community Savings Bank, Durham, NC

Lynn Turner
Glass, Lewis, LLP

Rachel Woods
PricewaterhouseCoopers

Arthur Wyatt
Arthur Anderson & Co., and the University of Illinois—Urbana

Finally, we appreciate the exemplary support and professional commitment given us by the development, marketing, production, and editorial staffs of John Wiley & Sons, including the following: George Hoffman, Susan Elbe, Chris DeJohn, Michael McDonald, Amy Scholz, Karolina Zarychta Honsa, Trish McFadden, Brian Kamins, Jackie Kepping, Allie Morris, Greg Chaput, Harry Nolan, and Jim O'Shea. Thanks, too, to Suzanne Ingrao for her production work, to Denise Showers and the staff at Aptara®, Inc. for their work on the textbook, Cyndy Taylor, and to Danielle Urban and the staff at Elm Street Publishing Services for their work on the solutions manual.

We also appreciate the cooperation of the American Institute of Certified Public Accountants and the Financial Accounting Standards Board in permitting us to quote from their pronouncements. We thank The Procter & Gamble Company for permitting us to use its 2009 annual report for our specimen financial statements. We also acknowledge permission from the American Institute of Certified Public Accountants, the Institute of Management Accountants, and the Institute of Internal Auditors to adapt and use material from the Uniform CPA Examinations, the CMA Examinations, and the CIA Examination, respectively.

Suggestions and comments from users of this book will be appreciated. Please feel free to e-mail any one of us at *AccountingAuthors@yahoo.com.*

Donald E. Kieso
Somonauk, Illinois

Jerry J. Weygandt
Madison, Wisconsin

Terry D. Warfield
Madison, Wisconsin

Brief Contents

Contents

15 ▶ Stockholders' Equity

It's a Global Market

As mentioned in prior chapters, we are moving rapidly toward one set of global financial reporting standards and one "common language" for financial information. This change will probably lead to more consolidation of our capital markets. To understand how quickly the global financial world is changing, let's examine a few trends occurring on stock exchanges around the world.

In 2007, the New York Stock Exchange (NYSE) merged with Paris-based Euronext, creating the world's first transatlantic stock exchange. NYSE Euronext is the world's largest exchange group, now with 8,000 listed issuers representing over 40 percent of global equity trading in 2010. Similarly, NASDAQ, the world's largest electronic stock market, merged with OMX, the Nordic stock market operator. This electronic exchange operates in 29 countries, on six continents, and has over 4,000 listed issuers, with a market value of approximately $5.5 trillion.

Another reason behind the movement to international financial reporting standards can be found in recent initial public offerings (IPOs). The emerging markets are driving the global IPO market. As shown in the following table, in the first three months of 2008, only one of the top ten IPOs occurred on the NYSE.

Top 10 IPOs by amount of capital raised, January–March 2008

Ranking	Issuer Name	Domicile Nation	Industry Description	Proceeds (US$m)	Primary Exchange
1	Visa Inc	United States	Financials	19,650	NYSE
2	China Railway Construction Corp	China	Industrials	5,709	Shanghai, HKEx
3	Reliance Power Ltd	India	Energy and power	2,964	Bombay
4	Mobile Telecommunications Company Saudi Arabia	Saudi Arabia	Telecommunications	1,867	Riyadh
5	Rabigh Refining & Petrochemical Company	Saudi Arabia	Materials	1,228	Riyadh
6	Want Want China Holdings	China	Consumer staples	1,046	Hong Kong
7	Seven Bank Ltd	Japan	Financials	486	JASDAQ
8	TGK-7 (Volzhskaya TGK)	Russia	Energy and power	464	RTS
9	Rural Electrification Corp	India	Energy and power	417	Bombay
10	Honghua Group Ltd	China	Energy and power	409	Hong Kong

See the **International Perspectives** on pages 844 and 845.

Read the **IFRS Insights** on pages 895–902 for a discussion of:

—Equity

—Accounting for preference shares

—Presentation of equity

The trend continued in 2009, with Euronext leading world markets with the amount of capital raised in IPOs. As another example, Brazil, Russia, India, and China—often referred to as the *BRIC countries*—generated 41 percent of total IPO proceeds in 2007, compared with just 14 percent for the BRIC countries in 2004.

Finally, consider the international sales of some of the largest U.S. corporations: **General Electric** now has approximately 50 percent of its sales overseas, **Boeing** in a recent year sold more planes overseas than in the United States, and **Ford Motor Company**'s sales would be much less except for success in the European market.

Source: Ernst and Young, *Growth During Economic Uncertainty: Global IPO Trends Report* (2008), and *www.euronext.com.*

PREVIEW OF CHAPTER 15 As our opening story indicates, the growth of global equity capital markets indicates that investors around the world need useful information. In this chapter, we explain the accounting issues related to the stockholders' equity of a corporation. The content and organization of the chapter are as follows.

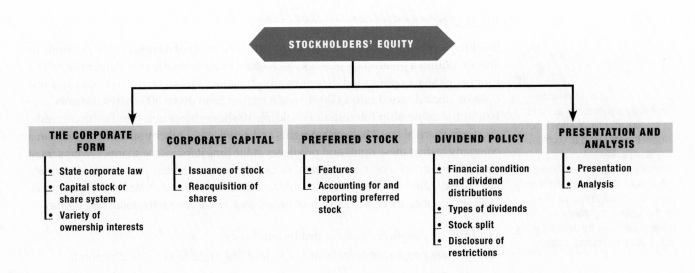

STOCKHOLDERS' EQUITY

THE CORPORATE FORM
- State corporate law
- Capital stock or share system
- Variety of ownership interests

CORPORATE CAPITAL
- Issuance of stock
- Reacquisition of shares

PREFERRED STOCK
- Features
- Accounting for and reporting preferred stock

DIVIDEND POLICY
- Financial condition and dividend distributions
- Types of dividends
- Stock split
- Disclosure of restrictions

PRESENTATION AND ANALYSIS
- Presentation
- Analysis

THE CORPORATE FORM OF ORGANIZATION

Of the three **primary forms of business organization**—the proprietorship, the partnership, and the corporation—the corporate form dominates. The corporation is by far the leader in terms of the aggregate amount of resources controlled, goods and services produced, and people employed. All of the "Fortune 500" largest industrial firms are corporations. Although the corporate form has a number of advantages (as well as disadvantages) over the other two forms, its principal advantage is its facility for attracting and accumulating large amounts of capital.

The special characteristics of the corporate form that affect accounting include:

1. Influence of state corporate law.
2. Use of the capital stock or share system.
3. Development of a variety of ownership interests.

State Corporate Law

Anyone who wishes to establish a corporation must submit **articles of incorporation** to the state in which incorporation is desired. After fulfilling requirements, the state issues a corporation charter, thereby recognizing the company as a legal entity subject to state law. Regardless of the number of states in which a corporation has operating divisions, it is incorporated in only one state.

It is to the company's advantage to incorporate in a state whose laws favor the corporate form of business organization. General Motors, for example, is incorporated in Delaware; U.S. Steel is a New Jersey corporation. Some corporations have increasingly been incorporating in states with laws favorable to existing management. For example, to thwart possible unfriendly takeovers, at one time, Gulf Oil changed its state of incorporation to Delaware. There, the board of directors alone, without a vote of the shareholders, may approve certain tactics against takeovers.

Each state has its own business incorporation act. The accounting for stockholders' equity follows the provisions of these acts. In many cases, states have adopted the principles contained in the Model Business Corporate Act prepared by the American Bar Association. State laws are complex and vary both in their provisions and in their definitions of certain terms. Some laws fail to define technical terms. As a result, terms often mean one thing in one state and another thing in a different state. These problems may be further compounded because legal authorities often interpret the effects and restrictions of the laws differently.

Capital Stock or Share System

Stockholders' equity in a corporation generally consists of a large number of units or shares. Within a given class of stock, each share exactly equals every other share. The number of shares possessed determines each owner's interest. If a company has one class of stock divided into 1,000 shares, a person who owns 500 shares controls one-half of the ownership interest. One holding 10 shares has a one-hundredth interest.

Each share of stock has certain rights and privileges. Only by special contract can a company restrict these rights and privileges at the time it issues the shares. Owners must examine the articles of incorporation, stock certificates, and the provisions of the state law to ascertain such restrictions on or variations from the standard rights and privileges. In the absence of restrictive provisions, each share carries the following rights:

1. To share proportionately in profits and losses.
2. To share proportionately in management (the right to vote for directors).

3. To share proportionately in corporate assets upon liquidation.

4. To share proportionately in any new issues of stock of the same class—called the preemptive right.[1]

The first three rights are self-explanatory. The last right is used to protect each stockholder's proportional interest in the company. **The preemptive right protects an existing stockholder from involuntary dilution of ownership interest.** Without this right, stockholders might find their interest reduced by the issuance of additional stock without their knowledge, and at prices unfavorable to them. However, many corporations have eliminated the preemptive right. Why? Because this right makes it inconvenient for corporations to issue large amounts of additional stock, as they frequently do in acquiring other companies.

The share system easily allows one individual to transfer an interest in a company to another investor. For example, individuals owning shares in Best Buy **may sell them to others at any time and at any price without obtaining the consent of the company or other stockholders**. Each share is personal property of the owner, who may dispose of it at will. Best Buy simply maintains a list or subsidiary ledger of stockholders as a guide to dividend payments, issuance of stock rights, voting proxies, and the like. Because owners freely and frequently transfer shares, Best Buy must revise the subsidiary ledger of stockholders periodically, generally in advance of every dividend payment or stockholders' meeting.

In addition, the major stock exchanges require ownership controls that the typical corporation finds uneconomic to provide. Thus, corporations often use **registrars and transfer agents** who specialize in providing services for recording and transferring stock. The Uniform Stock Transfer Act and the Uniform Commercial Code govern the negotiability of stock certificates.

Variety of Ownership Interests

In every corporation, one class of stock must represent the basic ownership interest. That class is called common stock. Common stock is the residual corporate interest that bears the ultimate risks of loss and receives the benefits of success. It is guaranteed neither dividends nor assets upon dissolution. But common stockholders generally control the management of the corporation and tend to profit most if the company is successful. In the event that a corporation has only one authorized issue of capital stock, that issue is by definition common stock, whether so designated in the charter or not.

In an effort to broaden investor appeal, corporations may offer two or more classes of stock, each with different rights or privileges. In the preceding section we pointed out that each share of stock of a given issue has the same four inherent rights as other shares of the same issue. By special stock contracts between the corporation and its stockholders, however, the stockholder may sacrifice certain of these rights in return for other special rights or privileges. Thus special classes of stock, usually called preferred stock, are created. In return for any special preference, the preferred stockholder always sacrifices some of the inherent rights of common stock ownership.

A common type of preference is to give the preferred stockholders a prior claim on earnings. The corporation thus assures them a dividend, usually at a stated rate, before it distributes any amount to the common stockholders. In return for this preference, the preferred stockholders may sacrifice their right to a voice in management or their right to share in profits beyond the stated rate.

> **INTERNATIONAL PERSPECTIVE**
>
> The U.S. and British systems of corporate governance and finance depend to a large extent on equity financing and the widely dispersed ownership of shares traded in highly liquid markets. The German and Japanese systems have relied more on debt financing, interlocking stock ownership, banker/directors, and worker/shareholder rights.

---

[1]This privilege is referred to as a **stock right** or **warrant**. The warrants issued in these situations are of short duration, unlike the warrants issued with other securities.

What do the numbers mean?

A CLASS (B) ACT

Some companies grant preferences to different shareholders by issuing different classes of common stock. Recent stock bids put the spotlight on dual-class stock structures. For example, ownership of Dow Jones & Co. was controlled by family members who owned Class B shares, which carry super voting powers. The same is true for the Ford family's control of Ford Motor Co. Class B shares are often criticized for protecting owners' interest at the expense of shareholder return. These shares often can determine if a takeover deal gets done, or not. Here are some notable companies with two-tiered shares.

Company	Votes Controlled by Class B Shareholders	Company	Votes Controlled by Class B Shareholders
Ford	40%	Estée Lauder	88%
New York Times	70%	Polo Ralph Lauren	88%
Meredith	71%	Martha Stewart Living	91%
Cablevision Systems	73%	1-800-Flowers	93%
Google	78%		

Data: Bloomberg Financial Markets, *BusinessWeek*, company documents.

For most retail investors, voting rights are not that important. But for family-controlled companies, issuing newer classes of lower or nonvoting stock effectively creates currency for acquisitions, increases liquidity, or puts a public value on the company without diluting the family's voting control. This was one of the main reasons Facebook gave when it created a dual-class share structure in 2009. Thus, investors must carefully compare the apparent bargain prices for some classes of stock—they may end up as second-class citizens with no voting rights.

Source: Adapted from Andy Serwer, "Dual-Listed Companies Aren't Fair or Balanced," *Fortune* (September 20, 2004), p. 83; Alex Halperin, "A Class (B) Act," *BusinessWeek* (May 28, 2007), p. 12; and J. Vascellaro, "Facebook Creates Dual-Class Stock Structure," *Wall Street Journal* (November 24, 2009).

CORPORATE CAPITAL

LEARNING OBJECTIVE
Identify the key components of stockholders' equity.

Owner's equity in a corporation is defined as stockholders' equity, shareholders' equity, or corporate capital. The following three categories normally appear as part of stockholders' equity:

1. Capital stock.
2. Additional paid-in capital.
3. Retained earnings.

The first two categories, capital stock and additional paid-in capital, constitute contributed (paid-in) capital. Retained earnings represents the earned capital of the company. Contributed (paid-in) capital is the total amount paid in on capital stock—the amount provided by stockholders to the corporation for use in the business. Contributed capital includes items such as the par value of all outstanding stock and premiums less discounts on issuance. Earned capital is the capital that develops from profitable operations. It consists of all undistributed income that remains invested in the company.

Stockholders' equity is the difference between the assets and the liabilities of the company. That is, the owners' or stockholders' interest in a company like Walt Disney Co. is a residual interest.[2] Stockholders' (owners') equity represents the cumulative net

---

[2]"Elements of Financial Statements," *Statement of Financial Accounting Concepts No. 6* (Stamford, Conn.: FASB, 1985), par. 60.

contributions by stockholders plus retained earnings. As a residual interest, stockholders' equity has no existence apart from the assets and liabilities of Disney—stockholders' equity equals net assets. Stockholders' equity is not a claim to specific assets but a claim against a portion of the total assets. Its amount is not specified or fixed; it depends on Disney's profitability. Stockholders' equity grows if it is profitable. It shrinks, or may disappear entirely, if Disney loses money.

Issuance of Stock

In issuing stock, companies follow these procedures: First, the state must authorize the stock, generally in a certificate of incorporation or charter. Next, the corporation offers shares for sale, entering into contracts to sell stock. Then, after receiving amounts for the stock, the corporation issues shares. The corporation generally makes no entry in the general ledger accounts when it receives its stock authorization from the state of incorporation.

3 LEARNING OBJECTIVE

Explain the accounting procedures for issuing shares of stock.

We discuss the accounting problems involved in the issuance of stock under the following topics.

1. Accounting for par value stock.

2. Accounting for no-par stock.

3. Accounting for stock issued in combination with other securities (lump-sum sales).

4. Accounting for stock issued in noncash transactions.

5. Accounting for costs of issuing stock.

Par Value Stock

The par value of a stock has no relationship to its fair value. At present, the par value associated with most capital stock issuances is very low. For example, **PepsiCo**'s par value is 1⅔¢, **Kellogg**'s is $0.25, and **Hershey**'s is $1. Such values contrast dramatically with the situation in the early 1900s, when practically all stock issued had a par value of $100. Low par values help companies avoid the contingent liability associated with stock sold below par.[3]

To show the required information for issuance of par value stock, corporations maintain accounts for each class of stock as follows.

1. *Preferred Stock or Common Stock.* Together, these two stock accounts reflect the par value of the corporation's issued shares. The company credits these accounts when it originally issues the shares. It makes no additional entries in these accounts unless it issues additional shares or retires them.

2. *Paid-in Capital in Excess of Par (also called Additional Paid-in Capital).* The Paid-in Capital in Excess of Par account indicates any excess over par value paid in by stockholders in return for the shares issued to them. Once paid in, the excess over par becomes a part of the corporation's additional paid-in capital. The individual stockholder has no greater claim on the excess paid in than all other holders of the same class of shares.

No-Par Stock

Many states permit the issuance of capital stock without par value, called no-par stock. The reasons for issuance of no-par stock are twofold: First, issuance of no-par stock

---

[3]Companies rarely, if ever, issue stock at a value below par value. If issuing stock below par, the company records the discount as a debit to Additional Paid-in Capital. In addition, the corporation may call on the original purchaser or the current holder of the shares issued below par to pay in the amount of the discount to prevent creditors from sustaining a loss upon liquidation of the corporation.

avoids the contingent liability (see footnote 3) that might occur if the corporation issued par value stock at a discount. Second, some confusion exists over the relationship (or rather the absence of a relationship) between the par value and fair value. If shares have no-par value, **the questionable treatment of using par value as a basis for fair value never arises.** This is particularly advantageous whenever issuing stock for property items such as intangible or tangible fixed assets.

A major disadvantage of no-par stock is that some states levy a high tax on these issues. In addition, in some states the total issue price for no-par stock may be considered legal capital, which could reduce the flexibility in paying dividends.

Corporations sell no-par shares, like par value shares, for whatever price they will bring. However, unlike par value shares, corporations issue them without a premium or a discount. The exact amount received represents the credit to common or preferred stock. For example, Video Electronics Corporation is organized with authorized common stock of 10,000 shares without par value. Video Electronics makes only a memorandum entry for the authorization, inasmuch as no amount is involved. If Video Electronics then issues 500 shares for cash at $10 per share, it makes the following entry.

Cash	5,000	
Common Stock (no-par value)		5,000

If it issues another 500 shares for $11 per share, Video Electronics makes this entry:

Cash	5,500	
Common Stock (no-par value)		5,500

True no-par stock should be carried in the accounts at issue price without any additional paid-in capital or discount reported. But some states require that no-par stock have a stated value. The stated value is a minimum value below which a company cannot issue it. Thus, instead of being no-par stock, such stated-value stock becomes, in effect, stock with a very low par value. It thus is open to all the criticism and abuses that first encouraged the development of no-par stock.[4]

If no-par stock has a stated value of $5 per share but sells for $11, all such amounts in excess of $5 are recorded as additional paid-in capital, which in many states is fully or partially available for dividends. Thus, no-par value stock, with a low stated value, permits a new corporation to commence its operations with additional paid-in capital that may exceed its stated capital. For example, if a company issued 1,000 of the shares with a $5 stated value at $15 per share for cash, it makes the following entry.

Cash	15,000	
Common Stock		5,000
Paid-in Capital in Excess of Stated Value—Common Stock		10,000

Most corporations account for no-par stock with a stated value as if it were par value stock with par equal to the stated value.

Stock Issued with Other Securities (Lump-Sum Sales)

Generally, corporations sell classes of stock separately from one another. The reason to do so is to track the proceeds relative to each class, as well as relative to each lot. Occasionally, a corporation issues two or more classes of securities for a single payment or lump sum (e.g., in the acquisition of another company). The accounting problem in such lump-sum sales is how to allocate the proceeds among the several classes of securities. Companies use one of two methods of allocation: (1) the proportional method and (2) the incremental method.

---

[4]*Accounting Trends and Techniques—2010* indicates that its 500 surveyed companies reported 478 issues of outstanding common stock, 467 par value issues, and 52 no-par issues; 5 of the no-par issues were shown at their stated (assigned) values.

Proportional Method. If the fair value or other sound basis for determining relative value is available for each class of security, **the company allocates the lump sum received among the classes of securities on a proportional basis**. For instance, assume a company issues 1,000 shares of $10 stated value common stock having a fair value of $20 a share, and 1,000 shares of $10 par value preferred stock having a fair value of $12 a share, for a lump sum of $30,000. Illustration 15-1 shows how the company allocates the $30,000 to the two classes of stock.

ILLUSTRATION 15-1
Allocation in Lump-Sum Securities Issuance—Proportional Method

```
Fair value of common (1,000 × $20) =  $20,000
Fair value of preferred (1,000 × $12) =   12,000
Aggregate fair value                    $32,000

Allocated to common:    $20,000  × $30,000 = $18,750
                        $32,000

Allocated to preferred:  $12,000  × $30,000 = $11,250
                        $32,000

Total allocation                        $30,000
```

Incremental Method. In instances where a company cannot determine the fair value of all classes of securities, it may use the incremental method. It uses the fair value of the securities as a basis for those classes that it knows, and allocates the remainder of the lump sum to the class for which it does not know the fair value. For instance, if a company issues 1,000 shares of $10 stated value common stock having a fair value of $20, and 1,000 shares of $10 par value preferred stock having no established fair value, for a lump sum of $30,000, it allocates the $30,000 to the two classes as shown in Illustration 15-2.

ILLUSTRATION 15-2
Allocation in Lump-Sum Securities Issuance—Incremental Method

```
Lump-sum receipt                        $30,000
Allocated to common (1,000 × $20)      (20,000)
Balance allocated to preferred          $10,000
```

If a company cannot determine fair value for any of the classes of stock involved in a lump-sum exchange, it may need to use other approaches. It may rely on an expert's appraisal. Or, if the company knows that one or more of the classes of securities issued will have a determinable fair value in the near future, it may use a best estimate basis with the intent to adjust later, upon establishment of the future fair value.

Stock Issued in Noncash Transactions

Accounting for the issuance of shares of stock for property or services involves an issue of valuation. **The general rule is: Companies should record stock issued for services or property other than cash at either the fair value of the stock issued or the fair value of the noncash consideration received, whichever is more clearly determinable.**

If a company can readily determine both, and the transaction results from an arm's-length exchange, there will probably be little difference in their fair values. In such cases, the basis for valuing the exchange should not matter.

If a company cannot readily determine either the fair value of the stock it issues or the property or services it receives, it should employ an appropriate valuation technique. Depending on available data, the valuation may be based on market transactions involving comparable assets or the use of discounted expected future cash flows. Companies should avoid the use of the book, par, or stated values as a basis of valuation for these transactions.

A company may exchange unissued stock or treasury stock (issued shares that it has reacquired but not retired) for property or services. If it uses treasury shares, the cost of the treasury shares **should not** be considered the decisive factor in establishing the fair value of the property or services. Instead, it should use the fair value of the treasury stock, if known, to value the property or services. Otherwise, if it does not know the fair value of the treasury stock, it should use the fair value of the property or services received, if determinable.

The following series of transactions illustrates the procedure for recording the issuance of 10,000 shares of $10 par value common stock for a patent for Marlowe Company, in various circumstances.

1. Marlowe cannot readily determine the fair value of the patent, but it knows the fair value of the stock is $140,000.

Patents	140,000	
Common Stock (10,000 shares × $10 per share)		100,000
Paid-in Capital in Excess of Par—Common Stock		40,000

2. Marlowe cannot readily determine the fair value of the stock, but it determines the fair value of the patent is $150,000.

Patents	150,000	
Common Stock (10,000 shares × $10 per share)		100,000
Paid-in Capital in Excess of Par—Common Stock		50,000

3. Marlowe cannot readily determine the fair value of the stock nor the fair value of the patent. An independent consultant values the patent at $125,000 based on discounted expected cash flows.

Patents	125,000	
Common Stock (10,000 shares × $10 share)		100,000
Paid-in Capital in Excess of Par—Common Stock		25,000

In corporate law, the board of directors has the power to set the value of noncash transactions. However, boards sometimes abuse this power. The issuance of stock for property or services has resulted in cases of overstated corporate capital through intentional overvaluation of the property or services received. The overvaluation of the stockholders' equity resulting from inflated asset values creates **watered stock**. The corporation should eliminate the "water" by simply writing down the overvalued assets.

If, as a result of the issuance of stock for property or services, a corporation undervalues the recorded assets, it creates **secret reserves**. An understated corporate structure (secret reserve) may also result from other methods: excessive depreciation or amortization charges, expensing capital expenditures, excessive write-downs of inventories or receivables, or any other understatement of assets or overstatement of liabilities. An example of a liability overstatement is an excessive provision for estimated product warranties that ultimately results in an understatement of owners' equity, thereby creating a secret reserve.

Costs of Issuing Stock

When a company like Walgreens issues stock, it should report direct costs incurred to sell stock, such as underwriting costs, accounting and legal fees, printing costs, and taxes, as a reduction of the amounts paid in. Walgreens therefore debits issue costs to Paid-in Capital in Excess of Par—Common Stock because they are unrelated to corporate operations. In effect, **issue costs are a cost of financing.** As such, issue costs should reduce the proceeds received from the sale of the stock.

Walgreens should expense management salaries and other indirect costs related to the stock issue because it is difficult to establish a relationship between these costs and the sale proceeds. In addition, Walgreens expenses recurring costs, primarily registrar and transfer agents' fees, as incurred.

THE CASE OF THE DISAPPEARING RECEIVABLE

What do the numbers mean?

Sometimes companies issue stock but may not receive cash in return. As a result, a company records a receivable.

Controversy existed regarding the presentation of this receivable on the balance sheet. Some argued that the company should report the receivable as an asset similar to other receivables. Others argued that the company should report the receivable as a deduction from stockholders' equity (similar to the treatment of treasury stock). The SEC settled this issue: It requires companies to use the contra-equity approach because the risk of collection in this type of transaction is often very high.

This accounting issue surfaced in Enron's accounting. Starting in early 2000, Enron issued shares of its common stock to four "special-purpose entities," in exchange for which it received a note receivable. Enron then increased its assets (by recording a receivable) and stockholders' equity, a move the company now calls an accounting error. As a result of this accounting treatment, Enron overstated assets and stockholders' equity by $172 million in its 2000 audited financial statements and by $828 million in its unaudited 2001 statements. This $1 billion overstatement was 8.5 percent of Enron's previously reported stockholders' equity at that time.

As Lynn Turner, former chief accountant of the SEC, noted, "It is a basic accounting principle that you don't record equity until you get cash, and a note doesn't count as cash." Situations like this led investors, creditors, and suppliers to lose faith in the credibility of Enron, which eventually caused its bankruptcy.

Source: Adapted from Jonathan Weil, "Basic Accounting Tripped Up Enron—Financial Statements Didn't Add Up—Auditors Overlook a Simple Rule," *Wall Street Journal* (November 11, 2001), p. C1.

Reacquisition of Shares

Companies often buy back their own shares. In fact, share buybacks now exceed dividends as a form of distribution to stockholders. For example, oil producer ConocoPhillips, health-care–products giant Johnson & Johnson, and discount retailer Wal-Mart Stores have ambitious buyback plans.

4 LEARNING OBJECTIVE
Describe the accounting for treasury stock.

Buybacks more than doubled from 2004 to 2007. However, as a result of the financial crisis, the buyback trend slowed in 2008, with buybacks declining 40 percent from 2007 highs. But 2009 buybacks rebounded, led by major companies like IBM, which announced a $5 billion buyback.[5]

Corporations purchase their outstanding stock for several reasons:

1. *To provide tax-efficient distributions of excess cash to shareholders.* Capital gain rates on sales of stock to the company by the stockholders have been approximately half the ordinary tax rate for many investors. This advantage has been somewhat diminished by recent changes in the tax law related to dividends.

2. *To increase earnings per share and return on equity.* Reducing both shares outstanding and stockholders' equity often enhances certain performance ratios. However, strategies to hype performance measures might increase performance in the short-run, but these tactics add no real long-term value.

3. *To provide stock for employee stock compensation contracts or to meet potential merger needs.* Honeywell Inc. reported that it would use part of its purchase of one million common shares for employee stock option contracts. Other companies acquire shares to have them available for business acquisitions.

[5]"R. Waters, "IBM Plans to Boost Buybacks by $5 Billion," *Financial Times* (October 27, 2009). In the early 1990s, share buybacks were less than half the level of dividends. Companies are extremely reluctant to reduce or eliminate their dividends, because they believe that the market negatively views this action.

4. *To thwart takeover attempts or to reduce the number of stockholders.* By reducing the number of shares held by the public, existing owners and managements bar "outsiders" from gaining control or significant influence. When Ted Turner attempted to acquire CBS, CBS started a substantial buyback of its stock. Companies may also use stock purchases to eliminate dissident stockholders.

5. *To make a market in the stock.* As one company executive noted, "Our company is trying to establish a floor for the stock." Purchasing stock in the marketplace creates a demand. This may stabilize the stock price or, in fact, increase it.

Some publicly held corporations have chosen to "go private," that is, to eliminate public (outside) ownership entirely by purchasing all of their outstanding stock. Companies often accomplish such a procedure through a leveraged buyout (LBO), in which the company borrows money to finance the stock repurchases.

After reacquiring shares, a company may either retire them or hold them in the treasury for reissue. If not retired, such shares are referred to as treasury stock (**treasury shares**). Technically, treasury stock is a corporation's own stock, reacquired after having been issued and fully paid.

Treasury stock is not an asset. When a company purchases treasury stock, a reduction occurs in both assets and stockholders' equity. It is inappropriate to imply that a corporation can own a part of itself. A corporation may sell treasury stock to obtain funds, but that does not make treasury stock a balance sheet asset. When a corporation buys back some of its own outstanding stock, it has not acquired an asset; it reduces net assets.

The possession of treasury stock does not give the corporation the right to vote, to exercise preemptive rights as a stockholder, to receive cash dividends, or to receive assets upon corporate liquidation. **Treasury stock is essentially the same as unissued capital stock.** No one advocates classifying unissued capital stock as an asset in the balance sheet.[6]

> **Underlying Concepts**
>
> As we indicated in Chapter 2, an asset should have probable future economic benefits. Treasury stock simply reduces common stock outstanding.

SIGNALS TO BUY?

What do the numbers mean?

Market analysts sometimes look to stock buybacks as a buy signal for a stock. That strategy is not that surprising if you look at the performance of companies that did buybacks. For example, in one study, buyback companies outperformed similar companies without buybacks by an average of 23 percent. In a recent three-year period, companies followed by Buybackletter.com were up 16.4 percent, while the S&P 500 Stock Index was up just 7.1 percent in that period. Why the premium? Well, the conventional wisdom is that companies who buy back shares believe their shares are undervalued. Thus, analysts view the buyback announcement as an important piece of inside information about future company prospects.

On the other hand, buybacks can actually hurt businesses and their shareholders over the long-run. For example, drug-makers Merck, Pfizer, and Amgen spent heavily on stock repurchases, possibly at the expense of research and development. Whether the buyback is a good thing appears to depend a lot on why the company did the buyback and what the repurchased shares were used for. One study found that companies often increased their buybacks when earnings growth slowed. This allowed the companies to prop up earnings per share (based on fewer shares outstanding). Furthermore, many buybacks do not actually result in a net reduction in shares outstanding. For example, companies such as Microsoft and Broadcom bought back shares to meet share demands for stock option exercises, resulting in higher net shares outstanding when it reissued the repurchased shares to the option holders upon exercise. In

---

[6]The possible justification for classifying these shares as assets is that the company will use them to liquidate a specific liability that appears on the balance sheet. *Accounting Trends and Techniques—2010* reported that out of 500 companies surveyed, 340 disclosed treasury stock, but none classified it as an asset.

this case, the buyback actually indicated a further dilution in the share ownership in the buy-back company.

This does not mean you should never trust a buyback signal. But if the buyback is intended to manage the company's earnings or if the buyback results in dilution, take a closer look.

Source: Adapted from Ann Tergesen, "When Buybacks Are Signals to Buy," *Business Week Online* (October 1, 2001); Rachel Beck, "Stock BuyBacks Not Always Good for the Company, Shareholders," *Naples [FL] Daily News* (March 7, 2004). p. I1; and W. Lazonick, "The Buyback Boondoggle," *BusinessWeek* (August 24, 2009).

What do the numbers mean? (continued)

Purchase of Treasury Stock

Companies use two general methods of handling treasury stock in the accounts: the cost method and the par value method. Both methods are generally acceptable. The cost method enjoys more widespread use.[7]

Gateway to the Profession

Discussion of Using Par or Stated Value for Treasury Stock Transactions

- The cost method results in debiting the Treasury Stock account for the reacquisition cost and in reporting this account as a deduction from the total paid-in capital **and** retained earnings on the balance sheet.

- The par or stated value method records all transactions in treasury shares at their par value and reports the treasury stock as a deduction from capital stock only.

No matter which method a company uses, most states consider the cost of the treasury shares acquired as a restriction on retained earnings.

Companies generally use the cost method to account for treasury stock. This method derives its name from the fact that a company maintains the Treasury Stock account at the cost of the shares purchased.[8] Under the cost method, the company debits the Treasury Stock account for the cost of the shares acquired. Upon reissuance of the shares, it credits the account for this same cost. The original price received for the stock does not affect the entries to record the acquisition and reissuance of the treasury stock.

To illustrate, assume that Pacific Company issued 100,000 shares of $1 par value common stock at a price of $10 per share. In addition, it has retained earnings of $300,000. Illustration 15-3 shows the stockholders' equity section on December 31, 2011, before purchase of treasury stock.

Stockholders' equity		
Paid-in capital		
Common stock, $1 par value, 100,000 shares		
issued and outstanding		$ 100,000
Additional paid-in capital		900,000
Total paid-in capital		1,000,000
Retained earnings		300,000
Total stockholders' equity		$1,300,000

ILLUSTRATION 15-3
Stockholders' Equity with No Treasury Stock

On January 20, 2012, Pacific acquires 10,000 shares of its stock at $11 per share. Pacific records the reacquisition as follows.

January 20, 2012

Treasury Stock	110,000	
Cash		110,000

Note that Pacific debited Treasury Stock for the cost of the shares purchased. The original paid-in capital account, Common Stock, is not affected because the number of issued

---

[7]*Accounting Trends and Techniques—2010* indicates that of its selected list of 500 companies, 321 carried common stock in treasury at cost and only 19 at par or stated value; no companies carried preferred stock in treasury.

[8]If making numerous acquisitions of blocks of treasury shares at different prices, a company may use inventory costing methods—such as specific identification, average cost, or FIFO—to identify the cost at date of reissuance.

shares does not change. The same is true for the Paid-in Capital in Excess of Par—Common Stock account. Pacific deducts treasury stock from total paid-in capital and retained earnings in the stockholders' equity section.

Illustration 15-4 shows the stockholders' equity section for Pacific after purchase of the treasury stock.

ILLUSTRATION 15-4
Stockholders' Equity
with Treasury Stock

Stockholders' equity		
Paid-in capital		
Common stock, $1 par value, 100,000 shares		
issued and 90,000 outstanding	$ 100,000	
Additional paid-in capital	900,000	
Total paid-in capital	1,000,000	
Retained earnings	300,000	
Total paid-in capital and retained earnings	1,300,000	
Less: Cost of treasury stock (10,000 shares)	110,000	
Total stockholders' equity	$1,190,000	

Pacific subtracts the cost of the treasury stock from the total of common stock, additional paid-in capital, and retained earnings. It therefore reduces stockholders' equity. Many states require a corporation to restrict retained earnings for the cost of treasury stock purchased. The restriction keeps intact the corporation's legal capital that it temporarily holds as treasury stock. When the corporation sells the treasury stock, it lifts the restriction.

Pacific discloses both the number of shares issued (100,000) and the number in the treasury (10,000). The difference is the number of shares of stock outstanding (90,000). The term **outstanding stock** means the number of shares of issued stock that stockholders own.

Sale of Treasury Stock

Companies usually reissue or retire treasury stock. When selling treasury shares, the accounting for the sale depends on the price. If the selling price of the treasury stock equals its cost, the company records the sale of the shares by debiting Cash and crediting Treasury Stock. In cases where the selling price of the treasury stock is not equal to cost, then accounting for treasury stock sold **above cost** differs from the accounting for treasury stock sold **below cost**. However, the sale of treasury stock either above or below cost increases both total assets and stockholders' equity.

Sale of Treasury Stock above Cost. When the selling price of shares of treasury stock exceeds its cost, a company credits the difference to Paid-in Capital from Treasury Stock. To illustrate, assume that Pacific acquired 10,000 shares of its treasury stock at $11 per share. It now sells 1,000 shares at $15 per share on March 10. Pacific records the entry as follows.

March 10, 2012		
Cash	15,000	
Treasury Stock		11,000
Paid-in Capital from Treasury Stock		4,000

There are two reasons why Pacific does not credit $4,000 to Gain on Sale of Treasury Stock: (1) Gains on sales occur when selling **assets**; treasury stock is not an asset. (2) A gain or loss should not be recognized from stock transactions with its own stockholders. Thus, Pacific should not include paid-in capital arising from the sale of treasury stock in the measurement of net income. Instead, it lists paid-in capital from treasury stock separately on the balance sheet, as a part of paid-in capital.

Sale of Treasury Stock below Cost. When a corporation sells treasury stock below its cost, it usually debits the excess of the cost over selling price to Paid-in Capital from Treasury Stock. Thus, if Pacific sells an additional 1,000 shares of treasury stock on March 21 at $8 per share, it records the sale as follows.

March 21, 2012

Cash	8,000	
Paid-in Capital from Treasury Stock	3,000	
Treasury Stock		11,000

We can make several observations based on the two sale entries (sale above cost and sale below cost): (1) Pacific credits Treasury Stock at cost in each entry. (2) Pacific uses Paid-in Capital from Treasury Stock for the difference between the cost and the resale price of the shares. (3) Neither entry affects the original paid-in capital account, Common Stock.

After eliminating the credit balance in Paid-in Capital from Treasury Stock, the corporation debits any additional excess of cost over selling price to Retained Earnings. To illustrate, assume that Pacific sells an additional 1,000 shares at $8 per share on April 10. Illustration 15-5 shows the balance in the Paid-in Capital from Treasury Stock account (before the April 10 purchase).

Paid-in Capital from Treasury Stock				
Mar. 21	3,000	Mar. 10	4,000	
		Balance	1,000	

ILLUSTRATION 15-5
Treasury Stock Transactions in Paid-in Capital Account

In this case, Pacific debits $1,000 of the excess to Paid-in Capital from Treasury Stock. It debits the remainder to Retained Earnings. The entry is:

April 10, 2012

Cash	8,000	
Paid-in Capital from Treasury Stock	1,000	
Retained Earnings	2,000	
Treasury Stock		11,000

Retiring Treasury Stock

The board of directors may approve the retirement of treasury shares. This decision results in cancellation of the treasury stock and a reduction in the number of shares of issued stock. Retired treasury shares have the status of authorized and unissued shares. The accounting effects are similar to the sale of treasury stock except that corporations debit the **paid-in capital accounts applicable to the retired shares** instead of cash. For example, if a corporation originally sells the shares at par, it debits Common Stock for the par value per share. If it originally sells the shares at $3 above par value, it also debits Paid-in Capital in Excess of Par—Common Stock for $3 per share at retirement.

NOT SO GOOD ANYMORE

Volatility in the markets can lead to wide swings in share repurchase activity. For example, share buybacks—following a long run of high buyback activity—tumbled 66 percent in a recent quarter from a year earlier among companies in the S&P 500 Index. Specifically, buybacks fell 42 percent in all of 2008 from the record that $589.1 billion members spent on buybacks in 2007. Why the pullback in buybacks? One experienced analyst reasoned that many companies have eliminated buybacks in a bid to boost liquidity and preserve cash in the face of tight credit markets and as many incur huge losses or have debt coming due that they are unable to refinance. Indeed, cash levels recently hit a record among index members as they cut spending in a host of areas. The reluctance of U.S. companies to spend money on share repurchases reflects what another analyst called a "storm-center mentality." Financial officers, watching companies teeter because of arid credit conditions and slowing business, have prioritized cash preservation above all else. And share repurchases are considered more "discretionary" than quarterly dividends from a corporate perspective.

What do the numbers mean?

Source: K. Grace and R. Curran, "Stock Buybacks Plummet," *Wall Street Journal* (March 27, 2009), p. C9.

PREFERRED STOCK

LEARNING OBJECTIVE 5
Explain the accounting for and
reporting of preferred stock.

As noted earlier, **preferred stock** is a special class of shares that possesses certain preferences or features not possessed by the common stock.[9] The following features are those most often associated with preferred stock issues.

1. Preference as to dividends.
2. Preference as to assets in the event of liquidation.
3. Convertible into common stock.
4. Callable at the option of the corporation.
5. Nonvoting.

The features that distinguish preferred from common stock may be of a more restrictive and negative nature than preferences. For example, the preferred stock may be nonvoting, noncumulative, and nonparticipating.

Companies usually issue preferred stock with a par value, expressing the dividend preference as a **percentage of the par value**. Thus, holders of 8 percent preferred stock with a $100 par value are entitled to an annual dividend of $8 per share. This stock is commonly referred to as 8 percent preferred stock. In the case of no-par preferred stock, a corporation expresses a dividend preference as a **specific dollar amount** per share, for example, $7 per share. This stock is commonly referred to as $7 preferred stock.

A preference as to dividends does not assure the payment of dividends. It merely assures that **the corporation must pay the stated dividend rate or amount applicable to the preferred stock before paying any dividends on the common stock**.

A company often issues preferred stock (instead of debt) because of a high debt-to-equity ratio. In other instances, it issues preferred stock through private placements with other corporations at a lower-than-market dividend rate because the acquiring corporation receives largely tax-free dividends (owing to the IRS's 70 percent or 80 percent dividends received deduction).

Features of Preferred Stock

A corporation may attach whatever preferences or restrictions, in whatever combination it desires, to a preferred stock issue, as long as it does not specifically violate its state incorporation law. Also, it may issue more than one class of preferred stock. We discuss the most common features attributed to preferred stock below.

Cumulative Preferred Stock

Cumulative preferred stock requires that if a corporation fails to pay a dividend in any year, it must make it up in a later year before paying any dividends to common stockholders. If the directors fail to declare a dividend at the normal date for dividend action, the dividend is said to have been "passed." Any passed dividend on cumulative preferred stock constitutes a **dividend in arrears**. Because no liability exists until the board of directors declares a dividend, a corporation does not record a dividend in arrears as a liability but discloses it in a note to the financial statements. A corporation seldom issues noncumulative preferred stock because a passed dividend is lost forever to the preferred stockholder. As a result, this stock issue would be less marketable.

Participating Preferred Stock

Holders of **participating preferred stock** share ratably with the common stockholders in any profit distributions beyond the prescribed rate. That is, 5 percent preferred stock,

---

[9]*Accounting Trends and Techniques—2010* reports that of its 500 surveyed companies, 39 had one class of preferred stock, and 8 had two or more classes. Of these companies, just 36 had preferred stock outstanding.

if fully participating, will receive not only its 5 percent return, but also dividends at the same rates as those paid to common stockholders if paying amounts in excess of 5 percent of par or stated value to common stockholders. Note that participating preferred stock may be only partially participating. Although seldom used, examples of companies that have issued participating preferred stock are LTV Corporation, Southern California Edison, and Allied Products Corporation.

Convertible Preferred Stock

Convertible preferred stock allows stockholders, at their option, to exchange preferred shares for common stock at a predetermined ratio. The convertible preferred stockholder not only enjoys a preferred claim on dividends but also has the option of converting into a common stockholder with unlimited participation in earnings.

Callable Preferred Stock

Callable preferred stock permits the corporation at its option to call or redeem the outstanding preferred shares at specified future dates and at stipulated prices. Many preferred issues are callable. The corporation usually sets the call or redemption price slightly above the original issuance price and commonly states it in terms related to the par value. The callable feature permits the corporation to use the capital obtained through the issuance of such stock until the need has passed or it is no longer advantageous.

The existence of a call price or prices tends to set a ceiling on the market value of the preferred shares unless they are convertible into common stock. When a corporation redeems preferred stock, it must pay any dividends in arrears.

Redeemable Preferred Stock

Recently, more and more issuances of preferred stock have features that make the security more like debt (legal obligation to pay) than an equity instrument. For example, redeemable preferred stock has a mandatory redemption period or a redemption feature that the issuer cannot control.

Previously, public companies were not permitted to report these debt-like preferred stock issues in equity, but they were not required to report them as a liability either. There were concerns about classification of these debt-like securities, which may have been reported as equity or in the "mezzanine" section of balance sheets between debt and equity. There also was diversity in practice as to how dividends on these securities were reported. The FASB now requires debt-like securities, like redeemable preferred stock, to be classified as liabilities and be measured and accounted for similar to liabilities. [1]

 See the FASB Codification section (page 876).

Accounting for and Reporting Preferred Stock

The accounting for preferred stock at issuance is similar to that for common stock. A corporation allocates proceeds between the par value of the preferred stock and additional paid-in capital. To illustrate, assume that Bishop Co. issues 10,000 shares of $10 par value preferred stock for $12 cash per share. Bishop records the issuance as follows.

Cash	120,000	
Preferred Stock		100,000
Paid-in Capital in Excess of Par—Preferred Stock		20,000

Thus, Bishop maintains separate accounts for these different classes of shares.

In contrast to convertible bonds (recorded as a liability on the date of issue) corporations consider convertible preferred stock as a part of stockholders' equity. In addition, when exercising convertible preferred stock, there is no theoretical justification for recognition of a gain or loss. A company recognizes no gain or loss when dealing with stockholders in their capacity as business owners. Instead, the company **employs the book value method**: debit Preferred Stock, along with any related Paid-in Capital in Excess of Par—Preferred Stock; credit Common Stock and Paid-in Capital in Excess of Par—Common Stock (if an excess exists).

Preferred stock generally has no maturity date. Therefore, no legal obligation exists to pay the preferred stockholder. As a result, companies classify preferred stock as part of stockholders' equity. Companies generally report preferred stock at par value as the first item in the stockholders' equity section. They report any excess over par value as part of additional paid-in capital. They also consider dividends on preferred stock as a distribution of income and not an expense. Companies must disclose the pertinent rights of the preferred stock outstanding. [2]

DIVIDEND POLICY

LEARNING OBJECTIVE 6
Describe the policies used in distributing dividends.

Dividend payouts can be important signals to the market. The practice of paying dividends declined sharply in the 1980s and 1990s as companies focused on growth and plowed profits back into the business. A resurgence in dividend payouts is due in large part to the dividend tax cut of 2003, which reduced the rate of tax on dividends to 15 percent (quite a bit lower than the ordinary income rate charged in the past). In addition, investors who were burned by accounting scandals in recent years began demanding higher payouts in the form of dividends. Why? A dividend check provides proof that at least some portion of a company's profits is genuine.[10]

Determining the proper amount of dividends to pay is a difficult financial management decision. Companies that are paying dividends are extremely reluctant to reduce or eliminate their dividend. They fear that the securities market might negatively view this action. As a consequence, companies that have been paying cash dividends will make every effort to continue to do so. In addition, the type of shareholder the company has (taxable or nontaxable, retail investor or institutional investor) plays a large role in determining dividend policy.

Very few companies pay dividends in amounts equal to their legally available retained earnings. The major reasons are as follows.

1. To maintain agreements (bond covenants) with specific creditors, to retain all or a portion of the earnings, in the form of assets, to build up additional protection against possible loss.

2. To meet state corporation requirements, that earnings equivalent to the cost of treasury shares purchased be restricted against dividend declarations.

3. To retain assets that would otherwise be paid out as dividends, to finance growth or expansion. This is sometimes called internal financing, reinvesting earnings, or "plowing" the profits back into the business.

4. To smooth out dividend payments from year to year by accumulating earnings in good years and using such accumulated earnings as a basis for dividends in bad years.

5. To build up a cushion or buffer against possible losses or errors in the calculation of profits.

The reasons above are self-explanatory except for the second. The laws of some states require that the corporation restrict its legal capital from distribution to stockholders, to protect against loss for creditors.[11] The applicable state law determines the legality of a dividend.

[10]Jeff Opdyke, "Tax Cut, Shareholder Pressure Stoke Surge in Dividends," *Wall Street Journal Online* (January 18, 2005). From January 1972 through July 2007, stocks paying dividends had an average price increase of 10.2 percent a year, versus 2.4 percent for nondividend-paying stocks, as indicated in a recent study (A. Blackman, "How Well Do You Know . . . Dividends?" *Wall Street Journal* (September 10, 2007), p. R5).

[11]If the corporation buys its own outstanding stock, it reduces its legal capital and distributes assets to stockholders. If permitted, the corporation could, by purchasing treasury stock at any price desired, return to the stockholders their investments and leave creditors with little or no protection against loss.

Financial Condition and Dividend Distributions

Effective management of a company requires attention to more than the legality of dividend distributions. Management must also consider economic conditions, most importantly, liquidity. Assume an extreme situation as shown in Illustration 15-6.

ILLUSTRATION 15-6
Balance Sheet, Showing a
Lack of Liquidity

BALANCE SHEET			
Plant assets	$500,000	Capital stock	$400,000
	$500,000	Retained earnings	100,000
			$500,000

The depicted company has a retained earnings credit balance. Unless restricted, it can declare a dividend of $100,000. But because all its assets are plant assets used in operations, payment of a cash dividend of $100,000 would require the sale of plant assets or borrowing.

Even if a balance sheet shows current assets, as in Illustration 15-7, the question remains as to whether the company needs its cash for other purposes.

ILLUSTRATION 15-7
Balance Sheet, Showing
Cash but Minimal
Working Capital

BALANCE SHEET				
Cash	$100,000	Current liabilities		$ 60,000
Plant assets	460,000	Capital stock	$400,000	
	$560,000	Retained earnings	100,000	500,000
				$560,000

The existence of current liabilities strongly implies that the company needs some of the cash to meet current debts as they mature. In addition, day-to-day cash requirements for payrolls and other expenditures not included in current liabilities also require cash.

Thus, before declaring a dividend, management must consider **availability of funds to pay the dividend**. A company should not pay a dividend unless both the present and future financial position warrant the distribution.

The SEC encourages companies to disclose their dividend policy in their annual report, especially those that (1) have earnings but fail to pay dividends, or (2) do not expect to pay dividends in the foreseeable future. In addition, the SEC encourages companies that consistently pay dividends to indicate whether they intend to continue this practice in the future.

Types of Dividends

Companies generally base dividend distributions either on accumulated profits (that is, retained earnings) or on some other capital item such as additional paid-in capital. Dividends are of the following types.

7 LEARNING OBJECTIVE
Identify the various forms of
dividend distributions.

1. Cash dividends.
2. Property dividends.
3. Liquidating dividends.
4. Stock dividends.

Although commonly paid in cash, companies occasionally pay dividends in stock or some other asset.[12] **All dividends, except for stock dividends, reduce the total stockholders' equity in the corporation.** When declaring a stock dividend, the corporation does not pay out assets or incur a liability. It issues additional shares of stock to each stockholder and nothing more.

The natural expectation of any stockholder who receives a dividend is that the corporation has operated successfully. As a result, he or she is receiving a share of its profits. A company should disclose a liquidating dividend—that is, a dividend not based on retained earnings—to the stockholders so that they will not misunderstand its source.

Cash Dividends

The board of directors votes on the declaration of cash dividends. Upon approval of the resolution, the board declares a dividend. Before paying it, however, the company must prepare a current list of stockholders. For this reason, there is usually a time lag between declaration and payment. For example, the board of directors might approve a resolution at the January 10 (**date of declaration**) meeting, and declare it payable February 5 (**date of payment**) to all stockholders of record January 25 (**date of record**).[13] In this example, the period from January 10 to January 25 gives time for the company to complete and register any transfers in process. The time from January 25 to February 5 provides an opportunity for the transfer agent or accounting department, depending on who does this work, to prepare a list of stockholders as of January 25 and to prepare and mail dividend checks.

A declared cash dividend is a liability. Because payment is generally required very soon, it is usually a current liability. Companies use the following entries to record the declaration and payment of an ordinary dividend payable in cash. For example, Roadway Freight Corp. on June 10 declared a cash dividend of 50 cents a share on 1.8 million shares payable July 16 to all stockholders of record June 24.

At date of declaration (June 10)

Retained Earnings (Cash Dividends Declared)	900,000	
Dividends Payable		900,000

At date of record (June 24)

No entry

At date of payment (July 16)

Dividends Payable	900,000	
Cash		900,000

To set up a ledger account that shows the amount of dividends declared during the year, Roadway Freight might debit Cash Dividends Declared instead of Retained Earnings at the time of declaration. It then closes this account to Retained Earnings at year-end.

A company may declare dividends either as a certain percent of par, such as a 6 percent dividend on preferred stock, or as an amount per share, such as 60 cents per share on no-par common stock. In the first case, the rate multiplied by the par value of

---

[12]*Accounting Trends and Techniques—2010* reported that of its 500 surveyed companies, 328 paid a cash dividend on common stock, 22 paid a cash dividend on preferred stock, none issued stock dividends, and 3 issued or paid dividends in kind. Some companies declare more than one type of dividend in a given year.

[13]Theoretically, the ex-dividend date is the day after the date of record. However, to allow time for transfer of the shares, the stock exchanges generally advance the ex-dividend date two to four days. Therefore, the party who owns the stock on the day prior to the expressed ex-dividend date receives the dividends. The party who buys the stock on and after the ex-dividend date does not receive the dividend. Between the declaration date and the ex-dividend date, the market price of the stock includes the dividend.

outstanding shares equals the total dividend. In the second, the dividend equals the amount per share multiplied by the number of shares outstanding. **Companies do not declare or pay cash dividends on treasury stock.**

Dividend policies vary among corporations. Some companies, such as JP Morgan Chase, Clorox Co., and Tootsie Roll Industries, take pride in a long, unbroken string of quarterly dividend payments. They would lower or pass the dividend only if forced to do so by a sustained decline in earnings or a critical shortage of cash.

"Growth" companies, on the other hand, pay little or no cash dividends because their policy is to expand as rapidly as internal and external financing permit. For example, Questcor Pharmaceuticals Inc. has never paid cash dividends to its common stockholders. These investors hope that the price of their shares will appreciate in value. The investors will then realize a profit when they sell their shares. Many companies focus more on increasing share price, stock repurchase programs, and corporate earnings than on dividend payout.

Property Dividends

Dividends payable in assets of the corporation other than cash are called property dividends or **dividends in kind.** Property dividends may be merchandise, real estate, or investments, or whatever form the board of directors designates. Ranchers Exploration and Development Corp. reported one year that it would pay a fourth-quarter dividend in gold bars instead of cash. Because of the obvious difficulties of divisibility of units and delivery to stockholders, the usual property dividend is in the form of securities of other companies that the distributing corporation holds as an investment.

For example, after ruling that DuPont's 23 percent stock interest in General Motors (GM) violated antitrust laws, the Supreme Court ordered DuPont to divest itself of the GM stock within 10 years. The stock represented 63 million shares of GM's 281 million shares then outstanding. DuPont could not sell the shares in one block of 63 million. Further, it could not sell 6 million shares annually for the next 10 years without severely depressing the value of the GM stock. DuPont solved its problem by declaring a property dividend and distributing the GM shares as a dividend to its own stockholders.

When declaring a property dividend, the corporation should **restate at fair value the property it will distribute**, **recognizing any gain or loss** as the difference between the property's fair value and carrying value at date of declaration. The corporation may then record the declared dividend as a debit to Retained Earnings (or Property Dividends Declared) and a credit to Property Dividends Payable, at an amount equal to the fair value of the distributed property. Upon distribution of the dividend, the corporation debits Property Dividends Payable and credits the account containing the distributed asset (restated at fair value).

For example, Trendler, Inc. transferred to stockholders some of its equity investments costing $1,250,000 by declaring a property dividend on December 28, 2011, to be distributed on January 30, 2012, to stockholders of record on January 15, 2012. At the date of declaration, the securities have a market price of $2,000,000. Trendler makes the following entries.

At date of declaration (December 28, 2011)

Equity Investments	750,000	
Unrealized Holding Gain or Loss—Income		750,000
Retained Earnings (property dividends declared)	2,000,000	
Property Dividends Payable		2,000,000

At date of distribution (January 30, 2012)

Property Dividends Payable	2,000,000	
Equity Investments		2,000,000

Liquidating Dividends

Some corporations use paid-in capital as a basis for dividends. Without proper disclosure of this fact, stockholders may erroneously believe the corporation has been operating at a profit. To avoid this type of deception, intentional or unintentional, a clear statement of the source of every dividend should accompany the dividend check.

Dividends based on other than retained earnings are sometimes described as liquidating dividends. This term implies that such dividends are a return of the stockholder's investment rather than of profits. In other words, **any dividend not based on earnings reduces corporate paid-in capital and to that extent, it is a liquidating dividend**. Companies in the extractive industries may pay dividends equal to the total of accumulated income and depletion. The portion of these dividends in excess of accumulated income represents a return of part of the stockholder's investment.

For example, McChesney Mines Inc. issued a "dividend" to its common stockholders of $1,200,000. The cash dividend announcement noted that stockholders should consider $900,000 as income and the remainder a return of capital. McChesney Mines records the dividend as follows.

At date of declaration

Retained Earnings	900,000	
Paid-in Capital in Excess of Par—Common Stock	300,000	
Dividends Payable		1,200,000

At date of payment

Dividends Payable	1,200,000	
Cash		1,200,000

In some cases, management simply decides to cease business and declares a liquidating dividend. In these cases, liquidation may take place over a number of years to ensure an orderly and fair sale of assets. For example, when Overseas National Airways dissolved, it agreed to pay a liquidating dividend to its stockholders over a period of years equivalent to $8.60 per share. Each liquidating dividend payment in such cases reduces paid-in capital.

Stock Dividends

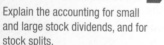

LEARNING OBJECTIVE 8

Explain the accounting for small and large stock dividends, and for stock splits.

Underlying Concepts

By requiring fair value, the intent was to punish companies that used stock dividends. This approach violates the neutrality concept (that is, that standards-setting should be even-handed).

If management wishes to "capitalize" part of the earnings (i.e., reclassify amounts from earned to contributed capital), and thus retain earnings in the business on a permanent basis, it may issue a stock dividend. In this case, **the company distributes no assets**. Each stockholder maintains exactly the same proportionate interest in the corporation and the same total book value after the company issues the stock dividend. Of course, the book value per share is lower because each stockholder holds more shares.

A stock dividend therefore is the issuance by a corporation of its own stock to its stockholders on a pro rata basis, without receiving any consideration. In recording a stock dividend, some believe that the company should transfer the **par value of the stock issued** as a dividend from retained earnings to capital stock. Others believe that it should transfer the **fair value of the stock issued**—its market value at the declaration date—from retained earnings to capital stock and additional paid-in capital.

The fair value position was adopted, at least in part, in order to influence the stock dividend policies of corporations. Evidently in 1941, both the New York Stock Exchange and many in the accounting profession regarded periodic stock dividends as objectionable. They believed that the term dividend when used with a distribution of additional stock was misleading because investors' net assets did not increase as a result of this "dividend." As a result, these groups decided to make it more difficult for corporations to sustain a series of such stock dividends out of their accumulated earnings, by requiring the use of fair value when it substantially exceeded book value.[14]

When the stock dividend is less than 20–25 percent of the common shares outstanding at the time of the dividend declaration, the company is therefore required to transfer the **fair value** of the stock issued from retained earnings. Stock dividends of less than 20–25 percent are often referred to as small (ordinary) stock dividends. This method of handling stock dividends is justified on the grounds that "many recipients of stock dividends look upon them as distributions of corporate earnings and usually in an amount equivalent to the fair value of the additional shares received." [3] We consider this argument unconvincing. It is generally agreed that stock dividends are not income to the recipients. Therefore, sound accounting should not recommend procedures simply because some recipients think they are income.[15]

To illustrate a small stock dividend, assume that Vine Corporation has outstanding 1,000 shares of $100 par value capital stock and retained earnings of $50,000. If Vine declares a 10 percent stock dividend, it issues 100 additional shares to current stockholders. If the fair value of the stock at the time of the stock dividend is $130 per share, the entry is:

At date of declaration

Retained Earnings	13,000	
Common Stock Dividend Distributable		10,000
Paid-in Capital in Excess of Par—Common Stock		3,000

Note that the stock dividend does not affect any asset or liability. **The entry merely reflects a reclassification of stockholders' equity**. If Vine prepares a balance sheet between the dates of declaration and distribution, it should show the common stock dividend distributable in the stockholders' equity section as an addition to capital stock (whereas it shows cash or property dividends payable as current liabilities).

When issuing the stock, the entry is:

At date of distribution

Common Stock Dividend Distributable	10,000	
Common Stock		10,000

No matter what the fair value is at the time of the stock dividend, each stockholder retains the same proportionate interest in the corporation.

Some state statutes specifically prohibit the issuance of stock dividends on treasury stock. In those states that permit treasury shares to participate in the distribution accompanying a stock dividend or stock split, the planned use of the treasury shares influences corporate practice. For example, if a corporation issues treasury shares in connection with employee stock options, the treasury shares may participate in the distribution because the corporation usually adjusts the number of shares under option for any stock dividends or splits. But no useful purpose is served by issuing additional shares to the treasury stock without a specific purpose, since they are essentially equivalent to authorized but unissued shares.

To continue with our example of the effect of the small stock dividend, note in Illustration 15-8 (on page 864) that the stock dividend does not change the total

[14]This was perhaps the earliest instance of "economic consequences" affecting an accounting pronouncement. The Committee on Accounting Procedure described its action as required by "proper accounting and corporate policy." See Stephen A. Zeff, "The Rise of 'Economic Consequences,'" *The Journal of Accountancy* (December 1978), pp. 53–66.

[15]One study concluded that *small* stock dividends do not always produce significant amounts of extra value on the date after issuance (ex date) and that *large* stock dividends almost always fail to generate extra value on the ex-dividend date. Taylor W. Foster III and Don Vickrey, "The Information Content of Stock Dividend Announcements," *The Accounting Review*, Vol. LIII, No. 2 (April 1978), pp. 360–370.

ILLUSTRATION 15-8
Effects of a Small (10%)
Stock Dividend

Before dividend	
Common stock, 1,000 shares of $100 par	$100,000
Retained earnings	50,000
Total stockholders' equity	$150,000
Stockholders' interests:	
A. 400 shares, 40% interest, book value	$ 60,000
B. 500 shares, 50% interest, book value	75,000
C. 100 shares, 10% interest, book value	15,000
	$150,000

After declaration but before distribution of 10% stock dividend

If fair value ($130) is used as basis for entry:	
Common stock, 1,000 shares at $100 par	$100,000
Common stock distributable, 100 shares at $100 par	10,000
Paid-in capital in excess of par	3,000
Retained earnings ($50,000 − $13,000)	37,000
Total stockholders' equity	$150,000

After declaration and distribution of 10% stock dividend

If fair value ($130) is used as basis for entry:	
Common stock, 1,100 shares at $100 par	$110,000
Paid-in capital in excess of par	3,000
Retained earnings ($50,000 − $13,000)	37,000
Total stockholders' equity	$150,000
Stockholders' interest:	
A. 440 shares, 40% interest, book value	$ 60,000
B. 550 shares, 50% interest, book value	75,000
C. 110 shares, 10% interest, book value	15,000
	$150,000

stockholders' equity. Also note that it does not change the proportion of the total shares outstanding held by each stockholder.

Stock Split

If a company has undistributed earnings over several years, and accumulates a sizable balance in retained earnings, the market value of its outstanding shares likely increases. Stock issued at prices less than $50 a share can easily attain a market price in excess of $200 a share. The higher the market price of a stock, however, the less readily some investors can purchase it.

The managements of many corporations believe that better public relations depend on wider ownership of the corporation stock. They therefore target a market price sufficiently low to be within range of the majority of potential investors. To reduce the market price of shares, they use the common device of a stock split. For example, after its stock price increased by 25-fold, Qualcomm Inc. split its stock 4-for-1. Qualcomm's stock had risen above $500 per share, raising concerns that Qualcomm could not meet an analyst target of $1,000 per share. The split reduced the analysts' target to $250, which it could better meet with wider distribution of shares at lower trading prices.

From an accounting standpoint, Qualcomm **records no entry for a stock split**. However, it enters a memorandum note to indicate the changed par value of the shares and the increased number of shares. Illustration 15-9 shows the lack of change in stockholders' equity for a 2-for-1 stock split on 1,000 shares of $100 par value stock with the par being halved upon issuance of the additional shares.

ILLUSTRATION 15-9
Effects of a Stock Split

Stockholders' Equity before 2-for-1 Split	
Common stock, 1,000 shares	
at $100 par	$100,000
Retained earnings	50,000
	$150,000

Stockholders' Equity after 2-for-1 Split	
Common stock, 2,000 shares	
at $50 par	$100,000
Retained earnings	50,000
	$150,000

SPLITSVILLE

What do the numbers mean?

Stock splits were all the rage in the booming stock market of the 1990s. Of major companies on the New York Stock Exchange, fewer than 80 companies split shares in 1990. By 1998, with stock prices soaring, over 200 companies split shares. Although the split does not increase a stockholder's proportionate ownership of the company, studies show that split shares usually outperform those that don't split, as well as the market as a whole, for several years after the split. In addition, the splits help the company keep the shares in more attractive price ranges.

What about when the market "turns south"? A number of companies who split their shares in the boom markets of the 1990s have since seen their share prices decline to a point considered too low. For example, since Ameritrade's 12-for-1 split in 1999, its stock price declined over 74 percent, so that it was trading around $6 per share in March 2002. Lucent traded at less than $5 a share following a 4-for-1 split. For some investors, these low-priced stocks are unattractive because some brokerage commissions rely on the number of shares traded, not the dollar amount. Others are concerned that low-priced shares are easier for would-be scamsters to manipulate. And if a company's per share price falls below $1 for 30 consecutive days, it is a violation of stock exchange listing requirements.

Some companies are considering reverse stock splits in which, say, 5 shares are consolidated into one. Thus, a stock previously trading at $5 per share would be part of an unsplit share trading at $25. Unsplitting might thus avoid some of the negative consequences of a low trading price. The downside to this strategy is that analysts might view reverse splits as additional bad news about the direction of the stock price. For example, Webvan, a failed Internet grocer, did a 1-for-25 reverse split just before it entered bankruptcy. And struggling banking giant Citigroup has contemplated a 1-for-30 reverse stock split in an attempt to get its price into a favorable trading range.

Source: Adapted from David Henry, "Stocks: The Case for Unsplitting," *BusinessWeek Online* (April 1, 2002); and L. Kulikowski, "Citigroup: Contemplating Reverse Split," *www.thestreet.com* (May 24, 2010).

Stock Split and Stock Dividend Differentiated

From a legal standpoint, a stock split differs from a stock dividend. How? A stock split increases the number of shares outstanding and decreases the par or stated value per share. **A stock dividend, although it increases the number of shares outstanding, does not decrease the par value; thus, it increases the total par value of outstanding shares.**

The reasons for issuing a stock dividend are numerous and varied. Stock dividends can be primarily a publicity gesture **because many consider stock dividends as dividends.** Another reason is that the corporation may simply wish to retain profits in the business by capitalizing a part of retained earnings. In such a situation, it makes a transfer on declaration of a stock dividend from earned capital to contributed capital.

A corporation may also use a stock dividend, like a stock split, to increase the marketability of the stock, although marketability is often a secondary consideration. If the stock dividend is large, it has the same effect on market price as a stock split. **Whenever corporations issue additional shares for the purpose of reducing the unit market price, then the distribution more closely resembles a stock split than a stock dividend. This effect usually results only if the number of shares issued is more than 20–25 percent of the number of shares previously outstanding.** [4] A stock dividend of more than 20–25 percent of the number of shares previously outstanding is called a large stock dividend.[16] Such a distribution should not be called a stock dividend but instead "a split-up effected in the form of a dividend" or "stock split."

Also, since a split-up effected in the form of a dividend does not alter the par value per share, companies generally are required to transfer the par value amount from retained earnings. In other words, companies transfer from retained earnings to capital stock **the par value of the stock issued**, as opposed to a transfer of the market price of the shares issued as in the case of a small stock dividend.[17] For example, Brown Group, Inc. at one time authorized a 2-for-1 split, effected in the form of a stock dividend. As a result of this authorization, it distributed approximately 10.5 million shares, and transferred more than $39 million representing the par value of the shares issued from Retained Earnings to the Common Stock account.

To illustrate a large stock dividend (stock split-up effected in the form of a dividend), Rockland Steel, Inc. declared a 30 percent stock dividend on November 20, payable December 29 to stockholders of record December 12. At the date of declaration, 1,000,000 shares, par value $10, are outstanding and with a fair value of $200 per share. The entries are:

At date of declaration (November 20)

Retained Earnings	3,000,000	
Common Stock Dividend Distributable		3,000,000

Computation: 1,000,000 shares	300,000 Additional shares
× 30%	× $10 Par value
300,000	$3,000,000

At date of distribution (December 29)

Common Stock Dividend Distributable	3,000,000	
Common Stock		3,000,000

Illustration 15-10 summarizes and compares the effects in the balance sheet and related items of various types of dividends and stock splits.

ILLUSTRATION 15-10
Effects of Dividends and Stock Splits on Financial Statement Elements

Effect on:	Declaration of Cash Dividend	Payment of Cash Dividend	Declaration and Distribution of		
			Small Stock Dividend	Large Stock Dividend	Stock Split
Retained earnings	Decrease	–0–	Decrease[a]	Decrease[b]	–0–
Capital stock	–0–	–0–	Increase[b]	Increase[b]	–0–
Additional paid-in capital	–0–	–0–	Increase[c]	–0–	–0–
Total stockholders' equity	Decrease	–0–	–0–	–0–	–0–
Working capital	Decrease	–0–	–0–	–0–	–0–
Total assets	–0–	Decrease	–0–	–0–	–0–
Number of shares outstanding	–0–	–0–	Increase	Increase	Increase

[a]Market price of shares. [b]Par or stated value of shares. [c]Excess of market price over par.

[16]The SEC has added more precision to the 20–25 percent rule. Specifically, the SEC indicates that companies should consider distributions of 25 percent or more as a "split-up effected in the form of a dividend." Companies should account for distributions of less than 25 percent as a stock dividend. The SEC more precisely defined GAAP here. As a result, public companies follow the SEC rule.

[17]Often, a company records a split-up effected in the form of a dividend as a debit to Paid-in Capital instead of Retained Earnings to indicate that this transaction should affect only paid-in capital accounts. No reduction of retained earnings is required except as indicated by legal requirements. *For homework purposes, assume that the debit is to Retained Earnings.* See, for example, Taylor W. Foster III and Edmund Scribner, "Accounting for Stock Dividends and Stock Splits: Corrections to Textbook Coverage," *Issues in Accounting Education* (February 1998).

DIVIDENDS UP, DIVIDENDS DOWN

Recently, the number of companies paying dividends is down—really down. As indicated in the chart below, for the first time in at least half a century, companies announced more dividend cuts than increases in 2009. But by the end of the year, positive actions were beginning to predominate.

What do the numbers mean?

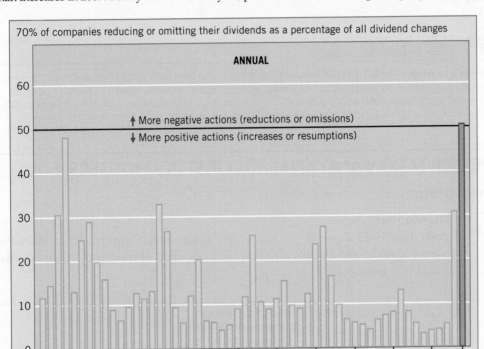

In a normal year, companies announce 10 to 20 times more favorable than unfavorable dividend changes, but the last two years have been anything but normal. Why? Well, it appears the financial crisis forced many financial companies to cut or suspend payments, and the credit crisis and recession led many other companies to cut back wherever they could. Thus, this has not been a good time to be an investor hoping to get a return on your shares through dividends.

However, just as dividends can go down, they can recover. Indeed, by the end of the year, there were indications that the recession was over and the number of negative dividend decisions began to decline. As one analyst noted, "The fourth quarter was in no way a good period for dividends, but compared to recent history it marks a significant improvement, and when added to the stabilization in increases, the worst may be over."

In fact, the sheer rapidity of the plunge could provide an indication that the dividend recovery will be fast. It is possible that some companies made cuts fearing much worse conditions than actually arrived and will therefore be able to raise payouts even without much improvement in business.

Source: F. Norris, "As Dividends Have Fallen, So May They Rise," *New York Times* (January 9, 2010).

Disclosure of Restrictions on Retained Earnings

Many corporations restrict retained earnings or dividends, without any formal journal entries. Such restrictions are **best disclosed by note**. Parenthetical notations are sometimes used, but restrictions imposed by bond indentures and loan agreements commonly require an extended explanation. Notes provide a medium for more complete explanations and free the financial statements from abbreviated notations. The note disclosure should reveal the source of the restriction, pertinent provisions, and the amount of retained earnings subject to restriction, or the amount not restricted.

Restrictions may be based on the retention of a certain retained earnings balance, the ability to maintain certain working capital requirements, additional borrowing, and other considerations. The example from the annual report of Alberto-Culver Company in Illustration 15-11 shows a note disclosing potential restrictions on retained earnings and dividends.

ILLUSTRATION 15-11
Disclosure of
Restrictions on Retained
Earnings and Dividends

Alberto-Culver Company
Note 3 (in part): The $200 million revolving credit facility, the term note, and the receivables agreement impose restrictions on such items as total debt, working capital, dividend payments, treasury stock purchases, and interest expense. At year-end, the company was in compliance with these arrangements, and $220 million of consolidated retained earnings was not restricted as to the payment of dividends.

PRESENTATION AND ANALYSIS OF STOCKHOLDERS' EQUITY

Presentation

LEARNING OBJECTIVE 9
Indicate how to present and analyze stockholders' equity.

Balance Sheet

Illustration 15-12 shows a comprehensive stockholders' equity section from the balance sheet of Frost Company that includes most of the equity items we discussed in this chapter.

ILLUSTRATION 15-12
Comprehensive
Stockholders' Equity
Presentation

FROST COMPANY STOCKHOLDERS' EQUITY DECEMBER 31, 2012		
Capital stock		
Preferred stock, $100 par value, 7% cumulative, 100,000 shares authorized, 30,000 shares issued and outstanding		$ 3,000,000
Common stock, no-par, stated value $10 per share, 500,000 shares authorized, 400,000 shares issued		4,000,000
Common stock dividend distributable, 20,000 shares		200,000
Total capital stock		7,200,000
Additional paid-in capital[18]		
Excess over par—preferred	$150,000	
Excess over stated value—common	840,000	990,000
Total paid-in capital		8,190,000
Retained earnings		4,360,000
Total paid-in capital and retained earnings		12,550,000
Less: Cost of treasury stock (2,000 shares, common)		190,000
Accumulated other comprehensive loss[19]		360,000
Total stockholders' equity		$12,000,000

[18]*Accounting Trends and Techniques—2010* reports that of its 500 surveyed companies, 452 had additional paid-in capital, 285 used the caption "Additional paid-in capital," 76 used "Capital in excess of par or stated value" as the caption, 65 used "Paid-in capital" or "Additional capital," and 26 used other captions.

[19]Companies may include a number of items in the "Accumulated other comprehensive loss." Among these items are "Foreign currency translation adjustments" (covered in advanced accounting), "Unrealized holding gains and losses for available-for-sale securities" (covered in Chapter 17), "Guarantees of employee stock option plan (ESOP) debt," "Unearned or deferred compensation related to employee stock award plans," and others.

Accounting Trends and Techniques—2010 reports that of its 500 surveyed companies, 23 reported cumulative translation adjustments, 23 reported defined benefit postretirement plan adjustments, 13 reported changes in the fair value of derivatives, and 14 reported unrealized losses/gains on certain investments. A number of companies had more than one item.

Frost should disclose the pertinent rights and privileges of the various securities outstanding. For example, companies must disclose all of the following: dividend and liquidation preferences, participation rights, call prices and dates, conversion or exercise prices and pertinent dates, sinking fund requirements, unusual voting rights, and significant terms of contracts to issue additional shares. Liquidation preferences should be disclosed in the equity section of the balance sheet, rather than in the notes to the financial statements, to emphasize the possible effect of this restriction on future cash flows. [5]

Statement of Stockholders' Equity

The statement of stockholders' equity is frequently presented in the following basic format.

1. Balance at the beginning of the period.
2. Additions.
3. Deductions.
4. Balance at the end of the period.

Companies must disclose changes in the separate accounts comprising stockholders' equity, to make the financial statements sufficiently informative.[20] Such changes may be disclosed in separate statements or in the basic financial statements or notes thereto.[21]

A **columnar format** for the presentation of changes in stockholders' equity items in published annual reports is gaining in popularity. An example is Kellogg Company's statement of stockholders' equity, shown in Illustration 15-13.

Kellogg Company and Subsidiaries
Consolidated Statement of Shareholders' Equity

(millions)	Common Stock		Capital in Excess of Par Value	Retained Earnings	Treasury Stock		Accumulated Other Comprehensive Income/(loss)	Total Shareholders' Equity	Total Comprehensive Income
	Shares	Amount			Shares	Amount			
Balance, January 3, 2009	419	$105	$438	$4,836	37	$(1,790)	$(2,141)	$1,448	$ (168)
Common stock repurchases					4	(187)		(187)	
Net income (loss)				1,212				1,212	1,212
Dividends				(546)				(546)	
Other comprehensive income (loss)							175	175	175
Stock compensation			37					37	
Stock options exercised and other			(3)	(21)	(3)	157		133	
Balance, January 2, 2010	419	$105	$472	$5,481	38	$(1,820)	$(1,966)	$2,272	$1,387

ILLUSTRATION 15-13
Columnar Format for Statement of Stockholders' Equity

[20]If a company has other comprehensive income, and computes total comprehensive income only in the statement of stockholders' equity, it must display the statement of stockholders' equity with the same prominence as other financial statements. [6]

[21]*Accounting Trends and Techniques—2010* reports that of the 500 companies surveyed, 490 presented statements of stockholders' equity, 2 presented separate statements of retained earnings only, 2 presented combined statements of income and retained earnings, and 6 presented changes in equity items in the notes only.

Analysis

Analysts use stockholders' equity ratios to evaluate a company's profitability and long-term solvency. We discuss and illustrate the following three ratios below.

1. Rate of return on common stock equity.
2. Payout ratio.
3. Book value per share.

Rate of Return on Common Stock Equity

Gateway to the Profession

Financial Analysis Primer

The **rate of return on common stock equity** measures profitability from the common stockholders' viewpoint. This ratio shows how many dollars of net income the company earned for each dollar invested by the owners. Return on equity (ROE) also helps investors judge the worthiness of a stock when the overall market is not doing well. For example, **Best Buy** shares dropped nearly 40 percent, along with the broader market in 2001–2002. But a review of its return on equity during this period and since shows a steady return of 20 to 22 percent while the overall market ROE declined from 16 percent to 8 percent. More importantly, Best Buy and other stocks, such as **3M** and **Procter & Gamble**, recovered their lost market value, while other stocks with less robust ROEs stayed in the doldrums.

Return on equity equals net income less preferred dividends, divided by average common stockholders' equity. For example, assume that Gerber's Inc. had net income of $360,000, declared and paid preferred dividends of $54,000, and average common stockholders' equity of $2,550,000. Illustration 15-14 shows how to compute Gerber's ratio.

ILLUSTRATION 15-14
Computation of Rate of Return on Common Stock Equity

$$\text{Rate of Return on Common Stock Equity} = \frac{\text{Net income} - \text{Preferred dividends}}{\text{Average common stockholders' equity}}$$

$$= \frac{\$360,000 - \$54,000}{\$2,550,000}$$

$$= 12\%$$

As shown in Illustration 15-14, when preferred stock is present, income available to common stockholders equals net income less preferred dividends. Similarly, the amount of common stock equity used in this ratio equals total stockholders' equity less the par value of preferred stock.

A company can improve its return on common stock equity through the prudent use of debt or preferred stock financing. **Trading on the equity** describes the practice of using borrowed money or issuing preferred stock in hopes of obtaining a higher rate of return on the money used. Shareholders win if return on the assets is higher than the cost of financing these assets. When this happens, the rate of return on common stock equity will exceed the rate of return on total assets. In short, the company is "trading on the equity at a gain." In this situation, the money obtained from bondholders or preferred stockholders earns enough to pay the interest or preferred dividends and leaves a profit for the common stockholders. On the other hand, if the cost of the financing is higher that the rate earned on the assets, the company is trading on equity at a loss and stockholders lose.

Payout Ratio

Another ratio of interest to investors, the **payout ratio**, is the ratio of cash dividends to net income. If preferred stock is outstanding, this ratio equals cash dividends paid to common stockholders, divided by net income available to common stockholders. For example, assume that Troy Co. has cash dividends of $100,000 and net income of $500,000, and no preferred stock outstanding. Illustration 15-15 shows the payout ratio computation.

$$\text{Payout ratio} = \frac{\text{Cash dividends}}{\text{Net income} - \text{Preferred dividends}}$$
$$= \frac{\$100,000}{\$500,000}$$
$$= 20\%$$

ILLUSTRATION 15-15
Computation of Payout Ratio

Recently, the payout ratio has plummeted. In 1982, more than half of earnings were converted to dividends. In the second quarter of 2007, just 29 percent of the earnings of the S&P 500 was distributed via dividends.[22]

Book Value per Share

A much-used basis for evaluating net worth is found in the book value or equity value per share of stock. Book value per share of stock is the amount each share would receive if the company were liquidated **on the basis of amounts reported on the balance sheet.** However, the figure loses much of its relevance if the valuations on the balance sheet fail to approximate fair value of the assets. Book value per share equals common stockholders' equity divided by outstanding common shares. Assume that Chen Corporation's common stockholders' equity is $1,000,000 and it has 100,000 shares of common stock outstanding. Illustration 15-16 shows its book value per share computation.

$$\frac{\text{Book value}}{\text{per share}} = \frac{\text{Common stockholders' equity}}{\text{Outstanding shares}}$$
$$= \frac{\$1,000,000}{100,000}$$
$$= \$10 \text{ per share}$$

ILLUSTRATION 15-16
Computation of Book Value per Share

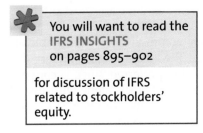

You will want to read the **IFRS INSIGHTS** on pages 895–902

for discussion of IFRS related to stockholders' equity.

[22]Andrew Blackman, "How Well Do You Know . . . Dividends?" *Wall Street Journal* (September 10, 2007), p. R5.

SUMMARY OF LEARNING OBJECTIVES

1 **Discuss the characteristics of the corporate form of organization.** Among the specific characteristics of the corporate form that affect accounting are the: (1) influence of state corporate law, (2) use of the capital stock or share system, and (3) development of a variety of ownership interests. In the absence of restrictive provisions, each share of stock carries the right to share proportionately in: (1) profits and losses; (2) management (the right to vote for directors); (3) corporate assets upon liquidation; (4) any new issues of stock of the same class (called the preemptive right).

2 **Identify the key components of stockholders' equity.** Stockholders' or owners' equity is classified into two categories: contributed capital and earned capital. Contributed capital (paid-in capital) describes the total amount paid in on capital stock. Put another way, it is the amount that stockholders advance to the corporation for use in the business. Contributed capital includes items such as the par value of all outstanding capital stock and premiums less any discounts on issuance. Earned capital is the capital that develops if the business operates profitably; it consists of all undistributed income that remains invested in the company.

3 **Explain the accounting procedures for issuing shares of stock.** Accounts are kept for the following different types of stock: *Par value stock:* (a) preferred stock or common stock; (b) paid-in capital in excess of par or additional paid-in capital; and (c) discount on stock. *No-par stock:* common stock or common stock and additional paid-in capital, if stated value used. Stock issued in combination with other securities (lump-sum sales): The two methods of allocation available are (a) the proportional method; and (b) the incremental method. Stock issued in noncash transactions: When issuing stock for services or property other than cash, the company should record the property or services at either the fair value of the stock issued, or the fair value of the noncash consideration received, whichever is more clearly determinable.

4 **Describe the accounting for treasury stock.** The cost method is generally used in accounting for treasury stock. This method derives its name from the fact that a company maintains the Treasury Stock account at the cost of the shares purchased. Under the cost method, a company debits the Treasury Stock account for the cost of the shares acquired and credits it for this same cost upon reissuance. The price received for the stock when originally issued does not affect the entries to record the acquisition and reissuance of the treasury stock.

5 **Explain the accounting for and reporting of preferred stock.** Preferred stock is a special class of shares that possesses certain preferences or features not possessed by the common stock. The features that are most often associated with preferred stock issues are: (1) preference as to dividends; (2) preference as to assets in the event of liquidation; (3) convertible into common stock; (4) callable at the option of the corporation; (5) nonvoting. At issuance, the accounting for preferred stock is similar to that for common stock. When convertible preferred stock is converted, a company uses the book value method: It debits Preferred Stock, along with any related Paid-in Capital in Excess of Par—Preferred Stock and credits Common Stock and Paid-in Capital in Excess of Par—Common Stock (if an excess exists).

6 **Describe the policies used in distributing dividends.** The state incorporation laws normally provide information concerning the legal restrictions related to the payment of dividends. Corporations rarely pay dividends in an amount equal to the legal limit. This is due, in part, to the fact that companies use assets represented by undistributed earnings to finance future operations of the business. If a company is considering declaring a dividend, it must ask two preliminary questions: (1) Is the condition of the corporation such that the dividend is **legally permissible**? (2) Is the condition of the corporation such that a dividend is **economically sound**?

7 Identify the various forms of dividend distributions. Dividends are of the following types: (1) cash dividends, (2) property dividends, (3) liquidating dividends (dividends based on other than retained earnings), (4) stock dividends (the issuance by a corporation of its own stock to its stockholders on a pro rata basis, but without receiving consideration).

8 Explain the accounting for small and large stock dividends, and for stock splits. Generally accepted accounting principles require that the accounting for small stock dividends (less than 20 or 25 percent) rely on the fair value of the stock issued. When declaring a stock dividend, a company debits Retained Earnings at the fair value of the stock it distributes. The entry includes a credit to Common Stock Dividend Distributable at par value times the number of shares, with any excess credited to Paid-in Capital in Excess of Par. If the number of shares issued exceeds 20 or 25 percent of the shares outstanding (large stock dividend), it debits Retained Earnings at par value and credits Common Stock Distributable—there is no additional paid-in capital.

A stock dividend is a capitalization of retained earnings that reduces retained earnings and increases certain contributed capital accounts. The par value per share and total stockholders' equity remain unchanged with a stock dividend, and all stockholders retain their same proportionate share of ownership. A stock split results in an increase or decrease in the number of shares outstanding, with a corresponding decrease or increase in the par or stated value per share. No accounting entry is required for a stock split.

9 Indicate how to present and analyze stockholders' equity. The stockholders' equity section of a balance sheet includes capital stock, additional paid-in capital, and retained earnings. A company might also present additional items such as treasury stock and accumulated other comprehensive income. Companies often provide a statement of stockholders' equity. Common ratios that use stockholders' equity amounts are: rate of return on common stock equity, payout ratio, and book value per share.

Gateway to the Profession

Expanded Discussion of Quasi-Reorganization

| APPENDIX **15A** | DIVIDEND PREFERENCES AND BOOK VALUE PER SHARE |

DIVIDEND PREFERENCES

Illustrations 15A-1 to 15A-4 indicate the **effects** of various **dividend preferences** on dividend distributions to common and preferred stockholders. Assume that in 2012, Mason Company is to distribute $50,000 as cash dividends, its outstanding common stock has a par value of $400,000, and its 6 percent preferred stock has a par value of $100,000. Mason would distribute dividends to each class, employing the assumptions given, as follows.

10 LEARNING OBJECTIVE
Explain the different types of preferred stock dividends and their effect on book value per share.

1. If the preferred stock is noncumulative and nonparticipating:

	Preferred	Common	Total
6% of $100,000	$6,000		$ 6,000
The remainder to common		$44,000	44,000
Totals	$6,000	$44,000	$50,000

ILLUSTRATION 15A-1
Dividend Distribution, Noncumulative and Nonparticipating Preferred

2. If the preferred stock is cumulative and nonparticipating, and Mason Company did not pay dividends on the preferred stock in the preceding two years:

ILLUSTRATION 15A-2
Dividend Distribution, Cumulative and Nonparticipating Preferred, with Dividends in Arrears

	Preferred	Common	Total
Dividends in arrears, 6% of $100,000 for 2 years	$12,000		$12,000
Current year's dividend, 6% of $100,000	6,000		6,000
The remainder to common		$32,000	32,000
Totals	$18,000	$32,000	$50,000

3. If the preferred stock is noncumulative and is fully participating:[23]

ILLUSTRATION 15A-3
Dividend Distribution, Noncumulative and Fully Participating Preferred

	Preferred	Common	Total
Current year's dividend, 6%	$ 6,000	$24,000	$30,000
Participating dividend of 4%	4,000	16,000	20,000
Totals	$10,000	$40,000	$50,000

The participating dividend was determined as follows.
Current year's dividend:
  Preferred, 6% of $100,000 = $ 6,000
  Common, 6% of $400,000 = 24,000 $ 30,000
Amount available for participation ($50,000 − $30,000) $ 20,000
Par value of stock that is to participate ($100,000 + $400,000) $500,000
Rate of participation ($20,000 ÷ $500,000)   4%
Participating dividend:
  Preferred, 4% of $100,000 $ 4,000
  Common, 4% of $400,000   16,000
                   $ 20,000

4. If the preferred stock is cumulative and is fully participating, and Mason Company did not pay dividends on the preferred stock in the preceding two years:

ILLUSTRATION 15A-4
Dividend Distribution, Cumulative and Fully Participating Preferred, with Dividends in Arrears

	Preferred	Common	Total
Dividends in arrears, 6% of $100,000 for 2 years	$12,000		$12,000
Current year's dividend, 6%	6,000	$24,000	30,000
Participating dividend, 1.6% ($8,000 ÷ $500,000)	1,600	6,400	8,000
Totals	$19,600	$30,400	$50,000

BOOK VALUE PER SHARE

Book value per share in its simplest form is computed as net assets divided by outstanding shares at the end of the year. The computation of book value per share becomes more complicated if a company has preferred stock in its capital structure. For example,

---

[23]When preferred stock is participating, there may be different agreements as to how the participation feature is to be executed. However, in the absence of any specific agreement the following procedure is recommended:

  a. After the preferred stock is assigned its current year's dividend, the common stock will receive a "like" percentage of par value outstanding. In example (3), this amounts to 6 percent of $400,000.

  b. In example (3), shown in Illustration 15A-3, the remainder of the declared dividend is $20,000. We divide this amount by total par value ($500,000) to find the rate of participation to be applied to each class of stock. In this case, the rate of participation is 4% ($20,000 ÷ $500,000), which we then multiply by the par value of each class of stock to determine the amount of participation.

if preferred dividends are in arrears, if the preferred stock is participating, or if preferred stock has a redemption or liquidating value higher than its carrying amount, the company must allocate retained earnings between the preferred and common stockholders in computing book value.

To illustrate, assume that the following situation exists.

Stockholders' equity	Preferred	Common
Preferred stock, 5%	$300,000	
Common stock		$400,000
Excess of issue price over par of common stock		37,500
Retained earnings		162,582
Totals	$300,000	$600,082
Shares outstanding		4,000
Book value per share		$150.02

ILLUSTRATION 15A-5
Computation of Book Value per Share—No Dividends in Arrears

The situation in Illustration 15A-5 assumes that no preferred dividends are in arrears and that the preferred is not participating. Now assume that the same facts exist except that the 5 percent preferred is cumulative, participating up to 8 percent, and that dividends for three years before the current year are in arrears. Illustration 15A-6 shows how to compute the book value of the common stock, assuming that no action has yet been taken concerning dividends for the current year.

Stockholders' equity	Preferred	Common
Preferred stock, 5%	$300,000	
Common stock		$400,000
Excess of issue price over par of common stock		37,500
Retained earnings:		
Dividends in arrears (3 years at 5% a year)	45,000	
Current year requirement at 5%	15,000	20,000
Participating—additional 3%	9,000	12,000
Remainder to common		61,582
Totals	$369,000	$531,082
Shares outstanding		4,000
Book value per share		$132.77

ILLUSTRATION 15A-6
Computation of Book Value per Share—with Dividends in Arrears

In connection with the book value computation, the analyst must know how to handle the following items: the number of authorized and unissued shares; the number of treasury shares on hand; any commitments with respect to the issuance of unissued shares or the reissuance of treasury shares; and the relative rights and privileges of the various types of stock authorized. As an example, if the liquidating value of the preferred stock is higher than its carrying amount, the liquidating amount should be used in the book value computation.

SUMMARY OF LEARNING OBJECTIVE FOR APPENDIX 15A

10 Explain the different types of preferred stock dividends and their effect on book value per share. The dividend preferences of preferred stock affect the dividends paid to stockholders. Preferred stock can be (1) cumulative or noncumulative, and (2) fully participating, partially participating, or nonparticipating. If preferred dividends are in arrears, if the preferred stock is participating, or if preferred stock has a redemption or liquidation value higher than its carrying amount, allocate retained earnings between preferred and common stockholders in computing book value per share.

FASB CODIFICATION

FASB Codification References

[1] FASB ASC 480-10-05. [Predecessor literature: "Accounting for Certain Financial Instruments with Characteristics of Both Liabilities and Equity," *Statement of Financial Accounting Standards No. 150* (Norwalk Conn.: FASB, 2003).]

[2] FASB ASC 505-10-50-3. [Predecessor literature: "Disclosure of Information about Capital Structure," *Statement of Financial Accounting Standards No. 129* (Norwalk, Conn.: FASB, 1997).]

[3] FASB ASC 505-20-05-2. [Predecessor literature: American Institute of Certified Public Accountants, *Accounting Research and Terminology Bulletins, No. 43* (New York: AICPA, 1961), Ch. 7, par. 10.]

[4] FASB ASC 505-20-25-3. [Predecessor literature: American Institute of Certified Public Accountants, *Accounting Research and Terminology Bulletins, No. 43* (New York: AICPA, 1961), par. 13.]

[5] FASB ASC 505-10-50-3. [Predecessor literature: "Disclosure of Information about Capital Structure," *Statement of Financial Accounting Standards No. 129* (Norwalk, Conn.: FASB, February 1997), par. 4.]

[6] FASB ASC 220-10-05. [Predecessor literature: "Reporting Comprehensive Income," *Statement of Financial Accounting Standards No. 130* (Norwalk, Conn.: FASB, June 1997).]

Exercises

If your school has a subscription to the FASB Codification, go to *http://aaahq.org/ascLogin.cfm* to log in and prepare responses to the following. Provide Codification references for your responses.

CE15-1 Access the glossary ("Master Glossary") to answer the following.

(a) What is a "convertible security"?
(b) What is a "stock dividend"?
(c) What is a "stock split"?
(d) What are "participation rights"?

CE15-2 At what percentage point can the issuance of additional shares still qualify as a stock dividend, as opposed to a stock split?

CE15-3 A company plans to issue shares and wants to know the SEC's stance on the accounting treatment for the costs of issuing stock. Can these costs be deferred, or must they be expensed immediately?

CE15-4 If a company chooses to purchase its own shares and then either (1) retires the repurchased shares and issues additional shares, or (2) resells the repurchased shares, can a gain or loss be recognized by the company? Why or why not?

An additional Codification case can be found in the Using Your Judgment section, on page 894.

Be sure to check the book's companion website for a Review and Analysis Exercise, with solution.

Questions, Brief Exercises, Exercises, Problems, and many more resources are available for practice in WileyPLUS.

Note: All asterisked Questions, Exercises, and Problems relate to material in the appendix to the chapter.

QUESTIONS

1. In the absence of restrictive provisions, what are the basic rights of stockholders of a corporation?

2. Why is a preemptive right important?

3. Distinguish between common and preferred stock.

4. Why is the distinction between paid-in capital and retained earnings important?

5. Explain each of the following terms: authorized capital stock, unissued capital stock, issued capital stock, outstanding capital stock, and treasury stock.

6. What is meant by par value, and what is its significance to stockholders?

7. Describe the accounting for the issuance for cash of no-par value common stock at a price in excess of the stated value of the common stock.

8. Explain the difference between the proportional method and the incremental method of allocating the proceeds of lump-sum sales of capital stock.

9. What are the different bases for stock valuation when assets other than cash are received for issued shares of stock?

10. Explain how underwriting costs and accounting and legal fees associated with the issuance of stock should be recorded.

11. For what reasons might a corporation purchase its own stock?

12. Discuss the propriety of showing:

(a) Treasury stock as an asset.

(b) "Gain" or "loss" on sale of treasury stock as additions to or deductions from income.

(c) Dividends received on treasury stock as income.

13. What features or rights may alter the character of preferred stock?

14. Dagwood Inc. recently noted that its 4% preferred stock and 4% participating preferred stock, which are both cumulative, have priority as to dividends up to 4% of their par value. Its participating preferred stock participates equally with the common stock in any dividends in excess of 4%. What is meant by the term participating? Cumulative?

15. Where in the financial statements is preferred stock normally reported?

16. List possible sources of additional paid-in capital.

17. Satchel Inc. purchases 10,000 shares of its own previously issued $10 par common stock for $290,000. Assuming the shares are held in the treasury with intent to reissue, what effect does this transaction have on (a) net income,

(b) total assets, (c) total paid-in capital, and (d) total stockholders' equity?

18. Indicate how each of the following accounts should be classified in the stockholders' equity section.

(a) Common Stock

(b) Retained Earnings

(c) Paid-in Capital in Excess of Par—Common Stock

(d) Treasury Stock

(e) Paid-in Capital from Treasury Stock

(f) Paid-in Capital in Excess of Stated Value—Common Stock

(g) Preferred Stock

19. What factors influence the dividend policy of a company?

20. What are the principal considerations of a board of directors in making decisions involving dividend declarations? Discuss briefly.

21. Dividends are sometimes said to have been paid "out of retained earnings." What is the error, if any, in that statement?

22. Distinguish among: cash dividends, property dividends, liquidating dividends, and stock dividends.

23. Describe the accounting entry for a stock dividend, if any. Describe the accounting entry for a stock split, if any.

24. Stock splits and stock dividends may be used by a corporation to change the number of shares of its stock outstanding.

(a) What is meant by a stock split effected in the form of a dividend?

(b) From an accounting viewpoint, explain how the stock split effected in the form of a dividend differs from an ordinary stock dividend.

(c) How should a stock dividend that has been declared but not yet issued be classified in a balance sheet? Why?

25. The following comment appeared in the notes of Colorado Corporation's annual report: "Such distributions, representing proceeds from the sale of Sarazan, Inc., were paid in the form of partial liquidating dividends and were in lieu of a portion of the Company's ordinary cash dividends." How would a partial liquidating dividend be accounted for in the financial records?

26. This comment appeared in the annual report of MacCloud Inc.: "The Company could pay cash or property dividends on the Class A common stock without paying cash or property dividends on the Class B common stock. But if the Company pays any cash or property dividends on the

Class B common stock, it would be required to pay at least the same dividend on the Class A common stock." How is a property dividend accounted for in the financial records?

27. For what reasons might a company restrict a portion of its retained earnings?

28. How are restrictions of retained earnings reported?

*29. McNabb Corp. had $100,000 of 7%, $20 par value preferred stock and 12,000 shares of $25 par value common stock outstanding throughout 2012.

(a) Assuming that total dividends declared in 2012 were $64,000, and that the preferred stock is not cumulative but is fully participating, common stockholders should receive 2012 dividends of what amount?

(b) Assuming that total dividends declared in 2012 were $64,000, and that the preferred stock is fully participating and cumulative with preferred dividends in arrears for 2011, preferred stockholders should receive 2012 dividends totaling what amount?

(c) Assuming that total dividends declared in 2012 were $30,000, that the preferred stock is cumulative, nonparticipating, and was issued on January 1, 2011, and that $5,000 of preferred dividends were declared and paid in 2011, the common stockholders should receive 2012 dividends totaling what amount?

BRIEF EXERCISES

BE15-1 Buttercup Corporation issued 300 shares of $10 par value common stock for $4,500. Prepare Buttercup's journal entry.

BE15-2 Swarten Corporation issued 600 shares of no-par common stock for $8,200. Prepare Swarten's journal entry if (a) the stock has no stated value, and (b) the stock has a stated value of $2 per share.

BE15-3 Wilco Corporation has the following account balances at December 31, 2012.

Common stock, $5 par value	$ 510,000
Treasury stock	90,000
Retained earnings	2,340,000
Paid-in capital in excess of par—common stock	1,320,000

Prepare Wilco's December 31, 2012, stockholders' equity section.

BE15-4 Ravonette Corporation issued 300 shares of $10 par value common stock and 100 shares of $50 par value preferred stock for a lump sum of $13,500. The common stock has a market price of $20 per share, and the preferred stock has a market price of $90 per share. Prepare the journal entry to record the issuance.

BE15-5 On February 1, 2012, Buffalo Corporation issued 3,000 shares of its $5 par value common stock for land worth $31,000. Prepare the February 1, 2012, journal entry.

BE15-6 Moonwalker Corporation issued 2,000 shares of its $10 par value common stock for $60,000. Moonwalker also incurred $1,500 of costs associated with issuing the stock. Prepare Moonwalker's journal entry to record the issuance of the company's stock.

BE15-7 Sprinkle Inc. has outstanding 10,000 shares of $10 par value common stock. On July 1, 2012, Sprinkle reacquired 100 shares at $87 per share. On September 1, Sprinkle reissued 60 shares at $90 per share. On November 1, Sprinkle reissued 40 shares at $83 per share. Prepare Sprinkle's journal entries to record these transactions using the cost method.

BE15-8 Arantxa Corporation has outstanding 20,000 shares of $5 par value common stock. On August 1, 2012, Arantxa reacquired 200 shares at $80 per share. On November 1, Arantxa reissued the 200 shares at $70 per share. Arantxa had no previous treasury stock transactions. Prepare Arantxa's journal entries to record these transactions using the cost method.

BE15-9 Hinges Corporation issued 500 shares of $100 par value preferred stock for $61,500. Prepare Hinges's journal entry.

BE15-10 Woolford Inc. declared a cash dividend of $1.00 per share on its 2 million outstanding shares. The dividend was declared on August 1, payable on September 9 to all stockholders of record on August 15. Prepare all journal entries necessary on those three dates.

BE15-11 Cole Inc. owns shares of Marlin Corporation stock classified as available-for-sale securities. At December 31, 2012, the available-for-sale securities were carried in Cole's accounting records at their cost of $875,000, which equals their fair value. On September 21, 2013, when the fair value of the securities was

$1,200,000, Cole declared a property dividend whereby the Marlin securities are to be distributed on October 23, 2013, to stockholders of record on October 8, 2013. Prepare all journal entries necessary on those three dates.

6 **7** **BE15-12** Graves Mining Company declared, on April 20, a dividend of $500,000 payable on June 1. Of this amount, $125,000 is a return of capital. Prepare the April 20 and June 1 entries for Graves.

8 **BE15-13** Green Day Corporation has outstanding 400,000 shares of $10 par value common stock. The corporation declares a 5% stock dividend when the fair value of the stock is $65 per share. Prepare the journal entries for Green Day Corporation for both the date of declaration and the date of distribution.

8 **BE15-14** Use the information from BE15-13, but assume Green Day Corporation declared a 100% stock dividend rather than a 5% stock dividend. Prepare the journal entries for both the date of declaration and the date of distribution.

10 *BE15-15** Nottebart Corporation has outstanding 10,000 shares of $100 par value, 6% preferred stock and 60,000 shares of $10 par value common stock. The preferred stock was issued in January 2012, and no dividends were declared in 2012 or 2013. In 2014, Nottebart declares a cash dividend of $300,000. How will the dividend be shared by common and preferred stockholders if the preferred is (a) noncumulative and (b) cumulative?

EXERCISES

3 **E15-1 (Recording the Issuances of Common Stock)** During its first year of operations, Sitwell Corporation had the following transactions pertaining to its common stock.

Jan. 10	Issued 80,000 shares for cash at $6 per share.
Mar. 1	Issued 5,000 shares to attorneys in payment of a bill for $35,000 for services rendered in helping the company to incorporate.
July 1	Issued 30,000 shares for cash at $8 per share.
Sept. 1	Issued 60,000 shares for cash at $10 per share.

Instructions

(a) Prepare the journal entries for these transactions, assuming that the common stock has a par value of $3 per share.

(b) Prepare the journal entries for these transactions, assuming that the common stock is no-par with a stated value of $2 per share.

3 **E15-2 (Recording the Issuance of Common and Preferred Stock)** Abernathy Corporation was organized on January 1, 2012. It is authorized to issue 10,000 shares of 8%, $50 par value preferred stock, and 500,000 shares of no-par common stock with a stated value of $2 per share. The following stock transactions were completed during the first year.

Jan. 10	Issued 80,000 shares of common stock for cash at $5 per share.
Mar. 1	Issued 5,000 shares of preferred stock for cash at $108 per share.
Apr. 1	Issued 24,000 shares of common stock for land. The asking price of the land was $90,000; the fair value of the land was $80,000.
May 1	Issued 80,000 shares of common stock for cash at $7 per share.
Aug. 1	Issued 10,000 shares of common stock to attorneys in payment of their bill of $50,000 for services rendered in helping the company organize.
Sept. 1	Issued 10,000 shares of common stock for cash at $9 per share.
Nov. 1	Issued 1,000 shares of preferred stock for cash at $112 per share.

Instructions
Prepare the journal entries to record the above transactions.

3 **E15-3 (Stock Issued for Land)** Twenty-five thousand shares reacquired by Pierce Corporation for $48 per share were exchanged for undeveloped land that has an appraised value of $1,700,000. At the time of the exchange, the common stock was trading at $60 per share on an organized exchange.

Instructions

(a) Prepare the journal entry to record the acquisition of land assuming that the purchase of the stock was originally recorded using the cost method.

(b) Briefly identify the possible alternatives (including those that are totally unacceptable) for quantifying the cost of the land and briefly support your choice.

3 **E15-4 (Lump-Sum Sale of Stock with Bonds)** Fogelberg Corporation is a regional company which is an SEC registrant. The corporation's securities are thinly traded on NASDAQ (National Association of Securities Dealers Quotes). Fogelberg has issued 10,000 units. Each unit consists of a $500 par, 12% subordinated debenture and 10 shares of $5 par common stock. The investment banker has retained 400 units as the underwriting fee. The other 9,600 units were sold to outside investors for cash at $850 per unit. Prior to this sale the 2-week ask price of common stock was $40 per share. Twelve percent is a reasonable market yield for the debentures, and therefore the par value of the bonds is equal to the fair value.

Instructions

(a) Prepare the journal entry to record Fogelberg's transaction, under the following conditions.
  (1) Employing the incremental method.
  (2) Employing the proportional method, assuming the recent price quote on the common stock reflects fair value.
(b) Briefly explain which method is, in your opinion, the better method.

3 **5** **E15-5 (Lump-Sum Sales of Stock with Preferred Stock)** Hartman Inc. issues 500 shares of $10 par value common stock and 100 shares of $100 par value preferred stock for a lump sum of $100,000.

Instructions

(a) Prepare the journal entry for the issuance when the market price of the common shares is $168 each and market price of the preferred is $210 each. (Round to nearest dollar.)
(b) Prepare the journal entry for the issuance when only the market price of the common stock is known and it is $170 per share.

3 **4** **E15-6 (Stock Issuances and Repurchase)** Loxley Corporation is authorized to issue 50,000 shares of $10 par value common stock. During 2012, Loxley took part in the following selected transactions.

1. Issued 5,000 shares of stock at $45 per share, less costs related to the issuance of the stock totaling $7,000.
2. Issued 1,000 shares of stock for land appraised at $50,000. The stock was actively traded on a national stock exchange at approximately $46 per share on the date of issuance.
3. Purchased 500 shares of treasury stock at $44 per share. The treasury shares purchased were issued in 2008 at $40 per share.

Instructions

(a) Prepare the journal entry to record item 1.
(b) Prepare the journal entry to record item 2.
(c) Prepare the journal entry to record item 3 using the cost method.

4 **E15-7 (Effect of Treasury Stock Transactions on Financials)** Sanborn Company has outstanding 40,000 shares of $5 par common stock which had been issued at $30 per share. Sanborn then entered into the following transactions.

1. Purchased 5,000 treasury shares at $45 per share.
2. Resold 500 of the treasury shares at $40 per share.
3. Resold 2,000 of the treasury shares at $49 per share.

Instructions

Use the following code to indicate the effect each of the three transactions has on the financial statement categories listed in the table below, assuming Sanborn Company uses the cost method: I = Increase; D = Decrease; NE = No effect.

#	Assets	Liabilities	Stockholders' Equity	Paid-in Capital	Retained Earnings	Net Income
1						
2						
3						

3 **5** **10** **E15-8 (Preferred Stock Entries and Dividends)** Weisberg Corporation has 10,000 shares of $100 par value, 6% preferred stock and 50,000 shares of $10 par value common stock outstanding at December 31, 2012.

Instructions

Answer the questions in each of the following independent situations.

(a) If the preferred stock is cumulative and dividends were last paid on the preferred stock on December 31, 2009, what are the dividends in arrears that should be reported on the December 31, 2012, balance sheet? How should these dividends be reported?

(b) If the preferred stock is convertible into seven shares of $10 par value common stock and 3,000 shares are converted, what entry is required for the conversion assuming the preferred stock was issued at par value?

(c) If the preferred stock was issued at $107 per share, how should the preferred stock be reported in the stockholders' equity section?

3 **4** **E15-9 (Correcting Entries for Equity Transactions)** Davison Inc. recently hired a new accountant with extensive experience in accounting for partnerships. Because of the pressure of the new job, the accountant was unable to review what he had learned earlier about corporation accounting. During the first month, he made the following entries for the corporation's capital stock.

May 2	Cash		192,000	
	Common Stock			192,000
	(Issued 12,000 shares of $10 par value common stock at $16 per share)			
10	Cash		600,000	
	Common Stock			600,000
	(Issued 10,000 shares of $30 par value preferred stock at $60 per share)			
15	Common Stock		14,000	
	Cash			14,000
	(Purchased 1,000 shares of common stock for the treasury at $14 per share)			
31	Cash		8,500	
	Common Stock			5,000
	Gain on Sale of Stock			3,500
	(Sold 500 shares of treasury stock at $17 per share)			

Instructions
On the basis of the explanation for each entry, prepare the entries that should have been made for the transactions.

3 **4** **E15-10 (Analysis of Equity Data and Equity Section Preparation)** For a recent 2-year period, the balance sheet of Franklin Company showed the following stockholders' equity data at December 31 in millions.

	2013	2012
Paid-in capital in excess of par—common stock	$ 891	$ 817
Common stock	545	540
Retained earnings	7,167	5,226
Treasury stock	1,428	918
Total stockholders' equity	$7,175	$5,665
Common stock shares issued	218	216
Common stock shares authorized	500	500
Treasury stock shares	34	27

Instructions
(a) Answer the following questions.
  (1) What is the par value of the common stock?
  (2) What is the cost per share of treasury stock at December 31, 2013, and at December 31, 2012?
(b) Prepare the stockholders' equity section at December 31, 2013.

7 **8** **E15-11 (Equity Items on the Balance Sheet)** The following are selected transactions that may affect stockholders' equity.

1. Recorded accrued interest earned on a note receivable.
2. Declared and distributed a stock split.
3. Declared a cash dividend.
4. Recorded a retained earnings restriction.
5. Recorded the expiration of insurance coverage that was previously recorded as prepaid insurance.
6. Paid the cash dividend declared in item 3 above.
7. Recorded accrued interest expense on a note payable.
8. Declared a stock dividend.
9. Distributed the stock dividend declared in item 8.

Instructions

In the following table, indicate the effect each of the nine transactions has on the financial statement elements listed. Use the following code:

I = Increase   D = Decrease   NE = No effect

Item	Assets	Liabilities	Stockholders' Equity	Paid-in Capital	Retained Earnings	Net Income

7 **E15-12 (Cash Dividend and Liquidating Dividend)** Addison Corporation has 10 million shares of common stock issued and outstanding. On June 1, the board of directors voted a 60 cents per share cash dividend to stockholders of record as of June 14, payable June 30.

Instructions

(a) Prepare the journal entry for each of the dates above assuming the dividend represents a distribution of earnings.

(b) How would the entry differ if the dividend were a liquidating dividend?

8 **E15-13 (Stock Split and Stock Dividend)** The common stock of Warner Inc. is currently selling at $110 per share. The directors wish to reduce the share price and increase share volume prior to a new issue. The per share par value is $10; book value is $70 per share. Five million shares are issued and outstanding.

Instructions

Prepare the necessary journal entries assuming the following.

(a) The board votes a 2-for-1 stock split.

(b) The board votes a 100% stock dividend.

(c) Briefly discuss the accounting and securities market differences between these two methods of increasing the number of shares outstanding.

8 **E15-14 (Entries for Stock Dividends and Stock Splits)** The stockholders' equity accounts of Lawrence Company have the following balances on December 31, 2012.

Common stock, $10 par, 200,000 shares issued and outstanding	$2,000,000
Paid-in capital in excess of par—common stock	1,200,000
Retained earnings	5,600,000

Shares of Lawrence Company stock are currently selling on the Midwest Stock Exchange at $37.

Instructions

Prepare the appropriate journal entries for each of the following cases.

(a) A stock dividend of 5% is declared and issued.

(b) A stock dividend of 100% is declared and issued.

(c) A 2-for-1 stock split is declared and issued.

 7 **8** **E15-15 (Dividend Entries)** The following data were taken from the balance sheet accounts of Wickham Corporation on December 31, 2012.

Current assets	$540,000
Debt investments	624,000
Common stock (par value $10)	600,000
Paid-in capital in excess of par—common stock	150,000
Retained earnings	840,000

Instructions

Prepare the required journal entries for the following unrelated items.

(a) A 5% stock dividend is declared and distributed at a time when the market price is $39 per share.

(b) The par value of the capital stock is reduced to $2 with a 5-for-1 stock split.

(c) A dividend is declared January 5, 2013, and paid January 25, 2013, in bonds held as an investment. The bonds have a book value of $90,000 and a fair value of $125,000.

6 **7** **E15-16 (Computation of Retained Earnings)** The following information has been taken from the ledger

8 accounts of Sampras Corporation.

Total income since incorporation	$287,000
Total cash dividends paid	60,000
Total value of stock dividends distributed	40,000
Gains on treasury stock transactions	18,000
Unamortized discount on bonds payable	32,000

Instructions

Determine the current balance of retained earnings.

9 **E15-17 (Stockholders' Equity Section)** Teller Corporation's post-closing trial balance at December 31, 2012, was as follows.

TELLER CORPORATION
POST-CLOSING TRIAL BALANCE
DECEMBER 31, 2012

	Dr.	Cr.
Accounts Payable		$ 310,000
Accounts Receivable	$ 480,000	
Accumulated Depreciation—Buildings		185,000
Paid-in Capital in Excess of Par—Common Stock		1,000,000
Paid-in Capital from Treasury Stock		160,000
Allowance for Doubtful Accounts		30,000
Bonds Payable		700,000
Buildings	1,450,000	
Cash	190,000	
Common Stock ($1 par value)		200,000
Dividends Payable (preferred stock)		4,000
Inventory	560,000	
Land	400,000	
Preferred Stock ($50 par value)		500,000
Prepaid Expenses	40,000	
Retained Earnings		201,000
Treasury Stock (common)	170,000	
Totals	$3,290,000	$3,290,000

At December 31, 2012, Teller had the following number of common and preferred shares.

	Common	Preferred
Authorized	600,000	60,000
Issued	200,000	10,000
Outstanding	190,000	10,000

The dividends on preferred stock are $4 cumulative. In addition, the preferred stock has a preference in liquidation of $50 per share.

Instructions

Prepare the stockholders' equity section of Teller's balance sheet at December 31, 2012.

(AICPA adapted)

E15-18 (Dividends and Stockholders' Equity Section) Elizabeth Company reported the following amounts in the stockholders' equity section of its December 31, 2012, balance sheet.

Preferred stock, 8%, $100 par (10,000 shares authorized, 2,000 shares issued)	$200,000
Common stock, $5 par (100,000 shares authorized, 20,000 shares issued)	100,000
Additional paid-in capital	125,000
Retained earnings	450,000
Total	$875,000

During 2013, Elizabeth took part in the following transactions concerning stockholders' equity.

1. Paid the annual 2012 $8 per share dividend on preferred stock and a $2 per share dividend on common stock. These dividends had been declared on December 31, 2012.
2. Purchased 2,700 shares of its own outstanding common stock for $40 per share. Elizabeth uses the cost method.
3. Reissued 700 treasury shares for land valued at $30,000.
4. Issued 500 shares of preferred stock at $105 per share.
5. Declared a 10% stock dividend on the outstanding common stock when the stock is selling for $45 per share.
6. Issued the stock dividend.
7. Declared the annual 2013 $8 per share dividend on preferred stock and the $2 per share dividend on common stock. These dividends are payable in 2014.

Instructions

(a) Prepare journal entries to record the transactions described above.
(b) Prepare the December 31, 2013, stockholders' equity section. Assume 2013 net income was $330,000.

E15-19 (Comparison of Alternative Forms of Financing) Shown below is the liabilities and stockholders' equity section of the balance sheet for Ingalls Company and Wilder Company. Each has assets totaling $4,200,000.

Ingalls Co.		Wilder Co.	
Current liabilities	$ 300,000	Current liabilities	$ 600,000
Long-term debt, 10%	1,200,000	Common stock ($20 par)	2,900,000
Common stock ($20 par)	2,000,000	Retained earnings (Cash	
Retained earnings (Cash		dividends, $328,000)	700,000
dividends, $220,000)	700,000		
	$4,200,000		$4,200,000

For the year, each company has earned the same income before interest and taxes.

	Ingalls Co.	Wilder Co.
Income before interest and taxes	$1,200,000	$1,200,000
Interest expense	120,000	–0–
	1,080,000	1,200,000
Income taxes (40%)	432,000	480,000
Net income	$ 648,000	$ 720,000

At year-end, the market price of Ingalls's stock was $101 per share, and Wilder's was $63.50. Assume balance sheet amounts are representative for the entire year.

Instructions

(a) Which company is more profitable in terms of return on total assets?
(b) Which company is more profitable in terms of return on stockholders' equity?
(c) Which company has the greater net income per share of stock? Neither company issued or reacquired shares during the year.
(d) From the point of view of net income, is it advantageous to the stockholders of Ingalls Co. to have the long-term debt outstanding? Why?
(e) What is the book value per share for each company?

9 **E15-20** **(Trading on the Equity Analysis)** Presented below is information from the annual report of Potter Plastics, Inc.

Operating income	$ 532,150
Bond interest expense	135,000
	397,150
Income taxes	183,432
Net income	$ 213,718
Bonds payable	$1,500,000
Common stock	875,000
Retained earnings	575,000

Instructions

(a) Compute the return on common stock equity and the rate of interest paid on bonds. (Assume balances for debt and equity accounts approximate averages for the year.)

(b) Is Potter Plastics, Inc. trading on the equity successfully? Explain.

10 *E15-21* **(Preferred Dividends)** The outstanding capital stock of Pennington Corporation consists of 2,000 shares of $100 par value, 6% preferred, and 5,000 shares of $50 par value common.

Instructions

Assuming that the company has retained earnings of $70,000, all of which is to be paid out in dividends, and that preferred dividends were not paid during the 2 years preceding the current year, determine how much each class of stock should receive under each of the following conditions.

(a) The preferred stock is noncumulative and nonparticipating.

(b) The preferred stock is cumulative and nonparticipating.

(c) The preferred stock is cumulative and participating. (Round dividend rate percentages to four decimal places.)

10 *E15-22* **(Preferred Dividends)** Martinez Company's ledger shows the following balances on December 31, 2012.

Preferred Stock (5%; $10 par value, outstanding 20,000 shares)	$ 200,000
Common Stock ($100 par value, outstanding 30,000 shares)	3,000,000
Retained Earnings	630,000

Instructions

Assuming that the directors decide to declare total dividends in the amount of $266,000, determine how much each class of stock should receive under each of the conditions stated below. One year's dividends are in arrears on the preferred stock.

(a) The preferred stock is cumulative and fully participating.

(b) The preferred stock is noncumulative and nonparticipating.

(c) The preferred stock is noncumulative and is participating in distributions in excess of a 7% dividend rate on the common stock.

10 *E15-23* **(Preferred Stock Dividends)** Hagar Company has outstanding 2,500 shares of $100 par, 6% preferred stock and 15,000 shares of $10 par value common. The schedule below shows the amount of dividends paid out over the last 4 years.

Instructions

Allocate the dividends to each type of stock under assumptions (a) and (b). Express your answers in per share amounts using the format shown below.

		Assumptions			
		(a) Preferred, noncumulative, and nonparticipating		(b) Preferred, cumulative, and fully participating	
Year	Paid-out	Preferred	Common	Preferred	Common
2011	$12,000				
2012	$26,000				
2013	$52,000				
2014	$76,000				

10 *E15-24 (Computation of Book Value per Share)** Johnstone Inc. began operations in January 2011 and reported the following results for each of its 3 years of operations.

2011 $260,000 net loss   2012 $40,000 net loss   2013 $700,000 net income

At December 31, 2013, Johnstone Inc. capital accounts were as follows.

6% cumulative preferred stock, par value $100; authorized, issued, and outstanding 5,000 shares	$500,000
Common stock, par value $1.00; authorized 1,000,000 shares; issued and outstanding 750,000 shares	$750,000

Johnstone Inc. has never paid a cash or stock dividend. There has been no change in the capital accounts since Johnstone began operations. The state law permits dividends only from retained earnings.

Instructions

(a) Compute the book value of the common stock at December 31, 2013.

(b) Compute the book value of the common stock at December 31, 2013, assuming that the preferred stock has a liquidating value of $106 per share.

See the book's companion website, www.wiley.com/college/kieso, for a set of B Exercises.

PROBLEMS

P15-1 (Equity Transactions and Statement Preparation) On January 5, 2012, Phelps Corporation received a charter granting the right to issue 5,000 shares of $100 par value, 8% cumulative and nonparticipating preferred stock, and 50,000 shares of $10 par value common stock. It then completed these transactions.

Jan. 11 Issued 20,000 shares of common stock at $16 per share.
Feb. 1 Issued to Sanchez Corp. 4,000 shares of preferred stock for the following assets: equipment with a fair value of $50,000; a factory building with a fair value of $160,000; and land with an appraised value of $270,000.
July 29 Purchased 1,800 shares of common stock at $17 per share. (Use cost method.)
Aug. 10 Sold the 1,800 treasury shares at $14 per share.
Dec. 31 Declared a $0.25 per share cash dividend on the common stock and declared the preferred dividend.
Dec. 31 Closed the Income Summary account. There was a $175,700 net income.

Instructions

(a) Record the journal entries for the transactions listed above.

(b) Prepare the stockholders' equity section of Phelps Corporation's balance sheet as of December 31, 2012.

P15-2 (Treasury Stock Transactions and Presentation) Clemson Company had the following stockholders' equity as of January 1, 2012.

Common stock, $5 par value, 20,000 shares issued	$100,000
Paid-in capital in excess of par—common stock	300,000
Retained earnings	320,000
Total stockholders' equity	$720,000

During 2012, the following transactions occurred.

Feb. 1 Clemson repurchased 2,000 shares of treasury stock at a price of $19 per share.
Mar. 1 800 shares of treasury stock repurchased above were reissued at $17 per share.
Mar. 18 500 shares of treasury stock repurchased above were reissued at $14 per share.
Apr. 22 600 shares of treasury stock repurchased above were reissued at $20 per share.

Instructions

(a) Prepare the journal entries to record the treasury stock transactions in 2012, assuming Clemson uses the cost method.

(b) Prepare the stockholders' equity section as of April 30, 2012. Net income for the first 4 months of 2012 was $130,000.

3 4 **P15-3 (Equity Transactions and Statement Preparation)** Hatch Company has two classes of capital stock
7 8 outstanding: 8%, $20 par preferred and $5 par common. At December 31, 2012, the following accounts were included in stockholders' equity.

Preferred Stock, 150,000 shares	$ 3,000,000
Common Stock, 2,000,000 shares	10,000,000
Paid-in Capital in Excess of Par—Preferred Stock	200,000
Paid-in Capital in Excess of Par—Common Stock	27,000,000
Retained Earnings	4,500,000

The following transactions affected stockholders' equity during 2013.

Jan.	1	30,000 shares of preferred stock issued at $22 per share.
Feb.	1	50,000 shares of common stock issued at $20 per share.
June	1	2-for-1 stock split (par value reduced to $2.50).
July	1	30,000 shares of common treasury stock purchased at $10 per share. Hatch uses the cost method.
Sept. 15		10,000 shares of treasury stock reissued at $11 per share.
Dec. 31		The preferred dividend is declared, and a common dividend of 50¢ per share is declared.
Dec. 31		Net income is $2,100,000.

Instructions

Prepare the stockholders' equity section for Hatch Company at December 31, 2013. Show all supporting computations.

3 5 **P15-4 (Stock Transactions—Lump Sum)** Seles Corporation's charter authorized issuance of 100,000 shares of $10 par value common stock and 50,000 shares of $50 preferred stock. The following transactions involving the issuance of shares of stock were completed. Each transaction is independent of the others.

1. Issued a $10,000, 9% bond payable at par and gave as a bonus one share of preferred stock, which at that time was selling for $106 a share.
2. Issued 500 shares of common stock for equipment. The equipment had been appraised at $7,100; the seller's book value was $6,200. The most recent market price of the common stock is $16 a share.
3. Issued 375 shares of common and 100 shares of preferred for a lump sum amounting to $10,800. The common had been selling at $14 and the preferred at $65.
4. Issued 200 shares of common and 50 shares of preferred for equipment. The common had a fair value of $16 per share; the equipment has a fair value of $6,500.

Instructions

Record the transactions listed above in journal entry form.

4 **P15-5 (Treasury Stock—Cost Method)** Before Gordon Corporation engages in the treasury stock transactions listed below, its general ledger reflects, among others, the following account balances (par value of its stock is $30 per share).

Paid-in Capital in Excess of Par—Common Stock	Common Stock	Retained Earnings
$99,000	$270,000	$80,000

Instructions

Record the treasury stock transactions (given below) under the cost method of handling treasury stock; use the FIFO method for purchase-sale purposes.

(a) Bought 380 shares of treasury stock at $40 per share.
(b) Bought 300 shares of treasury stock at $45 per share.
(c) Sold 350 shares of treasury stock at $42 per share.
(d) Sold 110 shares of treasury stock at $38 per share.

P15-6 (Treasury Stock—Cost Method—Equity Section Preparation) Washington Company has the following stockholders' equity accounts at December 31, 2012.

Common Stock ($100 par value, authorized 8,000 shares)	$480,000
Retained Earnings	294,000

Instructions

(a) Prepare entries in journal form to record the following transactions, which took place during 2013.
   (1) 280 shares of outstanding stock were purchased at $97 per share. (These are to be accounted for using the cost method.)
   (2) A $20 per share cash dividend was declared.
   (3) The dividend declared in (2) above was paid.
   (4) The treasury shares purchased in (1) above were resold at $102 per share.
   (5) 500 shares of outstanding stock were purchased at $105 per share.
   (6) 350 of the shares purchased in (5) above were resold at $96 per share.

(b) Prepare the stockholders' equity section of Washington Company's balance sheet after giving effect to these transactions, assuming that the net income for 2013 was $94,000. State law requires restriction of retained earnings for the amount of treasury stock.

P15-7 (Cash Dividend Entries) The books of Conchita Corporation carried the following account balances as of December 31, 2012.

Cash	$ 195,000
Preferred Stock (6% cumulative, nonparticipating, $50 par)	300,000
Common Stock (no-par value, 300,000 shares issued)	1,500,000
Paid-in Capital in Excess of Par—Preferred Stock	150,000
Treasury Stock (common 2,800 shares at cost)	33,600
Retained Earnings	105,000

The company decided not to pay any dividends in 2012.

The board of directors, at their annual meeting on December 21, 2013, declared the following: "The current year dividends shall be 6% on the preferred and $.30 per share on the common. The dividends in arrears shall be paid by issuing 1,500 shares of treasury stock." At the date of declaration, the preferred is selling at $80 per share, and the common at $12 per share. Net income for 2013 is estimated at $77,000.

Instructions

(a) Prepare the journal entries required for the dividend declaration and payment, assuming that they occur simultaneously.

(b) Could Conchita Corporation give the preferred stockholders 2 years' dividends and common stockholders a 30 cents per share dividend, all in cash?

P15-8 (Dividends and Splits) Myers Company provides you with the following condensed balance sheet information.

Assets		Liabilities and Stockholders' Equity		
Current assets	$ 40,000	Current and long-term liabilities		$100,000
Equity investments (ABC stock;		Stockholders' equity		
10,000 shares at cost)	60,000	Common stock ($5 par)	$ 20,000	
Equipment (net)	250,000	Paid-in capital in excess of par	110,000	
Intangibles	60,000	Retained earnings	180,000	310,000
Total assets	$410,000	Total liabilities and		
		stockholders' equity		$410,000

Instructions

For each transaction below, indicate the dollar impact (if any) on the following five items: (1) total assets, (2) common stock, (3) paid-in capital in excess of par, (4) retained earnings, and (5) stockholders' equity. (Each situation is independent.)

(a) Myers declares and pays a $0.50 per share cash dividend.

(b) Myers declares and issues a 10% stock dividend when the market price of the stock is $14 per share.

(c) Myers declares and issues a 30% stock dividend when the market price of the stock is $15 per share.

(d) Myers declares and distributes a property dividend. Myers gives one share of ABC stock for every two shares of Myers Company stock held. ABC is selling for $10 per share on the date the property dividend is declared.

(e) Myers declares a 2-for-1 stock split and issues new shares.

 P15-9 (Stockholders' Equity Section of Balance Sheet) The following is a summary of all relevant transactions of Vicario Corporation since it was organized in 2012.

In 2012, 15,000 shares were authorized and 7,000 shares of common stock ($50 par value) were issued at a price of $57. In 2013, 1,000 shares were issued as a stock dividend when the stock was selling for $60. Three hundred shares of common stock were bought in 2014 at a cost of $64 per share. These 300 shares are still in the company treasury.

In 2013, 10,000 preferred shares were authorized and the company issued 5,000 of them ($100 par value) at $113. Some of the preferred stock was reacquired by the company and later reissued for $4,700 more than it cost the company.

The corporation has earned a total of $610,000 in net income after income taxes and paid out a total of $312,600 in cash dividends since incorporation.

Instructions

Prepare the stockholders' equity section of the balance sheet in proper form for Vicario Corporation as of December 31, 2014. Account for treasury stock using the cost method.

 P15-10 (Stock Dividends and Stock Split) Oregon Inc. $10 par common stock is selling for $110 per share. Four million shares are currently issued and outstanding. The board of directors wishes to stimulate interest in Oregon common stock before a forthcoming stock issue but does not wish to distribute capital at this time. The board also believes that too many adjustments to the stockholders' equity section, especially retained earnings, might discourage potential investors.

The board has considered three options for stimulating interest in the stock:

1. A 20% stock dividend.
2. A 100% stock dividend.
3. A 2-for-1 stock split.

Instructions

Acting as financial advisor to the board, you have been asked to report briefly on each option and, considering the board's wishes, make a recommendation. Discuss the effects of each of the foregoing options.

 P15-11 (Stock and Cash Dividends) Earnhart Corporation has outstanding 3,000,000 shares of common stock of a par value of $10 each. The balance in its Retained Earnings account at January 1, 2012, was $24,000,000, and it then had Paid-in Capital in Excess of Par—Common Stock of $5,000,000. During 2012, the company's net income was $4,700,000. A cash dividend of $0.60 a share was declared on May 5, 2012, and was paid June 30, 2012, and a 6% stock dividend was declared on November 30, 2012, and distributed to stockholders of record at the close of business on December 31, 2012. You have been asked to advise on the proper accounting treatment of the stock dividend.

The existing stock of the company is quoted on a national stock exchange. The market price of the stock has been as follows.

October 31, 2012	$31
November 30, 2012	$34
December 31, 2012	$38

Instructions

(a) Prepare the journal entry to record the declaration and payment of the cash dividend.

(b) Prepare the journal entry to record the declaration and distribution of the stock dividend.

(c) Prepare the stockholders' equity section (including schedules of retained earnings and additional paid-in capital) of the balance sheet of Earnhart Corporation for the year 2012 on the basis of the foregoing information. Draft a note to the financial statements setting forth the basis of the accounting for the stock dividend, and add separately appropriate comments or explanations regarding the basis chosen.

 P15-12 (Analysis and Classification of Equity Transactions) Penn Company was formed on July 1, 2010. It was authorized to issue 300,000 shares of $10 par value common stock and 100,000 shares of 8% $25 par value, cumulative and nonparticipating preferred stock. Penn Company has a July 1–June 30 fiscal year.

The following information relates to the stockholders' equity accounts of Penn Company.

Common Stock

Prior to the 2012–13 fiscal year, Penn Company had 110,000 shares of outstanding common stock issued as follows.

1. 85,000 shares were issued for cash on July 1, 2010, at $31 per share.
2. On July 24, 2010, 5,000 shares were exchanged for a plot of land which cost the seller $70,000 in 2004 and had an estimated fair value of $220,000 on July 24, 2010.
3. 20,000 shares were issued on March 1, 2011, for $42 per share.

During the 2012–13 fiscal year, the following transactions regarding common stock took place.

November 30, 2012	Penn purchased 2,000 shares of its own stock on the open market at $39 per share. Penn uses the cost method for treasury stock.
December 15, 2012	Penn declared a 5% stock dividend for stockholders of record on January 15, 2013, to be issued on January 31, 2013. Penn was having a liquidity problem and could not afford a cash dividend at the time. Penn's common stock was selling at $52 per share on December 15, 2012.
June 20, 2013	Penn sold 500 shares of its own common stock that it had purchased on November 30, 2012, for $21,000.

Preferred Stock

Penn issued 40,000 shares of preferred stock at $44 per share on July 1, 2011.

Cash Dividends

Penn has followed a schedule of declaring cash dividends in December and June, with payment being made to stockholders of record in the following month. The cash dividends which have been declared since inception of the company through June 30, 2013, are shown below.

Declaration Date	Common Stock	Preferred Stock
12/15/11	$0.30 per share	$1.00 per share
6/15/12	$0.30 per share	$1.00 per share
12/15/12	—	$1.00 per share

No cash dividends were declared during June 2013 due to the company's liquidity problems.

Retained Earnings

As of June 30, 2012, Penn's retained earnings account had a balance of $690,000. For the fiscal year ending June 30, 2013, Penn reported net income of $40,000.

Instructions

Prepare the stockholders' equity section of the balance sheet, including appropriate notes, for Penn Company as of June 30, 2013, as it should appear in its annual report to the shareholders.

(CMA adapted)

CONCEPTS FOR ANALYSIS

CA15-1 (Preemptive Rights and Dilution of Ownership) Wallace Computer Company is a small, closely held corporation. Eighty percent of the stock is held by Derek Wallace, president. Of the remainder, 10% is held by members of his family and 10% by Kathy Baker, a former officer who is now retired. The balance sheet of the company at June 30, 2012, was substantially as shown below.

Assets		Liabilities and Stockholders' Equity	
Cash	$ 22,000	Current liabilities	$ 50,000
Other	450,000	Capital stock	250,000
	$472,000	Retained earnings	172,000
			$472,000

Additional authorized capital stock of $300,000 par value had never been issued. To strengthen the cash position of the company, Wallace issued capital stock with a par value of $100,000 to himself at par for cash. At the next stockholders' meeting, Baker objected and claimed that her interests had been injured.

Instructions

   (a) Which stockholder's right was ignored in the issue of shares to Derek Wallace?
   (b) How may the damage to Baker's interests be repaired most simply?
   (c) If Derek Wallace offered Baker a personal cash settlement and they agreed to employ you as an impartial arbitrator to determine the amount, what settlement would you propose? Present your calculations with sufficient explanation to satisfy both parties.

CA15-2 (Issuance of Stock for Land) Martin Corporation is planning to issue 3,000 shares of its own $10 par value common stock for two acres of land to be used as a building site.

Instructions

   (a) What general rule should be applied to determine the amount at which the land should be recorded?
   (b) Under what circumstances should this transaction be recorded at the fair value of the land?
   (c) Under what circumstances should this transaction be recorded at the fair value of the stock issued?
   (d) Assume Martin intentionally records this transaction at an amount greater than the fair value of the land and the stock. Discuss this situation.

CA15-3 (Conceptual Issues—Equity) Statements of Financial Accounting Concepts set forth financial accounting and reporting objectives and fundamentals that will be used by the Financial Accounting Standards Board in developing standards. *Concepts Statement No. 6* defines various elements of financial statements.

Instructions

Answer the following questions based on *SFAC No. 6*.

   (a) Define and discuss the term "equity."
   (b) What transactions or events change owners' equity?
   (c) Define "investments by owners" and provide examples of this type of transaction. What financial statement element other than equity is typically affected by owner investments?
   (d) Define "distributions to owners" and provide examples of this type of transaction. What financial statement element other than equity is typically affected by distributions?
   (e) What are examples of changes within owners' equity that do not change the total amount of owners' equity?

CA15-4 (Stock Dividends and Splits) The directors of Merchant Corporation are considering the issuance of a stock dividend. They have asked you to discuss the proposed action by answering the following questions.

Instructions

   (a) What is a stock dividend? How is a stock dividend distinguished from a stock split (1) from a legal standpoint, and (2) from an accounting standpoint?
   (b) For what reasons does a corporation usually declare a stock dividend? A stock split?
   (c) Discuss the amount, if any, of retained earnings to be capitalized in connection with a stock dividend.

(AICPA adapted)

CA15-5 (Stock Dividends) Kulikowski Inc., a client, is considering the authorization of a 10% common stock dividend to common stockholders. The financial vice president of Kulikowski wishes to discuss the accounting implications of such an authorization with you before the next meeting of the board of directors.

Instructions

   (a) The first topic the vice president wishes to discuss is the nature of the stock dividend to the recipient. Discuss the case against considering the stock dividend as income to the recipient.
   (b) The other topic for discussion is the propriety of issuing the stock dividend to all "stockholders of record" or to "stockholders of record exclusive of shares held in the name of the corporation as treasury stock." Discuss the case against issuing stock dividends on treasury shares.

(AICPA adapted)

CA15-6 (Stock Dividend, Cash Dividend, and Treasury Stock) Mask Company has 30,000 shares of $10 par value common stock authorized and 20,000 shares issued and outstanding. On August 15, 2012, Mask purchased 1,000 shares of treasury stock for $18 per share. Mask uses the cost method to account for treasury stock. On September 14, 2012, Mask sold 500 shares of the treasury stock for $20 per share.

In October 2012, Mask declared and distributed 1,950 shares as a stock dividend from unissued shares when the market price of the common stock was $21 per share.

On December 20, 2012, Mask declared a $1 per share cash dividend, payable on January 10, 2013, to shareholders of record on December 31, 2012.

Instructions

(a) How should Mask account for the purchase and sale of the treasury stock, and how should the treasury stock be presented in the balance sheet at December 31, 2012?

(b) How should Mask account for the stock dividend, and how would it affect the stockholders' equity at December 31, 2012? Why?

(c) How should Mask account for the cash dividend, and how would it affect the balance sheet at December 31, 2012? Why?

(AICPA adapted)

CA15-7 (Treasury Stock—Ethics) Lois Kenseth, president of Sycamore Corporation, is concerned about several large stockholders who have been very vocal lately in their criticisms of her leadership. She thinks they might mount a campaign to have her removed as the corporation's CEO. She decides that buying them out by purchasing their shares could eliminate them as opponents, and she is confident they would accept a "good" offer. Kenseth knows the corporation's cash position is decent, so it has the cash to complete the transaction. She also knows the purchase of these shares will increase earnings per share, which should make other investors quite happy. (Earnings per share is calculated by dividing net income available for the common shareholders by the weighted-average number of shares outstanding. Therefore, if the number of shares outstanding is decreased by purchasing treasury shares, earnings per share increases.)

Instructions

Answer the following questions.

(a) Who are the stakeholders in this situation?
(b) What are the ethical issues involved?
(c) Should Kenseth authorize the transaction?

USING YOUR JUDGMENT

FINANCIAL REPORTING

Financial Reporting Problem

 The Procter & Gamble Company (P&G)

The financial statements of P&G are presented in Appendix 5B or can be accessed at the book's companion website, **www.wiley.com/college/kieso**.

Instructions

Refer to these financial statements and the accompanying notes to answer the following questions.

(a) What is the par or stated value of P&G's preferred stock?

(b) What is the par or stated value of P&G's common stock?

(c) What percentage of P&G's authorized common stock was issued at June 30, 2009?

(d) How many shares of common stock were outstanding at June 30, 2009, and June 30, 2008?

(e) What was the dollar amount effect of the cash dividends on P&G's stockholders' equity?

(f) What is P&G's rate of return on common stock equity for 2009 and 2008?

(g) What is P&G's payout ratio for 2009 and 2008?

(h) What was the market price range (high/low) of P&G's common stock during the quarter ended June 30, 2009?

Comparative Analysis Case

The Coca-Cola Company and PepsiCo, Inc.

Instructions

Go to the book's companion website and use information found there to answer the following questions related to The Coca-Cola Company and PepsiCo, Inc.

(a) What is the par or stated value of Coca-Cola's and PepsiCo's common or capital stock?

(b) What percentage of authorized shares was issued by Coca-Cola at December 31, 2009, and by PepsiCo at December 26, 2009?

(c) How many shares are held as treasury stock by Coca-Cola at December 31, 2009, and by PepsiCo at December 26, 2009?

(d) How many Coca-Cola common shares are outstanding at December 31, 2009? How many PepsiCo shares of capital stock are outstanding at December 26, 2009?

(e) What amounts of cash dividends per share were declared by Coca-Cola and PepsiCo in 2009? What were the dollar amount effects of the cash dividends on each company's stockholders' equity?

(f) What are Coca-Cola's and PepsiCo's rate of return on common/capital stock equity for 2009 and 2008? Which company gets the higher return on the equity of its shareholders?

(g) What are Coca-Cola's and PepsiCo's payout ratios for 2009?

(h) What was the market price range (high/low) for Coca-Cola's common stock and PepsiCo's capital stock during the fourth quarter of 2009? Which company's (Coca-Cola's or PepsiCo's) stock price increased more (%) during 2009?

Financial Statement Analysis Cases

Case 1   Kellogg Company

Kellogg Company is the world's leading producer of ready-to-eat cereal products. In recent years, the company has taken numerous steps aimed at improving its profitability and earnings per share. Presented below are some basic facts for Kellogg.

	2009	2008
Net sales	$12,575	$12,822
Net earnings	1,212	1,148
Total assets	11,200	10,946
Total liabilities	8,925	9,491
Common stock, $0.25 par value	105	105
Capital in excess of par value	472	438
Retained earnings	5,481	4,836
Treasury stock, at cost	1,820	1,790
Number of shares outstanding (in millions)	419	419

Instructions

(a) What are some of the reasons that management purchases its own stock?

(b) Explain how earnings per share might be affected by treasury stock transactions.

(c) Calculate the ratio of debt to total assets for 2008 and 2009, and discuss the implications of the change.

Case 2   Wiebold, Incorporated

The following note related to stockholders' equity was reported in Wiebold, Inc.'s annual report.

On February 1, the Board of Directors declared a 3-for-2 stock split, distributed on February 22 to shareholders of record on February 10. Accordingly, all numbers of common shares, except unissued shares and treasury shares, and all per share data have been restated to reflect this stock split.

On the basis of amounts declared and paid, the annualized quarterly dividends per share were $0.80 in the current year and $0.75 in the prior year.

Instructions

(a) What is the significance of the date of record and the date of distribution?

(b) Why might Weibold have declared a 3-for-2 for stock split?

(c) What impact does Wiebold's stock split have on (1) total stockholders' equity, (2) total par value, (3) outstanding shares, and (4) book value per share?

Accounting, Analysis, and Principles

On January 1, 2012, Agassi Corporation had the following stockholders' equity accounts.

Common Stock ($10 par value, 60,000 shares issued and outstanding)	$600,000
Paid-in Capital in Excess of Par	500,000
Retained Earnings	620,000

During 2012, the following transactions occurred.

Jan. 15	Declared and paid a $1.05 cash dividend per share to stockholders.
Apr. 15	Declared and paid a 10% stock dividend. The market price of the stock was $14 per share.
May 15	Reacquired 2,000 common shares at a market price of $15 per share.
Nov. 15	Reissued 1,000 shares held in treasury at a price of $18 per share.
Dec. 31	Determined that net income for the year was $370,000.

Accounting

Journalize the above transactions. (Include entries to close net income to Retained Earnings.) Determine the ending balances for Paid-in Capital, Retained Earnings, and Stockholders' Equity.

Analysis

Calculate the payout ratio and the return on common stock equity ratio.

Principles

R. Federer is examining Agassi's financial statements and wonders whether the "gains" or "losses" on Agassi's treasury stock transactions should be included in income for the year. Briefly explain whether, and the conceptual reasons why, gains or losses on treasury stock transactions should be recorded in income.

BRIDGE TO THE PROFESSION

 ## Professional Research: FASB Codification

Recall from Chapter 13 that Hincapie Co. (a specialty bike-accessory manufacturer) is expecting growth in sales of some products targeted to the low-price market. Hincapie is contemplating a preferred stock issue to help finance this expansion in operations. The company is leaning toward participating preferred stock because ownership will not be diluted, but the investors will get an extra dividend if the company does well. The company management wants to be certain that its reporting of this transaction is transparent to its current shareholders and wants you to research the disclosure requirements related to its capital structure.

Instructions

If your school has a subscription to the FASB Codification, go to *http://aaahq.org/ascLogin.cfm* to log in and prepare responses to the following. Provide Codification references for your responses.

(a) Identify the authoritative literature that addresses disclosure of information about capital structure.

(b) Find definitions of the following:

(1) Securities.

(2) Participation rights.

(3) Preferred stock.

(c) What information about securities must companies disclose? Discuss how Hincapie should report the proposed preferred stock issue.

Professional Simulation

In this simulation, you are asked to address questions related to the accounting for stockholders, equity. Prepare responses to all parts.

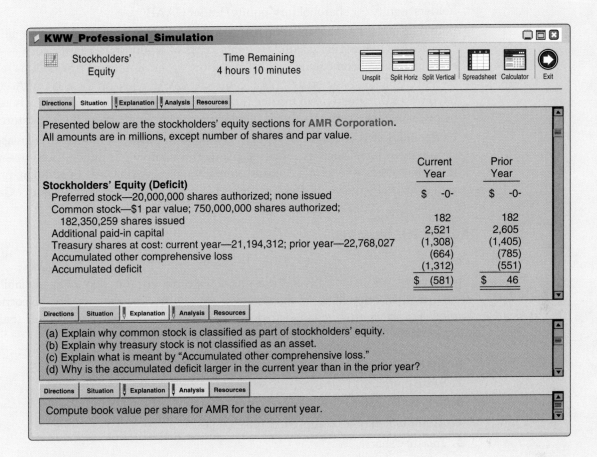

KWW_Professional_Simulation

Stockholders' Equity — Time Remaining 4 hours 10 minutes

Unsplit | Split Horiz | Split Vertical | Spreadsheet | Calculator | Exit

Directions | Situation | Explanation | Analysis | Resources

Presented below are the stockholders' equity sections for **AMR Corporation**. All amounts are in millions, except number of shares and par value.

	Current Year	Prior Year
Stockholders' Equity (Deficit)		
Preferred stock—20,000,000 shares authorized; none issued	$ -0-	$ -0-
Common stock—$1 par value; 750,000,000 shares authorized; 182,350,259 shares issued	182	182
Additional paid-in capital	2,521	2,605
Treasury shares at cost: current year—21,194,312; prior year—22,768,027	(1,308)	(1,405)
Accumulated other comprehensive loss	(664)	(785)
Accumulated deficit	(1,312)	(551)
	$ (581)	$ 46

Directions | Situation | Explanation | Analysis | Resources

(a) Explain why common stock is classified as part of stockholders' equity.
(b) Explain why treasury stock is not classified as an asset.
(c) Explain what is meant by "Accumulated other comprehensive loss."
(d) Why is the accumulated deficit larger in the current year than in the prior year?

Directions | Situation | Explanation | Analysis | Resources

Compute book value per share for AMR for the current year.

IFRS Insights

The primary IFRS related to stockholders' equity are *IAS 1* ("Presentation of Financial Statements"), *IAS 32* ("Financial Instruments: Presentation"), and *IAS 39* ("Financial Instruments: Recognition and Measurement"). The accounting for transactions related to stockholders' equity, such as issuance of shares, purchase of treasury stock, and declaration and payment of dividends, are similar under both IFRS and GAAP. Major differences relate to terminology used, introduction of terms such as revaluation surplus, and presentation of stockholders' equity information.

RELEVANT FACTS

- Many countries have different investor groups than the United States. For example, in Germany, financial institutions like banks are not only the major creditors but often are the largest shareholders as well. In the United States and the United Kingdom, many companies rely on substantial investment from private investors.

- The accounting for treasury share retirements differs between IFRS and GAAP. Under GAAP, a company has three options: (1) charge the excess of the cost of treasury shares over par value to retained earnings, (2) allocate the difference between paid-in capital and retained earnings, or (3) charge the entire amount to paid-in capital. Under IFRS, the excess may have to be charged to paid-in capital, depending on the original transaction related to the issuance of the shares.

- The statement of changes in equity is usually referred to as the statement of stockholders' equity (or shareholders' equity) under GAAP.

- Both IFRS and GAAP use the term retained earnings. However, IFRS relies on the term "reserve" as a dumping ground for other types of equity transactions, such as other comprehensive income items as well as various types of unusual transactions related to convertible debt and share option contracts. GAAP relies on the account Accumulated Other Comprehensive Income (Loss). We also use this account in the discussion below, as it appears this account is gaining prominence within the IFRS literature.

- Under IFRS, it is common to report "Revaluation Surplus" related to increases or decreases in items such as property, plant, and equipment; mineral resources; and intangible assets. The term surplus is generally not used in GAAP. In addition, unrealized gains on the above items are not reported in the financial statements under GAAP.

ABOUT THE NUMBERS

Equity

Equity is the residual interest in the assets of the company after deducting all liabilities. Equity is often referred to as shareholders' equity, stockholders' equity, or corporate capital. Equity is often subclassified on the statement of financial position (balance sheet) into the following categories (as discussed in Chapter 5).

1. Share capital.
2. Share premium.
3. Retained earnings.
4. Accumulated other comprehensive income.
5. Treasury shares.
6. Non-controlling interest (minority interest).

Such classifications help financial statement users to better understand the legal or other restrictions related to the ability of the company to pay dividends or otherwise use its equity for certain defined purposes. Companies often make a distinction between contributed capital (paid-in capital) and earned capital. **Contributed capital (paid-in capital)** is the total amount paid in on capital shares—the amount provided by shareholders to the corporation for use in the business. Contributed capital includes items such as the par value of all outstanding shares and premiums less discounts on issuance. **Earned capital** is the capital that develops from profitable operations. It consists of all undistributed income that remains invested in the company. **Retained earnings** represents the earned capital of the company.

As indicated above, equity is a **residual interest** and therefore its value is derived from the amount of the corporations' assets and liabilities. Only in unusual cases will a company's equity equal the total fair value of its shares. For example, BMW recently had total equity of €20,265 million and a market capitalization of €21,160 million. BMW's equity represents the net contributions from shareholders (from both majority and minority shareholders) plus retained earnings and accumulated other comprehensive income. As a residual interest, its equity has no existence apart from the assets and liabilities of BMW—equity equals net assets. Equity is not a claim to specific assets but a claim against a portion of the total assets. Its amount is not specified or fixed; it depends on BMW's profitability. Equity grows if it is profitable. It shrinks, or may disappear entirely, if BMW loses money.

Issuance of Ordinary Shares

Under IFRS, the accounting for share issuances is similar to GAAP. The primary difference is the account titles. GAAP uses an account, Common Stock, for the par value of shares, while IFRS uses an account labeled Share Capital. What about no-par shares? In some countries, as in the United States, the total issue price for no-par shares may be considered legal capital, which could reduce the flexibility in paying dividends. Corporations sell no-par shares, like par value shares, for whatever price they will bring. However, unlike par value shares, corporations issue them without a premium or a discount. The exact amount received represents the credit to ordinary or preference shares.

For example, Video Electronics Corporation is organized with 10,000 ordinary shares authorized without par value. Video Electronics makes only a memorandum entry for the authorization, inasmuch as no amount is involved. If Video Electronics then issues 500 shares for cash at $10 per share, it makes the following entry.

Cash	5,000	
Share Capital—Ordinary		5,000

If it issues another 500 shares for $11 per share, Video Electronics makes this entry.

Cash	5,500	
Share Capital—Ordinary		5,500

True no-par shares should be carried in the accounts at issue price without any share premium reported. But some countries require that no-par shares have a **stated value**. The stated value is a minimum value below which a company cannot issue it. Thus, instead of being no-par shares, such stated-value shares become, in effect, shares with a very low par value. It thus is open to all the criticism and abuses that first encouraged the development of no-par shares.

If no-par shares have a stated value of $5 per share but sell for $11, all such amounts in excess of $5 are recorded as share premium, which in many jurisdictions is fully or partially available for dividends. Thus, no-par value shares, with a low stated value, permit a new corporation to commence its operations with share premium that may exceed its stated capital. For example, if a company issued 1,000 of the shares with a $5 stated value at $15 per share for cash, it makes the following entry.

Cash	15,000	
Share Capital—Ordinary		5,000
Share Premium—Ordinary		10,000

Most corporations account for no-par shares with a stated value as if they were par value shares with par equal to the stated value.

Accounting for and Reporting Preference Shares

The accounting for preference shares at issuance is similar to that for ordinary shares. A corporation allocates proceeds between the par value of the preference shares and share premium. To illustrate, assume that Bishop Co. issues 10,000 shares of $10 par value preference shares for $12 cash per share. Bishop records the issuance as follows.

Cash	120,000	
Share Capital—Preference		100,000
Share Premium—Preference		20,000

Thus, Bishop maintains separate accounts for these different classes of shares. Corporations consider convertible preference shares as a part of equity. In addition, when exercising convertible preference shares, there is no theoretical justification for recognition of a gain or loss. A company recognizes no gain or loss when dealing with shareholders in their capacity as business owners. Instead, the company **employs the book value method**: debit Share Capital—Preference, along with any related Share Premium—Preference; credit Share Capital—Ordinary and Share Premium—Ordinary (if an excess exists).

Preference shares generally have no maturity date. Therefore, no legal obligation exists to pay the preference shareholder. As a result, companies classify preference shares as part of equity. Companies generally report preference shares at par value as the first item in the equity section. They report any excess over par value as part of share premium. They also consider dividends on preference shares as a distribution of income and not an expense. Companies must disclose the pertinent rights of the preference shares outstanding.

Presentation of Equity

Statement of Financial Position

Illustration IFRS15-1 shows a comprehensive equity section from the statement of financial position of Frost Company that includes the equity items we discussed previously.

ILLUSTRATION
IFRS15-1
Comprehensive Equity
Presentation

FROST COMPANY		
EQUITY		
DECEMBER 31, 2012		
Share capital—preference, $100 par value, 7% cumulative,		
100,000 shares authorized, 30,000 shares issued and outstanding	$3,000,000	
Share capital—ordinary, no-par, stated value $10 per share,		
500,000 shares authorized, 400,000 shares issued	4,000,000	
Ordinary share dividend distributable	200,000	$ 7,200,000
Share premium—preference	150,000	
Share premium—ordinary	840,000	990,000
Retained earnings		4,360,000
Treasury shares (2,000 ordinary shares)		(190,000)
Accumulated other comprehensive loss		(360,000)
Total equity		$12,000,000

Frost should disclose the pertinent rights and privileges of the various securities outstanding. For example, companies must disclose all of the following: dividend and liquidation preferences, participation rights, call prices and dates, conversion or exercise prices and pertinent dates, sinking fund requirements, unusual voting rights, and significant terms of contracts to issue additional shares. Liquidation preferences should be disclosed in the equity section of the statement of financial position, rather than in the notes to the financial statements, to emphasize the possible effect of this restriction on future cash flows.

Presentation of Statement of Changes in Equity

Companies are also required to present a **statement of changes in equity**. The statement of changes in equity includes the following.

1. Total comprehensive income for the period, showing separately the total amounts attributable to owners of the parent and to non-controlling interests.
2. For each component of equity, the effects of retrospective application or retrospective restatement.
3. For each component of equity, a reconciliation between the carrying amount at the beginning and the end of the period, separately disclosing changes resulting from:
   (a) Profit or loss;
   (b) Each item of other comprehensive income; and
   (c) Transactions with owners in their capacity as owners, showing separately contributions by and distributions to owners and changes in ownership interests in subsidiaries that do not result in a loss of control.

A typical statement of changes in equity is shown in Illustration IFRS15-2.

	Share Capital	Retained Earnings	Unrealized Holding Gain (Loss) on Non-Trading Equity Investments	Unrealized Holding Gain (Loss) on Property, Plant, and Equipment	Total
Balance—December 31, 2012	$600,000	$120,000	$22,000	$15,000	$ 757,000
Issue of Ordinary Shares	200,000				200,000
Total Comprehensive Income		70,000	11,000	8,000	89,000
Dividends		(20,000)			(20,000)
Balance—December 31, 2013	$800,000	$170,000	$33,000	$23,000	$1,026,000

ILLUSTRATION IFRS15-2
Statement of Changes in Equity

In addition, companies are required to present, either in the statement of changes in equity or in the notes, the amount of dividends recognized as distributions to owners during the period and the related amount per share.

ON THE HORIZON

As indicated in earlier discussions, the IASB and the FASB are currently working on a project related to financial statement presentation. An important part of this study is to determine whether certain line items, subtotals, and totals should be clearly defined and required to be displayed in the financial statements. For example, it is likely that the statement of changes in equity and its presentation will be examined closely. In addition, the options of how to present other comprehensive income under GAAP will change in any converged standard.

IFRS SELF-TEST QUESTIONS

1. Which of the following does *not* represent a pair of GAAP/IFRS-comparable terms?
   (a) Additional paid-in capital/Share premium.
   (b) Treasury stock/Repurchase reserve.
   (c) Common stock/Share capital—ordinary.
   (d) Preferred stock/Preference shares.

2. Under IFRS, the amount of capital received in excess of par value would be credited to:
   (a) Retained Earnings.
   (b) Contributed Capital.
   (c) Share Premium.
   (d) Par value is not used under IFRS.

3. The term *reserves* is used under IFRS with reference to all of the following *except:*
   (a) gains and losses on revaluation of property, plant, and equipment.
   (b) capital received in excess of the par value of issued shares.
   (c) retained earnings.
   (d) fair value differences.

4. Which of the following is *false*?
   (a) Under GAAP, companies cannot record gains on transactions involving their own shares.
   (b) Under IFRS, companies cannot record gains on transactions involving their own shares.
   (c) Under IFRS, the statement of stockholders' equity is a required statement.
   (d) Under IFRS, a company records a revaluation surplus when it experiences an increase in the price of its common stock.

5. Under IFRS, a purchase by a company of its own shares results in:
   (a) an increase in treasury shares.
   (b) a decrease in assets.
   (c) a decrease in equity.
   (d) All of the above.

IFRS CONCEPTS AND APPLICATION

IFRS15-1 Where can authoritative IFRS guidance related to stockholders' equity be found?

IFRS15-2 Briefly describe some of the similarities and differences between GAAP and IFRS with respect to the accounting for stockholders' equity.

IFRS15-3 Briefly discuss the implications of the financial statement presentation project for the reporting of stockholders' equity.

IFRS15-4 Mary Tokar is comparing a GAAP-based company to a company that uses IFRS. Both companies report equity investments. The IFRS company reports unrealized losses on these investments under the heading "Reserves" in its equity section. However, Mary can find no similar heading in the GAAP-based company financial statements. Can Mary conclude that the GAAP-based company has no unrealized gains or losses on its non-trading equity investments? Explain.

IFRS15-5 Explain each of the following terms: authorized ordinary shares, unissued ordinary shares, issued ordinary shares, outstanding ordinary shares, and treasury shares.

IFRS15-6 Indicate how each of the following accounts should be classified in the equity section.

   (a) Share Capital—Ordinary
   (b) Retained Earnings
   (c) Share Premium—Ordinary
   (d) Treasury Shares
   (e) Share Premium—Treasury
   (f) Share Capital—Preference
   (g) Accumulated Other Comprehensive Income

IFRS15-7 Kaymer Corporation issued 300 shares of $10 par value ordinary shares for $4,500. Prepare Kaymer's journal entry.

IFRS15-8 Wilco Corporation has the following account balances at December 31, 2012.

Share capital—ordinary, $5 par value	$ 510,000
Treasury shares	90,000
Retained earnings	2,340,000
Share premium—ordinary	1,320,000

Instructions

Prepare Wilco's December 31, 2012, equity section.

IFRS15-9 Ravonette Corporation issued 300 shares of $10 par value ordinary shares and 100 shares of $50 par value preference shares for a lump sum of $13,500. The ordinary shares have a market price of $20 per share, and the preference shares have a market price of $90 per share.

Instructions

Prepare the journal entry to record the issuance.

IFRS15-10 Weisberg Corporation has 10,000 shares of $100 par value, 6%, preference shares and 50,000 ordinary shares of $10 par value outstanding at December 31, 2012.

Instructions

Answer the questions in each of the following independent situations.

(a) If the preference shares are cumulative and dividends were last paid on the preference shares on December 31, 2009, what are the dividends in arrears that should be reported on the December 31, 2012, statement of financial position? How should these dividends be reported?

(b) If the preference shares are convertible into seven shares of $10 par value ordinary shares and 3,000 shares are converted, what entry is required for the conversion, assuming the preference shares were issued at par value?

(c) If the preference shares were issued at $107 per share, how should the preference shares be reported in the equity section?

IFRS15-11 Teller Corporation's post-closing trial balance at December 31, 2012, was as follows.

TELLER CORPORATION POST-CLOSING TRIAL BALANCE DECEMBER 31, 2012		
	Dr.	Cr.
Accounts payable		$ 310,000
Accounts receivable	$ 480,000	
Accumulated depreciation—building and equipment		185,000
Allowance for doubtful accounts		30,000
Bonds payable		700,000
Building and equipment	1,450,000	
Cash	190,000	
Dividends payable on preference shares—cash		4,000
Inventories	560,000	
Land	400,000	
Prepaid expenses	40,000	
Retained earnings		201,000
Share capital—ordinary ($1 par value)		200,000
Share capital—preference ($50 par value)		500,000
Share premium—ordinary		1,000,000
Share premium—treasury		160,000
Treasury shares—ordinary at cost	170,000	
Totals	$3,290,000	$3,290,000

At December 31, 2012, Teller had the following number of ordinary and preference shares.

	Ordinary	Preference
Authorized	600,000	60,000
Issued	200,000	10,000
Outstanding	190,000	10,000

The dividends on preference shares are $4 cumulative. In addition, the preference shares have a preference in liquidation of $50 per share.

Instructions

Prepare the equity section of Teller's statement of financial position at December 31, 2012.

Professional Research

IFRS15-12 Recall from Chapter 13 that Hincapie Co. (a specialty bike-accessory manufacturer) is expecting growth in sales of some products targeted to the low-price market. Hincapie is contemplating a preference share issue to help finance this expansion in operations. The company is leaning toward preference shares because ownership will not be diluted, but the investors will get an extra dividend if the company does well. The company management wants to be certain that its reporting of this transaction is transparent to its current shareholders and wants you to research the disclosure requirements related to its capital structure.

Instructions

Access the IFRS authoritative literature at the IASB website (*http://eifrs.iasb.org/*). When you have accessed the documents, you can use the search tool in your Internet browser to respond to the following questions. (Provide paragraph citations.)

(a) Identify the authoritative literature that addresses disclosure of information about capital structure.

(b) What information about share capital must companies disclose? Discuss how Hincapie should report the proposed preference share issue.

International Financial Reporting Problem:
Marks and Spencer plc

IFRS15-13 The financial statements of **Marks and Spencer plc (M&S)** are available at the book's companion website or can be accessed at *http://corporate.marksandspencer. com/documents/publications/2010/Annual_Report_2010*.

Instructions

Refer to M&S's financial statements and the accompanying notes to answer the following questions.

(a) What is the par or stated value of M&S's preference shares?

(b) What is the par or stated value of M&S's ordinary shares?

(c) What percentage of M&S's authorized ordinary shares was issued at April 3, 2010?

(d) How many ordinary shares were outstanding at December 31, 2010, and March 28, 2009?

(e) What was the pound amount effect of the cash dividends on M&S's equity?

(f) What is M&S's rate of return on ordinary share equity for 2010 and 2009?

(g) What is M&S's payout ratio for 2010 and 2009?

ANSWERS TO IFRS SELF-TEST QUESTIONS

1. b **2.** c **3.** b **4.** d **5.** d

16 Dilutive Securities and Earnings per Share

After studying this chapter, you should be able to:

1 Describe the accounting for the issuance, conversion, and retirement of convertible securities.

2 Explain the accounting for convertible preferred stock.

3 Contrast the accounting for stock warrants and for stock warrants issued with other securities.

4 Describe the accounting for stock compensation plans under generally accepted accounting principles.

5 Discuss the controversy involving stock compensation plans.

6 Compute earnings per share in a simple capital structure.

7 Compute earnings per share in a complex capital structure.

Kicking the Habit

Some habits die hard. Take stock options—called by some "the crack cocaine of incentives." Stock options are a form of compensation that gives key employees the choice to purchase shares at a given (usually lower-than-market) price. For many years, companies were hooked on these products. Why? The combination of a hot equity market and favorable accounting treatment made stock options the incentive of choice. They were compensation with no expense to the companies that granted them, and they were popular with key employees, so companies granted them with abandon. However, the accounting rules that took effect in 2005 required *expensing* the fair value of stock options. This new treatment has made it easier for companies to kick this habit.

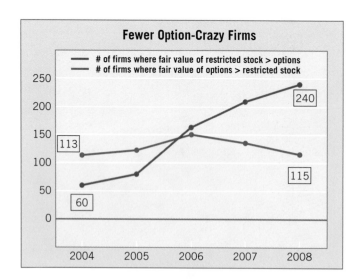

Fewer Option-Crazy Firms

— # of firms where fair value of restricted stock > options
— # of firms where fair value of options > restricted stock

As shown in the chart above, a review of option use for the U.S. companies in the S&P 500 indicates a decline in the use of option-based compensation and an increase in restricted-stock plans. Fewer companies are granting stock options, following implementation of stock-option expensing. As

IFRS IN THIS CHAPTER

See the **International Perspectives** on pages 912, 915, 918, 923, and 927.

Read the **IFRS Insights** on pages 965–973 for a discussion of:

—Accounting for convertible debt

—Employee share-purchase plans

a spokesperson at one company commented, "Once you begin expensing options, the attractiveness significantly drops."

In the 1990s, executives with huge option stockpiles had an almost irresistible incentive to do whatever it took to increase the stock price and cash in their options. By reining in options, many companies are taking the first steps toward curbing both out-of-control executive pay and the era of corporate corruption that it spawned.

As indicated earlier, some of the ways that companies are curbing option grants include replacing options with restricted shares. Further analysis of these trends indicates that restricted-stock use is more than 10 times the magnitude of options grants in the financial industry. Even after excluding nonfinancial companies from the statistics, restricted shares are now the plan of choice. And in the information technology area (where in the past, share options were heavily favored), the fair value of restricted-share plans exceeds that for share options. In this industry, some companies are simply reducing option grants, without offering a replacement, while others, like **Microsoft** and **Yahoo!**, have switched to restricted-stock plans completely. Is this a good trend? Most believe it is; the requirement to expense stock-based compensation similar to other forms of compensation has changed the focus of compensation plans to rewarding talent and performance without breaking the bank. The positive impact on corporate behavior, while hard to measure, should benefit investors in years to come.

Sources: Adapted from: Louis Lavelle, "Kicking the Stock-Options Habit," *BusinessWeek Online* (February 16, 2005). Graphs from J. Ciesielski, "S&P 500 Stock Compensation: Who Needs Options?" *The Analyst's Accounting Observer* (July 30, 2008), and J. Ciesielski, "S&P 500 Stock Compensation: Running Out of Options," *The Analyst's Accounting Observer* (August 25, 2009).

PREVIEW OF CHAPTER 16

As the opening story indicates, companies are rethinking the use of various forms of stock-based compensation. The purpose of this chapter is to discuss the proper accounting for stock-based compensation. In addition, the chapter examines issues related to other types of financial instruments, such as convertible securities, warrants, and contingent shares, including their effects on reporting earnings per share. The content and organization of the chapter are as follows.

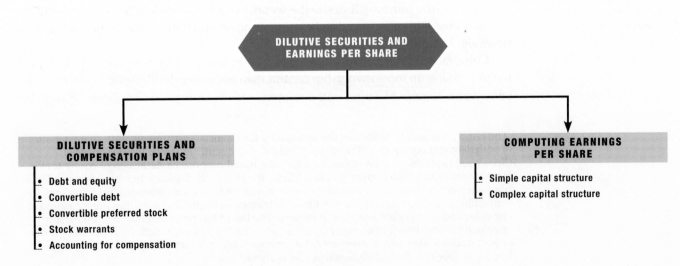

DILUTIVE SECURITIES AND EARNINGS PER SHARE

DILUTIVE SECURITIES AND COMPENSATION PLANS
- Debt and equity
- Convertible debt
- Convertible preferred stock
- Stock warrants
- Accounting for compensation

COMPUTING EARNINGS PER SHARE
- Simple capital structure
- Complex capital structure

SECTION 1 • DILUTIVE SECURITIES AND COMPENSATION PLANS

DEBT AND EQUITY

Many of the controversies related to the accounting for financial instruments such as stock options, convertible securities, and preferred stock relate to whether companies should report these instruments as a liability or as equity. For example, companies should classify nonredeemable common shares as equity because the issuer has no **obligation** to pay dividends or repurchase the stock. Declaration of dividends is at the issuer's discretion, as is the decision to repurchase the stock. Similarly, preferred stock that is not redeemable does not require the issuer to pay dividends or repurchase the stock. Thus, nonredeemable common or preferred stock lacks an important characteristic of a liability—an obligation to pay the holder of the common or preferred stock at some point in the future.

However the classification is not as clear-cut for other financial instruments. For example, in Chapter 15 we discussed the accounting for mandatorily redeemable preferred stock. Companies originally classified this security as part of equity. The SEC then prohibited equity classification, and most companies classified these securities between debt and equity on the balance sheet in a separate section often referred to as the "mezzanine section." The FASB now requires companies to report these types of securities as a liability.[1] [1]

 See the FASB Codification section (page 944).

In this chapter, we discuss securities that have characteristics of *both* debt and equity. For example, a convertible bond has both debt and equity characteristics. Should a company classify this security as debt, as equity, or as part debt and part equity? In addition, how should a company compute earnings per share if it has convertible bonds and other convertible securities in its capital structure? Convertible securities as well as options, warrants, and other securities are often called dilutive securities because upon exercise they may reduce (dilute) earnings per share.

ACCOUNTING FOR CONVERTIBLE DEBT

LEARNING OBJECTIVE 1
Describe the accounting for the issuance, conversion, and retirement of convertible securities.

Convertible bonds can be changed into other corporate securities during some specified period of time after issuance. A convertible bond combines the benefits of a bond with the privilege of exchanging it for stock at the holder's option. Investors who purchase it desire the security of a bond holding (guaranteed interest and principal) plus the added option of conversion if the value of the stock appreciates significantly.

Corporations issue convertibles for two main reasons. One is to raise equity capital without giving up more ownership control than necessary. To illustrate, assume a company wants to raise $1 million; its common stock is selling at $45 a share. To raise the

---

[1]The FASB continues to deliberate the accounting for financial instruments with characteristics of both debt and equity. In a "Preliminary Views" document, "*Financial Instruments with Characteristics of Equity*" (November 30, 2007), the Board proposed a definition of equity that is far more restrictive than current practice. Under the proposed "basic ownership approach," only common stock is classified as equity. All other instruments (such as preferred stock, options, and convertible debt) are classified as liabilities. Instruments classified as liabilities are measured at fair value and changes are reported in income. The Board has proposed the basic ownership approach because it requires a narrow definition of equity. A narrow definition provides fewer opportunities to structure instruments and arrangements to achieve a desired accounting treatment. (See *http://www.fasb.org/project/liabeq.shtml*.)

$1 million, the company would have to sell 22,222 shares (ignoring issue costs). By selling 1,000 bonds at $1,000 par, each convertible into 20 shares of common stock, the company could raise $1 million by committing only 20,000 shares of its common stock.

A second reason to issue convertibles is to obtain debt financing at cheaper rates. Many companies could issue debt only at high interest rates unless they attach a convertible covenant. The conversion privilege entices the investor to accept a lower interest rate than would normally be the case on a straight debt issue. For example, Amazon.com at one time issued convertible bonds that pay interest at an effective yield of 4.75 percent. This rate was much lower than Amazon.com would have had to pay by issuing straight debt. For this lower interest rate, the investor receives the right to buy Amazon.com's common stock at a fixed price until the bond's maturity.[2]

As indicated earlier, the accounting for convertible debt involves reporting issues at the time of (1) issuance, (2) conversion, and (3) retirement.

At Time of Issuance

The method for recording convertible bonds **at the date of issue follows the method used to record straight debt issues**. None of the proceeds are recorded as equity. Companies amortize to the maturity date any discount or premium that results from the issuance of convertible bonds. Why this treatment? Because it is difficult to predict when, if at all, conversion will occur. However, the accounting for convertible debt as a straight debt issue is controversial; we discuss it more fully later in the chapter.

At Time of Conversion

If converting bonds into other securities, a company uses the **book value method** to record the conversion. The book value method records the securities exchanged for the bond at the carrying amount (book value) of the bond.

To illustrate, assume that Hilton, Inc. has a $1,000 bond that is convertible into 10 shares of common stock (par value $10). At the time of conversion, the unamortized premium is $50. Hilton records the conversion of the bonds as follows.

Bonds Payable	1,000	
Premium on Bonds Payable	50	
Common Stock		100
Paid-in Capital in Excess of Par—Common Stock		950

Support for the book value approach is based on the argument that an agreement was established at the date of the issuance either to pay a stated amount of cash at maturity or to issue a stated number of shares of equity securities. Therefore, when the debtholder converts the debt to equity in accordance with the preexisting contract terms, the issuing company recognizes no gain or loss upon conversion.

Induced Conversions

Sometimes the issuer wishes to encourage prompt conversion of its convertible debt to equity securities in order to reduce interest costs or to improve its debt to equity ratio. Thus, the issuer may offer some form of additional consideration (such as cash or

[2]As with any investment, a buyer has to be careful. For example, Wherehouse Entertainment Inc., which had 6¼ percent convertibles outstanding, was taken private in a leveraged buyout. As a result, the convertible was suddenly as risky as a junk bond of a highly leveraged company with a coupon of only 6¼ percent. As one holder of the convertibles noted, "What's even worse is that the company will be so loaded down with debt that it probably won't have enough cash flow to make its interest payments. And the convertible debt we hold is subordinated to the rest of Wherehouse's debt." These types of situations make convertibles less attractive and lead to the introduction of takeover protection covenants in some convertible bond offerings. Or, sometimes convertibles are permitted to be called at par, and therefore the conversion premium may be lost.

common stock), called a "sweetener," to induce conversion. The issuing company reports the sweetener as an expense of the current period. Its amount is the fair value of the additional securities or other consideration given.

Assume that Helloid, Inc. has outstanding $1,000,000 par value convertible debentures convertible into 100,000 shares of $1 par value common stock. Helloid wishes to reduce its annual interest cost. To do so, Helloid agrees to pay the holders of its convertible debentures an additional $80,000 if they will convert. Assuming conversion occurs, Helloid makes the following entry.

Debt Conversion Expense	80,000	
Bonds Payable	1,000,000	
Common Stock		100,000
Paid-in Capital in Excess of Par—Common Stock		900,000
Cash		80,000

Helloid records the additional $80,000 as **an expense of the current period** and not as a reduction of equity.

Some argue that the cost of a conversion inducement is a cost of obtaining equity capital. As a result, they contend, companies should recognize the cost of conversion as a cost of (a reduction of) the equity capital acquired, and not as an expense. However, the FASB indicated that when an issuer makes an additional payment to encourage conversion, the payment is for a service (bondholders converting at a given time) and should be reported as an expense. The issuing company does not report this expense as an extraordinary item. [2]

Retirement of Convertible Debt

As indicated earlier, the method for recording the **issuance** of convertible bonds follows that used in recording straight debt issues. Specifically this means that issuing companies should not attribute any portion of the proceeds to the conversion feature, nor should it credit a paid-in capital account.

Although some raise theoretical objections to this approach, to be consistent, companies need to recognize a gain or loss on **retiring convertible debt in the same way that they recognize a gain or loss on retiring nonconvertible debt.** For this reason, companies should report differences between the cash acquisition price of debt and its carrying amount **in current income as a gain or loss.**

CONVERTIBLE PREFERRED STOCK

LEARNING OBJECTIVE 2
Explain the accounting for convertible preferred stock.

Convertible preferred stock includes an option for the holder to convert preferred shares into a fixed number of common shares. The major difference between accounting for a convertible bond and convertible preferred stock at the date of issue is their classification: Convertible bonds are considered liabilities, whereas convertible preferreds (unless mandatory redemption exists) are considered part of stockholders' equity.

In addition, when stockholders exercise convertible preferred stock, there is no theoretical justification for recognizing a gain or loss. A company does not recognize a gain or loss when it deals with stockholders in their capacity as business owners. Therefore, companies do not recognize a gain or loss when stockholders exercise convertible preferred stock.

In accounting for the exercise of convertible preferred stock, a company uses the **book value method**: It debits Preferred Stock, along with any related Paid-in Capital in Excess of Par—Preferred Stock, and it credits Common Stock and Paid-in Capital in Excess of Par—Common Stock (if an excess exists). The treatment differs when the par value of the common stock issued **exceeds** the book value of the preferred stock. In that case, the company usually debits Retained Earnings for the difference.

To illustrate, assume Host Enterprises issued 1,000 shares of common stock (par value $2) upon conversion of 1,000 shares of preferred stock (par value $1) that was originally issued for a $200 premium. The entry would be:

Convertible Preferred Stock	1,000	
Paid-in Capital in Excess of Par—Preferred Stock	200	
Retained Earnings	800	
Common Stock		2,000

The rationale for the debit to Retained Earnings is that Host has offered the preferred stockholders an **additional return** to facilitate their conversion to common stock. In this example, Host charges the additional return to retained earnings. Many states, however, require that this charge simply reduce additional paid-in capital from other sources.

HOW LOW CAN YOU GO?

What do the numbers mean?

Financial engineers are always looking for the next innovation in security design to meet the needs of both issuers and investors. Consider the convertible bonds issued by STMicroelectronics (STM). STM's 10-year bonds have a zero coupon and are convertible into STM common stock at an exercise price of $33.43. When issued, the bonds sold at an effective yield of −0.05 percent. That's right—a negative yield.

How could this happen? When STM issued the bonds, investors thought the options to convert were so valuable that they were willing to take zero interest payments and invest an amount *in excess of* the maturity value of the bonds. In essence, the investors are paying interest to STM, and STM records interest revenue. Why would investors do this? If the stock price rises, as many thought it would for STM and many tech companies at this time, these bond investors could convert and get a big gain in the stock.

Investors did get some additional protection in the deal: They can redeem the $1,000 bonds after three years and receive $975 (and after five and seven years, for lower amounts), if it looks like the bonds will never convert. In the end, STM has issued bonds with a significant equity component. And because the entire bond issue is classified as debt, STM records negative interest expense.

Source: STM Financial Reports. See also Floyd Norris, "Legal but Absurd: They Borrow a Billion and Report a Profit," *New York Times* (August 8, 2003), p. C1.

STOCK WARRANTS

Warrants are certificates entitling the holder to acquire shares of stock at a certain price within a stated period. This option is similar to the conversion privilege: Warrants, if exercised, become common stock and usually have a dilutive effect (reduce earnings per share) similar to that of the conversion of convertible securities. However, a substantial difference between convertible securities and stock warrants is that upon exercise of the warrants, the holder has to pay a certain amount of money to obtain the shares.

> **3 LEARNING OBJECTIVE**
> Contrast the accounting for stock warrants and for stock warrants issued with other securities.

The issuance of warrants or options to buy additional shares normally arises under three situations:

1. When issuing different types of securities, such as bonds or preferred stock, companies often include warrants **to make the security more attractive**—by providing an "equity kicker."

2. Upon the issuance of additional common stock, existing stockholders have a **preemptive right to purchase common stock** first. Companies may issue warrants to evidence that right.

3. Companies give warrants, often referred to as *stock options*, **to executives and employees** as a form of **compensation**.

The problems in accounting for stock warrants are complex and present many difficulties—some of which remain unresolved. The following sections address the accounting for stock warrants in the three situations listed on the previous page.

Stock Warrants Issued with Other Securities

Warrants issued with other securities are basically long-term options to buy common stock at a fixed price. Generally the life of warrants is five years, occasionally 10 years; very occasionally, a company may offer perpetual warrants.

A warrant works like this: Tenneco, Inc. offered a unit comprising one share of stock and one detachable warrant. As its name implies, the detachable stock warrant can be detached (separated) from the stock and traded as a separate security. The Tenneco warrant in this example is exercisable at $24.25 per share and good for five years. The unit (share of stock plus detachable warrant) sold for 22.75 ($22.75). Since the price of the common stock the day before the sale was 19.88 ($19.88), the difference suggests a price of 2.87 ($2.87) for the warrant.

The investor pays for the warrant in order to receive the right to buy the stock, at a fixed price of $24.25, sometime in the future. It would not be profitable at present for the purchaser to exercise the warrant and buy the stock, because the price of the stock was much below the exercise price.[3] But if, for example, the price of the stock rises to $30, the investor gains $2.88 ($30 − $24.25 − $2.87) on an investment of $2.87, a 100 percent increase! If the price never rises, the investor loses the full $2.87 per warrant.[4]

A company should allocate the proceeds from the sale of debt with detachable stock warrants **between the two securities**.[5] The profession takes the position that two separable instruments are involved, that is, (1) a bond and (2) a warrant giving the holder the right to purchase common stock at a certain price. Companies can trade detachable warrants separately from the debt. This allows the determination of a fair value. The two methods of allocation available are:

1. The proportional method.
2. The incremental method.

Proportional Method

At one time AT&T issued bonds with detachable five-year warrants to buy one share of common stock (par value $5) at $25. At the time, a share of AT&T stock was selling for approximately $50. These warrants enabled AT&T to price its bond offering at par with an 8¾ percent yield (quite a bit lower than prevailing rates at that time). To account for the proceeds from this offering, AT&T would place a value on the two securities: (1) the value of the bonds without the warrants, and (2) the value of the warrants. The proportional method then allocates the proceeds using the proportion of the two amounts, based on fair values.

For example, assume that AT&T's bonds (par $1,000) sold for 99 without the warrants soon after their issue. The market price of the warrants at that time was $30. (Prior

---

[3]Later in this discussion, we will show that the value of the warrant is normally determined on the basis of a relative fair-value approach because of the difficulty of imputing a warrant value in any other manner.

[4]From the illustration, it is apparent that buying warrants can be an "all or nothing" proposition.

[5]A detachable warrant means that the warrant can sell separately from the bond. GAAP makes a distinction between detachable and nondetachable warrants because companies must sell nondetachable warrants with the security as a complete package. Thus, no allocation is permitted. [3]

to sale the warrants will not have a fair value.) The allocation relies on an estimate of fair value, generally as established by an investment banker, or on the relative fair value of the bonds and the warrants soon after the company issues and trades them. The price paid for 10,000, $1,000 bonds with the warrants attached was par, or $10,000,000. Illustration 16-1 shows the proportional allocation of the bond proceeds between the bonds and warrants.

Fair value of bonds (without warrants) ($10,000,000 × .99)		$ 9,900,000
Fair value of warrants (10,000 × $30)		300,000
Aggregate fair value		$10,200,000
Allocated to bonds:	$\dfrac{\$9,900,000}{\$10,200,000} \times \$10,000,000 =$	$ 9,705,882
Allocated to warrants:	$\dfrac{\$300,000}{\$10,200,000} \times \$10,000,000 =$	$ 294,118
Total allocation		$10,000,000

ILLUSTRATION 16-1
Proportional Allocation of Proceeds between Bonds and Warrants

In this situation the bonds sell at a discount. AT&T records the sale as follows.

Cash	9,705,882	
Discount on Bonds Payable	294,118	
Bonds Payable		10,000,000

In addition, AT&T sells warrants that it credits to paid-in capital. It makes the following entry.

Cash	294,118	
Paid-in Capital—Stock Warrants		294,118

AT&T may combine the entries if desired. Here, we show them separately, to indicate that the purchaser of the bond is buying not only a bond, but also a possible future claim on common stock.

Assuming investors exercise all 10,000 warrants (one warrant per one share of stock), AT&T makes the following entry.

Cash (10,000 × $25)	250,000	
Paid-in Capital—Stock Warrants	294,118	
Common Stock (10,000 × $5)		50,000
Paid-in Capital in Excess of Par—Common Stock		494,118

What if investors fail to exercise the warrants? In that case, AT&T debits Paid-in Capital—Stock Warrants for $294,118, and credits Paid-in Capital—Expired Stock Warrants for a like amount. The additional paid-in capital reverts to the former stockholders.

Incremental Method

In instances where a company cannot determine the fair value of either the warrants or the bonds, it applies the **incremental method** used in lump-sum security purchases (as explained in Chapter 15, page 849). That is, the company uses the security for which it *can* determine the fair value. It allocates the remainder of the purchase price to the security for which it does not know the fair value.

For example, assume that the market price of the AT&T warrants is $300,000, but the company cannot determine the market price of the bonds without the warrants. Illustration 16-2 (on page 912) shows the amount allocated to the warrants and the stock in this case.

ILLUSTRATION 16-2
Incremental Allocation of
Proceeds between Bonds
and Warrants

Lump-sum receipt	$10,000,000
Allocated to the warrants	(300,000)
Balance allocated to bonds	$ 9,700,000

Conceptual Questions

The question arises whether the allocation of value to the warrants is consistent with the handling of convertible debt, in which companies allocate no value to the conversion privilege. The FASB stated that the features of a convertible security are **inseparable** in the sense that choices are mutually exclusive: The holder either converts the bonds or redeems them for cash, but cannot do both. No basis, therefore, exists for recognizing the conversion value in the accounts.

> **Underlying Concepts**
>
> Reporting a convertible bond solely as debt is not representationally faithful. However, the cost-benefit constraint is used to justify the failure to allocate between debt and equity.

The Board, however, indicated that the issuance of bonds with **detachable warrants** involves *two* securities, one a debt security, which will remain outstanding until maturity, and the other a warrant to purchase common stock. At the time of issuance, separable instruments exist. The existence of two instruments therefore justifies separate treatment. **Nondetachable warrants**, however, **do not require an allocation of the proceeds between the bonds and the warrants**. Similar to the accounting for convertible bonds, companies record the entire proceeds from nondetachable warrants as debt.

Many argue that the conversion feature of a convertible bond is not significantly different in nature from the call represented by a warrant. The question is whether, although the legal forms differ, sufficient similarities of substance exist to support the same accounting treatment. Some contend that inseparability *per se* is an insufficient basis for restricting allocation between identifiable components of a transaction. Examples of allocation between assets of value in a single transaction *do* exist, such as allocation of values in basket purchases and separation of principal and interest in capitalizing long-term leases. Critics of the current accounting for convertibles say that to deny recognition of value to the conversion feature merely looks to the form of the instrument and does not deal with the substance of the transaction.

> **INTERNATIONAL PERSPECTIVE**
>
> IFRS requires that the issuer of convertible debt record the liability and equity components separately.

In its current exposure draft on this subject, the FASB indicates that companies should separate the debt and equity components of securities such as convertible debt or bonds issued with nondetachable warrants. We agree with this position. In both situations (convertible debt and debt issued with warrants), the investor has made a payment to the company for an equity feature—the right to acquire an equity instrument in the future. The only real distinction between them is that the additional payment made when the equity instrument is formally acquired takes different forms. The warrant holder pays additional cash to the issuing company; the convertible debt holder pays for stock by forgoing the receipt of interest from conversion date until maturity date and by forgoing the receipt of the maturity value itself. Thus, the difference is one of method or form of payment only, rather than one of substance. However, until the profession officially reverses its stand in regard to accounting for convertible debt, companies will continue to report convertible debt and bonds issued with nondetachable warrants solely as debt.[6]

---

[6]A recent FASB Staff Position requires that convertible debt that can be settled in cash should account for the liability and equity components separately. [4] Academic research indicates that estimates of the debt and equity components of convertible bonds are subject to considerable measurement error. See Mary Barth, Wayne Landsman, and Richard Rendleman, Jr., "Option Pricing–Based Bond Value Estimates and a Fundamental Components Approach to Account for Corporate Debt," *The Accounting Review* (January 1998). This and other challenges explain in part the extended time needed to develop new standards in this area.

Rights to Subscribe to Additional Shares

If the directors of a corporation decide to issue new shares of stock, the old stockholders generally have the right (**preemptive privilege**) to purchase newly issued shares in proportion to their holdings. This privilege, referred to as a stock right, saves existing stockholders from suffering a dilution of voting rights without their consent. Also, it may allow them to purchase stock somewhat below its fair value. Unlike the warrants issued with other securities, the warrants issued for stock rights are of short duration.

The certificate representing the stock right states the number of shares the holder of the right may purchase. Each share of stock owned ordinarily gives the owner one stock right. The certificate also states the price at which the new shares may be purchased. The price is normally less than the current market price of such shares, which gives the rights a value in themselves. From the time they are issued until they expire, holders of stock rights may purchase and sell them like any other security.

Companies make only a memorandum entry when they issue rights to existing stockholders. This entry indicates the number of rights issued to existing stockholders in order to ensure that the company has additional unissued stock registered for issuance in case the rights are exercised. Companies make no formal entry at this time because they have not yet issued stock nor received cash.

If holders exercise the stock rights, a cash payment of some type usually is involved. If the company receives cash equal to the par value, it makes an entry crediting Common Stock at par value. If the company receives cash in excess of par value, it credits Paid-in Capital in Excess of Par—Common Stock. If it receives cash less than par value, a debit to Paid-in Capital in Excess of Par—Common Stock is appropriate.

Stock Compensation Plans

The third form of warrant arises in stock compensation plans to pay and motivate employees. This warrant is a stock option, which gives key employees the option to purchase common stock at a given price over an extended period of time.

A consensus of opinion is that effective compensation programs are ones that do the following: (1) base compensation on employee and company performance, (2) motivate employees to high levels of performance, (3) help retain executives and allow for recruitment of new talent, (4) maximize the employee's after-tax benefit and minimize the employer's after-tax cost, and (5) use performance criteria over which the employee has control. Straight cash-compensation plans (salary and perhaps a bonus), though important, are oriented to the short run. Many companies recognize that they need a longer-term compensation plan in addition to the cash component.

Long-term compensation plans attempt to develop company loyalty among key employees by giving them "a piece of the action"—that is, an equity interest. These plans, generally referred to as stock-based compensation plans, come in many forms. Essentially, they provide the employee with the opportunity to receive stock if the performance of the company (by whatever measure) is satisfactory. Typical performance measures focus on long-term improvements that are readily measurable and that benefit the company as a whole, such as increases in earnings per share, revenues, stock price, or market share.

As indicated in our opening story, companies are changing the way they use stock-based compensation. Illustration 16-3 (on page 914) indicates that option expense is on the decline and that another form of stock-based compensation, **restricted stock**, is on the rise. The major reasons for this change are two-fold. Critics often cited the indiscriminate use of stock options as a reason why company executives manipulated accounting numbers in an attempt to achieve higher share price. As a result, many responsible companies decided to cut back on the issuance of options, both to avoid such accounting manipulations and to head off investor doubts. In addition, GAAP now results in companies recording a higher expense when stock options are granted.

ILLUSTRATION 16-3
Stock-Option
Compensation Expense

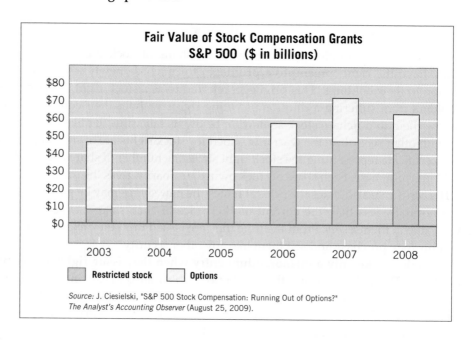

**Fair Value of Stock Compensation Grants
S&P 500 ($ in billions)**

Source: J. Ciesielski, "S&P 500 Stock Compensation: Running Out of Options?"
The Analyst's Accounting Observer (August 25, 2009).

The data reported in Illustration 16-4 reinforce the point that the design of compensation plans is changing. The study documents recent compensation trends of 68 CEOs of companies in the S&P 500.

ILLUSTRATION 16-4
Compensation Elements

2009 Average CEO Pay at S&P 500 Companies	
Salary	$1,041,012
Bonus	203,714
Restricted-Stock Awards	2,630,574
Option Awards	2,284,595
Non-Equity Incentive Plan Compensation	1,790,703
Pension and Deferred Compensation Earnings	1,060,867
All Other Compensation	235,232
Total	9,246,697

Source: AFL-CIO analysis of pay data from 292 companies provided by *salary.com*.

Illustration 16-4 shows that cash compensation is about 10 percent of total compensation. Long-term incentives (stock and option awards and pension and deferred compensation) comprise two-thirds of total compensation. As indicated, restricted stock represents the largest component, although stock options remain an important means of compensating these CEOs.

The Major Reporting Issue

Suppose that, as an employee for Hurdle Inc., you receive options to purchase 10,000 shares of the firm's common stock as part of your compensation. The date you receive the options is referred to as the **grant date**. The options are good for 10 years. The market price and the exercise price for the stock are both $20 at the grant date. **What is the value of the compensation you just received?**

Some believe that what you have received has no value. They reason that because the difference between the market price and the exercise price is zero, no compensation results. Others argue these options do have value: If the stock price goes above $20 any time in the next 10 years and you exercise the options, you may earn substantial compensation. For example, if at the end of the fourth year, the market price of the stock is

$30 and you exercise your options, you earn $100,000 [10,000 options × ($30 − $20)], ignoring income taxes.

The question for Hurdle is how to report the granting of these options. One approach measures compensation cost by the excess of the market price of the stock over its exercise price at the grant date. This approach is referred to as the **intrinsic-value method**. It measures what the holder would receive today if the option was immediately exercised. That intrinsic value **is the difference between the market price of the stock and the exercise price of the options at the grant date**. Using the intrinsic-value method, Hurdle would not recognize any compensation expense related to your options because at the grant date the market price equaled the exercise price. (In the preceding paragraph, those who answered that the options had no value were looking at the question from the intrinsic-value approach.)

> **INTERNATIONAL PERSPECTIVE**
>
> IFRS follows the same model as GAAP for recognizing share-based compensation.

The second way to look at the question of how to report the granting of these options bases the cost of employee stock options on the **fair value** of the stock options granted. Under this fair value method, companies use acceptable option-pricing models to value the options at the date of grant. These models take into account the many factors that determine an option's underlying value.[7]

The FASB guidelines now require that companies recognize compensation cost using the fair value method. [5] The FASB position is that companies should base the accounting for the cost of employee services on the fair value of compensation paid. This amount is presumed to be a measure of the value of the services received. We will discuss more about the politics of GAAP in this area later (see "Debate over Stock-Option Accounting," page 919). Let's first describe the procedures involved.

ACCOUNTING FOR STOCK COMPENSATION

Stock-Option Plans

Stock-option plans involve two main accounting issues:

> **4 LEARNING OBJECTIVE**
> Describe the accounting for stock compensation plans under generally accepted accounting principles.

1. How to determine compensation expense.
2. Over what periods to allocate compensation expense.

Determining Expense

Under the fair value method, companies compute total compensation expense based on the fair value of the options expected to vest on the date they grant the options to the employee(s) (i.e., the **grant date**).[8] Public companies estimate fair value by using an option-pricing model, with some adjustments for the unique factors of employee stock options. No adjustments occur after the grant date in response to subsequent changes in the stock price—either up or down.

Allocating Compensation Expense

In general, a company recognizes compensation expense in the periods in which its employees perform the service—the **service period**. Unless otherwise specified, the service period is the vesting period—the time between the grant date and the vesting date. Thus, the company determines total compensation cost at the grant date and allocates it to the periods benefited by its employees' services.

---

[7]These factors include the volatility of the underlying stock, the expected life of the options, the risk-free rate during the option life, and expected dividends during the option life.

[8]"To vest" means "to earn the rights to." An employee's award becomes vested at the date that the employee's right to receive or retain shares of stock or cash under the award is no longer contingent on remaining in the service of the employer.

Stock Compensation Example

An example will help show the accounting for a stock-option plan. Assume that on November 1, 2011, the stockholders of Chen Company approve a plan that grants the company's five executives options to purchase 2,000 shares each of the company's $1 par value common stock. The company grants the options on January 1, 2012. The executives may exercise the options at any time within the next 10 years. The option price per share is $60, and the market price of the stock at the date of grant is $70 per share.

Under the fair value method, the company computes total compensation expense by applying an acceptable fair value option-pricing model (such as the Black-Scholes option-pricing model). To keep this illustration simple, we assume that the fair value option-pricing model determines Chen's total compensation expense to be $220,000.

Basic Entries. Under the fair value method, a company recognizes the value of the options as an expense in the periods in which the employee performs services. In the case of Chen Company, assume that the expected period of benefit is two years, starting with the grant date. Chen would record the transactions related to this option contract as follows.

At date of grant (January 1, 2012)

No entry.

To record compensation expense for 2012 (December 31, 2012)

Compensation Expense	110,000	
Paid-in Capital—Stock Options ($220,000 ÷ 2)		110,000

To record compensation expense for 2013 (December 31, 2013)

Compensation Expense	110,000	
Paid-in Capital—Stock Options		110,000

As indicated, Chen allocates compensation expense evenly over the two-year service period.

Exercise. If Chen's executives exercise 2,000 of the 10,000 options (20 percent of the options) on June 1, 2015 (three years and five months after date of grant), the company records the following journal entry.

June 1, 2015

Cash (2,000 × $60)	120,000	
Paid-in Capital—Stock Options (20% × $220,000)	44,000	
Common Stock (2,000 × $1.00)		2,000
Paid-in Capital in Excess of Par—Common Stock		162,000

Expiration. If Chen's executives fail to exercise the remaining stock options before their expiration date, the company transfers the balance in the Paid-in Capital—Stock Options account to a more properly titled paid-in capital account, such as Paid-in Capital—Expired Stock Options. Chen records this transaction at the date of expiration as follows.

January 1, 2022 (expiration date)

Paid-in Capital—Stock Options	176,000	
Paid-in Capital—Expired Stock Options		176,000
(80% × $220,000)		

Adjustment. An unexercised stock option does not nullify the need to record the costs of services received from executives and attributable to the stock option plan. Under GAAP, a company therefore does not adjust compensation expense upon expiration of the options.

However, if an employee forfeits a stock option because **the employee fails to satisfy a service requirement** (e.g., leaves employment), the company should adjust the estimate of compensation expense recorded in the current period (as a change in estimate). A company records this change in estimate by debiting Paid-in Capital—Stock Options and crediting Compensation Expense for the amount of cumulative compensation expense recorded to date (thus decreasing compensation expense in the period of forfeiture.)

Restricted Stock

As indicated earlier, many companies are also using restricted stock (or replacing options altogether) to compensate employees. **Restricted-stock plans** transfer shares of stock to employees, subject to an agreement that the shares cannot be sold, transferred, or pledged until vesting occurs. These shares are subject to forfeiture if the conditions for vesting are not met.[9]

Major advantages of restricted-stock plans are:

1. Restricted stock never becomes completely worthless. In contrast, if the stock price does not exceed the exercise price for a stock option, the options are worthless. The restricted stock, however, still has value.

2. Restricted stock generally results in less dilution to existing stockholders. Restricted-stock awards are usually one-half to one-third the size of stock options. For example, if a company issues stock options on 1,000 shares, an equivalent restricted-stock offering might be 333 to 500 shares. The reason for the difference is that at the end of the vesting period, the restricted stock will have value, whereas the stock options may not. As a result, fewer shares are involved in restricted-stock plans, and therefore less dilution results if the stock price rises.

3. Restricted stock better aligns the employee incentives with the companies' incentives. The holder of restricted stock is essentially a stockholder and should be more interested in the long-term objectives of the company. In contrast, the recipients of stock options often have a short-run focus which leads to taking risks to hype the stock price for short-term gain to the detriment of the long-term.

The accounting for restricted stock follows the same general principles as accounting for stock options at the date of grant. That is, the company determines the fair value of the restricted stock at the date of grant (usually the fair value of a share of stock) and then expenses that amount over the service period. Subsequent changes in the fair value of the stock are ignored for purposes of computing compensation expense.

Restricted Stock Example

Assume that on January 1, 2012, Ogden Company issues 1,000 shares of restricted stock to its CEO, Christie DeGeorge. Ogden's stock has a fair value of $20 per share on January 1, 2012. Additional information is as follows.

1. The service period related to the restricted stock is five years.
2. Vesting occurs if DeGeorge stays with the company for a five-year period.
3. The par value of the stock is $1 per share.

Ogden makes the following entry on the grant date (January 1, 2012).

Unearned Compensation	20,000	
Common Stock (1,000 × $1)		1,000
Paid-in Capital in Excess of Par—Common Stock (1,000 × $19)		19,000

[9]Most companies base vesting on future service for a period of generally three to five years. Vesting may also be conditioned on some performance target such as revenue, net income, cash flows, or some combination of these three factors. The employee also collects dividends on the restricted stock, and these dividends generally must be repaid if forfeiture occurs.

The credits to Common Stock and Paid-in Capital in Excess of Par—Common Stock indicate that Ogden has issued shares of stock. The debit to Unearned Compensation (often referred to as Deferred Compensation Expense) identifies the total compensation expense the company will recognize over the five-year period. **Unearned Compensation represents the cost of services yet to be performed, which is not an asset.** Consequently, the company reports Unearned Compensation in stockholders' equity in the balance sheet, as a contra-equity account (similar to the reporting of treasury stock at cost).

At December 31, 2012, Ogden records compensation expense of $4,000 (1,000 shares $\times$ $20 $\times$ 20%) as follows.

Compensation Expense	4,000	
Unearned Compensation		4,000

Ogden records compensation expense of $4,000 for each of the next four years (2013, 2014, 2015, and 2016).

What happens if DeGeorge leaves the company before the five years has elapsed? In this situation, DeGeorge forfeits her rights to the stock, and Ogden reverses the compensation expense already recorded.

For example, assume that DeGeorge leaves on February 3, 2014 (before any expense has been recorded during 2014). The entry to record this forfeiture is as follows.

Common Stock	1,000	
Paid-in Capital in Excess of Par—Common Stock	19,000	
Compensation Expense ($4,000 $\times$ 2)		8,000
Unearned Compensation		12,000

In this situation, Ogden reverses the compensation expense of $8,000 recorded through 2013. In addition, the company debits Common Stock and Paid-in Capital in Excess of Par—Common Stock, reflecting DeGeorge's forfeiture. It credits the balance of Unearned Compensation since none remains when DeGeorge leaves Ogden.

This accounting is similar to accounting for stock options when employees do not fulfill vesting requirements. Recall that once compensation expense is recorded for stock options, it is not reversed. The only exception is if the employee does not fulfill the vesting requirement, by leaving the company early.

In Ogden's restricted-stock plan, vesting never occurred because DeGeorge left the company before she met the service requirement. Because DeGeorge was never vested, she had to forfeit her shares. Therefore, the company must reverse compensation expense recorded to date.[10]

Employee Stock-Purchase Plans

Employee stock-purchase plans (ESPPs) generally permit all employees to purchase stock at a discounted price for a short period of time. The company often uses such plans to secure equity capital or to induce widespread ownership of its common stock among employees. These plans are considered compensatory unless they satisfy **all three** conditions presented below.

1. Substantially all full-time employees may participate on an equitable basis.
2. The discount from market is small. That is, the discount does not exceed the per share amount of costs avoided by not having to raise cash in a public offering. If the amount of the discount is 5 percent or less, no compensation needs to be recorded.
3. The plan offers no substantive option feature.

For example, Masthead Company's stock-purchase plan allowed employees who met minimal employment qualifications to purchase its stock at a 5 percent reduction

---

[10]There are numerous variations on restricted-stock plans, including restricted-stock units (for which the shares are issued at the end of the vesting period) and restricted-stock plans with performance targets, such as EPS or stock price growth.

from market price for a short period of time. The reduction from market price is not considered compensatory. Why? Because the per share amount of the costs avoided by not having to raise the cash in a public offering equals 5 percent.

Companies that offer their employees a compensatory ESPP should record the compensation expense over the service life of the employees. It will be difficult for some companies to claim that their ESPPs are non-compensatory (and therefore not record compensation expense) unless they change their discount policy which in the past often was 15 percent. If they change their discount policy to 5 percent, participation in these plans will undoubtedly be lower. As a result, it is likely that some companies will end up dropping these plans.

Disclosure of Compensation Plans

Companies must fully disclose the status of their compensation plans at the end of the periods presented. To meet these objectives, companies must make extensive disclosures. Specifically, a company with one or more share-based payment arrangements must disclose information that enables users of the financial statements to understand:

1. The nature and terms of such arrangements that existed during the period and the potential effects of those arrangements on shareholders.
2. The effect on the income statement of compensation cost arising from share-based payment arrangements.
3. The method of estimating the fair value of the goods or services received, or the fair value of the equity instruments granted (or offered to grant), during the period.
4. The cash flow effects resulting from share-based payment arrangements.

Illustration 16-5 (on page 920) presents the type of information disclosed for compensation plans.

Debate over Stock-Option Accounting

The FASB faced considerable opposition when it proposed the fair value method for accounting for stock options. This is not surprising, given that the fair value method results in greater compensation costs relative to the intrinsic-value model. One study documented that, on average, companies in the Standard & Poor's 500 stock index overstated earnings in a recent year by 10 percent through the use of the intrinsic-value method. (See the "What Do the Numbers Mean" box on page 921.) Nevertheless, some companies, such as Coca-Cola, General Electric, Wachovia, Bank One, and The Washington Post, decided to use the fair value method. As the CFO of Coca-Cola stated, "There is no doubt that stock options are compensation. If they weren't, none of us would want them."

Yet many in corporate America resisted the fair value method. Many small high-technology companies have been especially vocal in their opposition, arguing that only through offering stock options can they attract top professional management. They contend that recognizing large amounts of compensation expense under these plans places them at a competitive disadvantage against larger companies that can withstand higher compensation charges. As one high-tech executive stated, "If your goal is to attack fat-cat executive compensation in multi-billion dollar firms, then please do so! But not at the expense of the people who are 'running lean and mean,' trying to build businesses and creating jobs in the process."

The stock-option saga is a classic example of the difficulty the FASB faces in issuing new accounting guidance. Many powerful interests aligned against the Board. Even some who initially appeared to support the Board's actions later reversed themselves. These efforts undermine the authority of the FASB, which in turn damages confidence in our financial reporting system.

Underlying Concepts

The stock-option controversy involves economic-consequence issues. The FASB believes companies should follow the neutrality concept. Others disagree, noting that factors other than accounting theory should be considered.

ILLUSTRATION 16-5
Stock-Option Plan
Disclosure

Description of plan

Valuation model
assumptions

Option plan activity
and balances

Option expense

Restricted-stock plan
details

Stock-Option Plan

The Company has a share-based compensation plan. The compensation cost that has been charged against income for the plan was $29.4 million, and $28.7 million for 2012 and 2011, respectively.

The Company's 2012 Employee Share-Option Plan (the Plan), which is shareholder-approved, permits the grant of share options and shares to its employees for up to 8 million shares of common stock. The Company believes that such awards better align the interests of its employees with those of its shareholders. Option awards are generally granted with an exercise price equal to the market price of the Company's stock at the date of grant; those option awards generally vest based on 5 years of continuous service and have 10-year contractual terms. Share awards generally vest over five years. Certain option and share awards provide for accelerated vesting if there is a change in control (as defined by the Plan).

The fair value of each option award is estimated on the date of grant using an option valuation model based on the assumptions noted in the following table.

	2012	2011
Expected volatility	25%–40%	24%–38%
Weighted-average volatility	33%	30%
Expected dividends	1.5%	1.5%
Expected term (in years)	5.3–7.8	5.5–8.0
Risk-free rate	6.3%–11.2%	6.0%–10.0%

A summary of option activity under the Plan as of December 31, 2012, and changes during the year then ended are presented below.

Options	Shares (000)	Weighted-Average Exercise Price	Weighted-Average Remaining Contractual Term	Aggregate Intrinsic Value ($000)
Outstanding at January 1, 2012	4,660	42		
Granted	950	60		
Exercised	(800)	36		
Forfeited or expired	(80)	59		
Outstanding at December 31, 2012	4,730	47	6.5	85,140
Exercisable at December 31, 2012	3,159	41	4.0	75,816

The weighted-average grant-date fair value of options granted during the years 2012 and 2011 was $19.57 and $17.46, respectively. The total intrinsic value of options exercised during the years ended December 31, 2012 and 2011, was $25.2 million, and $20.9 million, respectively.

As of December 31, 2012, there was $25.9 million of total unrecognized compensation cost related to nonvested share-based compensation arrangements granted under the Plan. That cost is expected to be recognized over a weighted-average period of 4.9 years. The total fair value of shares vested during the years ended December 31, 2012 and 2011, was $22.8 million and $21 million, respectively.

Restricted-Stock Awards

The Company also has a restricted-stock plan. The Plan is intended to retain and motivate the Company's Chief Executive Officer over the term of the award and to bring his total compensation package closer to median levels for Chief Executive Officers of comparable companies. The fair value of grants during the year was $1,889,000, or $35.68 per share, equivalent to 92% of the market price of a share of the Company's Common Stock on the date the award was granted.

Restricted-stock activity for the year ended 2012 is as follows.

	Shares	Price
Outstanding at December 31, 2011	57,990	—
Granted	149,000	$12.68
Vested	(19,330)	—
Forfeited	—	—
Outstanding at December 31, 2012	187,660	

Transparent financial reporting—including recognition of stock-based expense—should not be criticized because companies will report lower income. We may not like what the financial statements say, but we are always better off when the statements are representationally faithful to the underlying economic substance of transactions.

By leaving stock-based compensation expense out of income, reported income is biased. Biased reporting not only raises concerns about the credibility of companies' reports, but also of financial reporting in general. Even good companies get tainted by the biased reporting of a few "bad apples." If we write standards to achieve some social, economic, or public policy goal, financial reporting loses its credibility.

A LITTLE HONESTY GOES A LONG WAY

What do the numbers mean?

Before the change to required expensing of stock options, companies could choose whether to expense stock-based compensation or simply disclose the estimated costs in the notes to the financial statements. You might think investors would punish companies that decided to expense stock options. After all, most of corporate America has been battling for years to avoid having to expense them, worried that accounting for those perks would destroy earnings. And indeed, Merrill Lynch estimated that if all S&P 500 companies were to expense options, reported profits would fall by as much as 10 percent.

Yet, as a small but growing band of big-name companies voluntarily made the switch to expensing, investors for the most part showered them with love. With a few exceptions, the stock prices of the "expensers," from Cinergy to The Washington Post, outpaced the market after they announced the change.

| | Estimated EPS | | % change since announcement |
Company	Without options	With options expensed	Company stock price
Cinergy	$ 2.80	$ 2.77	22.4%
The Washington Post	20.48	20.10	16.4
Computer Associates	−0.46	−0.62	11.1
Fannie Mae	6.15	6.02	6.7
Bank One	2.77	2.61	2.6
General Motors	5.84	5.45	2.6
Procter & Gamble	3.57	3.35	−2.3
Coca-Cola	1.79	1.70	−6.2
General Electric	1.65	1.61	−6.2
Amazon.com	0.04	−0.99	−11.4

Data sources: Merrill Lynch; company reports.

Given the market's general positive reaction to the transparent reporting of stock options, it is puzzling why some companies continued to fight implementation of the expensing rule.

Source: David Stires, "A Little Honesty Goes a Long Way," *Fortune* (September 2, 2002), p. 186. Reprinted by permission. See also Troy Wolverton, "Foes of Expensing Welcome FASB Delay," *TheStreet.com* (October 15, 2004).

SECTION 2 • COMPUTING EARNINGS PER SHARE

As indicated earlier, stockholders and potential investors widely use earnings per share in evaluating the profitability of a company. As a result, much attention is given to earnings per share by the financial press. Earnings per share indicates the income earned by each share of common stock. Thus, **companies report earnings per share only for common stock**. For example, if Oscar Co. has net income of $300,000 and a weighted average of 100,000 shares of common stock outstanding for the year, earnings per share is $3 ($300,000 ÷ 100,000). Because of the importance of earnings per share information, most companies must report this information on the face of the income statement.[11] [6] The exception, due to cost-benefit considerations, is nonpublic companies.[12] Generally, companies report earnings per share information below net income in the income statement. Illustration 16-6 shows Oscar Co.'s income statement presentation of earnings per share.

ILLUSTRATION 16-6
Income Statement
Presentation of EPS

Net income	$300,000
Earnings per share	$3.00

When the income statement contains intermediate components of income (such as discontinued operations or extraordinary items), companies should disclose earnings per share for each component. The presentation in Illustration 16-7 is representative.

ILLUSTRATION 16-7
Income Statement
Presentation of EPS
Components

Earnings per share:	
Income from continuing operations	$4.00
Loss from discontinued operations, net of tax	0.60
Income before extraordinary item	3.40
Extraordinary gain, net of tax	1.00
Net income	$4.40

These disclosures enable the user of the financial statements to recognize the effects on EPS of income from continuing operations, as distinguished from income or loss from irregular items.[13]

EARNINGS PER SHARE—SIMPLE CAPITAL STRUCTURE

LEARNING OBJECTIVE 6
Compute earnings per share in a simple capital structure.

A corporation's capital structure is simple if it consists only of common stock or includes no **potential common stock** that upon conversion or exercise could dilute earnings per common share. A capital structure is complex if it includes securities that could have a dilutive effect on earnings per common share.

The computation of earnings per share for a simple capital structure involves two items (other than net income)—(1) preferred stock dividends and (2) weighted-average number of shares outstanding.

Preferred Stock Dividends

As we indicated earlier, earnings per share relates to earnings per common share. When a company has both common and preferred stock outstanding, **it subtracts the current-year preferred stock dividend from net income to arrive at** income available to common stockholders. Illustration 16-8 shows the formula for computing earnings per share.

ILLUSTRATION 16-8
Formula for Computing
Earnings per Share

$$\text{Earnings per Share} = \frac{\text{Net Income} - \text{Preferred Dividends}}{\text{Weighted-Average Number of Shares Outstanding}}$$

[11]For an article on the usefulness of reported EPS data and the application of the qualitative characteristics of accounting information to EPS data, see Lola W. Dudley, "A Critical Look at EPS," *Journal of Accountancy* (August 1985), pp. 102–111.

[12]A nonpublic enterprise is an enterprise (1) whose debt or equity securities are not traded in a public market on a foreign or domestic stock exchange or in the over-the-counter market (including securities quoted locally or regionally), or (2) that is not required to file financial statements with the SEC. An enterprise is not considered a nonpublic enterprise when its financial statements are issued in preparation for the sale of any class of securities in a public market.

[13]Companies should present, either on the face of the income statement or in the notes to the financial statements, per share amounts for discontinued operations and extraordinary items.

In reporting earnings per share information, a company must calculate income available to common stockholders. To do so, the company subtracts dividends on preferred stock from each of the intermediate components of income (income from continuing operations and income before extraordinary items) and finally from net income. If a company declares dividends on preferred stock and a net loss occurs, **the company adds the preferred dividend to the loss** for purposes of computing the loss per share.

If the preferred stock is cumulative and the company has net income but declares no dividend in the current year, it subtracts **an amount equal to the dividend that it should have declared for the current year only**. If the stock is cumulative and the company reports a net loss, but declares no dividend in the current year, it **adds** an amount equal to the dividend to the net loss. The company should have included dividends in arrears for previous years in the previous years' computations.

Weighted-Average Number of Shares Outstanding

In all computations of earnings per share, the weighted-average number of shares outstanding during the period constitutes the basis for the per share amounts reported. Shares issued or purchased during the period affect the amount outstanding. Companies must **weight the shares by the fraction of the period they are outstanding**. The rationale for this approach is to find the equivalent number of whole shares outstanding for the year.

To illustrate, assume that Franks Inc. has changes in its common stock shares outstanding for the period as shown in Illustration 16-9.

Date	Share Changes	Shares Outstanding
January 1	Beginning balance	90,000
April 1	Issued 30,000 shares for cash	30,000
		120,000
July 1	Purchased 39,000 shares	(39,000)
		81,000
November 1	Issued 60,000 shares for cash	60,000
December 31	Ending balance	141,000

ILLUSTRATION 16-9
Shares Outstanding, Ending Balance— Franks Inc.

Franks computes the weighted-average number of shares outstanding as follows.

Dates Outstanding	(A) Shares Outstanding	(B) Fraction of Year	(C) Weighted Shares (A × B)
Jan. 1–Apr. 1	90,000	3/12	22,500
Apr. 1–July 1	120,000	3/12	30,000
July 1–Nov. 1	81,000	4/12	27,000
Nov. 1–Dec. 31	141,000	2/12	23,500
Weighted-average number of shares outstanding			103,000

ILLUSTRATION 16-10
Weighted-Average Number of Shares Outstanding

As Illustration 16-10 shows, 90,000 shares were outstanding for three months, which is equivalent to 22,500 whole shares for the entire year. Because Franks issued additional shares on April 1, it must weight these shares for the time outstanding. When the company purchased 39,000 shares on July 1, it reduced the shares outstanding. Therefore, from July 1 to November 1, only 81,000 shares were outstanding, which is equivalent to 27,000 shares. The issuance of 60,000 shares increases shares outstanding for the last two months of the year. Franks then makes a new computation to determine the proper weighted shares outstanding.

Stock Dividends and Stock Splits

When **stock dividends** or **stock splits** occur, companies need to restate the shares outstanding before the stock dividend or split, in order to compute the weighted-average number of shares. For example, assume that Vijay Corporation had 100,000 shares outstanding on January 1 and issued a 25 percent stock dividend on June 30. For purposes of computing a weighted-average for the current year, it assumes the additional 25,000 shares outstanding as a result of the stock dividend to be **outstanding since the beginning of the year**. Thus, the weighted-average for the year for Vijay is 125,000 shares.

Companies restate the issuance of a stock dividend or stock split, but not the issuance or repurchase of stock for cash. Why? Because stock splits and stock dividends do not increase or decrease the net assets of the company. The company merely issues additional shares of stock. Because of the added shares, it must restate the weighted-average shares. Restating allows valid comparisons of earnings per share between periods before and after the stock split or stock dividend. Conversely, the issuance or purchase of stock for cash **changes the amount of net assets**. As a result, the company either earns more or less in the future as a result of this change in net assets. Stated another way, **a stock dividend or split does not change the shareholders' total investment**—it only increases (unless it is a reverse stock split) the number of common shares representing this investment.

To illustrate how a stock dividend affects the computation of the weighted-average number of shares outstanding, assume that Sabrina Company has the following changes in its common stock shares during the year.

ILLUSTRATION 16-11
Shares Outstanding,
Ending Balance—Sabrina
Company

Date	Share Changes	Shares Outstanding
January 1	Beginning balance	100,000
March 1	Issued 20,000 shares for cash	20,000
		120,000
June 1	60,000 additional shares (50% stock dividend)	60,000
		180,000
November 1	Issued 30,000 shares for cash	30,000
December 31	Ending balance	210,000

Sabrina computes the weighted-average number of shares outstanding as follows.

ILLUSTRATION 16-12
Weighted-Average
Number of Shares
Outstanding—Stock
Issue and Stock Dividend

Dates Outstanding	(A) Shares Outstanding	(B) Restatement	(C) Fraction of Year	(D) Weighted Shares (A × B × C)
Jan. 1–Mar. 1	100,000	1.50	2/12	25,000
Mar. 1–June 1	120,000	1.50	3/12	45,000
June 1–Nov. 1	180,000		5/12	75,000
Nov. 1–Dec. 31	210,000		2/12	35,000
Weighted-average number of shares outstanding				180,000

Sabrina must restate the shares outstanding prior to the stock dividend. The company adjusts the shares outstanding from January 1 to June 1 for the stock dividend, so that it now states these shares on the same basis as shares issued subsequent to the stock dividend. Sabrina does not restate shares issued after the stock dividend because they are on the new basis. The stock dividend simply restates existing shares. **The same type of treatment applies to a stock split.**

If a stock dividend or stock split occurs after the end of the year, but before issuing the financial statements, a company must restate the weighted-average number of shares outstanding for the year (and any other years presented in comparative form). For example, assume that Hendricks Company computes its weighted-average number of shares as 100,000 for the year ended December 31, 2012. On January 15, 2013, before issuing the financial statements, the company splits its stock 3 for 1. In this case, the weighted-average number of shares used in computing earnings per share for 2012 is now 300,000 shares. If providing earnings per share information for 2011 as comparative information, Hendricks must also adjust it for the stock split.

Comprehensive Example

Let's study a comprehensive illustration for a simple capital structure. Darin Corporation has income before extraordinary item of $580,000 and an extraordinary gain, net of tax, of $240,000. In addition, it has declared preferred dividends of $1 per share on 100,000 shares of preferred stock outstanding. Darin also has the following changes in its common stock shares outstanding during 2012.

Dates	Share Changes	Shares Outstanding
January 1	Beginning balance	180,000
May 1	Purchased 30,000 treasury shares	(30,000)
		150,000
July 1	300,000 additional shares (3-for-1 stock split)	300,000
		450,000
December 31	Issued 50,000 shares for cash	50,000
December 31	Ending balance	500,000

ILLUSTRATION 16-13
Shares Outstanding, Ending Balance— Darin Corp.

To compute the earnings per share information, Darin determines the weighted-average number of shares outstanding as follows.

Dates Outstanding	(A) Shares Outstanding	(B) Restatement	(C) Fraction of Year	(D) Weighted Shares (A × B × C)
Jan. 1–May 1	180,000	3	4/12	180,000
May 1–July 1	150,000	3	2/12	75,000
July 1–Dec. 31	450,000		6/12	225,000
Weighted-average number of shares outstanding				480,000

ILLUSTRATION 16-14
Weighted-Average Number of Shares Outstanding

In computing the weighted-average number of shares, the company ignores the shares sold on December 31, 2012, because they have not been outstanding during the year. Darin then divides the weighted-average number of shares into income before extraordinary item and net income to determine earnings per share. It subtracts its preferred dividends of $100,000 from income before extraordinary item ($580,000) to arrive at income before extraordinary item available to common stockholders of $480,000 ($580,000 − $100,000).

Deducting the preferred dividends from the income before extraordinary item also reduces net income without affecting the amount of the extraordinary item. The final amount is referred to as **income available to common stockholders**, as shown in Illustration 16-15.

ILLUSTRATION 16-15
Computation of Income Available to Common Stockholders

	(A) Income Information	(B) Weighted Shares	(C) Earnings per Share (A ÷ B)
Income before extraordinary item available to common stockholders	$480,000*	480,000	$1.00
Extraordinary gain (net of tax)	240,000	480,000	0.50
Income available to common stockholders	$720,000	480,000	$1.50

*$580,000 − $100,000

Darin must disclose the per share amount for the extraordinary item (net of tax) either on the face of the income statement or in the notes to the financial statements. Illustration 16-16 shows the income and per share information reported on the face of Darin's income statement.

ILLUSTRATION 16-16
Earnings per Share, with Extraordinary Item

Income before extraordinary item	$580,000
Extraordinary gain, net of tax	240,000
Net income	$820,000
Earnings per share:	
Income before extraordinary item	$1.00
Extraordinary item, net of tax	0.50
Net income	$1.50

EARNINGS PER SHARE—COMPLEX CAPITAL STRUCTURE

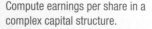

LEARNING OBJECTIVE 7

Compute earnings per share in a complex capital structure.

The EPS discussion to this point applies to basic EPS for a simple capital structure. One problem with a **basic EPS** computation is that it fails to recognize the potential impact of a corporation's dilutive securities. As discussed at the beginning of the chapter, dilutive securities are securities that can be converted to common stock.[14] Upon conversion or exercise by the holder, the dilutive securities reduce (dilute) earnings per share. This adverse effect on EPS can be significant and, more importantly, *unexpected* unless financial statements call attention to their potential dilutive effect.

As indicated earlier, a complex capital structure exists when a corporation has convertible securities, options, warrants, or other rights that upon conversion or exercise could dilute earnings per share. When a company has a complex capital structure, **it generally reports both basic and diluted earnings per share**.

Computing diluted EPS is similar to computing basic EPS. The difference is that diluted EPS includes the effect of all potential dilutive common shares that were outstanding during the period. The formula in Illustration 16-17 shows the relationship between basic EPS and diluted EPS.

[14]Issuance of these types of securities is typical in mergers and compensation plans.

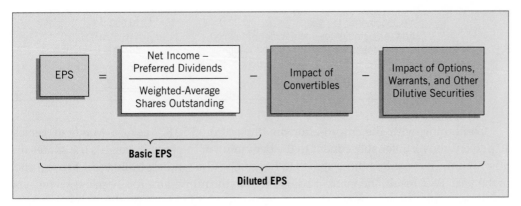

ILLUSTRATION 16-17
Relation between Basic and Diluted EPS

Some securities are antidilutive. Antidilutive securities are securities that upon conversion or exercise **increase** earnings per share (or reduce the loss per share). Companies with complex capital structures will not report diluted EPS if the securities in their capital structure are antidilutive. The purpose of presenting both basic and diluted EPS is to inform financial statement users of situations that will likely occur (basic EPS) and also to provide "worst case" dilutive situations (dilutive EPS). If the securities are antidilutive, the likelihood of conversion or exercise is considered remote. Thus, companies that have only antidilutive securities must report only the basic EPS number. We illustrated the computation of basic EPS in the prior section. In the following sections, we address the effects of convertible and other dilutive securities on EPS calculations.

> **INTERNATIONAL PERSPECTIVE**
>
> The provisions in GAAP are substantially the same as those in *International Accounting Standard No. 33*, "Earnings per Share," issued by the IASB.

Diluted EPS—Convertible Securities

At conversion, companies exchange convertible securities for common stock. Companies measure the dilutive effects of potential conversion on EPS using the if-converted method. This method for a convertible bond assumes: (1) the conversion of the convertible securities at the beginning of the period (or at the time of issuance of the security, if issued during the period), and (2) the elimination of related interest, net of tax. Thus the additional shares assumed issued increase the **denominator**—the weighted-average number of shares outstanding. The amount of interest expense, net of tax associated with those potential common shares, increases the **numerator**—net income.

Comprehensive Example—If-Converted Method

As an example, Mayfield Corporation has net income of $210,000 for the year and a weighted-average number of common shares outstanding during the period of 100,000 shares. The basic earnings per share is therefore $2.10 ($210,000 ÷ 100,000). The company has two convertible debenture bond issues outstanding. One is a 6 percent issue sold at 100 (total $1,000,000) in a prior year and convertible into 20,000 common shares. The other is a 10 percent issue sold at 100 (total $1,000,000) on April 1 of the current year and convertible into 32,000 common shares. The tax rate is 40 percent.

As Illustration 16-18 (on page 928) shows, to determine the numerator for diluted earnings per share, Mayfield adds back the interest on the if-converted securities, less the related tax effect. Because the if-converted method assumes conversion as of the beginning of the year, Mayfield assumes that it pays no interest on the convertibles during the year. The interest on the 6 percent convertibles is $60,000 for the year ($1,000,000 × 6%). The increased tax expense is $24,000 ($60,000 × 0.40). The interest added back net of taxes is $36,000 [$60,000 − $24,000, or simply $60,000 × (1 − 0.40)].

ILLUSTRATION 16-18
Computation of Adjusted
Net Income

Net income for the year	$210,000
Add: Adjustment for interest (net of tax)	
6% debentures ($60,000 × [1 − .40])	36,000
10% debentures ($100,000 × 9/12 × [1 − .40])	45,000
Adjusted net income	$291,000

Continuing with the information in Illustration 16-18, because Mayfield issues 10 percent convertibles subsequent to the beginning of the year, it weights the shares. In other words, it considers these shares to have been outstanding from April 1 to the end of the year. As a result, the interest adjustment to the numerator for these bonds reflects the interest for only nine months. Thus the interest added back on the 10 percent convertible is $45,000 [$1,000,000 × 10% × 9/12 year × (1 − 0.4)]. The final item in Illustration 16-18 shows the adjusted net income. This amount becomes the numerator for Mayfield's computation of diluted earnings per share.

Mayfield then calculates the weighted-average number of shares outstanding, as shown in Illustration 16-19. This number of shares becomes the denominator for Mayfield's computation of diluted earnings per share.

ILLUSTRATION 16-19
Computation of
Weighted-Average
Number of Shares

Weighted-average number of shares outstanding	100,000
Add: Shares assumed to be issued:	
6% debentures (as of beginning of year)	20,000
10% debentures (as of date of issue, April 1; 9/12 × 32,000)	24,000
Weighted-average number of shares adjusted for dilutive securities	144,000

In its income statement, Mayfield reports basic and diluted earnings per share.[15] Illustration 16-20 shows this dual presentation.

ILLUSTRATION 16-20
Earnings per Share
Disclosure

Net income for the year	$210,000
Earnings per Share (Note X)	
Basic earnings per share ($210,000 ÷ 100,000)	$2.10
Diluted earnings per share ($291,000 ÷ 144,000)	$2.02

Other Factors

The example above assumed that Mayfield sold its bonds at the face amount. If it instead sold the bonds at a premium or discount, the company must adjust the interest expense each period to account for this occurrence. Therefore, the interest expense reported on the income statement is the amount of interest expense, net of tax, added back to net income. (It is not the interest paid in cash during the period.)

In addition, the conversion rate on a dilutive security may change during the period in which the security is outstanding. For the diluted EPS computation in such a situation, the **company uses the most dilutive conversion rate available.** For example, assume that a company issued a convertible bond on January 1, 2011, with a conversion rate of 10 common shares for each bond starting January 1, 2013. Beginning January 1,

---

[15]Conversion of bonds is dilutive because EPS with conversion ($2.02) is less than basic EPS ($2.10). See Appendix 16B for a comprehensive evaluation of antidilution with multiple securities.

2016, the conversion rate is 12 common shares for each bond, and beginning January 1, 2020, it is 15 common shares for each bond. In computing diluted EPS in 2011, the company uses the conversion rate of 15 shares to one bond.

A final issue relates to preferred stock. For example, assume that Mayfield's 6 percent convertible debentures were instead 6 percent convertible *preferred stock.* In that case, Mayfield considers the convertible preferred as potential common shares. Thus, it includes them in its diluted EPS calculations as shares outstanding. The company does not subtract preferred dividends from net income in computing the numerator. Why not? Because for purposes of computing EPS, it assumes conversion of the convertible preferreds to outstanding common stock. The company uses net income as the numerator—it computes **no tax effect** because preferred dividends generally are not tax-deductible.

Diluted EPS—Options and Warrants

A company includes in diluted earnings per share stock options and warrants outstanding (whether or not presently exercisable), unless they are antidilutive. Companies use the treasury-stock method to include options and warrants and their equivalents in EPS computations.

The treasury-stock method assumes that the options or warrants are exercised at the beginning of the year (or date of issue if later), and that the company uses those proceeds to purchase common stock for the treasury. If the exercise price is lower than the market price of the stock, then the proceeds from exercise are insufficient to buy back all the shares. The company then adds the incremental shares remaining to the weighted-average number of shares outstanding for purposes of computing diluted earnings per share.

For example, if the exercise price of a warrant is $5 and the market price of the stock is $15, the treasury-stock method increases the shares outstanding. Exercise of the warrant results in one additional share outstanding, but the $5 received for the one share issued is insufficient to purchase one share in the market at $15. The company needs to exercise three warrants (and issue three additional shares) to produce enough money ($15) to acquire one share in the market. Thus, a net increase of two shares outstanding results.

To see this computation using larger numbers, assume 1,500 options outstanding at an exercise price of $30 for a common share and a common stock market price per share of $50. Through application of the treasury-stock method, the company would have 600 incremental shares outstanding, computed as shown in Illustration 16-21.[16]

Proceeds from exercise of 1,500 options (1,500 × $30)	$45,000
Shares issued upon exercise of options	1,500
Treasury shares purchasable with proceeds ($45,000 ÷ $50)	(900)
Incremental shares outstanding (potential common shares)	600

ILLUSTRATION 16-21
Computation of Incremental Shares

[16]The incremental number of shares may be more simply computed:

$$\frac{\text{Market price} - \text{Option price}}{\text{Market price}} \times \text{Number of options} = \text{Number of shares}$$

$$\frac{\$50 - \$30}{\$50} \times 1{,}500 \text{ options} = 600 \text{ shares}$$

Thus, if the exercise price of the option or warrant is **lower** than the market price of the stock, dilution occurs. An exercise price of the option or warrant **higher** than the market price of the stock reduces common shares. In this case, the options or warrants are **antidilutive** because their assumed exercise leads to an increase in earnings per share.

For both options and warrants, exercise is assumed only if the average market price of the stock exceeds the exercise price during the reported period.[17] As a practical matter, a simple average of the weekly or monthly prices is adequate, so long as the prices do not fluctuate significantly.

Comprehensive Example—Treasury-Stock Method

To illustrate application of the treasury-stock method, assume that Kubitz Industries, Inc. has net income for the period of $220,000. The average number of shares outstanding for the period was 100,000 shares. Hence, basic EPS—ignoring all dilutive securities—is $2.20. The average number of shares related to options outstanding (although not exercisable at this time), at an option price of $20 per share, is 5,000 shares. The average market price of the common stock during the year was $28. Illustration 16-22 shows the computation of EPS using the treasury-stock method.

ILLUSTRATION 16-22
Computation of Earnings per Share—Treasury-Stock Method

	Basic Earnings per Share	Diluted Earnings per Share
Average number of shares related to options outstanding:		5,000
Option price per share		× $20
Proceeds upon exercise of options		$100,000
Average market price of common stock		$28
Treasury shares that could be repurchased with proceeds ($100,000 ÷ $28)		3,571
Excess of shares under option over the treasury shares that could be repurchased (5,000 − 3,571)—potential common incremental shares		1,429
Average number of common shares outstanding	100,000	100,000
Total average number of common shares outstanding and potential common shares	100,000 (A)	101,429 (C)
Net income for the year	$220,000 (B)	$220,000 (D)
Earnings per share	$2.20 (B ÷ A)	$2.17 (D ÷ C)

Contingent Issue Agreement

In business combinations, the acquirer may promise to issue additional shares—referred to as **contingent shares**—under certain conditions. Sometimes the company issues these contingent shares as a result of a **passage-of-time condition** or upon the attainment of a **certain earnings or market price level**. If this passage-of-time condition occurs during the current year, or if the company meets the earnings or market price **by the end of the year**, the company considers the contingent shares as outstanding for the computation of diluted earnings per share.[18]

---

[17]Options and warrants have essentially the same assumptions and computational problems, although the warrants may allow or require the tendering of some other security, such as debt, in lieu of cash upon exercise. In such situations, the accounting becomes quite complex and is beyond the scope of this book.

[18]In addition to contingent issuances of stock, other situations that might lead to dilution are the issuance of participating securities and two-class common shares. The reporting of these types of securities in EPS computations is beyond the scope of this book.

For example, assume that Watts Corporation purchased Cardoza Company and agreed to give Cardoza's stockholders 20,000 additional shares in 2015 if Cardoza's net income in 2014 is $90,000. In 2013, Cardoza's net income is $100,000. Because Cardoza has already attained the 2014 stipulated earnings of $90,000, in computing diluted earnings per share for 2013, Watts would include the 20,000 contingent shares in the shares-outstanding computation.

Antidilution Revisited

In computing diluted EPS, a company must consider the aggregate of all dilutive securities. But first it must determine which potentially dilutive securities are in fact individually dilutive and which are antidilutive. **A company should exclude any security that is antidilutive**, nor can the company use such a security to offset dilutive securities.

Recall that including antidilutive securities in earnings per share computations increases earnings per share (or reduces net loss per share). With options or warrants, whenever the exercise price exceeds the market price, the security is antidilutive. Convertible debt is antidilutive if the addition to income of the interest (net of tax) causes a greater percentage increase in income (numerator) than conversion of the bonds causes a percentage increase in common and potentially dilutive shares (denominator). In other words, convertible debt is antidilutive if conversion of the security causes common stock earnings to increase by a greater amount per additional common share than earnings per share was before the conversion.

To illustrate, assume that Martin Corporation has a 6 percent, $1,000,000 debt issue that is convertible into 10,000 common shares. Net income for the year is $210,000, the weighted-average number of common shares outstanding is 100,000 shares, and the tax rate is 40 percent. In this case, assumed conversion of the debt into common stock at the beginning of the year requires the following adjustments of net income and the weighted-average number of shares outstanding.

Net income for the year	$210,000	Average number of shares outstanding	100,000
Add: Adjustment for interest (net of tax) on 6% debentures		Add: Shares issued upon assumed conversion of debt	10,000
$60,000 × (1 − .40)	36,000	Average number of common and	
Adjusted net income	$246,000	potential common shares	110,000

Basic EPS = $210,000 ÷ 100,000 = $2.10
Diluted EPS = $246,000 ÷ 110,000 = $2.24 = Antidilutive

ILLUSTRATION 16-23
Test for Antidilution

As a shortcut, Martin can also identify the convertible debt as antidilutive by comparing the EPS resulting from conversion, $3.60 ($36,000 additional earnings ÷ 10,000 additional shares), with EPS before inclusion of the convertible debt, $2.10.

Companies should ignore antidilutive securities in all calculations and in computing diluted earnings per share. This approach is reasonable. The profession's intent was to inform the investor of the possible dilution that might occur in reported earnings per share and not to be concerned with securities that, if converted or exercised, would result in an increase in earnings per share. Appendix 16B to this chapter provides an extended example of how companies consider antidilution in a complex situation with multiple securities.

EPS Presentation and Disclosure

A company with a complex capital structure would present its EPS information as follows.

ILLUSTRATION 16-24
EPS Presentation—
Complex Capital
Structure

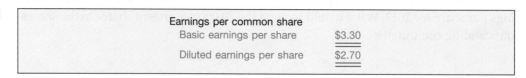

Earnings per common share	
Basic earnings per share	$3.30
Diluted earnings per share	$2.70

When the earnings of a period include irregular items, a company should show per share amounts (where applicable) for the following: income from continuing operations, income before extraordinary items, and net income. Companies that report a discontinued operation or an extraordinary item should present per share amounts **for those line items** either on the face of the income statement or in the notes to the financial statements. Illustration 16-25 shows a presentation reporting extraordinary items.

ILLUSTRATION 16-25
EPS Presentation, with
Extraordinary Item

Basic earnings per share	
Income before extraordinary item	$3.80
Extraordinary item	(0.80)
Net income	$3.00
Diluted earnings per share	
Income before extraordinary item	$3.35
Extraordinary item	(0.65)
Net income	$2.70

A company must show earnings per share amounts for all periods presented. Also, the company should restate all prior period earnings per share amounts presented for stock dividends and stock splits. If it reports diluted EPS data for at least one period, the company should report such data for all periods presented, even if it is the same as basic EPS. When a company restates results of operations of a prior period as a result of an error or a change in accounting principle, it should also restate the earnings per share data shown for the prior periods. Complex capital structures and dual presentation of earnings per share require the following additional disclosures in note form.

1. Description of pertinent rights and privileges of the various securities outstanding.
2. A reconciliation of the numerators and denominators of the basic and diluted per share computations, including individual income and share amount effects of all securities that affect EPS.
3. The effect given preferred dividends in determining income available to common stockholders in computing basic EPS.
4. Securities that could potentially dilute basic EPS in the future that were excluded in the computation because they would be antidilutive.
5. Effect of conversions subsequent to year-end, but before issuing statements.

Illustration 16-26 presents the reconciliation and the related disclosure to meet the requirements of this standard.[19] [7]

---

[19]Note that GAAP has specific disclosure requirements regarding stock-based compensation plans and earning per share disclosures as well.

ILLUSTRATION 16-26
Reconciliation for Basic
and Diluted EPS

	For the Year Ended 2012		
	Income (Numerator)	Shares (Denominator)	Per Share Amount
Income before extraordinary item	$7,500,000		
Less: Preferred stock dividends	45,000		
Basic EPS	7,455,000	3,991,666	$1.87
Warrants		30,768	
Convertible preferred stock	45,000	308,333	
4% convertible bonds (net of tax)	60,000	50,000	
Diluted EPS	$7,560,000	4,380,767	$1.73

Stock options to purchase 1,000,000 shares of common stock at $85 per share were outstanding during the second half of 2012 but were not included in the computation of diluted EPS because the options' exercise price was greater than the average market price of the common shares. The options were still outstanding at the end of year 2012 and expire on June 30, 2022.

PRO FORMA EPS CONFUSION

Many companies are reporting pro forma EPS numbers along with GAAP-based EPS numbers in the financial information provided to investors. Pro forma earnings generally exceed GAAP earnings because the pro forma numbers exclude such items as restructuring charges, impairments of assets, R&D expenditures, and stock compensation expense. Here are some examples.

What do the numbers mean?

Company	GAAP EPS	Pro Forma EPS
Adaptec	$(0.62)	$ 0.05
Corning	(0.24)	0.09
General Motors	(0.41)	0.85
Honeywell International	(0.38)	0.44
International Paper	(0.57)	0.14
Qualcomm	(0.06)	0.20
Broadcom	(6.36)	(0.13)
Lucent Technologies	(2.16)	(0.27)

Source: Company press releases.

The SEC has expressed concern that pro forma earnings may be misleading. For example, the SEC cited Trump Hotels & Casino Resorts (DJT) for abuses related to a recent third-quarter pro forma EPS release. It noted that the firm misrepresented its operating results by excluding a material, one-time $81.4 million charge in its pro forma EPS statement and including an undisclosed nonrecurring gain of $17.2 million. The gain enabled DJT to post a profit in the quarter. The SEC emphasized that DJT's pro forma EPS statement deviated from conservative GAAP reporting. Therefore, it was "fraudulent" because it created a "false and misleading impression" that DJT had actually (1) recorded a profit in the third quarter and (2) exceeded consensus earnings expectations by enhancing its operating fundamentals.

As discussed in Chapter 4, SEC Regulation G now requires companies to provide a clear reconciliation between pro forma and GAAP information. And this applies to EPS measures as well. This reconciliation will be especially important, given the expected spike in pro forma reporting by companies adding back employee stock-option expense.

Sources: See M. Moran, A. J. Cohen, and K. Shaustyuk, "Stock Option Expensing: The Battle Has Been Won; Now Comes the Aftermath," *Portfolio Strategy/Accounting.* Goldman Sachs (March 17, 2005).

Summary of EPS Computation

As you can see, computation of earnings per share is a complex issue. It is a controversial area because many securities, although technically not common stock, have many of its basic characteristics. Indeed, some companies have issued these other securities rather than common stock in order to avoid an adverse dilutive effect on earnings per share. Illustrations 16-27 and 16-28 display the elementary points of calculating earnings per share in a simple capital structure and in a complex capital structure.

ILLUSTRATION 16-27
Calculating EPS, Simple
Capital Structure

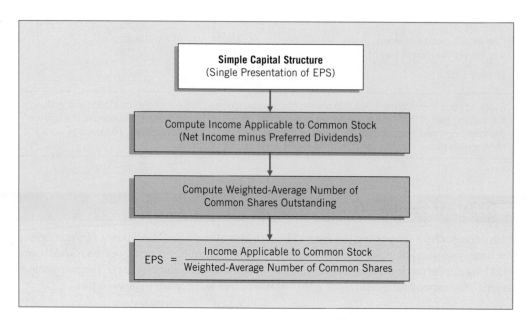

ILLUSTRATION 16-28
Calculating EPS, Complex
Capital Structure

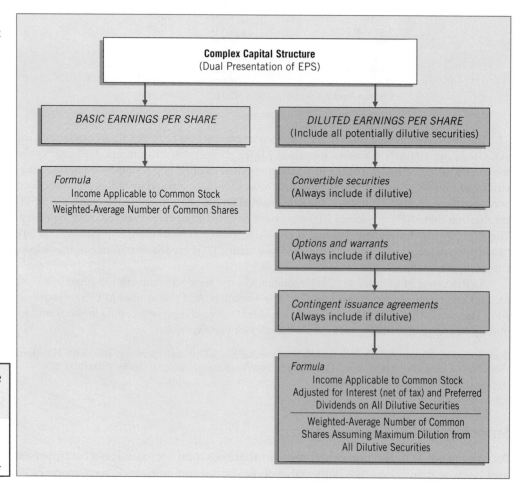

You will want to read the
IFRS INSIGHTS
on pages 965–973

for discussion of IFRS related to dilutive securities and earnings per share.

SUMMARY OF LEARNING OBJECTIVES

1 **Describe the accounting for the issuance, conversion, and retirement of convertible securities.** The method for recording convertible bonds at the date of issuance follows that used to record straight debt issues. Companies amortize any discount or premium that results from the issuance of convertible bonds, assuming the bonds will be held to maturity. If companies convert bonds into other securities, the principal accounting problem is to determine the amount at which to record the securities exchanged for the bonds. The book value method is considered GAAP. The retirement of convertible debt is considered a debt retirement, and the difference between the carrying amount of the retired convertible debt and the cash paid should result in a gain or loss.

2 **Explain the accounting for convertible preferred stock.** When convertible preferred stock is converted, a company uses the book value method: It debits Preferred Stock, along with any related Paid-in Capital in Excess of Par—Preferred Stock, and credits Common Stock and Paid-in Capital in Excess of Par—Common Stock (if an excess exists).

3 **Contrast the accounting for stock warrants and for stock warrants issued with other securities.** *Stock warrants*: Companies should allocate the proceeds from the sale of debt with detachable warrants between the two securities. Warrants that are detachable can be traded separately from the debt, and therefore companies can determine their fair value. Two methods of allocation are available: the proportional method and the incremental method. Nondetachable warrants do not require an allocation of the proceeds between the bonds and the warrants; companies record the entire proceeds as debt. *Stock rights*: No entry is required when a company issues rights to existing stockholders. The company needs only to make a memorandum entry to indicate the number of rights issued to existing stockholders and to ensure that the company has additional unissued stock registered for issuance in case the stockholders exercise the rights.

4 **Describe the accounting for stock compensation plans under generally accepted accounting principles.** Companies must use the fair value approach to account for stock-based compensation. Under this approach, a company computes total compensation expense based on the fair value of the options that it expects to vest on the grant date. Companies recognize compensation expense in the periods in which the employee performs the services. Restricted-stock plans follow the same general accounting principles as those for stock options. Companies estimate total compensation cost at the grant date based on the fair value of the restricted stock; they expense that cost over the service period. If vesting does not occur, companies reverse the compensation expense.

5 **Discuss the controversy involving stock compensation plans.** When first proposed, there was considerable opposition to the recognition provisions contained in the fair value approach. The reason: that approach could result in substantial, previously unrecognized compensation expense. Corporate America, particularly the high-technology sector, vocally opposed the proposed standard. They believed that the standard would place them at a competitive disadvantage with larger companies that can withstand higher compensation charges. Offsetting such opposition is the need for greater transparency in financial reporting, on which our capital markets depend.

6 **Compute earnings per share in a simple capital structure.** When a company has both common and preferred stock outstanding, it subtracts the current-year preferred stock dividend from net income to arrive at income available to common stockholders. The formula for computing earnings per share is net income less preferred stock dividends, divided by the weighted-average number of shares outstanding.

7 **Compute earnings per share in a complex capital structure.** A complex capital structure requires a dual presentation of earnings per share, each with equal prominence on the face of the income statement. These two presentations are referred to as basic earnings per share and diluted earnings per share. Basic earnings per share relies on the number of weighted-average common shares outstanding (i.e., equivalent to EPS for a simple capital structure). Diluted earnings per share indicates the dilution of earnings per share that will occur if all potential issuances of common stock that would reduce earnings per share takes place. Companies with complex capital structures should exclude antidilutive securities when computing earnings per share.

| APPENDIX **16A** | **ACCOUNTING FOR STOCK-APPRECIATION RIGHTS** |

LEARNING OBJECTIVE **8**
Explain the accounting for stock-appreciation rights plans.

A major disadvantage of many stock-option plans is that an executive must pay income tax on the difference between the market price of the stock and the option price at the **date of exercise**. This feature of stock-option plans (those referred to as **nonqualified**) can be a financial hardship for an executive who wishes to keep the stock (rather than sell it immediately) because he or she would have to pay not only income tax but the option price as well. In another type of plan (an **incentive plan**), the executive pays no taxes at exercise but may need to borrow to finance the exercise price, which leads to related interest cost.

One solution to this problem was the creation of stock-appreciation rights (SARs). In this type of plan, the company gives an executive the right to receive compensation equal to the share appreciation. Share appreciation is the excess of the market price of the stock at the date of exercise over a pre-established price. The company may pay the share appreciation in cash, shares, or a combination of both.

The major advantage of SARs is that the executive often does not have to make a cash outlay at the date of exercise, but receives a payment for the share appreciation. Unlike shares acquired under a stock-option plan, the company does not issue the shares that constitute the basis for computing the appreciation in a SARs plan. Rather, the company simply awards the executive cash or stock having a fair value equivalent to the appreciation. The accounting for stock-appreciation rights depends on whether the company classifies the rights as equity or as a liability.

SARS—SHARE-BASED EQUITY AWARDS

Companies classify SARs as **equity awards** if at the date of exercise, the holder receives shares of stock from the company upon exercise. In essence, SARs are essentially equivalent to a stock option. The major difference relates to the form of payment. With the stock option, the holder pays the exercise price and then receives the stock. In an equity SAR, the holder receives shares in an amount equal to the **share-price appreciation** (the difference between the market price and the pre-established price). The accounting for SARs when they are equity awards follows the accounting used for stock options. At the date of grant, the company determines a fair value for the SAR and then allocates this amount to compensation expense over the service period of the employees.

SARS—SHARE-BASED LIABILITY AWARDS

Companies classify SARs as liability awards if at the date of exercise, the holder receives a cash payment. In this case the holder is not receiving additional shares of stock but a cash payment equal to the amount of share-price appreciation. The company's compensation expense therefore changes as the value of the liability changes.

A company uses the following approach to record share-based liability awards:

1. Measure the fair value of the award at the grant date and accrue compensation over the service period.

2. Remeasure the fair value each reporting period, until the award is settled; adjust the compensation cost each period for changes in fair value pro-rated for the portion of the service period completed.

3. Once the service period is completed, determine compensation expense each subsequent period by reporting the full change in market price as an adjustment to compensation expense.

For liability awards, the company estimates the fair value of the SARs, using an option-pricing model. The company then allocates this total estimated compensation cost over the service period, recording expense (or a decrease in expense if fair value declines) in each period. At the end of each period, total compensation expense reported to date should equal the percentage of the total service period that has elapsed, multiplied by the total estimated compensation cost.

For example, assume that the service period is 40 percent complete, and total estimated compensation is $100,000. The company reports cumulative compensation expense to date of $40,000 ($100,000 × .40).

The method of allocating compensation expense is called the percentage approach. In this method, in the first year of, say, a four-year plan, the company charges one-fourth of the estimated cost to date. In the second year, it charges off two-fourths, or 50 percent, of the estimated cost to date, less the amount already recognized in the first year. In the third year, it charges off three-fourths of the estimated cost to date, less the amount recognized previously. In the fourth year it charges off the remaining compensation expense.

A special problem arises when the exercise date is later than the service period. In the previous example, if the stock-appreciation rights were not exercised at the end of four years, in the fifth year the company would have to account for the difference in the market price and the pre-established price. In this case, the company adjusts compensation expense whenever a change in the market price of the stock **occurs in subsequent reporting periods, until the rights expire or are exercised, whichever comes first**.

Increases or decreases in the fair value of the SAR between the date of grant and the exercise date, therefore, result in a change in the measure of compensation. Some periods will have credits to compensation expense if the fair value decreases from one period to the next. The credit to compensation expense, however, cannot exceed previously recognized compensation expense. In other words, **cumulative compensation expense cannot be negative**.

STOCK-APPRECIATION RIGHTS EXAMPLE

Assume that American Hotels, Inc. establishes a stock-appreciation rights plan on January 1, 2012. The plan entitles executives to receive cash at the date of exercise for the difference between the market price of the stock and the pre-established price of $10 on 10,000 SARs. The fair value of the SARs on December 31, 2012, is $3, and the service period runs for two years (2012–2013). Illustration 16A-1 (page 938) indicates the amount of compensation expense to be recorded each period, assuming that the executives hold the SARs for three years, at which time they exercise the rights.

In 2012, American Hotels records compensation expense of $15,000 because 50 percent of the $30,000 total compensation cost estimated at December 31, 2012, is allocable

STOCK-APPRECIATION RIGHTS							
SCHEDULE OF COMPENSATION EXPENSE							
(1)	(2)	(3)	(4)	(5)			
Date	Fair Value	Cumulative Compensation Recognizable^a	Percentage Accrued^b	Cumulative Compensation Accrued to Date	Expense 2012	Expense 2013	Expense 2014
12/31/12	$3	$30,000	50%	$ 15,000	$15,000		
				55,000		$55,000	
12/31/13	7	70,000	100%	70,000			
				(20,000)			$(20,000)
12/31/14	5	50,000	100%	$ 50,000			

^aCumulative compensation for unexercised SARs to be allocated to periods of service.
^bThe percentage accrued is based upon a two-year service period (2012–2013).

ILLUSTRATION 16A-1
Compensation Expense,
Stock-Appreciation Rights

to 2012. In 2013, the fair value increased to $7 per right ($70,000 total). The company recorded additional compensation expense of $55,000 ($70,000 minus $15,000).

The executives held the SARs through 2014, during which time the fair value declined to $5 (and the obligation to the executives equals $50,000). American Hotels recognizes the decrease by recording a $20,000 credit to compensation expense and a debit to Liability under Stock-Appreciation Plan. Note that after the service period ends, since the rights are still outstanding, the company adjusts the rights to market at December 31, 2014. Any such credit to compensation expense cannot exceed previous charges to expense attributable to that plan.

As the company records the compensation expense each period, the corresponding credit is to a liability account, because the company will pay the stock appreciation in cash. American Hotels records compensation expense in the first year as follows.

Compensation Expense	15,000	
Liability under Stock-Appreciation Plan		15,000

The company would credit the liability account for $55,000 again in 2013. In 2014, when it records negative compensation expense, American would debit the account for $20,000. The entry to record the negative compensation expense is as follows.

Liability under Stock-Appreciation Plan	20,000	
Compensation Expense		20,000

At December 31, 2014, the executives receive $50,000 (which equals the market price of the shares less the pre-established price). American would remove the liability with the following entry.

Liability under Stock-Appreciation Plan	50,000	
Cash		50,000

Compensation expense can increase or decrease substantially from one period to the next. The reason is that compensation expense is remeasured each year, which can lead to large swings in compensation expense.

KEY TERMS

percentage approach, *937*

share appreciation, *936*

stock-appreciation rights (SARs), *936*

SUMMARY OF LEARNING OBJECTIVE FOR APPENDIX 16A

8 ▸ **Explain the accounting for stock-appreciation rights plans.** The accounting for stock-appreciation rights depends on whether the rights are classified as equity- or liability-based. If equity-based, the accounting is similar to that used for stock options. If liability-based, companies remeasure compensation expense each period and allocate it over the service period using the percentage approach.

APPENDIX **16B** | COMPREHENSIVE EARNINGS PER SHARE EXAMPLE

This appendix illustrates the method of computing dilution when many securities are involved. We present the following section of the balance sheet of Webster Corporation for analysis. Assumptions related to the capital structure follow the balance sheet.

9 LEARNING OBJECTIVE
Compute earnings per share in a complex situation.

WEBSTER CORPORATION
BALANCE SHEET (PARTIAL)
AT DECEMBER 31, 2012

Long-term debt	
Notes payable, 14%	$ 1,000,000
8% convertible bonds payable	2,500,000
10% convertible bonds payable	2,500,000
Total long-term debt	$ 6,000,000
Stockholders' equity	
10% cumulative, convertible preferred stock, par value $100;	
100,000 shares authorized, 25,000 shares issued and outstanding	$ 2,500,000
Common stock, par value $1, 5,000,000 shares authorized,	
500,000 shares issued and outstanding	500,000
Additional paid-in capital	2,000,000
Retained earnings	9,000,000
Total stockholders' equity	$14,000,000

Notes and Assumptions
December 31, 2012

1. Options were granted in July 2010 to purchase 50,000 shares of common stock at $20 per share. The average market price of Webster's common stock during 2012 was $30 per share. All options are still outstanding at the end of 2012.
2. Both the 8 percent and 10 percent convertible bonds were issued in 2011 at face value. Each convertible bond is convertible into 40 shares of common stock. (Each bond has a face value of $1,000.)
3. The 10 percent cumulative, convertible preferred stock was issued at the beginning of 2012 at par. Each share of preferred is convertible into four shares of common stock.
4. The average income tax rate is 40 percent.
5. The 500,000 shares of common stock were outstanding during the entire year.
6. Preferred dividends were not declared in 2012.
7. Net income was $1,750,000 in 2012.
8. No bonds or preferred stock were converted during 2012.

ILLUSTRATION 16B-1
Balance Sheet for
Comprehensive
Illustration

The computation of basic earnings per share for 2012 starts with the amount based upon the weighted-average number of common shares outstanding, as shown in Illustration 16B-2.

Net income	$1,750,000
Less: 10% cumulative, convertible preferred stock dividend requirements	250,000
Income applicable to common stockholders	$1,500,000
Weighted-average number of common shares outstanding	$500,000
Earnings per common share ($1,500,000 ÷ 500,000)	$3.00

ILLUSTRATION 16B-2
Computation of Earnings
per Share—Simple
Capital Structure

Note the following points concerning this calculation.

1. When preferred stock is cumulative, the company subtracts the preferred dividend to arrive at income applicable to common stock, whether the dividend is declared or not.

2. The company must compute earnings per share of $3 as a starting point, because it is the per share amount that is subject to reduction due to the existence of convertible securities and options.

DILUTED EARNINGS PER SHARE

The steps for computing diluted earnings per share are:

1. Determine, for each dilutive security, the per share effect assuming exercise/conversion.

2. Rank the results from step 1 from smallest to largest earnings effect per share. That is, rank the results from most dilutive to least dilutive.

3. Beginning with the earnings per share based upon the weighted-average of common shares outstanding ($3), recalculate earnings per share by adding the smallest per share effects from step 2. If the results from this recalculation are less than $3, proceed to the next smallest per share effect and recalculate earnings per share. Continue this process so long as each recalculated earnings per share is smaller than the previous amount. The process will end either because there are no more securities to test or a particular security maintains or increases earnings per share (is antidilutive).

We'll now apply the three steps to Webster Corporation. (Note that net income and income available to common stockholders are not the same if preferred dividends are declared or cumulative.) Webster Corporation has four securities that could reduce EPS: options, 8 percent convertible bonds, 10 percent convertible bonds, and the convertible preferred stock.

The first step in the computation of diluted earnings per share is to determine a per share effect for each potentially dilutive security. Illustrations 16B-3 through 16B-6 illustrate these computations.

ILLUSTRATION 16B-3
Per Share Effect of Options (Treasury-Stock Method), Diluted Earnings per Share

Number of shares under option	50,000
Option price per share	× $20
Proceeds upon assumed exercise of options	$1,000,000
Average 2012 market price of common	$30
Treasury shares that could be acquired with proceeds ($1,000,000 ÷ $30)	33,333
Excess of shares under option over treasury shares that could be repurchased (50,000 − 33,333)	16,667

Per share effect:

$$\frac{\text{Incremental Numerator Effect}}{\text{Incremental Denominator Effect}} = \frac{\text{None}}{16,667 \text{ shares}} = \$0$$

ILLUSTRATION 16B-4
Per Share Effect of 8% Bonds (If-Converted Method), Diluted Earnings per Share

Interest expense for year (8% × $2,500,000)	$200,000
Income tax reduction due to interest (40% × $200,000)	80,000
Interest expense avoided (net of tax)	$120,000
Number of common shares issued assuming conversion of bonds (2,500 bonds × 40 shares)	100,000

Per share effect:

$$\frac{\text{Incremental Numerator Effect}}{\text{Incremental Denominator Effect}} = \frac{\$120,000}{100,000 \text{ shares}} = \$1.20$$

Interest expense for year (10% × $2,500,000)	$250,000
Income tax reduction due to interest (40% × $250,000)	100,000
Interest expense avoided (net of tax)	$150,000
Number of common shares issued assuming conversion of bonds (2,500 bonds × 40 shares)	100,000

Per share effect:

$$\frac{\text{Incremental Numerator Effect}}{\text{Incremental Denominator Effect}} = \frac{\$150,000}{100,000 \text{ shares}} = \$1.50$$

ILLUSTRATION 16B-5
Per Share Effect of 10%
Bonds (If-Converted
Method), Diluted
Earnings per Share

Dividend requirement on cumulative preferred (25,000 shares × $10)	$250,000
Income tax effect (dividends not a tax deduction)	none
Dividend requirement avoided	$250,000
Number of common shares issued assuming conversion of preferred (4 × 25,000 shares)	100,000

Per share effect:

$$\frac{\text{Incremental Numerator Effect}}{\text{Incremental Denominator Effect}} = \frac{\$250,000}{100,000 \text{ shares}} = \$2.50$$

ILLUSTRATION 16B-6
Per Share Effect of 10%
Convertible Preferred
(If-Converted Method),
Diluted Earnings per
Share

Illustration 16B-7 shows the ranking of all four potentially dilutive securities.

	Effect per Share
1. Options	$ 0
2. 8% convertible bonds	1.20
3. 10% convertible bonds	1.50
4. 10% convertible preferred	2.50

ILLUSTRATION 16B-7
Ranking of per Share
Effects (Smallest to
Largest), Diluted
Earnings per Share

The next step is to determine earnings per share giving effect to the ranking in Illustration 16B-7. Starting with the earnings per share of $3 computed previously, add the incremental effects of the options to the original calculation, as follows.

Options	
Income applicable to common stockholders	$1,500,000
Add: Incremental numerator effect of options	none
Total	$1,500,000
Weighted-average number of common shares outstanding	500,000
Add: Incremental denominator effect of options (Illustration 16B-3)	16,667
Total	516,667
Recomputed earnings per share ($1,500,000 ÷ 516,667 shares)	$2.90

ILLUSTRATION 16B-8
Recomputation of EPS
Using Incremental Effect
of Options

Since the recomputed earnings per share is reduced (from $3 to $2.90), the effect of the options is dilutive. Again, we could have anticipated this effect because the average market price ($30) exceeded the option price ($20).

Assuming that Webster converts the 8 percent bonds, recomputed earnings per share is as shown in Illustration 16B-9 (page 942).

ILLUSTRATION 16B-9
Recomputation of EPS
Using Incremental Effect
of 8% Convertible Bonds

8% Convertible Bonds	
Numerator from previous calculation	$1,500,000
Add: Interest expense avoided (net of tax)	120,000
Total	$1,620,000
Denominator from previous calculation (shares)	516,667
Add: Number of common shares assumed issued upon conversion of bonds	100,000
Total	616,667
Recomputed earnings per share ($1,620,000 ÷ 616,667 shares)	$2.63

Since the recomputed earnings per share is reduced (from $2.90 to $2.63), the effect of the 8 percent bonds is dilutive.

Next, assuming Webster converts the 10 percent bonds, the company recomputes earnings per share as shown in Illustration 16B-10.

ILLUSTRATION 16B-10
Recomputation of EPS
Using Incremental Effect
of 10% Convertible
Bonds

10% Convertible Bonds	
Numerator from previous calculation	$1,620,000
Add: Interest expense avoided (net of tax)	150,000
Total	$1,770,000
Denominator from previous calculation (shares)	616,667
Add: Number of common shares assumed issued upon conversion of bonds	100,000
Total	716,667
Recomputed earnings per share ($1,770,000 ÷ 716,667 shares)	$2.47

Since the recomputed earnings per share is reduced (from $2.63 to $2.47), the effect of the 10 percent convertible bonds is dilutive.

The final step is the recomputation that includes the 10 percent preferred stock. This is shown in Illustration 16B-11.

ILLUSTRATION 16B-11
Recomputation of EPS
Using Incremental Effect
of 10% Convertible
Preferred

10% Convertible Preferred	
Numerator from previous calculation	$1,770,000
Add: Dividend requirement avoided	250,000
Total	$2,020,000
Denominator from previous calculation (shares)	716,667
Add: Number of common shares assumed issued upon conversion of preferred	100,000
Total	816,667
Recomputed earnings per share ($2,020,000 ÷ 816,667 shares)	$2.47

Since the recomputed earnings per share is not reduced, the effect of the 10 percent convertible preferred is not dilutive. Diluted earnings per share is $2.47. The per share effects of the preferred are not used in the computation.

Finally, Illustration 16B-12 shows Webster Corporation's disclosure of earnings per share on its income statement.

ILLUSTRATION 16B-12
Income Statement
Presentation, EPS

Net income	$1,750,000
Basic earnings per common share (Note X)	$3.00
Diluted earnings per common share	$2.47

A company uses income from continuing operations (adjusted for preferred dividends) to determine whether potential common stock is dilutive or antidilutive. Some refer to this measure as the control number. To illustrate, assume that Barton Company provides the following information.

Income from continuing operations	$2,400,000
Loss from discontinued operations	3,600,000
Net loss	$1,200,000
Weighted-average shares of common stock outstanding	1,000,000
Potential common stock	200,000

ILLUSTRATION 16B-13
Barton Company Data

Barton reports basic and dilutive earnings per share as follows.

Basic earnings per share	
Income from continuing operations	$2.40
Loss from discontinued operations	3.60
Net loss	$1.20
Diluted earnings per share	
Income from continuing operations	$2.00
Loss from discontinued operations	3.00
Net loss	$1.00

ILLUSTRATION 16B-14
Basic and Diluted EPS

As Illustration 16B-14 shows, basic earnings per share from continuing operations is higher than the diluted earnings per share from continuing operations. The reason: The diluted earnings per share from continuing operations includes an additional 200,000 shares of potential common stock in its denominator.[20]

Companies use income from continuing operations as the control number because many of them show income from continuing operations (or a similar line item above net income if it appears on the income statement), but report a final net loss due to a loss on discontinued operations. If a company uses final net loss as the control number, basic and diluted earnings per share would be the same because the potential common shares are antidilutive.[21]

**Gateway to
the Profession**

*EPS Illustration with
Multiple Dilutive
Securities*

SUMMARY OF LEARNING OBJECTIVE FOR APPENDIX 16B

KEY TERM

control number, *943*

9 **Compute earnings per share in a complex situation.** For diluted EPS, make the following computations: (1) For each potentially dilutive security, determine the per share effect assuming exercise/conversion. (2) Rank the results from most dilutive to least dilutive. (3) Recalculate EPS starting with the most dilutive, and continue adding securities until EPS does not change or becomes larger.

---

[20]A company that does not report a discontinued operation but reports an extraordinary item should use that line item (for example, income before extraordinary items) as the control number.

[21]If a company reports a loss from continuing operations, basic and diluted earnings per share will be the same because potential common stock will be antidilutive, even if the company reports final net income. The FASB believes that comparability of EPS information will be improved by using income from continuing operations as the control number.

FASB CODIFICATION

FASB Codification References

[1] FASB ASC 480-10-25. [Predecessor literature: "Accounting for Certain Financial Instruments with Characteristics of Both Liabilities and Equity," *Statement of Financial Accounting Standards No. 150* (Norwalk Conn.: FASB, 2003), par. 23.]

[2] FASB ASC 470-20-45. [Predecessor literature: "Induced Conversions of Convertible Debt," *Statement of Financial Accounting Standards No. 84* (Stamford, Conn.: FASB, 1985).]

[3] FASB ASC 470-20-25-1 to 2. [Predecessor literature: "Accounting for Convertible Debt and Debt Issued with Stock Purchase Warrants," *Opinions of the Accounting Principles Board No. 14* (New York, NY: AICPA, 1973).]

[4] FASB ASC 470-20-30. [Predecessor literature: "Accounting for Convertible Debt Instruments that May be Settled in Cash Upon Conversion," *FASB Staff Position No. 14-1* (Norwalk, Conn: FASB, 2008).]

[5] FASB ASC 718-10-10. [Predecessor literature: "Accounting for Stock-Based Compensation," *Statement of Financial Accounting Standards No. 123* (Norwalk, Conn: FASB, 1995); and "Share-Based Payment," *Statement of Financial Accounting Standard No. 123(R)* (Norwalk, Conn: FASB, 2004).]

[6] FASB ASC 260-10-45-2. [Predecessor literature: "Earnings per Share," *Statement of Financial Accounting Standards No. 128* (Norwalk, Conn: FASB, 1997).]

[7] FASB ASC 260-10-50. [Predecessor literature: "Earnings per Share," *Statement of Financial Accounting Standards No. 128*, (Norwalk, Conn.: FASB, 1997.)]

Exercises

If your school has a subscription to the FASB Codification, go to *http://aaahq.org/ascLogin.cfm* to log in and prepare responses to the following. Provide Codification references for your responses.

CE16-1 Access the glossary ("Master Glossary") to answer the following.

 (a) What is the definition of "basic earnings per share"?

 (b) What is "dilution"?

 (c) What is a "warrant"?

 (d) What is a "grant date"?

CE16-2 For how many periods must a company present EPS data?

CE16-3 For each period that an income statement is presented, what must a company disclose about its EPS?

CE16-4 If a company's outstanding shares are increased through a stock dividend or a stock split, how would that alter the presentation of its EPS data?

An additional Codification case can be found in the Using Your Judgment section, on page 963.

Be sure to check the book's companion website for a Review and Analysis Exercise, with solution.

Questions, Brief Exercises, Exercises, Problems, and many more resources are available for practice in WileyPLUS.

Note: All asterisked Questions, Exercises, and Problems relate to material in the appendices to the chapter.

QUESTIONS

1. What is meant by a dilutive security?

2. Briefly explain why corporations issue convertible securities.

3. Discuss the similarities and the differences between convertible debt and debt issued with stock warrants.

4. Bridgewater Corp. offered holders of its 1,000 convertible bonds a premium of $160 per bond to induce conversion into shares of its common stock. Upon conversion of all the bonds, Bridgewater Corp. recorded the $160,000 premium as a reduction of paid-in capital. Comment on Bridgewater's treatment of the $160,000 "sweetener."

5. Explain how the conversion feature of convertible debt has a value (a) to the issuer and (b) to the purchaser.

6. What are the arguments for giving separate accounting recognition to the conversion feature of debentures?

7. Four years after issue, debentures with a face value of $1,000,000 and book value of $960,000 are tendered for conversion into 80,000 shares of common stock immediately after an interest payment date. At that time, the market price of the debentures is 104, and the common stock is selling at $14 per share (par value $10). The company records the conversion as follows.

Bonds Payable	1,000,000	
Discount on Bonds Payable		40,000
Common Stock		800,000
Paid-in Capital in Excess of Par—		
Common Stock		160,000

Discuss the propriety of this accounting treatment.

8. On July 1, 2012, Roberts Corporation issued $3,000,000 of 9% bonds payable in 20 years. The bonds include detachable warrants giving the bondholder the right to purchase for $30 one share of $1 par value common stock at any time during the next 10 years. The bonds were sold for $3,000,000. The value of the warrants at the time of issuance was $100,000. Prepare the journal entry to record this transaction.

9. What are stock rights? How does the issuing company account for them?

10. Briefly explain the accounting requirements for stock compensation plans under GAAP.

11. Cordero Corporation has an employee stock-purchase plan which permits all full-time employees to purchase 10 shares of common stock on the third anniversary of their employment and an additional 15 shares on each subsequent anniversary date. The purchase price is set at the market price on the date purchased and no commission is charged. Discuss whether this plan would be considered compensatory.

12. What date or event does the profession believe should be used in determining the value of a stock option? What arguments support this position?

13. Over what period of time should compensation cost be allocated?

14. How is compensation expense computed using the fair value approach?

15. What are the advantages of using restricted stock to compensate employees?

16. At December 31, 2012, Reid Company had 600,000 shares of common stock issued and outstanding, 400,000 of which had been issued and outstanding throughout the year and 200,000 of which were issued on October 1, 2012. Net income for 2012 was $2,000,000, and dividends declared on preferred stock were $400,000. Compute Reid's earnings per common share. (Round to the nearest penny.)

17. What effect do stock dividends or stock splits have on the computation of the weighted-average number of shares outstanding?

18. Define the following terms.

  (a) Basic earnings per share.

  (b) Potentially dilutive security.

  (c) Diluted earnings per share.

  (d) Complex capital structure.

  (e) Potential common stock.

19. What are the computational guidelines for determining whether a convertible security is to be reported as part of diluted earnings per share?

20. Discuss why options and warrants may be considered potentially dilutive common shares for the computation of diluted earnings per share.

21. Explain how convertible securities are determined to be potentially dilutive common shares and how those convertible securities that are not considered to be potentially dilutive common shares enter into the determination of earnings per share data.

22. Explain the treasury-stock method as it applies to options and warrants in computing dilutive earnings per share data.

23. Earnings per share can affect market prices of common stock. Can market prices affect earnings per share? Explain.

24. What is meant by the term antidilution? Give an example.

25. What type of earnings per share presentation is required in a complex capital structure?

*26. How is antidilution determined when multiple securities are involved?

BRIEF EXERCISES

1 **BE16-1** Archer Inc. issued $4,000,000 par value, 7% convertible bonds at 99 for cash. If the bonds had not included the conversion feature, they would have sold for 95. Prepare the journal entry to record the issuance of the bonds.

1 **BE16-2** Petrenko Corporation has outstanding 2,000 $1,000 bonds, each convertible into 50 shares of $10 par value common stock. The bonds are converted on December 31, 2012, when the unamortized discount is $30,000 and the market price of the stock is $21 per share. Record the conversion using the book value approach.

2 **BE16-3** Pechstein Corporation issued 2,000 shares of $10 par value common stock upon conversion of 1,000 shares of $50 par value preferred stock. The preferred stock was originally issued at $60 per share. The common stock is trading at $26 per share at the time of conversion. Record the conversion of the preferred stock.

3 **BE16-4** Eisler Corporation issued 2,000 $1,000 bonds at 101. Each bond was issued with one detachable stock warrant. After issuance, the bonds were selling in the market at 98, and the warrants had a market price of $40. Use the proportional method to record the issuance of the bonds and warrants.

3 **BE16-5** McIntyre Corporation issued 2,000 $1,000 bonds at 101. Each bond was issued with one detachable stock warrant. After issuance, the bonds were selling separately at 98. The market price of the warrants without the bonds cannot be determined. Use the incremental method to record the issuance of the bonds and warrants.

4 **BE16-6** On January 1, 2012, Barwood Corporation granted 5,000 options to executives. Each option entitles the holder to purchase one share of Barwood's $5 par value common stock at $50 per share at any time during the next 5 years. The market price of the stock is $65 per share on the date of grant. The fair value of the options at the grant date is $150,000. The period of benefit is 2 years. Prepare Barwood's journal entries for January 1, 2012, and December 31, 2012 and 2013.

4 **BE16-7** Refer to the data for Barwood Corporation in BE16-6. Repeat the requirements assuming that instead of options, Barwood granted 2,000 shares of restricted stock.

4 **BE16-8** On January 1, 2012 (the date of grant), Lutz Corporation issues 2,000 shares of restricted stock to its executives. The fair value of these shares is $75,000, and their par value is $10,000. The stock is forfeited if the executives do not complete 3 years of employment with the company. Prepare the journal entry (if any) on January 1, 2012, and on December 31, 2012, assuming the service period is 3 years.

6 **BE16-9** Kalin Corporation had 2012 net income of $1,000,000. During 2012, Kalin paid a dividend of $2 per share on 100,000 shares of preferred stock. During 2012, Kalin had outstanding 250,000 shares of common stock. Compute Kalin's 2012 earnings per share.

6 **BE16-10** Douglas Corporation had 120,000 shares of stock outstanding on January 1, 2012. On May 1, 2012, Douglas issued 60,000 shares. On July 1, Douglas purchased 10,000 treasury shares, which were reissued on October 1. Compute Douglas's weighted-average number of shares outstanding for 2012.

6 **BE16-11** Tomba Corporation had 300,000 shares of common stock outstanding on January 1, 2012. On May 1, Tomba issued 30,000 shares. (a) Compute the weighted-average number of shares outstanding if the 30,000 shares were issued for cash. (b) Compute the weighted-average number of shares outstanding if the 30,000 shares were issued in a stock dividend.

7 **BE16-12** Rockland Corporation earned net income of $300,000 in 2012 and had 100,000 shares of common stock outstanding throughout the year. Also outstanding all year was $800,000 of 10% bonds, which are convertible into 16,000 shares of common. Rockland's tax rate is 40 percent. Compute Rockland's 2012 diluted earnings per share.

7 **BE16-13** DiCenta Corporation reported net income of $270,000 in 2012 and had 50,000 shares of common stock outstanding throughout the year. Also outstanding all year were 5,000 shares of cumulative preferred stock, each convertible into 2 shares of common. The preferred stock pays an annual dividend of $5 per share. DiCenta's tax rate is 40%. Compute DiCenta's 2012 diluted earnings per share.

7 **BE16-14** Bedard Corporation reported net income of $300,000 in 2012 and had 200,000 shares of common stock outstanding throughout the year. Also outstanding all year were 45,000 options to purchase common stock at $10 per share. The average market price of the stock during the year was $15. Compute diluted earnings per share.

6 **BE16-15** The 2012 income statement of Wasmeier Corporation showed net income of $480,000 and an extraordinary loss of $120,000. Wasmeier had 100,000 shares of common stock outstanding all year. Prepare Wasmeier's income statement presentation of earnings per share.

8 *BE16-16 Ferraro, Inc. established a stock-appreciation rights (SAR) program on January 1, 2012, which entitles executives to receive cash at the date of exercise for the difference between the market price of the stock and the pre-established price of $20 on 5,000 SARs. The required service period is 2 years. The fair value of the SARs are determined to be $4 on December 31, 2012, and $9 on December 31, 2013. Compute Ferraro's compensation expense for 2012 and 2013.

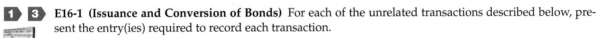

EXERCISES

1 **3** **E16-1 (Issuance and Conversion of Bonds)** For each of the unrelated transactions described below, present the entry(ies) required to record each transaction.

1. Coyle Corp. issued $10,000,000 par value 10% convertible bonds at 99. If the bonds had not been convertible, the company's investment banker estimates they would have been sold at 95. Expenses of issuing the bonds were $70,000.
2. Lambert Company issued $10,000,000 par value 10% bonds at 98. One detachable stock warrant was issued with each $100 par value bond. At the time of issuance, the warrants were selling for $4.
3. Sepracor, Inc. called its convertible debt in 2012. Assume the following related to the transaction: The 11%, $10,000,000 par value bonds were converted into 1,000,000 shares of $1 par value common stock on July 1, 2012. On July 1, there was $55,000 of unamortized discount applicable to the bonds, and the company paid an additional $75,000 to the bondholders to induce conversion of all the bonds. The company records the conversion using the book value method.

1 **E16-2 (Conversion of Bonds)** Schuss Inc. issued $3,000,000 of 10%, 10-year convertible bonds on June 1, 2012, at 98 plus accrued interest. The bonds were dated April 1, 2012, with interest payable April 1 and October 1. Bond discount is amortized semiannually on a straight-line basis.

On April 1, 2013, $1,000,000 of these bonds were converted into 30,000 shares of $20 par value common stock. Accrued interest was paid in cash at the time of conversion.

Instructions
(a) Prepare the entry to record the interest expense at October 1, 2012. Assume that accrued interest payable was credited when the bonds were issued. (Round to nearest dollar.)
(b) Prepare the entry(ies) to record the conversion on April 1, 2013. (The book value method is used.) Assume that the entry to record amortization of the bond discount and interest payment has been made.

1 **E16-3 (Conversion of Bonds)** Gabel Company has bonds payable outstanding in the amount of $400,000, and the Premium on Bonds Payable account has a balance of $6,000. Each $1,000 bond is convertible into 20 shares of preferred stock of par value of $50 per share. All bonds are converted into preferred stock.

Instructions
Assuming that the book value method was used, what entry would be made?

1 **E16-4 (Conversion of Bonds)** On January 1, 2012, when its $30 par value common stock was selling for $80 per share, Bartz Corp. issued $10,000,000 of 8% convertible debentures due in 20 years. The conversion option allowed the holder of each $1,000 bond to convert the bond into five shares of the corporation's common stock. The debentures were issued for $10,600,000. The present value of the bond payments at the time of issuance was $8,500,000, and the corporation believes the difference between the present value and the amount paid is attributable to the conversion feature. On January 1, 2013, the corporation's $30 par value common stock was split 2 for 1, and the conversion rate for the bonds was adjusted accordingly. On January 1, 2014, when the corporation's $15 par value common stock was selling for $135 per share, holders of 20% of the convertible debentures exercised their conversion options. The corporation uses the straight-line method for amortizing any bond discounts or premiums.

Instructions

(a) Prepare the entry to record the original issuance of the convertible debentures.

(b) Prepare the entry to record the exercise of the conversion option, using the book value method. Show supporting computations in good form.

E16-5 (Conversion of Bonds) The December 31, 2012, balance sheet of Osygus Corp. is as follows.

10% callable, convertible bonds payable (semiannual interest dates April 30 and October 31; convertible into 6 shares of $25 par value common stock per $1,000 of bond principal; maturity date April 30, 2018)	$600,000	
Discount on bonds payable	10,240	$589,760

On March 5, 2013, Osygus Corp. called all of the bonds as of April 30, for the principal plus interest through April 30. By April 30, all bondholders had exercised their conversion to common stock as of the interest payment date. Consequently, on April 30, Osygus Corp. paid the semiannual interest and issued shares of common stock for the bonds. The discount is amortized on a straight-line basis. Osygus uses the book value method.

Instructions

Prepare the entry(ies) to record the interest expense and conversion on April 30, 2013. Reversing entries were made on January 1, 2013.

E16-6 (Conversion of Bonds) On January 1, 2011, Trillini Corporation issued $3,000,000 of 10-year, 8% convertible debentures at 102. Interest is to be paid semiannually on June 30 and December 31. Each $1,000 debenture can be converted into eight shares of Trillini Corporation $100 par value common stock after December 31, 2012.

On January 1, 2013, $600,000 of debentures are converted into common stock, which is then selling at $110. An additional $600,000 of debentures are converted on March 31, 2013. The market price of the common stock is then $115. Accrued interest at March 31 will be paid on the next interest date.

Bond premium is amortized on a straight-line basis.

Instructions

Make the necessary journal entries for:

(a) December 31, 2012.   (c) March 31, 2013.

(b) January 1, 2013.   (d) June 30, 2013.

Record the conversions using the book value method.

E16-7 (Issuance of Bonds with Warrants) Prior Inc. has decided to raise additional capital by issuing $175,000 face value of bonds with a coupon rate of 10%. In discussions with investment bankers, it was determined that to help the sale of the bonds, detachable stock warrants should be issued at the rate of one warrant for each $100 bond sold. The value of the bonds without the warrants is considered to be $136,000, and the value of the warrants in the market is $24,000. The bonds sold in the market at issuance for $150,000.

Instructions

(a) What entry should be made at the time of the issuance of the bonds and warrants?

(b) If the warrants were nondetachable, would the entries be different? Discuss.

E16-8 (Issuance of Bonds with Detachable Warrants) On September 1, 2012, Jacob Company sold at 104 (plus accrued interest) 3,000 of its 8%, 10-year, $1,000 face value, nonconvertible bonds with detachable stock warrants. Each bond carried two detachable warrants. Each warrant was for one share of common stock at a specified option price of $15 per share. Shortly after issuance, the warrants were quoted on the market for $3 each. No fair value can be determined for the Jacob Company bonds. Interest is payable on December 1 and June 1. Bond issue costs of $30,000 were incurred.

Instructions

Prepare in general journal format the entry to record the issuance of the bonds.

(AICPA adapted)

E16-9 (Issuance of Bonds with Stock Warrants) On May 1, 2012, Barkley Company issued 3,000 $1,000 bonds at 102. Each bond was issued with one detachable stock warrant. Shortly after issuance, the bonds were selling at 98, but the fair value of the warrants cannot be determined.

Instructions

    (a) Prepare the entry to record the issuance of the bonds and warrants.

    (b) Assume the same facts as part (a), except that the warrants had a fair value of $20. Prepare the entry to record the issuance of the bonds and warrants.

E16-10 (Issuance and Exercise of Stock Options) On November 1, 2011, Olympic Company adopted a stock-option plan that granted options to key executives to purchase 40,000 shares of the company's $10 par value common stock. The options were granted on January 2, 2012, and were exercisable 2 years after the date of grant if the grantee was still an employee of the company. The options expired 6 years from date of grant. The option price was set at $40, and the fair value option-pricing model determines the total compensation expense to be $600,000.

    All of the options were exercised during the year 2014: 30,000 on January 3 when the market price was $67, and 10,000 on May 1 when the market price was $77 a share.

Instructions

Prepare journal entries relating to the stock-option plan for the years 2012, 2013, and 2014. Assume that the employee performs services equally in 2012 and 2013.

E16-11 (Issuance, Exercise, and Termination of Stock Options) On January 1, 2012, Magilla Inc. granted stock options to officers and key employees for the purchase of 20,000 shares of the company's $10 par common stock at $25 per share. The options were exercisable within a 5-year period beginning January 1, 2014, by grantees still in the employ of the company, and expiring December 31, 2016. The service period for this award is 2 years. Assume that the fair value option-pricing model determines total compensation expense to be $400,000.

    On April 1, 2013, 3,000 options were terminated when the employees resigned from the company. The market price of the common stock was $35 per share on this date.

    On March 31, 2014, 12,000 options were exercised when the market price of the common stock was $40 per share.

Instructions

Prepare journal entries to record issuance of the stock options, termination of the stock options, exercise of the stock options, and charges to compensation expense, for the years ended December 31, 2012, 2013, and 2014.

E16-12 (Issuance, Exercise, and Termination of Stock Options) On January 1, 2011, Scooby Corporation granted 10,000 options to key executives. Each option allows the executive to purchase one share of Scooby's $5 par value common stock at a price of $20 per share. The options were exercisable within a 2-year period beginning January 1, 2013, if the grantee is still employed by the company at the time of the exercise. On the grant date, Scooby's stock was trading at $25 per share, and a fair value option-pricing model determines total compensation to be $450,000.

    On May 1, 2013, 9,000 options were exercised when the market price of Scooby's stock was $30 per share. The remaining options lapsed in 2015 because executives decided not to exercise their options.

Instructions

Prepare the necessary journal entries related to the stock-option plan for the years 2011 through 2015.

E16-13 (Accounting for Restricted Stock) Derrick Company issues 4,000 shares of restricted stock to its CFO, Dane Yaping, on January 1, 2012. The stock has a fair value of $120,000 on this date. The service period related to this restricted stock is 4 years. Vesting occurs if Yaping stays with the company for 4 years. The par value of the stock is $5. At December 31, 2013, the fair value of the stock is $145,000.

Instructions

    (a) Prepare the journal entries to record the restricted stock on January 1, 2012 (the date of grant), and December 31, 2013.

    (b) On March 4, 2014, Yaping leaves the company. Prepare the journal entry (if any) to account for this forfeiture.

E16-14 (Accounting for Restricted Stock) Tweedie Company issues 10,000 shares of restricted stock to its CFO, Mary Tokar, on January 1, 2012. The stock has a fair value of $500,000 on this date. The service period related to this restricted stock is 5 years. Vesting occurs if Tokar stays with the company until December 31, 2016. The par value of the stock is $10. At December 31, 2012, the fair value of the stock is $450,000.

Instructions

    (a) Prepare the journal entries to record the restricted stock on January 1, 2012 (the date of grant), and December 31, 2013.

    (b) On July 25, 2016, Tokar leaves the company. Prepare the journal entry (if any) to account for this forfeiture.

E16-15 (Weighted-Average Number of Shares) Gogean Inc. uses a calendar year for financial reporting. The company is authorized to issue 9,000,000 shares of $10 par common stock. At no time has Gogean issued any potentially dilutive securities. Listed below is a summary of Gogean's common stock activities.

1. Number of common shares issued and outstanding at December 31, 2011	2,400,000
2. Shares issued as a result of a 10% stock dividend on September 30, 2012	240,000
3. Shares issued for cash on March 31, 2013	2,000,000
Number of common shares issued and outstanding at December 31, 2013	4,640,000
4. A 2-for-1 stock split of Gogean's common stock took place on March 31, 2014	

Instructions

(a) Compute the weighted-average number of common shares used in computing earnings per common share for 2012 on the 2013 comparative income statement.

(b) Compute the weighted-average number of common shares used in computing earnings per common share for 2013 on the 2013 comparative income statement.

(c) Compute the weighted-average number of common shares to be used in computing earnings per common share for 2013 on the 2014 comparative income statement.

(d) Compute the weighted-average number of common shares to be used in computing earnings per common share for 2014 on the 2014 comparative income statement.

(CMA adapted)

E16-16 (EPS: Simple Capital Structure) On January 1, 2012, Chang Corp. had 480,000 shares of common stock outstanding. During 2012, it had the following transactions that affected the Common Stock account.

February 1	Issued 120,000 shares
March 1	Issued a 20% stock dividend
May 1	Acquired 100,000 shares of treasury stock
June 1	Issued a 3-for-1 stock split
October 1	Reissued 60,000 shares of treasury stock

Instructions

(a) Determine the weighted-average number of shares outstanding as of December 31, 2012.

(b) Assume that Chang Corp. earned net income of $3,256,000 during 2012. In addition, it had 100,000 shares of 9%, $100 par nonconvertible, noncumulative preferred stock outstanding for the entire year. Because of liquidity considerations, however, the company did not declare and pay a preferred dividend in 2012. Compute earnings per share for 2012, using the weighted-average number of shares determined in part (a).

(c) Assume the same facts as in part (b), except that the preferred stock was cumulative. Compute earnings per share for 2012.

(d) Assume the same facts as in part (b), except that net income included an extraordinary gain of $864,000 and a loss from discontinued operations of $432,000. Both items are net of applicable income taxes. Compute earnings per share for 2012.

E16-17 (EPS: Simple Capital Structure) Ott Company had 210,000 shares of common stock outstanding on December 31, 2012. During the year 2013, the company issued 8,000 shares on May 1 and retired 14,000 shares on October 31. For the year 2013, Ott Company reported net income of $229,690 after a casualty loss of $40,600 (net of tax).

Instructions

What earnings per share data should be reported at the bottom of its income statement, assuming that the casualty loss is extraordinary?

E16-18 (EPS: Simple Capital Structure) Kendall Inc. presented the following data.

Net income	$2,200,000
Preferred stock: 50,000 shares outstanding,	
$100 par, 8% cumulative, not convertible	5,000,000
Common stock: Shares outstanding 1/1	600,000
Issued for cash, 5/1	300,000
Acquired treasury stock for cash, 8/1	150,000
2-for-1 stock split, 10/1	

Instructions

Compute earnings per share.

6 **E16-19 (EPS: Simple Capital Structure)** A portion of the statement of income and retained earnings of Pierson Inc. for the current year follows.

Income before extraordinary item		$15,000,000
Extraordinary loss, net of applicable		
income tax (Note 1)		1,340,000
Net income		13,660,000
Retained earnings at the beginning of the year		83,250,000
		96,910,000
Dividends declared:		
On preferred stock—$6.00 per share	$ 300,000	
On common stock—$1.75 per share	14,000,000	14,300,000
Retained earnings at the end of the year		$82,610,000

Note 1. During the year, Pierson Inc. suffered a major casualty loss of $1,340,000 after applicable income tax reduction of $1,200,000.

At the end of the current year, Pierson Inc. has outstanding 8,000,000 shares of $10 par common stock and 50,000 shares of 6% preferred.

On April 1 of the current year, Pierson Inc. issued 1,000,000 shares of common stock for $32 per share to help finance the casualty.

Instructions
Compute the earnings per share on common stock for the current year as it should be reported to stockholders.

6 **E16-20 (EPS: Simple Capital Structure)** On January 1, 2012, Bailey Industries had stock outstanding as follows.

6% Cumulative preferred stock, $100 par value,	
issued and outstanding 10,000 shares	$1,000,000
Common stock, $10 par value, issued and	
outstanding 200,000 shares	2,000,000

To acquire the net assets of three smaller companies, Bailey authorized the issuance of an additional 170,000 common shares. The acquisitions took place as shown below.

Date of Acquisition	Shares Issued
Company A April 1, 2012	60,000
Company B July 1, 2012	80,000
Company C October 1, 2012	30,000

On May 14, 2012, Bailey realized a $90,000 (before taxes) insurance gain on the expropriation of investments originally purchased in 2000.

On December 31, 2012, Bailey recorded net income of $300,000 before tax and exclusive of the gain.

Instructions
Assuming a 40% tax rate, compute the earnings per share data that should appear on the financial statements of Bailey Industries as of December 31, 2012. Assume that the expropriation is extraordinary.

6 **E16-21 (EPS: Simple Capital Structure)** At January 1, 2012, Cameron Company's outstanding shares included the following.

280,000 shares of $50 par value, 7% cumulative preferred stock
800,000 shares of $1 par value common stock

Net income for 2012 was $2,830,000. No cash dividends were declared or paid during 2012. On February 15, 2013, however, all preferred dividends in arrears were paid, together with a 5% stock dividend on common shares. There were no dividends in arrears prior to 2012.

On April 1, 2012, 450,000 shares of common stock were sold for $10 per share, and on October 1, 2012, 110,000 shares of common stock were purchased for $20 per share and held as treasury stock.

Instructions
Compute earnings per share for 2012. Assume that financial statements for 2012 were issued in March 2013.

7 **E16-22 (EPS with Convertible Bonds, Various Situations)** In 2012, Buraka Enterprises issued, at par, 75 $1,000, 8% bonds, each convertible into 100 shares of common stock. Buraka had revenues of $17,500 and expenses other than interest and taxes of $8,400 for 2013. (Assume that the tax rate is 40%.) Throughout 2013, 2,000 shares of common stock were outstanding; none of the bonds was converted or redeemed.

Instructions
(a) Compute diluted earnings per share for 2013.
(b) Assume the same facts as those assumed for part (a), except that the 75 bonds were issued on September 1, 2013 (rather than in 2012), and none have been converted or redeemed.
(c) Assume the same facts as assumed for part (a), except that 25 of the 75 bonds were actually converted on July 1, 2013.

7 **E16-23 (EPS with Convertible Bonds)** On June 1, 2011, Bluhm Company and Amanar Company merged to form Davenport Inc. A total of 800,000 shares were issued to complete the merger. The new corporation reports on a calendar-year basis.

On April 1, 2013, the company issued an additional 600,000 shares of stock for cash. All 1,400,000 shares were outstanding on December 31, 2013.

Davenport Inc. also issued $600,000 of 20-year, 8% convertible bonds at par on July 1, 2013. Each $1,000 bond converts to 40 shares of common at any interest date. None of the bonds have been converted to date.

Davenport Inc. is preparing its annual report for the fiscal year ending December 31, 2013. The annual report will show earnings per share figures based upon a reported after-tax net income of $1,540,000. (The tax rate is 40%.)

Instructions
Determine the following for 2013.
(a) The number of shares to be used for calculating:
(1) Basic earnings per share.
(2) Diluted earnings per share.
(b) The earnings figures to be used for calculating:
(1) Basic earnings per share.
(2) Diluted earnings per share.

(CMA adapted)

2 **7** **E16-24 (EPS with Convertible Bonds and Preferred Stock)** The Ottey Corporation issued 10-year, $4,000,000 par, 7% callable convertible subordinated debentures on January 2, 2012. The bonds have a par value of $1,000, with interest payable annually. The current conversion ratio is 14:1, and in 2 years it will increase to 18:1. At the date of issue, the bonds were sold at 98. Bond discount is amortized on a straight-line basis. Ottey's effective tax was 35%. Net income in 2012 was $7,500,000, and the company had 2,000,000 shares outstanding during the entire year.

Instructions
(a) Prepare a schedule to compute both basic and diluted earnings per share.
(b) Discuss how the schedule would differ if the security was convertible preferred stock.

2 **7** **E16-25 (EPS with Convertible Bonds and Preferred Stock)** On January 1, 2012, Lindsey Company issued 10-year, $3,000,000 face value, 6% bonds, at par. Each $1,000 bond is convertible into 15 shares of Lindsey common stock. Lindsey's net income in 2013 was $240,000, and its tax rate was 40%. The company had 100,000 shares of common stock outstanding throughout 2012. None of the bonds were converted in 2012.

Instructions
(a) Compute diluted earnings per share for 2012.
(b) Compute diluted earnings per share for 2012, assuming the same facts as above, except that $1,000,000 of 6% convertible preferred stock was issued instead of the bonds. Each $100 preferred share is convertible into 5 shares of Lindsey common stock.

7 **E16-26 (EPS with Options, Various Situations)** Zambrano Company's net income for 2012 is $40,000. The only potentially dilutive securities outstanding were 1,000 options issued during 2011, each exercisable for one share at $8. None has been exercised, and 10,000 shares of common were outstanding during 2012. The average market price of Zambrano's stock during 2012 was $20.

Instructions

(a) Compute diluted earnings per share. (Round to the nearest cent.)

(b) Assume the same facts as those assumed for part (a), except that the 1,000 options were issued on October 1, 2012 (rather than in 2011). The average market price during the last 3 months of 2012 was $20.

E16-27 (EPS with Contingent Issuance Agreement) Brooks Inc. recently purchased Donovan Corp., a large midwestern home painting corporation. One of the terms of the merger was that if Donovan's income for 2013 was $110,000 or more, 10,000 additional shares would be issued to Donovan's stockholders in 2014. Donovan's income for 2012 was $125,000.

Instructions

(a) Would the contingent shares have to be considered in Brooks's 2012 earnings per share computations?

(b) Assume the same facts, except that the 10,000 shares are contingent on Donovan's achieving a net income of $130,000 in 2013. Would the contingent shares have to be considered in Brooks's earnings per share computations for 2012?

E16-28 (EPS with Warrants) Werth Corporation earned $260,000 during a period when it had an average of 100,000 shares of common stock outstanding. The common stock sold at an average market price of $15 per share during the period. Also outstanding were 30,000 warrants that could be exercised to purchase one share of common stock for $10 for each warrant exercised.

Instructions

(a) Are the warrants dilutive?

(b) Compute basic earnings per share.

(c) Compute diluted earnings per share.

***E16-29 (Stock-Appreciation Rights)** On December 31, 2009, Flessel Company issues 120,000 stock-appreciation rights to its officers entitling them to receive cash for the difference between the market price of its stock and a pre-established price of $10. The fair value of the SARs is estimated to be $4 per SAR on December 31, 2010; $1 on December 31, 2011; $11 on December 31, 2012; and $9 on December 31, 2013. The service period is 4 years, and the exercise period is 7 years.

Instructions

(a) Prepare a schedule that shows the amount of compensation expense allocable to each year affected by the stock-appreciation rights plan.

(b) Prepare the entry at December 31, 2013, to record compensation expense, if any, in 2013.

(c) Prepare the entry on December 31, 2013, assuming that all 120,000 SARs are exercised.

***E16-30 (Stock-Appreciation Rights)** Derrick Company establishes a stock-appreciation rights program that entitles its new president, Dan Scott, to receive cash for the difference between the market price of the stock and a pre-established price of $30 (also market price) on January 1, 2011, on 40,000 SARs. The date of grant is January 1, 2011, and the required employment (service) period is 4 years. President Scott exercises all of the SARs in 2016. The fair value of the SARs is estimated to be $6 per SAR on December 31, 2011; $9 on December 31, 2012; $15 on December 31, 2013; $8 on December 31, 2014; and $18 on December 31, 2015.

Instructions

(a) Prepare a 5-year (2011–2015) schedule of compensation expense pertaining to the 40,000 SARs granted to president Scott.

(b) Prepare the journal entry for compensation expense in 2011, 2014, and 2015 relative to the 40,000 SARs.

See the book's companion website, www.wiley.com/college/kieso, for a set of B Exercises.

PROBLEMS

  P16-1 (Entries for Various Dilutive Securities) The stockholders' equity section of Martino Inc. at the beginning of the current year appears below.

Common stock, $10 par value, authorized 1,000,000 shares, 300,000 shares issued and outstanding	$3,000,000
Paid-in capital in excess of par—common stock	600,000
Retained earnings	570,000

During the current year, the following transactions occurred.

1. The company issued to the stockholders 100,000 rights. Ten rights are needed to buy one share of stock at $32. The rights were void after 30 days. The market price of the stock at this time was $34 per share.
2. The company sold to the public a $200,000, 10% bond issue at 104. The company also issued with each $100 bond one detachable stock purchase warrant, which provided for the purchase of common stock at $30 per share. Shortly after issuance, similar bonds without warrants were selling at 96 and the warrants at $8.
3. All but 5,000 of the rights issued in (1) were exercised in 30 days.
4. At the end of the year, 80% of the warrants in (2) had been exercised, and the remaining were outstanding and in good standing.
5. During the current year, the company granted stock options for 10,000 shares of common stock to company executives. The company, using a fair value option-pricing model, determines that each option is worth $10. The option price is $30. The options were to expire at year-end and were considered compensation for the current year.
6. All but 1,000 shares related to the stock-option plan were exercised by year-end. The expiration resulted because one of the executives failed to fulfill an obligation related to the employment contract.

Instructions
(a) Prepare general journal entries for the current year to record the transactions listed above.
(b) Prepare the stockholders' equity section of the balance sheet at the end of the current year. Assume that retained earnings at the end of the current year is $750,000.

 P16-2 (Entries for Conversion, Amortization, and Interest of Bonds) Volker Inc. issued $2,500,000 of convertible 10-year bonds on July 1, 2012. The bonds provide for 12% interest payable semiannually on January 1 and July 1. The discount in connection with the issue was $54,000, which is being amortized monthly on a straight-line basis.

The bonds are convertible after one year into 8 shares of Volker Inc.'s $100 par value common stock for each $1,000 of bonds.

On August 1, 2013, $250,000 of bonds were turned in for conversion into common stock. Interest has been accrued monthly and paid as due. At the time of conversion, any accrued interest on bonds being converted is paid in cash.

Instructions
Prepare the journal entries to record the conversion, amortization, and interest in connection with the bonds as of the following dates. (Round to the nearest dollar.)

(a) August 1, 2013. (Assume the book value method is used.)
(b) August 31, 2013.
(c) December 31, 2013, including closing entries for end-of-year.

(AICPA adapted)

 P16-3 (Stock-Option Plan) Berg Company adopted a stock-option plan on November 30, 2011, that provided that 70,000 shares of $5 par value stock be designated as available for the granting of options to officers of the corporation at a price of $9 a share. The market price was $12 a share on November 30, 2012.

On January 2, 2012, options to purchase 28,000 shares were granted to president Tom Winter—15,000 for services to be rendered in 2012 and 13,000 for services to be rendered in 2013. Also on that date, options to purchase 14,000 shares were granted to vice president Michelle Bennett—7,000 for services to be rendered in 2012 and 7,000 for services to be rendered in 2013. The market price of the stock was $14 a share on January 2, 2012. The options were exercisable for a period of one year following the year in which the services were rendered. The fair value of the options on the grant date was $4 per option.

In 2013, neither the president nor the vice president exercised their options because the market price of the stock was below the exercise price. The market price of the stock was $8 a share on December 31, 2013, when the options for 2012 services lapsed.

On December 31, 2014, both president Winter and vice president Bennett exercised their options for 13,000 and 7,000 shares, respectively, when the market price was $16 a share.

Instructions

Prepare the necessary journal entries in 2011 when the stock-option plan was adopted, in 2012 when options were granted, in 2013 when options lapsed, and in 2014 when options were exercised.

4 **P16-4 (Stock-Based Compensation)** Assume that Amazon has a stock-option plan for top management. Each stock option represents the right to purchase a share of Amazon $1 par value common stock in the future at a price equal to the fair value of the stock at the date of the grant. Amazon has 5,000 stock options outstanding, which were granted at the beginning of 2012. The following data relate to the option grant.

Exercise price for options	$40
Market price at grant date (January 1, 2012)	$40
Fair value of options at grant date (January 1, 2012)	$6
Service period	5 years

Instructions

(a) Prepare the journal entry(ies) for the first year of the stock-option plan.

(b) Prepare the journal entry(ies) for the first year of the plan assuming that, rather than options, 700 shares of restricted stock were granted at the beginning of 2012.

(c) Now assume that the market price of Amazon stock on the grant date was $45 per share. Repeat the requirements for (a) and (b).

(d) Amazon would like to implement an employee stock-purchase plan for rank-and-file employees, but it would like to avoid recording expense related to this plan. Which of the following provisions must be in place for the plan to avoid recording compensation expense?

(1) Substantially all employees may participate.

(2) The discount from market is small (less than 5%).

(3) The plan offers no substantive option feature.

(4) There is no preferred stock outstanding.

7 **P16-5 (EPS with Complex Capital Structure)** Amy Dyken, controller at Fitzgerald Pharmaceutical Industries, a public company, is currently preparing the calculation for basic and diluted earnings per share and the related disclosure for Fitzgerald's financial statements. Below is selected financial information for the fiscal year ended June 30, 2012.

FITZGERALD PHARMACEUTICAL INDUSTRIES
SELECTED BALANCE SHEET
INFORMATION
JUNE 30, 2012

Long-term debt	
Notes payable, 10%	$ 1,000,000
8% convertible bonds payable	5,000,000
10% bonds payable	6,000,000
Total long-term debt	$12,000,000
Shareholders' equity	
Preferred stock, 6% cumulative, $50 par value,	
100,000 shares authorized, 25,000 shares issued	
and outstanding	$ 1,250,000
Common stock, $1 par, 10,000,000 shares authorized,	
1,000,000 shares issued and outstanding	1,000,000
Additional paid-in capital	4,000,000
Retained earnings	6,000,000
Total shareholders' equity	$12,250,000

The following transactions have also occurred at Fitzgerald.

1. Options were granted on July 1, 2011, to purchase 200,000 shares at $15 per share. Although no options were exercised during fiscal year 2012, the average price per common share during fiscal year 2012 was $20 per share.
2. Each bond was issued at face value. The 8% convertible bonds will convert into common stock at 50 shares per $1,000 bond. The bonds are exercisable after 5 years and were issued in fiscal year 2011.
3. The preferred stock was issued in 2011.
4. There are no preferred dividends in arrears; however, preferred dividends were not declared in fiscal year 2012.
5. The 1,000,000 shares of common stock were outstanding for the entire 2012 fiscal year.
6. Net income for fiscal year 2012 was $1,500,000, and the average income tax rate is 40%.

Instructions

For the fiscal year ended June 30, 2012, calculate the following for Fitzgerald Pharmaceutical Industries.

(a) Basic earnings per share.
(b) Diluted earnings per share.

6 **P16-6 (Basic EPS: Two-Year Presentation)** Melton Corporation is preparing the comparative financial statements for the annual report to its shareholders for fiscal years ended May 31, 2012, and May 31, 2013. The income from operations for each year was $1,800,000 and $2,500,000, respectively. In both years, the company incurred a 10% interest expense on $2,400,000 of debt, an obligation that requires interest-only payments for 5 years. The company experienced a loss of $600,000 from a fire in its Scotsland facility in February 2013, which was determined to be an extraordinary loss. The company uses a 40% effective tax rate for income taxes.

The capital structure of Melton Corporation on June 1, 2011, consisted of 1 million shares of common stock outstanding and 20,000 shares of $50 par value, 6%, cumulative preferred stock. There were no preferred dividends in arrears, and the company had not issued any convertible securities, options, or warrants.

On October 1, 2011, Melton sold an additional 500,000 shares of the common stock at $20 per share. Melton distributed a 20% stock dividend on the common shares outstanding on January 1, 2012. On December 1, 2012, Melton was able to sell an additional 800,000 shares of the common stock at $22 per share. These were the only common stock transactions that occurred during the two fiscal years.

Instructions

(a) Identify whether the capital structure at Melton Corporation is a simple or complex capital structure, and explain why.
(b) Determine the weighted-average number of shares that Melton Corporation would use in calculating earnings per share for the fiscal year ended:
   (1) May 31, 2012.
   (2) May 31, 2013.
(c) Prepare, in good form, a comparative income statement, beginning with income from operations, for Melton Corporation for the fiscal years ended May 31, 2012, and May 31, 2013. This statement will be included in Melton's annual report and should display the appropriate earnings per share presentations.

(CMA adapted)

7 **P16-7 (Computation of Basic and Diluted EPS)** Charles Austin of the controller's office of Thompson Corporation was given the assignment of determining the basic and diluted earnings per share values for the year ending December 31, 2013. Austin has compiled the information listed below.

1. The company is authorized to issue 8,000,000 shares of $10 par value common stock. As of December 31, 2012, 2,000,000 shares had been issued and were outstanding.
2. The per share market prices of the common stock on selected dates were as follows.

	Price per Share
July 1, 2012	$20.00
January 1, 2013	21.00
April 1, 2013	25.00
July 1, 2013	11.00
August 1, 2013	10.50
November 1, 2013	9.00
December 31, 2013	10.00

3. A total of 700,000 shares of an authorized 1,200,000 shares of convertible preferred stock had been issued on July 1, 2012. The stock was issued at its par value of $25, and it has a cumulative dividend of $3 per share. The stock is convertible into common stock at the rate of one share of convertible preferred for one share of common. The rate of conversion is to be automatically adjusted for stock splits and stock dividends. Dividends are paid quarterly on September 30, December 31, March 31, and June 30.

4. Thompson Corporation is subject to a 40% income tax rate.

5. The after-tax net income for the year ended December 31, 2013, was $11,550,000.

The following specific activities took place during 2013.

1. January 1—A 5% common stock dividend was issued. The dividend had been declared on December 1, 2012, to all stockholders of record on December 29, 2012.

2. April 1—A total of 400,000 shares of the $3 convertible preferred stock was converted into common stock. The company issued new common stock and retired the preferred stock. This was the only conversion of the preferred stock during 2013.

3. July 1—A 2-for-1 split of the common stock became effective on this date. The board of directors had authorized the split on June 1.

4. August 1—A total of 300,000 shares of common stock were issued to acquire a factory building.

5. November 1—A total of 24,000 shares of common stock were purchased on the open market at $9 per share. These shares were to be held as treasury stock and were still in the treasury as of December 31, 2013.

6. Common stock cash dividends—Cash dividends to common stockholders were declared and paid as follows.

> April 15—$0.30 per share
> October 15—$0.20 per share

7. Preferred stock cash dividends—Cash dividends to preferred stockholders were declared and paid as scheduled.

Instructions
(a) Determine the number of shares used to compute basic earnings per share for the year ended December 31, 2013.
(b) Determine the number of shares used to compute diluted earnings per share for the year ended December 31, 2013.
(c) Compute the adjusted net income to be used as the numerator in the basic earnings per share calculation for the year ended December 31, 2013.

7 ▶ **P16-8 (Computation of Basic and Diluted EPS)** The information below pertains to Barkley Company for 2013.

Net income for the year	$1,200,000
8% convertible bonds issued at par ($1,000 per bond); each bond is convertible into 30 shares of common stock	2,000,000
6% convertible, cumulative preferred stock, $100 par value; each share is convertible into 3 shares of common stock	4,000,000
Common stock, $10 par value	6,000,000
Tax rate for 2013	40%
Average market price of common stock	$25 per share

There were no changes during 2013 in the number of common shares, preferred shares, or convertible bonds outstanding. There is no treasury stock. The company also has common stock options (granted in a prior year) to purchase 75,000 shares of common stock at $20 per share.

Instructions
(a) Compute basic earnings per share for 2013.
(b) Compute diluted earnings per share for 2013.

6 ▶ **P16-9 (EPS with Stock Dividend and Extraordinary Items)** Agassi Corporation is preparing the comparative financial statements to be included in the annual report to stockholders. Agassi employs a fiscal year ending May 31.

Income from operations before income taxes for Agassi was $1,400,000 and $660,000, respectively, for fiscal years ended May 31, 2013 and 2012. Agassi experienced an extraordinary loss of $400,000 because of an earthquake on March 3, 2013. A 40% combined income tax rate pertains to any and all of Agassi Corporation's profits, gains, and losses.

Agassi's capital structure consists of preferred stock and common stock. The company has not issued any convertible securities or warrants and there are no outstanding stock options.

Agassi issued 40,000 shares of $100 par value, 6% cumulative preferred stock in 2009. All of this stock is outstanding, and no preferred dividends are in arrears.

There were 1,000,000 shares of $1 par common stock outstanding on June 1, 2011. On September 1, 2011, Agassi sold an additional 400,000 shares of the common stock at $17 per share. Agassi distributed a 20% stock dividend on the common shares outstanding on December 1, 2012. These were the only common stock transactions during the past 2 fiscal years.

Instructions

(a) Determine the weighted-average number of common shares that would be used in computing earnings per share on the current comparative income statement for:
   (1) The year ended May 31, 2012.
   (2) The year ended May 31, 2013.

(b) Starting with income from operations before income taxes, prepare a comparative income statement for the years ended May 31, 2013 and 2012. The statement will be part of Agassi Corporation's annual report to stockholders and should include appropriate earnings per share presentation.

(c) The capital structure of a corporation is the result of its past financing decisions. Furthermore, the earnings per share data presented on a corporation's financial statements is dependent upon the capital structure.
   (1) Explain why Agassi Corporation is considered to have a simple capital structure.
   (2) Describe how earnings per share data would be presented for a corporation that has a complex capital structure.

(CMA adapted)

CONCEPTS FOR ANALYSIS

CA16-1 (Warrants Issued with Bonds and Convertible Bonds) Incurring long-term debt with an arrangement whereby lenders receive an option to buy common stock during all or a portion of the time the debt is outstanding is a frequent corporate financing practice. In some situations, the result is achieved through the issuance of convertible bonds; in others, the debt instruments and the warrants to buy stock are separate.

Instructions

(a) (1) Describe the differences that exist in current accounting for original proceeds of the issuance of convertible bonds and of debt instruments with separate warrants to purchase common stock.
   (2) Discuss the underlying rationale for the differences described in (a)(1) above.
   (3) Summarize the arguments that have been presented in favor of accounting for convertible bonds in the same manner as accounting for debt with separate warrants.

(b) At the start of the year, Huish Company issued $18,000,000 of 12% bonds along with warrants to buy 1,200,000 shares of its $10 par value common stock at $18 per share. The bonds mature over the next 10 years, starting one year from date of issuance, with annual maturities of $1,800,000. At the time, Huish had 9,600,000 shares of common stock outstanding, and the market price was $23 per share. The company received $20,040,000 for the bonds and the warrants. For Huish Company, 12% was a relatively low borrowing rate. If offered alone, at this time, the bonds would have been issued at a 22% discount. Prepare the journal entry (or entries) for the issuance of the bonds and warrants for the cash consideration received.

(AICPA adapted)

CA16-2 (Ethical Issues—Compensation Plan) The executive officers of Rouse Corporation have a performance-based compensation plan. The performance criteria of this plan is linked to growth in earnings per share. When annual EPS growth is 12%, the Rouse executives earn 100% of the shares; if growth is 16%, they earn 125%. If EPS growth is lower than 8%, the executives receive no additional compensation.

In 2012, Gail Devers, the controller of Rouse, reviews year-end estimates of bad debt expense and warranty expense. She calculates the EPS growth at 15%. Kurt Adkins, a member of the executive group, remarks over lunch one day that the estimate of bad debt expense might be decreased, increasing EPS growth to 16.1%. Devers is not sure she should do this because she believes that the current estimate of bad debts is sound. On the other hand, she recognizes that a great deal of subjectivity is involved in the computation.

Instructions

Answer the following questions.

(a) What, if any, is the ethical dilemma for Devers?

(b) Should Devers's knowledge of the compensation plan be a factor that influences her estimate?

(c) How should Devers respond to Adkins's request?

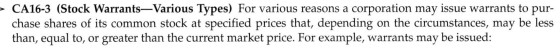 **CA16-3 (Stock Warrants—Various Types)** For various reasons a corporation may issue warrants to purchase shares of its common stock at specified prices that, depending on the circumstances, may be less than, equal to, or greater than the current market price. For example, warrants may be issued:

1. To existing stockholders on a pro rata basis.

2. To certain key employees under an incentive stock-option plan.

3. To purchasers of the corporation's bonds.

Instructions

For each of the three examples of how stock warrants are used:

(a) Explain why they are used.

(b) Discuss the significance of the price (or prices) at which the warrants are issued (or granted) in relation to (1) the current market price of the company's stock, and (2) the length of time over which they can be exercised.

(c) Describe the information that should be disclosed in financial statements, or notes thereto, that are prepared when stock warrants are outstanding in the hands of the three groups listed above.

(AICPA adapted)

CA16-4 (Stock Compensation Plans) The following two items appeared on the Internet concerning the GAAP requirement to expense stock options.

> *WASHINGTON, D.C.—February 17, 2005* Congressman David Dreier (R–CA), Chairman of the House Rules Committee, and Congresswoman Anna Eshoo (D–CA) reintroduced legislation today that will preserve broad-based employee stock option plans and give investors critical information they need to understand how employee stock options impact the value of their shares.
>
> "Last year, the U.S. House of Representatives overwhelmingly voted for legislation that would have ensured the continued ability of innovative companies to offer stock options to rank-and-file employees," Dreier stated. "Both the Financial Accounting Standards Board (FASB) and the Securities and Exchange Commission (SEC) continue to ignore our calls to address legitimate concerns about the impact of FASB's new standard on workers' ability to have an ownership stake in the New Economy, and its failure to address the real need of shareholders: accurate and meaningful information about a company's use of stock options."
>
> "In December 2004, FASB issued a stock option expensing standard that will render a huge blow to the 21st century economy," Dreier said. "Their action and the SEC's apparent lack of concern for protecting shareholders, requires us to once again take a firm stand on the side of investors and economic growth. Giving investors the ability to understand how stock options impact the value of their shares is critical. And equally important is preserving the ability of companies to use this innovative tool to attract talented employees."

> *"Here We Go Again!" by Jack Ciesielski* (2/21/2005, *http://www.accountingobserver.com/blog/2005/02/here-we-go-again*) On February 17, Congressman David Dreier (R–CA), and Congresswoman Anna Eshoo (D–CA), officially entered Silicon Valley's bid to gum up the launch of honest reporting of stock option compensation: They co-sponsored a bill to "preserve broad-based employee stock option plans and give investors critical information they need to understand how employee stock options impact the value of their shares." You know what "critical information" they mean: stuff like the stock compensation for the top five officers in a company, with a rigged value set as close to zero as possible. Investors *crave* this kind of information. Other ways the good Congresspersons want to "help" investors: The bill "also requires the SEC to study the effectiveness of those disclosures over three years, during which time, no new accounting standard related to the treatment of stock options could be recognized. Finally, the bill requires the Secretary of Commerce to conduct a study and report to Congress on the impact of broad-based employee stock option plans on expanding employee corporate ownership, skilled worker recruitment and retention, research and innovation, economic growth, and international competitiveness."
>
> It's the old "four corners" basketball strategy: stall, stall, stall. In the meantime, hope for regime change at your opponent, the FASB.

Instructions

(a) What are the major recommendations of the stock-based compensation pronouncement?

(b) How do the provisions of GAAP in this area differ from the bill introduced by members of Congress (Dreier and Eshoo), which would require expensing for options issued to only the top five officers in a company? Which approach do you think would result in more useful information? (Focus on comparability.)

(c) The bill in Congress urges the FASB to develop a rule that preserves "the ability of companies to use this innovative tool to attract talented employees." Write a response to these Congress-people explaining the importance of neutrality in financial accounting and reporting.

CA16-5 (EPS: Preferred Dividends, Options, and Convertible Debt) "Earnings per share" (EPS) is the most featured, single financial statistic about modern corporations. Daily published quotations of stock prices have recently been expanded to include for many securities a "times earnings" figure that is based on EPS. Stock analysts often focus their discussions on the EPS of the corporations they study.

Instructions

(a) Explain how dividends or dividend requirements on any class of preferred stock that may be outstanding affect the computation of EPS.

(b) One of the technical procedures applicable in EPS computations is the "treasury-stock method." Briefly describe the circumstances under which it might be appropriate to apply the treasury-stock method.

(c) Convertible debentures are considered potentially dilutive common shares. Explain how convertible debentures are handled for purposes of EPS computations.

(AICPA adapted)

CA16-6 (EPS Concepts and Effect of Transactions on EPS) Chorkina Corporation, a new audit client of yours, has not reported earnings per share data in its annual reports to stockholders in the past. The treasurer, Beth Botsford, requested that you furnish information about the reporting of earnings per share data in the current year's annual report in accordance with generally accepted accounting principles.

Instructions

(a) Define the term "earnings per share" as it applies to a corporation with a capitalization structure composed of only one class of common stock. Explain how earnings per share should be computed and how the information should be disclosed in the corporation's financial statements.

(b) Discuss the treatment, if any, that should be given to each of the following items in computing earnings per share of common stock for financial statement reporting.

(1) Outstanding preferred stock issued at a premium with a par value liquidation right.

(2) The exercise at below market price but above book value of a common stock option issued during the current fiscal year to officers of the corporation.

(3) The replacement of a machine immediately prior to the close of the current fiscal year at a cost 20% above the original cost of the replaced machine. The new machine will perform the same function as the old machine that was sold for its book value.

(4) The declaration of current dividends on cumulative preferred stock.

(5) The acquisition of some of the corporation's outstanding common stock during the current fiscal year. The stock was classified as treasury stock.

(6) A 2-for-1 stock split of common stock during the current fiscal year.

(7) A provision created out of retained earnings for a contingent liability from a possible lawsuit.

CA16-7 (EPS, Antidilution) Brad Dolan, a stockholder of Rhode Corporation, has asked you, the firm's accountant, to explain why his stock warrants were not included in diluted EPS. In order to explain this situation, you must briefly explain what dilutive securities are, why they are included in the EPS calculation, and why some securities are antidilutive and thus not included in this calculation.

Rhode Corporation earned $228,000 during the period, when it had an average of 100,000 shares of common stock outstanding. The common stock sold at an average market price of $25 per share during the period. Also outstanding were 30,000 warrants that could be exercised to purchase one share of common stock at $30 per warrant.

Instructions

Write Mr. Dolan a 1–1.5 page letter explaining why the warrants are not included in the calculation.

USING YOUR JUDGMENT

FINANCIAL REPORTING

Financial Reporting Problem

P&G The Procter & Gamble Company (P&G)

The financial statements of P&G are presented in Appendix 5B or can be accessed at the book's companion website, **www.wiley.com/college/kieso**.

Instructions

Refer to P&G's financial statements and accompanying notes to answer the following questions.

(a) Under P&G's stock-based compensation plan, stock options are granted annually to key managers and directors.

  (1) How many options were granted during 2009 under the plan?

  (2) How many options were exercisable at June 30, 2009?

  (3) How many options were exercised in 2009, and what was the average price of those exercised?

  (4) How many years from the grant date do the options expire?

  (5) To what accounts are the proceeds from these option exercises credited?

  (6) What was the number of outstanding options at June 30, 2009, and at what average exercise price?

(b) What number of diluted weighted-average common shares outstanding was used by P&G in computing earnings per share for 2009, 2008, and 2007? What was P&G's diluted earnings per share in 2009, 2008, and 2007?

(c) What other stock-based compensation plans does P&G have?

Comparative Analysis Case

The Coca-Cola Company and PepsiCo, Inc.

Instructions

Go to the book's companion website and use information found there to answer the following questions related to The Coca-Cola Company and PepsiCo, Inc.

(a) What employee stock-option compensation plans are offered by Coca-Cola and PepsiCo?

(b) How many options are outstanding at year-end 2009 for both Coca-Cola and PepsiCo?

(c) How many options were granted by Coca-Cola and PepsiCo to officers and employees during 2009?

(d) How many options were exercised during 2009?

(e) What was the average exercise price for Coca-Cola and PepsiCo employees during 2009?

(f) What are the weighted-average number of shares used by Coca-Cola and PepsiCo in 2009, 2008, and 2007 to compute diluted earnings per share?

(g) What was the diluted net income per share for Coca-Cola and PepsiCo for 2009, 2008, and 2007?

Financial Statement Analysis Cases

Case 1 Kellogg Company

Kellogg Company in its 2004 Annual Report in Note 1—Accounting Policies made the comment on page 962 about its accounting for employee stock options and other stock-based compensation. This was the annual report issued the year before the FASB mandated expensing stock options.

Stock compensation (in part) The Company currently uses the intrinsic value method prescribed by *Accounting Principles Board Opinion (APB) No. 25*, "Accounting for Stock Issued to Employees," to account for its employee stock options and other stock-based compensation. Under this method, because the exercise price of the Company's employee stock options equals the market price of the underlying stock on the date of the grant, no compensation expense is recognized. The following table presents the pro forma results for the current and prior years, as if the Company had used the alternate fair value method of accounting for stock-based compensation, prescribed by *SFAS No. 123*, "Accounting for Stock-Based Compensation" (as amended by *SFAS No. 148*).

Stock-based compensation expense, net of tax:

(millions, except per share data)	2004	2003	2002
As reported	$11.4	$12.5	$10.7
Pro forma	$41.8	$42.1	$52.8
Net earnings:			
As reported	$890.6	$787.1	$720.9
Pro forma	$860.2	$757.5	$678.8
Basic net earnings per share:			
As reported	$2.16	$1.93	$1.77
Pro forma	$2.09	$1.86	$1.66
Diluted net earnings per share:			
As reported	$2.14	$1.92	$1.75
Pro forma	$2.07	$1.85	$1.65

Under this pro forma method, the fair value of each option grant (net of estimated unvested forfeitures) was estimated at the date of grant using an option-pricing model and was recognized over the vesting period, generally two years. Refer to Note 8 for further information on the Company's stock compensation programs. In December 2004, the FASB issued *SFAS No. 123(Revised)*, "Share-Based Payment," which generally requires public companies to measure the cost of employee services received in exchange for an award of equity instruments based on the grant-date fair value and to recognize this cost over the requisite service period. The Company plans to adopt *SFAS No. 123(Revised)*, as of the beginning of its 2005 fiscal third quarter and is currently considering retrospective restatement to the beginning of its 2005 fiscal year. Once this standard is adopted, management believes full-year fiscal 2005 net earnings per share will be reduced by approximately $.08.

Instructions

(a) Briefly discuss how Kellogg's financial statements were affected by the adoption of the new standard.

(b) Some companies argued that the recognition provisions of the standard are not needed because the computation of earnings per share takes into account dilutive securities such as stock options. Do you agree? Explain, using the Kellogg disclosure provided above.

Case 2 Sepracor, Inc.

Sepracor, Inc., a drug company, reported the following information. The company prepares its financial statements in accordance with GAAP.

	2007 (,000)
Current liabilities	$ 554,114
Convertible subordinated debt	648,020
Total liabilities	1,228,313
Stockholders' equity	176,413
Net income	58,333

Analysts attempting to compare Sepracor to drug companies that issue debt with detachable warrants may face a challenge due to differences in accounting for convertible debt.

Instructions

(a) Compute the following ratios for Sepracor, Inc. (Assume that year-end balances approximate annual averages.)

   (1) Return on assets.

   (2) Return on stockholders' equity.

   (3) Debt to assets ratio.

(b) Briefly discuss the operating performance and financial position of Sepracor. Industry averages for these ratios in 2007 were: ROA 3.5%; return on equity 16%; and debt to assets 75%. Based on this analysis, would you make an investment in the company's 5% convertible bonds? Explain.

(c) Assume you want to compare Sepracor to an IFRS company like Merck (which issues nonconvertible debt with detachable warrants). Assuming that the fair value of the equity component of Sepracor's convertible bonds is $150,000, how would you adjust the analysis above to make valid comparisons between Sepracor and Merck?

Accounting, Analysis, and Principles

On January 1, 2011, Garner issued 10-year, $200,000 face value, 6% bonds at par. Each $1,000 bond is convertible into 30 shares of Garner $2 par value common stock. The company has had 10,000 shares of common stock (and no preferred stock) outstanding throughout its life. None of the bonds have been converted as of the end of 2012. (Ignore all tax effects.)

Accounting

(a) Prepare the journal entry Garner would have made on January 1, 2011, to record the issuance of the bonds.

(b) Garner's net income in 2012 was $30,000 and was $27,000 in 2011. Compute basic and diluted earnings per share for Garner for 2012 and 2011.

(c) Assume that 75 percent of the holders of Garner's convertible bonds convert their bonds to stock on June 30, 2013, when Garner's stock is trading at $32 per share. Garner pays $50 per bond to induce bondholders to convert. Prepare the journal entry to record the conversion.

Analysis

Show how Garner will report income and EPS for 2012 and 2011. Briefly discuss the importance of GAAP for EPS to analysts evaluating companies based on price-earnings ratios. Consider comparisons for a company over time, as well as comparisons between companies at a point in time.

Principles

In order to converge GAAP and IFRS, the FASB is considering whether the equity element of a convertible bond should be reported as equity. Describe how the journal entry you made in part (a) above would differ under IFRS. In terms of the accounting principles discussed in Chapter 2, what does IFRS for convertible debt accomplish that GAAP potentially sacrifices? What does GAAP for convertible debt accomplish that IFRS potentially sacrifices?

BRIDGE TO THE PROFESSION

Professional Research: FASB Codification

Richardson Company is contemplating the establishment of a share-based compensation plan to provide long-run incentives for its top management. However, members of the compensation committee of the board of directors have voiced some concerns about adopting these plans, based on news accounts related to a recent accounting standard in this area. They would like you to conduct some research on this recent standard so they can be better informed about the accounting for these plans.

Instructions

If your school has a subscription to the FASB Codification, go to *http://aaahq.org/ascLogin.cfm* to log in and prepare responses to the following. Provide Codification references for your responses.

(a) Identify the authoritative literature that addresses the accounting for share-based payment compensation plans.

(b) Briefly discuss the objectives for the accounting for stock compensation. What is the role of fair value measurement?

(c) The Richardson Company board is also considering an employee share-purchase plan, but the Board does not want to record expense related to the plan. What criteria must be met to avoid recording expense on an employee stock-purchase plan?

Professional Simulation

In this simulation, you are asked to address questions related to the accounting for stock options and earnings per share computations. Prepare responses to all parts.

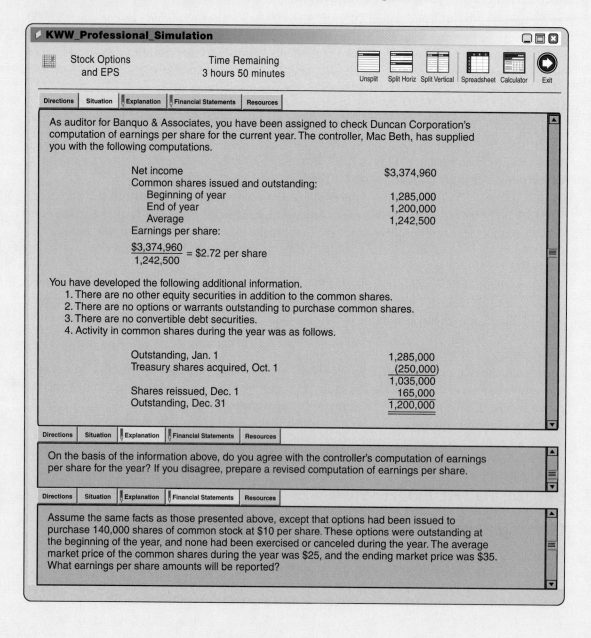

KWW_Professional_Simulation

| Stock Options and EPS | Time Remaining 3 hours 50 minutes | Unsplit | Split Horiz | Split Vertical | Spreadsheet | Calculator | Exit |

Directions | **Situation** | **Explanation** | **Financial Statements** | **Resources**

As auditor for Banquo & Associates, you have been assigned to check Duncan Corporation's computation of earnings per share for the current year. The controller, Mac Beth, has supplied you with the following computations.

Net income	$3,374,960
Common shares issued and outstanding:	
Beginning of year	1,285,000
End of year	1,200,000
Average	1,242,500
Earnings per share:	

$$\frac{\$3,374,960}{1,242,500} = \$2.72 \text{ per share}$$

You have developed the following additional information.
1. There are no other equity securities in addition to the common shares.
2. There are no options or warrants outstanding to purchase common shares.
3. There are no convertible debt securities.
4. Activity in common shares during the year was as follows.

Outstanding, Jan. 1	1,285,000
Treasury shares acquired, Oct. 1	(250,000)
	1,035,000
Shares reissued, Dec. 1	165,000
Outstanding, Dec. 31	1,200,000

Directions | **Situation** | **Explanation** | **Financial Statements** | **Resources**

On the basis of the information above, do you agree with the controller's computation of earnings per share for the year? If you disagree, prepare a revised computation of earnings per share.

Directions | **Situation** | **Explanation** | **Financial Statements** | **Resources**

Assume the same facts as those presented above, except that options had been issued to purchase 140,000 shares of common stock at $10 per share. These options were outstanding at the beginning of the year, and none had been exercised or canceled during the year. The average market price of the common shares during the year was $25, and the ending market price was $35. What earnings per share amounts will be reported?

IFRS ⟩ Insights

The primary IFRS related to financial instruments, including dilutive securities, is *IAS 39*, "Financial Instruments: Recognition and Measurement." The accounting for various forms of stock-based compensation under IFRS is found in *IFRS 2*, "Share-Based Payment." This standard was recently amended, resulting in significant convergence between IFRS and GAAP in this area. The IFRS addressing accounting and reporting for earnings per share computations is *IAS 33*, "Earnings per Share."

RELEVANT FACTS

- A significant difference between IFRS and GAAP is the accounting for securities with characteristics of debt and equity, such as convertible debt. Under GAAP, all of the proceeds of convertible debt are recorded as long-term debt. Under IFRS, convertible bonds are "bifurcated"—separated into the equity component (the value of the conversion option) of the bond issue and the debt component.

- Both IFRS and GAAP follow the same model for recognizing stock-based compensation: The fair value of shares and options awarded to employees is recognized over the period to which the employees' services relate.

- Related to employee share-purchase plans, under IFRS all employee share-purchase plans are deemed to be compensatory; that is, compensation expense is recorded for the amount of the discount. Under GAAP, these plans are often considered noncompensatory and therefore no compensation is recorded. Certain conditions must exist before a plan can be considered noncompensatory—the most important being that the discount generally cannot exceed 5%.

- Modification of a share option results in the recognition of any incremental fair value under both IFRS and GAAP. However, if the modification leads to a reduction, IFRS does not permit the reduction but GAAP does.

- Although the calculation of basic and diluted earnings per share is similar between IFRS and GAAP, the Boards are working to resolve the few minor differences in EPS reporting. One proposal in the FASB project concerns contracts that can be settled in either cash or shares. IFRS requires that share settlement must be used, while GAAP gives companies a choice. The FASB project proposes adopting the IFRS approach, thus converging GAAP and IFRS in this regard.

- Other EPS differences relate to (1) the treasury-stock method and how the proceeds from extinguishment of a liability should be accounted for, and (2) how to compute the weighted average of contingently issuable shares.

ABOUT THE NUMBERS

Accounting for Convertible Debt

Convertible debt is accounted for as a **compound instrument** because it contains both a liability and an equity component. IFRS requires that compound instruments be separated into their liability and equity components for purposes of accounting. Companies use the **"with-and-without" method** to value compound instruments. Illustration IFRS16-1 identifies the components used in the with-and-without method.

Fair value of convertible debt at date of issuance (with both debt and equity components)	−	Fair value of liability component at date of issuance, based on present value of cash flows	=	Equity component at date of issuance (without the debt component)

ILLUSTRATION IFRS16-1
Convertible Debt Components

As indicated, the equity component is the residual amount after subtracting the liability component. IFRS does not permit companies to assign a value to the equity amount first and then determine the liability component. To do so would be inconsistent with the definition of equity, which is considered a residual amount. To implement the with-and-without approach, companies do the following.

1. First, the company determines the total fair value of the convertible debt *with* both the liability and equity component. **This is straightforward, as this amount is the proceeds received upon issuance.**

2. The company then determines the liability component by computing the net present value of all contractual future cash flows discounted at the market rate of interest. This market rate is the rate the company would pay on similar nonconvertible debt.

3. In the final step, the company subtracts the liability component estimated in the second step from the fair value of the convertible debt (issue proceeds) to arrive at the equity component. That is, the equity component is the fair value of the convertible debt *without* the liability component

Accounting at Time of Issuance

To illustrate the accounting for convertible debt, assume that Roche Group issues 2,000 convertible bonds at the beginning of 2011. The bonds have a four-year term with a stated rate of interest of 6 percent, and are issued at par with a face value of $1,000 per bond (the total proceeds received from issuance of the bonds are $2,000,000). Interest is payable annually at December 31. Each bond is convertible into 250 ordinary shares with a par value of $1. The market rate of interest on similar nonconvertible debt is 9 percent. The time diagram in Illustration IFRS16-2 depicts both the interest and principal cash flows.

ILLUSTRATION IFRS16-2
Time Diagram for Convertible Bond

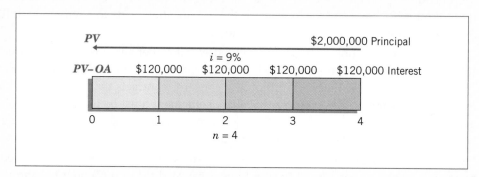

The liability component of the convertible debt is computed as shown in Illustration IFRS16-3.

ILLUSTRATION IFRS16-3
Fair Value of Liability Component of Convertible Bond

Present value of principal: $2,000,000 × .70843 (Table 6-2; $n = 4$, $i = 9\%$)	$1,416,860
Present value of the interest payments: $120,000 × 3.23972 (Table 6-4; $n = 4$, $i = 9\%$)	388,766
Present value of the liability component	$1,805,626

The equity component of Roche's convertible debt is then computed as shown in Illustration IFRS16-4.

ILLUSTRATION IFRS16-4
Equity Component of Convertible Bond

Fair value of convertible debt at date of issuance	$2,000,000
Less: Fair value of liability component at date of issuance	1,805,626
Fair value of equity component at date of issuance	$ 194,374

The journal entry to record this transaction is as follows.

Cash	2,000,000	
Bonds Payable		1,805,626
Share Premium—Conversion Equity		194,374

The liability component of Roche's convertible debt issue is recorded as Bonds Payable. As shown in Chapter 14, the amount of the discount relative to the face value of the bond is amortized at each reporting period so at maturity, the Bonds Payable account is reported at $2,000,000 (face value). The equity component of the convertible bond is recorded in the Share Premium—Conversion Equity account and is reported in the equity section of the statement of financial position. Because this amount is considered part of contributed capital, it does not change over the life of the convertible. **Transaction costs related to the liability and equity components are allocated in proportion to the proceeds received from the two components.** *For purposes of homework, use the Share Premium—Conversion Equity account to record the equity component.* **In practice, there may be considerable variation in the accounts used to record this component.**

Settlement of Convertible Bonds

We illustrate four settlement situations: (1) repurchase at maturity, (2) conversion at maturity, (3) conversion before maturity, and (4) repurchase before maturity.

Repurchase at Maturity. If the bonds are not converted at maturity, Roche makes the following entry to pay off the convertible debtholders.

Bonds Payable	2,000,000	
Cash		2,000,000
(To record the purchase of bonds at maturity)		

Because the carrying value of the bonds equals the face value, there is no gain or loss on repurchase at maturity. The amount originally allocated to equity of $194,384 either remains in the Share Premium—Conversion Equity account or is transferred to Share Premium—Ordinary.

Conversion of Bonds at Maturity. If the bonds are converted at maturity, Roche makes the following entry.

Share Premium—Conversion Equity	194,374	
Bonds Payable	2,000,000	
Share Capital—Ordinary		500,000
Share Premium—Ordinary		1,694,374
(To record the conversion of bonds at maturity)		

As indicated, Roche records a credit to Share Capital—Ordinary for $500,000 (2,000 bonds × 250 shares × $1 par) and the remainder to Share Premium—Ordinary for $1,694,374. There is no gain or loss on conversion at maturity. The original amount allocated to equity ($194,374) is transferred to the Share Premium—Ordinary account. As a result, Roche's equity has increased by a total of $2,194,374 through issuance and conversion of the convertible bonds. This accounting approach is often referred to as the **book value method** in that the carrying amount (book value) of the bond and related conversion equity determines the amount in the ordinary equity accounts.

Conversion of Bonds before Maturity. What happens if bonds are converted before maturity? To understand the accounting, we again use the Roche Group example. A schedule of bond amortization related to Roche's convertible bonds is shown in Illustration IFRS16-5 (page 968).

ILLUSTRATION IFRS16-5
Convertible Bond Amortization Schedule

		SCHEDULE OF BOND AMORTIZATION EFFECTIVE-INTEREST METHOD 6% BOND DISCOUNTED AT 9%		
Date	Cash Paid	Interest Expense	Discount Amortized	Carrying Amount of Bonds
1/1/11				$1,805,626
12/31/11	$120,000	$162,506	$42,506	1,848,132
12/31/12	120,000	166,332	46,332	1,894,464
12/31/13	120,000	170,502	50,502	1,944,966
12/31/14	120,000	175,034*	55,034	2,000,000

*$13 difference due to rounding.

Assuming that Roche converts its bonds into ordinary shares on December 31, 2012, Roche debits the Bonds Payable account for its carrying value of $1,894,464 (see Illustration IFRS16-5). In addition, Roche credits Share Capital—Ordinary for $500,000 (2,000 × 250 × $1) and credits Share Premium—Ordinary for $1,588,838. The entry to record this conversion is as follows.

Share Premium—Conversion Equity	194,374	
Bonds Payable	1,894,464	
Share Capital—Ordinary		500,000
Share Premium—Ordinary		1,588,838
(To record the conversion of bonds before maturity)		

There is no gain or loss on conversion before maturity: The original amount allocated to equity ($194,374) is transferred to the Share Premium—Ordinary account.

Repurchase before Maturity. In some cases, companies decide to repurchase the convertible debt before maturity. The approach used for allocating the amount paid upon repurchase follows the approach used when the convertible bond was originally issued. That is, Roche determines the fair value of the liability component of the convertible bonds at December 31, 2012, and then subtracts this amount from the fair value of the convertible bond issue (including the equity component) to arrive at the value for the equity. After this allocation is completed:

1. The difference between the consideration allocated to the liability component and the carrying amount of the liability is recognized as a gain or loss, and

2. The amount of consideration relating to the equity component is recognized (as a reduction) in equity.

To illustrate, instead of converting the bonds on December 31, 2012, assume that Roche repurchases the convertible bonds from the bondholders. Pertinent information related to this conversion is as follows.

- Fair value of the convertible debt (including both liability and equity components), based on market prices at December 31, 2012, is $1,965,000.

- The fair value of the liability component is $1,904,900. This amount is based on computing the present value of a nonconvertible bond with a two-year term (which corresponds to the shortened time to maturity of the repurchased bonds).

We first determine the gain or loss on the liability component, as computed in Illustration IFRS16-6.

ILLUSTRATION IFRS16-6
Gain or Loss on Debt Repurchase

Present value of liability component at December 31, 2012 (given above)	$ 1,904,900
Carrying value of liability component at December 31, 2012 (per Illustration IFRS16-5)	(1,894,464)
Loss on repurchase	$ 10,436

Roche has a loss on this repurchase because the value of the debt extinguished is greater than its carrying amount. To determine any adjustment to the equity, we compute the value of the equity as shown in Illustration IFRS16-7.

Fair value of convertible debt at December 31, 2012 (**with equity component**)	$1,965,000
Less: Fair value of liability component at December 31, 2012 (similar 2-year nonconvertible debt)	1,904,900
Fair value of equity component at December 31, 2012 (**without debt component**)	$ 60,100

ILLUSTRATION IFRS16-7
Equity Adjustment on Repurchase of Convertible Bonds

Roche makes the following compound journal entry to record the entire repurchase transaction.

Bonds Payable	1,894,464	
Share Premium—Conversion Equity	60,100	
Loss on Repurchase	10,436	
Cash		1,965,000
(To record the repurchase of convertible bonds)		

In summary, the repurchase results in a loss related to the liability component and a reduction in Share Premium—Conversion Equity. The remaining balance in Share Premium—Conversion Equity of $134,274 ($194,374 − $60,100) is often transferred to Share Premium—Ordinary upon the repurchase.

Employee Share-Purchase Plans

Employee share-purchase plans (ESPPs) generally permit all employees to purchase shares at a discounted price for a short period of time. The company often uses such plans to secure equity capital or to induce widespread ownership of its ordinary shares among employees. **These plans are considered compensatory and should be recorded as expense over the service period.**

To illustrate, assume that Masthead Company offers all its 1,000 employees the opportunity to participate in an employee share-purchase plan. Under the terms of the plan, the employees are entitled to purchase 100 ordinary shares (par value $1 per share) at a 20 percent discount. The purchase price must be paid immediately upon acceptance of the offer. In total, 800 employees accept the offer, and each employee purchases on average 80 shares. That is, the employees purchase a total of 64,000 shares. The weighted-average market price of the shares at the purchase date is $30 per share, and the weighted-average purchase price is $24 per share. The entry to record this transaction is as follows.

Cash (64,000 × $24)	1,536,000	
Compensation Expense [64,000 × ($30 − $24)]	384,000	
Share Capital—Ordinary (64,000 × $1)		64,000
Share Premium—Ordinary		1,856,000
(Issue shares in an employee share-purchase plan)		

The IASB indicates that there is no reason to treat broad-based employee share plans differently from other employee share plans. Some have argued that because these plans are used to raise capital, they should not be compensatory. However, IFRS requires recording expense for these arrangements. The Board notes that because these arrangements are available only to employees, it is sufficient to conclude that the benefits provided represent employee compensation.

ON THE HORIZON

The FASB has been working on a standard that will likely converge to IFRS in the accounting for convertible debt. Similar to the FASB, the IASB is examining the classification of hybrid securities; the IASB is seeking comment on a discussion document similar to the FASB Preliminary Views document, *"Financial Instruments with Characteristics of Equity."* It is hoped that the Boards will develop a converged standard in this area. While GAAP and IFRS are similar as to the presentation of EPS, the Boards have been working together to resolve remaining differences related to earnings per share computations.

IFRS SELF-TEST QUESTIONS

1. All of the following are key similarities between GAAP and IFRS with respect to accounting for dilutive securities and EPS *except:*
   (a) the model for recognizing stock-based compensation.
   (b) the calculation of basic and diluted EPS.
   (c) the accounting for convertible debt.
   (d) the accounting for modifications of share options, when the value increases.

2. Which of the following statements is *correct*?
   (a) IFRS separates the proceeds of a convertible bond between debt and equity by determining the fair value of the debt component before the equity component.
   (b) Both IFRS and GAAP assume that when there is choice of settlement of an option for cash or shares, share settlement is assumed.
   (c) IFRS separates the proceeds of a convertible bond between debt and equity, based on relative fair values.
   (d) Both GAAP and IFRS separate the proceeds of convertible bonds between debt and equity.

3. Under IFRS, convertible bonds:
   (a) are separated into the bond component and the expense component.
   (b) are separated into debt and equity components.
   (c) are separated into their components based on relative fair values.
   (d) All of the above.

4. Mae Jong Corp. issues $1,000,000 of 10% bonds payable which may be converted into 10,000 shares of $2 par value ordinary shares. The market rate of interest on similar bonds is 12%. Interest is payable annually on December 31, and the bonds were issued for total proceeds of $1,000,000. In accounting for these bonds, Mae Jong Corp. will:
   (a) first assign a value to the equity component, then determine the liability component.
   (b) assign no value to the equity component since the conversion privilege is not separable from the bond.
   (c) first assign a value to the liability component based on the face amount of the bond.
   (d) use the "with-and-without" method to value the compound instrument.

5. Anazazi Co. offers all its 10,000 employees the opportunity to participate in an employee share-purchase plan. Under the terms of the plan, the employees are entitled to purchase 100 ordinary shares (par value $1 per share) at a 20 percent discount. The purchase price must be paid immediately upon acceptance of the offer. In total, 8,500 employees accept the offer, and each employee purchases on average 80 shares at $22 share (market price $27.50). Under IFRS, Anazazi Co. will record:
   (a) no compensation since the plan is used to raise capital, not compensate employees.
   (b) compensation expense of $5,500,000.
   (c) compensation expense of $18,700,000.
   (d) compensation expense of $3,740,000.

IFRS CONCEPTS AND APPLICATION

IFRS16-1 Where can authoritative IFRS be found related to dilutive securities, stock-based compensation, and earnings per share?

IFRS16-2 Briefly describe some of the similarities and differences between GAAP and IFRS with respect to the accounting for dilutive securities, stock-based compensation, and earnings per share.

IFRS16-3 Norman Co., a fast-growing golf equipment company, uses GAAP. It is considering the issuance of convertible bonds. The bonds mature in 10 years, have a face value of $400,000, and pay interest annually at a rate of 4%. The estimated fair value of the equity portion of the bond issue is $35,000. Greg Shark is curious as to the difference in accounting for these bonds if the company were to use IFRS. (a) Prepare the entry to record issuance of the bonds at par under GAAP. (b) Repeat the requirement for part (a), assuming application of IFRS to the bond issuance. (c) Which approach provides the better accounting? Explain.

IFRS16-4 Briefly discuss the convergence efforts that are under way by the IASB and FASB in the area of dilutive securities and earnings per share.

IFRS16-5 Explain how the conversion feature of convertible debt has a value (a) to the issuer and (b) to the purchaser.

IFRS16-6 What are the arguments for giving separate accounting recognition to the conversion feature of debentures?

IFRS16-7 Four years after issue, debentures with a face value of $1,000,000 and book value of $960,000 are tendered for conversion into 80,000 ordinary shares immediately after an interest payment date. At that time, the market price of the debentures is 104, and the ordinary shares are selling at $14 per share (par value $10). At date of issue, the company needed Share Premium—Conversion Equity of $50,000. The company records the conversion as follows.

Bonds Payable	960,000	
Share Premium—Conversion Equity	50,000	
Share Capital—Ordinary		800,000
Share Premium—Ordinary		210,000

Discuss the propriety of this accounting treatment.

IFRS16-8 Cordero Corporation has an employee share-purchase plan which permits all full-time employees to purchase 10 ordinary shares on the third anniversary of their employment and an additional 15 shares on each subsequent anniversary date. The purchase price is set at the market price on the date purchased less a 10% discount. How is this discount accounted for by Cordero?

IFRS16-9 Archer Company issued $4,000,000 par value, 7% convertible bonds at 99 for cash. The net present value of the debt without the conversion feature is $3,800,000. Prepare the journal entry to record the issuance of the convertible bonds.

IFRS16-10 Petrenko Corporation has outstanding 2,000 $1,000 bonds, each convertible into 50 shares of $10 par value ordinary shares. The bonds are converted on December 31, 2012. The bonds payable has a carrying value of $1,950,000 and conversion equity of $20,000. Record the conversion using the book value method.

IFRS16-11 Angela Corporation issues 2,000 convertible bonds at January 1, 2011. The bonds have a three-year life, and are issued at par with a face value of $1,000 per bond, giving total proceeds of $2,000,000. Interest is payable annually at 6 percent. Each bond is convertible into 250 ordinary shares (par value of $1). When the bonds are issued, the market rate of interest for similar debt without the conversion option is 8%.

Instructions

(a) Compute the liability and equity component of the convertible bond on January 1, 2011.

(b) Prepare the journal entry to record the issuance of the convertible bond on January 1, 2011.

(c) Prepare the journal entry to record the repurchase of the convertible bond for cash at January 1, 2014, its maturity date.

IFRS16-12 Assume the same information in IFRS16-11, except that Angela Corporation converts its convertible bonds on January 1, 2012.

Instructions

(a) Compute the carrying value of the bond payable on January 1, 2012.

(b) Prepare the journal entry to record the conversion on January 1, 2012.

(c) Assume that the bonds were repurchased on January 1, 2012, for $1,940,000 cash instead of being converted. The net present value of the liability component of the convertible bonds on January 1, 2012, is $1,900,000. Prepare the journal entry to record the repurchase on January 1, 2012.

IFRS16-13 Assume that Sarazan Company has a share-option plan for top management. Each share option represents the right to purchase a $1 par value ordinary share in the future at a price equal to the fair value of the shares at the date of the grant. Sarazan has 5,000 share options outstanding, which were granted at the beginning of 2012. The following data relate to the option grant.

Exercise price for options	$40
Market price at grant date (January 1, 2012)	$40
Fair value of options at grant date (January 1, 2012)	$6
Service period	5 years

Instructions

(a) Prepare the journal entry(ies) for the first year of the share-option plan.

(b) Prepare the journal entry(ies) for the first year of the plan assuming that, rather than options, 700 shares of restricted shares were granted at the beginning of 2012.

(c) Now assume that the market price of Sarazan shares on the grant date was $45 per share. Repeat the requirements for (a) and (b).

(d) Sarazan would like to implement an employee share-purchase plan for rank-and-file employees, but it would like to avoid recording expense related to this plan. Explain how employee share-purchase plans are recorded.

Professional Research

IFRS16-14 Richardson Company is contemplating the establishment of a share-based compensation plan to provide long-run incentives for its top management. However, members of the compensation committee of the board of directors have voiced some concerns about adopting these plans, based on news accounts related to a recent accounting standard in this area. They would like you to conduct some research on this recent standard so they can be better informed about the accounting for these plans.

Instructions

Access the IFRS authoritative literature at the IASB website (*http://eifrs.iasb.org/*). When you have accessed the documents, you can use the search tool in your Internet browser to respond to the following questions. (Provide paragraph citations.)

(a) Identify the authoritative literature that addresses the accounting for share-based payment compensation plans.

(b) Briefly discuss the objectives for the accounting for share-based compensation. What is the role of fair value measurement?

(c) The Richardson Company board is also considering an employee share-purchase plan, but the Board does not want to record expense related to the plan. What are the IFRS requirements for the accounting for an employee share-purchase plan?

International Financial Reporting Problem:
Marks and Spencer plc

IFRS16-15 The financial statements of Marks and Spencer plc (M&S) are available at the books' companion website or can be accessed at *http://corporate.marksandspencer.com/documents/publications/2010/Annual_Report_2010.*

Instructions

Refer to M&S's financial statements and the accompanying notes to answer the following questions.

(a) Under M&S's share-based compensation plan, share options are granted annually to key managers and directors.

  (1) How many options were granted during 2010 under the plan?

  (2) How many options were exercisable at April 3, 2010?

  (3) How many options were exercised in 2010, and what was the average price of those exercised?

  (4) How many years from the grant date do the options expire?

  (5) To what accounts are the proceeds from these option exercises credited?

  (6) What was the number of outstanding options at April 3, 2010, and at what average exercise price?

(b) What number of diluted weighted-average shares outstanding was used by M&S in computing earnings per share for 2010 and 2009? What was M&S's diluted earnings per share in 2010 and 2009?

(c) What other share-based compensation plans does M&S have?

ANSWERS TO IFRS SELF-TEST QUESTIONS
1. c **2.** a **3.** b **4.** d **5.** d

Remember to check the book's companion website to find additional resources for this chapter.

17 Investments

What to Do?

Recently, a bank reported an $87.3 million write-down on its mortgage-backed securities for the third quarter of 2008; however, the bank stated that it expected its actual losses to be only $44,000. The loss of $44,000 was equal to a modest loss on a condo foreclosure. The bank's regulator found "the accounting result absurd." However, the rest of the story is that the bank, in the third quarter of 2009, raised its credit-loss estimate by **$263.1 million**, quite a difference from its original loss estimate of **$44,000**.

The discussion above highlights the challenge of valuing financial assets such as loans, derivatives, and other debt investments. The fundamental question that arose out of the example above and, more significantly, the recent financial crisis is: Should financial instruments be valued at amortized cost, fair value, or some other measure(s)? As one writer noted, the opinion that fair value accounting weakens financial and economic stability has persisted among many regulators and politicians, mostly in Europe but also in Asia. But some investors and others, particularly in the United States, believe that fair value is the right answer because it is more transparent information. OK, so what to do?

Well, the FASB has issued a proposal to account for just about all financial assets at fair value with gains and losses recorded in income (amortized cost would be disclosed for some financial assets). The FASB believes this approach will provide the most relevant and transparent information about financial assets. In contrast, the IASB has issued a new standard on financial assets *(IFRS 9)* that uses a mixed-attribute approach. Some of the financial assets are valued at amortized cost and others at fair value. Thus, at this point the two bodies do not agree as to how these instruments should be accounted for and reported.

A survey by the Chartered Financial Analysts association on *IFRS 9* contained the following question on the IASB's new standard: "Do you agree that the IASB's new standard requiring classification into amortized cost or fair value will improve the decision-usefulness of overall financial instrument accounting?" The survey results indicate that just 47 percent believe the IASB's approach improves the decision-usefulness of information. This less-than-strong support for the new rule is somewhat troubling, given that the group surveyed is representative of the IASB's key constituency—investors and creditors.

Interestingly, the European Union refused to consider adopting the requirements of *IFRS 9*, arguing that it contained **too much** fair value information. Nevertheless, the standard was issued and other countries that follow IFRS will soon be implementing the new standard. At the same time, as soon as the FASB issues its new standard, the IASB has indicated that it may revisit the valuation issue once again. Thus, the early reaction to *IFRS 9* indicates that, unfortunately, once again politics is raising its ugly head on an accounting issue. Some European regulators have suggested that the IASB's future funding may even depend on the Board putting more regulators on it. Such an intrusion could lead to the end of the convergence efforts between the IASB and the FASB. What do you think? Should the FASB implement its proposal or move to the mixed-attribute IASB approach?

Source: Adapted from Jonathan Weil, "Suing Wall Street Banks Never Looked So Shady," *http://www.bloomberg.com/* (February 28, 2010); Rachel Sanderson and Jennifer Hughes, "Carried Forward," *Financial Times Online* (April 20, 2010); and CFA Institute, *Survey on Proposed Financial Instrument Accounting Changes and International Convergence* (November 2009).

See the **International Perspectives** on pages 976, 977, 989, 990, 992, 1010, 1013, and 1018.

Read the **IFRS Insights** on pages 1048–1062 for a discussion of:

—Accounting for financial assets

—Debt investments

—Equity investments

—Impairments

PREVIEW OF CHAPTER 17 As indicated in the opening story, the accounting for financial assets is highly controversial. How to measure, recognize, and disclose this information is now being debated and discussed extensively. In this chapter, we address the accounting for debt and equity investments. Appendices to this chapter discuss the accounting for derivative instruments, variable-interest entities, and fair value disclosures. The content and organization of this chapter are as follows.

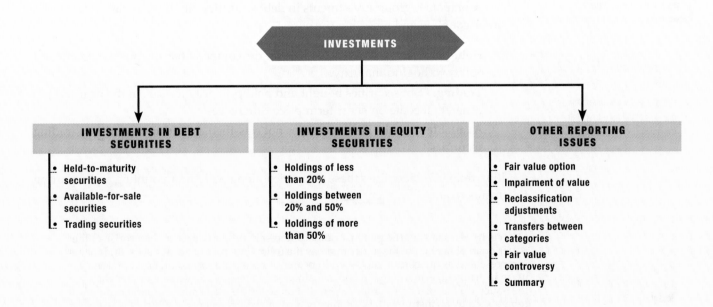

INVESTMENTS

INVESTMENTS IN DEBT SECURITIES	INVESTMENTS IN EQUITY SECURITIES	OTHER REPORTING ISSUES
• Held-to-maturity securities	• Holdings of less than 20%	• Fair value option
• Available-for-sale securities	• Holdings between 20% and 50%	• Impairment of value
• Trading securities	• Holdings of more than 50%	• Reclassification adjustments
		• Transfers between categories
		• Fair value controversy
		• Summary

INVESTMENT ACCOUNTING APPROACHES

Companies have different motivations for investing in securities issued by other companies.[1] **One motivation is to earn a high rate of return.** For example, companies like Coca-Cola and PepsiCo can receive interest revenue from a debt investment or dividend revenue from an equity investment. In addition, they can realize capital gains on both types of securities. **Another motivation for investing (in equity securities) is to secure certain operating or financing arrangements with another company.** As in the opening story, Coca-Cola and PepsiCo are able to exercise some control over bottler companies based on their significant (but not controlling) equity investments.

To provide useful information, companies account for investments based on the type of security (debt or equity) and their intent with respect to the investment. As indicated in Illustration 17-1, we organize our study of investments by type of security. Within each section, we explain how the accounting for investments in debt and equity securities varies according to management intent.

ILLUSTRATION 17-1
Summary of Investment Accounting Approaches

Type of Security	Management Intent	Valuation Approach
Debt (Section 1)	No plans to sell	Amortized cost
	Plan to sell	Fair value
Equity (Section 2)	Plan to sell	Fair value
	Exercise some control	Equity method

SECTION 1 • INVESTMENTS IN DEBT SECURITIES

LEARNING OBJECTIVE 1
Identify the three categories of debt securities and describe the accounting and reporting treatment for each category.

Debt securities represent a creditor relationship with another entity. Debt securities include U.S. government securities, municipal securities, corporate bonds, convertible debt, and commercial paper. Trade accounts receivable and loans receivable are not debt securities because they do not meet the definition of a security.

Companies group investments in debt securities into three separate categories for accounting and reporting purposes:

INTERNATIONAL PERSPECTIVE

Under IFRS, debt investments are classified as either held-for-collection or trading.

- **Held-to-maturity:** Debt securities that the company has the positive intent and ability to hold to maturity.
- **Trading:** Debt securities bought and held primarily for sale in the near term to generate income on short-term price differences.
- **Available-for-sale:** Debt securities not classified as held-to-maturity or trading securities.

Illustration 17-2 identifies these categories, along with the accounting and reporting treatments required for each.

See the FASB Codification section (page 1026).

[1]A **security** is a share, participation, or other interest in property or in an enterprise of the issuer or an obligation of the issuer that has the following three characteristics: (a) It either is represented by an instrument issued in bearer or registered form or, if not represented by an instrument, is registered in books maintained to record transfers by or on behalf of the issuer. (b) It is of a type commonly traded on securities exchanges or markets or, when represented by an instrument, is commonly recognized in any area in which it is issued or dealt in as a medium for investment. (c) It either is one of a class or series or by its terms is divisible into a class or series of shares, participations, interests, or obligations. [1]

ILLUSTRATION 17-2
Accounting for Debt
Securities by Category

Category	Valuation	Unrealized Holding Gains or Losses	Other Income Effects
Held-to-maturity	Amortized cost	Not recognized	Interest when earned; gains and losses from sale.
Trading securities	Fair value	Recognized in net income	Interest when earned; gains and losses from sale.
Available-for-sale	Fair value	Recognized as other comprehensive income and as separate component of stockholders' equity	Interest when earned; gains and losses from sale.

INTERNATIONAL PERSPECTIVE

Under IFRS, held-for-collection debt investments are valued at amortized cost; all other investments are measured at fair value.

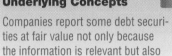

Underlying Concepts

Companies report some debt securities at fair value not only because the information is relevant but also because it is representationally faithful.

Amortized cost is the acquisition cost adjusted for the amortization of discount or premium, if appropriate. **Fair value** is the price that would be received to sell an asset or paid to transfer a liability in an orderly transaction between market participants at the measurement date. [2]

HELD-TO-MATURITY SECURITIES

Only debt securities can be classified as held-to-maturity. By definition, equity securities have no maturity date. A company like Starbucks should classify a debt security as **held-to-maturity** only if it has **both (1) the positive intent** and **(2) the ability to hold those securities to maturity**. It should not classify a debt security as held-to-maturity if it intends to hold the security for an indefinite period of time. Likewise, if Starbucks anticipates that a sale may be necessary due to changes in interest rates, foreign currency risk, liquidity needs, or other asset-liability management reasons, it should not classify the security as held-to-maturity.[2]

Companies account for held-to-maturity securities **at amortized cost**, not fair value. If management intends to hold certain investment securities to maturity and has no plans to sell them, fair values (selling prices) are not relevant for measuring and evaluating the cash flows associated with these securities. Finally, because companies do not adjust held-to-maturity securities to fair value, these securities do not increase the volatility of either reported earnings or reported capital as do trading securities and available-for-sale securities.

To illustrate the accounting for held-to-maturity debt securities, assume that Robinson Company purchased $100,000 of 8 percent bonds of Evermaster Corporation on January 1, 2011, at a discount, paying $92,278. The bonds mature January 1, 2016 and

2 LEARNING OBJECTIVE
Understand the procedures for discount and premium amortization on bond investments.

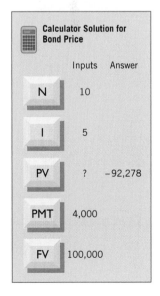

Calculator Solution for Bond Price

	Inputs	Answer
N	10	
I	5	
PV	?	−92,278
PMT	4,000	
FV	100,000	

---

[2]The FASB defines situations where, even though a company sells a security before maturity, it has constructively held the security to maturity, and thus does not violate the held-to-maturity requirement. These include selling a security close enough to maturity (such as three months) so that interest rate risk is no longer an important pricing factor.

However, companies must be extremely careful with debt securities held to maturity. If a company prematurely sells a debt security in this category, the sale may "taint" the entire held-to-maturity portfolio. That is, a management's statement regarding "intent" is no longer credible. Therefore the company may have to reclassify the securities. This could lead to unfortunate consequences. An interesting by-product of this situation is that companies that wish to retire their debt securities early are finding it difficult to do so. The holder will not sell because the securities are classified as held-to-maturity.

yield 10%; interest is payable each July 1 and January 1. Robinson records the investment as follows.

January 1, 2011

Debt Investments	92,278	
Cash		92,278

Robinson uses a Debt Investments account to indicate the type of debt security purchased.

As indicated in Chapter 14, companies must amortize premium or discount using the **effective-interest method** unless some other method—such as the straight-line method—yields a similar result. They apply the effective-interest method to bond investments in a way similar to that for bonds payable. To compute interest revenue, companies compute the effective-interest rate or yield at the time of investment and apply that rate to the beginning carrying amount (book value) for each interest period. The investment carrying amount is increased by the amortized discount or decreased by the amortized premium in each period.

Illustration 17-3 shows the effect of the discount amortization on the interest revenue that Robinson records each period for its investment in Evermaster bonds.

ILLUSTRATION 17-3
Schedule of Interest Revenue and Bond Discount Amortization—Effective-Interest Method

	8% BONDS PURCHASED TO YIELD 10%			
Date	Cash Received	Interest Revenue	Bond Discount Amortization	Carrying Amount of Bonds
1/1/11				$ 92,278
7/1/11	$ 4,000ᵃ	$ 4,614ᵇ	$ 614ᶜ	92,892ᵈ
1/1/12	4,000	4,645	645	93,537
7/1/12	4,000	4,677	677	94,214
1/1/13	4,000	4,711	711	94,925
7/1/13	4,000	4,746	746	95,671
1/1/14	4,000	4,783	783	96,454
7/1/14	4,000	4,823	823	97,277
1/1/15	4,000	4,864	864	98,141
7/1/15	4,000	4,907	907	99,048
1/1/16	4,000	4,952	952	100,000
	$40,000	$47,722	$7,722	

ᵃ$4,000 = $100,000 × .08 × ⁶⁄₁₂
ᵇ$4,614 = $92,278 × .10 × ⁶⁄₁₂
ᶜ$614 = $4,614 − $4,000
ᵈ$92,892 = $92,278 + $614

Robinson records the receipt of the first semiannual interest payment on July 1, 2011 (using the data in Illustration 17-3), as follows.

July 1, 2011

Cash	4,000	
Debt Investments	614	
Interest Revenue		4,614

Because Robinson is on a calendar-year basis, it accrues interest and amortizes the discount at December 31, 2011, as follows.

December 31, 2011

Interest Receivable	4,000	
Debt Investments	645	
Interest Revenue		4,645

Again, Illustration 17-3 shows the interest and amortization amounts.

Robinson reports its investment in Evermaster bonds in its December 31, 2011, financial statements, as follows.

ILLUSTRATION 17-4
Reporting of Held-to-Maturity Securities

Balance Sheet	
Current assets	
Interest receivable	$ 4,000
Long-term investments	
Debt investments (held-to-maturity)	$93,537
Income Statement	
Other revenues and gains	
Interest revenue	$ 9,259

Sometimes, a company sells a held-to-maturity debt security so close to its maturity date that a change in the market interest rate would not significantly affect the security's fair value. Such a sale may be considered a sale at maturity and would not call into question the company's original intent to hold the investment to maturity. Let's assume, as an example, that Robinson Company sells its investment in Evermaster bonds on November 1, 2015, at 99³/4 plus accrued interest. The discount amortization from July 1, 2015, to November 1, 2015, is $635 ($4/6 \times$ $952). Robinson records this discount amortization as follows.

November 1, 2015

Debt Investments	635	
Interest Revenue		635

Illustration 17-5 shows the computation of the realized gain on the sale.

ILLUSTRATION 17-5
Computation of Gain on Sale of Bonds

Selling price of bonds (exclusive of accrued interest)		$99,750
Less: Book value of bonds on November 1, 2015:		
Amortized cost, July 1, 2015	$99,048	
Add: Discount amortized for the period July 1, 2015,		
to November 1, 2015	635	
		99,683
Gain on sale of bonds		$ 67

Robinson records the sale of the bonds as:

November 1, 2015

Cash	102,417	
Interest Revenue (4/6 × $4,000)		2,667
Debt Investments		99,683
Gain on Sale of Investments		67

The credit to Interest Revenue represents accrued interest for four months, for which the purchaser pays cash. The debit to Cash represents the selling price of the bonds plus accrued interest ($99,750 + $2,667). The credit to Debt Investments represents the book value of the bonds on the date of sale. The credit to Gain on Sale of Investments represents the excess of the selling price over the book value of the bonds.

AVAILABLE-FOR-SALE SECURITIES

Underlying Concepts

Recognizing unrealized gains and losses is an application of the concept of comprehensive income.

Companies, like **Amazon.com**, report **available-for-sale** securities at fair value. It records the unrealized gains and losses related to changes in the fair value of available-for-sale debt securities in an unrealized holding gain or loss account. Amazon adds (subtracts) this amount to other comprehensive income for the

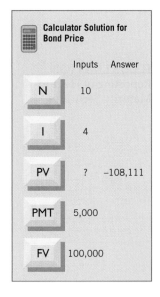

Calculator Solution for Bond Price

	Inputs	Answer
N	10	
I	4	
PV	?	−108,111
PMT	5,000	
FV	100,000	

period. Other comprehensive income is then added to (subtracted from) accumulated other comprehensive income, which is shown as a separate component of stockholders' equity until realized. Thus, **companies report available-for-sale securities at fair value on the balance sheet, but do not report changes in fair value as part of net income until after selling the security**. This approach reduces the volatility of net income.

Example: Single Security

To illustrate the accounting for available-for-sale securities, assume that Graff Corporation purchases $100,000, 10 percent, five-year bonds on January 1, 2011, with interest payable on July 1 and January 1. The bonds sell for $108,111, which results in a bond premium of $8,111 and an effective interest rate of 8 percent.

Graff records the purchase of the bonds as follows.[3]

January 1, 2011

Debt Investments	108,111	
Cash		108,111

Illustration 17-6 discloses the effect of the premium amortization on the interest revenue Graff records each period using the effective-interest method.

ILLUSTRATION 17-6
Schedule of Interest
Revenue and Bond
Premium Amortization—
Effective-Interest Method

			10% BONDS PURCHASED TO YIELD 8%		
Date	Cash Received	Interest Revenue	Bond Premium Amortization	Carrying Amount of Bonds	
1/1/11				$108,111	
7/1/11	$ 5,000[a]	$ 4,324[b]	$ 676[c]	107,435[d]	
1/1/12	5,000	4,297	703	106,732	
7/1/12	5,000	4,269	731	106,001	
1/1/13	5,000	4,240	760	105,241	
7/1/13	5,000	4,210	790	104,451	
1/1/14	5,000	4,178	822	103,629	
7/1/14	5,000	4,145	855	102,774	
1/1/15	5,000	4,111	889	101,885	
7/1/15	5,000	4,075	925	100,960	
1/1/16	5,000	4,040	960	100,000	
	$50,000	$41,889	$8,111		

[a]$5,000 = $100,000 × .10 × 6/12
[b]$4,324 = $108,111 × .08 × 6/12
[c]$676 = $5,000 − $4,324
[d]$107,435 = $108,111 − $676

The entry to record interest revenue on July 1, 2011, is as follows.

July 1, 2011

Cash	5,000	
Debt Investments		676
Interest Revenue		4,324

At December 31, 2011, Graff makes the following entry to recognize interest revenue.

December 31, 2011

Interest Receivable	5,000	
Debt Investments		703
Interest Revenue		4,297

As a result, Graff reports revenue for 2011 of $8,621 ($4,324 + $4,297).

---

[3]Companies generally record investments acquired at par, at a discount, or at a premium in the accounts at cost, including brokerage and other fees but excluding the accrued interest. They generally do not record investments at maturity value. The use of a separate discount or premium account as a valuation account is acceptable procedure for investments, but in practice companies do not widely use it.

To apply the fair value method to these debt investments, assume that at year-end the fair value of the bonds is $105,000 and that the carrying amount of the investments is $106,732. Comparing this fair value with the carrying amount (amortized cost) of the bonds at December 31, 2011, Graff recognizes an unrealized holding loss of $1,732 ($106,732 − $105,000). It reports this loss as other comprehensive income. Graff makes the following entry.

December 31, 2011		
Unrealized Holding Gain or Loss—Equity	1,732	
Fair Value Adjustment (available-for-sale)		1,732

Graff uses a valuation account instead of crediting the Debt Investments account. The use of the **Fair Value Adjustment** account enables the company to maintain a record of its amortized cost. Because the adjustment account has a credit balance in this case, Graff subtracts it from the balance of the Debt Investments account to determine fair value. Graff reports this fair value amount on the balance sheet. At each reporting date, Graff reports the bonds at fair value with an adjustment to the Unrealized Holding Gain or Loss—Equity account.

Example: Portfolio of Securities

To illustrate the accounting for a portfolio of securities, assume that Webb Corporation has two debt securities classified as available-for-sale. Illustration 17-7 identifies the amortized cost, fair value, and the amount of the unrealized gain or loss.

AVAILABLE-FOR-SALE DEBT SECURITY PORTFOLIO DECEMBER 31, 2012			
Investments	Amortized Cost	Fair Value	Unrealized Gain (Loss)
Watson Corporation 8% bonds	$ 93,537	$103,600	$ 10,063
Anacomp Corporation 10% bonds	200,000	180,400	(19,600)
Total of portfolio	$293,537	$284,000	(9,537)
Previous fair value adjustment balance			–0–
Fair value adjustment—Cr.			$ (9,537)

ILLUSTRATION 17-7 Computation of Fair Value Adjustment—Available-for-Sale Securities (2012)

The fair value of Webb's available-for-sale portfolio totals $284,000. The gross unrealized gains are $10,063, and the gross unrealized losses are $19,600, resulting in a net unrealized loss of $9,537. That is, the fair value of available-for-sale securities is $9,537 lower than its amortized cost. Webb makes an adjusting entry to a valuation allowance to record the decrease in value and to record the loss as follows.

December 31, 2012		
Unrealized Holding Gain or Loss—Equity	9,537	
Fair Value Adjustment (available-for-sale)		9,537

Webb reports the unrealized holding loss of $9,537 as other comprehensive income and a reduction of stockholders' equity. Recall that companies exclude from net income any unrealized holding gains and losses related to available-for-sale securities.

Sale of Available-for-Sale Securities

If a company sells bonds carried as investments in available-for-sale securities before the maturity date, it must make entries to remove from the Debt Investments account the amortized cost of bonds sold. To illustrate, assume that Webb Corporation sold the Watson bonds (from Illustration 17-7) on July 1, 2013, for $90,000, at which time it had an amortized cost of $94,214. Illustration 17-8 (on page 982) shows the computation of the realized loss.

ILLUSTRATION 17-8
Computation of Loss on
Sale of Bonds

Amortized cost (Watson bonds)	$94,214
Less: Selling price of bonds	90,000
Loss on sale of bonds	$ 4,214

Webb records the sale of the Watson bonds as follows.

July 1, 2013

Cash	90,000	
Loss on Sale of Investments	4,214	
Debt Investments		94,214

Webb reports this realized loss in the "Other expenses and losses" section of the income statement. Assuming no other purchases and sales of bonds in 2013, Webb on December 31, 2013, prepares the information shown in Illustration 17-9.

ILLUSTRATION 17-9
Computation of Fair
Value Adjustment—
Available-for-Sale (2013)

AVAILABLE-FOR-SALE DEBT SECURITY PORTFOLIO DECEMBER 31, 2013			
Investments	Amortized Cost	Fair Value	Unrealized Gain (Loss)
Anacomp Corporation 10% bonds (total portfolio)	$200,000	$195,000	$(5,000)
Previous fair value adjustment balance—Cr.			(9,537)
Fair value adjustment—Dr.			$ 4,537

Webb has an unrealized holding loss of $5,000. However, the Fair Value Adjustment account already has a credit balance of $9,537. To reduce the adjustment account balance to $5,000, Webb debits it for $4,537, as follows.

December 31, 2013

Fair Value Adjustment (available-for-sale)	4,537	
Unrealized Holding Gain or Loss—Equity		4,537

Financial Statement Presentation

Webb's December 31, 2013, balance sheet and the 2013 income statement include the following items and amounts (the Anacomp bonds are long-term investments but are not intended to be held to maturity).

ILLUSTRATION 17-10
Reporting of Available-
for-Sale Securities

Balance Sheet	
Current assets	
Interest receivable	$ xxx
Investments	
Debt investments (available-for-sale)	$195,000
Stockholders' equity	
Accumulated other comprehensive loss	$ 5,000
Income Statement	
Other revenues and gains	
Interest revenue	$ xxx
Other expenses and losses	
Loss on sale of investments	$ 4,214

Some favor including the unrealized holding gain or loss in net income rather than showing it as other comprehensive income.[4] However, some companies, particularly financial institutions, note that recognizing gains and losses on assets, but not liabilities, introduces substantial volatility in net income. They argue that hedges often exist between assets and liabilities so that gains in assets are offset by losses in liabilities, and vice versa. In short, to recognize gains and losses only on the asset side is unfair and not representative of the economic activities of the company.

This argument convinced the FASB. As a result, companies **do not include in net income** these unrealized gains and losses. [3] However, even this approach solves only some of the problems because **volatility of capital** still results. This is of concern to financial institutions because regulators restrict financial institutions' operations based on their level of capital. In addition, companies can still manage their net income by engaging in gains trading (i.e., selling the winners and holding the losers).

WHAT IS FAIR VALUE?

What do the numbers mean?

In the fall of 2000, Wall Street brokerage firm Morgan Stanley told investors that rumor of big losses in its bond portfolio were "greatly exaggerated." As it turns out, Morgan Stanley also was exaggerating.

As a result, the SEC accused Morgan Stanley of violating securities laws by overstating the value of certain bonds by $75 million. The overvaluations stemmed more from wishful thinking than reality, in violation of generally accepted accounting principles, the SEC said. "In effect, Morgan Stanley valued its positions at the price at which it thought a willing buyer and seller should enter into an exchange, rather than at a price at which a willing buyer and a willing seller would enter into a current exchange," the SEC wrote.

Especially egregious, stated one accounting expert, were the SEC's findings that Morgan Stanley in some instances used its own more optimistic assumptions as a substitute for external pricing sources. "What that is saying is: 'Fair value is what you want the value to be. Pick a number . . .' That's especially troublesome."

As indicated in the opening story, both the FASB and the IASB are assessing what is fair and what isn't when it comes to assigning valuations. Concerns over the issue caught fire after the collapses of Enron Corp. and other energy traders that abused the wide discretion given them under fair value accounting. Investors have expressed similar worries about some financial companies, which use internal—and subjectively designed—mathematical models to come up with valuations when market quotes aren't available.

Source: Adapted from Susanne Craig and Jonathan Weil, "SEC Targets Morgan Stanley Values," *Wall Street Journal* (November 8, 2004), p. C3. See also *http://www.iasb.org/Current_Projects/IASB_ Projects/Fair_Value_Measurement/Fair_Value_Measurement.htm* for the latest information on the IASB fair value project.

TRADING SECURITIES

Companies hold **trading securities** with the intention of selling them in a short period of time. "Trading" in this context means frequent buying and selling. Companies thus use trading securities to generate profits from short-term differences in price. Companies generally hold these securities for less than three months, some for merely days or hours.

Companies report trading securities at fair value, with unrealized holding gains and losses reported as part of net income. Similar to held-to-maturity or available-for-sale investments, they are required to amortize any discount or premium. A holding gain or loss is the net change in the fair value of a security from one period to another, exclusive

[4]In Chapter 4, we discussed the reporting of other comprehensive income and the concept of comprehensive income.

of dividend or interest revenue recognized but not received. In short, the FASB says to adjust the trading securities to fair value, at each reporting date. In addition, companies report the change in value as part of net income, not other comprehensive income.

To illustrate, assume that on December 31, 2012, Western Publishing Corporation determined its trading securities portfolio to be as shown in Illustration 17-11. (Assume that 2012 is the first year that Western Publishing held trading securities.) At the date of acquisition, Western Publishing recorded these trading securities at cost, including brokerage commissions and taxes, in the account entitled Debt Investments. This is the first valuation of this recently purchased portfolio.

ILLUSTRATION 17-11
Computation of Fair Value Adjustment—Trading Securities Portfolio (2012)

TRADING DEBT SECURITY PORTFOLIO DECEMBER 31, 2012			
Investments	Cost	Fair Value	Unrealized Gain (Loss)
Burlington Northern 10% bonds	$ 43,860	$ 51,500	$ 7,640
GM Corporation 11% bonds	184,230	175,200	(9,030)
Time Warner 8% bonds	86,360	91,500	5,140
Total of portfolio	$314,450	$318,200	3,750
Previous fair value adjustment balance			–0–
Fair value adjustment—Dr.			$ 3,750

The total cost of Western Publishing's trading portfolio is $314,450. The gross unrealized gains are $12,780 ($7,640 + $5,140), and the gross unrealized losses are $9,030, resulting in a net unrealized gain of $3,750. The fair value of trading securities is $3,750 greater than its cost.

At December 31, Western Publishing makes an adjusting entry to a valuation allowance, referred to as Fair Value Adjustment (trading), to record the increase in value and to record the unrealized holding gain.

December 31, 2012

Fair Value Adjustment (trading)	3,750	
Unrealized Holding Gain or Loss—Income		3,750

Because the Fair Value Adjustment account balance is a debit, Western Publishing adds it to the cost of the Debt Investments account to arrive at a fair value for the trading securities. Western Publishing reports this fair value amount on the balance sheet.

As with other debt investments, when a trading investment is sold, the Debt Investments account is reduced by the amount of the amortized cost of the bonds. Any realized gain or loss is recorded in the "Other expenses and losses" section of the income statement. The Fair Value Adjustment account is then adjusted at year-end for the unrealized gains or losses on the remaining securities in the trading investment portfolio.

When securities are actively traded, the FASB believes that the investments should be reported at fair value on the balance sheet. In addition, changes in fair value (unrealized gains and losses) should be reported in income. Such reporting on trading securities provides more relevant information to existing and prospective stockholders.

SECTION 2 • INVESTMENTS IN EQUITY SECURITIES

LEARNING OBJECTIVE 3
Identify the categories of equity securities and describe the accounting and reporting treatment for each category.

Equity securities represent ownership interests such as common, preferred, or other capital stock. They also include rights to acquire or dispose of ownership interests at an agreed-upon or determinable price, such as in warrants, rights, and call or put options. Companies do not treat convertible debt securities as equity securities. Nor do they treat as equity securities redeemable preferred stock (which must be redeemed for common stock). The cost of equity securities includes the purchase price of the security plus broker's commissions and other fees incidental to the purchase.

The degree to which one corporation (investor) acquires an interest in the common stock of another corporation (investee) generally determines the accounting treatment for the investment subsequent to acquisition. The classification of such investments depends on the percentage of the investee voting stock that is held by the investor:

1. Holdings of less than 20 percent (**fair value method**)—investor has passive interest.
2. Holdings between 20 percent and 50 percent (**equity method**)—investor has significant influence.
3. Holdings of more than 50 percent (**consolidated statements**)—investor has controlling interest.

Illustration 17-12 lists these levels of interest or influence and the corresponding valuation and reporting method that companies must apply to the investment.

Percentage of Ownership	0% ⟷ 20% ⟷ 50% ⟷ 100%		
Level of Influence	Little or None	Significant	Control
Valuation Method	Fair Value Method	Equity Method	Consolidation

ILLUSTRATION 17-12
Levels of Influence Determine Accounting Methods

The accounting and reporting for equity securities therefore depend on the level of influence and the type of security involved, as shown in Illustration 17-13.

ILLUSTRATION 17-13
Accounting and Reporting for Equity Securities by Category

Category	Valuation	Unrealized Holding Gains or Losses	Other Income Effects
Holdings less than 20%			
1. Available-for-sale	Fair value	Recognized in "Other comprehensive income" and as separate component of stockholders' equity	Dividends declared; gains and losses from sale.
2. Trading	Fair value	Recognized in net income	Dividends declared; gains and losses from sale.
Holdings between 20% and 50%	Equity	Not recognized	Proportionate share of investee's net income.
Holdings more than 50%	Consolidation	Not recognized	Not applicable.

HOLDINGS OF LESS THAN 20%

When an investor has an interest of less than 20 percent, it is presumed that the investor has little or no influence over the investee. In such cases, if market prices are available subsequent to acquisition, the company values and reports the investment using the fair value method.[5] The fair value method requires that companies classify equity securities at acquisition as **available-for-sale securities** or **trading securities**. Because equity securities have no maturity date, companies cannot classify them as held-to-maturity.

[5]If an equity investment is not publicly traded, a company values the investment and reports it at cost in periods subsequent to acquisition. This approach is often referred to as the cost method. Companies recognize dividends when received. They value the portfolio and report it at acquisition cost. Companies only recognize gains or losses after selling the securities.

Available-for-Sale Securities

Upon acquisition, companies record available-for-sale securities at cost.[6] To illustrate, assume that on November 3, 2012, Republic Corporation purchased common stock of three companies, each investment representing less than a 20 percent interest.

	Cost
Northwest Industries, Inc.	$259,700
Campbell Soup Co.	317,500
St. Regis Pulp Co.	141,350
Total cost	$718,550

Republic records these investments as follows.

November 3, 2012

Equity Investments	718,550	
Cash		718,550

On December 6, 2012, Republic receives a cash dividend of $4,200 on its investment in the common stock of Campbell Soup Co. It records the cash dividend as follows.

December 6, 2012

Cash	4,200	
Dividend Revenue		4,200

All three of the investee companies reported net income for the year, but only Campbell Soup declared and paid a dividend to Republic. But, recall that when an investor owns less than 20 percent of the common stock of another corporation, it is presumed that the investor has relatively little influence on the investee. As a result, **net income earned by the investee is not a proper basis for recognizing income from the investment by the investor**. Why? Because the increased net assets resulting from profitable operations may be permanently retained for use in the investee's business. Therefore, **the investor earns net income only when the investee declares cash dividends**.

At December 31, 2012, Republic's available-for-sale equity security portfolio has the cost and fair value shown in Illustration 17-14.

ILLUSTRATION 17-14
Computation of Fair
Value Adjustment—
Available-for-Sale Equity
Security Portfolio (2012)

AVAILABLE-FOR-SALE EQUITY SECURITY PORTFOLIO DECEMBER 31, 2012			
Investments	Cost	Fair Value	Unrealized Gain (Loss)
Northwest Industries, Inc.	$259,700	$275,000	$ 15,300
Campbell Soup Co.	317,500	304,000	(13,500)
St. Regis Pulp Co.	141,350	104,000	(37,350)
Total of portfolio	$718,550	$683,000	(35,550)
Previous fair value adjustment balance			–0–
Fair value adjustment—Cr.			$(35,550)

[6]Companies should record equity securities acquired in exchange for noncash consideration (property or services) at (1) the fair value of the consideration given, or (2) the fair value of the security received, whichever is more clearly determinable. Accounting for numerous purchases of securities requires the preservation of information regarding the cost of individual purchases, as well as the dates of purchases and sales. If specific identification is not possible, companies may use an average cost for multiple purchases of the same class of security. The **first-in, first-out method** (FIFO) of assigning costs to investments at the time of sale is also acceptable and normally employed.

For Republic's available-for-sale equity securities portfolio, the gross unrealized gains are $15,300, and the gross unrealized losses are $50,850 ($13,500 + $37,350), resulting in a net unrealized loss of $35,550. The fair value of the available-for-sale securities portfolio is below cost by $35,550.

As with available-for-sale **debt** securities, Republic records the net unrealized gains and losses related to changes in the fair value of available-for-sale **equity** securities in an Unrealized Holding Gain or Loss—Equity account. Republic reports this amount as a **part of other comprehensive income and as a component of other accumulated comprehensive income (reported in stockholders' equity) until realized**. In this case, Republic prepares an adjusting entry debiting the Unrealized Holding Gain or Loss—Equity account and crediting the Fair Value Adjustment account to record the decrease in fair value and to record the loss as follows.

December 31, 2012

Unrealized Holding Gain or Loss—Equity	35,550	
Fair Value Adjustment (available-for-sale)		35,550

On January 23, 2013, Republic sold all of its Northwest Industries, Inc. common stock receiving net proceeds of $287,220. Illustration 17-15 shows the computation of the realized gain on the sale.

Net proceeds from sale	$287,220
Cost of Northwest shares	259,700
Gain on sale of stock	$ 27,520

ILLUSTRATION 17-15
Computation of Gain on Sale of Stock

Republic records the sale as follows.

January 23, 2013

Cash	287,220	
Equity Investments		259,700
Gain on Sale of Investments		27,520

In addition, assume that on February 10, 2013, Republic purchased 20,000 shares of Continental Trucking at a market price of $12.75 per share plus brokerage commissions of $1,850 (total cost, $256,850).

Illustration 17-16 lists Republic's portfolio of available-for-sale securities, as of December 31, 2013.

ILLUSTRATION 17-16
Computation of Fair Value Adjustment—Available-for-Sale Equity Security Portfolio (2013)

AVAILABLE-FOR-SALE EQUITY SECURITY PORTFOLIO
DECEMBER 31, 2013

Investments	Cost	Fair Value	Unrealized Gain (Loss)
Continental Trucking	$256,850	$278,350	$ 21,500
Campbell Soup Co.	317,500	362,550	45,050
St. Regis Pulp Co.	141,350	139,050	(2,300)
Total of portfolio	$715,700	$779,950	64,250
Previous fair value adjustment balance—Cr.			(35,550)
Fair value adjustment—Dr.			$ 99,800

At December 31, 2013, the fair value of Republic's available-for-sale equity securities portfolio exceeds cost by $64,250 (unrealized gain). The Fair Value Adjustment account had a credit balance of $35,550 at December 31, 2013. To adjust its December 31, 2013, available-for-sale portfolio to fair value, the company debits the Fair Value Adjustment account for $99,800 ($35,550 + $64,250). Republic records this adjustment as follows.

December 31, 2013

Fair Value Adjustment (available-for-sale)	99,800	
Unrealized Holding Gain or Loss—Equity		99,800

Trading Securities

The accounting entries to record trading equity securities are the same as for available-for-sale equity securities, except for recording the unrealized holding gain or loss. For trading equity securities, companies **report the unrealized holding gain or loss as part of net income**. Thus, the account titled Unrealized Holding Gain or Loss—Income is used.

HOLDINGS BETWEEN 20% AND 50%

An investor corporation may hold an interest of less than 50 percent in an investee corporation and thus not possess legal control. However, an investment in voting stock of less than 50 percent can still give the investor the ability to exercise significant influence over the operating and financial policies of its bottlers. **[4] Significant influence** may be indicated in several ways. Examples include representation on the board of directors, participation in policy-making processes, material intercompany transactions, interchange of managerial personnel, or technological dependency.

Another important consideration is the extent of ownership by an investor in relation to the concentration of other shareholdings. To achieve a reasonable degree of uniformity in application of the "significant influence" criterion, the profession concluded that an investment (direct or indirect) of 20 percent or more of the voting stock of an investee should lead to a presumption that in the absence of evidence to the contrary, an investor has the ability to exercise significant influence over an investee.[7]

In instances of "significant influence" (generally an investment of 20 percent or more), the investor must account for the investment using the **equity method**.

Equity Method

LEARNING OBJECTIVE 4
Explain the equity method of accounting and compare it to the fair value method for equity securities.

Under the equity method, the investor and the investee acknowledge a substantive economic relationship. The company originally records the investment at the cost of the shares acquired but subsequently adjusts the amount each period for changes in the investee's net assets. That is, **the investor's proportionate share of the earnings (losses) of the investee periodically increases (decreases) the investment's carrying amount. All cash dividends received by the investor from the investee also decrease the investment's carrying amount.** The equity method recognizes that investee's earnings increase investee's net assets, and that investee's losses and dividends decrease these net assets.

[7]Cases in which an investment of 20 percent or more might not enable an investor to exercise significant influence include:
 (1) The investee opposes the investor's acquisition of its stock.
 (2) The investor and investee sign an agreement under which the investor surrenders significant shareholder rights.
 (3) The investor's ownership share does not result in "significant influence" because majority ownership of the investee is concentrated among a small group of shareholders who operate the investee without regard to the views of the investor.
 (4) The investor tries and fails to obtain representation on the investee's board of directors. **[5]**

To illustrate the equity method and compare it with the fair value method, assume that Maxi Company purchases a 20 percent interest in Mini Company. To apply the fair value method in this example, assume that Maxi does not have the ability to exercise significant influence, and classifies the securities as available-for-sale. Where this example applies the equity method, assume that the 20 percent interest permits Maxi to exercise significant influence. Illustration 17-17 shows the entries.

ILLUSTRATION 17-17
Comparison of Fair Value Method and Equity Method

ENTRIES BY MAXI COMPANY

Fair Value Method		Equity Method	

On January 2, 2012, Maxi Company acquired 48,000 shares (20% of Mini Company common stock) at a cost of $10 a share.

Fair Value Method		Equity Method	
Equity Investments	480,000	Equity Investments	480,000
Cash	480,000	Cash	480,000

For the year 2012, Mini Company reported net income of $200,000; Maxi Company's share is 20%, or $40,000.

Fair Value Method		Equity Method	
No entry		Equity Investments	40,000
		Revenue from Investment	40,000

At December 31, 2012, the 48,000 shares of Mini Company have a fair value (market price) of $12 a share, or $576,000.

Fair Value Method		Equity Method	
Fair Value Adjustment (available-for-sale)	96,000	No entry	
Unrealized Holding Gain or Loss—Equity	96,000		

On January 28, 2013, Mini Company announced and paid a cash dividend of $100,000; Maxi Company received 20%, or $20,000.

Fair Value Method		Equity Method	
Cash	20,000	Cash	20,000
Dividend Revenue	20,000	Equity Investments	20,000

For the year 2013, Mini reported a net loss of $50,000; Maxi Company's share is 20%, or $10,000.

Fair Value Method		Equity Method	
No entry		Loss on Investment	10,000
		Equity Investments	10,000

At December 31, 2013, the Mini Company 48,000 shares have a fair value (market price) of $11 a share, or $528,000.

Fair Value Method		Equity Method	
Unrealized Holding Gain or Loss—Equity	48,000	No entry	
Fair Value Adjustment (available-for-sale)	48,000		

Note that under the fair value method, Maxi reports as revenue only the cash dividends received from Mini. **The earning of net income by Mini (the investee) is not considered a proper basis for recognition of income from the investment by Maxi (the investor).** Why? Mini may permanently retain in the business any increased net assets resulting from its profitable operation. Therefore, Maxi only earns revenue when it receives dividends from Mini.

Under the equity method, Maxi reports as revenue its share of the net income reported by Mini. Maxi records the cash dividends received from Mini as a decrease in the investment carrying value. As a result, Maxi records its share of the net income of Mini in the year when it is earned. With significant influence, Maxi can ensure that Mini will pay dividends, if desired, on any net asset increases resulting from net income. To wait until receiving a dividend ignores the fact that Maxi is better off if the investee has earned income.

INTERNATIONAL PERSPECTIVE

IFRS has similar accounting rules for significant influence equity investments.

Using dividends as a basis for recognizing income poses an additional problem. For example, assume that the investee reports a net loss. However, the investor exerts influence to force a dividend payment from the investee. In this case, the investor reports income, even though the investee is experiencing a loss. **In other words, using dividends as a basis for recognizing income fails to report properly the economics of the situation**.

For some companies, equity accounting can be a real pain to the bottom line. For example, Amazon.com, the pioneer of Internet retailing, at one time struggled to turn a profit. Furthermore, some of Amazon's equity investments had resulted in Amazon's earnings performance going from bad to worse. In a recent year, Amazon.com disclosed equity stakes in such companies as Altera International, Basis Technology, Drugstore.com, and Eziba.com. These equity investees reported losses that made Amazon's already bad bottom line even worse, accounting for up to 22 percent of its reported loss in one year alone.

Investee Losses Exceed Carrying Amount

If an investor's share of the investee's losses exceeds the carrying amount of the investment, should the investor recognize additional losses? Ordinarily, the investor should discontinue applying the equity method and not recognize additional losses.

If the investor's potential loss is not limited to the amount of its original investment (by guarantee of the investee's obligations or other commitment to provide further financial support), or if imminent return to profitable operations by the investee appears to be assured, the investor should recognize additional losses. [6]

Underlying Concepts

Revenue to be recognized should be earned and realized or realizable. A low level of ownership indicates that a company should defer the income from an investee until cash is received.

WHO'S IN CONTROL HERE?

What do the numbers mean?

Molson Coors Brewing Company owns 42 percent of the MillerCoors brewing venture operating in the United States and Puerto Rico. As part of the agreement, Molson helps the MillerCoors unit produce and sell its products in the U.S. and Puerto Rican markets. Lenovo Group owns a significant percentage (45 percent) of the shares of Beijing Lenovo Parasaga Information Technology Co. (which develops and distributes computer software). Beijing Lenovo is important to Lenovo because it develops and sells the software that is used with Lenovo computers. In return, Beijing Lenovo depends on Lenovo to provide the products that make its software and services valuable, as well as significant customer and market support. Indeed, it can be said that to some extent, Lenovo controls Beijing Lenovo, which would likely not exist without the support of Lenovo.

As you have learned, because a company like Lenovo own less than 50 percent of the shares, it does not consolidate Beijing Lenovo but instead accounts for its investment using the *equity method*. Under the equity method, Lenovo reports a single income item for its profits from Beijing Lenovo and only the net amount of its investment in the statement of financial position. Equity method accounting gives Lenovo a pristine statement of financial position and income statement, by separating the assets and liabilities and the profit margins of the related companies from its laptop-computer businesses.

Some are critical of equity method accounting; they argue that some investees, like Beijing Lenovo, should be consolidated. The FASB has issued rules to consider other factors, in addition to voting interests, when determining whether an entity should be consolidated. We discuss these rules in Appendix 17B. The FASB has a project to tighten up consolidation rules, so that companies will be more likely to consolidate more of their 20–50 percent owned investments. Consolidation of entities, such as MillerCoors and Beijing Lenovo, is warranted if Molson and Lenovo effectively control their equity method investments. See *http://www.fasb.org/jsp/FASB/Page/SectionPage&cid= 1218820137074* for more information on these consolidation projects.

HOLDINGS OF MORE THAN 50%

When one corporation acquires a voting interest of more than 50 percent in another corporation, it is said to have a controlling interest. In such a relationship, the investor corporation is referred to as the parent and the investee corporation as the subsidiary. Companies present the investment in the common stock of the subsidiary as a long-term investment on the separate financial statements of the parent.

When the parent treats the investment as a subsidiary, the parent generally prepares consolidated financial statements. Consolidated financial statements treat the parent and subsidiary corporations as a single economic entity. (Advanced accounting courses extensively discuss the subject of when and how to prepare consolidated financial statements.) Whether or not consolidated financial statements are prepared, the parent company generally accounts for the investment in the subsidiary **using the equity method** as explained in the previous section of this chapter.

> **INTERNATIONAL PERSPECTIVE**
>
> In contrast to U.S. firms, financial statements of non-U.S. companies often include both consolidated (group) statements and parent company financial statements.

SECTION 3 • OTHER REPORTING ISSUES

We have identified the basic issues involved in accounting for investments in debt and equity securities. In addition, the following issues relate to both of these types of securities.

1. Fair value option.

2. Impairment of value.

3. Reclassification adjustments.

4. Transfers between categories.

5. Fair value controversy.

FAIR VALUE OPTION

As indicated in earlier chapters, companies have the option to report most financial instruments at fair value, with all gains and losses related to changes in fair value reported in the income statement. This option is applied on an instrument-by-instrument basis. The fair value option is generally available only at the time a company first purchases the financial asset or incurs a financial liability. If a company chooses to use the fair value option, it must measure this instrument at fair value until the company no longer has ownership.

> **5 LEARNING OBJECTIVE**
> Describe the accounting for the fair value option.

For example, assume that Abbott Laboratories purchased debt securities in 2012 that it classified as held-to-maturity. Abbott does not choose to report this security using the fair value option. In 2013, Abbott buys another held-to-maturity debt security. Abbott decides to report this security using the fair value option. Once it chooses the fair value option for the security bought in 2013, the decision is irrevocable (may not be changed). In addition, Abbott does not have the option to value the held-to- maturity security purchased in 2012 at fair value in 2013 or in subsequent periods.

Many support the use of the fair value option as a step closer to total fair value reporting for financial instruments. They believe this treatment leads to an improvement in financial reporting. Others argue that the fair value option is confusing. A company can choose from period to period whether to use the fair value option for any new investment in a financial instrument. By permitting an instrument-by-instrument approach, companies are able to report some financial instruments at fair value but not others. To illustrate the accounting issues related to the fair value option, we discuss two different situations.

Available-for-Sale Securities

Available-for-sale securities are presently reported at fair value, and any unrealized gains and losses are recorded as part of other comprehensive income. Assume that Hardy Company purchases stock in Fielder Company during 2012 that it classifies as available-for-sale. At December 31, 2012, the cost of this security is $100,000; its fair value at December 31, 2012, is $125,000. If Hardy chooses the fair value option to account for the Fielder Company stock, it makes the following entry at December 31, 2012.

Equity Investments	25,000	
Unrealized Holding Gain or Loss—Income		25,000

In this situation, Hardy uses an account titled Equity Investments to record the change in fair value at December 31. It does not use a Fair Value Adjustment account because the accounting for a fair value option is on an investment-by-investment basis rather than on a portfolio basis. Because Hardy selected the fair value option, the unrealized gain or loss is recorded as part of net income. Hardy must continue to use the fair value method to record this investment until it no longer has ownership of the security.

Equity Method of Accounting

Companies may also use the fair value option for investments that otherwise follow the equity method of accounting. To illustrate, assume that Durham Company holds a 28 percent stake in Suppan Inc. Durham purchased the investment in 2012 for $930,000. At December 31, 2012, the fair value of the investment is $900,000. Durham elects to report the investment in Suppan using the fair value option. The entry to record this investment is as follows.

Unrealized Holding Gain or Loss—Income	30,000	
Equity Investments		30,000

In contrast to equity method accounting, if the fair value option is chosen, Durham does not report its pro rata share of the income or loss from Suppan. In addition, any dividend payments are credited to Dividend Revenue and therefore do not reduce the Equity Investments account.

One major advantage of using the fair value option for this type of investment is that it addresses confusion about the equity method of accounting. In other words, what exactly does the one-line consolidation related to the equity method of accounting on the balance sheet tell investors? Many believe it does not provide information about liquidity or solvency, nor does it provide an indication of the worth of the company.

INTERNATIONAL PERSPECTIVE

IFRS does not allow the use of the fair value option for equity method investments. The FASB is considering a proposal to converge to IFRS in this area.

IMPAIRMENT OF VALUE

LEARNING OBJECTIVE **6**
Discuss the accounting for impairments of debt and equity investments.

A company should evaluate every investment, at each reporting date, to determine if it has suffered impairment—a loss in value that is other than temporary. For example, if an investee experiences a bankruptcy or a significant liquidity crisis, the investor may suffer a permanent loss. **If the decline is judged to be other than temporary, a company writes down the cost basis of the individual security to a new cost basis.** The company accounts for the write-down as a realized loss. Therefore, it includes the amount in net income.

For debt securities, a company uses the impairment test to determine whether "it is probable that the investor will be unable to collect all amounts due according to the contractual terms."

For equity securities, the guideline is less precise. Any time realizable value is lower than the carrying amount of the investment, a company must consider an impairment. Factors involved include the length of time and the extent to which the fair value has been less than cost; the financial condition and near-term prospects of the issuer; and the intent and ability of the investor company to retain its investment to allow for any anticipated recovery in fair value.

To illustrate an impairment, assume that Strickler Company holds available-for-sale bond securities with a par value and amortized cost of $1 million. The fair value of these securities is $800,000. Strickler has previously reported an unrealized loss on these securities of $200,000 as part of other comprehensive income. In evaluating the securities, Strickler now determines that it probably will not collect all amounts due. In this case, it reports the unrealized loss of $200,000 as a loss on impairment of $200,000. Strickler includes this amount in income, with the bonds stated at their new cost basis. It records this impairment as follows.

Loss on Impairment	200,000	
Debt Investments		200,000

The new cost basis of the investment in debt securities is $800,000. Strickler includes subsequent increases and decreases in the fair value of impaired available-for-sale securities as other comprehensive income.[8]

Companies base impairment for debt and equity securities on a fair value test. This test differs slightly from the impairment test for loans that we discuss in Appendix 7B. The FASB rejected the discounted cash flow alternative for securities because of the availability of market price information.

An example of the criteria used by Caterpillar to assess impairment is provided in Illustration 17-18.

ILLUSTRATION 17-18
Disclosure of Impairment
Assessment Criteria

Caterpillar, Inc.
Notes to Financial Statements

Note 1. Impairment of available-for-sale securities
Available-for-sale securities are reviewed monthly to identify market values below cost of 20% or more. If a decline for a debt security is in excess of 20% for six months, the investment is evaluated to determine if the decline is due to general declines in the marketplace or if the investment has been impaired and should be written down to market value. . . . After the six-month period, debt securities with declines from cost in excess of 20% are evaluated monthly for impairment. For equity securities, if a decline from cost of 20% or more continues for a 12-month period, an other than temporary impairment is recognized without continued analysis.

RECLASSIFICATION ADJUSTMENTS

As we indicated in Chapter 4, companies report changes in unrealized holding gains and losses related to available-for-sale securities as part of other comprehensive income. Companies may display the components of other comprehensive income in one of three ways: (1) in a combined statement of income and

7 LEARNING OBJECTIVE
Explain why companies report
reclassification adjustments.

---

[8]In addition, any balance in the Unrealized Gain or Loss—Equity and Fair Value Adjustment accounts related to the impaired security would be eliminated. Companies may not amortize any discount related to the debt securities after recording the impairment. The new cost basis of impaired held-to-maturity securities does not change unless additional impairment occurs.

comprehensive income, (2) in a separate statement of comprehensive income that begins with net income, or (3) in a statement of stockholders' equity.[9]

The reporting of changes in unrealized gains or losses in comprehensive income is straightforward unless a company sells securities during the year. In that case, double counting results when the company reports realized gains or losses as part of net income but also shows the amounts as part of other comprehensive income in the current period or in previous periods.

To ensure that gains and losses are not counted twice when a sale occurs, a **reclassification adjustment** is necessary. To illustrate, assume that Open Company has the following two available-for-sale securities in its portfolio at the end of 2011 (its first year of operations).

ILLUSTRATION 17-19
Available-for-Sale
Security Portfolio (2011)

Investments	Cost	Fair Value	Unrealized Holding Gain (Loss)
Lehman Inc. common stocks	$ 80,000	$105,000	$25,000
Woods Co. common stocks	120,000	135,000	15,000
Total of portfolio	$200,000	$240,000	40,000
Previous fair value adjustment balance			–0–
Fair value adjustment—Dr.			$40,000

If Open Company reports net income in 2011 of $350,000, it presents a statement of comprehensive income as follows.

ILLUSTRATION 17-20
Statement of
Comprehensive
Income (2011)

OPEN COMPANY
STATEMENT OF COMPREHENSIVE INCOME
FOR THE YEAR ENDED DECEMBER 31, 2011

Net income	$350,000
Other comprehensive income	
Holding gains arising during period	40,000
Comprehensive income	$390,000

During 2012, Open Company sold the Lehman Inc. common stock for $105,000 and realized a gain on the sale of $25,000 ($105,000 – $80,000). At the end of 2012, the fair value of the Woods Co. common stock increased an additional $20,000, to $155,000. Illustration 17-21 shows the computation of the change in the fair value adjustment account.

ILLUSTRATION 17-21
Available-for-Sale
Security Portfolio (2012)

Investments	Cost	Fair Value	Unrealized Holding Gain (Loss)
Woods Co. common stocks	$120,000	$155,000	$35,000
Previous fair value adjustment balance—Dr.			(40,000)
Fair value adjustment—Cr.			$ (5,000)

[9]The FASB (and IASB) have a proposal to simplify comprehensive income reporting. If adopted, all components of comprehensive income will be reported in a continuous financial statement that displays the components of net income and the components of other comprehensive income within comprehensive income [Proposed Accounting Standards Update—*Comprehensive Income (Topic 220): Statement of Comprehensive Income* (May 26, 2010)].

Illustration 17-21 indicates that Open should report an unrealized holding loss of $5,000 in comprehensive income in 2012. In addition, Open realized a gain of $25,000 on the sale of the Lehman common stock. **Comprehensive income includes both realized and unrealized components.** Therefore, Open recognizes a total holding gain (loss) in 2012 of $20,000, computed as follows.

Unrealized holding gain (loss)	$ (5,000)
Realized holding gain	25,000
Total holding gain recognized	$20,000

ILLUSTRATION 17-22
Computation of Total Holding Gain (Loss)

Open reports net income of $720,000 in 2012, which includes the realized gain on sale of the Lehman securities. Illustration 17-23 shows a statement of comprehensive income for 2012, indicating how Open reported the components of holding gains (losses).

OPEN COMPANY
STATEMENT OF COMPREHENSIVE INCOME
FOR THE YEAR ENDED DECEMBER 31, 2012

Net income (includes $25,000 realized gain on Lehman shares)		$720,000
Other comprehensive income		
Total holding gains arising during period [$(5,000) + $25,000]	$20,000	
Less: Reclassification adjustment for gains included in net income	25,000	(5,000)
Comprehensive income		$715,000

ILLUSTRATION 17-23
Statement of Comprehensive Income (2012)

In 2011, Open included the unrealized gain on the Lehman Co. common stock in comprehensive income. In 2012, Open sold the stock. It reported the realized gain in net income, which increased comprehensive income again. To avoid double-counting this gain, Open makes a reclassification adjustment to eliminate the realized gain from the computation of comprehensive income in 2012.

A company may display reclassification adjustments on the face of the financial statement in which it reports comprehensive income. Or, it may disclose these reclassification adjustments in the notes to the financial statements.

Comprehensive Example

To illustrate the reporting of investment securities and related gain or loss on available-for-sale securities, assume that on January 1, 2012, Hinges Co. had cash and common stock of $50,000.[10] At that date, the company had no other asset, liability, or equity balance. On January 2, Hinges purchased for cash $50,000 of equity securities classified as available-for-sale. On June 30, Hinges sold part of the available-for-sale security portfolio, realizing a gain as shown in Illustration 17-24.

Fair value of securities sold	$22,000
Less: Cost of securities sold	20,000
Realized gain	$ 2,000

ILLUSTRATION 17-24
Computation of Realized Gain

[10]We adapted this example from Dennis R. Beresford, L. Todd Johnson, and Cheri L. Reither, "Is a Second Income Statement Needed?" *Journal of Accountancy* (April 1996), p. 71.

Hinges did not purchase or sell any other securities during 2012. It received $3,000 in dividends during the year. At December 31, 2012, the remaining portfolio is as shown in Illustration 17-25.

ILLUSTRATION 17-25
Computation of
Unrealized Gain

Fair value of portfolio	$34,000
Less: Cost of portfolio	30,000
Unrealized gain	$ 4,000

Illustration 17-26 shows the company's income statement for 2012.

ILLUSTRATION 17-26
Income Statement

HINGES CO.
INCOME STATEMENT
FOR THE YEAR ENDED DECEMBER 31, 2012

Dividend revenue	$3,000
Realized gains on investment in securities	2,000
Net income	$5,000

The company reports its change in the unrealized holding gain in a statement of comprehensive income as follows.

ILLUSTRATION 17-27
Statement of
Comprehensive Income

HINGES CO.
STATEMENT OF COMPREHENSIVE INCOME
FOR THE YEAR ENDED DECEMBER 31, 2012

Net income		$5,000
Other comprehensive income:		
Holding gains arising during the period ($4,000 + $2,000)	$6,000	
Less: Reclassification adjustment for gains included in net income	2,000	4,000
Comprehensive income		$9,000

Its statement of stockholders' equity appears in Illustration 17-28.

ILLUSTRATION 17-28
Statement of
Stockholders' Equity

HINGES CO.
STATEMENT OF STOCKHOLDERS' EQUITY
FOR THE YEAR ENDED DECEMBER 31, 2012

	Common Stock	Retained Earnings	Accumulated Other Comprehensive Income	Total
Beginning balance	$50,000	$ –0–	$–0–	$50,000
Add: Net income		5,000		5,000
Other comprehensive income			4,000	4,000
Ending balance	$50,000	$5,000	$4,000	$59,000

The comparative balance sheet is shown on the next page in Illustration 17-29.

ILLUSTRATION 17-29
Comparative Balance
Sheet

HINGES CO. COMPARATIVE BALANCE SHEET	1/1/12	12/31/12
Assets		
Cash	$50,000	$25,000
Equity investments (available-for-sale)		34,000
Total assets	$50,000	$59,000
Stockholders' equity		
Common stock	$50,000	$50,000
Retained earnings		5,000
Accumulated other comprehensive income		4,000
Total stockholders' equity	$50,000	$59,000

This example indicates how an unrealized gain or loss on available-for-sale securities affects all the financial statements. Note that a company must disclose the components that comprise accumulated other comprehensive income.

TRANSFERS BETWEEN CATEGORIES

Companies account for transfers between any of the categories at fair value. Thus, if a company transfers available-for-sale securities to held-to-maturity investments, it records the new investment (held-to-maturity) at the date of transfer at **fair value** in the new category. Similarly, if it transfers held-to-maturity investments to available-for-sale investments, it records the new investments (available-for-sale) at **fair value**. This **fair value** rule assures that a company cannot omit recognition of fair value simply by transferring securities to the held-to-maturity category. Illustration 17-30 summarizes the accounting treatment for transfers.

8 LEARNING OBJECTIVE
Describe the accounting for transfer of investment securities between categories.

ILLUSTRATION 17-30
Accounting for Transfers

Type of Transfer	Measurement Basis	Impact of Transfer on Stockholders' Equity*	Impact of Transfer on Net Income*
Transfer from trading to available-for-sale	Security transferred at fair value at the date of transfer, which is the new cost basis of the security.	The unrealized gain or loss at the date of transfer increases or decreases stockholders' equity.	The unrealized gain or loss at the date of transfer is recognized in income.
Transfer from available-for-sale to trading	Security transferred at fair value at the date of transfer, which is the new cost basis of the security.	The unrealized gain or loss at the date of transfer increases or decreases stockholders' equity.	The unrealized gain or loss at the date of transfer is recognized in income.
Transfer from held-to-maturity to available-for-sale**	Security transferred at fair value at the date of transfer.	The separate component of stockholders' equity is increased or decreased by the unrealized gain or loss at the date of transfer.	None
Transfer from available-for-sale to held-to-maturity	Security transferred at fair value at the date of transfer.	The unrealized gain or loss at the date of transfer carried as a separate component of stockholders' equity is amortized over the remaining life of the security.	None
	*Assumes that adjusting entries to report changes in fair value for the current period are not yet recorded. **According to GAAP, these types of transfers should be rare.		

Gateway to the Profession

Examples of the Entries for Recording Transfers Between Categories

FAIR VALUE CONTROVERSY

The reporting of investment securities is controversial. Some believe that all securities should be reported at fair value; others believe they all should be stated at amortized cost. Others favor the present approach. In this section, we look at some of the major unresolved issues.

Measurement Based on Intent

Companies classify debt securities as held-to-maturity, available-for-sale, or trading. As a result, companies can report three identical debt securities in three different ways in the financial statements. Some argue such treatment is confusing. Furthermore, the held-to-maturity category relies solely on intent, a subjective evaluation. What is not subjective is the fair value of the debt instrument. In other words, the three classifications are subjective, resulting in arbitrary classifications.

Gains Trading

Companies can classify certain debt securities as held-to-maturity and therefore report them at amortized cost. Companies can classify other debt and equity securities as available-for-sale and report them at fair value with the unrealized gain or loss reported as other comprehensive income. In either case, a company can become involved in "gains trading" (also referred to as "cherry picking," "snacking," or "sell the best and keep the rest"). In gains trading, companies sell their "winners," reporting the gains in income, and hold on to the losers.

Liabilities Not Fairly Valued

Many argue that if companies report investment securities at fair value, they also should report liabilities at fair value. Why? By recognizing changes in value on only one side of the balance sheet (the asset side), a high degree of volatility can occur in the income and stockholders' equity amounts. Further, financial institutions are involved in asset and liability management (not just asset management). Viewing only one side may lead managers to make uneconomic decisions as a result of the accounting. The fair value option may address this concern to some extent. However, as we discussed in Chapter 14, there is debate on the usefulness of fair value estimates for liabilities.

Fair Values—Final Comment

The FASB (and the IASB) believe that fair value information for financial assets and financial liabilities provides more useful and relevant information than a cost-based system. The Boards take this position because fair value reflects the current cash equivalent of the financial instrument rather that the cost of a past transaction. As a consequence, only fair value provides an understanding of the current worth of the investment.

Companies must report fair values for some types of financial instruments. In addition, they have the option to record fair values for any of their financial instruments. As discussed in the opening story, the IASB has already issued rules (*IFRS 9*) which retain a mixed-attribute model with some financial assets measured at fair value and some measured at amortized cost. Whether the FASB expands fair accounting for financial assets beyond that in *IFRS 9* remains to be seen. We hope it does because such an approach would result in fair value accounting for all financial instruments.

SUMMARY OF REPORTING TREATMENT OF SECURITIES

Illustration 17-31 summarizes the major debt and equity securities and their reporting treatment.

Category*	Balance Sheet	Income Statement
Trading (debt and equity securities)	Investments shown at fair value. Current assets.	Interest and dividends are recognized as revenue. Unrealized holding gains and losses are included in net income.
Available-for-sale (debt and equity securities)	Investments shown at fair value. Current or long-term assets. Unrealized holding gains and losses are a separate component of stockholders' equity.	Interest and dividends are recognized as revenue. Unrealized holding gains and losses are **not** included in net income but in other comprehensive income.
Held-to-maturity (debt securities)	Investments shown at amortized cost. Current or long-term assets.	Interest is recognized as revenue.
Equity method and/or consolidation (equity securities)	Investments originally are carried at cost, are periodically adjusted by the investor's share of the investee's earnings or losses, and are decreased by all dividends received from the investee. Classified as long-term.	Revenue is recognized to the extent of the investee's earnings or losses reported subsequent to the date of investment.

*Companies have the option to report financial instruments at fair value with all gains and losses related to changes in fair value reported in the income statement. If a company chooses to use the fair option for some of its financial instruments, these assets or liabilities should be reported separately from other financial instruments that use a different valuation basis. To accomplish separate reporting, a company may either (a) report separate line items for the fair value and non–fair value amounts or (b) report the total fair value and non–fair value amounts in one line and parenthetically report the fair value amount in that line also.[11]

ILLUSTRATION 17-31
Summary of Treatment of Major Debt and Equity Securities

Gateway to the Profession

Discussion of Special Issues Related to Investments

MORE DISCLOSURE, PLEASE

As indicated in the last two sections, the level of disclosure for investment securities is extensive. How to account for investment securities is a particularly sensitive area, given the large amounts of equity investments involved. And presently companies report investments in equity securities at cost, equity, fair value, and full consolidation, depending on the circumstances. As a recent SEC study noted, "there are so many different accounting treatments for investments that it raises the question of whether they are all needed."

Presented below is an estimate of the percentage of companies on the major exchanges that have investments in the equity of other entities.

What do the numbers mean?

Investments in the Equity of Other Companies	
Categorized by Accounting Treatment	Percent of Companies
Presenting consolidated financial statements	91.1%
Reporting equity method investments	23.5
Reporting cost method investments*	17.4
Reporting available-for-sale investments	37.4
Reporting trading investments	6.2

*If the equity investments are not publicly traded, the company often accounts for the investment under the cost method. Changes in value are therefore not recognized unless there is impairment.

As the table indicates, many companies have equity investments of some type. These investments can be substantial. For example, based on the table above, the total amount of equity-method investments appearing on company balance sheets is approximately $403 billion, and the amount shown in the income statements in any one year for all companies is approximately $38 billion.

Source: "Report and Recommendations Pursuant to Section 401(c) of the Sarbanes-Oxley Act of 2002 on Arrangements with Off-Balance Sheet Implications, Special Purpose Entities, and Transparency of Filings by Issuers," United States Securities and Exchange Commission—Office of Chief Accountant, Office of Economic Analyses, Division of Corporation Finance (June 2005), pp. 36–39.

You will want to read the **IFRS INSIGHTS** on pages 1048–1062

for discussion of IFRS related to the accounting for investments.

[11]Not surprisingly, the disclosure requirements for investments and other financial assets and liabilities are extensive. We provide an expanded discussion with examples of these disclosure requirements in Appendix 17C.

SUMMARY OF LEARNING OBJECTIVES

1 **Identify the three categories of debt securities and describe the accounting and reporting treatment for each category.** (1) Carry and report *held-to-maturity debt securities* at amortized cost. (2) Value *trading debt securities* for reporting purposes at fair value, with unrealized holding gains or losses included in net income. (3) Value *available-for-sale debt securities* for reporting purposes at fair value, with unrealized holding gains or losses reported as other comprehensive income and as a separate component of stockholders' equity.

2 **Understand the procedures for discount and premium amortization on bond investments.** Similar to bonds payable, companies should amortize discount or premium on bond investments using the effective-interest method. They apply the effective interest rate or yield to the beginning carrying value of the investment for each interest period in order to compute interest revenue.

3 **Identify the categories of equity securities and describe the accounting and reporting treatment for each category.** The degree to which one corporation (investor) acquires an interest in the common stock of another corporation (investee) generally determines the accounting treatment for the investment. Long-term investments by one corporation in the common stock of another can be classified according to the percentage of the voting stock of the investee held by the investor.

4 **Explain the equity method of accounting and compare it to the fair value method for equity securities.** Under the equity method the investor and the investee acknowledge a substantive economic relationship. The company originally records the investment at cost but subsequently adjusts the amount each period for changes in the net assets of the investee. That is, the investor's proportionate share of the earnings (losses) of the investee periodically increases (decreases) the investment's carrying amount. All dividends received by the investor from the investee decrease the investment's carrying amount. Under the fair value method a company reports the equity investment at fair value each reporting period irrespective of the investee's earnings or dividends paid to it. A company applies the equity method to investment holdings between 20 percent and 50 percent of ownership. It applies the fair value method to holdings below 20 percent.

5 **Describe the accounting for the fair value option.** Companies have the option to report most financial instruments at fair value, with all gains and losses related to changes in fair value reported in the income statement. This option is applied on an instrument-by-instrument basis. The fair value option is generally available only at the time a company first purchases the financial asset or incurs a financial liability. If a company chooses to use the fair value option, it must measure this instrument at fair value until the company no longer has ownership.

6 **Discuss the accounting for impairments of debt and equity investments.** Impairments of debt and equity securities are losses in value that are determined to be other than temporary, are based on a fair value test, and are charged to income.

7 **Explain why companies report reclassification adjustments.** A company needs a reclassification adjustment when it reports realized gains or losses as part of net income but also shows the amounts as part of other comprehensive income in the current or in previous periods. Companies should report unrealized holding gains or losses related to available-for-sale securities in other comprehensive income and the aggregate balance as accumulated comprehensive income on the balance sheet.

8 **Describe the accounting for transfer of investment securities between categories.** Transfers of securities between categories of investments should be accounted for at fair value, with unrealized holding gains or losses treated in accordance with the nature of the transfer.

APPENDIX **17A**	ACCOUNTING FOR DERIVATIVE INSTRUMENTS

Until the early 1970s, most financial managers worked in a cozy, if unthrilling, world. Since then, constant change caused by volatile markets, new technology, and deregulation has increased the risks to businesses. In response, the financial community developed products to manage these risks.

These products—called derivative financial instruments or simply, derivatives—are useful for managing risk. Companies use the fair values or cash flows of these instruments to offset the changes in fair values or cash flows of the at-risk assets. The development of powerful computing and communication technology has aided the growth in derivative use. This technology provides new ways to analyze information about markets as well as the power to process high volumes of payments.

DEFINING DERIVATIVES

In order to understand derivatives, consider the following examples.

Example 1—Forward Contract. Assume that a company like Dell believes that the price of Google's stock will increase substantially in the next 3 months. Unfortunately, it does not have the cash resources to purchase the stock today. Dell therefore enters into a contract with a broker for delivery of 10,000 shares of Google stock in 3 months at the price of $110 per share.

Dell has entered into a forward contract, a type of derivative. As a result of the contract, Dell **has received the right** to receive 10,000 shares of Google stock in 3 months. Further, it **has an obligation** to pay $110 per share at that time. What is the benefit of this derivative contract? Dell can buy Google stock today and take delivery in 3 months. If the price goes up, as it expects, Dell profits. If the price goes down, Dell loses.

Example 2—Option Contract. Now suppose that Dell needs 2 weeks to decide whether to purchase Google stock. It therefore enters into a different type of contract, one that gives it the right to purchase Google stock at its current price any time within the next 2 weeks. As part of the contract, the broker charges $3,000 for holding the contract open for 2 weeks at a set price.

Dell has now entered into an option contract, another type of derivative. As a result of this contract, **it has received the right**, **but not the obligation** to purchase this stock. If the price of the Google stock increases in the next 2 weeks, Dell exercises its option. In this case, the cost of the stock is the price of the stock stated in the contract, plus the cost of the option contract. If the price does not increase, Dell does not exercise the contract, but still incurs the cost for the option.

The forward contract and the option contract both involve a future delivery of stock. The value of the contract relies on the underlying asset—the Google stock. Thus, these financial instruments are known as derivatives because they **derive their value from** values of other assets (e.g., stocks, bonds, or commodities). Or, put another way, their value relates to a market-determined indicator (e.g., stock price, interest rates, or the Standard and Poor's 500 stock composite index).

In this appendix, we discuss the accounting for three different types of derivatives:

1. Financial forwards or financial futures.

2. Options.

3. Swaps.

WHO USES DERIVATIVES, AND WHY?

LEARNING OBJECTIVE 9

Explain who uses derivatives and why.

Whether to protect for changes in interest rates, the weather, stock prices, oil prices, or foreign currencies, derivative contracts help to smooth the fluctuations caused by various types of risks. A company that wants to ensure against certain types of business risks often uses derivative contracts to achieve this objective.[12]

Producers and Consumers

To illustrate, assume that Heartland Ag is a large producer of potatoes for the consumer market. The present price for potatoes is excellent. Unfortunately, Heartland needs two months to harvest its potatoes and deliver them to the market. Because Heartland expects the price of potatoes to drop in the coming months, it signs a forward contract. It agrees to sell its potatoes today at the current market price for delivery in 2 months.

Who would buy this contract? Suppose on the other side of the contract is McDonald's Corporation. McDonald's wants to have potatoes (for French fries) in 2 months and believes that prices will increase. McDonald's is therefore agreeable to accepting delivery in 2 months at current prices. It knows that it will need potatoes in 2 months, and that it can make an acceptable profit at this price level.

In this situation, if the price of potatoes increases before delivery, Heartland loses and McDonald's wins. Conversely, if the price decreases, Heartland wins and McDonald's loses. However, the objective is not to gamble on the outcome. Regardless of which way the price moves, both Heartland and McDonald's have received a price at which they obtain an acceptable profit. In this case, although Heartland is a **producer** and McDonald's is a **consumer**, both companies are **hedgers**. They both **hedge their positions** to ensure an acceptable financial result.

Commodity prices are volatile. They depend on weather, crop production, and general economic conditions. For the producer and the consumer to plan effectively, it makes good sense to lock in specific future revenues or costs in order to run their businesses successfully.

Speculators and Arbitrageurs

In some cases, instead of McDonald's taking a position in the forward contract, a speculator may purchase the contract from Heartland. The speculator bets that the price of potatoes will rise, thereby increasing the value of the forward contract. The speculator, who may be in the market for only a few hours, will then sell the forward contract to another speculator or to a company like McDonald's.

Arbitrageurs also use derivatives. These market players attempt to exploit inefficiencies in markets. They seek to lock in profits by simultaneously entering into transactions in two or more markets. For example, an arbitrageur might trade in a futures contract. At the same time, the arbitrageur will also trade in the commodity underlying the futures contract, hoping to achieve small price gains on the difference between the two. Markets rely on speculators and arbitrageurs to keep the market liquid on a daily basis.

In these illustrations, we explained why Heartland (the producer) and McDonald's (the consumer) would become involved in a derivative contract. Consider other types of situations that companies face.

1. Airlines, like Delta, Southwest, and United, are affected by changes in the price of jet fuel.

---

[12]Derivatives are traded on many exchanges throughout the world. In addition, many derivative contracts (primarily interest rate swaps) are privately negotiated.

2. Financial institutions, such as Citigroup, Bankers Trust, and M&I Bank, are involved in borrowing and lending funds that are affected by changes in interest rates.

3. Multinational corporations, like Cisco Systems, Coca-Cola, and General Electric, are subject to changes in foreign exchange rates.

In fact, most corporations are involved in some form of derivatives transactions. Companies give these reasons (in their annual reports) as to why they use derivatives:

1. ExxonMobil uses derivatives to hedge its exposure to fluctuations in interest rates, foreign currency exchange rates, and hydrocarbon prices.

2. Caterpillar uses derivatives to manage foreign currency exchange rates, interest rates, and commodity price exposure.

3. Johnson & Johnson uses derivatives to manage the impact of interest rate and foreign exchange rate changes on earnings and cash flows.

Many corporations use derivatives extensively and successfully. However, derivatives can be dangerous. All parties involved must understand the risks and rewards associated with these contracts.[13]

BASIC PRINCIPLES IN ACCOUNTING FOR DERIVATIVES

The FASB concluded that derivatives such as forwards and options are assets and liabilities. It also concluded that companies should report them in the balance sheet **at fair value**.[14] The Board believes that fair value will provide statement users the best information about derivatives. Relying on some other basis of valuation for derivatives, such as historical cost, does not make sense. Why? Because many derivatives have a historical cost of zero. Furthermore, the markets for derivatives, and the assets upon which derivatives' values rely, are well developed. As a result, the Board believes that companies can determine reliable fair value amounts for derivatives.[15]

> **10 LEARNING OBJECTIVE**
> Understand the basic guidelines for accounting for derivatives.

On the income statement, a company should recognize any unrealized gain or loss in income, if it uses the derivative for speculation purposes. If using the derivative for hedging purposes, the accounting for any gain or loss depends on the type of hedge used. We discuss the accounting for hedged transactions later in the appendix.

---

[13]There are some well-publicized examples of companies that have suffered considerable losses using derivatives. For example, companies such as Fannie Mae (U.S.), Enron (U.S.), Showa Shell Sekiyu (Japan), Metallgesellschaft (Germany), Procter & Gamble (U.S.), and Air Products & Chemicals (U.S.) incurred significant losses from investments in derivative instruments.

[14]GAAP covers accounting and reporting for all derivative instruments, whether financial or not. In this appendix we focus on derivative financial instruments because of their widespread use in practice. [7]

[15]As discussed in earlier chapters, fair value is defined as "the price that would be received to sell an asset or paid to transfer a liability in an orderly transaction between market participants at the measurement date." Fair value is therefore a market-based measure. The FASB has also developed a fair value hierarchy, which indicates the priority of valuation techniques to use to determine fair value. *Level 1* fair value measures are based on observable inputs that reflect quoted prices for identical assets or liabilities in active markets. *Level 2* measures are based on inputs other than quoted prices included in Level 1 but that can be corroborated with observable data. *Level 3* fair values are based on unobservable inputs (for example, a company's own data or assumptions). Thus, Level 1 is the most reliable because it is based on quoted prices, like a closing stock price in the *Wall Street Journal*. Level 2 is the next most reliable and would rely on evaluating similar assets or liabilities in active markets. For Level 3 (the least reliable), much judgment is needed, based on the best information available, to arrive at a relevant and reliable fair value measurement. [8]

In summary, companies follow these guidelines in accounting for derivatives.

1. Recognize derivatives in the financial statements as assets and liabilities.

2. Report derivatives at fair value.

3. Recognize gains and losses resulting from speculation in derivatives immediately in income.

4. Report gains and losses resulting from hedge transactions differently, depending on the type of hedge.

Example of Derivative Financial Instrument—Speculation

LEARNING OBJECTIVE 11
Describe the accounting for derivative financial instruments.

To illustrate the measurement and reporting of a derivative for speculative purposes, we examine a derivative whose value depends on the market price of Laredo Inc. common stock. A company can realize a gain from the increase in the value of the Laredo shares with the use of a derivative, such as a call option.[16] A **call option** gives the holder the right, but not the obligation, to buy shares at a preset price. This price is often referred to as the **strike price** or the **exercise price**.

For example, assume a company enters into a call option contract with Baird Investment Co., which gives it the option to purchase Laredo stock at $100 per share.[17] If the price of Laredo stock increases above $100, the company can exercise this option and purchase the shares for $100 per share. If Laredo's stock never increases above $100 per share, the call option is worthless.

Accounting Entries. To illustrate the accounting for a call option, assume that the company purchases a call option contract on January 2, 2012, when Laredo shares are trading at $100 per share. The contract gives it the option to purchase 1,000 shares (referred to as the **notional amount**) of Laredo stock at an option price of $100 per share. The option expires on April 30, 2012. The company purchases the call option for $400 and makes the following entry.

January 2, 2012

Call Option	400	
Cash		400

This payment is referred to as the **option premium**. It is generally much less than the cost of purchasing the shares directly. The option premium consists of two amounts: (1) intrinsic value and (2) time value. Illustration 17A-1 shows the formula to compute the option premium.

ILLUSTRATION 17A-1
Option Premium Formula

Intrinsic value is the difference between the market price and the preset strike price at any point in time. It represents the amount realized by the option holder, if exercising the option immediately. On January 2, 2012, the intrinsic value is zero because the market price equals the preset strike price.

---

[16]Investors can use a different type of option contract—a **put option**—to realize a gain if anticipating a decline in the Laredo stock value. A put option gives the holder the option to sell shares at a preset price. Thus, a put option **increases** in value when the underlying asset **decreases** in value.

[17]Baird Investment Co. is referred to as the **counterparty**. Counterparties frequently are investment bankers or other companies that hold inventories of financial instruments.

Time value refers to the option's value over and above its intrinsic value. Time value reflects the possibility that the option has a fair value greater than zero. How? Because there is some expectation that the price of Laredo shares will increase above the strike price during the option term. As indicated, the time value for the option is $400.[18]

The following additional data are available with respect to the call option.

Date	Market Price of Laredo Shares	Time Value of Call Option
March 31, 2012	$120 per share	$100
April 16, 2012	$115 per share	$ 60

As indicated, on March 31, 2012, the price of Laredo shares increases to $120 per share. The intrinsic value of the call option contract is now $20,000. That is, the company can exercise the call option and purchase 1,000 shares from Baird Investment for $100 per share. It can then sell the shares in the market for $120 per share. This gives the company a gain of $20,000 ($120,000 − $100,000) on the option contract.[19] It records the increase in the intrinsic value of the option as follows.

March 31, 2012

Call Option	20,000	
Unrealized Holding Gain or Loss—Income		20,000

A market appraisal indicates that the time value of the option at March 31, 2012, is $100.[20] The company records this change in value of the option as follows.

March 31, 2012

Unrealized Holding Gain or Loss—Income	300	
Call Option ($400 − $100)		300

At March 31, 2012, the company reports the call option in its balance sheet at fair value of $20,100.[21] The unrealized holding gain increases net income for the period. The loss on the time value of the option decreases net income.

On April 16, 2012, the company settles the option before it expires. To properly record the settlement, it updates the value of the option for the decrease in the intrinsic value of $5,000 ([$20 − $15]) × 1,000) as follows.

April 16, 2012

Unrealized Holding Gain or Loss—Income	5,000	
Call Option		5,000

The decrease in the time value of the option of $40 ($100 − $60) is recorded as follows.

April 16, 2012

Unrealized Holding Gain or Loss—Income	40	
Call Option		40

---

[18]This cost is estimated using option-pricing models, such as the Black-Scholes model. The volatility of the underlying stock, the expected life of the option, the risk-free rate of interest, and expected dividends on the underlying stock during the option term affect the Black-Scholes fair value estimate.

[19]In practice, investors generally do not have to actually buy and sell the Laredo shares to settle the option and realize the gain. This is referred to as the net settlement feature of option contracts.

[20]The decline in value reflects both the decreased likelihood that the Laredo shares will continue to increase in value over the option period and the shorter time to maturity of the option contract.

[21]As indicated earlier, the total value of the option at any point in time equals the intrinsic value plus the time value.

Thus, at the time of the settlement, the call option's carrying value is as follows.

Call Option

January 2, 2012	400	March 31, 2012	300
March 31, 2012	20,000	April 16, 2012	5,000
		April 16, 2012	40
Balance, April 16, 2012	15,060		

The company records the settlement of the option contract with Baird as follows.

April 16, 2012

Cash	15,000	
Loss on Settlement of Call Option	60	
Call Option		15,060

Illustration 17A-2 summarizes the effects of the call option contract on net income.

ILLUSTRATION 17A-2
Effect on Income—
Derivative Financial
Instrument

Date	Transaction	Income (Loss) Effect
March 31, 2012	Net increase in value of call option ($20,000 − $300)	$19,700
April 16, 2012	Decrease in value of call option ($5,000 + $40)	(5,040)
April 16, 2012	Settle call option	(60)
	Total net income	$14,600

The accounting summarized in Illustration 17A-2 is in accord with GAAP. That is, because the call option meets the definition of an asset, the company records it in the balance sheet on March 31, 2012. Furthermore, it reports the call option at fair value, with any gains or losses reported in income.

Differences Between Traditional and Derivative Financial Instruments

How does a traditional financial instrument differ from a derivative one? A derivative financial instrument has the following three basic characteristics. [9]

1. *The instrument has (1) one or more underlyings and (2) an identified payment provision.* An underlying is a specified interest rate, security price, commodity price, index of prices or rates, or other market-related variable. The interaction of the underlying, with the face amount or the number of units specified in the derivative contract (the notional amounts), determines payment. For example, the value of the call option increased in value when the value of the Laredo stock increased. In this case, the underlying is the stock price. To arrive at the payment provision, multiply the change in the stock price by the number of shares (notional amount).

2. *The instrument requires little or no investment at the inception of the contract.* To illustrate, the company paid a small premium to purchase the call option—an amount much less than if purchasing the Laredo shares as a direct investment.

3. *The instrument requires or permits net settlement.* As indicated in the call option example, the company could realize a profit on the call option without taking possession of the shares. This **net settlement** feature reduces the transaction costs associated with derivatives.

Illustration 17A-3 summarizes the differences between traditional and derivative financial instruments. Here, we use a trading security for the traditional financial instrument and a call option as an example of a derivative one.

Feature	Traditional Financial Instrument (Trading Security)	Derivative Financial Instrument (Call Option)
Payment provision	Stock price times the number of shares.	Change in stock price (underlying) times number of shares (notional amount).
Initial investment	Investor pays full cost.	Initial investment is much less than full cost.
Settlement	Deliver stock to receive cash.	Receive cash equivalent, based on changes in stock price times the number of shares.

ILLUSTRATION 17A-3
Features of Traditional and Derivative Financial Instruments

RISKY BUSINESS

As shown in the graph below, use of derivatives has grown substantially in the past 10 years. In fact, over *$450 trillion* (in notional amounts) in derivative contracts were in play at the end of 2009. The primary players in the market for derivatives are large companies and various financial institutions, which continue to find new uses for derivatives for speculation and risk management

What do the numbers mean?

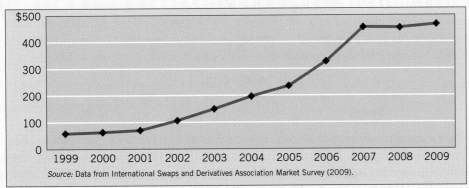

Total Swaps and Equity Derivatives
($ in trillions)

Source: Data from International Swaps and Derivatives Association Market Survey (2009).

Financial engineers continue to develop new uses for derivatives, many times through the use of increasingly complex webs of transactions, spanning a number of markets. As new uses for derivatives appear, the financial system as a whole can be dramatically affected. As a result, some market-watchers are concerned about the risk that a crisis in one company or sector could bring the entire financial system to its knees.

This was the case recently when credit default swaps were used to facilitate the sales of mortgage-backed securities (MBS). However, when the real estate market went south, the MBS defaulted, exposing large international financial institutions, like Barclays, AIG, and Bank of America, to massive losses. The losses were so widespread that government bailouts were required to prevent international securities markets from collapsing. In response, market regulators are proposing new rules to mitigate risks to broader markets from derivatives trading.

Source: P. Eavis, "Bill on Derivatives Overhaul Is Long Overdue," *Wall Street Journal* (April 14, 2010).

DERIVATIVES USED FOR HEDGING

Flexibility in use, and the low-cost features of derivatives relative to traditional financial instruments, explain the popularity of derivatives. An additional use for derivatives is in risk management. For example, companies such as Coca-Cola, ExxonMobil, and General Electric borrow and lend substantial amounts in credit markets. In doing so, they are exposed to significant **interest rate risk**. That is, they face substantial risk that the fair values or cash flows of interest-sensitive assets or liabilities will change if interest rates increase or decrease. These same companies also have significant international operations. As such, they are also exposed to **exchange rate risk**—the risk that changes in foreign currency exchange rates will negatively impact the profitability of their international businesses.

Companies can use derivatives to offset the negative impacts of changes in interest rates or foreign currency exchange rates. This use of derivatives is referred to as hedging.

GAAP established accounting and reporting standards for derivative financial instruments used in hedging activities. The FASB allows special accounting for two types of hedges—fair value and cash flow hedges.[22]

Fair Value Hedge

In a **fair value hedge**, a company uses a derivative to hedge (offset) the exposure to changes in the fair value of a recognized asset or liability or of an unrecognized commitment. In a perfectly hedged position, the gain or loss on the fair value of the derivative equals and offsets that of the hedged asset or liability.

Companies commonly use several types of fair value hedges. For example, companies use interest rate swaps to hedge the risk that changes in interest rates will impact the fair value of debt obligations. Or, they use put options to hedge the risk that an equity investment will decline in value.

To illustrate a fair value hedge, assume that on April 1, 2012, Hayward Co. purchases 100 shares of Sonoma stock at a market price of $100 per share. Hayward does not intend to actively trade this investment. It consequently classifies the Sonoma investment as available-for-sale. Hayward records this available-for-sale investment as follows.

April 1, 2012

Equity Investments	10,000	
Cash		10,000

Hayward records available-for-sale securities at fair value on the balance sheet. It reports unrealized gains and losses in equity as part of other comprehensive income.[23] Fortunately for Hayward, the value of the Sonoma shares increases to $125 per share during 2012. Hayward records the gain on this investment as follows.

December 31, 2013

Fair Value Adjustment (available-for-sale)	2,500	
Unrealized Holding Gain or Loss—Equity		2,500

Illustration 17A-4 indicates how Hayward reports the Sonoma investment in its balance sheet.

ILLUSTRATION 17A-4
Balance Sheet Presentation of Available-for-Sale Securities

HAYWARD CO. BALANCE SHEET (PARTIAL) DECEMBER 31, 2012	
Assets	
Equity investments (available-for-sale)	$12,500
Stockholders' Equity	
Accumulated other comprehensive income	
Unrealized holding gain	$2,500

[22]GAAP also addresses the accounting for certain foreign currency hedging transactions. In general, these transactions are special cases of the two hedges we discuss here. [10] Understanding of foreign currency hedging transactions requires knowledge related to consolidation of multinational entities, which is beyond the scope of this textbook.

[23]We discussed the distinction between trading and available-for-sale investments in the chapter.

While Hayward benefits from an increase in the price of Sonoma shares, it is exposed to the risk that the price of the Sonoma stock will decline. To hedge this risk, Hayward locks in its gain on the Sonoma investment by purchasing a put option on 100 shares of Sonoma stock.

Hayward enters into the put option contract on January 2, 2013, and designates the option as a fair value hedge of the Sonoma investment. This put option (which expires in two years) gives Hayward the option to sell Sonoma shares at a price of $125. Since the exercise price equals the current market price, no entry is necessary at inception of the put option.[24]

January 2, 2013

No entry required. A memorandum indicates the signing of the put option contract and its designation as a fair value hedge for the Sonoma investment.

At December 31, 2013, the price of the Sonoma shares has declined to $120 per share. Hayward records the following entry for the Sonoma investment.

December 31, 2013

Unrealized Holding Gain or Loss—Income	500	
Fair Value Adjustment (available-for-sale)		500

Note that upon designation of the hedge, the accounting for the available-for-sale security changes from regular GAAP. That is, Hayward records the unrealized holding loss in income, not in equity. If Hayward had not followed this accounting, a mismatch of gains and losses in the income statement would result. Thus, special accounting for the hedged item (in this case, an available-for-sale security) is necessary in a fair value hedge.

The following journal entry records the increase in value of the put option on Sonoma shares.

December 31, 2013

Put Option	500	
Unrealized Holding Gain or Loss—Income		500

The decline in the price of Sonoma shares results in an increase in the fair value of the put option. That is, Hayward could realize a gain on the put option by purchasing 100 shares in the open market for $120 and then exercise the put option, selling the shares for $125. This results in a gain to Hayward of $500 (100 shares × [$125 − $120]).[25]

Illustration 17A-5 indicates how Hayward reports the amounts related to the Sonoma investment and the put option.

HAYWARD CO. **BALANCE SHEET (PARTIAL)** **DECEMBER 31, 2013**	
Assets	
Equity investments (available-for-sale)	$12,000
Put option	500

ILLUSTRATION 17A-5
Balance Sheet Presentation of Fair Value Hedge

The increase in fair value on the option offsets or hedges the decline in value on Hayward's available-for-sale security. By using fair value accounting for both financial instruments, the financial statements reflect the underlying substance of Hayward's net exposure to the risks of holding Sonoma stock. By using fair value accounting for both

---

[24]To simplify the example, we assume no premium is paid for the option.

[25]In practice, Hayward generally does not have to actually buy and sell the Sonoma shares to realize this gain. Rather, unless the counterparty wants to hold Hayward shares, Hayward can "close out" the contract by having the counterparty pay it $500 in cash. This is an example of the net settlement feature of derivatives.

these financial instruments, the balance sheet reports the amount that Hayward would receive on the investment and the put option contract if Hayward sold and settled them, respectively.

Illustration 17A-6 illustrates the reporting of the effects of the hedging transaction on income for the year ended December 31, 2013.

ILLUSTRATION 17A-6
Income Statement
Presentation of Fair Value
Hedge

HAYWARD CO.
INCOME STATEMENT (PARTIAL)
FOR THE YEAR ENDED DECEMBER 31, 2013

Other Income	
Unrealized holding gain—put option	$ 500
Unrealized holding loss—available-for-sale securities	(500)

The income statement indicates that the gain on the put option offsets the loss on the available-for-sale securities.[26] The reporting for these financial instruments, even when they reflect a hedging relationship, illustrates why the FASB argued that fair value accounting provides the most relevant information about financial instruments, including derivatives.

Cash Flow Hedge

LEARNING OBJECTIVE 13
Explain how to account for a cash flow hedge.

Companies use **cash flow hedges** to hedge exposures to **cash flow risk**, which results from the variability in cash flows. The FASB allows special accounting for cash flow hedges. Generally, companies measure and report derivatives at fair value on the balance sheet. They report gains and losses directly in net income.

However, companies account for derivatives used in cash flow hedges at fair value on the balance sheet, but they **record gains or losses in equity, as part of other comprehensive income**.

INTERNATIONAL
PERSPECTIVE

Under IFRS, companies record unrealized holding gains or losses on cash flow hedges as adjustments to the value of the hedged item, not as "Other comprehensive income."

To illustrate, assume that in September 2012, Allied Can Co. anticipates purchasing 1,000 metric tons of aluminum in January 2013. Concerned that prices for aluminum will increase in the next few months, Allied wants to hedge the risk that it might pay higher prices for inventory in January 2013. As a result, Allied enters into an aluminum futures contract.

A **futures contract** gives the holder the right and the obligation to purchase an asset at a preset price for a specified period of time.[27] In this case, the aluminum futures contract gives Allied the right and the obligation to purchase 1,000 metric tons of aluminum for $1,550 per ton. This contract price is good until the contract expires in January 2013. The underlying for this derivative is the price of aluminum. If the price of aluminum rises above $1,550, the value of the futures contract to Allied increases. Why? Because Allied will be able to purchase the aluminum at the lower price of $1,550 per ton.[28]

Allied enters into the futures contract on September 1, 2012. Assume that the price to be paid today for inventory to be delivered in January—the **spot price**—equals the contract price. With the two prices equal, the futures contract has no value. Therefore, no entry is necessary.

[26]Note that the fair value changes in the option contract will not offset increases in the value of the Hayward investment. Should the price of Sonoma stock increase above $125 per share, Hayward would have no incentive to exercise the put option.

[27]A **futures contract** is a firm contractual agreement between a buyer and seller for a specified asset on a fixed date in the future. The contract also has a standard specification so both parties know exactly what is being traded. A **forward** is similar but is not traded on an exchange and does not have standardized conditions.

[28]As with the earlier call option example, the actual aluminum does not have to be exchanged. Rather, the parties to the futures contract settle by paying the cash difference between the futures price and the price of aluminum on each settlement date.

September 2012
No entry required. A memorandum indicates
the signing of the futures contract.

At December 31, 2012, the price for January delivery of aluminum increases to $1,575 per metric ton. Allied makes the following entry to record the increase in the value of the futures contract.

December 31, 2012

Futures Contract	25,000	
Unrealized Holding Gain or Loss—Equity		
([$1,575 − $1,550] × 1,000 tons)		25,000

Allied reports the futures contract in the balance sheet as a current asset. It reports the gain on the futures contract as part of other comprehensive income.

Since Allied has not yet purchased and sold the inventory, this gain arises from an anticipated transaction. In this type of transaction, a company accumulates in equity gains or losses on the futures contract as part of other comprehensive income until the period in which it sells the inventory, thereby affecting earnings.

In January 2013, Allied purchases 1,000 metric tons of aluminum for $1,575 and makes the following entry.[29]

January 2013

Aluminum Inventory	1,575,000	
Cash ($1,575 × 1,000 tons)		1,575,000

At the same time, Allied makes final settlement on the futures contract. It records the following entry.

January 2013

Cash	25,000	
Futures Contract ($1,575,000 − $1,550,000)		25,000

Through use of the futures contract derivative, Allied fixes the cost of its inventory. The $25,000 futures contract settlement offsets the amount paid to purchase the inventory at the prevailing market price of $1,575,000. The result: net cash outflow of $1,550 per metric ton, as desired. As Illustration 17A-7 shows, Allied has therefore effectively hedged the cash flow for the purchase of inventory.

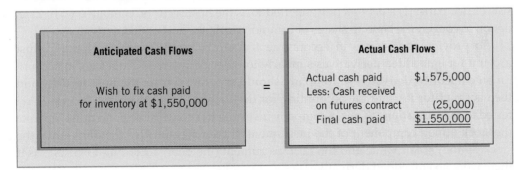

ILLUSTRATION 17A-7
Effect of Hedge on Cash Flows

There are no income effects at this point. Allied accumulates in equity the gain on the futures contract as part of other comprehensive income until the period when it sells the inventory, affecting earnings through cost of goods sold.

For example, assume that Allied processes the aluminum into finished goods (cans). The total cost of the cans (including the aluminum purchases in January 2013)

---

[29]In practice, futures contracts are settled on a daily basis. For our purposes, we show only one settlement for the entire amount.

is $1,700,000. Allied sells the cans in July 2013 for $2,000,000, and records this sale as follows.

July 2013

Cash	2,000,000	
Sales Revenue		2,000,000
Cost of Goods Sold	1,700,000	
Inventory (cans)		1,700,000

Since the effect of the anticipated transaction has now affected earnings, Allied makes the following entry related to the hedging transaction.

July 2013

Unrealized Holding Gain or Loss—Equity	25,000	
Cost of Goods Sold		25,000

The gain on the futures contract, which Allied reported as part of other comprehensive income, now reduces cost of goods sold. As a result, the cost of aluminum included in the overall cost of goods sold is $1,550,000. The futures contract has worked as planned. Allied has managed the cash paid for aluminum inventory and the amount of cost of goods sold.

OTHER REPORTING ISSUES

The preceding examples illustrate the basic reporting issues related to the accounting for derivatives. Next, we discuss the following additional issues:

1. The accounting for embedded derivatives.
2. Qualifying hedge criteria.

Embedded Derivatives

As we indicated at the beginning of this appendix, rapid innovation in the development of complex financial instruments drove efforts toward unifying and improving the accounting standards for derivatives. In recent years, this innovation has led to the development of **hybrid securities**. These securities have characteristics of both debt and equity. They often combine traditional and derivative financial instruments.

For example, a convertible bond (discussed in Chapter 16) is a hybrid instrument. It consists of two parts: (1) a debt security, referred to as the **host security**, combined with (2) an option to convert the bond to shares of common stock, the **embedded derivative**.

To provide consistency in accounting for similar derivatives, a company must account for embedded derivatives similarly to other derivatives. Therefore, to account for an embedded derivative, a company **should separate it from the host security** and then account for it using the accounting for derivatives. This separation process is referred to as **bifurcation**.[30] Thus, a company investing in a convertible bond must separate the stock option component of the instrument. It then accounts for the derivative (the stock option) at fair value and the host instrument (the debt) according to GAAP, as if there were no embedded derivative.[31]

---

[30]A company can also designate such a derivative as a hedging instrument. The company would apply the hedge accounting provisions outlined earlier in the chapter.

[31]The issuer of the convertible bonds would not bifurcate the option component of the convertible bonds payable. GAAP explicitly precludes embedded derivative accounting for an embedded derivative that is indexed to a company's own common stock. If the conversion feature was tied to **another company's** stock, then the derivative would be bifurcated.

Qualifying Hedge Criteria

The FASB identified certain criteria that hedging transactions must meet before requiring the special accounting for hedges. The FASB designed these criteria to ensure the use of hedge accounting in a consistent manner across different hedge transactions. The general criteria relate to the following areas.

INTERNATIONAL PERSPECTIVE

IFRS qualifying hedge criteria are similar to those used in GAAP.

1. *Documentation, risk management, and designation.* At inception of the hedge, there must be formal documentation of the hedging relationship, the company's risk management objective, and the strategy for undertaking the hedge. Designation refers to identifying the hedging instrument, the hedged item or transaction, the nature of the risk being hedged, and how the hedging instrument will offset changes in the fair value or cash flows attributable to the hedged risk.

   The FASB decided that documentation and designation are critical to the implementation of the special accounting for hedges. Without these requirements, companies might try to apply the hedge accounting provisions retroactively, only in response to negative changes in market conditions, to offset the negative impact of a transaction on the financial statements. Allowing special hedge accounting in such a setting could mask the speculative nature of the original transaction.

2. *Effectiveness of the hedging relationship.* At inception and on an ongoing basis, the hedging relationship should be highly effective in achieving offsetting changes in fair value or cash flows. Companies must assess effectiveness whenever preparing financial statements.

   The general guideline for effectiveness is that the fair values or cash flows of the hedging instrument (the derivative) and the hedged item exhibit a high degree of correlation. In practice, high effectiveness is assumed when the correlation is close to one (e.g., within plus or minus .10). In our earlier hedging examples (put option and the futures contract on aluminum inventory), the fair values and cash flows are perfectly correlated. That is, when the cash payment for the inventory purchase increased, it offset, dollar for dollar, the cash received on the futures contract.

   If the effectiveness criterion is not met, either at inception or because of changes following inception of the hedging relationship, the FASB no longer allows special hedge accounting. The company should then account for the derivative as a free-standing derivative.[32]

3. *Effect on reported earnings of changes in fair values or cash flows.* A change in the fair value of a hedged item or variation in the cash flow of a hedged forecasted transaction must have the potential to change the amount recognized in reported earnings.[33] There is no need for special hedge accounting if a company accounts for both the hedging instrument and the hedged item at fair value under existing GAAP. In this case, earnings will properly reflect the offsetting gains and losses.

   For example, special accounting is not needed for a fair value hedge of a trading security, because a company accounts for both the investment and the derivative at fair value on the balance sheet with gains or losses reported in earnings. Thus, "special"

---

[32]The accounting for the part of a derivative that is not effective in a hedge is at fair value, with gains and losses recorded in income.

[33]GAAP gives companies the option to measure most types of financial instruments—from equity investments to debt issued by the company—at fair value. Changes in fair value are recognized in net income each reporting period. Thus, GAAP provides companies with the opportunity to hedge their financial instruments without the complexity inherent in applying hedge accounting provisions. For example, if the fair value option is used, bifurcation of an embedded derivative is not required. [11]

hedge accounting is necessary only when there is a mismatch of the accounting effects for the hedging instrument and the hedged item under GAAP.[34]

Summary of Derivatives Accounting

Illustration 17A-8 summarizes the accounting provisions for derivatives and hedging transactions.

ILLUSTRATION 17A-8
Summary of Derivative Accounting under GAAP

Derivative Use	Accounting for Derivative	Accounting for Hedged Item	Common Example
Speculation	At fair value with unrealized holding gains and losses recorded in income.	Not applicable	Call or put option on an equity security.
Hedging Fair value	At fair value with holding gains and losses recorded in income.	At fair value with gains and losses recorded in income.	Put option to hedge an equity investment.
Cash flow	At fair value with unrealized holding gains and losses from the hedge recorded in other comprehensive income, and reclassified in income when the hedged transaction's cash flows affect earnings.	Use other generally accepted accounting principles for the hedged item.	Use of a futures contract to hedge a forecasted purchase of inventory.

As indicated, the general accounting for derivatives relies on fair values. GAAP also establishes special accounting guidance when companies use derivatives **for hedging purposes**. For example, when a company uses a put option to hedge price changes in an available-for-sale stock investment in a fair value hedge (see the Hayward example earlier), it records unrealized gains on the investment in earnings, which is not GAAP for available-for-sale securities without such a hedge. This special accounting is justified in order to accurately report the nature of the hedging relationship in the balance sheet (recording both the put option and the investment at fair value) and in the income statement (reporting offsetting gains and losses in the same period).

Special accounting also is used for cash flow hedges. Companies account for derivatives used in qualifying cash flow hedges at fair value on the balance sheet, but record unrealized holding gains or losses in other comprehensive income until selling or settling the hedged item. In a cash flow hedge, a company continues to record the hedged item at its historical cost.

Disclosure requirements for derivatives are complex. Recent pronouncements on fair value information and financial instruments provide a helpful disclosure framework for reporting derivative instruments. Appendix 17C illustrates many of these disclosures, except for discussion of hedging issues. In general, companies that have derivatives are required to disclose the objectives for holding or issuing those instruments (speculation or hedging), the hedging context (fair value or cash flow), and the strategies for achieving risk-management objectives.

---

[34]An important criterion specific to cash flow hedges is that the forecasted transaction in a cash flow hedge "is likely to occur." A company should support this probability (defined as significantly greater than the term "more likely than not") by observable facts such as frequency of similar past transactions and its financial and operational ability to carry out the transaction.

COMPREHENSIVE HEDGE ACCOUNTING EXAMPLE

To provide a comprehensive example of hedge accounting, we examine the use of an interest rate swap. First, let's consider how swaps work and why companies use them.

Options and futures trade on organized securities exchanges. Because of this, options and futures have standardized terms. Although that standardization makes the trading easier, it limits the flexibility needed to tailor contracts to specific circumstances. In addition, most types of derivatives have relatively short time horizons, thereby excluding their use for reducing long-term risk exposure.

As a result, many corporations instead turn to the swap, a very popular type of derivative. A **swap** is a transaction between two parties in which the first party promises to make a payment to the second party. Similarly, the second party promises to make a simultaneous payment to the first party.

The most common type of swap is the **interest rate swap**. In this type, one party makes payments based on a fixed or floating rate, and the second party does just the opposite. In most cases, large money-center banks bring together the two parties. These banks handle the flow of payments between the parties, as shown in Illustration 17A-9.

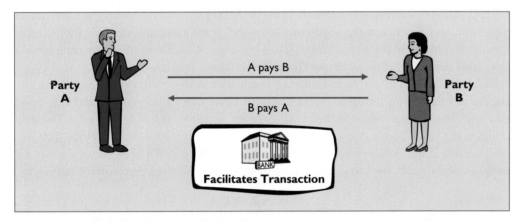

ILLUSTRATION 17A-9
Swap Transaction

Fair Value Hedge

To illustrate the use of a swap in a fair value hedge, assume that Jones Company issues $1,000,000 of five-year, 8 percent bonds on January 2, 2012. Jones records this transaction as follows.

	January 2, 2012	
Cash	1,000,000	
Bonds Payable		1,000,000

Jones offered a fixed interest rate to appeal to investors. But Jones is concerned that if market interest rates decline, the fair value of the liability will increase. The company will then suffer an economic loss.[35] To protect against the risk of loss, Jones hedges the risk of a decline in interest rates by entering into a five-year interest rate swap contract. Jones agrees to the following terms:

1. Jones will receive fixed payments at 8 percent (based on the $1,000,000 amount).
2. Jones will pay variable rates, based on the market rate in effect for the life of the swap contract. The variable rate at the inception of the contract is 6.8 percent.

---

[35]This economic loss arises because Jones is locked into the 8 percent interest payments even if rates decline.

As Illustration 17A-10 shows, this swap allows Jones to change the interest on the bonds payable from a fixed rate to a variable rate.

ILLUSTRATION 17A-10
Interest Rate Swap

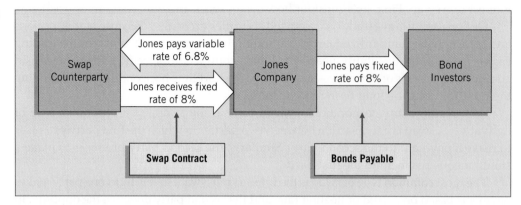

The settlement dates for the swap correspond to the interest payment dates on the debt (December 31). On each interest payment (settlement) date, Jones and the counterparty compute the difference between current market interest rates and the fixed rate of 8 percent, and determine the value of the swap.[36] If interest rates decline, the value of the swap contract to Jones increases (Jones has a gain), while at the same time Jones's fixed-rate debt obligation increases (Jones has an economic loss).

The swap is an effective risk-management tool in this setting. Its value relates to the same underlying (interest rates) that will affect the value of the fixed-rate bond payable. Thus, if the value of the swap goes up, it offsets the loss related to the debt obligation.

Assuming that Jones enters into the swap on January 2, 2012 (the same date as the issuance of the debt), the swap at this time has no value. Therefore no entry is necessary.

January 2, 2012

No entry required. A memorandum indicates the signing of the swap contract.

At the end of 2012, Jones makes the interest payment on the bonds. It records this transaction as follows.

December 31, 2012

Interest Expense	80,000	
Cash (8% × $1,000,000)		80,000

At the end of 2012, market interest rates have declined substantially. Therefore, the value of the swap contract increases. Recall (see Illustration 17A-9) that in the swap, Jones receives a fixed rate of 8 percent, or $80,000 ($1,000,000 × 8%), and pays a variable rate (6.8%), or $68,000. Jones therefore receives $12,000 ($80,000 − $68,000) as a settlement payment on the swap contract on the first interest payment date. Jones records this transaction as follows.

December 31, 2012

Cash	12,000	
Interest Expense		12,000

---

[36]The underlying for an interest rate swap is some index of market interest rates. The most commonly used index is the London Interbank Offer Rate, or LIBOR. In this example, we assume the LIBOR is 6.8 percent.

In addition, a market appraisal indicates that the value of the interest rate swap has increased $40,000. Jones records this increase in value as follows.[37]

	December 31, 2012	
Swap Contract	40,000	
Unrealized Holding Gain or Loss—Income		40,000

Jones reports this swap contract in the balance sheet. It reports the gain on the hedging transaction in the income statement. Because interest rates have declined, the company records a loss and a related increase in its liability as follows.

	December 31, 2012	
Unrealized Holding Gain or Loss—Income	40,000	
Bonds Payable		40,000

Jones reports the loss on the hedging activity in net income. It adjusts bonds payable in the balance sheet to fair value.

Financial Statement Presentation of an Interest Rate Swap

Illustration 17A-11 indicates how Jones reports the asset and liability related to this hedging transaction on the balance sheet.

<table>
<tr><td colspan="2" align="center">JONES COMPANY
BALANCE SHEET (PARTIAL)
DECEMBER 31, 2012</td></tr>
<tr><td>Current assets</td><td></td></tr>
<tr><td>   Swap contract</td><td>$40,000</td></tr>
<tr><td>Long-term liabilities</td><td></td></tr>
<tr><td>   Bonds payable</td><td>$1,040,000</td></tr>
</table>

ILLUSTRATION 17A-11
Balance Sheet Presentation of Fair Value Hedge

The effect on Jones's balance sheet is the addition of the swap asset and an increase in the carrying value of the bonds payable. Illustration 17A-12 indicates how Jones reports the effects of this swap transaction in the income statement.

<table>
<tr><td colspan="3" align="center">JONES COMPANY
INCOME STATEMENT (PARTIAL)
FOR THE YEAR ENDED DECEMBER 31, 2012</td></tr>
<tr><td>Interest expense ($80,000 − $12,000)</td><td></td><td>$68,000</td></tr>
<tr><td>Other income</td><td></td><td></td></tr>
<tr><td>Unrealized holding gain—swap contract</td><td>$40,000</td><td></td></tr>
<tr><td>Unrealized holding loss—bonds payable</td><td>(40,000)</td><td></td></tr>
<tr><td>   Net gain (loss)</td><td></td><td>$–0–</td></tr>
</table>

ILLUSTRATION 17A-12
Income Statement Presentation of Fair Value Hedge

On the income statement, Jones reports interest expense of $68,000. Jones has effectively changed the debt's interest rate from fixed to variable. That is, by receiving a fixed

---

[37]Theoretically, this fair value change reflects the present value of expected future differences in variable and fixed interest rates.

rate and paying a variable rate on the swap, the company converts the fixed rate on the bond payable to variable. This results in an effective interest rate of 6.8 percent in 2012.[38] Also, the gain on the swap offsets the loss related to the debt obligation. Therefore the net gain or loss on the hedging activity is zero.

Illustration 17A-13 shows the overall impact of the swap transaction on the financial statements.

ILLUSTRATION 17A-13
Impact on Financial
Statements of Fair
Value Hedge

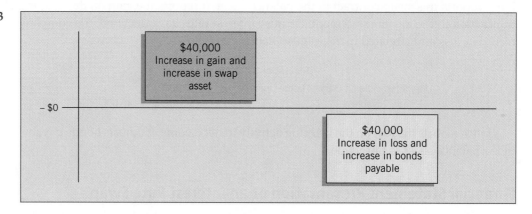

In summary, to account for fair value hedges (as illustrated in the Jones example) **record the derivative at its fair value in the balance sheet, and record any gains and losses in income**. Thus, the gain on the swap offsets or hedges the loss on the bond payable, due to the decline in interest rates.

By adjusting the hedged item (the bond payable in the Jones case) to fair value, with the gain or loss recorded in earnings, the accounting for the Jones bond payable deviates from amortized cost. This special accounting is justified in order to report accurately the nature of the hedging relationship between the swap and the bond payable in the balance sheet (both the swap and the debt obligation are recorded at fair value) and in the income statement (offsetting gains and losses are reported in the same period).[39]

INTERNATIONAL PERSPECTIVE

International accounting for hedges (*IAS 39*) is similar to the provisions of GAAP.

CONTROVERSY AND CONCLUDING REMARKS

Companies need rules to properly measure and report derivatives in financial statements. However, some argue that reporting derivatives at fair value results in unrealized gains and losses that are difficult to interpret. Still, others raise concerns about the complexity and cost of implementing GAAP in this area.

However, we believe that the long-term benefits of using fair value and reporting derivatives at fair value will far outweigh any short-term implementation costs. As the volume and complexity of derivatives and hedging transactions continue to grow, so does the risk that investors and creditors will be exposed to unexpected losses arising from derivative transactions. Statement readers must have comprehensive information concerning many derivative financial instruments and the effects of hedging transactions using derivatives.

---

[38]Jones will apply similar accounting and measurement at future interest payment dates. Thus, if interest rates increase, Jones will continue to receive 8 percent on the swap (records a loss) but will also be locked into the fixed payments to the bondholders at an 8 percent rate (records a gain).

[39]An interest rate swap can also be used in a cash flow hedge. A common setting is the cash flow risk inherent in having variable rate debt as part of a company's debt structure. In this situation, the variable debt issuer can hedge the cash flow risk by entering into a swap contract to receive variable rate cash flows but pay fixed rate. The cash received on the swap contract will offset the variable cash flows to be paid on the debt obligation.

SUMMARY OF LEARNING OBJECTIVES FOR APPENDIX 17A

9 **Explain who uses derivatives and why.** Any company or individual that wants to ensure against different types of business risks may use derivative contracts to achieve this objective. In general, these transactions involve some type of hedge. Speculators also use derivatives, attempting to find an enhanced return. Speculators are very important to the derivatives market because they keep it liquid on a daily basis. Arbitrageurs attempt to exploit inefficiencies in various derivative contracts. A company primarily uses derivatives for purposes of hedging its exposure to fluctuations in interest rates, foreign currency exchange rates, and commodity prices.

10 **Understand the basic guidelines for accounting for derivatives.** Companies should recognize derivatives in the financial statements as assets and liabilities, and report them at fair value. Companies should recognize gains and losses resulting from speculation immediately in income. They report gains and losses resulting from hedge transactions in different ways, depending on the type of hedge.

11 **Describe the accounting for derivative financial instruments.** Companies report derivative financial instruments in the balance sheet, and record them at fair value. Except for derivatives used in hedging, companies record realized and unrealized gains and losses on derivative financial instruments in income.

12 **Explain how to account for a fair value hedge.** A company records the derivative used in a qualifying fair value hedge at its fair value in the balance sheet, recording any gains and losses in income. In addition, the company also accounts for the item being hedged with the derivative at fair value. By adjusting the hedged item to fair value, with the gain or loss recorded in earnings, the accounting for the hedged item may deviate from GAAP in the absence of a hedge relationship. This special accounting is justified in order to report accurately the nature of the hedging relationship between the derivative hedging instruments and the hedged item. A company reports both in the balance sheet, reporting offsetting gains and losses in income in the same period.

13 **Explain how to account for a cash flow hedge.** Companies account for derivatives used in qualifying cash flow hedges at fair value on the balance sheet, but record gains or losses in equity as part of other comprehensive income. Companies accumulate these gains or losses, and reclassify them in income when the hedged transaction's cash flows affect earnings. Accounting is according to GAAP for the hedged item.

14 **Identify special reporting issues related to derivative financial instruments that cause unique accounting problems.** A company should separate a derivative that is embedded in a hybrid security from the host security, and account for it using the accounting for derivatives. This separation process is referred to as bifurcation. Special hedge accounting is allowed only for hedging relationships that meet certain criteria. The main criteria are: (1) There is formal documentation of the hedging relationship, the company's risk management objective, and the strategy for undertaking the hedge, and the company designates the derivative as either a cash flow or fair value hedge. (2) The company expects the hedging relationship to be highly effective in achieving offsetting changes in fair value or cash flows. (3) "Special" hedge accounting is necessary only when there is a mismatch of the accounting effects for the hedging instrument and the hedged item under GAAP.

KEY TERMS

anticipated transaction, *1011*

arbitrageurs, *1002*

bifurcation, *1012*

call option, *1004*

cash flow hedge, *1010*

counterparty, *1004* (*n*)

derivative financial instrument, derivative, *1001*

designation, *1013*

documentation, *1013*

embedded derivative, *1012*

fair value hedge, *1008*

forward contract, *1001*

futures contract, *1010*

hedging, *1008*

highly effective, *1013*

host security, *1012*

hybrid security, *1012*

interest rate swap, *1015*

intrinsic value, *1004*

net settlement, *1005* (*n*)

notional amount, *1004*

option contract, *1001*

option premium, *1004*

put option, *1004* (*n*)

risk management, *1013*

speculators, *1002*

spot price, *1010*

strike (exercise) price, *1004*

swap, *1015*

time value, *1005*

underlying, *1006*

APPENDIX **17B**	**VARIABLE-INTEREST ENTITIES**

LEARNING OBJECTIVE **15**
Describe the accounting for variable-interest entitles.

The FASB has issued rules to address the concern that some companies are not reporting the risks and rewards of certain investments and other financial arrangements in their consolidated financial statements. [12] As one analyst noted, Enron showed the world the power of the idea that "if investors can't see it, they can't ask you about it—the 'it' being assets and liabilities."

What exactly did Enron do? First, it created a number of entities whose purpose was to hide debt, avoid taxes, and enrich certain management personnel to the detriment of the company and its stockholders. In effect, these entities, called **special-purpose entities (SPEs)**, appeared to be separate entities for which Enron had a limited economic interest. For many of these arrangements, Enron actually had a substantial economic interest; the risks and rewards of ownership were not shifted to the entities but remained with Enron. In short, Enron was obligated to repay investors in these SPEs when they were unsuccessful. Once Enron's problems were discovered, it soon became apparent that many other companies had similar problems.

WHAT ABOUT GAAP?

A reasonable question to ask with regard to SPEs is, "Why didn't GAAP prevent companies from hiding SPE debt and other risks, by forcing companies to include these obligations in their consolidated financial statements?" To understand why, we have to look at the basic rules of consolidation.

The GAAP rules indicate that consolidated financial statements are "usually necessary for a fair presentation when one of the companies in the group directly or indirectly has a controlling financial interest in other companies." They further note that "the usual condition for a controlling financial interest is ownership of a majority voting interest."[40] In other words, if a company, like Intel, owns more than 50 percent of the voting stock of another company, Intel consolidates that company. GAAP also indicates that controlling financial interest may be achieved through arrangements that do not involve voting interests. However, applying these guidelines in practice is difficult.

Whenever GAAP uses a clear line, like "greater than 50 percent," companies sometimes exploit the criterion. For example, some companies set up joint ventures in which each party owns exactly 50 percent. In that case, neither party consolidates. Or like Coca-Cola, a company may own less than 50 percent of the voting stock but maintain effective control through board of director relationships, supply relationships, or through some other type of financial arrangement.

So the FASB realized that changes had to be made to GAAP for consolidations, and it issued expanded consolidation guidelines. These guidelines define when a company should use factors other than voting interest to determine controlling financial interest. In this pronouncement, the FASB created a new risk-and-reward model to be used in situations where voting interests were unclear. The risk-and-reward model answers the basic questions of who stands to gain or lose the most from ownership in an SPE when ownership is uncertain.

In other words, we now have two models for consolidation:

1. **Voting-interest model**—If a company owns more than 50 percent of another company, then consolidate in most cases.

2. **Risk-and-reward model**—If a company is involved substantially in the economics of another company, then consolidate.

[40]"Consolidation of Certain Special Purpose Entities," Proposed Interpretation (Norwalk, Conn.: FASB, June 28, 2002).

Operationally, the voting-interest model is easy to apply: It sets a "bright line" ownership standard of more than 50 percent of the voting stock. However, if companies cannot determine control based on voting interest, they may use the risk-and-reward model.

CONSOLIDATION OF VARIABLE-INTEREST ENTITIES

To answer the question of who gains or loses when voting rights do not determine consolidation, the FASB developed the risk-and-reward model. In this model, the FASB introduced the notion of a variable-interest entity. A **variable-interest entity (VIE)** is an entity that has one of the following characteristics:

1. *Insufficient equity investment at risk.* Stockholders are assumed to have sufficient capital investment to support the entity's operations. If thinly capitalized, the entity is considered a VIE and is subject to the risk-and-reward model.

2. *Stockholders lack decision-making rights.* In some cases, stockholders do not have the influence to control the company's destiny.

3. *Stockholders do not absorb the losses or receive the benefits of a normal stockholder.* In some entities, stockholders are shielded from losses related to their primary risks, or their returns are capped or must be shared with other parties.

Once the company determines that an entity is a variable-interest entity, it no longer can use the voting-interest model. The question that must then be asked is, "What party is exposed to the majority of the risks and rewards associated with the VIE?" This party is called the primary beneficiary and must consolidate the VIE. Illustration 17B-1 shows the decision model for the VIE consolidation model.[41]

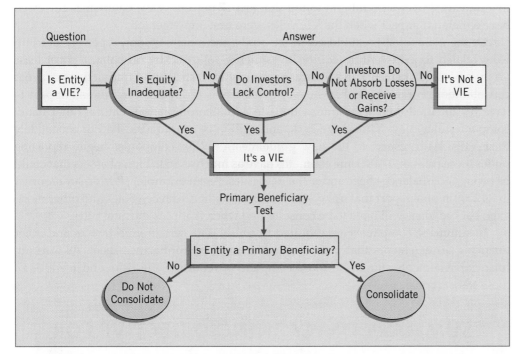

ILLUSTRATION 17B-1
VIE Consolidation Model

[41]In a recent amendment to the VIE consolidation rules, the FASB expanded the factors to be considered when deciding whether a VIE should be consolidated. The new guidelines require evaluation of qualitative factors related to the power to direct activities of the VIE and assessment of obligations to absorb losses or rights to receive benefits from the VIE. These qualitative factors must be considered in addition to the quantitative analysis of the expected losses of the entity to determine consolidation. [13] As discussed earlier in the chapter (see the "What Do the Numbers Mean?" box on page 990), the FASB and IASB deliberations on consolidation accounting may further modify these rules.

Some Examples

Let's look at a couple of examples to illustrate how this process works.

Example 1

Assume that Citigroup sells notes receivable to another entity called RAKO. RAKO's assets are financed in two ways: Lenders provide 90 percent, and investors provide the remaining 10 percent as an equity investment. If Citigroup does not guarantee the debt, Citigroup has low or nonexistent risk. Therefore, Citigroup would not consolidate the assets and liabilities of RAKO. On the other hand, if Citigroup guarantees RAKO's debt, then RAKO is a VIE, and Citigroup is the primary beneficiary. In that case, Citigroup must consolidate.

Example 2

San Diego Gas and Electric (SDGE) is required by law to buy power from small, local producers. In some cases, SDGE has contracts requiring it to purchase substantially all the power generated by these local companies over their lifetime. Because SDGE controls the outputs of the producers, they are VIEs. In this case, the risks and rewards related to ownership apply to SDGE. In other words, it is the primary beneficiary, and SDGE should include these producers in the consolidated financial statements.

Note that the primary beneficiary may have the risks and rewards of ownership through use of a variety of instruments and financial arrangements, such as equity investments, loans to the VIE, leases, derivatives, and guarantees. Potential VIEs include the following: corporations, partnerships, limited liability companies, and majority-owned subsidiaries.

What Is Happening in Practice?

For most companies, the reporting related to VIEs will not materially affect their financial statements. As shown in Illustration 17B-2, one study of 509 companies with total market values over $500 million found that just 17 percent of the companies reviewed have a material impact when the VIE rules were first implemented.

Of the material VIEs disclosed in the study, the most common types (42 percent) were related to joint-venture equity investments, followed by off-balance-sheet lease arrangements (22 percent). In some cases, companies restructured transactions to avoid consolidation. For example, Pep Boys, Choice Point, Inc., and Anadarko all appear to have restructured their lease transactions to avoid consolidation. On the other hand, companies like eBay, Kimberly-Clark, and Williams-Sonoma Inc. had to consolidate their VIEs. With respect to the new guidelines for VIEs, companies began reporting under these rules in 2010. Some estimates have as much as $5 trillion of assets that could be brought on-balance-sheet under the new rules. As an example, JP Morgan reported in its 2009 annual report that up to $160 billion of credit card receivables and other mortgage-backed loans will have to be consolidated when it adopts the new rules.

In summary, companies are required to consolidate certain investments and other financing arrangements that previously were reported off-balance-sheet. As a result, financial statements should be more complete in reporting the risks and rewards of these transactions.

ILLUSTRATION 17B-2
Impact of Rule Involving
Risk-and-Reward Model

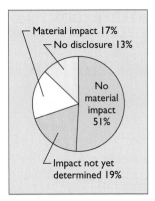

- Material impact 17%
- No disclosure 13%
- No material impact 51%
- Impact not yet determined 19%

Source: Company Reports, *Glass, Lewis, & Co. Research Report* (November 6, 2003).

KEY TERMS

risk-and-reward model, *1020*

special-purpose entity (SPE), *1020*

variable-interest entity (VIE), *1021*

voting-interest model, *1020*

SUMMARY OF LEARNING OBJECTIVE FOR APPENDIX 17B

15 **Describe the accounting for variable-interest entities.** Special variable-interest accounting is used in situations where control cannot be determined based on voting rights. A company is required to consolidate a variable-interest entity if it is the primary beneficiary of the variable-interest entity.

APPENDIX 17C   **FAIR VALUE MEASUREMENTS AND DISCLOSURES**

As indicated in the chapter, the FASB believes that fair value information is relevant for making effective business decisions. However, others express concern about fair value measurements for two reasons: (1) the lack of reliability related to the fair value measurement in certain cases, and (2) the ability to manipulate fair value measurements to achieve financial results inconsistent with the underlying economics of the situation.

The Board recognizes these concerns and has attempted to develop a sound conceptual basis for measuring and reporting fair value information. In addition, it has placed emphasis on developing guidelines for reporting fair value information for financial instruments, because many of these instruments have relatively active markets for which valuations can be reliably determined. The purpose of this appendix is to explain the disclosure requirements for financial instruments related to fair value information.

DISCLOSURE OF FAIR VALUE INFORMATION: FINANCIAL INSTRUMENTS—NO FAIR VALUE OPTION

One requirement related to fair value disclosure is that both the cost and the fair value of all financial instruments be reported in the notes to the financial statements. [14] This enables readers of the financial statements to understand the fair value of the company's financial instruments and the potential gains and losses that might occur in the future as a result of these instruments.

The Board also decided that companies should disclose information that enables users to determine the extent of usage of fair value and the inputs used to implement fair value measurement. Two reasons for additional disclosure beyond the simple itemization of fair values are:

1. Differing levels of reliability exist in the measurement of fair value information; it therefore is important to understand the varying risks involved in measurement. It is difficult to incorporate these levels of uncertainty into the financial statements. Disclosure provides a framework for addressing the qualitative aspects related to risk and measurement.

2. Changes in the fair value of financial instruments are reported differently in the financial statements, depending upon the type of financial instrument involved and whether the fair value option is employed. Note disclosure provides an opportunity to explain more precisely the impact that changes in the value of financial instruments have on financial results. In assessing the inputs, the Board recognizes that the reliability of the fair value measurement is of extreme importance. Many financial instruments are traded in active markets, and their valuation is not difficult. Other instruments are complex/illiquid, and their valuation is difficult.

To highlight these levels of reliability in valuation, the FASB established a fair value hierarchy. As discussed in Chapter 2 (page 59), this hierarchy identifies three broad levels—1, 2, and 3—related to the measurement of fair values. Level 1 is the most reliable measurement because fair value is based on quoted prices in active markets *for identical assets or liabilities*. Level 2 is less reliable; it is not based on quoted market prices for identical assets and liabilities but instead may be based on *similar assets or liabilities*. Level 3 is least reliable; it uses unobservable inputs that reflect the company's assumption as to the value of the financial instrument.

Illustration 17C-1 is an example of a fair value note disclosure for Sabathia Company. It includes both the fair value amounts and the reliability level. (A similar disclosure would be presented for liabilities.)

ILLUSTRATION 17C-1
Example of Fair Value Hierarchy

		SABATHIA COMPANY		
		NOTES TO THE FINANCIAL STATEMENTS		
($ in 000s)		Fair Value Measurements at Reporting Data Using		
Description	Fair Value 12/31/12	Quoted Prices in Active Markets for Identical Assets (Level 1)	Significant Other Observable Inputs (Level 2)	Significant Unobservable Inputs (Level 3)
Trading securities	$115	$105	$10	
Available-for-sale securities	75	75		
Derivatives	60	25	15	$20
Venture capital investments	10			10
Total	$260	$205	$25	$30

For assets and liabilities measured at fair value and classified as Level 3, a reconciliation of Level 3 changes for the period is required. In addition, companies should report an analysis of how Level 3 changes in fair value affect total gains and losses and their impact on net income. Illustration 17C-2 is an example of this disclosure.

ILLUSTRATION 17C-2
Reconciliation of Level 3 Inputs

	SABATHIA COMPANY		
	NOTES TO THE FINANCIAL STATEMENTS		
($ in 000s)	Fair Value Measurements Using Significant Unobservable Inputs (Level 3)		
	Derivatives	Venture Capital Investments	Total
Beginning balance	$14	$11	$25
Total gains or losses (realized/unrealized)			
Included in earnings (or changes in net assets)	11	(3)	8
Included in other comprehensive income	4		4
Purchases, issuances, and settlements	(7)	2	(5)
Transfers in and/or out of Level 3	(2)		(2)
Ending balance	$20	$10	$30
The amount of total gains or losses for the period included in earnings (or changes in net assets) attributable to the change in unrealized gains or losses relating to assets still held at the reporting date	$7	$2	$9

Gains and losses (realized and unrealized) included in earnings (or changes in net assets) for the period (above) are reported in trading revenues and in other revenues as follows.

	Trading Revenues	Other Revenues
Total gains or losses included in earnings (or changes in net assets) for the period (as shown in the table above)	$11	$(3)
Change in unrealized gains or losses relating to assets still held at reporting date	$7	$2

Sabathia Company's disclosure provides to the user of the financial statements an understanding of the following:

1. The carrying amount and the fair value of the company's financial instruments segregated by level of reliability. Thus the reader of the financial statements has a basis for judging what credence should be given to the fair value amounts.

2. For Level 3 financial instruments, a reconciliation of the balance from the beginning to the end of the period. This reconciliation enables the reader to understand the composition of the change. It is important because these calculations are most affected by subjective estimates and could be subject to manipulation.

3. The impact of changes in fair value on the net assets of the company from one period to the next.

DISCLOSURE OF FAIR VALUE INFORMATION: FINANCIAL INSTRUMENTS—FAIR VALUE OPTION

Some companies may choose to use the fair value option for some or all of their financial instruments. [15] In that case, companies have the option of incorporating the entire guidelines related to fair value measurement into one master schedule, or they can provide in a separate schedule information related solely to the fair value option. Illustration 17C-3 for Sheets Company includes only information related to the fair value option. It integrates the disclosure of the carrying amount in addition to the fair value disclosure.

ILLUSTRATION 17C-3
Disclosure of Fair Value Option

SHEETS COMPANY							
NOTES TO THE FINANCIAL STATEMENTS							
($ in 000s)		Fair Value Measurements at December 31, 2012, Using			Changes in Fair Values for the 12-Month Period Ended December 31, 2012, for Items Measured at Fair Value Pursuant to Election of the Fair Value Option		
Description	Fair Value Measure-ments 12/31/12	Quoted Prices in Active Markets for Identical Assets (Level 1)	Significant Other Observable Inputs (Level 2)	Significant Unobservable Inputs (Level 3)	Other Gains and Losses	Interest Income on Loans	Interest Expense on Long-Term Debt	Total Changes in Fair Values Included in Current-Period Earnings
Trading securities	$115	$105	$ 10					
Available-for-sale securities	75	75						
Loans	150	0	100	$ 50	$ (3)	$10		$ 7
Derivatives	60	25	15	20				
Private equity investments*	75	0	25	50	(18)			(18)
Long-term debt	(60)	(30)	(10)	(20)	13		$(4)	9

*Represents investments that would otherwise be accounted for under the equity method of accounting.

Loans are included in loans and lease receivables in the statement of financial position. As of December 31, 2012, approximately $160,000 of lease receivables are included in loans and lease receivables in the statement of financial position and are not eligible for the fair value option.

Source: Adapted from *FASB ASC 825-10-25* (Norwalk, Conn.: FASB, February 2007), Table 2, p. 47.

DISCLOSURE OF FAIR VALUES: IMPAIRED ASSETS OR LIABILITIES

In addition to financial instruments, companies often have assets or liabilities that are remeasured on a nonrecurring basis due to impairment. In this case the fair value hierarchy can highlight the reliability of the measurement, coupled with the related gain or loss for the period. Illustration 17C-4 highlights this disclosure for McClung Company.

ILLUSTRATION 17C-4
Disclosure of Fair Value, with Impairment

McCLUNG COMPANY
NOTES TO THE FINANCIAL STATEMENTS

($ in millions)		Fair Value Measurements Using		
Description	Year Ended 12/31/12	Quoted Prices in Active Markets for Identical Assets (Level 1)	Significant Other Observable Inputs (Level 2)	Significant Unobservable Inputs (Level 3)
Long-lived assets held and used	$75		$75	
Goodwill	30			$30
Long-lived assets held for sale	26		26	

Long-lived assets held and used with a carrying amount of $100 million were written down to their fair value of $75 million, resulting in an impairment charge of $25 million, which was included in earnings for the period.

Goodwill with a carrying amount of $65 million was written down to its implied fair value of $30 million, resulting in an impairment charge of $35 million, which was included in earnings for the period.

In accordance with the provisions of the Impairment or Disposal of Long-Lived Assets Subsections of FASB Codification Subtopic 360-10, long-lived assets held for sale with a carrying amount of $35 million were written down to their fair value of $26 million, less cost to sell of $6 million (or $20 million), resulting in a loss of $15 million, which was included in earnings for the period.

FASB CODIFICATION

FASB Codification References

[1] FASB ASC Glossary. [Predecessor literature: "Accounting for Certain Investments in Debt and Equity Securities," *Statement of Financial Accounting Standards No. 115* (Norwalk, Conn.: FASB 1993), par. 137.]

[2] FASB ASC 820-10-20. [Predecessor literature: "Fair Value Measurement," *Statement of Financial Accounting Standards No. 157* (Norwalk, Conn.: FASB, September 2006).]

[3] FASB ASC 220. [Predecessor literature: "Reporting Comprehensive Income," *Statement of Financial Accounting Standards No. 130* (Norwalk, Conn.: FASB, 1997).]

[4] FASB ASC 323-10-15. [Predecessor literature: "The Equity Method of Accounting for Investments in Common Stock," *Opinions of the Accounting Principles Board No. 18* (New York: AICPA, 1971), par. 17.]

[5] FASB ASC 323-10-15-10. [Predecessor literature: "Criteria for Applying the Equity Method of Accounting for Investments in Common Stock," *Interpretations of the Financial Accounting Standards Board No. 35* (Stamford, Conn.: FASB, 1981).]

[6] FASB ASC 323-10-35. [Predecessor literature: "The Equity Method of Accounting for Investments in Common Stock," *Opinions of the Accounting Principles Board No. 18* (New York: AICPA, 1971), par. 19(i).]

[7] FASB ASC 815-10-05. [Predecessor literature: "Accounting for Derivative Instruments and Hedging Activities," *Statement of Financial Accounting Standards No. 133* (Stamford, Conn.: FASB, 1998).]

[8] FASB ASC 820-10. [Predecessor literature: "Fair Value Measurement," *Statement of Financial Accounting Standards No. 157* (Norwalk, Conn.: FASB, September 2006).]

[9] FASB ASC 815-10-05-4. [Predecessor literature: "Accounting for Derivative Instruments and Hedging Activities," *Statement of Financial Accounting Standards No. 133* (Stamford, Conn.: FASB, 1998), par. 249.]

[10] FASB ASC 815-10-05-4. [Predecessor literature: "Accounting for Derivative Instruments and Hedging Activities," *Statement of Financial Accounting Standards No. 133* (Stamford, Conn.: FASB, 1998).]

[11] FASB ASC 825-10-25-1. [Predecessor literature: "The Fair Value Option for Financial Assets and Liabilities, Including an Amendment of FASB Statement No. 115," *Statement of Financial Accounting Standards No. 159* (Norwalk, Conn.: FASB, February 2007).]

[12] FASB ASC 810-10-05. [Predecessor literature: "Consolidation of Variable Interest Entities (revised)—An Interpretation of *ARB No. 51*," *Financial Accounting Standards Interpretation No. 46(R)* (Norwalk, Conn.: FASB, December 2003).]

[13] FASB ASC 810-10-15. [Predecessor literature: "Consolidation of Variable Interest Entities (revised)—An Interpretation of *ARB No. 51*," *Financial Accounting Standards Interpretation No. 46(R)* (Norwalk, Conn.: FASB, December 2003.).]

[14] FASB ASC 820-10. [Predecessor literature: "Fair Value Measurement," *Statement of Financial Accounting Standards No. 157* (Norwalk, Conn.: FASB, September 2006).]

[15] FASB ASC 825-10-25-1. (Predecessor literature: "The Fair Value Option for Financial Assets and Liabilities, Including an Amendment of FASB Statement No. 115," *Statement of Financial Accounting Standards No. 159* (Norwalk, Conn.: FASB, February 2007).]

Exercises

If your school has a subscription to the FASB Codification, go to *http://aaahq.org/ascLogin.cfm* to log in and prepare responses to the following. Provide Codification references for your responses.

CE17-1 Access the glossary ("Master Glossary") to answer the following.
    (a) What are trading securities?
    (b) What is the definition of "holding gain or loss"?
    (c) What is a cash flow hedge?
    (d) What is a fair value hedge?

CE17-2 What guidance does the SEC give for disclosures regarding accounting policies used for derivatives?

CE17-3 When would an investor discontinue applying the equity method in an investment? Are there any exceptions to this rule?

CE17-4 For balance sheet purposes, can the fair value of a derivative in a loss position be netted against the fair value of a derivative in a gain position?

An additional Codification case can be found in the Using Your Judgment section, on page 1047.

Be sure to check the book's companion website for a Review and Analysis Exercise, with solution.

 Questions, Brief Exercises, Exercises, Problems, and many more resources are available for practice in WileyPLUS.

Note: All asterisked Questions, Exercises, and Problems relate to material in the appendices to the chapter.

QUESTIONS

1. Distinguish between a debt security and an equity security.

2. What purpose does the variety in bond features (types and characteristics) serve?

3. What is the cost of a long-term investment in bonds?

4. Identify and explain the three types of classifications for investments in debt securities.

5. When should a debt security be classified as held-to-maturity?

6. Explain how trading securities are accounted for and reported.

7. At what amount should trading, available-for-sale, and held-to-maturity securities be reported on the balance sheet?

8. On July 1, 2012, Wheeler Company purchased $4,000,000 of Duggen Company's 8% bonds, due on July 1, 2019. The bonds, which pay interest semiannually on January 1 and July 1, were purchased for $3,500,000 to yield 10%. Determine the amount of interest revenue Wheeler should report on its income statement for the year ended December 31, 2012.

9. If the bonds in question 8 are classified as available-for-sale and they have a fair value at December 31, 2012, of $3,604,000, prepare the journal entry (if any) at December 31, 2012, to record this transaction.

10. Indicate how unrealized holding gains and losses should be reported for investments securities classified as trading, available-for-sale, and held-to-maturity.

11. (a) Assuming no Fair Value Adjustment (available-for-sale) account balance at the beginning of the year, prepare the adjusting entry at the end of the year if Laura Company's available-for-sale securities have a fair value $60,000 below cost. (b) Assume the same information as part (a), except that Laura Company has a debit balance in its Fair Value Adjustment account of $10,000 at the beginning of the year. Prepare the adjusting entry at year-end.

12. Identify and explain the different types of classifications for investment in equity securities.

13. Why are held-to-maturity investments applicable only to debt securities?

14. Hayes Company sold 10,000 shares of Kenyon Co. common stock for $27.50 per share, incurring $1,770 in brokerage commissions. These securities were classified as trading and originally cost $260,000. Prepare the entry to record the sale of these securities.

15. Distinguish between the accounting treatment for available-for-sale equity securities and trading equity securities.

16. What constitutes "significant influence" when an investor's financial interest is below the 50% level?

17. Explain how the investment account is affected by investee activities under the equity method.

18. When the equity method is applied, what disclosures should be made in the investor's financial statements?

19. Hiram Co. uses the equity method to account for investments in common stock. What accounting should be made for dividends received from these investments subsequent to the date of investment?

20. Raleigh Corp. has an investment with a carrying value (equity method) on its books of $170,000 representing a 30% interest in Borg Company, which suffered a $620,000 loss this year. How should Raleigh Corp. handle its proportionate share of Borg's loss?

21. Where on the asset side of the balance sheet are trading securities, available-for-sale securities, and held-to-maturity securities reported? Explain.

22. Explain why reclassification adjustments are necessary.

23. Briefly discuss how a transfer of securities from the available-for-sale category to the trading category affects stockholders' equity and income.

24. When is a debt security considered impaired? Explain how to account for the impairment of an available-for-sale debt security.

25. What is the GAAP definition of fair value?

26. What is the fair value option?

27. Franklin Corp. has an investment that it has held for several years. When it purchased the investment, Franklin classified and accounted for it as available-for-sale. Can Franklin use the fair value option for this investment? Explain.

*28. What is meant by the term underlying as it relates to derivative financial instruments?

*29. What are the main distinctions between a traditional financial instrument and a derivative financial instrument?

*30. What is the purpose of a fair value hedge?

*31. In what situation will the unrealized holding gain or loss on an available-for-sale security be reported in income?

*32. Why might a company become involved in an interest rate swap contract to receive fixed interest payments and pay variable?

*33. What is the purpose of a cash flow hedge?

*34. Where are gains and losses related to cash flow hedges involving anticipated transactions reported?

*35. What are hybrid securities? Give an example of a hybrid security.

*36. Explain the difference between the voting-interest model and the risk-and-reward model used for consolidation.

*37. What is a variable-interest entity?

BRIEF EXERCISES

BE17-1 Garfield Company purchased, as a held-to-maturity investment, $80,000 of the 9%, 5-year bonds of Chester Corporation for $74,086, which provides an 11% return. Prepare Garfield's journal entries for (a) the purchase of the investment, and (b) the receipt of annual interest and discount amortization. Assume effective-interest amortization is used.

BE17-2 Use the information from BE17-1, but assume the bonds are purchased as an available-for-sale security. Prepare Garfield's journal entries for (a) the purchase of the investment, (b) the receipt of annual interest and discount amortization, and (c) the year-end fair value adjustment. The bonds have a year-end fair value of $75,500.

2 **BE17-3** Carow Corporation purchased, as a held-to-maturity investment, $60,000 of the 8%, 5-year bonds of Harrison, Inc. for $65,118, which provides a 6% return. The bonds pay interest semiannually. Prepare Carow's journal entries for (a) the purchase of the investment, and (b) the receipt of semiannual interest and premium amortization. Assume effective-interest amortization is used.

2 **BE17-4** Hendricks Corporation purchased trading investment bonds for $50,000 at par. At December 31, Hendricks received annual interest of $2,000, and the fair value of the bonds was $47,400. Prepare Hendricks' journal entries for (a) the purchase of the investment, (b) the interest received, and (c) the fair value adjustment.

3 **BE17-5** Fairbanks Corporation purchased 400 shares of Sherman Inc. common stock as an available-for-sale investment for $13,200. During the year, Sherman paid a cash dividend of $3.25 per share. At year-end, Sherman stock was selling for $34.50 per share. Prepare Fairbanks's journal entries to record (a) the purchase of the investment, (b) the dividends received, and (c) the fair value adjustment.

3 **BE17-6** Use the information from BE17-5 but assume the stock was purchased as a trading security. Prepare Fairbanks's journal entries to record (a) the purchase of the investment, (b) the dividends received, and (c) the fair value adjustment.

4 **BE17-7** Zoop Corporation purchased for $300,000 a 30% interest in Murphy, Inc. This investment enables Zoop to exert significant influence over Murphy. During the year, Murphy earned net income of $180,000 and paid dividends of $60,000. Prepare Zoop's journal entries related to this investment.

3 **BE17-8** Cleveland Company has a stock portfolio valued at $4,000. Its cost was $3,300. If the Fair Value Adjustment account has a debit balance of $200, prepare the journal entry at year-end.

7 **BE17-9** The following information relates to Starbucks for the year ended September 30, 2009: net income $390.8 million; unrealized holding gain of $9.8 million related to available-for-sale securities during the year; accumulated other comprehensive income of $48.4 million on September 28, 2008. Assuming no other changes in accumulated other comprehensive income, determine (a) other comprehensive income for 2009, (b) comprehensive income for 2009, and (c) accumulated other comprehensive income at September 30, 2009.

6 **BE17-10** Hillsborough Co. has an available-for-sale investment in the bonds of Schuyler Corp. with a carrying (and fair) value of $70,000. Hillsborough determined that due to poor economic prospects for Schuyler, the bonds have decreased in value to $60,000. It is determined that this loss in value is other-than-temporary. Prepare the journal entry, if any, to record the reduction in value.

EXERCISES

1 **3** **E17-1 (Investment Classifications)** For the following investments, identify whether they are:

1. Trading
2. Available-for-Sale
3. Held-to-Maturity

Each case is independent of the other.

(a) A bond that will mature in 4 years was bought 1 month ago when the price dropped. As soon as the value increases, which is expected next month, it will be sold.
(b) 10% of the outstanding stock of Farm-Co was purchased. The company is planning on eventually getting a total of 30% of its outstanding stock.
(c) 10-year bonds were purchased this year. The bonds mature at the first of next year.
(d) Bonds that will mature in 5 years are purchased. The company would like to hold them until they mature, but money has been tight recently and they may need to be sold.
(e) A bond that matures in 10 years was purchased. The company is investing money set aside for an expansion project planned 10 years from now.
(f) Preferred stock was purchased for its constant dividend. The company is planning to hold the preferred stock for a long time.

2 **E17-2 (Entries for Held-to-Maturity Securities)** On January 1, 2012, Jennings Company purchased at par 10% bonds having a maturity value of $300,000. They are dated January 1, 2012, and mature January 1, 2017, with interest receivable December 31 of each year. The bonds are classified in the held-to-maturity category.

Instructions

(a) Prepare the journal entry at the date of the bond purchase.

(b) Prepare the journal entry to record the interest received for 2012.

(c) Prepare the journal entry to record the interest received for 2013.

E17-3 (Entries for Held-to-Maturity Securities) On January 1, 2011, Roosevelt Company purchased 12% bonds, having a maturity value of $500,000, for $537,907.40. The bonds provide the bondholders with a 10% yield. They are dated January 1, 2011, and mature January 1, 2016, with interest receivable December 31 of each year. Roosevelt Company uses the effective-interest method to allocate unamortized discount or premium. The bonds are classified in the held-to-maturity category.

Instructions

(a) Prepare the journal entry at the date of the bond purchase.

(b) Prepare a bond amortization schedule.

(c) Prepare the journal entry to record the interest received and the amortization for 2011.

(d) Prepare the journal entry to record the interest received and the amortization for 2012.

E17-4 (Entries for Available-for-Sale Securities) Assume the same information as in E17-3 except that the securities are classified as available-for-sale. The fair value of the bonds at December 31 of each year-end is as follows.

2011	$534,200	2014	$517,000
2012	$515,000	2015	$500,000
2013	$513,000		

Instructions

(a) Prepare the journal entry at the date of the bond purchase.

(b) Prepare the journal entries to record the interest received and recognition of fair value for 2011.

(c) Prepare the journal entry to record the recognition of fair value for 2012.

E17-5 (Effective-Interest versus Straight-Line Bond Amortization) On January 1, 2012, Morgan Company acquires $300,000 of Nicklaus, Inc., 9% bonds at a price of $278,384. The interest is payable each December 31, and the bonds mature December 31, 2014. The investment will provide Morgan Company a 12% yield. The bonds are classified as held-to-maturity.

Instructions

(a) Prepare a 3-year schedule of interest revenue and bond discount amortization, applying the straight-line method. (Round to nearest dollar.)

(b) Prepare a 3-year schedule of interest revenue and bond discount amortization, applying the effective-interest method. (Round to nearest cent.)

(c) Prepare the journal entry for the interest receipt of December 31, 2013, and the discount amortization under the straight-line method.

(d) Prepare the journal entry for the interest receipt of December 31, 2013, and the discount amortization under the effective-interest method.

E17-6 (Entries for Available-for-Sale and Trading Securities) The following information is available for Kinney Company at December 31, 2012, regarding its investments.

Securities	Cost	Fair Value
3,000 shares of Petty Corporation Common Stock	$40,000	$46,000
1,000 shares of Dowe Incorporated Preferred Stock	25,000	22,000
	$65,000	$68,000

Instructions

(a) Prepare the adjusting entry (if any) for 2012, assuming the securities are classified as trading.

(b) Prepare the adjusting entry (if any) for 2012, assuming the securities are classified as available-for-sale.

(c) Discuss how the amounts reported in the financial statements are affected by the entries in (a) and (b).

E17-7 (Trading Securities Entries) On December 21, 2012, Zurich Company provided you with the following information regarding its trading securities.

December 31, 2012

Investments (Trading)	Cost	Fair Value	Unrealized Gain (Loss)
Stargate Corp. stock	$20,000	$19,000	$(1,000)
Carolina Co. stock	10,000	9,000	(1,000)
Vectorman Co. stock	20,000	20,600	600
Total of portfolio	$50,000	$48,600	(1,400)
Previous fair value adjustment balance			–0–
Fair value adjustment—Cr.			$(1,400)

During 2013, Carolina Company stock was sold for $9,500. The fair value of the stock on December 31, 2013, was: Stargate Corp. stock—$19,300; Vectorman Co. stock—$20,500.

Instructions
(a) Prepare the adjusting journal entry needed on December 31, 2012.
(b) Prepare the journal entry to record the sale of the Carolina Company stock during 2013.
(c) Prepare the adjusting journal entry needed on December 31, 2013.

3 **E17-8 (Available-for-Sale Securities Entries and Reporting)** Player Corporation purchases equity securities costing $73,000 and classifies them as available-for-sale securities. At December 31, the fair value of the portfolio is $67,000.

Instructions
Prepare the adjusting entry to report the securities properly. Indicate the statement presentation of the accounts in your entry.

3 **E17-9 (Available-for-Sale Securities Entries and Financial Statement Presentation)** At December 31, 2012, the available-for-sale equity portfolio for Wenger, Inc. is as follows.

Security	Cost	Fair Value	Unrealized Gain (Loss)
A	$17,500	$15,000	($2,500)
B	12,500	14,000	1,500
C	23,000	25,500	2,500
Total	$53,000	$54,500	1,500
Previous fair value adjustment balance—Dr.			200
Fair value adjustment—Dr.			$1,300

On January 20, 2013, Wenger, Inc. sold security A for $15,300. The sale proceeds are net of brokerage fees.

Instructions
(a) Prepare the adjusting entry at December 31, 2012, to report the portfolio at fair value.
(b) Show the balance sheet presentation of the investment related accounts at December 31, 2012. (Ignore notes presentation.)
(c) Prepare the journal entry for the 2013 sale of security A.

7 **E17-10 (Comprehensive Income Disclosure)** Assume the same information as E17-9 and that Wenger, Inc. reports net income in 2012 of $120,000 and in 2013 of $140,000. Total holding gains (including any realized holding gain or loss) arising during 2013 total $30,000.

Instructions
(a) Prepare a statement of comprehensive income for 2012 starting with net income.
(b) Prepare a statement of comprehensive income for 2013 starting with net income.

3 **E17-11 (Equity Securities Entries)** Capriati Corporation made the following cash purchases of securities during 2012, which is the first year in which Capriati invested in securities.

1. On January 15, purchased 9,000 shares of Gonzalez Company's common stock at $33.50 per share plus commission $1,980.
2. On April 1, purchased 5,000 shares of Belmont Co.'s common stock at $52.00 per share plus commission $3,370.
3. On September 10, purchased 7,000 shares of Thep Co.'s preferred stock at $26.50 per share plus commission $4,910.

On May 20, 2012, Capriati sold 3,000 shares of Gonzalez Company's common stock at a market price of $35 per share less brokerage commissions, taxes, and fees of $2,850. The year-end fair values per share were: Gonzalez $30, Belmont $55, and Thep $28. In addition, the chief accountant of Capriati told you that Capriati Corporation plans to hold these securities for the long term but may sell them in order to earn profits from appreciation in prices.

Instructions
(a) Prepare the journal entries to record the above three security purchases.
(b) Prepare the journal entry for the security sale on May 20.
(c) Compute the unrealized gains or losses and prepare the adjusting entries for Capriati on December 31, 2012.

3 **4** **E17-12 (Journal Entries for Fair Value and Equity Methods)** Presented on page 1032 are two independent situations.

Situation 1

Hatcher Cosmetics acquired 10% of the 200,000 shares of common stock of Ramirez Fashion at a total cost of $14 per share on March 18, 2012. On June 30, Ramirez declared and paid a $75,000 cash dividend. On December 31, Ramirez reported net income of $122,000 for the year. At December 31, the market price of Ramirez Fashion was $15 per share. The securities are classified as available-for-sale.

Situation 2

Holmes, Inc. obtained significant influence over Nadal Corporation by buying 25% of Nadal's 30,000 outstanding shares of common stock at a total cost of $9 per share on January 1, 2012. On June 15, Nadal declared and paid a cash dividend of $36,000. On December 31, Nadal reported a net income of $85,000 for the year.

Instructions

Prepare all necessary journal entries in 2012 for both situations.

4 **E17-13 (Equity Method)** Gator Co. invested $1,000,000 in Demo Co. for 25% of its outstanding stock. Demo Co. pays out 40% of net income in dividends each year.

Instructions

Use the information in the following T-account for the investment in Demo to answer the following questions.

Equity Investments (Demo Co.)

1,000,000	
130,000	
	52,000

(a) How much was Gator Co.'s share of Demo Co.'s net income for the year?
(b) How much was Gator Co.'s share of Demo Co.'s dividends for the year?
(c) What was Demo Co.'s total net income for the year?
(d) What was Demo Co.'s total dividends for the year?

3 **E17-14 (Equity Investment—Trading)** Feiner Co. had purchased 300 shares of Guttman Co. for $40 each this year and classified the investment as a trading security. Feiner Co. sold 100 shares of the stock for $43 each. At year-end, the price per share of the Guttman Co. stock had dropped to $35.

Instructions

Prepare the journal entries for these transactions and any year-end adjustments.

3 **E17-15 (Equity Investments—Trading)** Swanson Company has the following securities in its trading portfolio of securities on December 31, 2012.

Investments (Trading)	Cost	Fair Value
1,500 shares of Parker, Inc., Common	$ 71,500	$ 69,000
5,000 shares of Beilman Corp., Common	180,000	175,000
400 shares of Duncan, Inc., Preferred	60,000	61,600
	$311,500	$305,600

All of the securities were purchased in 2012.

In 2013, Swanson completed the following securities transactions.

March 1   Sold the 1,500 shares of Parker, Inc., Common, @ $45 less fees of $1,200.
April 1   Bought 700 shares of McDowell Corp., Common, @ $75 plus fees of $1,300.

Swanson Company's portfolio of trading securities appeared as follows on December 31, 2013.

Investments (Trading)	Cost	Fair Value
5,000 shares of Beilman Corp., Common	$180,000	$175,000
700 shares of McDowell Corp., Common	53,800	50,400
400 shares of Duncan, Inc., Preferred	60,000	58,000
	$293,800	$283,400

Instructions

Prepare the general journal entries for Swanson Company for:

(a) The 2012 adjusting entry.
(b) The sale of the Parker stock.
(c) The purchase of the McDowell stock.
(d) The 2013 adjusting entry for the trading portfolio.

3 **4** **E17-16 (Fair Value and Equity Method Compared)** Gregory Inc. acquired 20% of the outstanding common stock of Handerson Inc. on December 31, 2012. The purchase price was $1,250,000 for 50,000 shares. Handerson Inc. declared and paid an $0.80 per share cash dividend on June 30 and on December 31, 2013. Handerson reported net income of $730,000 for 2013. The fair value of Handerson's stock was $27 per share at December 31, 2013.

Instructions
(a) Prepare the journal entries for Gregory Inc. for 2012, and 2013, assuming that Gregory cannot exercise significant influence over Handerson. The securities should be classified as available-for-sale.
(b) Prepare the journal entries for Gregory Inc. for 2012 and 2013, assuming that Gregory can exercise significant influence over Handerson.
(c) At what amount is the investment in securities reported on the balance sheet under each of these methods at December 31, 2013? What is the total net income reported in 2013 under each of these methods?

4 **E17-17 (Equity Method)** On January 1, 2012, Meredith Corporation purchased 25% of the common shares of Pirates Company for $200,000. During the year, Pirates earned net income of $80,000 and paid dividends of $20,000.

Instructions
Prepare the entries for Meredith to record the purchase and any additional entries related to this investment in Pirates Company in 2012.

6 **E17-18 (Impairment of Debt Securities)** Cairo Corporation has municipal bonds classified as available-for-sale at December 31, 2012. These bonds have a par value of $800,000, an amortized cost of $800,000, and a fair value of $740,000. The unrealized loss of $60,000 previously recognized as other comprehensive income and as a separate component of stockholders' equity is now determined to be other than temporary. That is, the company believes that impairment accounting is now appropriate for these bonds.

Instructions
(a) Prepare the journal entry to recognize the impairment.
(b) What is the new cost basis of the municipal bonds? Given that the maturity value of the bonds is $800,000, should Cairo Corporation amortize the difference between the carrying amount and the maturity value over the life of the bonds?
(c) At December 31, 2013, the fair value of the municipal bonds is $760,000. Prepare the entry (if any) to record this information.

3 **5** **E17-19 (Fair Value Measurement)** Presented below is information related to the purchases of common stock by Lilly Company during 2012.

	Cost (at purchase date)	Fair Value (at December 31)
Investment in Arroyo Company stock	$100,000	$ 80,000
Investment in Lee Corporation stock	250,000	300,000
Investment in Woods Inc. stock	180,000	190,000
Total	$530,000	$570,000

Instructions
(a) What entry would Lilly make at December 31, 2012, to record the investment in Arroyo Company stock if it chooses to report this security using the fair value option?
(b) What entry would Lilly make at December 31, 2012, to record the investment in Lee Corporation, assuming that Lilly wants to classify this security as available-for-sale? This security is the only available-for-sale security that Lilly presently owns.
(c) What entry would Lilly make at December 31, 2012, to record the investment in Woods Inc., assuming that Lilly wants to classify this investment as a trading security?

3 **5** **E17-20 (Fair Value Measurement Issues)** Assume the same information as in E17-19 for Lilly Company. In addition, assume that the investment in the Woods Inc. stock was sold during 2013 for $195,000. At December 31, 2013, the following information relates to its two remaining investments of common stock.

	Cost (at purchase date)	Fair Value (at December 31)
Investment in Arroyo Company stock	$100,000	$140,000
Investment in Lee Corporation stock	250,000	310,000
Total	$350,000	$450,000

Net income before any security gains and losses for 2013 was $905,000.

Instructions

(a) Compute the amount of net income or net loss that Lilly should report for 2013, taking into consideration Lilly's security transactions for 2013.

(b) Prepare the journal entry to record unrealized gain or loss related to the investment in Arroyo Company stock at December 31, 2013.

2 3 5 **E17-21 (Fair Value Option)** Presented below is selected information related to the financial instruments of Dawson Company at December 31, 2012. This is Dawson Company's first year of operations.

	Carrying Amount	Fair Value (at December 31)
Investment in debt securities (intent is to hold to maturity)	$ 40,000	$ 41,000
Investment in Chen Company stock	800,000	910,000
Bonds payable	220,000	195,000

Instructions

(a) Dawson elects to use the fair value option whenever possible. Assuming that Dawson's net income is $100,000 in 2012 before reporting any securities gains or losses, determine Dawson's net income for 2012.

(b) Record the journal entry, if any, necessary at December 31, 2012, to record the fair value option for the bonds payable.

11 *E17-22 (Derivative Transaction)** On January 2, 2012, Jones Company purchases a call option for $300 on Merchant common stock. The call option gives Jones the option to buy 1,000 shares of Merchant at a strike price of $50 per share. The market price of a Merchant share is $50 on January 2, 2012 (the intrinsic value is therefore $0). On March 31, 2012, the market price for Merchant stock is $53 per share, and the time value of the option is $200.

Instructions

(a) Prepare the journal entry to record the purchase of the call option on January 2, 2012.

(b) Prepare the journal entry(ies) to recognize the change in the fair value of the call option as of March 31, 2012.

(c) What was the effect on net income of entering into the derivative transaction for the period January 2 to March 31, 2012? (Ignore tax effects.)

12 *E17-23 (Fair Value Hedge)** On January 2, 2012, MacCloud Co. issued a 4-year, $100,000 note at 6% fixed interest, interest payable semiannually. MacCloud now wants to change the note to a variable-rate note.

As a result, on January 2, 2012, MacCloud Co. enters into an interest rate swap where it agrees to receive 6% fixed and pay LIBOR of 5.7% for the first 6 months on $100,000. At each 6-month period, the variable rate will be reset. The variable rate is reset to 6.7% on June 30, 2012.

Instructions

(a) Compute the net interest expense to be reported for this note and related swap transaction as of June 30, 2012.

(b) Compute the net interest expense to be reported for this note and related swap transaction as of December 31, 2012.

13 *E17-24 (Cash Flow Hedge)** On January 2, 2012, Parton Company issues a 5-year, $10,000,000 note at LIBOR, with interest paid annually. The variable rate is reset at the end of each year. The LIBOR rate for the first year is 5.8%.

Parton Company decides it prefers fixed-rate financing and wants to lock in a rate of 6%. As a result, Parton enters into an interest rate swap to pay 6% fixed and receive LIBOR based on $10 million. The variable rate is reset to 6.6% on January 2, 2013.

Instructions

(a) Compute the net interest expense to be reported for this note and related swap transactions as of December 31, 2012.

(b) Compute the net interest expense to be reported for this note and related swap transactions as of December 31, 2013.

12 *E17-25 (Fair Value Hedge)** Sarazan Company issues a 4-year, 7.5% fixed-rate interest only, non-prepayable $1,000,000 note payable on December 31, 2012. It decides to change the interest rate from a fixed rate to variable rate and enters into a swap agreement with M&S Corp. The swap agreement specifies that Sarazan will receive a fixed rate at 7.5% and pay variable with settlement dates that match the interest payments on the debt. Assume that interest rates have declined during 2013 and that Sarazan received $13,000 as an adjustment to interest expense for the settlement at December 31, 2013. The loss related to the debt (due to interest rate changes) was $48,000. The value of the swap contract increased $48,000.

Instructions

(a) Prepare the journal entry to record the payment of interest expense on December 31, 2013.

(b) Prepare the journal entry to record the receipt of the swap settlement on December 31, 2013.

(c) Prepare the journal entry to record the change in the fair value of the swap contract on December 31, 2013.

(d) Prepare the journal entry to record the change in the fair value of the debt on December 31, 2013.

11 *****E17-26 (Call Option)** On August 15, 2012, Outkast Co. invested idle cash by purchasing a call option on Counting Crows Inc. common shares for $360. The notional value of the call option is 400 shares, and the option price is $40. (Market price of an Outkast share is $40.) The option expires on January 31, 2013. The following data are available with respect to the call option.

Date	Market Price of Counting Crows Shares	Time Value of Call Option
September 30, 2012	$48 per share	$180
December 31, 2012	$46 per share	65
January 15, 2013	$47 per share	30

Instructions

Prepare the journal entries for Outkast for the following dates.

(a) Investment in call option on Counting Crows shares on August 15, 2012.

(b) September 30, 2012—Outkast prepares financial statements.

(c) December 31, 2012—Outkast prepares financial statements.

(d) January 15, 2013—Outkast settles the call option on the Counting Crows shares.

13 *****E17-27 (Cash Flow Hedge)** Hart Golf Co. uses titanium in the production of its specialty drivers. Hart anticipates that it will need to purchase 200 ounces of titanium in October 2012, for clubs that will be shipped in the holiday shopping season. However, if the price of titanium increases, this will increase the cost to produce the clubs, which will result in lower profit margins.

To hedge the risk of increased titanium prices, on May 1, 2012, Hart enters into a titanium futures contract and designates this futures contract as cash flow hedge of the anticipated titanium purchase. The notional amount of the contract is 200 ounces, and the terms of the contract give Hart the right and the obligation to purchase titanium at a price of $500 per ounce. The price will be good until the contract expires on November 30, 2012.

Assume the following data with respect to the price of the call options and the titanium inventory purchase.

Date	Spot Price for November Delivery
May 1, 2012	$500 per ounce
June 30, 2012	520 per ounce
September 30, 2013	525 per ounce

Instructions

Present the journal entries for the following dates/transactions.

(a) May 1, 2012—Inception of futures contract, no premium paid.

(b) June 30, 2012—Hart prepares financial statements.

(c) September 30, 2012—Hart prepares financial statements.

(d) October 5, 2012—Hart purchases 200 ounces of titanium at $525 per ounce and settles the futures contract.

(e) December 15, 2012—Hart sells clubs containing titanium purchased in October 2012 for $250,000. The cost of the finished goods inventory is $140,000.

(f) Indicate the amount(s) reported in the income statement related to the futures contract and the inventory transactions on December 31, 2012.

See the book's companion website, www.wiley.com/college/kieso, for a set of B Exercises.

PROBLEMS

2 **P17-1 (Debt Securities)** Presented below is an amortization schedule related to Spangler Company's 5-year, $100,000 bond with a 7% interest rate and a 5% yield, purchased on December 31, 2010, for $108,660.

Date	Cash Received	Interest Revenue	Bond Premium Amortization	Carrying Amount of Bonds
12/31/10				$108,660
12/31/11	$7,000	$5,433	$1,567	107,093
12/31/12	7,000	5,354	1,646	105,447
12/31/13	7,000	5,272	1,728	103,719
12/31/14	7,000	5,186	1,814	101,905
12/31/15	7,000	5,095	1,905	100,000

The following schedule presents a comparison of the amortized cost and fair value of the bonds at year-end.

	12/31/11	12/31/12	12/31/13	12/31/14	12/31/15
Amortized cost	$107,093	$105,447	$103,719	$101,905	$100,000
Fair value	$106,500	$107,500	$105,650	$103,000	$100,000

Instructions

(a) Prepare the journal entry to record the purchase of these bonds on December 31, 2010, assuming the bonds are classified as held-to-maturity securities.

(b) Prepare the journal entry(ies) related to the held-to-maturity bonds for 2011.

(c) Prepare the journal entry(ies) related to the held-to-maturity bonds for 2013.

(d) Prepare the journal entry(ies) to record the purchase of these bonds, assuming they are classified as available-for-sale.

(e) Prepare the journal entry(ies) related to the available-for-sale bonds for 2011.

(f) Prepare the journal entry(ies) related to the available-for-sale bonds for 2013.

2 **P17-2 (Available-for-Sale Debt Securities)** On January 1, 2012, Novotna Company purchased $400,000, 8% bonds of Aguirre Co. for $369,114. The bonds were purchased to yield 10% interest. Interest is payable semiannually on July 1 and January 1. The bonds mature on January 1, 2017. Novotna Company uses the effective-interest method to amortize discount or premium. On January 1, 2014, Novotna Company sold the bonds for $370,726 after receiving interest to meet its liquidity needs.

Instructions

(a) Prepare the journal entry to record the purchase of bonds on January 1. Assume that the bonds are classified as available-for-sale.

(b) Prepare the amortization schedule for the bonds.

(c) Prepare the journal entries to record the semiannual interest on July 1, 2012, and December 31, 2012.

(d) If the fair value of Aguirre bonds is $372,726 on December 31, 2013, prepare the necessary adjusting entry. (Assume the fair value adjustment balance on January 1, 2013, is a debit of $3,375.)

(e) Prepare the journal entry to record the sale of the bonds on January 1, 2014.

2 **3** **P17-3 (Available-for-Sale Investments)** Cardinal Paz Corp. carries an account in its general ledger called Investments, which contained debits for investment purchases, and no credits, with the following descriptions.

Feb. 1, 2012	Sharapova Company common stock, $100 par, 200 shares	$ 37,400
April 1	U.S. government bonds, 11%, due April 1, 2022, interest payable April 1 and October 1, 110 bonds of $1,000 par each	110,000
July 1	McGrath Company 12% bonds, par $50,000, dated March 1, 2012, purchased at 104 plus accrued interest, interest payable annually on March 1, due March 1, 2032	54,000

Instructions

(Round all computations to the nearest dollar.)

(a) Prepare entries necessary to classify the amounts into proper accounts, assuming that all the securities are classified as available-for-sale.

(b) Prepare the entry to record the accrued interest and the amortization of premium on December 31, 2012, using the straight-line method.

(c) The fair values of the investments on December 31, 2012, were:

Sharapova Company common stock	$ 31,800
U.S. government bonds	124,700
McGrath Company bonds	58,600

What entry or entries, if any, would you recommend be made?

(d) The U.S. government bonds were sold on July 1, 2013, for $119,200 plus accrued interest. Give the proper entry.

P17-4 (Available-for-Sale Debt Investments) Presented below is information taken from a bond investment amortization schedule with related fair values provided. These bonds are classified as available-for-sale.

	12/31/12	12/31/13	12/31/14
Amortized cost	$491,150	$519,442	$550,000
Fair value	$497,000	$509,000	$550,000

Instructions

(a) Indicate whether the bonds were purchased at a discount or at a premium.

(b) Prepare the adjusting entry to record the bonds at fair value at December 31, 2012. The Fair Value Adjustment account has a debit balance of $1,000 prior to adjustment.

(c) Prepare the adjusting entry to record the bonds at fair value at December 31, 2013.

P17-5 (Equity Securities Entries and Disclosures) Parnevik Company has the following securities in its investment portfolio on December 31, 2012 (all securities were purchased in 2012): (1) 3,000 shares of Anderson Co. common stock which cost $58,500, (2) 10,000 shares of Munter Ltd. common stock which cost $580,000, and (3) 6,000 shares of King Company preferred stock which cost $255,000. The Fair Value Adjustment account shows a credit of $10,100 at the end of 2012.

In 2013, Parnevik completed the following securities transactions.

1. On January 15, sold 3,000 shares of Anderson's common stock at $22 per share less fees of $2,150.
2. On April 17, purchased 1,000 shares of Castle's common stock at $33.50 per share plus fees of $1,980.

On December 31, 2013, the market values per share of these securities were: Munter $61, King $40, and Castle $29. In addition, the accounting supervisor of Parnevik told you that, even though all these securities have readily determinable fair values, Parnevik will not actively trade these securities because the top management intends to hold them for more than one year.

Instructions

(a) Prepare the entry for the security sale on January 15, 2013.

(b) Prepare the journal entry to record the security purchase on April 17, 2013.

(c) Compute the unrealized gains or losses and prepare the adjusting entry for Parnevik on December 31, 2013.

(d) How should the unrealized gains or losses be reported on Parnevik's balance sheet?

P17-6 (Trading and Available-for-Sale Securities Entries) McElroy Company has the following portfolio of investment securities at September 30, 2012, its last reporting date.

Trading Securities	Cost	Fair Value
Horton, Inc. common (5,000 shares)	$215,000	$200,000
Monty, Inc. preferred (3,500 shares)	133,000	140,000
Oakwood Corp. common (1,000 shares)	180,000	179,000

On October 10, 2012, the Horton shares were sold at a price of $54 per share. In addition, 3,000 shares of Patriot common stock were acquired at $54.50 per share on November 2, 2012. The December 31, 2012, fair values were: Monty $106,000, Patriot $132,000, and the Oakwood common $193,000. All the securities are classified as trading.

Instructions

(a) Prepare the journal entries to record the sale, purchase, and adjusting entries related to the trading securities in the last quarter of 2012.

(b) How would the entries in part (a) change if the securities were classified as available-for-sale?

P17-7 (Available-for-Sale and Held-to-Maturity Debt Securities Entries) The following information relates to the debt securities investments of Wildcat Company.

1. On February 1, the company purchased 10% bonds of Gibbons Co. having a par value of $300,000 at 100 plus accrued interest. Interest is payable April 1 and October 1.
2. On April 1, semiannual interest is received.

3. On July 1, 9% bonds of Sampson, Inc. were purchased. These bonds with a par value of $200,000 were purchased at 100 plus accrued interest. Interest dates are June 1 and December 1.
4. On September 1, bonds with a par value of $60,000, purchased on February 1, are sold at 99 plus accrued interest.
5. On October 1, semiannual interest is received.
6. On December 1, semiannual interest is received.
7. On December 31, the fair value of the bonds purchased February 1 and July 1 are 95 and 93, respectively.

Instructions

(a) Prepare any journal entries you consider necessary, including year-end entries (December 31), assuming these are available-for-sale securities.
(b) If Wildcat classified these as held-to-maturity investments, explain how the journal entries would differ from those in part (a).

3 4 5 **P17-8 (Fair Value and Equity Methods)** Brooks Corp. is a medium-sized corporation specializing in quarrying stone for building construction. The company has long dominated the market, at one time achieving a 70% market penetration. During prosperous years, the company's profits, coupled with a conservative dividend policy, resulted in funds available for outside investment. Over the years, Brooks has had a policy of investing idle cash in equity securities. In particular, Brooks has made periodic investments in the company's principal supplier, Norton Industries. Although the firm currently owns 12% of the outstanding common stock of Norton Industries, Brooks does not have significant influence over the operations of Norton Industries.

Cheryl Thomas has recently joined Brooks as assistant controller, and her first assignment is to prepare the 2012 year-end adjusting entries for the accounts that are valued by the "fair value" rule for financial reporting purposes. Thomas has gathered the following information about Brooks's pertinent accounts.

1. Brooks has trading securities related to Delaney Motors and Patrick Electric. During this fiscal year, Brooks purchased 100,000 shares of Delaney Motors for $1,400,000; these shares currently have a market value of $1,600,000. Brooks' investment in Patrick Electric has not been profitable; the company acquired 50,000 shares of Patrick in April 2012 at $20 per share, a purchase that currently has a value of $720,000.
2. Prior to 2012, Brooks invested $22,500,000 in Norton Industries and has not changed its holdings this year. This investment in Norton Industries was valued at $21,500,000 on December 31, 2011. Brooks' 12% ownership of Norton Industries has a current market value of $22,225,000.

Instructions

(a) Prepare the appropriate adjusting entries for Brooks as of December 31, 2012, to reflect the application of the "fair value" rule for both classes of securities described above.
(b) For both classes of securities presented above, describe how the results of the valuation adjustments made in (a) would be reflected in the body of and notes to Brooks' 2012 financial statements.
(c) Prepare the entries for the Norton investment, assuming that Brooks owns 25% of Norton's shares. Norton reported income of $500,000 in 2012 and paid cash dividends of $100,000.

3 5 **P17-9 (Financial Statement Presentation of Available-for-Sale Investments)** Kennedy Company has the following portfolio of available-for-sale securities at December 31, 2012.

Security	Quantity	Percent Interest	Per Share Cost	Per Share Price
Frank, Inc.	2,000 shares	8%	$11	$16
Ellis Corp.	5,000 shares	14%	23	19
Mendota Company	4,000 shares	2%	31	24

Instructions

(a) What should be reported on Kennedy's December 31, 2012, balance sheet relative to these long-term available-for-sale securities?

On December 31, 2013, Kennedy's portfolio of available-for-sale securities consisted of the following common stocks.

Security	Quantity	Percent Interest	Per Share Cost	Per Share Price
Ellis Corp.	5,000 shares	14%	$23	$28
Mendota Company	4,000 shares	2%	31	23
Mendota Company	2,000 shares	1%	25	23

At the end of year 2013, Kennedy Company changed its intent relative to its investment in Frank, Inc. and reclassified the shares to trading securities status when the shares were selling for $8 per share.

(b) What should be reported on the face of Kennedy's December 31, 2013, balance sheet relative to available-for-sale securities investments? What should be reported to reflect the transactions above in Kennedy's 2013 income statement?

(c) Assuming that comparative financial statements for 2012 and 2013 are presented, draft the footnote necessary for full disclosure of Kennedy's transactions and position in equity securities.

3 5 P17-10 (Gain on Sale of Investments and Comprehensive Income) On January 1, 2012, Acker Inc. had the following balance sheet.

<table>
<tr><td colspan="4" align="center">**ACKER INC.**
BALANCE SHEET
AS OF JANUARY 1, 2012</td></tr>
<tr><td colspan="2" align="center">Assets</td><td colspan="2" align="center">Equity</td></tr>
<tr><td>Cash</td><td>$ 50,000</td><td>Common stock</td><td>$260,000</td></tr>
<tr><td>Equity investments (available-for-sale)</td><td>240,000</td><td>Accumulated other comprehensive income</td><td>30,000</td></tr>
<tr><td>Total</td><td>$290,000</td><td>Total</td><td>$290,000</td></tr>
</table>

The accumulated other comprehensive income related to unrealized holding gains on available-for-sale securities. The fair value of Acker Inc.'s available-for-sale securities at December 31, 2012, was $190,000; its cost was $140,000. No securities were purchased during the year. Acker Inc.'s income statement for 2012 was as follows. (Ignore income taxes.)

<table>
<tr><td colspan="2" align="center">**ACKER INC.**
INCOME STATEMENT
FOR THE YEAR ENDED DECEMBER 31, 2012</td></tr>
<tr><td>Dividend revenue</td><td>$ 5,000</td></tr>
<tr><td>Gain on sale of investments</td><td>30,000</td></tr>
<tr><td>Net income</td><td>$35,000</td></tr>
</table>

Instructions
(Assume all transactions during the year were for cash.)

(a) Prepare the journal entry to record the sale of the available-for-sale securities in 2012.
(b) Prepare a statement of comprehensive income for 2012.
(c) Prepare a balance sheet as of December 31, 2012.

3 P17-11 (Equity Investments—Available-for-Sale) Castleman Holdings, Inc. had the following available-for-sale investment portfolio at January 1, 2012.

Evers Company	1,000 shares @ $15 each	$15,000
Rogers Company	900 shares @ $20 each	18,000
Chance Company	500 shares @ $9 each	4,500
Equity investments (available-for-sale) @ cost		37,500
Fair value adjustment (available-for-sale)		(7,500)
Equity investments (available-for-sale) @ fair value		$30,000

During 2012, the following transactions took place.

1. On March 1, Rogers Company paid a $2 per share dividend.
2. On April 30, Castleman Holdings, Inc. sold 300 shares of Chance Company for $11 per share.
3. On May 15, Castleman Holdings, Inc. purchased 100 more shares of Evers Co. stock at $16 per share.
4. At December 31, 2012, the stocks had the following price per share values: Evers $17, Rogers $19, and Chance $8.

During 2013, the following transactions took place.

5. On February 1, Castleman Holdings, Inc. sold the remaining Chance shares for $8 per share.
6. On March 1, Rogers Company paid a $2 per share dividend.
7. On December 21, Evers Company declared a cash dividend of $3 per share to be paid in the next month.
8. At December 31, 2013, the stocks had the following price per shares values: Evers $19 and Rogers $21.

Instructions
(a) Prepare journal entries for each of the above transactions.
(b) Prepare a partial balance sheet showing the investment-related amounts to be reported at December 31, 2012 and 2013.

P17-12 (Available-for-Sale Securities—Statement Presentation) Fernandez Corp. invested its excess cash in available-for-sale securities during 2012. As of December 31, 2012, the portfolio of available-for-sale securities consisted of the following common stocks.

Security	Quantity	Cost	Fair Value
Lindsay Jones, Inc.	1,000 shares	$ 15,000	$ 21,000
Poley Corp.	2,000 shares	40,000	42,000
Arnold Aircraft	2,000 shares	72,000	60,000
Totals		$127,000	$123,000

Instructions
(a) What should be reported on Fernandez's December 31, 2012, balance sheet relative to these securities? What should be reported on Fernandez's 2012 income statement?

On December 31, 2013, Fernandez's portfolio of available-for-sale securities consisted of the following common stocks.

Security	Quantity	Cost	Fair Value
Lindsay Jones, Inc.	1,000 shares	$ 15,000	$20,000
Lindsay Jones, Inc.	2,000 shares	33,000	40,000
Duff Company	1,000 shares	16,000	12,000
Arnold Aircraft	2,000 shares	72,000	22,000
Totals		$136,000	$94,000

During the year 2013, Fernandez Corp. sold 2,000 shares of Poley Corp. for $38,200 and purchased 2,000 more shares of Lindsay Jones, Inc. and 1,000 shares of Duff Company.

(b) What should be reported on Fernandez's December 31, 2013, balance sheet? What should be reported on Fernandez's 2013 income statement?

On December 31, 2014, Fernandez's portfolio of available-for-sale securities consisted of the following common stocks.

Security	Quantity	Cost	Fair Value
Arnold Aircraft	2,000 shares	$72,000	$82,000
Duff Company	500 shares	8,000	6,000
Totals		$80,000	$88,000

During the year 2014, Fernandez Corp. sold 3,000 shares of Lindsay Jones, Inc. for $39,900 and 500 shares of Duff Company at a loss of $2,700.

(c) What should be reported on the face of Fernandez's December 31, 2014, balance sheet? What should be reported on Fernandez's 2014 income statement?
(d) What would be reported in a statement of comprehensive income at (1) December 31, 2012, and (2) December 31, 2013?

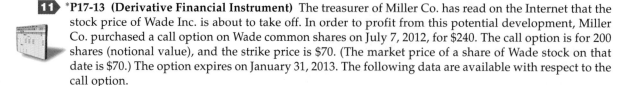

*P17-13 (Derivative Financial Instrument) The treasurer of Miller Co. has read on the Internet that the stock price of Wade Inc. is about to take off. In order to profit from this potential development, Miller Co. purchased a call option on Wade common shares on July 7, 2012, for $240. The call option is for 200 shares (notional value), and the strike price is $70. (The market price of a share of Wade stock on that date is $70.) The option expires on January 31, 2013. The following data are available with respect to the call option.

Date	Market Price of Wade Shares	Time Value of Call Option
September 30, 2012	$77 per share	$180
December 31, 2012	75 per share	65
January 4, 2013	76 per share	30

Instructions

Prepare the journal entries for Miller Co. for the following dates.

(a) July 7, 2012—Investment in call option on Wade shares.
(b) September 30, 2012—Miller prepares financial statements.
(c) December 31, 2012—Miller prepares financial statements.
(d) January 4, 2013—Miller settles the call option on the Wade shares.

11 *P17-14 (Derivative Financial Instrument)** Johnstone Co. purchased a put option on Ewing common shares on July 7, 2012, for $240. The put option is for 200 shares, and the strike price is $70. (The market price of a share of Ewing stock on that date is $70.) The option expires on January 31, 2013. The following data are available with respect to the put option.

Date	Market Price of Ewing Shares	Time Value of Put Option
September 30, 2012	$77 per share	$125
December 31, 2012	75 per share	50
January 31, 2013	78 per share	0

Instructions

Prepare the journal entries for Johnstone Co. for the following dates.

(a) July 7, 2012—Investment in put option on Ewing shares.
(b) September 30, 2012—Johnstone prepares financial statements.
(c) December 31, 2012—Johnstone prepares financial statements.
(d) January 31, 2013—Put option expires.

11 *P17-15 (Free-Standing Derivative)** Warren Co. purchased a put option on Echo common shares on January 7, 2012, for $360. The put option is for 400 shares, and the strike price is $85 (which equals the price of an Echo share on the purchase date). The option expires on July 31, 2012. The following data are available with respect to the put option.

Date	Market Price of Echo Shares	Time Value of Put Option
March 31, 2012	$80 per share	$200
June 30, 2012	82 per share	90
July 6, 2012	77 per share	25

Instructions

Prepare the journal entries for Warren Co. for the following dates.

(a) January 7, 2012—Investment in put option on Echo shares.
(b) March 31, 2012—Warren prepares financial statements.
(c) June 30, 2012—Warren prepares financial statements.
(d) July 6, 2012—Warren settles the put option on the Echo shares.

12 *P17-16 (Fair Value Hedge Interest Rate Swap)** On December 31, 2012, Mercantile Corp. had a $10,000,000, 8% fixed-rate note outstanding, payable in 2 years. It decides to enter into a 2-year swap with Chicago First Bank to convert the fixed-rate debt to variable-rate debt. The terms of the swap indicate that Mercantile will receive interest at a fixed rate of 8.0% and will pay a variable rate equal to the 6-month LIBOR rate, based on the $10,000,000 amount. The LIBOR rate on December 31, 2012, is 7%. The LIBOR rate will be reset every 6 months and will be used to determine the variable rate to be paid for the following 6-month period.

Mercantile Corp. designates the swap as a fair value hedge. Assume that the hedging relationship meets all the conditions necessary for hedge accounting. The 6-month LIBOR rate and the swap and debt fair values are as follows.

Date	6-Month LIBOR Rate	Swap Fair Value	Debt Fair Value
December 31, 2012	7.0%	—	$10,000,000
June 30, 2013	7.5%	(200,000)	9,800,000
December 31, 2013	6.0%	60,000	10,060,000

Instructions

(a) Present the journal entries to record the following transactions.
   (1) The entry, if any, to record the swap on December 31, 2012.
   (2) The entry to record the semiannual debt interest payment on June 30, 2013.

(3) The entry to record the settlement of the semiannual swap amount receivables at 8%, less amount payable at LIBOR, 7%.

(4) The entry to record the change in the fair value of the debt on June 30, 2013.

(5) The entry to record the change in the fair value of the swap at June 30, 2013.

(b) Indicate the amount(s) reported on the balance sheet and income statement related to the debt and swap on December 31, 2012.

(c) Indicate the amount(s) reported on the balance sheet and income statement related to the debt and swap on June 30, 2013.

(d) Indicate the amount(s) reported on the balance sheet and income statement related to the debt and swap on December 31, 2013.

13 *P17-17 (Cash Flow Hedge)** LEW Jewelry Co. uses gold in the manufacture of its products. LEW anticipates that it will need to purchase 500 ounces of gold in October 2012, for jewelry that will be shipped for the holiday shopping season. However, if the price of gold increases, LEW's cost to produce its jewelry will increase, which would reduce its profit margins.

To hedge the risk of increased gold prices, on April 1, 2012, LEW enters into a gold futures contract and designates this futures contract as a cash flow hedge of the anticipated gold purchase. The notional amount of the contract is 500 ounces, and the terms of the contract give LEW the right and the obligation to purchase gold at a price of $300 per ounce. The price will be good until the contract expires on October 31, 2012.

Assume the following data with respect to the price of the call options and the gold inventory purchase.

Date	Spot Price for October Delivery
April 1, 2012	$300 per ounce
June 30, 2012	310 per ounce
September 30, 2012	315 per ounce

Instructions

Prepare the journal entries for the following transactions.

(a) April 1, 2012—Inception of the futures contract, no premium paid.

(b) June 30, 2012—LEW Co. prepares financial statements.

(c) September 30, 2012—LEW Co. prepares financial statements.

(d) October 10, 2012—LEW Co. purchases 500 ounces of gold at $315 per ounce and settles the futures contract.

(e) December 20, 2012—LEW sells jewelry containing gold purchased in October 2012 for $350,000. The cost of the finished goods inventory is $200,000.

(f) Indicate the amount(s) reported on the balance sheet and income statement related to the futures contract on June 30, 2012.

(g) Indicate the amount(s) reported in the income statement related to the futures contract and the inventory transactions on December 31, 2012.

12 *P17-18 (Fair Value Hedge)** On November 3, 2012, Sprinkle Co. invested $200,000 in 4,000 shares of the common stock of Pratt Co. Sprinkle classified this investment as available-for-sale. Sprinkle Co. is considering making a more significant investment in Pratt Co. at some point in the future but has decided to wait and see how the stock does over the next several quarters.

To hedge against potential declines in the value of Pratt stock during this period, Sprinkle also purchased a put option on the Pratt stock. Sprinkle paid an option premium of $600 for the put option, which gives Sprinkle the option to sell 4,000 Pratt shares at a strike price of $50 per share. The option expires on July 31, 2013. The following data are available with respect to the values of the Pratt stock and the put option.

Date	Market Price of Pratt Shares	Time Value of Put Option
December 31, 2012	$50 per share	$375
March 31, 2013	45 per share	175
June 30, 2013	43 per share	40

Instructions

(a) Prepare the journal entries for Sprinkle Co. for the following dates.

(1) November 3, 2012—Investment in Pratt stock and the put option on Pratt shares.

(2) December 31, 2012—Sprinkle Co. prepares financial statements.

(3) March 31, 2013—Sprinkle prepares financial statements.

(4) June 30, 2013—Sprinkle prepares financial statements.

(5) July 1, 2013—Sprinkle settles the put option and sells the Pratt shares for $43 per share.

(b) Indicate the amount(s) reported on the balance sheet and income statement related to the Pratt investment and the put option on December 31, 2012.

(c) Indicate the amount(s) reported on the balance sheet and income statement related to the Pratt investment and the put option on June 30, 2013.

CONCEPTS FOR ANALYSIS

CA17-1 (Issues Raised about Investment Securities) You have just started work for Warren Co. as part of the controller's group involved in current financial reporting problems. Jane Henshaw, controller for Warren, is interested in your accounting background because the company has experienced a series of financial reporting surprises over the last few years. Recently, the controller has learned from the company's auditors that there is authoritative literature that may apply to its investment in securities. She assumes that you are familiar with this pronouncement and asks how the following situations should be reported in the financial statements.

Situation 1
Trading securities in the current assets section have a fair value that is $4,200 lower than cost.

Situation 2
A trading security whose fair value is currently less than cost is transferred to the available-for-sale category.

Situation 3
An available-for-sale security whose fair value is currently less than cost is classified as noncurrent but is to be reclassified as current.

Situation 4
A company's portfolio of available-for-sale securities consists of the common stock of one company. At the end of the prior year, the fair value of the security was 50% of original cost, and this reduction in fair value was reported as an other than temporary impairment. However, at the end of the current year the fair value of the security had appreciated to twice the original cost.

Situation 5
The company has purchased some convertible debentures that it plans to hold for less than a year. The fair value of the convertible debentures is $7,700 below its cost.

Instructions
What is the effect upon carrying value and earnings for each of the situations above? Assume that these situations are unrelated.

CA17-2 (Equity Securities) Lexington Co. has the following available-for-sale securities outstanding on December 31, 2012 (its first year of operations).

	Cost	Fair Value
Greenspan Corp. Stock	$20,000	$19,000
Summerset Company Stock	9,500	8,800
Tinkers Company Stock	20,000	20,600
	$49,500	$48,400

During 2013, Summerset Company stock was sold for $9,200, the difference between the $9,200 and the "fair value" of $8,800 being recorded as a "Gain on Sale of Investments." The market price of the stock on December 31, 2013, was: Greenspan Corp. stock $19,900; Tinkers Company stock $20,500.

Instructions
  (a) What justification is there for valuing available-for-sale securities at fair value and reporting the unrealized gain or loss as part of stockholders' equity?
  (b) How should Lexington Company apply this rule on December 31, 2012? Explain.
  (c) Did Lexington Company properly account for the sale of the Summerset Company stock? Explain.
  (d) Are there any additional entries necessary for Lexington Company at December 31, 2013, to reflect the facts on the financial statements in accordance with generally accepted accounting principles? Explain.

(AICPA adapted)

CA17-3 (Financial Statement Effect of Equity Securities) Presented below are three unrelated situations involving equity securities.

Situation 1
An equity security, whose fair value is currently less than cost, is classified as available-for-sale but is to be reclassified as trading.

Situation 2
A noncurrent portfolio with an aggregate fair value in excess of cost includes one particular security whose fair value has declined to less than one-half of the original cost. The decline in value is considered to be other than temporary.

Situation 3

The portfolio of trading securities has a cost in excess of fair value of $13,500. The available-for-sale portfolio has a fair value in excess of cost of $28,600.

Instructions

What is the effect upon carrying value and earnings for each of the situations above?

CA17-4 (Equity Securities) The Financial Accounting Standards Board issued accounting guidance to clarify accounting methods and procedures with respect to certain debt and all equity securities. An important part of the statement concerns the distinction between held-to-maturity, available-for-sale, and trading securities.

Instructions

(a) Why does a company maintain an investment portfolio of held-to-maturity, available-for-sale, and trading securities?

(b) What factors should be considered in determining whether investments in securities should be classified as held-to-maturity, available-for-sale, and trading? How do these factors affect the accounting treatment for unrealized losses?

CA17-5 (Investment Accounted for under the Equity Method) On July 1, 2013, Fontaine Company purchased for cash 40% of the outstanding capital stock of Knoblett Company. Both Fontaine Company and Knoblett Company have a December 31 year-end. Knoblett Company, whose common stock is actively traded in the over-the-counter market, reported its total net income for the year to Fontaine Company and also paid cash dividends on November 15, 2013, to Fontaine Company and its other stockholders.

Instructions

How should Fontaine Company report the above facts in its December 31, 2013, balance sheet and its income statement for the year then ended? Discuss the rationale for your answer.

(AICPA adapted)

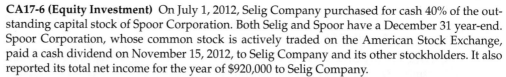

CA17-6 (Equity Investment) On July 1, 2012, Selig Company purchased for cash 40% of the outstanding capital stock of Spoor Corporation. Both Selig and Spoor have a December 31 year-end. Spoor Corporation, whose common stock is actively traded on the American Stock Exchange, paid a cash dividend on November 15, 2012, to Selig Company and its other stockholders. It also reported its total net income for the year of $920,000 to Selig Company.

Instructions

Prepare a one-page memorandum of instructions on how Selig Company should report the above facts in its December 31, 2012, balance sheet and its 2012 income statement. In your memo, identify and describe the method of valuation you recommend. Provide rationale where you can. Address your memo to the chief accountant at Selig Company.

CA17-7 (Fair Value) Addison Manufacturing holds a large portfolio of debt and equity securities as an investment. The fair value of the portfolio is greater than its original cost, even though some securities have decreased in value. Sam Beresford, the financial vice president, and Angie Nielson, the controller, are near year-end in the process of classifying for the first time this securities portfolio in accordance with GAAP. Beresford wants to classify those securities that have increased in value during the period as trading securities in order to increase net income this year. He wants to classify all the securities that have decreased in value as available-for-sale (the equity securities) and as held-to-maturity (the debt securities).

Nielson disagrees. She wants to classify those securities that have decreased in value as trading securities and those that have increased in value as available-for-sale (equity) and held-to-maturity (debt). She contends that the company is having a good earnings year and that recognizing the losses will help to smooth the income this year. As a result, the company will have built-in gains for future periods when the company may not be as profitable.

Instructions

Answer the following questions.

(a) Will classifying the portfolio as each proposes actually have the effect on earnings that each says it will?

(b) Is there anything unethical in what each of them proposes? Who are the stakeholders affected by their proposals?

(c) Assume that Beresford and Nielson properly classify the entire portfolio into trading, available-for-sale, and held-to-maturity categories. But then each proposes to sell just before year-end the securities with gains or with losses, as the case may be, to accomplish their effect on earnings. Is this unethical?

USING YOUR JUDGMENT

FINANCIAL REPORTING

Financial Reporting Problem

P&G The Procter & Gamble Company (P&G)

The financial statements of P&G are presented in Appendix 5B or can be accessed at the book's companion website, **www.wiley.com/college/kieso**.

Instructions

Refer to P&G's financial statements and the accompanying notes to answer the following questions.

(a) What investments does P&G report in 2009, and how are these investments accounted for in its financial statements?

(b) How are P&G's investments valued? How does P&G determine fair value?

(c) How does P&G use derivative financial instruments?

Comparative Analysis Case

The Coca-Cola Company and PepsiCo, Inc.

 PEPSICO

Instructions

Go to the book's companion website and use information found there to answer the following questions related to The Coca-Cola Company and PepsiCo, Inc.

(a) Based on the information contained in these financial statements, determine each of the following for each company.

    (1) Cash used in (for) investing activities during 2009 (from the statement of cash flows).

    (2) Cash used for acquisitions and investments in unconsolidated affiliates (or principally bottling companies) during 2009.

    (3) Total investment in unconsolidated affiliates (or investments and other assets) at the end of 2009.

    (4) What conclusions concerning the management of investments can be drawn from these data?

(b) (1) Briefly identify from Coca-Cola's December 31, 2009, balance sheet the investments it reported as being accounted for under the equity method. (2) What is the amount of investments that Coca-Cola reported in its 2009 balance sheet as "cost method investments," and what is the nature of these investments?

(c) In its Note 2 on Investments, what total amounts did Coca-Cola report at December 31, 2009, as: (1) trading securities, (2) available-for-sale securities, and (3) held-to-maturity securities?

Financial Statement Analysis Case

Union Planters

Union Planters is a Tennessee bank holding company (that is, a corporation that owns banks). (Union Planters is now part of Regions Bank.) Union Planters manages $32 billion in assets, the largest of which is its loan portfolio of $19 billion. In addition to its loan portfolio, however, like other banks it has significant debt investments. The nature of these investments varies from short-term in nature to long-term in nature. As a consequence, consistent with the requirements of accounting rules, Union Planters reports its investments in two different categories—trading and available-for-sale. The following facts were found in a recent Union Planters' annual report.

(all dollars in millions)	Amortized Cost	Gross Unrealized Gains	Gross Unrealized Losses	Fair Value
Trading account assets	$ 275	—	—	$ 275
Securities available for sale	8,209	$108	$15	8,302
Net income				224
Net securities gains (losses)				(9)

Instructions

(a) Why do you suppose Union Planters purchases investments, rather than simply making loans? Why does it purchase investments that vary in nature both in terms of their maturities and in type (debt versus stock)?

(b) How must Union Planters account for its investments in each of the two categories?

(c) In what ways does classifying investments into two different categories assist investors in evaluating the profitability of a company like Union Planters?

(d) Suppose that the management of Union Planters was not happy with its net income for the year. What step could it have taken with its investment portfolio that would have definitely increased reported profit? How much could it have increased reported profit? Why do you suppose it chose not to do this?

Accounting, Analysis, and Principles

Instar Company has several investments in the securities of other companies. The following information regarding these investments is available at December 31, 2012.

1. Instar holds bonds issued by Dorsel Corp. The bonds have an amortized cost of $320,000 and their fair value at December 31, 2012, is $400,000. Instar intends to hold the bonds until they mature on December 31, 2020.

2. Instar has invested idle cash in the equity securities of several publicly traded companies. Instar intends to sell these securities during the first quarter of 2013, when it will need the cash to acquire seasonal inventory. These equity securities have a cost basis of $800,000 and a fair value of $920,000 at December 31, 2012.

3. Instar has a significant ownership stake in one of the companies that supplies Instar with various components Instar uses in its products. Instar owns 6% of the common stock of the supplier, does not have any representation on the supplier's board of directors, does not exchange any personnel with the supplier, and does not consult with the supplier on any of the supplier's operating, financial, or strategic decisions. The cost basis of the investment in the supplier is $1,200,000 and the fair value of the investment at December 31, 2012, is $1,550,000. Instar does not intend to sell the investment in the foreseeable future. The supplier reported net income of $80,000 for 2012 and paid no dividends.

4. Instar owns some common stock of Forter Corp. The cost basis of the investment in Forter is $200,000 and the fair value at December 31, 2012, is $50,000. Instar believes the decline in the value of its investment in Forter is other than temporary, but Instar does not intend to sell its investment in Forter in the foreseeable future.

5. Instar purchased 25% of the stock of Slobbaer Co. for $900,000. Instar has significant influence over the operating activities of Slobbaer Co. During 2012, Slobbaer Co. reported net income of $300,000 and paid a dividend of $100,000.

Accounting

(a) Determine whether each of the investments described above should be classified as available-for-sale, held-to-maturity, trading, or equity method.

(b) Prepare any December 31, 2012, journal entries needed for Instar relating to Instar's various investments in other companies. Assume 2012 is Instar's first year of operations.

Analysis

What is the effect on Instar's 2012 net income (as reported on Instar's income statement) of Instar's investments in other companies?

Principles

Briefly explain the different rationales for the different accounting and reporting rules for different types of investments in the securities of other companies.

BRIDGE TO THE PROFESSION

Professional Research: FASB Codification

Your client, Cascade Company, is planning to invest some of its excess cash in 5-year revenue bonds issued by the county and in the stock of one of its suppliers, Teton Co. Teton's shares trade on the over-the-counter market. Cascade plans to classify these investments as available-for-sale. They would like you to conduct some research on the accounting for these investments.

Instructions

If your school has a subscription to the FASB Codification, go to *http://aaahq.org/ascLogin.cfm* to log in and prepare responses to the following. Provide Codification references for your responses.

(a) Since the Teton shares do not trade on one of the large stock markets, Cascade argues that the fair value of this investment is not readily available. According to the authoritative literature, when is the fair value of a security "readily determinable"?

(b) How is an impairment of a security accounted for?

(c) To avoid volatility in their financial statements due to fair value adjustments, Cascade debated whether the bond investment could be classified as held-to-maturity; Cascade is pretty sure it will hold the bonds for 5 years. How close to maturity could Cascade sell an investment and still classify it as held-to-maturity?

(d) What disclosures must be made for any sale or transfer from securities classified as held-to-maturity?

Professional Simulation

In this simulation, you are asked to address questions related to investments. Prepare responses to all parts.

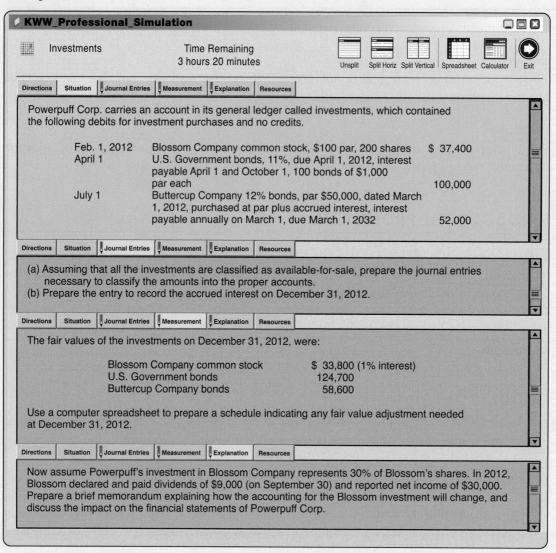

The fair values of the investments on December 31, 2012, were:

Blossom Company common stock	$ 33,800 (1% interest)
U.S. Government bonds	124,700
Buttercup Company bonds	58,600

Use a computer spreadsheet to prepare a schedule indicating any fair value adjustment needed at December 31, 2012.

IFRS Insights

The accounting for investments is discussed in *IAS 27* ("Consolidated and Separate Financial Statements"), *IAS 28* ("Accounting for Investments in Associates"), *IAS 39* ("Financial Instruments: Recognition and Measurement"), and *IFRS 9* ("Financial Instruments"). Until recently, when the IASB issued *IFRS 9*, the accounting and reporting for investments under IFRS and GAAP were for the most part very similar. However, *IFRS 9* introduces new investment classifications and increases the situations when investments are accounted for at fair value, with gains and losses recorded in income.

RELEVANT FACTS

- GAAP classifies investments as trading, available-for-sale (both debt and equity investments), and held-to-maturity (only for debt investments). IFRS uses held-for-collection (debt investments), trading (both debt and equity investments), and non-trading equity investment classifications.

- The accounting for trading investments is the same between GAAP and IFRS. Held-to-maturity (GAAP) and held-for-collection investments are accounted for at amortized cost. Gains and losses related to available-for-sale securities (GAAP) and non-trading equity investments (IFRS) are reported in other comprehensive income.

- Both GAAP and IFRS use the same test to determine whether the equity method of accounting should be used—that is, significant influence with a general guide of over 20 percent ownership.

- The basis for consolidation under IFRS is control. Under GAAP, a bipolar approach is used, which is a risk-and-reward model (often referred to as a variable-entity approach) and a voting-interest approach. However, under both systems, for consolidation to occur, the investor company must generally own 50 percent of another company.

- GAAP and IFRS are similar in the accounting for the fair value option. That is, the option to use the fair value method must be made at initial recognition, the selection is irrevocable, and gains and losses are reported as part of income. One difference is that GAAP permits the fair value option for equity method investments.

- While measurement of impairments is similar, GAAP does not permit the reversal of an impairment charge related to available-for-sale debt and equity investments. IFRS allows reversals of impairments of held-for-collection investments.

ABOUT THE NUMBERS

Accounting for Financial Assets

A **financial asset** is cash, an equity investment of another company (e.g., ordinary or preference shares), or a contractual right to receive cash from another party (e.g., loans, receivables, and bonds). The accounting for cash is relatively straightforward and is discussed in Chapter 7. The accounting and reporting for equity and debt investments, as discussed in the opening story, is extremely contentious, particularly in light of the credit crisis in the latter part of 2008.

IFRS requires that companies determine how to measure their financial assets based on two criteria:

- The company's business model for managing its financial assets; and
- The contractual cash flow characteristics of the financial asset.

If a company has (1) a business model whose objective is to hold assets in order to collect contractual cash flows and (2) the contractual terms of the financial asset provides specified dates to cash flows that are solely payments of principal and interest on the principal amount outstanding, then the company should use amortized cost.

For example, assume that Mitsubishi purchases a bond investment that it intends to hold to maturity. Its business model for this type of investment is to collect interest and then principal at maturity. The payment dates for the interest rate and principal are stated on the bond. In this case, Mitsubishi accounts for the investment at amortized cost. If, on the other hand, Mitsubishi purchased the bonds as part of a trading strategy to speculate on interest rate changes (a trading investment), then the debt investment is reported at fair value. As a result, only debt investments such as receivables, loans, and bond investments that meet the two criteria above are recorded at amortized cost. All other debt investments are recorded and reported at fair value.

Equity investments are generally recorded and reported at fair value. Equity investments do not have a fixed interest or principal payment schedule and therefore cannot be accounted for at amortized cost. In summary, companies account for investments based on the type of security, as indicated in Illustration IFRS17-1.

ILLUSTRATION IFRS17-1
Summary of Investment Accounting Approaches

Type of Investment	Assessment of Accounting Criteria	Valuation Approach
Debt (Section 1)	Meets business model (held-for-collection) and contractual cash flow tests.	Amortized cost
	Does not meet the business model test (not held-for-collection).	Fair value
Equity (Section 2)	Does not meet contractual cash flow test.	Fair value
	Exercises some control.	Equity method

Debt Investments

Debt Investments—Amortized Cost

Only debt investments can be measured at amortized cost. If a company like Carrefour makes an investment in the bonds of Nokia, it will receive contractual cash flows of interest over the life of the bonds and repayment of the principal at maturity. If it is Carrefour's strategy to hold this investment in order to receive these cash flows over the life of the bond, it has a held-for-collection strategy and it will measure the investment at amortized cost.[42]

Example: Debt Investment at Amortized Cost. To illustrate the accounting for a debt investment at amortized cost, assume that Robinson Company purchased $100,000 of 8 percent bonds of Evermaster Corporation on January 1, 2012, at a discount, paying $92,278. The bonds mature January 1, 2017, and yield 10 percent; interest is payable each July 1 and January 1. Robinson records the investment as follows.

January 1, 2012

Debt Investments	92,278	
Cash		92,278

As indicated in Chapter 14, companies must amortize premiums or discounts using the **effective-interest method**. They apply the effective-interest method to bond investments in a way similar to that for bonds payable. To compute interest revenue, companies compute the effective-interest rate or yield at the time of investment and apply that rate to the beginning carrying amount (book value) for each interest period. The investment carrying amount is increased by the amortized discount or decreased by the amortized premium in each period.

Illustration IFRS17-2 shows the effect of the discount amortization on the interest revenue that Robinson records each period for its investment in Evermaster bonds.

---

[42]Classification as held-for-collection does not mean the security must be held to maturity. For example, a company may sell an investment before maturity if (1) the security does not meet the company's investment strategy (e.g., the company has a policy to invest in only AAA-rated bonds but the bond investment has a decline in its credit rating), (2) a company changes its strategy to invest only in securities within a certain maturity range, or (3) the company needs to sell a security to fund certain capital expenditures. However, if a company begins trading held-for-collection investments on a regular basis, it should assess whether such trading is consistent with the held-for-collection classification.

ILLUSTRATION
IFRS17-2
Schedule of Interest
Revenue and Bond
Discount Amortization—
Effective-Interest Method

			8% Bonds Purchased to Yield 10%		
Date	Cash Received	Interest Revenue	Bond Discount Amortization	Carrying Amount of Bonds	
1/1/12				$ 92,278	
7/1/12	$ 4,000ᵃ	$ 4,614ᵇ	$ 614ᶜ	92,892ᵈ	
1/1/13	4,000	4,645	645	93,537	
7/1/13	4,000	4,677	677	94,214	
1/1/14	4,000	4,711	711	94,925	
7/1/14	4,000	4,746	746	95,671	
1/1/15	4,000	4,783	783	96,454	
7/1/15	4,000	4,823	823	97,277	
1/1/16	4,000	4,864	864	98,141	
7/1/16	4,000	4,907	907	99,048	
1/1/17	4,000	4,952	952	100,000	
	$40,000	$47,722	$7,722		

ᵃ$4,000 = $100,000 × 08 × $^6\!/_{12}$
ᵇ$4,614 = $92,278 × .10 × $^6\!/_{12}$
ᶜ$614 = $4,614 − $4,000
ᵈ$92,892 = $92,278 + $614

Robinson records the receipt of the first semiannual interest payment on July 1, 2012 (using the data in Illustration IFRS17-2), as follows.

July 1, 2012

Cash	4,000	
Debt Investments	614	
Interest Revenue		4,614

Because Robinson is on a calendar-year basis, it accrues interest and amortizes the discount at December 31, 2012, as follows.

December 31, 2012

Interest Receivable	4,000	
Debt Investments	645	
Interest Revenue		4,645

Again, Illustration IFRS17-2 shows the interest and amortization amounts. Thus, the accounting for held-for-collection investments in IFRS is the same as held-to-maturity investments under GAAP.

Debt Investments—Fair Value

In some cases, companies both manage and evaluate investment performance on a fair value basis. In these situations, these investments are managed and evaluated based on a documented risk-management or investment strategy based on fair value information. For example, some companies often hold debt investments with the intention of selling them in a short period of time. These debt investments are often referred to as **trading investments** because companies frequently buy and sell these investments to generate profits in short-term differences in price.

Companies that account for and report debt investments at fair value follow the same accounting entries as debt investments held-for-collection during the reporting period. That is, they are recorded at amortized cost. However, **at each reporting date, companies adjust the amortized cost to fair value, with any unrealized holding gain or loss reported as part of net income (fair value method)**. An **unrealized holding gain or loss** is the net change in the fair value of a debt investment from one period to another.

Example: Debt Investment at Fair Value. To illustrate the accounting for debt investments using the fair value approach, assume the same information as in our previous illustration for Robinson Company. Recall that Robinson Company purchased $100,000 of 8 percent bonds of Evermaster Corporation on January 1, 2012, at a discount, paying $92,278.[43] The bonds mature January 1, 2017, and yield 10 percent; interest is payable each July 1 and January 1.

The journal entries in 2012 are exactly the same as those for amortized cost. These entries are as follows.

January 1, 2012

Debt Investments	92,278	
Cash		92,278

July 1, 2012

Cash	4,000	
Debt Investments	614	
Interest Revenue		4,614

December 31, 2012

Interest Receivable	4,000	
Debt Investments	645	
Interest Revenue		4,645

Again, Illustration IFRS17-2 shows the interest and amortization amounts. If the debt investment is held-for-collection, no further entries are necessary. To apply the fair value approach, Robinson determines that, due to a decrease in interest rates, the fair value of the debt investment increased to $95,000 at December 31, 2012. Comparing the fair value with the carrying amount of these bonds at December 31, 2012, Robinson has an unrealized holding gain of $1,463, as shown in Illustration IFRS17-3.

ILLUSTRATION IFRS17-3
Computation of Unrealized Gain on Fair Value Debt Investment (2012)

Fair value at December 31, 2012	$95,000
Amortized cost at December 31, 2012 (per Illustration IFRS17-2)	93,537
Unrealized holding gain or (loss)	$ 1,463

Robinson therefore makes the following entry to record the adjustment of the debt investment to fair value at December 31, 2012.

Fair Value Adjustment	1,463	
Unrealized Holding Gain or Loss—Income		1,463

Robinson uses a valuation account (**Fair Value Adjustment**) instead of debiting Debt Investments to record the investment at fair value. The use of the Fair Value Adjustment account enables Robinson to maintain a record at amortized cost in the accounts. Because the valuation account has a debit balance, in this case the fair value of Robinson's debt investment is higher than its amortized cost.

The Unrealized Holding Gain or Loss—Income account is reported in the other income and expense section of the income statement as part of net income. This account is closed to net income each period. The Fair Value Adjustment account is not closed each period and is simply adjusted each period to its proper valuation. The Fair Value Adjustment balance is not shown on the statement of financial position but is simply used to restate the debt investment account to fair value.

[43]Companies may incur brokerage and transaction costs in purchasing securities. For investments accounted for at fair value (both debt and equity), IFRS requires that these costs be recorded in net income as other income and expense and not as an adjustment to the carrying value of the investment.

Robinson reports its investment in Evermaster bonds in its December 31, 2012, financial statements as shown in Illustration IFRS17-4.

Statement of Financial Position	
Current assets	
Interest receivable	$ 4,000
Debt investments (trading)	95,000
Income Statement	
Other income and expense	
Interest revenue ($4,614 + $4,645)	$ 9,259
Unrealized holding gain or (loss)	1,463

ILLUSTRATION IFRS17-4
Financial Statement Presentation of Debt Investments at Fair Value

As you can see from this example, the accounting for trading debt investments under IFRS is the same as GAAP.

Equity Investments

As in GAAP, under IFRS, the degree to which one corporation (**investor**) acquires an interest in the shares of another corporation (**investee**) generally determines the accounting treatment for the investment subsequent to acquisition. To review, the classification of such investments depends on the percentage of the investee voting shares that is held by the investor:

1. Holdings of less than 20 percent (**fair value method**)—investor has passive interest.
2. Holdings between 20 percent and 50 percent (**equity method**)—investor has significant influence.
3. Holdings of more than 50 percent (**consolidated statements**)—investor has controlling interest.

The accounting and reporting for equity investments therefore depend on the level of influence and the type of security involved, as shown in Illustration IFRS17-5.

Category	Valuation	Unrealized Holding Gains or Losses	Other Income Effects
Holdings less than 20%			
1. Trading	Fair value	Recognized in net income	Dividends declared; gains and losses from sale.
2. Non-Trading	Fair value	Recognized in "Other comprehensive income" and as separate component of equity	Dividends declared; gains and losses from sale.
Holdings between 20% and 50%	Equity	Not recognized	Proportionate share of investee's net income.
Holdings more than 50%	Consolidation	Not recognized	Not applicable.

ILLUSTRATION IFRS17-5
Accounting and Reporting for Equity Investments by Category

Equity Investments at Fair Value

When an investor has an interest of less than 20 percent, it is presumed that the investor has little or no influence over the investee. As indicated in Illustration IFRS17-5, there are two classifications for holdings less than 20 percent. Under IFRS, the presumption is that equity investments are held-for-trading. That is, companies hold these securities to profit from price changes. As with debt investments that are held-for-trading, the general accounting and reporting rule for these investments is to value the securities at fair value and record unrealized gains and losses in net income (**fair value method**).[44]

However, some equity investments are held for purposes other than trading. For example, a company may be required to hold an equity investment in order to sell its products in a particular area. In this situation, the recording of unrealized gains and losses in income, as is required for trading investments, is not indicative of the company's performance with respect to this investment. As a result, IFRS allows companies to classify some equity investments as non-trading. **Non-trading equity investments** are recorded at fair value on the statement of financial position, with unrealized gains and losses reported in other comprehensive income.

Example: Equity Investment (Income). Upon acquisition, companies record equity investments at fair value. To illustrate, assume that on November 3, 2012, Republic Corporation purchased ordinary shares of three companies, each investment representing less than a 20 percent interest.

	Cost
Burberry	$259,700
Nestlé	317,500
St. Regis Pulp Co.	141,350
Total cost	$718,550

Republic records these investments as follows.

November 3, 2012

Equity Investments	718,550	
Cash		718,550

On December 6, 2012, Republic receives a cash dividend of $4,200 on its investment in the ordinary shares of Nestlé. It records the cash dividend as follows.

December 6, 2012

Cash	4,200	
Dividend Revenue		4,200

All three of the investee companies reported net income for the year, but only Nestlé declared and paid a dividend to Republic. But, recall that when an investor owns less than 20 percent of the shares of another corporation, it is presumed that the investor has relatively little influence on the investee. As a result, **net income earned by the investee is not a proper basis for recognizing income from the investment by the investor**. Why? Because the increased net assets resulting from profitable operations may be permanently retained for use in the investee's business. Therefore, **the investor earns net income only when the investee declares cash dividends**.

At December 31, 2012, Republic's equity investment portfolio has the carrying value and fair value shown in Illustration IFRS17-6.

---

[44]Fair value at initial recognition is the transaction price (exclusive of brokerage and other transaction costs). Subsequent fair value measurements should be based on market prices, if available. For non-traded investments, a valuation technique based on discounted expected cash flows can be used to develop a fair value estimate. While IFRS requires that all equity investments be measured at fair value, in certain limited cases, cost may be an appropriate estimate of fair value for an equity investment.

EQUITY INVESTMENT PORTFOLIO DECEMBER 31, 2012			
Investments	Carrying Value	Fair Value	Unrealized Gain (Loss)
Burberry	$259,700	$275,000	$ 15,300
Nestlé	317,500	304,000	(13,500)
St. Regis Pulp Co.	141,350	104,000	(37,350)
Total of portfolio	$718,550	$683,000	(35,550)
Previous fair value adjustment balance			–0–
Fair value adjustment—Cr.			$(35,550)

ILLUSTRATION IFRS17-6 Computation of Fair Value Adjustment— Equity Investment Portfolio (2012)

For Republic's equity investment portfolio, the gross unrealized gains are $15,300, and the gross unrealized losses are $50,850 ($13,500 + $37,350), resulting in a net unrealized loss of $35,550. The fair value of the equity investment portfolio is below cost by $35,550.

As with **debt** investments, Republic records the net unrealized gains and losses related to changes in the fair value of **equity** investments in an Unrealized Holding Gain or Loss—Income account. Republic reports this amount as other income and expense. In this case, Republic prepares an adjusting entry debiting the Unrealized Holding Gain or Loss—Income account and crediting the Fair Value Adjustment account to record the decrease in fair value and to record the loss as follows.

December 31, 2012

Unrealized Holding Gain or Loss—Income	35,550	
Fair Value Adjustment		35,550

On January 23, 2013, Republic sold all of its Burberry ordinary shares, receiving $287,220. Illustration IFRS17-7 shows the computation of the realized gain on the sale.

Net proceeds from sale	$287,220
Cost of Burberry shares	259,700
Gain on sale of shares	$ 27,520

ILLUSTRATION IFRS17-7 Computation of Gain on Sale of Burberry Shares

Republic records the sale as follows.

January 23, 2013

Cash	287,220	
Equity Investments		259,700
Gain on Sale of Equity Investment		27,520

As indicated in this example, the fair value method accounting for trading equity investments under IFRS is the same as GAAP for trading equity investments. As shown in the next section the accounting for *non-trading* equity investments under IFRS is similar to the accounting for available-for-sale equity investments under GAAP.

Example: Equity Investments (OCI). The accounting entries to record non-trading equity investments are the same as for trading equity investments, except for recording the unrealized holding gain or loss. For non-trading equity investments, companies **report the unrealized holding gain or loss as other comprehensive income (OCI).** Thus, the account titled Unrealized Holding Gain or Loss—Equity is used.

To illustrate, assume that on December 10, 2012, Republic Corporation purchased $20,750 of 1,000 ordinary shares of Hawthorne Company for $20.75 per share (which represents less than a 20 percent interest). Hawthorne is a distributor for Republic products in certain locales, the laws of which require a minimum level of share owner-ship of a company in that region. The investment in Hawthorne meets this regulatory requirement. As a result, Republic accounts for this investment at fair value, with unrealized gains and losses recorded in OCI.[45] Republic records this investment as follows.

December 10, 2012

Equity Investments	20,750	
Cash		20,750

On December 27, 2012, Republic receives a cash dividend of $450 on its invest-ment in the ordinary shares of Hawthorne Company. It records the cash dividend as follows.

December 27, 2012

Cash	450	
Dividend Revenue		450

Similar to the accounting for trading investments, when an investor owns less than 20 percent of the ordinary shares of another corporation, it is presumed that the investor has relatively little influence on the investee. Therefore, **the investor earns income when the investee declares cash dividends**.

At December 31, 2012, Republic's investment in Hawthorne has the carrying value and fair value shown in Illustration IFRS17-8.

ILLUSTRATION IFRS17-8
Computation of Fair Value Adjustment—Non-Trading Equity Investment (2012)

Non-Trading Equity Investment	Carrying Value	Fair Value	Unrealized Gain (Loss)
Hawthorne Company	$20,750	$24,000	$3,250
Previous fair value adjustment balance			0
Fair value adjustment (Dr.)			$3,250

For Republic's non-trading investment, the unrealized gain is $3,250. That is, the fair value of the Hawthorne investment exceeds cost by $3,250. Because Republic has classified this investment as non-trading, Republic records the unrealized gains and losses related to changes in the fair value of this non-trading **equity** investment in an Unrealized Holding Gain or Loss—Equity account. Republic reports this amount as **a part of other comprehensive income and as a component of other accumulated com-prehensive income (reported in equity) until realized**. In this case, Republic prepares an adjusting entry crediting the Unrealized Holding Gain or Loss—Equity account and debiting the Fair Value Adjustment account to record the decrease in fair value and to record the loss as follows.

December 31, 2012

Fair Value Adjustment	3,250	
Unrealized Holding Gain or Loss—Equity		3,250

Republic reports its equity investments in its December 31, 2012, financial statements as shown in Illustration IFRS17-9.

---

[45]The classification of an equity investment as non-trading is irrevocable. This approach is designed to provide some discipline to the application of the non-trading classification, which allows unrealized gains and losses to bypass net income.

ILLUSTRATION
IFRS17-9
Financial Statement
Presentation of Equity
Investments at Fair Value
(2012)

Statement of Financial Position	
Investments	
Equity investments (non-trading)	$24,000
Equity	
Accumulated other comprehensive gain	$ 3,250
Statement of Comprehensive Income	
Other income and expense	
Dividend revenue	$ 450
Other comprehensive income	
Unrealized holding gain	$ 3,250

During 2013, sales of Republic products through Hawthorne as a distributor did not meet management's goals. As a result, Republic withdrew from these markets and on December 20, 2013, Republic sold all of its Hawthorne Company ordinary shares, receiving net proceeds of $22,500. Illustration IFRS17-10 shows the computation of the realized gain on the sale.

Net proceeds from sale	$22,500
Cost of Hawthorne shares	20,750
Gain on sale of shares	$ 1,750

Republic records the sale as follows.

December 20, 2013		
Cash	22,500	
Equity Investments		20,750
Gain on Sale of Equity Investment		1,750

Because Republic no longer holds any equity investments, it makes the following entry to eliminate the Fair Value Adjustment account.

Unrealized Holding Gain or Loss—Equity	3,250	
Fair Value Adjustment		3,250

In summary, the accounting for non-trading equity investments deviates from the general provisions for equity investments. The IASB noted that while fair value provides the most useful information about investments in equity investments, recording unrealized gains or losses in other comprehensive income is more representative for non-trading equity investments.

Impairments

A company should evaluate every held-for-collection investment, at each reporting date, to determine if it has suffered **impairment**—a loss in value such that the fair value of the investment is below its carrying value.[46] For example, if an investee experiences a bankruptcy or a significant liquidity crisis, the investor may suffer a permanent loss. **If the company determines that an investment is impaired, it writes down the amortized cost basis of the individual security to reflect this loss in value.** The company accounts for the write-down as a realized loss, and it includes the amount in net income.

For debt investments, a company uses the impairment test to determine whether "it is probable that the investor will be unable to collect all amounts due according to the contractual terms." If an investment is impaired, the company should measure the loss due to the **impairment**. This impairment loss is calculated as the difference between the

---

[46]Note that impairments tests are conducted only for debt investments that are held-for-collection (which are accounted for at amortized cost). Other debt and equity investments are measured at fair value each period; thus, an impairment test is not needed.

carrying amount plus accrued interest and the expected future cash flows discounted at the investment's historical effective-interest rate.

Example: Impairment Loss

At December 31, 2011, Mayhew Company has a debt investment in Bellovary Inc., purchased at par for $200,000. The investment has a term of four years, with annual interest payments at 10 percent, paid at the end of each year (the historical effective-interest rate is 10 percent). This debt investment is classified as held-for-collection. Unfortunately, Bellovary is experiencing significant financial difficulty and indicates that it will be unable to make all payments according to the contractual terms. Mayhew uses the present value method for measuring the required impairment loss. Illustration IFRS17-11 shows the cash flow schedule prepared for this analysis.

ILLUSTRATION IFRS17-11
Investment Cash Flows

Dec. 31	Contractual Cash Flows	Expected Cash Flows	Loss of Cash Flows
2012	$ 20,000	$ 16,000	$ 4,000
2013	20,000	16,000	4,000
2014	20,000	16,000	4,000
2015	220,000	216,000	4,000
Total cash flows	$280,000	$264,000	$16,000

As indicated, the expected cash flows of $264,000 are less than the contractual cash flows of $280,000. The amount of the impairment to be recorded equals the difference between the recorded investment of $200,000 and the present value of the expected cash flows, as shown in Illustration IFRS17-12.

ILLUSTRATION IFRS17-12
Computation of Impairment Loss

Recorded investment		$200,000
Less: Present value of $200,000 due in 4 years at 10% (Table 6-2); FV(PVF$_{4,10\%}$); ($200,000 × .68301)	$136,602	
Present value of $16,000 interest receivable annually for 4 years at 10% (Table 6-4); R(PVF-OA$_{4,10\%}$); ($16,000 × 3.16986)	50,718	187,320
Loss on impairment		$ 12,680

The loss due to the impairment is $12,680. Why isn't it $16,000 ($280,000 − $264,000)? A loss of $12,680 is recorded because Mayhew must measure the loss at a present value amount, not at an undiscounted amount. Mayhew recognizes an impairment loss of $12,680 by debiting Loss on Impairment for the expected loss. At the same time, it reduces the overall value of the investment. The journal entry to record the loss is therefore as follows.

Loss on Impairment	12,680	
Debt Investments		12,680

Recovery of Impairment Loss

Subsequent to recording an impairment, events or economic conditions may change such that the extent of the impairment loss decreases (e.g., due to an improvement in the debtor's credit rating). In this situation, some or all of the previously recognized impairment loss shall be reversed with a debit to the Debt Investments account and a credit to Recovery of Impairment Loss. Similar to the accounting for impairments of receivables shown in Chapter 7, the reversal of impairment losses shall not result in a carrying amount of the investment that exceeds the amortized cost that would have been reported had the impairment not been recognized.

ON THE HORIZON

At one time, both the FASB and IASB have indicated that they believe that all financial instruments should be reported at fair value and that changes in fair value should be reported as part of net income. However, the recently issued IFRS indicates that the IASB believes that certain debt investments should not be reported at fair value. The IASB's decision to issue new rules on investments, prior to the FASB's completion of its deliberations on financial instrument accounting, could create obstacles for the Boards in converging the accounting in this area.

IFRS SELF-TEST QUESTIONS

1. All of the following are key similarities between GAAP and IFRS with respect to accounting for investments *except:*
   (a) IFRS and GAAP have a held-to-maturity investment classification.
   (b) IFRS and GAAP apply the equity method to significant influence equity investments.
   (c) IFRS and GAAP have a fair value option for financial instruments.
   (d) the accounting for impairment of investments is similar, although IFRS allows recovery of impairment losses.

2. Which of the following statements is *correct*?
   (a) GAAP has a held-for-collection investment classification.
   (b) GAAP permits recovery of impairment losses.
   (c) Under IFRS, non-trading equity investments are accounted for at amortized cost
   (d) IFRS and GAAP both have a trading investment classification.

3. IFRS requires companies to measure their financial assets at fair value based on:
   (a) the company's business model for managing its financial assets.
   (b) whether the financial asset is a debt investment.
   (c) whether the financial asset is an equity investment.
   (d) All of the choices are IFRS requirements.

4. Select the investment accounting approach with the correct valuation approach:

	Not Held-for-Collection	Held-for-Collection
(a)	Amortized cost	Amortized cost
(b)	Fair value	Fair value
(c)	Fair value	Amortized cost
(d)	Amortized cost	Fair value

5. Under IFRS, a company:
   (a) should evaluate only equity investments for impairment.
   (b) accounts for an impairment as an unrealized loss, and includes it as a part of other comprehensive income and as a component of other accumulated comprehensive income until realized.
   (c) calculates the impairment loss on debt investments as the difference between the carrying amount plus accrued interest and the expected future cash flows discounted at the investment's historical effective-interest rate.
   (d) All of the above.

IFRS CONCEPTS AND APPLICATION

IFRS17-1 Where can authoritative IFRS be found related to investments?

IFRS17-2 Briefly describe some of the similarities and differences between GAAP and IFRS with respect to the accounting for investments.

IFRS17-3 Describe the two criteria for determining the valuation of financial assets.

IFRS17-4 Which types of investments are valued at amortized cost? Explain the rationale for this accounting.

IFRS17-5 Lady Gaga Co. recently made an investment in the bonds issued by Chili Peppers Inc. Lady Gaga's business model for this investment is to profit from trading in response to changes in market interest rates. How should this investment be classified by Lady Gaga? Explain.

IFRS17-6 Consider the bond investment by Lady Gaga in IFRS17-5. Discuss the accounting for this investment if Lady Gaga's business model is to hold the investment to collect interest while outstanding and to receive the principal at maturity.

IFRS17-7 Indicate how unrealized holding gains and losses should be reported for investments classified as trading and held for-collection.

IFRS17-8 Ramirez Company has a held-for-collection investment in the 6%, 20-year bonds of Soto Company. The investment was originally purchased for $1,200,000 in 2011. Early in 2012, Ramirez recorded an impairment of $300,000 on the Soto investment, due to Soto's financial distress. In 2013, Soto returned to profitability and the Soto investment was no longer impaired. What entry does Ramirez make in 2013 under (a) GAAP and (b) IFRS?

IFRS17-9 Carow Corporation purchased, as a held-for-collection investment, $60,000 of the 8%, 5-year bonds of Harrison, Inc. for $65,118, which provides a 6% return. The bonds pay interest semiannually. Prepare Carow's journal entries for (a) the purchase of the investment, and (b) the receipt of semiannual interest and premium amortization.

IFRS17-10 Fairbanks Corporation purchased 400 ordinary shares of Sherman Inc. as a trading investment for $13,200. During the year, Sherman paid a cash dividend of $3.25 per share. At year-end, Sherman shares were selling for $34.50 per share. Prepare Fairbanks's journal entries to record (a) the purchase of the investment, (b) the dividends received, and (c) the fair value adjustment.

IFRS17-11 Use the information from IFRS17-10 but assume the shares were purchased to meet a non-trading regulatory requirement. Prepare Fairbanks's journal entries to record (a) the purchase of the investment, (b) the dividends received, and (c) the fair value adjustment.

IFRS17-12 On January 1, 2012, Roosevelt Company purchased 12% bonds, having a maturity value of $500,000, for $537,907.40. The bonds provide the bondholders with a 10% yield. They are dated January 1, 2012, and mature January 1, 2017, with interest receivable December 31 of each year. Roosevelt's business model is to hold these bonds to collect contractual cash flows.

Instructions

(a) Prepare the journal entry at the date of the bond purchase.
(b) Prepare a bond amortization schedule.
(c) Prepare the journal entry to record the interest received and the amortization for 2012.
(d) Prepare the journal entry to record the interest received and the amortization for 2013.

IFRS17-13 Assume the same information as in IFRS17-12 except that Roosevelt has an active trading strategy for these bonds. The fair value of the bonds at December 31 of each year-end is as follows.

2012	$534,200	2015	$517,000
2013	$515,000	2016	$500,000
2014	$513,000		

Instructions

(a) Prepare the journal entry at the date of the bond purchase.

(b) Prepare the journal entries to record the interest received and recognition of fair value for 2012.

(c) Prepare the journal entry to record the recognition of fair value for 2013.

IFRS17-14 On December 21, 2012, Zurich Company provided you with the following information regarding its trading investments.

December 31, 2012

Investments (Trading)	Cost	Fair Value	Unrealized Gain (Loss)
Stargate Corp. shares	$20,000	$19,000	$(1,000)
Carolina Co. shares	10,000	9,000	(1,000)
Vectorman Co. shares	20,000	20,600	600
Total of portfolio	$50,000	$48,600	$(1,400)
Previous fair value adjustment balance	–0–		
Fair value adjustment—Cr.	$ (1,400)		

During 2013, Carolina Company shares were sold for $9,500. The fair value of the shares on December 31, 2013, was Stargate Corp. shares—$19,300; Vectorman Co. shares—$20,500.

Instructions

(a) Prepare the adjusting journal entry needed on December 31, 2012.

(b) Prepare the journal entry to record the sale of the Carolina Company shares during 2013.

(c) Prepare the adjusting journal entry needed on December 31, 2013.

IFRS17-15 Komissarov Company has a debt investment in the bonds issued by Keune Inc. The bonds were purchased at par for $400,000 and, at the end of 2012, have a remaining life of 3 years with annual interest payments at 10%, paid at the end of each year. This debt investment is classified as held-for-collection. Keune is facing a tough economic environment and informs all of its investors that it will be unable to make all payments according to the contractual terms. The controller of Komissarov has prepared the following revised expected cash flow forecast for this bond investment.

Dec. 31	Expected Cash Flows
2013	$ 35,000
2014	35,000
2015	385,000
Total cash flows	$455,000

Instructions

(a) Determine the impairment loss for Komissarov at December 31, 2012.

(b) Prepare the entry to record the impairment loss for Komissarov at December 31, 2012.

(c) On January 15, 2013, Keune receives a major capital infusion from a private equity investor. It informs Komissarov that the bonds now will be paid according to the contractual terms. Briefly describe how Komissarov would account for the bond investment in light of this new information.

Professional Research

IFRS17-16 Your client, Cascade Company, is planning to invest some of its excess cash in 5-year revenue bonds issued by the county and in the shares of one of its suppliers, Teton Co. Teton's shares trade on the over-the-counter market. Cascade plans to classify these investments as trading. They would like you to conduct some research on the accounting for these investments.

Instructions

Access the IFRS authoritative literature at the IASB website (*http://eifrs.iasb.org/*). When you have accessed the documents, you can use the search tool in your Internet browser to respond to the following questions. (Provide paragraph citations.)

- **(a)** Since the Teton shares do not trade on one of the large securities exchanges, Cascade argues that the fair value of this investment is not readily available. According to the authoritative literature, when is the fair value of a security "readily determinable"?
- **(b)** How is an impairment of a debt investment accounted for?
- **(c)** To avoid volatility in their financial statements due to fair value adjustments, Cascade debated whether the bond investment could be classified as held-for-collection; Cascade is pretty sure it will hold the bonds for 5 years. What criteria must be met for Cascade to classify it as held-for-collection?

International Financial Reporting Problem:
Marks and Spencer plc

IFRS17-17 The financial statements of Marks and Spencer plc (M&S) are available at the book's companion website or can be accessed at *http://corporate.marksandspencer.com/documents/publications/2010/Annual_Report_2010*.

Instructions

Refer to M&S's financial statements and the accompanying notes to answer the following questions.

- **(a)** What investments does M&S report in 2010, and where are these investments reported in its financial statements?
- **(b)** How are M&S's investments valued? How does M&S determine fair value?
- **(c)** How does M&S use derivative financial instruments?

ANSWERS TO IFRS SELF-TEST QUESTIONS

1. a   **2.** d   **3.** a   **4.** c   **5.** c

Remember to check the book's companion website to find additional resources for this chapter.

18 ▸ Revenue Recognition

LEARNING OBJECTIVES ▸

After studying this chapter, you should be able to:

1 Apply the revenue recognition principle.

2 Describe accounting issues for revenue recognition at point of sale.

3 Apply the percentage-of-completion method for long-term contracts.

4 Apply the completed-contract method for long-term contracts.

5 Identify the proper accounting for losses on long-term contracts.

6 Describe the installment-sales method of accounting.

7 Explain the cost-recovery method of accounting.

It's Back

Several years after passage, the accounting world continues to be preoccupied with the Sarbanes-Oxley Act of 2002 (SOX). Unfortunately, SOX did not solve one of the classic accounting issues—how to properly account for revenue. In fact, revenue recognition practices are the most prevalent reasons for accounting restatements. A number of the revenue recognition issues relate to possible fraudulent behavior by company executives and employees.

As a result of such revenue recognition problems, the SEC has increased its enforcement actions in this area. In some of these cases, companies made significant adjustments to previously issued financial statements. As Lynn Turner, a former chief accountant of the SEC, indicated, "When people cross over the boundaries of legitimate reporting, the Commission will take appropriate action to ensure the fairness and integrity that investors need and depend on every day."

Consider some SEC actions:

- The SEC charged the former co-chairman and CEO of **Qwest Communications International Inc.** and eight other former Qwest officers and employees with fraud and other violations of the federal securities laws. Three of these people fraudulently characterized nonrecurring revenue from one-time sales as revenue from recurring data and Internet services. The SEC release notes that internal correspondence likened Qwest's dependence on these transactions to fill the gap between actual and projected revenue to an addiction.

- The SEC filed a complaint against three former senior officers of **iGo Corp.**, alleging that the defendants collectively caused iGo to improperly recognize revenue on consignment sales and products that were not shipped or that were shipped after the end of a fiscal quarter.

- The SEC filed a complaint against the former CEO and chairman of **Homestore Inc.** and its former executive vice president of business development, alleging that they engaged in a fraudulent scheme to overstate advertising and subscription revenues. The scheme involved a complex structure of "round-trip" transactions using various third-party companies that, in essence, allowed Homestore to recognize its own cash as revenue.

- The SEC claims that **Lantronix** deliberately sent excessive product to distributors and granted them generous return rights and extended payment terms. In addition, as part of its alleged channel

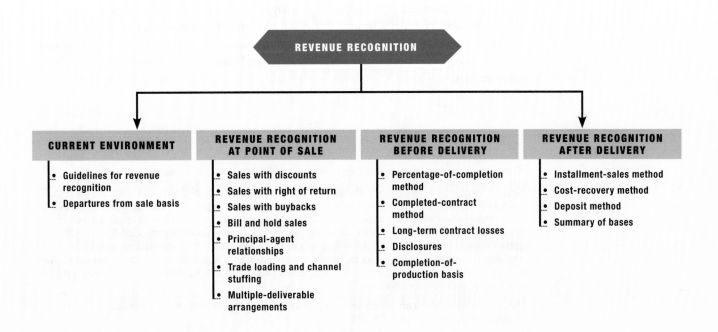
stuffing and to prevent product returns, Lantronix loaned funds to a third party to purchase Lantronix products from one of its distributors. The third party later returned the product. The SEC also asserted that Lantronix engaged in other improper revenue recognition practices, including shipping without a purchase order and recognizing revenue on a contingent sale.

Though the cases cited involved fraud and irregularity, not all revenue recognition errors are intentional. For example, in April 2005 **American Home Mortgage Investment Corp.** announced that it would reverse revenue recognized from its fourth-quarter 2004 loan securitization and would recognize it in the first quarter of 2005 instead. As a result, American Home restated its financial results for 2004.

So, how does a company ensure that revenue transactions are recorded properly? Some answers will become apparent after you study this chapter.

Sources: Cheryl de Mesa Graziano, "Revenue Recognition: A Perennial Problem," *Financial Executive* (July 14, 2005), *www.fei.org/mag/articles/7-2005_revenue.cfm;* and S. Taub, "SEC Accuses Ex-CFO of Channel Stuffing," *CFO.com* (September 30, 2006).

PREVIEW OF CHAPTER 18 As indicated in the opening story, the issue of when revenue should be recognized is complex. The many methods of marketing products and services make it difficult to develop guidelines that will apply to all situations. This chapter provides you with general guidelines used in most business transactions. The content and organization of the chapter are as follows.

REVENUE RECOGNITION

CURRENT ENVIRONMENT	REVENUE RECOGNITION AT POINT OF SALE	REVENUE RECOGNITION BEFORE DELIVERY	REVENUE RECOGNITION AFTER DELIVERY
• Guidelines for revenue recognition • Departures from sale basis	• Sales with discounts • Sales with right of return • Sales with buybacks • Bill and hold sales • Principal-agent relationships • Trade loading and channel stuffing • Multiple-deliverable arrangements	• Percentage-of-completion method • Completed-contract method • Long-term contract losses • Disclosures • Completion-of-production basis	• Installment-sales method • Cost-recovery method • Deposit method • Summary of bases

CURRENT ENVIRONMENT

Most revenue transactions pose few problems for revenue recognition. This is because, in many cases, the transaction is initiated and completed at the same time. However, not all transactions are that simple. For example, consider a customer who enters into a mobile phone contract with a company such as Verizon. The customer is often provided with a package that may include a handset, free minutes of talk time, data downloads, and text messaging service. In addition, some providers will bundle that with a fixed-line broadband service. At the same time, customers may pay for these services in a variety of ways, possibly receiving a discount on the handset, then paying higher prices for connection fees, and so forth. In some cases, depending on the package purchased, the company may provide free applications in subsequent periods. How then should the various pieces of this sale be reported by Verizon? The answer is not obvious.

It is therefore not surprising that a recent survey of financial executives noted that the revenue recognition process is increasingly more complex to manage, prone to error, and material to financial statements compared to any other area in financial reporting. The report went on to note that revenue recognition is a top fraud risk and that regardless of the accounting rules followed (GAAP or IFRS), the risk or errors and inaccuracies in revenue reporting is significant.[1]

INTERNATIONAL PERSPECTIVE

The FASB and IASB have a joint project to improve the accounting for revenue.

Indeed, both the FASB and the IASB indicate that the present state of reporting for revenue is unsatisfactory. IFRS is criticized because it lacks guidance in a number of areas. For example, IFRS has one basic standard on revenue recognition—*IAS 18*—plus some limited guidance related to certain minor topics. In contrast, GAAP has numerous standards related to revenue recognition (by some counts over 100), but many believe the standards are often inconsistent with one another. Thus, the accounting for revenues provides a most fitting contrast of the principles-based (IFRS) and rules-based (GAAP) approaches. While both sides have their advocates, the FASB and IASB recognize a number of deficiencies in this area.[2]

Unfortunately, inappropriate recognition of revenue can occur in any industry. Products that are sold to distributors for resale pose different risks than products or services that are sold directly to customers. Sales in high-technology industries, where rapid product obsolescence is a significant issue, pose different risks than sales of inventory with a longer life, such as farm or construction equipment, automobiles, trucks, and appliances.[3] As a consequence, restatements for improper revenue recognition are relatively common and can lead to significant share price adjustments.

---

[1]See *www.prweb.com/releases/RecognitionRevenue/IFRS/prweb1648994.htm.*

[2]See, for example, "Preliminary Views on Revenue Recognition in Contracts with Customers," *IASB/FASB Discussion Paper* (December 19, 2008). Some of the problems noted are that GAAP has so many standards that at times they are inconsistent with each other in applying basic principles. In addition, even with the many standards, no guidance is provided for service transactions. Conversely, IFRS has a lack of guidance in certain fundamental areas such as multiple-deliverable arrangements, which are becoming increasingly common. In addition, there is inconsistency in applying revenue recognition principles to long-term contracts versus other elements of revenue recognition.

[3]Adapted from American Institute of Certified Public Accountants, Inc., *Audit Issues in Revenue Recognition* (New York: AICPA, 1999).

Guidelines for Revenue Recognition

Revenue arises from ordinary operations and is referred to by various names such as sales, fees, rent, interest, royalties, and service revenue. Gains, on the other hand, may or may not arise in the normal course of operations. Typical gains are gains on sale of noncurrent assets or unrealized gains related to investments or noncurrent assets. The primary issue related to revenue recognition is when to recognize the revenue.

1 LEARNING OBJECTIVE
Apply the revenue recognition principle.

In general, the guidelines for revenue recognition are quite broad. On top of the broad guidelines, certain industries have specific additional guidelines that provide further insight into when revenue should be recognized. The **revenue recognition principle** provides that companies should recognize revenue[4] (1) when it is realized or realizable, and (2) when it is earned.[5] Therefore, proper revenue recognition revolves around three terms:

> Revenues are **realized** when a company exchanges goods and services for cash or claims to cash (receivables).
>
> Revenues are **realizable** when assets a company receives in exchange are readily convertible to known amounts of cash or claims to cash.
>
> Revenues are **earned** when a company has substantially accomplished what it must do to be entitled to the benefits represented by the revenues—that is, when the earnings process is complete or virtually complete.[6]

Four revenue transactions are recognized in accordance with this principle:

Underlying Concepts

Revenues are inflows of assets and/or settlements of liabilities from delivering or producing goods, providing services, or other earning activities that constitute a company's ongoing major or central operations during a period.

1. Companies recognize revenue from selling products at the date of sale. This date is usually interpreted to mean the date of delivery to customers.

2. Companies recognize revenue from services provided, when services have been performed and are billable.

3. Companies recognize revenue from permitting others to use enterprise assets, such as interest, rent, and royalties, as time passes or as the assets are used.

4. Companies recognize revenue from disposing of assets other than products at the date of sale.

---

[4]Recognition is "the process of formally recording or incorporating an item in the accounts and financial statements of an entity" (*SFAC No. 3*, par. 83). "Recognition includes depiction of an item in both words and numbers, with the amount included in the totals of the financial statements" (*SFAC No. 5*, par. 6). For an asset or liability, recognition involves recording not only acquisition or incurrence of the item but also later changes in it, including removal from the financial statements previously recognized.

Recognition is not the same as realization, although the two are sometimes used interchangeably in accounting literature and practice. *Realization* is "the process of converting noncash resources and rights into money and is most precisely used in accounting and financial reporting to refer to sales of assets for cash or claims to cash" (*SFAC No. 3*, par. 83).

[5]"Recognition and Measurement in Financial Statements of Business Enterprises," *Statement of Financial Accounting Concepts No. 5* (Stamford, Conn.: FASB, 1984), par. 83.

[6]Gains (as contrasted to revenues) commonly result from transactions and other events that do not involve an "earning process." For gain recognition, being earned is generally less significant than being realized or realizable. Companies commonly recognize gains at the time of an asset's sale, disposition of a liability, or when prices of certain assets change.

These revenue transactions are diagrammed in Illustration 18-1.

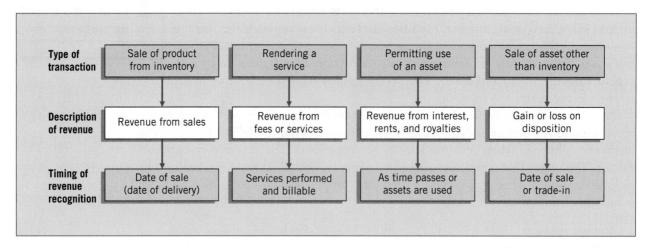

ILLUSTRATION 18-1
Revenue Recognition
Classified by Nature of
Transaction

The preceding statements are the basis of accounting for revenue transactions. Yet, in practice there are departures from the revenue recognition principle. Companies sometimes recognize revenue at other points in the earning process, owing in great measure to the considerable variety of revenue transactions.[7]

Departures from the Sale Basis

An FASB study found some common **reasons for departures from the sale basis**.[8] One reason is a desire to **recognize earlier** than the time of sale the effect of earning activities. Earlier recognition is appropriate if there is a high degree of certainty about the amount of revenue earned. A second reason is a desire to **delay recognition** of revenue beyond the time of sale. Delayed recognition is appropriate if the degree of uncertainty concerning the amount of either revenue or costs is sufficiently high or if the sale does not represent substantial completion of the earnings process.

This chapter focuses on two of the four general types of revenue transactions described earlier: (1) selling products and (2) providing services. Both of these are **sales transactions**. (In several other sections of the textbook, we discuss the other two types of revenue transactions—revenue from permitting others to use enterprise assets, and revenue from disposing of assets other than products.) Our discussion of product sales transactions in this chapter is organized around the following topics:

1. Revenue recognition at point of sale (delivery).
2. Revenue recognition before delivery.
3. Revenue recognition after delivery.

---

[7]The FASB and IASB are now involved in a joint project on revenue recognition. The purpose of this project is to develop comprehensive conceptual guidance on when to recognize revenue. Presently, the Boards are evaluating a customer-consideration model. In this model, a company accounts for the contract asset or liability that arises from the rights and performance obligations in an enforceable contract with the customer. At contract inception, the rights in the contract are measured at the amount of the promised customer payment (that is, the customer consideration). That amount is then allocated to the individual performance obligations identified within the contract in proportion to the standalone selling price of each good or service underlying the performance obligation. It is hoped that this approach (rather than using the earned and realized or realized criteria) will lead to a better basis for revenue recognition. See *www.fasb.org/project/ revenue_recognition.shtml.*

[8]Henry R. Jaenicke, *Survey of Present Practices in Recognizing Revenues, Expenses, Gains, and Losses, A Research Report* (Stamford, Conn.: FASB, 1981), p. 11.

Illustration 18-2 depicts this organization of revenue recognition topics.

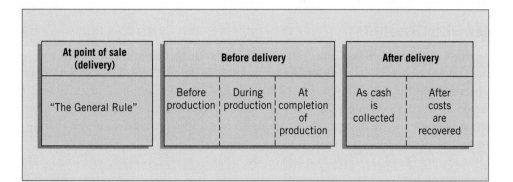

ILLUSTRATION 18-2
Revenue Recognition
Alternatives

LIABILITY OR REVENUE?

Suppose you purchased a gift card for spa services at Sundara Spa for $300. The gift card expires at the end of six months. When should Sundara record the revenue? Here are two choices:

1. At the time Sundara receives the cash for the gift card.
2. At the time Sundara provides the service to the gift-card holder.

What do the numbers mean?

If you answered number 2, you would be right. Companies should recognize revenue when the obligation is satisfied—which is when Sundara performs the service.

Now let's add a few more facts. Suppose that the gift-card holder fails to use the card in the six-month period. Statistics show that between 2 and 15 percent of gift-card holders never redeem their cards. So, do you still believe that Sundara should record the revenue at the expiration date?

If you say you are not sure, you are probably right. Here is why: Certain states do not recognize expiration dates, and therefore the customer has the right to redeem an otherwise expired gift card at any time. Let's say for the moment we are in one of these states. Because the card holder may never redeem, when can Sundara recognize the revenue? In that case, Sundara would have to show statistically that after a certain period of time, the likelihood of redemption is remote. If it can make that case, it can recognize the revenue. Otherwise, it may have to wait a long time.

Unfortunately, Sundara may still have a problem. It may be required to turn over the value of the spa services to the state. The treatment for unclaimed gift cards may fall under the abandoned-and-unclaimed-property laws. Most common unclaimed items are required to be remitted to the states after a five-year period. Failure to report and remit the property can result in additional fines and penalties. So if Sundara is in a state where unclaimed property must be sent state to the state, Sundara should report a liability on its balance sheet.

Source: PricewaterhouseCoopers, "Issues Surrounding the Recognition of Gift Card Sales and Escheat Liabilities," *Quick Brief* (December 2004).

REVENUE RECOGNITION AT POINT OF SALE (DELIVERY)

According to the FASB's *Concepts Statement No. 5*, companies usually meet the two conditions for recognizing revenue (being realized or realizable and being earned) by the time they deliver products or render services to customers.[9] Therefore, companies commonly recognize revenues from manufacturing and selling

> **2 LEARNING OBJECTIVE**
> Describe accounting issues for revenue recognition at point of sale.

[9]The SEC believes that revenue is realized or realizable and earned when all of the following criteria are met: (1) Persuasive evidence of an arrangement exists; (2) delivery has occurred or services have been provided; (3) the seller's price to the buyer is fixed or determinable; and (4) collectibility is reasonably assured. [1] The SEC provided more specific guidance because the general criteria were difficult to interpret.

See the FASB
Codification section
(page 1109).

activities at **point of sale** (usually meaning delivery).[10] Implementation problems, however, can arise. We discuss some of these problematic situations on the following pages.

Sales with Discounts

Any trade discounts or volume rebates should reduce consideration received and reduce revenue earned. In addition, if the payment is delayed, the seller should impute an interest rate for the difference between the cash or cash equivalent price and the deferred amount. In essence, the seller is financing the sale and should record interest revenue over the payment term. Illustrations 18-3 and 18-4 provide examples of transactions that illustrate these points.

ILLUSTRATION 18-3
Revenue Measurement—
Volume Discount

VOLUME DISCOUNT

Facts: Sansung Company has an arrangement with its customers that it will provide a 3% volume discount to its customers if they purchase at least $2 million of its product during the calendar year. On March 31, 2012, Sansung has made sales of $700,000 to Artic Co. In the previous two years, Sansung sold over $3,000,000 to Artic in the period April 1 to December 31.

Question: How much revenue should Sansung recognize for the first three months of 2012?

Solution: In this case, Sansung should reduce its revenue by $21,000 ($700,000 × 3%) because it is probable that it will provide this rebate. Revenue should therefore be reported at $679,000 ($700,000 − $21,000). To not recognize this volume discount overstates Sansung's revenue for the first three months of 2012. In other words, the realizable revenue is $679,000, not $700,000.

In this case, Sansung makes the following entry on March 31, 2012.

Accounts Receivable	679,000	
Sales Revenue		679,000

Assuming that Sansung's customers **meet the discount threshold**, Sansung makes the following entry.

Cash	679,000	
Accounts Receivable		679,000

If Sansung's customers **fail to meet the discount threshold**, Sansung makes the following entry upon payment.

Cash	700,000	
Accounts Receivable		679,000
Sales Discounts Forfeited		21,000

As indicated in Chapter 7 (page 372), Sales Discounted Forfeited is reported in the other revenue and expense section of the income statement.

In some cases, companies provide cash discounts to customers for a short period of time (often referred to as prompt settlement discounts). For example, assume that terms are payment due in 60 days, but if payment is made within 5 days, a 2 percent discount is given. These prompt settlement discounts should reduce revenues, if material. In most cases, companies record the revenue at full price (gross) and record a sales discount if payment is made within the discount period.

When a sales transaction involves a financing arrangement, the fair value is determined either by measuring the consideration received or by discounting the payment using an imputed interest rate. The imputed interest rate is the more clearly determinable of either (1) the prevailing rate for a similar instrument of an issuer with a similar credit

---

[10]*Statement of Financial Accounting Concepts No. 5*, op. cit., par. 84.

rating, or (2) a rate of interest that discounts the nominal amount of the instrument to the current sales price of the goods or services. [2] This issue is addressed in Illustration 18-4.

ILLUSTRATION 18-4
Revenue Measurement—
Deferred Payment

EXTENDED PAYMENT TERMS

Facts: On July 1, 2012, SEK Company sold goods to Grant Company for $900,000 in exchange for a 4-year zero-interest-bearing note in the face amount of $1,416,163. The goods have an inventory cost on SEK's books of $590,000.

Questions: (a) How much revenue should SEK Company record on July 1, 2012? (b) How much revenue should it report related to this transaction on December 31, 2012?

Solution:
(a) SEK should record revenue of $900,000 on July 1, 2012, which is the fair value of the inventory in this case.
(b) SEK is also financing this purchase and records interest revenue on the note over the 4-year period. In this case, the interest rate is imputed and is determined to be 12%. SEK records interest revenue of $54,000 (12% $\times$ ½ $\times$ $900,000) at December 31, 2012.

The journal entry to record SEK's sale to Grant Company is as follows (ignoring the cost of goods sold entry).

	July 1, 2012	
Notes Receivable	1,416,163	
Sales Revenue		900,000
Discount on Notes Receivable		516,163

SEK makes the following entry to record interest revenue.

	December 31, 2012	
Discount on Notes Receivable	54,000	
Interest Revenue (12% $\times$ ½ $\times$ $900,00)		54,000

Sales with Right of Return

Whether cash or credit sales are involved, a special problem arises with claims for returns and allowances. In Chapter 7, we presented the accounting treatment for normal returns and allowances. However, certain companies experience such a high rate of returns—a high ratio of returned merchandise to sales—that they find it necessary to postpone reporting sales until the return privilege has substantially expired.

For example, in the publishing industry, the rate of return approaches 25 percent for hardcover books and 65 percent for some magazines. Other types of companies that experience high return rates are perishable food dealers, distributors who sell to retail outlets, recording-industry companies, and some toy and sporting goods manufacturers. Returns in these industries are frequently made either through a right of contract or as a matter of practice involving "guaranteed sales" agreements or consignments.

Three alternative revenue recognition methods are available when the right of return exposes the seller to continued risks of ownership. These are (1) not recording a sale until all return privileges have expired; (2) recording the sale, but reducing sales by an estimate of future returns; and (3) recording the sale and accounting for the returns as they occur. The FASB concluded that if a company sells its product but gives the buyer the right to return it, the company should **recognize revenue** from the sales transactions at the time of sale **only if all of the following six conditions** have been met. [3]

1. The seller's price to the buyer is substantially fixed or determinable at the date of sale.

2. The buyer has paid the seller, or the buyer is obligated to pay the seller, and the obligation is not contingent on resale of the product.

3. The buyer's obligation to the seller would not be changed in the event of theft or physical destruction or damage of the product.

4. The buyer acquiring the product for resale has economic substance apart from that provided by the seller.

5. The seller does not have significant obligations for future performance to directly bring about resale of the product by the buyer.

6. The seller can reasonably estimate the amount of future returns.

What if the six conditions are not met? In that case, the company must recognize sales revenue and cost of sales either when the return privilege has substantially expired or when those six conditions subsequently are met, **whichever occurs first**. In the income statement, the company must reduce sales revenue and cost of sales by the amount of the estimated returns.[11]

An example of a return situation is presented in Illustration 18-5.

ILLUSTRATION 18-5
Recognition—Returns

SALES WITH RETURNS

Facts: Pesido Company is in the beta-testing stage for new laser equipment that will help patients who have acid reflux problems. The product that Pesido is selling has been very successful in trials to date. As a result, Pesido has received regulatory authority to sell this equipment to various hospitals. Because of the uncertainty surrounding this product, Pesido has granted to the participating hospitals the right to return the device and receive full reimbursement for a period of 9 months.

Question: When should Pesido recognize the revenue for the sale of the new laser equipment?

Solution: Given that the hospital has the right to rescind the purchase for a reason specified in the sales contract and Pesido is uncertain about the probability of return, Pesido should not record revenue at the time of delivery. If there is uncertainty about the possibility of return, revenue is recognized when the goods have been delivered and the time period for rejection has elapsed. Only at that time have the risks and rewards of ownership transferred.

Companies may retain only an insignificant risk of ownership when a refund or right of return is provided. For example, revenue is recognized at the time of sale (even though a right of return exists or refund is permitted), provided the seller can reliably estimate future returns. In this case, the seller recognizes an allowance for returns based on previous experience and other relevant factors.

Returning to the Pesido example, assume that Pesido sold $300,000 of laser equipment on August 1, 2012, and retains only an insignificant risk of ownership. On October 15, 2012, $10,000 in equipment was returned. In this case, Pesido makes the following entries.

	August 1, 2012	
Accounts Receivable	300,000	
Sales Revenue		300,000

	October 15, 2012	
Sales Returns and Allowances	10,000	
Accounts Receivable		10,000

At December 31, 2012, based on prior experience, Pesido estimates that returns on the remaining balance will be 4 percent. Pesido makes the following entry to record the expected returns.

---

[11]Here is an example where GAAP provides detailed guidelines beyond the general revenue recognition principle.

December 31, 2012

Sales Returns and Allowances		
[($300,000 − $10,000) × 4%]	11,600	
Allowance for Sales Returns and Allowances		11,600

The Sales Returns and Allowances account is reported as contra revenue in the income statement, and Allowance for Sales Returns and Allowances is reported as a contra account to Accounts Receivable in the balance sheet. As a result, the net revenue and net accounts receivable recognized are adjusted for the amount of the expected returns.

Sales with Buybacks

If a company sells a product in one period and agrees to buy it back in the next period, has the company sold the product? As indicated in Chapter 8, legal title has transferred in this situation. However, the economic substance of this transaction is that the seller retains the risks of ownership. Illustration 18-6 provides an example of a sale with a buyback provision.

ILLUSTRATION 18-6
Recognition—Sale with Buyback

SALE WITH BUYBACK

Facts: Morgan Inc., an equipment dealer, sells equipment to Lane Company for $135,000. The equipment has a cost of $115,000. Morgan agrees to repurchase the equipment at the end of 2 years at its fair value. Lane Company pays full price at the sales date, and there are no restrictions on the use of the equipment over the 2 years.

Question: How should Morgan record this transaction?

Solution: For a sale and repurchase agreement, the terms of the agreement need to be analyzed to ascertain whether, in substance, the seller has transferred the risks and rewards of ownership to the buyer. In this case, it appears that the risks and rewards of ownership are transferred to Lane Company and therefore a sale should be recorded. That is, Lane will receive fair value at the date of repurchase, which indicates Morgan has transferred risks of ownership. Furthermore, Lane has no restrictions on use of the equipment, which indicates that Morgan has transferred the rewards of ownership.

Morgan records the sale and related cost of goods sold as follows.

Cash	135,000	
Sales Revenue		135,000
Cost of Goods Sold	115,000	
Inventory		115,000

Now assume that Morgan requires Lane to sign a note with repayment to be made in 24 monthly payments. Lane is also required to maintain the equipment at a certain level. Morgan sets the payment schedule such that it receives a normal lender's rate of return on the transaction. In addition, Morgan agrees to repurchase the equipment after two years for $95,000.

In this case, this arrangement appears to be a financing transaction rather than a sale. That is, Lane is required to maintain the equipment at a certain level and Morgan agrees to repurchase at a set price, resulting in a lender's return. Thus, the risks and rewards of ownership are to a great extent still with Morgan. When the seller has retained the risks and rewards of ownership, even though legal title has been transferred, the transaction is a financing arrangement and does not give rise to revenue.[12]

---

[12]In essence, Lane is renting the equipment from Morgan for two years. We discuss the accounting for such rental or lease arrangements in Chapter 21.

Bill and Hold Sales

Bill and hold sales result when the buyer is not yet ready to take delivery but does take title and accept billing. For example, a customer may request a company to enter into such an arrangement because of (1) lack of available space for the product, (2) delays in its production schedule, or (3) more than sufficient inventory in its distribution channel.[13] Illustration 18-7 provides an example of a bill and hold arrangement.

ILLUSTRATION 18-7
Recognition—Bill and Hold

BILL AND HOLD

Facts: Butler Company sells $450,000 of fireplaces to a local coffee shop, Baristo, which is planning to expand its locations around the city. Under the agreement, Baristo asks Butler to retain these fireplaces in its warehouses until the new coffee shops that will house the fireplaces are ready. Title passes to Baristo at the time the agreement is signed.

Question: Should Butler report the revenue from this bill and hold arrangement when the agreement is signed, or should revenue be deferred and reported when the fireplaces are delivered?

Solution: When to recognize revenue in a bill and hold situation depends on the circumstances. Butler should record the revenue at the time title passes, provided (1) the risks of ownership have passed to Baristo, that is, Butler does not have specific performance obligations other than storage; (2) Baristo makes a fixed commitment to purchase the goods, requests that the transaction be on a bill and hold basis, and sets a fixed delivery date; and (3) goods must be segregated, complete, and ready for shipment. Otherwise, if these conditions are not met, it is assumed that the risks and rewards of ownership remain with the seller even though title has passed. In this case, it appears that these conditions were probably met and therefore revenue recognition should be permitted at the time the agreement is signed.

Butler makes the following entry to record the bill and hold sale.

Accounts Receivable	450,000	
Sales Revenue		450,000

If a significant period of time elapses before payment, the accounts receivable is discounted. In addition, it is likely that one of the conditions above is violated (such as the normal payment terms). In this case, the most appropriate approach for bill and hold sales is to defer revenue recognition until the goods are delivered because the risks and rewards of ownership usually do not transfer until that point. [4]

Principal-Agent Relationships

In a **principal-agent relationship**, amounts collected on behalf of the principal are not revenue of the agent. Instead, revenue for the agent is the amount of the commission it receives (usually a percentage of the total revenue).

Classic Example

An example of principal-agent relationships is an airline that sells tickets through a travel agent. For example, assume that Fly-Away Travels sells airplane tickets for British Airways (BA) to various customers. In this case, the principal is BA and the agent is Fly-Away Travels. BA is acting as a principal because it has exposure to the significant risks and rewards associated with the sale of its services. Fly-Away is acting as an agent because it does not have exposure to significant risks and rewards related to the tickets. Although Fly-Away collects the full airfare from the client, it then remits this amount to BA less a commission. Fly-Away therefore should not record the full amount of the fare as revenue on its books—to do so overstates its revenue. **Its revenue is the commission—not**

---

[13]Proposed Accounting Standards Update, "Revenue from Contracts with Customers" (Stamford, Conn.: FASB, June 24, 2010), p. 54.

the full fare price. The risks and rewards of ownership are not transferred to Fly-Away because it does not bear any inventory risk as it sells tickets to customers.

This distinction is very important for revenue recognition purposes. Some might argue that there is no harm in letting Fly-Away record revenue for the full price of the ticket and then charging the cost of the ticket against the revenue (often referred to as the **gross method** of recognizing revenue). Others note that this approach overstates the agent's revenue and is misleading. The revenue received is the commission for providing the travel services, not the full fare price (often referred to as the **net approach**). The profession believes the net approach is the correct method for recognizing revenue in a principal-agent relationship. As a result, the FASB has developed specific criteria to determine when a principal-agent relationship exists.[14] An important feature in deciding whether Fly-Away is acting as an agent is whether the amount it earns is predetermined, being either a fixed fee per transaction or a stated percentage of the amount billed to the customer.

GROSSED OUT

Consider Priceline.com, the company made famous by William Shatner's ads about "naming your own price" for airline tickets and hotel rooms. In one quarter, Priceline reported that it earned $152 million in revenues. But, that included the full amount customers paid for tickets, hotel rooms, and rental cars. Traditional travel agencies call that amount "gross bookings," not revenues. And, much like regular travel agencies, Priceline keeps only a small portion of gross bookings—namely, the spread between the customers' accepted bids and the price it paid for the merchandise. The rest, which Priceline calls "product costs," it pays to the airlines and hotels that supply the tickets and rooms.

However, Priceline's product costs came to $134 million, leaving Priceline just $18 million of what it calls "gross profit" and what most other companies would call revenues. And, that's before all of Priceline's other costs—like advertising and salaries—which netted out to a loss of $102 million. The difference isn't academic: Priceline shares traded at about 23 times its reported revenues but at a mind-boggling 214 times its "gross profit." This and other aggressive recognition practices explains the stricter revenue recognition guidance, indicating that if a company performs as an agent or broker without assuming the risks and rewards of ownership of the goods, the company should report sales on a net (fee) basis.

Source: Jeremy Kahn, "Presto Chango! Sales Are Huge," *Fortune* (March 20, 2000), p. 44.

What do the number mean?

Consignments

Another common principal-agent relationship involves consignments. In these cases, manufacturers (or wholesalers) deliver goods but retain title to the goods until they are sold. This specialized method of marketing certain types of products makes use of a device known as a **consignment**. Under this arrangement, the **consignor** (manufacturer or wholesaler) ships merchandise to the **consignee** (dealer), who is to act as an agent for the consignor in selling the merchandise. Both consignor and consignee are interested in selling—the former to make a profit or develop a market, the latter to make a commission on the sale.

---

[14]Common principal-agent arrangements include (but are not limited to) (1) arrangements with third-party suppliers to drop-ship merchandise on behalf of the entity, (2) services offered by a company that will be provided by a third-party service provider, (3) shipping and handling fees and costs billed to customers, and (4) reimbursements for out-of-pocket expenses (expenses often include, but are not limited to, expenses related to airfare, mileage, hotel stays, out-of-town meals, photocopies, and telecommunications and facsimile charges). Principal-agent accounting guidance is not limited to entities that sell products or services over the Internet but also to transactions related to advertisements, mailing lists, event tickets, travel tickets, auctions (and reverse auctions), magazine subscription brokers, and catalog, consignment, or special-order retail sales. [5]

The consignee accepts the merchandise and agrees to exercise due diligence in caring for and selling it. The consignee remits to the consignor cash received from customers, after deducting a sales commission and any chargeable expenses.

In consignment sales, the consignor uses a modified version of the sale basis of revenue recognition. That is, the consignor recognizes revenue only after receiving notification of sale and the cash remittance from the consignee. The consignor carries the merchandise as inventory throughout the consignment, separately classified as Inventory (consignments). **The consignee does not record the merchandise as an asset on its books.** Upon sale of the merchandise, the consignee has **a liability for the net amount due the consignor.** The consignor periodically receives from the consignee a report called **account sales** that shows the merchandise received, merchandise sold, expenses chargeable to the consignment, and the cash remitted. Revenue is then recognized by the consignor. Analysis of a consignment arrangement is provided in Illustration 18-8.

ILLUSTRATION 18-8
Entries for Consignment
Sales

SALES ON CONSIGNMENT

Facts: Nelba Manufacturing Co. ships merchandise costing $36,000 on consignment to Best Value Stores. Nelba pays $3,750 of freight costs, and Best Value pays $2,250 for local advertising costs that are reimbursable from Nelba. By the end of the period, Best Value has sold two-thirds of the consigned merchandise for $40,000 cash. Best Value notifies Nelba of the sales, retains a 10% commission, and remits the cash due Nelba.

Question: **What are the journal entries that the consignor (Nelba) and the consignee (Best Value) make to record this transaction?**

Solution:

	NELBA MFG. CO. (CONSIGNOR)			**BEST VALUE STORES** (CONSIGNEE)	
Shipment of consigned merchandise					
Inventory (consignments)	36,000		No entry (record memo of merchandise received).		
Finished Goods Inventory		36,000			
Payment of freight costs by consignor					
Inventory (consignments)	3,750		No entry.		
Cash		3,750			
Payment of advertising by consignee					
No entry until notified.			Receivable from Consignor	2,250	
			Cash		2,250
Sales of consigned merchandise					
No entry until notified.			Cash	40,000	
			Payable to Consignor		40,000
Notification of sales and expenses and remittance of amount due					
Cash	33,750		Payable to Consignor	40,000	
Advertising Expense	2,250		Receivable from		
Commission Expense	4,000		Consignor		2,250
Revenue from			Commission Revenue		4,000
Consignment Sales		40,000	Cash		33,750
Adjustment of inventory on consignment for cost of sales					
Cost of Goods Sold	26,500		No entry.		
Inventory (consignments)		26,500			
[2/3 ($36,000 + $3,750) = $26,500]					

Under the consignment arrangement, the consignor accepts the risk that the merchandise might not sell and relieves the consignee of the need to commit part of its working capital to inventory. Companies use a variety of different systems and account titles to record consignments, but they all share the common goal of postponing the recognition of revenue until it is known that a sale to a third party has occurred.

Trade Loading and Channel Stuffing

One commentator describes **trade loading** this way: "Trade loading is a crazy, uneconomic, insidious practice through which manufacturers—trying to show sales, profits, and market share they don't actually have—induce their wholesale customers, known as the trade, to buy more product than they can promptly resell." For example, the cigarette industry appears to have exaggerated a couple years' operating profits by as much as $600 million by taking the profits from future years.

In the computer software industry, a similar practice is referred to as **channel stuffing**. When a software maker needed to make its financial results look good, it offered deep discounts to its distributors to overbuy and then recorded revenue when the software left the loading dock. Of course, the distributors' inventories become bloated and the marketing channel gets too filled with product, but the software maker's current-period financials are improved. However, financial results in future periods will suffer, unless the company repeats the process.

Trade loading and channel stuffing distort operating results and "window dress" financial statements. In addition, similar to consignment transactions or sales with buy-back agreements, these arrangements generally do not transfer the risks and rewards of ownership. If used without an appropriate allowance for sales returns, channel stuffing is a classic example of booking tomorrow's revenue today. Business managers need to be aware of the ethical dangers of misleading the financial community by engaging in such practices to improve their financial statements.

NO TAKE-BACKS

What do the numbers mean?

Investors in Lucent Technologies were negatively affected when Lucent violated one of the fundamental criteria for revenue recognition—the "no take-back" rule. This rule holds that revenue should not be booked on inventory that is shipped if the customer can return it at some point in the future. In this particular case, Lucent agreed to take back shipped inventory from its distributors if the distributors were unable to sell the items to their customers.

In essence, Lucent was "stuffing the channel." By booking sales when goods were shipped, even though they most likely would get them back, Lucent was able to report continued sales growth. However, Lucent investors got a nasty surprise when distributors returned those goods and Lucent had to restate its financial results. The restatement erased $679 million in revenues, turning an operating profit into a loss. In response to this bad news, Lucent's share price declined $1.31 per share, or 8.5 percent. Lucent is not alone in this practice. Sunbeam got caught stuffing the sales channel with barbeque grills and other outdoor items, which contributed to its troubles when it was forced to restate its earnings.

Investors can be tipped off to potential channel stuffing by carefully reviewing a company's revenue recognition policy for generous return policies and by watching inventory and receivables levels. When sales increase along with receivables, that's one sign that customers are not paying for goods shipped on credit. And growing inventory levels are an indicator that customers have all the goods they need. Both scenarios suggest a higher likelihood of goods being returned and revenues and income being restated. So remember, no take-backs!

Source: Adapted from S. Young, "Lucent Slashes First Quarter Outlook, Erases Revenue from Latest Quarter," *Wall Street Journal Online* (December 22, 2000); and Tracey Byrnes, "Too Many Thin Mints: Spotting the Practice of Channel Stuffing," *Wall Street Journal Online* (February 7, 2002).

Multiple-Deliverable Arrangements

One of the most difficult issues related to revenue recognition involves **multiple-deliverable arrangements** (MDAs). MDAs provide multiple products or services to customers as part of a single arrangement. The major accounting issues related to this type of arrangement are how to allocate the revenue to the various products and services and how to allocate the revenue to the proper period.

These issues are particularly complex in the technology area. Many devices have contracts that typically include such multiple deliverables as hardware, software, professional services, maintenance, and support—all of which are valued and accounted for differently. A classic example relates to the **Apple** iPhone and its AppleTV product. Basically, until a recent rule change, revenues and related costs were accounted for on a subscription basis over a period of years. The reason was that Apple provides future unspecified software upgrades and other features without charge. It was argued that Apple should defer a significant portion of the cash received for the iPhone and recognize it over future periods. At the same time, engineering, marketing, and warranty costs were expensed as incurred. As a result, Apple reported conservative numbers related to its iPhone revenue. However, as a result of efforts to more clearly define the various services related to an item such as the iPhone, Apple is now able to report more revenue at the point of sale.

In general, all units in a multiple-deliverable arrangement are considered separate units of accounting, provided that:

1. A delivered item has value to the customer on a standalone basis; and
2. The arrangement includes a general right of return relative to the delivered item; and
3. Delivery or performance of the undelivered item is considered probable and substantially in the control of the seller.

Once the separate units of accounting are determined, the amount paid for the arrangement is allocated among the separate units based on **relative fair value**. A company determines fair value based on what the vendor could sell the component for on a standalone basis. If this information is not available, the seller may rely on third-party evidence or if not available, the seller may use its best estimate of what the item might sell for as a standalone unit. [6] Illustration 18-9 identifies the steps in the evaluation process.

ILLUSTRATION 18-9
Multiple-Deliverable
Evaluation Process

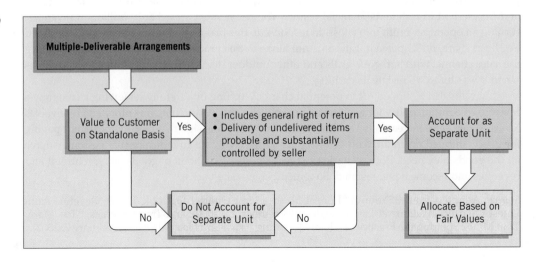

Presented in Illustrations 18-10 and 18-11 are two examples of the accounting for MDAs.

ILLUSTRATION 18-10
MDA—Equipment and
Maintenance

MULTIPLE DELIVERABLES

Facts: Lopez Company enters into a contract to build, run, and maintain a highly complex piece of electronic equipment for a period of 5 years, commencing upon delivery of the equipment. There is a fixed fee for each of the build, run, and maintenance deliverables, and any progress payments made are not refundable. In addition, there is a right of return in the arrangement. All the deliverables have a standalone value, and there is verifiable evidence of the selling price for the building and maintenance but not for running the equipment.

Questions: **Should Lopez separate and then measure and allocate the amounts paid for the MDA?**

Solution: Assuming delivery (performance) is probable and Lopez controls any undelivered items, Lopez determines whether the components have standalone value. The components of the MDA are the equipment, maintenance of the equipment, and running the equipment; each component has a standalone value. Lopez can determine standalone values of equipment and the maintenance agreement by third-party evidence of fair values. The company then makes a best estimate of the selling price for running of the equipment. Lopez next applies the relative fair value method at the inception of the MDA to determine the proper allocation to each component. Once the allocation is performed, the company recognizes revenue independently for each component using regular revenue recognition criteria.

ILLUSTRATION 18-11
MDA—Product,
Installation, and Service

PRODUCT, INSTALLATION, AND SERVICE

Facts: Handler Company is an experienced manufacturer of equipment used in the construction industry. Handler's products range from small to large individual pieces of automated machinery to complex systems containing numerous components. Unit selling prices range from $600,000 to $4,000,000 and are quoted inclusive of installation and training. The installation process does not involve changes to the features of the equipment and does not require proprietary information about the equipment in order for the installed equipment to perform to specifications. Handler has the following arrangement with Chai Company.

- Chai purchases equipment from Handler for a price of $2,000,000 and chooses Handler to do the installation. Handler charges the same price for the equipment irrespective of whether it does the installation or not. (Some companies do the installation themselves because they either prefer their own employees to do the work or because of relationships with other customers.) The price of the installation service is estimated to have a fair value of $20,000.
- The fair value of the training sessions is estimated at $50,000.
- Chai is obligated to pay Handler the $2,000,000 upon the delivery and installation of the equipment. Handler delivers the equipment on September 1, 2012, and completes the installation of the equipment on November 1, 2012. Training related to the equipment starts once the installation is completed and lasts for 1 year. The equipment has a useful life of 10 years.

Questions: **(a) What are the standalone units for purposes of accounting for the sale of the equipment? (b) If there is more than one standalone unit, how should the fee of $2,000,000 be allocated to various components?**

Solution:
(a) The first condition for separation into a standalone unit for the equipment is met. That is, the equipment, installation, and training are three separate components.
(b) The total revenue of $2,000,000 should be allocated to the three components based on their relative fair values. In this case, the fair value of the equipment should be considered $2,000,000, the installation fee is $20,000, and the training is $50,000. The total fair value to consider is $2,070,000 ($2,000,000 + $20,000 + $50,000). The allocation is as follows.

Equipment	$1,932,367	($2,000,000 ÷ $2,070,000) × $2,000,000
Installation	19,324	($20,000 ÷ $2,070,000) × $2,000,000
Training	48,309	($50,000 ÷ $2,070,000) × $2,000,000

Handler makes the following entries on November 1, 2012.

November 1, 2012

Cash	2,000,000	
Service Revenue (installation)		19,324
Unearned Service Revenue		48,309
Sales Revenue		1,932,367

The sale of the equipment should be recognized once the installation is completed on November 1, 2012, and the installation fee also should be recognized because these services have been provided. The training revenues should be allocated on a straight-line basis starting on November 1, 2012, or $4,026 ($48,309 ÷ 12) per month for one year (unless a more appropriate method such as the percentage-of-completion method is warranted). The journal entry to recognize the training revenue for two months in 2012 is as follows.

December 31, 2012

Unearned Service Revenue	8,052	
Service Revenue (training) ($4,026 × 2)		8,052

Therefore, the total revenue recognized at December 31, 2012, is $1,959,743 ($1,932,367 + $19,324 + $8,052). Handler makes the following journal entry to recognize the training revenue in 2013, assuming adjusting entries are made at year-end.

December 31, 2013

Unearned Service Revenue	40,257	
Service Revenue (training) ($48,309 − $8,052)		40,257

Summary of Revenue Recognition Methods

ILLUSTRATION 18-12
Revenue Recognition at the Point of Sale

Illustration 18-12 provides a summary of revenue recognition methods and related accounting guidance.

General Principles	
Recognize revenue (1) when it is realized or realizable, and (2) when it is earned. In numerous cases, GAAP provides additional specific guidance to help determine proper revenue recognition.	

Specific Transactions	Accounting Guidance
Sales with discounts	Trade, volume, and cash discounts reduce sales revenue.
Sales with extended payment terms	The fair value measurement of revenue is determined by using the fair value of the consideration received or by discounting the future payments using an imputed interest rate.
Sales with right of return	If there is uncertainty about the possibility of return, recognize revenue when the goods are delivered and the return period has lapsed. If the company can reliably estimate future returns, revenue (less estimated returns) is recognized at the point of sale.
Sales with buyback	Terms of the buyback agreement must be analyzed to determine if, in substance, the seller has transferred the risks and rewards of ownership.
Bill and hold sales	Recognition depends on the circumstances. Recognize revenue when title passes if (1) the risks of ownership have passed to the customer, and the seller does not have specific obligations other than storage; (2) the customer makes a fixed commitment to purchase the goods, requests that the transaction be on a bill and hold basis, and sets a fixed delivery date; and (3) goods must be segregated, complete, and ready for shipment.
Sales involving principal-agent relationship (general)	Amounts collected by the agent on behalf of the principal are not revenue of the agent. Instead, revenue to the agent is the amount of commission it receives.
Sales involving principal-agent relationship (consignments)	Consignor recognizes revenue (sales and cost of goods sold) when goods are sold by consignee. Consignee recognizes revenue for commissions received.
Trade loading and channel stuffing	Unless returns can be reliably measured, revenue should not be recognized until the goods are sold (by the distributor) to third parties.
Multiple-deliverable arrangements	Apply general revenue recognition principles to each element of the arrangement that has stand-alone value. Once the separate units of accounting are determined, the amount paid for the arrangement is allocated among the separate units based on relative fair value.

REVENUE RECOGNITION BEFORE DELIVERY

For the most part, companies recognize revenue at the point of sale (delivery) because at point of sale most of the uncertainties in the earning process are removed and the exchange price is known. Under certain circumstances, however, companies recognize revenue prior to completion and delivery. The most notable example is long-term construction contract accounting, which uses the percentage-of-completion method.

Long-term contracts frequently provide that the seller (builder) may bill the purchaser at intervals, as it reaches various points in the project. Examples of long-term contracts are construction-type contracts, development of military and commercial aircraft, weapons-delivery systems, and space exploration hardware. When the project consists of separable units, such as a group of buildings or miles of roadway, contract provisions may provide for delivery in installments. In that case, the seller would bill the buyer and transfer title at stated stages of completion, such as the completion of each building unit or every 10 miles of road. The accounting records should record sales when installments are "delivered."[15]

Two distinctly different methods of accounting for long-term construction contracts are recognized.[16] They are:

- **Percentage-of-completion method.** Companies recognize revenues and gross profits each period based upon the progress of the construction—that is, the percentage of completion. The company accumulates construction costs **plus gross profit earned to date** in an inventory account (Construction in Process), and it accumulates progress billings in a contra inventory account (Billings on Construction in Process).

- **Completed-contract method.** Companies recognize revenues and gross profit **only** when the contract is completed. The company accumulates construction costs in an inventory account (Construction in Process), and it accumulates progress billings in a contra inventory account (Billings on Construction in Process).

The rationale for using percentage-of-completion accounting is that under most of these contracts the buyer and seller have enforceable rights. The buyer has the legal right to require specific performance on the contract. The seller has the right to require progress payments that provide evidence of the buyer's ownership interest. As a result, a continuous sale occurs as the work progresses. Companies should recognize revenue according to that progression.

Companies *must* use the percentage-of-completion method when estimates of progress toward completion, revenues, and costs are reasonably dependable and **all of the following conditions** exist. [7]

Underlying Concepts

The percentage-of-completion method recognizes revenue from long-term contracts in the periods in which the revenue is earned. The firm contract fixes the selling price. And, if costs are estimable and collection reasonably assured, the revenue recognition concept is not violated.

1. The contract clearly specifies the enforceable rights regarding goods or services to be provided and received by the parties, the consideration to be exchanged, and the manner and terms of settlement.
2. The buyer can be expected to satisfy all obligations under the contract.
3. The contractor can be expected to perform the contractual obligations.

---

[15]*Statement of Financial Accounting Concepts No. 5*, par. 84, item c.

[16]*Accounting Trends and Techniques—2010* reports that of the 86 of its 500 sample companies that referred to long-term construction contracts, 63 used the percentage-of-completion method and 20 used the completed-contract method.

Companies should use the completed-contract method when one of the following conditions applies:

- When a company has primarily short-term contracts, *or*
- When a company cannot meet the conditions for using the percentage-of-completion method, *or*
- When there are inherent hazards in the contract beyond the normal, recurring business risks.

The presumption is that percentage-of-completion is the better method. Therefore, companies should use the completed-contract method only when the percentage-of-completion method is inappropriate. We discuss the two methods in more detail in the following sections.

Percentage-of-Completion Method

> **LEARNING OBJECTIVE 3**
>
> Apply the percentage-of-completion method for long-term contracts

The **percentage-of-completion method** recognizes revenues, costs, and gross profit as a company makes progress toward completion on a long-term contract. To defer recognition of these items until completion of the entire contract is to misrepresent the efforts (costs) and accomplishments (revenues) of the accounting periods during the contract. In order to apply the percentage-of-completion method, a company must have some basis or standard for measuring the progress toward completion at particular interim dates.

Measuring the Progress toward Completion

As one practicing accountant wrote, "The big problem in applying the percentage-of-completion method . . . has to do with the ability to make reasonably accurate estimates of completion and the final gross profit."[17] Companies use various methods to determine the **extent of progress toward completion**. The most common are the *cost-to-cost* and *units-of-delivery* methods.[18]

The objective of all these methods is to measure the extent of progress in terms of costs, units, or value added. Companies identify the various measures (costs incurred, labor hours worked, tons produced, floors completed, etc.) and classify them as input or output measures. **Input measures** (costs incurred, labor hours worked) are efforts devoted to a contract. **Output measures** (with units of delivery measured as tons produced, floors of a building completed, miles of a highway completed) track results. Neither are universally applicable to all long-term projects. Their use requires the exercise of judgment and careful tailoring to the circumstances.

Both input and output measures have certain disadvantages. The input measure is based on an established relationship between a unit of input and productivity. If inefficiencies cause the productivity relationship to change, inaccurate measurements result. Another potential problem is front-end loading, in which significant up-front costs result in higher estimates of completion. To avoid this problem, companies should disregard some early-stage construction costs—for example, costs of uninstalled materials or costs of subcontracts not yet performed—if they do not relate to contract performance.

Similarly, output measures can produce inaccurate results if the units used are not comparable in time, effort, or cost to complete. For example, using floors (stories) completed can be deceiving. Completing the first floor of an eight-story building may require more than one-eighth the total cost because of the substructure and foundation construction.

The most popular input measure used to determine the progress toward completion is the **cost-to-cost basis**. Under this basis, a company like **EDS** measures the

---

[17]Richard S. Hickok, "New Guidance for Construction Contractors: 'A Credit Plus,'" *The Journal of Accountancy* (March 1982), p. 46.

[18]R. K. Larson and K. L. Brown, "Where Are We with Long-Term Contract Accounting?" *Accounting Horizons* (September 2004), pp. 207–219.

percentage of completion by comparing costs incurred to date with the most recent estimate of the total costs required to complete the contract. Illustration 18-13 shows the formula for the cost-to-cost basis.

$$\frac{\text{Costs incurred to date}}{\text{Most recent estimate of total costs}} = \text{Percent complete}$$

ILLUSTRATION 18-13
Formula for Percentage-of-Completion, Cost-to-Cost Basis

Once EDS knows the percentage that costs incurred bear to total estimated costs, it applies that percentage to the total revenue or the estimated total gross profit on the contract. The resulting amount is the revenue or the gross profit to be recognized to date. Illustration 18-14 shows this computation.

$$\begin{array}{ccc} \text{Percent} \\ \text{complete} \end{array} \times \begin{array}{c} \text{Estimated} \\ \text{total revenue} \\ \text{(or gross profit)} \end{array} = \begin{array}{c} \text{Revenue (or gross} \\ \text{profit) to be} \\ \text{recognized to date} \end{array}$$

ILLUSTRATION 18-14
Formula for Total Revenue to Be Recognized to Date

To find the amounts of revenue and gross profit recognized each period, EDS subtracts total revenue or gross profit recognized in prior periods, as shown in Illustration 18-15.

$$\begin{array}{c} \text{Revenue (or gross} \\ \text{profit) to be} \\ \text{recognized to date} \end{array} - \begin{array}{c} \text{Revenue (or gross} \\ \text{profit) recognized} \\ \text{in prior periods} \end{array} = \begin{array}{c} \text{Current-period} \\ \text{revenue} \\ \text{(or gross profit)} \end{array}$$

ILLUSTRATION 18-15
Formula for Amount of Current-Period Revenue, Cost-to-Cost Basis

Because **the cost-to-cost method is widely used** (without excluding other bases for measuring progress toward completion), we have adopted it for use in our examples. [8]

Example of Percentage-of-Completion Method—Cost-to-Cost Basis

To illustrate the percentage-of-completion method, assume that Hardhat Construction Company has a contract to construct a $4,500,000 bridge at an estimated cost of $4,000,000. The contract is to start in July 2012, and the bridge is to be completed in October 2014. The following data pertain to the construction period. (Note that by the end of 2013, Hardhat has revised the estimated total cost from $4,000,000 to $4,050,000.)

	2012	2013	2014
Costs to date	$1,000,000	$2,916,000	$4,050,000
Estimated costs to complete	3,000,000	1,134,000	—
Progress billings during the year	900,000	2,400,000	1,200,000
Cash collected during the year	750,000	1,750,000	2,000,000

Hardhat would compute the percentage complete as shown in Illustration 18-16.

	2012	2013	2014
Contract price	$4,500,000	$4,500,000	$4,500,000
Less estimated cost:			
Costs to date	1,000,000	2,916,000	4,050,000
Estimated costs to complete	3,000,000	1,134,000	—
Estimated total costs	4,000,000	4,050,000	4,050,000
Estimated total gross profit	$ 500,000	$ 450,000	$ 450,000
Percent complete	25%	72%	100%
	$\left(\dfrac{\$1,000,000}{\$4,000,000}\right)$	$\left(\dfrac{\$2,916,000}{\$4,050,000}\right)$	$\left(\dfrac{\$4,050,000}{\$4,050,000}\right)$

ILLUSTRATION 18-16
Application of Percentage-of-Completion Method, Cost-to-Cost Basis

On the basis of the data above, Hardhat would make the following entries to record (1) the costs of construction, (2) progress billings, and (3) collections. These entries appear as summaries of the many transactions that would be entered individually as they occur during the year.

ILLUSTRATION 18-17
Journal Entries—
Percentage-of-Completion
Method, Cost-to-Cost
Basis

	2012		2013		2014	
To record cost of construction:						
Construction in Process	1,000,000		1,916,000		1,134,000	
Materials, Cash, Payables, etc.		1,000,000		1,916,000		1,134,000
To record progress billings:						
Accounts Receivable	900,000		2,400,000		1,200,000	
Billings on Construction in Process		900,000		2,400,000		1,200,000
To record collections:						
Cash	750,000		1,750,000		2,000,000	
Accounts Receivable		750,000		1,750,000		2,000,000

In this example, the costs incurred to date are a measure of the extent of progress toward completion. To determine this, Hardhat evaluates the costs incurred to date as a proportion of the estimated total costs to be incurred on the project. The estimated revenue and gross profit that Hardhat will recognize for each year are calculated as shown in Illustration 18-18.

ILLUSTRATION 18-18
Percentage-of-Completion
Revenue, Costs, and
Gross Profit by Year

	To Date	Recognized in Prior Years	Recognized in Current Year
2012			
Revenues ($4,500,000 × 25%)	$1,125,000		$1,125,000
Costs	1,000,000		1,000,000
Gross profit	$ 125,000		$ 125,000
2013			
Revenues ($4,500,000 × 72%)	$3,240,000	$1,125,000	$2,115,000
Costs	2,916,000	1,000,000	1,916,000
Gross profit	$ 324,000	$ 125,000	$ 199,000
2014			
Revenues ($4,500,000 × 100%)	$4,500,000	$3,240,000	$1,260,000
Costs	4,050,000	2,916,000	1,134,000
Gross profit	$ 450,000	$ 324,000	$ 126,000

Illustration 18-19 shows Hardhat's entries to recognize revenue and gross profit each year and to record completion and final approval of the contract.

ILLUSTRATION 18-19
Journal Entries to
Recognize Revenue and
Gross Profit and to
Record Contract
Completion—Percentage-
of-Completion Method,
Cost-to-Cost Basis

	2012		2013		2014	
To recognize revenue and gross profit:						
Construction in Process (gross profit)	125,000		199,000		126,000	
Construction Expenses	1,000,000		1,916,000		1,134,000	
Revenue from Long-Term Contracts		1,125,000		2,115,000		1,260,000
To record completion of the contract:						
Billings on Construction in Process					4,500,000	
Construction in Process						4,500,000

Note that Hardhat debits gross profit (as computed in Illustration 18-18) to Construction in Process. Similarly, it credits Revenue from Long-Term Contracts for the amounts computed in Illustration 18-18. Hardhat then debits the difference between the amounts recognized each year for revenue and gross profit to a nominal account, Construction Expenses (similar to Cost of Goods Sold in a manufacturing company). It reports that amount in the income statement as the actual cost of construction incurred in that period. For example, Hardhat uses the actual costs of $1,000,000 to compute both the gross profit of $125,000 and the percent complete (25 percent).

Hardhat continues to accumulate costs in the Construction in Process account, in order to maintain a record of total costs incurred (plus recognized gross profit) to date. Although theoretically a series of "sales" takes place using the percentage-of-completion method, the selling company cannot remove the inventory cost until the construction is completed and transferred to the new owner. Hardhat's Construction in Process account for the bridge would include the following summarized entries over the term of the construction project.

Construction in Process				
2012 construction costs	$1,000,000	12/31/14	to close	
2012 recognized gross profit	125,000		completed	
2013 construction costs	1,916,000		project	$4,500,000
2013 recognized gross profit	199,000			
2014 construction costs	1,134,000			
2014 recognized gross profit	126,000			
Total	$4,500,000	Total		$4,500,000

ILLUSTRATION 18-20
Content of Construction in Process Account—Percentage-of-Completion Method

Recall that the Hardhat Construction Company example contained a **change in estimate**: In the second year, 2013, it increased the estimated total costs from $4,000,000 to $4,050,000. The change in estimate is accounted for in a **cumulative catch-up manner**. This is done by first adjusting the percent completed to the new estimate of total costs. Next, Hardhat deducts the amount of revenues and gross profit recognized in prior periods from revenues and gross profit computed for progress to date. That is, it accounts for the change in estimate in the period of change. That way, the balance sheet at the end of the period of change and the accounting in subsequent periods are as they would have been if the revised estimate had been the original estimate.

Financial Statement Presentation—Percentage-of-Completion

Generally, when a company records a receivable from a sale, it reduces the Inventory account. Under the percentage-of-completion method, however, the company continues to carry both the receivable and the inventory. Subtracting the balance in the Billings account from Construction in Process avoids double-counting the inventory. During the life of the contract, Hardhat reports in the balance sheet the difference between the Construction in Process and the Billings on Construction in Process accounts. If that amount is a debit, Hardhat reports it **as a current asset**; if it is a credit, it reports it **as a current liability**.

At times, the costs incurred plus the gross profit recognized to date (the balance in Construction in Process) exceed the billings. In that case, Hardhat reports this excess as a current asset entitled "Cost and recognized profit in excess of billings." Hardhat can at any time calculate the unbilled portion of revenue recognized to date by subtracting the billings to date from the revenue recognized to date, as illustrated for 2012 for Hardhat Construction in Illustration 18-21.

Contract revenue recognized to date: $4,500,000 × $\dfrac{\$1,000,000}{\$4,000,000}$		$1,125,000
Billings to date		(900,000)
Unbilled revenue		$ 225,000

ILLUSTRATION 18-21
Computation of Unbilled Contract Price at 12/31/12

At other times, the billings exceed costs incurred and gross profit to date. In that case, Hardhat reports this excess as a current liability entitled "Billings in excess of costs and recognized profit."

It probably has occurred to you that companies often have more than one project going at a time. When a company has a number of projects, costs exceed billings on some contracts and billings exceed costs on others. In such a case, the company segregates the contracts. The asset side includes only those contracts on which costs and recognized profit exceed billings. The liability side includes only those on which billings exceed costs and recognized profit. Separate disclosures of the dollar volume of billings and costs are preferable to a summary presentation of the net difference.

Using data from the bridge example, Hardhat Construction Company would report the status and results of its long-term construction activities under the percentage-of-completion method as shown in Illustration 18-22.

ILLUSTRATION 18-22
Financial Statement
Presentation—Percentage-
of-Completion Method
(2012)

HARDHAT CONSTRUCTION COMPANY		
Income Statement (from Illustration 18-8)		2012
Revenue from long-term contracts		$1,125,000
Costs of construction		1,000,000
Gross profit		$ 125,000

Balance Sheet (12/31)		2012
Current assets		
Accounts receivable ($900,000 − $750,000)		$ 150,000
Inventory		
Construction in process	$1,125,000	
Less: Billings	900,000	
Costs and recognized profit in excess of billings		225,000

In 2013, its financial statement presentation is as follows.

ILLUSTRATION 18-23
Financial Statement
Presentation—Percentage-
of-Completion Method
(2013)

HARDHAT CONSTRUCTION COMPANY		
Income Statement (from Illustration 18-8)		2013
Revenue from long-term contracts		$2,115,000
Costs of construction		1,916,000
Gross profit		$ 199,000

Balance Sheet (12/31)		
Current assets		
Accounts receivable ($150,000 + $2,400,000 − $1,750,000)		$ 800,000
Current liabilities		
Billings	$3,300,000	
Less: Construction in process	3,240,000	
Billings in excess of costs and recognized profits		60,000

In 2014, Hardhat's financial statements only include an income statement because the bridge project was completed and settled.

HARDHAT CONSTRUCTION COMPANY

Income Statement (from Illustration 18-18)	2014
Revenue from long-term contracts	$1,260,000
Costs of construction	1,134,000
Gross profit	$ 126,000

ILLUSTRATION 18-24
Financial Statement
Presentation—Percentage-
of-Completion Method
(2014)

In addition, Hardhat should disclose the following information in each year.

Note 1.   Summary of significant accounting policies.
Long-Term Construction Contracts.   The company recognizes revenues and reports profits from long-term construction contracts, its principal business, under the percentage-of-completion method of accounting. These contracts generally extend for periods in excess of one year. The amounts of revenues and profits recognized each year are based on the ratio of costs incurred to the total estimated costs. Costs included in construction in process include direct materials, direct labor, and project-related overhead. Corporate general and administrative expenses are charged to the periods as incurred and are not allocated to construction contracts.

ILLUSTRATION 18-25
Percentage-of-
Completion Method
Note Disclosure

Completed-Contract Method

Under the **completed-contract method**, companies recognize revenue and gross profit only at point of sale—that is, when the contract is completed. Under this method, companies accumulate costs of long-term contracts in process, but they make no interim charges or credits to income statement accounts for revenues, costs, or gross profit.

> **4 LEARNING OBJECTIVE**
> Apply the completed-contract method for long-term contracts.

The principal advantage of the completed-contract method is that reported revenue reflects final results rather than *estimates* of unperformed work. Its major disadvantage is that it does not reflect current performance when the period of a contract extends into more than one accounting period. Although operations may be fairly uniform during the period of the contract, the company will not report revenue until the year of completion, creating a distortion of earnings.

Under the completed-contract method, the company would make the same **annual entries** to record costs of construction, progress billings, and collections from customers as those illustrated under the percentage-of-completion method. The significant difference is that the company **would not make entries to recognize revenue and gross profit**.

> **INTERNATIONAL PERSPECTIVE**
>
> IFRS prohibits the use of the completed-contract method of accounting for long-term construction contracts. Companies must use the percentage-of-completion method. If revenues and costs are difficult to estimate, then companies recognize revenue only to the extant of the cost incurred—a zero-profit approach.

For example, under the completed-contract method for the bridge project illustrated on the preceding pages, Hardhat Construction Company would make the following entries in 2014 to recognize revenue and costs and to close out the inventory and billing accounts.

Billings on Construction in Process	4,500,000	
Revenue from Long-Term Contracts		4,500,000
Costs of Construction	4,050,000	
Construction in Process		4,050,000

Illustration 18-26 compares the amount of gross profit that Hardhat Construction Company would recognize for the bridge project under the two revenue-recognition methods.

	Percentage-of-Completion	Completed-Contract
2012	$125,000	$ 0
2013	199,000	0
2014	126,000	450,000

ILLUSTRATION 18-26
Comparison of Gross
Profit Recognized under
Different Methods

Under the completed-contract method, Hardhat Construction would report its long-term construction activities as follows.

ILLUSTRATION 18-27
Financial Statement
Presentation—Completed-
Contract Method

HARDHAT CONSTRUCTION COMPANY			
	2012	2013	2014
Income Statement			
Revenue from long-term contracts	–	–	$4,500,000
Costs of construction	–	–	4,050,000
Gross profit	–	–	$ 450,000

Balance Sheet (12/31)				
Current assets				
Accounts receivable		$150,000	$800,000	$ –0–
Inventory				
Construction in process	$1,000,000			
Less: Billings	900,000			
Costs in excess of billings		100,000		–0–
Current liabilities				
Billings ($3,300,000) in excess of				
costs ($2,916,000)			384,000	–0–

Note 1.   Summary of significant accounting policies.
Long-Term Construction Contracts.   The company recognizes revenues and reports profits from long-term construction contracts, its principal business, under the completed-contract method. These contracts generally extend for periods in excess of one year. Contract costs and billings are accumulated during the periods of construction, but no revenues or profits are recognized until completion of the contract. Costs included in construction in process include direct material, direct labor, and project-related overhead. Corporate general and administrative expenses are charged to the periods as incurred.

Long-Term Contract Losses

LEARNING OBJECTIVE **5**
Identify the proper accounting for losses on long-term contracts.

Two types of losses can become evident under long-term contracts:[19]

1. *Loss in the current period on a profitable contract.* This condition arises when, during construction, there is a significant increase in the estimated total contract costs but the increase does not eliminate all profit on the contract. Under the percentage-of-completion method only, the estimated cost increase requires a current-period adjustment of excess gross profit recognized on the project in prior periods. The company records this adjustment as a loss in the current period because it is a **change in accounting estimate** (discussed in Chapter 22).

2. *Loss on an unprofitable contract.* Cost estimates at the end of the current period may indicate that a loss will result on completion of the *entire* contract. Under both the percentage-of-completion and the completed-contract methods, the company must recognize in the current period the entire expected contract loss.

The treatment described for unprofitable contracts is consistent with the accounting custom of anticipating foreseeable losses to avoid overstatement of current and future income (conservatism).

Loss in Current Period

To illustrate a loss in the current period on a contract expected to be profitable upon completion, we'll continue with the Hardhat Construction Company bridge project.

---

[19]Sak Bhamornsiri, "Losses from Construction Contracts," *The Journal of Accountancy* (April 1982), p. 26.

Assume that on December 31, 2013, Hardhat estimates the costs to complete the bridge contract at $1,468,962 instead of $1,134,000 (refer to page 1083). Assuming all other data are the same as before, Hardhat would compute the percentage complete and recognize the loss as shown in Illustration 18-28. Compare these computations with those for 2013 in Illustration 18-16 (page 1083). The "percent complete" has dropped, from 72 percent to 66½ percent, due to the increase in estimated future costs to complete the contract.

Cost to date (12/31/13)		$2,916,000
Estimated costs to complete (revised)		1,468,962
Estimated total costs		$4,384,962
Percent complete ($2,916,000 ÷ $4,384,962)		66½%
Revenue recognized in 2013		
($4,500,000 × 66½%) − $1,125,000		$1,867,500
Costs incurred in 2013		1,916,000
Loss recognized in 2013		$ (48,500)

ILLUSTRATION 18-28
Computation of Recognizable Loss, 2013—Loss in Current Period

The 2013 loss of $48,500 is a cumulative adjustment of the "excessive" gross profit recognized on the contract in 2012. Instead of restating the prior period, the company absorbs the prior period misstatement entirely in the current period. In this illustration, the adjustment was large enough to result in recognition of a loss.

Hardhat Construction would record the loss in 2013 as follows.

Construction Expenses	1,916,000	
Construction in Process (loss)		48,500
Revenue from Long-Term Contracts		1,867,500

Hardhat will report the loss of $48,500 on the 2013 income statement as the difference between the reported revenues of $1,867,500 and the costs of $1,916,000.[20] **Under the completed-contract method, the company does not recognize a loss in 2013.** Why not? Because the company still expects the contract **to result in a profit**, to be recognized in the year of completion.

Loss on an Unprofitable Contract

To illustrate the accounting for an **overall loss on a long-term contract**, assume that at December 31, 2013, Hardhat Construction Company estimates the costs to complete the bridge contract at $1,640,250 instead of $1,134,000. Revised estimates for the bridge contract are as follows.

	2012	2013
	Original Estimates	Revised Estimates
Contract price	$4,500,000	$4,500,000
Estimated total cost	4,000,000	4,556,250*
Estimated gross profit	$ 500,000	
Estimated loss		$ (56,250)

*($2,916,000 + $1,640,250)

[20]In 2014, Hardhat Construction will recognize the remaining 33½ percent of the revenue ($1,507,500), with costs of $1,468,962 as expected, and will report a gross profit of $38,538. The total gross profit over the three years of the contract would be $115,038 [$125,000 (2012) − $48,500 (2013) + $38,538 (2014)]. This amount is the difference between the total contract revenue of $4,500,000 and the total contract costs of $4,384,962.

Under the percentage-of-completion method, Hardhat recognized $125,000 of gross profit in 2012 (see Illustration 18-18 on page 1084). This amount must be offset in 2013 because it is no longer expected to be realized. In addition, since losses must be recognized as soon as estimable, the company must recognize the total estimated loss of $56,250 in 2013. Therefore, Hardhat must recognize a total loss of $181,250 ($125,000 + $56,250) in 2013.

Illustration 18-29 shows Hardhat's computation of the revenue to be recognized in 2013.

ILLUSTRATION 18-29
Computation of Revenue Recognizable, 2013—Unprofitable Contract

Revenue recognized in 2013:		
Contract price		$4,500,000
Percent complete		× 64%*
Revenue recognizable to date		2,880,000
Less: Revenue recognized prior to 2013		1,125,000
Revenue recognized in 2013		$1,755,000
*Cost to date (12/31/13)	$2,916,000	
Estimated cost to complete	1,640,250	
Estimated total costs	$4,556,250	
Percent complete: $2,916,000 ÷ $4,556,250 = 64%		

To compute the construction costs to be expensed in 2013, Hardhat adds the total loss to be recognized in 2013 ($125,000 + $56,250) to the revenue to be recognized in 2013. Illustration 18-30 shows this computation.

ILLUSTRATION 18-30
Computation of Construction Expense, 2013—Unprofitable Contract

Revenue recognized in 2013 (computed above)		$1,755,000
Total loss recognized in 2013:		
Reversal of 2012 gross profit	$125,000	
Total estimated loss on the contract	56,250	181,250
Construction cost expensed in 2013		$1,936,250

Hardhat Construction would record the long-term contract revenues, expenses, and loss in 2013 as follows.

Construction Expenses	1,936,250	
Construction in Process (loss)		181,250
Revenue from Long-Term Contracts		1,755,000

At the end of 2013, Construction in Process has a balance of $2,859,750 as shown below.[21]

ILLUSTRATION 18-31
Content of Construction in Process Account at End of 2013—Unprofitable Contract

Construction in Process			
2012 Construction costs	1,000,000		
2012 Recognized gross profit	125,000		
2013 Construction costs	1,916,000	2013 Recognized loss	181,250
Balance	**2,859,750**		

[21]If the costs in 2014 are $1,640,250 as projected, at the end of 2014 the Construction in Process account will have a balance of $1,640,250 + $2,859,750, or $4,500,000, equal to the contract price. When the company matches the revenue remaining to be recognized in 2014 of $1,620,000 [$4,500,000 (total contract price) − $1,125,000 (2012) − $1,755,000 (2013)] with the construction expense to be recognized in 2014 of $1,620,000 [total costs of $4,556,250 less the total costs recognized in prior years of $2,936,250 (2012, $1,000,000; 2013, $1,936,250)], a zero profit results. Thus, the total loss has been recognized in 2013, the year in which it first became evident.

Under the completed-contract method, Hardhat also would recognize the contract loss of $56,250 through the following entry in 2013 (the year in which the loss first became evident).

Loss from Long-Term Contracts	56,250	
Construction in Process (loss)		56,250

Just as the Billings account balance cannot exceed the contract price, neither can the balance in Construction in Process exceed the contract price. In circumstances where the Construction in Process balance exceeds the billings, the company can deduct the recognized loss from such accumulated costs on the balance sheet. That is, under both the percentage-of-completion and the completed-contract methods, the provision for the loss (the credit) may be combined with Construction in Process, thereby reducing the inventory balance. In those circumstances, however (as in the 2013 example above), where the billings exceed the accumulated costs, Hardhat must report separately on the balance sheet, as a current liability, the amount of the estimated loss. That is, under both the percentage-of-completion and the completed-contract methods, Hardhat would take the $56,250 loss, as estimated in 2013, from the Construction in Process account and report it separately as a current liability titled "Estimated liability from long-term contracts." [9]

Disclosures in Financial Statements

Construction contractors usually make some unique financial statement disclosures in addition to those required of all businesses. Generally, these additional disclosures are made in the notes to the financial statements. For example, a construction contractor should disclose the following: the method of recognizing revenue, [10] the basis used to classify assets and liabilities as current (the nature and length of the operating cycle), the basis for recording inventory, the effects of any revision of estimates, the amount of backlog on uncompleted contracts, and the details about receivables (billed and unbilled, maturity, interest rates, retainage provisions, and significant individual or group concentrations of credit risk).

LESS CONSERVATIVE

What do the numbers mean?

Halliburton provides engineering- and construction-related services in jobs around the world. Much of the company's work is completed under contract over long periods of time. The company uses percentage-of-completion accounting. The SEC started enforcement proceedings against the company related to its accounting for contract claims and disagreements with customers, including those arising from change orders and disputes about billable amounts and costs associated with a construction delay.

Prior to 1998, Halliburton took a very conservative approach to its accounting for disputed claims. As stated in the company's 1997 annual report, "Claims for additional compensation are recognized during the period such claims are resolved." That is, the company waited until all disputes were resolved before recognizing associated revenues. In contrast, in 1998 the company recognized revenue for disputed claims before their resolution, using estimates of amounts expected to be recovered. Such revenue and its related profit are more tentative and are subject to possible later adjustment than revenue and profit recognized when all claims have been resolved. As a case in point, the company noted that it incurred losses of $99 million in 1998 related to customer claims.

The accounting method put in place in 1998 is more aggressive than the company's former policy, but it is still within the boundaries of generally accepted accounting principles. However, the SEC noted that over six quarters, Halliburton failed to disclose its change in accounting

What do the numbers mean? (continued)

practice. In the absence of any disclosure, the SEC believed the investing public was misled about the precise nature of Halliburton's income in comparison to prior periods. The Halliburton situation illustrates the difficulty of using estimates in percentage-of-completion accounting and the impact of those estimates on the financial statements.

Source: "Failure to Disclose a 1998 Change in Accounting Practice," SEC (August 3, 2004), *www.sec.gov/news/press/2004-104.htm*. See also "Accounting Ace Charles Mulford Answers Accounting Questions," *Wall Street Journal Online* (June 7, 2002).

Completion-of-Production Basis

Underlying Concepts

This is not an exception to the revenue recognition principle. At the completion of production, realization is virtually assured and the earning process is substantially completed.

In certain cases, companies recognize revenue at the completion of **production** even though no sale has been made. Examples of such situations involve precious metals or agricultural products with assured prices. Under the **completion-of-production basis**, companies recognize revenue when these metals are mined or agricultural crops harvested because the sales price is reasonably assured, the units are interchangeable, and no significant costs are involved in distributing the product.[22] (See discussion in Chapter 9, page 501, "Valuation at Net Realizable Value.")

Likewise, when sale or cash receipt precedes production and delivery, as in the case of magazine subscriptions, companies recognize revenues as earned by production and delivery.[23]

REVENUE RECOGNITION AFTER DELIVERY

In some cases, the collection of the sales price is not reasonably assured and revenue recognition is deferred. One of two methods is generally employed to defer revenue recognition until the company receives cash: the **installment-sales method** or the **cost-recovery method**. A third method, the **deposit method**, applies in situations in which a company receives cash prior to delivery or transfer of the property; the company records that receipt as a deposit because the sales transaction is incomplete. This section examines these three methods.

Installment-Sales Method

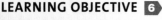

LEARNING OBJECTIVE 6

Describe the installment-sales method of accounting.

The **installment-sales method** recognizes income in the periods of collection rather than in the period of sale. The logic underlying this method is that when there is no reasonable approach for estimating the degree of collectibility, companies should not recognize revenue until cash is collected.

The expression "installment sales" generally describes any type of sale for which payment is required in periodic installments over an extended period of time. All types of farm and home equipment as well as home furnishings are sold on an installment basis. The heavy equipment industry also sometimes uses the method for machine installations paid for over a long period. Another application of the method is in land-development sales.

---

[22]Such revenue satisfies the criteria of *Concepts Statement No. 5* since the assets are readily realizable and the earning process is virtually complete (see par. 84, item c).

[23]*Statement of Financial Accounting Concepts No. 5*, par. 84, item b.

Because payment is spread over a relatively long period, the risk of loss resulting from uncollectible accounts is greater in installment-sales transactions than in ordinary sales. Consequently, selling companies use various devices to protect themselves. Two common devices are (1) the use of a *conditional sales contract*, which specifies that title to the item sold does not pass to the purchaser until all payments are made, and (2) use of notes secured by a *chattel* (personal property) *mortgage* on the article sold. Either of these permits the seller to "repossess" the goods sold if the purchaser defaults on one or more payments. The seller can then resell the repossessed merchandise at whatever price it will bring to compensate for the uncollected installments and the expense of repossession.

Underlying Concepts

Realization is a critical part of revenue recognition. Thus, if a high degree of uncertainty exists about collectibility, a company must defer revenue recognition.

Under the installment-sales method of accounting, companies defer income recognition until the period of cash collection. They recognize both revenues and costs of sales in the period of sale, but defer the related gross profit to those periods in which they collect the cash. Thus, **instead of deferring the sale, along with related costs and expenses, to the future periods of anticipated collection, the company defers only the proportional gross profit**. This approach is equivalent to deferring both sales and cost of sales. Other expenses—that is, selling expense, administrative expense, and so on—are not deferred.

Thus, the installment-sales method matches cost and expenses against sales through the gross profit figure, but no further. Companies using the installment-sales method generally record operating expenses without regard to the fact that they will defer some portion of the year's gross profit. This practice is often justified on the basis that (1) these expenses do not follow sales as closely as does the cost of goods sold, and (2) accurate apportionment among periods would be so difficult that it could not be justified by the benefits gained.[24]

Acceptability of the Installment-Sales Method

The use of the installment-sales method for revenue recognition has fluctuated widely. At one time, it was widely accepted for installment-sales transactions. Somewhat paradoxically, as installment-sales transactions increased in popularity, acceptance and use of the installment-sales method decreased. Finally, the profession concluded that except in special circumstances, "the installment method of recognizing revenue is not acceptable." **[11]** The rationale for this position is simple: Because the installment method recognizes no income until cash is collected, it is not in accordance with the accrual-accounting concept.

Use of the installment-sales method was often justified on the grounds that the risk of not collecting an account receivable may be so great that the sale itself is not sufficient evidence that recognition should occur. In some cases, this reasoning is valid but not in a majority of cases. The general approach is that a company should recognize a completed sale. If the company expects bad debts, it should record this possibility as separate estimates of uncollectibles. Although collection expenses, repossession expenses, and bad debts are an unavoidable part of installment-sales activities, the incurrence of these costs and the collectibility of the receivables are reasonably predictable.

We study this topic in intermediate accounting because the method is acceptable in cases where a company believes there to be no reasonable basis of estimating the degree of collectibility. In addition, the sales method of revenue recognition has certain weaknesses when used for franchise and land-development operations. Application of the

---

[24]In addition, other theoretical deficiencies of the installment-sales method could be cited. For example, see Richard A. Scott and Rita K. Scott, "Installment Accounting: Is It Inconsistent?" *The Journal of Accountancy* (November 1979).

sales method to **franchise and license operations** has resulted in the abuse described earlier as "front-end loading." In some cases, franchisors recognized revenue prematurely, when they granted a franchise or issued a license, rather than when revenue was earned or the cash is received. Many **land-development** ventures were susceptible to the same abuses. As a result, the FASB prescribes application of the installment-sales method of accounting for sales of real estate under certain circumstances. [12][25]

Procedure for Deferring Revenue and Cost of Sales of Merchandise

One could work out a procedure that deferred both the uncollected portion of the sales price and the proportionate part of the cost of the goods sold. Instead of apportioning both sales price and cost over the period of collection, however, the installment-sales method defers **only the gross profit**. This procedure has exactly the same effect as deferring both sales and cost of sales, but it requires only one deferred account rather than two.

For the **sales in any one year**, the steps companies use to defer gross profit are as follows.

1. During the year, record both sales and cost of sales in the regular way, using the special accounts described later, and compute the rate of gross profit on installment-sales transactions.

2. At the end of the year, apply the rate of gross profit to the cash collections of the current year's installment sales, to arrive at the realized gross profit.

3. Defer to future years the gross profit not realized.

For **sales made in prior years**, companies apply the gross profit rate of each year's sales against cash collections of accounts receivable resulting from that year's sales, to arrive at the realized gross profit.

Special accounts must be used in the installment-sales method. These accounts provide certain information required to determine the realized and unrealized gross profit in each year of operations. In computing net income under the installment-sales method as generally applied, the only peculiarity is the **deferral of gross profit until realized by accounts receivable collection**. We will use the following data to illustrate the installment-sales method in accounting for the sales of merchandise.

	2012	2013	2014
Installment sales	$200,000	$250,000	$240,000
Cost of installment sales	150,000	190,000	168,000
Gross profit	$ 50,000	$ 60,000	$ 72,000
Rate of gross profit on sales	25%[a]	24%[b]	30%[c]
Cash receipts			
2012 sales	$ 60,000	$100,000	$ 40,000
2013 sales		100,000	125,000
2014 sales			80,000
	[a] $50,000	[b] $60,000	[c] $72,000
	$200,000	$250,000	$240,000

To simplify this example, we have excluded interest charges. Summary entries in general journal form for the year 2012 are as follows.

[25]The installment-sales method of accounting must be applied to a retail land sale that meets all of the following criteria: (1) the period of cancellation of the sale with refund of the down payment and any subsequent payments has expired; (2) cumulative cash payments equal or exceed 10 percent of the sales value; and (3) the seller is financially capable of providing all promised contract representations (e.g., land improvements, off-site facilities).

2012

Installment Accounts Receivable, 2012	200,000	
Installment Sales		200,000
(To record sales made on installment in 2012)		
Cash	60,000	
Installment Accounts Receivable, 2012		60,000
(To record cash collected on installment receivables)		
Cost of Installment Sales	150,000	
Inventory (or Purchases)		150,000
(To record cost of goods sold on installment in 2012 on either a perpetual or a periodic inventory basis)		
Installment Sales	200,000	
Cost of Installment Sales		150,000
Deferred Gross Profit, 2012		50,000
(To close installment sales and cost of installment sales for the year)		
Deferred Gross Profit, 2012	15,000	
Realized Gross Profit		15,000
(To remove from deferred gross profit the profit realized through cash collections; $60,000 × 25%)		
Realized Gross Profit	15,000	
Income Summary		15,000
(To close profits realized by collections)		

Illustration 18-32 shows computation of the realized and deferred gross profit for the year 2012.

2012	
Rate of gross profit current year	25%
Cash collected on current year's sales	$60,000
Realized gross profit (25% of $60,000)	15,000
Gross profit to be deferred ($50,000 − $15,000)	35,000

ILLUSTRATION 18-32
Computation of Realized and Deferred Gross Profit, 2012

Summary entries in journal form for year 2 (2013) are as follows.

2013

Installment Accounts Receivable, 2013	250,000	
Installment Sales		250,000
(To record sales made on installment in 2013)		
Cash	200,000	
Installment Accounts Receivable, 2012		100,000
Installment Accounts Receivable, 2013		100,000
(To record cash collected on installment receivables)		
Cost of Installment Sales	190,000	
Inventory (or Purchases)		190,000
(To record cost of goods sold on installment in 2013)		
Installment Sales	250,000	
Cost of Installment Sales		190,000
Deferred Gross Profit, 2013		60,000
(To close installment sales and cost of installment sales for the year)		
Deferred Gross Profit, 2012 ($100,000 × 25%)	25,000	
Deferred Gross Profit, 2013 ($100,000 × 24%)	24,000	
Realized Gross Profit		49,000
(To remove from deferred gross profit the profit realized through cash collections)		
Realized Gross Profit	49,000	
Income Summary		49,000
(To close profits realized by collections)		

Illustration 18-33 shows computation of the realized and deferred gross profit for the year 2013.

ILLUSTRATION 18-33
Computation of Realized and Deferred Gross Profit, 2013

2013	
Current year's sales	
Rate of gross profit	24%
Cash collected on current year's sales	$100,000
Realized gross profit (24% of $100,000)	24,000
Gross profit to be deferred ($60,000 − $24,000)	36,000
Prior year's sales	
Rate of gross profit—2012	25%
Cash collected on 2012 sales	$100,000
Gross profit realized in 2013 on 2012 sales (25% of $100,000)	25,000
Total gross profit realized in 2013	
Realized on collections of 2012 sales	$ 25,000
Realized on collections of 2013 sales	24,000
Total	$ 49,000

The entries in 2014 would be similar to those of 2013, and the total gross profit taken up or realized would be $64,000, as shown by the computations in Illustration 18-34.

ILLUSTRATION 18-34
Computation of Realized and Deferred Gross Profit, 2014

2014	
Current year's sales	
Rate of gross profit	30%
Cash collected on current year's sales	$ 80,000
Gross profit realized on 2014 sales (30% of $80,000)	24,000
Gross profit to be deferred ($72,000 − $24,000)	48,000
Prior years' sales	
2012 sales	
Rate of gross profit	25%
Cash collected	$ 40,000
Gross profit realized in 2014 on 2012 sales (25% of $40,000)	10,000
2013 sales	
Rate of gross profit	24%
Cash collected	$125,000
Gross profit realized in 2014 on 2013 sales (24% of $125,000)	30,000
Total gross profit realized in 2014	
Realized on collections of 2012 sales	$ 10,000
Realized on collections of 2013 sales	30,000
Realized on collections of 2014 sales	24,000
Total	$ 64,000

In summary, here are the basic concepts you should understand about accounting for installment sales:

1. How to compute a proper gross profit percentage.
2. How to record installment sales, cost of installment sales, and deferred gross profit.
3. How to compute realized gross profit on installment receivables.
4. How the deferred gross profit balance at the end of the year results from applying the gross profit rate to the installment accounts receivable.

Additional Problems of Installment-Sales Accounting

In addition to computing realized and deferred gross profit currently, other problems are involved in accounting for installment-sales transactions. These problems are related to:

1. Interest on installment contracts.
2. Uncollectible accounts.
3. Defaults and repossessions.

Interest on Installment Contracts. Because the collection of installment receivables is spread over a long period, it is customary to charge the buyer interest on the unpaid balance. The seller and buyer set up a schedule of equal payments consisting of interest and principal. Each successive payment is attributable to a smaller amount of interest and a correspondingly larger amount of principal, as shown in Illustration 18-35. This illustration assumes that a company sells for $3,000 an asset costing $2,400 (rate of gross profit = 20%), with interest of 8 percent included in the three installments of $1,164.10.

Date	Cash (Debit)	Interest Earned (Credit)	Installment Receivables (Credit)	Installment Unpaid Balance	Realized Gross Profit (20%)
1/2/12	–	–	–	$3,000.00	–
1/2/13	$1,164.10[a]	$240.00[b]	$ 924.10[c]	2,075.90[d]	$184.82[e]
1/2/14	1,164.10	166.07	998.03	1,077.87	199.61
1/2/15	1,164.10	86.23	1,077.87	–0–	215.57
					$600.00

[a]Periodic payment = Original unpaid balance ÷ PV of an annuity of $1.00 for three periods at 8%;
$1,164.10 = $3,000 ÷ 2.57710.
[b]$3,000.00 × .08 = $240.
[c]$1,164.10 − $240.00 = $924.10.
[d]$3,000.00 − $924.10 = $2,075.90.
[e]$924.10 × .20 = $184.82.

ILLUSTRATION 18-35
Installment Payment Schedule

The company accounts for interest separate from the gross profit recognized on the installment-sales collections during the period, by recognizing interest revenue at the time of its cash receipt.

Uncollectible Accounts. The problem of bad debts or uncollectible accounts receivable is somewhat different for concerns selling on an installment basis because of a repossession feature commonly incorporated in the sales agreement. This feature gives the selling company an opportunity to recoup an uncollectible account through repossession and resale of repossessed merchandise. If the experience of the company indicates that repossessions do not, as a rule, compensate for uncollectible balances, it may be advisable to provide for such losses through charges to a special bad debt expense account, just as is done for other credit sales.

Defaults and Repossessions. Depending on the terms of the sales contract and the policy of the credit department, the seller can repossess merchandise sold under an installment arrangement if the purchaser fails to meet payment requirements. The seller may then recondition repossessed merchandise before offering it for re-sale, for either cash or installment payments.

The accounting for **repossessions** recognizes that the company is not likely to collect the related installment receivable and should write it off. Along with the installment account receivable, the company must remove the applicable deferred gross profit using the following entry.

Repossessed Merchandise (an inventory account)	xxx	
Deferred Gross Profit	xxx	
Installment Accounts Receivable		xxx

This entry assumes that the company will record the repossessed merchandise at exactly the amount of the uncollected account less the deferred gross profit applicable. This assumption may or may not be proper. To determine the correct amount, the company should consider the condition of the repossessed merchandise, the cost of reconditioning, and the market for secondhand merchandise of that particular type. The objective should be to put any asset acquired on the books at its fair value, or at the best possible approximation of fair value when fair value is not determinable. A loss can occur if the fair value of the repossessed merchandise is less than the uncollected balance less the deferred gross profit. In that case, the company should record a "loss on repossession" at the date of repossession.[26]

To illustrate the required entry, assume that Klein Brothers sells a refrigerator to Marilyn Hunt for $1,500 on September 1, 2012. Terms require a down payment of $600 and $60 on the first of every month for 15 months, starting October 1, 2012. It is further assumed that the refrigerator cost $900 and that Klein Brothers priced it to provide a 40 percent rate of gross profit on selling price. At the year-end, December 31, 2012, Klein Brothers should have collected a total of $180 in addition to the original down payment.

If Hunt makes her January and February payments in 2013 and then defaults, the account balances applicable to Hunt at time of default are as shown in Illustration 18-36.

ILLUSTRATION 18-36
Computation of Installment Receivable Balances

Installment accounts receivable (September 1, 2012)		$1,500
Less: Down payment:	$600	
Payments to date ($60 × 5)	300	900
Installment accounts receivable (March 1, 2013)		$ 600
Installment accounts receivable (March 1, 2013)		$ 600
Gross profit rate		× 40%
Deferred gross profit		$ 240

As indicated, Klein Brothers compute the balance of deferred gross profit applicable to Hunt's account by applying the gross profit rate for the year of sale to the balance of Hunt's account receivable: 40 percent of $600, or $240. The account balances are therefore:

Installment Account Receivable, 2012	600 (Dr.)
Deferred Gross Profit, 2012	240 (Cr.)

[26]Some contend that a company should record repossessed merchandise at a valuation that will permit the company to make its regular rate of gross profit on resale. If the company enters the value at its approximated cost to purchase, the regular rate of gross profit could be provided for upon its ultimate sale, but that is completely a secondary consideration. It is more important that the company record the repossessed asset at fair value. This accounting would be in accordance with the general practice of carrying assets at acquisition price, as represented by the fair value at the date of acquisition.

Klein repossesses the refrigerator following Hunt's default. If Klein sets the estimated fair value of the repossessed article at $150, it would make the following entry to record the repossession.

Deferred Gross Profit, 2012	240	
Repossessed Merchandise	150	
Loss on Repossession	210	
Installment Accounts Receivable, 2012		600

Klein determines the amount of the loss in two steps: (1) It subtracts the deferred gross profit from the amount of the account receivable, to determine the unrecovered cost (or book value) of the merchandise repossessed. (2) It then subtracts the estimated fair value of the merchandise repossessed from the unrecovered cost, to get the amount of the loss on repossession. Klein Brothers computes the loss on the refrigerator as shown in Illustration 18-37.

ILLUSTRATION 18-37
Computation of Loss on Repossession

Balance of account receivable (representing uncollected selling price)	$600
Less: Deferred gross profit	240
Unrecovered cost	360
Less: Estimated fair value of merchandise repossessed	150
Loss (Gain) on repossession	$210

As pointed out earlier, the loss on repossession may be charged to Allowance for Doubtful Accounts if a company carries such an account.

Financial Statement Presentation of Installment-Sales Transactions

If installment-sales transactions represent a significant part of total sales, it is desirable to make full disclosure of installment sales, the cost of installment sales, and any expenses allocable to installment sales. However, if installment-sales transactions constitute an insignificant part of total sales, it may be satisfactory to include only the realized gross profit in the income statement as a special item following the gross profit on sales. Illustration 18-38 shows this simpler presentation.

ILLUSTRATION 18-38
Disclosure of Installment-Sales Transactions—Insignificant Amount

HEALTH MACHINE COMPANY	
INCOME STATEMENT	
FOR THE YEAR ENDED DECEMBER 31, 2013	

Sales	$620,000
Cost of goods sold	490,000
Gross profit	130,000
Gross profit realized on installment sales	51,000
Total gross profit	$181,000

If a company wants more complete disclosure of installment-sales transactions, it would use a presentation similar to that shown in Illustration 18-39 (page 1100).

ILLUSTRATION 18-39
Disclosure of Installment-
Sales Transactions—
Significant Amount

HEALTH MACHINE COMPANY
INCOME STATEMENT
FOR THE YEAR ENDED DECEMBER 31, 2013

	Installment Sales	Other Sales	Total
Sales	$248,000	$620,000	$868,000
Cost of goods sold	182,000	490,000	672,000
Gross profit	66,000	130,000	196,000
Less: Deferred gross profit on installment sales of this year	47,000		47,000
Realized gross profit on this year's sales	19,000	130,000	149,000
Add: Gross profit realized on installment sales of prior years	32,000		32,000
Gross profit realized this year	$ 51,000	$130,000	$181,000

The presentation in Illustration 18-39 is awkward. Yet the awkwardness of this method is difficult to avoid if a company wants to provide full disclosure of installment-sales transactions in the income statement. One solution, of course, is to prepare a separate schedule showing installment-sales transactions, with only the final figure carried into the income statement.

In the balance sheet, it is generally considered desirable to classify installment accounts receivable by year of collectibility. There is some question as to whether companies should include in current assets installment accounts that are not collectible for two or more years. Yet if installment sales are **part of normal operations**, companies may consider them as current assets because they are collectible within the operating cycle of the business. Little confusion should result from this practice if the company fully discloses maturity dates, as illustrated in the following example.

ILLUSTRATION 18-40
Disclosure of Installment
Accounts Receivable,
by Year

Current assets		
Notes and accounts receivable		
Trade customers	$78,800	
Less: Allowance for doubtful accounts	3,700	
	75,100	
Installment accounts collectible in 2013	22,600	
Installment accounts collectible in 2014	47,200	$144,900

On the other hand, a company may have receivables from an installment contract, resulting from a transaction not related to normal operations. In that case, the company should report such receivables in the "Other assets" section if due beyond one year.

Repossessed merchandise is a part of inventory, and companies should report it as such in the "Current assets" section of the balance sheet. They should include any gain or loss on repossession in the income statement in the "Other revenues and gains" or "Other expenses and losses" section.

If a company has **deferred gross profit on installment sales**, it generally treats it as unearned revenue and classifies it as a current liability. Theoretically, deferred gross profit consists of three elements: (1) income tax liability to be paid when the sales are reported as realized revenue (current liability); (2) allowance for collection expense, bad debts, and repossession losses (deduction from installment accounts receivable); and (3) net income (retained earnings, restricted as to dividend availability). Because of the difficulty in allocating deferred gross profit among these three elements, however, companies frequently report the whole amount as unearned revenue.

In contrast, the FASB in *SFAC No. 6* states that "no matter how it is displayed in financial statements, deferred gross profit on installment sales is conceptually an asset valuation—that is, a reduction of an asset."[27] We support the FASB position, but we recognize that until an official standard on this topic is issued, financial statements will probably continue to report such deferred gross profit as a current liability.

Cost-Recovery Method

Under the **cost-recovery method**, a company recognizes no profit until cash payments by the buyer exceed the cost of the merchandise sold. After the seller has recovered all costs, it includes in income any additional cash collections. The seller's income statement for the period reports sales revenue, the cost of goods sold, and the gross profit—both the amount (if any) that is recognized during the period and the amount that is deferred. The deferred gross profit is offset against the related receivable—reduced by collections—on the balance sheet. Subsequent income statements report the gross profit as a separate item of revenue when the company recognizes it as earned.

> **7 LEARNING OBJECTIVE**
> Explain the cost-recovery method of accounting.

A seller is permitted to use the cost-recovery method to account for sales in which "there is no reasonable basis for estimating collectibility." In addition, use of this method is required where a high degree of uncertainty exists related to the collection of receivables. [13], [14], [15]

To illustrate the cost-recovery method, assume that early in 2012, Fesmire Manufacturing sells inventory with a cost of $25,000 to Higley Company for $36,000. Higley will make payments of $18,000 in 2012, $12,000 in 2013, and $6,000 in 2014. If the cost-recovery method applies to this transaction and Higley makes the payments as scheduled, Fesmire recognizes cash collections, revenue, cost, and gross profit as follows.[28]

	2012	2013	2014
Cash collected	$18,000	$12,000	$6,000
Revenue	$36,000	–0–	–0–
Cost of goods sold	25,000	–0–	–0–
Deferred gross profit	11,000	11,000	6,000
Less: Recognized gross profit	–0–	5,000*	6,000
Deferred gross profit balance (end of period)	$11,000	$ 6,000	$ –0–

*$25,000 − $18,000 = $7,000 of unrecovered cost at the end of 2012; $12,000 − $7,000 = $5,000, the excess of cash received in 2013 over unrecovered cost.

ILLUSTRATION 18-41
Computation of Gross Profit—Cost-Recovery Method

---

[27] See *Statement of Financial Accounting Concepts No. 6*, paras. 232–234.

[28] An alternative format for computing the amount of gross profit recognized annually is shown below.

Year	Cash Received	Original Cost Recovered	Balance of Unrecovered Cost	Gross Profit Realized
Beginning balance	—	—	$25,000	—
12/31/12	$18,000	$18,000	7,000	$ –0–
12/31/13	12,000	7,000	–0–	5,000
12/31/14	6,000	–0–	–0–	6,000

Under the cost-recovery method, Fesmire reports total revenue and cost of goods sold in the period of sale, similar to the installment-sales method. However, unlike the installment-sales method, which recognizes income as cash is collected, Fesmire recognizes profit under the cost-recovery method **only when cash collections exceed the total cost of the goods sold**.

Therefore, Fesmire's journal entry to record the deferred gross profit on the Higley sales transaction (after recording the sale and the cost of sales in the normal manner) at the end of 2012 is as follows.

2012

Sales Revenue	36,000	
Cost of Sales		25,000
Deferred Gross Profit		11,000
(To close sales and cost of sales and to record deferred gross profit on sales accounted for under the cost-recovery method)		

In 2013 and 2014, the deferred gross profit becomes realized gross profit as the cumulative cash collections exceed the total costs, by recording the following entries.

2013

Deferred Gross Profit	5,000	
Realized Gross Profit		5,000
(To recognize gross profit to the extent that cash collections in 2013 exceed costs)		

2014

Deferred Gross Profit	6,000	
Realized Gross Profit		6,000
(To recognize gross profit to the extent that cash collections in 2014 exceed costs)		

Deposit Method

In some cases, a company receives cash from the buyer before it transfers the goods or property. In such cases, the seller has not performed under the contract and has no claim against the purchaser. There is not sufficient transfer of the risks and rewards of ownership for a sale to be recorded. The method of accounting for these incomplete transactions is the **deposit method**.

Under the deposit method, the seller reports the cash received from the buyer as a deposit on the contract and classifies it on the balance sheet as a liability (refundable deposit or customer advance). The seller continues to report the property as an asset on its balance sheet, along with any related existing debt. Also, the seller continues to charge depreciation expense as a period cost for the property. **The seller does not recognize revenue or income until the sale is complete.** [16] At that time, it closes the deposit account and applies one of the revenue recognition methods discussed in this chapter to the sale.

The **major difference between the installment-sales and cost-recovery methods and the deposit method** relates to contract performance. In the installment-sales and cost-recovery methods, it is assumed that the seller has performed on the contract but cash collection is highly uncertain. In the deposit method, the seller has *not* performed and no legitimate claim exists. The deposit method postpones recognizing a sale until the company determines that a sale has occurred for accounting purposes. If there has not been sufficient transfer of risks and rewards of ownership, even if the selling company has received a deposit, the company postpones recognition of the sale until sufficient transfer has occurred. In that sense, the deposit method is not a revenue recognition method as are the installment-sales and cost-recovery methods.

Summary of Product Revenue Recognition Bases

Illustration 18-42 summarizes the revenue recognition bases or methods, the criteria for their use, and the reasons for departing from the sale basis.

Specific Transactions	Accounting Guidance
Point of sale	See Illustration 18–12 (page 1080).
Long-term contracts (construction)	
(a) Percentage-of-completion method	Long-term construction of property; dependable estimates of extent of progress and cost to complete; reasonable assurance of collectibility of contract price; expectation that both contractor and buyer can meet obligations; and absence of inherent hazards that make estimates doubtful.
(b) Completed-contract method	Use on short-term contracts and whenever percentage-of-completion cannot be used on long-term contracts. Existence of inherent hazards in the contract beyond the normal, recurring business risks; conditions for using the percentage-of-completion method are absent.
Completion-of-production basis	Immediate marketability at quoted prices; unit interchangeability; and no significant distribution costs.
Installment-sales method and cost-recovery method	Absence of reasonable basis for estimating degree of collectibility and costs of collection. Collectibility of the receivable is so uncertain that gross profit (or income) is not recognized until cash is actually received.
Deposit method	Cash received before the sales transaction is completed. No recognition of revenue and income because there is not sufficient transfer of the risks and rewards of ownership.

ILLUSTRATION 18-42
Revenue Recognition Bases

CONCLUDING REMARKS

As indicated, revenue recognition principles are sometimes difficult to apply and often vary by industry. Recently, the SEC has attempted to provide more guidance in this area because of concern that the revenue recognition principle is sometimes being incorrectly applied. Many cases of intentional misstatement of revenue to achieve better financial results have recently come to light. Such practices are fraudulent, and the SEC is vigorously prosecuting these situations.

For our capital markets to be efficient, investors must have confidence that the financial information provided is both relevant and reliable. As a result, it is imperative that the accounting profession, regulators, and companies eliminate aggressive revenue recognition practices. It is our hope that recent efforts by the SEC and the accounting profession will lead to higher-quality reporting in this area.

INTERNATIONAL PERSPECTIVE

There is no international enforcement body comparable to the U.S. SEC.

You will want to read the
IFRS INSIGHTS
on pages 1134–1140

for discussion of IFRS related to revenue recognition.

SUMMARY OF LEARNING OBJECTIVES

1 **Apply the revenue recognition principle.** The revenue recognition principle provides that a company should recognize revenue (1) when revenue is realized or realizable and (2) when it is earned. Revenues are realized when goods or services are exchanged for cash or claims to cash. Revenues are realizable when assets received in exchanges are readily convertible to known amounts of cash or claims to cash. Revenues are earned when a company has substantially accomplished what it must do to be entitled to the benefits represented by the revenues—that is, when the earnings process is complete or virtually complete.

2 **Describe accounting issues for revenue recognition at point of sale.** The two conditions for recognizing revenue are usually met by the time a company delivers products or merchandise or provides services to customers. Companies commonly recognize revenue from manufacturing and selling activities at time of sale. Problems of implementation can arise because of (1) sales with discounts, (2) sales with extended payment terms, (3) sales with right of return, (4) sales with buyback, (5) bill and hold sales, (6) principal-agent relationships, (7) trade loading and channel stuffing, and (8) multiple-deliverable arrangements. Illustration 18-12 (page 1080) summarizes accounting guidance in these areas.

3 **Apply the percentage-of-completion method for long-term contracts.** To apply the percentage-of-completion method to long-term contracts, a company must have some basis for measuring the progress toward completion at particular interim dates. One of the most popular input measures used to determine the progress toward completion is the cost-to-cost basis. Using this basis, a company measures the percentage of completion by comparing costs incurred to date with the most recent estimate of the total costs to complete the contract. The company applies that percentage to the total revenue or the estimated total gross profit on the contract, to arrive at the amount of revenue or gross profit to be recognized to date.

4 **Apply the completed-contract method for long-term contracts.** Under this method, companies recognize revenue and gross profit only at point of sale—that is, when the company completes the contract. The company accumulates costs of long-term contracts in process and current billings. It makes no interim charges or credits to income statement accounts for revenues, costs, and gross profit. The annual entries to record costs of construction, progress billings, and collections from customers would be identical to those for the percentage-of-completion method—with the significant exclusion of the recognition of revenue and gross profit.

5 **Identify the proper accounting for losses on long-term contracts.** Two types of losses can become evident under long-term contracts: (1) *Loss in current period on a profitable contract:* Under the percentage-of-completion method only, the estimated cost increase requires a current-period adjustment of excess gross profit recognized on the project in prior periods. The company records this adjustment as a loss in the current period because it is a change in accounting estimate. (2) *Loss on an unprofitable contract:* Under both the percentage-of-completion and the completed-contract methods, the company must recognize the entire expected contract loss in the current period.

6 **Describe the installment-sales method of accounting.** The installment-sales method recognizes income in the periods of collection rather than in the period of sale. The installment-sales method of accounting is justified on the basis that when there is no reasonable approach for estimating the degree of collectibility, a company should not recognize revenue until it has collected cash.

7 **Explain the cost-recovery method of accounting.** Under the cost-recovery method, companies do not recognize profit until cash payments by the buyer exceed the seller's cost of the merchandise sold. After the seller has recovered all costs, it includes in income any additional cash collections. The income statement for the period of sale reports sales revenue, the cost of goods sold, and the gross profit—both the amount recognized during the period and the amount deferred. The deferred gross profit is offset against the related receivable on the balance sheet. Subsequent income statements report the gross profit as a separate item of revenue when revenue is recognized as earned.

APPENDIX **18A**	REVENUE RECOGNITION FOR FRANCHISES

In this appendix, we cover a common yet unique type of business transaction—**franchises**. As indicated throughout this chapter, companies recognize revenue on the basis of two criteria: (1) when it is realized or realizable (occurrence of an exchange for cash or claims to cash), and (2) when it is earned (completion or virtual completion of the earnings process). These criteria are appropriate for most business activities. For some sales transactions, though, they do not adequately define when a company should recognize revenue. The fast-growing franchise industry is of special concern and challenge.

8 **LEARNING OBJECTIVE**
Explain revenue recognition for franchises.

In accounting for franchise sales, a company must analyze the transaction and, considering all the circumstances, use judgment in selecting one or more of the revenue recognition bases, and then possibly must monitor the situation over a long period of time.

Four types of franchising arrangements have evolved: (1) manufacturer-retailer, (2) manufacturer-wholesaler, (3) service sponsor-retailer, and (4) wholesaler-retailer. The fastest-growing category of franchising, and the one that caused a reexamination of appropriate accounting, has been the third category, **service sponsor-retailer**. Included in this category are such industries and businesses as:

Soft ice cream/frozen yogurt stores (Tastee Freez, TCBY, Dairy Queen)

Food drive-ins (McDonald's, KFC, Burger King)

Restaurants (TGI Friday's, Pizza Hut, Denny's)

Motels (Holiday Inn, Marriott, Best Western)

Auto rentals (Avis, Hertz, National)

Others (H & R Block, Meineke Mufflers, 7-Eleven Stores, Kelly Services)

Franchise companies derive their revenue from one or both of two sources: (1) from the sale of initial franchises and related assets or services, and (2) from continuing fees based on the operations of franchises. The franchisor (the party who grants business rights under the franchise) normally provides the franchisee (the party who operates the franchised business) with the following services.

1. Assistance in site selection: (a) analyzing location and (b) negotiating lease.
2. Evaluation of potential income.
3. Supervision of construction activity: (a) obtaining financing, (b) designing building, and (c) supervising contractor while building.
4. Assistance in the acquisition of signs, fixtures, and equipment.
5. Bookkeeping and advisory services: (a) setting up franchisee's records; (b) advising on income, real estate, and other taxes; and (c) advising on local regulations of the franchisee's business.
6. Employee and management training.

7. Quality control.

8. Advertising and promotion.[29]

In the past, it was standard practice for franchisors to recognize the entire franchise fee at the date of sale, whether the fee was received then or was collectible over a long period of time. Frequently, franchisors recorded the entire amount as revenue in the year of sale, even though many of the services were yet to be performed and uncertainty existed regarding the collection of the entire fee.[30] (In effect, the franchisors were counting their fried chickens before they were hatched.) However, a **franchise agreement** may provide for refunds to the franchisee if certain conditions are not met, and franchise fee profit can be reduced sharply by future costs of obligations and services to be rendered by the franchisor. To curb the abuses in revenue recognition that existed and to standardize the accounting and reporting practices in the franchise industry, the FASB issued rules which form the basis for the accounting discussed below.

INITIAL FRANCHISE FEES

The **initial franchise fee** is payment for establishing the franchise relationship and providing some initial services. Franchisors record initial franchise fees as revenue only when and as they make "substantial performance" of the services they are obligated to perform and when collection of the fee is reasonably assured. **Substantial performance** occurs when the franchisor has no remaining obligation to refund any cash received or excuse any nonpayment of a note and has performed all the initial services required under the contract. Commencement of operations by the franchisee shall be presumed to be the earliest point at which substantial performance has occurred, unless it can be demonstrated that substantial performance of all obligations, including services rendered voluntarily, has occurred before that time. [17]

Example of Entries for Initial Franchise Fee

To illustrate, assume that Tum's Pizza Inc. charges an initial franchise fee of $50,000 for the right to operate as a franchisee of Tum's Pizza. Of this amount, $10,000 is payable when the franchisee signs the agreement, and the balance is payable in five annual payments of $8,000 each. In return for the initial franchise fee, Tum's will help locate the site, negotiate the lease or purchase of the site, supervise the construction activity, and provide the bookkeeping services. The credit rating of the franchisee indicates that money can be borrowed at 8 percent. The present value of an ordinary annuity of five annual receipts of $8,000 each discounted at 8 percent is $31,941.68. The discount of $8,058.32 represents the interest revenue to be accrued by the franchisor over the payment period. The following examples show the entries that Tum's Pizza Inc. would make under various conditions.

1. If there is reasonable expectation that Tum's Pizza Inc. may refund the down payment and if substantial future services remain to be performed by Tum's Pizza Inc., the entry should be:

Cash	10,000.00	
Notes Receivable	40,000.00	
Discount on Notes Receivable		8,058.32
Unearned Franchise Fees		41,941.68

---

[29]Archibald E. MacKay, "Accounting for Initial Franchise Fee Revenue," *The Journal of Accountancy* (January 1970), pp. 66–67.

[30]In 1987 and 1988, the SEC ordered a half-dozen fast-growing startup franchisors, including Jiffy Lube International, Moto Photo, Inc., Swensen's, Inc., and LePeep Restaurants, Inc., to defer their initial franchise fee recognition until earned. See "Claiming Tomorrow's Profits Today," *Forbes* (October 17, 1988), p. 78.

2. If the probability of refunding the initial franchise fee is extremely low, the amount of future services to be provided to the franchisee is minimal, collectibility of the note is reasonably assured, and substantial performance has occurred, the entry should be:

Cash	10,000.00	
Notes Receivable	40,000.00	
Discount on Notes Receivable		8,058.32
Revenue from Franchise Fees		41,941.68

3. If the initial down payment is not refundable, represents a fair measure of the services already provided, with a significant amount of services still to be performed by Tum's Pizza in future periods, and collectibility of the note is reasonably assured, the entry should be:

Cash	10,000.00	
Notes Receivable	40,000.00	
Discount on Notes Receivable		8,058.32
Revenue from Franchise Fees		10,000.00
Unearned Franchise Fees		31,941.68

4. If the initial down payment is not refundable and no future services are required by the franchisor, but collection of the note is so uncertain that recognition of the note as an asset is unwarranted, the entry should be:

Cash	10,000.00	
Revenue from Franchise Fees		10,000.00

5. Under the same conditions as those listed in case 4 above, except that the down payment is refundable or substantial services are yet to be performed, the entry should be:

Cash	10,000.00	
Unearned Franchise Fees		10,000.00

In cases 4 and 5—where collection of the note is extremely uncertain—franchisors may recognize cash collections using the installment-sales method or the cost-recovery method.[31]

CONTINUING FRANCHISE FEES

Continuing franchise fees are received in return for the continuing rights granted by the franchise agreement and for providing such services as management training, advertising and promotion, legal assistance, and other support. Franchisors report continuing fees as revenue when they are earned and receivable from the franchisee, unless a portion of them has been designated for a particular purpose, such as providing a specified amount for building maintenance or local advertising. In that case, the portion deferred shall be an amount sufficient to cover the estimated cost in excess of continuing franchise fees and provide a reasonable profit on the continuing services.

BARGAIN PURCHASES

In addition to paying continuing franchise fees, franchisees frequently purchase some or all of their equipment and supplies from the franchisor. The franchisor would account for these sales as it would for any other product sales.

---

[31] A study that compared four revenue recognition procedures—installment-sales basis, spreading recognition over the contract life, percentage-of-completion basis, and substantial performance—for franchise sales concluded that the percentage-of-completion method is the most acceptable revenue recognition method; the substantial-performance method was found sometimes to yield ultra-conservative results. See Charles H. Calhoun III, "Accounting for Initial Franchise Fees: Is It a Dead Issue?" *The Journal of Accountancy* (February 1975), pp. 60–67.

Sometimes, however, the franchise agreement grants the franchisee the right to make **bargain purchases** of equipment or supplies after the franchisee has paid the initial franchise fee. If the bargain price is lower than the normal selling price of the same product, or if it does not provide the franchisor a reasonable profit, then the franchisor should defer a portion of the initial franchise fee. The franchisor would account for the deferred portion as an adjustment of the selling price when the franchisee subsequently purchases the equipment or supplies.

OPTIONS TO PURCHASE

A franchise agreement may give the franchisor an **option to purchase** the franchisee's business. As a matter of management policy, the franchisor may reserve the right to purchase a profitable franchise outlet, or to purchase one that is in financial difficulty.

If it is **probable** at the time the option is given that the franchisor will ultimately purchase the outlet, then the franchisor should not recognize the initial franchise fee as revenue but should instead record it as a liability. When the franchisor exercises the option, the liability would reduce the franchisor's investment in the outlet.

FRANCHISOR'S COST

Franchise accounting also involves proper accounting for the **franchisor's cost**. The objective is to match related costs and revenues by reporting them as components of income in the same accounting period. Franchisors should ordinarily defer **direct costs** (usually incremental costs) relating to specific franchise sales for which revenue has not yet been recognized. They should not, however, defer costs without reference to anticipated revenue and its realizability. [18] **Indirect costs** of a regular and recurring nature, such as selling and administrative expenses that are incurred irrespective of the level of franchise sales, should be expensed as incurred.

DISCLOSURES OF FRANCHISORS

Franchisors must disclose all significant commitments and obligations resulting from franchise agreements, including a description of services that have not yet been substantially performed. They also should disclose any resolution of uncertainties regarding the collectibility of franchise fees. Franchisors segregate initial franchise fees from other franchise fee revenue if they are significant. Where possible, revenues and costs related to franchisor-owned outlets should be distinguished from those related to franchised outlets.

KEY TERMS

continuing franchise
  fees, *1107*
franchisee, *1105*
franchisor, *1105*
initial franchise fee, *1106*
substantial performance,
  1106

SUMMARY OF LEARNING OBJECTIVE FOR APPENDIX 18A

8 **Explain revenue recognition for franchises.** In a franchise arrangement, the franchisor records as revenue the initial franchise fee as it makes substantial performance of the services it is obligated to perform and collection of the fee is reasonably assured. Franchisors recognize continuing franchise fees as revenue when they are earned and receivable from the franchisee.

FASB CODIFICATION

FASB Codification References

[1] FASB ASC 605-10-S99-1. [Predecessor literature: "Revenue Recognition in Financial Statements," *SEC Staff Accounting Bulletin No. 101* December 3, 1999), and "Revenue Recognition," *SEC Staff Accounting Bulletin No. 104* (December 17, 2003).]

[2] FASB ASC 470-40-25. [Predecessor literature: "Accounting for Product Financing Arrangements," *Statement of Financial Accounting Standards No. 49* (Stamford, Conn.: FASB, 1981).]

[3] FASB ASC 605-15-25-1. [Predecessor literature: "Revenue Recognition When Right of Return Exists," *Statement of Financial Accounting Standards No. 48* (Stamford, Conn.: FASB, 1981), par. 6.]

[4] FASB ASC 605-10-S99-1. [Predecessor literature: "Revenue Recognition in Financial Statements," *SEC Staff Accounting Bulletin No. 101* (December 3, 1999), and "Revenue Recognition," *SEC Staff Accounting Bulletin No. 104* (December 17, 2003).]

[5] FASB ASC 605-45-15. [Predecessor literature: "Revenue Recognition in Financial Statements," *SEC Staff Accounting Bulletin No. 101* (December 3, 1999), and "Revenue Recognition," *SEC Staff Accounting Bulletin No. 104* (December 17, 2003).]

[6] FASB ASC 605-25-05. [Predecessor literature: "EITF 00-21 Revenue Arrangements with Multiple Deliverables" (May 15, 2003).]

[7] FASB ASC 605-35-25-57. [Predecessor literature: "Accounting for Performance of Construction-Type and Certain Production-Type Contracts," *Statement of Position 81-1* (New York: AICPA, 1981), par. 23.]

[8] FASB ASC 605-35-05-7. [Predecessor literature: Committee on Accounting Procedure, "Long-Term Construction-Type Contracts," *Accounting Research Bulletin No. 45* (New York: AICPA, 1955), p. 7.]

[9] FASB ASC 910-405. [Predecessor literature: *Construction Contractors*, Audit and Accounting Guide (New York: AICPA, 1981), pp. 148–149.]

[10] FASB ASC 910-605-50-1. [Predecessor literature: *Construction Contractors*, Audit and Accounting Guide (New York: AICPA, 1981), p. 30.]

[11] FASB ASC 605-10-25-3. [Predecessor literature: "Omnibus Opinion," *Opinions of the Accounting Principles Board No. 10* (New York: AICPA, 1966), par. 12.]

[12] FASB ASC 976-605-25. [Predecessor literature: "Accounting for Sales of Real Estate," *Statement of Financial Accounting Standards No. 66* (Norwalk, Conn.: FASB, 1982), paras. 45–47.]

[13] FASB ASC 605-10-25-4. [Predecessor literature: "Omnibus Opinion," *Opinions of the Accounting Principles Board No. 10* (New York: AICPA, 1966), footnote 8, p. 149.]

[14] FASB ASC 952-605-25-7. [Predecessor literature: "Accounting for Franchise Fee Revenue," *Statement of Financial Accounting Standards No. 45* (Stamford, Conn.: FASB, 1981), par. 6.]

[15] FASB ASC 360-20-55-13. [Predecessor literature: "Accounting for Sales of Real Estate," *Statement of Financial Accounting Standards No. 66*, paras. 62 and 63.]

[16] FASB ASC 360-20-55-17. [Predecessor literature: "Accounting for Sales of Real Estate," *Statement of Financial Accounting Standards No. 66*, par. 65.]

[17] FASB ASC 952-605-25-3. [Predecessor literature: "Accounting for Franchise Fee Revenue," *Statement of Financial Accounting Standards No. 45* (Stamford, Conn.: FASB, 1981), par. 5.]

[18] FASB ASC 952-340-25. [Predecessor literature: "Accounting for Franchise Fee Revenue," *Statement of Financial Accounting Standards No. 45* (Stamford, Conn.: FASB, 1981), p. 17.]

Exercises

If your school has a subscription to the FASB Codification, go to *http://aaahq.org/asclogin.cfm* to log in and prepare responses to the following. Provide Codification references for your responses.

CE18-1 Access the glossary ("Master Glossary") to answer the following.
- **(a)** What is the cost-recovery method?
- **(b)** What is the percentage-of-completion method?
- **(c)** What is the deposit method?
- **(d)** What is the installment method?

CE18-2 Is the installment-sales method of recognizing revenue generally acceptable? Why or why not?

CE18-3 When would a construction company be allowed to use the completed-contract method?

CE18-4 When is it appropriate to use the cost-recovery method?

An additional Codification case can be found in the Using Your Judgment section, on page 1133.

Be sure to check the book's companion website for a Review and Analysis Exercise, with solution.

Questions, Brief Exercises, Exercises, Problems, and many more resources are available for practice in WileyPLUS.

Note: All asterisked Questions, Exercises, and Problems relate to material in the appendix to the chapter.

QUESTIONS

1. Explain the current environment regarding revenue recognition.

2. What is viewed as a major criticism of GAAP as regards revenue recognition?

3. What is the revenue recognition principle?

4. When is revenue recognized in the following situations: (a) Revenue from selling products? (b) Revenue from services rendered? (c) Revenue from permitting others to use enterprise assets? (d) Revenue from disposing of assets other than products?

5. What is the proper accounting for volume discounts on sales of products?

6. What are the three alternative accounting methods available to a seller that is exposed to continued risks of ownership through return of the product?

7. Under what conditions may a seller who is exposed to continued risks of a high rate of return of the product sold recognize sales transactions as current revenue?

8. Explain a bill and hold sale. When is revenue recognized in these situations?

9. What are the reporting issues in a sale and buyback agreement?

10. Explain a principal-agent relationship and its significance to revenue recognition.

11. What is the nature of a sale on consignment?

12. Explain a multiple-deliverable arrangement. What is the major accounting issue related to these arrangements?

13. Explain how multiple-deliverable arrangements are measured and reported.

14. What are the two basic methods of accounting for long-term construction contracts? Indicate the circumstances that determine when one or the other of these methods should be used.

15. Hawkins Construction Co. has a $60 million contract to construct a highway overpass and cloverleaf. The total estimated cost for the project is $50 million. Costs incurred in the first year of the project are $8 million. Hawkins Construction Co. appropriately uses the percentage-of-completion method. How much revenue and gross profit should Hawkins recognize in the first year of the project?

16. For what reasons should the percentage-of-completion method be used over the completed-contract method whenever possible?

17. What methods are used in practice to determine the extent of progress toward completion? Identify some "input measures" and some "output measures" that might be used to determine the extent of progress.

18. What are the two types of losses that can become evident in accounting for long-term contracts? What is the nature of each type of loss? How is each type accounted for?

19. Under the percentage-of-completion method, how are the Construction in Process and the Billings on Construction in Process accounts reported in the balance sheet?

20. Explain the differences between the installment-sales method and the cost-recovery method.

21. Identify and briefly describe the two methods generally employed to account for the cash received in situations where the collection of the sales price is not reasonably assured.

22. What is the deposit method and when might it be applied?

23. What is the nature of an installment sale? How do installment sales differ from ordinary credit sales?

24. Describe the installment-sales method of accounting.

25. How are operating expenses (not included in cost of goods sold) handled under the installment-sales method of accounting? What is the justification for such treatment?

26. Mojave sold her condominium for $500,000 on September 14, 2012; she had paid $330,000 for it in 2004. Mojave collected the selling price as follows: 2012, $80,000; 2013, $320,000; and 2014, $100,000. Mojave appropriately uses the installment-sales method. Prepare a schedule to determine the gross profit for 2012, 2013, and 2014 from the installment sale.

27. When interest is involved in installment-sales transactions, how should it be treated for accounting purposes?

28. How should the results of installment sales be reported on the income statement?

29. At what time is it proper to recognize income in the following cases: (a) Installment sales with no reasonable basis for estimating the degree of collectibility? (b) Sales for future delivery? (c) Merchandise shipped on consignment? (d) Profit on incomplete construction contracts? (e) Subscriptions to publications?

30. When is revenue recognized under the cost-recovery method?

31. When is revenue recognized under the deposit method? How does the deposit method differ from the installment-sales and cost-recovery methods?

*32. Why in franchise arrangements may it not be proper to recognize the entire franchise fee as revenue at the date of sale?

*33. How does the concept of "substantial performance" apply to accounting for franchise sales?

*34. How should a franchisor account for continuing franchise fees and routine sales of equipment and supplies to franchisees?

*35 What changes are made in the franchisor's recording of the initial franchise fee when the franchise agreement:

(a) Contains an option allowing the franchisor to purchase the franchised outlet, and it is likely that the option will be exercised?

(b) Allows the franchisee to purchase equipment and supplies from the franchisor at bargain prices?

BRIEF EXERCISES

BE18-1 Manual Company sells goods to Nolan Company during 2012. It offers Nolan the following rebates based on total sales to Nolan. If total sales to Nolan are 10,000 units, it will grant a rebate of 2%. If it sells up to 20,000 units, it will grant a rebate of 4%. If it sells up to 30,000 units, it will grant a rebate of 6%. In the first quarter of the year, Manual sells 11,000 units to Nolan at a sales price of $110,000. Manual, based on past experience, has sold over 40,000 units to Nolan and these sales normally take place in the third quarter of the year. Prepare the journal entry to record the sale of the 11,000 units in the first quarter of the year.

BE18-2 Adani Inc. sells goods to Geo Company for $11,000 on January 2, 2012, with payment due in 12 months. The fair value of the goods at the date of sale is $10,000. Prepare the journal entry to record this transaction on January 2, 2012. How much total revenue should be recognized on this sale in 2012?

BE18-3 Travel Inc. sells tickets for a Caribbean cruise to Carmel Company employees. The total cruise package costs Carmel $70,000 from ShipAway cruise liner. Travel Inc. receives a commission of 6% of the total price. Travel Inc. therefore remits $65,800 to ShipAway. Prepare the entry to record the revenue recognized by Travel Inc. on this transaction.

2 **BE18-4** Aamodt Music sold CDs to retailers and recorded sales revenue of $700,000. During 2012, retailers returned CDs to Aamodt and were granted credit of $78,000. Past experience indicates that the normal return rate is 15%. Prepare Aamodt's entries to record (a) the $78,000 of returns and (b) estimated returns at December 31, 2012.

2 **BE18-5** Jansen Corporation shipped $20,000 of merchandise on consignment to Gooch Company. Jansen paid freight costs of $2,000. Gooch Company paid $500 for local advertising, which is reimbursable from Jansen. By year-end, 60% of the merchandise had been sold for $21,500. Gooch notified Jansen, retained a 10% commission, and remitted the cash due to Jansen. Prepare Jansen's entry when the cash is received.

2 **BE18-6** Telephone Sellers Inc. sells prepaid telephone cards to customers. Telephone Sellers then pays the telecommunications company, TeleExpress, for the actual use of its telephone lines. Assume that Telephone Sellers sells $4,000 of prepaid cards in January 2012. It then pays TeleExpress based on usage, which turns out to be 50% in February, 30% in March, and 20% in April. The total payment by Telephone Sellers for TeleExpress lines over the 3 months is $3,000. Indicate how much income Telephone Sellers should recognize in January, February, March, and April.

3 **BE18-7** Turner, Inc. began work on a $7,000,000 contract in 2012 to construct an office building. During 2012, Turner, Inc. incurred costs of $1,700,000, billed its customers for $1,200,000, and collected $960,000. At December 31, 2012, the estimated future costs to complete the project total $3,300,000. Prepare Turner's 2012 journal entries using the percentage-of-completion method.

3 **BE18-8** O'Neil, Inc. began work on a $7,000,000 contract in 2012 to construct an office building. O'Neil uses the percentage-of-completion method. At December 31, 2012, the balances in certain accounts were Construction in Process $2,450,000; Accounts Receivable $240,000; and Billings on Construction in Process $1,400,000. Indicate how these accounts would be reported in O'Neil's December 31, 2012, balance sheet.

4 **BE18-9** Use the information from BE18-7, but assume Turner uses the completed-contract method. Prepare the company's 2012 journal entries.

4 **BE18-10** Guillen, Inc. began work on a $7,000,000 contract in 2012 to construct an office building. Guillen uses the completed-contract method. At December 31, 2012, the balances in certain accounts were Construction in Process $1,715,000; Accounts Receivable $240,000; and Billings on Construction in Process $1,000,000. Indicate how these accounts would be reported in Guillen's December 31, 2012, balance sheet.

5 **BE18-11** Archer Construction Company began work on a $420,000 construction contract in 2012. During 2012, Archer incurred costs of $278,000, billed its customer for $215,000, and collected $175,000. At December 31, 2012, the estimated future costs to complete the project total $162,000. Prepare Archer's journal entry to record profit or loss using (a) the percentage-of-completion method and (b) the completed-contract method, if any.

6 **BE18-12** Gordeeva Corporation began selling goods on the installment basis on January 1, 2012. During 2012, Gordeeva had installment sales of $150,000; cash collections of $54,000; cost of installment sales of $102,000. Prepare the company's entries to record installment sales, cash collected, cost of installment sales, deferral of gross profit, and gross profit recognized, using the installment-sales method.

6 **BE18-13** Lazaro Inc. sells goods on the installment basis and uses the installment-sales method. Due to a customer default, Lazaro repossessed merchandise that was originally sold for $800, resulting in a gross profit rate of 40%. At the time of repossession, the uncollected balance is $520, and the fair value of the repossessed merchandise is $275. Prepare Lazaro's entry to record the repossession.

6 **BE18-14** At December 31, 2012, Grinkov Corporation had the following account balances.

Installment Accounts Receivable, 2011	$ 65,000
Installment Accounts Receivable, 2012	110,000
Deferred Gross Profit, 2011	23,400
Deferred Gross Profit, 2012	41,800

Most of Grinkov's sales are made on a 2-year installment basis. Indicate how these accounts would be reported in Grinkov's December 31, 2012, balance sheet. The 2011 accounts are collectible in 2013, and the 2012 accounts are collectible in 2014.

7 **BE18-15** Schuss Corporation sold equipment to Potsdam Company for $20,000. The equipment is on Schuss's books at a net amount of $13,000. Schuss collected $10,000 in 2012, $5,000 in 2013, and $5,000 in 2014. If Schuss uses the cost-recovery method, what amount of gross profit will be recognized in each year?

8 *BE18-16** Frozen Delight, Inc. charges an initial franchise fee of $75,000 for the right to operate as a franchisee of Frozen Delight. Of this amount, $25,000 is collected immediately. The remainder is collected in 4 equal annual installments of $12,500 each. These installments have a present value of $41,402. There is reasonable expectation that the down payment may be refunded and substantial future services be performed by Frozen Delight, Inc. Prepare the journal entry required by Frozen Delight to record the franchise fee.

EXERCISES

2 **E18-1 (Revenue Recognition—Point of Sale)** Jupiter Company sells goods on January 1 that have a cost of $500,000 to Danone Inc. for $700,000, with payment due in 1 year. The cash price for these goods is $610,000, with payment due in 30 days. If Danone paid immediately upon delivery, it would receive a cash discount of $10,000.

Instructions
(a) Prepare the journal entry to record this transaction at the date of sale.
(b) How much revenue should Jupiter report for the entire year?

2 **E18-2 (Revenue Recognition—Point of Sale)** Shaw Company sells goods that cost $300,000 to Ricard Company for $410,000 on January 2, 2012. The sales price includes an installation fee, which is valued at $40,000. The fair value of the goods is $370,000. The installation is expected to take 6 months.

Instructions
(a) Prepare the journal entry (if any) to record the sale on January 2, 2012.
(b) Shaw prepares an income statement for the first quarter of 2012, ending on March 31, 2012. How much revenue should Shaw recognize related to its sale to Ricard?

2 **E18-3 (Revenue Recognition—Point of Sale)** Presented below are three revenue recognition situations.

(a) Grupo sells goods to MTN for $1,000,000, payment due at delivery.
(b) Grupo sells goods on account to Grifols for $800,000, payment due in 30 days.
(c) Grupo sells goods to Magnus for $500,000, payment due in two installments: the first installment payable in 6 months and the second payment due 3 months later.

Instructions
Indicate how each of these transactions is reported.

2 **E18-4 (Revenue Recognition—Point of Sale)** Wood-Mode Company is involved in the design, manufacture, and installation of various types of wood products for large construction projects. Wood-Mode recently completed a large contract for Stadium Inc., which consisted of building 35 different types of concession counters for a new soccer arena under construction. The terms of the contract are that upon completion of the counters, Stadium would pay $2,000,000. Unfortunately, due to the depressed economy, the completion of the new soccer arena is now delayed. Stadium has therefore asked Wood-Mode to hold the counters at its manufacturing plant until the arena is completed. Stadium acknowledges in writing that it ordered the counters and that they now have ownership. The time that Wood-Mode Company must hold the counters is totally dependent on when the arena is completed. Because Wood-Mode has not received additional progress payments for the arena due to the delay, Stadium has provided a deposit of $300,000.

Instructions
(a) Explain this type of revenue recognition transaction.
(b) What factors should be considered in determining when to recognize revenue in this transaction?
(c) Prepare the journal entry(ies) that Wood-Mode should make, assuming it signed a valid sales contract to sell the counters and received at the time of sale the $300,000 payment.

2 **E18-5 (Right of Return)** Organic Growth Company is presently testing a number of new agricultural seeds that it has recently harvested. To stimulate interest, it has decided to grant to five of its largest customers the unconditional right of return to these products if not fully satisfied. The right of return extends for 4 months. Organic Growth sells these seeds on account for $1,500,000 on January 2, 2012. Companies are required to pay the full amount due by March 15, 2012.

Instructions
(a) Prepare the journal entry for Organic Growth at January 2, 2012, assuming Organic Growth estimates returns of 20% based on prior experience. (Ignore cost of goods sold.)

(b) Assume that one customer returns the seeds on March 1, 2012, due to unsatisfactory performance. Prepare the journal entry to record this transaction, assuming this customer purchased $100,000 of seeds from Organic Growth.

(c) Briefly describe the accounting for these sales, if Organic Growth is unable to reliably estimate returns.

E18-6 (Revenue Recognition on Book Sales with High Returns) Uddin Publishing Co. publishes college textbooks that are sold to bookstores on the following terms. Each title has a fixed wholesale price, terms f.o.b. shipping point, and payment is due 60 days after shipment. The retailer may return a maximum of 30% of an order at the retailer's expense. Sales are made only to retailers who have good credit ratings. Past experience indicates that the normal return rate is 12%, and the average collection period is 72 days.

Instructions

(a) Identify alternative revenue recognition criteria that Uddin could employ concerning textbook sales.

(b) Briefly discuss the reasoning for your answers in (a) above.

(c) In late July, Uddin shipped books invoiced at $15,000,000. Prepare the journal entry to record this event that best conforms to GAAP and your answer to part (b).

(d) In October, $2 million of the invoiced July sales were returned according to the return policy, and the remaining $13 million was paid. Prepare the entries for the return and payment.

E18-7 (Sales Recorded Both Gross and Net) On June 3, Hunt Company sold to Ann Mount merchandise having a sales price of $8,000 with terms of 2/10, n/60, f.o.b. shipping point. An invoice totaling $120, terms n/30, was received by Mount on June 8 from the Olympic Transport Service for the freight cost. Upon receipt of the goods, June 5, Mount notified Hunt Company that merchandise costing $600 contained flaws that rendered it worthless. The same day, Hunt Company issued a credit memo covering the worthless merchandise and asked that it be returned at company expense. The freight on the returned merchandise was $24, paid by Hunt Company on June 7. On June 12, the company received a check for the balance due from Mount.

Instructions

(a) Prepare journal entries for Hunt Company to record all the events noted above under each of the following bases.

(1) Sales and receivables are entered at gross selling price.

(2) Sales and receivables are entered net of cash discounts.

(b) Prepare the journal entry under basis (2), assuming that Ann Mount did not remit payment until August 5.

E18-8 (Revenue Recognition on Marina Sales with Discounts) Taylor Marina has 300 available slips that rent for $800 per season. Payments must be made in full at the start of the boating season, April 1, 2013. Slips for the next season may be reserved if paid for by December 31, 2012. Under a new policy, if payment is made by December 31, 2012, a 5% discount is allowed. The boating season ends October 31, and the marina has a December 31 year-end. To provide cash flow for major dock repairs, the marina operator is also offering a 20% discount to slip renters who pay for the 2014 season.

For the fiscal year ended December 31, 2012, all 300 slips were rented at full price. Two hundred slips were reserved and paid for the 2013 boating season, and 60 slips for the 2014 boating season were reserved and paid for.

Instructions

(a) Prepare the appropriate journal entries for fiscal 2012.

(b) Assume the marina operator is unsophisticated in business. Explain the managerial significance of the accounting above to this person.

E18-9 (Consignment Computations) On May 3, 2012, Eisler Company consigned 80 freezers, costing $500 each, to Remmers Company. The cost of shipping the freezers amounted to $840 and was paid by Eisler Company. On December 30, 2012, a report was received from the consignee, indicating that 40 freezers had been sold for $750 each. Remittance was made by the consignee for the amount due, after deducting a commission of 6%, advertising of $200, and total installation costs of $320 on the freezers sold.

Instructions

(a) Compute the inventory value of the units unsold in the hands of the consignee.

(b) Compute the profit for the consignor for the units sold.

(c) Compute the amount of cash that will be remitted by the consignee.

2 **E18-10 (Multiple-Deliverable Arrangement)** Appliance Center is an experienced home appliance dealer. Appliance Center also offers a number of services together with the home appliances that it sells. Assume that Appliance Center sells ovens on a standalone basis. Appliance Center also sells installation services and maintenance services for ovens. However, Appliance Center does not offer installation or maintenance services to customers who buy ovens from other vendors. Pricing for ovens is as follows.

Oven only	$ 800
Oven with installation service	850
Oven with maintenance services	975
Oven with installation and maintenance services	1,000

In each instance in which maintenance services are provided, the maintenance service is separately priced within the arrangement at $175. Additionally, the incremental amount charged by Appliance Center for installation approximates the amount charged by independent third parties. Ovens are sold subject to a general right of return. If a customer purchases an oven with installation and/or maintenance services, in the event Appliance Center does not complete the service satisfactorily, the customer is only entitled to a refund of the portion of the fee that exceeds $800.

Instructions
(a) Assume that a customer purchases an oven with both installation and maintenance services for $1,000. Based on its experience, Appliance Center believes that it is probable that the installation of the equipment will be performed satisfactorily to the customer. Assume that the maintenance services are priced separately. Explain whether the conditions for a multiple-deliverable arrangement exist in this situation.
(b) Indicate the amount of revenues that should be allocated to the oven, the installation, and to the maintenance contract.

2 **E18-11 (Multiple-Deliverable Arrangement)** On December 31, 2012, Grando Company sells production equipment to Fargo Inc. for $50,000. Grando includes a 1-year warranty service with the sale of all its equipment. The customer receives and pays for the equipment on December 31, 2012. Grando estimates the prices to be $48,800 for the equipment and $1,200 for the warranty.

Instructions
(a) Prepare the journal entry to record this transaction on December 31, 2012.
(b) Indicate how much (if any) revenue should be recognized on January 31, 2013, and for the year 2013.

3 **4** **E18-12 (Recognition of Profit on Long-Term Contracts)** During 2012, Nilsen Company started a construction job with a contract price of $1,600,000. The job was completed in 2014. The following information is available.

	2012	2013	2014
Costs incurred to date	$400,000	$825,000	$1,070,000
Estimated costs to complete	600,000	275,000	–0–
Billings to date	300,000	900,000	1,600,000
Collections to date	270,000	810,000	1,425,000

Instructions
(a) Compute the amount of gross profit to be recognized each year, assuming the percentage-of-completion method is used.
(b) Prepare all necessary journal entries for 2013.
(c) Compute the amount of gross profit to be recognized each year, assuming the completed-contract method is used.

3 **E18-13 (Analysis of Percentage-of-Completion Financial Statements)** In 2012, Steinrotter Construction Corp. began construction work under a 3-year contract. The contract price was $1,000,000. Steinrotter uses the percentage-of-completion method for financial accounting purposes. The income to be recognized each year is based on the proportion of cost incurred to total estimated costs for completing the contract. The financial statement presentations relating to this contract at December 31, 2012, are shown on the next page.

Balance Sheet

Accounts receivable—construction contract billings		$18,000
Construction in process	$65,000	
Less: Contract billings	61,500	
Cost of uncompleted contract in excess of billings		3,500

Income Statement

Income (before tax) on the contract recognized in 2012	$19,500

Instructions

(a) How much cash was collected in 2012 on this contract?

(b) What was the initial estimated total income before tax on this contract?

(AICPA adapted)

E18-14 (Gross Profit on Uncompleted Contract) On April 1, 2012, Dougherty Inc. entered into a cost-plus-fixed-fee contract to construct an electric generator for Altom Corporation. At the contract date, Dougherty estimated that it would take 2 years to complete the project at a cost of $2,000,000. The fixed fee stipulated in the contract is $450,000. Dougherty appropriately accounts for this contract under the percentage-of-completion method. During 2012, Dougherty incurred costs of $800,000 related to the project. The estimated cost at December 31, 2012, to complete the contract is $1,200,000. Altom was billed $600,000 under the contract.

Instructions

Prepare a schedule to compute the amount of gross profit to be recognized by Dougherty under the contract for the year ended December 31, 2012. Show supporting computations in good form.

(AICPA adapted)

E18-15 (Recognition of Profit, Percentage-of-Completion) In 2012, Gurney Construction Company agreed to construct an apartment building at a price of $1,200,000. The information relating to the costs and billings for this contract is shown below.

	2012	2013	2014
Costs incurred to date	$280,000	$600,000	$ 785,000
Estimated costs yet to be incurred	520,000	200,000	–0–
Customer billings to date	150,000	500,000	1,200,000
Collection of billings to date	120,000	320,000	940,000

Instructions

(a) Assuming that the percentage-of-completion method is used, (1) compute the amount of gross profit to be recognized in 2012 and 2013, and (2) prepare journal entries for 2013.

(b) For 2013, show how the details related to this construction contract would be disclosed on the balance sheet and on the income statement.

E18-16 (Recognition of Revenue on Long-Term Contract and Entries) Hamilton Construction Company uses the percentage-of-completion method of accounting. In 2012, Hamilton began work under contract #E2-D2, which provided for a contract price of $2,200,000. Other details follow:

	2012	2013
Costs incurred during the year	$640,000	$1,425,000
Estimated costs to complete, as of December 31	960,000	–0–
Billings during the year	420,000	1,680,000
Collections during the year	350,000	1,500,000

Instructions

(a) What portion of the total contract price would be recognized as revenue in 2012? In 2013?

(b) Assuming the same facts as those above except that Hamilton uses the completed-contract method of accounting, what portion of the total contract price would be recognized as revenue in 2013?

(c) Prepare a complete set of journal entries for 2012 (using the percentage-of-completion method).

E18-17 (Recognition of Profit and Balance Sheet Amounts for Long-Term Contracts) Yanmei Construction Company began operations January 1, 2012. During the year, Yanmei Construction entered into a contract with Lundquist Corp. to construct a manufacturing facility. At that time, Yanmei estimated that it would take 5 years to complete the facility at a total cost of $4,500,000. The total contract price for construction of the facility is $6,000,000. During the year, Yanmei incurred $1,185,800 in construction costs related to the construction project. The estimated cost to complete the contract is $4,204,200. Lundquist Corp. was billed and paid 25% of the contract price.

Instructions

Prepare schedules to compute the amount of gross profit to be recognized for the year ended December 31, 2012, and the amount to be shown as "costs and recognized profit on uncompleted contract in excess of related billings" or "billings on uncompleted contract in excess of related costs and recognized profit" at December 31, 2012, under each of the following methods.

(a) Completed-contract method.
(b) Percentage-of-completion method.

Show supporting computations in good form.

(AICPA adapted)

4 **5** **E18-18 (Long-Term Contract Reporting)** Berstler Construction Company began operations in 2012. Construction activity for the first year is shown below. All contracts are with different customers, and any work remaining at December 31, 2012, is expected to be completed in 2013.

Project	Total Contract Price	Billings through 12/31/12	Cash Collections through 12/31/12	Contract Costs Incurred through 12/31/12	Estimated Additional Costs to Complete
1	$ 560,000	$ 360,000	$340,000	$450,000	$130,000
2	670,000	220,000	210,000	126,000	504,000
3	520,000	500,000	440,000	330,000	–0–
	$1,750,000	$1,080,000	$990,000	$906,000	$634,000

Instructions

Prepare a partial income statement and balance sheet to indicate how the above information would be reported for financial statement purposes. Berstler Construction Company uses the completed-contract method.

6 **E18-19 (Installment-Sales Method Calculations, Entries)** Coffin Corporation appropriately uses the installment-sales method of accounting to recognize income in its financial statements. The following information is available for 2012 and 2013.

	2012	2013
Installment sales	$900,000	$1,000,000
Cost of installment sales	594,000	680,000
Cash collections on 2012 sales	370,000	350,000
Cash collections on 2013 sales	–0–	450,000

Instructions

(a) Compute the amount of realized gross profit recognized in each year.
(b) Prepare all journal entries required in 2013.

6 **E18-20 (Analysis of Installment-Sales Accounts)** Samuels Co. appropriately uses the installment-sales method of accounting. On December 31, 2014, the books show balances as follows.

Installment Receivables		Deferred Gross Profit		Gross Profit on Sales	
2012	$12,000	2012	$ 7,000	2012	35%
2013	40,000	2013	26,000	2013	33%
2014	80,000	2014	95,000	2014	32%

Instructions

(a) Prepare the adjusting entry or entries required on December 31, 2014 to recognize 2014 realized gross profit. (Installment receivables have already been credited for cash receipts during 2014.)
(b) Compute the amount of cash collected in 2014 on accounts receivable from each year.

6 **E18-21 (Gross Profit Calculations and Repossessed Merchandise)** Basler Corporation, which began business on January 1, 2012, appropriately uses the installment-sales method of accounting. The following data were obtained for the years 2012 and 2013.

	2012	2013
Installment sales	$750,000	$840,000
Cost of installment sales	510,000	588,000
General & administrative expenses	70,000	84,000
Cash collections on sales of 2012	310,000	300,000
Cash collections on sales of 2013	–0–	400,000

Instructions

(a) Compute the balance in the deferred gross profit accounts on December 31, 2012, and on December 31, 2013.

(b) A 2012 sale resulted in default in 2014. At the date of default, the balance on the installment receivable was $12,000, and the repossessed merchandise had a fair value of $8,000. Prepare the entry to record the repossession.

(AICPA adapted)

6 **E18-22 (Interest Revenue from Installment Sale)** Becker Corporation sells farm machinery on the installment plan. On July 1, 2012, Becker entered into an installment-sales contract with Valente Inc. for an 8-year period. Equal annual payments under the installment sale are $100,000 and are due on July 1. The first payment was made on July 1, 2012.

Additional information:

1. The amount that would be realized on an outright sale of similar farm machinery is $586,842.
2. The cost of the farm machinery sold to Valente Inc. is $425,000.
3. The finance charges relating to the installment period are based on a stated interest rate of 10%, which is appropriate.
4. Circumstances are such that the collection of the installments due under the contract is reasonably assured.

Instructions

What income or loss before income taxes should Becker record for the year ended December 31, 2012, as a result of the transaction above?

(AICPA adapted)

6 **7** **E18-23 (Installment-Sales Method and Cost-Recovery Method)** Swift Corp., a capital goods manufacturing business that started on January 4, 2012, and operates on a calendar-year basis, uses the installment-sales method of profit recognition in accounting for all its sales. The following data were taken from the 2012 and 2013 records.

	2012	2013
Installment sales	$480,000	$620,000
Gross profit as a percent of costs	25%	28%
Cash collections on sales of 2012	$130,000	$240,000
Cash collections on sales of 2013	–0–	$160,000

The amounts given for cash collections exclude amounts collected for interest charges.

Instructions

(a) Compute the amount of realized gross profit to be recognized on the 2013 income statement, prepared using the installment-sales method. (Round percentages to three decimal places.)

(b) State where the balance of Deferred Gross Profit would be reported on the financial statements for 2013.

(c) Compute the amount of realized gross profit to be recognized on the income statement, prepared using the cost-recovery method.

(CIA adapted)

6 **7** **E18-24 (Installment-Sales Method and Cost-Recovery Method)** On January 1, 2012, Wetzel Company sold property for $250,000. The note will be collected as follows: $120,000 in 2012, $90,000 in 2013, and $40,000 in 2014. The property had cost Wetzel $150,000 when it was purchased in 2010.

Instructions

(a) Compute the amount of gross profit realized each year, assuming Wetzel uses the cost-recovery method.

(b) Compute the amount of gross profit realized each year, assuming Wetzel uses the installment-sales method.

6 **E18-25 (Installment Sales—Default and Repossession)** Crawford Imports Inc. was involved in two default and repossession cases during the year:

1. A refrigerator was sold to Cindy McClary for $1,800, including a 30% markup on selling price. McClary made a down payment of 20%, four of the remaining 16 equal payments, and then defaulted on further payments. The refrigerator was repossessed, at which time the fair value was determined to be $800.

2. An oven that cost $1,200 was sold to Travis Longman for $1,500 on the installment basis. Longman made a down payment of $240 and paid $80 a month for six months, after which he defaulted. The oven was repossessed and the estimated fair value at time of repossession was determined to be $750.

Instructions

Prepare journal entries to record each of these repossessions using a fair value approach. (Ignore interest charges.)

6 **E18-26 (Installment Sales—Default and Repossession)** Seaver Company uses the installment-sales method in accounting for its installment sales. On January 1, 2012, Seaver Company had an installment account receivable from Jan Noble with a balance of $1,800. During 2012, $500 was collected from Noble. When no further collection could be made, the merchandise sold to Noble was repossessed. The merchandise had a fair value of $650 after the company spent $60 for reconditioning of the merchandise. The merchandise was originally sold with a gross profit rate of 30%.

Instructions

Prepare the entries on the books of Seaver Company to record all transactions related to Noble during 2012. (Ignore interest charges.)

8 *E18-27 (Franchise Entries)** Pacific Crossburgers Inc. charges an initial franchise fee of $70,000. Upon the signing of the agreement, a payment of $28,000 is due. Thereafter, three annual payments of $14,000 are required. The credit rating of the franchisee is such that it would have to pay interest at 10% to borrow money.

Instructions

Prepare the entries to record the initial franchise fee on the books of the franchisor under the following assumptions. (Round to the nearest dollar.)

(a) The down payment is not refundable, no future services are required by the franchisor, and collection of the note is reasonably assured.

(b) The franchisor has substantial services to perform, the down payment is refundable, and the collection of the note is very uncertain.

(c) The down payment is not refundable, collection of the note is reasonably certain, the franchisor has yet to perform a substantial amount of services, and the down payment represents a fair measure of the services already performed.

8 *E18-28 (Franchise Fee, Initial Down Payment)** On January 1, 2012, Lesley Benjamin signed an agreement to operate as a franchisee of Campbell Inc. for an initial franchise fee of $50,000. The amount of $10,000 was paid when the agreement was signed, and the balance is payable in five annual payments of $8,000 each, beginning January 1, 2013. The agreement provides that the down payment is not refundable and that no future services are required of the franchisor. Lesley Benjamin's credit rating indicates that she can borrow money at 11% for a loan of this type.

Instructions

(a) How much should Campbell record as revenue from franchise fees on January 1, 2012? At what amount should Benjamin record the acquisition cost of the franchise on January 1, 2012?

(b) What entry would be made by Campbell on January 1, 2012, if the down payment is refundable and substantial future services remain to be performed by Campbell?

(c) How much revenue from franchise fees would be recorded by Campbell on January 1, 2012, if:

(1) The initial down payment is not refundable, it represents a fair measure of the services already provided, a significant amount of services is still to be performed by Campbell in future periods, and collectibility of the note is reasonably assured?

(2) The initial down payment is not refundable and no future services are required by the franchisor, but collection of the note is so uncertain that recognition of the note as an asset is unwarranted?

(3) The initial down payment has not been earned and collection of the note is so uncertain that recognition of the note as an asset is unwarranted?

See the book's companion website, www.wiley.com/college/kieso, for a set of B Exercises.

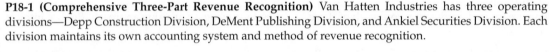

PROBLEMS

P18-1 (Comprehensive Three-Part Revenue Recognition) Van Hatten Industries has three operating divisions—Depp Construction Division, DeMent Publishing Division, and Ankiel Securities Division. Each division maintains its own accounting system and method of revenue recognition.

Depp Construction Division

During the fiscal year ended November 30, 2012, Depp Construction Division had one construction project in process. A $30,000,000 contract for construction of a civic center was granted on June 19, 2012, and construction began on August 1, 2012. Estimated costs of completion at the contract date were $25,000,000 over a 2-year time period from the date of the contract. On November 30, 2012, construction costs of $7,200,000 had been incurred and progress billings of $9,500,000 had been made. The construction costs to complete the remainder of the project were reviewed on November 30, 2012, and were estimated to amount to only $16,800,000 because of an expected decline in raw materials costs. Revenue recognition is based upon a percentage-of-completion method.

DeMent Publishing Division

The DeMent Publishing Division sells large volumes of novels to a few book distributors, which in turn sell to several national chains of bookstores. DeMent allows distributors to return up to 30% of sales, and distributors give the same terms to bookstores. While returns from individual titles fluctuate greatly, the returns from distributors have averaged 20% in each of the past 5 years. A total of $7,000,000 of paperback novel sales were made to distributors during fiscal 2012. On November 30, 2012 (the end of the fiscal year), $1,500,000 of fiscal 2012 sales were still subject to return privileges over the next 6 months. The remaining $5,500,000 of fiscal 2012 sales had actual returns of 21%. Sales from fiscal 2011 totaling $2,000,000 were collected in fiscal 2012 less 18% returns. This division records revenue according to the method referred to as revenue recognition when the right of return exists.

Ankiel Securities Division

Ankiel Securities Division works through manufacturers' agents in various cities. Orders for alarm systems and down payments are forwarded from agents, and the division ships the goods f.o.b. factory directly to customers (usually police departments and security guard companies). Customers are billed directly for the balance due plus actual shipping costs. The company received orders for $6,000,000 of goods during the fiscal year ended November 30, 2012. Down payments of $600,000 were received, and $5,200,000 of goods were billed and shipped. Actual freight costs of $100,000 were also billed. Commissions of 10% on product price are paid to manufacturing agents after goods are shipped to customers. Such goods are warranted for 90 days after shipment, and warranty returns have been about 1% of sales. Revenue is recognized at the point of sale by this division.

Instructions

(a) There are a variety of methods of revenue recognition. Define and describe each of the following methods of revenue recognition, and indicate whether each is in accordance with generally accepted accounting principles.
  (1) Point of sale.
  (2) Completion-of-production.
  (3) Percentage-of-completion.
  (4) Installment-sales.

(b) Compute the revenue to be recognized in fiscal year 2012 for each of the three operating divisions of Van Hatten Industries in accordance with generally accepted accounting principles.

3 **4** **P18-2 (Recognition of Profit on Long-Term Contract)** Shanahan Construction Company has entered into a contract beginning January 1, 2012, to build a parking complex. It has been estimated that the complex will cost $600,000 and will take 3 years to construct. The complex will be billed to the purchasing company at $900,000. The following data pertain to the construction period.

	2012	2013	2014
Costs to date	$270,000	$450,000	$610,000
Estimated costs to complete	330,000	150,000	–0–
Progress billings to date	270,000	550,000	900,000
Cash collected to date	240,000	500,000	900,000

Instructions

(a) Using the percentage-of-completion method, compute the estimated gross profit that would be recognized during each year of the construction period.

(b) Using the completed-contract method, compute the estimated gross profit that would be recognized during each year of the construction period.

3 **4** **P18-3 (Recognition of Profit and Entries on Long-Term Contract)** On March 1, 2012, Chance Company entered into a contract to build an apartment building. It is estimated that the building will cost $2,000,000 and will take 3 years to complete. The contract price was $3,000,000. The following information pertains to the construction period.

	2012	2013	2014
Costs to date	$ 600,000	$1,560,000	$2,100,000
Estimated costs to complete	1,400,000	520,000	–0–
Progress billings to date	1,050,000	2,000,000	3,000,000
Cash collected to date	950,000	1,950,000	2,850,000

Instructions

(a) Compute the amount of gross profit to be recognized each year, assuming the percentage-of-completion method is used.

(b) Prepare all necessary journal entries for 2014.

(c) Prepare a partial balance sheet for December 31, 2013, showing the balances in the receivables and inventory accounts.

3 **P18-4 (Recognition of Profit and Balance Sheet Presentation, Percentage-of-Completion)** On February 1, 2012, Hewitt Construction Company obtained a contract to build an athletic stadium. The stadium was to be built at a total cost of $5,400,000 and was scheduled for completion by September 1, 2014. One clause of the contract stated that Hewitt was to deduct $15,000 from the $6,600,000 billing price for each week that completion was delayed. Completion was delayed 6 weeks, which resulted in a $90,000 penalty. Below are the data pertaining to the construction period.

	2012	2013	2014
Costs to date	$1,620,000	$3,850,000	$5,500,000
Estimated costs to complete	3,780,000	1,650,000	–0–
Progress billings to date	1,200,000	3,300,000	6,510,000
Cash collected to date	1,000,000	2,800,000	6,510,000

Instructions

(a) Using the percentage-of-completion method, compute the estimated gross profit recognized in the years 2012–2014.

(b) Prepare a partial balance sheet for December 31, 2013, showing the balances in the receivables and inventory accounts.

3 **4** **P18-5 (Completed-Contract and Percentage-of-Completion with Interim Loss)** Reynolds Custom **5** Builders (RCB) was established in 1987 by Avery Conway and initially built high-quality customized homes under contract with specific buyers. In the 1990s, Conway's two sons joined the company and expanded RCB's activities into the high-rise apartment and industrial plant markets. Upon the retirement of RCB's long-time financial manager, Conway's sons recently hired Ed Borke as controller for RCB. Borke, a former college friend of Conway's sons, has been associated with a public accounting firm for the last 6 years.

Upon reviewing RCB's accounting practices, Borke observed that RCB followed the completed-contract method of revenue recognition, a carryover from the years when individual home building was the majority of RCB's operations. Several years ago, the predominant portion of RCB's activities shifted to the high-rise and industrial building areas. From land acquisition to the completion of construction, most building contracts cover several years. Under the circumstances, Borke believes that RCB should follow the percentage-of-completion method of accounting. From a typical building contract, Borke developed the following data.

BLUESTEM TRACTOR PLANT

Contract price: $8,000,000

	2012	2013	2014
Estimated costs	$1,600,000	$2,880,000	$1,920,000
Progress billings	1,000,000	2,500,000	4,500,000
Cash collections	800,000	2,300,000	4,900,000

Instructions

(a) Explain the difference between completed-contract revenue recognition and percentage-of-completion revenue recognition.

(b) Using the data provided for the Bluestem Tractor Plant and assuming the percentage-of-completion method of revenue recognition is used, calculate RCB's revenue and gross profit for 2012, 2013, and 2014, under **each** of the following circumstances.

   (1) Assume that all costs are incurred, all billings to customers are made, and all collections from customers are received within 30 days of billing, as planned.

   (2) Further assume that, as a result of unforeseen local ordinances and the fact that the building site was in a wetlands area, RCB experienced cost overruns of $800,000 in 2012 to bring the site into compliance with the ordinances and to overcome wetlands barriers to construction.

   (3) Further assume that, in addition to the cost overruns of $800,000 for this contract incurred under part (b)(2), inflationary factors over and above those anticipated in the development of the original contract cost have caused an additional cost overrun of $850,000 in 2013. It is not anticipated that any cost overruns will occur in 2014.

(CMA adapted)

3 4 5 P18-6 (Long-Term Contract with Interim Loss) On March 1, 2012, Pechstein Construction Company contracted to construct a factory building for Fabrik Manufacturing Inc. for a total contract price of $8,400,000. The building was completed by October 31, 2014. The annual contract costs incurred, estimated costs to complete the contract, and accumulated billings to Fabrik for 2012, 2013, and 2014 are given below.

	2012	2013	2014
Contract costs incurred during the year	$2,880,000	$2,230,000	$2,190,000
Estimated costs to complete the contract at 12/31	3,520,000	2,190,000	–0–
Billings to Fabrik during the year	3,200,000	3,500,000	1,700,000

Instructions

(a) Using the percentage-of-completion method, prepare schedules to compute the profit or loss to be recognized as a result of this contract for the years ended December 31, 2012, 2013, and 2014. (Ignore income taxes.)

(b) Using the completed-contract method, prepare schedules to compute the profit or loss to be recognized as a result of this contract for the years ended December 31, 2012, 2013, and 2014. (Ignore incomes taxes.)

3 4 5 P18-7 (Long-Term Contract with an Overall Loss) On July 1, 2012, Torvill Construction Company Inc. contracted to build an office building for Gumbel Corp. for a total contract price of $1,900,000. On July 1, Torvill estimated that it would take between 2 and 3 years to complete the building. On December 31, 2014, the building was deemed substantially completed. Following are accumulated contract costs incurred, estimated costs to complete the contract, and accumulated billings to Gumbel for 2012, 2013, and 2014.

	At 12/31/12	At 12/31/13	At 12/31/14
Contract costs incurred to date	$ 300,000	$1,200,000	$2,100,000
Estimated costs to complete the contract	1,200,000	800,000	–0–
Billings to Gumbel	300,000	1,100,000	1,850,000

Instructions

(a) Using the percentage-of-completion method, prepare schedules to compute the profit or loss to be recognized as a result of this contract for the years ended December 31, 2012, 2013, and 2014. (Ignore income taxes.)

(b) Using the completed-contract method, prepare schedules to compute the profit or loss to be recognized as a result of this contract for the years ended December 31, 2012, 2013, and 2014. (Ignore income taxes.)

6 **P18-8 (Installment-Sales Computations and Entries)** Presented below is summarized information for Johnston Co., which sells merchandise on the installment basis.

	2012	2013	2014
Sales (on installment plan)	$250,000	$260,000	$280,000
Cost of sales	155,000	163,800	182,000
Gross profit	$ 95,000	$ 96,200	$ 98,000
Collections from customers on:			
2012 installment sales	$ 75,000	$100,000	$ 50,000
2013 installment sales		100,000	120,000
2014 installment sales			100,000

Instructions

(a) Compute the realized gross profit for each of the years 2012, 2013, and 2014.

(b) Prepare in journal form all entries required in 2014, applying the installment-sales method of accounting. (Ignore interest charges.)

6 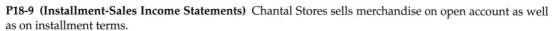 **P18-9 (Installment-Sales Income Statements)** Chantal Stores sells merchandise on open account as well as on installment terms.

	2012	2013	2014
Sales on account	$385,000	$426,000	$525,000
Installment sales	320,000	275,000	380,000
Collections on installment sales			
Made in 2012	100,000	90,000	40,000
Made in 2013		110,000	140,000
Made in 2014			125,000
Cost of sales			
Sold on account	270,000	277,000	341,000
Sold on installment	214,400	176,000	228,000
Selling expenses	77,000	87,000	92,000
Administrative expenses	50,000	51,000	52,000

Instructions

From the data above, which cover the 3 years since Chantal Stores commenced operations, determine the net income for each year, applying the installment-sales method of accounting. (Ignore interest charges.)

6 **P18-10 (Installment-Sales Computations and Entries)** Paul Dobson Stores sell appliances for cash and also on the installment plan. Entries to record cost of sales are made monthly.

PAUL DOBSON STORES
TRIAL BALANCE
DECEMBER 31, 2013

	Dr.	Cr.
Cash	$153,000	
Installment Accounts Receivable, 2012	56,000	
Installment Accounts Receivable, 2013	91,000	
Inventory—New Merchandise	123,200	
Inventory—Repossessed Merchandise	24,000	
Accounts Payable		$ 98,500
Deferred Gross Profit, 2012		45,600
Capital Stock		170,000
Retained Earnings		93,900
Sales		343,000
Installment Sales		200,000
Cost of Goods Sold	255,000	
Cost of Installment Sales	120,000	
Loss on Repossession	800	
Operating Expenses	128,000	
	$951,000	$951,000

The accounting department has prepared the following analysis of cash receipts for the year.

Cash sales (including repossessed merchandise)	$424,000
Installment accounts receivable, 2012	96,000
Installment accounts receivable, 2013	109,000
Other	36,000
Total	$665,000

Repossessions recorded during the year are summarized as follows.

	2012
Uncollected balance	$8,000
Loss on repossession	800
Repossessed merchandise	4,800

Instructions

From the trial balance and accompanying information:

(a) Compute the rate of gross profit on installment sales for 2012 and 2013.

(b) Prepare closing entries as of December 31, 2013, under the installment-sales method of accounting.

(c) Prepare an income statement for the year ended December 31, 2013. Include only the realized gross profit in the income statement.

6 **P18-11 (Installment-Sales Entries)** The following summarized information relates to the installment-sales activity of Phillips Stores, Inc. for the year 2012.

Installment sales during 2012	$500,000
Cost of goods sold on installment basis	350,000
Collections from customers	180,000
Unpaid balances on merchandise repossessed	24,000
Estimated value of merchandise repossessed	11,200

Instructions

(a) Prepare journal entries at the end of 2012 to record on the books of Phillips Stores, Inc. the summarized data above.

(b) Prepare the entry to record the gross profit realized during 2012.

6 **P18-12 (Installment-Sales Computation and Entries—Periodic Inventory)** Mantle Inc. sells merchandise for cash and also on the installment plan. Entries to record cost of goods sold are made at the end of each year.

Repossessions of merchandise (sold in 2012) were made in 2013 and were recorded correctly as follows.

Deferred Gross Profit, 2012	7,200	
Repossessed Merchandise	8,000	
Loss on Repossession	2,800	
Installment Accounts Receivable, 2012		18,000

Part of this repossessed merchandise was sold for cash during 2013, and the sale was recorded by a debit to Cash and a credit to Sales Revenue.

The inventory of repossessed merchandise on hand December 31, 2013, is $4,000; of new merchandise, $127,400. There was no repossessed merchandise on hand January 1, 2013.

Collections on accounts receivable during 2013 were:

Installment Accounts Receivable, 2012	$80,000
Installment Accounts Receivable, 2013	50,000

The cost of the merchandise sold under the installment plan during 2013 was $111,600. The rate of gross profit on 2012 and on 2013 installment sales can be computed from the information given.

MANTLE INC.
TRIAL BALANCE
DECEMBER 31, 2013

	Dr.	Cr.
Cash	$118,400	
Installment Accounts Receivable, 2012	80,000	
Installment Accounts Receivable, 2013	130,000	
Inventory, Jan. 1, 2013	120,000	
Repossessed Merchandise	8,000	
Accounts Payable		$ 47,200
Deferred Gross Profit, 2012		64,000
Common Stock		200,000
Retained Earnings		40,000
Sales Revenue		400,000
Installment Sales		180,000
Purchases	360,000	
Loss on Repossession	2,800	
Operating Expenses	112,000	
	$931,200	$931,200

Instructions
(a) From the trial balance and other information given above, prepare adjusting and closing entries as of December 31, 2013.
(b) Prepare an income statement for the year ended December 31, 2013. Include only the realized gross profit in the income statement.

P18-13 (Installment Repossession Entries) Selected transactions of TV Land Company are presented below.

1. A television set costing $540 is sold to Jack Matre on November 1, 2012, for $900. Matre makes a down payment of $300 and agrees to pay $30 on the first of each month for 20 months thereafter.
2. Matre pays the $30 installment due December 1, 2012.
3. On December 31, 2012, the appropriate entries are made to record profit realized on the installment sales.
4. The first seven 2013 installments of $30 each are paid by Matre. (Make one entry.)
5. In August 2013, the set is repossessed after Matre fails to pay the August 1 installment and indicates that he will be unable to continue the payments. The estimated fair value of the repossessed set is $100.

Instructions
Prepare journal entries to record the transactions above on the books of TV Land Company. Closing entries should not be made.

P18-14 (Installment-Sales Computations and Schedules) Saprano Company, on January 2, 2012, entered into a contract with a manufacturing company to purchase room-size air conditioners and to sell the units on an installment plan with collections over approximately 30 months with no carrying charge.

For income tax purposes Saprano Company elected to report income from its sales of air conditioners according to the installment-sales method.

Purchases and sales of new units were as follows.

	Units Purchased		Units Sold	
Year	Quantity	Price Each	Quantity	Price Each
2012	1,400	$130	1,100	$200
2013	1,200	112	1,500	170
2014	900	136	800	205

Collections on installment sales were as follows.

	Collections Received		
	2012	2013	2014
2012 sales	$42,000	$88,000	$ 80,000
2013 sales		51,000	110,000
2014 sales			34,600

In 2014, 50 units from the 2013 sales were repossessed and sold for $120 each on the installment plan. At the time of repossession, $2,000 had been collected from the original purchasers, and the units had a fair value of $3,000.

General and administrative expenses for 2014 were $60,000. No charge has been made against current income for the applicable insurance expense from a 3-year policy expiring June 30, 2015, costing $7,200, and for an advance payment of $12,000 on a new contract to purchase air conditioners beginning January 2, 2015.

Instructions

Assuming that the weighted-average method is used for determining the inventory cost, including repossessed merchandise, prepare schedules computing for 2012, 2013, and 2014:

(a) (1) The cost of goods sold on installments.
    (2) The average unit cost of goods sold on installments for each year.
(b) The gross profit percentages for 2012, 2013, and 2014.
(c) The gain or loss on repossessions in 2014.
(d) The net income from installment sales for 2014. (Ignore income taxes.)

(AICPA adapted)

P18-15 (Completed-Contract Method) Monat Construction Company, Inc., entered into a firm fixed-price contract with Hyatt Clinic on July 1, 2012, to construct a four-story office building. At that time, Monat estimated that it would take between 2 and 3 years to complete the project. The total contract price for construction of the building is $4,400,000. Monat appropriately accounts for this contract under the completed-contract method in its financial statements and for income tax reporting. The building was deemed substantially completed on December 31, 2014. Estimated percentage of completion, accumulated contract costs incurred, estimated costs to complete the contract, and accumulated billings to the Hyatt Clinic under the contract are shown below.

	At December 31, 2012	At December 31, 2013,	At December 31, 2014
Percentage of completion	30%	70%	100%
Contract costs incurred	$1,140,000	$3,290,000	$4,800,000
Estimated costs to complete the contract	$2,660,000	$1,410,000	–0–
Billings to Hyatt Clinic	$1,400,000	$2,500,000	$4,300,000

Instructions

(a) Prepare schedules to compute the amount to be shown as "Cost of uncompleted contract in excess of related billings" or "Billings on uncompleted contract in excess of related costs" at December 31, 2012, 2013, and 2014. (Ignore income taxes.) Show supporting computations in good form.
(b) Prepare schedules to compute the profit or loss to be recognized as a result of this contract for the years ended December 31, 2012, 2013, and 2014. (Ignore income taxes.) Show supporting computations in good form.

(AICPA adapted)

 P18-16 (Revenue Recognition Methods—Comparison) Sue's Construction is in its fourth year of business. Sue performs long-term construction projects and accounts for them using the completed-contract method. Sue built an apartment building at a price of $1,100,000. The costs and billings for this contract for the first three years are as follows.

	2012	2013	2014
Costs incurred to date	$240,000	$600,000	$ 790,000
Estimated costs yet to be incurred	560,000	200,000	–0–
Customer billings to date	150,000	410,000	1,100,000
Collection of billings to date	120,000	340,000	950,000

Sue has contacted you, a certified public accountant, about the following concern. She would like to attract some investors, but she believes that in order to recognize revenue she must first "deliver" the product. Therefore, on her balance sheet, she did not recognize any gross profits from the above contract until 2014, when she recognized the entire $310,000. That looked good for 2014, but the preceding years looked grim by comparison. She wants to know about an alternative to this completed-contract revenue recognition.

Instructions

Draft a letter to Sue, telling her about the percentage-of-completion method of recognizing revenue. Compare it to the completed-contract method. Explain the idea behind the percentage-of-completion method. In addition, illustrate how much revenue she could have recognized in 2012, 2013, and 2014 if she had used this method.

P18-17 (Comprehensive Problem—Long-Term Contracts) You have been engaged by Buhl Construction Company to advise it concerning the proper accounting for a series of long-term contracts. Buhl commenced doing business on January 1, 2012. Construction activities for the first year of operations are shown below. All contract costs are with different customers, and any work remaining at December 31, 2012, is expected to be completed in 2013.

Project	Total Contract Price	Billings Through 12/31/12	Cash Collections Through 12/31/12	Contract Costs Incurred Through 12/31/12	Estimated Additional Costs to Complete
A	$ 300,000	$200,000	$180,000	$248,000	$ 72,000
B	350,000	110,000	105,000	67,800	271,200
C	280,000	280,000	255,000	186,000	–0–
D	200,000	35,000	25,000	118,000	87,000
E	240,000	205,000	200,000	190,000	10,000
	$1,370,000	$830,000	$765,000	$809,800	$440,200

Instructions

(a) Prepare a schedule to compute gross profit (loss) to be reported, unbilled contract costs and recognized profit, and billings in excess of costs and recognized profit using the percentage-of-completion method.

(b) Prepare a partial income statement and balance sheet to indicate how the information would be reported for financial statement purposes.

(c) Repeat the requirements for part (a), assuming Buhl uses the completed-contract method.

(d) Using the responses above for illustrative purposes, prepare a brief report comparing the conceptual merits (both positive and negative) of the two revenue recognition approaches.

CONCEPTS FOR ANALYSIS

CA18-1 (Revenue Recognition—Alternative Methods) Peterson Industries has three operating divisions—Farber Mining, Glesen Paperbacks, and Enyart Protection Devices. Each division maintains its own accounting system and method of revenue recognition.

Farber Mining

Farber Mining specializes in the extraction of precious metals such as silver, gold, and platinum. During the fiscal year ended November 30, 2012, Farber entered into contracts worth $2,250,000 and shipped metals worth $2,000,000. A quarter of the shipments were made from inventories on hand at the beginning of the fiscal year, and the remainder were made from metals that were mined during the year. Mining totals for the year, valued at market prices, were silver at $750,000, gold at $1,400,000, and platinum at $490,000. Farber uses the completion-of-production method to recognize revenue because its operations meet the specified criteria, i.e., reasonably assured sales prices, interchangeable units, and insignificant distribution costs.

Enyart Paperbacks

Enyart Paperbacks sells large quantities of novels to a few book distributors that in turn sell to several national chains of bookstores. Enyart allows distributors to return up to 30% of sales, and distributors give the same terms to bookstores. While returns from individual titles fluctuate greatly, the returns from distributors have averaged 20% in each of the past 5 years. A total of $7,000,000 of paperback novel sales were made to distributors during the fiscal year. On November 30, 2012, $2,200,000 of fiscal 2012 sales were still subject to return privileges over the next 6 months. The remaining $4,800,000 of fiscal 2012 sales had actual returns of 21%. Sales from fiscal 2011 totaling $2,500,000 were collected in fiscal 2012, with less than 18% of sales returned. Enyart records revenue according to the method referred to as revenue recognition when the right of return exits, because all applicable criteria for use of this method are met by Enyart's operations.

Glesen Protection Devices

Glesen Protection Devices works through manufacturers' agents in various cities. Orders for alarm systems and down payments are forwarded from agents, and Glesen ships the goods f.o.b. shipping point. Customers are billed for the balance due plus actual shipping costs. The firm received orders for $6,000,000 of goods during the fiscal year ended November 30, 2012. Down payments of $600,000 were received, and $5,000,000 of goods were billed and shipped. Actual freight costs of $100,000 were also billed. Commissions of 10% on product price were paid to manufacturers' agents after the goods were shipped to customers. Such goods are warranted for 90 days after shipment, and warranty returns have been about 1% of sales. Revenue is recognized at the point of sale by Glesen.

Instructions

(a) There are a variety of methods for revenue recognition. Define and describe each of the following methods of revenue recognition, and indicate whether each is in accordance with generally accepted accounting principles.

   (1) Completion-of-production method.

   (2) Percentage-of-completion method.

   (3) Installment-sales method.

(b) Compute the revenue to be recognized in the fiscal year ended November 30, 2012, for

   (1) Farber Mining.

   (2) Enyart Paperbacks.

   (3) Glesen Protection Devices.

(CMA adapted)

CA18-2 (Recognition of Revenue—Theory) Revenue is usually recognized at the point of sale. Under special circumstances, however, bases other than the point of sale are used for the timing of revenue recognition.

Instructions

(a) Why is the point of sale usually used as the basis for the timing of revenue recognition?

(b) Disregarding the special circumstances when bases other than the point of sale are used, discuss the merits of each of the following objections to the sale basis of revenue recognition:

   (1) It is too conservative because revenue is earned throughout the entire process of production.

   (2) It is not conservative enough because accounts receivable do not represent disposable funds, sales returns and allowances may be made, and collection and bad debt expenses may be incurred in a later period.

(c) Revenue may also be recognized (1) during production and (2) when cash is received. For each of these two bases of timing revenue recognition, give an example of the circumstances in which it is properly used and discuss the accounting merits of its use in lieu of the sale basis.

(AICPA adapted)

CA18-3 (Recognition of Revenue—Theory) The earning of revenue by a business enterprise is recognized for accounting purposes when the transaction is recorded. In some situations, revenue is recognized approximately as it is earned in the economic sense. In other situations, however, accountants have developed guidelines for recognizing revenue by other criteria, such as at the point of sale.

Instructions

(Ignore income taxes.)

(a) Explain and justify why revenue is often recognized as earned at time of sale.

(b) Explain in what situations it would be appropriate to recognize revenue as the productive activity takes place.

(c) At what times, other than those included in (a) and (b) above, may it be appropriate to recognize revenue? Explain.

CA18-4 (Recognition of Revenue—Bonus Dollars) Griseta & Dubel Inc. was formed early this year to sell merchandise credits to merchants who distribute the credits free to their customers. For example, customers can earn additional credits based on the dollars they spend with a merchant (e.g., airlines and hotels). Accounts for accumulating the credits and catalogs illustrating the merchandise for which the credits may be exchanged are maintained online. Centers with inventories of merchandise premiums have been established for redemption of the credits. Merchants may not return unused credits to Griseta & Dubel.

The following schedule expresses Griseta & Dubel's expectations as to percentages of a normal month's activity that will be attained. For this purpose, a "normal month's activity" is defined as the level of operations expected when expansion of activities ceases or tapers off to a stable rate. The company expects that this level will be attained in the third year and that sales of credits will average $6,000,000 per month throughout the third year.

Month	Actual Credit Sales Percent	Merchandise Premium Purchases Percent	Credit Redemptions Percent
6th	30%	40%	10%
12th	60	60	45
18th	80	80	70
24th	90	90	80
30th	100	100	95

Griseta & Dubel plans to adopt an annual closing date at the end of each 12 months of operation.

Instructions

(a) Discuss the factors to be considered in determining when revenue should be recognized in measuring the income of a business enterprise.

(b) Discuss the accounting alternatives that should be considered by Griseta & Dubel Inc. for the recognition of its revenues and related expenses.

(c) For each accounting alternative discussed in (b), give balance sheet accounts that should be used and indicate how each should be classified.

(AICPA adapted)

CA18-5 (Recognition of Revenue from Subscriptions) *Cutting Edge* is a monthly magazine that has been on the market for 18 months. It currently has a circulation of 1.4 million copies. Negotiations are underway to obtain a bank loan in order to update the magazine's facilities. They are producing close to capacity and expect to grow at an average of 20% per year over the next 3 years.

After reviewing the financial statements of *Cutting Edge*, Andy Rich, the bank loan officer, had indicated that a loan could be offered to *Cutting Edge* only if it could increase its current ratio and decrease its debt to equity ratio to a specified level.

Jonathan Embry, the marketing manager of *Cutting Edge*, has devised a plan to meet these requirements. Embry indicates that an advertising campaign can be initiated to immediately increase circulation. The potential customers would be contacted after the purchase of another magazine's mailing list. The campaign would include:

1. An offer to subscribe to *Cutting Edge* at 3/4 the normal price.
2. A special offer to all new subscribers to receive the most current world atlas whenever requested at a guaranteed price of $2.
3. An unconditional guarantee that any subscriber will receive a full refund if dissatisfied with the magazine.

Although the offer of a full refund is risky, Embry claims that few people will ask for a refund after receiving half of their subscription issues. Embry notes that other magazine companies have tried this sales promotion technique and experienced great success. Their average cancellation rate was 25%. On average, each company increased its initial circulation threefold and in the long run increased circulation to twice that which existed before the promotion. In addition, 60% of the new subscribers are expected to take advantage of the atlas premium. Embry feels confident that the increased subscriptions from the advertising campaign will increase the current ratio and decrease the debt to equity ratio.

You are the controller of *Cutting Edge* and must give your opinion of the proposed plan.

Instructions

(a) When should revenue from the new subscriptions be recognized?

(b) How would you classify the estimated sales returns stemming from the unconditional guarantee?

(c) How should the atlas premium be recorded? Is the estimated premium claims a liability? Explain.

(d) Does the proposed plan achieve the goals of increasing the current ratio and decreasing the debt to equity ratio?

CA18-6 (Long-Term Contract—Percentage-of-Completion) Widjaja Company is accounting for a long-term construction contract using the percentage-of-completion method. It is a 4-year contract that is currently in its second year. The latest estimates of total contract costs indicate that the contract will be completed at a profit to Widjaja Company.

Instructions

(a) What theoretical justification is there for Widjaja Company's use of the percentage-of-completion method?

(b) How would progress billings be accounted for? Include in your discussion the classification of progress billings in Widjaja Company financial statements.

(c) How would the income recognized in the second year of the 4-year contract be determined using the cost-to-cost method of determining percentage of completion?

(d) What would be the effect on earnings per share in the second year of the 4-year contract of using the percentage-of-completion method instead of the completed-contract method? Discuss.

(AICPA adapted)

CA18-7 (Revenue Recognition—Real Estate Development) Lillehammer Lakes is a new recreational real estate development which consists of 500 lake-front and lake-view lots. As a special incentive to the first 100 buyers of lake-view lots, the developer is offering 3 years of free financing on 10-year, 12% notes, no down payment, and one week at a nearby established resort (to be used in the next 3 months)—"a $1,200 value." The normal price per lot is $15,000. The cost per lake-view lot to the developer is an estimated average of $3,000.

The development costs continue to be incurred; the actual average cost per lot is not known at this time. The resort promotion cost is $700 per lot. The notes are held by Harper Corp., a wholly owned subsidiary.

Instructions

(a) Discuss the revenue recognition and gross profit measurement issues raised by this situation.

(b) How would the developer's past financial and business experience influence your decision concerning the recording of these transactions?

(c) Assume 50 people have accepted the offer, signed 10-year notes, and have stayed at the local resort. Prepare the journal entries that you believe are proper.

(d) What should be disclosed in the notes to the financial statements?

CA18-8 (Revenue Recognition) Nimble Health and Racquet Club (NHRC), which operates eight clubs in the Chicago metropolitan area, offers one-year memberships. The members may use any of the eight facilities but must reserve racquetball court time and pay a separate fee before using the court. As an incentive to new customers, NHRC advertised that any customers not satisfied for any reason could receive a refund of the remaining portion of unused membership fees. Membership fees are due at the beginning of the individual membership period. However, customers are given the option of financing the membership fee over the membership period at a 9% interest rate.

Some customers have expressed a desire to take only the regularly scheduled aerobic classes without paying for a full membership. During the current fiscal year, NHRC began selling coupon books for aerobic classes to accommodate these customers. Each book is dated and contains 50 coupons that may be redeemed for any regularly scheduled aerobics class over a one-year period. After the one-year period, unused coupons are no longer valid.

During 2010, NHRC expanded into the health equipment market by purchasing a local company that manufactures rowing machines and cross-country ski machines. These machines are used in NHRC's facilities and are sold through the clubs and mail order catalogs. Customers must make a 20% down payment when placing an equipment order; delivery is 60–90 days after order placement. The machines are sold with a 2-year unconditional guarantee. Based on past experience, NHRC expects the costs to repair machines under guarantee to be 4% of sales.

NHRC is in the process of preparing financial statements as of May 31, 2013, the end of its fiscal year. Marvin Bush, corporate controller, expressed concern over the company's performance for the year and decided to review the preliminary financial statements prepared by Joyce Kiley, NHRC's assistant controller. After reviewing the statements, Bush proposed that the following changes be reflected in the May 31, 2013, published financial statements.

1. Membership revenue should be recognized when the membership fee is collected.
2. Revenue from the coupon books should be recognized when the books are sold.
3. Down payments on equipment purchases and expenses associated with the guarantee on the rowing and cross-country machines should be recognized when paid.

Kiley indicated to Bush that the proposed changes are not in accordance with generally accepted accounting principles, but Bush insisted that the changes be made. Kiley believes that Bush wants to manage income to forestall any potential financial problems and increase his year-end bonus. At this point, Kiley is unsure what action to take.

Instructions

(a) (1) Describe when Nimble Health and Racquet Club (NHRC) should recognize revenue from membership fees, court rentals, and coupon book sales.

(2) Describe how NHRC should account for the down payments on equipment sales, explaining when this revenue should be recognized.

(3) Indicate when NHRC should recognize the expense associated with the guarantee of the rowing and cross-country machines.

(b) Discuss why Marvin Bush's proposed changes and his insistence that the financial statement changes be made is unethical. Structure your answer around or to include the following aspects of ethical conduct: competence, confidentiality, integrity, and/or objectivity.

(c) Identify some specific actions Joyce Kiley could take to resolve this situation.

(CMA adapted)

CA18-9 (Revenue Recognition—Membership Fees) Midwest Health Club (MHC) offers one-year memberships. Membership fees are due in full at the beginning of the individual membership period. As an incentive to new customers, MHC advertised that any customers not satisfied for any reason could receive a refund of the remaining portion of unused membership fees. As a result of this policy, Richard Nies, corporate controller, recognized revenue ratably over the life of the membership.

MHC is in the process of preparing its year-end financial statements. Rachel Avery, MHC's treasurer, is concerned about the company's lackluster performance this year. She reviews the financial statements Nies prepared and tells Nies to recognize membership revenue when the fees are received.

Instructions
Answer the following questions.

   (a) What are the ethical issues involved?
   (b) What should Nies do?

*CA18-10 (Franchise Revenue)** Amigos Burrito Inc. sells franchises to independent operators throughout the northwestern part of the United States. The contract with the franchisee includes the following provisions.

  1. The franchisee is charged an initial fee of $120,000. Of this amount, $20,000 is payable when the agreement is signed, and a $20,000 non-interest-bearing note is payable at the end of each of the 5 subsequent years.
  2. All of the initial franchise fee collected by Amigos is to be refunded and the remaining obligation canceled if, for any reason, the franchisee fails to open his or her franchise.
  3. In return for the initial franchise fee, Amigos agrees to (a) assist the franchisee in selecting the location for the business, (b) negotiate the lease for the land, (c) obtain financing and assist with building design, (d) supervise construction, (e) establish accounting and tax records, and (f) provide expert advice over a 5-year period relating to such matters as employee and management training, quality control, and promotion.
  4. In addition to the initial franchise fee, the franchisee is required to pay to Amigos a monthly fee of 2% of sales for menu planning, receipt innovations, and the privilege of purchasing ingredients from Amigos at or below prevailing market prices.

Management of Amigos Burrito estimates that the value of the services rendered to the franchisee at the time the contract is signed amounts to at least $20,000. All franchisees to date have opened their locations at the scheduled time, and none have defaulted on any of the notes receivable.

   The credit ratings of all franchisees would entitle them to borrow at the current interest rate of 10%. The present value of an ordinary annuity of five annual receipts of $20,000 each discounted at 10% is $75,816.

Instructions
  (a) Discuss the alternatives that Amigos Burrito Inc. might use to account for the initial franchise fees, evaluate each by applying generally accepted accounting principles, and give illustrative entries for each alternative.
  (b) Given the nature of Amigos Burrito's agreement with its franchisees, when should revenue be recognized? Discuss the question of revenue recognition for both the initial franchise fee and the additional monthly fee of 2% of sales, and give illustrative entries for both types of revenue.
  (c) Assume that Amigos Burrito sells some franchises for $100,000, which includes a charge of $20,000 for the rental of equipment for its useful life of 10 years; that $50,000 of the fee is payable immediately and the balance on non-interest-bearing notes at $10,000 per year; that no portion of the $20,000 rental payment is refundable in case the franchisee goes out of business; and that title to the equipment remains with the franchisor. Under those assumptions, what would be the preferable method of accounting for the rental portion of the initial franchise fee? Explain.

(AICPA adapted)

USING YOUR JUDGMENT

FINANCIAL REPORTING

Financial Reporting Problem

 The Procter & Gamble Company (P&G)

The financial statements of P&G are presented in Appendix 5B or can be accessed at the book's companion website, **www.wiley.com/college/kieso**.

Instructions
Refer to P&G's financial statements and the accompanying notes to answer the following questions.

(a) What were P&G's sales for 2009?

(b) What was the percentage of increase or decrease in P&G's sales from 2008 to 2009? From 2007 to 2008? From 2005 to 2009?

(c) In its notes to the financial statements, what criteria does P&G use to recognize revenue?

(d) How does P&G account for trade promotions? Does the accounting conform to accrual accounting concepts? Explain.

Comparative Analysis Case

The Coca-Cola Company and PepsiCo, Inc.

PEPSICO

Instructions

Go to book's companion website and use information found there to answer the following questions related to The Coca-Cola Company and PepsiCo, Inc.

(a) What were Coca-Cola's and PepsiCo's net revenues (sales) for the year 2009? Which company increased its revenues more (dollars and percentage) from 2008 to 2009?

(b) Are the revenue recognition policies of Coca-Cola and PepsiCo similar? Explain.

(c) In which foreign countries (geographic areas) did Coca-Cola and PepsiCo experience significant revenues in 2009? Compare the amounts of foreign revenues to U.S. revenues for both Coca-Cola and PepsiCo.

Financial Statement Analysis Case

Westinghouse Electric Corporation

The following note appears in the "Summary of Significant Accounting Policies" section of the Annual Report of Westinghouse Electric Corporation.

Note 1 (in part): Revenue Recognition. Sales are primarily recorded as products are shipped and services are rendered. The percentage-of-completion method of accounting is used for nuclear steam supply system orders with delivery schedules generally in excess of five years and for certain construction projects where this method of accounting is consistent with industry practice.

WFSI revenues are generally recognized on the accrual method. When accounts become delinquent for more than two payment periods, usually 60 days, income is recognized only as payments are received. Such delinquent accounts for which no payments are received in the current month, and other accounts on which income is not being recognized because the receipt of either principal or interest is questionable, are classified as nonearning receivables.

Instructions

(a) Identify the revenue recognition methods used by Westinghouse Electric as discussed in its note on significant accounting policies.

(b) Under what conditions are the revenue recognition methods identified in the first paragraph of Westinghouse's note above acceptable?

(c) From the information provided in the second paragraph of Westinghouse's note, identify the type of operation being described and defend the acceptability of the revenue recognition method.

Accounting, Analysis, and Principles

Diversified Products, Inc. operates in several lines of business, including the construction and real estate industries. While the majority of its revenues are recognized at point of sale, Diversified appropriately recognizes revenue on long-term construction contracts using the percentage-of-completion method. It recognizes sales of some properties using the installment-sales approach. Income data for 2012 from operations other than construction and real estate are as follows.

Revenues	$9,500,000
Expenses	7,750,000

1. Diversified started a construction project during 2011. The total contract price is $1,000,000, and $200,000 in costs were incurred in both 2011 and 2012. In 2013, Diversified recognized $50,000 gross profit on the project. Estimated costs to complete the project in 2013 were $400,000.
2. During 2012, Diversified sold real-estate parcels at a price of $630,000. Gross profit at a 25% rate is recognized when cash is received. Diversified collected $500,000 during the year on these sales.

Accounting

Determine Diversified Products' 2012 net income. (Ignore taxes.)

Analysis

Determine free cash flow (see Chapter 5) for Diversified Products for 2012. In 2012, Diversified had depreciation expense of $175,000 and a net increase in working capital (changes in accounts receivable and accounts payable) of $250,000. In 2012, capital expenditures were $500,000; Diversified paid dividends of $120,000.

Principles

"Application of the percentage-of-completion and installment-sales method revenue recognition approaches illustrates the trade-off between relevance and faithful representation of accounting information." Explain.

BRIDGE TO THE PROFESSION

Professional Research: FASB Codification

Employees at your company disagree about the accounting for sales returns. The sales manager believes that granting more generous return provisions can give the company a competitive edge and increase sales revenue. The controller cautions that, depending on the terms granted, loose return provisions might lead to non-GAAP revenue recognition. The company CFO would like you to research the issue to provide an authoritative answer.

Instructions

If your school has a subscription to the FASB Codification, go to *http://aaa.hq.org/asclogin.cfm* to log in and prepare responses to the following. Provide Codification references for your responses.

(a) What is the authoritative literature addressing revenue recognition when right of return exists?
(b) What is meant by "right of return"?
(c) When there is a right of return, what conditions must the company meet to recognize the revenue at the time of sale?
(d) What factors may impair the ability to make a reasonable estimate of future returns?

Professional Simulation

In this simulation, you are asked to address questions related to revenue recognition issues. Prepare responses to all parts.

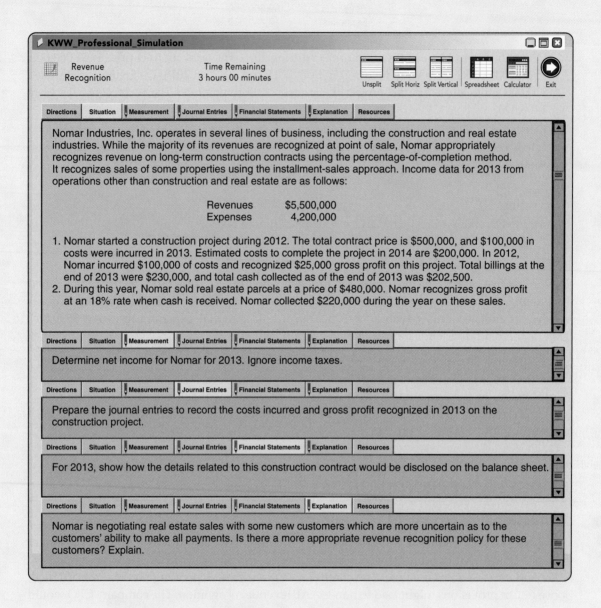

KWW_Professional_Simulation

Revenue Recognition   Time Remaining 3 hours 00 minutes

Unsplit Split Horiz Split Vertical Spreadsheet Calculator Exit

Directions | Situation | Measurement | Journal Entries | Financial Statements | Explanation | Resources

Nomar Industries, Inc. operates in several lines of business, including the construction and real estate industries. While the majority of its revenues are recognized at point of sale, Nomar appropriately recognizes revenue on long-term construction contracts using the percentage-of-completion method. It recognizes sales of some properties using the installment-sales approach. Income data for 2013 from operations other than construction and real estate are as follows:

Revenues	$5,500,000
Expenses	4,200,000

1. Nomar started a construction project during 2012. The total contract price is $500,000, and $100,000 in costs were incurred in 2013. Estimated costs to complete the project in 2014 are $200,000. In 2012, Nomar incurred $100,000 of costs and recognized $25,000 gross profit on this project. Total billings at the end of 2013 were $230,000, and total cash collected as of the end of 2013 was $202,500.
2. During this year, Nomar sold real estate parcels at a price of $480,000. Nomar recognizes gross profit at an 18% rate when cash is received. Nomar collected $220,000 during the year on these sales.

Directions | Situation | Measurement | Journal Entries | Financial Statements | Explanation | Resources

Determine net income for Nomar for 2013. Ignore income taxes.

Directions | Situation | Measurement | Journal Entries | Financial Statements | Explanation | Resources

Prepare the journal entries to record the costs incurred and gross profit recognized in 2013 on the construction project.

Directions | Situation | Measurement | Journal Entries | Financial Statements | Explanation | Resources

For 2013, show how the details related to this construction contract would be disclosed on the balance sheet.

Directions | Situation | Measurement | Journal Entries | Financial Statements | Explanation | Resources

Nomar is negotiating real estate sales with some new customers which are more uncertain as to the customers' ability to make all payments. Is there a more appropriate revenue recognition policy for these customers? Explain.

IFRS Insights

The general concepts and principles used for revenue recognition are similar between IFRS and GAAP. Where they differ is in the details. As indicated in the chapter, GAAP provides specific guidance related to revenue recognition for many different industries. That is not the case for IFRS.

RELEVANT FACTS

- The IASB defines revenue to include both revenues and gains. GAAP provides separate definitions for revenues and gains.

- Revenue recognition fraud is a major issue in U.S. financial reporting. The same situation occurs overseas as evidenced by revenue recognition breakdowns at Dutch software company Baan NV, Japanese electronics giant NEC, and Dutch grocer AHold NV.

- In general, the IFRS revenue recognition principle is based on the probability that the economic benefits associated with the transaction will flow to the company selling the goods, rendering the service, or receiving investment income. In addition, the revenues and costs must be capable of being measured reliably. GAAP uses concepts such as realized, realizable, and earned as a basis for revenue recognition.

- IFRS has one basic standard on revenue recognition—*IAS 18*. GAAP has numerous standards related to revenue recognition (by some counts over 100).

- Accounting for revenue provides a most fitting contrast of the principles-based (IFRS) and rules-based (GAAP) approaches. While both sides have their advocates, the IASB and the FASB have identified a number of areas for improvement in this area.

- Under IFRS, revenue should be measured at fair value of the consideration received or receivable. GAAP measures revenue based on the fair value of what is given up (goods or services) or the fair value of what is received—whichever is more clearly evident.

- In general, the accounting at point of sale is similar between IFRS and GAAP. As indicated earlier, GAAP often provides detailed guidance, such as in the accounting for right of return and multiple-deliverable arrangements.

- IFRS prohibits the use of the completed-contract method of accounting for long-term construction contracts *(IAS 13)*. Companies must use the percentage-of-completion method. If revenues and costs are difficult to estimate, then companies recognize revenue only to the extent of the cost incurred—a cost-recovery (zero-profit) approach.

- In long-term construction contracts, IFRS requires recognition of a loss immediately if the overall contract is going to be unprofitable. In other words, GAAP and IFRS are the same regarding this issue.

ABOUT THE NUMBERS

Long-Term Contracts (Construction)

Under IFRS, two distinctly different methods of accounting for long-term construction contracts are recognized. They are:

- **Percentage-of-completion method.** Companies recognize revenues and gross profits each period based on the progress of the construction—that is, the percentage of completion. The company accumulates construction costs **plus gross profit earned to date** in an inventory account (Construction in Process), and it accumulates progress billings in a contra inventory account (Billings on Construction in Process). This approach is the same as GAAP.

- **Cost-recovery (zero-profit) method.** In some cases, contract revenue is recognized only to the extent of costs incurred that are expected to be recoverable. Once all costs are recognized, profit is recognized. The company accumulates construction costs in an inventory account (Construction in Process), and it accumulates progress billings in a contra inventory account (Billings on Construction in Process).

The rationale for using percentage-of-completion accounting is that under most of these contracts, the buyer and seller have enforceable rights. The buyer has the legal right to require specific performance on the contract. The seller has the right to require progress payments that provide evidence of the buyer's ownership interest. As a result, a continuous sale occurs as the work progresses. Companies should recognize revenue according to that progression. Companies *must* use the percentage-of-completion method when estimates of progress toward completion, revenues, and costs can be estimated reliably and **all of the following conditions** exist.

1. Total contract revenue can be measured reliably;
2. It is probable that the economic benefits associated with the contract will flow to the company;
3. Both the contract costs to complete the contract and the stage of contract completion at the end of the reporting period can be measured reliably; and
4. The contract costs attributable to the contract can be clearly identified and measured reliably so the actual contract costs incurred can be compared with prior estimates.

Companies should use the cost-recovery method when **one of the following conditions** applies:

- When a company cannot meet the conditions for using the percentage-of-completion method, or
- When there are inherent hazards in the contract beyond the normal, recurring business risks.

The presumption is that percentage-of-completion is the better method. Therefore, companies should use the cost-recovery method only when the percentage-of-completion method is inappropriate.

Cost-Recovery (Zero-Profit) Method

During the early stages of a contract, a company like Alcatel-Lucent may not be able to estimate reliably the outcome of a long-term construction contract. Nevertheless, Alcatel-Lucent is confident that it will recover the contract costs incurred. In this case, Alcatel-Lucent uses the **cost-recovery method** (sometimes referred to as the zero-profit method). This method recognizes revenue only to the extent of costs incurred that are expected to be recoverable. Only after all costs are incurred is gross profit recognized.

To illustrate the cost-recovery method for a bridge project, recall the Hardhat Construction example on pages 1083–1088. Under the cost-recovery method, Hardhat would report the following revenues and costs for 2012–2014, as shown in Illustration IFRS18-1.

ILLUSTRATION IFRS18-1
Cost-Recovery Method Revenue, Costs, and Gross Profit by Year

	To Date	Recognized in Prior Years	Recognized in Current Year
2012			
Revenues (costs incurred)	$1,000,000		$1,000,000
Costs	1,000,000		1,000,000
Gross profit	$ 0		$ 0
2013			
Revenues (costs incurred)	$2,916,000	$1,000,000	$1,916,000
Costs	2,916,000	1,000,000	1,916,000
Gross profit	$ 0	$ 0	$ 0
2014			
Revenues ($4,500,000 × 100%)	$4,500,000	$2,916,000	$1,584,000
Costs	4,050,000	2,916,000	1,134,000
Gross profit	$ 450,000	$ 0	$ 450,000

Illustration IFRS18-2 shows Hardhat's entries to recognize revenue and gross profit each year and to record completion and final approval of the contract.

	2012	2013	2014
Construction Expenses	1,000,000	1,916,000	
Revenue from Long-Term Contracts	1,000,000	1,916,000	
(To recognize costs and related expenses)			
Construction in Process (Gross Profit)			450,000
Construction Expenses			1,134,000
Revenue from Long-Term Contracts			1,584,000
(To recognize costs and related expenses)			
Billings on Construction in Process			4,500,000
Construction in Process			4,500,000
(To record completion of the contract)			

ILLUSTRATION IFRS18-2
Journal Entries—Cost-Recovery Method

As indicated, no gross profit is recognized in 2012 and 2013. In 2014, Hardhat then recognizes gross profit and closes the Billings and Construction in Process accounts.

Illustration IFRS18-3 compares the amount of gross profit that Hardhat Construction Company would recognize for the bridge project under the two revenue recognition methods.

	Percentage-of-Completion	Cost-Recovery
2012	$125,000	$ 0
2013	199,000	0
2014	126,000	450,000

ILLUSTRATION IFRS18-3
Comparison of Gross Profit Recognized under Different Methods

Under the cost-recovery method, Hardhat Construction would report its long-term construction activities as shown in Illustration IFRS18-4.

ILLUSTRATION IFRS18-4
Financial Statement Presentation—Cost-Recovery Method

HARDHAT CONSTRUCTION COMPANY

Income Statement	2012	2013	2014
Revenue from long-term contracts	$1,000,000	$1,916,000	$1,584,000
Costs of construction	1,000,000	1,916,000	1,134,000
Gross profit	$ 0	$ 0	$ 450,000

Statement of Financial Position (12/31)		2012	2013	2014
Current assets				
Inventories				
Construction in process	$1,000,000			
Less: Billings	900,000			
Costs in excess of billings		$ 100,000		$ –0–
Accounts receivable		150,000	$ 800,000	–0–
Current liabilities				
Billings	3,300,000			
Less: Construction in process	2,916,000			
Billings in excess of costs				
and recognized profits			384,000	–0–

Note 1. Summary of significant accounting policies.

Long-Term Construction Contracts. The company recognizes revenues and reports profits from long-term construction contracts, its principal business, under the cost-recovery method. These contracts generally extend for periods in excess of one year. Contract costs and billings are accumulated during the periods of construction, and revenues are recognized only to the extent of costs incurred that are expected to be recoverable. Only after all costs are incurred is net income recognized. Costs included in construction in process include direct material, direct labor, and project-related overhead. Corporate general and administrative expenses are charged to the periods as incurred.

ON THE HORIZON

The FASB and IASB are now involved in a joint project on revenue recognition. The objective of the project is to develop coherent conceptual guidance for revenue recognition and a comprehensive statement on revenue recognition based on those concepts. In particular, the project is intended to improve financial reporting by (1) converging U.S. and international standards on revenue recognition, (2) eliminating inconsistencies in the existing conceptual guidance on revenue recognition, (3) providing conceptual guidance that would be useful in addressing future revenue recognition issues, (4) eliminating inconsistencies in existing standards-level authoritative literature and accepted practices, (5) filling voids in revenue recognition guidance that have developed over time, and (6) establishing a single, comprehensive standard on revenue recognition. Presently, the Boards are evaluating a "customer-consideration" model. It is hoped that this approach (rather than using the earned and realized or realized criteria) will lead to a better basis for revenue recognition. For more on this topic, see *http://www.fasb.org/project/revenue_recognition.shtml.*

IFRS SELF-TEST QUESTIONS

1. The IASB:
   (a) has issued over 100 standards related to revenue recognition.
   (b) has issued one standard related to revenue recognition.
   (c) indicates that the present state of reporting for revenue is satisfactory.
   (d) All of the above.

2. Under IFRS, the revenue recognition principle indicates that revenue is recognized when:
   I. the benefits can be measured reliably.
   II. the sales transaction is initiated and completed.
   III. it is probable the benefits will flow to the company.
   IV. the date of sale, date of delivery, and billing have all occurred.

   (a) I, II, and III.
   (b) II and III.
   (c) I and III.
   (d) I, II, III and IV.

3. Lark Corp. has a contract to construct a $5,000,000 cruise ship at an estimated cost of $4,000,000. The company will begin construction of the cruise ship in early January 2011 and expects to complete the project sometime in late 2012. Lark Corp. has never constructed a cruise ship before, and the customer has never operated a cruise ship. Due to this and other circumstances, Lark Corp. believes there are inherent hazards in the contract beyond the normal, recurring business risks. Lark Corp. expects to recover all its costs under the contract. Under these circumstances, Lark Corp. should:
   (a) wait until the completion of construction before it recognizes revenue.
   (b) use the percentage-of-completion method and measure progress toward completion using the units-of-delivery method.
   (c) use the percentage-of-completion method and measure progress toward completion using the cost-to-cost method.
   (d) use the cost-recovery (zero-profit) method.

4. Swallow Corp. has a contract to construct a $5,000,000 cruise ship at an estimated cost of $4,000,000. The company will begin construction of the cruise ship in early January 2011 and expects to complete the project sometime in late 2014. Swallow Corp. has never constructed a cruise ship before, and the customer has never operated a cruise ship. Due to this and other circumstances, Swallow Corp. believes there are inherent hazards in the contract beyond the normal, recurring business risks. Swallow Corp. expects to recover all its costs under the contract. During 2011 and 2012, the company has the following activity:

	2011	2012
Costs to date	$ 980,000	$2,040,000
Estimated costs to complete	3,020,000	1,960,000
Progress billings during the year	1,000,000	1,000,000
Cash collected during the year	648,000	1,280,000

For the year ended December 31, 2012, how much revenue should Swallow Corp. recognize on its income statement?

(a) $980,000.   (c) $1,300,000.

(b) $2,040,000.   (d) $1,060,000.

5. Given the information in question 4 above, on its statement of financial position at December 31, 2012, what amount is reported in the cost of construction and billings presentation by Swallow?

(a) $40,000 costs in excess of billings.

(b) $1,020,000 costs in excess of billings.

(c) $40,000 billings in excess of costs.

(d) $20,000 billings in excess of costs.

IFRS CONCEPTS AND APPLICATION

IFRS18-1 What is a major difference between IFRS and GAAP as regards revenue recognition practices?

IFRS18-2 IFRS prohibits the use of the completed-contract method in accounting for long-term contracts. If revenues and costs are difficult to estimate, how must companies account for long-term contracts?

IFRS18-3 Livesey Company has signed a long-term contract to build a new basketball arena. The total revenue related to the contract is $120 million. Estimated costs for building the arena are $40 million in the first year and $30 million in both the second and third years. The costs cannot be reliably estimated. How much revenue should Livesey Company report in the first year under IFRS?

IFRS18-4 What are the two basic methods of accounting for long-term construction contracts? Indicate the circumstances that determine when one or the other of these methods should be used.

IFRS18-5 When is revenue recognized under the cost-recovery method?

IFRS18-6 Turner, Inc. began work on a $7,000,000 contract in 2012 to construct an office building. During 2012, Turner, Inc. incurred costs of $1,700,000, billed its customers for $1,200,000, and collected $960,000. At December 31, 2012, the estimated future costs to complete the project total $3,300,000. Prepare Turner's 2012 journal entries using the percentage-of-completion method.

IFRS18-7 Use the information from IFRS18-6, but assume Turner uses the cost-recovery method. Prepare the company's 2012 journal entries.

IFRS18-8 Hamilton Construction Company uses the percentage-of-completion method of accounting. In 2012, Hamilton began work under contract #E2-D2, which provided for a contract price of $2,200,000. Other details are as follows.

	2012	2013
Costs incurred during the year	$640,000	$1,425,000
Estimated costs to complete, as of December 31	960,000	–0–
Billings during the year	420,000	1,680,000
Collections during the year	350,000	1,500,000

Instructions

(a) What portion of the total contract price would be recognized as revenue in 2012? In 2013?

(b) Assuming the same facts as those shown on page 1139 except that Hamilton uses the cost-recovery method of accounting, what portion of the total contract price would be recognized as revenue in 2013?

Professional Research

IFRS18-9 Employees at your company disagree about the accounting for sales returns. The sales manager believes that granting more generous return provisions and allowing customers to order items on a bill and hold basis can give the company a competitive edge and increase sales revenue. The controller cautions that, depending on the terms granted, loose return or bill and hold provisions might lead to non-IFRS revenue recognition. The company CFO would like you to research the issue to provide an authoritative answer.

Instructions

Access the IFRS authoritative literature at the IASB website (*http:/eifrs.iasb.org/*). When you have accessed the documents, you can use the search tool in your Internet browser to respond to the following questions. (Provide paragraph citations.)

(a) What is the authoritative literature addressing revenue recognition when right of return exists?

(b) What is meant by "right of return"? "Bill and hold"?

(c) When there is a right of return, what conditions must the company meet to recognize the revenue at the time of sale?

(d) What factors may impair the ability to make a reasonable estimate of future returns?

(e) When goods are sold on a bill and hold basis, what conditions must be met to recognize revenue upon receipt of the order?

International Financial Reporting Problem:
Marks and Spencer plc

IFRS18-10 The financial statements of Marks and Spencer plc (M&S) are available at the book's companion website or can be accessed at *http:/corporate.marksandspencer.com/documents/publications/2010/Annual_Report_2010.*

Instructions

Refer to M&S's financial statements and the accompanying notes to answer the following questions.

(a) What were M&S's sales for 2010?

(b) What was the percentage of increase or decrease in M&S's sales from 2009 to 2010? From 2008 to 2009? From 2008 to 2010?

(c) In its notes to the financial statements, what criteria does M&S use to recognize revenue?

(d) How does M&S account for discounts and loyalty schemes? Does the accounting conform to accrual-accounting concepts? Explain.

ANSWERS TO IFRS SELF-TEST QUESTIONS

1. b 2. c 3. d 4. d 5. a

Remember to check the book's companion website to find additional resources for this chapter.

19 Accounting for Income Taxes

After studying this chapter, you should be able to:

1 Identify differences between pretax financial income and taxable income.

2 Describe a temporary difference that results in future taxable amounts.

3 Describe a temporary difference that results in future deductible amounts.

4 Explain the purpose of a deferred tax asset valuation allowance.

5 Describe the presentation of income tax expense in the income statement.

6 Describe various temporary and permanent differences.

7 Explain the effect of various tax rates and tax rate changes on deferred income taxes.

8 Apply accounting procedures for a loss carryback and a loss carryforward.

9 Describe the presentation of deferred income taxes in financial statements.

10 Indicate the basic principles of the asset-liability method.

How Much Is Enough?

In the wake of the economic downturn due to the financial crisis, a number of companies and numerous banks have reported operating losses. As you will learn in this chapter, the tax code allows companies that report operating losses to claim a tax credit related to these losses for taxes paid in the past (referred to as "carrybacks") and to offset taxable income in periods following the operating loss (referred to as "carryforwards"). When companies use these offsets, they reduce income tax expense, which increases net income. For tax carryforwards, companies also record a deferred tax asset, which measures the expected future net cash inflows from lower taxable income in future periods.

Citigroup is a good example of a company that has used operating loss credits to reduce its tax bill. In 2008, it had deferred tax assets (DTAs) of $28.5 billion, which represents 80 percent of stockholders' equity and nearly eclipsed the bank's market value of equity. Some analysts have raised concerns about Citi's DTAs and whether these assets will ever be realized by Citi. Why the concerns?

Well, in order receive the tax deductions in future years, a company like Citigroup needs to be reasonably sure it will have taxable income in the future. In Citi's case, analysts predict that the struggling bank will need to earn $99 billion in taxable income over the next 20 years. Given that Citigroup recorded operating losses of $60 billion in 2008 and 2009, some are skeptical that the DTAs will be realized. As a result, market watchers are debating whether Citi should set up an allowance to reduce its deferred tax asset due to the possibility that the assets will not be realized. Not surprisingly, Citigroup has resisted setting up an allowance since the allowance reduces DTAs and increases income tax expense.

This accounting does not sit well with some market observers. As one critic noted, "Why should auditors, investors, regulators and others rely on Citigroup's projections . . . to justify the use (realizability) of their DTAs?" Former SEC chief accountant, Lynn Turner, agrees: "Citi's position defies imagination and logic. Instead of talking about making money, what Citi ought to do is to reserve for at least part of the deferred tax assets and reap the benefit of reducing the reserves once it actually makes money."

In response, Citigroup, which accumulated deferred tax assets partly because of its huge losses during the financial crisis, said it was "very comfortable with the recording of our deferred tax assets." And some market analysts sided with the bank, remarking that Citi's accounts were not out of order due to a misstatement of its DTAs. The Citigroup debate has arisen because accounting standards on DTAs are vague, stating that an allowance is not needed if management believes it is "more likely than not" the company will earn enough taxable income in the future.

This debate over Citigroup's accounting highlights the extent to which management judgment plays an important role in the accounting for taxes. After studying this chapter, you should be better able to evaluate Citigroup's accounting as well as the other judgments inherent in the accounting for income taxes.

Source: Adapted from J. Weil, "Citigroup's Capital Was All Casing, No Meat," *www.bloomberg.net* (November 24, 2008); and F. Guerra and J. Eaglesham, "Citi Under Fire Over Deferred Tax Assets," *Financial Times* (September 6, 2010).

IFRS IN THIS CHAPTER

▶ See the **International Perspectives** on pages 1145, 1154, 1163, 1165, and 1171.

▶ Read the **IFRS Insights** on pages 1199–1206 for a discussion of:

— Deferred tax asset (non-recognition)

— Statement of financial position classification

PREVIEW OF CHAPTER 19

As our opening story indicates, the accounting for income taxes involves significant judgment. Investors need to be knowledgeable of the accounting provisions related to taxes to be able to evaluate these judgments. Thus, companies must present financial information to the investment community that provides a clear picture of present and potential tax obligations and tax benefits. In this chapter, we discuss the basic guidelines that companies must follow in reporting income taxes. The content and organization of the chapter are as follows.

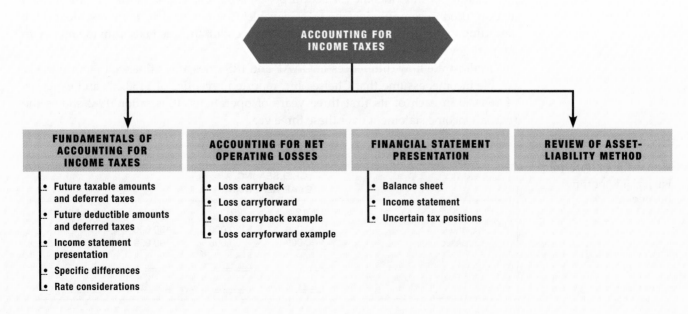

ACCOUNTING FOR INCOME TAXES

FUNDAMENTALS OF ACCOUNTING FOR INCOME TAXES	ACCOUNTING FOR NET OPERATING LOSSES	FINANCIAL STATEMENT PRESENTATION	REVIEW OF ASSET-LIABILITY METHOD
• Future taxable amounts and deferred taxes • Future deductible amounts and deferred taxes • Income statement presentation • Specific differences • Rate considerations	• Loss carryback • Loss carryforward • Loss carryback example • Loss carryforward example	• Balance sheet • Income statement • Uncertain tax positions	

FUNDAMENTALS OF ACCOUNTING FOR INCOME TAXES

LEARNING OBJECTIVE **1**

Identify differences between pretax financial income and taxable income.

Up to this point, you have learned the basic guidelines that corporations use to report information to investors and creditors. Corporations also must file income tax returns following the guidelines developed by the Internal Revenue Service (IRS). Because GAAP and tax regulations differ in a number of ways, so frequently do pretax financial income and taxable income. Consequently, the amount that a company reports as tax expense will differ from the amount of taxes payable to the IRS. Illustration 19-1 highlights these differences.

ILLUSTRATION 19-1
Fundamental Differences between Financial and Tax Reporting

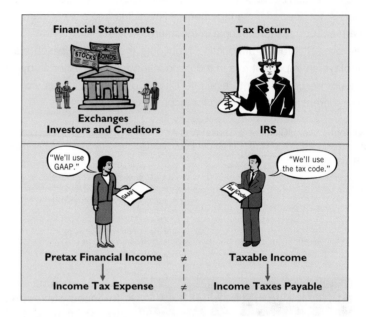

Pretax financial income is a *financial reporting* term. It also is often referred to as *income before taxes, income for financial reporting purposes,* or *income for book purposes.* Companies determine pretax financial income according to GAAP. They measure it with the objective of providing useful information to investors and creditors.

Taxable income (income for tax purposes) is a *tax accounting* term. It indicates the amount used to compute income taxes payable. Companies determine taxable income according to the Internal Revenue Code (the tax code). Income taxes provide money to support government operations.

To illustrate how differences in GAAP and IRS rules affect financial reporting and taxable income, assume that Chelsea Inc. reported revenues of $130,000 and expenses of $60,000 in each of its first three years of operations. Illustration 19-2 shows the (partial) income statement over these three years.

ILLUSTRATION 19-2
Financial Reporting Income

CHELSEA INC.				
GAAP REPORTING				
	2012	2013	2014	Total
Revenues	$130,000	$130,000	$130,000	
Expenses	60,000	60,000	60,000	
Pretax financial income	$ 70,000	$ 70,000	$ 70,000	$210,000
Income tax expense (40%)	$ 28,000	$ 28,000	$ 28,000	$ 84,000

For tax purposes (following the tax code), Chelsea reported the same expenses to the IRS in each of the years. But, as Illustration 19-3 shows, Chelsea reported taxable revenues of $100,000 in 2012, $150,000 in 2013, and $140,000 in 2014.

ILLUSTRATION 19-3
Tax Reporting Income

| | | **CHELSEA INC.** | | |
| | | **TAX REPORTING** | | |
	2012	2013	2014	Total
Revenues	$100,000	$150,000	$140,000	
Expenses	60,000	60,000	60,000	
Taxable income	$ 40,000	$ 90,000	$ 80,000	$210,000
Income taxes payable (40%)	$ 16,000	$ 36,000	$ 32,000	$ 84,000

Income tax expense and income taxes payable differed over the three years, but were equal **in total**, as Illustration 19-4 shows.

ILLUSTRATION 19-4
Comparison of Income Tax Expense to Income Taxes Payable

	CHELSEA INC.			
	INCOME TAX EXPENSE AND			
	INCOME TAXES PAYABLE			
	2012	2013	2014	Total
Income tax expense	$28,000	$28,000	$28,000	$84,000
Income taxes payable	16,000	36,000	32,000	84,000
Difference	$12,000	$ (8,000)	$ (4,000)	$ 0

The differences between income tax expense and income taxes payable in this example arise for a simple reason. For financial reporting, companies use the full accrual method to report revenues. For tax purposes, they use a modified cash basis. As a result, Chelsea reports pretax financial income of $70,000 and income tax expense of $28,000 for each of the three years. However, taxable income fluctuates. For example, in 2012 taxable income is only $40,000, so Chelsea owes just $16,000 to the IRS that year. Chelsea classifies the income taxes payable as a current liability on the balance sheet.

As Illustration 19-4 indicates, for Chelsea the $12,000 ($28,000 − $16,000) difference between income tax expense and income taxes payable in 2012 reflects taxes that it will pay in future periods. This $12,000 difference is often referred to as a **deferred tax amount**. In this case it is a **deferred tax liability**. In cases where taxes will be lower in the future, Chelsea records a **deferred tax asset**. We explain the measurement and accounting for deferred tax liabilities and assets in the following two sections.[1]

INTERNATIONAL PERSPECTIVE

In some countries, taxable income equals pretax financial income. As a consequence, accounting for differences between tax and book income is insignificant.

Future Taxable Amounts and Deferred Taxes

The example summarized in Illustration 19-4 shows how income taxes payable can differ from income tax expense. This can happen when there are temporary differences between the amounts reported for tax purposes and those reported for book purposes. A temporary difference is the difference between the tax basis of an asset or liability and its reported (carrying or book) amount in the financial statements, which will result in taxable amounts or deductible amounts in future

2 LEARNING OBJECTIVE
Describe a temporary difference that results in future taxable amounts.

---

[1]Determining the amount of tax to pay the IRS is a costly exercise for both individuals and companies. For example, a recent study documented that the average person spends about $200 annually collecting, calculating, and compiling tax data. U.S. corporations had a total cost of compliance of $170 billion. This is not surprising, when you consider that General Electric filed a return equivalent to 24,000 printed pages. J. Abrams, "Americans Spend 27 Hours, $200," *Naples (FL) Daily News* (April 15, 2008), p. 3a.

years. Taxable amounts increase taxable income in future years. Deductible amounts decrease taxable income in future years.

In Chelsea's situation, the only difference between the book basis and tax basis of the assets and liabilities relates to accounts receivable that arose from revenue recognized for book purposes. Illustration 19-5 indicates that Chelsea reports accounts receivable at $30,000 in the December 31, 2012, GAAP-basis balance sheet. However, the receivables have a zero tax basis.

ILLUSTRATION 19-5
Temporary Difference, Sales Revenue

Per Books	12/31/12	Per Tax Return	12/31/12
Accounts receivable	$30,000	Accounts receivable	$-0-

What will happen to the $30,000 temporary difference that originated in 2012 for Chelsea? Assuming that Chelsea expects to collect $20,000 of the receivables in 2013 and $10,000 in 2014, this collection results in future taxable amounts of $20,000 in 2013 and $10,000 in 2014. These future taxable amounts will cause taxable income to exceed pretax financial income in both 2013 and 2014.

An assumption inherent in a company's GAAP balance sheet is that companies recover and settle the assets and liabilities at their reported amounts (carrying amounts). This assumption creates a requirement under accrual accounting to recognize *currently* the deferred tax consequences of temporary differences. That is, companies recognize the amount of income taxes that are payable (or refundable) when they recover and settle the reported amounts of the assets and liabilities, respectively. Illustration 19-6 shows the reversal of the temporary difference described in Illustration 19-5 and the resulting taxable amounts in future periods.

ILLUSTRATION 19-6
Reversal of Temporary Difference, Chelsea Inc.

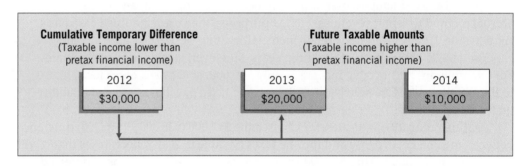

Chelsea assumes that it will collect the accounts receivable and report the $30,000 collection as taxable revenues in future tax returns. A payment of income tax in both 2013 and 2014 will occur. Chelsea should therefore record in its books in 2012 the deferred tax consequences of the revenue and related receivables reflected in the 2012 financial statements. Chelsea does this by recording a deferred tax liability.

Deferred Tax Liability

A deferred tax liability is the deferred tax consequences attributable to taxable temporary differences. In other words, **a deferred tax liability represents the increase in taxes payable in future years as a result of taxable temporary differences existing at the end of the current year**.

Recall from the Chelsea example that income taxes payable is $16,000 ($40,000 × 40%) in 2012 (Illustration 19-4 on page 1145). In addition, a temporary difference exists at year-end because Chelsea reports the revenue and related accounts receivable differently for book and tax purposes. The book basis of accounts receivable is $30,000, and the tax basis is zero. Thus, the total deferred tax liability at the end of 2012 is $12,000, computed as shown in Illustration 19-7.

Book basis of accounts receivable	$30,000
Tax basis of accounts receivable	–0–
Cumulative temporary difference at the end of 2012	30,000
Tax rate	40%
Deferred tax liability at the end of 2012	$12,000

ILLUSTRATION 19-7
Computation of Deferred Tax Liability, End of 2012

Companies may also compute the deferred tax liability by preparing a schedule that indicates the future taxable amounts due to existing temporary differences. Such a schedule, as shown in Illustration 19-8, is particularly useful when the computations become more complex.

	Future Years		
	2013	2014	Total
Future taxable amounts	$20,000	$10,000	$30,000
Tax rate	40%	40%	
Deferred tax liability at the end of 2012	$ 8,000	$ 4,000	$12,000

ILLUSTRATION 19-8
Schedule of Future Taxable Amounts

Because it is the first year of operations for Chelsea, there is no deferred tax liability at the beginning of the year. Chelsea computes the income tax expense for 2012 as shown in Illustration 19-9.

Deferred tax liability at end of 2012	$12,000
Deferred tax liability at beginning of 2012	–0–
Deferred tax expense for 2012	12,000
Current tax expense for 2012 (income taxes payable)	16,000
Income tax expense (total) for 2012	$28,000

ILLUSTRATION 19-9
Computation of Income Tax Expense, 2012

This computation indicates that income tax expense has two components—**current tax expense** (the amount of income taxes payable for the period) and deferred tax expense. **Deferred tax expense** is the increase in the deferred tax liability balance from the beginning to the end of the accounting period.

Companies credit taxes due and payable to Income Taxes Payable, and credit the increase in deferred taxes to Deferred Tax Liability. They then debit the sum of those two items to Income Tax Expense. For Chelsea, it makes the following entry at the end of 2012.

Income Tax Expense	28,000	
Income Taxes Payable		16,000
Deferred Tax Liability		12,000

At the end of 2013 (the second year), the difference between the book basis and the tax basis of the accounts receivable is $10,000. Chelsea multiplies this difference by the applicable tax rate to arrive at the deferred tax liability of $4,000 ($10,000 × 40%), which it reports at the end of 2013. Income taxes payable for 2013 is $36,000 (Illustration 19-3 on page 1145), and the income tax expense for 2013 is as shown in Illustration 19-10.

Deferred tax liability at end of 2013	$ 4,000
Deferred tax liability at beginning of 2013	12,000
Deferred tax expense (benefit) for 2013	(8,000)
Current tax expense for 2013 (income taxes payable)	36,000
Income tax expense (total) for 2013	$28,000

ILLUSTRATION 19-10
Computation of Income Tax Expense, 2013

Chelsea records income tax expense, the change in the deferred tax liability, and income taxes payable for 2013 as follows.

Income Tax Expense	28,000	
Deferred Tax Liability	8,000	
Income Taxes Payable		36,000

The entry to record income taxes at the end of 2014 reduces the Deferred Tax Liability by $4,000. The Deferred Tax Liability account appears as follows at the end of 2014.

ILLUSTRATION 19-11
Deferred Tax Liability
Account after Reversals

Deferred Tax Liability			
2013	8,000	2012	12,000
2014	4,000		

The Deferred Tax Liability account has a zero balance at the end of 2014.

"REAL LIABILITIES"

What do the numbers mean?

Some analysts dismiss deferred tax liabilities when assessing the financial strength of a company. But the FASB indicates that the deferred tax liability meets the definition of a liability established in *Statement of Financial Accounting Concepts No. 6*, "Elements of Financial Statements" because:

1. *It results from a past transaction.* In the Chelsea example, the company performed services for customers and recognized revenue in 2012 for financial reporting purposes but deferred it for tax purposes.

2. *It is a present obligation.* Taxable income in future periods will exceed pretax financial income as a result of this temporary difference. Thus, a present obligation exists.

3. *It represents a future sacrifice.* Taxable income and taxes due in future periods will result from past events. The payment of these taxes when they come due is the future sacrifice.

A study by B. Ayers indicates that the market views deferred tax assets and liabilities similarly to other assets and liabilities. Further, the study concludes that the FASB rules in this area increased the usefulness of deferred tax amounts in financial statements.

Source: B. Ayers, "Deferred Tax Accounting Under *SFAS No. 109*: An Empirical Investigation of Its Incremental Value-Relevance Relative to *APB No. 11*," *The Accounting Review* (April 1998).

Summary of Income Tax Accounting Objectives

One objective of accounting for income taxes is to recognize the amount of taxes payable or refundable for the current year. In Chelsea's case, income taxes payable is $16,000 for 2012.

A **second objective** is to recognize deferred tax liabilities and assets for the future tax consequences of events already recognized in the financial statements or tax returns. For example, Chelsea sold services to customers that resulted in accounts receivable of $30,000 in 2012. It reported that amount on the 2012 income statement, but not on the tax return as income. That amount will appear on future tax returns as income for the period **when collected**. As a result, a $30,000 temporary difference exists at the end of 2012, which will cause future taxable amounts. Chelsea reports a deferred tax liability of $12,000 on the balance sheet at the end of 2012, which represents the increase in taxes payable in future years ($8,000 in 2013 and $4,000 in 2014) as a result of a temporary difference existing at the end of the current year. The related deferred tax liability is reduced by $8,000 at the end of 2013 and by another $4,000 at the end of 2014.

In addition to affecting the balance sheet, deferred taxes impact income tax expense in each of the three years affected. In 2012, taxable income ($40,000) is less than pretax financial income ($70,000). Income taxes payable for 2012 is therefore $16,000 (based on taxable income). Deferred tax expense of $12,000 results from the increase in the Deferred Tax Liability account on the balance sheet. Income tax expense is then $28,000 for 2012.

In 2013 and 2014, however, taxable income will exceed pretax financial income, due to the reversal of the temporary difference ($20,000 in 2013 and $10,000 in 2014). Income taxes payable will therefore exceed income tax expense in 2013 and 2014. Chelsea will debit the Deferred Tax Liability account for $8,000 in 2013 and $4,000 in 2014. It records credits for these amounts in Income Tax Expense. These credits are often referred to as a **deferred tax benefit** (which we discuss again later on).

Future Deductible Amounts and Deferred Taxes

Assume that during 2012, Cunningham Inc. estimated its warranty costs related to the sale of microwave ovens to be $500,000, paid evenly over the next two years. For book purposes, in 2012 Cunningham reported warranty expense and a related estimated liability for warranties of $500,000 in its financial statements. For tax purposes, **the warranty tax deduction is not allowed until paid**. Therefore, Cunningham recognizes no warranty liability on a tax-basis balance sheet. Illustration 19-12 shows the balance sheet difference at the end of 2012.

3 LEARNING OBJECTIVE
Describe a temporary difference that results in future deductible amounts.

Per Books	12/31/12	Per Tax Return	12/31/12
Estimated liability for warranties	$500,000	Estimated liability for warranties	$-0-

ILLUSTRATION 19-12
Temporary Difference, Warranty Liability

When Cunningham pays the warranty liability, it reports an expense (deductible amount) for tax purposes. Because of this temporary difference, Cunningham should recognize in 2012 the tax benefits (positive tax consequences) for the tax deductions that will result from the future settlement of the liability. Cunningham reports this future tax benefit in the December 31, 2012, balance sheet as a **deferred tax asset**.

We can think about this situation another way. Deductible amounts occur in future tax returns. These **future deductible amounts** cause taxable income to be less than pretax financial income in the future as a result of an existing temporary difference. Cunningham's temporary difference originates (arises) in one period (2012) and reverses over two periods (2013 and 2014). Illustration 19-13 diagrams this situation.

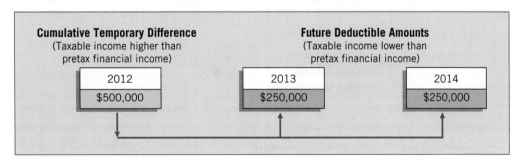

ILLUSTRATION 19-13
Reversal of Temporary Difference, Cunningham Inc.

Deferred Tax Asset

A deferred tax asset is the deferred tax consequence attributable to deductible temporary differences. In other words, a **deferred tax asset represents the increase in taxes refundable (or saved) in future years as a result of deductible temporary differences existing at the end of the current year**.

To illustrate, assume that Hunt Co. accrues a loss and a related liability of $50,000 in 2012 for financial reporting purposes because of pending litigation. Hunt cannot deduct this amount for tax purposes until the period it pays the liability, expected in 2013. As a result, a deductible amount will occur in 2013 when Hunt settles the liability (Estimated Litigation Liability), causing taxable income to be lower than pretax financial income. Illustration 19-14 (on page 1150) shows the computation of the deferred tax asset at the end of 2012 (assuming a 40 percent tax rate).

ILLUSTRATION 19-14
Computation of Deferred
Tax Asset, End of 2012

Book basis of litigation liability	$50,000
Tax basis of litigation liability	–0–
Cumulative temporary difference at the end of 2012	50,000
Tax rate	40%
Deferred tax asset at the end of 2012	$20,000

Hunt can also compute the deferred tax asset by preparing a schedule that indicates the future deductible amounts due to deductible temporary differences. Illustration 19-15 shows this schedule.

ILLUSTRATION 19-15
Schedule of Future
Deductible Amounts

	Future Years
Future deductible amounts	$50,000
Tax rate	40%
Deferred tax asset at the end of 2012	$20,000

Assuming that 2012 is Hunt's first year of operations, and income taxes payable is $100,000, Hunt computes its income tax expense as follows.

ILLUSTRATION 19-16
Computation of Income
Tax Expense, 2012

Deferred tax asset at end of 2012	$ 20,000
Deferred tax asset at beginning of 2012	–0–
Deferred tax expense (benefit) for 2012	(20,000)
Current tax expense for 2012 (income taxes payable)	100,000
Income tax expense (total) for 2012	$ 80,000

The **deferred tax benefit** results from the increase in the deferred tax asset from the beginning to the end of the accounting period (similar to the Chelsea example earlier). The deferred tax benefit is a negative component of income tax expense. The total income tax expense of $80,000 on the income statement for 2012 thus consists of two elements—current tax expense of $100,000 and a deferred tax benefit of $20,000. For Hunt, it makes the following journal entry at the end of 2012 to record income tax expense, deferred income taxes, and income taxes payable.

Income Tax Expense	80,000	
Deferred Tax Asset	20,000	
Income Taxes Payable		100,000

At the end of 2013 (the second year), the difference between the book value and the tax basis of the litigation liability is zero. Therefore, there is no deferred tax asset at this date. Assuming that income taxes payable for 2013 is $140,000, Hunt computes income tax expense for 2013 as shown in Illustration 19-17.

ILLUSTRATION 19-17
Computation of Income
Tax Expense, 2013

Deferred tax asset at the end of 2013	$ –0–
Deferred tax asset at the beginning of 2013	20,000
Deferred tax expense (benefit) for 2013	20,000
Current tax expense for 2013 (income taxes payable)	140,000
Income tax expense (total) for 2013	$160,000

The company records income taxes for 2013 as follows.

Income Tax Expense	160,000	
Deferred Tax Asset		20,000
Income Taxes Payable		140,000

The total income tax expense of $160,000 on the income statement for 2013 thus consists of two elements—current tax expense of $140,000 and deferred tax expense of $20,000. Illustration 19-18 shows the Deferred Tax Asset account at the end of 2013.

Deferred Tax Asset			
2012	20,000	2013	20,000

ILLUSTRATION 19-18
Deferred Tax Asset
Account after Reversals

"REAL ASSETS"

A key issue in accounting for income taxes is whether a company should recognize a deferred tax asset in the financial records. Based on the conceptual definition of an asset, a deferred tax asset meets the three main conditions for an item to be recognized as an asset:

What do the numbers mean?

1. **It results from a past transaction.** In the Hunt example, the accrual of the loss contingency is the past event that gives rise to a future deductible temporary difference.

3. **It gives rise to a probable benefit in the future.** Taxable income exceeds pretax financial income in the current year (2012). However, in the next year the exact opposite occurs. That is, taxable income is lower than pretax financial income. Because this deductible temporary difference reduces taxes payable in the future, a probable future benefit exists at the end of the current period.

3. **The entity controls access to the benefits.** Hunt can obtain the benefit of existing deductible temporary differences by reducing its taxes payable in the future. Hunt has the exclusive right to that benefit and can control others' access to it.

Market analysts' reactions to the **write-off** of deferred tax assets also supports their treatment as assets. When Bethlehem Steel reported a $1 billion charge in a recent year to write off a deferred tax asset, analysts believed that Bethlehem was signaling that it would not realize the future benefits of the tax deductions. Thus, Bethlehem should write down the asset like other assets.

Source: J. Weil and S. Liesman, "Stock Gurus Disregard Most Big Write-Offs but They Often Hold Vital Clues to Outlook," *Wall Street Journal Online* (December 31, 2001).

Deferred Tax Asset—Valuation Allowance

Companies recognize a deferred tax asset for all deductible temporary differences. However, based on available evidence, a company should reduce a deferred tax asset by a valuation allowance if **it is more likely than not** that it **will not realize** some portion or all of the deferred tax asset. "More likely than not" means a level of likelihood of at least slightly more than 50 percent.

4 LEARNING OBJECTIVE
Explain the purpose of a deferred tax asset valuation allowance.

Assume that Jensen Co. has a deductible temporary difference of $1,000,000 at the end of its first year of operations. Its tax rate is 40 percent, which means it records a deferred tax asset of $400,000 ($1,000,000 × 40%). Assuming $900,000 of income taxes payable, Jensen records income tax expense, the deferred tax asset, and income taxes payable as follows.

Income Tax Expense	500,000	
Deferred Tax Asset	400,000	
Income Taxes Payable		900,000

After careful review of all available evidence, Jensen determines that it is more likely than not that it will not realize $100,000 of this deferred tax asset. Jensen records this reduction in asset value as follows.

Income Tax Expense	100,000	
Allowance to Reduce Deferred Tax Asset to Expected Realizable Value		100,000

This journal entry increases income tax expense in the current period because Jensen does not expect to realize a favorable tax benefit for a portion of the deductible temporary difference. Jensen **simultaneously establishes a valuation allowance to recognize the reduction in the carrying amount of the deferred tax asset**. This valuation account is a contra account. Jensen reports it on the financial statements in the following manner.

ILLUSTRATION 19-19
Balance Sheet Presentation of Valuation Allowance Account

Deferred tax asset	$400,000
Less: Allowance to reduce deferred tax asset to expected realizable value	100,000
Deferred tax asset (net)	$300,000

Jensen then evaluates this allowance account at the end of each accounting period. If, at the end of the next period, the deferred tax asset is still $400,000, but now it expects to realize $350,000 of this asset, Jensen makes the following entry to adjust the valuation account.

Allowance to Reduce Deferred Tax Asset to Expected Realizable Value	50,000	
Income Tax Expense		50,000

Jensen should consider all available evidence, both positive and negative, to determine whether, based on the weight of available evidence, it needs a valuation allowance. For example, if Jensen has been experiencing a series of loss years, it reasonably assumes that these losses will continue. Therefore, Jensen will lose the benefit of the future deductible amounts. We discuss the use of a valuation account under other conditions later in the chapter.

Income Statement Presentation

LEARNING OBJECTIVE 5
Describe the presentation of income tax expense in the income statement.

Circumstances dictate whether a company should add or subtract the change in deferred income taxes to or from income taxes payable in computing income tax expense. For example, a company adds an increase in a deferred tax liability to income taxes payable. On the other hand, it subtracts an increase in a deferred tax asset from income taxes payable. The formula in Illustration 19-20 is used to compute income tax expense (benefit).

ILLUSTRATION 19-20
Formula to Compute Income Tax Expense

Income Taxes Payable or Refundable	±	Change in Deferred Income Taxes	=	Total Income Tax Expense or Benefit

In the income statement or in the notes to the financial statements, a company should disclose the significant components of income tax expense attributable to continuing operations. Given the information related to Chelsea on page 1145, Chelsea reports its income statement as follows.

ILLUSTRATION 19-21
Income Statement Presentation of Income Tax Expense

CHELSEA INC.
INCOME STATEMENT
FOR THE YEAR ENDING DECEMBER 31, 2012

Revenues		$130,000
Expenses		60,000
Income before income taxes		70,000
Income tax expense		
Current	$16,000	
Deferred	12,000	28,000
Net income		$ 42,000

As illustrated, Chelsea reports both the current portion (amount of income taxes payable for the period) and the deferred portion of income tax expense. Another option is to simply report the total income tax expense on the income statement, and then indicate in the notes to the financial statements the current and deferred portions. Income tax expense is often referred to as "Provision for income taxes." Using this terminology, the current provision is $16,000, and the provision for deferred taxes is $12,000.

Specific Differences

Numerous items create differences between pretax financial income and taxable income. For purposes of accounting recognition, these differences are of two types: (1) temporary, and (2) permanent.

6 LEARNING OBJECTIVE
Describe various temporary and permanent differences.

Temporary Differences

Taxable temporary differences are temporary differences that will result in taxable amounts in future years when the related assets are recovered. Deductible temporary differences are temporary differences that will result in deductible amounts in future years, when the related book liabilities are settled. Taxable temporary differences give rise to recording deferred tax liabilities. Deductible temporary differences give rise to recording deferred tax assets. Illustration 19-22 provides examples of temporary differences.

ILLUSTRATION 19-22
Examples of Temporary Differences

Revenues or gains are taxable after they are recognized in financial income.

An asset (e.g., accounts receivable or investment) may be recognized for revenues or gains that will result in **taxable amounts in future years** when the asset is recovered. Examples:
1. Sales accounted for on the accrual basis for financial reporting purposes and on the installment (cash) basis for tax purposes.
2. Contracts accounted for under the percentage-of-completion method for financial reporting purposes and a portion of related gross profit deferred for tax purposes.
3. Investments accounted for under the equity method for financial reporting purposes and under the cost method for tax purposes.
4. Gain on involuntary conversion of nonmonetary asset which is recognized for financial reporting purposes but deferred for tax purposes.
5. Unrealized holding gains for financial reporting purposes (including use of the fair value option), but deferred for tax purposes.

Expenses or losses are deductible after they are recognized in financial income.

A liability (or contra asset) may be recognized for expenses or losses that will result in **deductible amounts in future years** when the liability is settled. Examples:
1. Product warranty liabilities.
2. Estimated liabilities related to discontinued operations or restructurings.
3. Litigation accruals.
4. Bad debt expense recognized using the allowance method for financial reporting purposes; direct write-off method used for tax purposes.
5. Stock-based compensation expense.
6. Unrealized holding losses for financial reporting purposes (including use of the fair value option), but deferred for tax purposes.

Revenues or gains are taxable before they are recognized in financial income.

A liability may be recognized for an advance payment for goods or services to be provided in future years. For tax purposes, the advance payment is included in taxable income upon the receipt of cash. Future sacrifices to provide goods or services (or future refunds to those who cancel their orders) that settle the liability will result in **deductible amounts in future years**. Examples:
1. Subscriptions received in advance.
2. Advance rental receipts.
3. Sales and leasebacks for financial reporting purposes (income deferral) but reported as sales for tax purposes.
4. Prepaid contracts and royalties received in advance.

Expenses or losses are deductible before they are recognized in financial income.

The cost of an asset may have been deducted for tax purposes faster than it was expensed for financial reporting purposes. Amounts received upon future recovery of the amount of the asset for financial reporting (through use or sale) will exceed the remaining tax basis of the asset and thereby result in **taxable amounts in future years**. Examples:
1. Depreciable property, depletable resources, and intangibles.
2. Deductible pension funding exceeding expense.
3. Prepaid expenses that are deducted on the tax return in the period paid.

Determining a company's temporary differences may prove difficult. A company should prepare a balance sheet for tax purposes that it can compare with its GAAP balance sheet. Many of the differences between the two balance sheets are temporary differences.

Originating and Reversing Aspects of Temporary Differences. An **originating temporary difference** is the initial difference between the book basis and the tax basis of an asset or liability, regardless of whether the tax basis of the asset or liability exceeds or is exceeded by the book basis of the asset or liability. A **reversing difference**, on the other hand, occurs when eliminating a temporary difference that originated in prior periods and then removing the related tax effect from the deferred tax account.

For example, assume that Sharp Co. has tax depreciation in excess of book depreciation of $2,000 in 2010, 2011, and 2012. Further, it has an excess of book depreciation over tax depreciation of $3,000 in 2013 and 2014 for the same asset. Assuming a tax rate of 30 percent for all years involved, the Deferred Tax Liability account reflects the following.

ILLUSTRATION 19-23
Tax Effects of Originating and Reversing Differences

	Deferred Tax Liability				
Tax Effects	2013	900	2010	600	Tax Effects
of	2014	900	2011	600	of
Reversing Differences			2012	600	Originating Differences

The originating differences for Sharp in each of the first three years are $2,000. The related tax effect of each originating difference is $600. The reversing differences in 2013 and 2014 are each $3,000. The related tax effect of each is $900.

Permanent Differences

INTERNATIONAL PERSPECTIVE

If companies switch to IFRS, the impact on tax accounting methods will require consideration. For example, in cases in which GAAP and tax rules are the same, what happens if IFRS is different from GAAP? Should the tax method change to IFRS? And what might happen at the state level, due to changes in the financial reporting rules?

Some differences between taxable income and pretax financial income are permanent. **Permanent differences** result from items that (1) enter into pretax financial income but **never** into taxable income, or (2) enter into taxable income but **never** into pretax financial income.

Congress has enacted a variety of tax law provisions to attain certain political, economic, and social objectives. Some of these provisions exclude certain revenues from taxation, limit the deductibility of certain expenses, and permit the deduction of certain other expenses in excess of costs incurred. A corporation that has tax-free income, nondeductible expenses, or allowable deductions in excess of cost, has an effective tax rate that differs from its statutory (regular) tax rate.

Since permanent differences affect only the period in which they occur, they do not give rise to future taxable or deductible amounts. As a result, **companies recognize no deferred tax consequences**. Illustration 19-24 shows examples of permanent differences.

ILLUSTRATION 19-24
Examples of Permanent Differences

Items are recognized for financial reporting purposes but not for tax purposes.

Examples:
1. Interest received on state and municipal obligations.
2. Expenses incurred in obtaining tax-exempt income.
3. Proceeds from life insurance carried by the company on key officers or employees.
4. Premiums paid for life insurance carried by the company on key officers or employees (company is beneficiary).
5. Fines and expenses resulting from a violation of law.

Items are recognized for tax purposes but not for financial reporting purposes.

Examples:
1. "Percentage depletion" of natural resources in excess of their cost.
2. The deduction for dividends received from U.S. corporations, generally 70% or 80%.

Examples of Temporary and Permanent Differences

To illustrate the computations used when both temporary and permanent differences exist, assume that Bio-Tech Company reports pretax financial income of $200,000 in each of the years 2010, 2011, and 2013. The company is subject to a 30 percent tax rate, and has the following differences between pretax financial income and taxable income.

1. Bio-Tech reports an installment sale of $18,000 in 2010 for tax purposes over an 18-month period at a constant amount per month beginning January 1, 2011. It recognizes the entire sale for book purposes in 2010.

2. It pays life insurance premiums for its key officers of $5,000 in 2011 and 2012. Although not tax-deductible, Bio-Tech expenses the premiums for book purposes.

The installment sale is a temporary difference, whereas the life insurance premium is a permanent difference. Illustration 19-25 shows the reconciliation of Bio-Tech's pretax financial income to taxable income and the computation of income taxes payable.

	2010	2011	2012
Pretax financial income	$200,000	$200,000	$200,000
Permanent difference			
Nondeductible expense		5,000	5,000
Temporary difference			
Installment sale	(18,000)	12,000	6,000
Taxable income	182,000	217,000	211,000
Tax rate	30%	30%	30%
Income taxes payable	$ 54,600	$ 65,100	$ 63,300

ILLUSTRATION 19-25
Reconciliation and Computation of Income Taxes Payable

Note that Bio-Tech **deducts** the installment sales revenue from pretax financial income to arrive at taxable income. The reason: pretax financial income includes the installment sales revenue; taxable income does not. Conversely, it **adds** the $5,000 insurance premium to pretax financial income to arrive at taxable income. The reason: pretax financial income records an expense for this premium, but for tax purposes the premium is not deductible. As a result, pretax financial income is lower than taxable income. Therefore, the life insurance premium must be added back to pretax financial income to reconcile to taxable income.

Bio-Tech records income taxes for 2010, 2011, and 2012 as follows.

December 31, 2010

Income Tax Expense ($54,600 + $5,400)	60,000	
Deferred Tax Liability ($18,000 × 30%)		5,400
Income Taxes Payable ($182,000 × 30%)		54,600

December 31, 2011

Income Tax Expense ($65,100 − $3,600)	61,500	
Deferred Tax Liability ($12,000 × 30%)	3,600	
Income Taxes Payable ($217,000 × 30%)		65,100

December 31, 2012

Income Tax Expense ($63,300 − $1,800)	61,500	
Deferred Tax Liability ($6,000 × 30%)	1,800	
Income Taxes Payable ($211,000 × 30%)		63,300

Bio-Tech has one temporary difference, which originates in 2010 and reverses in 2011 and 2012. It recognizes a deferred tax liability at the end of 2010 because the temporary difference causes future taxable amounts. As the temporary difference reverses, Bio-Tech reduces the deferred tax liability. There is no deferred tax amount associated with the difference caused by the nondeductible insurance expense because it is a permanent difference.

Although an enacted tax rate of 30 percent applies for all three years, the effective rate differs from the enacted rate in 2011 and 2012. Bio-Tech computes the **effective tax rate** by dividing total income tax expense for the period by pretax financial income. The effective rate is 30 percent for 2010 ($60,000 ÷ $200,000 = 30%) and 30.75 percent for 2011 and 2012 ($61,500 ÷ $200,000 = 30.75%).

Tax Rate Considerations

<table>
<tr><td>

LEARNING OBJECTIVE ▶ **7**

Explain the effect of various tax rates and tax rate changes on deferred income taxes.

</td></tr>
</table>

In our previous illustrations, the enacted tax rate did not change from one year to the next. Thus, to compute the deferred income tax amount to report on the balance sheet, a company simply multiplies the cumulative temporary difference by the current tax rate. Using Bio-Tech as an example, it multiplies the cumulative temporary difference of $18,000 by the enacted tax rate, 30 percent in this case, to arrive at a deferred tax liability of $5,400 ($18,000 × 30%) at the end of 2010.

Future Tax Rates

What happens if tax rates are expected to change in the future? In this case, a company should use the **enacted tax rate** expected to apply. Therefore, a company must consider presently enacted changes in the tax rate that become effective for a particular future year(s) when determining the tax rate to apply to existing temporary differences. For example, assume that Warlen Co. at the end of 2009 has the following cumulative temporary difference of $300,000, computed as shown in Illustration 19-26.

ILLUSTRATION 19-26
Computation of Cumulative Temporary Difference

Book basis of depreciable assets	$1,000,000
Tax basis of depreciable assets	700,000
Cumulative temporary difference	$ 300,000

Furthermore, assume that the $300,000 will reverse and result in taxable amounts in the future, with the enacted tax rates shown in Illustration 19-27.

ILLUSTRATION 19-27
Deferred Tax Liability Based on Future Rates

	2010	2011	2012	2013	2014	Total
Future taxable amounts	$80,000	$70,000	$60,000	$50,000	$40,000	$300,000
Tax rate	40%	40%	35%	30%	30%	
Deferred tax liability	$32,000	$28,000	$21,000	$15,000	$12,000	$108,000

The total deferred tax liability at the end of 2009 is $108,000. Warlen may only use tax rates other than the current rate when the future tax rates have been enacted, as is the case in this example. **If new rates are not yet enacted for future years, Warlen should use the current rate.**

In determining the appropriate enacted tax rate for a given year, companies must use the **average tax rate**. The Internal Revenue Service and other taxing jurisdictions tax income on a graduated tax basis. For a U.S. corporation, the IRS taxes the first $50,000 of taxable income at 15 percent, the next $25,000 at 25 percent, with higher incremental levels of income at rates as high as 39 percent. In computing deferred income taxes, companies for which graduated tax rates are a significant factor must therefore **determine the average tax rate and use that rate**.

Revision of Future Tax Rates

When a change in the tax rate is enacted, companies should record its effect on the existing deferred income tax accounts immediately. **A company reports the effect as an adjustment to income tax expense in the period of the change.**

Assume that on December 10, 2009, a new income tax act is signed into law that lowers the corporate tax rate from 40 percent to 35 percent, effective January 1, 2011. If

Hostel Co. has one temporary difference at the beginning of 2009 related to $3 million of excess tax depreciation, then it has a Deferred Tax Liability account with a balance of $1,200,000 ($3,000,000 × 40%) at January 1, 2009. If taxable amounts related to this difference are scheduled to occur equally in 2010, 2011, and 2012, the deferred tax liability at the end of 2009 is $1,100,000, computed as follows.

ILLUSTRATION 19-28
Schedule of Future
Taxable Amounts and
Related Tax Rates

	2010	2011	2012	Total
Future taxable amounts	$1,000,000	$1,000,000	$1,000,000	$3,000,000
Tax rate	40%	35%	35%	
Deferred tax liability	$ 400,000	$ 350,000	$ 350,000	$1,100,000

Hostel, therefore, recognizes the decrease of $100,000 ($1,200,000 − $1,100,000) at the end of 2009 in the deferred tax liability as follows.

Deferred Tax Liability	100,000	
Income Tax Expense		100,000

Corporate tax rates do not change often. Therefore, companies usually employ the current rate. However, state and foreign tax rates change more frequently, and they require adjustments in deferred income taxes accordingly.[2]

GLOBAL TAX RATES

What do the numbers mean?

If you are concerned about your tax rate and the taxes you pay, you might want to consider moving to Switzerland, which has a personal tax rate of anywhere from zero percent to 13.2 percent. You don't want to move to Denmark though. Yes, the people of Denmark are regularly voted to be the happiest people on Earth but it's uncertain how many of these polls take place at tax time. The government in Denmark charges income tax rates ranging from 38 percent to 59 percent. So, taxes are a major item to many individuals, wherever they reside.

Taxes are also a big deal to corporations. For example, the Organisation for Economic Co-operation and Development (OECD) is an international organization of 30 countries that accept the principles of a free-market economy. Most OECD members are high-income economies and are regarded as developed countries. However, companies in the OECD can be subject to significant tax levies, as indicated in the following list of the ten highest corporate income tax rates for the OECD countries.

Japan	39.54%	Germany	30.18%
United States	39.25	Australia	30.00
France	34.43	New Zealand	30.00
Belgium	33.99	Spain	30.00
Canada	33.50	OECD Average	26.60
Luxembourg	30.38		

On the low end of the tax rate spectrum are Iceland and Ireland, with tax rates of 15 percent and 12.5 percent, respectively. Indeed, corporate tax rates have been dropping around the world as countries attempt to spur capital investment, which in turn spurs international tax competition. However, with stagnant global economic growth, there is concern that governments will target increases in corporate tax rates as a source of revenues to address budget shortfalls. In addition, further expansion of value-added taxes (VAT) is being considered. Indirect taxes such as VAT are charged on consumption of goods and services, which is much more stable than the corporate tax.

If these tax proposals result in changes in the tax rates applied to future deductible and taxable amounts, be prepared for significant re-measurement of deferred tax assets and liabilities.

Source: P. Toscano, "The World's Highest Tax Rates," *http://www.cnbc.com/id/30727913* (May 13, 2009).

---

[2]Tax rate changes nearly always will substantially impact income numbers and the reporting of deferred income taxes on the balance sheet. As a result, you can expect to hear an economic consequences argument every time that Congress decides to change the tax rates. For example, when Congress raised the corporate rate from 34 percent to 35 percent in 1993, companies took an additional "hit" to earnings if they were in a deferred tax liability position.

ACCOUNTING FOR NET OPERATING LOSSES

Every management hopes its company will be profitable. But hopes and profits may not materialize. For a start-up company, it is common to accumulate operating losses while expanding its customer base but before realizing economies of scale. For an established company, a major event such as a labor strike, rapidly changing regulatory and competitive forces, a disaster such as 9/11, or a general economic recession can cause expenses to exceed revenues—a net operating loss.

A **net operating loss (NOL)** occurs for tax purposes in a year when tax-deductible expenses exceed taxable revenues. An inequitable tax burden would result if companies were taxed during profitable periods without receiving any tax relief during periods of net operating losses. Under certain circumstances, therefore, the federal tax laws permit taxpayers to use the losses of one year to offset the profits of other years.

Companies accomplish this income-averaging provision through the **carryback and carryforward of net operating losses**. Under this provision, a company pays no income taxes for a year in which it incurs a net operating loss. In addition, it may select one of the two options discussed below and on the following pages.

Loss Carryback

Through use of a **loss carryback**, a company may carry the net operating loss back two years and receive refunds for income taxes paid in those years. The company must apply the loss to the earlier year first and then to the second year. It may **carry forward** any loss remaining after the two-year carryback up to 20 years to offset future taxable income. Illustration 19-29 diagrams the loss carryback procedure, assuming a loss in 2012.

ILLUSTRATION 19-29
Loss Carryback Procedure

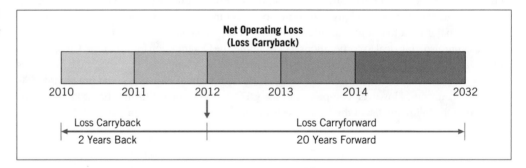

Loss Carryforward

A company may forgo the loss carryback and use only the **loss carryforward** option, offsetting future taxable income for up to 20 years. Illustration 19-30 shows this approach.

ILLUSTRATION 19-30
Loss Carryforward
Procedure

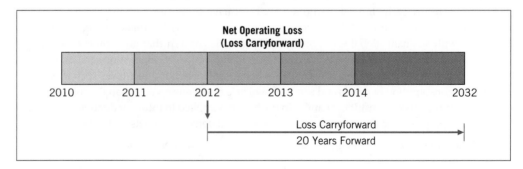

Operating losses can be substantial. For example, **Yahoo!** had net operating losses of approximately $5.4 billion in a recent year. That amount translates into tax savings of $1.4 billion if Yahoo! is able to generate taxable income before the NOLs expire.

Loss Carryback Example

To illustrate the accounting procedures for a net operating loss carryback, assume that Groh Inc. has no temporary or permanent differences. Groh experiences the following.

Year	Taxable Income or Loss	Tax Rate	Tax Paid
2009	$ 50,000	35%	$17,500
2010	100,000	30%	30,000
2011	200,000	40%	80,000
2012	(500,000)	—	–0–

In 2012, Groh incurs a net operating loss that it decides to carry back. Under the law, Groh must apply the carryback first to the **second year preceding the loss year**. Therefore, it carries the loss back first to 2010. Then, Groh carries back any unused loss to 2011. Accordingly, Groh files amended tax returns for 2010 and 2011, receiving refunds for the $110,000 ($30,000 + $80,000) of taxes paid in those years.

For accounting as well as tax purposes, the $110,000 represents the tax effect (tax benefit) of the loss carryback. Groh should recognize this tax effect in 2012, the loss year. Since the tax loss gives rise to a refund that is both measurable and currently realizable, Groh should recognize the associated tax benefit in this loss period.

Groh makes the following journal entry for 2012.

Income Tax Refund Receivable	110,000	
Benefit Due to Loss Carryback (Income Tax Expense)		110,000

Groh reports the account debited, Income Tax Refund Receivable, on the balance sheet as a current asset at December 31, 2012. It reports the account credited on the income statement for 2012 as shown in Illustration 19-31.

GROH INC. INCOME STATEMENT (PARTIAL) FOR 2012	
Operating loss before income taxes	$(500,000)
Income tax benefit	
Benefit due to loss carryback	110,000
Net loss	$(390,000)

ILLUSTRATION 19-31
Recognition of Benefit of the Loss Carryback in the Loss Year

Since the $500,000 net operating loss for 2012 exceeds the $300,000 total taxable income from the 2 preceding years, Groh carries forward the remaining $200,000 loss.

Loss Carryforward Example

If a carryback fails to fully absorb a net operating loss, or if the company decides not to carry the loss back, then it can carry forward the loss for up to 20 years.[3] Because companies use carryforwards to offset future taxable income, the **tax effect of a loss carryforward** represents **future tax savings**. Realization of the future tax benefit depends on future earnings, an uncertain prospect.

The key accounting issue is whether there should be different requirements for recognition of a deferred tax asset for (a) deductible temporary differences, and (b) operating

---

[3]The length of the carryforward and carryback periods has varied. The carryforward period has increased from 7 years to 20 years over a period of time. As part of the Economic Recovery Act of 2009, Congress enacted a temporary extension of the carryback period from two to five years for operating losses incurred in 2008 and 2009. It is estimated that the companies in the S&P 500 will reap a refund of $5 billion due to this change. See D. Zion, A. Varshney, and C. Cornett, "Spinning Losses into Gold," *Equity Research—Accounting and Tax*, Credit Suisse (November 12, 2009).

loss carryforwards. The FASB's position is that in substance these items are the same—both are tax-deductible amounts in future years. As a result, the Board concluded that there **should not be different requirements** for recognition of a deferred tax asset from deductible temporary differences and operating loss carryforwards.[4]

Carryforward without Valuation Allowance

To illustrate the accounting for an operating loss carryforward, return to the Groh example from the preceding section. In 2012, the company records the tax effect of the $200,000 loss carryforward as a deferred tax asset of $80,000 ($200,000 × 40%), assuming that the enacted future tax rate is 40 percent. Groh records the benefits of the carryback and the carryforward in 2012 as follows.

To recognize benefit of loss carryback

Income Tax Refund Receivable	110,000	
Benefit Due to Loss Carryback (Income Tax Expense)		110,000

To recognize benefit of loss carryforward

Deferred Tax Asset	80,000	
Benefit Due to Loss Carryforward (Income Tax Expense)		80,000

Groh realizes the income tax refund receivable of $110,000 immediately as a refund of taxes paid in the past. It establishes a Deferred Tax Asset for the benefits of future tax savings. The two accounts credited are contra income tax expense items, which Groh presents on the 2012 income statement shown in Illustration 19-32.

ILLUSTRATION 19-32
Recognition of the Benefit of the Loss Carryback and Carryforward in the Loss Year

GROH INC.		
INCOME STATEMENT (PARTIAL) FOR 2012		
Operating loss before income taxes		$(500,000)
Income tax benefit		
Benefit due to loss carryback	$110,000	
Benefit due to loss carryforward	80,000	190,000
Net loss		$(310,000)

The current tax benefit of $110,000 is the income tax refundable for the year. Groh determines this amount by applying the carryback provisions of the tax law to the taxable loss for 2012. The $80,000 is the **deferred tax benefit** for the year, which results from an increase in the deferred tax asset.

For 2013, assume that Groh returns to profitable operations and has taxable income of $250,000 (prior to adjustment for the NOL carryforward), subject to a 40 percent tax rate. Groh then realizes the benefits of the carryforward for tax purposes in 2013, which it recognized for accounting purposes in 2012. Groh computes the income taxes payable for 2013 as shown in Illustration 19-33.

ILLUSTRATION 19-33
Computation of Income Taxes Payable with Realized Loss Carryforward

Taxable income prior to loss carryforward	$ 250,000
Loss carryforward deduction	(200,000)
Taxable income for 2013	50,000
Tax rate	40%
Income taxes payable for 2013	$ 20,000

Groh records income taxes in 2013 as follows.

Income Tax Expense	100,000	
Deferred Tax Asset		80,000
Income Taxes Payable		20,000

---

[4]This requirement is controversial because many believe it is inappropriate to recognize deferred tax assets except when assured beyond a reasonable doubt. Others argue that companies should never recognize deferred tax assets for loss carryforwards until realizing the income in the future.

The benefits of the NOL carryforward, realized in 2013, reduce the Deferred Tax Asset account to zero.

The 2013 income statement that appears in Illustration 19-34 does **not report** the tax effects of either the loss carryback or the loss carryforward, because Groh had reported both previously.

GROH INC.
INCOME STATEMENT (PARTIAL) FOR 2013

Income before income taxes		$250,000
Income tax expense		
Current	$20,000	
Deferred	80,000	100,000
Net income		$150,000

ILLUSTRATION 19-34
Presentation of the Benefit of Loss Carryforward Realized in 2013, Recognized in 2012

Carryforward with Valuation Allowance

Let us return to the Groh example. Assume that it is more likely than not that Groh will *not* realize the entire NOL carryforward in future years. In this situation, Groh records the tax benefits of $110,000 associated with the $300,000 NOL carryback, as we previously described. In addition, it records a Deferred Tax Asset of $80,000 ($200,000 × 40%) for the potential benefits related to the loss carryforward, and an allowance to reduce the deferred tax asset by the same amount. Groh makes the following journal entries in 2012.

To recognize benefit of loss carryback

Income Tax Refund Receivable	110,000	
Benefit Due to Loss Carryback (Income Tax Expense)		110,000

To recognize benefit of loss carryforward

Deferred Tax Asset	80,000	
Benefit Due to Loss Carryforward (Income Tax Expense)		80,000

To record allowance amount

Benefit Due to Loss Carryforward (Income Tax Expense)	80,000	
Allowance to Reduce Deferred Tax Asset to Expected Realizable Value		80,000

The latter entry indicates that because positive evidence of sufficient quality and quantity is unavailable to counteract the negative evidence, Groh needs a valuation allowance.

Illustration 19-35 shows Groh's 2012 income statement presentation.

GROH INC.
INCOME STATEMENT (PARTIAL) FOR 2012

Operating loss before income taxes	$(500,000)
Income tax benefit	
Benefit due to loss carryback	110,000
Net loss	$(390,000)

ILLUSTRATION 19-35
Recognition of Benefit of Loss Carryback Only

In 2013, assuming that Groh has taxable income of $250,000 (before considering the carryforward), subject to a tax rate of 40 percent, it realizes the deferred tax asset. It thus no longer needs the allowance. Groh records the following entries.

To record current and deferred income taxes

Income Tax Expense	100,000	
Deferred Tax Asset		80,000
Income Taxes Payable		20,000

To eliminate allowance and recognize loss carryforward

Allowance to Reduce Deferred Tax Asset to Expected Realizable Value	80,000	
Benefit Due to Loss Carryforward (Income Tax Expense)		80,000

Groh reports the $80,000 Benefit Due to the Loss Carryforward on the 2013 income statement. The company did not recognize it in 2012 because it was more likely than not that it would not be realized. Assuming that Groh derives the income for 2013 from continuing operations, it prepares the income statement as shown in Illustration 19-36.

ILLUSTRATION 19-36
Recognition of Benefit of
Loss Carryforward When
Realized

GROH INC.		
INCOME STATEMENT (PARTIAL) FOR 2013		
Income before income taxes		$250,000
Income tax expense		
Current	$ 20,000	
Deferred	80,000	
Benefit due to loss carryforward	(80,000)	20,000
Net income		$230,000

Another method is to report only one line for total income tax expense of $20,000 on the face of the income statement and disclose the components of income tax expense in the notes to the financial statements.

Valuation Allowance Revisited

A company should consider all positive and negative information in determining whether it needs a valuation allowance. Whether the company will realize a deferred tax asset depends on whether sufficient taxable income exists or will exist within the carryforward period available under tax law. Illustration 19-37 shows possible sources of taxable income that may be available under the tax law to realize a tax benefit for deductible temporary differences and carryforwards.[5]

ILLUSTRATION 19-37
Possible Sources of
Taxable Income

See the FASB
Codification section
(page 1180).

Taxable Income Sources
a. Future reversals of existing taxable temporary differences
b. Future taxable income exclusive of reversing temporary differences and carryforwards
c. Taxable income in prior carryback year(s) if carryback is permitted under the tax law
d. **Tax-planning strategies** that would, if necessary, be implemented to: (1) Accelerate taxable amounts to utilize expiring carryforwards   (2) Change the character of taxable or deductible amounts from ordinary income or loss to capital gain or loss   (3) Switch from tax-exempt to taxable investments. [1]

If any one of these sources is sufficient to support a conclusion that a valuation allowance is unnecessary, a company need not consider other sources.

Forming a conclusion that a valuation allowance is not needed is difficult when there is negative evidence such as cumulative losses in recent years. Companies may also cite positive evidence indicating that a valuation allowance is not needed. Illustration 19-38 presents examples (not prerequisites) of evidence to consider when determining the need for a valuation allowance.[6]

---

[5]Companies implement a tax-planning strategy to realize a tax benefit for an operating loss or tax credit carryforward before it expires. Companies consider tax-planning strategies when assessing the need for and amount of a valuation allowance for deferred tax assets.

[6]In contrast to the valuation allowance issue for Citigroup in the opening story, General Motors announced that it would record a charge of $39 billion for the third quarter of 2007 related to establishing a valuation allowance against its deferred assets in the United States, Canada, and Germany. The company noted that this large loss was taken because of the company's three-year historical loss up to the third quarter of 2007, its losses related to its mortgage business in GMAC financial services, and the challenging near-term automotive market conditions in the United States. and Germany. These all indicate that it will be more likely than not that GM will not realize its deferred tax asset.

Negative Evidence
a. A history of operating loss or tax credit carryforwards expiring unused
b. Losses expected in early future years (by a presently profitable entity)
c. Unsettled circumstances that, if unfavorably resolved, would adversely affect future operations and profit levels on a continuing basis in future years
d. A carryback, carryforward period that is so brief that it would limit realization of tax benefits if (1) a significant deductible temporary difference is expected to reverse in a single year or (2) the enterprise operates in a traditionally cyclical business.

Positive Evidence
a. Existing contracts or firm sales backlog that will produce more than enough taxable income to realize the deferred tax asset based on existing sale prices and cost structures
b. An excess of appreciated asset value over the tax basis of the entity's net assets in an amount sufficient to realize the deferred tax asset
c. A strong earnings history exclusive of the loss that created the future deductible amount (tax loss carryforward or deductible temporary difference) coupled with evidence indicating that the loss is an aberration rather than a continuing condition (for example, the result of an unusual, infrequent, or extraordinary item). [2]

ILLUSTRATION 19-38
Evidence to Consider in Evaluating the Need for a Valuation Account

The use of a valuation allowance provides a company with an opportunity to manage its earnings. As one accounting expert notes, "The 'more likely than not' provision is perhaps the most judgmental clause in accounting." Some companies may set up a valuation account and then use it to increase income as needed. Others may take the income immediately to increase capital or to offset large negative charges to income.

INTERNATIONAL PERSPECTIVE

Under IFRS *(IAS 12)*, a company may not recognize a deferred tax asset unless realization is "probable." However, "probable" is not defined in the standard, leading to diversity in the recognition of deferred tax assets.

NOLs: GOOD NEWS OR BAD?

Here are some net operating loss numbers reported by several notable companies.

What do the numbers mean?

NOLs ($ in millions)

Company	Income (Loss)	Operating Loss Carryforward	Tax Benefit (Deferred Tax Asset)	Comment
Delta Airlines, Inc.	($5,198.00)	$7,500.00	$2,848.00	Begins to expire in 2022. Valuation allowance recorded.
Goodyear	114.80	1,306.60	457.30	Begins to expire in next year. Full valuation allowance.
Kodak	556.00	509.00	234.00	Begins to expire in next year. Valuation allowance on foreign credits only.
Yahoo Inc.	42.82	5,400.00	1,443.50	State and federal carryforwards. Begins to expire in next year. Valuation allowance recorded.

All of these companies are using the carryforward provisions of the tax code for their NOLs. For many of them, the NOL is an amount far exceeding their reported profits. Why carry forward the loss to get the tax deduction? First, the company may have already used up the carryback provision, which allows only a two-year carryback period. (Carryforwards can be claimed up to 20 years in the future.) In some cases, management expects the tax rates in the future to be higher. This difference in expected rates provides a bigger tax benefit if the losses are carried forward and matched against future income. Is there a downside? To realize the benefits of carryforwards, a company must have future taxable income in the carryforward period in order to claim the NOL deductions. As we learned, if it is more likely than not that a company will not have taxable income, it must record a valuation allowance (and increased tax expense). As the data above indicate, recording a valuation allowance to reflect the uncertainty of realizing the tax benefits has merit. But for some, the NOL benefits begin to expire in the following year, which may be not enough time to generate sufficient taxable income in order to claim the NOL deduction.

Source: Company annual reports.

FINANCIAL STATEMENT PRESENTATION

Balance Sheet

Deferred tax accounts are reported on the balance sheet as assets and liabilities. Companies should classify these accounts as a net current amount and a net noncurrent amount. **An individual deferred tax liability or asset is classified as current or noncurrent based on the classification of the related asset or liability for financial reporting purposes.**

A company considers a deferred tax asset or liability to be related to an asset or liability, if reduction of the asset or liability causes the temporary difference to reverse or turn around. A company should classify a deferred tax liability or asset that is unrelated to an asset or liability for financial reporting, including a deferred tax asset related to a loss carryforward, according to the expected reversal date of the temporary difference.

To illustrate, assume that Morgan Inc. records bad debt expense using the allowance method for accounting purposes and the direct write-off method for tax purposes. It currently has Accounts Receivable and Allowance for Doubtful Accounts balances of $2 million and $100,000, respectively. In addition, given a 40 percent tax rate, Morgan has a debit balance in the Deferred Tax Asset account of $40,000 (40% × $100,000). It considers the $40,000 debit balance in the Deferred Tax Asset account to be related to the Accounts Receivable and the Allowance for Doubtful Accounts balances because collection or write-off of the receivables will cause the temporary difference to reverse. Therefore, Morgan classifies the Deferred Tax Asset account as current, the same as the Accounts Receivable and Allowance for Doubtful Accounts balances.

In practice, most companies engage in a large number of transactions that give rise to deferred taxes. Companies should classify the balances in the deferred tax accounts on the balance sheet in two categories: one for the net current amount, and one for the net noncurrent amount. We summarize this procedure as follows.

1. *Classify the amounts as current or noncurrent.* If related to a specific asset or liability, classify the amounts in the same manner as the related asset or liability. If not related, classify them on the basis of the expected reversal date of the temporary difference.

2. *Determine the net current amount* by summing the various deferred tax assets and liabilities classified as current. If the net result is an asset, report it on the balance sheet as a current asset; if a liability, report it as a current liability.

3. *Determine the net noncurrent amount* by summing the various deferred tax assets and liabilities classified as noncurrent. If the net result is an asset, report it on the balance sheet as a noncurrent asset; if a liability, report it as a long-term liability.

To illustrate, assume that K. Scott Company has four deferred tax items at December 31, 2012. Illustration 19-39 shows an analysis of these four temporary differences as current or noncurrent.

K. Scott classifies as current a deferred tax asset of $9,000 ($42,000 + $12,000 − $45,000). It also reports as noncurrent a deferred tax liability of $214,000. Consequently, K. Scott's December 31, 2012, balance sheet reports deferred income taxes as shown in Illustration 19-40.

Temporary Difference	Resulting Deferred Tax (Asset)	Liability	Related Balance Sheet Account	Classification
1. Rent collected in advance: recognized when earned for accounting purposes and when received for tax purposes.	$(42,000)		Unearned Rent	Current
2. Use of straight-line depreciation for accounting purposes and accelerated depreciation for tax purposes.		$214,000	Equipment	Noncurrent
3. Recognition of profits on installment sales during period of sale for accounting purposes and during period of collection for tax purposes.		45,000	Installment Accounts Receivable	Current
4. Warranty liabilities: recognized for accounting purposes at time of sale; for tax purpose at time paid.	(12,000)		Estimated Liability under Warranties	Current
Totals	$(54,000)	$259,000		

ILLUSTRATION 19-39
Classification of Temporary Differences as Current or Noncurrent

Current assets	
Deferred tax asset	$ 9,000
Long-term liabilities	
Deferred tax liability	$214,000

ILLUSTRATION 19-40
Balance Sheet Presentation of Deferred Income Taxes

As we indicated earlier, a deferred tax asset or liability **may not be related** to an asset or liability for financial reporting purposes. One example is an operating loss carryforward. In this case, a company records a deferred tax asset, but there is no related, identifiable asset or liability for financial reporting purposes. In these limited situations, deferred income taxes are classified according to the **expected reversal date** of the temporary difference. That is, a company should report the tax effect of any temporary difference reversing next year as current, and the remainder as non-current. If a deferred tax asset is noncurrent, a company should classify it in the "Other assets" section.

The total of all deferred tax liabilities, the total of all deferred tax assets, and the total valuation allowance should be disclosed. In addition, companies should disclose the following: (1) any net change during the year in the total valuation allowance, and (2) the types of temporary differences, carryforwards, or carrybacks that give rise to significant portions of deferred tax liabilities and assets.

Income taxes payable is reported as a current liability on the balance sheet. Corporations make estimated tax payments to the Internal Revenue Service quarterly. They record these estimated payments by a debit to Prepaid Income Taxes. As a result, the balance of the Income Taxes Payable offsets the balance of the Prepaid Income Taxes account when reporting income taxes on the balance sheet.

INTERNATIONAL PERSPECTIVE

IFRS requires that deferred tax assets and liabilities be classified as noncurrent, regardless of the classification of the underlying asset or liability.

Income Statement

Companies should allocate income tax expense (or benefit) to continuing operations, discontinued operations, extraordinary items, and prior period adjustments. This approach is referred to as intraperiod tax allocation.

Gateway to the Profession

Expanded Discussion of Intraperiod Tax Allocation

In addition, companies should disclose the significant components of income tax expense attributable to continuing operations:

1. Current tax expense or benefit.

2. Deferred tax expense or benefit, exclusive of other components listed below.

3. Investment tax credits.

4. Government grants (if recognized as a reduction of income tax expense).

5. The benefits of operating loss carryforwards (resulting in a reduction of income tax expense).

6. Tax expense that results from allocating tax benefits either directly to paid-in capital or to reduce goodwill or other noncurrent intangible assets of an acquired entity.

7. Adjustments of a deferred tax liability or asset for enacted changes in tax laws or rates or a change in the tax status of a company.

8. Adjustments of the beginning-of-the-year balance of a valuation allowance because of a change in circumstances that causes a change in judgment about the realizability of the related deferred tax asset in future years.

In the notes, companies must also reconcile (using percentages or dollar amounts) income tax expense attributable to continuing operations with the amount that results from applying domestic federal statutory tax rates to pretax income from continuing significant reconciling items. Illustration 19-41 presents an example from the 2009 annual report of **PepsiCo, Inc.**

These income tax disclosures are required for several reasons:

1. *Assessing quality of earnings.* Many investors seeking to assess the quality of a company's earnings are interested in the reconciliation of pretax financial income to taxable income. Analysts carefully examine earnings that are enhanced by a favorable tax effect, particularly if the tax effect is nonrecurring. For example, the tax disclosure in Illustration 19-41 indicates that PepsiCo's effective tax rate decreased from 26.7 percent in 2008 to 26% percent in 2009 (due to lower foreign taxes and "other"). This decrease in the effective tax rate increased income for 2009.

2. *Making better predictions of future cash flows.* Examination of the deferred portion of income tax expense provides information as to whether taxes payable are likely to be higher or lower in the future. In PepsiCo's case, analysts expect future taxable amounts and higher tax payments, due to realization of gains on equity investments, lower deprecation in the future, and higher payments for pension expense. PepsiCo expects future deductible amounts and lower tax payments due to deductions for carryforwards, employee benefits, and state taxes. These deferred tax items indicate that actual tax payments for PepsiCo will be higher than the tax expense reported on the income statement in the future.[7]

---

[7]An article by R. P. Weber and J. E. Wheeler, "Using Income Tax Disclosures to Explore Significant Economic Transactions," *Accounting Horizons* (September 1992), discusses how analysts use deferred tax disclosures to assess the quality of earnings and to predict future cash flows.

PepsiCo, Inc.
(in millions)

ILLUSTRATION 19-41
Disclosure of Income
Taxes—PepsiCo, Inc.

Note 5—Income Taxes (in part)	2009	2008
Income before income taxes		
U.S.	$4,209	$3,274
Foreign	3,870	3,771
	$8,079	$7,045
Provision for income taxes		
Current: U.S. Federal	$1,238	$ 815
Foreign	473	732
State	124	87
	1,835	1,634
Deferred: U.S. Federal	223	313
Foreign	21	(69)
State	21	1
	265	245
	$2,100	$1,879
Tax rate reconciliation		
U.S. Federal statutory tax rate	35.0%	35.0%
State income tax, net of U.S. Federal tax benefit	1.2	0.8
Lower taxes on foreign results	(7.9)	(8.0)
Other, net	(2.3)	(1.1)
Annual tax rate	26.0%	26.7%
Deferred tax liabilities		
Investments in noncontrolled affiliates	$1,120	$1,193
Property, plant and equipment	1,056	881
Intangible assets other than nondeductible goodwill	417	295
Other	68	73
Gross deferred tax liabilities	2,661	2,442
Deferred tax assets		
Net carryforwards	624	682
Stock-based compensation	410	410
Retiree medical benefits	508	495
Other employee-related benefits	442	428
Pension benefits	179	345
Deductible state tax and interest benefits	256	230
Other	560	677
Gross deferred tax assets	2,979	3,267
Valuation allowances	(586)	(657)
Deferred tax assets, net	2,393	2,610
Net deferred tax liabilities (assets)	$ 268	$ (168)
Deferred taxes included within:		
Assets:		
Prepaid expenses and other current assets	$ 391	$ 372
Other assets	–	$ 22
Liabilities:		
Deferred income taxes	$ 659	$ 226
Analysis of valuation allowances		
Balance, beginning of year	$ 657	$ 695
(Benefit/provision)	(78)	(5)
Other additions/(deductions)	7	(33)
Balance, end of year	$ 586	$ 667

Labels at right of table:
- Current and deferred tax expense
- Tax rate reconciliation
- Deferred tax liabilities and deferred tax assets
- Valuation allowance adjustments

Carryforwards and allowances

Operating loss carryforwards totaling $6.4 billion at year-end 2009 are being carried forward in a number of foreign and state jurisdictions where we are permitted to use tax operating losses from prior periods to reduce future taxable income. These operating losses will expire as follows: $0.2 billion in 2010, $5.5 billion between 2011 and 2029 and $0.7 billion may be carried forward indefinitely. We establish valuation allowances for our deferred tax assets if, based on the available evidence, it is more likely than not that some portion or all of the deferred tax assets will not be realized.

3. *Predicting future cash flows for operating loss carryforwards.* Companies should disclose the amounts and expiration dates of any operating loss carryforwards for tax purposes. From this disclosure, analysts determine the amount of income that the company may recognize in the future on which it will pay no income tax. For example, the PepsiCo disclosure in Illustration 19-41 indicates that PepsiCo has $6.4 billion in net operating loss carryforwards that it can use to reduce future taxes. However, the valuation allowance indicates that $586 million of deferred tax assets may not be realized in the future.

Loss carryforwards can be valuable to a potential acquirer. For example, as mentioned earlier, Yahoo! has a substantial net operating loss carryforward. A potential acquirer would find Yahoo more valuable as a result of these carryforwards. That is, the acquirer may be able to use these carryforwards to shield future income. However the acquiring company has to be careful, because the structure of the deal may lead to a situation where the deductions will be severely limited.

Much the same issue arises in companies emerging from bankruptcy. In many cases these companies have large NOLs, but the value of the losses may be limited. This is because any gains related to the cancellation of liabilities in bankruptcy must be offset against the NOLs. For example, when Kmart Holding Corp. emerged from bankruptcy in early 2004, it disclosed NOL carryforwards approximating $3.8 billion. At the same time, Kmart disclosed cancellation of debt gains that reduced the value of the NOL carryforward. These reductions soured the merger between Kmart and Sears Roebuck because the cancellation of the indebtedness gains reduced the value of the Kmart carryforwards to the merged company by $3.74 billion.[8]

Uncertain Tax Positions

Whenever there is a contingency, companies determine if the contingency is *probable* and can be reasonably estimated. If both of these criteria are met, the company records the contingency in the financial statements. These guidelines also apply to uncertain tax positions. Uncertain tax positions are tax positions for which the tax authorities may disallow a deduction in whole or in part. Uncertain tax positions often arise when a company takes an aggressive approach in its tax planning. Examples are instances in which the tax law is unclear or the company may believe that the risk of audit is low. Uncertain tax positions give rise to tax benefits either by reducing income tax expense or related payables or by increasing an income tax refund receivable or deferred tax asset.

Unfortunately, companies have not applied these provisions consistently in accounting and reporting of uncertain tax positions. Some companies have not recognized a tax benefit unless it is probable that the benefit will be realized and can be reasonably estimated. Other companies have used a lower threshold, such as that found in the existing authoritative literature. As we have learned, the lower threshold—described as *"more likely than not"*—means that the company believes it has at least a 51 percent chance that the uncertain tax position will pass muster with the taxing authorities. Thus, there has been diversity in practice concerning the accounting and reporting of uncertain tax positions.

---

[8]P. McConnell, J. Pegg, C. Senyak, and D. Mott, "The ABCs of NOLs," *Accounting Issues*, Bear Stearns Equity Research (June 2005). In addition, some U.S. banks hope to cash in tax credits by acquiring weaker banks with operating losses and housing credits, arising from the credit crisis. See D. Palletta, "Goldman Looks to Buy Fannie Tax Credits," *Wall Street Journal* (November 2, 2009). The IRS frowns on acquisitions done solely to obtain operating loss carryforwards. If it determines that the merger is solely tax-motivated, the IRS disallows the deductions. But because it is very difficult to determine whether a merger is or is not tax-motivated, the "purchase of operating loss carryforwards" continues.

As a result, the FASB has issued rules for companies to follow to determine whether it is "more likely than not" that tax positions will be sustained upon audit. [3] If the probability is more than 50 percent, companies may reduce their liability or increase their assets. If the probability is less that 50 percent, companies may not record the tax benefit. In determining "more likely than not," companies must assume that they will be audited by the tax authorities. If the recognition threshold is passed, companies must then estimate the amount to record as an adjustment to their tax assets and liabilities. (This estimation process is complex and is beyond the scope of this textbook.)

Companies will experience varying financial statement effects upon adoption of these rules. Those with a history of conservative tax strategies may have their tax liabilities decrease or their tax assets increase. Others that followed more aggressive tax planning may have to increase their liabilities or reduce their assets, with a resulting negative effect on net income. For example, in 2007, PepsiCo recorded a $7 million increase to retained earnings upon adoption of the guidelines.

SHELTERED

What do the numbers mean?

Companies employ various tax strategies to reduce their tax bills and their effective tax rates. The following table reports some high-profile cases in which profitable companies paid little income tax and, in some cases, got tax refunds.

Company	Pretax income ($ millions)	Federal Tax Paid (Refund) ($ millions)	Tax Rate (%)
Enron	$ 1,785	$(381)	(21.34)%
El Paso Energy	1,638	(254)	(15.51)
Goodyear	442	(23)	(5.20)
Navistar	1,368	28	2.05
General Motors	12,468	740	5.94

These companies used various tools to lower their tax bills, including off-shore tax shelters, tax deferrals, and hefty use of stock options, the cost of which reduce taxable income but do not affect pretax financial income. Thus, companies can use various provisions in the tax code to reduce their effective tax rate well below the statutory rate of 35 percent.

One IRS provision designed to curb excessive tax avoidance is the alternative minimum tax (AMT). Companies compute their potential tax liability under the AMT, adjusting for various preference items that reduce their tax bills under the regular tax code. (Examples of such preference items are accelerated depreciation methods and the installment method for revenue recognition.) Companies must pay the higher of the two tax obligations computed under the AMT and the regular tax code. But, as indicated by the cases above, some profitable companies avoid high tax bills, even in the presence of the AMT. Indeed, a recent study by the Government Accounting Office found that roughly two-thirds of U.S. and foreign corporations paid no federal income taxes from 1998–2005. Many citizens and public-interest groups cite corporate avoidance of income taxes as a reason for more tax reform.

Source: H. Gleckman, D. Foust, M. Arndt, and K. Kerwin, "Tax Dodging: Enron Isn't Alone," *BusinessWeek* (March 4, 2002), pp. 40–41; and L. Browning, "Study Tallies Corporations Not Paying Income Tax," *New York Times* (August 13, 2008), p. C3.

REVIEW OF THE ASSET-LIABILITY METHOD

The FASB believes that the asset-liability method (sometimes referred to as the **liability approach**) is the most consistent method for accounting for income taxes. One objective of this approach is to recognize the amount of taxes payable or refundable for the current year. A second objective is to recognize **deferred tax**

10 LEARNING OBJECTIVE
Indicate the basic principles of the asset-liability method.

liabilities and assets for the **future tax consequences** of events that have been recognized in the financial statements or tax returns.

To implement the objectives, companies apply some basic principles in accounting for income taxes at the date of the financial statements, as listed in Illustration 19-42. **[4]**

ILLUSTRATION 19-42
Basic Principles of the
Asset-Liability Method

Basic Principles
a. A current tax liability or asset is recognized for the estimated taxes payable or refundable on the tax return for the current year.
b. A deferred tax liability or asset is recognized for the estimated future tax effects attributable to temporary differences and carryforwards.
c. The measurement of current and deferred tax liabilities and assets is based on provisions of the enacted tax law; the effects of future changes in tax laws or rates are not anticipated.
d. The measurement of deferred tax assets is reduced, if necessary, by the amount of any tax benefits that, based on available evidence, are not expected to be realized.

Illustration 19-43 diagrams the procedures for implementing the asset-liability method.

ILLUSTRATION 19-43
Procedures for
Computing and Reporting
Deferred Income Taxes

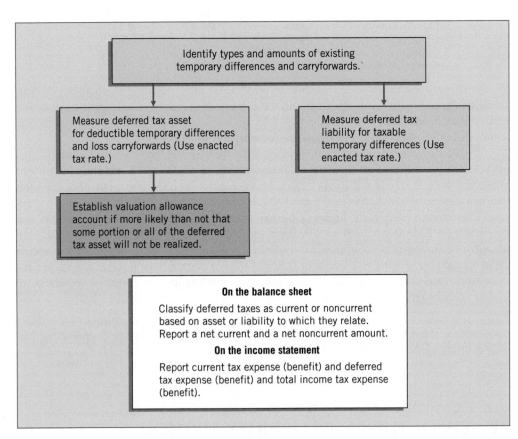

**Gateway to
the Profession**

*Discussion of
Conceptual Approaches
to Interperiod Tax
Allocation*

As an aid to understanding deferred income taxes, we provide the following glossary.

KEY DEFERRED INCOME TAX TERMS

CARRYBACKS. Deductions or credits that cannot be utilized on the tax return during a year and that may be carried back to reduce taxable income or taxes paid in a prior year. An **operating loss carryback** is an excess of tax deductions over gross income in a year. A **tax credit carryback** is the amount by which tax credits available for utilization exceed statutory limitations.

CARRYFORWARDS. Deductions or credits that cannot be utilized on the tax return during a year and that may be carried forward to reduce taxable income or taxes payable in a future year. An **operating loss carryforward** is an excess of tax deductions over gross income in a year. A **tax credit carryforward** is the amount by which tax credits available for utilization exceed statutory limitations.

CURRENT TAX EXPENSE (BENEFIT). The amount of income taxes paid or payable (or refundable) for a year as determined by applying the provisions of the enacted tax law to the taxable income or excess of deductions over revenues for that year.

DEDUCTIBLE TEMPORARY DIFFERENCE. Temporary differences that result in deductible amounts in future years when recovering or settling the related asset or liability, respectively.

DEFERRED TAX ASSET. The deferred tax consequences attributable to deductible temporary differences and carryforwards.

DEFERRED TAX CONSEQUENCES. The future effects on income taxes as measured by the enacted tax rate and provisions of the enacted tax law resulting from temporary differences and carryforwards at the end of the current year.

DEFERRED TAX EXPENSE (BENEFIT). The change during the year in a company's deferred tax liabilities and assets.

DEFERRED TAX LIABILITY. The deferred tax consequences attributable to taxable temporary differences.

INCOME TAXES. Domestic and foreign federal (national), state, and local (including franchise) taxes based on income.

INCOME TAXES CURRENTLY PAYABLE (REFUNDABLE). Refer to current tax expense (benefit).

INCOME TAX EXPENSE (BENEFIT). The sum of current tax expense (benefit) and deferred tax expense (benefit).

TAXABLE INCOME. The excess of taxable revenues over tax deductible expenses and exemptions for the year as defined by the governmental taxing authority.

TAXABLE TEMPORARY DIFFERENCE. Temporary differences that result in taxable amounts in future years when recovering or settling the related asset or liability, respectively.

TAX-PLANNING STRATEGY. An action that meets certain criteria and that a company implements to realize a tax benefit for an operating loss or tax credit carryforward before it expires. Companies consider tax-planning strategies when assessing the need for and amount of a valuation allowance for deferred tax assets.

TEMPORARY DIFFERENCE. A difference between the tax basis of an asset or liability and its reported amount in the financial statements that will result in taxable or deductible amounts in future years when recovering or settling the reported amount of the asset or liability, respectively.

VALUATION ALLOWANCE. The portion of a deferred tax asset for which it is more likely than not that a company will not realize a tax benefit.

INTERNATIONAL PERSPECTIVE

IFRS on income taxes is based on the same principles as GAAP—comprehensive recognition of deferred tax assets and liabilities.

You will want to read the **IFRS INSIGHTS** on pages 1199–1206

for discussion of IFRS related to income taxes.

SUMMARY OF LEARNING OBJECTIVES

1 **Identify differences between pretax financial income and taxable income.** Companies compute pretax financial income (or income for book purposes) in accordance with generally accepted accounting principles. They compute taxable income (or income for tax purposes) in accordance with prescribed tax regulations. Because tax regulations and GAAP differ in many ways, so frequently do pretax financial income and taxable income. Differences may exist, for example, in the timing of revenue recognition and the timing of expense recognition.

2 **Describe a temporary difference that results in future taxable amounts.** Revenue recognized for book purposes in the period earned but deferred and reported as revenue for tax purposes when collected results in future taxable amounts. The future taxable amounts will occur in the periods the company recovers the receivable and reports the collections as revenue for tax purposes. This results in a deferred tax liability.

3 **Describe a temporary difference that results in future deductible amounts.** An accrued warranty expense that a company pays for and deducts for tax purposes, in a period later than the period in which it incurs and recognizes it for book purposes, results in future deductible amounts. The future deductible amounts will occur in the periods during which the company settles the related liability for book purposes. This results in a deferred tax asset.

4 **Explain the purpose of a deferred tax asset valuation allowance.** A deferred tax asset should be reduced by a valuation allowance if, based on all available evidence, it is more likely than not (a level of likelihood that is at least slightly more than 50 percent) that it will not realize some portion or all of the deferred tax asset. The company should carefully consider all available evidence, both positive and negative, to determine whether, based on the weight of available evidence, it needs a valuation allowance.

5 **Describe the presentation of income tax expense in the income statement.** Significant components of income tax expense should be disclosed in the income statement or in the notes to the financial statements. The most commonly encountered components are the current expense (or benefit) and the deferred expense (or benefit).

6 **Describe various temporary and permanent differences.** Examples of temporary differences are: (1) revenue or gains that are taxable after recognition in financial income; (2) expenses or losses that are deductible after recognition in financial income; (3) revenues or gains that are taxable before recognition in financial income; (4) expenses or losses that are deductible before recognition in financial income. Examples of permanent differences are: (1) items recognized for financial reporting purposes but not for tax purposes, and (2) items recognized for tax purposes but not for financial reporting purposes.

7 **Explain the effect of various tax rates and tax rate changes on deferred income taxes.** Companies may use tax rates other than the current rate only after enactment of the future tax rates. When a change in the tax rate is enacted, a company should immediately recognize its effect on the deferred income tax accounts. The company reports the effects as an adjustment to income tax expense in the period of the change.

8 **Apply accounting procedures for a loss carryback and a loss carryforward.** A company may carry a net operating loss back two years and receive refunds for income taxes paid in those years. The loss is applied to the earlier year first and then to the second year. Any loss remaining after the two-year carryback may be carried forward up to 20 years to offset future taxable income. A company may forgo the loss carryback and use the loss carryforward, offsetting future taxable income for up to 20 years.

9 **Describe the presentation of deferred income taxes in financial statements.**
Companies report deferred tax accounts on the balance sheet as assets and liabilities.
These deferred tax accounts are classified as a net current and a net noncurrent amount.
Companies classify an individual deferred tax liability or asset as current or noncurrent
based on the classification of the related asset or liability for financial reporting. A deferred tax liability or asset that is not related to an asset or liability for financial reporting, including a deferred tax asset related to a loss carryforward, is classified according
to the expected reversal date of the temporary difference.

10 **Indicate the basic principles of the asset-liability method.** Companies apply
the following basic principles in accounting for income taxes at the date of the financial
statements: (1) Recognize a current tax liability or asset for the estimated taxes payable
or refundable on the tax return for the current year. (2) Recognize a deferred tax liability
or asset for the estimated future tax effects attributable to temporary differences and
carryforwards using the enacted tax rate. (3) Base the measurement of current and deferred tax liabilities and assets on provisions of the enacted tax law. (4) Reduce the measurement of deferred tax assets, if necessary, by the amount of any tax benefits that,
based on available evidence, companies do not expect to realize.

APPENDIX 19A   **COMPREHENSIVE EXAMPLE OF INTERPERIOD TAX ALLOCATION**

This appendix presents a comprehensive illustration of a deferred income tax
problem with several temporary and permanent differences. The example follows
one company through two complete years (2011 and 2012). **Study it carefully.** It
should help you understand the concepts and procedures presented in the
chapter.

11 LEARNING OBJECTIVE
Understand and apply the concepts and
procedures of interperiod tax allocation.

FIRST YEAR—2011

Allman Company, which began operations at the beginning of 2011, produces various
products on a contract basis. Each contract generates a gross profit of $80,000. Some of
Allman's contracts provide for the customer to pay on an installment basis. Under these
contracts, Allman collects one-fifth of the contract revenue in each of the following four
years. For financial reporting purposes, the company recognizes gross profit in the year
of completion (accrual basis); for tax purposes, Allman recognizes gross profit in the
year cash is collected (installment basis).
  Presented below is information related to Allman's operations for 2011.

1. In 2011, the company completed seven contracts that allow for the customer to pay
on an installment basis. Allman recognized the related gross profit of $560,000 for
financial reporting purposes. It reported only $112,000 of gross profit on installment
sales on the 2011 tax return. The company expects future collections on the related
installment receivables to result in taxable amounts of $112,000 in each of the next
four years.

2. At the beginning of 2011, Allman Company purchased depreciable assets with a cost
of $540,000. For financial reporting purposes, Allman depreciates these assets using
the straight-line method over a six-year service life. For tax purposes, the assets fall in
the five-year recovery class, and Allman uses the MACRS system. The depreciation
schedules for both financial reporting and tax purposes are shown on page 1174.

Year	Depreciation for Financial Reporting Purposes	Depreciation for Tax Purposes	Difference
2011	$ 90,000	$108,000	$(18,000)
2012	90,000	172,800	(82,800)
2013	90,000	103,680	(13,680)
2014	90,000	62,208	27,792
2015	90,000	62,208	27,792
2016	90,000	31,104	58,896
	$540,000	$540,000	$ –0–

3. The company warrants its product for two years from the date of completion of a contract. During 2011, the product warranty liability accrued for financial reporting purposes was $200,000, and the amount paid for the satisfaction of warranty liability was $44,000. Allman expects to settle the remaining $156,000 by expenditures of $56,000 in 2012 and $100,000 in 2013.

4. In 2011, nontaxable municipal bond interest revenue was $28,000.

5. During 2011, nondeductible fines and penalties of $26,000 were paid.

6. Pretax financial income for 2011, amounts to $412,000.

7. Tax rates enacted before the end of 2011 were:

2011	50%
2012 and later years	40%

8. The accounting period is the calendar year.

9. The company is expected to have taxable income in all future years.

Taxable Income and Income Taxes Payable—2011

The first step is to determine Allman Company's income taxes payable for 2011 by calculating its taxable income. Illustration 19A-1 shows this computation.

ILLUSTRATION 19A-1
Computation of Taxable Income, 2011

Pretax financial income for 2011	$412,000
Permanent differences:	
Nontaxable revenue—municipal bond interest	(28,000)
Nondeductible expenses—fines and penalties	26,000
Temporary differences:	
Excess gross profit per books ($560,000 − $112,000)	(448,000)
Excess depreciation per tax ($108,000 − $90,000)	(18,000)
Excess warranty expense per books ($200,000 − $44,000)	156,000
Taxable income for 2011	$100,000

Allman computes income taxes payable on taxable income for $100,000 as follows.

ILLUSTRATION 19A-2
Computation of Income Taxes Payable, End of 2011

Taxable income for 2011	$100,000
Tax rate	50%
Income taxes payable (current tax expense) for 2011	$ 50,000

Computing Deferred Income Taxes—End of 2011

The schedule in Illustration 19A-3 summarizes the temporary differences and the resulting future taxable and deductible amounts.

	Future Years					
	2012	2013	2014	2015	2016	Total
Future taxable (deductible) amounts:						
Installment sales	$112,000	$112,000	$112,000	$112,000		$448,000
Depreciation	(82,800)	(13,680)	27,792	27,792	$58,896	18,000
Warranty costs	(56,000)	(100,000)				(156,000)

ILLUSTRATION 19A-3
Schedule of Future Taxable and Deductible Amounts, End of 2011

Allman computes the amounts of deferred income taxes to be reported at the end of 2011 as shown in Illustration 19A-4.

Temporary Difference	Future Taxable (Deductible) Amounts	Tax Rate	Deferred Tax (Asset)	Liability
Installment sales	$448,000	40%		$179,200
Depreciation	18,000	40%		7,200
Warranty costs	(156,000)	40%	$(62,400)	
Totals	$310,000		$(62,400)	$186,400*

*Because only a single tax rate is involved in all relevant years, these totals can be reconciled: $310,000 × 40% = ($62,400) + $186,400.

ILLUSTRATION 19A-4
Computation of Deferred Income Taxes, End of 2011

A temporary difference is caused by the use of the accrual basis for financial reporting purposes and the installment method for tax purposes. This temporary difference will result in future taxable amounts, and hence, a deferred tax liability. Because of the installment contracts completed in 2011, a temporary difference of $448,000 originates that will reverse in equal amounts over the next four years. The company expects to have taxable income in all future years, and there is only one enacted tax rate applicable to all future years. Allman uses that rate (40 percent) to compute the entire deferred tax liability resulting from this temporary difference.

The temporary difference caused by different depreciation policies for books and for tax purposes originates over three years and then reverses over three years. This difference will cause deductible amounts in 2012 and 2013 and taxable amounts in 2014, 2015, and 2016. These amounts sum to a net future taxable amount of $18,000 (which is the cumulative temporary difference at the end of 2011). Because the company expects to have taxable income in all future years and because there is only one tax rate enacted for all of the relevant future years, Allman applies that rate to the net future taxable amount to determine the related net deferred tax liability.

The third temporary difference is caused by different methods of accounting for warranties. This difference will result in deductible amounts in each of the two future years it takes to reverse. Because the company expects to report a positive income on all future tax returns and because there is only one tax rate enacted for each of the relevant future years, Allman uses that 40 percent rate to calculate the resulting deferred tax asset.

Deferred Tax Expense (Benefit) and the Journal Entry to Record Income Taxes—2011

To determine the deferred tax expense (benefit), we need to compare the beginning and ending balances of the deferred income tax accounts. Illustration 19A-5 (on page 1476) shows that computation.

ILLUSTRATION 19A-5
Computation of Deferred
Tax Expense (Benefit),
2011

Deferred tax asset at the end of 2011	$ 62,400
Deferred tax asset at the beginning of 2011	–0–
Deferred tax expense (benefit)	$(62,400)
Deferred tax liability at the end of 2011	$186,400
Deferred tax liability at the beginning of 2011	–0–
Deferred tax expense (benefit)	$186,400

The $62,400 increase in the deferred tax asset causes a deferred tax benefit to be reported in the income statement. The $186,400 increase in the deferred tax liability during 2011 results in a deferred tax expense. These two amounts **net** to a deferred tax expense of $124,000 for 2011.

ILLUSTRATION 19A-6
Computation of Net
Deferred Tax Expense,
2011

Deferred tax expense (benefit)	$ (62,400)
Deferred tax expense (benefit)	186,400
Net deferred tax expense for 2011	$124,000

Allman then computes the total income tax expense as follows.

ILLUSTRATION 19A-7
Computation of Total
Income Tax Expense,
2011

Current tax expense for 2011	$ 50,000
Deferred tax expense for 2011	124,000
Income tax expense (total) for 2011	$174,000

Allman records income taxes payable, deferred income taxes, and income tax expense as follows.

Income Tax Expense	174,000	
Deferred Tax Asset	62,400	
Income Taxes Payable		50,000
Deferred Tax Liability		186,400

Financial Statement Presentation—2011

Companies should classify deferred tax assets and liabilities as current and noncurrent on the balance sheet based on the classifications of related assets and liabilities. Multiple categories of deferred taxes are classified into a net current amount and a net noncurrent amount. Illustration 19A-8 shows the classification of Allman's deferred tax accounts at the end of 2011.

ILLUSTRATION 19A-8
Classification of Deferred
Tax Accounts, End of
2011

Temporary Difference	Resulting Deferred Tax (Asset)	Liability	Related Balance Sheet Account	Classification
Installment sales		$179,200	Installment Receivable	Current
Depreciation		7,200	Plant Assets	Noncurrent
Warranty costs	$(62,400)		Warranty Obligation	Current
Totals	$(62,400)	$186,400		

For the first temporary difference, there is a related asset on the balance sheet, installment accounts receivable. Allman classifies that asset as current because it has a trade practice of selling to customers on an installment basis. Allman therefore classifies the resulting deferred tax liability as a current liability.

Certain assets on the balance sheet are related to the depreciation difference—the property, plant, and equipment being depreciated. Allman would classify the plant assets as noncurrent. Therefore, it also classifies the resulting deferred tax liability as noncurrent. Since the company's operating cycle is at least four years in length, Allman classifies the entire $156,000 warranty obligation as a current liability. Thus, it also classifies the related deferred tax asset of $62,400 as current.[9]

The balance sheet at the end of 2011 reports the following amounts.

Current liabilities	
Income taxes payable	$ 50,000
Deferred tax liability ($179,200 − $62,400)	116,800
Long-term liabilities	
Deferred tax liability	$ 7,200

ILLUSTRATION 19A-9
Balance Sheet
Presentation of Deferred
Taxes, 2011

Allman's income statement for 2011 reports the following.

Income before income taxes		$412,000
Income tax expense		
Current	$ 50,000	
Deferred	124,000	174,000
Net income		$238,000

ILLUSTRATION 19A-10
Income Statement
Presentation of Income
Tax Expense, 2011

SECOND YEAR—2012

1. During 2012, Allman collected $112,000 from customers for the receivables arising from contracts completed in 2011. The company expects recovery of the remaining receivables to result in taxable amounts of $112,000 in each of the following three years.

2. In 2012, the company completed four new contracts that allow for the customer to pay on an installment basis. These installment sales created new installment receivables. Future collections of these receivables will result in reporting gross profit of $64,000 for tax purposes in each of the next four years.

3. During 2012, Allman continued to depreciate the assets acquired in 2011 according to the depreciation schedules appearing on page 1174. Thus, depreciation amounted to $90,000 for financial reporting purposes and $172,800 for tax purposes.

4. An analysis at the end of 2012, of the product warranty liability account showed the following details.

Balance of liability at beginning of 2012	$156,000
Expense for 2012 income statement purposes	180,000
Amount paid for contracts completed in 2011	(56,000)
Amount paid for contracts completed in 2012	(50,000)
Balance of liability at end of 2012	$230,000

[9]If Allman's operating cycle were less than one year in length, the company would expect to settle $56,000 of the warranty obligation within one year of the December 31, 2011, balance sheet and would use current assets to do so. Thus $56,000 of the warranty obligation would be a current liability and the remaining $100,000 warranty obligation would be a long-term (noncurrent) liability. This would mean that Allman would classify $22,400 ($56,000 × 40%) of the related deferred tax asset as a current asset, and $40,000 ($100,000 × 40%) of the deferred tax asset as a noncurrent asset. *In doing homework problems, unless it is evident otherwise, assume a company's operating cycle is not longer than a year.*

The balance of the liability is expected to require expenditures in the future as follows.

$100,000 in 2013 due to 2011 contracts
$ 50,000 in 2013 due to 2012 contracts
$ 80,000 in 2014 due to 2012 contracts
$230,000

5. During 2012, nontaxable municipal bond interest revenue was $24,000.

6. Allman accrued a loss of $172,000 for financial reporting purposes because of pending litigation. This amount is not tax-deductible until the period the loss is realized, which the company estimates to be 2020.

7. Pretax financial income for 2012 amounts to $504,800.

8. The enacted tax rates still in effect are:

2011	50%
2012 and later years	40%

Taxable Income and Income Taxes Payable—2012

Allman computes taxable income for 2012 as follows.

ILLUSTRATION 19A-11
Computation of Taxable
Income, 2012

Pretax financial income for 2012	$504,800
Permanent difference:	
Nontaxable revenue—municipal bond interest	(24,000)
Reversing temporary differences:	
Collection on 2011 installment sales	112,000
Payments on warranties from 2011 contracts	(56,000)
Originating temporary differences:	
Excess gross profit per books—2012 contracts	(256,000)
Excess depreciation per tax	(82,800)
Excess warranty expense per books—2012 contracts	130,000
Loss accrual per books	172,000
Taxable income for 2012	$500,000

Income taxes payable for 2012 are as follows.

ILLUSTRATION 19A-12
Computation of Income
Taxes Payable, End of
2012

Taxable income for 2012	$500,000
Tax rate	40%
Income taxes payable (current tax expense) for 2012	$200,000

ILLUSTRATION 19A-13
Schedule of Future
Taxable and Deductible
Amounts, End of 2012

Computing Deferred Income Taxes—End of 2012

The schedule in Illustration 19A-13 summarizes the temporary differences existing at the end of 2012 and the resulting future taxable and deductible amounts.

	Future Years					
	2013	2014	2015	2016	2020	Total
Future taxable (deductible) amounts:						
Installment sales—2011	$112,000	$112,000	$112,000			$336,000
Installment sales—2012	64,000	64,000	64,000	$64,000		256,000
Depreciation	(13,680)	27,792	27,792	58,896		100,800
Warranty costs	(150,000)	(80,000)				(230,000)
Loss accrual					$(172,000)	(172,000)

Allman computes the amounts of deferred income taxes to be reported at the end of 2012 as follows.

Temporary Difference	Future Taxable (Deductible) Amounts	Tax Rate	Deferred Tax (Asset)	Liability
Installment sales	$592,000*	40%		$236,800
Depreciation	100,800	40%		40,320
Warranty costs	(230,000)	40%	$ (92,000)	
Loss accrual	(172,000)	40%	(68,800)	
Totals	$290,800		$(160,800)	$277,120**

*Cumulative temporary difference = $336,000 + $256,000
**Because of a flat tax rate, these totals can be reconciled: $290,800 × 40% = $(160,800) + $277,120

ILLUSTRATION 19A-14
Computation of Deferred Income Taxes, End of 2012

Deferred Tax Expense (Benefit) and the Journal Entry to Record Income Taxes—2012

To determine the deferred tax expense (benefit), Allman must compare the beginning and ending balances of the deferred income tax accounts, as shown in Illustration 19A-15.

Deferred tax asset at the end of 2012	$160,800
Deferred tax asset at the beginning of 2012	62,400
Deferred tax expense (benefit)	$ (98,400)
Deferred tax liability at the end of 2012	$277,120
Deferred tax liability at the beginning of 2012	186,400
Deferred tax expense (benefit)	$ 90,720

ILLUSTRATION 19A-15
Computation of Deferred Tax Expense (Benefit), 2012

The deferred tax expense (benefit) and the total income tax expense for 2012 are, therefore, as follows.

Deferred tax expense (benefit)	$ (98,400)
Deferred tax expense (benefit)	90,720
Deferred tax benefit for 2012	(7,680)
Current tax expense for 2012	200,000
Income tax expense (total) for 2012	$192,320

ILLUSTRATION 19A-16
Computation of Total Income Tax Expense, 2012

The deferred tax expense of $90,720 and the deferred tax benefit of $98,400 net to a deferred tax benefit of $7,680 for 2012.

Allman records income taxes for 2012 with the following journal entry.

Income Tax Expense	192,320	
Deferred Tax Asset	98,400	
Income Taxes Payable		200,000
Deferred Tax Liability		90,720

Financial Statement Presentation—2012

Illustration 19A-17 (on page 1180) shows the classification of Allman's deferred tax accounts at the end of 2012.

ILLUSTRATION 19A-17
Classification of Deferred Tax Accounts, End of 2012

Temporary Difference	Resulting Deferred Tax (Asset)	Liability	Related Balance Sheet Account	Classification
Installment sales		$236,800	Installment Receivables	Current
Depreciation		40,320	Plant Assets	Noncurrent
Warranty costs	$ (92,000)		Warranty Obligation	Current
Loss accrual	(68,800)		Litigation Obligation	Noncurrent
Totals	$(160,800)	$277,120		

The new temporary difference introduced in 2012 (due to the litigation loss accrual) results in a litigation obligation that is classified as a long-term liability. Thus, the related deferred tax asset is noncurrent.

Allman's balance sheet at the end of 2012 reports the following amounts.

ILLUSTRATION 19A-18
Balance Sheet Presentation of Deferred Taxes, End of 2012

Other assets (noncurrent)	
Deferred tax asset ($68,800 − $40,320)	$ 28,480
Current liabilities	
Income taxes payable	$200,000
Deferred tax liability ($236,800 − $92,000)	144,800

The income statement for 2012 reports the following.

ILLUSTRATION 19A-19
Income Statement Presentation of Income Tax Expense, 2012

Income before income taxes		$504,800
Income tax expense		
Current	$200,000	
Deferred	(7,680)	192,320
Net income		$312,480

SUMMARY OF LEARNING OBJECTIVE FOR APPENDIX 19A

11 **Understand and apply the concepts and procedures of interperiod tax allocation.** Accounting for deferred taxes involves the following steps: Calculate taxable income and income taxes payable for the year. Compute deferred income taxes at the end of the year. Determine deferred tax expense (benefit) and make the journal entry to record income taxes. Classify deferred tax assets and liabilities as current or noncurrent in the financial statements.

FASB CODIFICATION

FASB Codification References

[1] FASB ASC 740-10-30-18. [Predecessor literature: "Accounting for Income Taxes," *Statement of Financial Accounting Standards No. 109* (Norwalk, Conn.: FASB, 1992).]

[2] FASB ASC 740-10-30-21 & 22. [Predecessor literature: "Accounting for Income Taxes," *Statement of Financial Accounting Standards No. 109* (Norwalk, Conn.: FASB, 1992), paras. 23 and 24.]

[3] FASB ASC 740-10-25-6. [Predecessor literature: "Accounting for Uncertainty in Income Taxes," *FASB Interpretation No. 48* (Norwalk, Conn.: FASB, 2006).]

[4] FASB ASC 740-10-05. [Predecessor literature: "Accounting for Income Taxes," *Statement of Financial Accounting Standards No. 109* (Norwalk, Conn.: FASB, 1992), paras. 6 and 8.]

Exercises

If your school has a subscription to the FASB Codification, go to *http://aaahq.org/ascLogin.cfm* to log in and prepare responses to the following. Provide Codification references for your responses.

CE19-1 Access the glossary ("Master Glossary") to answer the following.

    (a) What is a deferred tax asset?

    (b) What is taxable income?

    (c) What is the definition of valuation allowance?

    (d) What is a deferred tax liability?

CE19-2 What are the two basic requirements applied to the measurement of current and deferred income taxes at the date of the financial statements?

CE19-3 A company wishes to conduct business in a foreign country that attracts businesses by granting "holidays" from income taxes for a certain period of time. Would the company have to disclose this "holiday" to the SEC? If so, what information must be disclosed?

CE19-4 When is a company allowed to initially recognize the financial statement effects of a tax position?

An additional Codification case can be found in the Using Your Judgment section, on page 1198.

Be sure to check the book's companion website for a Review and Analysis Exercise, with solution.

 Questions, Brief Exercises, Exercises, Problems, and many more resources are available for practice in WileyPLUS.

QUESTIONS

1. Explain the difference between pretax financial income and taxable income.

2. What are the two objectives of accounting for income taxes?

3. Interest on municipal bonds is referred to as a permanent difference when determining the proper amount to report for deferred taxes. Explain the meaning of permanent differences, and give two other examples.

4. Explain the meaning of a temporary difference as it relates to deferred tax computations, and give three examples.

5. Differentiate between an originating temporary difference and a reversing difference.

6. The book basis of depreciable assets for Erwin Co. is $900,000, and the tax basis is $700,000 at the end of 2013. The enacted tax rate is 34% for all periods. Determine the amount of deferred taxes to be reported on the balance sheet at the end of 2013.

7. Roth Inc. has a deferred tax liability of $68,000 at the beginning of 2013. At the end of 2013, it reports accounts receivable on the books at $90,000 and the tax basis at zero (its only temporary difference). If the enacted tax rate is

34% for all periods, and income taxes payable for the period is $230,000, determine the amount of total income tax expense to report for 2013.

8. What is the difference between a future taxable amount and a future deductible amount? When is it appropriate to record a valuation account for a deferred tax asset?

9. Pretax financial income for Lake Inc. is $300,000, and its taxable income is $100,000 for 2013. Its only temporary difference at the end of the period relates to a $70,000 difference due to excess depreciation for tax purposes. If the tax rate is 40% for all periods, compute the amount of income tax expense to report in 2013. No deferred income taxes existed at the beginning of the year.

10. How are deferred tax assets and deferred tax liabilities reported on the balance sheet?

11. Describe the procedures involved in segregating various deferred tax amounts into current and noncurrent categories.

12. How is it determined whether deferred tax amounts are considered to be "related" to specific asset or liability amounts?

13. At the end of the year, Falabella Co. has pretax financial income of $550,000. Included in the $550,000 is $70,000 interest income on municipal bonds, $25,000 fine for dumping hazardous waste, and depreciation of $60,000. Depreciation for tax purposes is $45,000. Compute income taxes payable, assuming the tax rate is 30% for all periods.

14. Addison Co. has one temporary difference at the beginning of 2012 of $500,000. The deferred tax liability established for this amount is $150,000, based on a tax rate of 30%. The temporary difference will provide the following taxable amounts: $100,000 in 2013, $200,000 in 2014, and $200,000 in 2015. If a new tax rate for 2015 of 20% is enacted into law at the end of 2012, what is the journal entry necessary in 2012 (if any) to adjust deferred taxes?

15. What are some of the reasons that the components of income tax expense should be disclosed and a reconciliation between the effective tax rate and the statutory tax rate be provided?

16. Differentiate between "loss carryback" and "loss carryforward." Which can be accounted for with the greater certainty when it arises? Why?

17. What are the possible treatments for tax purposes of a net operating loss? What are the circumstances that determine the option to be applied? What is the proper treatment of a net operating loss for financial reporting purposes?

18. What controversy relates to the accounting for net operating loss carryforwards?

19. What is an uncertain tax position, and what are the general guidelines for accounting for uncertain tax positions?

BRIEF EXERCISES

1 2 BE19-1 In 2012, Amirante Corporation had pretax financial income of $168,000 and taxable income of $120,000. The difference is due to the use of different depreciation methods for tax and accounting purposes. The effective tax rate is 40%. Compute the amount to be reported as income taxes payable at December 31, 2012.

1 2 BE19-2 Oxford Corporation began operations in 2012 and reported pretax financial income of $225,000 for the year. Oxford's tax depreciation exceeded its book depreciation by $40,000. Oxford's tax rate for 2012 and years thereafter is 30%. In its December 31, 2012, balance sheet, what amount of deferred tax liability should be reported?

9 BE19-3 Using the information from BE19-2, assume this is the only difference between Oxford's pretax financial income and taxable income. Prepare the journal entry to record the income tax expense, deferred income taxes, and income taxes payable, and show how the deferred tax liability will be classified on the December 31, 2012, balance sheet.

2 5 BE19-4 At December 31, 2012, Appaloosa Corporation had a deferred tax liability of $25,000. At December 31, 2013, the deferred tax liability is $42,000. The corporation's 2013 current tax expense is $48,000. What amount should Appaloosa report as total 2013 income tax expense?

1 3 BE19-5 At December 31, 2012, Suffolk Corporation had an estimated warranty liability of $105,000 for accounting purposes and $0 for tax purposes. (The warranty costs are not deductible until paid.) The effective tax rate is 40%. Compute the amount Suffolk should report as a deferred tax asset at December 31, 2012.

3 5 BE19-6 At December 31, 2012, Percheron Inc. had a deferred tax asset of $30,000. At December 31, 2013, the deferred tax asset is $59,000. The corporation's 2013 current tax expense is $61,000. What amount should Percheron report as total 2013 income tax expense?

4 BE19-7 At December 31, 2012, Hillyard Corporation has a deferred tax asset of $200,000. After a careful review of all available evidence, it is determined that it is more likely than not that $60,000 of this deferred tax asset will not be realized. Prepare the necessary journal entry.

5 BE19-8 Mitchell Corporation had income before income taxes of $195,000 in 2012. Mitchell's current income tax expense is $48,000, and deferred income tax expense is $30,000. Prepare Mitchell's 2012 income statement, beginning with Income before income taxes.

2 3 BE19-9 Shetland Inc. had pretax financial income of $154,000 in 2012. Included in the computation of that amount is insurance expense of $4,000 which is not deductible for tax purposes. In addition, depreciation for tax purposes exceeds accounting depreciation by $10,000. Prepare Shetland's journal entry to record 2012 taxes, assuming a tax rate of 45%.

2 BE19-10 Clydesdale Corporation has a cumulative temporary difference related to depreciation of $580,000 at December 31, 2012. This difference will reverse as follows: 2013, $42,000; 2014, $244,000; and 2015,

$294,000. Enacted tax rates are 34% for 2013 and 2014, and 40% for 2015. Compute the amount Clydesdale should report as a deferred tax liability at December 31, 2012.

7 **BE19-11** At December 31, 2012, Fell Corporation had a deferred tax liability of $680,000, resulting from future taxable amounts of $2,000,000 and an enacted tax rate of 34%. In May 2013, a new income tax act is signed into law that raises the tax rate to 40% for 2013 and future years. Prepare the journal entry for Fell to adjust the deferred tax liability.

8 **BE19-12** Conlin Corporation had the following tax information.

Year	Taxable Income	Tax Rate	Taxes Paid
2010	$300,000	35%	$105,000
2011	$325,000	30%	$ 97,500
2012	$400,000	30%	$120,000

In 2013, Conlin suffered a net operating loss of $480,000, which it elected to carry back. The 2013 enacted tax rate is 29%. Prepare Conlin's entry to record the effect of the loss carryback.

8 **BE19-13** Rode Inc. incurred a net operating loss of $500,000 in 2012. Combined income for 2010 and 2011 was $350,000. The tax rate for all years is 40%. Rode elects the carryback option. Prepare the journal entries to record the benefits of the loss carryback and the loss carryforward.

4 **8** **BE19-14** Use the information for Rode Inc. given in BE19-13. Assume that it is more likely than not that the entire net operating loss carryforward will not be realized in future years. Prepare all the journal entries necessary at the end of 2012.

9 **BE19-15** Youngman Corporation has temporary differences at December 31, 2012, that result in the following deferred taxes.

Deferred tax liability—current	$38,000
Deferred tax asset—current	$(62,000)
Deferred tax liability—noncurrent	$96,000
Deferred tax asset—noncurrent	$(27,000)

Indicate how these balances would be presented in Youngman's December 31, 2012, balance sheet.

EXERCISES

---

2 **5** **E19-1 (One Temporary Difference, Future Taxable Amounts, One Rate, No Beginning Deferred Taxes)** Starfleet Corporation has one temporary difference at the end of 2012 that will reverse and cause taxable amounts of $55,000 in 2013, $60,000 in 2014, and $75,000 in 2015. Starfleet's pretax financial income for 2012 is $400,000, and the tax rate is 30% for all years. There are no deferred taxes at the beginning of 2012.

Instructions
    (a) Compute taxable income and income taxes payable for 2012.
    (b) Prepare the journal entry to record income tax expense, deferred income taxes, and income taxes payable for 2012.
    (c) Prepare the income tax expense section of the income statement for 2012, beginning with the line "Income before income taxes."

2 **E19-2 (Two Differences, No Beginning Deferred Taxes, Tracked through 2 Years)** The following information is available for McKee Corporation for 2012.

    1. Excess of tax depreciation over book depreciation, $40,000. This $40,000 difference will reverse equally over the years 2013–2016.
    2. Deferral, for book purposes, of $25,000 of rent received in advance. The rent will be earned in 2013.
    3. Pretax financial income, $350,000.
    4. Tax rate for all years, 40%.

Instructions
    (a) Compute taxable income for 2012.
    (b) Prepare the journal entry to record income tax expense, deferred income taxes, and income taxes payable for 2012.
    (c) Prepare the journal entry to record income tax expense, deferred income taxes, and income taxes payable for 2013, assuming taxable income of $325,000.

E19-3 (One Temporary Difference, Future Taxable Amounts, One Rate, Beginning Deferred Taxes)
Brennan Corporation began 2012 with a $90,000 balance in the Deferred Tax Liability account. At the end of 2012, the related cumulative temporary difference amounts to $350,000, and it will reverse evenly over the next 2 years. Pretax accounting income for 2012 is $525,000, the tax rate for all years is 40%, and taxable income for 2012 is $400,000.

Instructions
(a) Compute income taxes payable for 2012.
(b) Prepare the journal entry to record income tax expense, deferred income taxes, and income taxes payable for 2012.
(c) Prepare the income tax expense section of the income statement for 2012, beginning with the line "Income before income taxes."

E19-4 (Three Differences, Compute Taxable Income, Entry for Taxes) Havaci Company reports pretax financial income of $80,000 for 2012. The following items cause taxable income to be different than pretax financial income.

1. Depreciation on the tax return is greater than depreciation on the income statement by $16,000.
2. Rent collected on the tax return is greater than rent earned on the income statement by $27,000.
3. Fines for pollution appear as an expense of $11,000 on the income statement.

Havaci's tax rate is 30% for all years, and the company expects to report taxable income in all future years. There are no deferred taxes at the beginning of 2012.

Instructions
(a) Compute taxable income and income taxes payable for 2012.
(b) Prepare the journal entry to record income tax expense, deferred income taxes, and income taxes payable for 2012.
(c) Prepare the income tax expense section of the income statement for 2012, beginning with the line "Income before income taxes."
(d) Compute the effective income tax rate for 2012.

E19-5 (Two Temporary Differences, One Rate, Beginning Deferred Taxes) The following facts relate to Alschuler Corporation.

1. Deferred tax liability, January 1, 2012, $40,000.
2. Deferred tax asset, January 1, 2012, $0.
3. Taxable income for 2012, $115,000.
4. Pretax financial income for 2012, $200,000.
5. Cumulative temporary difference at December 31, 2012, giving rise to future taxable amounts, $220,000.
6. Cumulative temporary difference at December 31, 2012, giving rise to future deductible amounts, $35,000.
7. Tax rate for all years, 40%.
8. The company is expected to operate profitably in the future.

Instructions
(a) Compute income taxes payable for 2012.
(b) Prepare the journal entry to record income tax expense, deferred income taxes, and income taxes payable for 2012.
(c) Prepare the income tax expense section of the income statement for 2012, beginning with the line "Income before income taxes."

E19-6 (Identify Temporary or Permanent Differences) Listed below are items that are commonly accounted for differently for financial reporting purposes than they are for tax purposes.

Instructions
For each item below, indicate whether it involves:

(1) A temporary difference that will result in future deductible amounts and, therefore, will usually give rise to a deferred income tax asset.
(2) A temporary difference that will result in future taxable amounts and, therefore, will usually give rise to a deferred income tax liability.
(3) A permanent difference.

Use the appropriate number to indicate your answer for each.

(a) _____ The MACRS depreciation system is used for tax purposes, and the straight-line depreciation method is used for financial reporting purposes for some plant assets.

(b) _____ A landlord collects some rents in advance. Rents received are taxable in the period when they are received.

(c) _____ Expenses are incurred in obtaining tax-exempt income.

(d) _____ Costs of guarantees and warranties are estimated and accrued for financial reporting purposes.

(e) _____ Installment sales of investments are accounted for by the accrual method for financial reporting purposes and the installment-sales method for tax purposes.

(f) _____ Interest is received on an investment in tax-exempt municipal obligations.

(g) _____ For some assets, straight-line depreciation is used for both financial reporting purposes and tax purposes, but the assets' lives are shorter for tax purposes.

(h) _____ Proceeds are received from a life insurance company because of the death of a key officer. (The company carries a policy on key officers.)

(i) _____ The tax return reports a deduction for 80% of the dividends received from U.S. corporations. The cost method is used in accounting for the related investments for financial reporting purposes.

(j) _____ Estimated losses on pending lawsuits and claims are accrued for books. These losses are tax-deductible in the period(s) when the related liabilities are settled.

(k) _____ Expenses on stock options are accrued for financial reporting purposes.

2 **3** **E19-7 (Terminology, Relationships, Computations, Entries)**

4 **6** **Instructions**

Complete the following statements by filling in the blanks.

(a) In a period in which a taxable temporary difference reverses, the reversal will cause taxable income to be _____ (less than, greater than) pretax financial income.

(b) If a $68,000 balance in Deferred Tax Asset was computed by use of a 40% rate, the underlying cumulative temporary difference amounts to $_____.

(c) Deferred taxes _____ (are, are not) recorded to account for permanent differences.

(d) If a taxable temporary difference originates in 2013, it will cause taxable income for 2013 to be _____ (less than, greater than) pretax financial income for 2013.

(e) If total tax expense is $50,000 and deferred tax expense is $65,000, then the current portion of the expense computation is referred to as current tax _____ (expense, benefit) of $_____.

(f) If a corporation's tax return shows taxable income of $105,000 for Year 2 and a tax rate of 40%, how much will appear on the December 31, Year 2, balance sheet for "Income taxes payable" if the company has made estimated tax payments of $36,500 for Year 2? $_____.

(g) An increase in the Deferred Tax Liability account on the balance sheet is recorded by a _____ (debit, credit) to the Income Tax Expense account.

(h) An income statement that reports current tax expense of $82,000 and deferred tax benefit of $23,000 will report total income tax expense of $_____.

(i) A valuation account is needed whenever it is judged to be _____ that a portion of a deferred tax asset _____ (will be, will not be) realized.

(j) If the tax return shows total taxes due for the period of $75,000 but the income statement shows total income tax expense of $55,000, the difference of $20,000 is referred to as deferred tax _____ (expense, benefit).

2 **3** **E19-8 (Two Temporary Differences, One Rate, 3 Years)** Gordon Company has two temporary differences

5 **9** between its pretax financial income and taxable income. The information is shown below.

	2012	2013	2014
Pretax financial income	$840,000	$910,000	$945,000
Excess depreciation expense on tax return	(30,000)	(40,000)	(20,000)
Excess warranty expense in financial income	20,000	10,000	8,000
Taxable income	$830,000	$880,000	$933,000

The income tax rate for all years is 40%.

Instructions

(a) Prepare the journal entry to record income tax expense, deferred income taxes, and income taxes payable for 2012, 2013, and 2014.

(b) Assuming there were no temporary differences prior to 2012, indicate how deferred taxes will be reported on the 2014 balance sheet. Gordon's product warranty is for 12 months.

(c) Prepare the income tax expense section of the income statement for 2014, beginning with the line "Pretax financial income."

8 **E19-9 (Carryback and Carryforward of NOL, No Valuation Account, No Temporary Differences)** The pretax financial income (or loss) figures for Synergetics Company are as follows.

2008	$160,000
2009	250,000
2010	90,000
2011	(160,000)
2012	(350,000)
2013	120,000
2014	100,000

Pretax financial income (or loss) and taxable income (loss) were the same for all years involved. Assume a 45% tax rate for 2008 and 2009 and a 40% tax rate for the remaining years.

Instructions
Prepare the journal entries for the years 2010 to 2014 to record income tax expense and the effects of the net operating loss carrybacks, and carryforwards, assuming Synergetics Company uses the carryback provision. All income and losses relate to normal operations. (In recording the benefits of a loss carryforward, assume that no valuation account is deemed necessary.)

8 **E19-10 (Two NOLs, No Temporary Differences, No Valuation Account, Entries and Income Statement)** Lanier Corporation has pretax financial income (or loss) equal to taxable income (or loss) from 2005 through 2013 as follows.

	Income (Loss)	Tax Rate
2005	$29,000	30%
2006	40,000	30%
2007	22,000	35%
2008	48,000	50%
2009	(150,000)	40%
2010	90,000	40%
2011	30,000	40%
2012	105,000	40%
2013	(50,000)	45%

Pretax financial income (loss) and taxable income (loss) were the same for all years since Lanier has been in business. Assume the carryback provision is employed for net operating losses. In recording the benefits of a loss carryforward, assume that it is more likely than not that the related benefits will be realized.

Instructions
(a) What entry(ies) for income taxes should be recorded for 2009?

(b) Indicate what the income tax expense portion of the income statement for 2009 should look like. Assume all income (loss) relates to continuing operations.

(c) What entry for income taxes should be recorded in 2010?

(d) How should the income tax expense section of the income statement for 2010 appear?

(e) What entry for income taxes should be recorded in 2013?

(f) How should the income tax expense section of the income statement for 2013 appear?

2 3 9 **E19-11 (Three Differences, Classify Deferred Taxes)** At December 31, 2012, Cascade Company had a net deferred tax liability of $450,000. An explanation of the items that compose this balance is as follows.

Temporary Differences	Resulting Balances in Deferred Taxes
1. Excess of tax depreciation over book depreciation	$200,000
2. Accrual, for book purposes, of estimated loss contingency from pending lawsuit that is expected to be settled in 2013. The loss will be deducted on the tax return when paid.	(50,000)
3. Accrual method used for book purposes and installment-sales method used for tax purposes for an isolated installment sale of an investment.	300,000
	$450,000

In analyzing the temporary differences, you find that $30,000 of the depreciation temporary difference will reverse in 2013, and $120,000 of the temporary difference due to the installment sale will reverse in 2013. The tax rate for all years is 40%.

Instructions

Indicate the manner in which deferred taxes should be presented on Cascade Company's December 31, 2012, balance sheet.

2 3 5 E19-12 (Two Temporary Differences, One Rate, Beginning Deferred Taxes, Compute Pretax Financial Income) The following facts relate to McKane Corporation.

1. Deferred tax liability, January 1, 2012, $60,000.
2. Deferred tax asset, January 1, 2012, $20,000.
3. Taxable income for 2012, $115,000.
4. Cumulative temporary difference at December 31, 2012, giving rise to future taxable amounts, $210,000.
5. Cumulative temporary difference at December 31, 2012, giving rise to future deductible amounts, $95,000.
6. Tax rate for all years, 40%. No permanent differences exist.
7. The company is expected to operate profitably in the future.

Instructions

(a) Compute the amount of pretax financial income for 2012.
(b) Prepare the journal entry to record income tax expense, deferred income taxes, and income taxes payable for 2012.
(c) Prepare the income tax expense section of the income statement for 2012, beginning with the line "Income before income taxes."
(d) Compute the effective tax rate for 2012.

2 7 E19-13 (One Difference, Multiple Rates, Effect of Beginning Balance versus No Beginning Deferred Taxes) At the end of 2012, Wasicsko Company has $180,000 of cumulative temporary differences that will result in reporting future taxable amounts as follows.

2013	$ 70,000
2014	50,000
2015	40,000
2016	20,000
	$180,000

Tax rates enacted as of the beginning of 2011 are:

2011 and 2012	40%
2013 and 2014	30%
2015 and later	25%

Wasicsko's taxable income for 2012 is $340,000. Taxable income is expected in all future years.

Instructions

(a) Prepare the journal entry for Wasicsko to record income taxes payable, deferred income taxes, and income tax expense for 2012, assuming that there were no deferred taxes at the end of 2011.
(b) Prepare the journal entry for Wasicsko to record income taxes payable, deferred income taxes, and income tax expense for 2012, assuming that there was a balance of $22,000 in a Deferred Tax Liability account at the end of 2011.

3 4 E19-14 (Deferred Tax Asset with and without Valuation Account) Callaway Corp. has a deferred tax asset account with a balance of $150,000 at the end of 2012 due to a single cumulative temporary difference of $375,000. At the end of 2013, this same temporary difference has increased to a cumulative amount of $500,000. Taxable income for 2013 is $850,000. The tax rate is 40% for all years. No valuation allowance related to the deferred tax asset is in existence at the end of 2012.

Instructions

(a) Record income tax expense, deferred income taxes, and income taxes payable for 2013, assuming that it is more likely than not that the deferred tax asset will be realized.
(b) Assuming that it is more likely than not that $30,000 of the deferred tax asset will not be realized, prepare the journal entry at the end of 2013 to record the valuation account.

3 4 5 E19-15 (Deferred Tax Asset with Previous Valuation Account) Assume the same information as E19-14, except that at the end of 2012, Callaway Corp. had a valuation account related to its deferred tax asset of $40,000.

Instructions

(a) Record income tax expense, deferred income taxes, and income taxes payable for 2013, assuming that it is more likely than not that the deferred tax asset will be realized in full.

(b) Record income tax expense, deferred income taxes, and income taxes payable for 2013, assuming that it is more likely than not that none of the deferred tax asset will be realized.

2 **5** **E19-16 (Deferred Tax Liability, Change in Tax Rate, Prepare Section of Income Statement)** Sharrer Inc.'s
7 **9** only temporary difference at the beginning and end of 2012 is caused by a $2 million deferred gain for tax purposes for an installment sale of a plant asset, and the related receivable (only one-half of which is classified as a current asset) is due in equal installments in 2013 and 2014. The related deferred tax liability at the beginning of the year is $800,000. In the third quarter of 2012, a new tax rate of 34% is enacted into law and is scheduled to become effective for 2014. Taxable income for 2012 is $5,000,000, and taxable income is expected in all future years.

Instructions

(a) Determine the amount reported as a deferred tax liability at the end of 2012. Indicate proper classification(s).

(b) Prepare the journal entry (if any) necessary to adjust the deferred tax liability when the new tax rate is enacted into law.

(c) Draft the income tax expense portion of the income statement for 2012. Begin with the line "Income before income taxes." Assume no permanent differences exist.

2 **3** **E19-17 (Two Temporary Differences, Tracked through 3 Years, Multiple Rates)** Taxable income and pre-
7 tax financial income would be identical for Jones Co. except for its treatments of gross profit on installment sales and estimated costs of warranties. The following income computations have been prepared.

Taxable income	2012	2013	2014
Excess of revenues over expenses (excluding two temporary differences)	$160,000	$210,000	$90,000
Installment income collected	8,000	8,000	8,000
Expenditures for warranties	(5,000)	(5,000)	(5,000)
Taxable income	$163,000	$213,000	$93,000

Pretax financial income	2012	2013	2014
Excess of revenues over expenses (excluding two temporary differences)	$160,000	$210,000	$90,000
Installment gross profit earned	24,000	–0–	–0–
Estimated cost of warranties	(15,000)	–0–	–0–
Income before taxes	$169,000	$210,000	$90,000

The tax rates in effect are: 2012, 45%; 2013 and 2014, 40%. All tax rates were enacted into law on January 1, 2012. No deferred income taxes existed at the beginning of 2012. Taxable income is expected in all future years.

Instructions

Prepare the journal entry to record income tax expense, deferred income taxes, and income taxes payable for 2012, 2013, and 2014.

2 **3** **E19-18 (Three Differences, Multiple Rates, Future Taxable Income)** During 2012, Graham Co.'s first
7 year of operations, the company reports pretax financial income of $250,000. Graham's enacted tax rate is 40% for 2012 and 35% for all later years. Graham expects to have taxable income in each of the next 5 years. The effects on future tax returns of temporary differences existing at December 31, 2012, are summarized below.

	Future Years					
	2013	2014	2015	2016	2017	Total
Future taxable (deductible) amounts:						
Installment sales	$32,000	$32,000	$32,000			$ 96,000
Depreciation	6,000	6,000	6,000	$6,000	$6,000	30,000
Unearned rent	(50,000)	(50,000)				(100,000)

Instructions

(a) Complete the schedule below to compute deferred taxes at December 31, 2012.

(b) Compute taxable income for 2012.

(c) Prepare the journal entry to record income taxes payable, deferred taxes, and income tax expense for 2012.

	Future Taxable (Deductible) Amounts	Tax Rate	December 31, 2012 Deferred Tax	
Temporary Difference			(Asset)	Liability
Installment sales	$ 96,000			
Depreciation	30,000			
Unearned rent	(100,000)			
Totals	$			

E19-19 (Two Differences, One Rate, Beginning Deferred Balance, Compute Pretax Financial Income) Shamess Co. establishes a $90 million liability at the end of 2012 for the estimated litigation settlement for manufacturing defects. All related costs will be paid and deducted on the tax return in 2013. Also, at the end of 2012, the company has $50 million of temporary differences due to excess depreciation for tax purposes, $7 million of which will reverse in 2013.

The enacted tax rate for all years is 40%, and the company pays taxes of $64 million on $160 million of taxable income in 2012. Shamess expects to have taxable income in 2013.

Instructions

(a) Determine the deferred taxes to be reported at the end of 2012.

(b) Indicate how the deferred taxes computed in (a) are to be reported on the balance sheet.

(c) Assuming that the only deferred tax account at the beginning of 2012 was a deferred tax liability of $10,000,000, draft the income tax expense portion of the income statement for 2012, beginning with the line "Income before income taxes." (*Hint:* You must first compute (1) the amount of temporary difference underlying the beginning $10,000,000 deferred tax liability, then (2) the amount of temporary differences originating or reversing during the year, then (3) the amount of pretax financial income.)

E19-20 (Two Differences, No Beginning Deferred Taxes, Multiple Rates) Macinski Inc., in its first year of operations, has the following differences between the book basis and tax basis of its assets and liabilities at the end of 2012.

	Book Basis	Tax Basis
Equipment (net)	$400,000	$340,000
Estimated warranty liability	$150,000	$ –0–

It is estimated that the warranty liability will be settled in 2013. The difference in equipment (net) will result in taxable amounts of $20,000 in 2013, $30,000 in 2014, and $10,000 in 2015. The company has taxable income of $550,000 in 2012. As of the beginning of 2012, the enacted tax rate is 34% for 2012–2014, and 30% for 2015. Macinski expects to report taxable income through 2015.

Instructions

(a) Prepare the journal entry to record income tax expense, deferred income taxes, and income taxes payable for 2012.

(b) Indicate how deferred income taxes will be reported on the balance sheet at the end of 2012.

E19-21 (Two Temporary Differences, Multiple Rates, Future Taxable Income) Flynn Inc. has two temporary differences at the end of 2012. The first difference stems from installment sales, and the second one results from the accrual of a loss contingency. Flynn's accounting department has developed a schedule of future taxable and deductible amounts related to these temporary differences as follows.

	2013	2014	2015	2016
Taxable amounts	$40,000	$50,000	$60,000	$90,000
Deductible amounts		(15,000)	(19,000)	
	$40,000	$35,000	$41,000	$90,000

As of the beginning of 2012, the enacted tax rate is 34% for 2012 and 2013, and 38% for 2014–2017. At the beginning of 2012, the company had no deferred income taxes on its balance sheet. Taxable income for 2012 is $400,000. Taxable income is expected in all future years.

Instructions

(a) Prepare the journal entry to record income tax expense, deferred income taxes, and income taxes payable for 2012.

(b) Indicate how deferred income taxes would be classified on the balance sheet at the end of 2012.

2 3
9
E19-22 (Two Differences, One Rate, First Year) The differences between the book basis and tax basis of the assets and liabilities of Morgan Corporation at the end of 2012 are presented below.

	Book Basis	Tax Basis
Accounts receivable	$50,000	$-0-
Litigation liability	20,000	-0-

It is estimated that the litigation liability will be settled in 2013. The difference in accounts receivable will result in taxable amounts of $30,000 in 2013 and $20,000 in 2014. The company has taxable income of $300,000 in 2012 and is expected to have taxable income in each of the following 2 years. Its enacted tax rate is 34% for all years. This is the company's first year of operations. The operating cycle of the business is 2 years.

Instructions

(a) Prepare the journal entry to record income tax expense, deferred income taxes, and income taxes payable for 2012.

(b) Indicate how deferred income taxes will be reported on the balance sheet at the end of 2012.

4 7
8
E19-23 (NOL Carryback and Carryforward, Valuation Account versus No Valuation Account) Sondgeroth Inc. reports the following pretax income (loss) for both financial reporting purposes and tax purposes. (Assume the carryback provision is used for a net operating loss.)

Year	Pretax Income (Loss)	Tax Rate
2011	$110,000	34%
2012	90,000	34%
2013	(260,000)	38%
2014	220,000	38%

The tax rates listed were all enacted by the beginning of 2011.

Instructions

(a) Prepare the journal entries for the years 2011–2014 to record income tax expense (benefit), income taxes payable (refundable), and the tax effects of the loss carryback and carryforward, assuming that at the end of 2013 the benefits of the loss carryforward are judged more likely than not to be realized in the future.

(b) Using the assumption in (a), prepare the income tax section of the 2013 income statement, beginning with the line "Operating loss before income taxes."

(c) Prepare the journal entries for 2013 and 2014, assuming that based on the weight of available evidence, it is more likely than not that one-fourth of the benefits of the loss carryforward will not be realized.

(d) Using the assumption in (c), prepare the income tax section of the 2013 income statement, beginning with the line "Operating loss before income taxes."

4 7
8
E19-24 (NOL Carryback and Carryforward, Valuation Account Needed) Nielson Inc. reports the following pretax income (loss) for both book and tax purposes. (Assume the carryback provision is used where possible for a net operating loss.)

Year	Pretax Income (Loss)	Tax Rate
2011	$100,000	40%
2012	90,000	40%
2013	(240,000)	45%
2014	120,000	45%

The tax rates listed were all enacted by the beginning of 2011.

Instructions

(a) Prepare the journal entries for the years 2011–2014 to record income tax expense (benefit), income taxes payable (refundable), and the tax effects of the loss carryback and loss carryforward, assuming that based on the weight of available evidence, it is more likely than not that one-half of the benefits of the loss carryforward will not be realized.

(b) Prepare the income tax section of the 2013 income statement, beginning with the line "Operating loss before income taxes."

(c) Prepare the income tax section of the 2014 income statement, beginning with the line "Income before income taxes."

4 7 8 **E19-25 (NOL Carryback and Carryforward, Valuation Account Needed)** Hayes Co. reported the following pretax financial income (loss) for the years 2011–2015.

2011	$240,000
2012	350,000
2013	90,000
2014	(550,000)
2015	180,000

Pretax financial income (loss) and taxable income (loss) were the same for all years involved. The enacted tax rate was 34% for 2011 and 2012, and 40% for 2013–2015. Assume the carryback provision is used first for net operating losses.

Instructions

(a) Prepare the journal entries for the years 2013–2015 to record income tax expense, income taxes payable (refundable), and the tax effects of the loss carryback and loss carryforward, assuming that based on the weight of available evidence, it is more likely than not that one-fifth of the benefits of the loss carryforward will not be realized.

(b) Prepare the income tax section of the 2014 income statement, beginning with the line "Income (loss) before income taxes."

> **See the book's companion website, www.wiley.com/college/kieso, for a set of B Exercises.**

PROBLEMS

2 3 5 **P19-1 (Three Differences, No Beginning Deferred Taxes, Multiple Rates)** The following information is available for Remmers Corporation for 2012.

1. Depreciation reported on the tax return exceeded depreciation reported on the income statement by $120,000. This difference will reverse in equal amounts of $30,000 over the years 2013–2016.
2. Interest received on municipal bonds was $10,000.
3. Rent collected in advance on January 1, 2012, totaled $60,000 for a 3-year period. Of this amount, $40,000 was reported as unearned at December 31, 2012, for book purposes.
4. The tax rates are 40% for 2012 and 35% for 2013 and subsequent years.
5. Income taxes of $320,000 are due per the tax return for 2012.
6. No deferred taxes existed at the beginning of 2012.

Instructions

(a) Compute taxable income for 2012.
(b) Compute pretax financial income for 2012.
(c) Prepare the journal entries to record income tax expense, deferred income taxes, and income taxes payable for 2012 and 2013. Assume taxable income was $980,000 in 2013.
(d) Prepare the income tax expense section of the income statement for 2012, beginning with "Income before income taxes."

3 5 6 **P19-2 (One Temporary Difference, Tracked for 4 Years, One Permanent Difference, Change in Rate)** The pretax financial income of Truttman Company differs from its taxable income throughout each of 4 years as follows.

Year	Pretax Financial Income	Taxable Income	Tax Rate
2012	$290,000	$180,000	35%
2013	320,000	225,000	40%
2014	350,000	260,000	40%
2015	420,000	560,000	40%

Pretax financial income for each year includes a nondeductible expense of $30,000 (never deductible for tax purposes). The remainder of the difference between pretax financial income and taxable income in each period is due to one depreciation temporary difference. No deferred income taxes existed at the beginning of 2012.

Instructions

(a) Prepare journal entries to record income taxes in all 4 years. Assume that the change in the tax rate to 40% was not enacted until the beginning of 2013.

(b) Prepare the income statement for 2013, beginning with Income before income taxes.

2 5 6 9 **P19-3 (Second Year of Depreciation Difference, Two Differences, Single Rate, Extraordinary Item)** The following information has been obtained for the Gocker Corporation.

1. Prior to 2012, taxable income and pretax financial income were identical.
2. Pretax financial income is $1,700,000 in 2012 and $1,400,000 in 2013.
3. On January 1, 2012, equipment costing $1,200,000 is purchased. It is to be depreciated on a straight-line basis over 5 years for tax purposes and over 8 years for financial reporting purposes. (*Hint:* Use the half-year convention for tax purposes, as discussed in Appendix 11A.)
4. Interest of $60,000 was earned on tax-exempt municipal obligations in 2013.
5. Included in 2013 pretax financial income is an extraordinary gain of $200,000, which is fully taxable.
6. The tax rate is 35% for all periods.
7. Taxable income is expected in all future years.

Instructions

(a) Compute taxable income and income taxes payable for 2013.

(b) Prepare the journal entry to record 2013 income tax expense, income taxes payable, and deferred taxes.

(c) Prepare the bottom portion of Gocker's 2013 income statement, beginning with "Income before income taxes and extraordinary item."

(d) Indicate how deferred income taxes should be presented on the December 31, 2013, balance sheet.

2 3 5 **P19-4 (Permanent and Temporary Differences, One Rate)** The accounting records of Shinault Inc. show the following data for 2012.

1. Life insurance expense on officers was $9,000.
2. Equipment was acquired in early January for $300,000. Straight-line depreciation over a 5-year life is used, with no salvage value. For tax purposes, Shinault used a 30% rate to calculate depreciation.
3. Interest revenue on State of New York bonds totaled $4,000.
4. Product warranties were estimated to be $50,000 in 2012. Actual repair and labor costs related to the warranties in 2012 were $10,000. The remainder is estimated to be paid evenly in 2013 and 2014.
5. Sales on an accrual basis were $100,000. For tax purposes, $75,000 was recorded on the installment-sales method.
6. Fines incurred for pollution violations were $4,200.
7. Pretax financial income was $750,000. The tax rate is 30%.

Instructions

(a) Prepare a schedule starting with pretax financial income in 2012 and ending with taxable income in 2012.

(b) Prepare the journal entry for 2012 to record income taxes payable, income tax expense, and deferred income taxes.

5 7 8 9 **P19-5 (NOL without Valuation Account)** Jennings Inc. reported the following pretax income (loss) and related tax rates during the years 2008–2014.

	Pretax Income (loss)	Tax Rate
2008	$ 40,000	30%
2009	25,000	30%
2010	50,000	30%
2011	80,000	40%
2012	(180,000)	45%
2013	70,000	40%
2014	100,000	35%

Pretax financial income (loss) and taxable income (loss) were the same for all years since Jennings began business. The tax rates from 2011–2014 were enacted in 2011.

Instructions

(a) Prepare the journal entries for the years 2012–2014 to record income taxes payable (refundable), income tax expense (benefit), and the tax effects of the loss carryback and carryforward. Assume that Jennings elects the carryback provision where possible and expects to realize the benefits of any loss carryforward in the year that immediately follows the loss year.

(b) Indicate the effect the 2012 entry(ies) has on the December 31, 2012, balance sheet.

    (c) Prepare the portion of the income statement, starting with "Operating loss before income taxes," for 2012.

    (d) Prepare the portion of the income statement, starting with "Income before income taxes," for 2013.

P19-6 (Two Differences, Two Rates, Future Income Expected) Presented below are two independent situations related to future taxable and deductible amounts resulting from temporary differences existing at December 31, 2012.

    1. Mooney Co. has developed the following schedule of future taxable and deductible amounts.

	2013	2014	2015	2016	2017
Taxable amounts	$300	$300	$300	$ 300	$300
Deductible amount	—	—	—	(1,600)	—

    2. Roesch Co. has the following schedule of future taxable and deductible amounts.

	2013	2014	2015	2016
Taxable amounts	$300	$300	$ 300	$300
Deductible amount	—	—	(2,300)	—

Both Mooney Co. and Roesch Co. have taxable income of $4,000 in 2012 and expect to have taxable income in all future years. The tax rates enacted as of the beginning of 2012 are 30% for 2012–2015 and 35% for years thereafter. All of the underlying temporary differences relate to noncurrent assets and liabilities.

Instructions
For each of these two situations, compute the net amount of deferred income taxes to be reported at the end of 2012, and indicate how it should be classified on the balance sheet.

P19-7 (One Temporary Difference, Tracked 3 Years, Change in Rates, Income Statement Presentation) Crosley Corp. sold an investment on an installment basis. The total gain of $60,000 was reported for financial reporting purposes in the period of sale. The company qualifies to use the installment-sales method for tax purposes. The installment period is 3 years; one-third of the sale price is collected in the period of sale. The tax rate was 40% in 2012, and 35% in 2013 and 2014. The 35% tax rate was not enacted in law until 2013. The accounting and tax data for the 3 years is shown below.

	Financial Accounting	Tax Return
2012 (40% tax rate)		
Income before temporary difference	$ 70,000	$70,000
Temporary difference	60,000	20,000
Income	$130,000	$90,000
2013 (35% tax rate)		
Income before temporary difference	$ 70,000	$70,000
Temporary difference	–0–	20,000
Income	$ 70,000	$90,000
2014 (35% tax rate)		
Income before temporary difference	$ 70,000	$70,000
Temporary difference	–0–	20,000
Income	$ 70,000	$90,000

Instructions
    (a) Prepare the journal entries to record the income tax expense, deferred income taxes, and the income taxes payable at the end of each year. No deferred income taxes existed at the beginning of 2012.

    (b) Explain how the deferred taxes will appear on the balance sheet at the end of each year. (Assume Installment Accounts Receivable is classified as a current asset.)

    (c) Draft the income tax expense section of the income statement for each year, beginning with "Income before income taxes."

P19-8 (Two Differences, 2 Years, Compute Taxable Income and Pretax Financial Income) The information below and on page 1194 was disclosed during the audit of Elbert Inc.

    1.

Year	Amount Due per Tax Return
2012	$130,000
2013	104,000

2. On January 1, 2012, equipment costing $600,000 is purchased. For financial reporting purposes, the company uses straight-line depreciation over a 5-year life. For tax purposes, the company uses the elective straight-line method over a 5-year life. (*Hint:* For tax purposes, the half-year convention as discussed in Appendix 11A must be used.)

3. In January 2013, $225,000 is collected in advance rental of a building for a 3-year period. The entire $225,000 is reported as taxable income in 2013, but $150,000 of the $225,000 is reported as unearned revenue in 2013 for financial reporting purposes. The remaining amount of unearned revenue is to be earned equally in 2014 and 2015.

4. The tax rate is 40% in 2012 and all subsequent periods. (*Hint:* To find taxable income in 2012 and 2013, the related income taxes payable amounts will have to be "grossed up.")

5. No temporary differences existed at the end of 2011. Elbert expects to report taxable income in each of the next 5 years.

Instructions

(a) Determine the amount to report for deferred income taxes at the end of 2012, and indicate how it should be classified on the balance sheet.

(b) Prepare the journal entry to record income taxes for 2012.

(c) Draft the income tax section of the income statement for 2012, beginning with "Income before income taxes." (*Hint:* You must compute taxable income and then combine that with changes in cumulative temporary differences to arrive at pretax financial income.)

(d) Determine the deferred income taxes at the end of 2013, and indicate how they should be classified on the balance sheet.

(e) Prepare the journal entry to record income taxes for 2013.

(f) Draft the income tax section of the income statement for 2013, beginning with "Income before income taxes."

   P19-9 (Five Differences, Compute Taxable Income and Deferred Taxes, Draft Income Statement) Wise Company began operations at the beginning of 2013. The following information pertains to this company.

1. Pretax financial income for 2013 is $100,000.

2. The tax rate enacted for 2013 and future years is 40%.

3. Differences between the 2013 income statement and tax return are listed below:

(a) Warranty expense accrued for financial reporting purposes amounts to $7,000. Warranty deductions per the tax return amount to $2,000.

(b) Gross profit on construction contracts using the percentage-of-completion method per books amounts to $92,000. Gross profit on construction contracts for tax purposes amounts to $67,000.

(c) Depreciation of property, plant, and equipment for financial reporting purposes amounts to $60,000. Depreciation of these assets amounts to $80,000 for the tax return.

(d) A $3,500 fine paid for violation of pollution laws was deducted in computing pretax financial income.

(e) Interest revenue earned on an investment in tax-exempt municipal bonds amounts to $1,500. (Assume (a) is short-term in nature; assume (b) and (c) are long-term in nature.)

4. Taxable income is expected for the next few years.

Instructions

(a) Compute taxable income for 2013.

(b) Compute the deferred taxes at December 31, 2013, that relate to the temporary differences described above. Clearly label them as deferred tax asset or liability.

(c) Prepare the journal entry to record income tax expense, deferred taxes, and income taxes payable for 2013.

(d) Draft the income tax expense section of the income statement, beginning with "Income before income taxes."

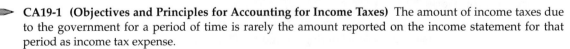

CONCEPTS FOR ANALYSIS

CA19-1 (Objectives and Principles for Accounting for Income Taxes) The amount of income taxes due to the government for a period of time is rarely the amount reported on the income statement for that period as income tax expense.

Instructions

(a) Explain the objectives of accounting for income taxes in general-purpose financial statements.

(b) Explain the basic principles that are applied in accounting for income taxes at the date of the financial statements to meet the objectives discussed in (a).

(c) List the steps in the annual computation of deferred tax liabilities and assets.

CA19-2 (Basic Accounting for Temporary Differences) Dexter Company appropriately uses the asset-liability method to record deferred income taxes. Dexter reports depreciation expense for certain machinery purchased this year using the modified accelerated cost recovery system (MACRS) for income tax purposes and the straight-line basis for financial reporting purposes. The tax deduction is the larger amount this year.

Dexter received rent revenues in advance this year. These revenues are included in this year's taxable income. However, for financial reporting purposes, these revenues are reported as unearned revenues, a current liability.

Instructions
(a) What are the principles of the asset-liability approach?
(b) How would Dexter account for the temporary differences?
(c) How should Dexter classify the deferred tax consequences of the temporary differences on its balance sheet?

CA19-3 (Identify Temporary Differences and Classification Criteria) The asset-liability approach for recording deferred income taxes is an integral part of generally accepted accounting principles.

Instructions
(a) Indicate whether each of the following independent situations should be treated as a temporary difference or as a permanent difference, and explain why.
   (1) Estimated warranty costs (covering a 3-year warranty) are expensed for financial reporting purposes at the time of sale but deducted for income tax purposes when paid.
   (2) Depreciation for book and income tax purposes differs because of different bases of carrying the related property, which was acquired in a trade-in. The different bases are a result of different rules used for book and tax purposes to compute the basis of property acquired in a trade-in.
   (3) A company properly uses the equity method to account for its 30% investment in another company. The investee pays dividends that are about 10% of its annual earnings.
   (4) A company reports a gain on an involuntary conversion of a nonmonetary asset to a monetary asset. The company elects to replace the property within the statutory period using the total proceeds so the gain is not reported on the current year's tax return.
(b) Discuss the nature of the deferred income tax accounts and possible classifications in a company's balance sheet. Indicate the manner in which these accounts are to be reported.

CA19-4 (Accounting and Classification of Deferred Income Taxes)

Part A
This year, Gumowski Company has each of the following items in its income statement.

1. Gross profits on installment sales.
2. Revenues on long-term construction contracts.
3. Estimated costs of product warranty contracts.
4. Premiums on officers' life insurance policies with Gumowski as beneficiary.

Instructions
(a) Under what conditions would deferred income taxes need to be reported in the financial statements?
(b) Specify when deferred income taxes would need to be recognized for each of the items above, and indicate the rationale for such recognition.

Part B
Gumowski Company's president has heard that deferred income taxes can be classified in different ways in the balance sheet.

Instructions
Identify the conditions under which deferred income taxes would be classified as a noncurrent item in the balance sheet. What justification exists for such classification?

(AICPA adapted)

CA19-5 (Explain Computation of Deferred Tax Liability for Multiple Tax Rates) At December 31, 2012, Higley Corporation has one temporary difference which will reverse and cause taxable amounts in 2013. In 2012, a new tax act set taxes equal to 45% for 2012, 40% for 2013, and 34% for 2014 and years thereafter.

Instructions
Explain what circumstances would call for Higley to compute its deferred tax liability at the end of 2012 by multiplying the cumulative temporary difference by:
(a) 45%.
(b) 40%.
(c) 34%.

CA19-6 (Explain Future Taxable and Deductible Amounts, How Carryback and Carryforward Affects Deferred Taxes) Maria Rodriquez and Lynette Kingston are discussing accounting for income taxes. They are currently studying a schedule of taxable and deductible amounts that will arise in the future as a result of existing temporary differences. The schedule is as follows.

	Current Years	Future Years			
	2012	2013	2014	2015	2016
Taxable income	$850,000				
Taxable amounts		$375,000	$375,000	$375,000	$375,000
Deductible amounts				(2,400,000)	
Enacted tax rate	50%	45%	40%	35%	30%

Instructions

(a) Explain the concept of future taxable amounts and future deductible amounts as illustrated in the schedule.

(b) How do the carryback and carryforward provisions affect the reporting of deferred tax assets and deferred tax liabilities?

CA19-7 (Deferred Taxes, Income Effects) Stephanie Delaney, CPA, is the newly hired director of corporate taxation for Acme Incorporated, which is a publicly traded corporation. Ms. Delaney's first job with Acme was the review of the company's accounting practices on deferred income taxes. In doing her review, she noted differences between tax and book depreciation methods that permitted Acme to realize a sizable deferred tax liability on its balance sheet. As a result, Acme paid very little in income taxes at that time.

Delaney also discovered that Acme has an explicit policy of selling off plant assets before they reversed in the deferred tax liability account. This policy, coupled with the rapid expansion of its plant asset base, allowed Acme to "defer" all income taxes payable for several years, even though it always has reported positive earnings and an increasing EPS. Delaney checked with the legal department and found the policy to be legal, but she's uncomfortable with the ethics of it.

Instructions

Answer the following questions.

(a) Why would Acme have an explicit policy of selling plant assets before the temporary differences reversed in the deferred tax liability account?

(b) What are the ethical implications of Acme's "deferral" of income taxes?

(c) Who could be harmed by Acme's ability to "defer" income taxes payable for several years, despite positive earnings?

(d) In a situation such as this, what are Ms. Delaney's professional responsibilities as a CPA?

USING YOUR JUDGMENT

FINANCIAL REPORTING

Financial Reporting Problem

The Procter & Gamble Company (P&G)

The financial statements of **P&G** are presented in Appendix 5B or can be accessed at the book's companion website, **www.wiley.com/college/kieso**.

Instructions

Refer to P&G's financial statements and the accompanying notes to answer the following questions.

(a) What amounts relative to income taxes does P&G report in its:

(1) 2009 income statement?

(2) June 30, 2009, balance sheet?

(3) 2009 statement of cash flows?

(b) P&G's provision for income taxes in 2007, 2008, and 2009 was computed at what effective tax rates? (See the notes to the financial statements.)

(c) How much of P&G's 2009 total provision for income taxes was current tax expense, and how much was deferred tax expense?

(d) What did P&G report as the significant components (the details) of its June 30, 2009, deferred tax assets and liabilities?

Comparative Analysis Case

The Coca-Cola Company and PepsiCo, Inc.

Instructions

Go to the book's companion website and use information found there to answer the following questions related to The Coca-Cola Company and PepsiCo, Inc.

(a) What are the amounts of Coca-Cola's and PepsiCo's provision for income taxes for the year 2009? Of each company's 2009 provision for income taxes, what portion is current expense and what portion is deferred expense?

(b) What amount of cash was paid in 2009 for income taxes by Coca-Cola and by PepsiCo?

(c) What was the U.S. federal statutory tax rate in 2009? What was the effective tax rate in 2009 for Coca-Cola and PepsiCo? Why might their effective tax rates differ?

(d) For year-end 2009, what amounts were reported by Coca-Cola and PepsiCo as (1) gross deferred tax assets and (2) gross deferred tax liabilities?

(e) Do either Coca-Cola or PepsiCo disclose any net operating loss carrybacks and/or carryforwards at year-end 2009? What are the amounts, and when do the carryforwards expire?

Financial Statement Analysis Case

Homestake Mining Company

Homestake Mining Company is a 120-year-old international gold mining company with substantial gold mining operations and exploration in the United States, Canada, and Australia. At year-end, Homestake reported the following items related to income taxes (thousands of dollars).

Total current taxes	$ 26,349
Total deferred taxes	(39,436)
Total income and mining taxes (the provision for taxes per its income statement)	(13,087)
Deferred tax liabilities	$303,050
Deferred tax assets, net of valuation allowance of $207,175	95,275
Net deferred tax liability	$207,775

Note 6: The classification of deferred tax assets and liabilities is based on the related asset or liability creating the deferred tax. Deferred taxes not related to a specific asset or liability are classified based on the estimated period of reversal.

Tax loss carryforwards (U.S., Canada, Australia, and Chile)	$71,151
Tax credit carryforwards	$12,007

Instructions

(a) What is the significance of Homestake's disclosure of "Current taxes" of $26,349 and "Deferred taxes" of $(39,436)?

(b) Explain the concept behind Homestake's disclosure of gross deferred tax liabilities (future taxable amounts) and gross deferred tax assets (future deductible amounts).

(c) Homestake reported tax loss carryforwards of $71,151 and tax credit carryforwards of $12,007. How do the carryback and carryforward provisions affect the reporting of deferred tax assets and deferred tax liabilities?

Accounting, Analysis, and Principles

Allman Company, which began operations at the beginning of 2010, produces various products on a contract basis. Each contract generates a gross profit of $80,000. Some of Allman's contracts provide for the customer to pay on an installment basis. Under these contracts, Allman collects one-fifth of the contract revenue in each of the following four years. For financial reporting purposes, the company recognizes gross profit in the year of completion (accrual basis); for tax purposes, Allman recognizes gross profit in the year cash is collected (installment basis).

Presented below is information related to Allman's operations for 2012:

1. In 2012, the company completed seven contracts that allow for the customer to pay on an installment basis. Allman recognized the related gross profit of $560,000 for financial reporting purposes. It reported only $112,000 of gross profit on installment sales on the 2012 tax return. The company expects future collections on the related installment receivables to result in taxable amounts of $112,000 in each of the next four years.
2. In 2012, nontaxable municipal bond interest revenue was $28,000.
3. During 2012, nondeductible fines and penalties of $26,000 were paid.
4. Pretax financial income for 2012 amounts to $500,000.
5. Tax rates (enacted before the end of 2012) are 50% for 2012 and 40% for 2013 and later.
6. The accounting period is the calendar year.
7. The company is expected to have taxable income in all future years.
8. The company has no deferred tax assets or liabilities at the end of 2011.

Accounting

Prepare the journal entry to record income taxes for 2012.

Analysis

Classify deferred income taxes on the balance sheet at December 31, 2012, and indicate, starting with income before income taxes, how income taxes are reported on the income statement. What is Allman's effective tax rate?

Principles

Explain how the conceptual framework is used as a basis for determining the proper accounting for deferred income taxes.

BRIDGE TO THE PROFESSION

Professional Research: FASB Codification

Kleckner Company started operations in 2009, and although it has grown steadily, the company reported accumulated operating losses of $450,000 in its first four years in business. In the most recent year (2013), Kleckner appears to have turned the corner and reported modest taxable income of $30,000. In addition to a deferred tax asset related to its net operating loss, Kleckner has recorded a deferred tax asset related to product warranties and a deferred tax liability related to accelerated depreciation.

Given its past operating results, Kleckner has established a full valuation allowance for its deferred tax assets. However, given its improved performance, Kleckner management wonders whether the company can now reduce or eliminate the valuation allowance. They would like you to conduct some research on the accounting for its valuation allowance.

Instructions

If your school has a subscription to the FASB Codification, go to *http://aaahq.org/ascLogin.cfm* to log in and prepare responses to the following. Provide Codification references for your responses.

(a) Briefly explain to Kleckner management the importance of future taxable income as it relates to the valuation allowance for deferred tax assets.

(b) What are the sources of income that may be relied upon to remove the need for a valuation allowance?

(c) What are tax-planning strategies? From the information provided, does it appear that Kleckner could employ a tax-planning strategy to support reducing its valuation allowance?

Professional Simulation

In this simulation, you are asked to address questions related to the accounting for taxes. Prepare responses to all parts.

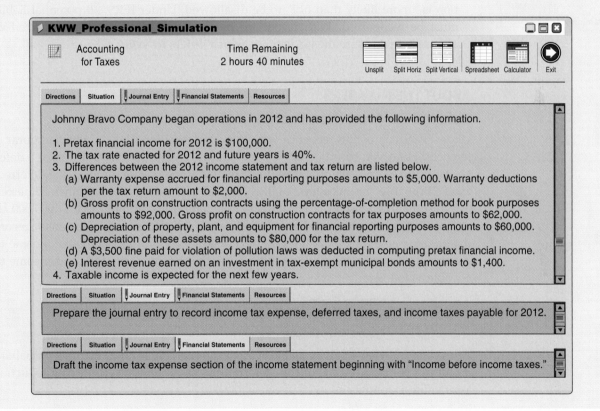

KWW_Professional_Simulation

Accounting for Taxes   Time Remaining 2 hours 40 minutes

Unsplit Split Horiz Split Vertical Spreadsheet Calculator Exit

Directions | Situation | Journal Entry | Financial Statements | Resources

Johnny Bravo Company began operations in 2012 and has provided the following information.

1. Pretax financial income for 2012 is $100,000.
2. The tax rate enacted for 2012 and future years is 40%.
3. Differences between the 2012 income statement and tax return are listed below.
   (a) Warranty expense accrued for financial reporting purposes amounts to $5,000. Warranty deductions per the tax return amount to $2,000.
   (b) Gross profit on construction contracts using the percentage-of-completion method for book purposes amounts to $92,000. Gross profit on construction contracts for tax purposes amounts to $62,000.
   (c) Depreciation of property, plant, and equipment for financial reporting purposes amounts to $60,000. Depreciation of these assets amounts to $80,000 for the tax return.
   (d) A $3,500 fine paid for violation of pollution laws was deducted in computing pretax financial income.
   (e) Interest revenue earned on an investment in tax-exempt municipal bonds amounts to $1,400.
4. Taxable income is expected for the next few years.

Directions | Situation | Journal Entry | Financial Statements | Resources

Prepare the journal entry to record income tax expense, deferred taxes, and income taxes payable for 2012.

Directions | Situation | Journal Entry | Financial Statements | Resources

Draft the income tax expense section of the income statement beginning with "Income before income taxes."

IFRS Insights

The accounting for income taxes in IFRS is covered in *IAS 12* ("Income Taxes"). Similar to GAAP, IFRS uses the asset and liability approach for recording deferred taxes. The differences between IFRS and GAAP involve a few exceptions to the asset-liability approach; some minor differences in the recognition, measurement, and disclosure criteria; and differences in implementation guidance.

RELEVANT FACTS

- The classification of deferred taxes under IFRS is always non-current. As indicated in the chapter, GAAP classifies deferred taxes based on the classification of the asset or liability to which it relates.
- Under IFRS, an affirmative judgment approach is used, by which a deferred tax asset is recognized up to the amount that is probable to be realized. GAAP uses an impairment approach. In this approach, the deferred tax asset is recognized in full. It is then reduced by a valuation account if it is more likely than not that all or a portion of the deferred tax asset will not be realized.
- IFRS uses the enacted tax rate or substantially enacted tax rate. ("Substantially enacted" means virtually certain.) For GAAP, the enacted tax rate must be used.
- The tax effects related to certain items are reported in equity under IFRS. That is not the case under GAAP, which charges or credits the tax effects to income.
- GAAP requires companies to assess the likelihood of uncertain tax positions being sustainable upon audit. Potential liabilities must be accrued and disclosed if the position is "more likely than not" to be disallowed. Under IFRS, all potential liabilities must be recognized. With respect to measurement, IFRS uses an expected-value approach to measure the tax liability, which differs from GAAP.

ABOUT THE NUMBERS

Deferred Tax Asset (Non-Recognition)

Under IFRS, companies recognize a deferred tax asset for all deductible temporary differences. However, based on available evidence, a company should reduce a deferred tax asset if it is probable that it **will not realize** some portion or all of the deferred tax asset. "**Probable**" means a level of likelihood of at least slightly more than 50 percent.

Assume that Jensen Co. has a deductible temporary difference of $1,000,000 at the end of its first year of operations. Its tax rate is 40 percent, which means it records a deferred tax asset of $400,000 ($1,000,000 × 40%). Assuming $900,000 of income taxes payable, Jensen records income tax expense, the deferred tax asset, and income taxes payable as follows.

Income Tax Expense	500,000	
Deferred Tax Asset	400,000	
Income Taxes Payable		900,000

After careful review of all available evidence, Jensen determines that it is probable that it will not realize $100,000 of this deferred tax asset. Jensen records this reduction in asset value as follows.

Income Tax Expense	100,000	
Deferred Tax Asset		100,000

This journal entry increases income tax expense in the current period because Jensen does not expect to realize a favorable tax benefit for a portion of the deductible temporary difference. Jensen **simultaneously recognizes a reduction in the carrying amount of the deferred tax asset**. Jensen then reports a deferred tax asset of $300,000 in its statement of financial position.

Jensen evaluates the deferred tax asset account at the end of each accounting period. If, at the end of the next period, it expects to realize $350,000 of this deferred tax asset, Jensen makes the following entry to adjust this account.

Deferred Tax Asset ($350,000 − $300,000)	50,000	
Income Tax Expense		50,000

Jensen should consider all available evidence, both positive and negative, to determine whether, based on the weight of available evidence, it needs to adjust the deferred tax asset. For example, if Jensen has been experiencing a series of loss years, it reasonably assumes that these losses will continue. Therefore, Jensen will lose the benefit of the future deductible amounts.

Generally, sufficient taxable income arises from temporary taxable differences that will reverse in the future or from a tax-planning strategy that will generate taxable income in the future. Illustration IFRS19-1 shows how **Ahold** describes its reporting of deferred assets.

Ahold
Note 11. Significant judgment is required in determining whether deferred tax assets are realizable. Ahold determines this on the basis of expected taxable profits arising from recognized deferred tax liabilities and on the basis of budgets, cash flow forecasts, and impairment models. Where utilization is not considered probable, deferred taxes are not recognized.

ILLUSTRATION IFRS19-1
Deferred Tax Asset Disclosure

Carryforward (Non-Recognition)

To illustrate non-recognition of a loss carryforward, assume that Groh Inc. has tax benefits of $110,000 associated with a NOL carryback and a potential deferred tax asset of $80,000 associated with an operating loss carryforward of $200,000, assuming a future tax rate of 40% ($200,000 × 40%). However, if it is probable that Groh will *not* realize the entire NOL carryforward in future years, it does not recognize this deferred tax asset. To illustrate, Groh makes the following journal entry in 2012 to record only the tax refund receivable.

To recognize benefit of loss carryback		
Income Tax Refund Receivable	110,000	
Benefit Due to Loss Carryback (Income Tax Expense)		110,000

Illustration IFRS19-2 shows Groh's 2012 income statement presentation.

GROH INC.	
INCOME STATEMENT (PARTIAL) FOR 2012	
Operating loss before income taxes	$(500,000)
Income tax benefit	
Benefit due to loss carryback	110,000
Net loss	$(390,000)

ILLUSTRATION IFRS19-2
Recognition of Benefit of Loss Carryback Only

In 2013, assuming that Groh has taxable income of $250,000 (before considering the carryforward), subject to a tax rate of 40 percent, it realizes the deferred tax asset. Groh records the following entries.

To recognize deferred tax asset and loss carryforward		
Deferred Tax Asset	80,000	
Benefit Due to Loss Carryforward (Income Tax Expense)		80,000

To record current and deferred income taxes		
Income Tax Expense	100,000	
Deferred Tax Asset		80,000
Income Taxes Payable		20,000

Groh reports the $80,000 Benefit Due to the Loss Carryforward on the 2013 income statement. The company did not recognize it in 2012 because it was probable that it would not be realized. Assuming that Groh derives the income for 2013 from continuing operations, it prepares the income statement as shown in Illustration IFRS19-3.

ILLUSTRATION IFRS19-3
Recognition of Benefit of Loss Carryforward When Realized

GROH INC. INCOME STATEMENT (PARTIAL) FOR 2013		
Income before income taxes		$250,000
Income tax expense		
Current	$ 20,000	
Deferred	80,000	
Benefit due to loss carryforward	(80,000)	20,000
Net income		$230,000

Another method is to report only one line for total income tax expense of $20,000 on the face of the income statement and disclose the components of income tax expense in the notes to the financial statements.

Statement of Financial Position Classification

Companies classify taxes receivable or payable as current assets or current liabilities. Although current tax assets and liabilities are separately recognized and measured, they are often offset in the statement of financial position. The offset occurs because companies normally have a legally enforceable right to offset a current tax asset (Taxes Receivable) against a current tax liability (Taxes Payable) when they relate to income taxes levied by the same taxation authority. Deferred tax assets and deferred tax liabilities are also separately recognized and measured but may be offset in the statement of financial position. Companies are permitted to offset deferred tax assets and deferred tax liabilities if, and only if: (1) the company has a legally enforceable right to offset current tax assets against current tax liabilities; and (2) the deferred tax assets and the deferred tax liabilities relate to income taxes levied by the same tax authority and for the same company.

The net deferred tax asset or net deferred tax liability is reported in the non-current section of the statement of financial position. Deferred tax amounts should not be discounted. The IASB apparently considers discounting to be an unnecessary complication even if the effects are material. To illustrate, assume that K. Scott Company has four deferred tax items at December 31, 2012, as shown in Illustration IFRS19-4.

ILLUSTRATION IFRS19-4
Classification of Temporary Differences

Temporary Difference	Resulting Deferred Tax (Asset)	Liability
1. Rent collected in advance: recognized when earned for accounting purposes and when received for tax purposes.	$(42,000)	
2. Use of straight-line depreciation for accounting purposes and accelerated depreciation for tax purposes.		$214,000
3. Recognition of profits on installment sales during period of sale for accounting purposes and during period of collection for tax purposes.		45,000
4. Warranty liabilities: recognized for accounting purposes at time of sale; for tax purposes at time paid.	(12,000)	
Totals	$(54,000)	$259,000

As indicated, K. Scott has a total deferred tax asset of $54,000 and a total deferred tax liability of $259,000. Assuming these two items can be offset, K. Scott reports a deferred tax liability of $205,000 ($259,000 − $54,000) in the non-current liability section of its statement of financial position.

ON THE HORIZON

The IASB and the FASB have been working to address some of the differences in the accounting for income taxes. Some of the issues under discussion are the term "probable" under IFRS for recognition of a deferred tax asset, which might be interpreted to mean "more likely than not." If the term is changed, the reporting for impairments of deferred tax assets will be essentially the same between GAAP and IFRS. In addition, the IASB is considering adoption of the classification approach used in GAAP for deferred assets and liabilities. Also, GAAP will likely continue to use the enacted tax rate in computing deferred taxes, except in situations where the taxing jurisdiction is not involved. In that case, companies should use IFRS, which is based on enacted rates or substantially enacted tax rates. Finally, the issue of allocation of deferred income taxes to equity for certain transactions under IFRS must be addressed in order to converge with GAAP, which allocates the effects to income. At the time of this printing, deliberations on the income tax project have been suspended indefinitely.

IFRS SELF-TEST QUESTIONS

1. Which of the following is *false*?
   (a) Under GAAP, deferred taxes are reported based on the classification of the asset or liability to which it relates.
   (b) Under IFRS, some potential liabilities are not recognized.
   (c) Under GAAP, the enacted tax rate is used to measure deferred tax assets and liabilities.
   (d) Under IFRS, all deferred tax assets and liabilities are classified as non-current.

2. Which of the following statements is *correct* with regard to IFRS and GAAP?
   (a) Under GAAP, all potential liabilities related to uncertain tax positions must be recognized.
   (b) The tax effects related to certain items are reported in equity under GAAP; under IFRS, the tax effects are charged or credited to income.
   (c) IFRS uses an affirmative judgment approach for deferred tax assets, whereas GAAP uses an impairment approach for deferred tax assets.
   (d) IFRS classifies deferred taxes based on the classification of the asset or liability to which it relates.

3. Under IFRS:
   (a) "probable" is defined as a level of likelihood of at least slightly more than 60%.
   (b) a company should reduce a deferred tax asset when it is likely that some or all of it will not be realized by using a valuation allowance.
   (c) a company considers only positive evidence when determining whether to recognize a deferred tax asset.
   (d) deferred tax assets must be evaluated at the end of each accounting period.

4. Stephens Company has a deductible temporary difference of $2,000,000 at the end of its first year of operations. Its tax rate is 40 percent. Stephens has $1,800,000 of income taxes payable. After a careful review of all available evidence, Stephens determines that it is probable that it will not realize $200,000 of this deferred tax asset. On Stephens Company's statement of financial position at the end of its first year of operations, what is the amount of deferred tax asset?
   (a) $2,000,000.   (c) $800,000.
   (b) $1,800,000.   (d) $600,000.

5. Lincoln Company has the following four deferred tax items at December 31, 2012. The deferred tax assets and the deferred tax liabilities relate to income taxes levied by the same tax authority.

Temporary Difference	Deferred Tax Asset	Deferred Tax Liability
Rent collected in advance: recognized when earned for accounting purposes and when received for tax purposes	$652,000	
Use of straight-line depreciation for accounting purposes and accelerated depreciation for tax purposes		$330,000
Recognition of profits on installment sales during period of sale for accounting purposes and during period of collection for tax purposes		64,000
Warranty liabilities: recognized for accounting purposes at time of sale; for tax purposes at time paid	37,000	

On Lincoln's December 31, 2012, statement of financial position, it will report:

(a) $394,000 non-current deferred tax liability and $689,000 non-current deferred tax asset.

(b) $330,000 non-current liability and $625,000 current deferred tax asset.

(c) $295,000 non-current deferred tax asset.

(d) $295,000 current tax receivable.

IFRS CONCEPTS AND APPLICATION

IFRS19-1 Where can authoritative IFRS related to the accounting for taxes be found?

IFRS19-2 Briefly describe some of the similarities and differences between GAAP and IFRS with respect to income tax accounting.

IFRS19-3 Describe the current convergence efforts of the FASB and IASB in the area of accounting for taxes.

IFRS19-4 How are deferred tax assets and deferred tax liabilities reported on the statement of financial position under IFRS?

IFRS19-5 Describe the procedure(s) involved in classifying deferred tax amounts on the statement of financial position under IFRS.

IFRS19-6 At December 31, 2012, Hillyard Corporation has a deferred tax asset of $200,000. After a careful review of all available evidence, it is determined that it is probable that $60,000 of this deferred tax asset will not be realized. Prepare the necessary journal entry.

IFRS19-7 Rode Inc. incurred a net operating loss of $500,000 in 2012. Combined income for 2010 and 2011 was $350,000. The tax rate for all years is 40%. Rode elects the carryback option. Prepare the journal entries to record the benefits of the loss carryback and the loss carryforward.

IFRS19-8 Use the information for Rode Inc. given in IFRS19-7. Assume that it is probable that the entire net operating loss carryforward will not be realized in future years. Prepare the journal entry(ies) necessary at the end of 2012.

IFRS19-9 Youngman Corporation has temporary differences at December 31, 2012, that result in the following deferred taxes.

Deferred tax asset	$24,000
Deferred tax liability	$69,000

Indicate how these balances would be presented in Youngman's December 31, 2012, statement of financial position.

IFRS19-10 At December 31, 2012, Cascade Company had a net deferred tax liability of $450,000. An explanation of the items that compose this balance is as follows.

Temporary Differences in Deferred Taxes	Resulting Balances
1. Excess of tax depreciation over book depreciation.	$200,000
2. Accrual, for book purposes, of estimated loss contingency from pending lawsuit that is expected to be settled in 2013. The loss will be deducted on the tax return when paid.	$ (50,000)
3. Accrual method used for book purposes and installment method used for tax purposes for an isolated installment sale of an investment.	$300,000

In analyzing the temporary differences, you find that $30,000 of the depreciation temporary difference will reverse in 2013, and $120,000 of the temporary difference due to the installment sale will reverse in 2013. The tax rate for all years is 40%.

Instructions

Indicate the manner in which deferred taxes should be presented on Cascade Company's December 31, 2012, statement of financial position.

IFRS19-11 Callaway Corp. has a deferred tax asset account with a balance of $150,000 at the end of 2012 due to a single cumulative temporary difference of $375,000. At the end of 2013, this same temporary difference has increased to a cumulative amount of $500,000. Taxable income for 2013 is $850,000. The tax rate is 40% for all years.

Instructions

(a) Record income tax expense, deferred income taxes, and income taxes payable for 2013, assuming that it is probable that the deferred tax asset will be realized.

(b) Assuming that it is probable that $30,000 of the deferred tax asset will not be realized, prepare the journal entry at the end of 2013 to recognize this probability.

Professional Research

IFRS19-12 Kleckner Company started operations in 2009, and although it has grown steadily, the company reported accumulated operating losses of $450,000 in its first four years in business. In the most recent year (2013), Kleckner appears to have turned the corner and reported modest taxable income of $30,000. In addition to a deferred tax asset related to its net operating loss, Kleckner has recorded a deferred tax asset related to product warranties and a deferred tax liability related to accelerated depreciation. Given its past operating results, Kleckner has determined that it is not probable that it will realize any of the deferred tax assets. However, given its improved performance, Kleckner management wonders whether there are any accounting consequences for its deferred tax assets. They would like you to conduct some research on the accounting for recognition of its deferred tax asset.

Instructions

Access the IFRS authoritative literature at the IASB website (*http://eifrs.iasb.org/*). When you have accessed the documents, you can use the search tool in your Internet browser to respond to the following questions. (Provide paragraph citations.)

(a) Briefly explain to Kleckner management the importance of future taxable income as it relates to the recognition of deferred tax assets.

(b) What are the sources of income that may be relied upon in assessing realization of a deferred tax asset?

(c) What are tax-planning strategies? From the information provided, does it appear that Kleckner could employ a tax-planning strategy in evaluating its deferred tax asset?

International Financial Reporting Problem:

Marks and Spencer plc

IFRS19-13 The financial statements of **Marks and Spencer plc (M&S)** are available at the book's companion website or can be accessed at *http://corporate.marksandspencer. com/documents/publications/2010/Annual_Report_2010.*

Instructions

Refer to M&S's financial statements and the accompanying notes to answer the following questions.

(a) What amounts relative to income taxes does M&S report in its:
   (1) 2010 income statement?
   (2) 3 April 2010 statement of financial position?
   (3) 2010 statement of cash flows?
(b) M&S's provision for income taxes in 2009 and 2010 was computed at what effective tax rates? (See the notes to the financial statements.)
(c) How much of M&S's 2010 total provision for income taxes was current tax expense, and how much was deferred tax expense?
(d) What did M&S report as the significant components (the details) of its 3 April 2010 deferred tax assets and liabilities?

ANSWERS TO IFRS SELF-TEST QUESTIONS

1. b 2. c 3. d 4. d 5. c

Accounting for Pensions and Postretirement Benefits

After studying this chapter, you should be able to:

1 Distinguish between accounting for the employer's pension plan and accounting for the pension fund.

2 Identify types of pension plans and their characteristics.

3 Explain alternative measures for valuing the pension obligation.

4 List the components of pension expense.

5 Use a worksheet for employer's pension plan entries.

6 Describe the amortization of prior service costs.

7 Explain the accounting for unexpected gains and losses.

8 Explain the corridor approach to amortizing gains and losses.

9 Describe the requirements for reporting pension plans in financial statements.

Where Have All the Pensions Gone?

Many companies have benefit plans that promise income and other benefits to retired employees in exchange for services during their working years. However, a shift is on from traditional defined benefit plans, in which employers bear the risk of meeting the benefit promises, to plans in which employees bear more of the risk. In some cases, employers are dropping retirement plans altogether. Here are some of the reasons for the shift.

Competition. Newer and foreign competitors do not have the same retiree costs that older U.S. companies do. **Southwest Airlines** does not offer a traditional pension plan, but **United** has a pension deficit exceeding $100,000 per employee.

Cost. Retirees are living longer, and the costs of retirement are higher. Combined with annual retiree healthcare costs, retirement benefits are costing the S&P 500 companies over $25 billion a year and are rising at double-digit rates.

Insurance. Pensions are backed by premiums paid to the **Pension Benefit Guarantee Corporation** (PBGC). When a company fails, the PBGC takes over the plan. But due to a number of significant company failures, the PBGC is running a deficit, and healthy companies are subsidizing the weak.

Accounting. To bring U.S. standards in line with international rules, accounting rule-makers are considering rules that will require companies to "mark their pensions to market" (value them at market rates). Such a move would increase the reported volatility of the retirement plan and of company financial statements. When Great Britain made this shift, 25 percent of British companies closed their plans to new entrants.

As a result of such factors, it is not hard to believe that experts can think of no major company that has instituted a traditional pension plan in the past decade.

What does this mean for you as you evaluate job offers and benefit packages in the not-too-distant future? To start, you should begin building *your own* retirement nest egg, rather than relying on your employer to provide postretirement income and health-care benefits. A look at recent data on retirees' financial position, summarized in the chart to the right, supports a strategy to become more self-reliant.

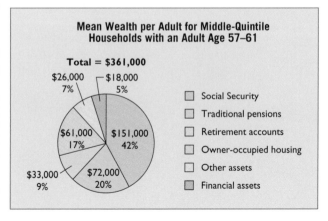

Mean Wealth per Adult for Middle-Quintile Households with an Adult Age 57–61

Total = $361,000

- $26,000 — 7%
- $18,000 — 5%
- $61,000 — 17%
- $151,000 — 42%
- $33,000 — 9%
- $72,000 — 20%

☐ Social Security
☐ Traditional pensions
☐ Retirement accounts
☐ Owner-occupied housing
☐ Other assets
☐ Financial assets

As indicated, the average person at retirement has about $360,000 in resources to sustain him or her in the retirement years. However, Social Security and traditional pension benefits comprise a substantial share of wealth for typical near-to-retirement households—nearly two-thirds of their $361,000 in total wealth. This wealth snapshot highlights the extraordinary importance of Social Security, traditional pensions, and owner-occupied housing (not very liquid) for typical near-retiree households today. Together, these assets comprise nearly four-fifths of wealth of those on the verge of retirement.

However, these sources of income are in decline and will likely continue to shrink as employers and governments wrestle with financial and other constraints discussed earlier. That means that retirement accounts, including individual retirement accounts and defined contribution pensions such as 401(k) plans, will need to become a bigger piece of the pie to fill the gap left by smaller government and employer-sponsored benefits. So get started now with a personal savings strategy to ensure an adequate nest egg at your retirement.

Sources: Story adapted from Nanette Byrnes with David Welch, "The Benefits Trap," *BusinessWeek* (July 19, 2004), pp. 54–72. *Source of chart:* G. Mermin, "Typical Wealth Held by Those at the Verge of Retirement," Urban Institute, *http://www.urban.org/url.cfm?ID=411618* (February 22, 2008).

PREVIEW OF CHAPTER 20

As our opening story indicates, the cost of retirement benefits is steep. For example, British Airways' pension and healthcare costs for retirees in a recent year totaled $195 million, or approximately $6 per passenger carried. Many other companies are also facing substantial pension and other postretirement expenses and obligations. In this chapter, we discuss the accounting issues related to these benefit plans. The content and organization of the chapter are as follows.

ACCOUNTING FOR PENSIONS AND POSTRETIREMENT BENEFITS

NATURE OF PENSION PLANS	ACCOUNTING FOR PENSIONS	USING A PENSION WORKSHEET	REPORTING PENSION PLANS IN FINANCIAL STATEMENTS
• Defined contribution plan	• Alternative measures of liability	• 2012 entries and worksheet	• Within the financial statements
• Defined benefit plan	• Recognition of net funded status	• Amortization of prior service cost	• Within the notes to the financial statements
• Role of actuaries	• Components of pension expense	• 2013 entries and worksheet	• Pension note disclosure
		• Gain or loss	• 2015 entries and worksheet—a comprehensive example
		• 2014 entries and worksheet	• Special issues

NATURE OF PENSION PLANS

A **pension plan** is an arrangement whereby an employer provides benefits (payments) to retired employees for services they provided in their working years. Pension accounting may be divided and separately treated as **accounting for the employer** and **accounting for the pension fund**. The *company* or *employer* is the organization sponsoring the pension plan. It incurs the cost and makes contributions to the pension fund. The *fund* or *plan* is the entity that receives the contributions from the employer, administers the pension assets, and makes the benefit payments to the retired employees (pension recipients). Illustration 20-1 shows the three entities involved in a pension plan and indicates the flow of cash among them.

ILLUSTRATION 20-1
Flow of Cash among
Pension Plan Participants

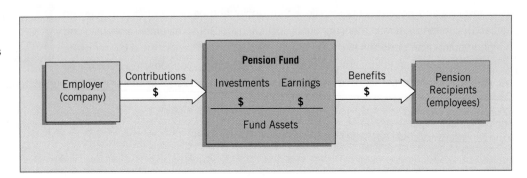

A pension plan is **funded** when the employer makes payments to a funding agency.[1] That agency accumulates the assets of the pension fund and makes payments to the recipients as the benefits come due.

Some pension plans are **contributory**. In these, the employees bear part of the cost of the stated benefits or voluntarily make payments to increase their benefits. Other plans are **noncontributory**. In these plans, the employer bears the entire cost. Companies generally design their pension plans so as to take advantage of federal income tax benefits. Plans that offer tax benefits are called **qualified pension plans**. They permit **deductibility of the employer's contributions to the pension fund and tax-free status of earnings from pension fund assets**.

The pension fund should be a separate legal and accounting entity. The pension fund, as a separate entity, maintains a set of books and prepares financial statements. Maintaining records and preparing financial statements for the fund, an activity known as "accounting for employee benefit plans," is not the subject of this chapter.[2] Instead, this chapter explains the pension accounting and reporting problems **of the employer** as the sponsor of a pension plan.

The need to properly administer and account for pension funds becomes apparent when you understand the size of these funds. Listed in Illustration 20-2 are the pension fund assets and pension expenses of six major companies.

[1]When used as a verb, **fund** means to pay to a funding agency (as to fund future pension benefits or to fund pension cost). Used as a noun, it refers to assets accumulated in the hands of a funding agency (trustee) for the purpose of meeting pension benefits when they become due.

[2]The FASB issued a separate standard covering the accounting and reporting for employee benefit plans. [1]

Company ($ in millions)	Size of Pension Fund	2009 Pension Expense	Pension Expense as % of Pretax Income
General Motors	$98,527	$3,405	3.32%
Hewlett-Packard	8,371	409	4.34%
Deere & Company	8,401	5	0.37%
Merck	10,835	407	2.66%
The Coca-Cola Company	3,032	218	2.44%
Molson Coors Brewing	2,783	11	1.48%

ILLUSTRATION 20-2
Pension Funds and
Pension Expense

As Illustration 20-2 indicates, pension expense is a substantial percentage of total pretax income for many companies.[3] The two most common types of pension plans are **defined contribution plans** and **defined benefit plans**, and we look at each of them in the following sections.

Defined Contribution Plan

In a defined contribution plan, the employer agrees to contribute to a pension trust a certain sum each period, based on a formula. This formula may consider such factors as age, length of employee service, employer's profits, and compensation level. **The plan defines only the employer's contribution.** It makes no promise regarding the ultimate benefits paid out to the employees. A common form of this plan is a **401(k) plan**.

2 LEARNING OBJECTIVE
Identify types of pension plans and their characteristics.

The size of the pension benefits that the employee finally collects under the plan depends on several factors: the amounts originally contributed to the pension trust, the income accumulated in the trust, and the treatment of forfeitures of funds caused by early terminations of other employees. A company usually turns over to an **independent third-party trustee** the amounts originally contributed. The trustee, acting on behalf of the beneficiaries (the participating employees), assumes ownership of the pension assets and is accountable for their investment and distribution. The trust is separate and distinct from the employer.

The accounting for a defined contribution plan is straightforward. The employee gets the benefit of gain (or the risk of loss) from the assets contributed to the pension plan. The employer simply contributes each year based on the formula established in the plan. As a result, the employer's annual cost (pension expense) is simply the amount that it is obligated to contribute to the pension trust. The employer reports a liability on its balance sheet only if it does not make the contribution in full. The employer reports an asset only if it contributes more than the required amount.

In addition to pension expense, the employer must disclose the following for a defined contribution plan: a plan description, including employee groups covered; the basis for determining contributions; and the nature and effect of significant matters affecting comparability from period to period. [2]

Defined Benefit Plan

A defined benefit plan outlines the benefits that employees will receive when they retire. These benefits typically are a function of an employee's years of service and of the compensation level in the years approaching retirement.

To meet the defined benefit commitments that will arise at retirement, a company must determine what the contribution should be today (a time value of money computation). Companies may use many different contribution approaches. However, the funding method should provide enough money at retirement to meet the benefits defined by the plan.

[3]Global pension funds (private and public) held or owned more assets than mutual funds, insurance companies, official reserves, sovereign wealth funds, and private equity. The enormous size (and social significance) of these funds is staggering. See "Asset-Backed Insecurity," *The Economist* (January 17, 2008).

INTERNATIONAL
PERSPECTIVE

Outside the United States, private pension plans are less common because many other nations rely on government-sponsored pension plans. Consequently, accounting for defined benefit pension plans is typically a less important issue elsewhere in the world.

The **employees** are the beneficiaries of a defined **contribution** trust, but the **employer** is the beneficiary of a defined **benefit** trust. Under a defined benefit plan, the trust's primary purpose is to safeguard and invest assets so that there will be enough to pay the employer's obligation to the employees. **In form**, the trust is a separate entity. **In substance**, the trust assets and liabilities belong to the employer. That is, **as long as the plan continues, the employer is responsible for the payment of the defined benefits (without regard to what happens in the trust)**. The employer must make up any shortfall in the accumulated assets held by the trust. On the other hand, the employer can recapture any excess accumulated in the trust, either through reduced future funding or through a reversion of funds.

Because a defined benefit plan specifies benefits in terms of uncertain future variables, a company must establish an appropriate funding pattern to ensure the availability of funds at retirement in order to provide the benefits promised. This funding level depends on a number of factors such as turnover, mortality, length of employee service, compensation levels, and interest earnings.

Employers are at risk with defined benefit plans because they must contribute enough to meet the cost of benefits that the plan defines. The expense recognized each period is not necessarily equal to the cash contribution. Similarly, the liability is controversial because its measurement and recognition relate to unknown future variables. Thus, the accounting issues related to this type of plan are complex. **Our discussion in the following sections deals primarily with defined benefit plans.**[4]

WHICH PLAN IS RIGHT FOR YOU?

What do the numbers mean?

Defined contribution plans have become much more popular with employers than defined benefit plans, as indicated in the chart below. One reason is that they are cheaper. Defined contribution plans often cost no more than 3 percent of payroll, whereas defined benefit plans can cost 5 to 6 percent of payroll.

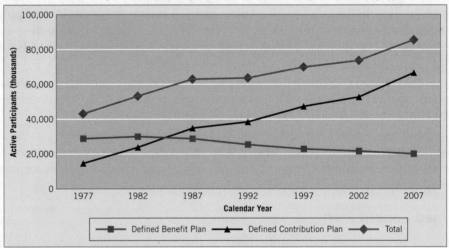

Number of Active Participants in Employer-Sponsored Retirement Plans (in thousands) by Type of Plan

Source: Department of Labor, Employee Benefits Security Administration, January 2010 "Private Pension Plan Bulletin" and February 2009 "Private Pension Plan Bulletin Historical Tables and Graphs."

Although many companies are changing to defined contribution plans, defined benefit plans had an average of almost $63,000 in assets per participant, while defined contribution plans had an average of about $42,000 per participant.

---

[4]A recent federal law requires employees to explicitly opt out of an employer-sponsored defined contribution plan. This should help employees build their own nest eggs (as suggested in the opening story) and will contribute to further growth in defined contribution plans. See D. Darlin, "On Making Enrollment in a 401(k) Automatic," *New York Times* (August 19, 2006), p. B1.

The Role of Actuaries in Pension Accounting

The problems associated with pension plans involve complicated mathematical considerations. Therefore, companies engage **actuaries** to ensure that a pension plan is appropriate for the employee group covered.[5] Actuaries are individuals trained through a long and rigorous certification program to assign probabilities to future events and their financial effects. The insurance industry employs actuaries to assess risks and to advise on the setting of premiums and other aspects of insurance policies. Employers rely heavily on actuaries for assistance in developing, implementing, and funding pension funds.

Actuaries make predictions (called *actuarial assumptions*) of mortality rates, employee turnover, interest and earnings rates, early retirement frequency, future salaries, and any other factors necessary to operate a pension plan. They also compute the various pension measures that affect the financial statements, such as the pension obligation, the annual cost of servicing the plan, and the cost of amendments to the plan. In summary, accounting for defined benefit pension plans relies heavily upon information and measurements provided by actuaries.

ACCOUNTING FOR PENSIONS

In accounting for a company's pension plan, two questions arise: (1) What is the pension obligation that a company should report in the financial statements? (2) What is the pension expense for the period? Attempting to answer the first question has produced much controversy.

> **3 LEARNING OBJECTIVE**
> Explain alternative measures for valuing the pension obligation.

Alternative Measures of the Liability

Most agree that an employer's **pension obligation** is the deferred compensation obligation it has to its employees for their service under the terms of the pension plan. Measuring that obligation is not so simple, though, because there are alternative ways of measuring it.[6]

One measure of the pension obligation is to base it only on the benefits vested to the employees. **Vested benefits** are those that the employee is entitled to receive even if he or she renders no additional services to the company. Most pension plans require a certain minimum number of years of service to the employer before an employee achieves vested benefits status. Companies compute the **vested benefit obligation** using only vested benefits, at current salary levels.

Another way to measure the obligation uses both vested and nonvested years of service. On this basis, the company computes the deferred compensation amount on all years of employees' service—**both vested and nonvested**—using current salary levels. This measurement of the pension obligation is called the **accumulated benefit obligation**.

---

[5] An actuary's primary purpose is to ensure that the company has established an appropriate funding pattern to meet its pension obligations. This computation involves developing a set of assumptions and continued monitoring of these assumptions to ensure their realism. That the general public has little understanding of what an actuary does is illustrated by the following excerpt from the *Wall Street Journal*: "A polling organization once asked the general public what an actuary was, and received among its more coherent responses the opinion that it was a place where you put dead actors."

[6] One measure of the pension obligation is to determine the amount that the **Pension Benefit Guaranty Corporation** would require the employer to pay if it defaulted. (This amount is limited to 30 percent of the employer's net worth.) The accounting profession rejected this approach for financial reporting because it is too hypothetical and ignores the going concern concept.

A third measure bases the deferred compensation amount on both vested and nonvested service **using future salaries**. This measurement of the pension obligation is called the **projected benefit obligation**. Because future salaries are expected to be higher than current salaries, this approach results in the largest measurement of the pension obligation.

The choice between these measures is critical. The choice affects the amount of a company's pension liability and the annual pension expense reported. The diagram in Illustration 20-3 presents the differences in these three measurements.

ILLUSTRATION 20-3
Different Measures of the Pension Obligation

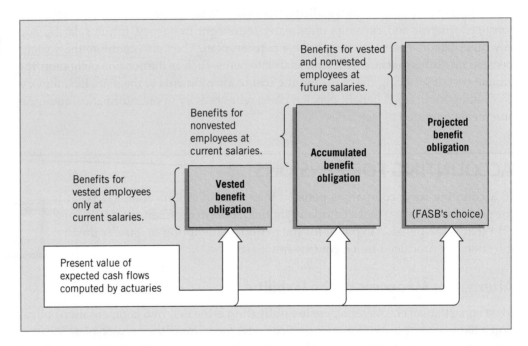

Which of these alternative measures of the pension liability does the profession favor? **The profession adopted the projected benefit obligation—the present value of vested and nonvested benefits accrued to date, based on employees' future salary levels.**[7] Those in favor of the projected benefit obligation contend that a promise by an employer to pay benefits based on a percentage of the employees' future salaries is far greater than a promise to pay a percentage of their current salary, and such a difference should be reflected in the pension liability and pension expense.

Moreover, companies discount to present value the estimated future benefits to be paid. Minor changes in the interest rate used to discount pension benefits can dramatically affect the measurement of the employer's obligation. For example, a 1 percent decrease in the discount rate can increase pension liabilities 15 percent. Accounting rules require that, at each measurement date, a company must determine the appropriate discount rate used to measure the pension liability, based on current interest rates.

Underlying Concepts

The FASB and IASB are studying whether the liability should include estimates of future salaries. This debate will center on whether a company can have a liability today that is based in part on future salaries that have not yet been earned.

---

[7]When we use the term "present value of benefits" throughout this chapter, we really mean the *actuarial* present value of benefits. **Actuarial present value** is the amount payable adjusted to reflect the time value of money *and* the probability of payment (by means of decrements for events such as death, disability, withdrawals, or retirement) between the present date and the expected date of payment. For simplicity, though, we use the term "present value" instead of "actuarial present value" in our discussion.

Recognition of the Net Funded Status of the Pension Plan

Companies must recognize on their balance sheet the full overfunded or underfunded status of their defined benefit pension plan.[8] [3] The overfunded or underfunded status is measured as the difference between the fair value of the plan assets and the projected benefit obligation.

> **INTERNATIONAL PERSPECTIVE**
>
> IFRS differs from GAAP in that companies have the option to report the funded status of their pension plans on the balance sheet.

To illustrate, assume that Coker Company has a projected benefit obligation of $300,000, and the fair value of its plan assets is $210,000. In this case, Coker Company's pension plan is underfunded, and therefore it reports a pension liability of $90,000 ($300,000 − $210,000) on its balance sheet. If, instead, the fair value of Coker's plan assets were $430,000, it would report a pension asset of $130,000 ($430,000 − $300,000).

In 2007, by slowing the growth of pension liabilities and increasing contributions to pension funds, the S&P 500 companies reported aggregate overfunding (assets exceeded liabilities) of $51.6 billion. However, by 2009, these same pension plans were underfunded by $263.7 billion as a result of the financial crisis of 2008.[9]

Components of Pension Expense

There is broad agreement that companies should account for pension cost on the **accrual basis**.[10] The profession recognizes that **accounting for pension plans requires measurement of the cost and its identification with the appropriate time periods**. The determination of pension cost, however, is extremely complicated because it is a function of the following components.

> **4 LEARNING OBJECTIVE**
> List the components of pension expense.

1. *Service cost.* Service cost is the expense caused by the increase in pension benefits payable (the **projected benefit obligation**) to employees because of their services rendered during the current year. Actuaries compute **service cost** as the present value of the new benefits earned by employees during the year.

> **Underlying Concepts**
>
> The expense recognition principle and the definition of a liability justify accounting for pension cost on the accrual basis. This requires recording an expense when employees earn the future benefits, and recognizing an existing obligation to pay pensions later based on current services received.

2. *Interest on the liability.* Because a pension is a deferred compensation arrangement, there is a time value of money factor. As a result, companies record the pension liability on a discounted basis. **Interest expense accrues each year on the projected benefit obligation just as it does on any discounted debt.** The actuary helps to select the interest rate, referred to as the **settlement rate**.

3. *Actual return on plan assets.* The return earned by the accumulated pension fund assets in a particular year is relevant in measuring the net cost to the employer of sponsoring an employee pension plan. Therefore, **a company should adjust annual pension expense for interest and dividends that accumulate within the fund, as well as increases and decreases in the fair value of the fund assets**.

4. *Amortization of prior service cost.* Pension plan amendments (including initiation of a pension plan) often include provisions to increase benefits (or in rare situations, to decrease benefits) for employee service provided in prior years. A company grants plan amendments with the expectation that it will realize economic benefits in future periods. Thus, **it allocates the cost (prior service cost) of providing these**

---

[8]Recognize that GAAP applies to pensions as well as other postretirement benefit plans (OPEBs). Appendix 20A addresses the accounting for OPEBs.

[9]J. Ciesielski, "Still NSFW? The State of Pensions, 2009," *The Analyst's Accounting Observer* (April 26, 2010).

[10]At one time, companies applied the **cash basis** of accounting to pension plans by recognizing the amount paid in a particular accounting period as the pension expense for the period. The problem was that the amount paid or funded in a fiscal period depended on financial management and was too often discretionary. For example, funding could depend on the availability of cash, the level of earnings, or other factors unrelated to the requirements of the plan. Application of the cash basis made it possible to manipulate the amount of pension expense appearing in the income statement simply by varying the cash paid to the pension fund.

retroactive benefits to pension expense in the future, specifically to the remaining service-years of the affected employees.

5. *Gain or loss.* Volatility in pension expense can result from sudden and large changes in the fair value of plan assets and by changes in the projected benefit obligation (which changes when actuaries modify assumptions or when actual experience differs from expected experience). Two items comprise this gain or loss: (1) the difference between the actual return and the expected return on plan assets, and (2) amortization of the net gain or loss from previous periods. We will discuss this complex computation later in the chapter.

Illustration 20-4 shows the **components of pension expense** and their effect on total pension expense (increase or decrease).

ILLUSTRATION 20-4
Components of Annual
Pension Expense

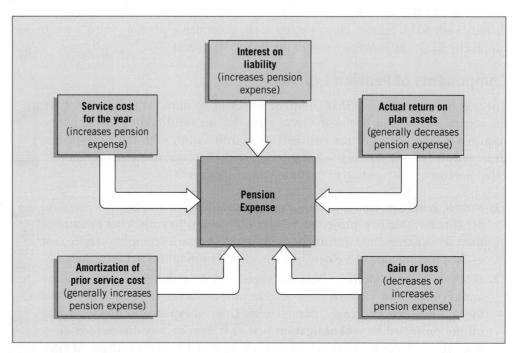

Service Cost

The service cost is the **actuarial present value of benefits attributed by the pension benefit formula to employee service during the period**. That is, the actuary predicts the additional benefits that an employer must pay under the plan's benefit formula as a result of the employees' current year's service, and then discounts the cost of those future benefits back to their present value.

The Board concluded that **companies must consider future compensation levels in measuring the present obligation and periodic pension expense if the plan benefit formula incorporates them**. In other words, the present obligation resulting from a promise to pay a benefit of 1 percent of an employee's **final pay** differs from the promise to pay 1 percent of **current pay**. To overlook this fact is to ignore an important aspect of pension expense. Thus, the FASB adopts the **benefits/years-of-service actuarial method, which determines pension expense based on future salary levels**.

Some object to this determination, arguing that a company should have more freedom to select an expense recognition pattern. Others believe that incorporating future salary increases into current pension expense is accounting for events that have not yet happened. They argue that if a company terminates the plan today, it pays only liabilities for accumulated benefits. **Nevertheless, the FASB indicates that the projected benefit obligation provides a more realistic measure of the employer's obligation under the plan on a going concern basis and, therefore, companies should use it as the basis for determining service cost.**

Interest on the Liability

The second component of pension expense is interest on the liability, or interest expense. Because a company defers paying the liability until maturity, the company records it on a discounted basis. The liability then accrues interest over the life of the employee. **The interest component is the interest for the period on the projected benefit obligation outstanding during the period.** The FASB did not address the question of how often to compound the interest cost. To simplify our illustrations and problem materials, we use a simple interest computation, applying it to the beginning-of-the-year balance of the projected benefit liability.

How do companies determine the interest rate to apply to the pension liability? The Board states that the assumed discount rate should **reflect the rates at which companies can effectively settle pension benefits**. In determining these settlement rates, companies should look to rates of return on high-quality fixed-income investments currently available, whose cash flows match the timing and amount of the expected benefit payments. The objective of selecting the assumed discount rates is to measure a single amount that, if invested in a portfolio of high-quality debt instruments, would provide the necessary future cash flows to pay the pension benefits when due.

Actual Return on Plan Assets

Pension plan assets are usually investments in stocks, bonds, other securities, and real estate that a company holds to earn a reasonable return, generally at minimum risk. Employer contributions and actual returns on pension plan assets increase pension plan assets. Benefits paid to retired employees decrease them. As we indicated, the actual return earned on these assets increases the fund balance and correspondingly reduces the employer's net cost of providing employees' pension benefits. That is, the higher the actual return on the pension plan assets, the less the employer has to contribute eventually and, therefore, the less pension expense that it needs to report.

The actual return on the plan assets is the increase in pension funds from interest, dividends, and realized and unrealized changes in the fair value of the plan assets. Companies compute the actual return by adjusting the change in the plan assets for the effects of contributions during the year and benefits paid out during the year. The equation in Illustration 20-5, or a variation thereof, can be used to compute the actual return.

$$\text{Actual Return} = \left(\begin{array}{c} \text{Plan Assets Ending Balance} \end{array} - \begin{array}{c} \text{Plan Assets Beginning Balance} \end{array} \right) - (\text{Contributions} - \text{Benefits Paid})$$

ILLUSTRATION 20-5
Equation for Computing Actual Return

Stated another way, the actual return on plan assets is the difference between the fair value of the plan assets at the beginning of the period and at the end of the period, adjusted for contributions and benefit payments. Illustration 20-6 uses the equation above to compute the actual return, using some assumed amounts.

Fair value of plan assets at end of period		$5,000,000
Deduct: Fair value of plan assets at beginning of period		4,200,000
Increase in fair value of plan assets		800,000
Deduct: Contributions to plan during period	$500,000	
Less benefits paid during period	300,000	200,000
Actual return on plan assets		$ 600,000

ILLUSTRATION 20-6
Computation of Actual Return on Plan Assets

If the actual return on the plan assets is positive (a gain) during the period, a company subtracts it when computing pension expense. If the actual return is negative (a loss) during the period, the company adds it when computing pension expense.[11]

---

[11]At this point, we use the actual rate of return. Later, for purposes of computing pension expense, we use the expected rate of return.

USING A PENSION WORKSHEET

We will now illustrate the basic computation of pension expense using the first three components: (1) service cost, (2) interest on the liability, and (3) actual return on plan assets. We discuss the other pension expense components (amortization of prior service cost, and gains and losses) in later sections.

Companies often use a worksheet to record pension-related information. As its name suggests, the worksheet is a working tool. A worksheet is **not** a permanent accounting record: It is neither a journal nor part of the general ledger. The worksheet is merely a device to make it easier to prepare entries and the financial statements.[12] Illustration 20-7 shows the format of the pension worksheet.

ILLUSTRATION 20-7
Basic Format of Pension Worksheet

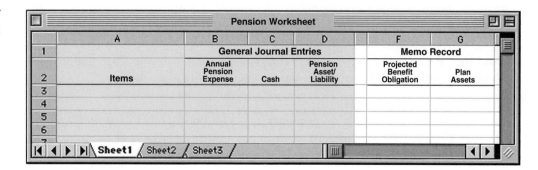

The "General Journal Entries" columns of the worksheet (near the left side) determine the entries to record in the formal general ledger accounts. The "Memo Record" columns (on the right side) maintain balances in the projected benefit obligation and the plan assets. The difference between the projected benefit obligation and the fair value of the plan assets is the pension asset/liability, which is shown in the balance sheet. If the projected benefit obligation is greater than the plan assets, a pension liability occurs. If the projected benefit obligation is less than the plan assets, a pension asset occurs.

On the first line of the worksheet, a company records the beginning balances (if any). It then records subsequent transactions and events related to the pension plan using debits and credits, using both sets of columns as if they were one. For each transaction or event, the debits must equal the credits. **The ending balance in the Pension Asset/Liability column should equal the net balance in the memo record.**

2012 Entries and Worksheet

To illustrate the use of a worksheet and how it helps in accounting for a pension plan, assume that on January 1, 2012, Zarle Company provides the following information related to its pension plan for the year 2012.

Plan assets, January 1, 2012, are $100,000.

Projected benefit obligation, January 1, 2012, is $100,000.

Annual service cost is $9,000.

Settlement rate is 10 percent.

Actual return on plan assets is $10,000.

Funding contributions are $8,000.

Benefits paid to retirees during the year are $7,000.

[12]The use of a pension entry worksheet is recommended and illustrated by Paul B. W. Miller, "The New Pension Accounting (Part 2)," *Journal of Accountancy* (February 1987), pp. 86–94.

Using the data presented on page 1218, the worksheet in Illustration 20-8 presents the beginning balances and all of the pension entries recorded by Zarle in 2012. Zarle records the beginning balances for the projected benefit obligation and the pension plan assets on the first line of the worksheet in the memo record. Because the projected benefit obligation and the plan assets are the same at January 1, 2012, the Pension Asset/Liability account has a zero balance at January 1, 2012.

ILLUSTRATION 20-8
Pension Worksheet—2012

	Pension Worksheet—2012					
	A	**B**	**C**	**D**	**F**	**G**
1		**General Journal Entries**			**Memo Record**	
2	**Items**	**Annual Pension Expense**	**Cash**	**Pension Asset/ Liability**	**Projected Benefit Obligation**	**Plan Assets**
3	Balance, Jan. 1, 2012			—	100,000 Cr.	100,000 Dr.
4	(a) Service cost	9,000 Dr.			9,000 Cr.	
5	(b) Interest cost	10,000 Dr.			10,000 Cr.	
6	(c) Actual return	10,000 Cr.				10,000 Dr.
7	(d) Contributions		8,000 Cr.			8,000 Dr.
8	(e) Benefits				7,000 Dr.	7,000 Cr.
9						
10						
11	Journal entry for 2012	9,000 Dr.	8,000 Cr.	1,000 Cr.*		
12	Balance, Dec. 31, 2012			1,000 Cr.**	112,000 Cr.	111,000 Dr.
13						
14	*$9,000 – $8,000 = $1,000					
15	**$112,000 – $111,000 = $1.000					

Sheet1 / Sheet2 / Sheet3

Entry (a) in Illustration 20-8 records the service cost component, which increases pension expense by $9,000 and increases the liability (projected benefit obligation) by $9,000. Entry (b) accrues the interest expense component, which increases both the liability and the pension expense by $10,000 (the beginning projected benefit obligation multiplied by the settlement rate of 10 percent). Entry (c) records the actual return on the plan assets, which increases the plan assets and decreases the pension expense. Entry (d) records Zarle's contribution (funding) of assets to the pension fund, thereby decreasing cash by $8,000 and increasing plan assets by $8,000. Entry (e) records the benefit payments made to retirees, which results in equal $7,000 decreases to the plan assets and the projected benefit obligation.

Zarle makes the "formal journal entry" on December 31, which records the pension expense in 2012, as follows.

2012

Pension Expense	9,000	
Cash		8,000
Pension Asset/Liability		1,000

The credit to Pension Asset/Liability for $1,000 represents the difference between the 2012 pension expense of $9,000 and the amount funded of $8,000. Pension Asset/Liability (credit) is a liability because Zarle underfunds the plan by $1,000. The Pension Asset/Liability account balance of $1,000 also equals the net of the balances in the memo accounts. Illustration 20-9 shows that the projected benefit obligation exceeds the plan assets by $1,000, which reconciles to the pension liability reported in the balance sheet.

Projected benefit obligation (Credit)	$(112,000)
Plan assets at fair value (Debit)	111,000
Pension asset/liability (Credit)	$ (1,000)

ILLUSTRATION 20-9
Pension Reconciliation Schedule—December 31, 2012

If the net of the memo record balances is a credit, the reconciling amount in the pension asset/liability column will be a credit equal in amount. If the net of the memo record balances is a debit, the pension asset/liability amount will be a debit equal in amount. The worksheet is designed to produce this reconciling feature, which is useful later in the preparation of the financial statements and required note disclosure related to pensions.

In this illustration (for 2012), the debit to Pension Expense exceeds the credit to Cash, resulting in a credit to Pension Asset/Liability—the recognition of a liability. If the credit to Cash exceeded the debit to Pension Expense, Zarle would debit Pension Asset/Liability—the recognition of an asset.

Amortization of Prior Service Cost (PSC)

LEARNING OBJECTIVE 6
Describe the amortization of prior service costs.

When either initiating (adopting) or amending a defined benefit plan, a company often provides benefits to employees for years of service before the date of initiation or amendment. As a result of this prior service cost, the projected benefit obligation is increased to recognize this additional liability. In many cases, the increase in the projected benefit obligation is substantial.

Should a company report an expense for these prior service costs (PSC) at the time it initiates or amends a plan? The FASB says no. The Board's rationale is that the employer would not provide credit for past years of service unless it expects to receive benefits in the future. As a result, a company should not recognize the retroactive benefits as pension expense in the year of amendment. Instead, **the employer initially records the prior service cost as an adjustment to other comprehensive income. The employer then recognizes the prior service cost as a component of pension expense over the remaining service lives of the employees who are expected to benefit from the change in the plan.**

The cost of the retroactive benefits (including any benefits provided to existing retirees) is the increase in the projected benefit obligation at the date of the amendment. An actuary computes the amount of the prior service cost. Amortization of the prior service cost is also an accounting function performed with the assistance of an actuary.

The Board prefers a years-of-service method that is similar to a units-of-production computation. First, the company computes the total number of service-years to be worked by all of the participating employees. Second, it divides the prior service cost by the total number of service-years, to obtain a cost per service-year (the unit cost). Third, the company multiplies the number of service-years consumed each year by the cost per service-year, to obtain the annual amortization charge.

To illustrate the amortization of the prior service cost under the years-of-service method, assume that Zarle Company's defined benefit pension plan covers 170 employees. In its negotiations with the employees, Zarle Company amends its pension plan on January 1, 2013, and grants $80,000 of prior service costs to its employees. The employees are grouped according to expected years of retirement, as shown below.

Group	Number of Employees	Expected Retirement on Dec. 31
A	40	2013
B	20	2014
C	40	2015
D	50	2016
E	20	2017
	170	

Illustration 20-10 shows computation of the service-years per year and the total service-years.

ILLUSTRATION 20-10
Computation of Service-
Years

			Service-Years			
Year	A	B	C	D	E	Total
2013	40	20	40	50	20	170
2014		20	40	50	20	130
2015			40	50	20	110
2016				50	20	70
2017					20	20
	40	40	120	200	100	500

Computed on the basis of a prior service cost of $80,000 and a total of 500 service-years for all years, the cost per service-year is $160 ($80,000 ÷ 500). The annual amount of amortization based on a $160 cost per service-year is computed as follows.

ILLUSTRATION 20-11
Computation of Annual
Prior Service Cost
Amortization

Year	Total Service-Years	×	Cost per Service-Year	=	Annual Amortization
2013	170		$160		$27,200
2014	130		160		20,800
2015	110		160		17,600
2016	70		160		11,200
2017	20		160		3,200
	500				$80,000

An alternative method of computing amortization of **prior service cost is permitted: Employers may use straight-line amortization over the average remaining service life of the employees.** In this case, with 500 service-years and 170 employees, the average would be 2.94 years (500 ÷ 170). The annual expense would be $27,211 ($80,000 ÷ 2.94). Using this method, Zarle Company would charge cost to expense in 2013, 2014, and 2015 as follows.

Year	Expense
2013	$27,211
2014	27,211
2015	25,578*
	$80,000

*.94 × $27,211

2013 Entries and Worksheet

Continuing the Zarle Company illustration into 2013, we note that the company amends the pension plan on January 1, 2013, to grant employees prior service benefits with a present value of $80,000. Zarle uses the annual amortization amounts, as computed in the previous section using the years-of-service approach ($27,200 for 2013). The following additional facts apply to the pension plan for the year 2013.

Annual service cost is $9,500.

Settlement rate is 10 percent.

Actual return on plan assets is $11,100.

Annual funding contributions are $20,000.

Benefits paid to retirees during the year are $8,000.

Amortization of prior service cost (PSC) using the years-of-service method is $27,200.

Accumulated other comprehensive income (hereafter referred to as accumulated OCI) on December 31, 2012, is zero.

Illustration 20-12 presents a worksheet of all the pension entries and information recorded by Zarle in 2013. We now add an additional column to the worksheet to record the prior service cost adjustment to other comprehensive income. In addition, as shown in rows 17 and 18, the other comprehensive income amount related to prior service cost is added to accumulated other comprehensive income ("Accumulated OCI") to arrive at a debit balance of $52,800 at December 31, 2013.

Pension Worksheet—2013

	A	B	C	D	E	G	H
1		General Journal Entries				Memo Record	
2				Other Comprehensive Income			
3	Items	Annual Pension Expense	Cash	Prior Service Cost	Pension Asset/Liability	Projected Benefit Obligation	Plan Assets
4	Balance, Dec. 31, 2012				1,000 Cr.	112,000 Cr.	111,000 Dr.
5	(f) Prior service cost			80,000 Dr.		80,000 Cr.	0
6							
7	Balance, Jan. 1, 2013					192,000 Cr.	111,000 Dr.
8	(g) Service cost	9,500 Dr.				9,500 Cr.	
9	(h) Interest cost	19,200 Dr.				19,200 Cr.	
10	(i) Actual return	11,100 Cr.					11,100 Dr.
11	(j) Amortization of PSC	27,200 Dr.		27,200 Cr.			
12	(k) Contributions		20,000 Cr.				20,000 Dr.
13	(l) Benefits					8,000 Dr.	8,000 Cr.
14							
15	Journal entry for 2013	44,800 Dr.	20,000 Cr.	52,800 Dr.	77,600 Cr.		
16							
17	Accumulated OCI, Dec. 31, 2012			0			
18	Balance, Dec. 31, 2013			52,800 Dr.	78,600 Cr.	212,700 Cr.	134,100 Dr.
19							

ILLUSTRATION 20-12
Pension Worksheet—2013

The first line of the worksheet shows the beginning balances of the Pension Asset/Liability account and the memo accounts. Entry (f) records Zarle's granting of prior service cost, by adding $80,000 to the projected benefit obligation and decreasing other comprehensive income—prior service cost by the same amount. Entries (g), (h), (i), (k), and (l) are similar to the corresponding entries in 2012. To compute the interest cost on the projected benefit obligation for entry (h), we use the beginning projected benefit balance of $192,000, which has been adjusted for the prior service cost amendment on January 1, 2013. Entry (j) records the 2013 amortization of prior service cost by debiting Pension Expense for $27,200 and crediting **Other Comprehensive Income (PSC)** for the same amount.

Zarle makes the following journal entry on December 31 to formally record the 2013 pension expense (the sum of the annual pension expense column), and related pension information.

2013

Pension Expense	44,800	
Other Comprehensive Income (PSC)	52,800	
Cash		20,000
Pension Asset/Liability		77,600

Because the debits to Pension Expense and to Other Comprehensive Income (PSC) exceed the funding, Zarle credits the Pension Asset/Liability account for the $77,600 difference. That account is a liability. In 2013, as in 2012, the balance of the Pension

Asset/Liability account ($78,600) is equal to the net of the balances in the memo accounts, as shown in Illustration 20-13.

Projected benefit obligation (Credit)	$(212,700)
Plan assets at fair value (Debit)	134,100
Pension asset/liability (Credit)	$ (78,600)

ILLUSTRATION 20-13
Pension Reconciliation
Schedule—December 31, 2013

The reconciliation is the formula that makes the worksheet work. It relates the components of pension accounting, recorded and unrecorded, to one another.

Gain or Loss

Of great concern to companies that have pension plans are the uncontrollable and unexpected swings in pension expense that can result from (1) sudden and large changes in the fair value of plan assets, and (2) changes in actuarial assumptions that affect the amount of the projected benefit obligation. If these gains or losses impact fully the financial statements in the period of realization or incurrence, substantial fluctuations in pension expense result.

7 LEARNING OBJECTIVE
Explain the accounting for unexpected gains and losses.

Therefore, the FASB decided to reduce the volatility associated with pension expense by using **smoothing techniques** that dampen and in some cases fully eliminate the fluctuations.

Smoothing Unexpected Gains and Losses on Plan Assets

One component of pension expense, actual return on plan assets, reduces pension expense (assuming the actual return is positive). A large change in the actual return can substantially affect pension expense for a year. Assume a company has a 40 percent return in the stock market for the year. Should this substantial, and perhaps one-time, event affect current pension expense?

Actuaries ignore current fluctuations when they develop a funding pattern to pay expected benefits in the future. They develop an expected rate of return and multiply it by an asset value weighted over a reasonable period of time to arrive at an expected return on plan assets. They then use this return to determine a company's funding pattern.

The FASB adopted the actuary's approach to dampen wide swings that might occur in the actual return. That is, a company includes the **expected return** on the plan assets as a component of pension expense, not the actual return in a given year. To achieve this goal, the company multiplies the expected rate of return by the market-related value of the plan assets. The market-related asset value of the plan assets is either the fair value of plan assets or a calculated value that recognizes changes in fair value in a systematic and rational manner. [4][13]

The difference between the expected return and the actual return is referred to as the unexpected gain or loss; the FASB uses the term asset gains and losses. **Asset gains** occur when actual return exceeds expected return; **asset losses** occur when actual return is less than expected return.

What happens to unexpected gains or losses in the accounting for pensions? Companies record asset gains and asset losses in an account, Other Comprehensive Income (G/L), combining them with gains and losses accumulated in prior years. This treatment

---

[13]Companies may use different ways of determining the calculated market-related value for different classes of assets. For example, an employer might use fair value for bonds and a five-year moving-average for equities. But companies should consistently apply the manner of determining market-related value from year to year for each asset class. Throughout our Zarle illustrations, we assume that market-related values based on a calculated value and the fair value of plan assets are equal. *For homework purposes, use the fair value of plan assets as the measure for the market-related value.*

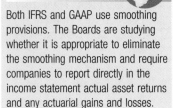

is similar to prior service cost. The Board believes this treatment is consistent with the practice of including in other comprehensive income certain changes in value that have not been recognized in net income (for example, unrealized gains and losses on available-for-sale securities). [5] In addition, the accounting is simple, transparent, and symmetrical.

To illustrate the computation of an unexpected gain or loss and its related accounting, assume that in 2014, Zarle Company has an actual return on plan assets of $12,000 when the expected return is $13,410 (the expected rate of return of 10% on plan assets times the beginning-of-the-year plan assets). The unexpected asset loss of $1,410 ($12,000 − $13,410) is debited to Other Comprehensive Income (G/L) and credited to Pension Expense.

PENSION COSTS UPS AND DOWNS

What do the numbers mean?

For some companies, pension plans generated real profits in the late 1990s. The plans not only paid for themselves but also increased earnings. This happens when the expected return on pension assets exceed the company's annual costs. At Norfolk Southern, pension income amounted to 12 percent of operating profit. It tallied 11 percent of operating profit at Lucent Technologies, Coastal Corp., and Unisys Corp. The issue is important because in these cases management is not driving the operating income—pension income is. And as a result, income can change quickly.

Unfortunately, when the stock market stops booming, pension expense substantially increases for many companies. The reason: Expected return on a smaller asset base no longer offsets pension service costs and interest on the projected benefit obligation. As a result, many companies find it difficult to meet their earnings targets, and at a time when meeting such targets is crucial to maintaining the stock price.

Smoothing Unexpected Gains and Losses on the Pension Liability

In estimating the projected benefit obligation (the liability), actuaries make assumptions about such items as mortality rate, retirement rate, turnover rate, disability rate, and salary amounts. Any change in these actuarial assumptions affects the amount of the projected benefit obligation. Seldom does actual experience coincide exactly with actuarial predictions. These unexpected gains or losses from changes in the projected benefit obligation are called liability gains and losses.

Companies report liability gains (resulting from unexpected decreases in the liability balance) and liability losses (resulting from unexpected increases) in Other Comprehensive Income (G/L). Companies combine the liability gains and losses in the same Other Comprehensive Income (G/L) account used for asset gains and losses. They accumulate the asset and liability gains and losses from year to year that are not amortized in Accumulated Other Comprehensive Income. This amount is reported on the balance sheet in the stockholders' equity section.

Corridor Amortization

LEARNING OBJECTIVE **8**

Explain the corridor approach to amortizing gains and losses.

The asset gains and losses and the liability gains and losses can offset each other. As a result, the Accumulated OCI account related to gains and losses may not grow very large. But, it is possible that no offsetting will occur and that the balance in the Accumulated OCI account related to gains and losses will continue to grow.

To limit the growth of the Accumulated OCI account, the FASB invented the corridor approach for amortizing the account's accumulated balance when it gets too large. How large is too large? The FASB set a limit of 10 percent of the larger of the beginning balances of the projected benefit obligation or the market-related value of the plan assets. **Above that size, the Accumulated OCI account related to gains and losses is considered too large and must be amortized.**

To illustrate the corridor approach, data for Callaway Co.'s projected benefit obligation and plan assets over a period of six years are shown in Illustration 20-14.

ILLUSTRATION 20-14
Computation of the
Corridor

Beginning-of-the-Year Balances	Projected Benefit Obligation	Market-Related Asset Value	Corridor* +/− 10%
2011	$1,000,000	$ 900,000	$100,000
2012	1,200,000	1,100,000	120,000
2013	1,300,000	1,700,000	170,000
2014	1,500,000	2,250,000	225,000
2015	1,700,000	1,750,000	175,000
2016	1,800,000	1,700,000	180,000

*The corridor becomes 10% of the larger (in colored type) of the projected benefit obligation or the market-related plan asset value.

How the corridor works becomes apparent when we portray the data graphically, as in Illustration 20-15.

ILLUSTRATION 20-15
Graphic Illustration of
the Corridor

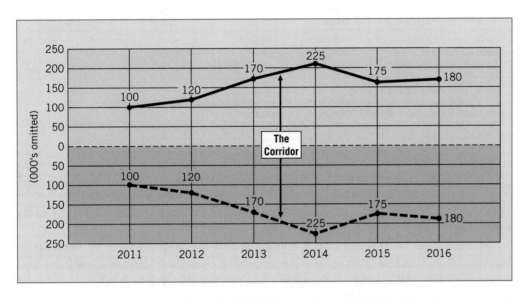

If the balance in the Accumulated OCI account related to gains and losses stays within the upper and lower limits of the corridor, no amortization is required. In that case, Callaway carries forward unchanged the accumulated OCI related to gains and losses.

If amortization is required, the minimum amortization is the excess divided by the average remaining service period of active employees who are expected to receive benefits under the plan. Callaway may use any systematic method of amortization of gains and losses in lieu of the minimum, provided it is greater than the minimum. It must use the method consistently for both gains and losses, and must disclose the amortization method used.

Example of Gains/Losses

In applying the corridor, companies should include amortization of the net gain or loss as a component of pension expense only if, at the **beginning of the year**, the net gain or loss in Accumulated OCI exceeded the corridor. That is, if no net gain or loss exists in Accumulated OCI at the beginning of the period, the company cannot recognize pension expense gains or losses in that period.

To illustrate the amortization of net gains and losses, assume the following information for Soft-White, Inc.

	2012	2013	2014
		(beginning of the year)	
Projected benefit obligation	$2,100,000	$2,600,000	$2,900,000
Market-related asset value	2,600,000	2,800,000	2,700,000

Soft-White recorded in Other Comprehensive Income actuarial losses of $400,000 in 2012 and $300,000 in 2013.

If the average remaining service life of all active employees is 5.5 years, the schedule to amortize the net gain or loss is as shown in Illustration 20-16.

ILLUSTRATION 20-16
Corridor Test and
Gain/Loss Amortization
Schedule

Year	Projected Benefit Obligation[a]	Plan Assets[a]	Corridor[b]	Accumulated OCI (G/L)[a]	Minimum Amortization of Loss (For Current Year)
2012	$2,100,000	$2,600,000	$260,000	$ –0–	$ –0–
2013	2,600,000	2,800,000	280,000	400,000	21,818[c]
2014	2,900,000	2,700,000	290,000	678,182[d]	70,579[d]

[a]All as of the beginning of the period.
[b]10% of the greater of projected benefit obligation or plan assets' market-related value.
[c]$400,000 − $280,000 = $120,000; $120,000 ÷ 5.5 = $21,818.
[d]$400,000 − $21,818 + $300,000 = $678,182; $678,182 − $290,000 = $388,182; $388,182 ÷ 5.5 = $70,579.

As Illustration 20-16 indicates, the loss recognized in 2013 increased pension expense by $21,818. This amount is small in comparison with the total loss of $400,000. It indicates that the corridor approach dampens the effects (reduces volatility) of these gains and losses on pension expense.

The rationale for the corridor is that gains and losses result from refinements in estimates as well as real changes in economic value; over time, some of these gains and losses will offset one another. It therefore seems reasonable that Soft-White should not fully recognize gains and losses as a component of pension expense in the period in which they arise.

However, Soft-White should immediately recognize in net income certain gains and losses—if they arise from a single occurrence not directly related to the operation of the pension plan and not in the ordinary course of the employer's business. For example, a gain or loss that is directly related to a plant closing, a disposal of a business component, or a similar event that greatly affects the size of the employee work force should be recognized as a part of the gain or loss associated with that event.

For example, at one time, Bethlehem Steel reported a quarterly loss of $477 million. A great deal of this loss was attributable to future estimated benefits payable to workers who were permanently laid off. In this situation, the loss should be treated as an adjustment to the gain or loss on the plant closing and should not affect pension cost for the current or future periods.

Summary of Calculations for Asset Gain or Loss

The difference between the actual return on plan assets and the expected return on plan assets is the **unexpected asset gain or loss** component. This component defers the difference between the actual return and expected return on plan assets in computing current-year pension expense. Thus, after considering this component, **it is really the expected return on plan assets (not the actual return) that determines current pension expense**.

Companies determine the amortized net gain or loss by amortizing the Accumulated OCI amount related to net gain or loss at the beginning of the year subject to the corridor limitation. In other words, **if the accumulated gain or loss is greater than the corridor, these net gains and losses are subject to amortization**. Soft-White computed this minimum amortization by dividing the net gains or losses subject to amortization by the average remaining service period. When the current-year unexpected gain or loss is combined with the amortized net gain or loss, we determine the current-year gain or loss. Illustration 20-17 summarizes these gain and loss computations.

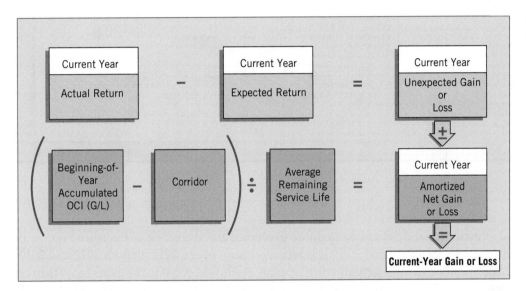

ILLUSTRATION 20-17
Graphic Summary of Gain
or Loss Computation

In essence, these gains and losses are subject to *triple* smoothing. That is, companies first smooth the asset gain or loss by using the expected return. Second, they do not amortize the accumulated gain or loss at the beginning of the year unless it is greater than the corridor. Finally, they spread the excess over the remaining service life of existing employees.

2014 Entries and Worksheet

Continuing the Zarle Company illustration, the following facts apply to the pension plan for 2014.

Annual service cost is $13,000.

Settlement rate is 10 percent; expected earnings rate is 10 percent.

Actual return on plan assets is $12,000.

Amortization of prior service cost (PSC) is $20,800.

Annual funding contributions are $24,000.

Benefits paid to retirees during the year are $10,500.

Changes in actuarial assumptions resulted in an end-of-year projected benefit obligation of $265,000.

The worksheet in Illustration 20-18 (on page 1228) presents all of Zarle's 2014 pension entries and related information. The first line of the worksheet records the beginning balances that relate to the pension plan. In this case, Zarle's beginning balances are the ending balances from its 2013 pension worksheet in Illustration 20-12 (page 1222).

		Pension Worksheet—2014						
	A	B	C	D	E	F	H	I
1		General Journal Entries					Memo Record	
2				Other Comprehensive Income				
3	**Items**	Annual Pension Expense	Cash	Prior Service Cost	Gains/Losses	Pension Asset/Liability	Projected Benefit Obligation	Plan Assets
4	Balance, Jan. 1, 2014					78,600 Cr.	212,700 Cr.	134,100 Dr.
5	(m) Service cost	13,000 Dr.					13,000 Cr.	
6	(n) Interest cost	21,270 Dr.					21,270 Cr.	
7	(o) Actual return	12,000 Cr.						12,000 Dr.
8	(p) Unexpected loss	1,410 Cr.			1,410 Dr.			
9	(q) Amortization of PSC	20,800 Dr.		20,800 Cr.				
10	(r) Contributions		24,000 Cr.					24,000 Dr.
11	(s) Benefits						10,500 Dr.	10,500 Cr.
12	(t) Liability increase				28,530 Dr.		28,530 Cr.	
13								
14	Journal entry for 2014	41,660 Dr.	24,000 Cr.	20,800 Cr.	29,940 Dr.	26,800 Cr.		
15								
16	Accumulated OCI, Dec. 31, 2013			52,800 Dr.	0			
17	Balance, Dec. 31, 2014*			32,000 Dr.	29,940 Dr.	105,400 Cr.	265,000 Cr.	159,600 Dr.
18								
19	*Accumulated OCI (PSC)	$32,000 Dr.						
20	Accumulated OCI (G/L)	29,940 Dr.						
21	Accumulated OCI, Dec. 31, 2014	$61,940 Dr.						

Sheet1 / Sheet2 / Sheet3

ILLUSTRATION 20-18
Pension Worksheet—2014

Entries (m), (n), (o), (q), (r), and (s) are similar to the corresponding entries in 2012 or 2013.

Entries (o) and (p) are related. We explained the recording of the actual return in entry (o) in both 2012 and 2013; it is recorded similarly in 2014. In both 2012 and 2013, Zarle assumed that the actual return on plan assets was equal to the expected return on plan assets. In 2014, the expected return of $13,410 (the expected rate of return of 10 percent times the beginning-of-the-year plan assets' balance of $134,100) is higher than the actual return of $12,000. To smooth pension expense, Zarle defers the unexpected loss of $1,410 ($13,410 − $12,000) by debiting the Other Comprehensive Income (G/L) account and crediting Pension Expense. **As a result of this adjustment, the expected return on the plan assets is the amount actually used to compute pension expense.**

Entry (t) records the change in the projected benefit obligation resulting from the change in the actuarial assumptions. As indicated, the actuary has now computed the ending balance to be $265,000. Given the PBO balance at December 31, 2013, and the related transactions during 2014, the PBO balance to date is computed as shown in Illustration 20-19.

ILLUSTRATION 20-19
Projected Benefit
Obligation Balance
(Unadjusted)

December 31, 2013, PBO balance	$212,700
Service cost [entry (m)]	13,000
Interest cost [entry (n)]	21,270
Benefits paid	(10,500)
December 31, 2014, PBO balance (before liability increases)	$236,470

The difference between the ending balance of $265,000 and the balance of $236,470 before the liability increase is $28,530 ($265,000 − $236,470). This $28,530 increase in the employer's liability is an unexpected loss. The journal entry on December 31, 2014, to record the pension information is as follows.

Pension Expense	41,660	
Other Comprehensive Income (G/L)	29,940	
Cash		24,000
Other Comprehensive Income (PSC)		20,800
Pension Asset/Liability		26,800

As the 2014 worksheet indicates, the $105,400 balance in the Pension Asset/Liability account at December 31, 2014, is equal to the net of the balances in the memo accounts. Illustration 20-20 shows this computation.

Projected benefit obligation (Credit)	$(265,000)
Plan assets at fair value (Debit)	159,600
Pension asset/liability	$(105,400)

ILLUSTRATION 20-20
Pension Reconciliation Schedule—December 31, 2014

ROLLER COASTER

What do the numbers mean?

The chart below shows what has happened to the financial health of pension plans over the last few years. It is a real roller coaster.

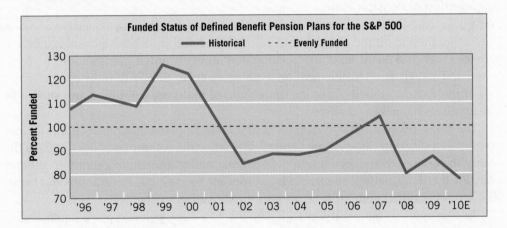

Funded Status of Defined Benefit Pension Plans for the S&P 500

At the turn of the century, when the stock market was strong, pension plans were over-funded. However the bubble burst, and by 2002 companies in the S&P 500 saw their pension plans funded at just 85 percent of reported liabilities. In recent years, plans have bounced back, and by 2007 pension plans were overfunded again. However, due to recent downturns, plans are now underfunded again and the future is highly uncertain.

A number of factors cause a fund to change from being overfunded to underfunded. First, low interest rates decimate returns on pension plan assets. As a result, pension fund assets have not grown; in some cases, they have declined in value. Second, using low interest rates to discount the projected benefit payments leads to a higher pension liability. Finally, more individuals are retiring, which leads to a depletion of the pension plan assets.

Source: D. Zion and A. Varshay, "Pension Headwinds," *Credit Suisse Equity Research* (September 21, 2010).

REPORTING PENSION PLANS IN FINANCIAL STATEMENTS

As you might suspect, a phenomenon as significant and complex as pensions involves extensive reporting and disclosure requirements. We will cover these requirements in two categories: (1) those within the financial statements, and (2) those within the notes to the financial statements.

9 LEARNING OBJECTIVE
Describe the requirements for reporting pension plans in financial statements.

Within the Financial Statements

Recognition of the Net Funded Status of the Pension Plan

Companies must recognize on their balance sheet the overfunded (pension asset) or underfunded (pension liability) status of their defined benefit pension plan. The overfunded or underfunded status is measured as the difference between the fair value of the plan assets and the projected benefit obligation.

Classification of Pension Asset or Pension Liability

No portion of a pension asset is reported as a current asset. The excess of the fair value of the plan assets over the benefit obligation is classified as a noncurrent asset. The rationale for noncurrent classification is that the pension plan assets are restricted. That is, these assets are used to fund the projected benefit obligation, and therefore noncurrent classification is appropriate.

The current portion of a net pension liability represents the amount of benefit payments to be paid in the next 12 months (or operating cycle, if longer), if that amount cannot be funded from existing plan assets. Otherwise, the pension liability is classified as a noncurrent liability.[14]

Aggregation of Pension Plans

Some companies have two or more pension plans. In such instances, a question arises as to whether these multiple plans should be combined and shown as one amount on the balance sheet. The Board takes the position that **all overfunded plans should be combined** and shown as a pension asset on the balance sheet. Similarly, if the company has two or more underfunded plans, the **underfunded plans are combined and shown as one amount** on the balance sheet.

The FASB rejected the alternative of combining *all* plans and representing the net amount as a single net asset or net liability. The rationale: A company does not have the ability to offset excess assets of one plan against underfunded obligations of another plan. Furthermore, netting all plans is inappropriate because offsetting assets and liabilities is not permitted under GAAP unless a right of offset exists.

To illustrate, assume that Cresci Company has three pension plans as shown in Illustration 20-21.

ILLUSTRATION 20-21
Multiple Pension Plans'
Funded Status

	Pension Assets (at Fair Value)	Projected Benefit Obligation	Pension Asset/Liability
Plan A	$400,000	$300,000	$100,000 Asset
Plan B	600,000	720,000	120,000 Liability
Plan C	550,000	700,000	150,000 Liability

In this case, Cresci reports a pension plan asset of $100,000 and a pension plan liability of $270,000 ($120,000 + $150,000).

Actuarial Gains and Losses/Prior Service Cost

Actuarial gains and losses not recognized as part of pension expense are recognized as increases and decreases in other comprehensive income. The same type of accounting is also used for prior service cost. The Board requires that the prior service cost arising in the year of the amendment (which increases the projected benefit obligation) be recognized by an offsetting debit to other comprehensive income. By recognizing both

[14]Recently, the FASB required more extensive disclosures related to pension plan assets. At a minimum, companies must disclose the amount of assets allocated to equities, government and corporate bonds, mortgage-backed securities, derivatives, and real estate. Also, information on concentrations of risk must be explained. Finally, fair value disclosures would be required, including classification of amounts into levels of the fair value hierarchy. [6]

actuarial gains and losses and prior service cost as part of other comprehensive income, the Board believes that the usefulness of financial statements is enhanced.

To illustrate the presentation of other comprehensive income and related accumulated OCI, assume that Obey Company provides the following information for the year 2012. None of the Accumulated OCI on January 1, 2012, should be amortized in 2012.

Net income for 2012	$100,000
Actuarial liability loss for 2012	60,000
Prior service cost adjustment to provide additional benefits in December 2012	15,000
Accumulated OCI, January 1, 2012	40,000

Both the actuarial liability loss and the prior service adjustment decrease the funded status of the plan on the balance sheet. This results because the projected benefit obligation increases. However, neither the actuarial liability loss nor the prior service cost adjustment affects pension expense in 2012. In subsequent periods, these items will impact pension expense through amortization.

For Obey Company, the computation of "Other comprehensive loss" for 2012 is as follows.

Actuarial liability loss	$60,000
Prior service cost benefit adjustment	15,000
Other comprehensive loss	$75,000

ILLUSTRATION 20-22
Computation of Other Comprehensive Income

The computation of "Comprehensive income" for 2012 is as follows.

Net income	$100,000
Other comprehensive loss	75,000
Comprehensive income	$ 25,000

ILLUSTRATION 20-23
Computation of Comprehensive Income

The components of other comprehensive income must be reported in one of three ways: (1) in a second income statement, (2) in a combined statement of comprehensive income, or (3) as a part of the statement of stockholders' equity. Regardless of the format used, net income must be added to other comprehensive income to arrive at comprehensive income. *For homework purposes, use the second income statement approach unless stated otherwise.* Earnings per share information related to comprehensive income is not required.

To illustrate the second income statement approach, assume that Obey Company has reported a traditional income statement. The comprehensive income statement is shown in Illustration 20-24.

ILLUSTRATION 20-24
Comprehensive Income Reporting

OBEY COMPANY COMPREHENSIVE INCOME STATEMENT FOR THE YEAR ENDED DECEMBER 31, 2012		
Net income		$100,000
Other comprehensive loss		
Actuarial liability loss	$60,000	
Prior service cost	15,000	75,000
Comprehensive income		$ 25,000

The computation of "Accumulated other comprehensive income" as reported in stockholders' equity at December 31, 2012, is as follows.

ILLUSTRATION 20-25
Computation of
Accumulated Other
Comprehensive Income

Accumulated other comprehensive income, January 1, 2012	$40,000
Other comprehensive loss	75,000
Accumulated other comprehensive loss, December 31, 2012	$35,000

Regardless of the display format for the income statement, the accumulated other comprehensive loss is reported in the stockholders' equity section of the balance sheet of Obey Company as shown in Illustration 20-26. (Illustration 20-26 uses assumed data for the common stock and retained earnings information.)

ILLUSTRATION 20-26
Reporting of
Accumulated OCI

OBEY COMPANY
BALANCE SHEET
AS OF DECEMBER 31, 2012
(STOCKHOLDERS' EQUITY SECTION)

Stockholders' equity	
Common stock	$100,000
Retained earnings	60,000
Accumulated other comprehensive loss	35,000
Total stockholders' equity	$125,000

By providing information on the components of comprehensive income as well as total accumulated other comprehensive income, the company communicates all changes in net assets.

In this illustration, it is assumed that the accumulated other comprehensive income at January 1, 2012, is not adjusted for the amortization of any prior service cost or actuarial gains and losses that would change pension expense. As discussed in the earlier examples, these items will be amortized into pension expense in future periods.

Within the Notes to the Financial Statements

Pension plans are frequently important to understanding a company's financial position, results of operations, and cash flows. Therefore, a company discloses the following information, either in the body of the financial statements or in the notes. [7]

1. A schedule showing all the major components of pension expense.
   Rationale: Information provided about the components of pension expense helps users better understand how a company determines pension expense. It also is useful in forecasting a company's net income.
2. A reconciliation showing how the projected benefit obligation and the fair value of the plan assets changed from the beginning to the end of the period.
   Rationale: Disclosing the projected benefit obligation, the fair value of the plan assets, and changes in them should help users understand the economics underlying the obligations and resources of these plans. Explaining the changes in the projected benefit obligation and fair value of plan assets in the form of a reconciliation provides a more complete disclosure and makes the financial statements more understandable.

3. A disclosure of the rates used in measuring the benefit amounts (discount rate, expected return on plan assets, rate of compensation).

Rationale: Disclosure of these rates permits users to determine the reasonableness of the assumptions applied in measuring the pension liability and pension expense.

4. A table indicating the allocation of pension plan assets by category (equity securities, debt securities, real estate, and other assets), and showing the percentage of the fair value to total plan assets. In addition, a company must include a narrative description of investment policies and strategies, including the target allocation percentages (if used by the company).

Rationale: Such information helps financial statement users evaluate the pension plan's exposure to market risk and possible cash flow demands on the company. It also will help users better assess the reasonableness of the company's expected rate of return assumption.

5. The **expected benefit payments** to be paid to current plan participants for each of the next five fiscal years and in the aggregate for the five fiscal years thereafter. Also required is disclosure of a company's best **estimate of expected contributions** to be paid to the plan during the next year.

Rationale: These disclosures provide information related to the cash outflows of the company. With this information, financial statement users can better understand the potential cash outflows related to the pension plan. They can better assess the liquidity and solvency of the company, which helps in assessing the company's overall financial flexibility.

6. The nature and amount of changes in plan assets and benefit obligations recognized in net income and in other comprehensive income of each period.

Rationale: This disclosure provides information on pension elements affecting the projected benefit obligation and plan assets and on whether those amounts have been recognized in income or deferred to future periods.

7. The accumulated amount of changes in plan assets and benefit obligations that have been recognized in other comprehensive income and that will be recycled into net income in future periods.

Rationale: This information indicates the pension-related balances recognized in stockholders' equity, which will affect future income.

8. The amount of estimated net actuarial gains and losses and prior service costs and credits that will be amortized from accumulated other comprehensive income into net income over the next fiscal year.

Rationale: This information helps users predict the impact of deferred pension expense items on next year's income.

In summary, the disclosure requirements are extensive, and purposely so. One factor that has been a challenge for useful pension reporting has been the lack of consistent terminology. Furthermore, a substantial amount of offsetting is inherent in the measurement of pension expense and the pension liability. These disclosures are designed to address these concerns and take some of the mystery out of pension reporting.

Example of Pension Note Disclosure

In the following sections, we provide examples and explain the key pension disclosure elements.

Components of Pension Expense

The FASB requires disclosure of the individual pension expense components (derived from the information in the pension expense worksheet column): (1) service cost,

(2) interest cost, (3) expected return on assets, (4) other gains or losses component, and (5) prior service cost component. The purpose of such disclosure is to clarify to more sophisticated readers how companies determine pension expense. Providing information on the components should also be useful in predicting future pension expense.

Illustration 20-27 presents an example of this part of the disclosure. It uses the information from the Zarle illustration, specifically the expense component information from the worksheets in Illustrations 20-8 (page 1219), 20-12 (page 1222), and 20-18 (page 1228).

ILLUSTRATION 20-27
Summary of Expense Components—2012, 2013, 2014

ZARLE COMPANY			
	2012	2013	2014
Components of Pension Expense			
Service cost	$ 9,000	$ 9,500	$13,000
Interest cost	10,000	19,200	21,270
Expected return on plan assets	(10,000)	(11,100)	(13,410)*
Amortization of prior service cost	–0–	27,200	20,800
Pension expense	$ 9,000	$44,800	$41,660

*Note that the expected return must be disclosed, not the actual return. In 2014, the expected return is $13,410, which is the actual gain ($12,000) adjusted by the unrecognized loss ($1,410).

Funded Status of Plan

Underlying Concepts

This represents another compromise between relevance and faithful representation. Disclosure attempts to balance these objectives.

Having a reconciliation of the changes in the assets and liabilities from the beginning of the year to the end of the year, statement readers can better understand the underlying economics of the plan. In essence, this disclosure contains the information in the pension worksheet for the projected benefit obligation and plan asset columns. Using the information for Zarle, the schedule in Illustration 20-28 provides an example of the reconciliation.

ILLUSTRATION 20-28
Pension Disclosure for Zarle Company—2012, 2013, 2014

ZARLE COMPANY **PENSION DISCLOSURE**			
	2012	2013	2014
Change in benefit obligation			
Benefit obligation at beginning of year	$100,000	$112,000	$ 212,700
Service cost	9,000	9,500	13,000
Interest cost	10,000	19,200	21,270
Amendments (Prior service cost)	–0–	80,000	–0–
Actuarial loss	–0–	–0–	28,530
Benefits paid	(7,000)	(8,000)	(10,500)
Benefit obligation at end of year	112,000	212,700	265,000
Change in plan assets			
Fair value of plan assets at beginning of year	100,000	111,000	134,100
Actual return on plan assets	10,000	11,100	12,000
Contributions	8,000	20,000	24,000
Benefits paid	(7,000)	(8,000)	(10,500)
Fair value of plan assets at end of year	111,000	134,100	159,600
Funded status (Pension asset/liability)	$ (1,000)	$ (78,600)	$(105,400)

The 2012 column reveals that Zarle underfunds the projected benefit obligation by $1,000. The 2013 column reveals that Zarle reports the underfunded liability of $78,600 in the balance sheet. Finally, the 2014 column indicates that Zarle recognizes the underfunded liability of $105,400 in the balance sheet.

2015 Entries and Worksheet—A Comprehensive Example

Incorporating the corridor computation and the required disclosures, we continue the Zarle Company pension plan accounting based on the following facts for 2015.

Underlying Concepts

Does it make a difference to users of financial statements whether companies recognize pension information in the financial statements or disclose it only in the notes? The FASB was unsure, so in accord with the full disclosure principle, it decided to provide extensive pension plan disclosures.

Service cost is $16,000.

Settlement rate is 10 percent; expected rate of return is 10 percent.

Actual return on plan assets is $22,000.

Amortization of prior service cost is $17,600.

Annual funding contributions are $27,000.

Benefits paid to retirees during the year are $18,000.

Average service life of all covered employees is 20 years.

Zarle prepares a worksheet to facilitate accumulation and recording of the components of pension expense and maintenance of amounts related to the pension plan. Illustration 20-29 shows that worksheet, which uses the basic data presented above. Beginning-of-the-year 2015 account balances are the December 31, 2014, balances from Zarle's revised 2014 pension worksheet in Illustration 20-18 (on page 1228).

ILLUSTRATION 20-29
Comprehensive Pension Worksheet—2015

	Comprehensive Pension Worksheet—2015							
	A	B	C	D	E	F	H	I
1				General Journal Entries				Memo Record	
2				Other Comprehensive Income					
3	Items	Annual Pension Expense	Cash	Prior Service Cost	Gains/Losses	Pension Asset/Liability	Projected Benefit Obligation	Plan Assets
4	Balance, Dec. 31, 2014					105,400 Cr.	265,000 Cr.	159,600 Dr.
5	(aa) Service cost	16,000 Dr.					16,000 Cr.	
6	(bb) Interest cost	26,500 Dr.					26,500 Cr.	
7	(cc) Actual return	22,000 Cr.						22,000 Dr.
8	(dd) Unexpected gain	6,040 Dr.			6,040 Cr.			
9	(ee) Amortization of PSC	17,600 Dr.		17,600 Cr.				
10	(ff) Contributions		27,000 Cr.					27,000 Dr.
11	(gg) Benefits						18,000 Dr.	18,000 Cr.
12	(hh) Amortization of loss	172 Dr.			172 Cr.			
13								
14	Journal entry for 2015	44,312 Dr.	27,000 Cr.	17,600 Cr.	6,212 Cr.	6,500 Dr.		
15								
16	Accumulated OCI, Dec. 31, 2014			32,000 Dr.	29,940 Dr.			
17	Balance, Dec. 31, 2015*			14,400 Dr.	23,728 Dr.	98,900 Cr.	289,500 Cr.	190,600 Dr.
18								
19	*Accumulated OCI (PSC)	$14,400 Dr.						
20	Accumulated OCI (G/L)	23,728 Dr.						
21	Accumulated OCI, Dec. 31, 2015	$38,128 Dr.						

Sheet1 / Sheet2 / Sheet3

Worksheet Explanations and Entries

Entries (aa) through (gg) are similar to the corresponding entries previously explained in the prior years' worksheets, with the exception of entry (dd). In 2014, the expected return on plan assets exceeded the actual return, producing an unexpected loss. In 2015, the actual return of $22,000 exceeds the expected return of $15,960 ($159,600 × 10%), resulting in an unexpected gain of $6,040, entry (dd). By netting the gain of $6,040 against the actual return of $22,000, pension expense is affected only by the expected return of $15,960.

A new entry (hh) in Zarle's worksheet results from application of the corridor test on the accumulated balance of net gain or loss in accumulated other comprehensive income.

Zarle Company begins 2015 with a balance in the net loss account of $29,940. The company applies the corridor criterion in 2015 to determine whether the balance is excessive and should be amortized. In 2015, the corridor is 10 percent of the larger of the beginning-of-the-year projected benefit obligation of $265,000 or the plan asset's $159,600 market-related asset value (assumed to be fair value). The corridor for 2015 is $26,500 ($265,000 × 10%). Because the balance in Accumulated OCI is a net loss of $29,940, the excess (outside the corridor) is $3,440 ($29,940 − $26,500). Zarle amortizes the $3,440 excess over the average remaining service life of all employees. Given an average remaining service life of 20 years, the amortization in 2015 is $172 ($3,440 ÷ 20). In the 2015 pension worksheet, Zarle debits Pension Expense for $172 and credits that amount to Other Comprehensive Income (G/L). Illustration 20-30 shows the computation of the $172 amortization charge.

ILLUSTRATION 20-30
Computation of 2015
Amortization Charge
(Corridor Test)

2015 Corridor Test	
Net (gain) or loss at beginning of year in accumulated OCI	$29,940
10% of larger of PBO or market-related asset value of plan assets	(26,500)
Amortizable amount	$ 3,440
Average service life of all employees	20 years
2015 amortization ($3,440 ÷ 20 years)	$172

Zarle formally records pension expense for 2015 as follows.

2015		
Pension Expense	44,312	
Pension Asset/Liability	6,500	
Cash		27,000
Other Comprehensive Income (G/L)		6,212
Other Comprehensive Income (PSC)		17,600

Note Disclosure

Illustration 20-31 (next page) shows the note disclosure of Zarle's pension plan for 2015. Note that this example assumes that the pension liability is noncurrent and that the 2016 adjustment for amortization of the net gain or loss and amortization of prior service cost are the same as 2015.

Underlying Concepts

Many plans are underfunded but still quite viable. For example, at one time **Loews Corp.** had a $159 million shortfall, but also had earnings of $594 million and a good net worth. Thus, the going concern assumption permits us to ignore pension underfundings in some cases because in the long run they are not significant.

Special Issues

The Pension Reform Act of 1974

The Employee Retirement Income Security Act of 1974—ERISA—affects virtually every private retirement plan in the United States. It attempts to safeguard employees' pension rights by mandating many pension plan requirements, including minimum funding, participation, and vesting.

These requirements can influence the employers' cash flows significantly. Under this legislation, annual funding is no longer discretionary. An employer now must fund the plan in accordance with an actuarial funding method that over time will be sufficient to pay for all pension obligations. If companies do not fund their plans in a reasonable manner, they may be subject to fines and/or loss of tax deductions.[15]

[15]In 2006, Congress passed the Pension Protection Act. This new law has many provisions. One important aspect of the act is that it forced many companies to expedite their contributions to their pension plans. One group estimates that companies in the S&P 500 would have had to contribute $47 billion to their pension plans if the new rules were fully phased in for 2006. That amount is about 57 percent more than the $30 billion that companies were expecting to contribute to their plans that year. However, in 2010, Congress passed the Preservation of Access to Medicare Beneficiaries and Pension Relief Act of 2010, which provides some relief for mandatory contributions to company pension plans. See Credit Suisse, "Pension Protection Act" (August 14, 2006), p. 1; and JPMorgan Chase, "Pension Risk Ratios" (October 12, 2010).

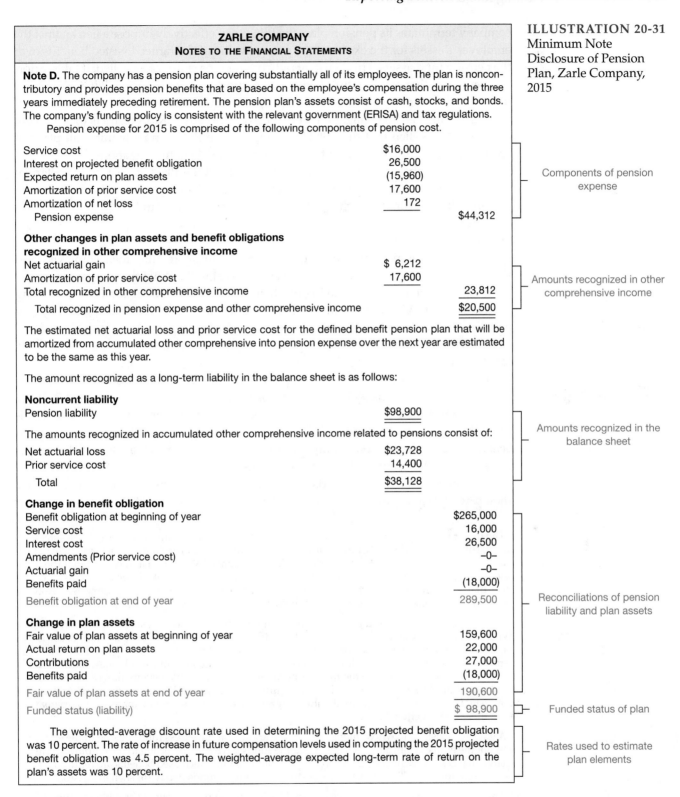

ILLUSTRATION 20-31
Minimum Note
Disclosure of Pension
Plan, Zarle Company,
2015

ZARLE COMPANY
NOTES TO THE FINANCIAL STATEMENTS

Note D. The company has a pension plan covering substantially all of its employees. The plan is noncontributory and provides pension benefits that are based on the employee's compensation during the three years immediately preceding retirement. The pension plan's assets consist of cash, stocks, and bonds. The company's funding policy is consistent with the relevant government (ERISA) and tax regulations.
   Pension expense for 2015 is comprised of the following components of pension cost.

Service cost	$16,000
Interest on projected benefit obligation	26,500
Expected return on plan assets	(15,960)
Amortization of prior service cost	17,600
Amortization of net loss	172
Pension expense	$44,312

Components of pension expense

Other changes in plan assets and benefit obligations recognized in other comprehensive income

Net actuarial gain	$ 6,212
Amortization of prior service cost	17,600
Total recognized in other comprehensive income	23,812
Total recognized in pension expense and other comprehensive income	$20,500

Amounts recognized in other comprehensive income

The estimated net actuarial loss and prior service cost for the defined benefit pension plan that will be amortized from accumulated other comprehensive into pension expense over the next year are estimated to be the same as this year.

The amount recognized as a long-term liability in the balance sheet is as follows:

Noncurrent liability

Pension liability	$98,900

The amounts recognized in accumulated other comprehensive income related to pensions consist of:

Net actuarial loss	$23,728
Prior service cost	14,400
Total	$38,128

Amounts recognized in the balance sheet

Change in benefit obligation

Benefit obligation at beginning of year	$265,000
Service cost	16,000
Interest cost	26,500
Amendments (Prior service cost)	–0–
Actuarial gain	–0–
Benefits paid	(18,000)
Benefit obligation at end of year	289,500

Change in plan assets

Fair value of plan assets at beginning of year	159,600
Actual return on plan assets	22,000
Contributions	27,000
Benefits paid	(18,000)
Fair value of plan assets at end of year	190,600
Funded status (liability)	$ 98,900

Reconciliations of pension liability and plan assets

Funded status of plan

   The weighted-average discount rate used in determining the 2015 projected benefit obligation was 10 percent. The rate of increase in future compensation levels used in computing the 2015 projected benefit obligation was 4.5 percent. The weighted-average expected long-term rate of return on the plan's assets was 10 percent.

Rates used to estimate plan elements

The law requires plan administrators to publish a comprehensive description and summary of their plans, along with detailed annual reports that include many supplementary schedules and statements.

Another important provision of the act is the creation of the Pension Benefit Guaranty Corporation (PBGC). **The PBGC's purpose is to administer terminated plans** and to impose liens on an employer's assets for certain unfunded pension liabilities. If a company terminates its pension plan, the PBGC can effectively impose a lien against the employer's assets for the excess of the present value of guaranteed vested benefits over the pension fund assets. This lien generally has had the status of a tax lien; it takes priority over most other creditorship claims. This section of the act gives the PBGC the power to force an involuntary termination of a pension plan whenever the risks related to non-payment of the pension obligation seem too great. Because ERISA restricts to 30 percent of net worth the lien that the PBGC can impose, the PBGC must monitor all plans to ensure that net worth is sufficient to meet the pension benefit obligations.[16]

A large number of terminated plans have caused the PBGC to pay out substantial benefits. Currently the PBGC receives its funding from employers, who contribute a certain dollar amount for each employee covered under the plan.[17]

Pension Terminations

A congressman at one time noted, "Employers are simply treating their employee pension plans like company piggy banks, to be raided at will." What this congressman was referring to is the practice of paying off the projected benefit obligation and pocketing any excess. ERISA prevents companies from recapturing excess assets unless they pay participants what is owed to them and then terminate the plan. As a result, companies were buying *annuities* to pay off the pension claimants and then used the excess funds for other corporate purposes.[18]

For example, at one time, pension plan terminations netted $363 million for Occidental Petroleum Corp., $95 million for Stroh's Brewery Co., $58 million for Kellogg Co., and $29 million for Western Airlines. Recently, many large companies have terminated their pension plans and captured billions in surplus assets. The U.S. Treasury also benefits: Federal legislation requires companies to pay an excise tax of anywhere from 20 percent to 50 percent on the gains. All of this is quite legal.[19]

The accounting issue that arises from these terminations is whether a company should recognize a gain when pension plan assets revert back to the company (often

---

[16]The major problems in underfunding are occurring in four labor-intensive industries—steel, autos, rubber, and airlines. For example, even after government funding, the pension plans at General Motors and Chrysler are underfunded by a total of $17 billion and could fail if the automakers do not return to profitability. Both companies need to make large payments into their plans within the next five years—$12.3 billion by GM and $2.6 billion by Chrysler. See Nick Bunkley, "Automakers Pensions Underfunded by $17 Billion," *New York Times* (April 6, 2010).

[17]Pan American Airlines is a good illustration of how difficult it is to assess when to terminate. When Pan Am filed for bankruptcy in 1991, it had a pension liability of $900 million. From 1983 to 1991, the IRS gave it six waivers so it did not have to make contributions. When Pan Am terminated the plan, there was little net worth left upon which to impose a lien. An additional accounting problem relates to the manner of disclosing the possible termination of a plan. For example, should Pan Am have disclosed a contingent liability for its struggling plan? At present this issue is unresolved, and considerable judgment would be needed to analyze a company with these contingent liabilities.

[18]A question exists as to whose money it is. Some argue that the excess funds belong to the employees, not the employer. In addition, given that the funds have been reverting to the employer, critics charge that cost-of-living increases and the possibility of other increased benefits are reduced, because companies will be reluctant to use those remaining funds to pay for such increases.

[19]Another way that companies have reduced their pension obligations is through adoption of cash-balance plans. These are *hybrid* plans combining features of defined benefit and defined contribution plans. Although these plans permit employees to transfer their pension benefits when they change employers (like a defined contribution plan), they are controversial because the change to a cash-balance plan often reduces benefits to older workers.

The accounting for cash-balance plans is similar to that for defined benefit plans, because employers bear the investment risk in cash-balance plans. When an employer adopts a cash-balance plan, the measurement of the future benefit obligation to employees generally is lower, compared to a traditional defined benefit plan. See A. T. Arcady and F. Mellors, "Cash-Balance Conversions," *Journal of Accountancy* (February 2000), pp. 22–28.

called **asset reversion** transactions). The issue is complex: In some cases, a company starts a new defined benefit plan after it eliminates the old one. Thus, some contend that there has been no change in substance but merely a change in form. However, the FASB disagrees. It requires recognition in earnings of a gain or loss when the employer settles a pension obligation either by lump-sum cash payments to participants or by purchasing nonparticipating annuity contracts. **[8]**[20]

BAILING OUT

The Pension Benefit Guaranty Corp. (PBGC) recently announced that it would take over responsibility for the pilots' pension plan at United Airlines, to the tune of $1.4 billion. This federal agency, which acts as an insurer for corporate pension plans, has spent much of the past few years securing pension plans for "Big Steel" (U.S. steel companies), and it looks as if airlines are next.

What do the numbers mean?

For example, the PBGC also became the trustee of US Airways pilots' pensions in 2003, and it may soon announce a takeover of that struggling carrier's other three pension plans. The grand total at US Airways? It's $2.8 billion—mere pocket change next to the $6.4 billion the PBGC will owe if it has to bail out all four of United Airlines' plans. To date, the airline industry, which makes up 2 percent of participants in the program, has made 20 percent of the claims. The chart below shows how a $6.4 billion bailout would compare with the PBGC's biggest payouts to date.

Pension Plan
year of termination   **Bailout** in billions

Pension Plan (year of termination)	Bailout (in billions)
Bethlehem Steel 2003	$3.6
LTV Steel 2002	$1.9
United Airlines pilots 2005	$1.4
National Steel 2003	$1.2
Pan American Airlines 1991	$0.84
US Airways pilots 2003	$0.73
Weirton Steel 2004	$0.69
TWA 2001	$0.67
Kaiser Aluminum 2004	$0.57
Eastern Air Lines 1991	$0.55

$0.0   0.5   1.0   1.5   2.0   2.5   3.0   3.5   4.0

Source: Kate Bonamici, "By the Numbers," *Fortune* (January 24, 2005), p. 24.

Concluding Observations

Hardly a day goes by without the financial press analyzing in depth some issue related to pension plans in the United States. This is not surprising, since pension funds exceed over $22 trillion in assets globally. As you have seen, the accounting issues related to pension plans are complex. Recent changes to GAAP have clarified many of these issues and should help users understand the financial implications of a company's pension plans on its financial position, results of operations, and cash flows.

You will want to read the
IFRS INSIGHTS
on pages 1274–1287

for discussion of IFRS related to pension accounting.

---

[20]Some companies have established *pension poison pills* as an anti-takeover measure. These plans require asset reversions from termination of a plan to benefit employees and retirees rather than the acquiring company. For a discussion of pension poison pills, see Eugene E. Comiskey and Charles W. Mulford, "Interpreting Pension Disclosures: A Guide for Lending Officers," *Commercial Lending Review* (Winter 1993–94), Vol. 9, No. 1.

SUMMARY OF LEARNING OBJECTIVES

1 **Distinguish between accounting for the employer's pension plan and accounting for the pension fund.** The company or employer is the organization sponsoring the pension plan. It incurs the cost and makes contributions to the pension fund. The fund or plan is the entity that receives the contributions from the employer, administers the pension assets, and makes the benefit payments to the pension recipients (retired employees). The fund should be a separate legal and accounting entity; it maintains a set of books and prepares financial statements.

2 **Identify types of pension plans and their characteristics.** The two most common types of pension arrangements are: (1) *Defined contribution plans:* The employer agrees to contribute to a pension trust a certain sum each period based on a formula. This formula may consider such factors as age, length of employee service, employer's profits, and compensation level. Only the employer's contribution is defined; no promise is made regarding the ultimate benefits paid out to the employees. (2) *Defined benefit plans:* These plans define the benefits that the employee will receive at the time of retirement. The formula typically provides for the benefits to be a function of the employee's years of service and the compensation level when he or she nears retirement.

3 **Explain alternative measures for valuing the pension obligation.** One measure bases the pension obligation only on the benefits vested to the employees. Vested benefits are those that the employee is entitled to receive even if he or she renders no additional services under the plan. Companies compute the *vested benefit pension obligation* using current salary levels; this obligation includes only vested benefits. Another measure of the obligation, called the *accumulated benefit obligation,* computes the deferred compensation amount based on all years of service performed by employees under the plan—both vested and nonvested—using current salary levels. A third measure, called the *projected benefit obligation,* bases the computation of the deferred compensation amount on both vested and nonvested service using future salaries.

4 **List the components of pension expense.** Pension expense is a function of the following components: (1) service cost, (2) interest on the liability, (3) return on plan assets, (4) amortization of prior service cost, and (5) gain or loss.

5 **Use a worksheet for employer's pension plan entries.** Companies may use a worksheet unique to pension accounting. This worksheet records both the formal entries and the memo entries to keep track of all the employer's relevant pension plan items and components.

6 **Describe the amortization of prior service costs.** An actuary computes the amount of the prior service cost, and the company then records it as an adjustment to the projected benefit obligation and other comprehensive income. It then amortizes it, generally using a "years-of-service" amortization method, similar to a units-of-production computation. First, the company computes total estimated number of service-years to be worked by all of the participating employees. Second, it divides the accumulated prior service cost by the total number of service-years, to obtain a cost per service-year (the unit cost). Third, the company multiplies the number of service-years consumed each year times the cost per service-year, to obtain the annual amortization charge.

7 **Explain the accounting for unexpected gains and losses.** In estimating the projected benefit obligation (the liability), actuaries make assumptions about such items as mortality rate, retirement rate, turnover rate, disability rate, and salary amounts. Any change in these actuarial assumptions affects the amount of the projected benefit obligation. These unexpected gains or losses from changes in the projected benefit obligation are liability gains and losses. Liability gains result from unexpected decreases in the liability balance; liability losses result from unexpected increases. Companies also incur asset gains or losses. Both types of actuarial gains and losses are recorded in other comprehensive income and adjust either the projected benefit obligation or the plan assets.

8 **Explain the corridor approach to amortizing gains and losses.** The FASB set a limit for the size of an accumulated net gain or loss balance. That arbitrarily selected limit (called a *corridor*) is 10 percent of the larger of the beginning balances of the projected benefit obligation or the market-related value of the plan assets. Beyond that limit, an accumulated net gain or loss balance is considered too large and must be amortized. If the balance of the accumulated net gain or loss account stays within the upper and lower limits of the corridor, no amortization is required.

9 **Describe the requirements for reporting pension plans in financial statements.** Currently, companies must disclose the following pension plan information in their financial statements: (1) The components of pension expense for the period. (2) A schedule showing changes in the benefit obligation and plan assets during the year. (3) The amount of prior service cost and net gains and losses in accumulated OCI, including the estimated prior service cost and gains and losses that will affect net income in the next year. (4) The weighted-average assumed discount rate, the rate of compensation increase used to measure the projected benefit obligation, and the weighted-average expected long-term rate of return on plan assets. (5) A table showing the allocation of pension plan assets by category and the percentage of the fair value to total plan assets. (6) The expected benefit payments for current plan participants for each of the next five fiscal years and for the following five years in aggregate, along with an estimate of expected contributions to the plan during the next year.

| APPENDIX **20A** | ACCOUNTING FOR POSTRETIREMENT BENEFITS |

IBM's adoption of the GAAP requirements on postretirement benefits resulted in a $2.3 billion charge and a historical curiosity—IBM's first-ever quarterly loss. General Electric disclosed that its charge for adoption of the same GAAP rules would be $2.7 billion. AT&T absorbed a $2.1 billion pretax hit for postretirement benefits upon adoption. What is GAAP in this area, and how could its adoption have so grave an impact on companies' earnings?

ACCOUNTING GUIDANCE

After a decade of study, the FASB in December 1990 issued GAAP for "Employers' Accounting for Postretirement Benefits Other Than Pensions." [9] It alone was the cause for the large charges to income cited above. These rules cover for healthcare and other "welfare benefits" provided to retirees, their spouses, dependents, and beneficiaries.[21] These other welfare benefits include life insurance offered outside a pension plan; medical, dental, and eye care; legal and tax services; tuition assistance; day care; and housing assistance.[22] Because healthcare benefits are the largest of the other postretirement benefits, we use this item to illustrate accounting for postretirement benefits.

---

[21]*Accounting Trends and Techniques—2010* reports that of its 500 surveyed companies, 317 reported benefit plans that provide postretirement healthcare benefits. In response to rising healthcare costs and higher premiums on healthcare insurance, companies are working to get their postretirement benefit costs under control.

[22]"OPEB" is the acronym frequently used to describe postretirement benefits other than pensions. This term came into being before the scope of guidance was narrowed from "other postemployment benefits" to "other postretirement benefits," thereby excluding postemployment benefits related to severance pay or wage continuation to disabled, terminated, or laid-off employees.

For many employers (about 95 percent), these GAAP rules required a change from the predominant practice of accounting for postretirement benefits on a pay-as-you-go (cash) basis to an accrual basis. Similar to pension accounting, the accrual basis necessitates measuring the employer's obligation to provide future benefits and accrual of the cost during the years that the employee provides service.

One of the reasons companies had not prefunded these benefit plans was that payments to prefund healthcare costs, unlike excess contributions to a pension trust, are not tax-deductible. Another reason was that postretirement healthcare benefits were once perceived to be a low-cost employee benefit that could be changed or eliminated at will and therefore were not a legal liability. Now, the accounting definition of a liability goes beyond the notion of a legally enforceable claim; the definition now encompasses equitable or constructive obligations as well, making it clear that the postretirement benefit promise is a liability.[23]

DIFFERENCES BETWEEN PENSION BENEFITS AND HEALTHCARE BENEFITS

LEARNING OBJECTIVE **10**

Identify the differences between pensions and postretirement healthcare benefits.

The FASB used the GAAP rules on pensions as a reference for the accounting prescribed for healthcare and other nonpension postretirement benefits.[24] Why didn't the FASB cover these other types of postretirement benefits in the earlier pension accounting statement? Because the apparent similarities between the two benefits mask some significant differences. Illustration 20A-1 shows these differences.[25]

ILLUSTRATION 20A-1
Differences between Pensions and Postretirement Healthcare Benefits

Item	Pensions	Healthcare Benefits
Funding	Generally funded.	Generally *NOT* funded.
Benefit	Well-defined and level dollar amount.	Generally uncapped and great variability.
Beneficiary	Retiree (maybe some benefit to surviving spouse).	Retiree, spouse, and other dependents.
Benefit payable	Monthly.	As needed and used.
Predictability	Variables are reasonably predictable.	Utilization difficult to predict. Level of cost varies geographically and fluctuates over time.

Two of the differences in Illustration 20A-1 highlight why measuring the future payments for healthcare benefit plans is so much more difficult than for pension plans.

1. Many postretirement plans do not set a limit on healthcare benefits. No matter how serious the illness or how long it lasts, the benefits continue to flow. (Even if the employer uses an insurance company plan, the premiums will escalate according to the increased benefits provided.)

2. The levels of healthcare benefit use and healthcare costs are difficult to predict. Increased longevity, unexpected illnesses (e.g., AIDS, SARS, and avian flu), along with new medical technologies and cures, cause changes in healthcare utilization.

---

[23]"Elements of Financial Statements," *Statement of Financial Accounting Concepts No. 6* (Stamford, Conn.: 1985), p. 13, footnote 21.

[24]Other postemployment (but before retirement) benefits include, but are not limited to, salary continuation, disability-related benefits, severance benefits, and continuance of healthcare benefits and life insurance for inactive or former (e.g., terminated, disabled, or deceased) employees or their beneficiaries. These benefits are accounted for similar to accounting for compensated absences (see Chapter 13). [10]

[25]D. Gerald Searfoss and Naomi Erickson, "The Big Unfunded Liability: Postretirement Health-Care Benefits," *Journal of Accountancy* (November 1988), pp. 28–39.

Additionally, although the fiduciary and reporting standards for employee benefit funds under government regulations generally cover healthcare benefits, the stringent minimum vesting, participation, and funding standards that apply to pensions do not apply to healthcare benefits. Nevertheless, as you will learn, many of the basic concepts of pensions, and much of the related accounting terminology and measurement methodology, do apply to other postretirement benefits. Therefore, in the following discussion and illustrations, we point out the similarities and differences in the accounting and reporting for these two types of postretirement benefits.

OPEBs—HOW BIG ARE THEY?

For many companies, *other postretirement benefit obligations* (OPEBs) are substantial. Generally, OPEBs are not well funded because companies are not permitted a tax deduction for contributions to the plan assets, as is the case with pensions. That is, the company may not claim a tax deduction until it makes a payment to the participant (pay-as-you-go).

Presented below are companies with the largest OPEB obligations, indicating their relationship with other financial items.

What do the numbers mean?

(For year ended 12/31/2009, $ in millions)	Obligation	% Underfunded	Obligation as a % of Stockholders' Equity
General Motors	$125,945	21.77%	592.71%
Ford Motor Company	6,053	100.00%	(−92.91%)
SBC Communications	50,850	7.82%	49.69%
Verizon Communications	31,818	10.14%	37.71%
General Electric	57,714	15.07%	46.12%
Lucent Technologies	25,910	3.80%	420.00%
Delphi Corp.	81	100.00%	1.51%

So, how big are OPEB obligations? REALLY big.

Source: Company reports.

POSTRETIREMENT BENEFITS ACCOUNTING PROVISIONS

Healthcare and other postretirement benefits for current and future retirees and their dependents are forms of deferred compensation. They are earned through employee service and are subject to accrual during the years an employee is working.

The period of time over which the postretirement benefit cost accrues is called the **attribution period**. It is the period of service during which the employee earns the benefits under the terms of the plan. The attribution period, shown in Illustration 20A-2 (page 1244) for a hypothetical employee, generally begins when an employee is hired and ends on the date the employee is eligible to receive the benefits and ceases to earn additional benefits by performing service, the vesting date.[26]

---

[26]This is a benefit-years-of-service approach (the projected unit credit actuarial cost method). The FASB found no compelling reason to switch from the traditional pension accounting approach. It rejected the employee's full service period (i.e., to the estimated retirement date) because it was unable to identify any approach that would appropriately attribute benefits beyond the date when an employee attains full eligibility for those benefits. Employees attain full eligibility by meeting specified age, service, or age and service requirements of the plan.

ILLUSTRATION 20A-2
Range of Possible
Attribution Periods

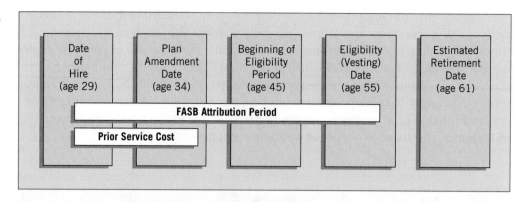

Obligations Under Postretirement Benefits

In defining the obligation for postretirement benefits, the FASB maintained many concepts similar to pension accounting. It also designed some new and modified terms specifically for postretirement benefits. Two of the most important of these specialized terms are (a) expected postretirement benefit obligation and (b) accumulated postretirement benefit obligation.

The **expected postretirement benefit obligation (EPBO)** is the actuarial present value as of a particular date of **all benefits a company expects to pay after retirement to employees and their dependents**. Companies do not record the EPBO in the financial statements, but they do use it in measuring periodic expense.

The **accumulated postretirement benefit obligation (APBO)** is the actuarial present value of **future benefits attributed to employees' services rendered to a particular date**. The APBO is equal to the EPBO for retirees and active employees fully eligible for benefits. Before the date an employee achieves full eligibility, the APBO is only a portion of the EPBO. Or stated another way, the difference between the APBO and the EPBO is the future service costs of active employees who are not yet fully eligible.

Illustration 20A-3 contrasts the EPBO and the APBO.

ILLUSTRATION 20A-3
APBO and EPBO
Contrasted

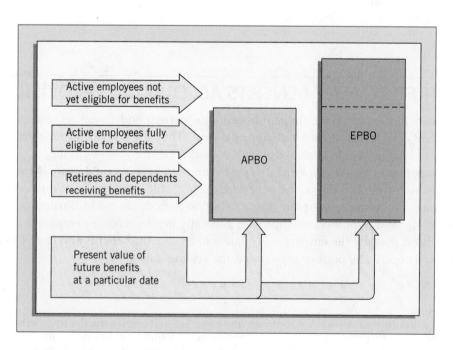

At the date an employee is fully eligible (the end of the attribution period), the APBO and the EPBO for that employee are equal.

Postretirement Expense

Postretirement expense is the employer's annual expense for postretirement benefits. Also called **net periodic postretirement benefit cost**, this expense consists of many of the familiar components used to compute annual pension expense. The components of net periodic postretirement benefit cost are as follows. [11][27]

1. *Service cost.* The portion of the EPBO attributed to employee service during the period.
2. *Interest cost.* The increase in the APBO attributable to the passage of time. Companies compute interest cost by applying the beginning-of-the-year discount rate to the beginning-of-the-year APBO, adjusted for benefit payments to be made during the period. The discount rate is based on the rates of return on high-quality, fixed-income investments that are currently available.[28]
3. *Actual return on plan assets.* The change in the fair value of the plan's assets adjusted for contributions and benefit payments made during the period. Because companies charge or credit the postretirement expense for the gain or loss on plan assets (the difference between the actual and the expected return), this component is actually the expected return.
4. *Amortization of prior service cost.* The amortization of the cost of retroactive benefits resulting from plan amendments. The typical amortization period, beginning at the date of the plan amendment, is the remaining service periods through the full eligibility date.
5. *Gains and losses.* In general, changes in the APBO resulting from changes in assumptions or from experience different from that assumed. For funded plans, this component also includes the difference between actual return and expected return on plan assets.

ILLUSTRATIVE ACCOUNTING ENTRIES

Like pension accounting, the accounting for postretirement plans must recognize in the accounts and in the financial statements effects of several significant items. These items are:

> **11 LEARNING OBJECTIVE**
>
> Contrast accounting for pensions to accounting for other postretirement benefits.

1. Expected postretirement benefit obligation (EPBO).
2. Accumulated postretirement benefit obligation (APBO).
3. Postretirement benefit plan assets.
4. Prior service cost.
5. Net gain or loss.

The EPBO is not recognized in the financial statements or disclosed in the notes. Companies recompute it each year, and the actuary uses it in measuring the annual

---

[27]See James R. Wilbert and Kenneth E. Dakdduk, "The New FASB 106: How to Account for Postretirement Benefits," *Journal of Accountancy* (August 1991), pp. 36–41.

[28]The FASB concluded that the discount rate for measuring the present value of the postretirement benefit obligation and the service cost component should be the same as that applied to pension measurements. It chose not to label it the *settlement rate*, in order to clarify that the objective of the discount rate is to measure the time value of money.

service cost. Because of the numerous assumptions and actuarial complexity involved in measuring annual service cost, we have omitted these computations of the EPBO.

Similar to pensions, companies must recognize in the financial statements items 2 through 5 listed above. In addition, as in pension accounting, companies must know the exact amount of these items in order to compute postretirement expense. Therefore, companies use the worksheet like that for pension accounting to record both the formal general journal entries and the memo entries.

2012 Entries and Worksheet

To illustrate the use of a worksheet in accounting for a postretirement benefits plan, assume that on January 1, 2012, Quest Company adopts a healthcare benefit plan. The following facts apply to the postretirement benefits plan for the year 2012.

Plan assets at fair value on January 1, 2012, are zero.

Actual and expected returns on plan assets are zero.

Accumulated postretirement benefit obligation (APBO), January 1, 2012, is zero.

Service cost is $54,000.

No prior service cost exists.

Interest cost on the APBO is zero.

Funding contributions during the year are $38,000.

Benefit payments to employees from plan are $28,000.

Using that data, the worksheet in Illustration 20A-4 presents the postretirement entries for 2012.

ILLUSTRATION 20A-4
Postretirement
Worksheet—2012

		General Journal Entries			Memo Record	
	Items	Annual Postretirement Expense	Cash	Postretirement Asset/Liability	APBO	Plan Assets
3	Balance, Jan. 1, 2012					
4	(a) Service cost	54,000 Dr.			54,000 Cr.	
5	(b) Contributions		38,000 Cr.			38,000 Dr.
6	(c) Benefits				28,000 Dr.	28,000 Cr.
7						
8	Journal entry for 2012	54,000 Dr.	38,000 Cr.	16,000 Cr.*		
9	Balance, Dec. 31, 2012			16,000 Cr.**	26,000 Cr.	10,000 Dr.
10						
11	*$54,000 – $38,000 = $16,000					
12	**$26,000 – $10,000 = $16,000					

Entry (a) records the service cost component, which increases postretirement expense $54,000 and increases the liability (APBO) $54,000. Entry (b) records Quest's funding of assets to the postretirement fund. The funding decreases cash $38,000 and increases plan assets $38,000. Entry (c) records the benefit payments made to retirees, which results in equal $28,000 decreases to the plan assets and the liability (APBO).

Quest's December 31 adjusting entry formally records the postretirement expense in 2012, as follows.

December 31, 2012

Postretirement Expense	54,000	
Cash		38,000
Postretirement Asset/Liability		16,000

The credit to Postretirement Asset/Liability for $16,000 represents the difference between the APBO and the plan assets. The $16,000 credit balance is a liability because the plan is underfunded. The Postretirement Asset/Liability account balance of $16,000 also equals the net of the balances in the memo accounts.

Illustration 20A-5 shows the funded status reported in the balance sheet. (Notice its similarity to the pension schedule.)

Accumulated postretirement benefit obligation (Credit)	$(26,000)
Plan assets at fair value (Debit)	10,000
Postretirement asset/liability (Credit)	$(16,000)

ILLUSTRATION 20A-5
Postretirement Reconciliation Schedule— December 31, 2012

Recognition of Gains and Losses

Gains and losses represent changes in the APBO or the value of plan assets. These changes result either from actual experience different from that expected or from changes in actuarial assumptions. The amortization of these gains and losses follows the approach used for pensions. That is, the gains and losses are recorded in other comprehensive income.

The Corridor Approach

Consistent with pension accounting, companies amortize the gains and losses in accumulated other comprehensive income as a component of postretirement expense if, at the beginning of the period, they exceed a "corridor" limit. The corridor is measured as the greater of 10 percent of the APBO or 10 percent of the market-related value of plan assets.

The intent of the corridor approach is to reduce volatility of postretirement expense by providing a reasonable opportunity for gains and losses to offset over time without affecting net periodic expense.

Amortization Methods

If the company must amortize gains and losses (beyond the corridor) on postretirement benefit plans, the **minimum amortization amount** is the excess gain or loss divided by the average remaining service life to expected retirement of all active employees. Companies may use any systematic method of amortization provided that: (1) the amount amortized in any period is equal to or greater than the minimum amount, (2) the company applies the method consistently, and (3) the company applies the method similarly for gains and losses.

The company must recompute the amount of gain or loss in accumulated other comprehensive income each year and amortize the gain or loss over the average remaining service life if the net amount exceeds the "corridor."

2013 Entries and Worksheet

Continuing the Quest Company illustration into 2013, the following facts apply to the postretirement benefits plan for the year 2013.

Actual return on plan assets is $600.

Expected return on plan assets is $800.

Discount rate is 8 percent.

Increase in APBO due to change in actuarial assumptions is $60,000.

Service cost is $26,000.

Funding contributions during the year are $18,000.

Benefit payments to employees during the year are $5,000.

Average remaining service to expected retirement: 25 years.

The worksheet in Illustration 20A-6 presents all of Quest's postretirement benefit entries and information for 2013. The beginning balances on the first line of the worksheet are the ending balances from Quest's 2012 postretirement benefits worksheet in Illustration 20A-4 (on page 1246).

Postretirement Benefits Worksheet—2013

Items	General Journal Entries					Memo Record	
	Annual Postretirement Expense	Cash	Other Comprehensive Income (G/L)	Postretirement Asset/Liability		APBO	Plan Assets
Balance, Jan. 1, 2013				16,000 Cr.		26,000 Cr.	10,000 Dr.
(d) Service cost	26,000 Dr.					26,000 Cr.	
(e) Interest cost	2,080 Dr.					2,080 Cr.	
(f) Actual return	600 Cr.						600 Dr.
(g) Unexpected loss	200 Cr.		200 Dr.				
(h) Contributions		18,000 Cr.					18,000 Dr.
(i) Benefits						5,000 Dr.	5,000 Cr.
(j) Increase in APBO (Loss)			60,000 Dr.			60,000 Cr.	
Journal entry for 2013	27,280 Dr.	18,000 Cr.	60,200 Dr.	69,480 Cr.			
Accumulated OCI, Dec. 31, 2012			0				
Balance, Dec. 31, 2013			60,200 Dr.	85,480 Cr.		109,080 Cr.	23,600 Dr.

ILLUSTRATION 20A-6
Postretirement Benefits
Worksheet—2013

Entries (d), (h), and (i) are similar to the corresponding entries previously explained for 2012. Entry (e) accrues the interest expense component, which increases both the liability and the postretirement expense by $2,080 (the beginning APBO multiplied by the discount rate of 8%). Entries (f) and (g) are related. The expected return of $800 is higher than the actual return of $600. To smooth postretirement expense, Quest defers the unexpected loss of $200 ($800 − $600) by debiting Other Comprehensive Income (G/L) and crediting Postretirement Expense. As a result of this adjustment, the expected return on the plan assets is the amount actually used to compute postretirement expense.

Entry (j) records the change in the APBO resulting from a change in actuarial assumptions. This $60,000 increase in the employer's accumulated liability is an unexpected loss. Quest debits this loss to Other Comprehensive Income (G/L).

On December 31 Quest formally records net periodic expense for 2013 as follows.

December 31, 2013

Postretirement Expense	27,280	
Other Comprehensive Income (G/L)	60,200	
Cash		18,000
Postretirement Asset/Liability		69,480

The balance of the Postretirement Asset/Liability account at December 31, 2013, is $85,480. This balance is equal to the net of the balances in the memo accounts as shown in the reconciliation schedule in Illustration 20A-7.

Accumulated postretirement benefit obligation (Credit)	$(109,080)
Plan assets at fair value (Debit)	23,600
Postretirement asset/liability (Credit)	$ (85,480)

ILLUSTRATION 20A-7
Postretirement Benefits
Reconciliation
Schedule—December 31,
2013

Amortization of Net Gain or Loss in 2014

Quest has a beginning balance in Accumulated OCI related to losses of $60,200. Therefore, Quest must apply the corridor test for amortization of the balance for 2014. Illustration 20A-8 shows the computation of the amortization charge for the loss.

2014 CORRIDOR TEST	
Accumulated OCI at beginning of year	$60,200
10% of greater of APBO or market-related value of plan assets ($109,080 × .10)	(10,908)
Amortizable amount	$49,292
Average remaining service to expected retirement	25 years
2014 amortization of loss ($49,292 ÷ 25)	$1,972

ILLUSTRATION 20A-8
Computation of
Amortization Charge
(Corridor Test)—2014

DISCLOSURES IN NOTES TO THE FINANCIAL STATEMENTS

The disclosures required for other postretirement benefit plans are similar to and just as detailed and extensive as those required for pensions. The note disclosure for Tootsie Roll, Inc. in Illustration 20A-9 (page 1250) provides a good example of the extensive disclosure required for other postretirement benefit plans.

As indicated in Illustration 20A-9, Tootsie Roll shows the impact of the postretirement benefit plan on income, the balance sheet, and the cash flow statement, and it provides information on important assumptions used in the measurement of the postretirement benefit obligation. Also note that given no tax incentives for funding, Tootsie Roll (like many companies) does not have any assets set aside for its other postretirement benefit obligations.

While Tootsie Roll has only an other postretirement benefit plan, many companies sponsor both defined benefit pension and other postretirement plans. Given the similarities in accounting for these plans, companies can combine pension and other postretirement benefit disclosures.

ACTUARIAL ASSUMPTIONS AND CONCEPTUAL ISSUES

Measurement of the EPBO, the APBO, and the net periodic postretirement benefit cost is involved and complex. Due to the uncertainties in forecasting healthcare costs, rates of use, changes in government health programs, and the differences employed in non-medical assumptions (e.g., discount rate, employee turnover, rate of pre-65 retirement, spouse-age difference), estimates of postretirement benefit costs may have a large margin of error. Is the information relevant, reliable, or verifiable? The FASB concluded that "the obligation to provide postretirement benefits meets the definition of a liability, is representationally faithful, is relevant to financial statement users, and can be measured with sufficient reliability at a justifiable cost." [12] Failure to accrue an obligation and an expense prior to payment of benefits would result in an unfaithful representation of what financial statements should represent.

ILLUSTRATION 20A-9
Postretirement Benefit
Disclosure

Tootsie Roll Industries, Inc.

Notes to Financial Statements

Note 7 Employee Benefit Plans (partial)

Postretirement health care and life insurance benefit plans ($000):

The Company provides certain postretirement health care and life insurance benefits for corporate office and management employees. Employees become eligible for these benefits based upon their age and service and if they agree to contribute a portion of the cost. The Company has the right to modify or terminate these benefits. The Company does not fund postretirement health care and life insurance benefits in advance of payments for benefit claims.

Amounts recognized in accumulated other comprehensive loss (pre-tax) at December 31, 2009 are as follows:

Amounts recognized in other comprehensive income

Prior service credit	$ (877)
Net actuarial loss	2,523
Net amount recognized in accumulated other comprehensive loss	$1,646

The estimated actuarial loss and prior service credit amortized from accumulated other comprehensive income into net periodic benefit cost during 2010 are $253 and $(125), respectively.

The changes in the accumulated postretirement benefit obligation at December 31, 2009 and 2008, consist of the following:

Reconciliation of OPEB liability

	December 31,	
	2009	**2008**
Benefit obligation, beginning of year	$15,468	$13,214
Service cost	704	646
Interest cost	853	740
Actuarial (gain)/loss	(38)	1,172
Benefits paid	(313)	(304)
Benefit obligation, end of year	$16,674	$15,468

Net periodic postretirement benefit cost included the following components:

Components of OPEB expense

	2009	**2008**	**2007**
Service cost—benefits attributed to service during the period	$ 704	$ 646	$ 667
Interest cost on the accumulated postretirement benefit obligation	853	740	694
Net amortization	140	33	90
Net periodic postretirement benefit cost	$1,697	$1,419	$1,451

Rates used to estimate plan elements

For measurement purposes, the 2009 annual rate of increase in the per capita cost of covered health care benefits was assumed to be 6.0% for pre-age 65 retirees, 7.5% for post-age 65 retirees and 9.0% for prescription drugs; these rates were assumed to decrease gradually to 5.0% for 2014 and remain at that level thereafter. The health care cost trend rate assumption has a significant effect on the amounts reported. The weighted-average discount rate used in determining the accumulated postretirement benefit obligation was 5.84% and 5.60% at December 31, 2009 and 2008, respectively.

Increasing or decreasing the health care trend rates by one percentage point in each year would have the following effect on:

	1% Increase	1% Decrease
Postretirement benefit obligation	$2,237	$(1,930)
Total of service and interest cost components	$ 258	$ (209)

The Company estimates future benefit payments will be $539, $584, $693, $782 and $911 in 2010 through 2014, respectively, and a total of $5,976 in 2015 through 2019. The future benefit payments are net of the annual Medicare Part D subsidy of approximately $1,062 beginning in 2010.

The FASB took a momentous step by requiring recognition of a postretirement liability. Many opposed the requirement, warning that the GAAP rules would devastate earnings. Others argued that putting these numbers on the balance sheet was inappropriate. Others noted that the requirement would force companies to curtail postretirement benefits to employees.

The authors believe that the FASB deserves special praise. Because the Board addressed this issue, companies now recognize the magnitude of these costs. This recognition has led to efforts to control escalating healthcare costs. As John Ruffle, a former president of the Financial Accounting Foundation noted, "The Board has done American industry a gigantic favor. Over the long term, industry will look back and say thanks."

GASB WHO?

The Governmental Accounting Standards Board (GASB) was organized in 1984 as an operating entity of the Financial Accounting Foundation (FAF) to establish standards of financial accounting and reporting for state and local governmental entities. Similar to the FASB, FAF Trustees are responsible for selecting the members of the GASB and its Advisory Council, funding their activities, and exercising general oversight (with the exception of the GASB's resolution of technical issues). The GASB's function is important because high-quality external financial reporting can demonstrate financial accountability of state and local governments to the public and is the basis for investment, credit, and many legislative and regulatory decisions.

Until recently, the GASB went about its work in relative obscurity. How did the GASB get everyone's attention? It recommended that governmental units recognize other postretirement benefits on their balance sheets on an accrual basis, similar to the accounting required for pensions. Some states do not like that recommendation and have proposed legislation that will allow them to ignore GASB standards. However, the GASB, with the support of users of government reports, has pushed for the change. They are concerned that without the new requirements, governments will continue to misrepresent the true cost of their retirement-related promises to public employees. In their view, the new accounting rules are in the best interests of municipal bondholders and the public in general. Thus, it appears that the FASB is not the only standard-setter subject to political pressure.

Source: R. H. Attmore, "Who Do Texas Elected Officials Think They Are Fooling?" *The Bond Buyer* (June 18, 2007). For more information on the GASB, go to *www.gasb.org/*.

What do the numbers mean?

SUMMARY OF LEARNING OBJECTIVES FOR APPENDIX 20A

10 **Identify the differences between pensions and postretirement healthcare benefits.** Pension plans are generally funded, but healthcare benefit plans are not. Pension benefits are generally well-defined and level in amount; healthcare benefits are generally uncapped and variable. Pension benefits are payable monthly; healthcare benefits are paid as needed and used. Pension plan variables are reasonably predictable, whereas healthcare plan variables are difficult to predict.

11 **Contrast accounting for pensions to accounting for other postretirement benefits.** Many of the basic concepts, accounting terminology, and measurement methodology that apply to pensions also apply to other postretirement benefit accounting. Because other postretirement benefit plans are unfunded, large obligations can occur. Two significant concepts peculiar to accounting for other postretirement benefits are (a) expected postretirement benefit obligation (EPBO), and (b) accumulated postretirement benefit obligation (APBO).

FASB CODIFICATION

FASB Codification References

[1] FASB ASC 960. [Predecessor literature: "Accounting and Reporting by Defined Benefit Pension Plans," *Statement of Financial Accounting Standards No. 35* (Stamford, Conn.: FASB, 1979).]

[2] FASB ASC 715-70-50-1. [Predecessor literature: "Employers' Accounting for Pension Plans," *Statement of Financial Accounting Standards No. 87* (Stamford, Conn.: FASB, 1985), paras. 63–66.]

[3] FASB ASC 715-30-25-1. [Predecessor literature: "Employers' Accounting for Defined Benefit Pension and Other Postretirement Plans: An Amendment to SFAS Nos. 87, 88, 106, and 132(R)," *Statement of Financial Accounting Standards No. 158* (Norwalk, CT: FASB, 2006).]

[4] FASB ASC 715-30-35-22. [Predecessor literature: "Employers' Accounting for Pension Plans," *Statement of Financial Accounting Standards No. 87* (Stamford, Conn.: FASB, 1985), par. 30.]

[5] FASB ASC 220-10-45-13. [Predecessor literature: "Employers' Accounting for Defined Benefit Pension and Other Postretirement Plans: An Amendment of SFAS Nos. 87, 88, 106, and 132(R)," *Statement of Financial Accounting Standards No. 158* (Norwalk, CT: FASB, 2006), par. B41.]

[6] FASB ASC 715-20-50-1. [Predecessor literature: None.]

[7] FASB ASC 715-20-50-1. [Predecessor literature: "Employers' Disclosure about Pensions and Other Postretirement Benefits," *Statement of Financial Accounting Standards No. 132* (Stamford, Conn.: FASB, 1998; revised 2003); and "Employers' Accounting for Defined Benefit Pension and Other Postretirement Plans: An Amendment of SFAS Nos. 87, 88, 106, and 132(R)," *Statement of Financial Accounting Standards No. 158* (Norwalk, CT: FASB, 2006).]

[8] FASB ASC 715-30-05-9. [Predecessor literature: "Employers' Accounting for Settlements and Curtailments of Defined Benefit Pension Plans and for Termination Benefits," *Statement of Financial Accounting Standards No. 88* (Stamford, Conn.: FASB, 1985).]

[9] FASB ASC 715-60. [Predecessor literature: "Employers' Accounting for Postretirement Benefits Other Than Pensions," *Statement of Financial Accounting Standards No. 106* (Norwalk, Conn.: FASB, 1990).]

[10] FASB ASC 712-10-05. [Predecessor literature: "Employers' Accounting for Postemployment Benefits," *Statement of Financial Accounting Standards No. 112* (Norwalk, Conn.: FASB, 1992).]

[11] FASB ASC 715-60-35-9. [Predecessor literature: "Employers' Accounting for Postretirement Benefits Other Than Pensions," *Statement of Financial Accounting Standards No. 106* (Norwalk, Conn.: FASB, 1990), paras. 46–66.]

[12] FASB ASC 715-60-25. [Predecessor literature: "Employers' Accounting for Postretirement Benefits Other Than Pensions," *Statement of Financial Accounting Standards No. 106* (Norwalk, Conn.: FASB, 1990), par. 163.]

Exercises

If your school has a subscription to the FASB Codification, go to *http://aaahq.org/ascLogin.cfm* to log in and prepare responses to the following. Provide Codification references for your responses.

CE20-1 Access the glossary ("Master Glossary") to answer the following.

    (a) What is an accumulated benefit obligation?

    (b) What is a defined benefit postretirement plan?

    (c) What is the definition of "actuarial present value"?

    (d) What is a prior service cost?

CE20-2 In general, how can an employer choose an appropriate discount rate for its pension plan? What information could an employer use in choosing a discount rate?

CE20-3 If an employer has a defined benefit pension plan, what components would make up its net periodic pension cost?

CE20-4 What information about its pension plan must a publicly traded company disclose in its interim financial statements?

An additional Codification case can be found in the Using Your Judgment section, on page 1273.

Be sure to check the book's companion website for a Review and Analysis Exercise, with solution.

 Questions, Brief Exercises, Exercises, Problems, and many more resources are available for practice in WileyPLUS.

Note: All asterisked Questions, Exercises, and Problems relate to material in the appendix to the chapter.

QUESTIONS

1. What is a private pension plan? How does a contributory pension plan differ from a noncontributory plan?

2. Differentiate between a defined contribution pension plan and a defined benefit pension plan. Explain how the employer's obligation differs between the two types of plans.

3. Differentiate between "accounting for the employer" and "accounting for the pension fund."

4. The meaning of the term "fund" depends on the context in which it is used. Explain its meaning when used as a noun. Explain its meaning when it is used as a verb.

5. What is the role of an actuary relative to pension plans? What are actuarial assumptions?

6. What factors must be considered by the actuary in measuring the amount of pension benefits under a defined benefit plan?

7. Name three approaches to measuring benefit obligations from a pension plan and explain how they differ.

8. Explain how cash-basis accounting for pension plans differs from accrual-basis accounting for pension plans. Why is cash-basis accounting generally considered unacceptable for pension plan accounting?

9. Identify the five components that comprise pension expense. Briefly explain the nature of each component.

10. What is service cost, and what is the basis of its measurement?

11. In computing the interest component of pension expense, what interest rates may be used?

12. Explain the difference between service cost and prior service cost.

13. What is meant by "prior service cost"? When is prior service cost recognized as pension expense?

14. What are "liability gains and losses," and how are they accounted for?

15. If pension expense recognized in a period exceeds the current amount funded by the employer, what kind of account arises, and how should it be reported in the financial statements? If the reverse occurs—that is, current funding by the employer exceeds the amount recognized as pension expense—what kind of account arises, and how should it be reported?

16. Given the following items and amounts, compute the actual return on plan assets: fair value of plan assets at the beginning of the period $9,500,000; benefits paid during the period $1,400,000; contributions made during the period $1,000,000; and fair value of the plan assets at the end of the period $10,150,000.

17. How does an "asset gain or loss" develop in pension accounting? How does a "liability gain or loss" develop in pension accounting?

18. What is the meaning of "corridor amortization"?

19. At the end of the current period, Agler Inc. had a projected benefit obligation of $400,000 and pension plan assets (at fair value) of $350,000. What are the accounts and amounts that will be reported on the company's balance sheet as pension assets or pension liabilities?

20. At the end of the current year, Pociek Co. has prior service cost of $9,150,000. Where should the prior service cost be reported on the balance sheet?

21. Describe the accounting for actuarial gains and losses.

22. Boey Company reported net income of $25,000 in 2013. It had the following amounts related to its pension plan in 2013: Actuarial liability gain $10,000; Unexpected asset loss $14,000; Accumulated other comprehensive income (G/L) (beginning balance), zero. Determine for 2013 (a) Boey's other comprehensive income, and (b) comprehensive income.

23. Describe the reporting of pension plans for a company with multiple plans, some of which are underfunded and some of which are overfunded.

24. Determine the meaning of the following terms.
   (a) Contributory plan.
   (b) Vested benefits.
   (c) Retroactive benefits.
   (d) Years-of-service method.

25. A headline in the *Wall Street Journal* stated, "Firms Increasingly Tap Their Pension Funds to Use Excess Assets." What is the accounting issue related to the use of these "excess assets" by companies?

****26.** What are postretirement benefits other than pensions?

****27.** Why didn't the FASB cover both types of postretirement benefits—pensions and healthcare—in the earlier pension accounting rules?

****28.** What are the major differences between postretirement healthcare benefits and pension benefits?

****29.** What is the difference between the APBO and the EPBO? What are the components of postretirement expense?

BRIEF EXERCISES

4 BE20-1 AMR Corporation (parent company of American Airlines) reported the following for 2009 (in millions).

Service cost	$333
Interest on P.B.O.	712
Return on plan assets	566
Amortization of prior service cost	13
Amortization of net loss	145

Compute AMR Corporation's 2009 pension expense.

4 BE20-2 For Warren Corporation, year-end plan assets were $2,000,000. At the beginning of the year, plan assets were $1,780,000. During the year, contributions to the pension fund were $120,000, and benefits paid were $200,000. Compute Warren's actual return on plan assets.

5 BE20-3 At January 1, 2012, Beaty Company had plan assets of $280,000 and a projected benefit obligation of the same amount. During 2012, service cost was $27,500, the settlement rate was 10%, actual and expected return on plan assets were $25,000, contributions were $20,000, and benefits paid were $17,500. Prepare a pension worksheet for Beaty Company for 2012.

4 BE20-4 For 2010, Campbell Soup Company had pension expense of $68 million and contributed $284 million to the pension fund. Prepare Campbell Soup Company's journal entry to record pension expense and funding.

6 BE20-5 Mancuso Corporation amended its pension plan on January 1, 2012, and granted $160,000 of prior service costs to its employees. The employees are expected to provide 2,000 service years in the future, with 350 service years in 2012. Compute prior service cost amortization for 2012.

9 BE20-6 At December 31, 2012, Besler Corporation had a projected benefit obligation of $560,000, plan assets of $322,000, and prior service cost of $127,000 in accumulated other comprehensive income. Determine the pension asset/liability at December 31, 2012.

8 **BE20-7** Shin Corporation had a projected benefit obligation of $3,100,000 and plan assets of $3,300,000 at January 1, 2012. Shin also had a net actuarial loss of $465,000 in accumulated OCI at January 1, 2012. The average remaining service period of Shin's employees is 7.5 years. Compute Shin's minimum amortization of the actuarial loss.

9 **BE20-8** Hawkins Corporation has the following balances at December 31, 2012.

Projected benefit obligation	$2,600,000
Plan assets at fair value	2,000,000
Accumulated OCI (PSC)	1,100,000

How should these balances be reported on Hawkins's balance sheet at December 31, 2012?

9 **BE20-9** Norton Co. had the following amounts related to its pension plan in 2012.

Actuarial liability loss for 2012	$28,000
Unexpected asset gain for 2012	18,000
Accumulated other comprehensive income (G/L) (beginning balance)	7,000 Cr.

Determine for 2012: (a) Norton's other comprehensive income (loss), and (b) comprehensive income. Net income for 2012 is $26,000; no amortization of gain or loss is necessary in 2012.

9 **BE20-10** Lahey Corp. has three defined benefit pension plans as follows.

	Pension Assets (at Fair Value)	Projected Benefit Obligation
Plan X	$600,000	$500,000
Plan Y	900,000	720,000
Plan Z	550,000	700,000

How will Lahey report these multiple plans in its financial statements?

10 **11** *****BE20-11** Manno Corporation has the following information available concerning its postretirement benefit plan for 2012.

Service cost	$40,000
Interest cost	47,400
Actual and expected return on plan assets	26,900

Compute Manno's 2012 postretirement expense.

10 **11** *****BE20-12** For 2012, Sampsell Inc. computed its annual postretirement expense as $240,900. Sampsell's contribution to the plan during 2012 was $180,000. Prepare Sampsell's 2012 entry to record postretirement expense.

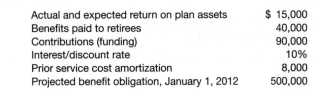

EXERCISES

4 **6** **E20-1 (Pension Expense, Journal Entries)** The following information is available for the pension plan of Radcliffe Company for the year 2012.

Actual and expected return on plan assets	$ 15,000
Benefits paid to retirees	40,000
Contributions (funding)	90,000
Interest/discount rate	10%
Prior service cost amortization	8,000
Projected benefit obligation, January 1, 2012	500,000
Service cost	60,000

Instructions

(a) Compute pension expense for the year 2012.

(b) Prepare the journal entry to record pension expense and the employer's contribution to the pension plan in 2012.

4 **6** **E20-2 (Computation of Pension Expense)** Veldre Company provides the following information about its defined benefit pension plan for the year 2012.

Service cost	$ 90,000
Contribution to the plan	105,000
Prior service cost amortization	10,000
Actual and expected return on plan assets	64,000
Benefits paid	40,000
Plan assets at January 1, 2012	640,000
Projected benefit obligation at January 1, 2012	700,000
Accumulated OCI (PSC) at January 1, 2012	150,000
Interest/discount (settlement) rate	10%

Instructions
Compute the pension expense for the year 2012.

5 **E20-3 (Preparation of Pension Worksheet)** Using the information in E20-2, prepare a pension worksheet inserting January 1, 2012, balances, showing December 31, 2012, balances, and the journal entry recording pension expense.

5 **E20-4 (Basic Pension Worksheet)** The following facts apply to the pension plan of Boudreau Inc. for the year 2012.

Plan assets, January 1, 2012	$490,000
Projected benefit obligation, January 1, 2012	490,000
Settlement rate	8%
Service cost	40,000
Contributions (funding)	25,000
Actual and expected return on plan assets	49,700
Benefits paid to retirees	33,400

Instructions
Using the preceding data, compute pension expense for the year 2012. As part of your solution, prepare a pension worksheet that shows the journal entry for pension expense for 2012 and the year-end balances in the related pension accounts.

6 **E20-5 (Application of Years-of-Service Method)** Andrews Company has five employees participating in its defined benefit pension plan. Expected years of future service for these employees at the beginning of 2012 are as follows.

Employee	Future Years of Service
Jim	3
Paul	4
Nancy	5
Dave	6
Kathy	6

On January 1, 2012, the company amended its pension plan, increasing its projected benefit obligation by $72,000.

Instructions
Compute the amount of prior service cost amortization for the years 2012 through 2017 using the years-of-service method, setting up appropriate schedules.

4 **E20-6 (Computation of Actual Return)** Gingrich Importers provides the following pension plan information.

Fair value of pension plan assets, January 1, 2012	$2,400,000
Fair value of pension plan assets, December 31, 2012	2,725,000
Contributions to the plan in 2012	280,000
Benefits paid retirees in 2012	350,000

Instructions
From the data above, compute the actual return on the plan assets for 2012.

5 **6** **E20-7 (Basic Pension Worksheet)** The following defined pension data of Rydell Corp. apply to the year 2012.

Projected benefit obligation, 1/1/12 (before amendment)	$560,000
Plan assets, 1/1/12	546,200
Pension liability	13,800
On January 1, 2012, Rydell Corp., through plan amendment, grants prior service benefits having a present value of	120,000
Settlement rate	9%
Service cost	58,000
Contributions (funding)	65,000
Actual (expected) return on plan assets	52,280
Benefits paid to retirees	40,000
Prior service cost amortization for 2012	17,000

Instructions

For 2012, prepare a pension worksheet for Rydell Corp. that shows the journal entry for pension expense and the year-end balances in the related pension accounts.

8 **E20-8 (Application of the Corridor Approach)** Kenseth Corp. has the following beginning-of-the-year present values for its projected benefit obligation and market-related values for its pension plan assets.

	Projected Benefit Obligation	Plan Assets Value
2011	$2,000,000	$1,900,000
2012	2,400,000	2,500,000
2013	2,950,000	2,600,000
2014	3,600,000	3,000,000

The average remaining service life per employee in 2011 and 2012 is 10 years and in 2013 and 2014 is 12 years. The net gain or loss that occurred during each year is as follows: 2011, $280,000 loss; 2012, $90,000 loss; 2013, $11,000 loss; and 2014, $25,000 gain. (In working the solution, the gains and losses must be aggregated to arrive at year-end balances.)

Instructions

Using the corridor approach, compute the amount of net gain or loss amortized and charged to pension expense in each of the four years, setting up an appropriate schedule.

9 **E20-9 (Disclosures: Pension Expense and Other Comprehensive Income)** Taveras Enterprises provides the following information relative to its defined benefit pension plan.

Balances or Values at December 31, 2012	
Projected benefit obligation	$2,737,000
Accumulated benefit obligation	1,980,000
Fair value of plan assets	2,278,329
Accumulated OCI (PSC)	210,000
Accumulated OCI—Net loss (1/1/12 balance, –0–)	45,680
Pension liability	458,671
Other pension plan data:	
Service cost for 2012	94,000
Prior service cost amortization for 2012	42,000
Actual return on plan assets in 2012	130,000
Expected return on plan assets in 2012	175,680
Interest on January 1, 2012, projected benefit obligation	253,000
Contributions to plan in 2012	93,329
Benefits paid	140,000

Instructions

(a) Prepare the note disclosing the components of pension expense for the year 2012.

(b) Determine the amounts of other comprehensive income and comprehensive income for 2012. Net income for 2012 is $35,000.

(c) Compute the amount of accumulated other comprehensive income reported at December 31, 2012.

5 **E20-10 (Pension Worksheet)** Webb Corp. sponsors a defined benefit pension plan for its employees. On January 1, 2012, the following balances relate to this plan.

Plan assets	$480,000
Projected benefit obligation	600,000
Pension asset/liability	120,000
Accumulated OCI (PSC)	100,000

As a result of the operation of the plan during 2012, the following additional data are provided by the actuary.

Service cost for 2012	$90,000
Settlement rate, 9%	
Actual return on plan assets in 2012	55,000
Amortization of prior service cost	19,000
Expected return on plan assets	52,000
Unexpected loss from change in projected benefit obligation,	
due to change in actuarial predictions	76,000
Contributions in 2012	99,000
Benefits paid retirees in 2012	85,000

Instructions

(a) Using the data above, compute pension expense for Webb Corp. for the year 2012 by preparing a pension worksheet.

(b) Prepare the journal entry for pension expense for 2012.

4 **9** **E20-11 (Pension Expense, Journal Entries, Statement Presentation)** Henning Company sponsors a defined benefit pension plan for its employees. The following data relate to the operation of the plan for the year 2012 in which no benefits were paid.

1. The actuarial present value of future benefits earned by employees for services rendered in 2012 amounted to $56,000.
2. The company's funding policy requires a contribution to the pension trustee amounting to $145,000 for 2012.
3. As of January 1, 2012, the company had a projected benefit obligation of $900,000, an accumulated benefit obligation of $800,000, and a balance of $400,000 in accumulated OCI (PSC). The fair value of pension plan assets amounted to $600,000 at the beginning of the year. The actual and expected return on plan assets was $54,000. The settlement rate was 9%. No gains or losses occurred in 2012 and no benefits were paid.
4. Amortization of prior service cost was $50,000 in 2012. Amortization of net gain or loss was not required in 2012.

Instructions

(a) Determine the amounts of the components of pension expense that should be recognized by the company in 2012.

(b) Prepare the journal entry or entries to record pension expense and the employer's contribution to the pension trustee in 2012.

(c) Indicate the amounts that would be reported on the income statement and the balance sheet for the year 2012.

4 **6** **7** **8** **9** **E20-12 (Pension Expense, Journal Entries, Statement Presentation)** Ferreri Company received the following selected information from its pension plan trustee concerning the operation of the company's defined benefit pension plan for the year ended December 31, 2012.

	January 1, 2012	December 31, 2012
Projected benefit obligation	$1,500,000	$1,527,000
Market-related and fair value of plan assets	800,000	1,130,000
Accumulated benefit obligation	1,600,000	1,720,000
Accumulated OCI (G/L)—Net gain	–0–	(200,000)

The service cost component of pension expense for employee services rendered in the current year amounted to $77,000 and the amortization of prior service cost was $120,000. The company's actual funding (contributions) of the plan in 2012 amounted to $250,000. The expected return on plan assets and the actual rate were both 10%; the interest/discount (settlement) rate was 10%. Accumulated other comprehensive income (PSC) had a balance of $1,200,000 on January 1, 2012. Assume no benefits paid in 2012.

Instructions

(a) Determine the amounts of the components of pension expense that should be recognized by the company in 2012.

(b) Prepare the journal entry to record pension expense and the employer's contribution to the pension plan in 2012.

(c) Indicate the pension-related amounts that would be reported on the income statement and the balance sheet for Ferreri Company for the year 2012.

4 **6** **E20-13 (Computation of Actual Return, Gains and Losses, Corridor Test, and Pension Expense)** Erickson
7 **8** Company sponsors a defined benefit pension plan. The corporation's actuary provides the following infor-
9 mation about the plan.

	January 1, 2012	December 31, 2012
Vested benefit obligation	$1,500	$1,900
Accumulated benefit obligation	1,900	2,730
Projected benefit obligation	2,500	3,300
Plan assets (fair value)	1,700	2,620
Settlement rate and expected rate of return		10%
Pension asset/liability	800	?
Service cost for the year 2012		400
Contributions (funding in 2012)		700
Benefits paid in 2012		200

Instructions
(a) Compute the actual return on the plan assets in 2012.
(b) Compute the amount of the other comprehensive income (G/L) as of December 31, 2012. (Assume the January 1, 2012, balance was zero.)
(c) Compute the amount of net gain or loss amortization for 2012 (corridor approach).
(d) Compute pension expense for 2012.

5 **E20-14 (Worksheet for E20-13)** Using the information in E20-13 about Erickson Company's defined benefit pension plan, prepare a 2012 pension worksheet with supplementary schedules of computations. Prepare the journal entries at December 31, 2012, to record pension expense and related pension transactions. Also, indicate the pension amounts reported in the balance sheet.

4 **E20-15 (Pension Expense, Journal Entries)** Latoya Company provides the following selected information related to its defined benefit pension plan for 2012.

Pension asset/liability (January 1)	$ 25,000 Cr.
Accumulated benefit obligation (December 31)	400,000
Actual and expected return on plan assets	10,000
Contributions (funding) in 2012	150,000
Fair value of plan assets (December 31)	800,000
Settlement rate	10%
Projected benefit obligation (January 1)	700,000
Service cost	80,000

Instructions
(a) Compute pension expense and prepare the journal entry to record pension expense and the employer's contribution to the pension plan in 2012. Preparation of a pension worksheet is not required. Benefits paid in 2012 were $35,000.
(b) Indicate the pension-related amounts that would be reported in the company's income statement and balance sheet for 2012.

8 **E20-16 (Amortization of Accumulated OCI (G/L), Corridor Approach, Pension Expense Computation)** The actuary for the pension plan of Gustafson Inc. calculated the following net gains and losses.

Incurred during the Year	(Gain) or Loss
2012	$300,000
2013	480,000
2014	(210,000)
2015	(290,000)

Other information about the company's pension obligation and plan assets is as follows.

As of January 1,	Projected Benefit Obligation	Plan Assets (market-related asset value)
2012	$4,000,000	$2,400,000
2013	4,520,000	2,200,000
2014	5,000,000	2,600,000
2015	4,240,000	3,040,000

Gustafson Inc. has a stable labor force of 400 employees who are expected to receive benefits under the plan. The total service-years for all participating employees is 5,600. The beginning balance of accumulated OCI (G/L) is zero on January 1, 2012. The market-related value and the fair value of plan assets are the same for the 4-year period. Use the average remaining service life per employee as the basis for amortization.

Instructions
(Round to the nearest dollar.)

Prepare a schedule which reflects the minimum amount of accumulated OCI (G/L) amortized as a component of net periodic pension expense for each of the years 2012, 2013, 2014, and 2015. Apply the "corridor" approach in determining the amount to be amortized each year.

8 **E20-17 (Amortization of Accumulated OCI Balances)** Keeton Company sponsors a defined benefit pension plan for its 600 employees. The company's actuary provided the following information about the plan.

	January 1,	December 31,	
	2012	2012	2013
Projected benefit obligation	$2,800,000	$3,650,000	$4,195,000
Accumulated benefit obligation	1,900,000	2,430,000	2,900,000
Plan assets (fair value and market-related asset value)	1,700,000	2,900,000	3,790,000
Accumulated net (gain) or loss (for purposes of the corridor calculation)	–0–	198,000	(24,000)
Discount rate (current settlement rate)		9%	8%
Actual and expected asset return rate		10%	10%
Contributions		1,030,000	660,000

The average remaining service life per employee is 10.5 years. The service cost component of net periodic pension expense for employee services rendered amounted to $400,000 in 2012 and $475,000 in 2013. The accumulated OCI (PSC) on January 1, 2012, was $1,260,000. No benefits have been paid.

Instructions
(Round to the nearest dollar.)

(a) Compute the amount of accumulated OCI (PSC) to be amortized as a component of net periodic pension expense for each of the years 2012 and 2013.

(b) Prepare a schedule which reflects the amount of accumulated OCI (G/L) to be amortized as a component of pension expense for 2012 and 2013.

(c) Determine the total amount of pension expense to be recognized by Keeton Company in 2012 and 2013.

5 **8** **E20-18 (Pension Worksheet—Missing Amounts)** The accounting staff of Usher Inc. has prepared the following pension worksheet. Unfortunately, several entries in the worksheet are not decipherable. The company has asked your assistance in completing the worksheet and completing the accounting tasks related to the pension plan for 2012.

	A	B	C	D	E	F		H	I
1		General Journal Entries						Memo Record	
2	Items	Annual Pension Expense	Cash	OCI—Prior Service Cost	OCI— Gain/Loss	Pension Asset/Liability		Projected Benefit Obligation	Plan Assets
3	Balance, Jan. 1, 2012					1,100 Cr.		2,800	1,700
4	Service cost	(1)						500	
5	Interest cost	(2)						280	
6	Actual return	(3)							220
7	Unexpected gain	150			(4)				
8	Amortization of PSC	(5)		55					
9	Contributions		800						800
10	Benefits							200	200
11	Liability increase				(6)			365	
12	Journal entry	(7)	(8)	(9)	(10)	(11)			
13									
14	Accumulated OCI, Dec. 31, 2011			1,100	0				
15	Balance, Dec. 31, 2012			1,045	215	1,225		3,745	2,520
16									

Pension Worksheet—Usher Inc.

Sheet1 / Sheet2 / Sheet3 /

Instructions

(a) Determine the missing amounts in the 2012 pension worksheet, indicating whether the amounts are debits or credits.

(b) Prepare the journal entry to record 2012 pension expense for Usher Inc.

(c) The accounting staff has heard of a pension accounting procedure called "corridor amortization." Is Usher required to record any amounts for corridor amortization in (1) 2012? In (2) 2013? Explain.

10 11 *E20-19 (Postretirement Benefit Expense Computation)** Kreter Co. provides the following information about its postretirement benefit plan for the year 2012.

Service cost	$ 45,000
Contribution to the plan	10,000
Actual and expected return on plan assets	11,000
Benefits paid	20,000
Plan assets at January 1, 2012	110,000
Accumulated postretirement benefit obligation at January 1, 2012	330,000
Discount rate	8%

Instructions

Compute the postretirement benefit expense for 2012.

10 11 *E20-20 (Postretirement Benefit Worksheet)** Using the information in E20-19, prepare a worksheet inserting January 1, 2012, balances, and showing December 31, 2012, balances. Prepare the journal entry recording postretirement benefit expense.

10 11 *E20-21 (Postretirement Benefit Expense Computation)** Garner Inc. provides the following information related to its postretirement benefits for the year 2012.

Accumulated postretirement benefit obligation at January 1, 2012	$710,000
Actual and expected return on plan assets	34,000
Prior service cost amortization	21,000
Discount rate	10%
Service cost	83,000

Instructions

Compute postretirement benefit expense for 2012.

10 11 *E20-22 (Postretirement Benefit Expense Computation)** Englehart Co. provides the following information about its postretirement benefit plan for the year 2012.

Service cost	$ 90,000
Prior service cost amortization	3,000
Contribution to the plan	56,000
Actual and expected return on plan assets	62,000
Benefits paid	40,000
Plan assets at January 1, 2012	710,000
Accumulated postretirement benefit obligation at January 1, 2012	760,000
Accumulated OCI (PSC) at January 1, 2012	100,000 Dr.
Discount rate	9%

Instructions

Compute the postretirement benefit expense for 2012.

10 11 *E20-23 (Postretirement Benefit Worksheet)** Using the information in E20-22, prepare a worksheet inserting January 1, 2012, balances, showing December 31, 2012, balances, and the journal entry recording postretirement benefit expense.

10 11 *E20-24 (Postretirement Benefit Worksheet—Missing Amounts)** The accounting staff of Holder Inc. has prepared the postretirement benefit worksheet on page 1262. Unfortunately, several entries in the worksheet are not decipherable. The company has asked your assistance in completing the worksheet and completing the accounting tasks related to the pension plan for 2012.

				General Journal Entries		**Memo Record**	

Postretirement Benefit Worksheet—Holder Inc.

	A	B	C	D	E	G	H
1				**General Journal Entries**		**Memo Record**	
2	Items	Annual Expense	Cash	Other Comprehensive Income—PSC	Postretirement Asset/Liability	APBO	Plan Assets
3	Balance, Jan. 1, 2012				290,000	410,000	120,000
4	Service cost	(1)				56,000	
5	Interest cost	(2)				36,900	
6	Actual/Expected return	(3)					2,000
7	Contributions		66,000				(4)
8	Benefits					5,000	5,000
9	Amortization of PSC	3,000		(5)			
10	Journal entry for 2012	(6)	(7)	(8)	(9)		
11							
12	Accumulated OCI, Dec. 31, 2011			30,000 Dr.			
13	Balance, Dec. 31, 2012			27,000 Dr.	314,900 Cr.	497,900 Cr.	183,000 Dr.
14							

Sheet1 / Sheet2 / Sheet3

Instructions

(a) Determine the missing amounts in the 2012 postretirement worksheet, indicating whether the amounts are debits or credits.

(b) Prepare the journal entry to record 2012 postretirement expense for Holder Inc.

(c) What discount rate is Holder using in accounting for the interest on its other postretirement benefit plan? Explain.

> **See the book's companion website, www.wiley.com/college/kieso, for a set of B Exercises.**

PROBLEMS

P20-1 (2-Year Worksheet) On January 1, 2012, Harrington Company has the following defined benefit pension plan balances.

Projected benefit obligation	$4,500,000
Fair value of plan assets	4,200,000

The interest (settlement) rate applicable to the plan is 10%. On January 1, 2013, the company amends its pension agreement so that prior service costs of $500,000 are created. Other data related to the pension plan are as follows.

	2012	2013
Service cost	$150,000	$180,000
Prior service cost amortization	–0–	90,000
Contributions (funding) to the plan	240,000	285,000
Benefits paid	200,000	280,000
Actual return on plan assets	252,000	260,000
Expected rate of return on assets	6%	8%

Instructions

(a) Prepare a pension worksheet for the pension plan for 2012 and 2013.

(b) For 2013, prepare the journal entry to record pension-related amounts.

P20-2 (3-Year Worksheet, Journal Entries, and Reporting) Jackson Company adopts acceptable accounting for its defined benefit pension plan on January 1, 2011, with the following beginning balances: plan assets $200,000; projected benefit obligation $250,000. Other data relating to 3 years' operation of the plan are shown on the next page.

	2011	2012	2013
Annual service cost	$16,000	$ 19,000	$ 26,000
Settlement rate and expected rate of return	10%	10%	10%
Actual return on plan assets	18,000	22,000	24,000
Annual funding (contributions)	16,000	40,000	48,000
Benefits paid	14,000	16,400	21,000
Prior service cost (plan amended, 1/1/12)		160,000	
Amortization of prior service cost		54,400	41,600
Change in actuarial assumptions establishes			
a December 31, 2013, projected benefit obligation of:			520,000

Instructions

(a) Prepare a pension worksheet presenting all 3 years' pension balances and activities.

(b) Prepare the journal entries (from the worksheet) to reflect all pension plan transactions and events at December 31 of each year.

(c) Indicate the pension-related amounts reported in the financial statements for 2013.

6 7 8 9 **P20-3 (Pension Expense, Journal Entries, Amortization of Loss)** Gottschalk Company sponsors a defined benefit plan for its 100 employees. On January 1, 2012, the company's actuary provided the following information.

Accumulated other comprehensive loss (PSC)	$150,000
Pension plan assets (fair value and market-related asset value)	200,000
Accumulated benefit obligation	260,000
Projected benefit obligation	380,000

The average remaining service period for the participating employees is 10 years. All employees are expected to receive benefits under the plan. On December 31, 2012, the actuary calculated that the present value of future benefits earned for employee services rendered in the current year amounted to $52,000; the projected benefit obligation was $490,000; fair value of pension assets was $276,000; the accumulated benefit obligation amounted to $365,000. The expected return on plan assets and the discount rate on the projected benefit obligation were both 10%. The actual return on plan assets is $11,000. The company's current year's contribution to the pension plan amounted to $65,000. No benefits were paid during the year.

Instructions

(a) Determine the components of pension expense that the company would recognize in 2012. (With only one year involved, you need not prepare a worksheet.)

(b) Prepare the journal entry to record the pension expense and the company's funding of the pension plan in 2012.

(c) Compute the amount of the 2012 increase/decrease in gains or losses and the amount to be amortized in 2012 and 2013.

(d) Indicate the pension amounts reported in the financial statement as of December 31, 2012.

5 6 7 8 **P20-4 (Pension Expense, Journal Entries for 2 Years)** Gordon Company sponsors a defined benefit pension plan. The following information related to the pension plan is available for 2012 and 2013.

	2012	2013
Plan assets (fair value), December 31	$699,000	$849,000
Projected benefit obligation, January 1	700,000	800,000
Pension asset/liability, January 1	140,000 Cr.	?
Prior service cost, January 1	250,000	240,000
Service cost	60,000	90,000
Actual and expected return on plan assets	24,000	30,000
Amortization of prior service cost	10,000	12,000
Contributions (funding)	115,000	120,000
Accumulated benefit obligation, December 31	500,000	550,000
Interest/settlement rate	9%	9%

Instructions

(a) Compute pension expense for 2012 and 2013.

(b) Prepare the journal entries to record the pension expense and the company's funding of the pension plan for both years.

7 **8** **P20-5 (Computation of Pension Expense, Amortization of Net Gain or Loss–Corridor Approach, Journal Entries for 3 Years)** Hiatt Toothpaste Company initiates a defined benefit pension plan for its 50 employees on January 1, 2012. The insurance company which administers the pension plan provided the following selected information for the years 2012, 2013, and 2014.

	For Year Ended December 31,		
	2012	2013	2014
Plan assets (fair value)	$50,000	$ 85,000	$180,000
Accumulated benefit obligation	45,000	165,000	292,000
Projected benefit obligation	60,000	200,000	324,000
Net (gain) loss (for purposes of corridor calculation)	–0–	78,400	86,121
Employer's funding contribution (made at end of year)	50,000	60,000	105,000

There were no balances as of January 1, 2012, when the plan was initiated. The actual and expected return on plan assets was 10% over the 3-year period, but the settlement rate used to discount the company's pension obligation was 13% in 2012, 11% in 2013, and 8% in 2014. The service cost component of net periodic pension expense amounted to the following: 2012, $60,000; 2013, $85,000; and 2014, $119,000. The average remaining service life per employee is 12 years. No benefits were paid in 2012, $30,000 of benefits were paid in 2013, and $18,500 of benefits were paid in 2014 (all benefits paid at end of year).

Instructions

(Round to the nearest dollar.)

(a) Calculate the amount of net periodic pension expense that the company would recognize in 2012, 2013, and 2014.

(b) Prepare the journal entries to record net periodic pension expense, employer's funding contribution, and related pension amounts for the years 2012, 2013, and 2014.

6 **7** **8** **P20-6 (Computation of Prior Service Cost Amortization, Pension Expense, Journal Entries, and Net Gain or Loss)** Aykroyd Inc. has sponsored a noncontributory, defined benefit pension plan for its employees since 1989. Prior to 2012, cumulative net pension expense recognized equaled cumulative contributions to the plan. Other relevant information about the pension plan on January 1, 2012, is as follows.

1. The company has 200 employees. All these employees are expected to receive benefits under the plan. The average remaining service life per employee is 12 years.
2. The projected benefit obligation amounted to $5,000,000 and the fair value of pension plan assets was $3,000,000. The market-related asset value was also $3,000,000. Unrecognized prior service cost was $2,000,000.

On December 31, 2012, the projected benefit obligation and the accumulated benefit obligation were $4,850,000 and $4,025,000, respectively. The fair value of the pension plan assets amounted to $4,100,000 at the end of the year. A 10% settlement rate and a 10% expected asset return rate were used in the actuarial present value computations in the pension plan. The present value of benefits attributed by the pension benefit formula to employee service in 2012 amounted to $200,000. The employer's contribution to the plan assets amounted to $775,000 in 2012. This problem assumes no payment of pension benefits.

Instructions

(Round all amounts to the nearest dollar.)

(a) Prepare a schedule, based on the average remaining life per employee, showing the prior service cost that would be amortized as a component of pension expense for 2012, 2013, and 2014.

(b) Compute pension expense for the year 2012.

(c) Prepare the journal entries required to report the accounting for the company's pension plan for 2012.

(d) Compute the amount of the 2012 increase/decrease in net gains or losses and the amount to be amortized in 2012 and 2013.

5 **6** **7** **P20-7 (Pension Worksheet)** Hanson Corp. sponsors a defined benefit pension plan for its employees. On January 1, 2012, the following balances related to this plan.

Plan assets (market-related value)	$520,000
Projected benefit obligation	700,000
Pension asset/liability	180,000 Cr.
Prior service cost	81,000
Net gain or loss (debit)	91,000

As a result of the operation of the plan during 2012, the actuary provided the following additional data at December 31, 2012.

Service cost for 2012	$108,000
Settlement rate, 9%; expected return rate, 10%	
Actual return on plan assets in 2012	48,000
Amortization of prior service cost	25,000
Contributions in 2012	133,000
Benefits paid retirees in 2012	85,000
Average remaining service life of active employees	10 years

Instructions

Using the preceding data, compute pension expense for Hanson Corp. for the year 2012 by preparing a pension worksheet that shows the journal entry for pension expense. Use the market-related asset value to compute the expected return and for corridor amortization.

  P20-8 (Comprehensive 2-Year Worksheet) Lemke Company sponsors a defined benefit pension plan for its employees. The following data relate to the operation of the plan for the years 2012 and 2013.

	2012	2013
Projected benefit obligation, January 1	$600,000	
Plan assets (fair value and market-related value), January 1	410,000	
Pension asset/liability, January 1	190,000 Cr.	
Prior service cost, January 1	160,000	
Service cost	40,000	$ 59,000
Settlement rate	10%	10%
Expected rate of return	10%	10%
Actual return on plan assets	36,000	61,000
Amortization of prior service cost	70,000	50,000
Annual contributions	97,000	81,000
Benefits paid retirees	31,500	54,000
Increase in projected benefit obligation due to changes in actuarial assumptions	87,000	–0–
Accumulated benefit obligation at December 31	721,800	789,000
Average service life of all employees		20 years
Vested benefit obligation at December 31		464,000

Instructions

(a) Prepare a pension worksheet presenting both years 2012 and 2013 and accompanying computations and amortization of the loss (2013) using the corridor approach.

(b) Prepare the journal entries (from the worksheet) to reflect all pension plan transactions and events at December 31 of each year.

(c) For 2013, indicate the pension amounts reported in the financial statements.

  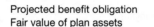 **P20-9 (Comprehensive 2-Year Worksheet)** Hobbs Co. has the following defined benefit pension plan balances on January 1, 2012.

Projected benefit obligation	$4,600,000
Fair value of plan assets	4,600,000

The interest (settlement) rate applicable to the plan is 10%. On January 1, 2013, the company amends its pension agreement so that prior service costs of $600,000 are created. Other data related to the pension plan are:

	2012	2013
Service cost	$150,000	$170,000
Prior service cost amortization	–0–	90,000
Contributions (funding) to the plan	200,000	184,658
Benefits paid	220,000	280,000
Actual return on plan assets	252,000	350,000
Expected rate of return on assets	6%	8%

Instructions

(a) Prepare a pension worksheet for the pension plan in 2012.

(b) Prepare any journal entries related to the pension plan that would be needed at December 31, 2012.

(c) Prepare a pension worksheet for 2013 and any journal entries related to the pension plan as of December 31, 2013.

(d) Indicate the pension-related amounts reported in the 2013 financial statements.

5 6 7 **P20-10 (Pension Worksheet – Missing Amounts)** Kramer Co. has prepared the following pension worksheet. Unfortunately, several entries in the worksheet are not decipherable. The company has asked your assistance in completing the worksheet and completing the accounting tasks related to the pension plan for 2012.

Pension Worksheet—Kramer Co.

	A	B	C	D	E	G	H
1		General Journal Entries				Memo Record	
2	**Items**	Annual Pension Expense	Cash	OCI—Prior Service Cost	OCI— Gain/Loss	Pension Asset/Liability	Projected Benefit Obligation	Plan Assets
3	Balance, Jan. 1, 2012					120,000	325,000	205,000 Dr.
4	Service cost	(1)					20,000	
5	Interest cost	(2)					26,000	
6	Actual return	(3)						18,000 Dr.
7	Unexpected loss	2,500			(4)			
8	Amortization of PSC	(5)		35,000				
9	Contributions		41,000					41,000 Dr.
10	Benefits						15,000	15,000 Cr.
11	Increase in PBO				(6)		43,500	
12	Journal entry for 2012	(7)	(8)	(9)	(10)	(11)		
13	Accumulated OCI, Dec. 31, 2011			80,000	0			
14	Balance, Dec. 31, 2012			45,000	46,000	150,500 Cr.	399,500 Cr.	249,000 Dr.

Instructions

(a) Determine the missing amounts in the 2012 pension worksheet, indicating whether the amounts are debits or credits.

(b) Prepare the journal entry to record 2012 pension expense for Kramer Co.

(c) Determine the following for Kramer for 2012: (1) settlement rate used to measure the interest on the liability and (2) expected return on plan assets.

5 6 7 8 9 **P20-11 (Pension Worksheet)** The following data relate to the operation of Kramer Co.'s pension plan in 2013. The pension worksheet for 2012 is provided in P20-10.

Service cost	$59,000
Actual return on plan assets	32,000
Amortization of prior service cost	28,000
Annual contributions	51,000
Benefits paid retirees	27,000
Average service life of all employees	25 years

For 2013, Kramer will use the same assumptions as 2012 for the expected rate of returns on plan assets. The settlement rate for 2013 is 10%.

Instructions

(a) Prepare a pension worksheet for 2013 and accompanying computations and amortization of the loss, if any, in 2013 using the corridor approach.

(b) Prepare the journal entries (from the worksheet) to reflect all pension plan transactions and events at December 31.

(c) Indicate the pension amounts reported in the financial statements.

5 6 7 8 9 **P20-12 (Pension Worksheet)** Larson Corp. sponsors a defined benefit pension plan for its employees. On January 1, 2013, the following balances related to this plan.

Plan assets (market-related value)	$270,000
Projected benefit obligation	340,000
Pension asset/liability	70,000 Cr.
Prior service cost	90,000
OCI—Loss	39,000

As a result of the operation of the plan during 2013, the actuary provided the following additional data at December 31, 2013.

Service cost for 2013	$45,000
Actual return on plan assets in 2013	27,000
Amortization of prior service cost	12,000
Contributions in 2013	65,000
Benefits paid retirees in 2013	41,000
Settlement rate	7%
Expected return on plan assets	8%
Average remaining service life of active employees	10 years

Instructions

(a) Compute pension expense for Larson Corp. for the year 2013 by preparing a pension worksheet that shows the journal entry for pension expense.

(b) Indicate the pension amounts reported in the financial statements.

10 11 *P20-13 (Postretirement Benefit Worksheet)** Hollenbeck Foods Inc. sponsors a postretirement medical and dental benefit plan for its employees. The following balances relate to this plan on January 1, 2012.

Plan assets	$200,000
Expected postretirement benefit obligation	820,000
Accumulated postretirement benefit obligation	200,000
No prior service costs exist.	

As a result of the plan's operation during 2012, the following additional data are provided by the actuary.

Service cost for 2012 is $70,000
Discount rate is 10%
Contributions to plan in 2012 are $65,000
Expected return on plan assets is $10,000
Actual return on plan assets is $15,000
Benefits paid to employees are $44,000
Average remaining service to full eligibility: 20 years

Instructions

(a) Using the preceding data, compute the net periodic postretirement benefit cost for 2012 by preparing a worksheet that shows the journal entry for postretirement expense and the year-end balances in the related postretirement benefit memo accounts. (Assume that contributions and benefits are paid at the end of the year.)

(b) Prepare any journal entries related to the postretirement plan for 2012 and indicate the postretirement amounts reported in the financial statements for 2012.

10 11 *P20-14 (Postretirement Benefit Worksheet—2 Years)** Elton Co. has the following postretirement benefit plan balances on January 1, 2012.

Accumulated postretirement benefit obligation	$2,250,000
Fair value of plan assets	2,250,000

The interest (settlement) rate applicable to the plan is 10%. On January 1, 2013, the company amends the plan so that prior service costs of $175,000 are created. Other data related to the plan are:

	2012	2013
Service costs	$ 75,000	$ 85,000
Prior service costs amortization	–0–	12,000
Contributions (funding) to the plan	45,000	35,000
Benefits paid	40,000	45,000
Actual return on plan assets	140,000	120,000
Expected rate of return on assets	8%	6%

Instructions

(a) Prepare a worksheet for the postretirement plan in 2012.

(b) Prepare any journal entries related to the postretirement plan that would be needed at December 31, 2012.

(c) Prepare a worksheet for 2013 and any journal entries related to the postretirement plan as of December 31, 2013.

(d) Indicate the postretirement-benefit–related amounts reported in the 2013 financial statements.

CONCEPTS FOR ANALYSIS

CA20-1 (Pension Terminology and Theory) Many business organizations have been concerned with providing for the retirement of employees since the late 1800s. During recent decades, a marked increase in this concern has resulted in the establishment of private pension plans in most large companies and in many medium- and small-sized ones.

The substantial growth of these plans, both in numbers of employees covered and in amounts of retirement benefits, has increased the significance of pension costs in relation to the financial position, results of operations, and cash flows of many companies. In examining the costs of pension plans, a CPA encounters certain terms. The components of pension costs that the terms represent must be dealt with appropriately if generally accepted accounting principles are to be reflected in the financial statements of entities with pension plans.

Instructions
- **(a)** Define a private pension plan. How does a contributory pension plan differ from a noncontributory plan?
- **(b)** Differentiate between "accounting for the employer" and "accounting for the pension fund."
- **(c)** Explain the terms "funded" and "pension liability" as they relate to:
  - **(1)** The pension fund.
  - **(2)** The employer.
- **(d)** **(1)** Discuss the theoretical justification for accrual recognition of pension costs.
  - **(2)** Discuss the relative objectivity of the measurement process of accrual versus cash (pay-as-you-go) accounting for annual pension costs.
- **(e)** Distinguish among the following as they relate to pension plans.
  - **(1)** Service cost.
  - **(2)** Prior service costs.
  - **(3)** Vested benefits.

CA20-2 (Pension Terminology) The following items appear on Brueggen Company's financial statements.

1. Under the caption Assets:
   Pension asset/liability.
2. Under the caption Liabilities:
   Pension asset/liability.
3. Under the caption Stockholders' Equity:
   Prior service cost as a component of Accumulated Other Comprehensive Income.
4. On the income statement:
   Pension expense.

Instructions
Explain the significance of each of the items above on corporate financial statements. (*Note:* All items set forth above are not necessarily to be found on the statements of a single company.)

CA20-3 (Basic Terminology) In examining the costs of pension plans, Helen Kaufman, CPA, encounters certain terms. The components of pension costs that the terms represent must be dealt with appropriately if generally accepted accounting principles are to be reflected in the financial statements of entities with pension plans.

Instructions
- **(a)** **(1)** Discuss the theoretical justification for accrual recognition of pension costs.
  - **(2)** Discuss the relative objectivity of the measurement process of accrual versus cash (pay-as-you-go) accounting for annual pension costs.
- **(b)** Explain the following terms as they apply to accounting for pension plans.
  - **(1)** Market-related asset value.
  - **(2)** Projected benefit obligation.
  - **(3)** Corridor approach.
- **(c)** What information should be disclosed about a company's pension plans in its financial statements and its notes?

(AICPA adapted)

CA20-4 (Major Pension Concepts) Davis Corporation is a medium-sized manufacturer of paperboard containers and boxes. The corporation sponsors a noncontributory, defined benefit pension plan that covers its 250 employees. Sid Cole has recently been hired as president of Davis Corporation. While reviewing last year's financial statements with Carol Dilbeck, controller, Cole expressed confusion about several of the items in the footnote to the financial statements relating to the pension plan. In part, the footnote reads as follows.

> **Note J.** The company has a defined benefit pension plan covering substantially all of its employees. The benefits are based on years of service and the employee's compensation during the last four years of employment. The company's funding policy is to contribute annually the maximum amount allowed under the federal tax code. Contributions are intended to provide for benefits expected to be earned in the future as well as those earned to date.

The net periodic pension expense on Davis Corporation's comparative income statement was $72,000 in 2012 and $57,680 in 2011.

The following are selected figures from the plan's funded status and amounts recognized in the Davis Corporation's Statement of Financial Position at December 31, 2012 ($000 omitted).

Actuarial present value of benefit obligations:	
Accumulated benefit obligation	
(including vested benefits of $636)	$ (870)
Projected benefit obligation	$(1,200)
Plan assets at fair value	1,050
Projected benefit obligation in	
excess of plan assets	$ (150)

Given that Davis Corporation's work force has been stable for the last 6 years, Cole could not understand the increase in the net periodic pension expense. Dilbeck explained that the net periodic pension expense consists of several elements, some of which may increase or decrease the net expense.

Instructions
- **(a)** The determination of the net periodic pension expense is a function of five elements. List and briefly describe each of the elements.
- **(b)** Describe the major difference and the major similarity between the accumulated benefit obligation and the projected benefit obligation.
- **(c)** **(1)** Explain why pension gains and losses are not recognized on the income statement in the period in which they arise.
    - **(2)** Briefly describe how pension gains and losses are recognized.

(CMA adapted)

CA20-5 (Implications of GAAP Rules on Pensions) Jill Vogel and Pete Dell have to do a class presentation on GAAP rules for reporting pension information. In developing the class presentation, they decided to provide the class with a series of questions related to pensions and then discuss the answers in class. Given that the class has all read the rules related to pension accounting and reporting, they felt this approach would provide a lively discussion. Here are the questions:

1. In an article in *Business Week* prior to new rules related to pensions, it was reported that the discount rates used by the largest 200 companies for pension reporting ranged from 5% to 11%. How can such a situation exist, and does GAAP alleviate this problem?
2. An article indicated that when new GAAP rules were issued related to pensions, it caused an increase in the liability for pensions for approximately 20% of companies. Why might this situation occur?
3. A recent article noted that while "smoothing" is not necessarily an accounting virtue, pension accounting has long been recognized as an exception—an area of accounting in which at least some dampening of market swings is appropriate. This is because pension funds are managed so that their performance is insulated from the extremes of short-term market swings. A pension expense that reflects the volatility of market swings might, for that reason, convey information of little relevance. Are these statements true?

4. Understanding the impact of the changes required in pension reporting requires detailed information about its pension plan(s) and an analysis of the relationship of many factors, particularly the:
   (a) Type of plan(s) and any significant amendments.
   (b) Plan participants.
   (c) Funding status.
   (d) Actuarial funding method and assumptions currently used.
   What impact does each of these items have on financial statement presentation?

5. An article noted "You also need to decide whether to amortize gains and losses using the corridor
method, or to use some other systematic method. Under the corridor approach, only gains and losses
in excess of 10% of the greater of the projected benefit obligation or the plan assets would have to be
amortized." What is the corridor method and what is its purpose?

Instructions
What answers do you believe Jill and Pete gave to each of these questions?

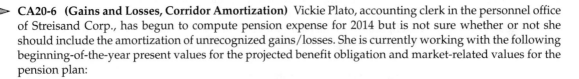

CA20-6 **(Gains and Losses, Corridor Amortization)** Vickie Plato, accounting clerk in the personnel office
of Streisand Corp., has begun to compute pension expense for 2014 but is not sure whether or not she
should include the amortization of unrecognized gains/losses. She is currently working with the following
beginning-of-the-year present values for the projected benefit obligation and market-related values for the
pension plan:

	Projected Benefit Obligation	Plan Assets Value
2011	$2,200,000	$1,900,000
2012	2,400,000	2,500,000
2013	2,900,000	2,600,000
2014	3,900,000	3,000,000

The average remaining service life per employee in 2011 and 2012 is 10 years and in 2013 and 2014 is
12 years. The net gain or loss that occurred during each year is as follows.

2011	$280,000 loss
2012	85,000 loss
2013	12,000 loss
2014	25,000 gain

(In working the solution, you must aggregate the unrecognized gains and losses to arrive at year-end
balances.)

Instructions
You are the manager in charge of accounting. Write a memo to Vickie Plato, explaining why in some years
she must amortize some of the net gains and losses and in other years she does not need to. In order to
explain this situation fully, you must compute the amount of net gain or loss that is amortized and charged
to pension expense in each of the 4 years listed above. Include an appropriate amortization schedule, referring to it whenever necessary.

CA20-7 (Nonvested Employees—An Ethical Dilemma) Thinken Technology recently merged with
College Electronix (CE), a computer graphics manufacturing firm. In performing a comprehensive audit of
CE's accounting system, Gerald Ott, internal audit manager for Thinken Technology, discovered that the
new subsidiary did not record pension assets and liabilities, subject to GAAP.

The net present value of CE's pension assets was $15.5 million, the vested benefit obligation was $12.9
million, and the projected benefit obligation was $17.4 million. Ott reported this audit finding to Julie
Habbe, the newly appointed controller of CE. A few days later, Habbe called Ott for his advice on what to
do. Habbe started her conversation by asking, "Can't we eliminate the negative income effect of our pension dilemma simply by terminating the employment of nonvested employees before the end of our fiscal
year?"

Instructions
How should Ott respond to Habbe's remark about firing nonvested employees?

USING YOUR JUDGMENT

FINANCIAL REPORTING

Financial Reporting Problem

The Procter & Gamble Company (P&G)

The financial statements of P&G are presented in Appendix 5B or can be accessed at the book's companion website, **www.wiley.com/college/kieso**.

Instructions

Refer to P&G's financial statements and the accompanying notes to answer the following questions.

(a) What kind of pension plan does P&G provide its employees in the United States?

(b) What was P&G's pension expense for 2009, 2008, and 2007 for the United States?

(c) What is the impact of P&G's pension plans for 2009 on its financial statements?

(d) What information does P&G provide on the target allocation of its pension assets? (Compare the asset allocation for "Pensions and Other Retiree Benefits.") How do the allocations relate to the expected returns on these assets?

Comparative Analysis Case

The Coca-Cola Company and PepsiCo, Inc.

Instructions

Go to the book's companion website and use information found there to answer the following questions related to The Coca-Cola Company and PepsiCo, Inc.

(a) What kind of pension plans do Coca-Cola and PepsiCo provide their employees?

(b) What net periodic pension expense (cost) did Coca-Cola and PepsiCo report in 2009?

(c) What is the year-end 2009 funded status of Coca-Cola's and PepsiCo's U.S. plans?

(d) What relevant rates were used by Coca-Cola and PepsiCo in computing their pension amounts?

(e) Compare the expected benefit payments and contributions for Coca-Cola and PepsiCo.

*Financial Statement Analysis Case

General Electric

A *Wall Street Journal* article discussed a $1.8 billion charge to income made by General Electric for postretirement benefit costs. It was attributed to previously unrecognized healthcare and life insurance cost. As financial vice president and controller for Peake, Inc., you found this article interesting because the president recently expressed interest in adopting a postemployment benefit program for Peake's employees, to complement the company's existing defined benefit plan. The president, Martha Beyerlein, wants to know how the expense on the new plan will be determined and what impact the accounting for the plan will have on Peake's financial statements.

Instructions

(a) As financial vice president and controller of Peake, Inc., explain the calculation of postemployment benefit expense under GAAP, and indicate how the accounting for the plan will affect Peake's financial statements.

(b) Discuss the similarities and differences in the accounting for the other postemployment benefit plan relative to the accounting for the defined benefit plan.

Accounting, Analysis, and Principles

PENCOMP's balance sheet at December 31, 2012, is as follows.

PENCOMP, INC.
BALANCE SHEET
AS OF DECEMBER 31, 2012

Assets		*Liabilities*	
Cash	$ 438	Notes payable	$1,000
Inventory	1,800	Pension liability	344
Total current assets	2,238	Total liabilities	1,344
Plant and equipment	2,000	*Stockholders' equity*	
Accumulated depreciation	(240)	Common stock	2,000
	1,760	Retained earnings	896
Total assets	$3,998	Accumulated other comprehensive income	(242)
		Total equity	2,654
		Total liabilities and stockholders' equity	$3,998

Additional information concerning PENCOMP's defined benefit pension plain is as follows.

Projected benefit obligation at 12/31/12	$ 820.5
Plan assets (fair value) at 12/31/12	476.5
Unamortized past service cost at 12/31/12	150.0
Amortization of past service cost during 2013	15.0
Service cost for 2013	42.0
Discount rate	10%
Expected rate of return on plan assets in 2013	12%
Actual return on plan assets in 2013	10.4
Contributions to pension fund in 2013	70.0
Benefits paid during 2013	40.0
Unamortized net loss due to changes in actuarial assumptions and deferred net losses on plan assets at 12/31/12	92.0
Expected remaining service life of employees	15.0
Average period to vesting of prior service costs	10.0

Other information about PENCOMP is as follows.

Salary expense, all paid with cash during 2013	$ 700.0
Sales, all for cash	3,000.0
Purchases, all for cash	2,000.0
Inventory at 12/31/13	1,800.0

Property originally cost $2,000 and is depreciated on a straight-line basis over 25 years with no residual value.

Interest on the note payable is 10% annually and is paid in cash on 12/31 of each year.

Dividends declared and paid are $200 in 2013.

Accounting

Prepare an income statement for 2013 and a balance sheet as of December 31, 2013. Also, prepare the pension expense journal entry for the year ended December 31, 2013. Round to the nearest tenth (e.g., round 2.87 to 2.9).

Analysis

Compute return on equity for PENCOMP for 2013 (assume stockholders' equity is equal to year-end average stockholders' equity). Do you think an argument can be made for including some or even all of the change in accumulated other comprehensive income (due to pensions) in the numerator of return on equity? Illustrate that calculation.

Principles

Explain a rationale for why the FASB has (so far) decided to exclude from the current period income statement the effects of pension plan amendments and gains and losses due to changes in actuarial assumptions.

BRIDGE TO THE PROFESSION

Professional Research: FASB Codification

Monat Company has grown rapidly since its founding in 2002. To instill loyalty in its employees, Monat is contemplating establishment of a defined benefit plan. Monat knows that lenders and potential investors will pay close attention to the impact of the pension plan on the company's financial statements, particularly any gains or losses that develop in the plan. Monat has asked you to conduct some research on the accounting for gains and losses in a defined benefit plan.

Instructions

If your school has a subscription to the FASB Codification, go to *http://aaahq.org/ascLogin.cfm* to log in and prepare responses to the following. Provide Codification references for your responses.

(a) Briefly describe how pension gains and losses are accounted for.

(b) Explain the rationale behind the accounting method described in part (a).

(c) What is the related pension asset or liability that will show up on the balance sheet? When will each of these situations occur?

Professional Simulation

In this simulation, you are asked to address questions regarding accounting for pensions. Prepare responses to all parts.

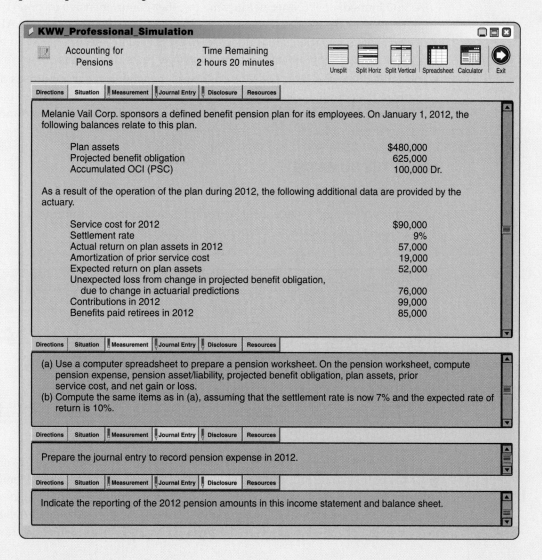

The accounting for various forms of compensation plans under IFRS is found in *IAS 19* ("Employee Benefits") and *IFRS 2* ("Share-Based Payment"). *IAS 19* addresses the accounting for a wide range of compensation elements—wages, bonuses, postretirement benefits, and compensated absences. The underlying concepts for the accounting for postretirement benefits are similar between GAAP and IFRS— both GAAP and IFRS view pensions and other postretirement benefits as forms of deferred compensation. At present, there are significant differences in the specific accounting provisions as applied to these plans.

RELEVANT FACTS

- IFRS and GAAP separate pension plans into defined contribution plans and defined benefit plans. The accounting for defined contribution plans is similar.
- Both IFRS and GAAP compute unrecognized past service costs (PSC) (referred to as prior service cost in GAAP) in the same manner. However, IFRS recognizes any vested amounts immediately and spreads unvested amounts over the average remaining period to vesting. GAAP amortizes PSC over the remaining service lives of employees.
- Under IFRS, companies have the choice of recognizing actuarial gains and losses in income immediately (either net income or other comprehensive income) or amortizing them over the expected remaining working lives of employees. GAAP does not permit choice; actuarial gains and losses are reported in "Accumulated other comprehensive income" and amortized to income over remaining service lives.
- For defined benefit plans, GAAP recognizes a pension asset or liability as the funded status of the plan (i.e., defined benefit obligation minus the fair value of plan assets). IFRS recognizes the funded status, net of unrecognized past service cost and unrecognized net gain or loss.

ABOUT THE NUMBERS

Using a Pension Worksheet

Companies often use a worksheet to record pension-related information. Illustration IFRS20-1 shows the format of the **pension worksheet**.

ILLUSTRATION IFRS20-1
Basic Format of Pension Worksheet

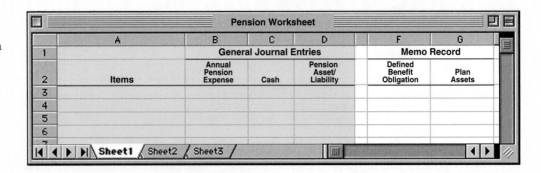

The "General Journal Entries" columns of the worksheet (near the left side) determine the entries to record in the formal general ledger accounts. The "Memo Record" columns (on the right side) maintain balances in the defined benefit obligation and the plan assets. Similar to GAAP, the difference between the defined benefit obligation and the fair value of the plan assets is the **pension asset/liability**, which is shown in the statement of financial position. If the defined benefit obligation is greater than the plan assets, a pension liability occurs. If the defined benefit obligation is less than the plan assets, a pension asset occurs.

On the first line of the worksheet, a company enters the beginning balances (if any). It then records subsequent transactions and events related to the pension plan using debits and credits, using both sets of columns as if they were one. For each transaction or event, the debits must equal the credits. **The ending balance in the Pension Asset/ Liability column should equal the net balance in the memo record.**

2012 Entries and Worksheet

To illustrate the use of a worksheet, and how it helps in accounting for a pension plan, assume that on January 1, 2012, Zarle Company provides the following information related to its pension plan for the year 2012.

Plan assets, January 1, 2012, are $100,000.

Defined benefit obligation, January 1, 2012, is $100,000.

Annual service cost is $9,000.

Discount rate is 10 percent.

Actual return on plan assets is $10,000.

Funding contributions are $8,000.

Benefits paid to retirees during the year are $7,000.

Using the data presented above, the worksheet in Illustration IFRS20-2 presents the beginning balances and all of the pension entries recorded by Zarle in 2012. Zarle records the beginning balances for the defined benefit obligation and the pension plan assets on the first line of the worksheet in the memo record. Because the defined benefit obligation and the plan assets are the same at January 1, 2012, the Pension Asset/Liability account has a zero balance at January 1, 2012.

ILLUSTRATION IFRS20-2
Pension Worksheet—2012

	General Journal Entries			Memo Record	
Items	Annual Pension Expense	Cash	Pension Asset/ Liability	Defined Benefit Obligation	Plan Assets
Balance, Jan. 1, 2012			—	100,000 Cr.	100,000 Dr.
(a) Service cost	9,000 Dr.			9,000 Cr.	
(b) Interest cost	10,000 Dr.			10,000 Cr.	
(c) Actual return	10,000 Cr.				10,000 Dr.
(d) Contributions		8,000 Cr.			8,000 Dr.
(e) Benefits				7,000 Dr.	7,000 Cr.
Journal entry for 2012	9,000 Dr.	8,000 Cr.	1,000 Cr.*		
Balance, Dec. 31, 2012			1,000 Cr.**	112,000 Cr.	111,000 Dr.

*$9,000 − $8,000 = $1,000
**$112,000 − $111,000 = $1.000

Sheet1 / Sheet2 / Sheet3

Entry (a) in Illustration IFRS20-2 records the service cost component, which increases pension expense by $9,000 and increases the liability (defined benefit obligation) by $9,000. Entry (b) accrues the interest expense component, which increases both the liability and the pension expense by $10,000 (the beginning defined benefit obligation multiplied by the discount rate of 10 percent). Entry (c) records the actual return on the plan assets, which increases the plan assets and decreases the pension expense. Entry (d) records Zarle's contribution (funding) of assets to the pension fund, thereby decreasing cash by $8,000 and increasing plan assets by $8,000. Entry (e) records the benefit payments made to retirees, which results in equal $7,000 decreases to the plan assets and the defined benefit obligation.

Zarle makes the "formal journal entry" on December 31, which records the pension expense in 2012, as follows.

2012

Pension Expense	9,000	
Cash		8,000
Pension Asset/Liability		1,000

The credit to Pension Asset/Liability for $1,000 represents the difference between the 2012 pension expense of $9,000 and the amount funded of $8,000. Pension Asset/Liability (credit) is a liability because Zarle underfunds the plan by $1,000. The Pension Asset/Liability account balance of $1,000 also equals the net of the balances in the memo accounts. Illustration IFRS20-3 shows that the defined benefit obligation exceeds the plan assets by $1,000, which reconciles to the pension liability reported in the statement of financial position.

ILLUSTRATION IFRS20-3
Pension Reconciliation Schedule—December 31, 2012

Defined benefit obligation (Credit)	$(112,000)
Plan assets at fair value (Debit)	111,000
Pension asset/liability (Credit)	$ (1,000)

If the net of the memo record balances is a credit, the reconciling amount in the Pension Asset/Liability column will be a credit equal in amount. If the net of the memo record balances is a debit, the Pension Asset/Liability amount will be a debit equal in amount. The worksheet is designed to produce this reconciling feature, which is useful later in the preparation of the financial statements and required note disclosure related to pensions.

In this illustration (for 2012), the debit to Pension Expense exceeds the credit to Cash, resulting in a credit to Pension Asset/Liability—the recognition of a liability. If the credit to Cash exceeded the debit to Pension Expense, Zarle would debit Pension Asset/Liability—the recognition of an asset.[29]

Amortization of Past Service Cost (PSC)

When either initiating (adopting) or amending a defined benefit plan, a company often provides benefits to employees for years of service before the date of initiation or amendment. As a result of this **past service cost (PSC)**, the defined benefit obligation is increased to recognize this additional liability. In many cases, the increase in the defined benefit obligation is substantial.

Should a company report an expense immediately for these past service costs? The IASB says it depends on when the benefits are vested. If the benefits from the amendment to the plan vest immediately, then the company should recognize the expense and related liability at the amendment date. If the benefits do not vest immediately, past service cost should be recognized as an expense on a straight-line basis over the average

---

[29]The IASB in *IAS 19* limits the amount of a pension asset that is recognized, based on a recoverability test. This test, which has been further clarified in *IFRIC 14*, limits the amount of the pension asset to the sum of unrecognized actuarial gains and losses (discussed later) and amounts that will be received by the company in the form of refunds or reduction of future contributions. *For purposes of homework, assume that a pension asset, if present, meets the criteria for full recognition.*

remaining period until the benefits become vested.[30] The rationale for using the vesting date as the target date for recognition is that is when the liability is established.

To illustrate, assume that Hitchcock plc amends its defined pension plan on January 1, 2012, resulting in $300,000 of past service cost. The company has 300 active employees, of which 60 vest immediately (20%) and the other 240 (80%) vest in four years. The past service cost applicable to the vested employees is $60,000 and vests immediately. The unrecognized past service cost related to the unvested employees is $240,000 and is amortized over four years ($60,000 per year). The amortization of the past service costs for Hitchcock for the four years is computed as shown in Illustration IFRS20-4.

Year	Beginning Balance in Unrecognized PSC	Amortization (Expense) Vested	Amortization (Expense) Unvested	Ending Balance in Unrecognized PSC
2012	$300,000	$60,000	$60,000	$180,000
2013			60,000	120,000
2014			60,000	60,000
2015			60,000	—0—

ILLUSTRATION IFRS20-4
Computation of Past Service Cost Amortization

As a result, Hitchcock reports amortization of past service cost of $120,000 in 2012 and $60,000 in each of the years 2013, 2014, and 2015.

As indicated earlier, Hitchcock measures past service cost due to an increase in the liability resulting from the amendment (referred to as positive past service cost). It is also possible to decrease past service costs by decreasing the defined benefit obligation (referred to as negative past service cost). Negative past service cost arises when an entity changes the benefits attributable to past service cost so that the present value of the defined benefit obligation decreases. Both positive and negative past service cost adjustments are handled in the same manner, that is, adjust income immediately if vested and amortize the unvested amount over the average remaining period until vesting occurs.

2013 Entries and Worksheet

Continuing the Zarle Company illustration into 2013, we note that the company amends the pension plan on January 1, 2013, to grant employees past service benefits with a present value of $81,600. The following additional facts apply to the pension plan for the year 2013.

Annual service cost is $9,500.

Discount rate is 10 percent.

Actual return on plan assets is $11,100.

Annual funding contributions are $20,000.

Benefits paid to retirees during the year are $8,000.

The past service cost (PSC) is not vested, and the average remaining period to vesting is three years. Amortization of PSC using the straight-line method is $27,200 ($81,600 ÷ 3).

Illustration IFRS20-5 (page 1278) presents a worksheet of all the pension entries and information recorded by Zarle in 2013.

The first line of the worksheet shows the beginning balances of the Pension Asset/Liability account and the memo accounts. Entry (f) records Zarle's granting of past service cost, by adding $81,600 to the defined benefit obligation and to the new Unrecognized Past Service Cost. Entries (g), (h), (i), (k), and (l) are similar to the corresponding entries in 2012. Entry (j) records the 2013 amortization of unrecognized past service cost

---

[30]*For purposes of homework, assume that all past service costs are non-vested, unless stated otherwise.* After initially establishing the amortization schedule for past service costs, companies do not revise the schedule (e.g., due to changes in employee service lives) unless there is a plan curtailment or settlement.

	A	B	C	D		F	G	H
		Pension Worksheet—2013						
1		General Journal Entries				Memo Record		
2	Items	Annual Pension Expense	Cash	Pension Asset/ Liability		Defined Benefit Obligation	Plan Assets	Unrecognized Past Service Cost
3	Balance, Dec. 31, 2012			1,000 Cr.		112,000 Cr.	111,000 Dr.	
4	(f) Past service cost					81,600 Cr.		81,600 Dr.
5	Balance, Jan. 1, 2013			1,000 Cr.		193,600 Cr.	111,000 Dr.	81,600 Dr.
6	(g) Service cost	9,500 Dr.				9,500 Cr.		
7	(h) Interest cost	19,360 Dr.[a]				19,360 Cr.		
8	(i) Actual return	11,100 Cr.					11,100 Dr.	
9	(j) Amortization of PSC	27,200 Dr.						27,200 Cr.
10	(k) Contributions		20,000 Cr.				20,000 Dr.	
11	(l) Benefits					8,000 Dr.	8,000 Cr.	
12								
13	Journal entry for 2013	44,960 Dr.	20,000 Cr.	24,960 Cr.				
14	Balance Dec. 31, 2013			25,960 Cr.		214,460 Cr.	134,100 Dr.	54,400 Dr.
15	[a]$19,360 = $193,600 × 10%							

ILLUSTRATION IFRS20-5
Pension Worksheet—2013

by debiting Pension Expense by $27,200 and crediting the Unrecognized Past Service Cost account by the same amount.

Zarle makes the following journal entry on December 31 to formally record the 2013 pension expense—the sum of the annual pension expense column.

2013

Pension Expense	44,960	
Cash		20,000
Pension Asset/Liability		24,960

Because the expense exceeds the funding, Zarle credits the Pension Asset/Liability account for the $24,960 difference. That account is a liability. In 2013, as in 2012, the balance of the Pension Asset/Liability account ($25,960) is equal to the net of the balances in the memo accounts, as shown in Illustration IFRS20-6.

ILLUSTRATION IFRS20-6
Pension Reconciliation Schedule—December 31, 2013

Defined benefit obligation (Credit)	$(214,460)
Plan assets at fair value (Debit)	134,100
Funded status	(80,360)
Unrecognized past service cost (Debit)	54,400
Pension asset/liability (Credit)	$ (25,960)

The reconciliation is the formula that makes the worksheet work. It relates the components of pension accounting, recorded and unrecorded, to one another. Note that in contrast to GAAP, the past service cost is recorded in the memo records, not in other comprehensive income.

Gain or Loss

Of great concern to companies that have pension plans are the uncontrollable and unexpected swings in pension expense that can result from (1) sudden and large changes in the fair value of plan assets, and (2) changes in actuarial assumptions that affect the amount of the defined benefit obligation. If these gains or losses impact fully the financial statements in the period of realization or incurrence, substantial fluctuations in pension expense result.

Therefore, the IASB decided to reduce the volatility associated with pension expense by using **smoothing techniques** that dampen and in some cases fully eliminate the fluctuations.

Smoothing Unexpected Gains and Losses on Plan Assets

One component of pension expense, actual return on plan assets, reduces pension expense (assuming the actual return is positive). A large change in the actual return can substantially affect pension expense for a year. Assume a company has a 40 percent return in the securities market for the year. Should this substantial, and perhaps one-time, event affect current pension expense?

Actuaries ignore current fluctuations when they develop a funding pattern to pay expected benefits in the future. They develop an **expected rate of return** and multiply it by an asset value weighted over a reasonable period of time to arrive at an **expected return on plan assets**. They then use this return to determine a company's funding pattern.

The IASB adopted the actuary's approach to dampen wide swings that might occur in the actual return. That is, a company includes the **expected return on the plan assets as a component of pension expense, not the actual return in a given year**. To achieve this goal, the company multiplies the expected rate of return by the fair value of the plan assets.

The difference between the expected return and the actual return is referred to as the **unexpected gain or loss**; the IASB uses the term **asset gains and losses**. **Asset gains** occur when actual return exceeds expected return; **asset losses** occur when actual return is less than expected return.

What happens to unexpected gains or losses in the accounting for pensions? Companies record asset gains and asset losses in an Unrecognized Net Gain or Loss account, combining them with unrecognized gains and losses accumulated in prior years.

To illustrate the computation of an unexpected gain or loss and its related accounting, assume that in 2014 Zarle Company has an actual return on plan assets of $12,000 when the expected return in $13,410 (the expected rate of return of 10 percent on plan assets times the beginning of the year plan assets). The unexpected asset loss of $1,410 ($12,000 − $13,410) is debited to Unrecognized Net Gain or Loss and credited to Pension Expense.

Smoothing Unexpected Gains and Losses on the Pension Liability

In estimating the defined benefit obligation (the liability), actuaries make assumptions about such items as mortality rate, retirement rate, turnover rate, disability rate, and salary amounts. Any change in these actuarial assumptions affects the amount of the defined benefit obligation. Seldom does actual experience coincide exactly with actuarial predictions. These unexpected gains or losses from changes in the defined benefit obligation are called **liability gains and losses**.

Companies defer liability gains (resulting from unexpected decreases in the liability balance) and liability losses (resulting from unexpected increases). Companies combine the liability gains and losses in the same **Unrecognized Net Gain or Loss** account used for asset gains and losses. They accumulate the asset and liability gains and losses from year to year, off-balance-sheet, in a memo account.[31]

Corridor Amortization

The asset gains and losses and the liability gains and losses can offset each other. As a result, the accumulated total unrecognized net gain or loss may not grow very large. But, it is possible that no offsetting will occur and that the balance in the Unrecognized Net Gain or Loss account will continue to grow.

To limit the growth of the Unrecognized Net Gain or Loss account, as in GAAP, the IASB uses the **corridor approach** for amortizing the account's accumulated balance when it gets too large. How large is too large? The IASB set a limit of 10 percent of the larger of the beginning balances of the defined benefit obligation or the fair value of the plan assets. **Above that size, the unrecognized net gain or loss balance is considered too large and must be amortized.**

---

[31]In *IAS 19*, asset gains and losses and liability gains and losses are collectively referred to as "actuarial gains and losses." [5] IFRS permits other accounting approaches for these gains and losses. We discuss these in a later section.

To illustrate the corridor approach, data for Callaway Co.'s defined benefit obligation and plan assets over a period of six years are shown in Illustration IFRS20-7.

ILLUSTRATION IFRS20-7
Computation of the Corridor

Beginning-of-the-Year Balances	Defined Benefit Obligation	Fair Value of Assets	Corridor* +/− 10%
2011	$1,000,000	$ 900,000	$100,000
2012	1,200,000	1,100,000	120,000
2013	1,300,000	1,700,000	170,000
2014	1,500,000	2,250,000	225,000
2015	1,700,000	1,750,000	175,000
2016	1,800,000	1,700,000	180,000

*The corridor becomes 10% of the larger (in colored type) of the defined benefit obligation or the fair value of plan assets.

How the corridor works becomes apparent when we portray the data graphically, as in Illustration IFRS20-8.

ILLUSTRATION IFRS20-8
Graphic Illustration of the Corridor

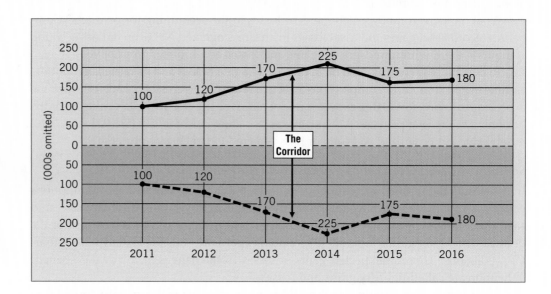

If the balance of the Unrecognized Net Gain or Loss account stays within the upper and lower limits of the corridor, no amortization is required. In that case, Callaway carries forward the unrecognized net gain or loss balance unchanged.

If amortization is required, the minimum amortization is the excess divided by the average remaining service period of active employees who are expected to receive benefits under the plan. Callaway may use any systematic method of amortization of unrecognized gains and losses in lieu of the minimum, provided it is greater than the minimum. It must use the method consistently for both gains and losses and must disclose the amortization method used.

Example of Unrecognized Gains/Losses

In applying the corridor, companies should include amortization of the excess unrecognized net gain or loss as a component of pension expense only if, at the **beginning of the year**, the unrecognized net gain or loss exceeded the corridor. That is, if no unrecognized net gain or loss exists at the beginning of the period, the company cannot recognize pension expense gains or losses in that period.

To illustrate the amortization of unrecognized net gains and losses, assume the following information for Soft-White, Inc.

	2012	2013	2014
		(beginning of the year)	
Defined benefit obligation	$2,100,000	$2,600,000	$2,900,000
Fair value of assets	2,600,000	2,800,000	2,700,000
Unrecognized net loss	–0–	400,000	300,000

If the average remaining service life of all active employees is 5.5 years, the schedule to amortize the unrecognized net loss is as shown in Illustration IFRS20-9.

Year	Defined Benefit Obligation[a]	Plan Assets[a]	Corridor[b]	Cumulative Unrecognized Net Loss[a]	Minimum Amortization of Loss (For Current Year)
2012	$2,100,000	$2,600,000	$260,000	$ –0–	$ –0–
2013	2,600,000	2,800,000	280,000	400,000	21,818[c]
2014	2,900,000	2,700,000	290,000	678,182[d]	70,579[d]

[a]All as of the beginning of the period.
[b]10% of the greater of defined benefit obligation or plan assets fair value.
[c]$400,000 − $280,000 = $120,000; $120,000 ÷ 5.5 = $21,818.
[d]$400,000 − $21,818 + $300,000 = $678,182; $678,182 − $290,000 = $388,182; $388,182 ÷ 5.5 = $70,579.

ILLUSTRATION IFRS20-9
Corridor Test and Gain/Loss Amortization Schedule

As Illustration IFRS20-9 indicates, the loss recognized in 2013 increased pension expense by $21,818. This amount is small in comparison with the total loss of $400,000. It indicates that the corridor approach dampens the effects (reduces volatility) of these gains and losses on pension expense.

The rationale for the corridor is that gains and losses result from refinements in estimates as well as real changes in economic value; over time, some of these gains and losses will offset one another. It therefore seems reasonable that Soft-White should not fully recognize gains and losses as a component of pension expense in the period in which they arise.

2014 Entries and Worksheet

Continuing the Zarle Company illustration, the following facts apply to the pension plan for 2014.

Annual service cost is $13,000.

Discount rate is 10 percent; expected return on plan assets is 10 percent.

Actual return on plan assets is $12,000.

Amortization of past service cost (PSC) is $27,200 ($81,600 ÷ 3).

Annual funding contributions are $24,000.

Benefits paid to retirees during the year are $10,500.

Changes in actuarial assumptions establish the end-of-year defined benefit obligation at $265,000.

The worksheet in Illustration IFRS20-10 (page 1282) presents all of Zarle's 2014 pension entries and related information. The first line of the worksheet records the beginning balances that relate to the pension plan. In this case, Zarle's beginning balances are the ending balances from its 2013 pension worksheet in Illustration IFRS20-5.

Entries (m), (n), (o), (q), (r), and (s) are similar to the corresponding entries in 2012 or 2013.

	General Journal Entries			Memo Record			
Items	Annual Pension Expense	Cash	Pension Asset/ Liability	Defined Benefit Obligation	Plan Assets	Unrecognized Past Service Cost	Unrecognized Net Gain or Loss
Balance, Dec. 31, 2013			25,960 Cr.	214,460 Cr.	134,100 Dr.	54,400 Dr.	
(m) Service cost	13,000 Dr.			13,000 Cr.			
(n) Interest cost	21,446 Dr.			21,446 Cr.			
(o) Actual return	12,000 Cr.				12,000 Dr.		
(p) Unexpected loss	1,410 Cr.						1,410 Dr.
(q) Amortization of PSC	27,200 Dr.					27,200 Cr.	
(r) Contributions		24,000 Cr.			24,000 Dr.		
(s) Benefits				10,500 Dr.	10,500 Cr.		
(t) Liability increase				26,594 Cr.			26,594 Dr.
Journal entry for 2014	48,236 Dr.	24,000 Cr.	24,236 Cr.				
Balance, Dec. 31, 2014			50,196 Cr.	265,000 Cr.	159,600 Dr.	27,200 Dr.	28,004 Dr.

ILLUSTRATION IFRS20-10
Pension Worksheet—2014

Entries (o) and (p) are related. We explained the recording of the actual return in entry (o) in both 2012 and 2013; it is recorded similarly in 2014. In both 2012 and 2013, Zarle's actual return on plan assets was equal to the expected return on plan assets. In 2014, the expected return of $13,410 (the expected rate of return of 10 percent times the beginning-of-the-year plan assets balance of $134,100) is higher than the actual return of $12,000. To smooth pension expense, Zarle defers the unexpected loss of $1,410 ($13,410 − $12,000) by debiting the Unrecognized Net Gain or Loss account and crediting Pension Expense. **As a result of this adjustment, the expected return on the plan assets is the amount actually used to compute pension expense.**

Entry (t) records the change in the defined benefit obligation resulting from a change in actuarial assumptions. As indicated, the actuary has now computed the ending balance to be $265,000. Given that the memo record balance at December 31 is $238,406 ($214,460 + $13,000 + $21,446 − $10,500), a difference of $26,594 ($265,000 − $238,406) exists. This $26,594 increase in the employer's liability is an unexpected loss. Zarle defers that amount by debiting it to the Unrecognized Net Gain or Loss account. The journal entry on December 31 to formally record pension expense for 2014 is as follows.

2014

Pension Expense	48,236	
Cash		24,000
Pension Asset/Liability		24,236

As the 2014 worksheet indicates, the $50,196 balance of the Pension Asset/Liability account at December 31, 2014, is equal to the net of the balances in the memo accounts. Illustration IFRS20-11 shows this computation.

ILLUSTRATION IFRS20-11
Pension Reconciliation Schedule—December 31, 2014

Defined benefit obligation (Credit)	$(265,000)
Plan assets at fair value (Debit)	159,600
Funded status	(105,400)
Unrecognized past service cost (Debit)	27,200
Unrecognized net loss (Debit)	28,004
Pension asset/liability (Credit)	$ (50,196)

Immediate Recognition of Actuarial Gains and Losses

The IASB indicates that the corridor approach results in the minimum amount recognized as an actuarial gain and loss. Companies may use any systematic method that is faster than the corridor approach provided it is used for both gains and losses and is used consistently from period to period. The IASB also indicates that it favors the immediate recognition of actuarial gains and losses.

If a company chooses the immediate recognition approach, the actuarial gain or loss can either adjust net income or other comprehensive income. To illustrate, assume that Wentworth Company has the following components of pension expense for 2012.

Service cost	$2,000
Interest on defined benefit obligation	210
Expected return on plan assets	(80)
Past service cost amortization	60
Actuarial loss recognized in full	100
Pension expense	$2,290

ILLUSTRATION IFRS20-12
Components of Pension Expense (in thousands)

Wentworth's 2012 revenues are $100,000, and expenses for 2012 (excluding pension expense) are $70,000. If Wentworth reports the adjustment of actuarial gains and losses in net income, its income statement is as shown in Illustration IFRS20-13.

Income Statement	
Revenues	$100,000
Expenses (excluding pension expense)	70,000
Pension expense	2,290
Net income	$ 27,710

ILLUSTRATION IFRS20-13
Income Excluding Pension Expense

If Wentworth decides to report the adjustment of actuarial gains and losses in other comprehensive income, its statement of comprehensive income is as follows.

Statement of Comprehensive Income	
Revenues	$100,000
Expenses (excluding pension expense)	70,000
Pension expense ($2,290 − $100)	2,190
Net income	27,810
Other comprehensive income	
Actuarial loss on defined benefit plan	100
Total comprehensive income	$ 27,710

ILLUSTRATION IFRS20-14
Comprehensive Income Reporting of Actuarial Gains and Losses

ON THE HORIZON

The IASB is proposing changes to its standard on accounting of pensions and other postretirement benefits. The proposal is not the result of a joint effort between the IASB and the FASB, but the IASB is moving closer to GAAP in this area. However, differences likely will continue to exist related to amortization polices for prior service costs and actuarial gains and losses. It is expected that the FASB will then reevaluate its standard after the IASB has completed its work in hopes of achieving convergence in this area.

IFRS SELF-TEST QUESTIONS

1. At the end of the current period, Oxford Ltd. has a defined benefit obligation of $195,000 and pension plan assets with a fair value of $110,000. The amount of the vested benefits for the plan is $105,000. What amount related to its pension plan will be reported on the company's statement of financial position?
   (a) $5,000.
   (b) $90,000.
   (c) $85,000.
   (d) $20,000.

2. At the end of the current year, Kennedy Co. has a defined benefit obligation of $335,000 and pension plan assets with a fair value of $245,000. The amount of the vested benefits for the plan is $225,000. Kennedy has unrecognized past service costs of $24,000 and an unrecognized actuarial gain of $8,300. What account and amount(s) related to its pension plan will be reported on the company's statement of financial position?
   (a) Pension Liability and $74,300.
   (b) Pension Liability and $90,000.
   (c) Pension Asset and $233,300.
   (d) Pension Asset and $110,000.

3. For 2012, Carson Majors Inc. had pension expense of $77 million and contributed $55 million to the pension fund. Which of the following is the journal entry that Carson Majors would make to record pension income and funding?

   (a) Pension Expense 77,000,000
         Pension Asset/Liability   22,000,000
         Cash   55,000,000

   (b) Pension Expense 77,000,000
         Pension Asset/Liability 22,000,000
         Cash   99,000,000

   (c) Pension Expense 55,000,000
         Pension Asset/Liability 22,000,000
         Cash   77,000,000

   (d) Pension Expense 22,000,000
         Pension Asset/Liability 55,000,000
         Cash   77,000,000

4. At January 1, 2012, Wembley Company had plan assets of $250,000 and a defined benefit obligation of the same amount. During 2012, service cost was $27,500, the discount rate was 10%, actual and expected return on plan assets were $25,000, contributions were $20,000, and benefits paid were $17,500. Based on this information, what would be the defined benefit obligation for Wembley Company at December 31, 2012?
   (a) $277,500.
   (b) $285,000.
   (c) $27,500.
   (d) $302,500.

5. Towson Ltd. has experienced tough competition, leading it to seek concessions from its employees in the company's pension plan. In exchange for promises to avoid layoffs and wage cuts, the employees agreed to receive lower pension benefits in the future. As a result, Towson amended its pension plan on January 1, 2012, and recorded negative unrecognized past service cost of $225,000. The average period to vesting for the benefits affected by this plan is 6 years. What is the unrecognized past service cost amortization for 2012?

(a) $225,000.

(b) $112,500.

(c) $1,350,000.

(d) $37,500.

IFRS CONCEPTS AND APPLICATION

IFRS20-1 What is meant by "past service cost"? When is past service cost recognized as pension expense?

IFRS20-2 What is the meaning of "corridor amortization"?

IFRS20-3 Describe the immediate recognition approach for unrecognized actuarial gains and losses.

IFRS20-4 Bill Haley is learning about pension accounting. He is convinced that, regardless of the method used to recognize actuarial gains and losses, total comprehensive income will always be the same. Is Bill correct? Explain.

IFRS20-5 At the end of the current year, Joshua Co. has a defined benefit obligation of $335,000 and pension plan assets with a fair value of $245,000. The amount of the vested benefits for the plan is $225,000. Joshua has unrecognized past service costs of $24,000 and an unrecognized actuarial gain of $8,300. What amount and account(s) related to its pension plan will be reported on the company's statement of financial position?

IFRS20-6 Villa Company has experienced tough competition, leading it to seek concessions from its employees in the company's pension plan. In exchange for promises to avoid layoffs and wage cuts, the employees agreed to receive lower pension benefits in the future. As a result, Villa amended its pension plan on January 1, 2012, and recorded negative unrecognized past service cost of $125,000. The average period to vesting for the benefits affected by this plan is 5 years. Compute unrecognized past service cost amortization for 2012. Discuss the impact of this amendment on Villa's pension expense in 2012 and 2013.

IFRS20-7 Tevez Company experienced an actuarial loss of $750 in its defined benefit plan in 2012. Tevez has elected to recognize these losses immediately. For 2012, Tevez's revenues are $125,000, and expenses (excluding pension expense of $14,000, which does not include the actuarial loss) are $85,000. Prepare Tevez's statement of comprehensive income for 2012, assuming Tevez recognizes the loss in (a) net income, and (b) other comprehensive income.

IFRS20-8 The following defined pension data of Doreen Corp. apply to the year 2012.

Defined benefit obligation, 1/1/12 (before amendment)	$560,000
Plan assets, 1/1/12	546,200
Pension asset/liability	13,800 Cr.
On January 1, 2012, Doreen Corp., through plan amendment, grants past service benefits having a present value of	100,000
Discount rate	9%
Service cost	58,000
Contributions (funding)	55,000
Actual (expected) return on plan assets	52,280
Benefits paid to retirees	40,000
Past service cost amortization for 2012	17,000

Instructions

For 2012, prepare a pension worksheet for Doreen Corp. that shows the journal entry for pension expense and the year-end balances in the related pension accounts.

IFRS20-9 Buhl Corp. sponsors a defined benefit pension plan for its employees. On January 1, 2012, the following balances relate to this plan.

Plan assets	$480,000
Defined benefit obligation	625,000
Pension asset/liability	45,000
Unrecognized past service cost	100,000

As a result of the operation of the plan during 2012, the following additional data are provided by the actuary.

Service cost for 2012	$90,000
Discount rate, 9%	
Actual return on plan assets in 2012	57,000
Amortization of past service cost	19,000
Expected return on plan assets	52,000
Unexpected loss from change in defined benefit obligation, due to change in actuarial predictions	76,000
Contributions in 2012	99,000
Benefits paid retirees in 2012	85,000

Instructions

(a) Using the data above, compute pension expense for Buhl Corp. for the year 2012 by preparing a pension worksheet that shows the journal entry for pension expense and the year-end balances in the related pension accounts.

(b) At December 31, 2012, prepare a schedule reconciling the funded status of the plan with the pension amount reported on the statement of financial position.

IFRS20-10 Linda Berstler Company sponsors a defined benefit pension plan. The corporation's actuary provides the following information about the plan.

	January 1, 2012	December 31, 2012
Vested benefit obligation	$1,500	$1,900
Defined benefit obligation	2,800	3,645
Plan assets (fair value)	1,700	2,620
Discount rate and expected rate of return		10%
Pension asset/liability	–0–	?
Unrecognized past service cost	1,100	?
Service cost for the year 2012		400
Contributions (funding in 2012)		800
Benefits paid in 2012		200

The average remaining service life per employee is 20 years. The average time to vesting past service costs is 10 years.

Instructions

(a) Compute the actual return on the plan assets in 2012.

(b) Compute the amount of the unrecognized net gain or loss as of December 31, 2012. (Assume the January 1, 2012, balance was zero.)

Professional Research

IFRS20-11 Jack Kelly Company has grown rapidly since its founding in 2002. To instill loyalty in its employees, Kelly is contemplating establishment of a defined benefit plan. Kelly knows that lenders and potential investors will pay close attention to the impact of the pension plan on the company's financial statements, particularly any gains or losses that develop in the plan. Kelly has asked you to conduct some research on the accounting for gains and losses in a defined benefit plan.

Instructions

Access the IFRS authoritative literature at the IASB website (*http://eifrs.iasb.org/*). When you have accessed the documents, you can use the search tool in your Internet browser to respond to the following questions. (Provide paragraph citations.)

(a) Briefly describe how pension gains and losses are accounted for.

(b) Explain the rationale behind the accounting method described in part (a).

(c) What is the related pension asset or liability that may show up on the statement of financial position? When will each of these situations occur?

International Financial Reporting Problem:
Marks and Spencer plc

IFRS20-12 The financial statements of **Marks and Spencer plc (M&S)** are available at the book's companion website or can be accessed at *http://corporate.marksandspencer.com/documents/publications/2010/Annual_Report_2010*.

Instructions

Refer to M&S's financial statements and the accompanying notes to answer the following questions.

(a) What kind of pension plan does M&S provide its employees?

(b) What was M&S's pension expense for 2010 and 2009?

(c) What is the impact of M&S's pension plans for 2010 on its financial statements?

(d) What information does M&S provide on the target allocation of its pension assets? How do the allocations relate to the expected returns on these assets?

ANSWERS TO IFRS SELF-TEST QUESTIONS

1. c **2.** a **3.** a **4.** b **5.** d

LEARNING OBJECTIVES

After studying this chapter, you should be able to:

1 Explain the nature, economic substance, and advantages of lease transactions.

2 Describe the accounting criteria and procedures for capitalizing leases by the lessee.

3 Contrast the operating and capitalization methods of recording leases.

4 Identify the classifications of leases for the lessor.

5 Describe the lessor's accounting for direct-financing leases.

6 Identify special features of lease arrangements that cause unique accounting problems.

7 Describe the effect of residual values, guaranteed and unguaranteed, on lease accounting.

8 Describe the lessor's accounting for sales-type leases.

9 List the disclosure requirements for leases.

More Companies Ask, "Why Buy?"

Leasing has grown tremendously in popularity. Today, it is the fastest growing form of capital investment. Instead of borrowing money to buy an airplane, computer, nuclear core, or satellite, a company makes periodic payments to lease these assets. Even gambling casinos lease their slot machines. Of the 500 companies surveyed by the AICPA in 2010, 488 disclosed lease data.*

A classic example is the airline industry. Many travelers on airlines such as **United**, **Delta**, and **Southwest** believe these airlines own the planes on which they are flying. Often, this is not the case. Airlines lease many of their airplanes due to the favorable accounting treatment they receive if they lease rather than purchase. Presented below are the lease percentages for the major U.S. airlines.

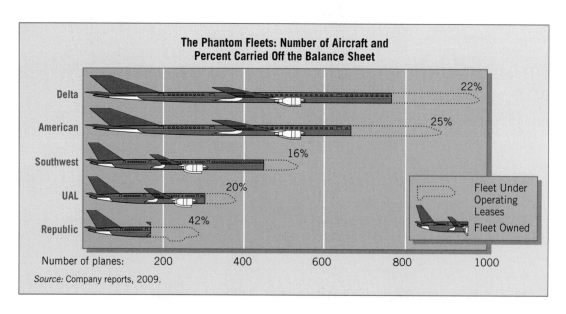

The Phantom Fleets: Number of Aircraft and Percent Carried Off the Balance Sheet

Delta — 22%
American — 25%
Southwest — 16%
UAL — 20%
Republic — 42%

Fleet Under Operating Leases
Fleet Owned

Number of planes: 200 400 600 800 1000

Source: Company reports, 2009.

*AICPA, *Accounting Trends and Techniques—2010*. Eight out of 10 U.S. companies lease all or some of their equipment. Companies that lease tend to be smaller, are high growth, and are in technology-oriented industries (see *www.techlease.com*).

IFRS IN THIS CHAPTER

See the **International Perspectives** on pages 1292, 1296, 1306, and 1324.

Read the **IFRS Insights** on pages 1355–1365 for a discussion of:

—Lessee accounting

—Lessor accounting

What about other companies? They are also exploiting the existing lease-accounting rules to keep assets and liabilities off the books. For example, **Krispy Kreme**, a chain of 217 doughnut shops, had been showing good growth and profitability, using a relatively small bit of capital. That's an impressive feat if you care about return on capital. But there's a hole in this doughnut. The company explained that it was building a $30 million new mixing plant and warehouse in Effingham, Illinois. Yet the financial statements failed to disclose the investments and obligations associated with that $30 million.

By financing through a synthetic lease, Krispy Kreme kept the investment and obligation off the books. In a synthetic lease, a financial institution like **Bank of America** sets up a *special-purpose entity* (SPE) that borrows money to build the plant and then leases it to Krispy Kreme. For accounting purposes, Krispy Kreme reports only rent expense, but for tax purposes Krispy Kreme can be considered the owner of the asset and gets depreciation tax deductions.

In response to negative publicity about the use of SPEs to get favorable financial reporting and tax benefits, Krispy Kreme announced it would change its method of financing construction of its dough-making plant.

Source: Adapted from Seth Lubore and Elizabeth MacDonald, "Debt? Who, Me?" *Forbes* (February 18, 2002), p. 56.

PREVIEW OF CHAPTER 21 Our opening story indicates the increased significance and prevalence of lease arrangements. As a result, the need for uniform accounting and informative reporting of these transactions has intensified. In this chapter, we look at the accounting issues related to leasing. The content and organization of this chapter are as follows.

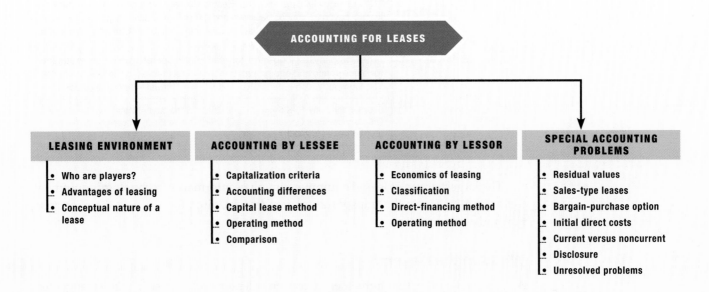

ACCOUNTING FOR LEASES

LEASING ENVIRONMENT	ACCOUNTING BY LESSEE	ACCOUNTING BY LESSOR	SPECIAL ACCOUNTING PROBLEMS
• Who are players?	• Capitalization criteria	• Economics of leasing	• Residual values
• Advantages of leasing	• Accounting differences	• Classification	• Sales-type leases
• Conceptual nature of a lease	• Capital lease method	• Direct-financing method	• Bargain-purchase option
	• Operating method	• Operating method	• Initial direct costs
	• Comparison		• Current versus noncurrent
			• Disclosure
			• Unresolved problems

THE LEASING ENVIRONMENT

Aristotle once said, "Wealth does not lie in ownership but in the use of things"! Clearly, many U.S. companies have decided that Aristotle is right, as they have become heavily involved in leasing assets rather than owning them. For example, according to the Equipment Leasing Association (ELA), the global equipment-leasing market is a $400–$500 billion business, with the United States accounting for about one-third of the global market. The ELA estimates that of the $850 billion in total fixed investment expected from domestic businesses in 2010, $521 billion (46 percent) will be financed through leasing. Remember that these statistics are just for equipment leasing; add in real estate leasing, which is probably larger, and we are talking about a very large and growing business, one that is at least in part driven by the accounting.

What types of assets are being leased? As the opening story indicated, any type of equipment can be leased, such as railcars, helicopters, bulldozers, barges, CT scanners, computers, and so on.

Illustration 21-1 summarizes, in their own words, what several major companies are leasing.

ILLUSTRATION 21-1
What Do Companies Lease?

Company (Ticker)	Description
Gap (GPS)	"We lease most of our store premises and some of our headquarters facilities and distribution centers."
ExxonMobil Corp. (XOM)	"Minimum commitments for operating leases, shown on an undiscounted basis, cover drilling equipment, tankers, service stations, and other properties."
JPMorgan Chase (JPM)	"JPMorgan Chase and its subsidiaries were obligated under a number of noncancelable operating leases for premises and equipment used primarily for banking purposes."
Maytag Corp. (MYG)	"The Company leases real estate, machinery, equipment, and automobiles under operating leases, some of which have renewal options."
McDonald's Corp. (MCD)	"The Company was the lessee at 15,235 restaurant locations through ground leases (the Company leases the land and the Company or franchisee owns the building) and through improved leases (the Company leases land and buildings)."
Starbucks Corp. (SBUX)	"Starbucks leases retail stores, roasting and distribution facilities, and office space under operating leases."
TXU Corp. (TXU)	"TXU Energy Holdings and TXU Electric Delivery have entered into operating leases covering various facilities and properties including generation plant facilities, combustion turbines, transportation equipment, mining equipment, data processing equipment, and office space."
Viacom Inc. (VIA.B)	"The Company has long-term non-cancelable operating lease commitments for office space and equipment, transponders, studio facilities, and vehicles. The Company also enters into capital leases for satellite transponders."

Source: Company 10-K filings; D. Zion, B. Carcache, and A. Varshney, "Bring It On: Off–Balance Sheet Operating Leases," *Credit Suisse Equity Research: Accounting and Tax* (April 19, 2006).

The largest group of leased equipment involves information technology equipment, followed by assets in the transportation area (trucks, aircraft, rail), and then construction and agriculture.

Who Are the Players?

A **lease** is a contractual agreement between a lessor and a lessee. This arrangement gives the **lessee** the right to use specific property, owned by the **lessor**, for a specified period of time. In return for the use of the property, the lessee makes rental payments over the lease term to the lessor.

Who are the lessors that own this property? They generally fall into one of three categories:

1. Banks.
2. Captive leasing companies.
3. Independents.

Banks

Banks are the largest players in the leasing business. They have low-cost funds, which give them the advantage of being able to purchase assets at less cost than their competitors. Banks also have been more aggressive in the leasing markets. They have decided that there is money to be made in leasing, and as a result they have expanded their product lines in this area. Finally, leasing transactions are now more standardized, which gives banks an advantage because they do not have to be as innovative in structuring lease arrangements. Thus, banks like Wells Fargo, Chase, Citigroup, and PNC have substantial leasing subsidiaries.

Captive Leasing Companies

Captive leasing companies are subsidiaries whose primary business is to perform leasing operations for the parent company. Companies like Caterpillar Financial Services Corp. (for Caterpillar), Ford Motor Credit (for Ford), and IBM Global Financing (for IBM) facilitate the sale of products to consumers. For example, suppose that Sterling Construction Co. wants to acquire a number of earthmovers from Caterpillar. In this case, Caterpillar Financial Services Corp. will offer to structure the transaction as a lease rather than as a purchase. Thus, Caterpillar Financial provides the financing rather than an outside financial institution.

Captive leasing companies have the point-of-sale advantage in finding leasing customers. That is, as soon as Caterpillar receives a possible order, its leasing subsidiary can quickly develop a lease-financing arrangement. Furthermore, the captive lessor has product knowledge that gives it an advantage when financing the parent's product.

The current trend is for captives to focus primarily on their companies' products rather than do general lease financing. For example, Boeing Capital and UPS Capital are two captives that have left the general finance business to focus exclusively on their parent companies' products.

Independents

Independents are the final category of lessors. Independents have not done well over the last few years. Their market share has dropped fairly dramatically as banks and captive leasing companies have become more aggressive in the lease-financing area. Independents do not have point-of-sale access, nor do they have a low cost of funds advantage. What they *are* often good at is developing innovative contracts for lessees. In addition, they are starting to act as captive finance companies for some companies that do not have a leasing subsidiary. For example, International Lease Finance Corp. is one of the world's largest independent lessors.

According to recent data at *www.ficinc.com* on new business volume by lessor type, banks hold about 47 percent of the market, followed by captives at 26 percent. Independents had the remaining 23 percent of new business. Data on changes in market share show that both banks and captives have increased business at the expense of the independents. That is, from 2008 to 2009, banks' and captives' market shares had grown by 9 percent and 3 percent, respectively, while the independents' market share declined by 10 percent.

Advantages of Leasing

The growth in leasing indicates that it often has some genuine advantages over owning property, such as:

1. *100% financing at fixed rates.* Leases are often signed without requiring any money down from the lessee. This helps the lessee conserve scarce cash—an especially desirable feature for new and developing companies. In addition, lease payments often remain fixed, which protects the lessee against inflation and increases in the cost of money. The following comment explains why companies choose a lease instead of a conventional loan: "Our local bank finally came up to 80 percent of the purchase price but wouldn't go any higher, and they wanted a floating interest rate. We just couldn't afford the down payment, and we needed to lock in a final payment rate we knew we could live with."

2. *Protection against obsolescence.* Leasing equipment reduces risk of obsolescence to the lessee, and in many cases passes the risk of residual value to the lessor. For example, Merck (a pharmaceutical maker) leases computers. Under the lease agreement, Merck may turn in an old computer for a new model at any time, canceling the old lease and writing a new one. The lessor adds the cost of the new lease to the balance due on the old lease, less the old computer's trade-in value. As one treasurer remarked, "Our instinct is to purchase." But if a new computer is likely to come along in a short time, "then leasing is just a heck of a lot more convenient than purchasing." Naturally, the lessor also protects itself by requiring the lessee to pay higher rental payments or provide additional payments if the lessee does not maintain the asset.

3. *Flexibility.* Lease agreements may contain less restrictive provisions than other debt agreements. Innovative lessors can tailor a lease agreement to the lessee's special needs. For instance, the duration of the lease—the lease term—may be anything from a short period of time to the entire expected economic life of the asset. The rental payments may be level from year to year, or they may increase or decrease in amount. The payment amount may be predetermined or may vary with sales, the prime interest rate, the Consumer Price Index, or some other factor. In most cases the rent is set to enable the lessor to recover the cost of the asset plus a fair return over the life of the lease.

4. *Less costly financing.* Some companies find leasing cheaper than other forms of financing. For example, start-up companies in depressed industries or companies in low tax brackets may lease to claim tax benefits that they might otherwise lose. Depreciation deductions offer no benefit to companies that have little if any taxable income. Through leasing, the leasing companies or financial institutions use these tax benefits. They can then pass some of these tax benefits back to the user of the asset in the form of lower rental payments.

5. *Tax advantages.* In some cases, companies can "have their cake and eat it too" with tax advantages that leases offer. That is, for financial reporting purposes, companies do not report an asset or a liability for the lease arrangement. For tax purposes, however, companies can capitalize and depreciate the leased asset. As a result, a company takes deductions earlier rather than later and also reduces its taxes. A common vehicle for this type of transaction is a "synthetic lease" arrangement, such as that described in the opening story for Krispy Kreme.

6. *Off–balance-sheet financing.* Certain leases do not add debt on a balance sheet or affect financial ratios. In fact, they may add to borrowing capacity.[1] Such off–balance-sheet financing is critical to some companies.

INTERNATIONAL PERSPECTIVE

Some companies "double dip" on the international level too. The leasing rules of the lessor's and lessee's countries may differ, permitting both parties to own the asset. Thus, both lessor and lessee receive the tax benefits related to depreciation.

[1]As demonstrated later in this chapter, certain types of lease arrangements are not capitalized on the balance sheet. The liabilities section is thereby relieved of large future lease commitments that, if recorded, would adversely affect the debt to equity ratio. The reluctance to record lease obligations as liabilities is one of the primary reasons some companies resist capitalized lease accounting.

OFF–BALANCE-SHEET FINANCING

As shown in our opening story, airlines use lease arrangements extensively. This results in a great deal of off–balance-sheet financing. The following chart indicates that many airlines that lease aircraft understate debt levels by a substantial amount.

What do the numbers mean?

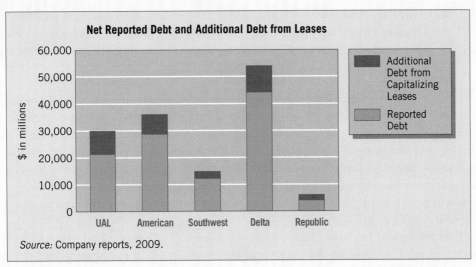

Net Reported Debt and Additional Debt from Leases

Legend:
- Additional Debt from Capitalizing Leases
- Reported Debt

Y-axis: $ in millions (0 to 60,000)

X-axis categories: UAL, American, Southwest, Delta, Republic

Source: Company reports, 2009.

Airlines are not the only ones playing the off–balance-sheet game. A recent study estimates that for S&P 500 companies, off–balance-sheet lease obligations total more than one-half trillion dollars, or roughly three percent of market value. Thus, analysts must adjust reported debt levels for the effects of non-capitalized leases. A methodology for making this adjustment is discussed in Eugene A. Imhoff, Jr., Robert C. Lipe, and David W. Wright, "Operating Leases: Impact of Constructive Capitalization," *Accounting Horizons* (March 1991).

Source: D. Zion and A. Varshney, "Leases Landing on Balance Sheets," *Credit Suisse Equity Research* (August 17, 2010).

Conceptual Nature of a Lease

If Delta borrows $47 million on a 10-year note from Bank of America to purchase a Boeing 737 jet plane, Delta should clearly report an asset and related liability at that amount on its balance sheet. Similarly, if Delta purchases the 737 for $47 million directly from Boeing through an installment purchase over 10 years, it should obviously report an asset and related liability (i.e., it should "capitalize" the installment transaction).

However, what if Delta **leases** the Boeing 737 for 10 years from International Lease Finance Corp. (ILFC)—the world's largest lessor of airplanes—through a noncancelable lease transaction with payments of the same amount as the installment purchase transaction? In that case, opinion differs over how to report this transaction. The various views on capitalization of leases are as follows.

1. *Do not capitalize any leased assets.* This view considers capitalization inappropriate, because Delta does not own the property. Furthermore, a lease is an **"executory" contract** requiring continuing performance by both parties. Because companies do not currently capitalize other executory contracts (such as purchase commitments and employment contracts), they should not capitalize leases either.

2. *Capitalize leases that are similar to installment purchases.* This view holds that companies should report transactions in accordance with their economic substance. Therefore, if companies capitalize installment purchases, they should also capitalize leases that have similar characteristics. For example, Delta Airlines makes the same payments over a 10-year period for either a lease or an installment purchase. Lessees make rental payments, whereas owners make mortgage payments.

Underlying Concepts

The issue of how to report leases is the classic case of substance versus form. Although legal title does not technically pass in lease transactions, the benefits from the use of the property do transfer.

Why should the financial statements not report these transactions in the same manner?

3. *Capitalize all long-term leases.* This approach requires only the long-term right to use the property in order to capitalize. This property-rights approach capitalizes all long-term leases.[2]

4. *Capitalize firm leases where the penalty for nonperformance is substantial.* A final approach advocates capitalizing only "firm" (noncancelable) contractual rights and obligations. "Firm" means that it is unlikely to avoid performance under the lease without a severe penalty.

In short, the various viewpoints range from no capitalization to capitalization of all leases. The FASB apparently agrees with the capitalization approach when the lease is similar to an installment purchase: It notes that Delta **should capitalize a lease that transfers substantially all of the benefits and risks of property ownership, provided the lease is noncancelable**. Noncancelable means that Delta can cancel the lease contract only upon the outcome of some remote contingency, or that the cancellation provisions and penalties of the contract are so costly to Delta that cancellation probably will not occur.

This viewpoint leads to three basic conclusions: (1) Companies must identify the characteristics that indicate the transfer of substantially all of the benefits and risks of ownership. (2) The same characteristics should apply consistently to the lessee and the lessor. (3) Those leases that do **not** transfer substantially all the benefits and risks of ownership are operating leases. Companies should not capitalize operating leases. Instead, companies should account for them as rental payments and receipts.

ACCOUNTING BY THE LESSEE

LEARNING OBJECTIVE **2**

Describe the accounting criteria and procedures for capitalizing leases by the lessee.

If Delta Airlines (the lessee) **capitalizes** a lease, it records an asset and a liability generally equal to the present value of the rental payments. ILFC (the lessor), having transferred substantially all the benefits and risks of ownership, recognizes a sale by removing the asset from the balance sheet and replacing it with a receivable. The typical journal entries for Delta and ILFC, assuming leased and capitalized equipment, appear as shown in Illustration 21-2.

ILLUSTRATION 21-2
Journal Entries for
Capitalized Lease

Delta (Lessee)			ILFC (Lessor)		
Leased Equipment	XXX		Lease Receivable	XXX	
Lease Liability		XXX	Equipment		XXX

Having capitalized the asset, Delta records depreciation on the leased asset. Both ILFC and Delta treat the lease rental payments as consisting of interest and principal.

If Delta does not capitalize the lease, it does not record an asset, nor does ILFC remove one from its books. When Delta makes a lease payment, it records rental expense; ILFC recognizes rental revenue.

[2]Capitalization of most leases (based on either a right of use or on noncancelable rights and obligations) has the support of financial analysts. See Peter H. Knutson, "Financial Reporting in the 1990s and Beyond," *Position Paper* (Charlottesville, Va.: AIMR, 1993); and Warren McGregor, "Accounting for Leases: A New Approach," Special Report (Norwalk, Conn.: FASB, 1996). The joint FASB/IASB project on lease accounting is based on a right-of-use model, which will require expanded capitalization of lease assets and liabilities. See *http://www.fasb.org/jsp/FASB/Page/SectionPage&cid=1218220137074*.

In order to record a lease as a capital lease, the lease must be noncancelable. Further, it must meet one or more of the four criteria listed in Illustration 21-3.

Capitalization Criteria (Lessee)

- The lease transfers ownership of the property to the lessee.
- The lease contains a bargain-purchase option.[3]
- The lease term is equal to 75 percent or more of the estimated economic life of the leased property.
- The present value of the minimum lease payments (excluding executory costs) equals or exceeds 90 percent of the fair value of the leased property. [1]

ILLUSTRATION 21-3
Capitalization Criteria for Lessee

See the FASB Codification section (page 1334).

Delta classifies and accounts for leases that **do not meet any of the four criteria** as operating leases. Illustration 21-4 shows that a lease meeting any one of the four criteria results in the lessee having a capital lease.

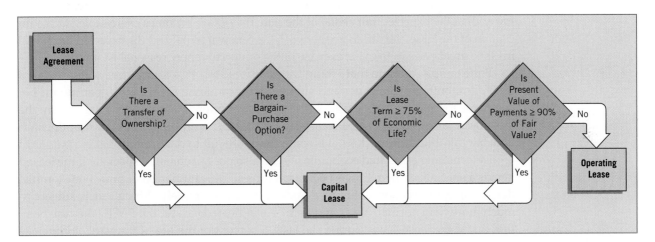

ILLUSTRATION 21-4
Diagram of Lessee's Criteria for Lease Classification

In keeping with the FASB's reasoning that a company consumes a significant portion of the value of the asset in the first 75 percent of its life, the lessee applies neither the third nor the fourth criterion when the inception of the lease occurs during the last 25 percent of the asset's life.

Capitalization Criteria

Three of the four capitalization criteria that apply to lessees are controversial and can be difficult to apply in practice. We discuss each of the criteria in detail on the following pages.

Transfer of Ownership Test

If the lease transfers ownership of the asset to the lessee, it is a capital lease. This criterion is not controversial and easily implemented in practice.

Bargain-Purchase Option Test

A bargain-purchase option allows the lessee to purchase the leased property for a price that is **significantly lower** than the property's expected fair value at the date the option becomes exercisable. At the inception of the lease, the difference between the option price and the expected fair value must be large enough to make exercise of the option reasonably assured.

---

[3]We define a bargain-purchase option in the next section.

For example, assume that Brett's Delivery Service was to lease a Honda Accord for $599 per month for 40 months, with an option to purchase for $100 at the end of the 40-month period. If the estimated fair value of the Honda Accord is $3,000 at the end of the 40 months, the $100 option to purchase is clearly a bargain. Therefore, Brett must capitalize the lease. In other cases, the criterion may not be as easy to apply, and determining *now* that a certain *future* price is a bargain can be difficult.

Economic Life Test (75% Test)

If the lease period equals or exceeds 75 percent of the asset's economic life, the lessor transfers most of the risks and rewards of ownership to the lessee. Capitalization is therefore appropriate. However, determining the lease term and the economic life of the asset can be troublesome.

The lease term is generally considered to be the fixed, noncancelable term of the lease. However, a bargain-renewal option, if provided in the lease agreement, can extend this period. A bargain-renewal option allows the lessee to renew the lease for a rental that is lower than the expected fair rental at the date the option becomes exercisable. At the inception of the lease, the difference between the renewal rental and the expected fair rental must be great enough to make exercise of the option to renew reasonably assured.

For example, assume that Home Depot leases Dell PCs for two years at a rental of $100 per month per computer and subsequently can lease them for $10 per month per computer for another two years. The lease clearly offers a bargain-renewal option; the lease term is considered to be four years. However, with bargain-renewal options, as with bargain-purchase options, it is sometimes difficult to determine what is a bargain.[4]

Determining estimated economic life can also pose problems, especially if the leased item is a specialized item or has been used for a significant period of time. For example, determining the economic life of a nuclear core is extremely difficult. It is subject to much more than normal "wear and tear." As indicated earlier, the FASB takes the position that if the lease starts during the last 25 percent of the life of the asset, companies cannot use the economic life test to classify a lease as a capital lease.

Recovery of Investment Test (90% Test)

INTERNATIONAL PERSPECTIVE

IFRS does not specify an exact percentage, such as 90%. Instead, it uses the term "substantially all." This difference illustrates the distinction between rules-based and principles-based standards.

If the present value of the minimum lease payments equals or exceeds 90 percent of the fair value of the asset, then a lessee like Delta should capitalize the leased asset. Why? If the present value of the minimum lease payments is reasonably close to the fair value of the aircraft, Delta is effectively purchasing the asset.

Determining the present value of the minimum lease payments involves three important concepts: (1) minimum lease payments, (2) executory costs, and (3) discount rate.

Minimum Lease Payments. Delta is obligated to make, or expected to make, minimum lease payments in connection with the leased property. These payments include the following.

1. *Minimum rental payments.* Minimum rental payments are those that Delta must make to ILFC under the lease agreement. In some cases, the minimum rental payments may equal the minimum lease payments. However, the minimum lease payments may also include a guaranteed residual value (if any), penalty for failure to renew, or a bargain-purchase option (if any), as we note on the next page.

---

[4]The original lease term is also extended for leases having the following: substantial penalties for nonrenewal; periods for which the lessor has the option to renew or extend the lease; renewal periods preceding the date a bargain-purchase option becomes exercisable; and renewal periods in which any lessee guarantees of the lessor's debt are expected to be in effect or in which there will be a loan outstanding from the lessee to the lessor. The lease term, however, can never extend beyond the time a bargain-purchase option becomes exercisable. [2]

2. *Guaranteed residual value.* The residual value is the estimated fair (market) value of the leased property at the end of the lease term. ILFC may transfer the risk of loss to Delta or to a third party by obtaining a guarantee of the estimated residual value. The guaranteed residual value is either (1) the certain or determinable amount that Delta will pay ILFC at the end of the lease to purchase the aircraft at the end of the lease, or (2) the amount Delta or the third party guarantees that ILFC will realize if the aircraft is returned. (Third-party guarantors are, in essence, insurers who for a fee assume the risk of deficiencies in leased asset residual value.) If not guaranteed in full, the **unguaranteed residual value** is the estimated residual value exclusive of any portion guaranteed.[5]

3. *Penalty for failure to renew or extend the lease.* The amount Delta must pay if the agreement specifies that it must extend or renew the lease, and it fails to do so.

4. *Bargain-purchase option.* As we indicated earlier (in item 1), an option given to Delta to purchase the aircraft at the end of the lease term at a price that is fixed sufficiently below the expected fair value, so that, at the inception of the lease, purchase is reasonably assured.

Delta excludes executory costs (defined below) from its computation of the present value of the minimum lease payments.

Executory Costs. Like most assets, leased tangible assets incur insurance, maintenance, and tax expenses—called executory costs—during their economic life. If ILFC retains responsibility for the payment of these "ownership-type costs," **it should exclude**, in computing the present value of the minimum lease payments, a portion of each lease payment that represents executory costs. Executory costs do not represent payment on or reduction of the obligation.

Many lease agreements specify that the lessee directly pays executory costs to the appropriate third parties. In these cases, the lessor can use the rental payment **without adjustment** in the present value computation.

Discount Rate. A lessee, like Delta, generally computes the present value of the minimum lease payments using its incremental borrowing rate. This rate is defined as: "The rate that, at the inception of the lease, the lessee would have incurred to borrow the funds necessary to buy the leased asset on a secured loan with repayment terms similar to the payment schedule called for in the lease." [4]

To determine whether the present value of these payments is less than 90 percent of the fair value of the property, Delta discounts the payments using its incremental borrowing rate. Determining the incremental borrowing rate often requires judgment because the lessee bases it on a hypothetical purchase of the property.

However, there is one exception to this rule. If (1) Delta knows the implicit interest rate **computed by ILFC** and (2) it is less than Delta's incremental borrowing rate, then Delta **must use ILFC's implicit rate**. What is the **interest rate implicit in the lease**? It is the discount rate that, when applied to the minimum lease payments and any unguaranteed residual value accruing to the lessor, causes the aggregate present value to equal the fair value of the leased property to the lessor. [5]

The purpose of this exception is twofold. First, **the implicit rate of ILFC is generally a more realistic rate** to use in determining the amount (if any) to report as the asset and related liability for Delta. Second, the guideline ensures that Delta **does not use an artificially high incremental borrowing rate** that would cause the present value of the minimum lease payments to be less than 90 percent of the fair value of the aircraft. Use of such a rate would thus make it possible to avoid capitalization of the asset and related liability.

---

[5]A lease provision requiring the lessee to make up a residual value deficiency that is attributable to damage, extraordinary wear and tear, or excessive usage is not included in the minimum lease payments. Lessees recognize such costs as period costs when incurred. [3]

Delta may argue that it cannot determine the implicit rate of the lessor and therefore should use the higher rate. However, in most cases, Delta can approximate the implicit rate used by ILFC. The determination of whether or not a reasonable estimate could be made will require judgment, particularly where the result from using the incremental borrowing rate comes close to meeting the 90 percent test. Because Delta **may not capitalize the leased property at more than its fair value** (as we discuss later), it cannot use an excessively low discount rate.

Asset and Liability Accounted for Differently

In a capital lease transaction, Delta uses the lease as a source of financing. ILFC finances the transaction (provides the investment capital) through the leased asset. Delta makes rent payments, which actually are installment payments. Therefore, over the life of the aircraft rented, **the rental payments to ILFC constitute a payment of principal plus interest.**

Asset and Liability Recorded

Under the capital lease method, Delta treats the lease transaction as if it purchases the aircraft in a financing transaction. That is, Delta acquires the aircraft and creates an obligation. Therefore, it records a capital lease as an asset and a liability at the lower of (1) the present value of the minimum lease payments (excluding executory costs) or (2) the fair value of the leased asset at the inception of the lease. The rationale for this approach is that companies should not record a leased asset for more than its fair value.

Depreciation Period

One troublesome aspect of accounting for the depreciation of the capitalized leased asset relates to the period of depreciation. If the lease agreement transfers ownership of the asset to Delta (criterion 1) or contains a bargain-purchase option (criterion 2), Delta depreciates the aircraft consistent with its normal depreciation policy for other aircraft, **using the economic life of the asset.**

On the other hand, if the lease does not transfer ownership or does not contain a bargain-purchase option, then Delta depreciates it over the **term of the lease.** In this case, the aircraft reverts to ILFC after a certain period of time.

Effective-Interest Method

Throughout the term of the lease, Delta uses the effective-interest method to allocate each lease payment between principal and interest. This method produces a periodic interest expense equal to a constant percentage of the carrying value of the lease obligation. When applying the effective-interest method to capital leases, Delta must use the same discount rate that determines the present value of the minimum lease payments.

Depreciation Concept

Although Delta computes the amounts initially capitalized as an asset and recorded as an obligation at the same present value, the **depreciation of the aircraft and the discharge of the obligation are independent accounting processes** during the term of the lease. It should depreciate the leased asset by applying conventional depreciation methods: straight-line, sum-of-the-years'-digits, declining-balance, units of production, etc. The FASB uses the term "amortization" more frequently than "depreciation" to recognize intangible leased property rights. We prefer "depreciation" to describe the write-off of a tangible asset's expired services.

Capital Lease Method (Lessee)

To illustrate a capital lease, assume that Caterpillar Financial Services Corp. (a subsidiary of Caterpillar) and Sterling Construction Corp. sign a lease agreement dated

January 1, 2012, that calls for Caterpillar to lease a front-end loader to Sterling beginning January 1, 2012. The terms and provisions of the lease agreement, and other pertinent data, are as follows.

- The term of the lease is five years. The lease agreement is noncancelable, requiring equal rental payments of $25,981.62 at the beginning of each year (annuity-due basis).
- The loader has a fair value at the inception of the lease of $100,000, an estimated economic life of five years, and no residual value.
- Sterling pays all of the executory costs directly to third parties except for the property taxes of $2,000 per year, which is included as part of its annual payments to Caterpillar.
- The lease contains no renewal options. The loader reverts to Caterpillar at the termination of the lease.
- Sterling's incremental borrowing rate is 11 percent per year.
- Sterling depreciates, on a straight-line basis, similar equipment that it owns.
- Caterpillar sets the annual rental to earn a rate of return on its investment of 10 percent per year; Sterling knows this fact.

The lease meets the criteria for classification as a capital lease for the following reasons.

1. The lease term of five years, being equal to the equipment's estimated economic life of five years, satisfies the 75 percent test.
2. The present value of the minimum lease payments ($100,000 as computed below) exceeds 90 percent of the fair value of the loader ($100,000).

The minimum lease payments are $119,908.10 ($23,981.62 × 5). Sterling computes the amount capitalized as leased assets as the present value of the minimum lease payments (excluding executory costs—property taxes of $2,000) as shown in Illustration 21-5.

Capitalized amount = ($25,981.62 − $2,000) × Present value of an annuity due of 1 for 5 periods at 10% (Table 6-5)

= $23,981.62 × 4.16986

= $100,000

ILLUSTRATION 21-5
Computation of Capitalized Lease Payments

Sterling uses Caterpillar's implicit interest rate of 10 percent instead of its incremental borrowing rate of 11 percent because (1) it is lower and (2) it knows about it.[6]

Sterling records the capital lease on its books on January 1, 2012, as:

Leased Equipment (under capital leases)	100,000	
Lease Liability		100,000

Note that the entry records the obligation at the net amount of $100,000 (the present value of the future rental payments) rather than at the gross amount of $119,908.10 ($23,981.62 × 5).

Sterling records the **first lease payment on January 1, 2012**, as follows.

Property Tax Expense	2,000.00	
Lease Liability	23,981.62	
Cash		25,981.62

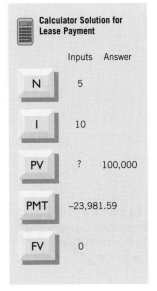

Calculator Solution for Lease Payment

	Inputs	Answer
N	5	
I	10	
PV	?	100,000
PMT	−23,981.59	
FV	0	

[6]If Sterling has an incremental borrowing rate of, say, 9 percent (lower than the 10 percent rate used by Caterpillar) and it did not know the rate used by Caterpillar, the present value computation would yield a capitalized amount of $101,675.35 ($23,981.62 × 4.23972). And, because this amount exceeds the $100,000 fair value of the equipment, Sterling would have to capitalize the $100,000 and use 10 percent as its effective rate for amortization of the lease obligation.

Each lease payment of $25,981.62 consists of three elements: (1) a reduction in the lease liability, (2) a financing cost (interest expense), and (3) executory costs (property taxes). The total financing cost (interest expense) over the term of the lease is $19,908.10. This amount is the difference between the present value of the lease payments ($100,000) and the actual cash disbursed, net of executory costs ($119,908.10). Therefore, the annual interest expense, applying the effective-interest method, is a function of the outstanding liability, as Illustration 21-6 shows.

ILLUSTRATION 21-6
Lease Amortization
Schedule for Lessee—
Annuity-Due Basis

STERLING CONSTRUCTION
LEASE AMORTIZATION SCHEDULE
ANNUITY-DUE BASIS

Date	Annual Lease Payment (a)	Executory Costs (b)	Interest (10%) on Liability (c)	Reduction of Lease Liability (d)	Lease Liability (e)
1/1/12					$100,000.00
1/1/12	$ 25,981.62	$ 2,000	$ –0–	$ 23,981.62	76,018.38
1/1/13	25,981.62	2,000	7,601.84	16,379.78	59,638.60
1/1/14	25,981.62	2,000	5,963.86	18,017.76	41,620.84
1/1/15	25,981.62	2,000	4,162.08	19,819.54	21,801.30
1/1/16	25,981.62	2,000	2,180.32*	21,801.30	–0–
	$129,908.10	$10,000	$19,908.10	$100,000.00	

(a) Lease payment as required by lease.
(b) Executory costs included in rental payment.
(c) Ten percent of the preceding balance of (e) except for 1/1/12; since this is an annuity due, no time has elapsed at the date of the first payment and no interest has accrued.
(d) (a) minus (b) and (c).
(e) Preceding balance minus (d).

*Rounded by 19 cents.

At the end of its fiscal year, December 31, 2012, Sterling records **accrued interest** as follows.

Interest Expense	7,601.84	
Interest Payable		7,601.84

Depreciation of the leased equipment over its five-year lease term, applying Sterling's normal depreciation policy (straight-line method), results in the following entry on December 31, 2012.

Depreciation Expense (capital leases)	20,000	
Accumulated Depreciation—Capital Leases		20,000
($100,000 ÷ 5 years)		

At December 31, 2012, Sterling separately identifies the assets recorded under capital leases on its balance sheet. Similarly, it separately identifies the related obligations. Sterling classifies the portion due within one year or the operating cycle, whichever is longer, with current liabilities, and the rest with noncurrent liabilities. For example, the current portion of the December 31, 2012, total obligation of $76,018.38 in Sterling's amortization schedule is the amount of the reduction in the obligation in 2013, or $16,379.78. Illustration 21-7 shows the liabilities section as it relates to lease transactions at December 31, 2012.

ILLUSTRATION 21-7
Reporting Current and
Noncurrent Lease
Liabilities

Current liabilities	
Interest payable	$ 7,601.84
Lease liability	16,379.78
Noncurrent liabilities	
Lease liability	$59,638.60

Sterling records the lease payment of January 1, 2013, as follows.

Property Tax Expense	2,000.00	
Interest Payable	7,601.84	
Lease Liability	16,379.78	
Cash		25,981.62

Entries through 2016 would follow the pattern above. Sterling records its other executory costs (insurance and maintenance) in a manner similar to how it records any other operating costs incurred on assets it owns.

Upon expiration of the lease, Sterling has fully amortized the amount capitalized as leased equipment. It also has fully discharged its lease obligation. If Sterling does not purchase the loader, it returns the equipment to Caterpillar. Sterling then removes the leased equipment and related accumulated depreciation accounts from its books.[7]

If Sterling purchases the equipment at termination of the lease, at a price of $5,000 and the estimated life of the equipment changes from five to seven years, it makes the following entry.

Equipment ($100,000 + $5,000)	105,000	
Accumulated Depreciation—Capital Leases	100,000	
Leased Equipment (under capital leases)		100,000
Accumulated Depreciation—Equipment		100,000
Cash		5,000

Operating Method (Lessee)

Under the **operating method**, rent expense (and the associated liability) accrues day by day to the lessee as it uses the property. **The lessee assigns rent to the periods benefiting from the use of the asset and ignores, in the accounting, any commitments to make future payments.** The lessee makes appropriate accruals or deferrals if the accounting period ends between cash payment dates.

For example, assume that the capital lease illustrated in the previous section did not qualify as a capital lease. Sterling therefore accounts for it as an operating lease. The first-year charge to operations is now $25,981.62, the amount of the rental payment. Sterling records this payment on January 1, 2012, as follows.

Rent Expense	25,981.62	
Cash		25,981.62

Sterling does not report the loader, as well as any long-term liability for future rental payments, on the balance sheet. Sterling reports rent expense on the income statement. And, as discussed later in the chapter, **Sterling must disclose all operating leases that have noncancelable lease terms in excess of one year**.

RESTATEMENTS ON THE MENU

What do the numbers mean?

Accounting for operating leases would appear routine, so it is unusual for a bevy of companies in a single industry—restaurants—to get caught up in the accounting rules for operating leases. Getting the accounting right is particularly important for restaurant chains, because they make extensive use of leases for their restaurants and equipment.

The problem stems from the way most property (and equipment) leases cover a specific number of years (the so-called *primary lease term*) as well as renewal periods (sometimes referred to as the *option term*). In some cases, companies were calculating their lease expense for the primary term but depreciating lease-related assets over both the primary and option terms. This practice resulted in understating the total cost of the lease and thus boosted earnings.

---

[7]If Sterling purchases the front-end loader during the term of a "capital lease," it accounts for it like a renewal or extension of a capital lease. "Any difference between the purchase price and the carrying amount of the lease obligation shall be recorded as an adjustment of the carrying amount of the asset." [6]

What do the numbers mean? (continued)

For example, the CFO at CKE Restaurants Inc., owner of the Hardee's, and Carl's Jr. chains, noted that CKE ran into trouble because it was not consistent in calculating the lease and depreciation expense. Correcting the error at CKE reduced earnings by nine cents a share in fiscal 2002, nine cents a share in fiscal 2003, and 10 cents a share in fiscal 2004. The company now uses the shorter, primary lease terms for calculating both lease expense and depreciation. The change increases depreciation annually, which in turn decreases total assets.

CKE was not alone in improper operating lease accounting. Notable restaurateurs who ran afoul of the lease rules included Brinker International Inc., operator of Chili's; Darden Restaurants Inc., which operates Red Lobster and Olive Garden; and Jack in the Box. To correct their operating lease accounting, these restaurants reported restatements that resulted in lower earnings and assets.

Source: Steven D. Jones and Richard Gibson, *Wall Street Journal* (January 26, 2005), p. C3.

Comparison of Capital Lease with Operating Lease

LEARNING OBJECTIVE 3

Contrast the operating and capitalization methods of recording leases.

As we indicated, if accounting for the lease as an operating lease, the first-year charge to operations is $25,981.62, the amount of the rental payment. Treating the transaction as a capital lease, however, results in a first-year charge of $29,601.84: depreciation of $20,000 (assuming straight-line), interest expense of $7,601.84 (per Illustration 21-6), and executory costs of $2,000. Illustration 21-8 shows that **while the total charges to operations are the same over the lease term whether accounting for the lease as a capital lease or as an operating lease, under the capital lease treatment the charges are higher in the earlier years and lower in the later years.**[8]

ILLUSTRATION 21-8
Comparison of Charges to Operations—Capital vs. Operating Leases

STERLING CONSTRUCTION
SCHEDULE OF CHARGES TO OPERATIONS
CAPITAL LEASE VERSUS OPERATING LEASE

| | Capital Lease | | | | Operating Lease | |
Year	Depreciation	Executory Costs	Interest	Total Charge	Charge	Difference
2012	$ 20,000	$ 2,000	$ 7,601.84	$ 29,601.84	$ 25,981.62	$3,620.22
2013	20,000	2,000	5,963.86	27,963.86	25,981.62	1,982.24
2014	20,000	2,000	4,162.08	26,162.08	25,981.62	180.46
2015	20,000	2,000	2,180.32	24,180.32	25,981.62	(1,801.30)
2016	20,000	2,000	—	22,000.00	25,981.62	(3,981.62)
	$100,000	$10,000	$19,908.10	$129,908.10	$129,908.10	$ –0–

If using an accelerated method of depreciation, the differences between the amounts charged to operations under the two methods would be even larger in the earlier and later years.

In addition, using the capital lease approach results in an asset and related liability of $100,000 initially reported on the balance sheet. The lessee would not report any asset

---

[8]The higher charges in the early years is one reason lessees are reluctant to adopt the capital lease accounting method. Lessees (especially those of real estate) claim that it is really no more costly to operate the leased asset in the early years than in the later years. Thus, they advocate an even charge similar to that provided by the operating method.

or liability under the operating method. Therefore, the following differences occur if using a capital lease instead of an operating lease.

1. An increase in the amount of reported debt (both short-term and long-term).
2. An increase in the amount of total assets (specifically long-lived assets).
3. A lower income early in the life of the lease and, therefore, lower retained earnings.

Thus, many companies believe that capital leases negatively impact their financial position: Their debt to total equity ratio increases, and their rate of return on total assets decreases. As a result, the business community resists capitalizing leases.

Whether this resistance is well founded is debatable. From a cash flow point of view, the company is in the same position whether accounting for the lease as an operating or a capital lease. Managers often argue against capitalization for several reasons. First, capitalization can more easily lead to **violation of loan covenants**. It also can affect the **amount of compensation received by owners** (for example, a stock compensation plan tied to earnings). Finally, capitalization can **lower rates of return** and **increase debt to equity relationships**, making the company less attractive to present and potential investors.[9]

ARE YOU LIABLE?

Under current accounting rules, companies can keep the obligations associated with operating leases off the balance sheet. (For example, see the "What Do the Numbers Mean?" box on page 1293 for the effects of this approach for airlines.) This approach may change if the FASB and IASB are able to craft a new lease-accounting rule. The current plans for a new rule in this area should result in many more operating leases on balance sheets. Analysts are beginning to estimate the expected impact of a new rule. As shown in the table below, if the FASB (and IASB) issue a new rule on operating leases, a company like Walgreen could see its liabilities jump a whopping 216 percent.

What do the numbers mean?

Ring It Up

Rule-makers are debating a change to lease accounting that would have a major impact on the balance sheets of some big-name retailers:

Retailer	Estimated Off–Balance-Sheet Lease Liabilities	Jump in Liabilities If They Were on the Balance Sheet
McDonalds	$ 7.996 billion	149%
Walgreen	23.212	216
Home Depot	5.846	27
Starbucks	3.685	146
CVS	26.913	104

---

[9]One study indicates that management's behavior did change as a result of the leasing rules. For example, many companies restructure their leases to avoid capitalization. Others increase their purchases of assets instead of leasing. Still others, faced with capitalization, postpone their debt offerings or issue stock instead. However, note that the study found no significant effect on stock or bond prices as a result of capitalization of leases. See A. Rashad Abdel-khalik, "The Economic Effects on Lessees of *FASB Statement No. 13,* Accounting for Leases," Research Report (Stamford, Conn.: FASB, 1981).

And it is not just retailers who be impacted. A PricewaterhouseCoopers survey of 3,000 international companies indicated the following impacts for several industries.

	Average Increase in Interest-Bearing Debt	Companies with over 25% Increase	Average Increase in Leverage
Retail and trade	213%	71%	64%
Other services	51	35	34
Transportation and warehousing	95	38	31
Professional services	158	52	19
Accommodation	101	41	18
All companies	58	24	13

As indicated, the expected effects are significant, with all companies expecting a 58 percent increase in their debt levels and a 13 percent increase in leverage ratios.

This is not a pretty picture, but investors need to see it if they are to fully understand a company's lease obligations.

Source: Nanette Byrnes, "You May Be Liable for That Lease," *BusinessWeek* (June 5, 2006), p. 76; PricewaterhouseCoopers, *The Future of Leasing: Research of Impact on Companies' Financial Ratios* (2009); and J. E. Ketz, "Operating Lease Obligations to Be Capitalized," *Smartpros* (August 2010), *http://accounting.smartpros.com/x70304.xml.*

ACCOUNTING BY THE LESSOR

Earlier in this chapter, we discussed leasing's advantages to the lessee. Three important benefits are available to the lessor:

1. *Interest revenue.* Leasing is a form of financing. Banks, captives, and independent leasing companies find leasing attractive because it provides competitive interest margins.

2. *Tax incentives.* In many cases, companies that lease cannot use the tax benefit of the asset, but leasing allows them to transfer such tax benefits to another party (the lessor) in return for a lower rental rate on the leased asset. To illustrate, Boeing Aircraft might sell one of its 737 jet planes to a wealthy investor who needed only the tax benefit. The investor then leased the plane to a foreign airline, for whom the tax benefit was of no use. Everyone gained. Boeing sold its airplane, the investor received the tax benefit, and the foreign airline cheaply acquired a 737.[10]

3. *High residual value.* Another advantage to the lessor is the return of the property at the end of the lease term. Residual values can produce very large profits. Citigroup at one time assumed that the commercial aircraft it was leasing to the airline industry would have a residual value of 5 percent of their purchase price. It turned out that they were worth 150 percent of their cost—a handsome profit. At the same time, if residual values decline, lessors can suffer losses when less-valuable leased assets are returned at the conclusion of the lease. Recently, automaker Ford took a $2.1 billion write-down on its lease portfolio, when rising gas prices spurred dramatic declines in the resale values of leased trucks and SUVs. Such residual value losses led Chrysler to get out of the leasing business altogether.

---

[10]Some would argue that there is a loser—the U.S. government. The tax benefits enable the profitable investor to reduce or eliminate taxable income.

Economics of Leasing

A lessor, such as Caterpillar Financial in our earlier example, determines the amount of the rental, basing it on the rate of return—the implicit rate—needed to justify leasing the front-end loader. In establishing the rate of return, Caterpillar considers the credit standing of Sterling Construction, the length of the lease, and the status of the residual value (guaranteed versus unguaranteed).

In the Caterpillar/Sterling example on pages 1298–1301, Caterpillar's implicit rate was 10 percent, the cost of the equipment to Caterpillar was $100,000 (also fair value), and the estimated residual value was zero. Caterpillar determines the amount of the lease payment as follows.

Fair value of leased equipment	$100,000.00
Less: Present value of the residual value	–0–
Amount to be recovered by lessor through lease payments	$100,000.00
Five beginning-of-the-year lease payments to yield a 10% return ($100,000 ÷ 4.16986[a])	$ 23,981.62

[a]PV of an annuity due of 1 for 5 years at 10% (Table 6-5).

ILLUSTRATION 21-9
Computation of Lease Payments

If a residual value is involved (whether guaranteed or not), Caterpillar would not have to recover as much from the lease payments. Therefore, the lease payments would be less. (Illustration 21-16, on page 1311, shows this situation.)

Classification of Leases by the Lessor

For accounting purposes, the **lessor** may classify leases as one of the following:

4 LEARNING OBJECTIVE
Identify the classifications of leases for the lessor.

1. Operating leases.
2. Direct-financing leases.
3. Sales-type leases.

Illustration 21-10 presents two groups of capitalization criteria for the lessor. If at the date of inception, the lessor agrees to a lease that meets **one or more** of the Group I criteria (1, 2, 3, and 4) and **both** of the Group II criteria (1 and 2), the lessor shall classify and account for the arrangement as a direct-financing lease or as a sales-type lease. [7] Note that the Group I criteria are identical to the criteria that must be met in order for a lessee to classify a lease as a capital lease, as shown in Illustration 21-3 (on page 1295).

ILLUSTRATION 21-10
Capitalization Criteria for Lessor

Capitalization Criteria (Lessor)

Group I
1. The lease transfers ownership of the property to the lessee.
2. The lease contains a bargain-purchase option.
3. The lease term is equal to 75 percent or more of the estimated economic life of the leased property.
4. The present value of the minimum lease payments (excluding executory costs) equals or exceeds 90 percent of the fair value of the leased property.

Group II
1. Collectibility of the payments required from the lessee is reasonably predictable.
2. No important uncertainties surround the amount of unreimbursable costs yet to be incurred by the lessor under the lease (lessor's performance is substantially complete or future costs are reasonably predictable).

Why the Group II requirements? The profession wants to ensure that the lessor has really transferred the risks and benefits of ownership. If collectibility of payments is not predictable or if performance by the lessor is incomplete, then the criteria for revenue recognition have not been met. The lessor should therefore account for the lease as an operating lease.

For example, computer leasing companies at one time used to buy IBM equipment, lease the equipment, and remove the leased assets from their balance sheets. In leasing the assets, the computer lessors stated that they would substitute new IBM equipment if obsolescence occurred. However, when IBM introduced a new computer line, IBM refused to sell it to the computer leasing companies. As a result, a number of the lessors could not meet their contracts with their customers and had to take back the old equipment. The computer leasing companies therefore had to reinstate the assets they had taken off the books. Such a case demonstrates one reason for the Group II requirements.

The distinction for the lessor between a direct-financing lease and a sales-type lease is the presence or absence of a manufacturer's or dealer's profit (or loss): A sales-type lease involves a manufacturer's or dealer's profit, and a direct-financing lease does not. The profit (or loss) to the lessor is evidenced by the difference between the fair value of the leased property at the inception of the lease and the lessor's cost or carrying amount (book value).

Normally, sales-type leases arise when manufacturers or dealers use leasing as a means of marketing their products. For example, a computer manufacturer will lease its computer equipment (possibly through a captive) to businesses and institutions. Direct-financing leases generally result from arrangements with lessors that are primarily engaged in financing operations (e.g., banks). However, a lessor need not be a manufacturer or dealer to recognize a profit (or loss) at the inception of a lease that requires application of sales-type lease accounting.

Lessors classify and account for all leases that do not qualify as direct-financing or sales-type leases as operating leases. Illustration 21-11 shows the circumstances under which a lessor classifies a lease as operating, direct-financing, or sales-type.

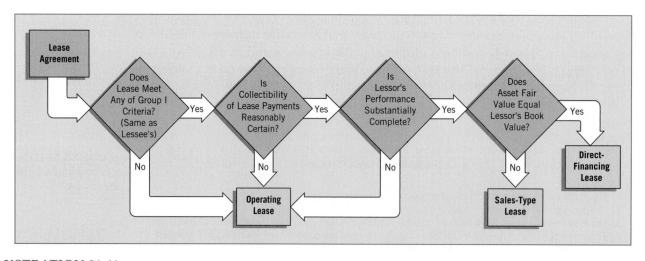

ILLUSTRATION 21-11
Diagram of Lessor's Criteria for Lease Classification

As a consequence of the additional Group II criteria for lessors, a lessor may classify a lease as an **operating** lease but the lessee may classify the same lease as a **capital** lease. In such an event, both the lessor and lessee will carry the asset on their books, and both will depreciate the capitalized asset.

For purposes of comparison with the lessee's accounting, we will illustrate only the operating and direct-financing leases in the following section. We will discuss the more complex sales-type lease later in the chapter.

Direct-Financing Method (Lessor)

Direct-financing leases are in substance the financing of an asset purchase by the lessee. In this type of lease, the lessor records a **lease receivable** instead of a leased asset. The lease receivable is the present value of the minimum lease payments. Remember that "minimum lease payments" include:

5 LEARNING OBJECTIVE
Describe the lessor's accounting for direct-financing leases.

1. Rental payments (excluding executory costs).
2. Bargain-purchase option (if any).
3. Guaranteed residual value (if any).
4. Penalty for failure to renew (if any).

Thus, the lessor records the residual value, whether guaranteed or not. Also, recall that if the lessor pays any executory costs, then it should reduce the rental payment by that amount in computing minimum lease payments.

The following presentation, using the data from the preceding Caterpillar/Sterling example on pages 1298–1301, illustrates the accounting treatment for a direct-financing lease. We repeat here the information relevant to Caterpillar in accounting for this lease transaction.

1. The term of the lease is five years beginning January 1, 2012, noncancelable, and requires equal rental payments of $25,981.62 at the beginning of each year. Payments include $2,000 of executory costs (property taxes).
2. The equipment (front-end loader) has a cost of $100,000 to Caterpillar, a fair value at the inception of the lease of $100,000, an estimated economic life of five years, and no residual value.
3. Caterpillar incurred no initial direct costs in negotiating and closing the lease transaction.
4. The lease contains no renewal options. The equipment reverts to Caterpillar at the termination of the lease.
5. Collectibility is reasonably assured and Caterpillar incurs no additional costs (with the exception of the property taxes being collected from Sterling).
6. Caterpillar sets the annual lease payments to ensure a rate of return of 10 percent (implicit rate) on its investment as shown in Illustration 21-12.

Fair value of leased equipment	$100,000.00
Less: Present value of residual value	–0–
Amount to be recovered by lessor through lease payments	$100,000.00
Five beginning-of-the-year lease payments to yield a 10% return ($100,000 ÷ 4.16986[a])	$ 23,981.62

[a]PV of an annuity due of 1 for 5 years at 10% (Table 6-5).

ILLUSTRATION 21-12
Computation of Lease Payments

The lease meets the criteria for classification as a direct-financing lease for several reasons: (1) The lease term exceeds 75 percent of the equipment's estimated economic life. (2) The present value of the minimum lease payments exceeds 90 percent of the equipment's fair value. (3) Collectibility of the payments is reasonably assured. And (4) Caterpillar incurs no further costs. It is not a sales-type lease because there is no difference between the fair value ($100,000) of the loader and Caterpillar's cost ($100,000).

The Lease Receivable is the present value of the minimum lease payments (excluding executory costs which are property taxes of $2,000). Caterpillar computes it as follows.

ILLUSTRATION 21-13
Computation of Lease
Receivable

Lease receivable = ($25,981.62 − $2,000) × Present value of an annuity due of 1 for 5
periods at 10% (Table 6-5)

= $23,981.62 × 4.16986

= $100,000

Caterpillar records the lease of the asset and the resulting receivable on January 1, 2012 (the inception of the lease), as follows.

Lease Receivable	100,000	
Equipment		100,000

Companies often **report** the lease receivable in the balance sheet as "Net investment in capital leases." Companies classify it either as current or noncurrent, depending on when they recover the net investment.[11]

Caterpillar replaces its investment (the leased front-end loader, a cost of $100,000), with a lease receivable. In a manner similar to Sterling's treatment of interest, Caterpillar applies the effective-interest method and recognizes interest revenue as a function of the lease receivable balance, as Illustration 21-14 shows.

ILLUSTRATION 21-14
Lease Amortization
Schedule for Lessor—
Annuity-Due Basis

CATERPILLAR FINANCIAL
LEASE AMORTIZATION SCHEDULE
ANNUITY-DUE BASIS

Date	Annual Lease Payment	Executory Costs	Interest (10%) on Lease Receivable	Lease Receivable Recovery	Lease Receivable
	(a)	(b)	(c)	(d)	(e)
1/1/12					$100,000.00
1/1/12	$ 25,981.62	$ 2,000.00	$ –0–	$ 23,981.62	76,018.38
1/1/13	25,981.62	2,000.00	7,601.84	16,379.78	59,638.60
1/1/14	25,981.62	2,000.00	5,963.86	18,017.76	41,620.84
1/1/15	25,981.62	2,000.00	4,162.08	19,819.54	21,801.30
1/1/16	25,981.62	2,000.00	2,180.32*	21,801.30	–0–
	$129,908.10	$10,000.00	$19,908.10	$100,000.00	

(a) Annual rental that provides a 10% return on net investment.
(b) Executory costs included in rental payment.
(c) Ten percent of the preceding balance of (e) except for 1/1/12.
(d) (a) minus (b) and (c).
(e) Preceding balance minus (d).

*Rounded by 19 cents.

[11]In the notes to the financial statements (see Illustration 21-32, pages 1322–1323, for lessor disclosures by Hewlett-Packard), the lease receivable is reported at its gross amount (minimum lease payments plus the unguaranteed residual value). In addition, the lessor also reports total unearned interest related to the lease. As a result, some lessors record lease receivable on a gross basis and record the unearned interest in a separate account. We illustrate the net approach here because it is consistent with the accounting for the lessee.

On January 1, 2012, Caterpillar records receipt of the first year's lease payment as follows.

Cash	25,981.62	
Lease Receivable		23,981.62
Property Tax Expense/Property Taxes Payable		2,000.00

On December 31, 2012, Caterpillar recognizes the interest revenue earned during the first year through the following entry.

Interest Receivable	7,601.84	
Interest Revenue (leases)		7,601.84

At December 31, 2012, Caterpillar reports the lease receivable in its balance sheet among current assets or noncurrent assets, or both. It classifies the portion due within one year or the operating cycle, whichever is longer, as a current asset, and the rest with noncurrent assets.

Illustration 21-15 shows the assets section as it relates to lease transactions at December 31, 2012.

Current assets		
Interest receivable	$ 7,601.84	
Lease receivable	16,379.78	
Noncurrent assets (investments)		
Lease receivable	$59,638.60	

ILLUSTRATION 21-15
Reporting Lease Transactions by Lessor

The following entries record receipt of the second year's lease payment and recognition of the interest earned.

January 1, 2013

Cash	25,981.62	
Lease Receivable		16,379.78
Interest Receivable		7,601.84
Property Tax Expense/Property Taxes Payable		2,000.00

December 31, 2013

Interest Receivable	5,963.86	
Interest Revenue (leases)		5,963.86

Journal entries through 2016 follow the same pattern except that Caterpillar records no entry in 2016 (the last year) for earned interest. Because it fully collects the receivable by January 1, 2016, no balance (investment) is outstanding during 2016. Caterpillar **recorded no depreciation**. If Sterling buys the loader for $5,000 upon expiration of the lease, Caterpillar recognizes disposition of the equipment as follows.

Cash	5,000	
Gain on Sale of Leased Equipment		5,000

Operating Method (Lessor)

Under the **operating method**, the lessor records each rental receipt as rental revenue. It **depreciates the leased asset in the normal manner**, with the depreciation expense of the period matched against the rental revenue. The amount of revenue recognized in each accounting period is a level amount (straight-line basis) regardless of the lease provisions, unless another systematic and rational basis better represents the time pattern in which the lessor derives benefit from the leased asset.

In addition to the depreciation charge, the lessor expenses maintenance costs and the cost of any other services rendered under the provisions of the lease that pertain to the current accounting period. The lessor **amortizes over the life of the lease** any costs paid to independent third parties, such as appraisal fees, finder's fees, and costs of credit checks, usually on a straight-line basis.

To illustrate the operating method, assume that the direct-financing lease illustrated in the previous section does not qualify as a capital lease. Therefore, Caterpillar accounts for it as an operating lease. It records the cash rental receipt, assuming the $2,000 was for property tax expense, as follows.

Cash	25,981.62	
Rent Revenue		25,981.62

Caterpillar records depreciation as follows (assuming a straight-line method, a cost basis of $100,000, and a five-year life).

Depreciation Expense (leased equipment)	20,000	
Accumulated Depreciation—Equipment		20,000

If Caterpillar pays property taxes, insurance, maintenance, and other operating costs during the year, it records them as expenses chargeable against the gross rental revenues.

If Caterpillar owns plant assets that it uses in addition to those leased to others, the company **separately classifies the leased equipment and accompanying accumulated depreciation** as Equipment Leased to Others or Investment in Leased Property. If significant in amount or in terms of activity, Caterpillar separates the rental revenues and accompanying expenses in the income statement from sales revenue and cost of goods sold.

SPECIAL ACCOUNTING PROBLEMS

LEARNING OBJECTIVE **6**

Identify special features of lease arrangements that cause unique accounting problems.

The features of lease arrangements that cause unique accounting problems are:

1. Residual values.
2. Sales-type leases (lessor).
3. Bargain-purchase options.
4. Initial direct costs.
5. Current versus noncurrent classification.
6. Disclosure.

We discuss each of these features on the following pages.

Residual Values

Up to this point, in order to develop the basic accounting issues related to lessee and lessor accounting, we have generally ignored residual values. Accounting for residual values is complex and will probably provide you with the greatest challenge in understanding lease accounting.

Meaning of Residual Value

The residual value is the estimated fair value of the leased asset at the end of the lease term. Frequently, a significant residual value exists at the end of the lease term, especially when the economic life of the leased asset exceeds the lease term. If title does not pass automatically to the lessee (criterion 1) and a bargain-purchase option does not exist (criterion 2), the lessee returns physical custody of the asset to the lessor at the end of the lease term.[12]

Guaranteed versus Unguaranteed

The residual value may be unguaranteed or guaranteed by the lessee. Sometimes the lessee agrees to make up any deficiency below a stated amount that the lessor realizes in residual value at the end of the lease term. In such a case, that stated amount is the guaranteed residual value.

> **7 LEARNING OBJECTIVE**
> Describe the effect of residual values, guaranteed and unguaranteed, on lease accounting.

The parties to a lease use guaranteed residual value in lease arrangements for two reasons. The first is a business reason: It protects the lessor against any loss in estimated residual value, thereby ensuring the lessor of the desired rate of return on investment. The second reason is an accounting benefit that you will learn from the discussion at the end of this chapter.

Lease Payments

A guaranteed residual value—by definition—has more assurance of realization than does an unguaranteed residual value. As a result, the lessor may adjust lease payments because of the increased certainty of recovery. After the lessor establishes this rate, it makes no difference from an accounting point of view whether the residual value is guaranteed or unguaranteed. The net investment that the lessor records (once the rate is set) will be the same.

Assume the same data as in the Caterpillar/Sterling illustrations except that Caterpillar estimates a residual value of $5,000 at the end of the five-year lease term. In addition, Caterpillar assumes a 10 percent return on investment (ROI),[13] whether the residual value is guaranteed or unguaranteed. Caterpillar would compute the amount of the lease payments as follows.

CATERPILLAR'S COMPUTATION OF LEASE PAYMENTS (10% ROI) GUARANTEED OR UNGUARANTEED RESIDUAL VALUE ANNUITY-DUE BASIS, INCLUDING RESIDUAL VALUE	
Fair value of leased asset to lessor	$100,000.00
Less: Present value of residual value ($5,000 × .62092, Table 6-2)	3,104.60
Amount to be recovered by lessor through lease payments	$ 96,895.40
Five periodic lease payments ($96,895.40 ÷ 4.16986, Table 6-5)	$ 23,237.09

ILLUSTRATION 21-16
Lessor's Computation of Lease Payments

Contrast the foregoing lease payment amount to the lease payments of $23,981.62 as computed in Illustration 21-9 (on page 1305), where no residual value existed. In the second example, the payments are less, because the present value of the residual value reduces Caterpillar's total recoverable amount from $100,000 to $96,895.40.

Lessee Accounting for Residual Value

Whether the estimated residual value is guaranteed or unguaranteed has both economic and accounting consequence to the lessee. We saw the economic consequence—lower

---

[12]When the lease term and the economic life are not the same, the residual value and the salvage value of the asset will probably differ. For simplicity, we will assume that residual value and salvage value are the same, even when the economic life and lease term vary.

[13]Technically, the rate of return Caterpillar demands would differ depending upon whether the residual value was guaranteed or unguaranteed. To simplify the illustrations, we are ignoring this difference in subsequent sections.

lease payments—in the preceding example. The accounting consequence is that the **minimum lease payments**, the basis for capitalization, include the guaranteed residual value but excludes the unguaranteed residual value.

Guaranteed Residual Value (Lessee Accounting). A guaranteed residual value affects the lessee's computation of minimum lease payments. Therefore, it also affects the amounts capitalized as a leased asset and a lease obligation. In effect, the guaranteed residual value **is an additional lease payment that the lessee will pay in property or cash, or both, at the end of the lease term**.

Using the rental payments as computed by the lessor in Illustration 21-16, the minimum lease payments are $121,185.45 ([$23,237.09 × 5] + $5,000). Illustration 21-17 shows the capitalized present value of the minimum lease payments (excluding executory costs) for Sterling Construction.

ILLUSTRATION 21-17
Computation of Lessee's
Capitalized Amount—
Guaranteed Residual
Value

| STERLING'S CAPITALIZED AMOUNT (10% RATE) | |
ANNUITY-DUE BASIS, INCLUDING GUARANTEED RESIDUAL VALUE	
Present value of five annual rental payments ($23,237.09 × 4.16986, Table 6-5)	$ 96,895.40
Present value of guaranteed residual value of $5,000 due five years after date of inception: ($5,000 × .62092, Table 6-2)	3,104.60
Lessee's capitalized amount	$100,000.00

Sterling prepares a schedule of interest expense and amortization of the $100,000 lease liability. That schedule, shown in Illustration 21-18, is based on a $5,000 final guaranteed residual value payment at the end of five years.

ILLUSTRATION 21-18
Lease Amortization
Schedule for Lessee—
Guaranteed Residual
Value

| STERLING CONSTRUCTION | | | | |
| LEASE AMORTIZATION SCHEDULE | | | | |
ANNUITY-DUE BASIS, GUARANTEED RESIDUAL VALUE—GRV				
Date	Lease Payment Plus GRV	Executory Costs	Interest (10%) on Liability	Reduction of Lease Liability	Lease Liability
	(a)	(b)	(c)	(d)	(e)
1/1/12					$100,000.00
1/1/12	$ 25,237.09	$ 2,000	–0–	$ 23,237.09	76,762.91
1/1/13	25,237.09	2,000	$ 7,676.29	15,560.80	61,202.11
1/1/14	25,237.09	2,000	6,120.21	17,116.88	44,085.23
1/1/15	25,237.09	2,000	4,408.52	18,828.57	25,256.66
1/1/16	25,237.09	2,000	2,525.67	20,711.42	4,545.24
12/31/16	5,000.00*		454.76**	4,545.24	–0–
	$131,185.45	$10,000	$21,185.45	$100,000.00	

(a) Annual lease payment as required by lease.
(b) Executory costs included in rental payment.
(c) Preceding balance of (e) × 10%, except 1/1/12.
(d) (a) minus (b) and (c).
(e) Preceding balance minus (d).

*Represents the guaranteed residual value.
**Rounded by 24 cents.

Sterling records the leased asset (front-end loader) and liability, depreciation, interest, property tax, and lease payments on the basis of a guaranteed residual value. (These journal entries are shown in Illustration 21-23, on page 1315.) The format of these entries is the same as illustrated earlier, although the amounts are different because of the guaranteed residual value. Sterling records the loader at $100,000 and depreciates it over five years. To compute depreciation, it subtracts the guaranteed residual value from the cost of the loader. Assuming that Sterling uses the straight-line method, the depreciation expense each year is $19,000 ([$100,000 − $5,000] ÷ 5 years).

At the end of the lease term, before the lessee transfers the asset to Caterpillar, the lease asset and liability accounts have the following balances.

Leased equipment (under capital leases)	$100,000.00	Interest payable	$ 454.76
Less: Accumulated depreciation—		Lease liability	4,545.24
capital leases	95,000.00		
	$ 5,000.00		$5,000.00

ILLUSTRATION 21-19
Account Balances on Lessee's Books at End of Lease Term—Guaranteed Residual Value

If, at the end of the lease, the fair value of the residual value is less than $5,000, Sterling will have to record a loss. Assume that Sterling depreciated the leased asset down to its residual value of $5,000 but that the fair value of the residual value at December 31, 2016, was $3,000. In this case, Sterling would have to report a loss of $2,000. Assuming that it pays cash to make up the residual value deficiency, Sterling would make the following journal entry.

Loss on Capital Lease	2,000.00	
Interest Expense (or Interest Payable)	454.76	
Lease Liability	4,545.24	
Accumulated Depreciation—Capital Leases	95,000.00	
Leased Equipment (under capital leases)		100,000.00
Cash		2,000.00

If the fair value *exceeds* $5,000, a gain may be recognized. Caterpillar and Sterling may apportion gains on guaranteed residual values in whatever ratio the parties initially agree.

When there is a guaranteed residual value, the lessee must be careful not to depreciate the total cost of the asset. For example, if Sterling mistakenly depreciated the total cost of the loader ($100,000), a misstatement would occur. That is, the carrying amount of the asset at the end of the lease term would be zero, but Sterling would show the liability under the capital lease at $5,000. In that case, if the asset was worth $5,000, Sterling would end up reporting a gain of $5,000 when it transferred the asset back to Caterpillar. As a result, Sterling would overstate depreciation and would understate net income in 2012–2015; in the last year (2016) net income would be overstated.

Unguaranteed Residual Value (Lessee Accounting). From the lessee's viewpoint, an unguaranteed residual value is the same as no residual value in terms of its effect upon the lessee's method of computing the minimum lease payments and the capitalization of the leased asset and the lease liability.

Assume the same facts as those above except that the $5,000 residual value is **unguaranteed** instead of guaranteed. The amount of the annual lease payments would be the same—$23,237.09. Whether the residual value is guaranteed or unguaranteed, Caterpillar will recover the same amount through lease rentals—that is, $96,895.40. The minimum lease payments are $116,185.45 ($23,237.09 × 5). Sterling would capitalize the amount shown in Illustration 21-20 (page 1314).

ILLUSTRATION 21-20
Computation of Lessee's
Capitalized Amount—
Unguaranteed Residual
Value

STERLING'S CAPITALIZED AMOUNT (10% RATE)
ANNUITY-DUE BASIS, INCLUDING **UNGUARANTEED** RESIDUAL VALUE

Present value of 5 annual rental payments of $23,237.09 × 4.16986 (Table 6-5)	$96,895.40
Unguaranteed residual value of $5,000 (not capitalized by lessee)	–0–
Lessee's capitalized amount	$96,895.40

Illustration 21-21 shows Sterling's schedule of interest expense and amortization of the lease liability of $96,895.40, assuming an unguaranteed residual value of $5,000 at the end of five years.

ILLUSTRATION 21-21
Lease Amortization
Schedule for Lessee—
Unguaranteed Residual
Value

STERLING CONSTRUCTION
LEASE AMORTIZATION SCHEDULE (10%)
ANNUITY-DUE BASIS, **UNGUARANTEED** RESIDUAL VALUE

Date	Annual Lease Payments	Executory Costs	Interest (10%) on Liability	Reduction of Lease Liability	Lease Liability
	(a)	(b)	(c)	(d)	(e)
1/1/12					$96,895.40
1/1/12	$ 25,237.09	$ 2,000	–0–	$23,237.09	73,658.31
1/1/13	25,237.09	2,000	$ 7,365.83	15,871.26	57,787.05
1/1/14	25,237.09	2,000	5,778.71	17,458.38	40,328.67
1/1/15	25,237.09	2,000	4,032.87	19,204.22	21,124.45
1/1/16	25,237.09	2,000	2,112.64*	21,124.45	–0–
	$126,185.45	$10,000	$19,290.05	$96,895.40	

(a) Annual lease payment as required by lease.
(b) Executory costs included in rental payment.
(c) Preceding balance of (e) × 10%.
(d) (a) minus (b) and (c).
(e) Preceding balance minus (d).

*Rounded by 19 cents.

Sterling records the leased asset and liability, depreciation, interest, property tax, and lease payments on the basis of an unguaranteed residual value. (These journal entries are shown in Illustration 21-23.) The format of these capital lease entries is the same as illustrated earlier. Note that Sterling records the leased asset at $96,895.40 and depreciates it over five years. Assuming that it uses the straight-line method, the depreciation expense each year is $19,379.08 ($96,895.40 ÷ 5 years). At the end of the lease term, before Sterling transfers the asset to Caterpillar, the lease asset and liability accounts have the following balances.

ILLUSTRATION 21-22
Account Balances on
Lessee's Books at
End of Lease Term—
Unguaranteed Residual
Value

Leased equipment (under capital leases)	$96,895		Lease liability	$–0–
Less: Accumulated depreciation— capital leases	96,895			
	$ –0–			

Assuming that Sterling has fully depreciated the leased asset and has fully amortized the lease liability, no entry is required at the end of the lease term, except to remove the asset from the books.

If Sterling depreciated the asset down to its unguaranteed residual value, a misstatement would occur. That is, the carrying amount of the leased asset would be $5,000 at the end of the lease, but the liability under the capital lease would be stated at zero before the transfer of the asset. Thus, Sterling would end up reporting a loss of $5,000 when it transferred the asset back to Caterpillar. Sterling would understate depreciation and would overstate net income in 2012–2015; in the last year (2016), net income would be understated because of the recorded loss.

Lessee Entries Involving Residual Values. Illustration 21-23 shows, in comparative form, Sterling's entries for both a guaranteed and an unguaranteed residual value.

Guaranteed Residual Value			Unguaranteed Residual Value		
Capitalization of lease (January 1, 2012):					
Leased Equipment			Leased Equipment		
(under capital leases)	100,000.00		(under capital leases)	96,895.40	
Lease Liability		100,000.00	Lease Liability		96,895.40
First payment (January 1, 2012):					
Property Tax Expense	2,000.00		Property Tax Expense	2,000.00	
Lease Liability	23,237.09		Lease Liability	23,237.09	
Cash		25,237.09	Cash		25,237.09
Adjusting entry for accrued interest (December 31, 2012):					
Interest Expense	7,676.29		Interest Expense	7,365.83	
Interest Payable		7,676.29	Interest Payable		7,365.83
Entry to record depreciation (December 31, 2012):					
Depreciation Expense			Depreciation Expense		
(capital leases)	19,000.00		(capital leases)	19,379.08	
Accumulated Depreciation—			Accumulated Depreciation—		
Capital Leases		19,000.00	Capital Leases		19,379.08
([$100,000 − $5,000] ÷ 5 years)			($96,895.40 ÷ 5 years)		
Second payment (January 1, 2013):					
Property Tax Expense	2,000.00		Property Tax Expense	2,000.00	
Lease Liability	15,560.80		Lease Liability	15,871.26	
Interest Expense			Interest Expense		
(or Interest Payable)	7,676.29		(or Interest Payable)	7,365.83	
Cash		25,237.09	Cash		25,237.09

ILLUSTRATION 21-23
Comparative Entries for Guaranteed and Unguaranteed Residual Values, Lessee Company

Lessor Accounting for Residual Value

As we indicated earlier, the lessor will recover the same net investment whether the residual value is guaranteed or unguaranteed. That is, the lessor works on the assumption that it will realize **the residual value at the end of the lease term whether guaranteed or unguaranteed**. The lease payments required in order for the company to earn a certain return on investment are the same (e.g., $23,237.09 in our example) whether the residual value is guaranteed or unguaranteed.

To illustrate, we again use the Caterpillar/Sterling data and assume classification of the lease as a direct-financing lease. With a residual value (either guaranteed or unguaranteed) of $5,000, Caterpillar determines the payments as shown in Illustration 21-24 (on page 1316).

ILLUSTRATION 21-24
Computation of Direct-
Financing Lease
Payments

Fair value of leased equipment	$100,000.00
Less: Present value of residual value ($5,000 × .62092, Table 6-2)	3,104.60
Amount to be recovered by lessor through lease payments	$ 96,895.40
Five beginning-of-the-year lease payments to yield a 10% return ($96,895.40 ÷ 4.16986, Table 6-5)	$ 23,237.09

The amortization schedule is the same for guaranteed or unguaranteed residual value, as Illustration 21-25 shows.

ILLUSTRATION 21-25
Lease Amortization
Schedule, for Lessor—
Guaranteed or
Unguaranteed Residual
Value

CATERPILLAR FINANCIAL
LEASE AMORTIZATION SCHEDULE
ANNUITY-DUE BASIS, GUARANTEED OR UNGUARANTEED RESIDUAL VALUE

Date	Annual Lease Payment Plus Residual Value (a)	Executory Costs (b)	Interest (10%) on Lease Receivable (c)	Lease Receivable Recovery (d)	Lease Receivable (e)
1/1/12					$100,000.00
1/1/12	$ 25,237.09	$ 2,000.00	$ –0–	$ 23,237.09	76,762.91
1/1/13	25,237.09	2,000.00	7,676.29	15,560.80	61,202.11
1/1/14	25,237.09	2,000.00	6,120.21	17,116.88	44,085.23
1/1/15	25,237.09	2,000.00	4,408.52	18,828.57	25,256.66
1/1/16	25,237.09	2,000.00	2,525.67	20,711.42	4,545.24
12/31/16	5,000.00	–0–	454.76*	4,545.24	–0–
	$131,185.45	$10,000.00	$21,185.45	$100,000.00	

(a) Annual lease payment as required by lease.
(b) Executory costs included in rental payment.
(c) Preceding balance of (e) × 10%, except 1/1/12.
(d) (a) minus (b) and (c).
(e) Preceding balance minus (d).

*Rounded by 24 cents.

Using the amounts computed above, Caterpillar would make the following entries for this direct-financing lease in the first year. Note the similarity to Sterling's entries in Illustration 21-23.

ILLUSTRATION 21-26
Entries for Either
Guaranteed or
Unguaranteed Residual
Value, Lessor Company

Inception of lease (January 1, 2012):

Lease Receivable	100,000.00	
Equipment		100,000.00

First payment received (January 1, 2012):

Cash	25,237.09	
Lease Receivable		23,237.09
Property Tax Expense/Property Taxes Payable		2,000.00

Adjusting entry for accrued interest (December 31, 2012):

Interest Receivable	7,676.29	
Interest Revenue		7,676.29

Sales-Type Leases (Lessor)

LEARNING OBJECTIVE 8
Describe the lessor's accounting for sales-type leases.

As already indicated, the primary difference between a direct-financing lease and a **sales-type lease** is the manufacturer's or dealer's gross profit (or loss). The diagram in Illustration 21-27 presents the distinctions between direct-financing and sales-type leases.

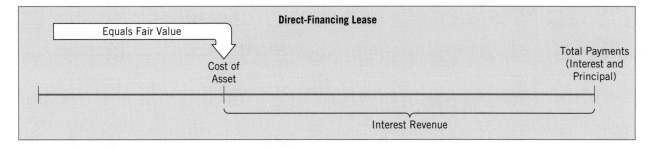

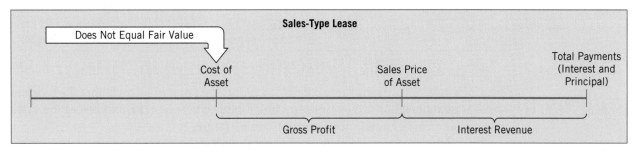

ILLUSTRATION 21-27
Direct-Financing versus
Sales-Type Leases

In a sales-type lease, the lessor records the sales price of the asset, the cost of goods sold and related inventory reduction, and the lease receivable. The information necessary to record the sales-type lease is as follows.

SALES-TYPE LEASE TERMS

LEASE RECEIVABLE (also referred to as NET INVESTMENT). The present value of the minimum lease payments plus the present value of any unguaranteed residual value. The lease receivable therefore includes the present value of the residual value, whether guaranteed or not.

SALES PRICE OF THE ASSET. The present value of the minimum lease payments.

COST OF GOODS SOLD. The cost of the asset to the lessor, less the present value of any unguaranteed residual value.

When recording sales revenue and cost of goods sold, there is a difference in the accounting for guaranteed and unguaranteed residual values. The guaranteed residual value can be considered part of sales revenue because the lessor knows that the entire asset has been sold. But there is less certainty that the unguaranteed residual portion of the asset has been "sold" (i.e., will be realized). Therefore, the lessor recognizes sales and cost of goods sold only for the portion of the asset for which realization is assured. However, **the gross profit amount on the sale of the asset is the same whether a guaranteed or unguaranteed residual value is involved**.

To illustrate a sales-type lease with a guaranteed residual value and with an unguaranteed residual value, assume the same facts as in the preceding direct-financing lease situation (pages 1307–1309). The estimated residual value is $5,000 (the present value of which is $3,104.60), and the leased equipment has an $85,000 cost to the dealer, Caterpillar. Assume that the fair value of the residual value is $3,000 at the end of the lease term.

Illustration 21-28 (page 1318) shows computation of the amounts relevant to a sales-type lease.

ILLUSTRATION 21-28
Computation of Lease
Amounts by Caterpillar
Financial—Sales-Type
Lease

	Sales-Type Lease	
	Guaranteed Residual Value	Unguaranteed Residual Value
Lease receivable	$100,000 [$23,237.09 × 4.16986 (Table 6-5) + $5,000 ×.62092 (Table 6-2)]	Same
Sales price of the asset	$100,000	$96,895.40 ($100,000 − $3,104.60)
Cost of goods sold	$85,000	$81,895.40 ($85,000 − $3,104.60)
Gross profit	$15,000 ($100,000 − $85,000)	$15,000 ($96,895.40 − $81,895.40)

Caterpillar records the same profit ($15,000) at the point of sale whether the residual value is guaranteed or unguaranteed. The difference between the two is that **the sales revenue and cost of goods sold amounts are different**.

In making this computation, we deduct the present value of the unguaranteed residual value from sales revenue and cost of goods sold for two reasons: (1) The criteria for revenue recognition have not been met. (2) It is improper to match expense against revenue not yet recognized. The revenue recognition criteria have not been met **because of the uncertainty surrounding the realization of the unguaranteed residual value**.

Caterpillar makes the following entries to record this transaction on January 1, 2012, and the receipt of the residual value at the end of the lease term.

ILLUSTRATION 21-29
Entries for Guaranteed
and Unguaranteed
Residual Values, Lessor
Company—Sales-Type
Lease

Guaranteed Residual Value			Unguaranteed Residual Value		
To record sales-type lease at inception (January 1, 2012):					
Cost of Goods Sold	85,000.00		Cost of Goods Sold	81,895.40	
Lease Receivable	100,000.00		Lease Receivable	100,000.00	
Sales Revenue		100,000.00	Sales Revenue		96,895.40
Inventory		85,000.00	Inventory		85,000.00
To record receipt of the first lease payment (January 1, 2012):					
Cash	25,237.09		Cash	25,237.09	
Lease Receivable		23,237.09	Lease Receivable		23,237.09
Property Tax Exp./Pay.		2,000.00	Property Tax Exp./Pay.		2,000.00
To recognize interest revenue earned during the first year (December 31, 2012):					
Interest Receivable	7,676.29		Interest Receivable	7,676.29	
Interest Revenue		7,676.29	Interest Revenue		7,676.29
(See lease amortization schedule, Illustration 21-25 on page 1316)					
To record receipt of the second lease payment (January 1, 2012):					
Cash	25,237.09		Cash	25,237.09	
Interest Receivable		7,676.29	Interest Receivable		7,676.29
Lease Receivable		15,560.80	Lease Receivable		15,560.80
Property Tax Exp./Pay.		2,000.00	Property Tax Exp./Pay.		2,000.00
To recognize interest revenue earned during the second year (December 31, 2013):					
Interest Receivable	6,120.21		Interest Receivable	6,120.21	
Interest Revenue		6,120.21	Interest Revenue		6,120.21
To record receipt of residual value at end of lease term (December 31, 2016):					
Inventory	3,000		Inventory	3,000	
Cash	2,000		Loss on Capital Lease	2,000	
Lease Receivable		5,000	Lease Receivable		5,000

Companies must periodically review the **estimated unguaranteed residual value in a sales-type lease**. If the estimate of the unguaranteed residual value declines, the company must revise the accounting for the transaction using the changed estimate. The decline represents a reduction in the lessor's lease receivable (net investment). The lessor recognizes the decline as a loss in the period in which it reduces the residual estimate. Companies do not recognize upward adjustments in estimated residual value.

XEROX TAKES ON THE SEC

What do the numbers mean?

Xerox derives much of its income from leasing equipment. Reporting such leases as sales leases, Xerox records a lease contract as a sale, therefore recognizing income immediately. One problem is that each lease receipt consists of payments for items such as supplies, services, financing, and equipment.

The SEC *accused* Xerox of inappropriately allocating lease receipts, which affects the timing of income that it reports. If Xerox applied SEC guidelines, it would report income in different time periods. Xerox contended that its methods were correct. It also noted that when the lease term is up, the bottom line is the same using either the SEC's recommended allocation method or its current method.

Although Xerox can refuse to change its method, the SEC has the right to prevent a company from selling stock or bonds to the public if the agency rejects filings of the company.

Apparently, being able to access public markets is very valuable to Xerox. The company agreed to change its accounting according to SEC wishes, and Xerox will pay $670 million to settle a shareholder lawsuit related to its lease transactions. Its former auditor, KPMG LLP, will pay $80 million.

Source: Adapted from "Xerox Takes on the SEC," *Accounting Web* (January 9, 2002) (*www. account-ingweb.com*); and K. Shwiff and M. Maremont, "Xerox, KPMG Settle Shareholder Lawsuit," *Wall Street Journal Online* (March 28, 2008), p. B3.

Bargain-Purchase Option (Lessee)

As stated earlier, a bargain-purchase option allows the lessee to purchase the leased property for a future price that is substantially lower than the property's expected future fair value. The price is so favorable at the lease's inception that the future exercise of the option appears to be reasonably assured. If a bargain-purchase option exists, **the lessee must increase the present value of the minimum lease payments by the present value of the option price**.

For example, assume that Sterling Construction in Illustration 21-18 on page 1312 had an option to buy the leased equipment for $5,000 at the end of the five-year lease term. At that point, Sterling and Caterpillar expect the fair value to be $18,000. The significant difference between the option price and the fair value creates a bargain-purchase option, and the exercise of that option is reasonably assured.

A bargain-purchase option affects the accounting for leases in essentially the same way as a guaranteed residual value. In other words, with a guaranteed residual value, the lessee must pay the residual value at the end of the lease. Similarly, a purchase option that is a bargain will almost certainly be paid by the lessee. Therefore, the computations, amortization schedule, and entries that would be prepared for this $5,000 bargain-purchase option are identical to those shown for the $5,000 guaranteed residual value (see Illustrations 21-16, 21-17, and 21-18 on pages 1311 and 1312).

The only difference between the accounting treatment for a bargain-purchase option and a guaranteed residual value of identical amounts and circumstances is in the **computation of the annual depreciation**. In the case of a guaranteed residual value, Sterling depreciates the asset over the lease term; in the case of a bargain-purchase option, it uses the **economic life** of the asset.

Initial Direct Costs (Lessor)

Initial direct costs are of two types: incremental and internal. [8] **Incremental direct costs** are paid to independent third parties for originating a lease arrangement. Examples include the cost of independent appraisal of collateral used to secure a lease, the cost of an outside credit check of the lessee, or a broker's fee for finding the lessee.

Internal direct costs are directly related to specified activities performed **by the lessor** on a given lease. Examples are evaluating the prospective lessee's financial condition; evaluating and recording guarantees, collateral, and other security arrangements; negotiating lease terms and preparing and processing lease documents; and closing the transaction. The costs directly related to an employee's time spent on a specific lease transaction are also considered initial direct costs.

However, initial direct costs should **not** include **internal indirect costs**. Such costs are related to activities the lessor performs for advertising, servicing existing leases, and establishing and monitoring credit policies. Nor should the lessor include the costs for supervision and administration or for expenses such as rent and depreciation.

The accounting for initial direct costs depends on the type of lease:

- For **operating leases**, the lessor should defer initial direct costs and **allocate them over the lease term** in proportion to the recognition of rental revenue.
- For **sales-type leases**, the lessor expenses the initial direct costs **in the period** in which it recognizes the profit on the sale.
- For a **direct-financing lease**, the lessor adds initial direct costs to the net investment in the lease and **amortizes them over the life of the lease as a yield adjustment**.

In a direct-financing lease, the lessor must disclose the unamortized deferred initial direct costs that are part of its investment in the direct-financing lease. For example, if the carrying value of the asset in the lease is $4,000,000 and the lessor incurs initial direct costs of $35,000, then the lease receivable (net investment in the lease) would be $4,035,000. The yield would be lower than the initial rate of return, and the lessor would adjust the yield to ensure proper amortization of the amount over the life of the lease.

Current versus Noncurrent

Earlier in the chapter, we presented the classification of the lease liability/receivable in an annuity-due situation. Illustration 21-7 (on page 1300) indicated that Sterling's current liability is the payment of $23,981.62 (excluding $2,000 of executory costs) to be made on January 1 of the next year. Similarly, as shown in Illustration 21-15 (on page 1309), Caterpillar's current asset is the $23,981.62 (excluding $2,000 of executory costs) it will collect on January 1 of the next year. In these annuity-due instances, the balance sheet date is December 31 and the due date of the lease payment is January 1 (less than one year), so the present value ($23,981.62) of the payment due the following January 1 is the same as the rental payment ($23,981.62).

What happens if the situation is an ordinary annuity rather than an annuity due? For example, assume that the rent is due at the **end of the year** (December 31) rather than at the beginning (January 1). GAAP does not indicate how to measure the current and noncurrent amounts. It requires that for the lessee the "obligations shall be separately identified on the balance sheet as obligations under capital leases and shall be subject to the same considerations as other obligations in classifying them with current and noncurrent liabilities in classified balance sheets." [9] **The most common method of measuring the current liability portion in ordinary annuity leases is the change-in-the-present-value method.**[14]

---

[14]For additional discussion on this approach and possible alternatives, see R. J. Swieringa, "When Current Is Noncurrent and Vice Versa!" *The Accounting Review* (January 1984), pp. 123–30; and A. W. Richardson, "The Measurement of the Current Portion of the Long-Term Lease Obligations—Some Evidence from Practice," *The Accounting Review* (October 1985), pp. 744–52.

To illustrate the change-in-the-present-value method, assume an ordinary-annuity situation with the same facts as the Caterpillar/Sterling case, excluding the $2,000 of executory costs. Because Sterling pays the rents at the end of the period instead of at the beginning, Caterpillar sets the five rents at $26,379.73, to have an effective-interest rate of 10 percent. Illustration 21-30 shows the ordinary-annuity amortization schedule.

		STERLING/CATERPILLAR LEASE AMORTIZATION SCHEDULE ORDINARY-ANNUITY BASIS		
Date	Annual Lease Payment	Interest 10%	Reduction of Lease Liability/Receivable	Balance of Lease Liability/Receivable
1/1/12				$100,000.00
12/31/12	$ 26,379.73	$10,000.00	$ 16,379.73	83,620.27
12/31/13	26,379.73	8,362.03	18,017.70	65,602.57
12/31/14	26,379.73	6,560.26	19,819.47	45,783.10
12/31/15	26,379.73	4,578.31	21,801.42	23,981.68
12/31/16	26,379.73	2,398.05*	23,981.68	–0–
	$131,898.65	$31,898.65	$100,000.00	

*Rounded by 12 cents.

ILLUSTRATION 21-30
Lease Amortization Schedule—Ordinary-Annuity Basis

The current portion of the lease liability/receivable under the **change-in-the-present-value method** as of December 31, 2012, would be $18,017.70 ($83,620.27 − $65,602.57). As of December 31, 2013, the current portion would be $19,819.47 ($65,602.57 − $45,783.10). At December 31, 2012, Caterpillar classifies $65,602.57 of the receivable as noncurrent.

Thus, both the annuity-due and the ordinary-annuity situations report the reduction of principal for the next period as a current liability/current asset. In the annuity-due situation, Caterpillar accrues interest during the year but is not paid until the next period. As a result, **a current asset arises for the receivable reduction and for the interest** that was earned in the preceding period.

In the ordinary-annuity situation, the interest accrued during the period is also paid in the same period. Consequently, the lessor shows as a current asset only the principal reduction.

Disclosing Lease Data

The FASB requires **lessees** and **lessors** to disclose certain information about leases in their financial statements or in the notes. These requirements vary based upon the type of lease (capital or operating) and whether the issuer is the lessor or lessee. These disclosure requirements provide investors with the following information.

 **9 LEARNING OBJECTIVE**
List the disclosure requirements for leases.

- General description of the nature of leasing arrangements.
- The nature, timing, and amount of cash inflows and outflows associated with leases, including payments to be paid or received for each of the five succeeding years.
- The amount of lease revenues and expenses reported in the income statement each period.
- Description and amounts of leased assets by major balance sheet classification and related liabilities.
- Amounts receivable and unearned revenues under lease agreements. [10]

Illustration 21-31 (on page 1322) presents financial statement excerpts from the 2009 annual report of Tasty Baking Company. These excerpts represent the statement and note disclosures typical of a lessee having both capital leases and operating leases.

ILLUSTRATION 21-31
Disclosure of Leases by
Lessee

Description and amount of lease obligations

Tasty Baking Company
(dollar amounts in thousands)

	2009	2008
Current Liabilities		
Current obligations under capital leases	$ 919	$ 720
Noncurrent Liabilities		
Long-term obligations under capital leases, less current portion	$1,387	$1,199

General description

Note 8: Commitments and Contingencies

The Company leases certain facilities, machinery, automotive equipment, computer equipment and facilities, including the new manufacturing and distribution facility at the Philadelphia Navy Yard under noncancelable lease agreements. The Company expects that in the normal course of business, leases that expire will be renewed or replaced by other leases. Property, plant and equipment related to capital leases were $3.8 million at December 26, 2009, and $2.6 million at December 27, 2008, with accumulated amortization of $1.5 million and $0.7 million, respectively. Depreciation and amortization of assets recorded under capital leases was $0.8 million in 2009 and $0.6 million in 2008.

Description and amounts of leased assets

The following is a schedule of future minimum lease payments as of December 26, 2009 (in thousands):

	Capital Leases	Noncancelable Operating Leases
2010	$1,066	$ 2,850
2011	799	6,298
2012	451	6,054
2013	167	6,112
2014	99	6,039
Later years	—	151,058
Total minimum lease payments	$2,582	$178,411
Less interest portion of payments	(276)	
Present value of future minimum lease payments	$2,306	

Nature, timing, and amounts of cash outflows

Amount of lease rental expense

Rental expense was approximately $4.5 million in 2009 and $2.2 million in 2008.

Illustration 21-32 presents the lease note disclosure from the 2009 annual report of Hewlett-Packard Company. The disclosure highlights required lessor disclosures.

ILLUSTRATION 21-32
Disclosure of Leases by
Lessor

Hewlett-Packard Company
Notes to Financial Statements
(in millions)

General description

Note 11: Financing Receivables and Operating Leases

Financing receivables represent sales-type and direct-financing leases resulting from the marketing of HP's and third-party products. These receivables typically have terms from two to five years and are usually collateralized by a security interest in the underlying assets. Financing receivables also include billed receivables from operating leases. The components of net financing receivables, which are included in financing receivables and long-term financing receivables and other assets, were as follows for the following fiscal years ended October 31:

	2009	2008
Minimum lease payments receivable	$6,413	$5,338
Allowance for doubtful accounts	(108)	(90)
Unguaranteed residual value	244	254
Unearned income	(571)	(466)
Financing receivables, net	5,978	5,036
Less current portion	(2,675)	(2,314)
Amounts due after one year, net	$3,303	$2,722

Amount receivable and unearned revenues

ILLUSTRATION 21-32
(Continued)

As of October 31, 2009, scheduled maturities of HP's minimum lease payments receivable were as follows for the following fiscal years ended October 31:

	2010	2011	2012	2013	Thereafter	Total
Scheduled maturities of minimum lease payments receivable	$2,956	$1,816	$1,007	$427	$207	$6,413

Nature, timing, and amounts of cash inflows

Equipment leased to customers under operating leases was $3.0 billion at October 31, 2009 and $2.3 billion at October 31, 2008 and is included in machinery and equipment. Accumulated depreciation on equipment under lease was $0.9 billion at October 31, 2009 and $0.5 billion at October 31, 2008. As of October 31, 2009, minimum future rentals on non-cancelable operating leases related to leased equipment were as follows for the following fiscal years ended October 31:

Description of leased assets

	2010	2011	2012	2013	Thereafter	Total
Minimum future rentals on non-cancelable operating leases	$976	$647	$336	$114	$49	$2,122

Amount of future rentals

LEASE ACCOUNTING—UNRESOLVED PROBLEMS

As we indicated at the beginning of this chapter, lease accounting is subject to abuse. Companies make strenuous efforts to circumvent GAAP in this area. In practice, the strong desires of lessees to resist capitalization have rendered the accounting rules for capitalizing leases partially ineffective. Leasing generally involves large dollar amounts that, when capitalized, materially increase reported liabilities and adversely affect the debt-to-equity ratio. Lessees also resist lease capitalization because charges to expense made in the early years of the lease term are higher under the capital lease method than under the operating method, frequently without tax benefit. As a consequence, "let's beat the lease standard" is one of the most popular games in town.[15]

To avoid leased asset capitalization, companies design, write, and interpret lease agreements to prevent satisfying any of the four capitalized lease criteria. Companies can easily devise lease agreements in such a way, by meeting the following specifications.

1. Ensure that the lease does not specify the transfer of title of the property to the lessee.

2. Do not write in a bargain-purchase option.

3. Set the lease term at something less than 75 percent of the estimated economic life of the leased property.

4. Arrange for the present value of the minimum lease payments to be less than 90 percent of the fair value of the leased property.

The real challenge lies in disqualifying the lease as a capital lease to the lessee, while having the same lease qualify as a capital (sales or financing) lease to the lessor. Unlike lessees, lessors try to avoid having lease arrangements classified as operating leases.[16]

---

[15]Richard Dieter, "Is Lessee Accounting Working?" *CPA Journal* (August 1979), pp. 13–19. This article provides interesting examples of abuses of GAAP in this area, discusses the circumstances that led to the current situation, and proposes a solution.

[16]The reason is that most lessors are banks, which are not permitted to hold these assets on their balance sheets except for relatively short periods of time. Furthermore, the capital lease transaction from the lessor's standpoint provides higher income flows in the earlier periods of the lease life.

Avoiding the first three criteria is relatively simple, but it takes a little ingenuity to avoid the "90 percent recovery test" for the lessee while satisfying it for the lessor. Two of the factors involved in this effort are: (1) the use of the incremental borrowing rate by the lessee when it is higher than the implicit interest rate of the lessor, by making information about the implicit rate unavailable to the lessee; and (2) residual value guarantees.

The lessee's use of the higher interest rate is probably the more popular subterfuge. Lessees are knowledgeable about the fair value of the leased property and, of course, the rental payments. However, they generally are unaware of the estimated residual value used by the lessor. Therefore, the lessee who does not know exactly the lessor's implicit interest rate might use a different (higher) incremental borrowing rate.

The residual value guarantee is the other unique, yet popular, device used by lessees and lessors. In fact, a whole new industry has emerged to circumvent symmetry between the lessee and the lessor in accounting for leases. The residual value guarantee has spawned numerous companies whose principal, or even sole, function is to guarantee the residual value of leased assets.

Because the minimum lease payments include the guaranteed residual value for the lessor, this satisfies the 90 percent recovery of the fair value test. The lease is a nonoperating lease to the lessor. **But because a third-party guarantees the residual value, the minimum lease payments of the lessee exclude the guarantee.** Thus, by merely transferring some of the risk to a third party, lessees can alter substantially the accounting treatment by converting what would otherwise be capital leases to operating leases.[17]

The nature of the criteria encourages much of this circumvention, stemming from weaknesses in the basic objective of the lease-accounting guidelines. Accounting rule-makers continue to have poor experience with arbitrary break points or other size and percentage criteria—such as rules like "90 percent of" and "75 percent of." Some believe that a more workable solution is to require capitalization of all leases that have noncancelable payment terms in excess of one year. Under this approach, the lessee acquires an asset (a property right) and a corresponding liability, rather than on the basis that the lease transfers substantially all the risks and rewards of ownership.

INTERNATIONAL PERSPECTIVE

Recently, the IASB and the FASB have agreed to jointly undertake a project to reconsider lease-accounting standards.

Three years after it issued a lease-accounting pronouncement, a majority of the FASB expressed "the tentative view that, if the lease-accounting rules were to be reconsidered, they would support a property right approach in which all leases are included as 'rights to use property' and as 'lease obligations' in the lessee's balance sheet."[18] The FASB and IASB have issued a proposal on lease accounting to address off-balance-sheet reporting of leases. As summarized in Illustration 21-33, early analysis of the potential impact of the proposed leasing rules indicates significant impacts.[19]

---

[17]As an aside, third-party guarantors have experienced some difficulty. Lloyd's of London, at one time, insured the fast-growing U.S. computer-leasing industry in the amount of $2 billion against revenue losses, and losses in residual value, for canceled leases. Because of "overnight" technological improvements and the successive introductions of more efficient and less expensive computers, lessees in abundance canceled their leases. As the market for secondhand computers became flooded, residual values plummeted, and third-party guarantor Lloyd's of London projected a loss of $400 million. The lessees' and lessors' desire to circumvent GAAP stimulated much of the third-party guarantee business.

[18]"Is Lessee Accounting Working?" op. cit., p. 19; and H. Nailor and A. Lennard, "Capital Leases: Implementation of a New Approach," *Financial Accounting Series No. 206A* (Norwalk, Conn.: FASB, 2000).

[19]See *http://www.fasb.org/project/leases.shtml* for the latest information on the lease-accounting project.

> **A quick look at the current leasing market, and some possible effects of the proposed rules:**
>
> - **$600 billion.** Annual volume of leased equipment.
> - **70%.** Volume of real estate leases as a percentage of all leases held by U.S. public companies.
> - **$1.3 trillion.** Amount of operating lease payments that U.S. public companies will bring back on balance sheets as capital leases under the proposed rule.
> - **7%.** Potential first-year average increase in lease expense for a 3-year lease.
> - **21%.** Potential first-year average increase in lease expense for a 10-year lease.
>
> *Source:* Equipment Leasing and Finance Association, 2009; PricewaterhouseCoopers and Rotterdam School of Management, 2009.

ILLUSTRATION 21-33
Leasing Statistics and
Accounting Impacts

As indicated, over $1.1 trillion of operating leases will come on-balance-sheet if the rules are adopted. In addition, there will be a significant negative impact on lessee income statements in the early years of leases. As shown in Illustration 21-34, the front-loading of lease expenses will be felt by lessees in several industry sectors.

ILLUSTRATION 21-34
Lease Expense Impacts—
By Industry Sector

Sector	Typical Lease Term (Years)	First-Year % Increase Prompted by New Rules*	Cumulative % Increase Through Peak Year*
Airline	17	26%	128%/yr. 9
Automotive fleet	3	4	N/A
Banking	10	21	64%/yr. 5
Copier/office equipment	3	7	7%/yr. 3
Industrial-equipment manufacturers	5	11	17%/yr. 2
Health-care equipment	5	11	17%/yr. 2
Information technology	3	7	7%/yr. 2
Rail	22	26	200%/yr. 12
Real estate	10	21	64%/yr. 5
Trucking	7	16	33%/yr. 4

*As compared with the straight-line method of accounting.

Source: Equipment Leasing and Finance Association, 2009.

Given these effects—increased reported debt and lower income—as a consequence of these proposed rules, it is not surprising that the FASB (and IASB) are receiving numerous comments opposing changes in lease-accounting rules. These concerns may be valid, but we hope that new accounting rules can be developed so that financial statements provide relevant and representationally faithful information about leasing arrangements.[20]

You will want to read the
IFRS INSIGHTS
on pages 1355–1365

for discussion of IFRS related
to lease accounting.

---

[20]M. Leone, "Taking the 'Ease' Out of 'Lease'?" *CFO Magazine* (December 1, 2010).

SUMMARY OF LEARNING OBJECTIVES

1 **Explain the nature, economic substance, and advantages of lease transactions.**
A lease is a contractual agreement between a lessor and a lessee that conveys to the lessee the right to use specific property (real or personal), owned by the lessor, for a specified period of time. In return, the lessee periodically pays cash (rent) to the lessor. The advantages of lease transactions are: (1) 100 percent financing, (2) protection against obsolescence, (3) flexibility, (4) less costly financing, (5) possible tax advantages, and (6) off-balance-sheet financing.

2 **Describe the accounting criteria and procedures for capitalizing leases by the lessee.** A lease is a capital lease if it meets one or more of the following criteria: (1) The lease transfers ownership of the property to the lessee. (2) The lease contains a bargain-purchase option. (3) The lease term is equal to 75 percent or more of the estimated economic life of the leased property. (4) The present value of the minimum lease payments (excluding executory costs) equals or exceeds 90 percent of the fair value of the leased property. For a capital lease, the lessee records an asset and a liability at the lower of (1) the present value of the minimum lease payments, or (2) the fair value of the leased asset at the inception of the lease.

3 **Contrast the operating and capitalization methods of recording leases.**
The total charges to operations are the same over the lease term whether accounting for the lease as a capital lease or as an operating lease. Under the capital lease treatment, the charges are higher in the earlier years and lower in the later years. If using an accelerated method of depreciation, the differences between the amounts charged to operations under the two methods would be even larger in the earlier and later years. If using a capital lease instead of an operating lease, the following occurs: (1) an increase in the amount of reported debt (both short-term and long-term), (2) an increase in the amount of total assets (specifically long-lived assets), and (3) lower income early in the life of the lease and, therefore, lower retained earnings.

4 **Identify the classifications of leases for the lessor.** A lessor may classify leases for accounting purposes as follows: (1) operating leases, (2) direct-financing leases, (3) sales-type leases. The lessor should classify and account for an arrangement as a direct-financing lease or a sales-type lease if, at the date of the lease agreement, the lease meets one or more of the Group I criteria (as shown in Learning Objective 2 for lessees) and *both* of the following Group II criteria. *Group II:* (1) Collectibility of the payments required from the lessee is reasonably predictable; and (2) no important uncertainties surround the amount of unreimbursable costs yet to be incurred by the lessor under the lease. The lessor classifies and accounts for all leases that fail to meet the criteria as operating leases.

5 **Describe the lessor's accounting for direct-financing leases.** Leases that are in substance the financing of an asset purchase by a lessee require the lessor to substitute a "lease receivable" for the leased asset. "Lease receivable" is the present value of the minimum lease payments plus the present value of the unguaranteed residual value. Therefore, lessors include the residual value, whether guaranteed or unguaranteed, as part of the lease receivable.

6 **Identify special features of lease arrangements that cause unique accounting problems.** The features of lease arrangements that cause unique accounting problems are: (1) residual values; (2) sales-type leases (lessor); (3) bargain-purchase options; (4) initial direct costs; (5) current versus noncurrent; and (6) disclosures.

7 **Describe the effect of residual values, guaranteed and unguaranteed, on lease accounting.** Whether the estimated residual value is guaranteed or unguaranteed is of both economic and accounting consequence to the lessee. The accounting consequence is that the minimum lease payments, the basis for capitalization, include the guaranteed residual value but exclude the unguaranteed residual value. A guaranteed residual value affects the lessee's computation of minimum lease payments and the amounts capitalized as a leased asset and a lease obligation. In effect, the guaranteed residual value is an additional lease payment that the lessee will pay in property or cash, or both, at the end of the lease term. An unguaranteed residual value from the lessee's viewpoint is the same as no residual value in terms of its effect upon the lessee's method of computing the minimum lease payments and the capitalization of the leased asset and the lease liability.

8 **Describe the lessor's accounting for sales-type leases.** A sales-type lease recognizes interest revenue like a direct-financing lease. It also recognizes a manufacturer's or dealer's profit. In a sales-type lease, the lessor records at the inception of the lease the sales price of the asset, the cost of goods sold and related inventory reduction, and the lease receivable. Sales-type leases differ from direct-financing leases in terms of the cost and fair value of the leased asset, which results in gross profit. Lease receivable and interest revenue are the same whether a guaranteed or an unguaranteed residual value is involved. The accounting for guaranteed and for unguaranteed residual values requires recording sales revenue and cost of goods sold differently. The guaranteed residual value can be considered part of sales revenue because the lessor knows that the entire asset has been sold. There is less certainty that the unguaranteed residual portion of the asset has been "sold"; therefore, lessors recognize sales and cost of goods sold only for the portion of the asset for which realization is assured. However, the gross profit amount on the sale of the asset is the same whether a guaranteed or unguaranteed residual value is involved.

9 **List the disclosure requirements for leases.** The disclosure requirements for the lessees and lessors vary based upon the type of lease (capital or operating) and whether the issuer is the lessor or lessee. These disclosure requirements provide investors with the following information: (1) general description of the nature of leasing arrangements; (2) the nature, timing, and amount of cash inflows and outflows associated with leases, including payments to be paid or received for each of the five succeeding years; (3) the amount of lease revenues and expenses reported in the income statement each period; (4) description and amounts of leased assets by major balance sheet classification and related liabilities; and (5) amounts receivable and unearned revenues under lease agreements.

Gateway to the Profession

Expanded Discussion of Real Estate Leases and Leveraged Leases

---

| APPENDIX **21A** | EXAMPLES OF LEASE ARRANGEMENTS |

To illustrate concepts discussed in this chapter, assume that Morgan Bakeries is involved in four different lease situations. Each of these leases is noncancelable, and in no case does Morgan receive title to the properties leased during or at the end of the lease term. All leases start on January 1, 2012, with the first rental due at the beginning of the year. The additional information is shown in Illustration 21A-1 (on page 1328).

10 LEARNING OBJECTIVE
Understand and apply lease-accounting concepts to various lease arrangements.

	Harmon, Inc.	Arden's Oven Co.	Mendota Truck Co.	Appleland Computer
Type of property	Cabinets	Oven	Truck	Computer
Yearly rental	$6,000	$15,000	$5,582.62	$3,557.25
Lease term	20 years	10 years	3 years	3 years
Estimated economic life	30 years	25 years	7 years	5 years
Purchase option	None	$75,000 at end of 10 years $4,000 at end of 15 years	None	$3,000 at end of 3 years, which approximates fair value
Renewal option	None	5-year renewal option at $15,000 per year	None	1 year at $1,500; no penalty for nonrenewal; standard renewal clause
Fair value at inception of lease	$60,000	$120,000	$20,000	$10,000
Cost of asset to lessor	$60,000	$120,000	$15,000	$10,000
Residual value				
Guaranteed	–0–	–0–	$7,000	–0–
Unguaranteed	$5,000	–0–	–0–	$3,000
Incremental borrowing rate of lessee	12%	12%	12%	12%
Executory costs paid by	*Lessee* $300 per year	*Lessee* $1,000 per year	*Lessee* $500 per year	*Lessor* Estimated to be $500 per year, included in lease payment
Present value of minimum lease payments				
Using incremental borrowing rate of lessee	$50,194.68	$115,153.35	$20,000	$8,224.16
Using implicit rate of lessor	Not known	Not known	Not known	Known by lessee, $8,027.48
Estimated fair value at end of lease	$5,000	$80,000 at end of 10 years $60,000 at end of 15 years	Not available	$3,000

ILLUSTRATION 21A-1
Illustrative Lease
Situations, Lessors

EXAMPLE 1: HARMON, INC.

The following is an analysis of the Harmon, Inc. lease.

1. Transfer of title? No.

2. Bargain-purchase option? No.

3. Economic life test (75% test). The lease term is 20 years and the estimated economic life is 30 years. Thus it **does not** meet the 75 percent test.

4. Recovery of investment test (90% test):

Fair value	$60,000	Rental payments	$	6,000
Rate	× 90%	PV of annuity due for		
90% of fair value	$54,000	20 years at 12%		× 8.36578
		PV of rental payments		$50,194.68

Because the present value of the minimum lease payments is less than 90 percent of the fair value, the lease does not meet the 90 percent test.

Both Morgan and Harmon should account for this lease as an operating lease, as indicated by the January 1, 2012, entries shown in Illustration 21A-2.

Morgan Bakeries (Lessee)		Harmon, Inc. (Lessor)	
Rent Expense	6,000	Cash	6,000
Cash	6,000	Rent Revenue	6,000

EXAMPLE 2: ARDEN'S OVEN CO.

The following is an analysis of the Arden's Oven Co. lease.

1. **Transfer of title?** No.
2. **Bargain-purchase option?** The $75,000 option at the end of 10 years does not appear to be sufficiently lower than the expected fair value of $80,000 to make it reasonably assured that it will be exercised. However, the $4,000 at the end of 15 years when the fair value is $60,000 does appear to be a bargain. From the information given, criterion 2 is therefore met. Note that both the guaranteed and the unguaranteed residual values are assigned zero values because the lessor does not expect to repossess the leased asset.
3. **Economic life test (75% test):** Given that a bargain-purchase option exists, the lease term is the initial lease period of 10 years plus the five-year renewal option since it precedes a bargain-purchase option. Even though the lease term is now considered to be 15 years, this test is still not met because 75 percent of the economic life of 25 years is 18.75 years.
4. **Recovery of investment test (90% test):**

Fair value	$120,000	Rental payments	$ 15,000.00
Rate	× 90%	PV of annuity due for 15 years at 12%	× 7.62817
90% of fair value	$108,000	PV of rental payments	$114,422.55

PV of bargain-purchase option: $= \$4,000 \times (PVF_{15,12\%}) = \$4,000 \times .18270 = \$730.80$

PV of rental payments	$114,422.55
PV of bargain-purchase option	730.80
PV of minimum lease payments	$115,153.35

The present value of the minimum lease payments is greater than 90 percent of the fair value; therefore, the lease does meet the 90 percent test.

Morgan Bakeries should account for this as a capital lease because the lease meets both criteria 2 and 4. Assuming that Arden's implicit rate is less than Morgan's incremental borrowing rate, the following entries are made on January 1, 2012.

Morgan Bakeries (Lessee)		Arden's Oven Co. (Lessor)	
Leased Equipment (oven)	115,153.35	Lease Receivable	120,000
Lease Liability	115,153.35	Equipment (oven)	120,000

Morgan Bakeries would depreciate the leased asset over its economic life of 25 years, given the bargain-purchase option. Arden's Oven Co. does not use sales-type accounting because the fair value and the cost of the asset are the same at the inception of the lease.

EXAMPLE 3: MENDOTA TRUCK CO.

The following is an analysis of the Mendota Truck Co. lease.

1. **Transfer of title?** No.
2. **Bargain-purchase option?** No.

3. Economic life test (75% test): The lease term is three years and the estimated economic life is seven years. Thus it **does not** meet the 75 percent test.

4. Recovery of investment test (90% test):

Fair value	$20,000	Rental payments	$ 5,582.62
Rate	× 90%	PV of annuity due for	
90% of fair value	$18,000	3 years at 12%	× 2.69005
		PV of rental payments	$15,017.54

(*Note:* Adjusted for $0.01 due to rounding.)

PV of guaranteed residual value: = $7,000 × (PVF$_{3,12\%}$) = $7,000 × .71178 = $4,982.46

PV of rental payments	$15,017.54
PV of guaranteed residual value	4,982.46
PV of minimum lease payments	$20,000.00

The present value of the minimum lease payments is greater than 90 percent of the fair value; therefore, the lease meets the 90 percent test.

Assuming that Mendota's implicit rate is the same as Morgan's incremental borrowing rate, the following entries are made on January 1, 2012.

ILLUSTRATION 21A-4
Comparative Entries for
Capital Lease

Morgan Bakeries (Lessee)			Mendota Truck Co. (Lessor)			
Leased Equipment (truck)	20,000		Lease Receivable	20,000		
Lease Liability		20,000	Cost of Goods Sold	15,000		
			Trucks			15,000
			Sales Revenue			20,000

Because the cost of the truck is less than the fair value, this is a sales-type lease for Mendota. Morgan depreciates the leased asset over three years to its guaranteed residual value.

EXAMPLE 4: APPLELAND COMPUTER

The following is an analysis of the Appleland Computer lease.

1. Transfer of title? No.

2. Bargain-purchase option? No. The option to purchase at the end of three years at approximate fair value is clearly not a bargain.

3. Economic life test (75% test): The lease term is three years, and no bargain-renewal period exists. Therefore the 75 percent test **is not** met.

4. Recovery of investment test (90% test):

Fair value	$10,000	Rental payments	$3,557.25
Rate	× 90%	Less executory costs	500.00
90% of fair value	$ 9,000		3,057.25
		PV of annuity-due factor	
		for 3 years at 12%	× 2.69005
		PV of minimum lease payments	
		using incremental borrowing rate	$8,224.16

The present value of the minimum lease payments using the incremental borrowing rate is $8,224.16; using the implicit rate, it is $8,027.48 (see Illustration 21A-1 on page 1328). The lessor's implicit rate is therefore higher than the incremental borrowing rate. Given this situation, the lessee uses the $8,224.16 (lower interest rate when discounting) when comparing with the 90 percent of fair value. Because the present value of the minimum lease payments is lower than 90 percent of the fair value, the lease does **not** meet the recovery of investment test.

The following entries are made on January 1, 2012, indicating an operating lease.

Morgan Bakeries (Lessee)		Appleland Computer (Lessor)	
Rent Expense	3,557.25	Cash	3,557.25
Cash	3,557.25	Rent Revenue	3,557.25

If the lease payments had been $3,557.25 with no executory costs involved, this lease arrangement would have qualified for capital-lease accounting treatment.

SUMMARY OF LEARNING OBJECTIVE FOR APPENDIX 21A

10 **Understand and apply lease-accounting concepts to various lease arrangements.** The classification of leases by lessees and lessors is based on criteria that assess whether the lessor has transferred to the lessee substantially all of the risks and benefits of ownership of the asset. In addition, lessors assess two additional criteria to ensure that payment is assured and that there are not uncertainties about lessor's future costs. Lessees capitalize leases that meet any of the criteria, recording a lease asset and related lease liability. For leases that are in substance a financing of an asset purchase, lessors substitute a lease receivable for the leased asset. In a sales-type lease, the fair value of the leased asset is greater than the cost, and lessors record gross profit. Leases that do not meet capitalization criteria are classified as operating leases, on which rent expense (revenue) is recognized by lessees (lessors) for lease payments.

APPENDIX 21B **SALE-LEASEBACKS**

The term **sale-leaseback** describes a transaction in which the owner of the property (seller-lessee) sells the property to another and simultaneously leases it back from the new owner. The use of the property is generally continued without interruption.

Sale-leasebacks are common. Financial institutions (e.g., **Bank of America** and **First Chicago**) have used this technique for their administrative offices, public utilities (**Ohio Edison** and **Pinnacle West Corporation**) for their generating plants, and airlines (**Continental** and **Alaska Airlines**) for their aircraft. The advantages of a sale-leaseback from the seller's viewpoint usually involve two primary considerations:

11 LEARNING OBJECTIVE
Describe the lessee's accounting for sale-leaseback transactions.

1. *Financing.* If the purchase of equipment has already been financed, a sale-leaseback can allow the seller to refinance at lower rates, assuming rates have dropped. In addition, a sale-leaseback can provide another source of working capital, particularly when liquidity is tight.

2. *Taxes.* At the time a company purchased equipment, it may not have known that it would be subject to an alternative minimum tax and that ownership might increase its minimum tax liability. By selling the property, the seller-lessee may deduct the entire lease payment, which is not subject to alternative minimum tax considerations.

DETERMINING ASSET USE

To the extent the **seller-lessee continues to use** the asset after the sale, the sale-leaseback is really a form of financing. Therefore, the lessor **should not recognize a gain or loss** on the transaction. In short, the seller-lessee is simply borrowing funds.

On the other hand, if the **seller-lessee gives up the right to the use** of the asset, the transaction is in substance a sale. In that case, **gain or loss recognition** is appropriate.

Underlying Concepts

A sale-leaseback is similar in substance to the parking of inventories (discussed in Chapter 8). The ultimate economic benefits remain under the control of the "seller," thus satisfying the definition of an asset.

Trying to ascertain when the lessee has given up the use of the asset is difficult, however, and the FASB has formulated complex rules to identify this situation.[21] To understand the profession's position in this area, we discuss the basic accounting for the lessee and lessor below.

Lessee

If the lease meets one of the four criteria for treatment as a capital lease (see Illustration 21-3 on page 1295), the **seller-lessee accounts for the transaction as a sale and the lease as a capital lease.** The seller-lessee should defer any profit or loss it experiences from the sale of the assets that are leased back under a capital lease; it should **amortize that profit over the lease term** (or the economic life if either criterion 1 or 2 is satisfied) in proportion to the amortization of the leased assets.

For example, assume Scott Paper sells equipment having a book value of $580,000 and a fair value of $623,110 to General Electric Credit for $623,110 and leases the equipment back for $50,000 a year for 20 years. Scott should amortize the profit of $43,110 over the 20-year period at the same rate that it depreciates the $623,110. [12] It credits the $43,110 ($623,110 − $580,000) to **Unearned Profit on Sale-Leaseback.**

If none of the capital lease criteria are satisfied, **the seller-lessee accounts for the transaction as a sale and the lease as an operating lease.** Under an operating lease, the lessee defers such profit or loss and amortizes it in proportion to the rental payments over the period when it expects to use the assets.

There are exceptions to these two general rules. They are:

1. *Losses recognized.* When the fair value of the asset is **less than the book value** (carrying amount), the lessee must recognize a loss immediately, up to the amount of the difference between the book value and fair value. For example, if Lessee, Inc. sells equipment having a book value of $650,000 and a fair value of $623,110, it should charge the difference of $26,890 to a loss account.[22]

2. *Minor leaseback.* Leasebacks in which the present value of the rental payments are 10 percent or less of the fair value of the asset are **minor leasebacks**. In this case, the seller-lessee gives up most of the rights to the use of the asset sold. Therefore, the transaction is a sale, and full gain or loss recognition is appropriate. It is not a financing transaction because the risks of ownership have been transferred.[23]

Lessor

If the lease meets one of the criteria in Group I and both of the criteria in Group II (see Illustration 21-10 on page 1305), the **purchaser-lessor** records the transaction as a purchase and a direct-financing lease. If the lease does not meet the criteria, the purchaser-lessor records the transaction as a purchase and an operating lease.

SALE-LEASEBACK EXAMPLE

To illustrate the accounting treatment accorded a sale-leaseback transaction, assume that American Airlines on January 1, 2012, sells a used Boeing 757 having a carrying amount on its books of $75,500,000 to CitiCapital for $80,000,000. American immediately leases the aircraft back under the following conditions:

[21]Sales and leasebacks of real estate are often accounted for differently. A discussion of the issues related to these transactions is beyond the scope of this textbook. [11]

[22]There can be two types of losses in sale-leaseback arrangements. One is a real economic loss that results when the carrying amount of the asset is higher than the fair value of the asset. In this case, the loss should be recognized. An artificial loss results when the sales price is below the carrying amount of the asset but the fair value is above the carrying amount. In this case, the loss is more in the form of prepaid rent, and the lessee should defer the loss and amortize it in the future.

[23]In some cases the seller-lessee retains more than a minor part but less than substantially all. The computations to arrive at these values are complex and beyond the scope of this textbook.

1. The term of the lease is 15 years, noncancelable, and requires equal rental payments of $10,487,443 at the beginning of each year.

2. The aircraft has a fair value of $80,000,000 on January 1, 2012, and an estimated economic life of 15 years.

3. American pays all executory costs.

4. American depreciates similar aircraft that it owns on a straight-line basis over 15 years.

5. The annual payments assure the lessor a 12 percent return.

6. American's incremental borrowing rate is 12 percent.

This lease is a capital lease to American because the lease term exceeds 75 percent of the estimated life of the aircraft and because the present value of the lease payments exceeds 90 percent of the fair value of the aircraft to CitiCapital. Assuming that collectibility of the lease payments is reasonably predictable and that no important uncertainties exist in relation to unreimbursable costs yet to be incurred by CitiCapital, it should classify this lease as a direct-financing lease.

Illustration 21B-1 presents the typical journal entries to record the sale-leaseback transactions for American and CitiCapital for the first year.

ILLUSTRATION 21B-1
Comparative Entries for Sale-Leaseback for Lessee and Lessor

American Airlines (Lessee)		CitiCapital (Lessor)	
Sale of Aircraft by American to CitiCapital (January 1, 2012):			
Cash	80,000,000	Aircraft	80,000,000
Aircraft	75,500,000	Cash	80,000,000
Unearned Profit on Sale-Leaseback	4,500,000	Lease Receivable	80,000,000
Leased Aircraft (under capital leases)	80,000,000	Aircraft	80,000,000
Lease Liability	80,000,000		
First Lease Payment (January 1, 2012):			
Lease Liability	10,487,443	Cash	10,487,443
Cash	10,487,443	Lease Receivable	10,487,443
Incurrence and Payment of Executory Costs by American Corp. throughout 2012:			
Insurance, Maintenance, Taxes, etc.	XXX	(No entry)	
Cash or Accounts Payable	XXX		
Depreciation Expense on the Aircraft (December 31, 2012):			
Depreciation Expense	5,333,333	(No entry)	
Accumulated Depr.— Capital Leases ($80,000,000 ÷ 15)	5,333,333		
Amortization of Profit on Sale-Leaseback by American (December 31, 2012):			
Unearned Profit on Sale-Leaseback	300,000	(No entry)	
Depreciation Expense ($4,500,000 ÷ 15)	300,000		
(*Note:* A case might be made for crediting Sales Revenue instead of Depreciation Expense.)			
Interest for 2012 (December 31, 2012):			
Interest Expense	8,341,507[a]	Interest Receivable	8,341,507
Interest Payable	8,341,507	Interest Revenue	8,341,507[a]

[a]Partial Lease Amortization Schedule:

Date	Annual Rental Payment	Interest 12%	Reduction of Balance	Balance
1/1/12				$80,000,000
1/1/12	$10,487,443	$ –0–	$10,487,443	69,512,557
1/1/13	10,487,443	8,341,507	2,145,936	67,366,621

KEY TERMS

minor leaseback, *1332*
sale-leaseback, *1331*

SUMMARY OF LEARNING OBJECTIVE FOR APPENDIX 21B

11 **Describe the lessee's accounting for sale-leaseback transactions.** If the lease meets one of the four criteria for treatment as a capital lease, the seller-lessee accounts for the transaction as a sale and the lease as a capital lease. The seller-lessee defers any profit it experiences from the sale of the assets that are leased back under a capital lease. The seller-lessee amortizes any profit over the lease term (or the economic life if either criterion 1 or 2 is satisfied) in proportion to the amortization of the leased assets. If the lease satisfies none of the capital lease criteria, the seller-lessee accounts for the transaction as a sale and the lease as an operating lease. Under an operating lease, the lessee defers such profit and amortizes it in proportion to the rental payments over the period of time that it expects to use the assets.

 FASB CODIFICATION

FASB Codification References

[1] FASB ASC 840-10-25-1. [Predecessor literature: "Accounting for Leases," *FASB Statement No. 13* as amended and interpreted through May 1980 (Stamford, Conn.: FASB, 1980), par. 7.]

[2] FASB ASC 840-10-25. [Predecessor literature: "Accounting for Leases: Sale-Leaseback Transactions Involving Real Estate; Sales-Type Leases of Real Estate; Definition of the Lease Term; Initial Direct Costs of Direct Financing Leases," *Statement of Financial Accounting Standards No. 98* (Stamford, Conn.: FASB, 1988).]

[3] FASB ASC 840-10-25-9. [Predecessor literature: "Lessee Guarantee of the Residual Value of Leased Property," *FASB Interpretation No. 19* (Stamford, Conn.: FASB, 1977), par. 3.]

[4] FASB ASC 840-10-25-22. [Predecessor literature: "Accounting for Leases," *FASB Statement No. 13* as amended and interpreted through May 1980 (Stamford, Conn.: FASB, 1980), par. 5 (l).]

[5] FASB ASC 840-10-25-31. [Predecessor literature: "Accounting for Leases," *FASB Statement No. 13* as amended and interpreted through May 1980 (Stamford, Conn.: FASB, 1980), par. 5 (k).]

[6] FASB ASC 840-30-35-14. [Predecessor literature: "Accounting for Purchase of a Leased Asset by the Lessee During the Term of the Lease," *FASB Interpretation No. 26* (Stamford, Conn.: FASB, 1978), par. 5.]

[7] FASB ASC 840-10-25-43. [Predecessor literature: "Accounting for Leases," *FASB Statement No. 13* as amended and interpreted through May 1980 (Stamford, Conn.: FASB, 1980), paras. 6, 7, and 8.]

[8] FASB ASC 840-30-30-12. [Predecessor literature: "Accounting for Nonrefundable Fees and Costs Associated with Originating or Acquiring Loans and Initial Direct Costs of Leases," *Statement of Financial Accounting Standards No. 91* (Stamford: Conn.: FASB, 1987).]

[9] FASB ASC 840-30-50-1. [Predecessor literature: "Accounting for Leases," *FASB Statement No. 13* as amended and interpreted through May 1980 (Stamford, Conn.: FASB, 1980), par. 16.]

[10] FASB ASC 840-30-50-4. [Predecessor literature: "Accounting for Leases," *FASB Statement No. 13* as amended and interpreted through May 1980 (Stamford, Conn.: FASB, 1980), paras. 16 and 23.]

[11] FASB ASC 840-40. [Predecessor literature: "Accounting for Leases: Sale-Leaseback Transactions Involving Real Estate; Sales-Type Leases of Real Estate; Definition of the Lease Term; Initial Direct Costs of Direct Financing Leases," *Statement of Financial Accounting Standards No. 98* (Stamford, Conn.: FASB, 1988).]

[12] FASB ASC 840-40. [Predecessor literature: *Statement of Financial Accounting Standards No. 28,* "Accounting for Sales with Leasebacks" (Stamford, Conn.: FASB, 1979).]

Exercises

If your school has a subscription to the FASB Codification, go to *http://aaahq.org/ascLogin.cfm* to log in and prepare responses to the following. Provide Codification references for your responses.

CE21-1 Access the glossary ("Master Glossary") to answer the following.

    (a) What is a bargain-purchase option?
    (b) What is the definition of "incremental borrowing rate"?
    (c) What is the definition of "estimated residual value"?
    (d) What is an unguaranteed residual value?

CE21-2 What comprises a lessee's minimum lease payments? What is excluded?

CE21-3 What information should a lessee disclose about its capital leases in its financial statements and footnotes?

CE21-4 How should a lessor measure its initial gross investment in either a sales-type lease or a direct-financing lease?

An additional Codification case can be found in the Using Your Judgment section, on page 1353.

Be sure to check the book's companion website for a Review and Analysis Exercise, with solution.

Questions, Brief Exercises, Exercises, Problems, and many more resources are available for practice in WileyPLUS.

Note: All asterisked Questions, Exercises, and Problems relate to material in the appendices to the chapter.

(Unless instructed otherwise, round all amounts to the nearest dollar.)

QUESTIONS

1. What are the major lessor groups in the United States? What advantage does a captive have in a leasing arrangement?

2. Bradley Co. is expanding its operations and is in the process of selecting the method of financing this program. After some investigation, the company determines that it may (1) issue bonds and with the proceeds purchase the needed assets or (2) lease the assets on a long-term basis. Without knowing the comparative costs involved, answer these questions:

    (a) What might be the advantages of leasing the assets instead of owning them?

    (b) What might be the disadvantages of leasing the assets instead of owning them?

    (c) In what way will the balance sheet be differently affected by leasing the assets as opposed to issuing bonds and purchasing the assets?

3. Identify the two recognized lease-accounting methods for lessees and distinguish between them.

4. Ballard Company rents a warehouse on a month-to-month basis for the storage of its excess inventory. The company periodically must rent space whenever its production greatly exceeds actual sales. For several years, the company officials have discussed building their own storage facility, but this enthusiasm wavers when sales increase sufficiently to absorb the excess inventory. What is the nature of this type of lease arrangement, and what accounting treatment should be accorded it?

5. Distinguish between minimum rental payments and minimum lease payments, and indicate what is included in minimum lease payments.

6. Explain the distinction between a direct-financing lease and a sales-type lease for a lessor.

7. Outline the accounting procedures involved in applying the operating method by a lessee.

8. Outline the accounting procedures involved in applying the capital lease method by a lessee.

9. Identify the lease classifications for lessors and the criteria that must be met for each classification.

10. Outline the accounting procedures involved in applying the direct-financing method.

11. Outline the accounting procedures involved in applying the operating method by a lessor.

12. Walker Company is a manufacturer and lessor of computer equipment. What should be the nature of its lease arrangements with lessees if the company wishes to account for its lease transactions as sales-type leases?

13. Metheny Corporation's lease arrangements qualify as sales-type leases at the time of entering into the transactions. How should the corporation recognize revenues and costs in these situations?

14. Alice Foyle, M.D. (lessee), has a noncancelable 20-year lease with Brownback Realty, Inc. (lessor) for the use of a medical building. Taxes, insurance, and maintenance are paid by the lessee in addition to the fixed annual payments, of which the present value is equal to the fair value of the leased property. At the end of the lease period, title becomes the lessee's at a nominal price. Considering the terms of the lease described above, comment on the nature of the lease transaction and the accounting treatment that should be accorded it by the lessee.

15. The residual value is the estimated fair value of the leased property at the end of the lease term.

(a) Of what significance is (1) an unguaranteed and (2) a guaranteed residual value in the lessee's accounting for a capitalized-lease transaction?

(b) Of what significance is (1) an unguaranteed and (2) a guaranteed residual value in the lessor's accounting for a direct-financing lease transaction?

16. How should changes in the estimated unguaranteed residual value be handled by the lessor?

17. Describe the effect of a "bargain-purchase option" on accounting for a capital lease transaction by a lessee.

18. What are "initial direct costs" and how are they accounted for?

19. What disclosures should be made by lessees and lessors related to future lease payments?

*20. What is the nature of a "sale-leaseback" transaction?

BRIEF EXERCISES

② **BE21-1** Callaway Golf Co. leases telecommunication equipment. Assume the following data for equipment leased from Photon Company. The lease term is 5 years and requires equal rental payments of $31,000 at the beginning of each year. The equipment has a fair value at the inception of the lease of $138,000, an estimated useful life of 8 years, and no residual value. Callaway pays all executory costs directly to third parties. Photon set the annual rental to earn a rate of return of 10%, and this fact is known to Callaway. The lease does not transfer title or contain a bargain-purchase option. How should Callaway classify this lease?

② **BE21-2** Waterworld Company leased equipment from Costner Company. The lease term is 4 years and requires equal rental payments of $43,019 at the beginning of each year. The equipment has a fair value at the inception of the lease of $150,000, an estimated useful life of 4 years, and no salvage value. Waterworld pays all executory costs directly to third parties. The appropriate interest rate is 10%. Prepare Waterworld's January 1, 2012, journal entries at the inception of the lease.

② **BE21-3** Rick Kleckner Corporation recorded a capital lease at $300,000 on January 1, 2012. The interest rate is 12%. Kleckner Corporation made the first lease payment of $53,920 on January 1, 2012. The lease requires eight annual payments. The equipment has a useful life of 8 years with no salvage value. Prepare Kleckner Corporation's December 31, 2012, adjusting entries.

② **BE21-4** Use the information for Rick Kleckner Corporation from BE21-3. Assume that at December 31, 2012, Kleckner made an adjusting entry to accrue interest expense of $29,530 on the lease. Prepare Kleckner's January 1, 2013, journal entry to record the second lease payment of $53,920.

③ **BE21-5** Jana Kingston Corporation enters into a lease on January 1, 2012, that does not transfer ownership or contain a bargain-purchase option. It covers 3 years of the equipment's 8-year useful life, and the present value of the minimum lease payments is less than 90% of the fair value of the asset leased. Prepare Jana Kingston's journal entry to record its January 1, 2012, annual lease payment of $35,000.

④ **⑤** **BE21-6** Assume that IBM leased equipment that was carried at a cost of $150,000 to Sharon Swander Company. The term of the lease is 6 years beginning January 1, 2012, with equal rental payments of $30,044 at the beginning of each year. All executory costs are paid by Swander directly to third parties. The fair value of the equipment at the inception of the lease is $150,000. The equipment has a useful life of 6 years with no salvage value. The lease has an implicit interest rate of 8%, no bargain-purchase option, and no transfer of title. Collectibility is reasonably assured with no additional cost to be incurred by IBM. Prepare IBM's January 1, 2012, journal entries at the inception of the lease.

4 **5** **BE21-7** Use the information for IBM from BE21-6. Assume the direct-financing lease was recorded at a present value of $150,000. Prepare IBM's December 31, 2012, entry to record interest.

4 **BE21-8** Jennifer Brent Corporation owns equipment that cost $80,000 and has a useful life of 8 years with no salvage value. On January 1, 2012, Jennifer Brent leases the equipment to Donna Havaci Inc. for one year with one rental payment of $15,000 on January 1. Prepare Jennifer Brent Corporation's 2012 journal entries.

6 **7** **BE21-9** Indiana Jones Corporation enters into a 6-year lease of equipment on January 1, 2012, which requires 6 annual payments of $40,000 each, beginning January 1, 2012. In addition, Indiana Jones guarantees the lessor a residual value of $20,000 at lease-end. The equipment has a useful life of 6 years. Prepare Indiana Jones' January 1, 2012, journal entries assuming an interest rate of 10%.

6 **7** **BE21-10** Use the information for Indiana Jones Corporation from BE21-9. Assume that for Lost Ark Company, the lessor, collectibility is reasonably predictable, there are no important uncertainties concerning costs, and the carrying amount of the equipment is $202,921. Prepare Lost Ark's January 1, 2012, journal entries.

8 **BE21-11** Geiberger Corporation manufactures replicators. On January 1, 2012, it leased to Althaus Company a replicator that had cost $110,000 to manufacture. The lease agreement covers the 5-year useful life of the replicator and requires 5 equal annual rentals of $40,800 payable each January 1, beginning January 1, 2012. An interest rate of 12% is implicit in the lease agreement. Collectibility of the rentals is reasonably assured, and there are no important uncertainties concerning costs. Prepare Geiberger's January 1, 2012, journal entries.

11 *BE21-12 On January 1, 2012, Irwin Animation sold a truck to Peete Finance for $33,000 and immediately leased it back. The truck was carried on Irwin's books at $28,000. The term of the lease is 5 years, and title transfers to Irwin at lease-end. The lease requires five equal rental payments of $8,705 at the end of each year. The appropriate rate of interest is 10%, and the truck has a useful life of 5 years with no salvage value. Prepare Irwin's 2012 journal entries.

EXERCISES

2 **E21-1 (Lessee Entries, Capital Lease with Unguaranteed Residual Value)** On January 1, 2012, Adams Corporation signed a 5-year noncancelable lease for a machine. The terms of the lease called for Adams to make annual payments of $9,968 at the beginning of each year, starting January 1, 2012. The machine has an estimated useful life of 6 years and a $5,000 unguaranteed residual value. The machine reverts back to the lessor at the end of the lease term. Adams uses the straight-line method of depreciation for all of its plant assets. Adams's incremental borrowing rate is 10%, and the lessor's implicit rate is unknown.

Instructions
    (a) What type of lease is this? Explain.
    (b) Compute the present value of the minimum lease payments.
    (c) Prepare all necessary journal entries for Adams for this lease through January 1, 2013.

2 **E21-2 (Lessee Computations and Entries, Capital Lease with Guaranteed Residual Value)** Brecker Company leases an automobile with a fair value of $10,906 from Emporia Motors, Inc., on the following terms.

    1. Noncancelable term of 50 months.
    2. Rental of $250 per month (at end of each month). (The present value at 1% per month is $9,800.)
    3. Estimated residual value after 50 months is $1,180. (The present value at 1% per month is $715.) Brecker Company guarantees the residual value of $1,180.
    4. Estimated economic life of the automobile is 60 months.
    5. Brecker Company's incremental borrowing rate is 12% a year (1% a month). Emporia's implicit rate is unknown.

Instructions

(Round amounts to the nearest cent.)

(a) What is the nature of this lease to Brecker Company?

(b) What is the present value of the minimum lease payments?

(c) Record the lease on Brecker Company's books at the date of inception.

(d) Record the first month's depreciation on Brecker Company's books (assume straight-line).

(e) Record the first month's lease payment.

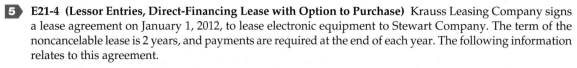

E21-3 (Lessee Entries, Capital Lease with Executory Costs and Unguaranteed Residual Value) Assume that on January 1, 2012, Kimberly-Clark Corp. signs a 10-year noncancelable lease agreement to lease a storage building from Trevino Storage Company. The following information pertains to this lease agreement.

1. The agreement requires equal rental payments of $90,000 beginning on January 1, 2012.

2. The fair value of the building on January 1, 2012 is $550,000.

3. The building has an estimated economic life of 12 years, with an unguaranteed residual value of $10,000. Kimberly-Clark depreciates similar buildings on the straight-line method.

4. The lease is nonrenewable. At the termination of the lease, the building reverts to the lessor.

5. Kimberly-Clark's incremental borrowing rate is 12% per year. The lessor's implicit rate is not known by Kimberly-Clark.

6. The yearly rental payment includes $3,088 of executory costs related to taxes on the property.

Instructions

Prepare the journal entries on the lessee's books to reflect the signing of the lease agreement and to record the payments and expenses related to this lease for the years 2012 and 2013. Kimberly-Clark's corporate year end is December 31.

 E21-4 (Lessor Entries, Direct-Financing Lease with Option to Purchase) Krauss Leasing Company signs a lease agreement on January 1, 2012, to lease electronic equipment to Stewart Company. The term of the noncancelable lease is 2 years, and payments are required at the end of each year. The following information relates to this agreement.

1. Stewart has the option to purchase the equipment for $16,000 upon termination of the lease.

2. The equipment has a cost and fair value of $240,000 to Krauss Leasing Company. The useful economic life is 2 years, with a salvage value of $16,000.

3. Stewart Company is required to pay $7,000 each year to the lessor for executory costs.

4. Krauss Leasing Company desires to earn a return of 10% on its investment.

5. Collectibility of the payments is reasonably predictable, and there are no important uncertainties surrounding the costs yet to be incurred by the lessor.

Instructions

(Round amounts to the nearest cent.)

(a) Prepare the journal entries on the books of Krauss Leasing to reflect the payments received under the lease and to recognize income for the years 2012 and 2013.

(b) Assuming that Stewart Company exercises its option to purchase the equipment on December 31, 2013, prepare the journal entry to reflect the sale on Krauss's books.

E21-5 (Type of Lease, Amortization Schedule) Jacobsen Leasing Company leases a new machine that has a cost and fair value of $75,000 to Stadler Corporation on a 3-year noncancelable contract. Stadler Corporation agrees to assume all risks of normal ownership including such costs as insurance, taxes, and maintenance. The machine has a 3-year useful life and no residual value. The lease was signed on January 1, 2012. Jacobsen Leasing Company expects to earn a 9% return on its investment. The annual rentals are payable on each December 31.

Instructions

(a) Discuss the nature of the lease arrangement and the accounting method that each party to the lease should apply.

(b) Prepare an amortization schedule that would be suitable for both the lessor and the lessee and that covers all the years involved.

 E21-6 (Lessor Entries, Sales-Type Lease) Wadkins Company, a machinery dealer, leased a machine to Romero Corporation on January 1, 2012. The lease is for an 8-year period and requires equal annual payments of $38,514 at the beginning of each year. The first payment is received on January 1, 2012. Wadkins had purchased the machine during 2011 for $170,000. Collectibility of lease payments is reasonably predictable, and no important uncertainties surround the amount of costs yet to be incurred by Wadkins. Wadkins set the annual rental to ensure an 11% rate of return. The machine has an economic life of 10 years with no residual value and reverts to Wadkins at the termination of the lease.

Instructions

(a) Compute the amount of the lease receivable.

(b) Prepare all necessary journal entries for Wadkins for 2012.

8 **E21-7 (Lessee-Lessor Entries, Sales-Type Lease)** On January 1, 2012, Palmer Company leased equipment to Woods Corporation. The following information pertains to this lease.

1. The term of the noncancelable lease is 6 years, with no renewal option. The equipment reverts to the lessor at the termination of the lease.
2. Equal rental payments are due on January 1 of each year, beginning in 2012.
3. The fair value of the equipment on January 1, 2012, is $200,000, and its cost is $150,000.
4. The equipment has an economic life of 8 years, with an unguaranteed residual value of $10,000. Woods depreciates all of its equipment on a straight-line basis.
5. Palmer sets the annual rental to ensure an 11% rate of return. Woods's incremental borrowing rate is 12%, and the implicit rate of the lessor is unknown.
6. Collectibility of lease payments is reasonably predictable, and no important uncertainties surround the amount of costs yet to be incurred by the lessor.

Instructions

(Both the lessor and the lessee's accounting period ends on December 31.)

(a) Discuss the nature of this lease to Palmer and Woods.

(b) Calculate the amount of the annual rental payment.

(c) Prepare all the necessary journal entries for Woods for 2012.

(d) Prepare all the necessary journal entries for Palmer for 2012.

6 **E21-8 (Lessee Entries with Bargain-Purchase Option)** The following facts pertain to a noncancelable lease agreement between Lennox Leasing Company and Gill Company, a lessee.

Inception date:	May 1, 2012
Annual lease payment due at the beginning of each year, beginning with May 1, 2012	$18,829.49
Bargain-purchase option price at end of lease term	$ 4,000.00
Lease term	5 years
Economic life of leased equipment	10 years
Lessor's cost	$65,000.00
Fair value of asset at May 1, 2012	$81,000.00
Lessor's implicit rate	10%
Lessee's incremental borrowing rate	10%

The collectibility of the lease payments is reasonably predictable, and there are no important uncertainties surrounding the costs yet to be incurred by the lessor. The lessee assumes responsibility for all executory costs.

Instructions

(Round all numbers to the nearest cent.)

(a) Discuss the nature of this lease to Gill Company.

(b) Discuss the nature of this lease to Lennox Company.

(c) Prepare a lease amortization schedule for Gill Company for the 5-year lease term.

(d) Prepare the journal entries on the lessee's books to reflect the signing of the lease agreement and to record the payments and expenses related to this lease for the years 2012 and 2013. Gill's annual accounting period ends on December 31. Reversing entries are used by Gill.

6 **E21-9 (Lessor Entries with Bargain-Purchase Option)** A lease agreement between Lennox Leasing Company and Gill Company is described in E21-8.

Instructions

Refer to the data in E21-8 and do the following for the lessor. (Round all numbers to the nearest cent.)

(a) Compute the amount of the lease receivable at the inception of the lease.

(b) Prepare a lease amortization schedule for Lennox Leasing Company for the 5-year lease term.

(c) Prepare the journal entries to reflect the signing of the lease agreement and to record the receipts and income related to this lease for the years 2012, 2013, and 2014. The lessor's accounting period ends on December 31. Reversing entries are not used by Lennox.

5 **E21-10 (Computation of Rental, Journal Entries for Lessor)** Fieval Leasing Company signs an agreement on January 1, 2012, to lease equipment to Reid Company. The following information relates to this agreement.

1. The term of the noncancelable lease is 6 years with no renewal option. The equipment has an estimated economic life of 6 years.
2. The cost of the asset to the lessor is $343,000. The fair value of the asset at January 1, 2012, is $343,000.
3. The asset will revert to the lessor at the end of the lease term at which time the asset is expected to have a residual value of $61,071, none of which is guaranteed.
4. Reid Company assumes direct responsibility for all executory costs.
5. The agreement requires equal annual rental payments, beginning on January 1, 2012.
6. Collectibility of the lease payments is reasonably predictable. There are no important uncertainties surrounding the amount of costs yet to be incurred by the lessor.

Instructions
(Round all numbers to the nearest cent.)

(a) Assuming the lessor desires a 10% rate of return on its investment, calculate the amount of the annual rental payment required.
(b) Prepare an amortization schedule that would be suitable for the lessor for the lease term.
(c) Prepare all of the journal entries for the lessor for 2012 and 2013 to record the lease agreement, the receipt of lease payments, and the recognition of income. Assume the lessor's annual accounting period ends on December 31.

2 **E21-11 (Amortization Schedule and Journal Entries for Lessee)** Grady Leasing Company signs an agreement on January 1, 2012, to lease equipment to Azure Company. The following information relates to this agreement.

1. The term of the noncancelable lease is 5 years with no renewal option. The equipment has an estimated economic life of 5 years.
2. The fair value of the asset at January 1, 2012, is $90,000.
3. The asset will revert to the lessor at the end of the lease term, at which time the asset is expected to have a residual value of $7,000, none of which is guaranteed.
4. Azure Company assumes direct responsibility for all executory costs, which include the following annual amounts: (1) $900 to Frontier Insurance Company for insurance and (2) $1,600 to Crawford County for property taxes.
5. The agreement requires equal annual rental payments of $20,541.11 to the lessor, beginning on January 1, 2012.
6. The lessee's incremental borrowing rate is 12%. The lessor's implicit rate is 10% and is known to the lessee.
7. Azure Company uses the straight-line depreciation method for all equipment.
8. Azure uses reversing entries when appropriate.

Instructions
(Round all numbers to the nearest cent.)

(a) Prepare an amortization schedule that would be suitable for the lessee for the lease term.
(b) Prepare all of the journal entries for the lessee for 2012 and 2013 to record the lease agreement, the lease payments, and all expenses related to this lease. Assume the lessee's annual accounting period ends on December 31.

3 **4** **E21-12 (Accounting for an Operating Lease)** On January 1, 2012, Secada Co. leased a building to Ryker Inc. The relevant information related to the lease is as follows.

1. The lease arrangement is for 10 years.
2. The leased building cost $3,600,000 and was purchased for cash on January 1, 2012.
3. The building is depreciated on a straight-line basis. Its estimated economic life is 50 years with no salvage value.
4. Lease payments are $220,000 per year and are made at the end of the year.
5. Property tax expense of $85,000 and insurance expense of $10,000 on the building were incurred by Secada in the first year. Payment on these two items was made at the end of the year.
6. Both the lessor and the lessee are on a calendar-year basis.

Instructions
(a) Prepare the journal entries that Secada Co. should make in 2012.
(b) Prepare the journal entries that Ryker Inc. should make in 2012.
(c) If Secada paid $30,000 to a real estate broker on January 1, 2012, as a fee for finding the lessee, how much should be reported as an expense for this item in 2012 by Secada Co.?

3 4 E21-13 (Accounting for an Operating Lease) On January 1, 2012, a machine was purchased for $900,000 by Floyd Co. The machine is expected to have an 8-year life with no salvage value. It is to be depreciated on a straight-line basis. The machine was leased to Crampton Inc. on January 1, 2012, at an annual rental of $180,000. Other relevant information is as follows.

1. The lease term is for 3 years.
2. Floyd Co. incurred maintenance and other executory costs of $25,000 in 2012 related to this lease.
3. The machine could have been sold by Floyd Co. for $940,000 instead of leasing it.
4. Crampton is required to pay a rent security deposit of $35,000 and to prepay the last month's rent of $15,000.

Instructions
(a) How much should Floyd Co. report as income before income tax on this lease for 2012?
(b) What amount should Crampton Inc. report for rent expense for 2012 on this lease?

3 4 E21-14 (Operating Lease for Lessee and Lessor) On February 20, 2012, Hooke Inc., purchased a machine for $1,200,000 for the purpose of leasing it. The machine is expected to have a 10-year life, no residual value, and will be depreciated on the straight-line basis. The machine was leased to Sage Company on March 1, 2012, for a 4-year period at a monthly rental of $15,600. There is no provision for the renewal of the lease or purchase of the machine by the lessee at the expiration of the lease term. Hooke paid $30,000 of commissions associated with negotiating the lease in February 2012:

Instructions
(a) What expense should Sage Company record as a result of the facts above for the year ended December 31, 2012? Show supporting computations in good form.
(b) What income or loss before income taxes should Hooke record as a result of the facts above for the year ended December 31, 2012? (*Hint:* Amortize commissions over the life of the lease.)

(AICPA adapted)

11 *E21-15 (Sale-Leaseback) Assume that on January 1, 2012, Elmer's Restaurants sells a computer system to Liquidity Finance Co. for $510,000 and immediately leases the computer system back. The relevant information is as follows.

1. The computer was carried on Elmer's books at a value of $450,000.
2. The term of the noncancelable lease is 10 years; title will transfer to Elmer.
3. The lease agreement requires equal rental payments of $83,000.11 at the end of each year.
4. The incremental borrowing rate for Elmer is 12%. Elmer is aware that Liquidity Finance Co. set the annual rental to ensure a rate of return of 10%.
5. The computer has a fair value of $680,000 on January 1, 2012, and an estimated economic life of 10 years.
6. Elmer pays executory costs of $9,000 per year.

Instructions
Prepare the journal entries for both the lessee and the lessor for 2012 to reflect the sale-leaseback agreement. No uncertainties exist, and collectibility is reasonably certain.

11 *E21-16 (Lessee-Lessor, Sale-Leaseback) Presented below are four independent situations.
(a) On December 31, 2012, Beard Inc. sold computer equipment to Barber Co. and immediately leased it back for 10 years. The sales price of the equipment was $560,000, its carrying amount is $400,000, and its estimated remaining economic life is 12 years. Determine the amount of deferred revenue to be reported from the sale of the computer equipment on December 31, 2012.
(b) On December 31, 2012, Nicklaus Co. sold a machine to Ozaki Co. and simultaneously leased it back for one year. The sales price of the machine was $480,000, the carrying amount is $420,000, and it had an estimated remaining useful life of 14 years. The present value of the rental payments for the one year is $35,000. At December 31, 2012, how much should Nicklaus report as deferred revenue from the sale of the machine?
(c) On January 1, 2012, Barone Corp. sold an airplane with an estimated useful life of 10 years. At the same time, Barone leased back the plane for 10 years. The sales price of the airplane was $500,000, the

carrying amount $401,000, and the annual rental $73,975. Barone Corp. intends to depreciate the leased asset using the sum-of-the-years'-digits depreciation method. Discuss how the gain on the sale should be reported at the end of 2012 in the financial statements.

(d) On January 1, 2012, Durocher Co. sold equipment with an estimated useful life of 5 years. At the same time, Durocher leased back the equipment for 2 years under a lease classified as an operating lease. The sales price (fair value) of the equipment was $212,700, the carrying amount is $300,000, the monthly rental under the lease is $6,000, and the present value of the rental payments is $115,753. For the year ended December 31, 2012, determine which items would be reported on its income statement for the sale-leaseback transaction.

See the book's companion website, www.wiley.com/college/kieso, for a set of B Exercises.

PROBLEMS

2 8 P21-1 (Lessee-Lessor Entries, Sales-Type Lease) Glaus Leasing Company agrees to lease machinery to Jensen Corporation on January 1, 2012. The following information relates to the lease agreement.

1. The term of the lease is 7 years with no renewal option, and the machinery has an estimated economic life of 9 years.
2. The cost of the machinery is $525,000, and the fair value of the asset on January 1, 2012, is $700,000.
3. At the end of the lease term, the asset reverts to the lessor and has a guaranteed residual value of $100,000. Jensen depreciates all of its equipment on a straight-line basis.
4. The lease agreement requires equal annual rental payments, beginning on January 1, 2012.
5. The collectibility of the lease payments is reasonably predictable, and there are no important uncertainties surrounding the amount of costs yet to be incurred by the lessor.
6. Glaus desires a 10% rate of return on its investments. Jensen's incremental borrowing rate is 11%, and the lessor's implicit rate is unknown.

Instructions

(Assume the accounting period ends on December 31.)

(a) Discuss the nature of this lease for both the lessee and the lessor.
(b) Calculate the amount of the annual rental payment required.
(c) Compute the present value of the minimum lease payments.
(d) Prepare the journal entries Jensen would make in 2012 and 2013 related to the lease arrangement.
(e) Prepare the journal entries Glaus would make in 2012 and 2013.

 3 4 P21-2 (Lessee-Lessor Entries, Operating Lease) Cleveland Inc. leased a new crane to Abriendo Construction under a 5-year noncancelable contract starting January 1, 2012. Terms of the lease require payments of $33,000 each January 1, starting January 1, 2012. Cleveland will pay insurance, taxes, and maintenance charges on the crane, which has an estimated life of 12 years, a fair value of $240,000, and a cost to Cleveland of $240,000. The estimated fair value of the crane is expected to be $45,000 at the end of the lease term. No bargain-purchase or renewal options are included in the contract. Both Cleveland and Abriendo adjust and close books annually at December 31. Collectibility of the lease payments is reasonably certain, and no uncertainties exist relative to unreimbursable lessor costs. Abriendo's incremental borrowing rate is 10%, and Cleveland's implicit interest rate of 9% is known to Abriendo.

Instructions
(a) Identify the type of lease involved and give reasons for your classification. Discuss the accounting treatment that should be applied by both the lessee and the lessor.
(b) Prepare all the entries related to the lease contract and leased asset for the year 2012 for the lessee and lessor, assuming the following amounts.
   (1) Insurance $500.
   (2) Taxes $2,000.
   (3) Maintenance $650.
   (4) Straight-line depreciation and salvage value $15,000.
(c) Discuss what should be presented in the balance sheet, the income statement, and the related notes of both the lessee and the lessor at December 31, 2012.

P21-3 (Lessee-Lessor Entries, Balance Sheet Presentation, Sales-Type Lease) Winston Industries and Ewing Inc. enter into an agreement that requires Ewing Inc. to build three diesel-electric engines to Winston's specifications. Upon completion of the engines, Winston has agreed to lease them for a period of 10 years and to assume all costs and risks of ownership. The lease is noncancelable, becomes effective on January 1, 2012, and requires annual rental payments of $413,971 each January 1, starting January 1, 2012.

Winston's incremental borrowing rate is 10%. The implicit interest rate used by Ewing Inc. and known to Winston is 8%. The total cost of building the three engines is $2,600,000. The economic life of the engines is estimated to be 10 years, with residual value set at zero. Winston depreciates similar equipment on a straight-line basis. At the end of the lease, Winston assumes title to the engines. Collectibility of the lease payments is reasonably certain; no uncertainties exist relative to unreimbursable lessor costs.

Instructions
(Round all numbers to the nearest dollar.)

(a) Discuss the nature of this lease transaction from the viewpoints of both lessee and lessor.
(b) Prepare the journal entry or entries to record the transaction on January 1, 2012, on the books of Winston Industries.
(c) Prepare the journal entry or entries to record the transaction on January 1, 2012, on the books of Ewing Inc.
(d) Prepare the journal entries for both the lessee and lessor to record the first rental payment on January 1, 2012.
(e) Prepare the journal entries for both the lessee and lessor to record interest expense (revenue) at December 31, 2012. (Prepare a lease amortization schedule for 2 years.)
(f) Show the items and amounts that would be reported on the balance sheet (not notes) at December 31, 2012, for both the lessee and the lessor.

 P21-4 (Balance Sheet and Income Statement Disclosure—Lessee) The following facts pertain to a noncancelable lease agreement between Alschuler Leasing Company and McKee Electronics, a lessee, for a computer system.

Inception date	October 1, 2012
Lease term	6 years
Economic life of leased equipment	6 years
Fair value of asset at October 1, 2012	$300,383
Residual value at end of lease term	–0–
Lessor's implicit rate	10%
Lessee's incremental borrowing rate	10%
Annual lease payment due at the beginning of each year, beginning with October 1, 2012	$62,700

The collectibility of the lease payments is reasonably predictable, and there are no important uncertainties surrounding the costs yet to be incurred by the lessor. The lessee assumes responsibility for all executory costs, which amount to $5,500 per year and are to be paid each October 1, beginning October 1, 2012. (This $5,500 is not included in the rental payment of $62,700.) The asset will revert to the lessor at the end of the lease term. The straight-line depreciation method is used for all equipment.

The following amortization schedule has been prepared correctly for use by both the lessor and the lessee in accounting for this lease. The lease is to be accounted for properly as a capital lease by the lessee and as a direct-financing lease by the lessor.

Date	Annual Lease Payment/ Receipt	Interest (10%) on Unpaid Liability/Receivable	Reduction of Lease Liability/Receivable	Balance of Lease Liability/Receivable
10/01/12				$300,383
10/01/12	$ 62,700		$ 62,700	237,683
10/01/13	62,700	$23,768	38,932	198,751
10/01/14	62,700	19,875	42,825	155,926
10/01/15	62,700	15,593	47,107	108,819
10/01/16	62,700	10,822	51,818	57,001
10/01/17	62,700	5,699*	57,001	–0–
	$376,200	$75,817	$300,383	

*Rounding error is $1.

Instructions

(Round all numbers to the nearest cent.)

(a) Assuming the lessee's accounting period ends on September 30, answer the following questions with respect to this lease agreement.

(1) What items and amounts will appear on the lessee's income statement for the year ending September 30, 2013?

(2) What items and amounts will appear on the lessee's balance sheet at September 30, 2013?

(3) What items and amounts will appear on the lessee's income statement for the year ending September 30, 2014?

(4) What items and amounts will appear on the lessee's balance sheet at September 30, 2014?

(b) Assuming the lessee's accounting period ends on December 31, answer the following questions with respect to this lease agreement.

(1) What items and amounts will appear on the lessee's income statement for the year ending December 31, 2012?

(2) What items and amounts will appear on the lessee's balance sheet at December 31, 2012?

(3) What items and amounts will appear on the lessee's income statement for the year ending December 31, 2013?

(4) What items and amounts will appear on the lessee's balance sheet at December 31, 2013?

5 9 P21-5 (Balance Sheet and Income Statement Disclosure—Lessor) Assume the same information as in P21-4.

Instructions

(Round all numbers to the nearest cent.)

(a) Assuming the lessor's accounting period ends on September 30, answer the following questions with respect to this lease agreement.

(1) What items and amounts will appear on the lessor's income statement for the year ending September 30, 2013?

(2) What items and amounts will appear on the lessor's balance sheet at September 30, 2013?

(3) What items and amounts will appear on the lessor's income statement for the year ending September 30, 2014?

(4) What items and amounts will appear on the lessor's balance sheet at September 30, 2014?

(b) Assuming the lessor's accounting period ends on December 31, answer the following questions with respect to this lease agreement.

(1) What items and amounts will appear on the lessor's income statement for the year ending December 31, 2012?

(2) What items and amounts will appear on the lessor's balance sheet at December 31, 2012?

(3) What items and amounts will appear on the lessor's income statement for the year ending December 31, 2013?

(4) What items and amounts will appear on the lessor's balance sheet at December 31, 2013?

2 7 P21-6 (Lessee Entries with Residual Value) The following facts pertain to a noncancelable lease agreement between Faldo Leasing Company and Vance Company, a lessee.

Inception date	January 1, 2012
Annual lease payment due at the beginning of each year, beginning with January 1, 2012	$124,798
Residual value of equipment at end of lease term, guaranteed by the lessee	$50,000
Lease term	6 years
Economic life of leased equipment	6 years
Fair value of asset at January 1, 2012	$600,000
Lessor's implicit rate	12%
Lessee's incremental borrowing rate	12%

The lessee assumes responsibility for all executory costs, which are expected to amount to $5,000 per year. The asset will revert to the lessor at the end of the lease term. The lessee has guaranteed the lessor a residual value of $50,000. The lessee uses the straight-line depreciation method for all equipment.

Instructions

(Round all numbers to the nearest cent.)

(a) Prepare an amortization schedule that would be suitable for the lessee for the lease term.

(b) Prepare all of the journal entries for the lessee for 2012 and 2013 to record the lease agreement, the lease payments, and all expenses related to this lease. Assume the lessee's annual accounting period ends on December 31 and reversing entries are used when appropriate.

P21-7 (Lessee Entries and Balance Sheet Presentation, Capital Lease) Ludwick Steel Company as lessee signed a lease agreement for equipment for 5 years, beginning December 31, 2012. Annual rental payments of $40,000 are to be made at the beginning of each lease year (December 31). The taxes, insurance, and the maintenance costs are the obligation of the lessee. The interest rate used by the lessor in setting the payment schedule is 9%; Ludwick's incremental borrowing rate is 10%. Ludwick is unaware of the rate being used by the lessor. At the end of the lease, Ludwick has the option to buy the equipment for $1, considerably below its estimated fair value at that time. The equipment has an estimated useful life of 7 years, with no salvage value. Ludwick uses the straight-line method of depreciation on similar owned equipment.

Instructions
(Round all numbers to the nearest dollar.)

(a) Prepare the journal entry or entries, with explanations, that should be recorded on December 31, 2012, by Ludwick.
(b) Prepare the journal entry or entries, with explanations, that should be recorded on December 31, 2013, by Ludwick. (Prepare the lease amortization schedule for all five payments.)
(c) Prepare the journal entry or entries, with explanations, that should be recorded on December 31, 2014, by Ludwick.
(d) What amounts would appear on Ludwick's December 31, 2014, balance sheet relative to the lease arrangement?

P21-8 (Lessee Entries and Balance Sheet Presentation, Capital Lease) On January 1, 2012, Cage Company contracts to lease equipment for 5 years, agreeing to make a payment of $137,899 (including the executory costs of $6,000) at the beginning of each year, starting January 1, 2012. The taxes, the insurance, and the maintenance, estimated at $6,000 a year, are the obligations of the lessee. The leased equipment is to be capitalized at $550,000. The asset is to be depreciated on a double-declining-balance basis, and the obligation is to be reduced on an effective-interest basis. Cage's incremental borrowing rate is 12%, and the implicit rate in the lease is 10%, which is known by Cage. Title to the equipment transfers to Cage when the lease expires. The asset has an estimated useful life of 5 years and no residual value.

Instructions
(Round all numbers to the nearest dollar.)

(a) Explain the probable relationship of the $550,000 amount to the lease arrangement.
(b) Prepare the journal entry or entries that should be recorded on January 1, 2012, by Cage Company.
(c) Prepare the journal entry to record depreciation of the leased asset for the year 2012.
(d) Prepare the journal entry to record the interest expense for the year 2012.
(e) Prepare the journal entry to record the lease payment of January 1, 2013, assuming reversing entries are not made.
(f) What amounts will appear on the lessee's December 31, 2012, balance sheet relative to the lease contract?

P21-9 (Lessee Entries, Capital Lease with Monthly Payments) Shapiro Inc. was incorporated in 2011 to operate as a computer software service firm with an accounting fiscal year ending August 31. Shapiro's primary product is a sophisticated online inventory-control system; its customers pay a fixed fee plus a usage charge for using the system.

Shapiro has leased a large, Alpha-3 computer system from the manufacturer. The lease calls for a monthly rental of $40,000 for the 144 months (12 years) of the lease term. The estimated useful life of the computer is 15 years.

Each scheduled monthly rental payment includes $3,000 for full-service maintenance on the computer to be performed by the manufacturer. All rentals are payable on the first day of the month beginning with August 1, 2012, the date the computer was installed and the lease agreement was signed. The lease is noncancelable for its 12-year term, and it is secured only by the manufacturer's chattel lien on the Alpha-3 system.

This lease is to be accounted for as a capital lease by Shapiro, and it will be depreciated by the straight-line method with no expected salvage value. Borrowed funds for this type of transaction would cost Shapiro 12% per year (1% per month). Following is a schedule of the present value of $1 for selected periods discounted at 1% per period when payments are made at the beginning of each period.

Periods (months)	Present Value of $1 per Period Discounted at 1% per Period
1	1.000
2	1.990
3	2.970
143	76.658
144	76.899

Instructions

Prepare, in general journal form, all entries Shapiro should have made in its accounting records during August 2012 relating to this lease. Give full explanations and show supporting computations for each entry. Remember, August 31, 2012, is the end of Shapiro's fiscal accounting period and it will be preparing financial statements on that date. Do not prepare closing entries.

(AICPA adapted)

P21-10 (Lessor Computations and Entries, Sales-Type Lease with Unguaranteed Residual Value) George Company manufactures a check-in kiosk with an estimated economic life of 12 years and leases it to National Airlines for a period of 10 years. The normal selling price of the equipment is $278,072, and its unguaranteed residual value at the end of the lease term is estimated to be $20,000. National will pay annual payments of $40,000 at the beginning of each year and all maintenance, insurance, and taxes. George incurred costs of $180,000 in manufacturing the equipment and $4,000 in negotiating and closing the lease. George has determined that the collectibility of the lease payments is reasonably predictable, that no additional costs will be incurred, and that the implicit interest rate is 10%.

Instructions

(Round all numbers to the nearest dollar.)

(a) Discuss the nature of this lease in relation to the lessor and compute the amount of each of the following items.
  (1) Lease receivable.
  (2) Sales price.
  (3) Cost of sales.
(b) Prepare a 10-year lease amortization schedule.
(c) Prepare all of the lessor's journal entries for the first year.

P21-11 (Lessee Computations and Entries, Capital Lease with Unguaranteed Residual Value) Assume the same data as in P21-10 with National Airlines Co. having an incremental borrowing rate of 10%.

Instructions

(Round all numbers to the nearest dollar.)

(a) Discuss the nature of this lease in relation to the lessee, and compute the amount of the initial obligation under capital leases.
(b) Prepare a 10-year lease amortization schedule.
(c) Prepare all of the lessee's journal entries for the first year.

P21-12 (Basic Lessee Accounting with Difficult PV Calculation) In 2011, Grishell Trucking Company negotiated and closed a long-term lease contract for newly constructed truck terminals and freight storage facilities. The buildings were erected to the company's specifications on land owned by the company. On January 1, 2012, Grishell Trucking Company took possession of the lease properties. On January 1, 2012 and 2013, the company made cash payments of $948,000 that were recorded as rental expenses.

Although the terminals have a composite useful life of 40 years, the noncancelable lease runs for 20 years from January 1, 2012, with a bargain-purchase option available upon expiration of the lease.

The 20-year lease is effective for the period January 1, 2012, through December 31, 2031. Advance rental payments of $800,000 are payable to the lessor on January 1 of each of the first 10 years of the lease term. Advance rental payments of $320,000 are due on January 1 for each of the last 10 years of the lease. The company has an option to purchase all of these leased facilities for $1 on December 31, 2031. It also must make annual payments to the lessor of $125,000 for property taxes and $23,000 for insurance. The lease was negotiated to assure the lessor a 6% rate of return.

Instructions

(Round all numbers to the nearest dollar.)

(a) Prepare a schedule to compute for Grishell Trucking Company the discounted present value of the terminal facilities and related obligation at January 1, 2012.
(b) Assuming that the discounted present value of terminal facilities and related obligation at January 1, 2012, was $7,600,000, prepare journal entries for Grishell Trucking Company to record the:
  (1) Cash payment to the lessor on January 1, 2014.
  (2) Amortization of the cost of the leased properties for 2014 using the straight-line method and assuming a zero salvage value.
  (3) Accrual of interest expense at December 31, 2014.

Selected present value factors are as follows.

Periods	For an Ordinary Annuity of $1 at 6%	For $1 at 6%
1	.943396	.943396
2	1.833393	.889996
8	6.209794	.627412
9	6.801692	.591898
10	7.360087	.558395
19	11.158117	.330513
20	11.469921	.311805

(AICPA adapted)

[4] [7] [8] P21-13 (Lessor Computations and Entries, Sales-Type Lease with Guaranteed Residual Value) Amirante Inc. manufactures an X-ray machine with an estimated life of 12 years and leases it to Chambers Medical Center for a period of 10 years. The normal selling price of the machine is $411,324, and its guaranteed residual value at the end of the noncancelable lease term is estimated to be $15,000. The hospital will pay rents of $60,000 at the beginning of each year and all maintenance, insurance, and taxes. Amirante Inc. incurred costs of $250,000 in manufacturing the machine and $14,000 in negotiating and closing the lease. Amirante Inc. has determined that the collectibility of the lease payments is reasonably predictable, that there will be no additional costs incurred, and that the implicit interest rate is 10%.

Instructions
(Round all numbers to the nearest dollar.)

(a) Discuss the nature of this lease in relation to the lessor and compute the amount of each of the following items.
   (1) Lease receivable at inception of the lease.
   (2) Sales price.
   (3) Cost of sales.
(b) Prepare a 10-year lease amortization schedule.
(c) Prepare all of the lessor's journal entries for the first year.

[2] [7] P21-14 (Lessee Computations and Entries, Capital Lease with Guaranteed Residual Value) Assume the same data as in P21-13 and that Chambers Medical Center has an incremental borrowing rate of 10%.

Instructions
(Round all numbers to the nearest dollar.)

(a) Discuss the nature of this lease in relation to the lessee, and compute the amount of the initial obligation under capital leases.
(b) Prepare a 10-year lease amortization schedule.
(c) Prepare all of the lessee's journal entries for the first year.

[2] [3] [7] P21-15 (Operating Lease vs. Capital Lease) You are auditing the December 31, 2012, financial statements of Hockney, Inc., manufacturer of novelties and party favors. During your inspection of the company garage, you discovered that a used automobile not listed in the equipment subsidiary ledger is parked there. You ask Stacy Reeder, plant manager, about the vehicle, and she tells you that the company did not list the automobile because the company was only leasing it. The lease agreement was entered into on January 1, 2012, with Crown New and Used Cars.

You decide to review the lease agreement to ensure that the lease should be afforded operating lease treatment, and you discover the following lease terms.

1. Noncancelable term of 4 years.
2. Rental of $3,240 per year (at the end of each year). (The present value at 8% per year is $10,731.)
3. Estimated residual value after 4 years is $1,100. (The present value at 8% per year is $809.) Hockney guarantees the residual value of $1,100.
4. Estimated economic life of the automobile is 5 years.
5. Hockney's incremental borrowing rate is 8% per year.

Instructions
You are a senior auditor writing a memo to your supervisor, the audit partner in charge of this audit, to discuss the above situation. Be sure to include (a) why you inspected the lease agreement, (b) what you determined about the lease, and (c) how you advised your client to account for this lease. Explain every journal entry that you believe is necessary to record this lease properly on the client's books. (It is also necessary to include the fact that you communicated this information to your client.)

P21-16 (Lessee-Lessor Accounting for Residual Values) Goring Dairy leases its milking equipment from King Finance Company under the following lease terms.

1. The lease term is 10 years, noncancelable, and requires equal rental payments of $30,300 due at the beginning of each year starting January 1, 2012.
2. The equipment has a fair value and cost at the inception of the lease (January 1, 2012) of $220,404, an estimated economic life of 10 years, and a residual value (which is guaranteed by Goring Dairy) of $20,000.
3. The lease contains no renewable options, and the equipment reverts to King Finance Company upon termination of the lease.
4. Goring Dairy's incremental borrowing rate is 9% per year. The implicit rate is also 9%.
5. Goring Dairy depreciates similar equipment that it owns on a straight-line basis.
6. Collectibility of the payments is reasonably predictable, and there are no important uncertainties surrounding the costs yet to be incurred by the lessor.

Instructions

(a) Evaluate the criteria for classification of the lease, and describe the nature of the lease. In general, discuss how the lessee and lessor should account for the lease transaction.
(b) Prepare the journal entries for the lessee and lessor at January 1, 2012, and December 31, 2012 (the lessee's and lessor's year-end). Assume no reversing entries.
(c) What would have been the amount capitalized by the lessee upon the inception of the lease if:
  (1) The residual value of $20,000 had been guaranteed by a third party, not the lessee?
  (2) The residual value of $20,000 had not been guaranteed at all?
(d) On the lessor's books, what would be the amount recorded as the Net Investment (Lease Receivable) at the inception of the lease, assuming:
  (1) The residual value of $20,000 had been guaranteed by a third party?
  (2) The residual value of $20,000 had not been guaranteed at all?
(e) Suppose the useful life of the milking equipment is 20 years. How large would the residual value have to be at the end of 10 years in order for the lessee to qualify for the operating method? (Assume that the residual value would be guaranteed by a third party.) (*Hint:* The lessee's annual payments will be appropriately reduced as the residual value increases.)

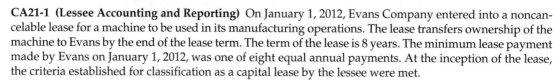

CONCEPTS FOR ANALYSIS

CA21-1 (Lessee Accounting and Reporting) On January 1, 2012, Evans Company entered into a noncancelable lease for a machine to be used in its manufacturing operations. The lease transfers ownership of the machine to Evans by the end of the lease term. The term of the lease is 8 years. The minimum lease payment made by Evans on January 1, 2012, was one of eight equal annual payments. At the inception of the lease, the criteria established for classification as a capital lease by the lessee were met.

Instructions

(a) What is the theoretical basis for the accounting standard that requires certain long-term leases to be capitalized by the lessee? Do not discuss the specific criteria for classifying a specific lease as a capital lease.
(b) How should Evans account for this lease at its inception and determine the amount to be recorded?
(c) What expenses related to this lease will Evans incur during the first year of the lease, and how will they be determined?
(d) How should Evans report the lease transaction on its December 31, 2012, balance sheet?

CA21-2 (Lessor and Lessee Accounting and Disclosure) Sylvan Inc. entered into a noncancelable lease arrangement with Breton Leasing Corporation for a certain machine. Breton's primary business is leasing; it is not a manufacturer or dealer. Sylvan will lease the machine for a period of 3 years, which is 50% of the machine's economic life. Breton will take possession of the machine at the end of the initial 3-year lease and lease it to another, smaller company that does not need the most current version of the machine. Sylvan does not guarantee any residual value for the machine and will not purchase the machine at the end of the lease term.

Sylvan's incremental borrowing rate is 10%, and the implicit rate in the lease is 9%. Sylvan has no way of knowing the implicit rate used by Breton. Using either rate, the present value of the minimum lease payments is between 90% and 100% of the fair value of the machine at the date of the lease agreement.

Sylvan has agreed to pay all executory costs directly, and no allowance for these costs is included in the lease payments.

Breton is reasonably certain that Sylvan will pay all lease payments, and because Sylvan has agreed to pay all executory costs, there are no important uncertainties regarding costs to be incurred by Breton. Assume that no indirect costs are involved.

Instructions

   (a) With respect to Sylvan (the lessee), answer the following.
   (1) What type of lease has been entered into? Explain the reason for your answer.
   (2) How should Sylvan compute the appropriate amount to be recorded for the lease or asset acquired?
   (3) What accounts will be created or affected by this transaction, and how will the lease or asset and other costs related to the transaction be matched with earnings?
   (4) What disclosures must Sylvan make regarding this leased asset?
   (b) With respect to Breton (the lessor), answer the following.
   (1) What type of leasing arrangement has been entered into? Explain the reason for your answer.
   (2) How should this lease be recorded by Breton, and how are the appropriate amounts determined?
   (3) How should Breton determine the appropriate amount of earnings to be recognized from each lease payment?
   (4) What disclosures must Breton make regarding this lease?

(AICPA adapted)

CA21-3 (Lessee Capitalization Criteria) On January 1, Santiago Company, a lessee, entered into three noncancelable leases for brand-new equipment, Lease L, Lease M, and Lease N. None of the three leases transfers ownership of the equipment to Santiago at the end of the lease term. For each of the three leases, the present value at the beginning of the lease term of the minimum lease payments, excluding that portion of the payments representing executory costs such as insurance, maintenance, and taxes to be paid by the lessor, is 75% of the fair value of the equipment.

   The following information is peculiar to each lease.

   1. Lease L does not contain a bargain-purchase option. The lease term is equal to 80% of the estimated economic life of the equipment.
   2. Lease M contains a bargain-purchase option. The lease term is equal to 50% of the estimated economic life of the equipment.
   3. Lease N does not contain a bargain-purchase option. The lease term is equal to 50% of the estimated economic life of the equipment.

Instructions

   (a) How should Santiago Company classify each of the three leases above, and why? Discuss the rationale for your answer.
   (b) What amount, if any, should Santiago record as a liability at the inception of the lease for each of the three leases above?
   (c) Assuming that the minimum lease payments are made on a straight-line basis, how should Santiago record each minimum lease payment for each of the three leases above?

(AICPA adapted)

CA21-4 (Comparison of Different Types of Accounting by Lessee and Lessor)

Part 1
Capital leases and operating leases are the two classifications of leases described in FASB pronouncements from the standpoint of the **lessee**.

Instructions

   (a) Describe how a capital lease would be accounted for by the lessee both at the inception of the lease and during the first year of the lease, assuming the lease transfers ownership of the property to the lessee by the end of the lease.
   (b) Describe how an operating lease would be accounted for by the lessee both at the inception of the lease and during the first year of the lease, assuming equal monthly payments are made by the lessee at the beginning of each month of the lease. Describe the change in accounting, if any, when rental payments are not made on a straight-line basis.

   Do **not** discuss the criteria for distinguishing between capital leases and operating leases.

Part 2
Sales-type leases and direct-financing leases are two of the classifications of leases described in FASB pronouncements from the standpoint of the **lessor**.

Instructions
Compare and contrast a sales-type lease with a direct-financing lease as follows.

(a) Lease receivable.
(b) Recognition of interest revenue.
(c) Manufacturer's or dealer's profit.

Do **not** discuss the criteria for distinguishing between the leases described above and operating leases.

(AICPA adapted)

CA21-5 (Lessee Capitalization of Bargain-Purchase Option) Albertsen Corporation is a diversified company with nationwide interests in commercial real estate developments, banking, copper mining, and metal fabrication. The company has offices and operating locations in major cities throughout the United States. Corporate headquarters for Albertsen Corporation is located in a metropolitan area of a midwestern state, and executives connected with various phases of company operations travel extensively. Corporate management is currently evaluating the feasibility of acquiring a business aircraft that can be used by company executives to expedite business travel to areas not adequately served by commercial airlines. Proposals for either leasing or purchasing a suitable aircraft have been analyzed, and the leasing proposal was considered to be more desirable.

The proposed lease agreement involves a twin-engine turboprop Viking that has a fair value of $1,000,000. This plane would be leased for a period of 10 years beginning January 1, 2012. The lease agreement is cancelable only upon accidental destruction of the plane. An annual lease payment of $141,780 is due on January 1 of each year; the first payment is to be made on January 1, 2012. Maintenance operations are strictly scheduled by the lessor, and Albertsen Corporation will pay for these services as they are performed. Estimated annual maintenance costs are $6,900. The lessor will pay all insurance premiums and local property taxes, which amount to a combined total of $4,000 annually and are included in the annual lease payment of $141,780. Upon expiration of the 10-year lease, Albertsen Corporation can purchase the Viking for $44,440. The estimated useful life of the plane is 15 years, and its salvage value in the used plane market is estimated to be $100,000 after 10 years. The salvage value probably will never be less than $75,000 if the engines are overhauled and maintained as prescribed by the manufacturer. If the purchase option is not exercised, possession of the plane will revert to the lessor, and there is no provision for renewing the lease agreement beyond its termination on December 31, 2021.

Albertsen Corporation can borrow $1,000,000 under a 10-year term loan agreement at an annual interest rate of 12%. The lessor's implicit interest rate is not expressly stated in the lease agreement, but this rate appears to be approximately 8% based on 10 net rental payments of $137,780 per year and the initial fair value of $1,000,000 for the plane. On January 1, 2012, the present value of all net rental payments and the purchase option of $44,440 is $888,890 using the 12% interest rate. The present value of all net rental payments and the $44,440 purchase option on January 1, 2012, is $1,022,226 using the 8% interest rate implicit in the lease agreement. The financial vice president of Albertsen Corporation has established that this lease agreement is a capital lease as defined in GAAP.

Instructions
(a) What is the appropriate amount that Albertsen Corporation should recognize for the leased aircraft on its balance sheet after the lease is signed?
(b) Without prejudice to your answer in part (a), assume that the annual lease payment is $141,780 as stated in the question, that the appropriate capitalized amount for the leased aircraft is $1,000,000 on January 1, 2012, and that the interest rate is 9%. How will the lease be reported in the December 31, 2012, balance sheet and related income statement? (Ignore any income tax implications.)

(CMA adapted)

CA21-6 (Lease Capitalization, Bargain-Purchase Option) Baden Corporation entered into a lease agreement for 10 photocopy machines for its corporate headquarters. The lease agreement qualifies as an operating lease in all terms except there is a bargain-purchase option. After the 5-year lease term, the corporation can purchase each copier for $1,000, when the anticipated fair value is $2,500.

Jerry Suffolk, the financial vice president, thinks the financial statements must recognize the lease agreement as a capital lease because of the bargain-purchase option. The controller, Diane Buchanan, disagrees: "Although I don't know much about the copiers themselves, there is a way to avoid recording the lease liability." She argues that the corporation might claim that copier technology advances rapidly and that by the end of the lease term the machines will most likely not be worth the $1,000 bargain price.

Instructions

Answer the following questions.

(a) What ethical issue is at stake?

(b) Should the controller's argument be accepted if she does not really know much about copier technology? Would it make a difference if the controller were knowledgeable about the pace of change in copier technology?

(c) What should Suffolk do?

*CA21-7 (Sale-Leaseback) On January 1, 2012, Perriman Company sold equipment for cash and leased it back. As seller-lessee, Perriman retained the right to substantially all of the remaining use of the equipment.

The term of the lease is 8 years. There is a gain on the sale portion of the transaction. The lease portion of the transaction is classified appropriately as a capital lease.

Instructions

(a) What is the theoretical basis for requiring lessees to capitalize certain long-term leases? **Do not discuss the specific criteria for classifying a lease as a capital lease**.

(b) (1) How should Perriman account for the sale portion of the sale-leaseback transaction at January 1, 2012?

(2) How should Perriman account for the leaseback portion of the sale-leaseback transaction at January 1, 2012?

(c) How should Perriman account for the gain on the sale portion of the sale-leaseback transaction during the first year of the lease? Why?

(AICPA adapted)

*CA21-8 (Sale-Leaseback) On December 31, 2012, Shellhammer Co. sold 6-month-old equipment at fair value and leased it back. There was a loss on the sale. Shellhammer pays all insurance, maintenance, and taxes on the equipment. The lease provides for eight equal annual payments, beginning December 31, 2013, with a present value equal to 85% of the equipment's fair value and sales price. The lease's term is equal to 80% of the equipment's useful life. There is no provision for Shellhammer to reacquire ownership of the equipment at the end of the lease term.

Instructions

(a) (1) Why is it important to compare an equipment's fair value to its lease payments' present value and its useful life to the lease term?

(2) Evaluate Shellhammer's leaseback of the equipment in terms of each of the four criteria for determination of a capital lease.

(b) How should Shellhammer account for the sale portion of the sale-leaseback transaction at December 31, 2012?

(c) How should Shellhammer report the leaseback portion of the sale-leaseback transaction on its December 31, 2013, balance sheet?

USING YOUR JUDGMENT

FINANCIAL REPORTING

Financial Reporting Problem

P&G The Procter & Gamble Company (P&G)

The financial statements of **P&G** are presented in Appendix 5B or can be accessed at the book's companion website, **www.wiley.com/college/kieso**.

Instructions

Refer to P&G's financial statements, accompanying notes, and management's discussion and analysis to answer the following questions.

(a) What types of leases are used by P&G?

(b) What amount of capital leases was reported by P&G in total and for less than one year?

(c) What minimum annual rental commitments under all noncancelable leases at June 30, 2009, did P&G disclose?

Comparative Analysis Case

UAL, Inc. and Southwest Airlines

Instructions

Go to the book's companion website or the company websites and use information found there to answer the following questions related to **UAL, Inc.** and **Southwest Airlines**.

(a) What types of leases are used by Southwest and on what assets are these leases primarily used?

(b) How long-term are some of Southwest's leases? What are some of the characteristics or provisions of Southwest's (as lessee) leases?

(c) What did Southwest report in 2009 as its future minimum annual rental commitments under noncancelable leases?

(d) At year-end 2009, what was the present value of the minimum rental payments under Southwest's capital leases? How much imputed interest was deducted from the future minimum annual rental commitments to arrive at the present value?

(e) What were the amounts and details reported by Southwest for rental expense in 2009, 2008, and 2007?

(f) How does UAL's use of leases compare with Southwest's?

Financial Statement Analysis Case

Tasty Baking Company

Presented in Illustration 21-31 are the financial statement disclosures from the 2009 annual report of **Tasty Baking Company**.

Instructions

Answer the following questions related to these disclosures.

(a) What is the total obligation under capital leases at December 26, 2009, for Tasty Baking Company?

(b) What is the book value of the assets under capital lease at December 26, 2009, for Tasty Baking Company? Explain why there is a difference between the amounts reported for assets and liabilities under capital leases.

(c) What is the total rental expense reported for leasing activity for the year ended December 26, 2009, for Tasty Baking Company?

(d) Estimate the off–balance-sheet liability due to Tasty Baking's operating leases at fiscal year-end 2009.

Accounting, Analysis, and Principles

Salaur Company is evaluating a lease arrangement being offered by TSP Company for use of a computer system. The lease is noncancelable, and in no case does Salaur receive title to the computers during or at the end of the lease term. The lease starts on January 1, 2012, with the first rental payment due on January 1, 2012. Additional information related to the lease is as follows.

Yearly rental	$3,557.25
Lease term	3 years
Estimated economic life	5 years
Purchase option	$3,000 at end of 3 years, which approximates fair value
Renewal option	1 year at $1,500; no penalty for nonrenewal; standard renewal clause
Fair value at inception of lease	$10,000
Cost of asset to lessor	$10,000
Residual value:	
Guaranteed	–0–
Unguaranteed	$3,000
Lessor's implicit rate (known by the lessee)	12%
Executory costs paid by:	Lessor; estimated to be $500 per year (included in rental equipment)
Estimated fair value at end of lease	$3,000

Accounting

Analyze the lease capitalization criteria for this lease for Salaur Company. Prepare the journal entry for Salaur on January 1, 2012.

Analysis

Briefly discuss the impact of the accounting for this lease for two common ratios: return on assets and debt to total assets.

Principles

What element of faithful representation (completeness, verifiability, neutrality, free from error) is being addressed when a company like Salaur evaluates lease capitalization criteria?

BRIDGE TO THE PROFESSION

Professional Research: FASB Codification

Daniel Hardware Co. is considering alternative financing arrangements for equipment used in its warehouses. Besides purchasing the equipment outright, Daniel is also considering a lease. Accounting for the outright purchase is fairly straightforward, but because Daniel has not used equipment leases in the past, the accounting staff is less informed about the specific accounting rules for leases.

The staff is aware of some lease rules related to a "90 percent of fair value," "75 percent of useful life," and "residual value deficiencies," but they are unsure about the meanings of these terms in lease accounting. Daniel has asked you to conduct some research on these items related to lease capitalization criteria.

Instructions

If your school has a subscription to the FASB Codification, go to *http://aaahq.org/ascLogin.cfm* to log in and prepare responses to the following. Provide Codification references for your responses.

(a) What is the objective of lease classification criteria?

(b) An important element of evaluating leases is determining whether substantially all of the risks and rewards of ownership are transferred in the lease. How is "substantially all" defined in the authoritative literature?

(c) Besides the noncancelable term of the lease, name at least three other considerations in determining the "lease term."

(d) A common issue in the accounting for leases concerns lease requirements that the lessee make up a residual value deficiency that is attributable to damage, extraordinary wear and tear, or excessive usage (e.g., excessive mileage on a leased vehicle). Do these features constitute a lessee guarantee of the residual value such that the estimated residual value of the leased property at the end of the lease term should be included in minimum lease payments? Explain.

Professional Simulations

Simulation 1

In this simulation, you are asked to address questions related to the accounting for leases. Prepare responses to all parts.

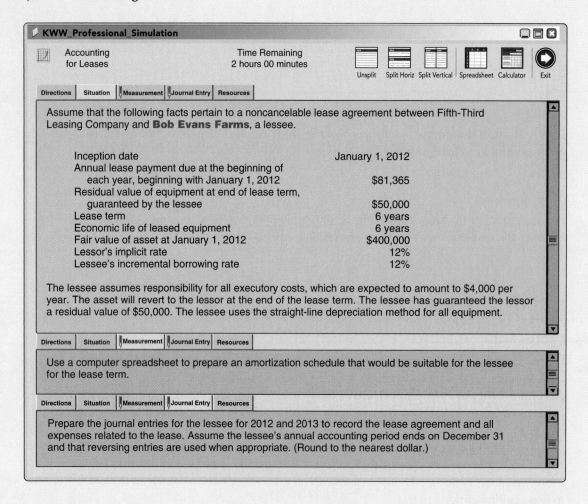

Simulation 2

In this simulation, you are asked to address questions related to the accounting for leases. Prepare responses to all parts. (Round amounts to the nearest cent.)

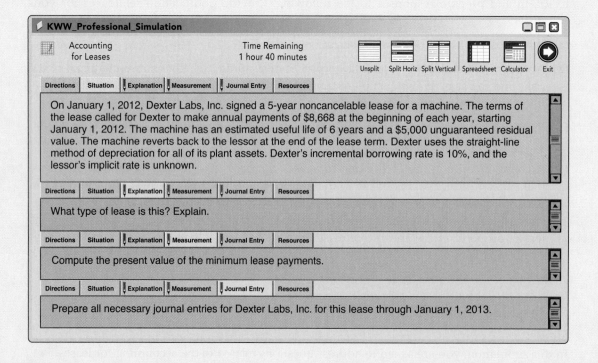

Leasing is a global business. Lessors and lessees enter into arrangements with one another without regard to national boundaries. Although GAAP and IFRS for leasing are similar, both the FASB and the IASB have decided that the existing accounting does not provide the most useful, transparent, and complete information about leasing transactions that should be provided in the financial statements.

RELEVANT FACTS

- Both GAAP and IFRS share the same objective of recording leases by lessees and lessors according to their economic substance—that is, according to the definitions of assets and liabilities.

- GAAP for leases uses bright-line criteria to determine if a lease arrangement transfers the risks and rewards of ownership; IFRS is more general in its provisions.

- Much of the terminology for lease accounting in IFRS and GAAP is the same. One difference is that finance leases are referred to as capital leases in GAAP.

- Under IFRS, lessees and lessors use the same general lease capitalization criteria to determine if the risks and rewards of ownership have been transferred in the lease. GAAP has additional lessor criteria that payments are collectible and there are no additional costs associated with a lease.

- IFRS requires that lessees use the implicit rate to record a lease, unless it is impractical to determine the lessor's implicit rate. GAAP requires use of the incremental rate, unless the implicit rate is known by the lessee and the implicit rate is lower than the incremental rate.

- Under GAAP, extensive disclosure of future noncancelable lease payments is required for each of the next five years and the years thereafter. Although some international companies (e.g., Nokia) provide a year-by-year breakout of payments due in years 1 through 5, IFRS does not require it.

- The FASB standard for leases was originally issued in 1976. The standard (*SFAS No. 13*) has been the subject of more than 30 interpretations since its issuance. The IFRS leasing standard is *IAS 17*, first issued in 1982. This standard is the subject of only three interpretations. One reason for this small number of interpretations is that IFRS does not specifically address a number of leasing transactions that are covered by GAAP. Examples include lease agreements for natural resources, sale-leasebacks, real estate leases, and leveraged leases.

ABOUT THE NUMBERS

Accounting by the Lessee

If Air France (the lessee) **capitalizes** a lease, it records an asset and a liability generally equal to the present value of the rental payments. ILFC (the lessor), having transferred substantially all the benefits and risks of ownership, recognizes a sale by removing the asset from the statement of financial position and replacing it with a receivable.

Under IFRS, a lease is classified as a **finance lease** if it transfers substantially all the risks and rewards incidental to ownership. In order to record a lease as a finance lease, the lease must be non-cancelable. The IASB identifies the four criteria listed in Illustration IFRS21-1 (page 1356) for assessing whether the risks and rewards have been transferred in the lease arrangement.

ILLUSTRATION
IFRS21-1
Capitalization Criteria
for Lessee

Capitalization Criteria (Lessee)
1. The lease transfers ownership of the property to the lessee.
2. The lease contains a bargain-purchase option.
3. The lease term is for the major part of the economic life of the asset.
4. The present value of the minimum lease payments amounts to substantially all of the fair value of the leased asset.

Air France classifies and accounts for leases that **do not meet any of the four criteria** as **operating leases**. Illustration IFRS21-2 shows that a lease meeting any one of the four criteria results in the lessee having a finance lease.

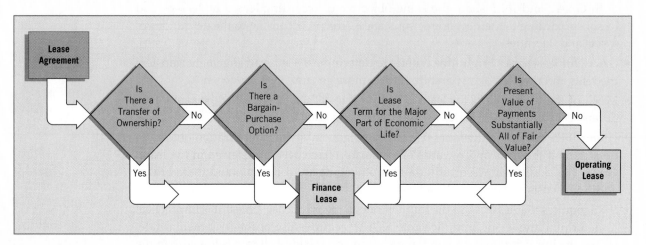

ILLUSTRATION
IFRS21-2
Diagram of Lessee's
Criteria for Lease
Classification

Thus, the proper classification of a lease is determined based on the substance of the lease transaction, rather than on its mere form. This determination often requires the use of professional judgment of whether the risks and rewards of ownership are transferred.

As indicated, the capitalization criteria for finance leases are similar to those used in GAAP for capital leases (see Illustration 21-3 on page 1295). The main differences relate to the economic life and recoverability tests, which we describe in the following sections.

Economic Life Test

If the lease period is for a major part of the asset's economic life, the lessor transfers most of the risks and rewards of ownership to the lessee. Capitalization is therefore appropriate. However, determining the lease term and what constitutes the major part of the economic life of the asset can be troublesome.

The IASB has not defined what is meant by the "major part" of an asset's economic life. In practice, following the IASB Hierarchy, it has been customary to look to GAAP, which has a 75 percent of economic life threshold for evaluating the economic life test. While the 75 percent guideline may be a useful reference point, it does not represent an automatic cutoff point. Rather, lessees and lessors should consider all relevant factors when assessing whether substantially all the risks and rewards of ownership have been transferred in the lease.[24] *For purposes of homework, assume a 75 percent threshold for the economic life test, unless otherwise stated.*

[24]See KPMG, *Insights into IFRS*, Fifth Edition (Thomson Reuters: London, 2008), p. 1011; and The International Financial Reporting Group of Ernst and Young, *International GAAP, 2009* (John Wiley and Sons: New York, 2009), p. 1356.

The **lease term** is generally considered to be the fixed, non-cancelable term of the lease. However, a bargain-renewal option, if provided in the lease agreement, can extend this period. A **bargain-renewal option** allows the lessee to renew the lease for a rental that is lower than the expected fair rental at the date the option becomes exercisable. At the inception of the lease, the difference between the renewal rental and the expected fair rental must be great enough to make exercise of the option to renew reasonably assured.

For example, assume that Carrefour leases Lenovo PCs for two years at a rental of $100 per month per computer and subsequently can lease them for $10 per month per computer for another two years. The lease clearly offers a bargain-renewal option; the lease term is considered to be four years. However, with bargain-renewal options, as with bargain-purchase options, it is sometimes difficult to determine what is a bargain.

Determining estimated economic life can also pose problems, especially if the leased item is a specialized item or has been used for a significant period of time. For example, determining the economic life of a nuclear core is extremely difficult. It is subject to much more than normal "wear and tear."

Recovery of Investment Test

If the present value of the minimum lease payments equals or exceeds substantially all of the fair value of the asset, then a lessee like Air France should capitalize the leased asset. Why? If the present value of the minimum lease payments is reasonably close to the fair value of the aircraft, Air France is effectively purchasing the asset.

As with the economic life test, the IASB has not defined what is meant by "substantially all" of an asset's fair value. In practice, it has been customary to look to GAAP, which has a 90 percent of fair value threshold for assessing the recovery of investment test. Again, rather than focusing on any single element of the lease classification indicators, lessees and lessors should consider all relevant factors when evaluating lease classification criteria.[25] *For purposes of homework, assume a 90 percent threshold for the recovery of investment test.*

Determining the present value of the minimum lease payments involves three important concepts: (1) minimum lease payments, (2) executory costs, and (3) discount rate. The IFRS guidelines for minimum lease payments and executory costs are the same as that of GAAP.

Discount Rate. A lessee, like Air France, computes the present value of the minimum lease payments using the **implicit interest rate**. This rate is defined as the discount rate that, at the inception of the lease, causes the aggregate present value of the minimum lease payments and the unguaranteed residual value to be equal to the fair value of the leased asset.

While Air France may argue that it cannot determine the implicit rate of the lessor, in most cases Air France can approximate the implicit rate used by ILFC. In the event that it is impracticable to determine the implicit rate, Air France should use its incremental borrowing rate. The incremental borrowing rate is the rate of interest the lessee would have to pay on a similar lease or the rate that, at the inception of the lease, the lessee would incur to borrow over a similar term the funds necessary to purchase the asset.

---

[25]*Ibid.* The 75 percent of useful life and 90 percent of fair value "bright-line" cutoffs in GAAP have been criticized. Many believe that lessees structure leases so as to just miss the 75 and 90 percent cutoffs, avoiding classifying leases as finance leases, thereby keeping leased assets and the related liabilities off the statement of financial position. See Warren McGregor, " Accounting for Leases: A New Approach," Special Report (Norwalk, Conn.: FASB, 1996).

If known or practicable to estimate, use of the implicit rate is preferred. This is because **the implicit rate of ILFC is generally a more realistic rate** to use in determining the amount (if any) to report as the asset and related liability for Air France. In addition, use of the implicit rate avoids use of **an artificially high incremental borrowing rate** that would cause the present value of the minimum lease payments to be lower, supporting an argument that the lease does not meet the recovery of investment test. Use of such a rate would thus make it more likely that the lessee avoids capitalization of the leased asset and related liability.

Air France may argue that it cannot determine the implicit rate of the lessor and therefore should use the higher incremental rate. However, in most cases, Air France can approximate the implicit rate used by ILFC. The determination of whether or not a reasonable estimate could be made will require judgment, particularly where the result from using the incremental borrowing rate comes close to meeting the fair value test. Because Air France **may not capitalize the leased property at more than its fair value** (as we discuss later), it cannot use an excessively low discount rate.

Finance Lease Method (Lessee)

To illustrate a finance lease, assume that CNH Capital (a subsidiary of CNH Global) and Ivanhoe Mines Ltd. sign a lease agreement dated January 1, 2012, that calls for CNH to lease a front-end loader to Ivanhoe beginning January 1, 2012. The terms and provisions of the lease agreement, and other pertinent data, are as follows.

- The term of the lease is five years. The lease agreement is non-cancelable, requiring equal rental payments of $25,981.62 at the beginning of each year (annuity-due basis).
- The loader has a fair value at the inception of the lease of $100,000, an estimated economic life of five years, and no residual value.
- Ivanhoe pays all of the executory costs directly to third parties except for the property taxes of $2,000 per year, which is included as part of its annual payments to CNH.
- The lease contains no renewal options. The loader reverts to CNH at the termination of the lease.
- Ivanhoe's incremental borrowing rate is 11 percent per year.
- Ivanhoe depreciates similar equipment that it owns on a straight-line basis.
- CNH sets the annual rental to earn a rate of return on its investment of 10 percent per year; Ivanhoe knows this fact.

The lease meets the criteria for classification as a finance lease for the following reasons:

1. The lease term of five years, being equal to the equipment's estimated economic life of five years, satisfies the economic life test.
2. The present value of the minimum lease payments ($100,000 as computed below) equals the fair value of the loader ($100,000).

The minimum lease payments are $119,908.10 ($23,981.62 × 5). Ivanhoe computes the amount capitalized as leased assets as the present value of the minimum lease payments (excluding executory costs—property taxes of $2,000) as shown in Illustration IFRS21-3.

ILLUSTRATION IFRS21-3
Computation of Capitalized Lease Payments

Capitalized amount = ($25,981.62 − $2,000) × Present value of an annuity due of 1 for
5 periods at 10% (Table 6-5)
= $23,981.62 × 4.16986
= $100,000

Ivanhoe uses CNH's implicit interest rate of 10 percent instead of its incremental borrowing rate of 11 percent because it knows about it.[26] Ivanhoe records the finance lease on its books on January 1, 2012, as:

Leased Equipment (under finance leases)	100,000	
Lease Liability		100,000

Note that the entry records the obligation at the net amount of $100,000 (the present value of the future rental payments) rather than at the gross amount of $119,908.10 ($23,981.62 × 5).

Ivanhoe records the **first lease payment on January 1, 2012**, as follows.

Property Tax Expense	2,000.00	
Lease Liability	23,981.62	
Cash		25,981.62

Each lease payment of $25,981.62 consists of three elements: (1) a reduction in the lease liability, (2) a financing cost (interest expense), and (3) executory costs (property taxes). The total financing cost (interest expense) over the term of the lease is $19,908.10. This amount is the difference between the present value of the lease payments ($100,000) and the actual cash disbursed, net of executory costs ($119,908.10). The annual interest expense, applying the effective-interest method, is a function of the outstanding liability, as Illustration IFRS21-4 shows.

Calculator Solution for Lease Payment

	Inputs	Answer
N	5	
I	10	
PV	?	100,000
PMT	−23,981.59	
FV	0	

IVANHOE MINES
LEASE AMORTIZATION SCHEDULE
ANNUITY-DUE BASIS

Date	Annual Lease Payment (a)	Executory Costs (b)	Interest (10%) on Liability (c)	Reduction of Lease Liability (d)	Lease Liability (e)
1/1/12					$100,000.00
1/1/12	$ 25,981.62	$ 2,000	$ –0–	$ 23,981.62	76,018.38
1/1/13	25,981.62	2,000	7,601.84	16,379.78	59,638.60
1/1/14	25,981.62	2,000	5,963.86	18,017.76	41,620.84
1/1/15	25,981.62	2,000	4,162.08	19,819.54	21,801.30
1/1/16	25,981.62	2,000	2,180.32*	21,801.30	–0–
	$129,908.10	$10,000	$19,908.10	$100,000.00	

(a) Lease payment as required by lease.
(b) Executory costs included in rental payment.
(c) Ten percent of the preceding balance of (e) except for 1/1/12; since this is an annuity due, no time has elapsed at the date of the first payment and no interest has accrued.
(d) (a) minus (b) and (c).
(e) Preceding balance minus (d).

*Rounded by 19 cents.

ILLUSTRATION IFRS21-4
Lease Amortization Schedule for Lessee—Annuity-Due Basis

At the end of its fiscal year, December 31, 2012, Ivanhoe records **accrued interest** as follows.

Interest Expense	7,601.84	
Interest Payable		7,601.84

Depreciation of the leased equipment over its five-year lease term, applying Ivanhoe's normal depreciation policy (straight-line method), results in the entry shown on page 1360 on December 31, 2012.

[26]If it is impracticable for Ivanhoe to determine the implicit rate and it has an incremental borrowing rate of, say, 9 percent (lower than the 10 percent rate used by CNH), the present value computation would yield a capitalized amount of $101,675.35 ($23,981.62 × 4.23972). Thus, use of an unrealistically low discount rate could lead to a lessee recording a leased asset at an amount exceeding the fair value of the equipment, which is generally prohibited in IFRS. This explains why the implicit rate should be used to capitalize the minimum lease payments.

Depreciation Expense (finance leases)	20,000	
Accumulated Depreciation—Finance Leases		
($100,000 ÷ 5 years)		20,000

At December 31, 2012, Ivanhoe separately identifies the assets recorded under finance leases on its statement of financial position. Similarly, it separately identifies the related obligations. Thus, once a lessee capitalizes a finance lease, the accounting under IFRS is the same as that applied for capital leases under GAAP.

Accounting by the Lessor

For accounting purposes, under IFRS the **lessor** also classifies leases as operating or finance leases. Finance leases may be further subdivided into direct-financing and sales-type leases.

As with lessee accounting, if the lease transfers substantially all the risks and rewards incidental to ownership, the lessor shall classify and account for the arrangement as a finance lease. Lessors evaluate the same criteria shown in Illustration IFRS21-1 to make this determination.

The distinction for the lessor between a direct-financing lease and a sales-type lease is the presence or absence of a manufacturer's or dealer's profit (or loss): A sales-type lease involves a manufacturer's or dealer's profit, and a direct-financing lease does not. The profit (or loss) to the lessor is evidenced by the difference between the fair value of the leased property at the inception of the lease and the lessor's cost or carrying amount (book value).

Normally, sales-type leases arise when manufacturers or dealers use leasing as a means of marketing their products. For example, a computer manufacturer will lease its computer equipment (possibly through a captive) to businesses and institutions. Direct-financing leases generally result from arrangements with lessors that are primarily engaged in financing operations (e.g., banks).

Lessors classify and account for all leases that do not qualify as direct-financing or sales-type leases as operating leases. Illustration IFRS21-5 shows the circumstances under which a lessor classifies a lease as operating, direct-financing, or sales-type.

ILLUSTRATION IFRS21-5
Diagram of Lessor's Criteria for Lease Classification

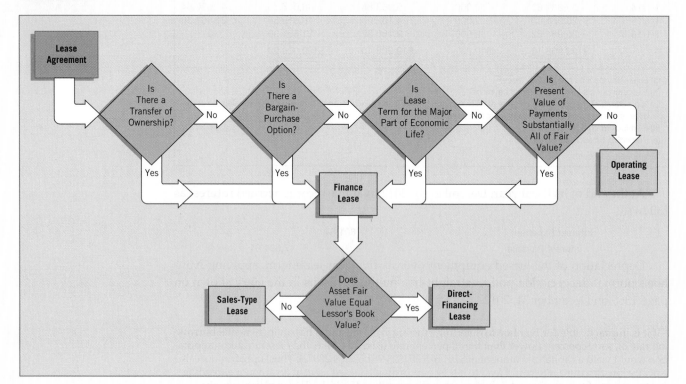

For purposes of comparison with the lessee's accounting, we will illustrate only the operating and direct-financing leases in the following section.

Direct-Financing Method (Lessor)

Direct-financing leases are in substance the financing of an asset purchase by the lessee. In this type of lease, the lessor records a **lease receivable** instead of a leased asset. The lease receivable is the present value of the minimum lease payments plus the present value of the unguaranteed residual value. Remember that "minimum lease payments" include: (1) rental payments (excluding executory costs), (2) bargain-purchase option (if any), (3) guaranteed residual value (if any), and (4) penalty for failure to renew (if any).

Thus, the lessor records the residual value, whether guaranteed or not. Also, recall that if the lessor pays any executory costs, then it should reduce the rental payment by that amount in computing minimum lease payments.

The following presentation, using the data from the preceding CNH/Ivanhoe example on pages 1358–1360, illustrates the accounting treatment for a direct-financing lease. We repeat here the information relevant to CNH in accounting for this lease transaction.

1. The term of the lease is five years beginning January 1, 2012, non-cancelable, and requires equal rental payments of $25,981.62 at the beginning of each year. Payments include $2,000 of executory costs (property taxes).

2. The equipment (front-end loader) has a cost of $100,000 to CNH, a fair value at the inception of the lease of $100,000, an estimated economic life of five years, and no residual value.

3. CNH incurred no initial direct costs in negotiating and closing the lease transaction.

4. The lease contains no renewal options. The equipment reverts to CNH at the termination of the lease.

5. CNH sets the annual lease payments to ensure a rate of return of 10 percent (implicit rate) on its investment, as shown in Illustration IFRS21-6.

Fair value of leased equipment		$100,000.00
Less: Present value of residual value		–0–
Amount to be recovered by lessor through lease payments		$100,000.00
Five beginning-of-the-year lease payments to yield a 10% return ($100,000 ÷ 4.16986ª)		$ 23,981.62

ªPV of an annuity due of 1 for 5 years at 10% (Table 6-5).

ILLUSTRATION IFRS21-6
Computation of Lease Payments

As shown in the earlier analysis, the lease meets the criteria for classification as a direct-financing lease for two reasons: (1) The lease term equals the equipment's estimated economic life, and (2) the present value of the minimum lease payments equals the equipment's fair value. It is not a sales-type lease because there is no difference between the fair value ($100,000) of the loader and CNH's cost ($100,000).

The Lease Receivable is the present value of the minimum lease payments (excluding executory costs which are property taxes of $2,000). CNH computes it as follows.

Lease receivable = ($25,981.62 − $2,000) × Present value of an annuity due of 1 for 5 periods at 10% (Table 6-5)
= $23,981.62 × 4.16986
= $100,000

ILLUSTRATION IFRS21-7
Computation of Lease Receivable

CNH records the lease of the asset and the resulting receivable on January 1, 2012 (the inception of the lease), as follows.

Lease Receivable	100,000	
Equipment		100,000

Companies often **report** the lease receivable in the statement of financial position as "Net investment in finance leases." Companies classify it either as current or noncurrent, depending on when they recover the net investment.

Under IFRS, once a lessor determines classification of a lease as either direct-financing or sales-type, the accounting for the lease arrangement is the same as GAAP (as shown on pages 1307–1309 and 1316–1319).

ON THE HORIZON

Lease accounting is one of the areas identified in the IASB/FASB Memorandum of Understanding. The Boards have issued proposed rules based on "right of use," which requires that all leases, regardless of their terms, be accounted for in a manner similar to how finance leases are treated today. That is, the notion of an operating lease will be eliminated, which will address the concerns under current rules in which no asset or liability is recorded for many operating leases. A final standard is expected in 2011. You can follow the lease project at either the FASB (*http://www.fasb.org*) or IASB (*http://www. iasb.org*) websites.

IFRS SELF-TEST QUESTIONS

1. Which of the following is *not* a criterion for a lease to be recorded as a finance lease?
  (a) There is transfer of ownership.
  (b) The lease is cancelable.
  (c) The lease term is for the major part of the economic life of the asset.
  (d) There is a bargain-purchase option.

2. Under IFRS, in computing the present value of the minimum lease payments, the lessee should:
  (a) use its incremental borrowing rate in all cases.
  (b) use either its incremental borrowing rate or the implicit rate of the lessor, whichever is higher, assuming that the implicit rate is known to the lessee.
  (c) use either its incremental borrowing rate or the implicit rate of the lessor, whichever is lower, assuming that the implicit rate is known to the lessee.
  (d) use the implicit rate of the lessor, unless it is impracticable to determine the implicit rate.

3. A lease that involves a manufacturer's or dealer's profit is a (an):
  (a) direct financing lease.
  (b) finance lease.
  (c) operating lease.
  (d) sales-type lease.

4. Which of the following statements is *true* when comparing the accounting for leasing transactions under GAAP with IFRS?
  (a) IFRS for leases is more "rules-based" than GAAP and includes many bright-line criteria to determine ownership.
  (b) IFRS requires that companies provide a year-by-year breakout of future noncancelable lease payments due in years 1 through 5.

(c) The IFRS leasing standard is the subject of over 30 interpretations since its issuance in 1982.

(d) IFRS does not provide detailed guidance for leases of natural resources, sale-leasebacks, and leveraged leases.

5. All of the following statements about lease accounting under IFRS and GAAP are true *except:*

(a) IFRS requires a year-by-year breakout of payments related to leasing arrangements.

(b) IFRS is more general in its lease accounting provisions than is GAAP.

(c) the IFRS leasing standard, *IAS 17*, is the subject of only three interpretations.

(d) Finance leases under IFRS are referred to as capital leases under GAAP.

IFRS CONCEPTS AND APPLICATION

IFRS21-1 Where can authoritative IFRS related to the accounting for leases be found?

IFRS21-2 Briefly describe some of the similarities and differences between GAAP and IFRS with respect to the accounting for leases.

IFRS21-3 Briefly discuss the IASB and FASB efforts to converge their accounting guidelines for leases.

IFRS21-4 Outline the accounting procedures involved in applying the operating lease method by a lessee.

IFRS21-5 Outline the accounting procedures involved in applying the finance lease method by a lessee.

IFRS21-6 Identify the lease classifications for lessors and the criteria that must be met for each classification.

IFRS21-7 Rick Kleckner Corporation recorded a finance lease at $300,000 on January 1, 2012. The interest rate is 12%. Kleckner Corporation made the first lease payment of $53,920 on January 1, 2012. The lease requires eight annual payments. The equipment has a useful life of 8 years with no residual value. Prepare Kleckner Corporation's December 31, 2012, adjusting entries.

IFRS21-8 Use the information for Rick Kleckner Corporation from IFRS21-7. Assume that at December 31, 2012, Kleckner made an adjusting entry to accrue interest expense of $29,530 on the lease. Prepare Kleckner's January 1, 2013, journal entry to record the second lease payment of $53,920.

IFRS21-9 Brecker Company leases an automobile with a fair value of $10,906 from Emporia Motors, Inc., on the following terms:

1. Non-cancelable term of 50 months.

2. Rental of $250 per month (at end of each month). (The present value at 1% per month is $9,800.)

3. Estimated residual value after 50 months is $1,180. (The present value at 1% per month is $715.) Brecker Company guarantees the residual value of $1,180.

4. Estimated economic life of the automobile is 60 months.

5. Brecker Company's incremental borrowing rate is 12% a year (1% a month). It is impracticable to determine Emporia's implicit rate.

Instructions

(a) What is the nature of this lease to Brecker Company?

(b) What is the present value of the minimum lease payments?

(c) Record the lease on Brecker Company's books at the date of inception.

   (d) Record the first month's depreciation on Brecker Company's books (assume straight-line).

   (e) Record the first month's lease payment.

IFRS21-10 The following facts pertain to a non-cancelable lease agreement between Lennox Leasing Company and Gill Company, a lessee. (Round all numbers to the nearest cent.)

Inception date: May 1, 2012

Annual lease payment due at the beginning of each year, beginning with May 1, 2012: $18,829.49

Bargain-purchase option price at end of lease term: $4,000.00

Lease term: 5 years

Economic life of leased equipment: 10 years

Lessor's cost: $65,000.00; fair value of asset at May 1, 2012, $81,000.00

Lessor's implicit rate: 10%; lessee's incremental borrowing rate 10%

The lessee assumes responsibility for all executory costs.

Instructions

   (a) Discuss the nature of this lease to Gill Company.

   (b) Discuss the nature of this lease to Lennox Company.

   (c) Prepare a lease amortization schedule for Gill Company for the 5-year lease term.

   (d) Prepare the journal entries on the lessee's books to reflect the signing of the lease agreement and to record the payments and expenses related to this lease for the years 2012 and 2013. Gill's annual accounting period ends on December 31. Reversing entries are used by Gill.

IFRS21-11 A lease agreement between Lennox Leasing Company and Gill Company is described in IFRS21-10. Refer to the data in IFRS21-10 and do the following for the lessor. (Round all numbers to the nearest cent.)

Instructions

   (a) Compute the amount of the lease receivable at the inception of the lease.

   (b) Prepare a lease amortization schedule for Lennox Leasing Company for the 5-year lease term.

   (c) Prepare the journal entries to reflect the signing of the lease agreement and to record the receipts and income related to this lease for the years 2012, 2013, and 2014. The lessor's accounting period ends on December 31. Reversing entries are not used by Lennox.

Professional Research

IFRS21-12 Daniel Hardware Co. is considering alternative financing arrangements for equipment used in its warehouses. Besides purchasing the equipment outright, Daniel is also considering a lease. Accounting for the outright purchase is fairly straightforward, but because Daniel has not used equipment leases in the past, the accounting staff is less informed about the specific accounting rules for leases. The staff is aware of some general lease rules related to "risks and rewards," but they are unsure about the meanings of these terms in lease accounting. Daniel has asked you to conduct some research on these items related to lease capitalization criteria.

Instructions

Access the IFRS authoritative literature at the IASB website (*http://eifrs.iasb.org/*). When you have accessed the documents, you can use the search tool in your Internet browser to respond to the following questions (Provide paragraph citations.)

(a) What is the objective of lease classification criteria?

(b) An important element of evaluating leases is determining whether substantially all of the risks and rewards of ownership are transferred in the lease. How is "substantially all" defined in the authoritative literature?

(c) Besides the non-cancelable term of the lease, name at least three other considerations in determining the "lease term."

International Financial Reporting Problem:
Marks and Spencer plc

IFRS21-13 The financial statements of Marks and Spencer plc (M&S) are available at the book's companion website or can be accessed at *http://corporate.marksandspencer. com/documents/publications/2010/Annual_Report_2010*.

Instructions

Refer to M&S's financial statements and the accompanying notes to answer the following questions.

(a) What types of leases are used by M&S?

(b) What amount of finance leases was reported by M&S in total and for less than one year?

(c) What minimum annual rental commitments under all non-cancelable leases at April 3, 2010, did M&S disclose?

ANSWERS TO IFRS SELF-TEST QUESTIONS
1. b **2.** d **3.** d **4.** d **5.** a

Accounting Changes and Error Analysis

After studying this chapter, you should be able to:

1 Identify the types of accounting changes.

2 Describe the accounting for changes in accounting principles.

3 Understand how to account for retrospective accounting changes.

4 Understand how to account for impracticable changes.

5 Describe the accounting for changes in estimates.

6 Identify changes in a reporting entity.

7 Describe the accounting for correction of errors.

8 Identify economic motives for changing accounting methods.

9 Analyze the effect of errors.

In the Dark

The FASB's conceptual framework describes comparability (including consistency) as one of the qualitative characteristics that contribute to the usefulness of accounting information. Unfortunately, companies are finding it difficult to maintain comparability and consistency due to the numerous changes in accounting principles mandated by the FASB. In addition, a number of companies have faced restatements due to errors in their financial statements. For example, the table below shows types and numbers of recent accounting changes.

Noncontrolling interests	96	Debt-equity financial instruments	20
Fair value measurements	51	Derivative and hedging	18
Business combinations	46	Earnings per share	17
Defined benefit pension and postretirement plans	44	Other, including tax uncertainties, inventories, impairments, asset retirement obligations	43

Although the percentage of companies reporting material changes or errors is small, readers of financial statements still must be careful. The reason: The amounts in the financial statements may have changed due to changing accounting principles and/or restatements. The chart below indicates the recent trends in restatements.

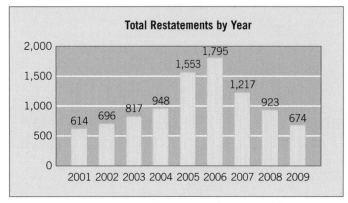

Total Restatements by Year

2001: 614
2002: 696
2003: 817
2004: 948
2005: 1,553
2006: 1,795
2007: 1,217
2008: 923
2009: 674

There is much good news in the chart. In 2007, restatements declined by 32.2 percent (from 1,795 to 1,217). In 2008, restatements declined another 24 percent (from 1,217 to 923). The declining trend

IFRS IN THIS CHAPTER

▶ See the **International Perspectives** on pages 1369 and 1379.

▶ Read the **IFRS Insights** on pages 1428–1432 for a discussion of:

—Direct and indirect effects of changes

—Impracticability

continued in 2009. However, investors can be in the dark when a company has an error that requires restatement. It may take some time for companies to sort out the source of an error, prepare corrected statements, and get auditor sign-off. Recent data indicate it takes on average about 3 months to resolve a restatement. The following table reports the range of periods when investors are in the dark due to a restatement.

Time to File Restated Financial Statements	% of All Restatements
Up to 3 Months	77
3–9 Months	11
Greater than 9 Months	12

While most companies (77%) resolve their errors within 3 months, 12 percent (or over 200 companies) take more than 9 months to file corrected statements.

These lengthy "dark periods" have caught the attention of policy-setters and were a topic of discussion of the Committee for Improvements in Financial Reporting (CIFR). As one member of CIFR noted, "The dark period is bad for users." As a result, the committee is proposing that for some errors, companies might not need to go through the pain of restatement, but enhanced disclosures about errors are needed.

Sources: Accounting change data from *Accounting Trends and Techniques—2010* (New York: AICPA, 2010). Restatement data from *2009 Financial Restatements: A Nine Year Comparison*, Audit Analytics (February 10, 2010), p. 3; and M. Leone, "Materiality Debate Emerges from the Dark," *CFO.com* (July 14, 2008).

PREVIEW OF CHAPTER 22 ▶ As our opening story indicates, changes in accounting principles and errors in financial information have increased substantially in recent years. When these changes occur, companies must follow specific accounting and reporting requirements. In addition, to ensure comparability among companies, the FASB has standardized reporting of accounting changes, accounting estimates, error corrections, and related earnings per share information. In this chapter, we discuss these reporting standards, which help investors better understand a company's financial condition. The content and organization of the chapter are as follows.

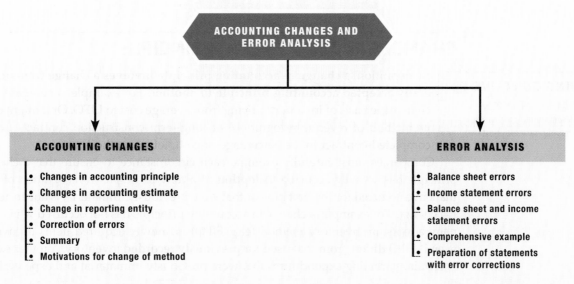

ACCOUNTING CHANGES AND ERROR ANALYSIS

ACCOUNTING CHANGES
- Changes in accounting principle
- Changes in accounting estimate
- Change in reporting entity
- Correction of errors
- Summary
- Motivations for change of method

ERROR ANALYSIS
- Balance sheet errors
- Income statement errors
- Balance sheet and income statement errors
- Comprehensive example
- Preparation of statements with error corrections

SECTION 1 • ACCOUNTING CHANGES

LEARNING OBJECTIVE 1
Identify the types of accounting changes.

Accounting alternatives diminish the comparability of financial information between periods and between companies; they also obscure useful historical trend data. For example, if **Ford** revises its estimates for equipment useful lives, depreciation expense for the current year will not be comparable to depreciation expense reported by Ford in prior years. Similarly, if **OfficeMax** changes to FIFO inventory pricing while **Staples** uses LIFO, it will be difficult to compare these companies' reported results. A reporting framework helps preserve comparability when there is an accounting change.

See the FASB Codification section (page 1404).

The FASB has established a reporting framework, which involves three types of accounting changes. [1] The three types of accounting changes are:

Underlying Concepts

While changes in accounting may enhance the qualitative characteristic of *usefulness*, these changes may adversely affect the characteristics of *comparability* and *consistency*.

1. *Change in accounting principle.* A change from one generally accepted accounting principle to another one. For example, a company may change its inventory valuation method from LIFO to average cost.

2. *Change in accounting estimate.* A change that occurs as the result of new information or additional experience. For example, a company may change its estimate of the useful lives of depreciable assets.

3. *Change in reporting entity.* A change from reporting as one type of entity to another type of entity. As an example, a company might change the subsidiaries for which it prepares consolidated financial statements.

A fourth category necessitates changes in accounting, though it is not classified as an accounting change.

4. *Errors in financial statements.* Errors result from mathematical mistakes, mistakes in applying accounting principles, or oversight or misuse of facts that existed when preparing the financial statements. For example, a company may incorrectly apply the retail inventory method for determining its final inventory value.

The FASB classifies changes in these categories because each category involves different methods of recognizing changes in the financial statements. In this chapter, we discuss these classifications. We also explain how to report each item in the accounts and how to disclose the information in comparative statements.

CHANGES IN ACCOUNTING PRINCIPLE

LEARNING OBJECTIVE 2
Describe the accounting for changes in accounting principles.

By definition, a change in accounting principle **involves a change from one generally accepted accounting principle to another**. For example, a company might change the basis of inventory pricing from average cost to LIFO. Or it might change its method of revenue recognition for long-term construction contracts from the completed-contract to the percentage-of-completion method.

Companies must carefully examine each circumstance to ensure that a change in principle has actually occurred. **Adoption of a new principle** in recognition of events that have occurred for the first time or that were previously immaterial is not an accounting change. For example, a change in accounting principle has not occurred when a company adopts an inventory method (e.g., FIFO) for **newly** acquired items of inventory, even if FIFO differs from that used for **previously recorded** inventory. Another example is certain marketing expenditures that were previously immaterial and expensed in the period incurred. It would not be considered a change in accounting principle if they become material and so may be acceptably deferred and amortized.

Finally, what if a company previously followed an accounting principle that was not acceptable? Or what if the company applied a principle incorrectly? In such cases, the profession considers a change to a generally accepted accounting principle **a correction of an error**. For example, a switch from the cash (income tax) basis of accounting to the accrual basis is a correction of an error. Or, if a company deducted salvage value when computing double-declining depreciation on plant assets and later recomputed depreciation without deducting estimated salvage value, it has corrected an error.

There are three possible approaches for reporting changes in accounting principles:

Report changes currently. In this approach, companies report the cumulative effect of the change in the current year's income statement as an irregular item. The cumulative effect is the difference in prior years' income between the newly adopted and prior accounting method. Under this approach, the effect of the change on prior years' income appears only in the current-year income statement. The company does not change **prior-year financial statements**.

Advocates of this position argue that changing prior years' financial statements results in a loss of confidence in financial reports. How do investors react when told that the earnings computed three years ago are now entirely different? Changing prior periods, if permitted, also might upset contractual arrangements based on the old figures. For example, profit-sharing arrangements computed on the old basis might have to be recomputed and completely new distributions made, creating numerous legal problems. Many practical difficulties also exist: The cost of changing prior period financial statements may be excessive, or determining the amount of the prior period effect may be impossible on the basis of available data.

Report changes retrospectively. Retrospective application refers to the application of a different accounting principle to recast previously issued financial statements—**as if the new principle had always been used**. In other words, the company "goes back" and adjusts **prior years' statements** on a basis consistent with the newly adopted principle. The company shows any cumulative effect of the change as an adjustment to beginning retained earnings of the earliest year presented.

Advocates of this position argue that retrospective application ensures comparability. Think for a moment what happens if this approach is not used: The year *previous* to the change will be on the old method; the year *of the change* will report the entire cumulative adjustment; and the *following* year will present financial statements on the new basis without the cumulative effect of the change. Such lack of consistency fails to provide meaningful earnings-trend data and other financial relationships necessary to evaluate the business.

Report changes prospectively (in the future). In this approach, previously reported results remain. As a result, companies do not adjust opening balances to reflect the change in principle. Advocates of this position argue that once management presents financial statements based on acceptable accounting principles, they are final; management cannot change prior periods by adopting a new principle. According to this line of reasoning, the current-period cumulative adjustment is not appropriate, because that approach includes amounts that have little or no relationship to the current year's income or economic events.

> **INTERNATIONAL PERSPECTIVE**
>
> IFRS (*IAS 8*) generally requires retrospective application to prior years for accounting changes. However, *IAS 8* permits the prospective method if a company cannot reasonably determine the amounts to which to restate prior periods.

Given these three possible approaches, which does the accounting profession prefer? The FASB **requires that companies use the retrospective approach.** Why? Because it provides financial statement users with more useful information than the cumulative-effect or prospective approaches. [2] The rationale is that changing the prior statements to be on the same basis as the newly adopted principle results in greater consistency across accounting periods. Users can then better compare results from one period to the next.[1]

QUITE A CHANGE

The cumulative-effect approach results in a loss of comparability. Also, reporting the cumulative adjustment in the period of the change can significantly affect net income, resulting in a misleading income figure. For example, at one time Chrysler Corporation changed its inventory accounting from LIFO to FIFO. If Chrysler had used the cumulative-effect approach, it would have reported a $53,500,000 adjustment to net income. That adjustment would have resulted in net income of $45,900,000, instead of a net loss of $7,600,000.

A second case: In the early 1980s, the railroad industry switched from the retirement-replacement method of depreciating railroad equipment to more generally used methods such as straight-line depreciation. Using cumulative treatment, railroad companies would have made substantial adjustments to income in the period of change. Many in the industry argued that including such large cumulative-effect adjustments in the current year would distort the information and make it less useful.

Such situations lend support to retrospective application so that comparability is maintained.

Retrospective Accounting Change Approach

A presumption exists that once a company adopts an accounting principle, it should not change. That presumption is understandable, given the idea that consistent use of an accounting principle enhances the usefulness of financial statements. However, the environment continually changes, and companies change in response. Recent standards on such subjects as stock options, exchanges of nonmonetary assets, and derivatives indicate that changes in accounting principle will continue to occur.

When a company changes an accounting principle, it should report the change using retrospective application. In general terms, here is what it must do:

1. It adjusts its financial statements for each prior period presented. Thus, financial statement information about prior periods is on the same basis as the new accounting principle.

2. It adjusts the carrying amounts of assets and liabilities as of the beginning of the first year presented. By doing so, these accounts reflect the cumulative effect on periods prior to those presented of the change to the new accounting principle. The company also makes an offsetting adjustment to the opening balance of retained earnings or other appropriate component of stockholders' equity or net assets as of the beginning of the first year presented.

For example, assume that Target decides to change its inventory valuation method in 2012 from the retail inventory method (FIFO) to the retail inventory (average cost). It provides comparative information for 2010 and 2011 based on the new method. Target would adjust its assets, liabilities, and retained earnings for periods prior to 2010 and report these amounts in the 2010 financial statements, when it prepares comparative financial statements.

[1]Adoption of the retrospective approach contributes to international accounting convergence. As discussed throughout the textbook, the FASB and the IASB are collaborating on a project in which they have agreed to converge around high-quality solutions to resolve differences between GAAP and IFRS. By adopting the retrospective approach, which is the method used in IFRS, the FASB agreed that this approach is superior to the current approach.

Retrospective Accounting Change: Long-Term Contracts

To illustrate the retrospective approach, assume that Denson Company has accounted for its income from long-term construction contracts using the completed-contract method. In 2012, the company changed to the percentage-of-completion method. Management believes this approach provides a more appropriate measure of the income earned. For tax purposes, the company uses the completed-contract method and plans to continue doing so in the future. (We assume a 40 percent enacted tax rate.)

Illustration 22-1 shows portions of three income statements for 2010–2012—for both the completed-contract and percentage-of-completion methods (2010 was Denson's first year of operations).

COMPLETED-CONTRACT METHOD
DENSON COMPANY
INCOME STATEMENT (PARTIAL)
FOR THE YEARS ENDED DECEMBER 31

	2010	2011	2012
Income before income tax	$400,000	$160,000	$190,000
Income tax (40%)	160,000	64,000	76,000
Net income	$240,000	$ 96,000	$114,000

PERCENTAGE-OF-COMPLETION METHOD
DENSON COMPANY
INCOME STATEMENT (PARTIAL)
FOR THE YEARS ENDED DECEMBER 31

	2010	2011	2012
Income before income tax	$600,000	$180,000	$200,000
Income tax (40%)	240,000	72,000	80,000
Net income	$360,000	$108,000	$120,000

ILLUSTRATION 22-1
Comparative Income Statements for Completed-Contract versus Percentage-of-Completion Methods

To record a change from the completed-contract to the percentage-of-completion method, we analyze the various effects, as Illustration 22-2 shows.

ILLUSTRATION 22-2
Data for Retrospective Change Example

	Pretax Income from			Difference in Income	
Year	Percentage-of-Completion	Completed-Contract	Difference	Tax Effect 40%	Income Effect (net of tax)
Prior to 2011	$600,000	$400,000	$200,000	$80,000	$120,000
In 2011	180,000	160,000	20,000	8,000	12,000
Total at beginning of 2012	$780,000	$560,000	$220,000	$88,000	$132,000
Total in 2012	$200,000	$190,000	$ 10,000	$ 4,000	$ 6,000

The entry to record the change at the beginning of 2012 would be:

Construction in Process	220,000	
Deferred Tax Liability		88,000
Retained Earnings		132,000

The Construction in Process account increases by $220,000 (as indicated in the first column under "Difference in Income" in Illustration 22-2). The credit to Retained Earnings of $132,000 reflects the cumulative income effects prior to 2012 (third column under "Difference in Income" in Illustration 22-2). The company credits Retained Earnings because prior years' income is closed to this account each year. The credit to Deferred Tax Liability represents the adjustment to prior years' tax expense. The company now recognizes that amount, $88,000, as a tax liability for future taxable amounts. That is, in future periods, taxable income will be higher than book income as a result of current temporary differences. Therefore, Denson must report a deferred tax liability in the current year.

CHANGE MANAGEMENT

What do the numbers mean?

Halliburton offers a case study in the importance of good reporting of an accounting change. Recall from Chapter 18 that Halliburton uses percentage-of-completion accounting for its long-term construction-services contracts. Recently, the SEC questioned the company about its change in accounting for disputed claims.

Prior to the year of the change, Halliburton took a very conservative approach to its accounting for disputed claims. That is, the company waited until all disputes were resolved before recognizing associated revenues. In contrast, in the year of the change, the company recognized revenue for disputed claims *before* their resolution, using estimates of amounts expected to be recovered. Such revenue and its related profit are more tentative and subject to possible later adjustment. The accounting method adopted is more aggressive than the company's former policy but is within the boundaries of GAAP.

It appears that the problem with Halliburton's accounting stems more from how the company handled its accounting change than from the new method itself. That is, Halliburton did not provide in its annual report in the year of the change an explicit reference to its change in accounting method. In fact, rather than stating its new policy, the company simply deleted the sentence that described how it accounted for disputed claims. Then later, in its next-year's annual report, the company stated its new accounting policy.

When companies make such changes in accounting, investors need to be informed about the change and about its effects on the financial results. With such information, investors and analysts can compare current results with those of prior periods and can make a more informed assessment about the company's future prospects.

Source: Adapted from "Accounting Ace Charles Mulford Answers Accounting Questions," *Wall Street Journal Online* (June 7, 2002).

Reporting a Change in Principle. The disclosure of accounting changes is particularly important. Users of the financial statements want consistent information from one period to the next. Such consistency ensures the usefulness of financial statements. The major disclosure requirements are as follows.

1. The nature of and reason for the change in accounting principle. This must include an explanation of why the newly adopted accounting principle is preferable.
2. The method of applying the change, and:
   a. A description of the prior period information that has been retrospectively adjusted, if any.
   b. The effect of the change on income from continuing operations, net income (or other appropriate captions of changes in net assets or performance indicators), any other affected line item, and any affected per share amounts for the current period and for any prior periods retrospectively adjusted.
   c. The cumulative effect of the change on retained earnings or other components of equity or net assets in the statement of financial position as of the beginning of the earliest period presented.[2]

To illustrate, Denson will prepare comparative financial statements for 2011 and 2012 using the percentage-of-completion method (the new-construction accounting method). Illustration 22-3 indicates how Denson presents this information.

[2]Presentation of the effect on financial statement subtotals and totals other than income from continuing operations and net income (or other appropriate captions of changes in the applicable net assets or performance indicator) is not required. [3]

DENSON COMPANY
INCOME STATEMENT (PARTIAL)
FOR THE YEAR ENDED

	2012	2011
		As Adjusted (Note A)
Income before income tax	$200,000	$180,000
Income tax (40%)	80,000	72,000
Net income	$120,000	$108,000

Note A: Change in Method of Accounting for Long-Term Contracts. The company has accounted for revenue and costs for long-term construction contracts by the percentage-of-completion method in 2012, whereas in all prior years revenue and costs were determined by the completed-contract method. The new method of accounting for long-term contracts was adopted to recognize . . . [state justification for change in accounting principle] . . ., and financial statements of prior years have been restated to apply the new method retrospectively. For income tax purposes, the completed-contract method has been continued. The effect of the accounting change on income of 2012 was an increase of $6,000 net of related taxes and on income of 2011 as previously reported was an increase of $12,000 net of related taxes. The balances of retained earnings for 2011 and 2012 have been adjusted for the effect of applying retroactively the new method of accounting. As a result of the accounting change, retained earnings as of January 1, 2011, increased by $120,000 compared to that reported using the completed-contract method.

As Illustration 22-3 shows, Denson Company reports net income under the newly adopted percentage-of-completion method for both 2011 and 2012. The company retrospectively adjusted the 2011 income statement to report the information on a percentage-of-completion basis. Also, the note to the financial statements indicates the nature of the change, why the company made the change, and the years affected.

In addition, companies are required to provide data on important differences between the amounts reported under percentage-of-completion versus completed-contract. When identifying the significant differences, some companies show the *entire* financial statements and line-by-line differences between percentage-of-completion and completed-contract. However, most companies will show only line-by-line differences. For example, Denson would show the differences in construction in process, retained earnings, gross profit, and net income for 2011 and 2012 under the completed-contract and percentage-of-completion methods.

Retained Earnings Adjustment. As indicated earlier, one of the disclosure requirements is to show the cumulative effect of the change on retained earnings as of the beginning of the earliest period presented. For Denson Company, that date is January 1, 2011. Denson disclosed that information by means of a narrative description (see Note A in Illustration 22-3). Denson also would disclose this information in its retained earnings statement. Assuming a retained earnings balance of $1,360,000 at the beginning of 2010, Illustration 22-4 shows Denson's retained earnings statement under the completed-contract method—that is, before giving effect to the change in accounting principle. (The income information comes from Illustration 22-1 on page 1371.)

ILLUSTRATION 22-4
Retained Earnings
Statement before
Retrospective Change

DENSON COMPANY
RETAINED EARNINGS STATEMENT
FOR THE YEAR ENDED

	2012	2011	2010
Retained earnings, January 1	$1,696,000	$1,600,000	$1,360,000
Net income	114,000	96,000	240,000
Retained earnings, December 31	$1,810,000	$1,696,000	$1,600,000

If Denson presents comparative statements for 2011 and 2012 under percentage-of-completion, then it must change the beginning balance of retained earnings at

January 1, 2011. The difference between the retained earnings balances under completed-contract and percentage-of-completion is computed as follows.

Retained earnings, January 1, 2011 (percentage-of-completion)	$1,720,000
Retained earnings, January 1, 2011 (completed-contract)	(1,600,000)
Cumulative-effect difference	$ 120,000

The $120,000 difference is the cumulative effect. Illustration 22-5 shows a comparative retained earnings statement for 2011 and 2012, giving effect to the change in accounting principle to percentage-of-completion.

ILLUSTRATION 22-5
Retained Earnings
Statement after
Retrospective Application

DENSON COMPANY
RETAINED EARNINGS STATEMENT
FOR THE YEAR ENDED

	2012	2011
Retained earnings, January 1, as reported	—	$1,600,000
Add: Adjustment for the cumulative effect on prior years of applying retrospectively the new method of accounting for construction contracts		120,000
Retained earnings, January 1, as adjusted	$1,828,000	1,720,000
Net income	120,000	108,000
Retained earnings, December 31	$1,948,000	$1,828,000

Denson adjusted the beginning balance of retained earnings on January 1, 2011, for the excess of percentage-of-completion net income over completed-contract net income in 2010. This comparative presentation indicates the type of adjustment that a company needs to make. It follows that this adjustment would be much larger if a number of prior periods were involved.

Retrospective Accounting Change: Inventory Methods

As a second illustration of the retrospective approach, assume that Lancer Company has accounted for its inventory using the LIFO method. In 2012, the company changes to the FIFO method because management believes this approach provides a more appropriate reporting of its inventory costs. Illustration 22-6 provides additional information related to Lancer Company.

ILLUSTRATION 22-6
Lancer Company
Information

1. Lancer Company started its operations on January 1, 2010. At that time, stockholders invested $100,000 in the business in exchange for common stock.

2. All sales, purchases, and operating expenses for the period 2010–2012 are cash transactions. Lancer's cash flows over this period are as follows.

	2010	2011	2012
Sales	$300,000	$300,000	$300,000
Purchases	90,000	110,000	125,000
Operating expenses	100,000	100,000	100,000
Cash flow from operations	$110,000	$ 90,000	$ 75,000

3. Lancer has used the LIFO method for financial reporting since its inception.

4. Inventory determined under LIFO and FIFO for the period 2010–2012 is as follows.

	LIFO Method	FIFO Method	Difference
January 1, 2010	$ 0	$ 0	$ 0
December 31, 2010	10,000	12,000	2,000
December 31, 2011	20,000	25,000	5,000
December 31, 2012	32,000	39,000	7,000

ILLUSTRATION 22-6
(Continued)

5. Cost of goods sold under LIFO and FIFO for the period 2010–2012 are as follows.

	Cost of Goods Sold LIFO	Cost of Goods Sold FIFO	Difference
2010	$ 80,000	$ 78,000	$2,000
2011	100,000	97,000	3,000
2012	113,000	111,000	2,000

6. Earnings per share information is not required on the income statement.
7. All tax effects for this illustration should be ignored.

Given the information about Lancer Company, Illustration 22-7 shows its income statement, retained earnings statement, balance sheet, and statement of cash flows for 2010–2012 under LIFO.

ILLUSTRATION 22-7
Lancer Financial
Statements (LIFO)

LANCER COMPANY
INCOME STATEMENT
FOR THE YEAR ENDED DECEMBER 31

	2010	2011	2012
Sales	$300,000	$300,000	$300,000
Cost of goods sold (LIFO)	80,000	100,000	113,000
Operating expenses	100,000	100,000	100,000
Net income	$120,000	$100,000	$ 87,000

LANCER COMPANY
RETAINED EARNINGS STATEMENT
FOR THE YEAR ENDED DECEMBER 31

	2010	2011	2012
Retained earnings (beginning)	$ 0	$120,000	$220,000
Add: Net income	120,000	100,000	87,000
Retained earnings (ending)	$120,000	$220,000	$307,000

LANCER COMPANY
BALANCE SHEET
AT DECEMBER 31

	2010	2011	2012
Cash	$210,000	$300,000	$375,000
Inventory (LIFO)	10,000	20,000	32,000
Total assets	$220,000	$320,000	$407,000
Common stock	$100,000	$100,000	$100,000
Retained earnings	120,000	220,000	307,000
Total liabilities and stockholders' equity	$220,000	$320,000	$407,000

LANCER COMPANY
STATEMENT OF CASH FLOWS
FOR THE YEAR ENDED DECEMBER 31

	2010	2011	2012
Cash flows from operating activities			
Sales	$300,000	$300,000	$300,000
Purchases	90,000	110,000	125,000
Operating expenses	100,000	100,000	100,000
Net cash provided by operating activities	110,000	90,000	75,000
Cash flows from financing activities			
Issuance of common stock	100,000	—	—
Net increase in cash	210,000	90,000	75,000
Cash at beginning of year	0	210,000	300,000
Cash at end of year	$210,000	$300,000	$375,000

As Illustration 22-7 indicates, under LIFO Lancer Company reports $120,000 net income in 2010, $100,000 net income in 2011, and $87,000 net income in 2012. The amount of inventory reported on Lancer's balance sheet reflects LIFO costing.

Illustration 22-8 shows Lancer's income statement, retained earnings statement, balance sheet, and statement of cash flows for 2010–2012 under **FIFO**. You can see that **the cash flow statement under FIFO is the same as under LIFO**. Although the net incomes are different in each period, there is no cash flow effect from these differences in net income. (If we considered income taxes, a cash flow effect would result.)

ILLUSTRATION 22-8
Lancer Financial
Statements (FIFO)

LANCER COMPANY
INCOME STATEMENT
FOR THE YEAR ENDED DECEMBER 31

	2010	2011	2012
Sales	$300,000	$300,000	$300,000
Cost of goods sold (FIFO)	78,000	97,000	111,000
Operating expenses	100,000	100,000	100,000
Net income	$122,000	$103,000	$ 89,000

LANCER COMPANY
RETAINED EARNINGS STATEMENT
FOR THE YEAR ENDED DECEMBER 31

	2010	2011	2012
Retained earnings (beginning)	$ 0	$122,000	$225,000
Add: Net income	122,000	103,000	89,000
Retained earnings (ending)	$122,000	$225,000	$314,000

LANCER COMPANY
BALANCE SHEET
AT DECEMBER 31

	2010	2011	2012
Cash	$210,000	$300,000	$375,000
Inventory (FIFO)	12,000	25,000	39,000
Total assets	$222,000	$325,000	$414,000
Common stock	$100,000	$100,000	$100,000
Retained earnings	122,000	225,000	314,000
Total liabilities and stockholders' equity	$222,000	$325,000	$414,000

LANCER COMPANY
STATEMENT OF CASH FLOWS
FOR THE YEAR ENDED DECEMBER 31

	2010	2011	2012
Cash flows from operating activities			
Sales	$300,000	$300,000	$300,000
Purchases	90,000	110,000	125,000
Operating expenses	100,000	100,000	100,000
Net cash provided by operating activities	110,000	90,000	75,000
Cash flows from financing activities			
Issuance of common stock	100,000	—	—
Net increase in cash	210,000	90,000	75,000
Cast at beginning of year	0	210,000	300,000
Cash at end of year	$210,000	$300,000	$375,000

Compare the financial statements reported in Illustration 22-7 and Illustration 22-8. You can see that, under retrospective application, the change to FIFO inventory valuation affects reported inventories, cost of goods sold, net income, and retained earnings. In the following sections, we discuss the accounting and reporting of Lancer's accounting change from LIFO to FIFO.

Given the information provided in Illustrations 22-6, 22-7, and 22-8, we now are ready to account for and report on the accounting change.

Our first step is to adjust the financial records for the change from LIFO to FIFO. To do so, we perform the analysis in Illustration 22-9.

Year	Net Income LIFO	Net Income FIFO	Difference in Income
2010	$120,000	$122,000	$2,000
2011	100,000	103,000	3,000
Total at beginning of 2012	$220,000	$225,000	$5,000
Total in 2012	$ 87,000	$ 89,000	$2,000

ILLUSTRATION 22-9
Data for Recording Change in Accounting Principle

The entry to record the change to the FIFO method at the beginning of 2012 is as follows.

Inventory	5,000	
Retained Earnings		5,000

The change increases the Inventory account by $5,000. This amount represents the difference between the ending inventory at December 31, 2011, under LIFO ($20,000) and the ending inventory under FIFO ($25,000). The credit to Retained Earnings indicates the amount needed to change prior-year's income, assuming that Lancer had used FIFO in previous periods.

Reporting a Change in Principle. Lancer Company will prepare comparative financial statements for 2011 and 2012 using FIFO (the new inventory method). Illustration 22-10 indicates how Lancer might present this information.

ILLUSTRATION 22-10
Comparative Information Related to Accounting Change (FIFO)

LANCER COMPANY
INCOME STATEMENT
FOR THE YEAR ENDED DECEMBER 31

	2012	2011 As adjusted (Note A)
Sales	$300,000	$300,000
Cost of goods sold	111,000	97,000
Operating expenses	100,000	100,000
Net income	$ 89,000	$103,000

Note A

Change in Method of Accounting for Inventory Valuation On January 1, 2012, Lancer Company elected to change its method of valuing its inventory to the FIFO method; in all prior years, inventory was valued using the LIFO method. The Company adopted the new method of accounting for inventory to better report cost of goods sold in the year incurred. Comparative financial statements of prior years have been adjusted to apply the new method retrospectively. The following financial statement line items for years 2012 and 2011 were affected by the change in accounting principle.

Nature and reason for change; description of prior period information adjusted

Balance Sheet	2012 LIFO	2012 FIFO	2012 Difference	2011 LIFO	2011 FIFO	2011 Difference
Inventory	$ 32,000	$ 39,000	$7,000	$ 20,000	$ 25,000	$5,000
Retained earnings	307,000	314,000	7,000	220,000	225,000	5,000
Income Statement						
Cost of goods sold	$113,000	$111,000	$2,000	$100,000	$ 97,000	$3,000
Net income	87,000	89,000	2,000	100,000	103,000	3,000
Statement of Cash Flows						
(no effect)						

Effect of change on key performance indicators

As a result of the accounting change, retained earnings as of January 1, 2011, increased from $120,000, as originally reported using the LIFO method, to $122,000 using the FIFO method.

Cumulative effect on retained earnings

As Illustration 22-10 shows, Lancer Company reports net income under the newly adopted FIFO method for both 2011 and 2012. The company retrospectively adjusted the 2011 income statement to report the information on a FIFO basis. In addition, the note to the financial statements indicates the nature of the change, why the company made the change, and the years affected. The note also provides data on important differences between the amounts reported under LIFO versus FIFO. (When identifying the significant differences, some companies show the *entire* financial statements and line-by-line differences between LIFO and FIFO.)

Retained Earnings Adjustment. As indicated earlier, one of the disclosure requirements is to show the cumulative effect of the change on retained earnings as of the beginning of the earliest period presented. For Lancer Company, that date is January 1, 2011. Lancer disclosed that information by means of a narrative description (see Note A in Illustration 22-10). Lancer also would disclose this information in its retained earnings statement. Illustration 22-11 shows Lancer's retained earnings statement under LIFO—that is, before giving effect to the change in accounting principle. (This information comes from Illustration 22-7 on page 1375.)

ILLUSTRATION 22-11
Retained Earnings
Statements (LIFO)

	2012	2011	2010
Retained earnings, January 1	$220,000	$120,000	$ 0
Net income	87,000	100,000	(120,000)
Retained earnings, December 31	$307,000	$220,000	$120,000

If Lancer presents comparative statements for 2011 and 2012 under FIFO, then it must change the beginning balance of retained earnings at January 1, 2011. The difference between the retained earnings balances under LIFO and FIFO is computed as follows.

Retained earnings, January 1, 2011 (FIFO)	$122,000
Retained earnings, January 1, 2011 (LIFO)	(120,000)
Cumulative effect difference	$ 2,000

The $2,000 difference is the cumulative effect. Illustration 22-12 shows a comparative retained earnings statement for 2011 and 2012, giving effect to the change in accounting principle to FIFO.

ILLUSTRATION 22-12
Retained Earnings
Statements after
Retrospective Application

	2012	2011
Retained earnings, January 1, as reported		$120,000
Add: Adjustment for the cumulative effect on prior years of applying retrospectively the new method of accounting for inventory		2,000
Retained earnings, January 1, as adjusted	$225,000	122,000
Net income	89,000	103,000
Retained earnings, December 31	$314,000	$225,000

Lancer adjusted the beginning balance of retained earnings on January 1, 2011, for the excess of FIFO net income over LIFO net income in 2010. This comparative presentation indicates the type of adjustment that a company needs to make. It follows that the amount of this adjustment would be much larger if a number of prior periods were involved.

Direct and Indirect Effects of Changes

Are there other effects that a company should report when it makes a change in accounting principle? For example, what happens when a company like Lancer has a bonus plan based on net income and the prior year's net income changes when FIFO is retrospectively applied? Should Lancer also change the reported amount of bonus expense? Or what happens if we had not ignored income taxes in the Lancer example? Should Lancer adjust net income, given that taxes will be different under LIFO and FIFO in prior periods? The answers depend on whether the effects are direct or indirect.

Direct Effects. The FASB takes the position that companies should retrospectively apply the **direct effects of a change in accounting principle**. An example of a **direct effect** is an adjustment to an inventory balance as a result of a change in the inventory valuation method. For example, Lancer Company should change the inventory amounts in prior periods to indicate the change to the FIFO method of inventory valuation. Another inventory-related example would be an impairment adjustment resulting from applying the lower-of-cost-or-market test to the adjusted inventory balance. Related changes, such as deferred income tax effects of the impairment adjustment, are also considered direct effects. This entry was illustrated in the Denson example, in which the change to percentage-of-completion accounting resulted in recording a deferred tax liability.

Indirect Effects. In addition to direct effects, companies can have **indirect effects related to a change in accounting principle**. An **indirect effect** is any change to current or future cash flows of a company that result from making a change in accounting principle that is applied retrospectively. An example of an indirect effect is a change in profit-sharing or royalty payment that is based on a reported amount such as revenue or net income. **Indirect effects do not change prior period amounts.**

INTERNATIONAL PERSPECTIVE

IFRS does not explicitly address the accounting and disclosure of indirect effects.

For example, let's assume that Lancer has an employee profit-sharing plan based on net income. As Illustration 22-9 showed (on page 1377), Lancer would report higher income in 2010 and 2011 if it used the FIFO method. In addition, let's assume that the profit-sharing plan requires that Lancer pay the incremental amount due based on the FIFO income amounts. In this situation, Lancer reports this additional expense **in the current period**; it would not change prior periods for this expense. If the company prepares comparative financial statements, it follows that it does not recast the prior periods for this additional expense.[3]

If the terms of the profit-sharing plan indicate that *no payment is necessary* in the current period due to this change, then the company need not recognize additional profit-sharing expense in the current period. Neither does it change amounts reported for prior periods.

When a company recognizes the indirect effects of a change in accounting principle, it includes in the financial statements a description of the indirect effects. In doing so, it discloses the amounts recognized in the current period and related per share information.

Impracticability

It is not always possible for companies to determine how they would have reported prior periods' financial information under retrospective application of an accounting principle change. Retrospective application is considered **impracticable** if a company cannot determine the prior period effects using every reasonable effort to do so.

---

[3]The rationale for this approach is that companies should recognize, in the period the adoption occurs (not the prior period), the effect on the cash flows that is caused by the adoption of the new accounting principle. That is, the accounting change is a necessary "past event" in the definition of an asset or liability that gives rise to the accounting recognition of the indirect effect in the current period. [4]

Companies should not use retrospective application if one of the following conditions exists:

1. The company cannot determine the effects of the retrospective application.
2. Retrospective application requires assumptions about management's intent in a prior period.
3. Retrospective application requires significant estimates for a prior period, and the company cannot objectively verify the necessary information to develop these estimates.

If any of the above conditions exists, it is deemed impracticable to apply the retrospective approach. In this case, the company **prospectively applies** the new accounting principle as of the earliest date it is practicable to do so. [5]

For example, assume that Williams Company changed its inventory method from FIFO to LIFO, effective January 1, 2013. Williams prepares statements on a calendar-year basis and has used the FIFO method since its inception. Williams judges it impracticable to retrospectively apply the new method. Determining prior period effects would require subjective assumptions about the LIFO layers established in prior periods. These assumptions would ordinarily result in the computation of a number of different earnings figures.

As a result, the only adjustment necessary may be to restate the beginning inventory to a cost basis from a lower-of-cost-or-market approach (which establishes the beginning LIFO layer). Williams must disclose only the effect of the change on the results of operations in the period of change. Also, the company should explain the reasons for omitting the computations of the cumulative effect for prior years. Finally, it should disclose the justification for the change to LIFO. [6][4] Illustration 22-13, from the annual report of Quaker Oats Company, shows the type of disclosure needed.

ILLUSTRATION 22-13
Disclosure of Change to LIFO

The Quaker Oats Company

Note 1 (In Part): Summary of Significant Accounting Policies

Inventories. Inventories are valued at the lower of cost or market, using various cost methods, and include the cost of raw materials, labor and overhead. The percentage of year-end inventories valued using each of the methods is as follows:

June 30	Current Year	Prior Year
Average quarterly cost	21%	54%
Last-in, first-out (LIFO)	65%	29%
First-in, first-out (FIFO)	14%	17%

Effective July 1, the Company adopted the LIFO cost flow assumption for valuing the majority of remaining U.S. Grocery Products inventories. The Company believes that the use of the LIFO method better matches current costs with current revenues. The cumulative effect of this change on retained earnings at the beginning of the year is not determinable, nor are the pro-forma effects of retroactive application of LIFO to prior years. The effect of this change on current-year fiscal results was to decrease net income by $16.0 million, or $.20 per share.

If the LIFO method of valuing certain inventories were not used, total inventories would have been $60.1 million higher in the current year, and $24.0 million higher in the prior year.

---

[4]In practice, many companies defer the formal adoption of LIFO until year-end. Management thus has an opportunity to assess the impact that a change to LIFO will have on the financial statements and to evaluate the desirability of a change for tax purposes. As indicated in Chapter 8, many companies use LIFO because of the advantages of this inventory valuation method in a period of inflation.

CHANGES IN ACCOUNTING ESTIMATE

To prepare financial statements, companies must estimate the effects of future conditions and events. For example, the following items require estimates.

5 LEARNING OBJECTIVE

Describe the accounting for changes in estimates.

1. Uncollectible receivables.
2. Inventory obsolescence.
3. Useful lives and salvage values of assets.
4. Periods benefited by deferred costs.
5. Liabilities for warranty costs and income taxes.
6. Recoverable mineral reserves.
7. Change in depreciation methods.

A company cannot perceive future conditions and events and their effects with certainty. Therefore, estimation requires the exercise of judgment. Accounting estimates will change as new events occur, as a company acquires more experience, or as it obtains additional information.

Prospective Reporting

Companies report prospectively changes in accounting estimates. That is, companies should not adjust previously reported results for changes in estimates. Instead, they account for the effects of all changes in estimates in (1) the period of change if the change affects that period only, or (2) the period of change and future periods if the change affects both. The FASB views changes in estimates as **normal recurring corrections and adjustments**, the natural result of the accounting process. It prohibits retrospective treatment.

The circumstances related to a change in estimate differ from those for a change in accounting principle. If companies reported changes in estimates retrospectively, continual adjustments of prior years' income would occur. It seems proper to accept the view that, because new conditions or circumstances exist, the revision fits the new situation (not the old one). Companies should therefore handle such a revision in the current and future periods.

To illustrate, Underwriters Labs Inc. purchased for $300,000 a building that it originally estimated to have a useful life of 15 years and no salvage value. It recorded depreciation for 5 years on a straight-line basis. On January 1, 2012, Underwriters Labs revises the estimate of the useful life. It now considers the asset to have a total life of 25 years. (Assume that the useful life for financial reporting and tax purposes and depreciation method are the same.) Illustration 22-14 shows the accounts at the beginning of the sixth year.

Buildings	$300,000
Less: Accumulated depreciation—buildings (5 × $20,000)	100,000
Book value of building	$200,000

ILLUSTRATION 22-14
Book Value after Five Years' Depreciation

Underwriters Labs records depreciation for the year 2012 as follows.

Depreciation Expense	10,000	
Accumulated Depreciation—Buildings		10,000

The company computes the $10,000 depreciation charge as shown in Illustration 22-15.

$$\text{Depreciation charge} = \frac{\text{Book value of asset}}{\text{Remaining service live}} = \frac{\$200,000}{25 \text{ years} - 5 \text{ years}} = \$10,000$$

ILLUSTRATION 22-15
Depreciation after Change in Estimate

Companies sometime find it difficult to differentiate between a change in estimate and a change in accounting principle. Is it a change in principle or a change in estimate when a company changes from deferring and amortizing marketing costs to expensing them as incurred because future benefits of these costs have become doubtful? If it is impossible to determine whether a change in principle or a change in estimate has occurred, the rule is this: **Consider the change as a change in estimate.** This is often referred to as a change in estimate effected by a change in accounting principle.

Another example of a change in estimate effected by a change in principle is a change in depreciation (as well as amortization or depletion) methods. Because companies change depreciation methods based on changes in estimates about future benefits from long-lived assets, it is not possible to separate the effect of the accounting principle change from that of the estimates. **As a result, companies account for a change in depreciation methods as a change in estimate effected by a change in accounting principle.** [7]

A similar problem occurs in differentiating between a change in estimate and a correction of an error, although here the answer is more clear-cut. How does a company determine whether it overlooked the information in earlier periods (an error), or whether it obtained new information (a change in estimate)? Proper classification is important because the accounting treatment differs for corrections of errors versus changes in estimates. The general rule is this: **Companies should consider careful estimates that later prove to be incorrect as changes in estimate.** Only when a company obviously computed the estimate incorrectly because of lack of expertise or in bad faith should it consider the adjustment an error. There is no clear demarcation line here. Companies must use good judgment in light of all the circumstances.[5]

Disclosures

Illustration 22-16 shows disclosure of a change in estimated useful lives, which appeared in the annual report of Ampco–Pittsburgh Corporation.

ILLUSTRATION 22-16
Disclosure of Change in
Estimated Useful Lives

Ampco–Pittsburgh Corporation

Note 11: Change in Accounting Estimate. The Corporation revised its estimate of the useful lives of certain machinery and equipment. Previously, all machinery and equipment, whether new when placed in use or not, were in one class and depreciated over 15 years. The change principally applies to assets purchased new when placed in use. Those lives are now extended to 20 years. These changes were made to better reflect the estimated periods during which such assets will remain in service. The change had the effect of reducing depreciation expense and increasing net income by approximately $991,000 ($.10 per share).

For the most part, companies need not disclose changes in accounting estimate made as part of normal operations, such as bad debt allowances or inventory obsolescence, unless such changes are material. However, for a change in estimate that affects several periods (such as a change in the service lives of depreciable assets), companies should disclose the effect on income from continuing operations and related per share

---

[5]In evaluating reasonableness, the auditor should use one or a combination of the following approaches.
  (a) Review and test the process used by management to develop the estimate.
  (b) Develop an independent expectation of the estimate to corroborate the reasonableness of management's estimate.
  (c) Review subsequent events or transactions occurring prior to completion of fieldwork.
"Auditing Accounting Estimates," *Statement on Auditing Standards No. 57* (New York: AICPA, 1988).

amounts of the current period. When a company has a change in estimate effected by a change in accounting principle, it must indicate why the new method is preferable. In addition, companies are subject to all other disclosure guidelines established for changes in accounting principle.

CHANGE IN REPORTING ENTITY

6 LEARNING OBJECTIVE
Identify changes in a reporting entity.

Occasionally companies make changes that result in different reporting entities. In such cases, companies report the change by **changing the financial statements of all prior periods presented**. The revised statements show the financial information for the **new reporting entity** for all periods.

Examples of a change in reporting entity are:

1. Presenting consolidated statements in place of statements of individual companies.
2. Changing specific subsidiaries that constitute the group of companies for which the entity presents consolidated financial statements.
3. Changing the companies included in combined financial statements.
4. Changing the cost, equity, or consolidation method of accounting for subsidiaries and investments.[6] In this case, a change in the reporting entity does not result from creation, cessation, purchase, or disposition of a subsidiary or other business unit.

In the year in which a company changes a reporting entity, it should disclose in the financial statements the nature of the change and the reason for it. It also should report, for all periods presented, the effect of the change on income before extraordinary items, net income, and earnings per share. These disclosures need not be repeated in subsequent periods' financial statements.

Illustration 22-17 shows a note disclosing a change in reporting entity, from the annual report of Hewlett-Packard Company.

ILLUSTRATION 22-17
Disclosure of Change in Reporting Entity

Hewlett-Packard Company

Note: Accounting and Reporting Changes (In Part)

Consolidation of Hewlett-Packard Finance Company. The company implemented a new accounting pronouncement on consolidations. With the adoption of this new pronouncement, the company consolidated the accounts of Hewlett-Packard Finance Company (HPFC), a wholly owned subsidiary previously accounted for under the equity method, with those of the company. The change resulted in an increase in consolidated assets and liabilities but did not have a material effect on the company's financial position. Since HPFC was previously accounted for under the equity method, the change did not affect net earnings. Prior years' consolidated financial information has been restated to reflect this change for comparative purposes.

CORRECTION OF ERRORS

7 LEARNING OBJECTIVE
Describe the accounting for correction of errors.

No business, large or small, is immune from errors. As the opening story discussed, the number of accounting errors that lead to restatement are beginning to decline. However, without accounting and disclosure guidelines for the reporting of errors, investors can be left in the dark about the effects of errors.

Certain errors, such as misclassifications of balances within a financial statement, are not as significant to investors as other errors. Significant errors would be those resulting in overstating assets or income, for example. However, investors should know

---

[6]An exception to retrospective application occurs when changing from the equity method. We provide an expanded illustration of the accounting for a change from or to the equity method in Appendix 22A.

the potential impact of all errors. Even "harmless" misclassifications can affect important ratios. Also, some errors could signal important weaknesses in internal controls that could lead to more significant errors.

In general, accounting errors include the following types:

1. A change from an accounting principle that is **not** generally accepted to an accounting principle that is acceptable. The rationale is that the company incorrectly presented prior periods because of the application of an improper accounting principle. For example, a company may change from the cash (income tax) basis of accounting to the accrual basis.

2. Mathematical mistakes, such as incorrectly totaling the inventory count sheets when computing the inventory value.

3. Changes in estimates that occur because a company did not prepare the estimates in good faith. For example, a company may have adopted a clearly unrealistic depreciation rate.

4. An oversight, such as the failure to accrue or defer certain expenses and revenues at the end of the period.

5. A misuse of facts, such as the failure to use salvage value in computing the depreciation base for the straight-line approach.

6. The incorrect classification of a cost as an expense instead of an asset, and vice versa.

ILLUSTRATION 22-18
Accounting-Error Types

Accounting errors occur for a variety of reasons. Illustration 22-18 indicates 11 major categories of accounting errors that drive restatements.

Accounting Category	Type of Restatement
Expense recognition	Recording expenses in the incorrect period or for an incorrect amount.
Revenue recognition	Improper revenue accounting. This category includes instances in which revenue was improperly recognized, questionable revenues were recognized, or any other number of related errors that led to misreported revenue.
Misclassification	Misclassifying significant accounting items on the balance sheet, income statement, or statement of cash flows. These include restatements due to misclassification of short- or long-term accounts or those that impact cash flows from operations.
Equity—other	Improper accounting for EPS, restricted stock, warrants, and other equity instruments.
Reserves/Contingencies	Errors involving accounts receivables bad debts, inventory reserves, income tax allowances, and loss contingencies.
Long-lived assets	Asset impairments of property, plant, and equipment; goodwill; or other related items.
Taxes	Errors involving correction of tax provision, improper treatment of tax liabilities, and other tax-related items.
Equity—other comprehensive income	Improper accounting for comprehensive income equity transactions including foreign currency items, minimum pension liability adjustments, unrealized gains and losses on certain investments in debt, equity securities, and derivatives.
Inventory	Inventory costing valuations, quantity issues, and cost of sales adjustments.
Equity—stock options	Improper accounting for employee stock options.
Other	Any restatement not covered by the listed categories including those related to improper accounting for acquisitions or mergers.

Source: T. Baldwin and D. Yoo, "Restatements—Traversing Shaky Ground," *Trend Alert*, Glass Lewis & Co. (June 2, 2005), p. 8.

As soon as a company discovers an error, it must correct the error. Companies record **corrections of errors** from prior periods as an adjustment to the beginning balance of retained earnings in the current period. Such corrections are called **prior period adjustments**.[7] [8]

[7]See Mark L. DeFord and James Jiambalvo, "Incidence and Circumstances of Accounting Errors," *The Accounting Review* (July 1991) for examples of different types of errors and why these errors might have occurred.

If it presents comparative statements, a company should restate the prior statements affected, to correct for the error.[8] The company need not repeat the disclosures in the financial statements of subsequent periods.

Example of Error Correction

To illustrate, in 2013 the bookkeeper for Selectro Company discovered an error: In 2012, the company failed to record $20,000 of depreciation expense on a newly constructed building. This building is the only depreciable asset Selectro owns. The company correctly included the depreciation expense in its tax return and correctly reported its income taxes payable. Illustration 22-19 presents Selectro's income statement for 2012 (starting with income before depreciation expense) with and without the error.

ILLUSTRATION 22-19
Error Correction
Comparison

SELECTRO COMPANY
INCOME STATEMENT
FOR THE YEAR ENDED, DECEMBER 31, 2012

		Without Error		With Error
Income before depreciation expense		$100,000		$100,000
Depreciation expense		20,000		0
Income before income tax		80,000		100,000
Current income tax expense	$32,000		$ 32,000	
Deferred income tax expense	–0–	32,000	8,000	40,000
Net income		$ 48,000		$ 60,000

Illustration 22-20 shows the entries that Selectro should have made and did make for recording depreciation expense and income taxes.

ILLUSTRATION 22-20
Error Entries

Entries Company Should Have Made (Without Error)			Entries Company Did Make (With Error)		
Depreciation Expense	20,000		No entry made for depreciation		
Accumulated Depreciation					
—Buildings		20,000			
Income Tax Expense	32,000		Income Tax Expense	40,000	
Income Taxes Payable		32,000	Deferred Tax Liability		8,000
			Income Taxes Payable		32,000

As Illustration 22-20 indicates, the $20,000 omission error in 2012 results in the following effects.

Income Statement Effects

Depreciation expense (2012) is understated $20,000.

Income tax expense (2012) is overstated $8,000 ($20,000 × 40%).

Net income (2012) is overstated $12,000 ($20,000 − $8,000).

Balance Sheet Effects

Accumulated depreciation—buildings is understated $20,000.

Deferred tax liability is overstated $8,000 ($20,000 × 40%).

To make the proper correcting entry in 2013, Selectro should recognize that net income in 2012 is overstated by $12,000, the Deferred Tax Liability is overstated by $8,000,

[8]The term restatement is used for the process of revising previously issued financial statements to reflect the correction of an error. This distinguishes an error correction from a change in accounting principle. [9]

and Accumulated Depreciation—Buildings is understated by $20,000. The entry to correct this error in 2013 is as follows.

Retained Earnings	12,000	
Deferred Tax Liability	8,000	
Accumulated Depreciation—Buildings		20,000

The debit to Retained Earnings results because net income for 2012 is overstated. The debit to Deferred Tax Liability is made to remove this account, which was caused by the error. The credit to Accumulated Depreciation—Buildings reduces the book value of the building to its proper amount. Selectro will make the same journal entry to record the correction of the error in 2013 whether it prepares single-period (noncomparative) or comparative financial statements.

Single-Period Statements

To demonstrate how to show this information in a single-period statement, assume that Selectro Company has a beginning retained earnings balance at January 1, 2013, of $350,000. The company reports net income of $400,000 in 2013. Illustration 22-21 shows Selectro's retained earnings statement for 2013.

ILLUSTRATION 22-21
Reporting an Error—
Single-Period Financial
Statement

SELECTRO COMPANY RETAINED EARNINGS STATEMENT FOR THE YEAR ENDED DECEMBER 31, 2013		
Retained earnings, January 1, as reported		$350,000
Correction of an error (depreciation)	$20,000	
Less: Applicable income tax reduction	8,000	(12,000)
Retained earnings, January 1, as adjusted		338,000
Add: Net income		400,000
Retained earnings, December 31		$738,000

The balance sheet in 2013 would not have any deferred tax liability related to the building, and Accumulated Depreciation—Buildings is now restated at a higher amount. The income statement would not be affected.

Comparative Statements

If preparing comparative financial statements, a company should make adjustments to correct the amounts for all affected accounts reported in the statements for **all periods** reported. The company should restate the data to the correct basis for each year presented. It should **show any catch-up adjustment as a prior period adjustment to retained earnings for the earliest period it reported**. These requirements are essentially the same as those for reporting a change in accounting principle.

For example, in the case of Selectro, the error of omitting the depreciation of $20,000 in 2012, discovered in 2013, results in the restatement of the 2012 financial statements. Illustration 22-22 shows the accounts that Selectro restates in the 2012 financial statements.

ILLUSTRATION 22-22
Reporting an Error—
Comparative Financial
Statements

In the balance sheet:	
Accumulated depreciation—buildings	$20,000 increase
Deferred tax liability	$ 8,000 decrease
Retained earnings, ending balance	$12,000 decrease
In the income statement:	
Depreciation expense—buildings	$20,000 increase
Income tax expense	$ 8,000 decrease
Net income	$12,000 decrease
In the retained earnings statement:	
Retained earnings, ending balance (due to lower net income for the period)	$12,000 decrease

Selectro prepares the 2013 financial statements in comparative form with those of 2012 **as if the error had not occurred**. In addition, Selectro must disclose that it has restated its previously issued financial statements, and it describes the nature of the error. Selectro also must disclose the following.

1. The effect of the correction on each financial statement line item and any per-share amounts affected for each prior period presented.

2. The cumulative effect of the change on retained earnings or other appropriate components of equity or net assets in the statement of financial position, as of the beginning of the earliest period presented. [10]

SUMMARY OF ACCOUNTING CHANGES AND CORRECTION OF ERRORS

Having guidelines for reporting accounting changes and corrections has helped resolve several significant and long-standing accounting problems. Yet, because of diversity in situations and characteristics of the items encountered in practice, use of professional judgment is of paramount importance. In applying these guidelines, the primary objective is to serve the users of the financial statements. Achieving this objective requires accuracy, full disclosure, and an absence of misleading inferences.

Illustration 22-23 summarizes the main distinctions and treatments presented in the discussion in this chapter.

ILLUSTRATION 22-23
Summary of Guidelines for Accounting Changes and Errors

Changes in accounting principle

Employ the retrospective approach by:
a. Changing the financial statements of all prior periods presented.
b. Disclosing in the year of the change the effect on net income and earnings per share for all prior periods presented.
c. Reporting an adjustment to the beginning retained earnings balance in the retained earnings statement in the earliest year presented.

If impracticable to determine the prior period effect (e.g., change to LIFO):
a. Do not change prior years' income.
b. Use opening inventory in the year the method is adopted as the base-year inventory for all subsequent LIFO computations.
c. Disclose the effect of the change on the current year, and the reasons for omitting the computation of the cumulative effect and pro forma amounts for prior years.

Changes in accounting estimate

Employ the current and prospective approach by:
a. Reporting current and future financial statements on the new basis.
b. Presenting prior period financial statements as previously reported.
c. Making no adjustments to current-period opening balances for the effects in prior periods.

Changes in reporting entity

Employ the retrospective approach by:
a. Restating the financial statements of all prior periods presented.
b. Disclosing in the year of change the effect on net income and earnings per share data for all prior periods presented.

Changes due to error

Employ the restatement approach by:
a. Correcting all prior period statements presented.
b. Restating the beginning balance of retained earnings for the first period presented when the error effects occur in a period prior to the first period presented.

Changes in accounting principle are appropriate **only** when a company demonstrates that the newly adopted generally accepted accounting principle is **preferable** to the existing one. Companies and accountants determine preferability on the basis of whether the new principle constitutes an **improvement in financial reporting**, not on the basis of the income tax effect alone.[9]

But it is not always easy to determine an improvement in financial reporting. **How does one measure preferability or improvement?** Such measurement varies from company to company. Quaker Oats Company, for example, argued that a change in accounting principle to LIFO inventory valuation "better matches current costs with current revenues" (see Illustration 22-13, page 1380). Conversely, another company might change from LIFO to FIFO because it wishes to report a more realistic ending inventory. How do you determine which is the better of these two arguments? Determining the preferable method requires some "standard" or "objective." Because no universal standard or objective is generally accepted, the problem of determining preferability continues to be difficult.

Initially, the SEC took the position that the auditor should indicate whether a change in accounting principle was preferable. The SEC has since modified this approach, noting that greater reliance may be placed on management's judgment in assessing preferability. Even though the preferability criterion is difficult to apply, the general guidelines have acted as a deterrent to capricious changes in accounting principles.[10] **If a FASB rule creates a new principle, expresses preference for, or rejects a specific accounting principle, a change is considered clearly acceptable.**

CAN I GET MY MONEY BACK?

What do the numbers mean?

When companies report restatements, investors usually lose money. What should investors do if a company misleads them by misstating its financial results? Join other investors in a class-action suit against the company and in some cases, the auditor.

Class-action activity has picked up in recent years, and settlements can be large. To find out about class actions, investors can go online to see if they are eligible to join any class actions. Below are some recent examples.

Company	Settlement Amount	Contact for Claim
Fifth-Third	$ 9.5 million	www.lawyersandsettlements.com
Huron Securities	$ 38 million	www.lawyersandsettlements.com
GlaxoSmithKline	$750 million	www.lawyersandsettlements.com

The amounts reported are *before* attorney's fees, which can range from 15 to 30 percent of the total. Also, investors may owe taxes if the settlement results in a capital gain on the investment. Thus, investors can get back some of the money they lost due to restatements, but they should be prepared to pay an attorney and the government first.

Source: Adapted from C. Coolidge, "Lost and Found," *Forbes* (October 1, 2001), pp. 124–125; data from *www.lawyersandsettlements.com* as of 12/13/10.

---

[9]A change in accounting principle, a change in the reporting entity (special type of change in accounting principle), and a correction of an error require an explanatory paragraph in the auditor's report discussing lack of consistency from one period to the next. A change in accounting estimate does not affect the auditor's opinion relative to consistency; however, if the change in estimate has a material effect on the financial statements, disclosure may still be required. Error correction not involving a change in accounting principle does not require disclosure relative to consistency.

[10]If management has not provided reasonable justification for the change in accounting principle, the auditor should express a qualified opinion. Or, if the effect of the change is sufficiently material, the auditor should express an adverse opinion on the financial statements. "Reports on Audited Financial Statements," *Statement on Auditing Standards No. 58* (New York: AICPA, 1988).

MOTIVATIONS FOR CHANGE OF ACCOUNTING METHOD

8 LEARNING OBJECTIVE
Identify economic motives for changing accounting methods.

Difficult as it is to determine which accounting standards have the strongest conceptual support, other complications make the process even more complex. These complications stem from the fact that managers have self-interest in how the financial statements make the company look. They naturally wish to show their financial performance in the best light. A **favorable profit picture** can influence investors, and a strong liquidity position can influence creditors. **Too favorable a profit picture**, however, can provide union negotiators and government regulators with ammunition during bargaining talks. Hence, managers might have varying motives for reporting income numbers.

Research has provided additional insight into why companies may prefer certain accounting methods.[11] Some of these reasons are as follows.

1. *Political costs.* As companies become larger and more politically visible, politicians and regulators devote more attention to them. The larger the firm, the more likely it is to become subject to regulation such as antitrust, and the more likely it is to be required to pay higher taxes. Therefore, companies that are politically visible may seek to report low income numbers, to avoid the scrutiny of regulators. In addition, other constituents, such as labor unions, may be less willing to ask for wage increases if reported income is low. Researchers have found that the larger the company, the more likely it is to adopt income-decreasing approaches in selecting accounting methods.

2. *Capital structure.* A number of studies have indicated that the capital structure of the company can affect the selection of accounting methods. For example, a company with a high debt to equity ratio is more likely to be constrained by debt covenants. The debt covenant may indicate that the company cannot pay dividends if retained earnings fall below a certain level. As a result, such a company is more likely to select accounting methods that will increase net income.

3. *Bonus payments.* Studies have found that if compensation plans tie managers' bonus payments to income, management will select accounting methods that maximize their bonus payments.

4. *Smooth earnings.* Substantial earnings increases attract the attention of politicians, regulators, and competitors. In addition, large increases in income are difficult to achieve in following years. Further, executive compensation plans would use these higher numbers as a baseline and make it difficult for managers to earn bonuses in subsequent years. Conversely, investors and competitors might view large decreases in earnings as a signal that the company is in financial trouble. Also, substantial decreases in income raise concerns on the part of stockholders, lenders, and other interested parties about the competency of management. For all these reasons, companies have an incentive to "manage" or "smooth" earnings. In general, management tends to believe that a steady 10 percent growth a year is much better than a 30 percent growth one year and a 10 percent decline the next.[12] In other words, managers usually prefer a gradually increasing income report and sometimes change accounting methods to ensure such a result.

[11]See Ross L. Watts and Jerold L. Zimmerman, "Positive Accounting Theory: A Ten-Year Perspective," *The Accounting Review* (January 1990) for an excellent review of research findings related to management incentives in selecting accounting methods.

[12]O. Douglas Moses, "Income Smoothing and Incentives: Empirical Tests Using Accounting Changes," *The Accounting Review* (April 1987). The findings provide evidence that earnings smoothing is associated with firm size, the existence of bonus plans, and the divergence of actual earnings from expectations.

Management pays careful attention to the accounting it follows and often changes accounting methods, not for conceptual reasons, but for economic reasons. As indicated throughout this textbook, such arguments have come to be known as **economic consequences** arguments. These arguments focus on the supposed impact of the accounting method on the behavior of investors, creditors, competitors, governments, or managers of the reporting companies themselves.[13]

To counter these pressures, standard-setters such as the FASB have declared, as part of their conceptual framework, that they will assess the merits of proposed standards from a position of **neutrality**. That is, they evaluate the soundness of standards on the basis of conceptual soundness, not on the grounds of possible impact on behavior. It is not the FASB's place to choose standards according to the kinds of behavior it wishes to promote and the kinds it wishes to discourage. At the same time, it must be admitted that some standards often **will have** the effect of influencing behavior. Yet their justification should be conceptual, and not viewed in terms of their economic impact.

SECTION 2 • ERROR ANALYSIS

LEARNING OBJECTIVE **9**
Analyze the effect of errors.

In this section, we show some additional types of accounting errors. Companies generally do not correct for errors that do not have a significant effect on the presentation of the financial statements. For example, should a company with a total annual payroll of $1,750,000 and net income of $940,000 correct its financial statements if it finds it failed to record accrued wages of $5,000? No—it would not consider this error significant.

Obviously, defining materiality is difficult, and managers and auditors must use experience and judgment to determine whether adjustment is necessary for a given error. We assume **all errors discussed in this section to be material and to require adjustment**. (Also, we ignore all tax effects in this section.)

Companies must answer three questions in error analysis:

1. What type of error is involved?
2. What entries are needed to correct for the error?
3. After discovery of the error, how are financial statements to be restated?

As indicated earlier, companies treat errors **as prior period adjustments and report them in the current year as adjustments to the beginning balance of Retained Earnings**. If a company presents comparative statements, it restates the prior affected statements to correct for the error.

BALANCE SHEET ERRORS

Balance sheet errors affect only the presentation of an asset, liability, or stockholders' equity account. Examples are the classification of a short-term receivable as part of the investment section, the classification of a note payable as an account payable, and the classification of plant assets as inventory.

---

[13]Lobbyists use economic consequences arguments—and there are many of them—to put pressure on standard-setters. We have seen examples of these arguments in the oil and gas industry about successful efforts versus full cost, in the technology area with the issue of mandatory expensing of research and developmental costs and stock options.

When the error is discovered, the company reclassifies the item to its proper position. If the company prepares comparative statements that include the error year, it should correctly restate the balance sheet for the error year.

INCOME STATEMENT ERRORS

Income statement errors involve the improper classification of revenues or expenses. Examples include recording interest revenue as part of sales, purchases as bad debt expense, and depreciation expense as interest expense. An income statement classification error has no effect on the balance sheet and **no effect on net income**.

A company must make a reclassification entry when it discovers the error, if it makes the discovery in the same year in which the error occurs. If the error occurred in prior periods, the company does not need to make a reclassification entry at the date of discovery because the accounts for the current year are correctly stated. (Remember that the company has closed the income statement accounts from the prior period to retained earnings.) If the company prepares comparative statements that include the error year, it restates the income statement for the error year.

BALANCE SHEET AND INCOME STATEMENT ERRORS

The third type of error involves both the balance sheet and income statement. For example, assume that the bookkeeper overlooked accrued wages payable at the end of the accounting period. The effect of this error is to understate expenses, understate liabilities, and overstate net income for that period of time. This type of error affects both the balance sheet and the income statement. We classify this type of error in one of two ways—counterbalancing or noncounterbalancing.

Counterbalancing errors are those that will be offset or corrected over two periods. For example, the failure to record accrued wages is a counterbalancing error because over a two-year period the error will no longer be present. In other words, the failure to record accrued wages in the previous period means: (1) net income for the first period is overstated; (2) accrued wages payable (a liability) is understated, and (3) wages expense is understated. In the next period, net income is understated; accrued wages payable (a liability) is correctly stated; and wages expense is overstated. For the two **years combined**: (1) net income is correct; (2) wages expense is correct; and (3) accrued wages payable at the end of the second year is correct. Most errors in accounting that affect both the balance sheet and income statement are counterbalancing errors.

Noncounterbalancing errors are those that are not offset in the next accounting period. An example would be the failure to capitalize equipment that has a useful life of five years. If we expense this asset immediately, expenses will be overstated in the first period but understated in the next four periods. At the end of the second period, the effect of the error is not fully offset. Net income is correct in the aggregate only at the end of five years, because the asset is fully depreciated at this point. Thus, **noncounterbalancing errors are those that take longer than two periods to correct themselves**.

Only in rare instances is an error never reversed. An example would be if a company initially expenses land. Because land is not depreciable, theoretically the error is never offset, unless the land is sold.

Counterbalancing Errors

We illustrate the usual types of counterbalancing errors on the following pages. In studying these illustrations, keep in mind a couple of points.

First, determine whether the company has closed the books for the period in which the error is found:

1. **If the company has closed the books in the current year:**
   (a) If the error is already counterbalanced, no entry is necessary.
   (b) If the error is not yet counterbalanced, make an entry to adjust the present balance of retained earnings.
2. **If the company has not closed the books in the current year:**
   (a) If the error is already counterbalanced, make an entry to correct the error in the current period and to adjust the beginning balance of Retained Earnings.
   (b) If the error is not yet counterbalanced, make an entry to adjust the beginning balance of Retained Earnings.

Second, if the company presents comparative statements, it must restate the amounts for comparative purposes. **Restatement is necessary even if a correcting journal entry is not required.**

To illustrate, assume that Sanford's Cement Co. failed to accrue revenue in 2010 when earned, but recorded the revenue in 2011 when received. The company discovered the error in 2013. It does not need to make an entry to correct for this error because the effects have been counterbalanced by the time Sanford discovered the error in 2013. However, if Sanford presents comparative financial statements for 2010 through 2013, it must **restate the accounts and related amounts for the years 2010 and 2011 for financial reporting purposes.**

The sections that follow demonstrate the accounting for the usual types of counterbalancing errors.

Failure to Record Accrued Wages

On December 31, 2012, Hurley Enterprises did not accrue wages in the amount of $1,500. The entry in 2013 to correct this error, assuming Hurley has not closed the books for 2013, is:

Retained Earnings	1,500	
Salaries and Wages Expense		1,500

The rationale for this entry is as follows: (1) When Hurley pays the 2012 accrued wages in 2013, it makes an additional debit of $1,500 to 2013 Salaries and Wages Expense. (2) Salaries and Wages Expense—2013 is overstated by $1,500. (3) Because the company did not record 2012 accrued wages as Salaries and Wages Expense in 2012, the net income for 2012 was overstated by $1,500. (4) Because 2012 net income is overstated by $1,500, the Retained Earnings account is overstated by $1,500 (because net income is closed to Retained Earnings).

If Hurley has closed the books for 2013, it makes no entry, because the error is counterbalanced.

Failure to Record Prepaid Expenses

In January 2012, Hurley Enterprises purchased a two-year insurance policy costing $1,000. It debited Insurance Expense, and credited Cash. The company made no adjusting entries at the end of 2012.

The entry on December 31, 2013, to correct this error, assuming Hurley has not closed the books for 2013, is:

Insurance Expense	500	
Retained Earnings		500

If Hurley has closed the books for 2013, it makes no entry, because the error is counterbalanced.

Understatement of Unearned Revenue

On December 31, 2012, Hurley Enterprises received $50,000 as a prepayment for renting certain office space for the following year. At the time of receipt of the rent payment, the company recorded a debit to Cash and a credit to Rent Revenue. It made no adjusting entry as of December 31, 2012. The entry on December 31, 2013, to correct for this error, assuming that Hurley has not closed the books for 2013, is:

Retained Earnings	50,000	
Rent Revenue		50,000

If Hurley has closed the books for 2013, it makes no entry, because the error is counterbalanced.

Overstatement of Accrued Revenue

On December 31, 2012, Hurley Enterprises accrued as interest revenue $8,000 that applied to 2013. On that date, the company recorded a debit to Interest Receivable and a credit to Interest Revenue. The entry on December 31, 2013, to correct for this error, assuming that Hurley has not closed the books for 2013, is:

Retained Earnings	8,000	
Interest Revenue		8,000

If Hurley has closed the books for 2013, it makes no entry, because the error is counterbalanced.

Overstatement of Purchases

Hurley's accountant recorded a purchase of merchandise for $9,000 in 2012 that applied to 2013. The physical inventory for 2012 was correctly stated. The company uses the periodic inventory method. The entry on December 31, 2013, to correct for this error, assuming that Harley has not closed the books for 2013, is:

Purchases	9,000	
Retained Earnings		9,000

If Hurley has closed the books for 2013, it makes no entry, because the error is counterbalanced.

Noncounterbalancing Errors

The entries for noncounterbalancing errors are more complex. Companies must make correcting entries, even if they have closed the books.

Failure to Record Depreciation

Assume that on January 1, 2012, Hurley Enterprises purchased a machine for $10,000 that had an estimated useful life of five years. The accountant incorrectly expensed this machine in 2012, but discovered the error in 2013. If we assume that Hurley uses straight-line depreciation on this asset, the entry on December 31, 2013, to correct for this error, given that Hurley has not closed the books, is:

Machinery	10,000	
Depreciation Expense	2,000	
Retained Earnings		8,000*
Accumulated Depreciation—Machinery (20% × $10,000 × 2)		4,000

*Computations:
Retained Earnings

Overstatement of expense in 2012	$10,000
Proper depreciation for 2012 (20% × $10,000)	(2,000)
Retained earnings understated as of Dec. 31, 2012	$ 8,000

If Hurley has closed the books for 2013, the entry is:

Machinery	10,000	
Retained Earnings		6,000*
Accumulated Depreciation—Machinery		4,000

*Computations:
Retained Earnings

Retained earnings understated as of Dec. 31, 2012	$ 8,000
Proper depreciation for 2013 (20% × $10,000)	(2,000)
Retained earnings understated as of Dec. 31, 2013	$ 6,000

Failure to Adjust for Bad Debts

Companies sometimes use a specific charge-off method in accounting for bad debt expense when a percentage of sales is more appropriate. They then make adjustments to change from the specific write-off to some type of allowance method. For example, assume that Hurley Enterprises has recognized bad debt expense when it has the following uncollectible debts.

	2012	2013
From 2012 sales	$550	$690
From 2013 sales		700

Hurley estimates that it will charge off an additional $1,400 in 2014, of which $300 is applicable to 2012 sales and $1,100 to 2013 sales. The entry on December 31, 2013, assuming that Hurley **has not closed the books for 2013**, is:

Bad Debt Expense	410	
Retained Earnings	990	
Allowance for Doubtful Accounts		1,400

Allowance for doubtful accounts: Additional $300 for 2012 sales and $1,100 for 2013 sales.
Bad debts and retained earnings balance:

	2012	2013
Bad debts charged for	$1,240*	$ 700
Additional bad debts anticipated in 2014	300	1,100
Proper bad debt expense	1,540	1,800
Charges currently made to each period	(550)	(1,390)
Bad debt adjustment	$ 990	$ 410

*$550 + $690 = $1,240

If Hurley **has closed the books for 2013**, the entry is:

Retained Earnings	1,400	
Allowance for Doubtful Accounts		1,400

COMPREHENSIVE EXAMPLE: NUMEROUS ERRORS

In some circumstances a combination of errors occurs. The company therefore prepares a worksheet to facilitate the analysis. The following problem demonstrates use of the worksheet. The mechanics of its preparation should be obvious from the solution format. The income statements of Hudson Company for the years ended December 31, 2011, 2012, and 2013, indicate the following net incomes.

2011	$17,400
2012	20,200
2013	11,300

An examination of the accounting records for these years indicates that Hudson Company made several errors in arriving at the net income amounts reported:

1. The company consistently omitted from the records wages earned by workers but not paid at December 31. The amounts omitted were:

December 31, 2011	$1,000
December 31, 2012	$1,400
December 31, 2013	$1,600

When paid in the year following that in which they were earned, Hudson recorded these amounts as expenses.

2. The company overstated merchandise inventory on December 31, 2011, by $1,900 as the result of errors made in the footings and extensions on the inventory sheets.

3. On December 31, 2012, Hudson expensed unexpired insurance of $1,200, applicable to 2013.

4. The company did not record on December 31, 2012, interest receivable in the amount of $240.

5. On January 2, 2012, Hudson sold for $1,800 a piece of equipment costing $3,900. At the date of sale, the equipment had accumulated depreciation of $2,400. The company recorded the cash received as Miscellaneous Income in 2012. In addition, the company continued to record depreciation for this equipment in both 2012 and 2013 at the rate of 10 percent of cost.

The first step in preparing the worksheet is to prepare a schedule showing the corrected net income amounts for the years ended December 31, 2011, 2012, and 2013. Each correction of the amount originally reported is clearly labeled. The next step is to indicate the balance sheet accounts affected as of December 31, 2013. Illustration 22-24 shows the completed worksheet for Hudson Company.

ILLUSTRATION 22-24
Worksheet to Correct Income and Balance Sheet Errors

HUDSON COMPANY
Worksheet to Correct Income and Balance Sheet Errors

	A	B	C	D	E	F	G	H
1		Worksheet Analysis of Changes in Net Income				Balance Sheet Correction at December 31, 2013		
2		2011	2012	2013	Totals	Debit	Credit	Account
3	Net income as reported	$17,400	$20,200	$11,300	$48,900			
4	Wages unpaid, 12/31/11	(1,000)	1,000		–0–			
5	Wages unpaid, 12/31/12		(1,400)	1,400	–0–			
6	Wages unpaid, 12/31/13			(1,600)	(1,600)		$1,600	Salaries and Wages Payable
7	Inventory overstatement, 12/31/11	(1,900)	1,900		–0–			
8	Unexpired insurance, 12/31/12		1,200	(1,200)	–0–			
9	Interest receivable, 12/31/12		240	(240)	–0–			
10	Correction for entry made upon sale of equipment, 1/2/12[a]		(1,500)		(1,500)	$2,400	3,900	Accumulated Depreciation—Machinery / Machinery
11	Overcharge of depreciation, 2012		390		390	390		Accumulated Depreciation—Machinery
12	Overcharge of depreciation, 2013			390	390	390		Accumulated Depreciation—Machinery
13	Corrected net income	$14,500	$22,030	$10,050	$46,580			
14	[a]Cost	$ 3,900						
15	Accumulated depreciation	2,400						
16	Book value	1,500						
17	Less: Proceeds from sale	1,800						
18	Gain on sale	300						
19	Income reported	(1,800)						
20	Adjustment	$(1,500)						

Sheet1 / Sheet2 / Sheet3

Assuming that Hudson Company **has not closed the books**, correcting entries on December 31, 2013, are:

Retained Earnings	1,400	
Salaries and Wages Expense		1,400
(To correct improper charge to Salaries and Wages Expense for 2013)		
Salaries and Wages Expense	1,600	
Salaries and Wages Payable		1,600
(To record proper wages expense for 2013)		
Insurance Expense	1,200	
Retained Earnings		1,200
(To record proper insurance expense for 2013)		
Interest Revenue	240	
Retained Earnings		240
(To correct improper credit to Interest Revenue in 2013)		
Retained Earnings	1,500	
Accumulated Depreciation—Machinery	2,400	
Machinery		3,900
(To record write-off of machinery in 2012 and adjustment of Retained Earnings)		
Accumulated Depreciation—Machinery	780	
Depreciation Expense		390
Retained Earnings		390
(To correct improper charge for depreciation expense in 2012 and 2013)		

If Hudson Company has closed the books for 2013, the correcting entries are:

Retained Earnings	1,600	
Salaries and Wages Payable		1,600
(To record proper wage expense for 2013)		
Retained Earnings	1,500	
Accumulated Depreciation—Machinery	2,400	
Machinery		3,900
(To record write-off of machinery in 2012 and adjustment of Retained Earnings)		
Accumulated Depreciation—Machinery	780	
Retained Earnings		780
(To correct improper charge for depreciation expense in 2012 and 2013)		

GUARD THE FINANCIAL STATEMENTS!

What do the numbers mean?

Restatements sometimes occur because of financial fraud. Financial frauds involve the intentional misstatement or omission of material information in the organization's financial reports. Common methods of financial fraud manipulation include recording fictitious revenues, concealing liabilities or expenses, and artificially inflating reported assets. Financial frauds made up only 5 percent of the frauds in a recent study on occupational fraud but caused a median loss of more than $4 million—by far the most costly category of fraud. Presented on the next page is a chart that compares loss amounts for 2010 versus 2008 for financial statement fraud, corruption, and asset misappropriation.

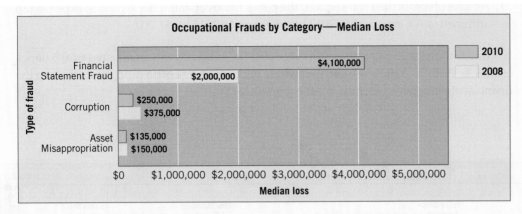

Unfortunately, the trend is going in the wrong direction (the median loss from financial state-ment fraud more than doubled). Therefore, companies must increase their efforts to protect their statements from the negative effects of fraud.

Source: Report to the Nations on Occupational Fraud and Abuse, 2010 Global Fraud Study, Association of Certified Fraud Examiners (2010), p. 11.

PREPARATION OF FINANCIAL STATEMENTS WITH ERROR CORRECTIONS

Up to now, our discussion of error analysis has focused on identifying the type of error involved and accounting for its correction in the records. We have noted that companies must present the correction of the error on comparative financial statements.

The following example illustrates how a company would restate a typical year's financial statements, given many different errors.

Dick & Wally's Outlet is a small retail outlet in the town of Holiday. Lacking exper-tise in accounting, the company does not keep adequate records, and numerous errors occurred in recording accounting information.

1. The bookkeeper inadvertently failed to record a cash receipt of $1,000 on the sale of merchandise in 2013.

2. Accrued wages expense at the end of 2012 was $2,500; at the end of 2013, $3,200. The company does not accrue for wages; all wages are charged to Administrative Ex-penses.

3. The company had not set up an allowance for estimated uncollectible receivables. Dick and Wally decided to set up such an allowance for the estimated probable losses, as of December 31, 2013, for 2012 accounts of $700, and for 2013 accounts of $1,500. They also decided to correct the charge against each year so that it shows the losses (actual and estimated) relating to that year's sales. The company has written off accounts to bad debt expense (selling expense) as follows.

	In 2012	In 2013
2012 accounts	$400	$2,000
2013 accounts		1,600

4. Unexpired insurance not recorded at the end of 2012 was $600, and at the end of 2013, $400. All insurance is charged to Administrative Expenses.

5. An account payable of $6,000 should have been a note payable.

6. During 2012, the company sold for $7,000 an asset that cost $10,000 and had a book value of $4,000. At the time of sale, Cash was debited and Miscellaneous Income was credited for $7,000.

7. As a result of the last transaction, the company overstated depreciation expense (an administrative expense) in 2012 by $800 and in 2013 by $1,200.

Illustration 22-25 presents a worksheet that begins with the unadjusted trial balance of Dick & Wally's Outlet. You can determine the correcting entries and their effect on the financial statements by examining the worksheet.

ILLUSTRATION 22-25
Worksheet to Analyze
Effect of Errors in
Financial Statements

DICK & WALLY'S OUTLET
Worksheet Analysis to Adjust Financial Statements for the Year 2013

A	Trial Balance Unadjusted Debit	Trial Balance Unadjusted Credit		Adjustments Debit		Adjustments Credit	Income Statement Adjusted Debit	Income Statement Adjusted Credit	Balance Sheet Adjusted Debit	Balance Sheet Adjusted Credit
Cash	3,100		(1)	1,000					4,100	
Accounts Receivable	17,600								17,600	
Notes Receivable	8,500								8,500	
Inventory	34,000								34,000	
Property, Plant, and Equipment	112,000				(6)	10,000ᵃ			102,000	
Accumulated Depreciation—Machinery		83,500	(6)	6,000ᵃ						75,500
			(7)	2,000						
Investments	24,300								24,300	
Accounts Payable		14,500	(5)	6,000						8,500
Notes Payable		10,000			(5)	6,000				16,000
Capital Stock		43,500								43,500
Retained Earnings		20,000	(3)	2,700ᵇ						
			(6)	4,000ᵃ	(4)	600				
			(2)	2,500	(7)	800				12,200
Sales Revenue		94,000			(1)	1,000		95,000		
Cost of Goods Sold	21,000						21,000			
Selling Expenses	22,000				(3)	500ᵇ	21,500			
Administrative Expenses	23,000		(2)	700	(4)	400	22,700			
			(4)	600	(7)	1,200				
Totals	265,500	265,500								
Salaries and Wages Payable					(2)	3,200				3,200
Allowance for Doubtful Accounts					(3)	2,200ᵇ				2,200
Unexpired Insurance			(4)	400					400	
Net Income							29,800			29,800
Totals				25,900		25,900	95,000	95,000	190,900	190,900

Sheet1 / Sheet2 / Sheet3

Computations:

ᵃMachinery	
Proceeds from sale	$ 7,000
Book value of machinery	(4,000)
Gain on sale	3,000
Less: Income credited	7,000
Retained earnings adjustment	$(4,000)

ᵇBad Debts	2012	2013
Bad debts charged for	$2,400	$1,600
Additional bad debts anticipated	700	1,500
	3,100	3,100
Charges currently made to each year	(400)	(3,600)
Bad debt adjustment	$2,700	$ (500)

You will want to read
IFRS INSIGHTS
on pages 1428–1432

for discussion of IFRS
related to accounting
changes and errors.

SUMMARY OF LEARNING OBJECTIVES

1 **Identify the types of accounting changes.** The three different types of accounting changes are: (1) *Change in accounting principle*: a change from one generally accepted accounting principle to another generally accepted accounting principle. (2) *Change in accounting estimate:* a change that occurs as the result of new information or as additional experience is acquired. (3) *Change in reporting entity:* a change from reporting as one type of entity to another type of entity.

2 **Describe the accounting for changes in accounting principles.** A change in accounting principle involves a change from one generally accepted accounting principle to another. A change in accounting principle is not considered to result from the adoption of a new principle in recognition of events that have occurred for the first time or that were previously immaterial. If the accounting principle previously followed was not acceptable or if the principle was applied incorrectly, a change to a generally accepted accounting principle is considered a correction of an error.

3 **Understand how to account for retrospective accounting changes.** The general requirement for changes in accounting principle is retrospective application. Under retrospective application, companies change prior years' financial statements on a basis consistent with the newly adopted principle. They treat any part of the effect attributable to years prior to those presented as an adjustment of the earliest retained earnings presented.

4 **Understand how to account for impracticable changes.** Retrospective application is impracticable if the prior period effect cannot be determined using every reasonable effort to do so. For example, in changing to LIFO, the base-year inventory for all subsequent LIFO calculations is generally the opening inventory in the year the company adopts the method. There is no restatement of prior years' income because it is often too impractical to do so.

5 **Describe the accounting for changes in estimates.** Companies report changes in estimates prospectively. That is, companies should make no changes in previously reported results. They do not adjust opening balances nor change financial statements of prior periods.

6 **Identify changes in a reporting entity.** An accounting change that results in financial statements that are actually the statements of a different entity should be reported by restating the financial statements of all prior periods presented, to show the financial information for the new reporting entity for all periods.

7 **Describe the accounting for correction of errors.** Companies must correct errors as soon as they discover them, by proper entries in the accounts, and report them in the financial statements. The profession requires that a company treat corrections of errors as prior period adjustments, record them in the year in which it discovered the errors, and report them in the financial statements in the proper periods. If presenting comparative statements, a company should restate the prior statements affected to correct for the errors. The company need not repeat the disclosures in the financial statements of subsequent periods.

8 **Identify economic motives for changing accounting methods.** Managers might have varying motives for income reporting, depending on economic times and whom they seek to impress. Some of the reasons for changing accounting methods are: (1) political costs, (2) capital structure, (3) bonus payments, and (4) smoothing of earnings.

KEY TERMS

change in accounting estimate, *1368, 1381*

change in accounting estimate effected by a change in accounting principle, *1382*

change in accounting principle, *1368*

change in reporting entity, *1368*

correction of an error, *1384*

counterbalancing errors, *1391*

cumulative effect, *1369*

direct effects of change in accounting principle, *1379*

economic consequences, *1390*

errors in financial statements, *1368*

impracticable, *1379*

indirect effects of change in accounting principle, *1379*

noncounterbalancing errors, *1391*

prior period adjustments, *1384*

prospectively, *1369*

restatement, *1385(n)*

retrospective application, *1369*

9 **Analyze the effect of errors.** Three types of errors can occur: (1) *Balance sheet errors*, which affect only the presentation of an asset, liability, or stockholders' equity account. (2) *Income statement errors*, which affect only the presentation of revenue, expense, gain, or loss accounts in the income statement. (3) *Balance sheet and income statement errors*, which involve both the balance sheet and income statement. Errors are classified into two types: (1) *Counterbalancing errors* are offset or corrected over two periods. (2) *Noncounterbalancing errors* are not offset in the next accounting period and take longer than two periods to correct themselves.

As an aid to understanding accounting changes, we provide the following glossary.

KEY TERMS RELATED TO ACCOUNTING CHANGES

ACCOUNTING CHANGE. A change in (1) an accounting principle, (2) an accounting estimate, or (3) the reporting entity. The correction of an error in previously issued financial statements is not an accounting change.

CHANGE IN ACCOUNTING PRINCIPLE. A change from one generally accepted accounting principle to another generally accepted accounting principle when two or more generally accepted accounting principles apply or when the accounting principle formerly used is no longer generally accepted.

CHANGE IN ACCOUNTING ESTIMATE. A change that has the effect of adjusting the carrying amount of an existing asset or liability or altering the subsequent accounting for existing or future assets or liabilities. Changes in accounting estimates result from new information.

CHANGE IN ACCOUNTING ESTIMATE EFFECTED BY A CHANGE IN ACCOUNTING PRINCIPLE. A change in accounting estimate that is inseparable from the effect of a related change in accounting principle.

CHANGE IN THE REPORTING ENTITY. A change that results in financial statements that, in effect, are those of a different reporting entity (see page 1383).

DIRECT EFFECTS OF A CHANGE IN ACCOUNTING PRINCIPLE. Those recognized changes in assets or liabilities necessary to effect a change in accounting principle.

ERROR IN PREVIOUSLY ISSUED FINANCIAL STATEMENTS. An error in recognition, measurement, presentation, or disclosure in financial statements resulting from mathematical mistakes, mistakes in the application of GAAP, or oversight or misuse of facts that existed at the time the financial statements were prepared. A change from an accounting principle that is not generally accepted to one that is generally accepted is a correction of an error.

INDIRECT EFFECTS OF A CHANGE IN ACCOUNTING PRINCIPLE. Any changes to current or future cash flows of an entity that result from making a change in accounting principle that is applied retrospectively.

RESTATEMENT. The process of revising previously issued financial statements to reflect the correction of an error in those financial statements.

RETROSPECTIVE APPLICATION. The application of a different accounting principle to one or more previously issued financial statements, or to the statement of financial position at the beginning of the current period, as if that principle had always been used, or a change to financial statements of prior accounting periods to present the financial statements of a new reporting entity as if it had existed in those prior years. [11]

APPENDIX **22A**	**CHANGING FROM OR TO THE EQUITY METHOD**

As noted in the chapter, companies generally should report an accounting change that results in financial statements for a different entity by **changing the financial statements of all prior periods presented**.

An example of a change in reporting entity is when a company's level of ownership or influence changes, such as when it changes from or to the equity method. When changing **to** the equity method, companies use retrospective application. Companies treat a change **from** the equity method prospectively. We present examples of these changes in entity in the following two sections.

CHANGE FROM THE EQUITY METHOD

If the investor level of influence or ownership falls below that necessary for continued use of the equity method, a company must change from the equity method to the fair value method. The earnings or losses that the investor previously recognized under the equity method should **remain as part of the carrying amount** of the investment, with no retrospective application to the new method.

> **10 LEARNING OBJECTIVE**
> Make the computations and prepare the entries necessary to record a change from or to the equity method of accounting.

When a company changes **from the equity method to the fair value method**, **the cost basis for accounting purposes is the carrying amount of the investment at the date of the change**. The investor applies the new method in its entirety once the equity method is no longer appropriate. At the next reporting date, the investor should record the unrealized holding gain or loss to recognize the difference between the carrying amount and fair value.[14]

Dividends in Excess of Earnings

In subsequent periods, dividends received by the investor company may exceed its share of the investee's earnings for such periods (all periods following the change in method). To the extent that they do so, the investor company should account for such dividends as a **reduction of the investment carrying amount**, rather than as revenue. The reason: Dividends in excess of earnings are viewed as a liquidating dividend, with this excess then accounted for as a reduction of the equity investment.

To illustrate, assume that on January 1, 2011, Investor Company purchased 250,000 shares of Investee Company's 1,000,000 shares of outstanding stock for $8,500,000. Investor correctly accounted for this investment using the equity method. After accounting for dividends received and investee net income, in 2011, Investor reported its investment in Investee Company at $8,780,000 at December 31, 2011. On January 2, 2012, Investee Company sold 1,500,000 additional shares of its own common stock to the public, thereby reducing Investor Company's ownership from 25 percent to 10 percent. Illustration 22A-1 shows the net income (or loss) and dividends of Investee Company for the years 2012 through 2014.

Year	Investor's Share of Investee Income (Loss)	Investee Dividends Received by Investor
2012	$600,000	$ 400,000
2013	350,000	400,000
2014	–0–	210,000
Totals	$950,000	$1,010,000

ILLUSTRATION 22A-1
Income Earned and
Dividends Received

[14]A retrospective application for this type of change is impracticable in many cases. Determining fair values on a portfolio basis for securities in previous periods may be quite difficult. As a result, prospective application is used.

Assuming a change from the equity method to the fair value method as of January 2, 2012, Investor Company's reported investment in Investee Company and its reported income would be as shown in Illustration 22A-2.

ILLUSTRATION 22A-2
Impact on Investment
Carrying Amount

Year	Dividend Revenue Recognized	Cumulative Excess of Share of Earnings over Dividends Received	Investment at December 31
2012	$400,000	$200,000[a]	$8,780,000
2013	400,000	150,000[b]	8,780,000
2014	150,000	(60,000)[c]	$8,780,000 − $60,000 = $8,720,000

[a]$600,000 − $400,000 = $200,000
[b]($350,000 − $400,000) + $200,000 = $150,000
[c]$150,000 − $210,000 = $(60,000)

Investor Company would record the dividends and earnings data for the three years subsequent to the change in methods as shown by the following entries.

2012 and 2013

Cash	400,000	
Dividend Revenue		400,000
(To record dividend received from Investee Company)		

2014

Cash	210,000	
Equity Investments (available-for-sale)		60,000
Dividend Revenue		150,000
(To record dividend revenue from Investee Company in 2014 and to recognize cumulative excess of dividends received over share of Investee earnings in periods subsequent to change from equity method)		

CHANGE TO THE EQUITY METHOD

When converting to the equity method, companies use retrospective application. Such a change involves adjusting the carrying amount of the investment, results of current and prior operations, and retained earnings of the investor **as if the equity method has been in effect during all of the previous periods in which this investment was held**. [12] When changing from the fair value method to the equity method, companies also must eliminate any balances in the Unrealized Holding Gain or Loss—Equity account and the Fair Value Adjustment account. In addition, they eliminate the available-for-sale classification for this investment, and they record the investment under the equity method.

For example, on January 2, 2012, Amsted Corp. purchased, for $500,000 cash, 10 percent of the outstanding shares of Cable Company common stock. On that date, the net identifiable assets of Cable Company had a fair value of $3,000,000. The excess of cost over the underlying equity in the net identifiable assets of Cable Company is goodwill. On January 2, 2014, Amsted Corp. purchased an additional 20 percent of Cable Company's stock for $1,200,000 cash when the fair value of Cable's net identifiable assets was $4,000,000. The excess of cost over fair value related to this additional investment is goodwill. Now having a 30 percent interest, Amsted Corp. must use the equity method.

From January 2, 2012, to January 2, 2014, Amsted Corp. used the fair value method and categorized these securities as available-for-sale. At January 2, 2014, Amsted has a credit balance of $92,000 in its Unrealized Holding Gain or Loss—Equity account and a debit balance in its Fair Value Adjustment account of the same amount. This change in fair value occurred in 2012 (Income tax effects are ignored.) Illustration 22A-3 shows the net income reported by Cable Company and the Cable Company dividends received by Amsted during the period 2012 through 2014.

Year	Cable Company Net Income	Cable Co. Dividends Paid to Amsted
2012	$ 500,000	$ 20,000
2013	1,000,000	30,000
2014	1,200,000	120,000

ILLUSTRATION 22A-3
Income Earned and
Dividends Received

Amsted makes the following journal entries from January 2, 2012, through December 31, 2014, relative to Amsted Corp.'s investment in Cable Company, reflecting the data above and a change from the fair value method to the equity method.[15]

January 2, 2012

Equity Investments (available-for-sale)	500,000	
Cash		500,000
(To record the purchase of a 10% interest in Cable Company)		

December 31, 2012

Cash	20,000	
Dividend Revenue		20,000
(To record the receipt of cash dividends from Cable Company)		
Fair Value Adjustment (available-for-sale)	92,000	
Unrealized Holding Gain or Loss—Equity		92,000
(To record increase in fair value of securities)		

December 31, 2013

Cash	30,000	
Dividend Revenue		30,000
(To record the receipt of cash dividends from Cable Company)		

January 2, 2014

Equity Investments (Cable stock)	1,300,000	
Cash		1,200,000
Retained Earnings		100,000
(To record the purchase of an additional interest in Cable Company and to reflect retrospectively a change from the fair value method to the equity method of accounting for the investment. The $100,000 adjustment is computed as follows:)		

	2012	2013	Total
Amsted Corp. equity in earnings of Cable Company (10%)	$50,000	$100,000	$150,000
Dividend received	(20,000)	(30,000)	(50,000)
Retrospective application	$30,000	$ 70,000	$100,000

January 2, 2014

Equity Investments (Cable stock)	500,000	
Equity Investments (available-for-sale)		500,000
(To reclassify initial 10% interest to equity method)		

January 2, 2014

Unrealized Holding Gain or Loss—Equity	92,000	
Fair Value Adjustment (available-for-sale)		92,000
(To eliminate fair value accounts for change to equity method)		

[15]Adapted from Paul A. Pacter, "Applying APB Opinion No. 18—Equity Method," *Journal of Accountancy* (September 1971), pp. 59–60.

	December 31, 2014		
Equity Investments (Cable stock)		360,000	
Revenue from Investment			360,000
[To record equity in earnings of Cable Company (30% of $1,200,000)]			
Cash		120,000	
Equity Investments (Cable stock)			120,000
(To record the receipt of cash dividends from Cable Company)			

Companies change to the equity method by placing the accounts related to and affected by the investment on the same basis **as if the equity method had always been the basis of accounting for that investment**. Thus, they report the effects of this accounting change using the retrospective approach.[16]

SUMMARY OF LEARNING OBJECTIVE FOR APPENDIX 22A

10 **Make the computations and prepare the entries necessary to record a change from or to the equity method of accounting.** When changing *from* the equity method to the fair value method, the cost basis for accounting purposes is the carrying amount used for the investment at the date of change. The investor company applies the new method in its entirety once the equity method is no longer appropriate. When changing *to* the equity method, the company adjusts the accounts to be on the same basis as if the equity method had always been used for that investment.

FASB CODIFICATION

FASB Codification References

[1] FASB ASC 250-10-05-1. [Predecessor literature: "Accounting Changes and Error Corrections," *Statement of Financial Accounting Standards No. 154* (Stamford, Conn.: FASB, 2005).]

[2] FASB ASC 250-10-05-2. [Predecessor literature: "Accounting Changes and Error Corrections," *Statement of Financial Accounting Standards No. 154* (Stamford, Conn.: FASB, 2005).]

[3] FASB ASC 250-10-50-1. [Predecessor literature: "Accounting Changes and Error Corrections," *Statement of Financial Accounting Standards No. 154* (Stamford, Conn.: FASB, 2005), par. 17.]

[4] FASB ASC 250-10-50-1. [Predecessor literature: "Accounting Changes and Error Corrections," *Statement of Financial Accounting Standards No. 154* (Stamford, Conn.: FASB, 2005), par. B19.]

[5] FASB ASC 250-10-45-6. [Predecessor literature: "Accounting Changes and Error Corrections," *Statement of Financial Accounting Standards No. 154* (Stamford, Conn.: FASB, 2005), paras. 8–11.]

[6] FASB ASC 250-10-50-1. [Predecessor literature: "Accounting Changes and Error Corrections," *Statement of Financial Accounting Standards No. 154* (Stamford, Conn.: FASB, 2005), par. 17.]

[7] FASB ASC 250-10-45-18. [Predecessor literature: "Accounting Changes and Error Corrections," *Statement of Financial Accounting Standards No. 154* (Stamford, Conn.: FASB, 2005), par. 20.]

[16]The change to the equity method illustration assumes that the fair value and the book value of the net identifiable assets of the investee are the same. However, the fair value of the net identifiable assets of the investee may be greater than their book value. In this case, this excess (if depreciable or amortizable) reduces the net income reported by the investor from the investee. For example, assume that the fair value of an investee's building is $1,000,000 and its book value is $800,000 at the time of change to the equity method. In that case, this difference of $200,000 is depreciated over the useful life of the building, thereby reducing the amount of investee's net income reported on the investor's books.

[8] FASB ASC 250-10-45-24. [Predecessor literature: "Prior Period Adjustments," *Statement of Financial Accounting Standards No. 16* (Stamford, Conn.: FASB, 1977), p. 5.]

[9] FASB ASC 250-10-50-4. [Predecessor literature: "Accounting Changes and Error Corrections," *Statement of Financial Accounting Standards No. 154* (Stamford, Conn.: FASB, 2005), par. 2.]

[10] FASB ASC 250-10-50-7. [Predecessor literature: "Accounting Changes and Error Corrections," *Statement of Financial Accounting Standards No. 154* (Stamford, Conn.: FASB, 2005), par. 26.]

[11] FASB ASC 250-10-50-1. [Predecessor literature: "Accounting Changes and Error Corrections," *Statement of Financial Accounting Standards No. 154* (Stamford, Conn.: FASB, 2005), par. 2.]

[12] FASB ASC 323-10-35-33. [Predecessor literature: "The Equity Method of Accounting for Investments in Common Stock," *Opinions of the Accounting Principles Board No. 18* (New York: AICPA, 1971), par. 17.]

Exercises

If your school has a subscription to the FASB Codification, go to *http://aaahq.org/ascLogin.cfm* to log in and prepare responses to the following. Provide Codification references for your responses.

CE22-1 Access the glossary ("Master Glossary") to answer the following.
  (a) What is a change in accounting estimate?
  (b) What is a change in accounting principle?
  (c) What is a restatement?
  (d) What is the definition of "retrospective application"?

CE22-2 When a company has to restate its financial statements to correct an error, what information must the company disclose?

CE22-3 What reporting requirements does retrospective application require?

CE22-4 If a company registered with the SEC justifies a change in accounting method as preferable under the circumstances, and the circumstances change, can that company switch back to its prior method of accounting before the change? Why or why not?

An additional Codification case can be found in the Using Your Judgment section, on page 1427.

Be sure to check the book's companion website for a Review and Analysis Exercise, with solution.

 Questions, Brief Exercises, Exercises, Problems, and many more resources are available for practice in WileyPLUS.

Note: All asterisked Questions, Exercises, and Problems relate to material in the appendix to the chapter.

QUESTIONS

1. In recent years, the *Wall Street Journal* has indicated that many companies have changed their accounting principles. What are the major reasons why companies change accounting methods?

2. State how each of the following items is reflected in the financial statements.
  (a) Change from FIFO to LIFO method for inventory valuation purposes.

  (b) Charge for failure to record depreciation in a previous period.
  (c) Litigation won in current year, related to prior period.
  (d) Change in the realizability of certain receivables.
  (e) Write-off of receivables.
  (f) Change from the percentage-of-completion to the completed-contract method for reporting net income.

3. Discuss briefly the three approaches that have been suggested for reporting changes in accounting principles.

4. Identify and describe the approach the FASB requires for reporting changes in accounting principles.

5. What is the indirect effect of a change in accounting principle? Briefly describe the reporting of the indirect effects of a change in accounting principle.

6. Define a change in estimate and provide an illustration. When is a change in accounting estimate effected by a change in accounting principle?

7. Lenexa State Bank has followed the practice of capitalizing certain marketing costs and amortizing these costs over their expected life. In the current year, the bank determined that the future benefits from these costs were doubtful. Consequently, the bank adopted the policy of expensing these costs as incurred. How should the bank report this accounting change in the comparative financial statements?

8. Indicate how the following items are recorded in the accounting records in the current year of Coronet Co.

(a) Impairment of goodwill.

(b) A change in depreciating plant assets from accelerated to the straight-line method.

(c) Large write-off of inventories because of obsolescence.

(d) Change from the cash basis to accrual basis of accounting.

(e) Change from LIFO to FIFO method for inventory valuation purposes.

(f) Change in the estimate of service lives for plant assets.

9. Whittier Construction Co. had followed the practice of expensing all materials assigned to a construction job without recognizing any salvage inventory. On December 31, 2012, it was determined that salvage inventory should be valued at $52,000. Of this amount, $29,000 arose during the current year. How does this information affect the financial statements to be prepared at the end of 2012?

10. Parsons Inc. wishes to change from the completed-contract to the percentage-of-completion method for financial reporting purposes. The auditor indicates that a change would be permitted only if it is to a preferable method. What difficulties develop in assessing preferability?

11. Discuss how a change to the LIFO method of inventory valuation is handled when it is impracticable to determine previous LIFO inventory amounts.

12. How should consolidated financial statements be reported this year when statements of individual companies were presented last year?

13. Simms Corp. controlled four domestic subsidiaries and one foreign subsidiary. Prior to the current year, Simms Corp. had excluded the foreign subsidiary from consolidation. During the current year, the foreign subsidiary was included in the financial statements. How should this change in accounting entity be reflected in the financial statements?

14. Distinguish between counterbalancing and noncounterbalancing errors. Give an example of each.

15. Discuss and illustrate how a correction of an error in previously issued financial statements should be handled.

16. Prior to 2012, Heberling Inc. excluded manufacturing overhead costs from work in process and finished goods inventory. These costs have been expensed as incurred. In 2012, the company decided to change its accounting methods for manufacturing inventories to full costing by including these costs as product costs. Assuming that these costs are material, how should this change be reflected in the financial statements for 2011 and 2012?

17. Elliott Corp. failed to record accrued salaries for 2011, $2,000; 2012, $2,100; and 2013, $3,900. What is the amount of the overstatement or understatement of Retained Earnings at December 31, 2014?

18. In January 2012, installation costs of $6,000 on new machinery were charged to Maintenance and Repairs Expense. Other costs of this machinery of $30,000 were correctly recorded and have been depreciated using the straight-line method with an estimated life of 10 years and no salvage value. At December 31, 2013, it is decided that the machinery has a remaining useful life of 20 years, starting with January 1, 2013. What entry(ies) should be made in 2013 to correctly record transactions related to machinery, assuming the machinery has no salvage value? The books have not been closed for 2013 and depreciation expense has not yet been recorded for 2013.

19. On January 2, 2012, $100,000 of 11%, 10-year bonds were issued for $97,000. The $3,000 discount was charged to Interest Expense. The bookkeeper, Mark Landis, records interest only on the interest payment dates of January 1 and July 1. What is the effect on reported net income for 2012 of this error, assuming straight-line amortization of the discount? What entry is necessary to correct for this error, assuming that the books are not closed for 2012?

20. An entry to record Purchases and related Accounts Payable of $13,000 for merchandise purchased on December 23, 2013, was recorded in January 2014. This merchandise was not included in inventory at December 31, 2013. What effect does this error have on reported net income for 2013? What entry should be made to correct for this error, assuming that the books are not closed for 2013?

21. Equipment was purchased on January 2, 2012, for $24,000, but no portion of the cost has been charged to depreciation. The corporation wishes to use the straight-line method for these assets, which have been estimated to have a life of 10 years and no salvage value. What effect does this error have on net income in 2012? What entry is necessary to correct for this error, assuming that the books are not closed for 2012?

BRIEF EXERCISES

3 **BE22-1** Wertz Construction Company decided at the beginning of 2012 to change from the completed-contract method to the percentage-of-completion method for financial reporting purposes. The company will continue to use the completed-contract method for tax purposes. For years prior to 2012, pretax income under the two methods was as follows: percentage-of-completion $120,000, and completed-contract $80,000. The tax rate is 35%. Prepare Wertz's 2012 journal entry to record the change in accounting principle.

3 **BE22-2** Refer to the accounting change by Wertz Construction Company in BE22-1. Wertz has a profit-sharing plan, which pays all employees a bonus at year-end based on 1% of pretax income. Compute the indirect effect of Wertz's change in accounting principle that will be reported in the 2012 income statement, assuming that the profit-sharing contract explicitly requires adjustment for changes in income numbers.

3 **BE22-3** Shannon, Inc., changed from the LIFO cost flow assumption to the FIFO cost flow assumption in 2012. The increase in the prior year's income before taxes is $1,200,000. The tax rate is 40%. Prepare Shannon's 2012 journal entry to record the change in accounting principle.

5 **BE22-4** Tedesco Company changed depreciation methods in 2012 from double-declining-balance to straight-line. Depreciation prior to 2012 under double-declining-balance was $90,000, whereas straight-line depreciation prior to 2012 would have been $50,000. Tedesco's depreciable assets had a cost of $250,000 with a $40,000 salvage value, and an 8-year remaining useful life at the beginning of 2012. Prepare the 2012 journal entries, if any, related to Tedesco's depreciable assets.

5 **BE22-5** Sesame Company purchased a computer system for $74,000 on January 1, 2011. It was depreciated based on a 7-year life and an $18,000 salvage value. On January 1, 2013, Sesame revised these estimates to a total useful life of 4 years and a salvage value of $10,000. Prepare Sesame's entry to record 2013 depreciation expense.

7 **BE22-6** In 2012, Bailey Corporation discovered that equipment purchased on January 1, 2010, for $50,000 was expensed at that time. The equipment should have been depreciated over 5 years, with no salvage value. The effective tax rate is 30%. Prepare Bailey's 2012 journal entry to correct the error.

7 **BE22-7** At January 1, 2012, Beidler Company reported retained earnings of $2,000,000. In 2012, Beidler discovered that 2011 depreciation expense was understated by $400,000. In 2012, net income was $900,000 and dividends declared were $250,000. The tax rate is 40%. Prepare a 2012 retained earnings statement for Beidler Company.

7 **BE22-8** Indicate the effect—Understate, Overstate, No Effect—that each of the following errors has on 2012 net income and 2013 net income.

	2012	2013
(a) Equipment purchased in 2010 was expensed.	___	___
(b) Wages payable were not recorded at 12/31/12.	___	___
(c) Equipment purchased in 2012 was expensed.	___	___
(d) 2012 ending inventory was overstated.	___	___
(e) Patent amortization was not recorded in 2013.	___	___

3 **5** **BE22-9** Roundtree Manufacturing Co. is preparing its year-end financial statements and is considering the accounting for the following items.

1. The vice president of sales had indicated that one product line has lost its customer appeal and will be phased out over the next 3 years. Therefore, a decision has been made to lower the estimated lives on related production equipment from the remaining 5 years to 3 years.
2. The Hightone Building was converted from a sales office to offices for the Accounting Department at the beginning of this year. Therefore, the expense related to this building will now appear as an administrative expense rather than a selling expense on the current year's income statement.
3. Estimating the lives of new products in the Leisure Products Division has become very difficult because of the highly competitive conditions in this market. Therefore, the practice of deferring and amortizing preproduction costs has been abandoned in favor of expensing such costs as they are incurred.

Identify and explain whether each of the above items is a change in principle, a change in estimate, or an error.

3 **7** **BE22-10** Palmer Co. is evaluating the appropriate accounting for the following items.

1. Management has decided to switch from the FIFO inventory valuation method to the LIFO inventory valuation method for all inventories.
2. When the year-end physical inventory adjustment was made for the current year, the controller discovered that the prior year's physical inventory sheets for an entire warehouse were mislaid and excluded from last year's count.
3. Palmer's Custom Division manufactures large-scale, custom-designed machinery on a contract basis. Management decided to switch from the completed-contract method to the percentage-of-completion method of accounting for long-term contracts.

Identify and explain whether each of the above items is a change in accounting principle, a change in estimate, or an error.

10 *BE22-11 Simmons Corporation owns stock of Armstrong, Inc. Prior to 2012, the investment was accounted for using the equity method. In early 2012, Simmons sold part of its investment in Armstrong, and began using the fair value method. In 2012, Armstrong earned net income of $80,000 and paid dividends of $95,000. Prepare Simmons's entries related to Armstrong's net income and dividends, assuming Simmons now owns 10% of Armstrong's stock.

10 *BE22-12 Oliver Corporation has owned stock of Conrad Corporation since 2009. At December 31, 2012, its balances related to this investment were:

Equity Investments	$185,000
Fair Value Adjustment (AFS)	34,000 Dr.
Unrealized Holding Gain or Loss—Equity	34,000 Cr.

On January 1, 2013, Oliver purchased additional stock of Conrad Company for $475,000 and now has significant influence over Conrad. If the equity method had been used in 2009–2012, Oliver's share of income would have been $33,000 greater than dividends received. Prepare Oliver's journal entries to record the purchase of the investment and the change to the equity method.

EXERCISES

---

3 **E22-1 (Change in Principle—Long-Term Contracts)** Cherokee Construction Company began operations in 2011 and changed from the completed-contract to the percentage-of-completion method of accounting for long-term construction contracts during 2012. For tax purposes, the company employs the completed-contract method and will continue this approach in the future. (*Hint:* Adjust all tax consequences through the Deferred Tax Liability account.) The appropriate information related to this change is as follows.

	Pretax Income from		
	Percentage-of-Completion	Completed-Contract	Difference
2011	$780,000	$610,000	$170,000
2012	700,000	480,000	220,000

Instructions
(a) Assuming that the tax rate is 35%, what is the amount of net income that would be reported in 2012?
(b) What entry(ies) are necessary to adjust the accounting records for the change in accounting principle?

3 **E22-2 (Change in Principle—Inventory Methods)** Whitman Company began operations on January 1, 2010, and uses the average cost method of pricing inventory. Management is contemplating a change in inventory methods for 2013. The following information is available for the years 2010–2012.

	Net Income Computed Using		
	Average Cost Method	FIFO Method	LIFO Method
2010	$16,000	$19,000	$12,000
2011	18,000	21,000	14,000
2012	20,000	25,000	17,000

Instructions
(Ignore all tax effects.)

(a) Prepare the journal entry necessary to record a change from the average cost method to the FIFO method in 2013.

(b) Determine net income to be reported for 2010, 2011, and 2012, after giving effect to the change in accounting principle.

(c) Assume Whitman Company used the LIFO method instead of the average cost method during the years 2010–2012. In 2013, Whitman changed to the FIFO method. Prepare the journal entry necessary to record the change in principle.

3 **E22-3 (Accounting Change)** Ramirez Co. decides at the beginning of 2012 to adopt the FIFO method of inventory valuation. Ramirez had used the LIFO method for financial reporting since its inception on January 1, 2010, and had maintained records adequate to apply the FIFO method retrospectively. Ramirez concluded that FIFO is the preferable inventory method because it reflects the current cost of inventory on the balance sheet. The table presents the effects of the change in accounting principle on inventory and cost of goods sold.

	Inventory Determined by		Cost of Goods Sold Determined by	
Date	LIFO Method	FIFO Method	LIFO Method	FIFO Method
January 1, 2010	$ 0	$ 0	$ 0	$ 0
December 31, 2010	100	80	800	820
December 31, 2011	200	240	1,000	940
December 31, 2012	320	390	1,130	1,100

Retained earnings reported under LIFO are as follows.

	Retained Earnings Balance
December 31, 2010	$2,200
December 31, 2011	4,200
December 31, 2012	6,070

Other information:

1. For each year presented, sales are $4,000 and operating expenses are $1,000.
2. Ramirez provides two years of financial statements. Earnings per share information is not required.

Instructions

(a) Prepare income statements under LIFO and FIFO for 2010, 2011, and 2012.

(b) Prepare income statements reflecting the retrospective application of the accounting change from the LIFO method to the FIFO method for 2012 and 2011.

(c) Prepare the note to the financial statements describing the change in method of inventory valuation. In the note, indicate the income statement line items for 2012 and 2011 that were affected by the change in accounting principle.

(d) Prepare comparative retained earnings statements for 2011 and 2012 under FIFO.

3 **E22-4 (Accounting Change)** Linden Company started operations on January 1, 2008, and has used the FIFO method of inventory valuation since its inception. In 2014, it decides to switch to the average cost method. You are provided with the following information.

	Net Income		Retained Earnings (Ending Balance)
	Under FIFO	Under Average Cost	Under FIFO
2008	$100,000	$ 92,000	$100,000
2009	70,000	65,000	160,000
2010	90,000	80,000	235,000
2011	120,000	130,000	340,000
2012	300,000	293,000	590,000
2013	305,000	310,000	780,000

Instructions

(a) What is the beginning retained earnings balance at January 1, 2010, if Linden prepares comparative financial statements starting in 2010?

(b) What is the beginning retained earnings balance at January 1, 2013, if Linden prepares comparative financial statements starting in 2013?

(c) What is the beginning retained earnings balance at January 1, 2014, if Linden prepares single-period financial statements for 2014?

(d) What is the net income reported by Linden in the 2013 income statement if it prepares comparative financial statements starting with 2011?

3 **E22-5 (Accounting Change)** Presented on page 1410 are income statements prepared on a LIFO and FIFO basis for Carlton Company, which started operations on January 1, 2011. The company presently uses the LIFO method of pricing its inventory and has decided to switch to the FIFO method in 2012. The FIFO income statement is computed in accordance with GAAP requirements. Carlton's profit-sharing agreement with its employees indicates that the company will pay employees 5% of income before profit sharing. Income taxes are ignored.

	LIFO Basis		FIFO Basis	
	2012	2011	2012	2011
Sales	$3,000	$3,000	$3,000	$3,000
Cost of goods sold	1,130	1,000	1,100	940
Operating expenses	1,000	1,000	1,000	1,000
Income before profit sharing	870	1,000	900	1,060
Profit sharing expense	44	50	45	53
Net income	$ 826	$ 950	$ 855	$1,007

Instructions
Answer the following questions.

(a) If comparative income statements are prepared, what net income should Carlton report in 2011 and 2012?
(b) Explain why, under the FIFO basis, Carlton reports $50 in 2011 and $48 in 2012 for its profit-sharing expense.
(c) Assume that Carlton has a beginning balance of retained earnings at January 1, 2012, of $8,000 using the LIFO method. The company declared and paid dividends of $2,500 in 2012. Prepare the retained earnings statement for 2012, assuming that Carlton has switched to the FIFO method.

5 **E22-6 (Accounting Changes—Depreciation)** Robillard Inc. acquired the following assets in January of 2009.

Equipment, estimated service life, 5 years; salvage value, $15,000	$465,000
Building, estimated service life, 30 years; no salvage value	$780,000

The equipment has been depreciated using the sum-of-the-years'-digits method for the first 3 years for financial reporting purposes. In 2012, the company decided to change the method of computing depreciation to the straight-line method for the equipment, but no change was made in the estimated service life or salvage value. It was also decided to change the total estimated service life of the building from 30 years to 40 years, with no change in the estimated salvage value. The building is depreciated on the straight-line method.

Instructions
(a) Prepare the journal entry to record depreciation expense for the equipment in 2012.
(b) Prepare the journal entry to record depreciation expense for the building in 2012. (Round to nearest dollar.)

5 **7** **E22-7 (Change in Estimate and Error; Financial Statements)** Presented below are the comparative income statements for Pannebecker Inc. for the years 2011 and 2012.

	2012	2011
Sales	$340,000	$270,000
Cost of sales	200,000	142,000
Gross profit	140,000	128,000
Expenses	88,000	50,000
Net income	$ 52,000	$ 78,000
Retained earnings (Jan. 1)	$125,000	$ 72,000
Net income	52,000	78,000
Dividends	(30,000)	(25,000)
Retained earnings (Dec. 31)	$147,000	$125,000

The following additional information is provided.

1. In 2012, Pannebecker Inc. decided to switch its depreciation method from sum-of-the-years'-digits to the straight-line method. The assets were purchased at the beginning of 2011 for $90,000 with an estimated useful life of 4 years and no salvage value. (The 2012 income statement contains depreciation expense of $27,000 on the assets purchased at the beginning of 2011.)
2. In 2012, the company discovered that the ending inventory for 2011 was overstated by $20,000; ending inventory for 2012 is correctly stated.

Instructions
Prepare the revised retained earnings statement for 2011 and 2012, assuming comparative statements. (Ignore income taxes.)

3 5 7 E22-8 (Accounting for Accounting Changes and Errors) Listed below are various types of accounting changes and errors.

_____ **1.** Change from FIFO to average cost inventory method.
_____ **2.** Change due to overstatement of inventory.
_____ **3.** Change from sum-of-the-years'-digits to straight-line method of depreciation.
_____ **4.** Change from presenting unconsolidated to consolidated financial statements.
_____ **5.** Change from LIFO to FIFO inventory method.
_____ **6.** Change in the rate used to compute warranty costs.
_____ **7.** Change from an unacceptable accounting principle to an acceptable accounting principle.
_____ **8.** Change in a patent's amortization period.
_____ **9.** Change from completed-contract to percentage-of-completion method on construction contracts.
_____ **10.** Change in a plant asset's salvage value.

Instructions

For each change or error, indicate how it would be accounted for using the following code letters:

(a) Accounted for prospectively.
(b) Accounted for retrospectively.
(c) Neither of the above.

5 7 **E22-9 (Error and Change in Estimate—Depreciation)** Tarkington Co. purchased a machine on January 1, 2009, for $440,000. At that time it was estimated that the machine would have a 10-year life and no salvage value. On December 31, 2012, the firm's accountant found that the entry for depreciation expense had been omitted in 2010. In addition, management has informed the accountant that the company plans to switch to straight-line depreciation, starting with the year 2012. At present, the company uses the sum-of-the-years'-digits method for depreciating equipment.

Instructions

Prepare the general journal entries that should be made at December 31, 2012, to record these events. (Ignore tax effects.)

5 E22-10 (Depreciation Changes) On January 1, 2008, McElroy Company purchased a building and equipment that have the following useful lives, salvage values, and costs.

> Building, 40-year estimated useful life, $50,000 salvage value, $1,200,000 cost
> Equipment, 12-year estimated useful life, $10,000 salvage value, $130,000 cost

The building has been depreciated under the double-declining-balance method through 2011. In 2012, the company decided to switch to the straight-line method of depreciation. McElroy also decided to change the total useful life of the equipment to 9 years, with a salvage value of $5,000 at the end of that time. The equipment is depreciated using the straight-line method.

Instructions

(a) Prepare the journal entry(ies) necessary to record the depreciation expense on the building in 2012.
(b) Compute depreciation expense on the equipment for 2012.

5 **E22-11 (Change in Estimate—Depreciation)** Thurber Co. purchased equipment for $710,000 which was estimated to have a useful life of 10 years with a salvage value of $10,000 at the end of that time. Depreciation has been entered for 7 years on a straight-line basis. In 2013, it is determined that the total estimated life should be 15 years with a salvage value of $4,000 at the end of that time.

Instructions

(a) Prepare the entry (if any) to correct the prior years' depreciation.
(b) Prepare the entry to record depreciation for 2013.

5 E22-12 (Change in Estimate—Depreciation) Frederick Industries changed from the double-declining-balance to the straight-line method in 2012 on all its plant assets. There was no change in the assets' salvage values or useful lives. Plant assets, acquired on January 2, 2011, had an original cost of $2,400,000, with a $100,000 salvage value and an 8-year estimated useful life. Income before depreciation expense was $370,000 in 2009 and $300,000 in 2012.

Instructions

(a) Prepare the journal entry(ies) to record the change in depreciation method in 2012.
(b) Starting with income before depreciation expense, prepare the remaining portion of the income statement for 2011 and 2012.

3 ▸ **E22-13 (Change in Principle—Long-Term Contracts)** Bryant Construction Company began operations in 2011 and changed from the completed-contract to the percentage-of-completion method of accounting for long-term construction contracts during 2012. For tax purposes, the company employs the completed-contract method and will continue this approach in the future. The appropriate information related to this change is as follows.

| | Pretax Income from | | |
	Percentage-of-Completion	Completed-Contract	Difference
2011	$980,000	$730,000	$250,000
2012	900,000	480,000	420,000

Instructions

(a) Assuming that the tax rate is 40%, what is the amount of net income that would be reported in 2012?

(b) What entry(ies) are necessary to adjust the accounting records for the change in accounting principle?

3 ▸ **E22-14 (Various Changes in Principle—Inventory Methods)** Below is the net income of Benchley Instrument Co., a private corporation, computed under the three inventory methods using a periodic system.

	FIFO	Average Cost	LIFO
2010	$26,000	$23,000	$20,000
2011	30,000	25,000	21,000
2012	29,000	27,000	24,000
2013	34,000	30,000	26,000

Instructions
(Ignore tax considerations.)

(a) Assume that in 2013 Benchley decided to change from the FIFO method to the average cost method of pricing inventories. Prepare the journal entry necessary for the change that took place during 2013, and show net income reported for 2010, 2011, 2012, and 2013.

(b) Assume that in 2013 Benchley, which had been using the LIFO method since incorporation in 2010, changed to the FIFO method of pricing inventories. Prepare the journal entry necessary to record the change in 2013 and show net income reported for 2010, 2011, 2012, and 2013.

7 ▸ **E22-15 (Error Correction Entries)** The first audit of the books of Fenimore Company was made for the year ended December 31, 2012. In examining the books, the auditor found that certain items had been overlooked or incorrectly handled in the last 3 years. These items are:

1. At the beginning of 2010, the company purchased a machine for $510,000 (salvage value of $51,000) that had a useful life of 5 years. The bookkeeper used straight-line depreciation, but failed to deduct the salvage value in computing the depreciation base for the 3 years.

2. At the end of 2011, the company failed to accrue sales salaries of $45,000.

3. A tax lawsuit that involved the year 2010 was settled late in 2012. It was determined that the company owed an additional $85,000 in taxes related to 2010. The company did not record a liability in 2010 or 2011 because the possibility of loss was considered remote, and debited the $85,000 to a loss account in 2012 and credited Cash for the same amount.

4. Fenimore Company purchased a copyright from another company early in 2010 for $50,000. Fenimore has not amortized the copyright because management believes that its value had not diminished. The copyright has a useful life at purchase of 20 years.

5. In 2012, the company wrote off $87,000 of inventory considered to be obsolete; this loss was charged directly to Retained Earnings and credited to Inventory.

Instructions
Prepare the journal entries necessary in 2012 to correct the books, assuming that the books have not been closed. Disregard effects of corrections on income tax.

7 ▸ **E22-16 (Error Analysis and Correcting Entry)** You have been engaged to review the financial statements of Longfellow Corporation. In the course of your examination, you conclude that the bookkeeper hired during the current year is not doing a good job. You notice a number of irregularities as follows.

1. Year-end wages payable of $3,400 were not recorded because the bookkeeper thought that "they were immaterial."

2. Accrued vacation pay for the year of $31,100 was not recorded because the bookkeeper "never heard that you had to do it."

3. Insurance for a 12-month period purchased on November 1 of this year was charged to insurance expense in the amount of $3,300 because "the amount of the check is about the same every year."

4. Reported sales revenue for the year is $1,908,000. This includes all sales taxes collected for the year. The sales tax rate is 6%. Because the sales tax is forwarded to the state's Department of Revenue, the Sales Tax Expense account is debited. The bookkeeper thought that "the sales tax is a selling expense." At the end of the current year, the balance in the Sales Tax Expense account is $103,400.

Instructions

Prepare the necessary correcting entries, assuming that Longfellow uses a calendar-year basis.

7 **E22-17 (Error Analysis and Correcting Entry)** The reported net incomes for the first 2 years of Sinclair Products, Inc., were as follows: 2012, $147,000; 2013, $185,000. Early in 2014, the following errors were discovered.

1. Depreciation of equipment for 2012 was overstated $19,000.
2. Depreciation of equipment for 2013 was understated $38,500.
3. December 31, 2012, inventory was understated $50,000.
4. December 31, 2013, inventory was overstated $14,200.

Instructions

Prepare the correcting entry necessary when these errors are discovered. Assume that the books for 2013 are closed. (Ignore income tax considerations.)

7 **9** **E22-18 (Error Analysis)** Emerson Tool Company's December 31 year-end financial statements contained the following errors.

	December 31, 2011	December 31, 2012
Ending inventory	$9,600 understated	$7,100 overstated
Depreciation expense	$2,300 understated	—

An insurance premium of $60,000 was prepaid in 2011 covering the years 2011, 2012, and 2013. The entire amount was charged to expense in 2011. In addition, on December 31, 2012, fully depreciated machinery was sold for $15,000 cash, but the entry was not recorded until 2013. There were no other errors during 2011 or 2012, and no corrections have been made for any of the errors. (Ignore income tax considerations.)

Instructions

(a) Compute the total effect of the errors on 2012 net income.
(b) Compute the total effect of the errors on the amount of Emerson's working capital at December 31, 2012.
(c) Compute the total effect of the errors on the balance of Emerson's retained earnings at December 31, 2012.

7 **9** **E22-19 (Error Analysis and Correcting Entries)** A partial trial balance of Dickinson Corporation is as follows on December 31, 2012.

	Dr.	Cr.
Supplies	$ 2,500	
Salaries and Wages Payable		$ 1,500
Interest Receivable	5,100	
Prepaid Insurance	90,000	
Unearned Rent		–0–
Interest Payable		15,000

Additional adjusting data:

1. A physical count of supplies on hand on December 31, 2012, totaled $1,100.
2. Through oversight, the Salaries and Wages Payable account was not changed during 2012. Accrued salaries and wages on December 31, 2012, amounted to $4,400.
3. The Interest Receivable account was also left unchanged during 2012. Accrued interest on investments amounts to $4,350 on December 31, 2012.
4. The unexpired portions of the insurance policies totaled $65,000 as of December 31, 2012.
5. $24,000 was received on January 1, 2012, for the rent of a building for both 2012 and 2013. The entire amount was credited to Rent Revenue.
6. Depreciation for the year was erroneously recorded as $5,000 rather than the correct figure of $50,000.
7. A further review of depreciation calculations of prior years revealed that depreciation of $7,200 was not recorded. It was decided that this oversight should be corrected by a prior period adjustment.

Instructions

(a) Assuming that the books have not been closed, what are the adjusting entries necessary at December 31, 2012? (Ignore income tax considerations.)

(b) Assuming that the books have been closed, what are the adjusting entries necessary at December 31, 2012? (Ignore income tax considerations.)

7 ▶ 9 ▶ E22-20 (Error Analysis) The before-tax income for Fitzgerald Co. for 2012 was $101,000 and $77,400 for 2013. However, the accountant noted that the following errors had been made.

1. Sales for 2012 included amounts of $38,200 which had been received in cash during 2012, but for which the related products were delivered in 2013. Title did not pass to the purchaser until 2013.
2. The inventory on December 31, 2012, was understated by $8,640.
3. The bookkeeper in recording interest expense for both 2012 and 2013 on bonds payable made the following entry on an annual basis.

Interest Expense	15,000	
Cash		15,000

The bonds have a face value of $250,000 and pay a stated interest rate of 6%. They were issued at a discount of $10,000 on January 1, 2012, to yield an effective-interest rate of 7%. (Assume that the effective-interest method should be used.)

4. Ordinary repairs to equipment had been erroneously charged to the Equipment account during 2012 and 2013. Repairs in the amount of $8,000 in 2012 and $9,400 in 2013 were so charged. The company applies a rate of 10% to the balance in the Equipment account at the end of the year in its determination of depreciation charges.

Instructions

Prepare a schedule showing the determination of corrected income before taxes for 2012 and 2013.

7 ▶ 9 ▶ E22-21 (Error Analysis) When the records of Archibald Corporation were reviewed at the close of 2013, the errors listed below were discovered. For each item, indicate by a check mark in the appropriate column whether the error resulted in an overstatement, an understatement, or had no effect on net income for the years 2012 and 2013.

	2012			2013		
Item	**Over-statement**	**Under-statement**	**No Effect**	**Over-statement**	**Under-statement**	**No Effect**
1. Failure to reflect supplies on hand on balance sheet at end of 2012.						
2. Failure to record the correct amount of ending 2012 inventory. The amount was understated because of an error in calculation.						
3. Failure to record merchandise purchased in 2012. Merchandise was also omitted from ending inventory in 2012 but was not yet sold.						
4. Failure to record accrued interest on notes payable in 2012; that amount was recorded when paid in 2013.						
5. Failure to record amortization of patent in 2013.						

10 *E22-22 **(Change from Fair Value to Equity)** On January 1, 2012, Sandburg Co. purchased 25,000 shares (a 10% interest) in Yevette Corp. for $1,400,000. At the time, the book value and the fair value of Yevette's net identifiable assets were $13,000,000.

On July 1, 2013, Sandburg paid $3,040,000 for 50,000 additional shares of Yevette common stock, which represented a 20% investment in Yevette. The fair value of Yevette's identifiable assets net of liabilities was equal to their carrying amount of $14,200,000. As a result of this transaction, Sandburg owns 30% of Yevette and can exercise significant influence over Yevette's operating and financial policies. Any excess of the cost over the fair value of the identifiable net assets is attributed to goodwill.

Yevette reported the following net income and declared and paid the following dividends.

	Net Income	Dividend per Share
Year ended 12/31/12	$900,000	None
Six months ended 6/30/13	500,000	None
Six months ended 12/31/13	815,000	$1.40

Instructions
Determine the ending balance that Sandburg Co. should report as its investment in Yevette Corp. at the end of 2013.

10 *E22-23 **(Change from Equity to Fair Value)** Gamble Corp. was a 30% owner of Sabrina Company, holding 210,000 shares of Sabrina's common stock on December 31, 2012. The investment account had the following entries.

Investment in Sabrina

1/1/11 Cost	$3,180,000	12/6/11 Dividend received	$150,000
12/31/11 Share of income	390,000	12/5/12 Dividend received	200,000
12/31/12 Share of income	510,000		

On January 2, 2013, Gamble sold 126,000 shares of Sabrina for $3,440,000, thereby losing its significant influence. During the year 2013, Sabrina experienced the following results of operations and paid the following dividends to Gamble.

	Sabrina Income (Loss)	Dividends Paid to Gamble
2013	$350,000	$50,400

At December 31, 2013, the fair value of Sabrina shares held by Gamble is $1,570,000. This is the first reporting date since the January 2 sale of Sabrina shares.

Instructions
(a) What effect does the January 2, 2013, transaction have upon Gamble's accounting treatment for its investment in Sabrina?
(b) Compute the carrying amount in Sabrina as of December 31, 2013.
(c) Prepare the adjusting entry on December 31, 2013, applying the fair value method to Gamble's long-term investment in Sabrina Company's securities.

See the book's companion website, www.wiley.com/college/kieso, for a set of B Exercises.

PROBLEMS

2 **5** P22-1 **(Change in Estimate and Error Correction)** Holtzman Company is in the process of preparing its
7 financial statements for 2012. Assume that no entries for depreciation have been recorded in 2012. The following information related to depreciation of fixed assets is provided to you.

1. Holtzman purchased equipment on January 2, 2009, for $85,000. At that time, the equipment had an estimated useful life of 10 years with a $5,000 salvage value. The equipment is depreciated on a straight-line basis. On January 2, 2012, as a result of additional information, the company determined that the equipment has a remaining useful life of 4 years with a $3,000 salvage value.
2. During 2012, Holtzman changed from the double-declining-balance method for its building to the straight-line method. The building originally cost $300,000. It had a useful life of 10 years and a

salvage value of $30,000. The following computations present depreciation on both bases for 2010 and 2011.

	2011	2010
Straight-line	$27,000	$27,000
Declining-balance	48,000	60,000

3. Holtzman purchased a machine on July 1, 2010, at a cost of $120,000. The machine has a salvage value of $16,000 and a useful life of 8 years. Holtzman's bookkeeper recorded straight-line depreciation in 2010 and 2011 but failed to consider the salvage value.

Instructions
(a) Prepare the journal entries to record depreciation expense for 2012 and correct any errors made to date related to the information provided.
(b) Show comparative net income for 2011 and 2012. Income before depreciation expense was $300,000 in 2012, and was $310,000 in 2011. (Ignore taxes.)

3 5 7 P22-2 (Comprehensive Accounting Change and Error Analysis Problem) Botticelli Inc. was organized in late 2010 to manufacture and sell hosiery. At the end of its fourth year of operation, the company has been fairly successful, as indicated by the following reported net incomes.

2010	$140,000[a]	2012	$205,000
2011	160,000[b]	2013	276,000

[a]Includes a $10,000 increase because of change in bad debt experience rate.
[b]Includes extraordinary gain of $30,000.

The company has decided to expand operations and has applied for a sizable bank loan. The bank officer has indicated that the records should be audited and presented in comparative statements to facilitate analysis by the bank. Botticelli Inc. therefore hired the auditing firm of Check & Doublecheck Co. and has provided the following additional information.

1. In early 2011, Botticelli Inc. changed its estimate from 2% to 1% on the amount of bad debt expense to be charged to operations. Bad debt expense for 2010, if a 1% rate had been used, would have been $10,000. The company therefore restated its net income for 2010.

2. In 2013, the auditor discovered that the company had changed its method of inventory pricing from LIFO to FIFO. The effect on the income statements for the previous years is as follows.

	2010	2011	2012	2013
Net income unadjusted—LIFO basis	$140,000	$160,000	$205,000	$276,000
Net income unadjusted—FIFO basis	155,000	165,000	215,000	260,000
	$ 15,000	$ 5,000	$ 10,000	$ (16,000)

3. In 2013, the auditor discovered that:
(a) The company incorrectly overstated the ending inventory by $14,000 in 2012.
(b) A dispute developed in 2011 with the Internal Revenue Service over the deductibility of entertainment expenses. In 2010, the company was not permitted these deductions, but a tax settlement was reached in 2013 that allowed these expenses. As a result of the court's finding, tax expenses in 2013 were reduced by $60,000.

Instructions
(a) Indicate how each of these changes or corrections should be handled in the accounting records. (Ignore income tax considerations.)
(b) Present comparative income statements for the years 2010 to 2013, starting with income before extraordinary items. (Ignore income tax considerations.)

3 5 7 P22-3 (Error Corrections and Accounting Changes) Penn Company is in the process of adjusting and correcting its books at the end of 2012. In reviewing its records, the following information is compiled.

1. Penn has failed to accrue sales commissions payable at the end of each of the last 2 years, as follows.

December 31, 2011	$3,500
December 31, 2012	$2,500

2. In reviewing the December 31, 2011, inventory, Penn discovered errors in its inventory-taking procedures that have caused inventories for the last 3 years to be incorrect, as follows.

December 31, 2010	Understated	$16,000
December 31, 2011	Understated	$19,000
December 31, 2012	Overstated	$ 6,700

Penn has already made an entry that established the incorrect December 31, 2012, inventory amount.

3. At December 31, 2012, Penn decided to change the depreciation method on its office equipment from double-declining-balance to straight-line. The equipment had an original cost of $100,000 when purchased on January 1, 2010. It has a 10-year useful life and no salvage value. Depreciation expense recorded prior to 2012 under the double-declining-balance method was $36,000. Penn has already recorded 2012 depreciation expense of $12,800 using the double-declining-balance method.

4. Before 2012, Penn accounted for its income from long-term construction contracts on the completed-contract basis. Early in 2012, Penn changed to the percentage-of-completion basis for accounting purposes. It continues to use the completed-contract method for tax purposes. Income for 2012 has been recorded using the percentage-of-completion method. The following information is available.

	Pretax Income	
	Percentage-of-Completion	Completed-Contract
Prior to 2012	$150,000	$105,000
2012	60,000	20,000

Instructions

Prepare the journal entries necessary at December 31, 2012, to record the above corrections and changes. The books are still open for 2012. The income tax rate is 40%. Penn has not yet recorded its 2012 income tax expense and payable amounts so current-year tax effects may be ignored. Prior-year tax effects must be considered in item 4.

P22-4 (Accounting Changes) Aston Corporation performs year-end planning in November of each year before its calendar year ends in December. The preliminary estimated net income is $3 million. The CFO, Rita Warren, meets with the company president, J. B. Aston, to review the projected numbers. She presents the following projected information.

ASTON CORPORATION
PROJECTED INCOME STATEMENT
FOR THE YEAR ENDED DECEMBER 31, 2012

Sales		$29,000,000
Cost of goods sold	$14,000,000	
Depreciation	2,600,000	
Operating expenses	6,400,000	23,000,000
Income before income tax		6,000,000
Income tax		3,000,000
Net income		$ 3,000,000

ASTON CORPORATION
SELECTED BALANCE SHEET INFORMATION
AT DECEMBER 31, 2012

Estimated cash balance	$ 5,000,000
Available-for-sale securities (at cost)	10,000,000
Fair value adjustment (1/1/12)	200,000

Estimated market value at December 31, 2012:

Security	Cost	Estimated Market
A	$ 2,000,000	$ 2,200,000
B	4,000,000	3,900,000
C	3,000,000	3,000,000
D	1,000,000	1,800,000
Total	$10,000,000	$10,900,000

Other information at December 31, 2012:

Equipment	$ 3,000,000
Accumulated depreciation (5-year SL)	1,200,000
New robotic equipment (purchased 1/1/12)	5,000,000
Accumulated depreciation (5-year DDB)	2,000,000

The corporation has never used robotic equipment before, and Warren assumed an accelerated method because of the rapidly changing technology in robotic equipment. The company normally uses straight-line depreciation for production equipment.

Aston explains to Warren that it is important for the corporation to show a $7,000,000 income before taxes because Aston receives a $1,000,000 bonus if the income before taxes and bonus reaches $7,000,000. Aston also does not want the company to pay more than $3,000,000 in income taxes to the government.

Instructions

(a) What can Warren do within GAAP to accommodate the president's wishes to achieve $7,000,000 in income before taxes and bonus? Present the revised income statement based on your decision.

(b) Are the actions ethical? Who are the stakeholders in this decision, and what effect do Warren's actions have on their interests?

P22-5 (Change in Principle—Inventory—Periodic) The management of Utrillo Instrument Company had concluded, with the concurrence of its independent auditors, that results of operations would be more fairly presented if Utrillo changed its method of pricing inventory from last-in, first-out (LIFO) to average cost in 2012. Given below is the 5-year summary of income under LIFO and a schedule of what the inventories would be if stated on the average cost method.

UTRILLO INSTRUMENT COMPANY
STATEMENT OF INCOME AND RETAINED EARNINGS
FOR THE YEARS ENDED MAY 31

	2008	2009	2010	2011	2012
Sales—net	$13,964	$15,506	$16,673	$18,221	$18,898
Cost of goods sold					
Beginning inventory	1,000	1,100	1,000	1,115	1,237
Purchases	13,000	13,900	15,000	15,900	17,100
Ending inventory	(1,100)	(1,000)	(1,115)	(1,237)	(1,369)
Total	12,900	14,000	14,885	15,778	16,968
Gross profit	1,064	1,506	1,788	2,443	1,930
Administrative expenses	700	763	832	907	989
Income before taxes	364	743	956	1,536	941
Income taxes (50%)	182	372	478	768	471
Net income	182	371	478	768	470
Retained earnings—beginning	1,206	1,388	1,759	2,237	3,005
Retained earnings—ending	$ 1,388	$ 1,759	$ 2,237	$ 3,005	$ 3,475
Earnings per share	$1.82	$3.71	$4.78	$7.68	$4.70

SCHEDULE OF INVENTORY BALANCES USING AVERAGE COST METHOD
FOR THE YEARS ENDED MAY 31

2007	2008	2009	2010	2011	2012
$1,010	$1,124	$1,101	$1,270	$1,500	$1,720

Instructions

Prepare comparative statements for the 5 years, assuming that Utrillo changed its method of inventory pricing to average cost. Indicate the effects on net income and earnings per share for the years involved. Utrillo Instruments started business in 2007. (All amounts except EPS are rounded up to the nearest dollar.)

P22-6 (Accounting Change and Error Analysis) On December 31, 2012, before the books were closed, the management and accountants of Madrasa Inc. made the following determinations about three depreciable assets.

1. Depreciable asset A was purchased January 2, 2009. It originally cost $540,000 and, for depreciation purposes, the straight-line method was originally chosen. The asset was originally expected to be useful for 10 years and have a zero salvage value. In 2012, the decision was made to change the depreciation method from straight-line to sum-of-the-years' digits, and the estimates relating to useful life and salvage value remained unchanged.

2. Depreciable asset B was purchased January 3, 2008. It originally cost $180,000 and, for depreciation purposes, the straight-line method was chosen. The asset was originally expected to be useful for 15

years and have a zero salvage value. In 2012, the decision was made to shorten the total life of this asset to 9 years and to estimate the salvage value at $3,000.

3. Depreciable asset C was purchased January 5, 2008. The asset's original cost was $160,000, and this amount was entirely expensed in 2008. This particular asset has a 10-year useful life and no salvage value. The straight-line method was chosen for depreciation purposes.

Additional data:

1. Income in 2012 before depreciation expense amounted to $400,000.
2. Depreciation expense on assets other than A, B, and C totaled $55,000 in 2012.
3. Income in 2011 was reported at $370,000.
4. Ignore all income tax effects.
5. 100,000 shares of common stock were outstanding in 2011 and 2012.

Instructions

(a) Prepare all necessary entries in 2012 to record these determinations.
(b) Prepare comparative retained earnings statements for Madrasa Inc. for 2011 and 2012. The company had retained earnings of $200,000 at December 31, 2010.

 P22-7 (Error Corrections) You have been assigned to examine the financial statements of Zarle Company for the year ended December 31, 2012. You discover the following situations.

1. Depreciation of $3,200 for 2012 on delivery vehicles was not recorded.
2. The physical inventory count on December 31, 2011, improperly excluded merchandise costing $19,000 that had been temporarily stored in a public warehouse. Zarle uses a periodic inventory system.
3. A collection of $5,600 on account from a customer received on December 31, 2012, was not recorded until January 2, 2013.
4. In 2012, the company sold for $3,700 fully depreciated equipment that originally cost $25,000. The company credited the proceeds from the sale to the Equipment account.
5. During November 2012, a competitor company filed a patent-infringement suit against Zarle claiming damages of $220,000. The company's legal counsel has indicated that an unfavorable verdict is probable and a reasonable estimate of the court's award to the competitor is $125,000. The company has not reflected or disclosed this situation in the financial statements.
6. Zarle has a portfolio of trading securities. No entry has been made to adjust to market. Information on cost and market value is as follows.

	Cost	Market
December 31, 2011	$95,000	$95,000
December 31, 2012	$84,000	$82,000

7. At December 31, 2012, an analysis of payroll information shows accrued salaries of $12,200. The accrued salaries account had a balance of $16,000 at December 31, 2012, which was unchanged from its balance at December 31, 2011.
8. A large piece of equipment was purchased on January 3, 2012, for $40,000 and was charged to Maintenance and Repairs Expense. The equipment is estimated to have a service life of 8 years and no residual value. Zarle normally uses the straight-line depreciation method for this type of equipment.
9. A $12,000 insurance premium paid on July 1, 2011, for a policy that expires on June 30, 2014, was charged to insurance expense.
10. A trademark was acquired at the beginning of 2011 for $50,000. No amortization has been recorded since its acquisition. The maximum allowable amortization period is 10 years.

Instructions
Assume the trial balance has been prepared but the books have not been closed for 2012. Assuming all amounts are material, prepare journal entries showing the adjustments that are required. (Ignore income tax considerations.)

 P22-8 (Comprehensive Error Analysis) On March 5, 2013, you were hired by Hemingway Inc., a closely held company, as a staff member of its newly created internal auditing department. While reviewing the company's records for 2011 and 2012, you discover that no adjustments have yet been made for the items listed below.

Items
1. Interest income of $14,100 was not accrued at the end of 2011. It was recorded when received in February 2012.

2. A computer costing $4,000 was expensed when purchased on July 1, 2011. It is expected to have a 4-year life with no salvage value. The company typically uses straight-line depreciation for all fixed assets.

3. Research and development costs of $33,000 were incurred early in 2011. They were capitalized and were to be amortized over a 3-year period. Amortization of $11,000 was recorded for 2011 and $11,000 for 2012.

4. On January 2, 2011, Hemingway leased a building for 5 years at a monthly rental of $8,000. On that date, the company paid the following amounts, which were expensed when paid.

Security deposit	$20,000
First month's rent	8,000
Last month's rent	8,000
	$36,000

5. The company received $36,000 from a customer at the beginning of 2011 for services that it is to perform evenly over a 3-year period beginning in 2011. None of the amount received was reported as unearned revenue at the end of 2011.

6. Merchandise inventory costing $18,200 was in the warehouse at December 31, 2011, but was incorrectly omitted from the physical count at that date. The company uses the periodic inventory method.

Instructions

Indicate the effect of any errors on the net income figure reported on the income statement for the year ending December 31, 2011, and the retained earnings figure reported on the balance sheet at December 31, 2012. Assume all amounts are material, and ignore income tax effects. Using the following format, enter the appropriate dollar amounts in the appropriate columns. Consider each item independent of the other items. It is not necessary to total the columns on the grid.

	Net Income for 2011		Retained Earnings at 12/31/12	
Item	Understand	Overstated	Understated	Overstated

(CIA adapted)

 P22-9 (Error Analysis) Lowell Corporation has used the accrual basis of accounting for several years. A review of the records, however, indicates that some expenses and revenues have been handled on a cash basis because of errors made by an inexperienced bookkeeper. Income statements prepared by the bookkeeper reported $29,000 net income for 2011 and $37,000 net income for 2012. Further examination of the records reveals that the following items were handled improperly.

1. Rent was received from a tenant in December 2011. The amount, $1,000, was recorded as revenue at that time even though the rental pertained to 2012.

2. Wages payable on December 31 have been consistently omitted from the records of that date and have been entered as expenses when paid in the following year. The amounts of the accruals recorded in this manner were:

December 31, 2010	$1,100
December 31, 2011	1,200
December 31, 2012	940

3. Invoices for office supplies purchased have been charged to expense accounts when received. Inventories of supplies on hand at the end of each year have been ignored, and no entry has been made for them.

December 31, 2010	$1,300
December 31, 2011	940
December 31, 2012	1,420

Instructions

Prepare a schedule that will show the corrected net income for the years 2011 and 2012. All items listed should be labeled clearly. (Ignore income tax considerations.)

P22-10 (Error Analysis and Correcting Entries) You have been asked by a client to review the records of Roberts Company, a small manufacturer of precision tools and machines. Your client is interested in buying the business, and arrangements have been made for you to review the accounting records. Your examination reveals the following information.

1. Roberts Company commenced business on April 1, 2010, and has been reporting on a fiscal year ending March 31. The company has never been audited, but the annual statements prepared by the bookkeeper reflect the following income before closing and before deducting income taxes.

Year Ended March 31	Income Before Taxes
2011	$ 71,600
2012	111,400
2013	103,580

2. A relatively small number of machines have been shipped on consignment. These transactions have been recorded as ordinary sales and billed as such. On March 31 of each year, machines billed and in the hands of consignees amounted to:

2011	$6,500
2012	none
2013	5,590

Sales price was determined by adding 25% to cost. Assume that the consigned machines are sold the following year.

3. On March 30, 2012, two machines were shipped to a customer on a C.O.D. basis. The sale was not entered until April 5, 2012, when cash was received for $6,100. The machines were not included in the inventory at March 31, 2012. (Title passed on March 30, 2012.)

4. All machines are sold subject to a 5-year warranty. It is estimated that the expense ultimately to be incurred in connection with the warranty will amount to ½ of 1% of sales. The company has charged an expense account for warranty costs incurred.

Sales per books and warranty costs were as follows.

Year Ended March 31	Sales	Warranty Expense for Sales Made in 2011	2012	2013	Total
2011	$ 940,000	$760			$ 760
2012	1,010,000	360	$1,310		1,670
2013	1,795,000	320	1,620	$1,910	3,850

5. Bad debts have been recorded on a direct write-off basis. Experience of similar enterprises indicates that losses will approximate ¼ of 1% of sales. Bad debts written off were:

	Bad Debts Incurred on Sales Made in 2011	2012	2013	Total
2011	$750			$ 750
2012	800	$ 520		1,320
2013	350	1,800	$1,700	3,850

6. The bank deducts 6% on all contracts financed. Of this amount, ½% is placed in a reserve to the credit of Roberts Company that is refunded to Roberts as finance contracts are paid in full. The reserve established by the bank has not been reflected in the books of Roberts. The excess of credits over debits (net increase) to the reserve account with Roberts on the books of the bank for each fiscal year were as follows.

2011	$ 3,000
2012	3,900
2013	5,100
	$12,000

7. Commissions on sales have been entered when paid. Commissions payable on March 31 of each year were as follows.

2011	$1,400
2012	900
2013	1,120

8. A review of the corporate minutes reveals the manager is entitled to a bonus of 1% of the income before deducting income taxes and the bonus. The bonuses have never been recorded or paid.

Instructions

(a) Present a schedule showing the revised income before income taxes for each of the years ended March 31, 2011, 2012, and 2013. Make computations to the nearest whole dollar.

(b) Prepare the journal entry or entries you would give the bookkeeper to correct the books. Assume the books have not yet been closed for the fiscal year ended March 31, 2013. Disregard correction of income taxes.

(AICPA adapted)

10 *P22-11 (Fair Value to Equity Method with Goodwill)** On January 1, 2012, Millay Inc. paid $700,000 for 10,000 shares of Genso Company's voting common stock, which was a 10% interest in Genso. At that date, the net assets of Genso totaled $6,000,000. The fair values of all of Genso's identifiable assets and liabilities were equal to their book values. Millay does not have the ability to exercise significant influence over the operating and financial policies of Genso. Millay received dividends of $1.50 per share from Genso on October 1, 2012. Genso reported net income of $550,000 for the year ended December 31, 2012.

On July 1, 2013, Millay paid $2,325,000 for 30,000 additional shares of Genso Company's voting common stock which represents a 30% investment in Genso. The fair values of all of Genso's identifiable assets net of liabilities were equal to their book values of $6,550,000. As a result of this transaction, Millay has the ability to exercise significant influence over the operating and financial policies of Genso. Millay received dividends of $2.00 per share from Genso on April 1, 2013, and $2.50 per share on October 1, 2013. Genso reported net income of $650,000 for the year ended December 31, 2013, and $350,000 for the 6 months ended December 31, 2013.

Instructions

(a) Prepare a schedule showing the income or loss before income taxes for the year ended December 31, 2012, that Millay should report from its investment in Genso in its income statement issued in March 2013.

(b) During March 2014, Millay issues comparative financial statements for 2012 and 2013. Prepare schedules showing the income or loss before income taxes for the years ended December 31, 2012 and 2013, that Millay should report from its investment in Genso.

(AICPA adapted)

10 *P22-12 (Change from Fair Value to Equity Method)** On January 3, 2011, Martin Company purchased for $500,000 cash a 10% interest in Renner Corp. On that date, the net assets of Renner had a book value of $3,700,000. The excess of cost over the underlying equity in net assets is attributable to undervalued depreciable assets having a remaining life of 10 years from the date of Martin's purchase.

The fair value of Martin's investment in Renner securities is as follows: December 31, 2011, $560,000, and December 31, 2012, $515,000.

On January 2, 2013, Martin purchased an additional 30% of Renner's stock for $1,545,000 cash when the book value of Renner's net assets was $4,150,000. The excess was attributable to depreciable assets having a remaining life of 8 years.

During 2011, 2012, and 2013, the following occurred.

	Renner Net Income	Dividends Paid by Renner to Martin
2011	$350,000	$15,000
2012	450,000	20,000
2013	550,000	70,000

Instructions

On the books of Martin Company, prepare all journal entries in 2011, 2012, and 2013 that relate to its investment in Renner Corp., reflecting the data above and a change from the fair value method to the equity method.

CONCEPTS FOR ANALYSIS

CA22-1 (Analysis of Various Accounting Changes and Errors) Joblonsky Inc. has recently hired a new independent auditor, Karen Ogleby, who says she wants "to get everything straightened out." Consequently, she has proposed the accounting changes shown below and on the next page in connection with Joblonsky Inc.'s 2012 financial statements.

1. At December 31, 2011, the client had a receivable of $820,000 from Hendricks Inc. on its balance sheet. Hendricks Inc. has gone bankrupt, and no recovery is expected. The client proposes to write off the receivable as a prior period item.

2. The client proposes the following changes in depreciation policies.
   (a) For office furniture and fixtures, it proposes to change from a 10-year useful life to an 8-year life. If this change had been made in prior years, retained earnings at December 31, 2011, would have been $250,000 less. The effect of the change on 2012 income alone is a reduction of $60,000.
   (b) For its equipment in the leasing division, the client proposes to adopt the sum-of-the-years'-digits depreciation method. The client had never used SYD before. The first year the client operated a leasing division was 2012. If straight-line depreciation were used, 2012 income would be $110,000 greater.

3. In preparing its 2011 statements, one of the client's bookkeepers overstated ending inventory by $235,000 because of a mathematical error. The client proposes to treat this item as a prior period adjustment.

4. In the past, the client has spread preproduction costs in its furniture division over 5 years. Because its latest furniture is of the "fad" type, it appears that the largest volume of sales will occur during the first 2 years after introduction. Consequently, the client proposes to amortize preproduction costs on a per-unit basis, which will result in expensing most of such costs during the first 2 years after the furniture's introduction. If the new accounting method had been used prior to 2012, retained earnings at December 31, 2011, would have been $375,000 less.

5. For the nursery division, the client proposes to switch from FIFO to LIFO inventories because it believes that LIFO will provide a better matching of current costs with revenues. The effect of making this change on 2012 earnings will be an increase of $320,000. The client says that the effect of the change on December 31, 2011, retained earnings cannot be determined.

6. To achieve a better matching of revenues and expenses in its building construction division, the client proposes to switch from the completed-contract method of accounting to the percentage-of-completion method. Had the percentage-of-completion method been employed in all prior years, retained earnings at December 31, 2011, would have been $1,075,000 greater.

Instructions
   (a) For each of the changes described above, decide whether:
      (1) The change involves an accounting principle, accounting estimate, or correction of an error.
      (2) Restatement of opening retained earnings is required.
   (b) What would be the proper adjustment to the December 31, 2011, retained earnings?

CA22-2 (Analysis of Various Accounting Changes and Errors) Various types of accounting changes can affect the financial statements of a business enterprise differently. Assume that the following list describes changes that have a material effect on the financial statements for the current year of your business enterprise.

1. A change from the completed-contract method to the percentage-of-completion method of accounting for long-term construction-type contracts.
2. A change in the estimated useful life of previously recorded fixed assets as a result of newly acquired information.
3. A change from deferring and amortizing preproduction costs to recording such costs as an expense when incurred because future benefits of the costs have become doubtful. The new accounting method was adopted in recognition of the change in estimated future benefits.
4. A change from including the employer share of FICA taxes with payroll tax expenses to including it with "Retirement benefits" on the income statement.
5. Correction of a mathematical error in inventory pricing made in a prior period.
6. A change from presentation of statements of individual companies to presentation of consolidated statements.
7. A change in the method of accounting for leases for tax purposes to conform with the financial accounting method. As a result, both deferred and current taxes payable changed substantially.
8. A change from the FIFO method of inventory pricing to the LIFO method of inventory pricing.

Instructions
Identify the type of change that is described in each item above and indicate whether the prior year's financial statements should be retrospectively applied or restated when presented in comparative form with the current year's financial statements.

CA22-3 (Analysis of Three Accounting Changes and Errors) Listed below and on the next page are three independent, unrelated sets of facts relating to accounting changes.

Situation 1
Sanford Company is in the process of having its first audit. The company has used the cash basis of accounting for revenue recognition. Sanford president, B. J. Jimenez, is willing to change to the accrual method of revenue recognition.

Situation 2
Hopkins Co. decides in January 2013 to change from FIFO to weighted-average pricing for its inventories.

Situation 3
Marshall Co. determined that the depreciable lives of its fixed assets are too long at present to fairly match the cost of the fixed assets with the revenue produced. The company decided at the beginning of the current year to reduce the depreciable lives of all of its existing fixed assets by 5 years.

Instructions
For each of the situations described, provide the information indicated below.

(a) Type of accounting change.
(b) Manner of reporting the change under current generally accepted accounting principles including a discussion, where applicable, of how amounts are computed.
(c) Effect of the change on the balance sheet and income statement.

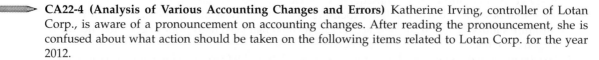 **CA22-4 (Analysis of Various Accounting Changes and Errors)** Katherine Irving, controller of Lotan Corp., is aware of a pronouncement on accounting changes. After reading the pronouncement, she is confused about what action should be taken on the following items related to Lotan Corp. for the year 2012.

1. In 2012, Lotan decided to change its policy on accounting for certain marketing costs. Previously, the company had chosen to defer and amortize all marketing costs over at least 5 years because Lotan believed that a return on these expenditures did not occur immediately. Recently, however, the time differential has considerably shortened, and Lotan is now expensing the marketing costs as incurred.
2. In 2012, the company examined its entire policy relating to the depreciation of plant equipment. Plant equipment had normally been depreciated over a 15-year period, but recent experience has indicated that the company was incorrect in its estimates and that the assets should be depreciated over a 20-year period.
3. One division of Lotan Corp., Hawthorne Co., has consistently shown an increasing net income from period to period. On closer examination of its operating statement, it is noted that bad debt expense and inventory obsolescence charges are much lower than in other divisions. In discussing this with the controller of this division, it has been learned that the controller has increased his net income each period by knowingly making low estimates related to the write-off of receivables and inventory.
4. In 2012, the company purchased new machinery that should increase production dramatically. The company has decided to depreciate this machinery on an accelerated basis, even though other machinery is depreciated on a straight-line basis.
5. All equipment sold by Lotan is subject to a 3-year warranty. It has been estimated that the expense ultimately to be incurred on these machines is 1% of sales. In 2012, because of a production breakthrough, it is now estimated that $\frac{1}{2}$ of 1% of sales is sufficient. In 2010 and 2011, warranty expense was computed as $64,000 and $70,000, respectively. The company now believes that these warranty costs should be reduced by 50%.
6. In 2012, the company decided to change its method of inventory pricing from average cost to the FIFO method. The effect of this change on prior years is to increase 2010 income by $65,000 and increase 2011 income by $20,000.

Instructions
Katherine Irving has come to you, as her CPA, for advice about the situations above. Prepare a report, indicating the appropriate accounting treatment that should be given each of these situations.

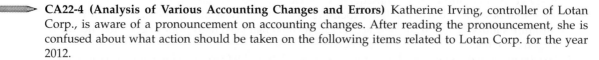 **CA22-5 (Change in Principle, Estimate)** As a certified public accountant, you have been contacted by Joe Davison, CEO of Sports-Pro Athletics, Inc., a manufacturer of a variety of athletic equipment. He has asked you how to account for the following changes.

1. Sports-Pro appropriately changed its depreciation method for its production machinery from the double-declining-balance method to the production method effective January 1, 2012.
2. Effective January 1, 2012, Sports-Pro appropriately changed the salvage values used in computing depreciation for its office equipment.
3. On December 31, 2012, Sports-Pro appropriately changed the specific subsidiaries constituting the group of companies for which consolidated financial statements are presented.

Instructions
Write a 1–1.5 page letter to Joe Davison explaining how each of the above changes should be presented in the December 31, 2012, financial statements.

CA22-6 (Change in Estimate) Mike Crane is an audit senior of a large public accounting firm who has just been assigned to the Frost Corporation's annual audit engagement. Frost has been a client of Crane's firm for many years. Frost is a fast-growing business in the commercial construction industry. In reviewing the fixed asset ledger, Crane discovered a series of unusual accounting changes, in which the useful lives of assets, depreciated using the straight-line method, were substantially lowered near the midpoint of the original estimate. For example, the useful life of one dump truck was changed from 10 to 6 years during its fifth year of service. Upon further investigation, Mike was told by Kevin James, Frost's accounting manager, "I don't really see your problem. After all, it's perfectly legal to change an accounting estimate. Besides, our CEO likes to see big earnings!"

Instructions
Answer the following questions.

   (a) What are the ethical issues concerning Frost's practice of changing the useful lives of fixed assets?
   (b) Who could be harmed by Frost's unusual accounting changes?
   (c) What should Crane do in this situation?

USING YOUR JUDGMENT

FINANCIAL REPORTING

Financial Reporting Problem

The Procter & Gamble Company (P&G)

The financial statements of P&G are provided in Appendix 5B or can be accessed at the book's companion website, **www.wiley.com/college/kieso.**

Instructions
Refer to P&G's financial statements and the accompanying notes to answer the following questions.

(a) Were there changes in accounting principles reported by P&G during the three years covered by its income statements (2007–2009)? If so, describe the nature of the change and the year of change.

(b) What types of estimates did P&G discuss in 2009?

Comparative Analysis Case

The Coca-Cola Company and PepsiCo, Inc.

Instructions
Go to the book's companion website and use information found there to answer the following questions related to The Coca-Cola Company and PepsiCo Inc.

(a) Identify the changes in accounting principles reported by Coca-Cola during the 3 years covered by its income statements (2007–2009). Describe the nature of the change and the year of change.

(b) Identify the changes in accounting principles reported by PepsiCo during the 3 years covered by its income statements (2007–2009). Describe the nature of the change and the year of change.

(c) For each change in accounting principle by Coca-Cola and PepsiCo, identify, if possible, the cumulative effect of each change on prior years and the effect on operating results in the year of change.

Accounting, Analysis, and Principles

In preparation for significant international operations, ABC Co. has adopted a plan to gradually shift to the same accounting methods as used by its international competitors. Part of this plan includes a switch from LIFO inventory accounting to FIFO (recall that IFRS does not allow LIFO). ABC decides to make the switch to FIFO at January 1, 2012. The following data pertains to ABC's 2012 financial statements.

Sales	$550
Inventory purchases	350
12/31/12 inventory (using FIFO)	580
Compensation expense	17

All sales and purchases were with cash. All of 2012's compensation expense was paid with cash. (Ignore taxes.) ABC's property, plant, and equipment cost $400 and has an estimated useful life of 10 years with no salvage value.

ABC Co. reported the following for fiscal 2011 (in millions of dollars):

ABC CO.
BALANCE SHEET AT DECEMBER 31, 2011

	2011	2010		2011	2010
Cash	$ 365	$ 200	Common stock	$ 500	$ 500
Inventory	500	480	Retained earnings	685	540
Property, plant, and equipment	400	400			
Accumulated depreciation	(80)	(40)			
Total assets	$1,185	$1,040	Total equity	$1,185	$1,040

ABC CO.
INCOME STATEMENT
FOR THE YEAR ENDED DECEMBER 31, 2011

	2011
Sales	$ 500
Cost of goods sold	(300)
Depreciation expense	(40)
Compensation expense	(15)
Net income	$ 145

Summary of Significant Accounting Policies
Inventory: The company accounts for inventory by the LIFO method. The current cost of the company's inventory, which approximates FIFO, was $60 and $50 higher at the end of fiscal 2011 and 2010, respectively, than those reported in the balance sheet.

Accounting

Prepare ABC's December 31, 2012, balance sheet and an income statement for the year ended December 31, 2012. In columns beside 2012's numbers, include 2011's numbers *as they would appear in the 2012 financial statements* for comparative purposes.

Analysis

Compute ABC's inventory turnover for 2011 and 2012 under both LIFO and FIFO. Assume averages are equal to year-end balances where necessary. What causes the differences in this ratio between LIFO and FIFO?

Principles

Briefly explain, in terms of the principles discussed in Chapter 2, why GAAP requires that companies that change accounting methods recast prior year's financial statement data.

BRIDGE TO THE PROFESSION

Professional Research: FASB Codification

As part of the year-end accounting process and review of operating policies, Cullen Co. is considering a change in the accounting for its equipment from the straight-line method to an accelerated method. Your supervisor wonders how the company will report this change in principle. He read in a newspaper article that the FASB has issued a standard in this area and has changed GAAP for a "change in estimate that is effected by a change in accounting principle." (Thus, the accounting may be different from that he learned in intermediate accounting.) Your supervisor wants you to research the authoritative guidance on a change in accounting principle related to depreciation methods.

Instructions

If your school has a subscription to the FASB Codification, go to *http://aaahq.org/ascLogin.cfm* to log in and prepare responses to the following. Provide Codification references for your responses.

(a) What are the accounting and reporting guidelines for a change in accounting principle related to depreciation methods?

(b) What are the conditions that justify a change in depreciation method, as contemplated by Cullen Co.?

(c) What guidance does the SEC provide concerning the impact that recently issued accounting standards will have on the financial statements in a future period?

Professional Simulation

In this simulation, you are asked questions about changes in accounting principle. Prepare responses to all parts.

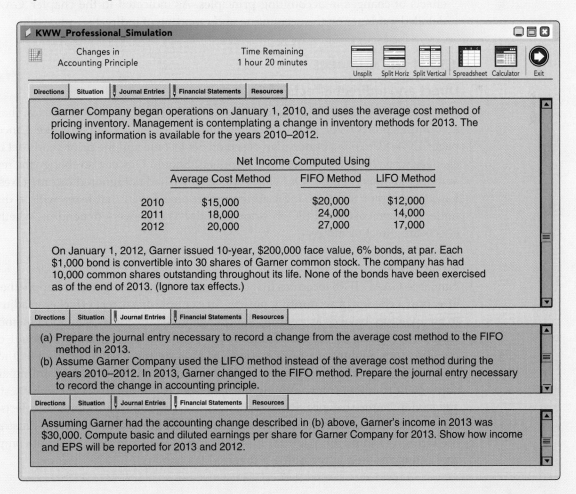

KWW_Professional_Simulation

Changes in Accounting Principle	Time Remaining 1 hour 20 minutes	Unsplit Split Horiz Split Vertical Spreadsheet Calculator Exit

| Directions | Situation | Journal Entries | Financial Statements | Resources |

Garner Company began operations on January 1, 2010, and uses the average cost method of pricing inventory. Management is contemplating a change in inventory methods for 2013. The following information is available for the years 2010–2012.

	Net Income Computed Using		
	Average Cost Method	FIFO Method	LIFO Method
2010	$15,000	$20,000	$12,000
2011	18,000	24,000	14,000
2012	20,000	27,000	17,000

On January 1, 2012, Garner issued 10-year, $200,000 face value, 6% bonds, at par. Each $1,000 bond is convertible into 30 shares of Garner common stock. The company has had 10,000 common shares outstanding throughout its life. None of the bonds have been exercised as of the end of 2013. (Ignore tax effects.)

| Directions | Situation | Journal Entries | Financial Statements | Resources |

(a) Prepare the journal entry necessary to record a change from the average cost method to the FIFO method in 2013.

(b) Assume Garner Company used the LIFO method instead of the average cost method during the years 2010–2012. In 2013, Garner changed to the FIFO method. Prepare the journal entry necessary to record the change in accounting principle.

| Directions | Situation | Journal Entries | Financial Statements | Resources |

Assuming Garner had the accounting change described in (b) above, Garner's income in 2013 was $30,000. Compute basic and diluted earnings per share for Garner Company for 2013. Show how income and EPS will be reported for 2013 and 2012.

IFRS › **Insights**

ACCOUNTING CHANGES AND ERRORS

The IFRS addressing accounting and reporting for changes in accounting principles, changes in estimates, and errors is *IAS 8* ("Accounting Policies, Changes in Accounting Estimates and Errors"). Various presentation issues related to restatements are addressed in *IAS 1* ("Presentation of Financial Statements"). As indicated in the chapter, the FASB has issued guidance on changes in accounting principles, changes in estimates, and corrections of errors, which essentially converges GAAP to *IAS 8*.

RELEVANT FACTS

- One area in which GAAP and IFRS differ is the reporting of error corrections in previously issued financial statements. While both sets of standards require restatement, GAAP is an absolute standard—that is, there is no exception to this rule.
- The accounting for changes in estimates is similar between GAAP and IFRS.
- Under GAAP and IFRS, if determining the effect of a change in accounting policy is considered impracticable, then a company should report the effect of the change in the period in which it believes it practicable to do so, which may be the current period.
- Under IFRS, the impracticality exception applies both to changes in accounting principles and to the correction of errors. Under GAAP, this exception applies only to changes in accounting principle.
- IFRS (*IAS 8*) does not specifically address the accounting and reporting for indirect effects of changes in accounting principles. As indicated in the chapter, GAAP has detailed guidance on the accounting and reporting of indirect effects.

ABOUT THE NUMBERS

Direct and Indirect Effects of Changes

Are there other effects that a company should report when it makes a change in accounting policy? For example, what happens when a company like Lancer (see pages 1374–1378) has a bonus plan based on net income and the prior year's net income changes when FIFO is retrospectively applied? Should Lancer also change the reported amount of bonus expense? Or, what happens if we had not ignored income taxes in the Lancer example? Should Lancer adjust net income, given that taxes will be different under average cost and FIFO in prior periods? The answers depend on whether the effects are direct or indirect.

Direct Effects

Similar to GAAP, IFRS indicates that companies should retrospectively apply the **direct effects of a change in accounting policy**. An example of a **direct effect** is an adjustment to an inventory balance as a result of a change in the inventory valuation method. For example, referring to Lancer Company on pages 1374–1378, Lancer should change the inventory amounts in prior periods to indicate the change to the FIFO method of inventory valuation. Another inventory-related example would be an impairment adjustment resulting from applying the lower-of-cost-or-net realizable value test to the adjusted inventory balance. Related changes, such as deferred income tax effects of the impairment adjustment, are also considered direct effects. This entry was illustrated in the Denson example on page 1371, in which the change to percentage-of-completion accounting resulted in recording a deferred tax liability.

Indirect Effects

In addition to direct effects, companies can have **indirect effects related to a change in accounting policy**. An **indirect effect** is any change to current or future cash flows of a company that results from making a change in accounting policy that is applied retrospectively. An example of an indirect effect is a change in profit-sharing or royalty payment that is based on a reported amount such as revenue or net income. The IASB is silent on what to do in this situation. GAAP (likely because its standard in this area was issued after *IAS 8*) requires that indirect effects do not change prior period amounts.

For example, let's assume that Lancer Company has an employee profit-sharing plan based on net income and it changed from the weighted-average inventory method to FIFO in 2012. Lancer reports higher income in 2011 and 2012 if it used the FIFO method. In addition, let's assume that the profit-sharing plan requires that Lancer pay the incremental amount due based on the FIFO income amounts. In this situation, Lancer reports this additional expense **in the current period**; it would not change prior periods for this expense. If the company prepares comparative financial statements, it follows that it does not recast the prior periods for this additional expense. If the terms of the profit-sharing plan indicate that *no payment is necessary* in the current period due to this change, then the company need not recognize additional profit-sharing expense in the current period. Neither does it change amounts reported for prior periods.

When a company recognizes the indirect effects of a change in accounting policy, it includes in the financial statements a description of the indirect effects. In doing so, it discloses the amounts recognized in the current period and related per share information.

Impracticability

It is not always possible for companies to determine how they would have reported prior periods' financial information under retrospective application of an accounting policy change. Retrospective application is considered **impracticable** if a company cannot determine the prior period effects using every reasonable effort to do so.

Companies should not use retrospective application if one of the following conditions exists:

1. The company cannot determine the effects of the retrospective application.

2. Retrospective application requires assumptions about management's intent in a prior period.

3. Retrospective application requires significant estimates for a prior period, and the company cannot objectively verify the necessary information to develop these estimates.

If any of the above conditions exists, it is deemed impracticable to apply the retrospective approach. In this case, the company **prospectively applies** the new accounting policy as of the earliest date it is practicable to do so.

For example, assume that Williams Company changed its accounting policy for depreciable assets so as to more fully apply component depreciation under revaluation accounting. Unfortunately, the company does not have detailed accounting records to establish a basis for the components of these assets. As a result, Williams determines it is not practicable to account for the change to full component depreciation using the retrospective application approach. It therefore applies the policy prospectively, starting at the beginning of the current year.

Williams must disclose only the effect of the change on the results of operations in the period of change. Also, the company should explain the reasons for omitting the computations of the cumulative effect for prior years. Finally, it should disclose the justification for the change to component depreciation.

ON THE HORIZON

For the most part, IFRS and GAAP are similar in the area of accounting changes and reporting the effects of errors. Thus, there is no active project in this area. A related development involves the presentation of comparative data. Under IFRS, when a company prepares financial statements on a new basis, two years of comparative data are reported. GAAP requires comparative information for a three-year period. Use of the shorter comparative data period must be addressed before U.S. companies can adopt IFRS.

IFRS SELF-TEST QUESTIONS

1. Which of the following is *false*?
   (a) GAAP and IFRS have the same absolute standard regarding the reporting of error corrections in previously issued financial statements.
   (b) The accounting for changes in estimates is similar between GAAP and IFRS.
   (c) Under IFRS, the impracticality exception applies both to changes in accounting principles and to the correction of errors.
   (d) GAAP has detailed guidance on the accounting and reporting of indirect effects; IFRS does not.

2. Which of the following is *not* classified as an accounting change by IFRS?
   (a) Change in accounting policy.
   (b) Change in accounting estimate.
   (c) Errors in financial statements.
   (d) None of the above.

3. IFRS requires companies to use which method for reporting changes in accounting policies?
   (a) Cumulative effect approach.
   (b) Retrospective approach.
   (c) Prospective approach.
   (d) Averaging approach.

4. Under IFRS, the retrospective approach should not be used if:
   (a) retrospective application requires assumptions about management's intent in a prior period.
   (b) the company does not have trained staff to perform the analysis.
   (c) the effects of the change have counterbalanced.
   (d) the effects of the change have not counterbalanced.

5. Which of the following is *true* regarding whether IFRS specifically addresses the accounting and reporting for effects of changes in accounting policies?

	Direct effects	Indirect effects
(a)	Yes	Yes
(b)	No	No
(c)	No	Yes
(d)	Yes	No

IFRS CONCEPTS AND APPLICATION

IFRS22-1 Where can authoritative IFRS related to accounting changes be found?

IFRS22-2 Briefly describe some of the similarities and differences between GAAP and IFRS with respect to reporting accounting changes.

IFRS22-3 How might differences in presentation of comparative data under GAAP and IFRS affect adoption of IFRS by U.S. companies?

IFRS22-4 What is the indirect effect of a change in accounting policy? Briefly describe the approach to reporting the indirect effects of a change in accounting policy under IFRS.

IFRS22-5 Discuss how a change in accounting policy is handled when it is impracticable to determine previous amounts.

IFRS22-6 Joblonsky Inc. has recently hired a new independent auditor, Karen Ogleby, who says she wants "to get everything straightened out." Consequently, she has proposed the following accounting changes in connection with Joblonsky Inc.'s 2012 financial statements.

1. At December 31, 2011, the client had a receivable of $820,000 from Hendricks Inc. on its statement of financial position. Hendricks Inc. has gone bankrupt, and no recovery is expected. The client proposes to write off the receivable as a prior period item.

2. The client proposes the following changes in depreciation policies.

    (a) For office furniture and fixtures, it proposes to change from a 10-year useful life to an 8-year life. If this change had been made in prior years, retained earnings at December 31, 2011, would have been $250,000 less. The effect of the change on 2012 income alone is a reduction of $60,000.

    (b) For its equipment in the leasing division, the client proposes to adopt the sum-of-the-years'-digits depreciation method. The client had never used SYD before. The first year the client operated a leasing division was 2012. If straight-line depreciation were used, 2012 income would be $110,000 greater.

3. In preparing its 2011 statements, one of the client's bookkeepers overstated ending inventory by $235,000 because of a mathematical error. The client proposes to treat this item as a prior period adjustment.

4. In the past, the client has spread preproduction costs in its furniture division over 5 years. Because its latest furniture is of the "fad" type, it appears that the largest volume of sales will occur during the first 2 years after introduction. Consequently, the client proposes to amortize preproduction costs on a per-unit basis, which will result in expensing most of such costs during the first 2 years after the furniture's introduction. If the new accounting method had been used prior to 2012, retained earnings at December 31, 2011, would have been $375,000 less.

5. For the nursery division, the client proposes to switch from FIFO to average cost inventories because it believes that average cost will provide a better matching of current costs with revenues. The effect of making this change on 2012 earnings will be an increase of $320,000. The client says that the effect of the change on December 31, 2011, retained earnings cannot be determined.

6. To achieve a better matching of revenues and expenses in its building construction division, the client proposes to switch from the cost-recovery method of accounting to the percentage-of-completion method. Had the percentage-of-completion method been employed in all prior years, retained earnings at December 31, 2011, would have been $1,075,000 greater.

Instructions

    (a) For each of the changes described above, decide whether:

        (1) The change involves an accounting policy, accounting estimate, or correction of an error.

        (2) Restatement of opening retained earnings is required.

    (b) What would be the proper adjustment to the December 31, 2011, retained earnings?

Professional Research

IFRS22-7 As part of the year-end accounting process and review of operating policies, Cullen Co. is considering a change in the accounting for its equipment from the straight-line method to an accelerated method. Your supervisor wonders how the company will report this change in accounting. It has been few years since he took intermediate accounting, and he cannot remember whether this change would be treated in a retrospective or prospective manner. Your supervisor wants you to research the authoritative guidance on a change in accounting policy related to depreciation methods.

Instructions

Access the IFRS authoritative literature at the IASB website (*http://eifrs.iasb.org/*). When you have accessed the documents, you can use the search tool in your Internet browser to respond to the following questions. (Provide paragraph citations.)

    (a) What are the accounting and reporting guidelines for a change in accounting policy related to depreciation methods?

    (b) What are the conditions that justify a change in depreciation method, as contemplated by Cullen Co.?

International Financial Reporting Problem:
Marks and Spencer plc

IFRS22-8 The financial statements of Marks and Spencer plc (M&S) are available at the book's companion website or can be accessed at *http://corporate.marksandspencer.com/documents/publications/2010/Annual_Report_2010*.

Instructions

Refer to M&S's financial statements and the accompanying notes to answer the following questions.

    (a) Were there changes in accounting policies reported by M&S during the two years covered by its income statements (2009–2010)? If so, describe the nature of the change and the year of change.

    (b) What types of estimates did M&S discuss in 2010?

ANSWERS TO IFRS SELF-TEST QUESTIONS

1. a **2.** c **3.** b **4.** a **5.** d

23 ▶ Statement of Cash Flows

Show Me the Money

Investors usually look to net income as a key indicator of a company's financial health and future prospects. The following graph shows the net income of one company over a seven-year period.

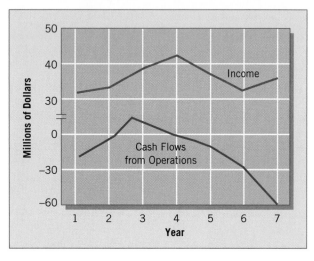

The company showed a pattern of consistent profitability and even some periods of income growth. Between years 1 and 4, net income for this company grew by 32 percent, from $31 million to $41 million. Would you expect its profitability to continue? The company had consistently paid dividends and interest. Would you expect it to continue to do so? Investors answered these questions by buying the company's stock. Eighteen months later, this company—**W. T. Grant**—filed for bankruptcy, in what was then the largest bankruptcy filing in the United States.

How could this happen? As indicated by the second line in the graph, the company had experienced several years of negative cash flow from its operations, even though it reported profits. How can a company have negative cash flows while reporting profits? The answer lays partly in the fact that W. T. Grant was having trouble collecting the receivables from its credit sales, causing cash flow to be less than the net income. Investors who analyzed the cash flows would have been likely to find an early warning signal of W. T. Grant's operating problems.

Investors can also look to cash flow information to sniff out companies that can be good buys. As one analyst stated when it comes to valuing stocks: "Show me the money!" Here's the thinking behind that statement. Start with the "cash flows from operations" reported in the statement of cash

See the **International Perspectives** on pages 1437, 1439, and 1458.

Read the **IFRS Insights** on pages 1505–1510 for a discussion of:

—Significant non-cash transactions

—Special disclosures

flows, which (as you will learn in this chapter) consists of net income with noncash charges (like depreciation and deferred taxes) added back and cash-draining events (like an inventory pile-up) taken out. Now subtract capital expenditures and dividends. What you're left with is free cash flow (as discussed in Chapter 5).

Many analysts like companies trading at low multiples of their free cash flow—low, that is, in relation to rivals today or the same company in past years. Why? They know that reported earnings can be misleading. Case in point: Computer-game firm **Activision Blizzard** reported net income of $113 million last year. But it did better than that. It took in an additional $300 million, mostly for subscriptions to online multiplayer games. It gets the cash now but records the revenue only over time, as the subscriptions run out. A couple of investment houses put this stock on their buy list on the strength of its cash flows. So watch cash flow—to get an indicator of companies headed for trouble, as well as companies that may be undervalued.

Source: Adapted from James A. Largay III and Clyde P. Stickney, "Cash Flows, Ratio Analysis, and the W. T. Grant Company Bankruptcy," *Financial Analysts Journal* (July–August 1980), p. 51; and D. Fisher, "Cash Doesn't Lie," *Forbes* (April 12, 2010), pp. 52–55.

PREVIEW OF CHAPTER 23 As the opening story indicates, examination of W. T. Grant's cash flows from operations would have shown the financial inflexibility that eventually caused the company's bankruptcy. This chapter explains the main components of a statement of cash flows and the types of information it provides. The content and organization of the chapter are as follows.

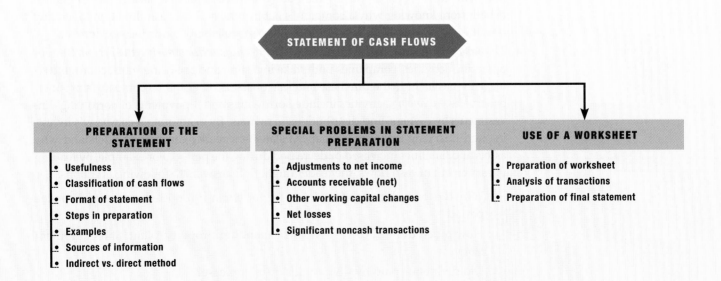

STATEMENT OF CASH FLOWS

PREPARATION OF THE STATEMENT
- Usefulness
- Classification of cash flows
- Format of statement
- Steps in preparation
- Examples
- Sources of information
- Indirect vs. direct method

SPECIAL PROBLEMS IN STATEMENT PREPARATION
- Adjustments to net income
- Accounts receivable (net)
- Other working capital changes
- Net losses
- Significant noncash transactions

USE OF A WORKSHEET
- Preparation of worksheet
- Analysis of transactions
- Preparation of final statement

SECTION 1 • PREPARATION OF THE STATEMENT OF CASH FLOWS

LEARNING OBJECTIVE **1**
Describe the purpose of the statement of cash flows.

The primary purpose of the 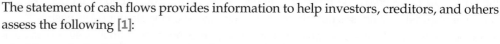statement of cash flows is to provide information about a company's cash receipts and cash payments during a period. A secondary objective is to provide cash-basis information about the company's operating, investing, and financing activities. The statement of cash flows therefore reports cash receipts, cash payments, and net change in cash resulting from a company's operating, investing, and financing activities during a period. Its format reconciles the beginning and ending cash balances for the period.

USEFULNESS OF THE STATEMENT OF CASH FLOWS

See the FASB Codification section (page 1478).

The statement of cash flows provides information to help investors, creditors, and others assess the following [1]:

1. *The entity's ability to generate future cash flows.* A primary objective of financial reporting is to provide information with which to predict the amounts, timing, and uncertainty of future cash flows. By examining relationships between items such as sales and net cash flow from operating activities, or net cash flow from operating activities and increases or decreases in cash, it is possible to better predict the future cash flows than is possible using accrual-basis data alone.

2. *The entity's ability to pay dividends and meet obligations.* Simply put, cash is essential. Without adequate cash, a company cannot pay employees, settle debts, pay out dividends, or acquire equipment. A statement of cash flows indicates where the company's cash comes from and how the company uses its cash. Employees, creditors, stockholders, and customers should be particularly interested in this statement, because it alone shows the flows of cash in a business.

3. *The reasons for the difference between net income and net cash flow from operating activities.* The net income number is important: It provides information on the performance of a company from one period to another. But some people are critical of accrual-basis net income because companies must make estimates to arrive at it. Such is not the case with cash. Thus, as the opening story showed, financial statement readers can benefit from knowing why a company's net income and net cash flow from operating activities differ, and can assess for themselves the reliability of the income number.

4. *The cash and noncash investing and financing transactions during the period.* Besides operating activities, companies undertake investing and financing transactions. *Investing* activities include the purchase and sale of assets other than a company's products or services. *Financing* activities include borrowings and repayments of borrowings, investments by owners, and distributions to owners. By examining a company's investing and financing activities, a financial statement reader can better understand why assets and liabilities increased or decreased during the period. For example, by reading the statement of cash flows, the reader might find answers to following questions:

> Why did cash decrease for Home Depot when it reported net income for the period?
>
> How much did Southwest Airlines spend on property, plant, and equipment last year?
>
> Did dividends paid by Campbell's Soup increase?
>
> How much money did Coca-Cola borrow last year?
>
> How much cash did Hewlett-Packard use to repurchase its common stock?

CLASSIFICATION OF CASH FLOWS

The statement of cash flows classifies cash receipts and cash payments by operating, investing, and financing activities.[1] Transactions and other events characteristic of each kind of activity is as follows.

2 LEARNING OBJECTIVE
Identify the major classifications of cash flows.

1. **Operating activities** involve the cash effects of transactions that enter into the determination of net income, such as cash receipts from sales of goods and services, and cash payments to suppliers and employees for acquisitions of inventory and expenses.
2. **Investing activities** generally involve long-term assets and include (a) making and collecting loans, and (b) acquiring and disposing of investments and productive long-lived assets.
3. **Financing activities** involve liability and stockholders' equity items and include (a) obtaining cash from creditors and repaying the amounts borrowed, and (b) obtaining capital from owners and providing them with a return on, and a return of, their investment.

Illustration 23-1 classifies the typical cash receipts and payments of a company according to operating, investing, and financing activities. The operating activities category is the most important. It shows the cash provided by company operations. This source of cash is generally considered to be the best measure of a company's ability to generate enough cash to continue as a going concern.

ILLUSTRATION 23-1
Classification of Typical Cash Inflows and Outflows

Operating	
Cash inflows	
From sales of goods or services.	
From returns on loans (interest) and on equity	Income
securities (dividends).	Statement
Cash outflows	Items
To suppliers for inventory.	
To employees for services.	
To government for taxes.	
To lenders for interest.	
To others for expenses.	
Investing	
Cash inflows	
From sale of property, plant, and equipment.	
From sale of debt or equity securities of other entities.	Generally
From collection of principal on loans to other entities.	Long-Term
Cash outflows	Asset Items
To purchase property, plant, and equipment.	
To purchase debt or equity securities of other entities.	
To make loans to other entities.	
Financing	
Cash inflows	Generally
From sale of equity securities.	Long-Term
From issuance of debt (bonds and notes).	Liability
Cash outflows	and Equity
To stockholders as dividends.	Items
To redeem long-term debt or reacquire capital stock.	

INTERNATIONAL PERSPECTIVE

According to IFRS, companies can define "cash and cash equivalents" as "net monetary assets"—that is, as "cash and demand deposits and highly liquid investments less short-term borrowings."

---

[1]The basis recommended by the FASB for the statement of cash flows is actually "cash and cash equivalents." **Cash equivalents** are short-term, highly liquid investments that are both: (a) readily convertible to known amounts of cash, and (b) so near their maturity that they present insignificant risk of changes in interest rates. Generally, only investments with original maturities of three months or less qualify under this definition. Examples of cash equivalents are Treasury bills, commercial paper, and money market funds purchased with cash that is in excess of immediate needs.

    Although we use the term "cash" throughout our discussion and illustrations, we mean cash and cash equivalents when reporting the cash flows and the net increase or decrease in cash.

Note the following general guidelines about the classification of cash flows.

1. Operating activities involve income statement items.
2. Investing activities involve cash flows resulting from changes in investments and long-term asset items.
3. Financing activities involve cash flows resulting from changes in long-term liability and stockholders' equity items.

Companies classify some cash flows relating to investing or financing activities as operating activities.[2] For example, companies classify receipts of investment income (interest and dividends) and payments of interest to lenders as operating activities. Why are these considered operating activities? Companies report these items in the income statement, where the results of operations are shown.

Conversely, companies classify some cash flows relating to operating activities as investing or financing activities. For example, a company classifies the cash received from the sale of property, plant, and equipment at a gain, although reported in the income statement, as an investing activity. It excludes the effects of the related gain in net cash flow from operating activities. Likewise, a gain or loss on the payment (extinguishment) of debt is generally part of the cash outflow related to the repayment of the amount borrowed. It therefore is a financing activity.

HOW'S MY CASH FLOW?

What do the numbers mean?

To evaluate overall cash flow, it is useful to understand where in the product life cycle a company is. Generally, companies move through several stages of development, which have implications for cash flow. As the graph below shows, the pattern of cash flows from operating, financing, and investing activities will vary depending on the stage of the product life cycle.

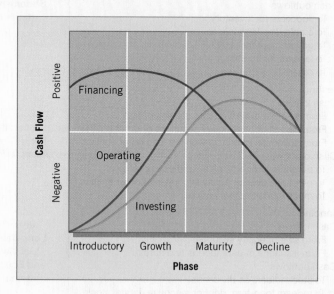

In the introductory phase, the product is likely not generating much revenue (operating cash flow is negative). Because the company is making heavy investments to get a product off the ground, cash flow from investment is negative, and financing cash flows are positive.

---

[2]Banks and brokers must classify cash flows from purchases and sales of loans and securities specifically for resale and carried at fair value **as operating activities**. This requirement recognizes that for these firms these assets are similar to inventory in other businesses. [2]

As the product moves to the growth and maturity phases, these cash flow relationships reverse. The product generates more cash flow from operations, which can be used to cover investments needed to support the product, and less cash is needed from financing. So is a negative operating cash flow bad? Not always. It depends on the product life cycle.

Source: Adapted from Paul D. Kimmel, Jerry J. Weygandt, and Donald E. Kieso, *Financial Accounting: Tools for Business Decision Making*, 6th ed. (New York: John Wiley & Sons, 2011), p. 628.

What do the numbers mean? (continued)

FORMAT OF THE STATEMENT OF CASH FLOWS

The three activities we discussed above constitute the general format of the statement of cash flows. The operating activities section always appears first. It is followed by the investing activities section and then the financing activities section.

A company reports the individual inflows and outflows from investing and financing activities separately. That is, a company reports them gross, not netted against one another. Thus, a cash outflow from the purchase of property is reported separately from the cash inflow from the sale of property. Similarly, a cash inflow from the issuance of debt is reported separately from the cash outflow from its retirement.

The net increase or decrease in cash reported during the period should reconcile the beginning and ending cash balances as reported in the comparative balance sheets. The general format of the statement of cash flows presents the results of the three activities discussed previously–operating, investing, and financing. Illustration 23-2 shows a widely used form of the statement of cash flows.

ILLUSTRATION 23-2
Format of the Statement of Cash Flows

COMPANY NAME		
STATEMENT OF CASH FLOWS		
PERIOD COVERED		
Cash flows from operating activities		
Net income		XXX
Adjustments to reconcile net income to net cash provided (used) by operating activities:		
(List of individual items)	XX	XX
Net cash provided (used) by operating activities		XXX
Cash flows from investing activities		
(List of individual inflows and outflows)	XX	
Net cash provided (used) by investing activities		XXX
Cash flows from financing activities		
(List of individual inflows and outflows)	XX	
Net cash provided (used) by financing activities		XXX
Net increase (decrease) in cash		XXX
Cash at beginning of period		XXX
Cash at end of period		XXX

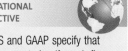

INTERNATIONAL PERSPECTIVE

Both IFRS and GAAP specify that companies must classify cash flows as operating, investing, or financing.

STEPS IN PREPARATION

Companies prepare the statement of cash flows differently from the three other basic financial statements. For one thing, it is not prepared from an adjusted trial balance. The cash flow statement requires detailed information concerning the changes in account balances that occurred between two points in time. An adjusted trial balance will not provide the necessary data. Second, the statement of cash flows deals with cash receipts and payments. As a result, the company must adjust the effects of the use of accrual accounting to determine cash flows. The information to prepare this statement usually comes from three sources:

1. **Comparative balance sheets** provide the amount of the changes in assets, liabilities, and equities from the beginning to the end of the period.
2. **Current income statement** data help determine the amount of cash provided by or used by operations during the period.
3. **Selected transaction data** from the general ledger provide additional detailed information needed to determine how the company provided or used cash during the period.

Preparing the statement of cash flows from the data sources above involves three major steps:

Step 1. *Determine the change in cash.* This procedure is straightforward. A company can easily compute the difference between the beginning and the ending cash balance from examining its comparative balance sheets.

Step 2. *Determine the net cash flow from operating activities.* This procedure is complex. It involves analyzing not only the current year's income statement but also comparative balance sheets as well as selected transaction data.

Step 3. *Determine net cash flows from investing and financing activities.* A company must analyze all other changes in the balance sheet accounts to determine their effects on cash.

On the following pages we work through these three steps in the process of preparing the statement of cash flows for Tax Consultants Inc. over several years.

FIRST EXAMPLE—2011

To illustrate a statement of cash flows, we use the **first year of operations** for Tax Consultants Inc. The company started on January 1, 2011, when it issued 60,000 shares of $1 par value common stock for $60,000 cash. The company rented its office space, furniture, and equipment, and performed tax consulting services throughout the first year. The comparative balance sheets at the beginning and end of the year 2011 appear in Illustration 23-3.

ILLUSTRATION 23-3
Comparative Balance Sheets, Tax Consultants Inc., Year 1

TAX CONSULTANTS INC. COMPARATIVE BALANCE SHEETS			
Assets	Dec. 31, 2011	Jan. 1, 2011	Change Increase/Decrease
Cash	$49,000	$–0–	$49,000 Increase
Accounts receivable	36,000	–0–	36,000 Increase
Total	$85,000	$–0–	
Liabilities and Stockholders' Equity			
Accounts payable	$ 5,000	$–0–	$ 5,000 Increase
Common stock ($1 par)	60,000	–0–	60,000 Increase
Retained earnings	20,000	–0–	20,000 Increase
Total	$85,000	$–0–	

Illustration 23-4 shows the income statement and additional information for Tax Consultants.

ILLUSTRATION 23-4
Income Statement, Tax
Consultants Inc., Year 1

TAX CONSULTANTS INC. INCOME STATEMENT FOR THE YEAR ENDED DECEMBER 31, 2011	
Revenues	$125,000
Operating expenses	85,000
Income before income taxes	40,000
Income tax expense	6,000
Net income	$ 34,000

Additional Information
Examination of selected data indicates that a dividend of $14,000 was declared and paid during the year.

Step 1: Determine the Change in Cash

To prepare a statement of cash flows, the first step is to **determine the change in cash.** This is a simple computation. Tax Consultants had no cash on hand at the beginning of the year 2011. It had $49,000 on hand at the end of 2011. Thus, cash changed (increased) in 2011 by $49,000.

Step 2: Determine Net Cash Flow from Operating Activities

To determine net cash flow from operating activities,[3] companies adjust net income in numerous ways. A useful starting point is to understand why net income must be converted to net cash provided by operating activities.

Under generally accepted accounting principles, most companies use the accrual basis of accounting. As you have learned, this basis requires that companies record revenue when earned and record expenses when incurred. Earned revenues may include credit sales for which the company has not yet collected cash. Expenses incurred may include some items that the company has not yet paid in cash. Thus, under the accrual basis of accounting, net income is not the same as net cash flow from operating activities.

To arrive at net cash flow from operating activities, a company must determine revenues and expenses on a **cash basis. It does this by eliminating the effects of income statement transactions that do not result in an increase or decrease in cash.** Illustration 23-5 shows the relationship between net income and net cash flow from operating activities.

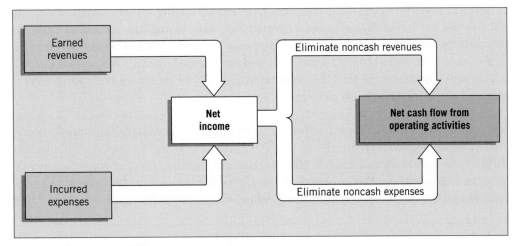

ILLUSTRATION 23-5
Net Income versus
Net Cash Flow from
Operating Activities

[3]"Net cash flow from operating activities" is a generic phrase, replaced in the statement of cash flows with either "Net cash **provided by** operating activities" if operations increase cash, or "Net cash **used by** operating activities" if operations decrease cash.

In this chapter, we use the term net income to refer to accrual-based net income. A company may convert net income to net cash flow from operating activities through either a direct method or an indirect method. We explain both methods in the following sections. The advantages and disadvantages of these two methods are discussed later in the chapter.

Direct Method

The **direct method** (also called the **income statement method**) reports cash receipts and cash disbursements from operating activities. The difference between these two amounts is the net cash flow from operating activities. In other words, the direct method deducts operating cash disbursements from operating cash receipts. The direct method results in the presentation of a condensed cash receipts and cash disbursements statement.

As indicated from the accrual-based income statement, Tax Consultants reported revenues of $125,000. However, because the company's accounts receivable increased during 2011 by $36,000, the company collected only $89,000 ($125,000 − $36,000) in cash from these revenues. Similarly, Tax Consultants reported operating expenses of $85,000. However, accounts payable increased during the period by $5,000. Assuming that these payables relate to operating expenses, cash operating expenses were $80,000 ($85,000 − $5,000). Because no taxes payable exist at the end of the year, the company must have paid $6,000 income tax expense for 2011 in cash during the year. Tax Consultants computes net cash flow from operating activities as shown in Illustration 23-6.

ILLUSTRATION 23-6
Computation of Net Cash Flow from Operating Activities, Year 1—Direct Method

Cash collected from revenues	$89,000
Cash payments for expenses	80,000
Income before income taxes	9,000
Cash payments for income taxes	6,000
Net cash provided by operating activities	$ 3,000

"Net cash provided by operating activities" is the equivalent of cash basis net income. ("Net cash used by operating activities" is equivalent to cash basis net loss.)

Indirect Method

The **indirect method** (or **reconciliation method**) starts with net income and converts it to net cash flow from operating activities. In other words, **the indirect method adjusts net income for items that affected reported net income but did not affect cash**. To compute net cash flow from operating activities, a company adds back noncash charges in the income statement to net income and deducts noncash credits. We explain the two adjustments to net income for Tax Consultants, namely, the increases in accounts receivable and accounts payable, as follows.

Increase in Accounts Receivable—Indirect Method. Tax Consultant's accounts receivable increased by $36,000 (from $0 to $36,000) during the year. For Tax Consultants, this means that cash receipts were $36,000 lower than revenues. The Accounts Receivable account in Illustration 23-7 shows that Tax Consultants had $125,000 in revenues (as reported on the income statement), but it collected only $89,000 in cash.

ILLUSTRATION 23-7
Analysis of Accounts Receivable

Accounts Receivable				
1/1/11	Balance	–0–	Receipts from customer	89,000
	Revenues	125,000		
12/31/11	Balance	36,000		

As shown in Illustration 23-8, to adjust net income to net cash provided by operating activities, Tax Consultants must deduct the increase of $36,000 in accounts receivable from net income. When the Accounts Receivable balance *decreases*, cash receipts are higher than revenue earned under the accrual basis. Therefore, the company adds to net income the amount of the decrease in accounts receivable to arrive at net cash provided by operating activities.

Increase in Accounts Payable—Indirect Method. When accounts payable increase during the year, expenses on an accrual basis exceed those on a cash basis. Why? Because Tax Consultants incurred expenses, but some of the expenses are not yet paid. To convert net income to net cash flow from operating activities, Tax Consultants must add back the increase of $5,000 in accounts payable to net income.

As a result of the accounts receivable and accounts payable adjustments, Tax Consultants determines net cash provided by operating activities is $3,000 for the year 2011. Illustration 23-8 shows this computation.

Net income		$ 34,000
Adjustments to reconcile net income to net		
cash provided by operating activities:		
Increase in accounts receivable	$(36,000)	
Increase in accounts payable	5,000	(31,000)
Net cash provided by operating activities		$ 3,000

ILLUSTRATION 23-8
Computation of Net Cash Flow from Operating Activities, Year 1—Indirect Method

Note that net cash provided by operating activities is the same whether using the direct (Illustration 23-6) or the indirect method (Illustration 23-8).

PUMPING UP CASH

What do the numbers mean?

Due to recent concerns about a decline in the quality of earnings, some investors have been focusing on cash flow. Management has an incentive to make operating cash flow look good because Wall Street has paid a premium for companies that generate a lot of cash from operations, rather than through borrowings. However, similar to earnings, companies have ways to pump up cash flow from operations.

One way that companies can boost their operating cash flow is by "securitizing" receivables. That is, companies can speed up cash collections by selling their receivables. For example, Federated Department Stores reported a $2.2 billion increase in cash flow from operations. This seems impressive until you read the fine print, which indicates that a big part of the increase was due to the sale of receivables. As discussed in this section, decreases in accounts receivable increase cash flow from operations. So while it appeared that Federated's core operations had improved, the company really did little more than accelerate collections of its receivables. In fact, the cash flow from the securitizations represented more than half of Federated's operating cash flow. Thus, just like earnings, cash flow can be of high or low quality.

Source: Adapted from Ann Tergesen, "Cash Flow Hocus Pocus," *BusinessWeek* (July 16, 2002), pp. 130–131. See also Bear Stearns Equity Research, *Accounting Issues: Cash Flow Metrics* (June 2006).

Step 3: Determine Net Cash Flows from Investing and Financing Activities

After Tax Consultants has computed the net cash provided by operating activities, the next step is to determine whether any other changes in balance sheet accounts caused an increase or decrease in cash.

For example, an examination of the remaining balance sheet accounts for Tax Consultants shows increases in both common stock and retained earnings. The

5 LEARNING OBJECTIVE
Determine net cash flows from investing and financing activities.

common stock increase of $60,000 resulted from the issuance of common stock for cash. The issuance of common stock is reported in the statement of cash flows as a receipt of cash from a financing activity.

Two items caused the retained earnings increase of $20,000:

1. Net income of $34,000 increased retained earnings.
2. Declaration of $14,000 of dividends decreased retained earnings.

Tax Consultants has converted net income into net cash flow from operating activities, as explained earlier. The additional data indicate that it paid the dividend. Thus, the company reports the dividend payment as a cash outflow, classified as a financing activity.

Statement of Cash Flows—2011

LEARNING OBJECTIVE 6
Prepare a statement of cash flows.

We are now ready to prepare the statement of cash flows. The statement starts with the operating activities section. Tax Consultants may use either the direct or indirect method to report net cash flow from operating activities.

The FASB **encourages** the use of the direct method over the indirect method. If a company uses the direct method of reporting net cash flow from operating activities, the FASB **requires** that the company provide in a separate schedule a reconciliation of net income to net cash flow from operating activities. If a company uses the indirect method, it can either report the reconciliation within the statement of cash flows or can provide it in a separate schedule, with the statement of cash flows reporting only the **net** cash flow from operating activities. [3] Throughout this chapter we use the indirect method, which is also used more extensively in practice.[4] *In doing homework assignments, you should follow instructions for use of either the direct or indirect method.*

Illustration 23-9 shows the statement of cash flows for Tax Consultants Inc., for year 1 (2011).

ILLUSTRATION 23-9
Statement of Cash Flows,
Tax Consultants Inc.,
Year 1

TAX CONSULTANTS INC. STATEMENT OF CASH FLOWS FOR THE YEAR ENDED DECEMBER 31, 2011 INCREASE (DECREASE) IN CASH		
Cash flows from operating activities		
Net income		$ 34,000
Adjustments to reconcile net income to net		
cash provided by operating activities:		
Increase in accounts receivable	$(36,000)	
Increase in accounts payable	5,000	(31,000)
Net cash provided by operating activities		3,000
Cash flows from financing activities		
Issuance of common stock	60,000	
Payment of cash dividends	(14,000)	
Net cash provided by financing activities		46,000
Net increase in cash		49,000
Cash, January 1, 2011		–0–
Cash, December 31, 2011		$ 49,000

As indicated, the $60,000 increase in common stock results in a financing-activity cash inflow. The payment of $14,000 in cash dividends is a financing-activity outflow of cash. The $49,000 increase in cash reported in the statement of cash flows agrees with the increase of $49,000 shown in the comparative balance sheets as the change in the cash account.

[4]*Accounting Trends and Techniques—2010* reports that out of its 500 surveyed companies, 495 (99 percent) used the indirect method, and only 5 used the direct method.

SECOND EXAMPLE—2012

Tax Consultants Inc. continued to grow and prosper in its second year of operations. The company purchased land, building, and equipment, and revenues and net income increased substantially over the first year. Illustrations 23-10 and 23-11 present information related to the second year of operations for Tax Consultants Inc.

ILLUSTRATION 23-10
Comparative Balance
Sheets, Tax Consultants
Inc., Year 2

TAX CONSULTANTS INC.
COMPARATIVE BALANCE SHEETS
AS OF DECEMBER 31

Assets	2012	2011	Change Increase/Decrease
Cash	$ 37,000	$ 49,000	$ 12,000 Decrease
Accounts receivable	26,000	36,000	10,000 Decrease
Prepaid expenses	6,000	–0–	6,000 Increase
Land	70,000	–0–	70,000 Increase
Buildings	200,000	–0–	200,000 Increase
Accumulated depreciation—buildings	(11,000)	–0–	11,000 Increase
Equipment	68,000	–0–	68,000 Increase
Accumulated depreciation—equipment	(10,000)	–0–	10,000 Increase
Total	$386,000	$ 85,000	
Liabilities and Stockholders' Equity			
Accounts payable	$ 40,000	$ 5,000	$ 35,000 Increase
Bonds payable	150,000	–0–	150,000 Increase
Common stock ($1 par)	60,000	60,000	–0–
Retained earnings	136,000	20,000	116,000 Increase
Total	$386,000	$ 85,000	

ILLUSTRATION 23-11
Income Statement, Tax
Consultants Inc., Year 2

TAX CONSULTANTS INC.
INCOME STATEMENT
FOR THE YEAR ENDED DECEMBER 31, 2012

Revenues		$492,000
Operating expenses (excluding depreciation)	$269,000	
Depreciation expense	21,000	290,000
Income from operations		202,000
Income tax expense		68,000
Net income		$134,000

Additional Information
(a) The company declared and paid an $18,000 cash dividend.
(b) The company obtained $150,000 cash through the issuance of long-term bonds.
(c) Land, building, and equipment were acquired for cash.

Step 1: Determine the Change in Cash

To prepare a statement of cash flows from the available information, the first step is to determine the change in cash. As indicated from the information presented, cash decreased $12,000 ($49,000 − $37,000).

Step 2: Determine Net Cash Flow from Operating Activities—Indirect Method

Using the indirect method, we adjust net income of $134,000 on an accrual basis to arrive at net cash flow from operating activities. Explanations for the adjustments to net income follow.

Decrease in Accounts Receivable. Accounts receivable decreased during the period, because cash receipts (cash-basis revenues) are higher than revenues reported on an accrual basis. To convert net income to net cash flow from operating activities, the decrease of $10,000 in accounts receivable must be added to net income.

Increase in Prepaid Expenses. When prepaid expenses (assets) increase during a period, expenses on an accrual-basis income statement are lower than they are on a cash-basis income statement. The reason: Tax Consultants has made cash payments in the current period, but expenses (as charges to the income statement) have been deferred to future periods. To convert net income to net cash flow from operating activities, the company must deduct from net income the increase of $6,000 in prepaid expenses. An increase in prepaid expenses results in a decrease in cash during the period.

Increase in Accounts Payable. Like the increase in 2011, Tax Consultants must add the 2012 increase of $35,000 in accounts payable to net income, to convert to net cash flow from operating activities. The company incurred a greater amount of expense than the amount of cash it disbursed.

Depreciation Expense (Increase in Accumulated Depreciation). The purchase of depreciable assets is a use of cash, shown in the investing section in the year of acquisition. Tax Consultant's depreciation expense of $21,000 (also represented by the increase in accumulated depreciation) is a noncash charge; the company adds it back to net income, to arrive at net cash flow from operating activities. The $21,000 is the sum of the $11,000 depreciation on the building plus the $10,000 depreciation on the equipment.

Certain other periodic charges to expense do not require the use of cash. Examples are the amortization of intangible assets and depletion expense. Such charges are treated in the same manner as depreciation. Companies frequently list depreciation and similar noncash charges as the first adjustments to net income in the statement of cash flows.

As a result of the foregoing items, net cash provided by operating activities is $194,000 as shown in Illustration 23-12.

ILLUSTRATION 23-12
Computation of Net
Cash Flow from
Operating Activities,
Year 2—Indirect Method

Net income		$134,000
Adjustments to reconcile net income to		
net cash provided by operating activities:		
Depreciation expense	$21,000	
Decrease in accounts receivable	10,000	
Increase in prepaid expenses	(6,000)	
Increase in accounts payable	35,000	60,000
Net cash provided by operating activities		$194,000

Step 3: Determine Net Cash Flows from Investing and Financing Activities

After you have determined the items affecting net cash provided by operating activities, the next step involves analyzing the remaining changes in balance sheet accounts. Tax Consultants Inc. analyzed the following accounts.

Increase in Land. As indicated from the change in the Land account, the company purchased land of $70,000 during the period. This transaction is an investing activity, reported as a use of cash.

Increase in Buildings and Related Accumulated Depreciation. As indicated in the additional data, and from the change in the Buildings account, Tax Consultants acquired an office building using $200,000 cash. This transaction is a cash outflow, reported in the investing section. The $11,000 increase in accumulated depreciation results from recording depreciation expense on the building. As indicated earlier, the reported depreciation expense has no effect on the amount of cash.

Increase in Equipment and Related Accumulated Depreciation. An increase in equipment of $68,000 resulted because the company used cash to purchase equipment. This transaction is an outflow of cash from an investing activity. The depreciation expense entry for the period explains the increase in Accumulated Depreciation—Equipment.

Increase in Bonds Payable. The Bonds Payable account increased $150,000. Cash received from the issuance of these bonds represents an inflow of cash from a financing activity.

Increase in Retained Earnings. Retained earnings increased $116,000 during the year. Two factors explain this increase: (1) Net income of $134,000 increased retained earnings, and (2) dividends of $18,000 decreased retained earnings. As indicated earlier, the company adjusts net income to net cash provided by operating activities in the operating activities section. Payment of the dividends is a financing activity that involves a cash outflow.

Statement of Cash Flows—2012

Combining the foregoing items, we get a statement of cash flows for 2012 for Tax Consultants Inc., using the indirect method to compute net cash flow from operating activities.

ILLUSTRATION 23-13
Statement of Cash Flows, Tax Consultants Inc., Year 2

TAX CONSULTANTS INC.
STATEMENT OF CASH FLOWS
FOR THE YEAR ENDED DECEMBER 31, 2012
INCREASE (DECREASE) IN CASH

Cash flows from operating activities		
Net income		$ 134,000
Adjustments to reconcile net income to net cash provided by operating activities:		
Depreciation expense	$ 21,000	
Decrease in accounts receivable	10,000	
Increase in prepaid expenses	(6,000)	
Increase in accounts payable	35,000	60,000
Net cash provided by operating activities		194,000
Cash flows from investing activities		
Purchase of land	(70,000)	
Purchase of building	(200,000)	
Purchase of equipment	(68,000)	
Net cash used by investing activities		(338,000)
Cash flows from financing activities		
Issuance of bonds	150,000	
Payment of cash dividends	(18,000)	
Net cash provided by financing activities		132,000
Net decrease in cash		(12,000)
Cash, January 1, 2012		49,000
Cash, December 31, 2012		$ 37,000

THIRD EXAMPLE—2013

Our third example, covering the 2013 operations of Tax Consultants Inc., is more complex. It again uses the indirect method to compute and present net cash flow from operating activities.

Tax Consultants Inc. experienced continued success in 2013 and expanded its operations to include the sale of computer software used in tax-return preparation and tax planning. Thus, inventory is a new asset appearing in the company's December 31, 2013, balance sheet. Illustrations 23-14 and 23-15 show the comparative balance sheets, income statements, and selected data for 2013.

ILLUSTRATION 23-14
Comparative Balance
Sheets, Tax Consultants
Inc., Year 3

TAX CONSULTANTS INC.
COMPARATIVE BALANCE SHEETS
AS OF DECEMBER 31

Assets	2013	2012	Change Increase/Decrease
Cash	$ 54,000	$ 37,000	$ 17,000 Increase
Accounts receivable	68,000	26,000	42,000 Increase
Inventory	54,000	–0–	54,000 Increase
Prepaid expenses	4,000	6,000	2,000 Decrease
Land	45,000	70,000	25,000 Decrease
Buildings	200,000	200,000	–0–
Accumulated depreciation—buildings	(21,000)	(11,000)	10,000 Increase
Equipment	193,000	68,000	125,000 Increase
Accumulated depreciation—equipment	(28,000)	(10,000)	18,000 Increase
Totals	$569,000	$386,000	
Liabilities and Stockholders' Equity			
Accounts payable	$ 33,000	$ 40,000	$ 7,000 Decrease
Bonds payable	110,000	150,000	40,000 Decrease
Common stock ($1 par)	220,000	60,000	160,000 Increase
Retained earnings	206,000	136,000	70,000 Increase
Totals	$569,000	$386,000	

ILLUSTRATION 23-15
Income Statement, Tax
Consultants Inc., Year 3

TAX CONSULTANTS INC.
INCOME STATEMENT
FOR THE YEAR ENDED DECEMBER 31, 2013

Revenues		$890,000
Cost of goods sold	$465,000	
Operating expenses	221,000	
Interest expense	12,000	
Loss on sale of equipment	2,000	700,000
Income from operations		190,000
Income tax expense		65,000
Net income		$125,000

Additional Information
(a) Operating expenses include depreciation expense of $33,000 and expiration of prepaid expenses of $2,000.
(b) Land was sold at its book value for cash.
(c) Cash dividends of $55,000 were declared and paid.
(d) Interest expense of $12,000 was paid in cash.
(e) Equipment with a cost of $166,000 was purchased for cash. Equipment with a cost of $41,000 and a book value of $36,000 was sold for $34,000 cash.
(f) Bonds were redeemed at their book value for cash.
(g) Common stock ($1 par) was issued for cash.

Step 1: Determine the Change in Cash

The first step in the preparation of the statement of cash flows is to determine the change in cash. As the comparative balance sheets show, cash increased $17,000 in 2013.

Step 2: Determine Net Cash Flow from Operating Activities—Indirect Method

We explain the adjustments to net income of $125,000 as follows.

Increase in Accounts Receivable. The increase in accounts receivable of $42,000 represents recorded accrual-basis revenues in excess of cash collections in 2013. The company deducts this increase from net income to convert from the accrual basis to the cash basis.

Increase in Inventory. The $54,000 increase in inventory represents an operating use of cash, not an expense. Tax Consultants therefore deducts this amount from net income, to arrive at net cash flow from operations. In other words, when inventory purchased exceeds inventory sold during a period, cost of goods sold on an accrual basis is lower than on a cash basis.

Decrease in Prepaid Expenses. The $2,000 decrease in prepaid expenses represents a charge to the income statement for which Tax Consultants made no cash payment in the current period. The company adds back the decrease to net income, to arrive at net cash flow from operating activities.

Decrease in Accounts Payable. When accounts payable decrease during the year, cost of goods sold and expenses on a cash basis are higher than they are on an accrual basis. To convert net income to net cash flow from operating activities, the company must deduct the $7,000 in accounts payable from net income.

Depreciation Expense (Increase in Accumulated Depreciation). Accumulated Depreciation—Buildings increased $10,000 ($21,000 − $11,000). The Buildings account did not change during the period, which means that Tax Consultants recorded depreciation expense of $10,000 in 2013.

Accumulated Depreciation—Equipment increased by $18,000 ($28,000 − $10,000) during the year. But Accumulated Depreciation—Equipment decreased by $5,000 as a result of the sale during the year. Thus, depreciation for the year was $23,000. The company reconciled Accumulated Depreciation—Equipment as follows.

Beginning balance	$10,000
Add: Depreciation for 2013	23,000
	33,000
Deduct: Sale of equipment	5,000
Ending balance	$28,000

The company must add back to net income the total depreciation of $33,000 ($10,000 + $23,000) charged to the income statement, to determine net cash flow from operating activities.

Loss on Sale of Equipment. Tax Consultants Inc. sold for $34,000 equipment that cost $41,000 and had a book value of $36,000. As a result, the company reported a loss of $2,000 on its sale. To arrive at net cash flow from operating activities, it must add back to net income the loss on the sale of the equipment. The reason is that the loss is a non-cash charge to the income statement. The loss did not reduce cash, but it did reduce net income.[5]

---

[5]A similar adjustment is required for unrealized gains or losses recorded on trading security investments or other financial assets and liabilities accounted for under the fair value option. Marking these assets and liabilities to fair value results in an increase or decrease in income, but there is no effect on cash flows.

From the foregoing items, the company prepares the operating activities section of the statement of cash flows, as shown in Illustration 23-16.

ILLUSTRATION 23-16
Operating Activities
Section of Cash Flows
Statement

Cash flows from operating activities		
Net income		$ 125,000
Adjustments to reconcile net income to		
net cash provided by operating activities:		
Depreciation expense	$ 33,000	
Loss on sale of equipment	2,000	
Increase in accounts receivable	(42,000)	
Increase in inventory	(54,000)	
Decrease in prepaid expenses	2,000	
Decrease in accounts payable	(7,000)	(66,000)
Net cash provided by operating activities		59,000

Step 3: Determine Net Cash Flows from Investing and Financing Activities

By analyzing the remaining changes in the balance sheet accounts, Tax Consultants identifies cash flows from investing and financing activities.

Land. Land decreased $25,000 during the period. As indicated from the information presented, the company sold land for cash at its book value. This transaction is an investing activity, reported as a $25,000 source of cash.

Equipment. An Analysis of the Equipment account indicates the following.

Beginning balance	$ 68,000
Purchase of equipment	166,000
	234,000
Sale of equipment	41,000
Ending balance	$193,000

The company used cash to purchase equipment with a fair value of $166,000—an investing transaction reported as a cash outflow. The sale of the equipment for $34,000 is also an investing activity, but one that generates a cash inflow.

Bonds Payable. Bonds payable decreased $40,000 during the year. As indicated from the additional information, the company redeemed the bonds at their book value. This financing transaction used $40,000 of cash.

Common Stock. The Common Stock account increased $160,000 during the year. As indicated from the additional information, Tax Consultants issued common stock of $160,000 at par. This financing transaction provided cash of $160,000.

Retained Earnings. Retained earnings changed $70,000 ($206,000 − $136,000) during the year. The $70,000 change in retained earnings results from net income of $125,000 from operations and the financing activity of paying cash dividends of $55,000.

Statement of Cash Flows—2013

Tax Consultants Inc. combines the foregoing items to prepare the statement of cash flows shown in Illustration 23-17.

TAX CONSULTANTS INC.
STATEMENT OF CASH FLOWS
FOR THE YEAR ENDED DECEMBER 31, 2013
INCREASE (DECREASE) IN CASH

Cash flows from operating activities		
Net income		$ 125,000
Adjustments to reconcile net income to		
net cash provided by operating activities:		
Depreciation expense	$ 33,000	
Loss on sale of equipment	2,000	
Increase in accounts receivable	(42,000)	
Increase in inventory	(54,000)	
Decrease in prepaid expenses	2,000	
Decrease in accounts payable	(7,000)	(66,000)
Net cash provided by operating activities		59,000
Cash flows from investing activities		
Sale of land	25,000	
Sale of equipment	34,000	
Purchase of equipment	(166,000)	
Net cash used by investing activities		(107,000)
Cash flows from financing activities		
Redemption of bonds	(40,000)	
Sale of common stock	160,000	
Payment of dividends	(55,000)	
Net cash provided by financing activities		65,000
Net increase in cash		17,000
Cash, January 1, 2013		37,000
Cash, December 31, 2013		$ 54,000

ILLUSTRATION 23-17
Statement of Cash Flows,
Tax Consultants Inc.,
Year 3

SOURCES OF INFORMATION FOR THE STATEMENT OF CASH FLOWS

7 LEARNING OBJECTIVE
Identify sources of information for a statement of cash flows.

Important points to remember in the preparation of the statement of cash flows are these:

1. Comparative balance sheets provide the basic information from which to prepare the report. Additional information obtained from analyses of specific accounts is also included.

2. An analysis of the Retained Earnings account is necessary. The net increase or decrease in Retained Earnings without any explanation is a meaningless amount in the statement. Without explanation, it might represent the effect of net income, dividends declared, or prior period adjustments.

3. The statement includes all changes that have passed through cash or have resulted in an increase or decrease in cash.

4. Write-downs, amortization charges, and similar "book" entries, such as depreciation of plant assets, represent neither inflows nor outflows of cash, because they have no effect on cash. To the extent that they have entered into the determination of net income, however, the company must add them back to or subtract them from net income, to arrive at net cash provided (used) by operating activities.

NET CASH FLOW FROM OPERATING ACTIVITIES— INDIRECT VERSUS DIRECT METHOD

As we discussed previously, the two different methods available to adjust income from operations on an accrual basis to net cash flow from operating activities are the indirect (reconciliation) method and the direct (income statement) method.

The FASB encourages use of the direct method and permits use of the indirect method. Yet, if the direct method is used, the Board requires that companies provide in a separate schedule a reconciliation of net income to net cash flow from operating activities. Therefore, under either method, companies must prepare and report information from the indirect (reconciliation) method.

Indirect Method

For consistency and comparability and because it is the most widely used method in practice, we used the indirect method in the examples just presented. We determined net cash flow from operating activities by adding back to or deducting from net income those items that had no effect on cash. Illustration 23-18 presents more completely the common types of adjustments that companies make to net income to arrive at net cash flow from operating activities.

ILLUSTRATION 23-18
Adjustments Needed to Determine Net Cash Flow from Operating Activities—Indirect Method

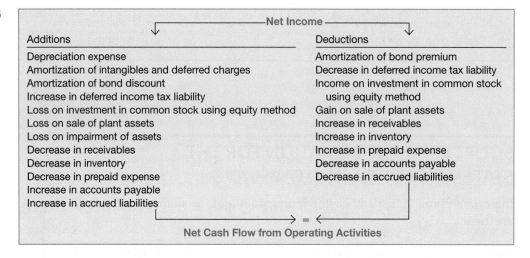

The additions and deductions in Illustration 23-18 reconcile net income to net cash flow from operating activities, illustrating why the indirect method is also called the reconciliation method.

Direct Method—An Example

Under the direct method the statement of cash flows reports net cash flow from operating activities as major classes of *operating cash receipts* (e.g., cash collected from customers and cash received from interest and dividends) and *cash disbursements* (e.g., cash paid to suppliers for goods, to employees for services, to creditors for interest, and to government authorities for taxes).

We illustrate the direct method here in more detail to help you understand the difference between accrual-based income and net cash flow from operating activities. This example also illustrates the data needed to apply the direct method. Emig Company, which began business on January 1, 2012, has the following selected balance sheet information.

	December 31, 2012	January 1, 2012
Cash	$159,000	–0–
Accounts receivable	15,000	–0–
Inventory	160,000	–0–
Prepaid expenses	8,000	–0–
Property, plant, and equipment (net)	90,000	–0–
Accounts payable	60,000	–0–
Accrued expenses payable	20,000	–0–

ILLUSTRATION 23-19
Balance Sheet Accounts, Emig Co.

Emig Company's December 31, 2012, income statement and additional information are as follows.

Sales revenue		$780,000
Cost of goods sold		450,000
Gross profit		330,000
Operating expenses	$160,000	
Depreciation	10,000	170,000
Income before income taxes		160,000
Income tax expense		48,000
Net income		$112,000

Additional Information
(a) Dividends of $70,000 were declared and paid in cash.
(b) The accounts payable increase resulted from the purchase of merchandise.
(c) Prepaid expenses and accrued expenses payable relate to operating expenses.

ILLUSTRATION 23-20
Income Statement, Emig Co.

Under the **direct method**, companies compute net cash provided by operating activities by **adjusting each item in the income statement** from the accrual basis to the cash basis. To simplify and condense the operating activities section, only major classes of operating cash receipts and cash payments are reported. As Illustration 23-21 shows, the difference between these major classes of cash receipts and cash payments is the net cash provided by operating activities.

ILLUSTRATION 23-21
Major Classes of Cash Receipts and Payments

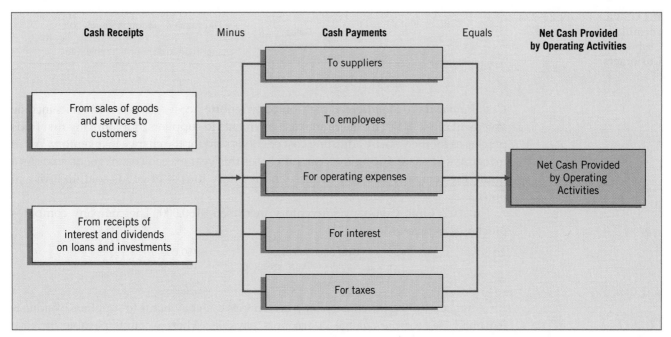

An efficient way to apply the direct method is to analyze the revenues and expenses reported in the income statement in the order in which they are listed. The company then determines cash receipts and cash payments related to these revenues and expenses. In the following sections, we present the direct method adjustments for Emig Company in 2012, to determine net cash provided by operating activities.

Cash Receipts from Customers. The income statement for Emig Company reported revenues from customers of $780,000. To determine cash receipts from customers, the company considers the change in accounts receivable during the year.

When accounts receivable increase during the year, revenues on an accrual basis are higher than cash receipts from customers. In other words, operations led to increased revenues, but not all of these revenues resulted in cash receipts. To determine the amount of increase in cash receipts, deduct the amount of the increase in accounts receivable from the total sales revenue. Conversely, a decrease in accounts receivable is added to sales revenue, because cash receipts from customers then exceed sales revenue.

For Emig Company, accounts receivable increased $15,000. Thus, cash receipts from customers were $765,000, computed as follows.

Sales revenue	$780,000
Deduct: Increase in accounts receivable	15,000
Cash receipts from customers	$765,000

Emig could also determine cash receipts from customers by analyzing the Accounts Receivable account as shown below.

Accounts Receivable

1/1/12	Balance	–0–	Receipts from customers	765,000
	Sales revenue	780,000		
12/31/12	Balance	15,000		

Illustration 23-22 shows the relationships between cash receipts from customers, sales revenue, and changes in accounts receivable.

ILLUSTRATION 23-22
Formula to Compute
Cash Receipts from
Customers

Cash Payments to Suppliers. Emig Company reported cost of goods sold on its income statement of $450,000. To determine cash payments to suppliers, the company first finds purchases for the year, by adjusting cost of goods sold for the change in inventory. When inventory increases during the year, purchases this year exceed cost of goods sold. As a result, the company adds the increase in inventory to cost of goods sold, to arrive at purchases.

In 2012, Emig Company's inventory increased $160,000. The company computes purchases as follows.

Cost of goods sold	$450,000
Add: Increase in inventory	160,000
Purchases	$610,000

After computing purchases, Emig determines cash payments to suppliers by adjusting purchases for the change in accounts payable. When accounts payable increase during the year, purchases on an accrual basis are higher than they are on a cash basis. As a result, it deducts from purchases the increase in accounts payable to arrive at cash payments to suppliers. Conversely, if cash payments to suppliers exceed purchases, Emig adds to purchases the decrease in accounts payable. Cash payments to suppliers were $550,000, computed as follows.

Purchases	$610,000
Deduct: Increase in accounts payable	60,000
Cash payments to suppliers	$550,000

Emig also can determine cash payments to suppliers by analyzing Accounts Payable, as shown below.

Accounts Payable

Payments to suppliers	550,000	1/1/12	Balance	–0–
			Purchases	610,000
		12/31/12	Balance	60,000

Illustration 23-23 shows the relationships between cash payments to suppliers, cost of goods sold, changes in inventory, and changes in accounts payable.

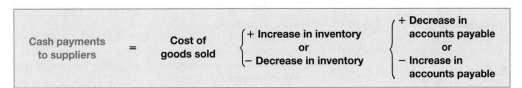

ILLUSTRATION 23-23
Formula to Compute Cash Payments to Suppliers

Cash Payments for Operating Expenses. Emig reported operating expenses of $160,000 on its income statement. To determine the cash paid for operating expenses, it must adjust this amount for any changes in prepaid expenses and accrued expenses payable.

For example, when prepaid expenses increased $8,000 during the year, cash paid for operating expenses was $8,000 higher than operating expenses reported on the income statement. To convert operating expenses to cash payments for operating expenses, the company adds to operating expenses the increase of $8,000. Conversely, if prepaid expenses decrease during the year, it deducts from operating expenses the amount of the decrease.

Emig also must adjust operating expenses for changes in accrued expenses payable. When accrued expenses payable increase during the year, operating expenses on an accrual basis are higher than they are on a cash basis. As a result, the company deducts from operating expenses an increase in accrued expenses payable, to arrive at cash payments for operating expenses. Conversely, it adds to operating expenses a decrease in accrued expenses payable, because cash payments exceed operating expenses.

Emig Company's cash payments for operating expenses were $148,000, computed as follows.

Operating expenses	$160,000
Add: Increase in prepaid expenses	8,000
Deduct: Increase in accrued expenses payable	(20,000)
Cash payments for operating expenses	$148,000

The relationships among cash payments for operating expenses, changes in prepaid expenses, and changes in accrued expenses payable are shown in Illustration 23-24 (page 1456).

ILLUSTRATION 23-24
Formula to Compute
Cash Payments for
Operating Expenses

Cash payments for operating expenses	=	Operating expenses	{ + Increase in prepaid expense or − Decrease in prepaid expense	{ + Decrease in accrued expenses payable or − Increase in accrued expenses payable

Note that the company did not consider depreciation expense, because it is a non-cash charge.

Cash Payments for Income Taxes. The income statement for Emig shows income tax expense of $48,000. This amount equals the cash paid. How do we know that? Because the comparative balance sheet indicated no income taxes payable at either the beginning or end of the year.

Summary of Net Cash Flow from Operating Activities—Direct Method
The following schedule summarizes the computations illustrated above.

ILLUSTRATION 23-25
Accrual Basis to Cash
Basis

Accrual Basis			Adjustment	Add (Subtract)	Cash Basis
Sales revenue	$780,000	−	Increase in accounts receivable	$ (15,000)	$765,000
Cost of goods sold	450,000	+	Increase in inventory	160,000	
		−	Increase in accounts payable	(60,000)	550,000
Operating expenses	160,000	+	Increase in prepaid expenses	8,000	
		−	Increase in accrued expenses payable	(20,000)	148,000
Depreciation expense	10,000	−	Depreciation expense	(10,000)	–0–
Income tax expense	48,000				48,000
Total expense	668,000				746,000
Net income	$112,000		Net cash provided by operating activities		$ 19,000

Illustration 23-26 shows the presentation of the direct method for reporting net cash flow from operating activities for the Emig Company illustration.

ILLUSTRATION 23-26
Operating Activities
Section—Direct Method,
2012

EMIG COMPANY STATEMENT OF CASH FLOWS (PARTIAL)		
Cash flows from operating activities		
Cash received from customers		$765,000
Cash payments:		
To suppliers	$550,000	
For operating expenses	148,000	
For income taxes	48,000	746,000
Net cash provided by operating activities		$ 19,000

If Emig Company uses the direct method to present the net cash flow from operating activities, it must provide in a separate schedule the reconciliation of net income to net cash provided by operating activities. The reconciliation assumes the identical form and content of the indirect method of presentation, as shown on the next page.

EMIG COMPANY RECONCILIATION		
Net income		$112,000
Adjustments to reconcile net income to net cash provided by operating activities:		
Depreciation expense	$ 10,000	
Increase in accounts receivable	(15,000)	
Increase in inventory	(160,000)	
Increase in prepaid expenses	(8,000)	
Increase in accounts payable	60,000	
Increase in accrued expense payable	20,000	(93,000)
Net cash provided by operating activities		$ 19,000

When the direct method is used, the company may present this reconciliation at the bottom of the statement of cash flows or in a separate schedule.

Direct versus Indirect Controversy

The most contentious decision that the FASB faced related to cash flow reporting was choosing between the direct method and the indirect method of determining net cash flow from operating activities. Companies lobbied *against* the direct method, urging adoption of the indirect method. Commercial lending officers expressed to the FASB a strong preference in favor of the direct method. In the next two sections, we consider the arguments in favor of each of the methods.

In Favor of the Direct Method

The principal advantage of the direct method is that **it shows operating cash receipts and payments**. Thus, it is more consistent with the objective of a statement of cash flows—to provide information about cash receipts and cash payments—than the indirect method, which does not report operating cash receipts and payments.

Supporters of the direct method contend that knowledge of the specific sources of operating cash receipts and the purposes for which operating cash payments were made in past periods is useful in estimating future operating cash flows. Furthermore, information about amounts of major classes of operating cash receipts and payments is more useful than information only about their arithmetic sum (the net cash flow from operating activities). Such information is more revealing of a company's ability (1) to generate sufficient cash from operating activities to pay its debts, (2) to reinvest in its operations, and (3) to make distributions to its owners. [4]

Many companies indicate that they do not currently collect information in a manner that allows them to determine amounts such as cash received from customers or cash paid to suppliers directly from their accounting systems. But supporters of the direct method contend that the incremental cost of determining operating cash receipts and payments is not significant.

In Favor of the Indirect Method

The principal advantage of the indirect method is that **it focuses on the differences between net income and net cash flow from operating activities**. That is, it provides a useful link between the statement of cash flows and the income statement and balance sheet.

Many companies contend that it is less costly to adjust net income to net cash flow from operating activities (indirect) than it is to report gross operating cash receipts and payments (direct). Supporters of the indirect method also state that the direct method, which effectively reports income statement information on a cash rather than an accrual basis, may erroneously suggest that net cash flow from operating activities is as good as, or better than, net income as a measure of performance.

Special Rules Applying to Direct and Indirect Methods

Companies that use the direct method are required, at a minimum, to report separately the following classes of operating cash receipts and payments:

Receipts

1. Cash collected from customers (including lessees, licensees, etc.).

2. Interest and dividends received.

3. Other operating cash receipts, if any.

Payments

1. Cash paid to employees and suppliers of goods or services (including suppliers of insurance, advertising, etc.).

2. Interest paid.

3. Income taxes paid.

4. Other operating cash payments, if any.

INTERNATIONAL
PERSPECTIVE

Consolidated statements of cash flows may be of limited use to analysts evaluating multinational companies. Without disaggregation, users of such statements are not able to determine "where in the world" the funds are sourced and used.

The FASB encourages companies to provide further breakdowns of operating cash receipts and payments that they consider meaningful.

Companies using the indirect method must disclose separately changes in inventory, receivables, and payables in order to reconcile net income to net cash flow from operating activities. In addition, they must disclose, elsewhere in the financial statements or in accompanying notes, interest paid (net of amount capitalized) and income taxes paid.[6] The FASB requires these separate and additional disclosures so that users may approximate the direct method. Also, an acceptable alternative presentation of the indirect method is to report net cash flow from operating activities as a single line item in the statement of cash flows and to present the reconciliation details elsewhere in the financial statements.

NOT WHAT IT SEEMS

What do the numbers mean?

The controversy over direct and indirect methods highlights the importance that the market attributes to operating cash flow. By showing an improving cash flow, a company can give a favorable impression of its ongoing operations. For example, WorldCom concealed declines in its operations by capitalizing certain operating expenses—to the tune of $3.8 billion! This practice not only "juiced up" income but also made it possible to report the cash payments in the investing section of the cash flow statement rather than as a deduction from operating cash flow.

The SEC recently addressed a similar cash flow classification issue with automakers like Ford, GM, and Chrysler. For years, automakers classified lease receivables and other dealer-financing arrangements as investment cash flows. Thus, they reported an increase in lease or loan receivables from cars sold as a use of cash in the investing section of the statement of cash flows. The SEC objected and now requires automakers to report these receivables as operating cash flows, since the leases and loans are used to facilitate car sales. At GM, these reclassifications reduced its operating cash flows from $7.6 billion to $3 billion in the year before the change. So while the overall cash flow—from operations, investing, and financing—remained the same, operating cash flow at these companies looked better than it really was.

Source: Peter Elstrom, "How to Hide $3.8 Billion in Expenses," *BusinessWeek Online* (July 8, 2002); and Judith Burns, "SEC Tells US Automakers to Retool Cash-Flow Accounting," *Wall Street Journal Online* (February 28, 2005).

---

[6]*Accounting Trends and Techniques—2010* reports that of the 500 companies surveyed, 244 disclosed interest paid in notes to the financial statements, 235 disclosed interest paid at the bottom of the statement of cash flows, 6 disclosed interest paid within the statement of cash flows, and 15 reported no separate amount. Income taxes paid during the year were disclosed in a manner similar to interest payments.

SECTION 2 • SPECIAL PROBLEMS IN STATEMENT PREPARATION

We discussed some of the special problems related to preparing the statement of cash flows in connection with the preceding illustrations. Other problems that arise with some frequency in the preparation of this statement include the following.

8 LEARNING OBJECTIVE
Discuss special problems in preparing a statement of cash flows.

1. Adjustments to net income.
2. Accounts receivable (net).
3. Other working capital changes.
4. Net losses.
5. Significant noncash transactions.

ADJUSTMENTS TO NET INCOME

Depreciation and Amortization

Depreciation expense is the most common adjustment to net income that companies make to arrive at net cash flow from operating activities. But there are numerous other noncash expense or revenue items. Examples of expense items that companies must add back to net income are the **amortization of limited-life intangible assets** such as patents, and the **amortization of deferred costs** such as bond issue costs. These charges to expense involve expenditures made in prior periods that a company amortizes currently. These charges reduce net income without affecting cash in the current period.

Also, **amortization of bond discount or premium** on long-term bonds payable affects the amount of interest expense. However, neither affects cash. As a result, a company should add back discount amortization and subtract premium amortization from net income to arrive at net cash flow from operating activities.

Postretirement Benefit Costs

If a company has postretirement costs such as an employee pension plan, chances are that the pension expense recorded during a period will either be higher or lower than the cash funded. It will be higher when there is an unfunded liability and will be lower when there is a prepaid pension cost. When the expense is higher or lower than the cash paid, **the company must adjust net income by the difference between cash paid and the expense reported** in computing net cash flow from operating activities.

Change in Deferred Income Taxes

Changes in deferred income taxes affect net income but have no effect on cash. For example, Delta Airlines reported an increase in its liability for deferred taxes of approximately $1.2 billion. This change in the liability increased tax expense and decreased net income, but did not affect cash. Therefore, Delta added back $1.2 billion to net income on its statement of cash flows.

Equity Method of Accounting

Another common adjustment to net income is **a change related to an investment in common stock** when recording income or loss under the equity method. Recall that under the equity method, the investor (1) debits the investment account and credits revenue for its share of the investee's net income, and (2) credits dividends received to the investment account. Therefore, the net increase in the investment account does not affect cash flow. A company must deduct the net increase from net income to arrive at net cash flow from operating activities.

Assume that Victor Co. owns 40 percent of Milo Inc. During the year Milo reports net income of $100,000 and pays a cash dividend of $30,000. Victor reports this in its statement of cash flows as a deduction from net income in the following manner—Equity in earnings of Milo, net of dividends, $28,000 [($100,000 − $30,000) × 40%].

Losses and Gains

Realized Losses and Gains

In the illustration for Tax Consultants, the company experienced a loss of $2,000 from the sale of equipment. The company added this loss to net income to compute net cash flow from operating activities because **the loss is a noncash charge in the income statement**.

If Tax Consultants experiences a **gain** from a sale of equipment, it too requires an adjustment to net income. Because a company reports the gain in the statement of cash flows as part of the cash proceeds from the sale of equipment under investing activities, **it deducts the gain from net income to avoid double-counting**—once as part of net income and again as part of the cash proceeds from the sale.

To illustrate, assume that Tax Consultants had land with a carrying value of $200,000, which was condemned by the state government for a highway project. The condemnation proceeds received were $205,000, resulting in a gain of $5,000. In the statement of cash flows (indirect method), the company would deduct the $5,000 gain from net income in the operating activities section. It would report the $205,000 cash inflow from the condemnation as an investing activity, as follows.

Cash flows from investing activities
Condemnation of land $205,000

Unrealized Losses and Gains

Unrealized losses and gains generally occur for debt investments and for equity investments. For example, assume that Target purchases the following two investments on January 10, 2012.

1. Debt investment for $1 million that is classified as trading. During 2012, the debt investment has an unrealized holding gain of $110,000 (recorded in net income).

2. Equity investment for $600,000 that is classified as available-for-sale. During 2012, the available-for-sale equity investment has an unrealized holding loss of $50,000 (recorded in other comprehensive income).

For Target, the unrealized holding gain of $110,000 on the debt investment increases net income but does not increase net cash flow from operating activities. As a result, the unrealized holding gain of $110,000 is deducted from net income to compute net cash flow from operating activities.

On the other hand, the unrealized holding loss of $50,000 that Target incurs on the available-for-sale equity investment does not affect net income or cash flows—this loss is reported in the other comprehensive income section. As a result, no adjustment to net income is necessary in computing net cash flow from operating activities.

Thus, the general rule is that unrealized holding gains or losses that affect net income must be adjusted to determine net cash flow from operating activities. Conversely, unrealized holding gains or losses that do not affect net income are not adjusted to determine net cash flow from operating activities.

Stock Options

Recall for share-based compensation plans that companies are required to use the fair value method to determine total compensation cost. The compensation cost is then recognized as an expense in the periods in which the employee provides services. When Compensation Expense is debited, Paid-in Capital—Stock Options is often credited. Cash is not affected by recording the expense. **Therefore, the company must increase net income by the amount of compensation expense from stock options in computing net cash flow from operating activities.**

To illustrate how this information should be reported on a statement of cash flows, assume that First Wave Inc. grants 5,000 options to its CEO, Ann Johnson. Each option entitles Johnson to purchase one share of First Wave's $1 par value common stock at $50 per share at any time in the next two years (the service period). The fair value of the options is $200,000. First Wave records compensation expense in the first year as follows.

Compensation Expense ($200,000 ÷ 2)	100,000	
Paid-in Capital—Stock Options		100,000

In addition, if we assume that First Wave has a 35 percent tax rate, it would recognize a deferred tax asset of $35,000 ($100,000 × 35%) in the first year as follows.

Deferred Tax Asset	35,000	
Income Tax Expense		35,000

Therefore, on the statement of cash flows for the first year, First Wave reports the following (assuming a net income of $600,000).

Net income	$600,000
Adjustments to reconcile net income to net cash provided by operating activities:	
Share-based compensation expense	100,000
Increase in deferred tax asset	(35,000)

As shown in First Wave's statement of cash flows, it adds the share-based compensation expense to net income because it is a noncash expense. The increase in the deferred tax asset and the related reduction in income tax expense increase net income. Although the negative income tax expense increases net income, it does not increase cash. Therefore, it should be deducted.

Subsequently, if Ann Johnson exercises her options, Third Wave reports "Cash provided by exercise of stock options" in the financing section of the statement of cash flows.[7]

Extraordinary Items

Companies should report **either as investing activities or as financing activities** cash flows from extraordinary transactions and other events whose effects are included in net income, but which are not related to operations.

---

[7]Companies receive a tax deduction related to share-based compensation plans at the time employees exercise their options. The amount of the deduction is equal to the difference between the market price of the stock and the exercise price at the date the employee purchases the stock, which in most cases is much larger than the total compensation expense recorded. When the tax deduction exceeds the total compensation recorded, this provides an additional cash inflow to the company. For example, in a recent year Cisco Systems reported an additional cash inflow related to its stock option plans equal to $537 million. Under GAAP, this tax-related cash inflow is reported in the financing section of the statement of cash flows. [5]

For example, assume that Tax Consultants had land with a carrying value of $200,000, which was condemned by the state of Maine for a highway project. The condemnation proceeds received were $205,000, resulting in a gain of $5,000 less $2,000 of taxes. In the statement of cash flows (indirect method), the company would deduct the $5,000 gain from net income in the operating activities section. It would report the $205,000 cash inflow from the condemnation as an investing activity, as follows.

Cash flows from investing activities	
Condemnation of land	$205,000

Underlying Concepts

By rejecting the requirement to allocate taxes to the various activities the FASB invoked the cost constraint. The information would be beneficial, but the cost of providing such information would exceed the benefits of providing it.

Note that Tax Consultants handles the gain at its **gross** amount ($5,000), not net of tax. The company reports the cash received in the condemnation as an investing activity at $205,000, also exclusive of the tax effect.

The FASB requires companies to classify **all income taxes paid as operating cash outflows**. Some suggested that income taxes paid be allocated to investing and financing transactions. But the Board decided that allocation of income taxes paid to operating, investing, and financing activities would be so complex and arbitrary that the benefits, if any, would not justify the costs involved. Under both the direct method and the indirect method, companies must disclose the total amount of income taxes paid.[8]

ACCOUNTS RECEIVABLE (NET)

Up to this point, we assumed no allowance for doubtful accounts—a contra account—to offset accounts receivable. However, if a company needs an allowance for doubtful accounts, how does that allowance affect the company's determination of net cash flow from operating activities? For example, assume that Redmark Co. reports net income of $40,000. It has the accounts receivable balances as shown in Illustration 23-28.

ILLUSTRATION 23-28
Accounts Receivable
Balances, Redmark Co.

	2012	2011	Change Increase/Decrease
Accounts receivable	$105,000	$90,000	$15,000 Increase
Allowance for doubtful accounts	(10,000)	(4,000)	6,000 Increase
Accounts receivable (net)	$ 95,000	$86,000	9,000 Increase

Indirect Method

Because an increase in Allowance for Doubtful Accounts results from a charge to bad debt expense, a company should add back an increase in Allowance for Doubtful Accounts to net income to arrive at net cash flow from operating activities. Illustration 23-29 shows one method for presenting this information in a statement of cash flows.

[8]For an insightful article on some weaknesses and limitations in the statement of cash flows, see Hugo Nurnberg, "Inconsistencies and Ambiguities in Cash Flow Statements Under *FASB Statement No. 95*," *Accounting Horizons* (June 1993), pp. 60–73. Nurnberg identifies the inconsistencies caused by the three-way classification of all cash receipts and cash payments, gross versus net of tax, the ambiguous disclosure requirements for noncash investing and financing transactions and the ambiguous presentation of third-party financing transactions. See also Paul B. W. Miller and Bruce P. Budge, "Nonarticulation in Cash Flow Statements and Implications for Education, Research, and Practice," *Accounting Horizons* (December 1996), pp. 1–15; and Charles Mulford and Michael Ely, "Calculating Sustainable Cash Flow: A Study of the S&P 100," *Georgia Tech Financial Analysis Lab* (October 2004).

REDMARK CO.
STATEMENT OF CASH FLOWS (PARTIAL)
FOR THE YEAR 2012

Cash flows from operating activities		
Net income		$40,000
Adjustments to reconcile net income to net		
cash provided by operating activities:		
Increase in accounts receivable	$(15,000)	
Increase in allowance for doubtful accounts	6,000	(9,000)
		$31,000

As we indicated, the increase in the Allowance for Doubtful Accounts balance results from a charge to bad debt expense for the year. Because bad debt expense is a noncash charge, a company must add it back to net income in arriving at net cash flow from operating activities.

Instead of separately analyzing the allowance account, a short-cut approach is to net the allowance balance against the receivable balance and compare the change in accounts receivable on a net basis. Illustration 23-30 shows this presentation.

REDMARK CO.
STATEMENT OF CASH FLOWS (PARTIAL)
FOR THE YEAR 2012

Cash flows from operating activities	
Net income	$40,000
Adjustments to reconcile net income to	
net cash provided by operating activities:	
Increase in accounts receivable (net)	(9,000)
	$31,000

This short-cut procedure works also if the change in the allowance account results from a write-off of accounts receivable. This reduces both Accounts Receivable and Allowance for Doubtful Accounts. No effect on cash flows occurs. *Because of its simplicity, use the net approach for your homework assignments.*

Direct Method

If using the direct method, a company **should not net** Allowance for Doubtful Accounts against Accounts Receivable. To illustrate, assume that Redmark Co.'s net income of $40,000 consisted of the items shown in Illustration 23-31.

ILLUSTRATION 23-31
Income Statement,
Redmark Co.

REDMARK CO.
INCOME STATEMENT
FOR THE YEAR 2012

Sales		$100,000
Expenses		
Salaries	$46,000	
Utilities	8,000	
Bad debts	6,000	60,000
Net income		$ 40,000

If Redmark deducts the $9,000 increase in accounts receivable (net) from sales for the year, it would report cash sales at $91,000 ($100,000 − $9,000) and cash payments for operating expenses at $60,000. Both items would be misstated: Cash sales should be reported at $85,000 ($100,000 − $15,000), and total cash payments for operating expenses should be reported at $54,000 ($60,000 − $6,000). Illustration 23-32 shows the proper presentation.

ILLUSTRATION 23-32
Bad Debts—Direct Method

REDMARK CO. STATEMENT OF CASH FLOWS (PARTIAL) FOR THE YEAR 2012		
Cash flows from operating activities		
Cash received from customers		$85,000
Salaries paid	$46,000	
Utilities paid	8,000	54,000
Net cash provided by operating activities		$31,000

An added complication develops when a company writes off accounts receivable. Simply adjusting sales for the change in accounts receivable will not provide the proper amount of cash sales. The reason is that the write-off of the accounts receivable is not a cash collection. Thus, an additional adjustment is necessary.

OTHER WORKING CAPITAL CHANGES

Up to this point, we showed how companies handled all of the changes in working capital items (current asset and current liability items) as adjustments to net income in determining net cash flow from operating activities. You must be careful, however, because **some changes in working capital, although they affect cash, do not affect net income**. Generally, these are investing or financing activities of a current nature.

One activity is the purchase of **short-term available-for-sale securities**. For example, the purchase of short-term available-for-sale securities for $50,000 cash has no effect on net income but it does cause a $50,000 decrease in cash. A company reports this transaction as a cash flow from investing activities as follows. [6]

Cash flows from investing activities	
Purchase of short-term available-for-sale securities	$(50,000)

What about **trading securities?** Because companies hold these investments principally for the purpose of selling them in the near term, companies should classify the cash flows from purchases and sales of trading securities as cash flows from **operating activities**. [7][9]

Another example is the issuance of a **short-term nontrade note payable** for cash. This change in a working capital item has no effect on income from operations but it increases cash by the amount of the note payable. For example, a company reports the

---

[9]If the basis of the statement of cash flows is **cash and cash equivalents** and the short-term investment is considered a cash equivalent, then a company reports nothing in the statement because the transaction does not affect the balance of cash and cash equivalents. The Board notes that cash purchases of short-term investments generally are part of the company's cash management activities rather than part of its operating, investing, or financing activities.

issuance of a $10,000 short-term note payable for cash in the statement of cash flows as follows.

Cash flows from financing activities	
Issuance of short-term note	$10,000

Another change in a working capital item that has no effect on income from operations or on cash is a **cash dividend payable**. Although a company will report the cash dividends when paid as a financing activity, it does not report the declared but unpaid dividend on the statement of cash flows.

NET LOSSES

If a company reports a net loss instead of a net income, it must adjust the net loss for those items that do not result in a cash inflow or outflow. The net loss, after adjusting for the charges or credits not affecting cash, may result in a negative or a positive cash flow from operating activities.

For example, if the net loss is $50,000 and the total amount of charges to add back is $60,000, then net cash provided by operating activities is $10,000. Illustration 23-33 shows this computation.

Net loss		$(50,000)
Adjustments to reconcile net income to net cash provided by operating activities:		
Depreciation of plant assets	$55,000	
Amortization of patents	5,000	60,000
Net cash provided by operating activities		$ 10,000

ILLUSTRATION 23-33
Computation of Net Cash Flow from Operating Activities—Cash Inflow

If the company experiences a net loss of $80,000 and the total amount of the charges to add back is $25,000, the presentation appears as follows.

Net loss	$(80,000)
Adjustments to reconcile net income to net cash used by operating activities:	
Depreciation of plant assets	25,000
Net cash used by operating activities	$(55,000)

ILLUSTRATION 23-34
Computation of Net Cash Flow from Operating Activities—Cash Outflow

Although not illustrated in this chapter, a negative cash flow may result even if the company reports a net income.

SIGNIFICANT NONCASH TRANSACTIONS

Because the statement of cash flows reports only the effects of operating, investing, and financing activities in terms of cash flows, it omits some significant noncash transactions and other events that are investing or financing activities. Among the more common of these noncash transactions that a company should report or disclose in some manner are the following.

1. Acquisition of assets by assuming liabilities (including capital lease obligations) or by issuing equity securities.
2. Exchanges of nonmonetary assets.
3. Refinancing of long-term debt.
4. Conversion of debt or preferred stock to common stock.
5. Issuance of equity securities to retire debt.

A company does not incorporate these noncash items in the statement of cash flows. If material in amount, these disclosures may be either narrative or summarized in a separate schedule at the bottom of the statement, or they may appear in a separate note or supplementary schedule to the financial statements.[10] Illustration 23-35 shows the presentation of these significant noncash transactions or other events in a separate schedule at the bottom of the statement of cash flows.

ILLUSTRATION 23-35
Schedule Presentation of Noncash Investing and Financing Activities

Net increase in cash	$3,717,000
Cash at beginning of year	5,208,000
Cash at end of year	$8,925,000
Noncash investing and financing activities	
Purchase of land and building through issuance of 250,000 shares of common stock	$1,750,000
Exchange of Steadfast, NY, land for Bedford, PA, land	$2,000,000
Conversion of 12% bonds to 50,000 shares of common stock	$500,000

Or, companies may present these noncash transactions in a separate note, as shown in Illustration 23-36.

ILLUSTRATION 23-36
Note Presentation of Noncash Investing and Financing Activities

Note G: Significant noncash transactions. During the year, the company engaged in the following significant noncash investing and financing transactions:	
Issued 250,000 shares of common stock to purchase land and building	$1,750,000
Exchanged land in Steadfast, NY, for land in Bedford, PA	$2,000,000
Converted 12% bonds to 50,000 shares of common stock	$500,000

Companies do not generally report certain other significant noncash transactions or other events in conjunction with the statement of cash flows. Examples of these types of transactions are **stock dividends, stock splits, and restrictions on retained earnings**. Companies generally report these items, neither financing nor investing activities, in conjunction with the statement of stockholders' equity or schedules and notes pertaining to changes in capital accounts.

---

[10]Some noncash investing and financing activities are part cash and part noncash. Companies should report only the cash portion on the statement of cash flows. The noncash component should be reported at the bottom of the statement or in a separate note.

CASH FLOW TOOL

By understanding the relationship between cash flow and income measures, analysts can gain better insights into company performance. Because earnings altered through creative accounting practices generally do not change operating cash flows, analysts can use the relationship between earnings and operating cash flow to detect suspicious accounting practices. Also, by monitoring the ratio between cash flow from operations and operating income, they can get a clearer picture of developing problems in a company.

For example, the chart below plots the ratio of operating cash flows to earnings for Xerox Corp. in the years leading up to the SEC singling it out in 2000 for aggressive revenue recognition practices on its leases.

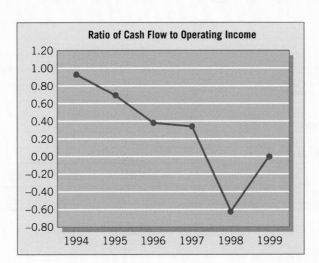

Ratio of Cash Flow to Operating Income

Similar to W. T. Grant in the chapter opening story, Xerox was reporting earnings growth in the years leading up to its financial breakdown in 2000 but teetering near bankruptcy in 2001. However, Xerox's ratio of cash flow to earnings showed a declining trend and became negative well before its revenue recognition practices were revealed. The trend revealed in the graph should have given any analyst reason to investigate Xerox further. As one analyst noted, "Earnings growth that exceeds the growth in operating cash flow cannot continue for extended periods and should be investigated."

Source: Adapted from Charles Mulford and Eugene Comiskey, *The Financial Numbers Game: Detecting Creative Accounting Practices* (New York: John Wiley & Sons, 2002), Chapter 11, by permission.

SECTION 3 • USE OF A WORKSHEET

When numerous adjustments are necessary or other complicating factors are present, companies often use **a worksheet to assemble and classify the data that will appear on the statement of cash flows**. The worksheet (a **spreadsheet** when using computer software) is merely a device that aids in the preparation of the statement. Its use is optional. Illustration 23-37 (page 1468) shows the skeleton format of the worksheet for preparation of the statement of cash flows using the indirect method.

9 LEARNING OBJECTIVE
Explain the use of a worksheet in preparing a statement of cash flows.

	XYZ COMPANY Statement of Cash Flows for the Year Ended...				
	A	**B**	**C**	**D**	**E**
		End of Prior Year Balances	Reconciling Items		End of Current Year Balances
1	Balance Sheet Accounts		Debits	Credits	
2	Debit balance accounts	XX	XX	XX	XX
3		XX	XX	XX	XX
4	Totals	XXX			XXX
5	Credit balance accounts	XX	XX	XX	XX
6		XX	XX	XX	XX
7	Totals	XXX			XXX
8	Statement of Cash Flows Effects				
9	Operating activities				
10	Net income		XX		
11	Adjustments		XX	XX	
12	Investing activities				
13	Receipts and payments		XX	XX	
14	Financing activities				
15	Receipts and payments		XX	XX	
16	Totals		XXX	XXX	
17	Increase (decrease) in cash		(XX)	XX	
18	Totals		XXX	XXX	

Sheet1 / Sheet2 / Sheet3

ILLUSTRATION 23-37
Format of Worksheet for
Preparation of Statement
of Cash Flows

The following guidelines are important in using a worksheet.

1. In the balance sheet accounts section, **list accounts with debit balances separately from those with credit balances**. This means, for example, that Accumulated Depreciation is listed under credit balances and not as a contra account under debit balances. Enter the beginning and ending balances of each account in the appropriate columns. Then, enter the transactions that caused the change in the account balance during the year as reconciling items in the two middle columns.

After all reconciling items have been entered, each line pertaining to a balance sheet account should foot across. That is, the beginning balance plus or minus the reconciling item(s) must equal the ending balance. When this agreement exists for all balance sheet accounts, all changes in account balances have been reconciled.

2. The bottom portion of the worksheet consists of the operating, investing, and financing activities sections. Accordingly, it provides the information necessary to prepare the formal statement of cash flows. **Enter inflows of cash as debits in the reconciling columns, and outflows of cash as credits in the reconciling columns.** Thus, in this section, a company would enter the sale of equipment for cash at book value as a debit under inflows of cash from investing activities. Similarly, it would enter the purchase of land for cash as a credit under outflows of cash from investing activities.

3. **Do not enter in any journal or post to any account the reconciling items shown in the worksheet.** These items do not represent either adjustments or corrections of the balance sheet accounts. They are used only to facilitate the preparation of the statement of cash flows.

PREPARATION OF THE WORKSHEET

The preparation of a worksheet involves the following steps.

Step 1. Enter the balance sheet accounts and their beginning and ending balances in the balance sheet accounts section.

Step 2. Enter the data that explain the changes in the balance sheet accounts (other than cash) and their effects on the statement of cash flows in the reconciling columns of the worksheet.

Step 3. Enter the increase or decrease in cash on the cash line and at the bottom of the worksheet. This entry should enable the totals of the reconciling columns to be in agreement.

To illustrate the preparation and use of a worksheet and to illustrate the reporting of some of the special problems discussed in the prior section, we present a comprehensive example for Satellite Corporation. Again, the indirect method serves as the basis for the computation of net cash provided by operating activities. Illustrations 23-38 and 23-39 present the balance sheet, combined statement of income and retained earnings, and additional information for Satellite Corporation.

ILLUSTRATION 23-38
Comparative Balance Sheet, Satellite Corporation

	SATELLITE CORPORATION Comparative Balance Sheet—December 31, 2012 and 2011			
	A	**B**	**C**	**D**
1	Assets	2012	2011	Increase or (Decrease)
2	Cash	$ 59,000	$ 66,000	$ (7,000)
3	Accounts receivable (net)	104,000	51,000	53,000
4	Inventory	493,000	341,000	152,000
5	Prepaid expenses	16,500	17,000	(500)
6	Investment in Porter Co. (equity method)	18,500	15,000	3,500
7	Land	131,500	82,000	49,500
8	Equipment	187,000	142,000	45,000
9	Accumulated depreciation—equipment	(29,000)	(31,000)	(2,000)
10	Buildings	262,000	262,000	—
11	Accumulated depreciation—buildings	(74,100)	(71,000)	3,100
12	Trademarks	7,600	10,000	(2,400)
13	Total assets	$1,176,000	$884,000	
14	Liabilities			
15	Accounts payable	$ 132,000	$ 131,000	1,000
16	Accrued liabilities	43,000	39,000	4,000
17	Income taxes payable	3,000	16,000	(13,000)
18	Notes payable (long-term)	60,000	—	60,000
19	Bonds payable	100,000	100,000	—
20	Premium on bonds payable	7,000	8,000	(1,000)
21	Deferred tax liability (long-term)	9,000	6,000	3,000
22	Total liabilities	354,000	300,000	
23	Stockholders' Equity			
24	Common stock ($1 par)	60,000	50,000	10,000
25	Paid-in capital in excess of par—common stock	187,000	38,000	149,000
26	Retained earnings	592,000	496,000	96,000
27	Treasury stock	(17,000)	—	17,000
28	Total stockholders' equity	822,000	584,000	
29	Total liabilities and stockholders' equity	$1,176,000	$884,000	

Sheet1 / Sheet2 / Sheet3

ILLUSTRATION 23-39
Income and Retained
Earnings Statements,
Satellite Corporation

SATELLITE CORPORATION
COMBINED STATEMENT OF INCOME AND RETAINED EARNINGS
FOR THE YEAR ENDED DECEMBER 31, 2012

Net sales		$526,500
Other revenue		3,500
Total revenues		530,000
Expense		
Cost of goods sold		310,000
Selling and administrative expenses		47,000
Other expenses and losses		12,000
Total expenses		369,000
Income before income tax and extraordinary item		161,000
Income tax		
Current	$47,000	
Deferred	3,000	50,000
Income before extraordinary item		111,000
Gain on condemnation of land (net of $2,000 tax)		6,000
Net income		117,000
Retained earnings, January 1		496,000
Less:		
Cash dividends	6,000	
Stock dividend	15,000	21,000
Retained earnings, December 31		$592,000
Per share:		
Income before extraordinary item		$2.02
Extraordinary item		.11
Net income		$2.13

Additional Information

(a) Other income of $3,500 represents Satellite's equity share in the net income of Porter Co., an equity investee. Satellite owns 22% of Porter Co.

(b) An analysis of the equipment account and related accumulated depreciation indicates the following:

	Equipment Dr./(Cr.)	Accum. Dep. Dr./(Cr.)	Gain or (Loss)
Balance at end of 2011	$142,000	$(31,000)	
Purchases of equipment	53,000		
Sale of equipment	(8,000)	2,500	$(1,500)
Depreciation for the period		(11,500)	
Major repair charged to accumulated depreciation		11,000	
Balance at end of 2012	$187,000	$(29,000)	

(c) Land in the amount of $60,000 was purchased through the issuance of a long-term note; in addition, certain parcels of land costing $10,500 were condemned. The state government paid Satellite $18,500, resulting in an $8,000 gain which has a $2,000 tax effect.

(d) The change in the Accumulated Depreciation—Buildings, Trademarks, and Premium on Bonds Payable accounts resulted from depreciation and amortization entries.

(e) An analysis of the paid-in capital accounts in stockholders' equity discloses the following.

	Common Stock	Paid-In Capital in Excess of Par—Common Stock
Balance at end of 2011	$50,000	$ 38,000
Issuance of 2% stock dividend	1,000	14,000
Sale of stock for cash	9,000	135,000
Balance at end of 2012	$60,000	$187,000

(f) Interest paid (net of amount capitalized) is $9,000; income taxes paid is $62,000.

The discussion that follows provides additional explanations related to the preparation of the worksheet.

ANALYSIS OF TRANSACTIONS

The following discussion explains the individual adjustments that appear on the worksheet in Illustration 23-40 (page 1475). Because cash is the basis for the analysis, Satellite reconciles the cash account last. Because income is the first item that appears on the statement of cash flows, it is handled first.

Change in Retained Earnings

Net income for the period is $117,000. The entry for it on the worksheet is as follows.

(1)

Operating—Net Income	117,000	
Retained Earnings		117,000

Satellite reports net income on the bottom section of the worksheet. This **is the starting point for preparation of the statement of cash flows (under the indirect method)**.

A stock dividend and a cash dividend also affected retained earnings. The retained earnings statement reports a stock dividend of $15,000. The worksheet entry for this transaction is as follows.

(2)

Retained Earnings	15,000	
Common Stock		1,000
Paid-in Capital in Excess of Par—Common Stock		14,000

The issuance of stock dividends is not a cash operating, investing, or financing item. Therefore, **although the company enters this transaction on the worksheet for reconciling purposes, it does not report it in the statement of cash flows**.

The $6,000 cash dividend paid represents a financing activity cash outflow. Satellite makes the following worksheet entry:

(3)

Retained Earnings	6,000	
Financing—Cash Dividends		6,000

The company reconciles the beginning and ending balances of retained earnings by entry of the three items above.

Accounts Receivable (Net)

The increase in accounts receivable (net) of $53,000 represents adjustments that did not result in cash inflows during 2012. As a result, the company would deduct from net income the increase of $53,000. Satellite makes the following worksheet entry.

(4)

Accounts Receivable (net)	53,000	
Operating—Increase in Accounts Receivable (net)		53,000

Inventory

The increase in inventory of $152,000 represents an operating use of cash. The incremental investment in inventory during the year reduces cash without increasing the cost of goods sold. Satellite makes the following worksheet entry.

(5)

Inventory	152,000	
Operating—Increase in Inventory		152,000

Prepaid Expense

The decrease in prepaid expenses of $500 represents a charge in the income statement for which there was no cash outflow in the current period. Satellite should add that amount back to net income through the following entry.

(6)

Operating—Decrease in Prepaid Expenses	500	
Prepaid Expenses		500

Investment in Stock

Satellite's investment in the stock of Porter Co. increased $3,500. This amount reflects Satellite's share of net income earned by Porter (its equity investee) during the current year. Although Satellite's revenue, and therefore its net income increased $3,500 by recording Satellite's share of Porter Co.'s net income, no cash (dividend) was provided. Satellite makes the following worksheet entry.

(7)

Equity Investments (Porter Co.)	3,500	
Operating—Equity in Earnings of Porter Co.		3,500

Land

Satellite purchased land in the amount of $60,000 through the issuance of a long-term note payable. This transaction did not affect cash. It is a significant noncash investing/financing transaction that the company would disclose either in a separate schedule below the statement of cash flows or in the accompanying notes. Satellite makes the following entry to reconcile the worksheet.

(8)

Land	60,000	
Notes Payable		60,000

In addition to the noncash transaction involving the issuance of a note to purchase land, the Land account was decreased by the condemnation proceedings. The following worksheet entry records the receipt of $18,500 for land having a book value of $10,500.

(9)

Investing—Proceeds from Condemnation of Land	18,500	
Land		10,500
Operating—Gain on Condemnation of Land		8,000

In reconciling net income to net cash flow from operating activities, Satellite deducts from net income the extraordinary gain of $8,000. The reason is that the transaction that gave rise to the gain is an item whose cash effect is already classified as an investing cash inflow. The Land account is now reconciled.

Equipment and Accumulated Depreciation

An analysis of Equipment and Accumulated Depreciation—Equipment shows that a number of transactions have affected these accounts. The company purchased equipment in the amount of $53,000 during the year. Satellite records this transaction on the worksheet as follows.

(10)

Equipment	53,000	
Investing—Purchase of Equipment		53,000

In addition, Satellite sold at a loss of $1,500 equipment with a book value of $5,500. It records this transaction as follows.

(11)

Investing—Sale of Equipment	4,000	
Operating—Loss on Sale of Equipment	1,500	
Accumulated Depreciation—Equipment	2,500	
Equipment		8,000

The proceeds from the sale of the equipment provided cash of $4,000. In addition, the loss on the sale of the equipment has reduced net income but did not affect cash. Therefore, the company adds back to net income the amount of the loss, in order to accurately report cash provided by operating activities.

Satellite reported depreciation on the equipment at $11,500 and recorded it on the worksheet as follows.

(12)

Operating—Depreciation Expense—Equipment	11,500	
Accumulated Depreciation—Equipment		11,500

The company adds depreciation expense back to net income because that expense reduced income but did not affect cash.

Finally, the company made a major repair to the equipment. It charged this expenditure, in the amount of $11,000, to Accumulated Depreciation—Equipment. This expenditure required cash, and so Satellite makes the following worksheet entry.

(13)

Accumulated Depreciation—Equipment	11,000	
Investing—Major Repairs of Equipment		11,000

After adjusting for the foregoing items, Satellite has reconciled the balances in the Equipment and related Accumulated Depreciation—Equipment accounts.

Building Depreciation and Amortization of Trademarks

Depreciation expense on the buildings of $3,100 and amortization of trademarks of $2,400 are both expenses in the income statement that reduced net income but did not require cash outflows in the current period. Satellite makes the following worksheet entry.

(14)

Operating—Depreciation Expense—Buildings	3,100	
Operating—Amortization of Trademarks	2,400	
Accumulated Depreciation—Buildings		3,100
Trademarks		2,400

Other Noncash Charges or Credits

Analysis of the remaining accounts indicates that changes in the Accounts Payable, Accrued Liabilities, Income Taxes Payable, Premium on Bonds Payable, and Deferred Tax Liability balances resulted from charges or credits to net income that did not affect cash. The company should individually analyze each of these items and enter them in the worksheet. The following compound entry summarizes these noncash, income-related items.

(15)

Income Taxes Payable	13,000	
Premium on Bonds Payable	1,000	
Operating—Increase in Accounts Payable	1,000	
Operating—Increase in Accrued Liabilities	4,000	
Operating—Increase in Deferred Tax Liability	3,000	
Operating—Decrease in Income Taxes Payable		13,000
Operating—Amortization of Bond Premium		1,000
Accounts Payable		1,000
Accrued Liabilities		4,000
Deferred Tax Liability		3,000

Common Stock and Related Accounts

Comparison of the Common Stock balances and the Paid-in Capital in Excess of Par—Common Stock balances shows that transactions during the year affected these accounts. First, Satellite issues a stock dividend of 2 percent to stockholders. As the discussion of worksheet entry (2) indicated, no cash was provided or used by the stock dividend transaction. In addition to the shares issued via the stock dividend, Satellite sold shares of common stock at $16 per share. The company records this transaction as follows.

(16)

Financing—Sale of Common Stock	144,000	
Common Stock		9,000
Paid-in Capital in Excess of Par—Common Stock		135,000

Also, the company purchased shares of its common stock in the amount of $17,000. It records this transaction on the worksheet as follows.

(17)

Treasury Stock	17,000	
Financing—Purchase of Treasury Stock		17,000

Final Reconciling Entry

The final entry to reconcile the change in cash and to balance the worksheet is shown below. The $7,000 amount is the difference between the beginning and ending cash balance.

(18)

Decrease in Cash	7,000	
Cash		7,000

Once the company has determined that the differences between the beginning and ending balances per the worksheet columns have been accounted for, it can total the reconciling transactions columns, and they should balance. Satellite can prepare the statement of cash flows entirely from the items and amounts that appear at the bottom of the worksheet under "Statement of Cash Flows Effects," as shown in Illustration 23-40.

SATELLITE CORPORATION
Worksheet for Preparation of Statement of Cash Flows for the Year Ended December 31, 2012

	A	B	C	D	E	F	G
1		Balance 12/31/11	Reconciling Items–2012				Balance 12/31/12
1				Debits		Credits	
2	Debits						
3	Cash	$ 66,000			(18)	7,000	$ 59,000
4	Accounts receivable (net)	51,000	(4)	$ 53,000			104,000
5	Inventory	341,000	(5)	152,000			493,000
6	Prepaid expenses	17,000			(6)	500	16,500
7	Investment in Porter Co. (equity method)	15,000	(7)	3,500			18,500
8	Land	82,000	(8)	60,000	(9)	10,500	131,500
9	Equipment	142,000	(10)	53,000	(11)	8,000	187,000
10	Buildings	262,000					262,000
11	Trademarks	10,000			(14)	2,400	7,600
12	Treasury stock		(17)	17,000			17,000
13	Total debits	$986,000					$1,296,100
14	Credits						
15	Accum. depr.–equipment	$ 31,000	(11)	2,500	(12)	11,500	
16			(13)	11,000			$ 29,000
17	Accum. depr.–buildings	71,000			(14)	3,100	74,100
18	Accounts payable	131,000			(15)	1,000	132,000
19	Accrued liabilities	39,000			(15)	4,000	43,000
20	Income taxes payable	16,000	(15)	13,000			3,000
21	Notes payable	-0-			(8)	60,000	60,000
22	Bonds payable	100,000					100,000
23	Premium on bonds payable	8,000	(15)	1,000			7,000
24	Deferred tax liability	6,000			(15)	3,000	9,000
25	Common stock	50,000			(2)	1,000	
26					(16)	9,000	60,000
27	Paid-in capital in excess of	38,000			(2)	14,000	
28	par—common stock				(16)	135,000	187,000
29	Retained earnings	496,000	(2)	15,000	(1)	117,000	
30			(3)	6,000			592,000
31	Total credits	$986,000					$1,296,100
32	Statement of Cash Flows Effects						
33	Operating activities						
34	Net income		(1)	117,000			
35	Increase in accounts receivable (net)				(4)	53,000	
36	Increase in inventory				(5)	152,000	
37	Decrease in prepaid expenses		(6)	500			
38	Equity in earnings of Porter Co.				(7)	3,500	
39	Gain on condemnation of land				(9)	8,000	
40	Loss on sale of equipment		(11)	1,500			
41	Depr. expense–equipment		(12)	11,500			
42	Depr. expense–buildings		(14)	3,100			
43	Amortization of trademarks		(14)	2,400			
44	Increase in accounts payable		(15)	1,000			
45	Increase in accrued liabilities		(15)	4,000			
46	Increase in deferred tax liability		(15)	3,000			
47	Decrease in income taxes payable				(15)	13,000	
48	Amortization of bond premium				(15)	1,000	
49	Investing activities						
50	Proceeds from condemnation of land		(9)	18,500			
51	Purchase of equipment				(10)	53,000	
52	Sale of equipment		(11)	4,000			
53	Major repairs of equipment				(13)	11,000	
54	Financing activities						
55	Payment of cash dividend				(3)	6,000	
56	Issuance of common stock		(16)	144,000			
57	Purchase of treasury stock				(17)	17,000	
58	Totals			697,500		704,500	
59	Decrease in cash		(18)	7,000			
60	Totals			$704,500		$704,500	

Sheet1 / Sheet2 / Sheet3

ILLUSTRATION 23-40
Completed Worksheet for Preparation of Statement of Cash Flows, Satellite Corporation

PREPARATION OF FINAL STATEMENT

Illustration 23-41 presents a formal statement of cash flows prepared from the data compiled in the lower portion of the worksheet.

ILLUSTRATION 23-41
Statement of Cash Flows, Satellite Corporation

Gateway to the Profession

Discussion of the T-Account Approach to Preparation of the Statement of Cash Flows

---

SATELLITE CORPORATION
STATEMENT OF CASH FLOWS
FOR THE YEAR ENDED DECEMBER 31, 2012
INCREASE (DECREASE) IN CASH

Cash flows from operating activities		
Net income		$117,000
Adjustments to reconcile net income to net cash used by operating activities:		
Depreciation expense	$ 14,600	
Amortization of trademarks	2,400	
Amortization of bond premium	(1,000)	
Equity in earnings of Porter Co.	(3,500)	
Gain on condemnation of land	(8,000)	
Loss on sale of equipment	1,500	
Increase in deferred tax liability	3,000	
Increase in accounts receivable (net)	(53,000)	
Increase in inventory	(152,000)	
Decrease in prepaid expenses	500	
Increase in accounts payable	1,000	
Increase in accrued liabilities	4,000	
Decrease in income taxes payable	(13,000)	(203,500)
Net cash used by operating activities		(86,500)
Cash flows from investing activities		
Proceeds from condemnation of land	18,500	
Purchase of equipment	(53,000)	
Sale of equipment	4,000	
Major repairs of equipment	(11,000)	
Net cash used by investing activities		(41,500)
Cash flows from financing activities		
Payment of cash dividend	(6,000)	
Issuance of common stock	144,000	
Purchase of treasury stock	(17,000)	
Net cash provided by financing activities		121,000
Net decrease in cash		(7,000)
Cash, January 1, 2012		66,000
Cash, December 31, 2012		$ 59,000

Supplemental Disclosures of Cash Flow Information:
Cash paid during the year for:		
Interest (net of amount capitalized)		$ 9,000
Income taxes		$ 62,000

Supplemental Schedule of Noncash Investing and Financing Activities:
Purchase of land for $60,000 in exchange for a $60,000 long-term note.

You will want to read
IFRS INSIGHTS
on pages 1505–1510

for discussion of IFRS related to the statement of cash flows.

SUMMARY OF LEARNING OBJECTIVES

1 **Describe the purpose of the statement of cash flows.** The primary purpose of the statement of cash flows is to provide information about cash receipts and cash payments of an entity during a period. A secondary objective is to report the entity's operating, investing, and financing activities during the period.

2 **Identify the major classifications of cash flows.** Companies classify cash flows as follows: (1) *Operating activities*—transactions that result in the revenues, expenses, gains, and losses that determine net income. (2) *Investing activities*—lending money and collecting on those loans, and acquiring and disposing of investments, plant assets, and intangible assets. (3) *Financing activities*—obtaining cash from creditors and repaying loans, issuing and reacquiring capital stock, and paying cash dividends.

3 **Differentiate between net income and net cash flow from operating activities.** Companies must adjust net income on an accrual basis to determine net cash flow from operating activities because some expenses and losses do not cause cash outflows, and some revenues and gains do not provide cash inflows.

4 **Contrast the direct and indirect methods of calculating net cash flow from operating activities.** Under the direct approach, companies calculate the major classes of operating cash receipts and cash disbursements. Companies summarize the computations in a schedule of changes from the accrual to the cash basis income statement. Presentation of the direct approach of reporting net cash flow from operating activities takes the form of a condensed cash-basis income statement. The indirect method adds back to net income the noncash expenses and losses and subtracts the noncash revenues and gains.

5 **Determine net cash flows from investing and financing activities.** Once a company has computed the net cash flow from operating activities, the next step is to determine whether any other changes in balance sheet accounts caused an increase or decrease in cash. Net cash flows from investing and financing activities can be determined by examining the changes in noncurrent balance sheet accounts.

6 **Prepare a statement of cash flows.** Preparing the statement involves three major steps: (1) *Determine the change in cash.* This is the difference between the beginning and the ending cash balance shown on the comparative balance sheets. (2) *Determine the net cash flow from operating activities.* This procedure is complex; it involves analyzing not only the current year's income statement but also the comparative balance sheets and the selected transaction data. (3) *Determine cash flows from investing and financing activities.* Analyze all other changes in the balance sheet accounts to determine the effects on cash.

7 **Identify sources of information for a statement of cash flows.** The information to prepare the statement usually comes from three sources: (1) *Comparative balance sheets.* Information in these statements indicates the amount of the changes in assets, liabilities, and equities during the period. (2) *Current income statement.* Information in this statement is used in determining the cash provided by operations during the period. (3) *Selected transaction data.* These data from the general ledger provide additional detailed information needed to determine how cash was provided or used during the period.

8 **Discuss special problems in preparing a statement of cash flows.** These special problems are: (1) adjustments to income (depreciation and amortization, post retirement benefit costs, change in deferred income taxes, equity method of accounting, losses and gains, stock options, extraordinary items); (2) accounts receivable (net); (3) other working capital changes; (4) net losses; and (5) significant noncash transactions.

9 **Explain the use of a worksheet in preparing a statement of cash flows.** When numerous adjustments are necessary, or other complicating factors are present, companies often use a worksheet to assemble and classify the data that will appear on the statement of cash flows. The worksheet is merely a device that aids in the preparation of the statement. Its use is optional.

 FASB CODIFICATION

FASB Codification References

[1] FASB ASC 230-10-10-2. [Predecessor literature: "The Statement of Cash Flows," *Statement of Financial Accounting Standards No. 95* (Stamford, Conn.: FASB, 1987), paras. 4 and 5.]

[2] FASB ASC 230-10-45-18 through 21. [Predecessor literature: "Statement of Cash Flows—Exemption of Certain Enterprises and Classification of Cash Flows from Certain Securities Acquired for Resale (amended)," *Statement of Financial Accounting Standards No. 102* (February 1989).]

[3] FASB ASC 230-10-45-31. [Predecessor literature: "The Statement of Cash Flows," *Statement of Financial Accounting Standards No. 95* (Stamford, Conn.: FASB, 1987), paras. 27 and 30.]

[4] FASB ASC 230-10-45-25. [Predecessor literature: "Statement of Cash Flows," *Statement of Financial Accounting Standards No. 95* (Stamford, Conn.: FASB, 1987), paras. 107 and 111.]

[5] FASB ASC 230-10-45-14. [Predecessor literature: "Share-Based Payment," *Statement of Financial Accounting Standard No. 123(R)* (Norwalk, Conn.: FASB, 2004), par. 68.]

[6] FASB ASC 320-10-45-11. [Predecessor literature: "Accounting for Certain Investments in Debt and Equity Securities," *Statement of Financial Accounting Standards No. 115* (Norwalk, Conn.: 1993), par. 118.]

[7] FASB ASC 320-10-45-11. [Predecessor literature: "Accounting for Certain Investments in Debt and Equity Securities," *Statement of Financial Accounting Standards No. 115* (Norwalk, Conn.: 1993), par. 118.]

Exercises

If your school has a subscription to the FASB Codification, go to *http://aaahq.org/ascLogin.cfm* to log in and prepare responses to the following. Provide Codification references for your responses.

CE23-1 Access the glossary ("Master Glossary") to answer the following.

(a) What are cash equivalents?

(b) What are financing activities?

(c) What are investing activities?

(d) What are operating activities?

CE23-2 Name five cash inflows that would qualify as a "financing activity."

CE23-3 How should cash flows from purchases, sales, and maturities of available-for-sale securities be classified and reported in the statement of cash flows?

CE23-4 Do companies need to disclose information about investing and financing activities that do not affect cash receipts or cash payments? If so, how should such information be disclosed?

An additional codification case can be found in the Using Your Judgment section, on page 1504.

Be sure to check the book's companion website for a Review and Analysis Exercise, with solution.

Questions, Brief Exercises, Exercises, Problems, and many more resources are available for practice in WileyPLUS.

QUESTIONS

1. What is the purpose of the statement of cash flows? What information does it provide?

2. Of what use is the statement of cash flows?

3. Differentiate between investing activities, financing activities, and operating activities.

4. What are the major sources of cash (inflows) in a statement of cash flows? What are the major uses (outflows) of cash?

5. Identify and explain the major steps involved in preparing the statement of cash flows.

6. Identify the following items as (1) operating, (2) investing, or (3) financing activities: purchase of land; payment of dividends; cash sales; and purchase of treasury stock.

7. Unlike the other major financial statements, the statement of cash flows is not prepared from the adjusted trial balance. From what sources does the information to prepare this statement come, and what information does each source provide?

8. Why is it necessary to convert accrual-based net income to a cash basis when preparing a statement of cash flows?

9. Differentiate between the direct method and the indirect method by discussing each method.

10. Broussard Company reported net income of $3.5 million in 2012. Depreciation for the year was $520,000; accounts receivable increased $500,000; and accounts payable increased $300,000. Compute net cash flow from operating activities using the indirect method.

11. Collinsworth Co. reported sales on an accrual basis of $100,000. If accounts receivable increased $30,000, and the allowance for doubtful accounts increased $9,000 after a write-off of $2,000, compute cash sales.

12. Your roommate is puzzled. During the last year, the company in which she is a stockholder reported a net loss of $675,000, yet its cash increased $321,000 during the same period of time. Explain to your roommate how this situation could occur.

13. The board of directors of Gifford Corp. declared cash dividends of $260,000 during the current year. If dividends payable was $85,000 at the beginning of the year and $90,000 at the end of the year, how much cash was paid in dividends during the year?

14. Explain how the amount of cash payments to suppliers is computed under the direct method.

15. The net income for Letterman Company for 2012 was $320,000. During 2012, depreciation on plant assets was $124,000, amortization of patent was $40,000, and the company incurred a loss on sale of plant assets of $21,000. Compute net cash flow from operating activities.

16. Each of the following items must be considered in preparing a statement of cash flows for Blackwell Inc. for the year ended December 31, 2012. State where each item is to be shown in the statement, if at all.

(a) Plant assets that had cost $18,000 6½ years before and were being depreciated on a straight-line basis over 10 years with no estimated scrap value were sold for $4,000.

(b) During the year, 10,000 shares of common stock with a stated value of $20 a share were issued for $41 a share.

(c) Uncollectible accounts receivable in the amount of $22,000 were written off against Allowance for Doubtful Accounts.

(d) The company sustained a net loss for the year of $50,000. Depreciation amounted to $22,000, and a gain of $9,000 was realized on the sale of available-for-sale securities for $38,000 cash.

17. Classify the following items as (1) operating, (2) investing, (3) financing, or (4) significant noncash investing and financing activities, using the direct method.

(a) Cash payments to employees.

(b) Redemption of bonds payable.

(c) Sale of building at book value.

(d) Cash payments to suppliers.

(e) Exchange of equipment for furniture.

(f) Issuance of preferred stock.

(g) Cash received from customers.

(h) Purchase of treasury stock.

(i) Issuance of bonds for land.

(j) Payment of dividends.

(k) Purchase of equipment.

(l) Cash payments for operating expenses.

18. Stan Conner and Mark Stein were discussing the presentation format of the statement of cash flows of Bombeck Co.

At the bottom of Bombeck's statement of cash flows was a separate section entitled "Noncash investing and financing activities." Give three examples of significant noncash transactions that would be reported in this section.

19. During 2012, Simms Company redeemed $2,000,000 of bonds payable for $1,880,000 cash. Indicate how this transaction would be reported on a statement of cash flows, if at all.

20. What are some of the arguments in favor of using the indirect (reconciliation) method as opposed to the direct method for reporting a statement of cash flows?

21. Why is it desirable to use a worksheet when preparing a statement of cash flows? Is a worksheet required to prepare a statement of cash flows?

BRIEF EXERCISES

5 **BE23-1** Wainwright Corporation had the following activities in 2012.

1. Sale of land $180,000
2. Purchase of inventory $845,000
3. Purchase of treasury stock $72,000
4. Purchase of equipment $415,000
5. Issuance of common stock $320,000
6. Purchase of available-for-sale securities $59,000

Compute the amount Wainwright should report as net cash provided (used) by investing activities in its statement of cash flows.

5 **BE23-2** Stansfield Corporation had the following activities in 2012.

1. Payment of accounts payable $770,000
2. Issuance of common stock $250,000
3. Payment of dividends $350,000
4. Collection of note receivable $100,000
5. Issuance of bonds payable $510,000
6. Purchase of treasury stock $46,000

Compute the amount Stansfield should report as net cash provided (used) by financing activities in its 2012 statement of cash flows.

2 **BE23-3** Novak Corporation is preparing its 2012 statement of cash flows, using the indirect method. Presented below is a list of items that may affect the statement. Using the code below, indicate how each item will affect Novak's 2012 statement of cash flows.

Code Letter	Effect
A	Added to net income in the operating section
D	Deducted from net income in the operating section
R-I	Cash receipt in investing section
P-I	Cash payment in investing section
R-F	Cash receipt in financing section
P-F	Cash payment in financing section
N	Noncash investing and financing activity

Items

____ **(a)** Purchase of land and building.
____ **(b)** Decrease in accounts receivable.
____ **(c)** Issuance of stock.
____ **(d)** Depreciation expense.
____ **(e)** Sale of land at book value.
____ **(f)** Sale of land at a gain.
____ **(g)** Payment of dividends.
____ **(h)** Increase in accounts receivable.
____ **(i)** Purchase of available-for-sale investment.

____ **(j)** Increase in accounts payable.
____ **(k)** Decrease in accounts payable.
____ **(l)** Loan from bank by signing note.
____ **(m)** Purchase of equipment using a note.
____ **(n)** Increase in inventory.
____ **(o)** Issuance of bonds.
____ **(p)** Retirement of bonds payable.
____ **(q)** Sale of equipment at a loss.
____ **(r)** Purchase of treasury stock.

3 **4** **BE23-4** Bloom Corporation had the following 2012 income statement.

Sales	$200,000
Cost of goods sold	120,000
Gross profit	80,000
Operating expenses (includes depreciation of $21,000)	50,000
Net income	$ 30,000

The following accounts increased during 2012: Accounts Receivable $12,000; Inventory $11,000; Accounts Payable $13,000. Prepare the cash flows from operating activities section of Bloom's 2012 statement of cash flows using the direct method.

BE23-5 Use the information from BE23-4 for Bloom Corporation. Prepare the cash flows from operating activities section of Bloom's 2012 statement of cash flows using the indirect method.

BE23-6 At January 1, 2012, Eikenberry Inc. had accounts receivable of $72,000. At December 31, 2012, accounts receivable is $54,000. Sales for 2012 total $420,000. Compute Eikenberry's 2012 cash receipts from customers.

BE23-7 Moxley Corporation had January 1 and December 31 balances as follows.

	1/1/12	12/31/12
Inventory	$95,000	$113,000
Accounts payable	61,000	69,000

For 2012, cost of goods sold was $500,000. Compute Moxley's 2012 cash payments to suppliers.

BE23-8 In 2012, Elbert Corporation had net cash provided by operating activities of $531,000; net cash used by investing activities of $963,000; and net cash provided by financing activities of $585,000. At January 1, 2012, the cash balance was $333,000. Compute December 31, 2012, cash.

BE23-9 Loveless Corporation had the following 2012 income statement.

Revenues	$100,000
Expenses	60,000
	$ 40,000

In 2012, Loveless had the following activity in selected accounts.

Accounts Receivable					Allowance for Doubtful Accounts			
1/1/12	20,000						1,200	1/1/12
Revenues	100,000	1,000	Write-offs		Write-offs	1,000	1,840	Bad debt expense
		90,000	Collections					
12/31/12	29,000						2,040	12/31/12

Prepare Loveless's cash flows from operating activities section of the statement of cash flows using (a) the direct method and (b) the indirect method.

BE23-10 Hendrickson Corporation reported net income of $50,000 in 2012. Depreciation expense was $17,000. The following working capital accounts changed.

Accounts receivable	$11,000 increase
Available-for-sale securities	16,000 increase
Inventory	7,400 increase
Nontrade note payable	15,000 decrease
Accounts payable	12,300 increase

Compute net cash provided by operating activities.

BE23-11 In 2012, Wild Corporation reported a net loss of $70,000. Wild's only net income adjustments were depreciation expense $81,000, and increase in accounts receivable $8,100. Compute Wild's net cash provided (used) by operating activities.

BE23-12 In 2012, Leppard Inc. issued 1,000 shares of $10 par value common stock for land worth $40,000.

(a) Prepare Leppard's journal entry to record the transaction.
(b) Indicate the effect the transaction has on cash.
(c) Indicate how the transaction is reported on the statement of cash flows.

BE23-13 Indicate in general journal form how the items below would be entered in a worksheet for the preparation of the statement of cash flows.

(a) Net income is $317,000.
(b) Cash dividends declared and paid totaled $120,000.
(c) Equipment was purchased for $114,000.
(d) Equipment that originally cost $40,000 and had accumulated depreciation of $32,000 was sold for $10,000.

EXERCISES

E23-1 **(Classification of Transactions)** Springsteen Co. had the following activity in its most recent year of operations.

(a) Pension expense exceeds amount funded.	(g) Amortization of intangible assets.
(b) Redemption of bonds payable.	(h) Purchase of treasury stock.
(c) Sale of building at book value.	(i) Issuance of bonds for land.
(d) Depreciation.	(j) Payment of dividends.
(e) Exchange of equipment for furniture.	(k) Increase in interest receivable on notes receivable.
(f) Issuance of capital stock.	(l) Purchase of equipment.

Instructions

Classify the items as (1) operating—add to net income; (2) operating—deduct from net income; (3) investing; (4) financing; or (5) significant noncash investing and financing activities. Use the indirect method.

E23-2 **(Statement Presentation of Transactions—Indirect Method)** Each of the following items must be considered in preparing a statement of cash flows (indirect method) for Granderson Inc. for the year ended December 31, 2012.

(a) Plant assets that had cost $25,000 6 years before and were being depreciated on a straight-line basis over 10 years with no estimated scrap value were sold at the beginning of the year for $5,300.

(b) During the year, 10,000 shares of common stock with a stated value of $10 a share were issued for $33 a share.

(c) Uncollectible accounts receivable in the amount of $27,000 were written off against Allowance for Doubtful Accounts.

(d) The company sustained a net loss for the year of $50,000. Depreciation amounted to $22,000, and a gain of $9,000 was realized on the sale of land for $39,000 cash.

(e) A 3-month U.S. Treasury bill was purchased for $100,000. The company uses a cash and cash-equivalent basis for its cash flow statement.

(f) Patent amortization for the year was $20,000.

(g) The company exchanged common stock for a 70% interest in Plumlee Co. for $900,000.

(h) During the year, treasury stock costing $47,000 was purchased.

Instructions

State where each item is to be shown in the statement of cash flows, if at all.

E23-3 **(Preparation of Operating Activities Section—Indirect Method, Periodic Inventory)** The income statement of Rodriquez Company is shown below.

RODRIQUEZ COMPANY
INCOME STATEMENT
FOR THE YEAR ENDED DECEMBER 31, 2012

Sales		$6,900,000
Cost of goods sold		
Beginning inventory	$1,900,000	
Purchases	4,400,000	
Goods available for sale	6,300,000	
Ending inventory	1,600,000	
Cost of goods sold		4,700,000
Gross profit		2,200,000
Operating expenses		
Selling expenses	450,000	
Administrative expenses	700,000	1,150,000
Net income		$1,050,000

Additional information:

1. Accounts receivable decreased $310,000 during the year.
2. Prepaid expenses increased $170,000 during the year.
3. Accounts payable to suppliers of merchandise decreased $275,000 during the year.
4. Accrued expenses payable decreased $120,000 during the year.
5. Administrative expenses include depreciation expense of $60,000.

Instructions
Prepare the operating activities section of the statement of cash flows for the year ended December 31, 2012, for Rodriquez Company, using the indirect method.

E23-4 (Preparation of Operating Activities Section—Direct Method) Data for the Rodriquez Company are presented in E23-3.

Instructions
Prepare the operating activities section of the statement of cash flows using the direct method.

E23-5 (Preparation of Operating Activities Section—Direct Method) Norman Company's income statement for the year ended December 31, 2012, contained the following condensed information.

Service revenue		$840,000
Operating expenses (excluding depreciation)	$624,000	
Depreciation expense	60,000	
Loss on sale of equipment	26,000	710,000
Income before income taxes		130,000
Income tax expense		40,000
Net income		$ 90,000

Norman's balance sheet contained the following comparative data at December 31.

	2012	2011
Accounts receivable	$37,000	$59,000
Accounts payable	46,000	31,000
Income taxes payable	4,000	8,500

(Accounts payable pertains to operating expenses.)

Instructions
Prepare the operating activities section of the statement of cash flows using the direct method.

E23-6 (Preparation of Operating Activities Section—Indirect Method) Data for Norman Company are presented in E23-5.

Instructions
Prepare the operating activities section of the statement of cash flows using the indirect method.

E23-7 (Computation of Operating Activities—Direct Method) Presented below are two independent situations.

Situation A:
Chenowith Co. reports revenues of $200,000 and operating expenses of $110,000 in its first year of operations, 2012. Accounts receivable and accounts payable at year-end were $71,000 and $39,000, respectively. Assume that the accounts payable related to operating expenses. Ignore income taxes.

Instructions
Using the direct method, compute net cash provided (used) by operating activities.

Situation B:
The income statement for Edgebrook Company shows cost of goods sold $310,000 and operating expenses (exclusive of depreciation) $230,000. The comparative balance sheet for the year shows that inventory increased $21,000, prepaid expenses decreased $8,000, accounts payable (related to merchandise) decreased $17,000, and accrued expenses payable increased $11,000.

Instructions
Compute (a) cash payments to suppliers and (b) cash payments for operating expenses.

E23-8 (Schedule of Net Cash Flow from Operating Activities—Indirect Method) Messner Co. reported $145,000 of net income for 2012. The accountant, in preparing the statement of cash flows, noted several items occurring during 2012 that might affect cash flows from operating activities. These items are listed below and on page 1484.

1. Messner purchased 100 shares of treasury stock at a cost of $20 per share. These shares were then resold at $25 per share.
2. Messner sold 100 shares of IBM common at $200 per share. The acquisition cost of these shares was $165 per share. This investment was shown on Messner's December 31, 2011, balance sheet as an available-for-sale security.

3. Messner revised its estimate for bad debts. Before 2012, Messner's bad debt expense was 1% of its net sales. In 2012, this percentage was increased to 2%. Net sales for 2012 were $500,000, and net accounts receivable decreased by $12,000 during 2012.
4. Messner issued 500 shares of its $10 par common stock for a patent. The market price of the shares on the date of the transaction was $23 per share.
5. Depreciation expense is $39,000.
6. Messner Co. holds 30% of the Sanchez Company's common stock as a long-term investment. Sanchez Company reported $27,000 of net income for 2012.
7. Sanchez Company paid a total of $2,000 of cash dividends to all investees in 2012.
8. Messner declared a 10% stock dividend. One thousand shares of $10 par common stock were distributed. The market price at date of issuance was $20 per share.

Instructions

Prepare a schedule that shows the net cash flow from operating activities using the indirect method. Assume no items other than those listed above affected the computation of 2012 net cash flow from operating activities.

6 **E23-9 (SCF—Direct Method)** Waubansee Corp. uses the direct method to prepare its statement of cash flows. Relevant balances for Waubansee at December 31, 2012 and 2011, are as follows.

	December 31	
	2012	2011
Debits		
Cash	$ 35,000	$ 32,000
Accounts receivable	33,000	30,000
Inventory	31,000	47,000
Property, plant, & equipment	100,000	95,000
Unamortized bond discount	4,500	5,000
Cost of goods sold	250,000	380,000
Selling expenses	141,500	172,000
General and administrative expenses	137,000	151,300
Interest expense	4,300	2,600
Income tax expense	20,400	61,200
	$756,700	$976,100
Credits		
Allowance for doubtful accounts	$ 1,300	$ 1,100
Accumulated depreciation	16,500	13,500
Trade accounts payable	25,000	17,000
Income taxes payable	21,000	29,100
Deferred income taxes	5,300	4,600
8% callable bonds payable	45,000	20,000
Common stock	50,000	40,000
Paid-in capital in excess of par—common stock	9,100	7,500
Retained earnings	44,700	64,600
Sales revenue	538,800	778,700
	$756,700	$976,100

Additional information:

1. Waubansee purchased $5,000 in equipment during 2012.
2. Waubansee allocated one-third of its depreciation expense to selling expenses and the remainder to general and administrative expenses.
3. Bad debt expense for 2012 was $5,000, and write-offs of uncollectible accounts totaled $3,800.

Instructions

Determine what amounts Waubansee should report in its statement of cash flows for the year ended December 31, 2012, for the following items.

(a) Cash collected from customers.
(b) Cash paid to suppliers.
(c) Cash paid for interest.
(d) Cash paid for income taxes.
(e) Cash paid for selling expenses.

2 **8** **E23-10 (Classification of Transactions)** Following are selected balance sheet accounts of Sander Bros. Corp. at December 31, 2012 and 2011, and the increases or decreases in each account from 2011 to 2012. Also presented is selected income statement information for the year ended December 31, 2012, and additional information.

Selected balance sheet accounts	2012	2011	Increase (Decrease)
Assets			
Accounts receivable	$ 34,000	$ 24,000	$ 10,000
Property, plant, and equipment	277,000	247,000	30,000
Accumulated depreciation	(178,000)	(167,000)	(11,000)

	2012	2011	Increase
Liabilities and stockholders' equity			
Bonds payable	$ 49,000	$46,000	$ 3,000
Dividends payable	8,000	5,000	3,000
Common stock, $1 par	22,000	19,000	3,000
Paid-in capital in excess of par—common stock	9,000	3,000	6,000
Retained earnings	104,000	91,000	13,000

Selected income statement information for the year ended December 31, 2012

Sales revenue	$155,000
Depreciation	38,000
Gain on sale of equipment	14,500
Net income	31,000

Additional information:

1. During 2012, equipment costing $45,000 was sold for cash.
2. Accounts receivable relate to sales of merchandise.
3. During 2012, $25,000 of bonds payable were issued in exchange for property, plant, and equipment. There was no amortization of bond discount or premium.

Instructions
Determine the category (operating, investing, or financing) and the amount that should be reported in the statement of cash flows for the following items.

(a) Payments for purchase of property, plant, and equipment.
(b) Proceeds from the sale of equipment.
(c) Cash dividends paid.
(d) Redemption of bonds payable.

E23-11 (SCF—Indirect Method) Condensed financial data of Fairchild Company for 2012 and 2011 are presented below and on page 1486.

FAIRCHILD COMPANY
COMPARATIVE BALANCE SHEET
AS OF DECEMBER 31, 2012 AND 2011

	2012	2011
Cash	$1,800	$1,100
Receivables	1,750	1,300
Inventory	1,600	1,900
Plant assets	1,900	1,700
Accumulated depreciation	(1,200)	(1,170)
Long-term investments (held-to-maturity)	1,300	1,470
	$7,150	$6,300
Accounts payable	$1,200	$ 800
Accrued liabilities	200	250
Bonds payable	1,400	1,650
Common stock	1,900	1,700
Retained earnings	2,450	1,900
	$7,150	$6,300

FAIRCHILD COMPANY
INCOME STATEMENT
FOR THE YEAR ENDED DECEMBER 31, 2012

Sales	$6,900	
Cost of goods sold	4,700	
Gross margin	2,200	
Selling and administrative expenses	930	
Income from operations	1,270	
Other revenues and gains		
Gain on sale of investments	80	
Income before tax	1,350	
Income tax expense	540	
Net income	$ 810	

Additional information:

During the year, $70 of common stock was issued in exchange for plant assets. No plant assets were sold in 2012. Cash dividends were $260.

Instructions
Prepare a statement of cash flows using the indirect method.

6 **E23-12 (SCF—Direct Method)** Data for Fairchild Company are presented in E23-11.

Instructions
Prepare a statement of cash flows using the direct method. (Do not prepare a reconciliation schedule.)

6 **E23-13 (SCF—Direct Method)** Andrews Inc., a greeting card company, had the following statements prepared as of December 31, 2012.

ANDREWS INC.
COMPARATIVE BALANCE SHEET
AS OF DECEMBER 31, 2012 AND 2011

	12/31/12	12/31/11
Cash	$ 6,000	$ 9,000
Accounts receivable	62,000	49,000
Short-term investments (available-for-sale)	35,000	18,000
Inventory	40,000	60,000
Prepaid rent	5,000	4,000
Equipment	154,000	130,000
Accumulated depr.—equipment	(35,000)	(25,000)
Copyrights	46,000	50,000
Total assets	$313,000	$295,000
Accounts payable	$ 46,000	$ 42,000
Income taxes payable	4,000	6,000
Salaries and wages payable	8,000	4,000
Short-term loans payable	8,000	10,000
Long-term loans payable	60,000	67,000
Common stock, $10 par	100,000	100,000
Contributed capital, common stock	30,000	30,000
Retained earnings	57,000	36,000
Total liabilities & stockholders' equity	$313,000	$295,000

ANDREWS INC.
INCOME STATEMENT
FOR THE YEAR ENDING DECEMBER 31, 2012

Sales		$338,150
Cost of goods sold		175,000
Gross margin		163,150
Operating expenses		120,000
Operating income		43,150
Interest expense	$11,400	
Gain on sale of equipment	2,000	(9,400)
Income before tax		33,750
Income tax expense		6,750
Net income		$ 27,000

Additional information:

1. Dividends in the amount of $6,000 were declared and paid during 2012.
2. Depreciation expense and amortization expense are included in operating expenses.
3. No unrealized gains or losses have occurred on the investments during the year.
4. Equipment that had a cost of $30,000 and was 70% depreciated was sold during 2012.

Instructions
Prepare a statement of cash flows using the direct method. (Do not prepare a reconciliation schedule.)

6 **E23-14 (SCF—Indirect Method)** Data for Andrews Inc. are presented in E23-13.

Instructions
Prepare a statement of cash flows using the indirect method.

6 **E23-15 (SCF—Indirect Method)** Presented below are data taken from the records of Morganstern Company.

	December 31, 2012	December 31, 2011
Cash	$ 15,000	$ 10,000
Current assets other than cash	85,000	58,000
Long-term investments	10,000	53,000
Plant assets	335,000	215,000
	$445,000	$336,000
Accumulated depreciation	$ 20,000	$ 40,000
Current liabilities	40,000	22,000
Bonds payable	75,000	–0–
Common stock	254,000	254,000
Retained earnings	56,000	20,000
	$445,000	$336,000

Additional information:

1. Held-to-maturity securities carried at a cost of $43,000 on December 31, 2011, were sold in 2012 for $34,000. The loss (not extraordinary) was incorrectly charged directly to Retained Earnings.
2. Plant assets that cost $60,000 and were 80% depreciated were sold during 2012 for $8,000. The loss (not extraordinary) was incorrectly charged directly to Retained Earnings.
3. Net income as reported on the income statement for the year was $59,000.
4. Dividends paid amounted to $10,000.
5. Depreciation charged for the year was $28,000.

Instructions
Prepare a statement of cash flows for the year 2012 using the indirect method.

2 **3** **5** **E23-16 (Cash Provided by Operating, Investing, and Financing Activities)** The balance sheet data of Wyeth Company at the end of 2012 and 2011 are shown on page 1488.

	2012	2011
Cash	$ 30,000	$ 35,000
Accounts receivable (net)	55,000	45,000
Inventory	65,000	45,000
Prepaid expenses	15,000	25,000
Equipment	90,000	75,000
Accumulated depreciation—equipment	(18,000)	(8,000)
Land	70,000	40,000
	$307,000	$257,000
Accounts payable	$ 65,000	$ 52,000
Accrued expenses	15,000	18,000
Notes payable—bank, long-term	–0–	23,000
Bonds payable	30,000	–0–
Common stock, $10 par	189,000	159,000
Retained earnings	8,000	5,000
	$307,000	$257,000

Land was acquired for $30,000 in exchange for common stock, par $30,000, during the year; all equipment purchased was for cash. Equipment costing $13,000 was sold for $3,000; book value of the equipment was $6,000. Cash dividends of $9,000 were declared and paid during the year.

Instructions

Compute net cash provided (used) by:

(a) Operating activities.

(b) Investing activities.

(c) Financing activities.

6 **E23-17 (SCF—Indirect Method and Balance Sheet)** Ochoa Inc., had the following condensed balance sheet at the end of operations for 2011.

OCHOA INC.
BALANCE SHEET
DECEMBER 31, 2011

Cash	$ 8,500	Current liabilities	$ 15,000
Current assets other than cash	29,000	Long-term notes payable	25,500
Investments	20,000	Bonds payable	25,000
Plant assets (net)	67,500	Common stock	75,000
Land	40,000	Retained earnings	24,500
	$165,000		$165,000

During 2012, the following occurred.

1. A tract of land was purchased for $11,000.
2. Bonds payable in the amount of $20,000 were retired at par.
3. An additional $10,000 in common stock was issued at par.
4. Dividends totaling $9,375 were paid to stockholders.
5. Net income was $30,250 after deducting depreciation of $13,500.
6. Land was purchased through the issuance of $22,500 in bonds.
7. Ochoa Inc. sold part of its investment portfolio for $12,875. This transaction resulted in a gain of $2,000 for the company. The company classifies the investments as available-for-sale.
8. Both current assets (other than cash) and current liabilities remained at the same amount.

Instructions

(a) Prepare a statement of cash flows for 2012 using the indirect method.

(b) Prepare the condensed balance sheet for Ochoa Inc. as it would appear at December 31, 2012.

6 **8** **E23-18 (Partial SCF—Indirect Method)** The following accounts appear in the ledger of Popovich Company.

Retained Earnings		Dr.	Cr.	Bal.
Jan. 1, 2012	Credit Balance			$ 42,000
Aug. 15	Dividends (cash)	$15,000		27,000
Dec. 31	Net Income for 2012		$50,000	77,000

Machinery	Dr.	Cr.	Bal.
Jan. 1, 2012 Debit Balance			$140,000
Aug. 3 Purchase of Machinery	$62,000		202,000
Sept. 10 Cost of Machinery Constructed	48,000		250,000
Nov. 15 Machinery Sold		$66,000	184,000

Accumulated Depreciation— Machinery	Dr.	Cr.	Bal.
Jan. 1, 2012 Credit Balance			$ 84,000
Apr. 8 Extraordinary Repairs	$21,000		63,000
Nov. 15 Accum. Depreciation on Machinery Sold	25,200		37,800
Dec. 31 Depreciation for 2012		$16,800	54,600

Instructions

From the postings in the accounts above, indicate how the information is reported on a statement of cash flows by preparing a partial statement of cash flows using the indirect method. The loss on sale of equipment (November 15) was $5,800.

9 **E23-19 (Worksheet Analysis of Selected Accounts)** Data for Popovich Company are presented in E23-18.

Instructions

Prepare entries in journal form for all adjustments that should be made on a worksheet for a statement of cash flows.

9 **E23-20 (Worksheet Analysis of Selected Transactions)** The transactions below took place during the year 2012.

1. Convertible bonds payable with a par value of $300,000 were exchanged for unissued common stock with a par value of $300,000. The market price of both types of securities was par.
2. The net income for the year was $360,000.
3. Depreciation expense for the building was $90,000.
4. Some old office equipment was traded in on the purchase of some newer office equipment and the following entry was made. (The exchange has commercial substance.)

Equipment	45,000	
Accum. Depreciation—Equipment	30,000	
Equipment		40,000
Cash		34,000
Gain on Disposal of Plant Assets		1,000

The Gain on Disposal of Plant Assets was credited to current operations as ordinary income.

5. Dividends in the amount of $123,000 were declared. They are payable in January of next year.

Instructions

Show by journal entries the adjustments that would be made on a worksheet for a statement of cash flows.

9 **E23-21 (Worksheet Preparation)** Below is the comparative balance sheet for Lowenstein Corporation.

	Dec. 31, 2012	Dec. 31, 2011
Cash	$ 16,500	$ 24,000
Short-term investments	25,000	19,000
Accounts receivable	43,000	45,000
Allowance for doubtful accounts	(1,800)	(2,000)
Prepaid expenses	4,200	2,500
Inventory	81,500	57,000
Land	50,000	50,000
Buildings	125,000	78,500
Accumulated depreciation—buildings	(30,000)	(23,000)
Equipment	53,000	46,000
Accumulated depreciation—equipment	(19,000)	(15,500)
Delivery equipment	39,000	39,000
Accumulated depreciation—delivery equipment	(22,000)	(20,500)
Patents	15,000	–0–
	$379,400	$300,000

	Dec. 31, 2012	Dec. 31, 2011
Accounts payable	$ 26,000	$ 16,000
Short-term notes payable (trade)	4,000	6,000
Accrued payables	3,000	4,600
Mortgage payable	73,000	53,400
Bonds payable	50,000	62,500
Common stock	140,000	102,000
Paid-in capital in excess of par—common stock	10,000	4,000
Retained earnings	73,400	51,500
	$379,400	$300,000

Dividends in the amount of $10,000 were declared and paid in 2012.

Instructions

From this information, prepare a worksheet for a statement of cash flows. Make reasonable assumptions as appropriate. The short-term investments are considered available-for-sale, and no unrealized gains or losses have occurred on these securities.

> **See the book's companion website, www.wiley.com/college/kieso, for a set of B Exercises.**

PROBLEMS

P23-1 (SCF—Indirect Method) The following are Sullivan Corp.'s comparative balance sheet accounts at December 31, 2012 and 2011, with a column showing the increase (decrease) from 2011 to 2012.

COMPARATIVE BALANCE SHEETS

	2012	2011	Increase (Decrease)
Cash	$ 815,000	$ 700,000	$115,000
Accounts receivable	1,128,000	1,168,000	(40,000)
Inventory	1,850,000	1,715,000	135,000
Property, plant, and equipment	3,307,000	2,967,000	340,000
Accumulated depreciation	(1,165,000)	(1,040,000)	(125,000)
Investment in Myers Co.	310,000	275,000	35,000
Loan receivable	250,000	—	250,000
Total assets	$6,495,000	$5,785,000	$710,000
Accounts payable	$1,015,000	$ 955,000	$ 60,000
Income taxes payable	30,000	50,000	(20,000)
Dividends payable	80,000	100,000	(20,000)
Capital lease obligation	400,000	—	400,000
Common stock, $1 par	500,000	500,000	—
Paid-in capital in excess of par—common stock	1,500,000	1,500,000	—
Retained earnings	2,970,000	2,680,000	290,000
Total liabilities and stockholders' equity	$6,495,000	$5,785,000	$710,000

Additional information:

1. On December 31, 2011, Sullivan acquired 25% of Myers Co.'s common stock for $275,000. On that date, the carrying value of Myers's assets and liabilities, which approximated their fair values, was $1,100,000. Myers reported income of $140,000 for the year ended December 31, 2012. No dividend was paid on Myers's common stock during the year.

2. During 2012, Sullivan loaned $300,000 to TLC Co., an unrelated company. TLC made the first semi-annual principal repayment of $50,000, plus interest at 10%, on December 31, 2012.

3. On January 2, 2012, Sullivan sold equipment costing $60,000, with a carrying amount of $38,000, for $40,000 cash.

4. On December 31, 2012, Sullivan entered into a capital lease for an office building. The present value of the annual rental payments is $400,000, which equals the fair value of the building. Sullivan made the first rental payment of $60,000 when due on January 2, 2013.

5. Net income for 2012 was $370,000.

6. Sullivan declared and paid cash dividends for 2012 and 2011 as shown on the next page.

	2012	2011
Declared	December 15, 2012	December 15, 2011
Paid	February 28, 2013	February 28, 2012
Amount	$80,000	$100,000

Instructions
Prepare a statement of cash flows for Sullivan Corp. for the year ended December 31, 2012, using the indirect method.

(AICPA adapted)

P23-2 (SCF—Indirect Method) The comparative balance sheets for Hinckley Corporation show the following information.

	December 31	
	2012	2011
Cash	$ 33,500	$13,000
Accounts receivable	12,250	10,000
Inventory	12,000	9,000
Investments	–0–	3,000
Buildings	–0–	29,750
Equipment	45,000	20,000
Patents	5,000	6,250
	$107,750	$91,000
Allowance for doubtful accounts	$ 3,000	$ 4,500
Accumulated depreciation—equipment	2,000	4,500
Accumulated depreciation—building	–0–	6,000
Accounts payable	5,000	3,000
Dividends payable	–0–	5,000
Notes payable, short-term (nontrade)	3,000	4,000
Long-term notes payable	31,000	25,000
Common stock	43,000	33,000
Retained earnings	20,750	6,000
	$107,750	$91,000

Additional data related to 2012 are as follows.

1. Equipment that had cost $11,000 and was 40% depreciated at time of disposal was sold for $2,500.
2. $10,000 of the long-term note payable was paid by issuing common stock.
3. Cash dividends paid were $5,000.
4. On January 1, 2012, the building was completely destroyed by a flood. Insurance proceeds on the building were $30,000 (net of $2,000 taxes).
5. Investments (available-for-sale) were sold at $1,700 above their cost. The company has made similar sales and investments in the past.
6. Cash was paid for the acquisition of equipment.
7. A long-term note for $16,000 was issued for the acquisition of equipment.
8. Interest of $2,000 and income taxes of $6,500 were paid in cash.

Instructions
Prepare a statement of cash flows using the indirect method. Flood damage is unusual and infrequent in that part of the country.

P23-3 (SCF—Direct Method) Mortonson Company has not yet prepared a formal statement of cash flows for the 2012 fiscal year. Comparative balance sheets as of December 31, 2011 and 2012, and a statement of income and retained earnings for the year ended December 31, 2012, are presented below and on page 1492.

MORTONSON COMPANY
STATEMENT OF INCOME AND RETAINED EARNINGS
FOR THE YEAR ENDED DECEMBER 31, 2012
($000 OMITTED)

Sales		$3,800
Expenses		
Cost of goods sold	$1,200	
Salaries and benefits	725	
Heat, light, and power	75	
Depreciation	80	
Property taxes	19	
Patent amortization	25	
Miscellaneous expenses	10	
Interest	30	2,164

MORTONSON COMPANY
STATEMENT OF INCOME AND RETAINED EARNINGS
FOR THE YEAR ENDED DECEMBER 31, 2012
(CONTINUED)

Income before income taxes	1,636
Income taxes	818
Net income	818
Retained earnings—Jan. 1, 2012	310
	1,128
Stock dividend declared and issued	600
Retained earnings—Dec. 31, 2012	$ 528

MORTONSON COMPANY
COMPARATIVE BALANCE SHEETS
AS OF DECEMBER 31
($000 OMITTED)

Assets	2012	2011
Current assets		
Cash	$ 333	$ 100
U.S. Treasury notes (available-for-sale)	10	50
Accounts receivable	780	500
Inventory	720	560
Total current assets	1,843	1,210
Long-term assets		
Land	150	70
Buildings and equipment	910	600
Accumulated depreciation	(200)	(120)
Patents (less amortization)	105	130
Total long-term assets	965	680
Total assets	$2,808	$1,890
Liabilities and Stockholders' Equity		
Current liabilities		
Accounts payable	$ 420	$ 330
Income taxes payable	40	30
Notes payable	320	320
Total current liabilities	780	680
Long-term notes payable—due 2014	200	200
Total liabilities	980	880
Stockholders' equity		
Common stock	1,300	700
Retained earnings	528	310
Total stockholders' equity	1,828	1,010
Total liabilities and stockholders' equity	$2,808	$1,890

Instructions

Prepare a statement of cash flows using the direct method. Changes in accounts receivable and accounts payable relate to sales and cost of goods sold. Do not prepare a reconciliation schedule.

(CMA adapted)

6 7 **P23-4 (SCF—Direct Method)** Michaels Company had available at the end of 2012 the information shown
8 below.

MICHAELS COMPANY
COMPARATIVE BALANCE SHEETS
AS OF DECEMBER 31, 2012 AND 2011

	2012	2011
Cash	$ 10,000	$ 4,000
Accounts receivable	20,500	12,950
Short-term investments	22,000	30,000
Inventory	42,000	35,000
Prepaid rent	3,000	12,000
Prepaid insurance	2,100	900
Supplies	1,000	750
Land	125,000	175,000
Buildings	350,000	350,000
Accumulated depreciation—buildings	(105,000)	(87,500)
Equipment	525,000	400,000
Accumulated depreciation—equipment	(130,000)	(112,000)
Patents	45,000	50,000
Total assets	$910,600	$871,100
Accounts payable	$ 22,000	$ 32,000
Income taxes payable	5,000	4,000
Salaries and wages payable	5,000	3,000
Short-term notes payable	10,000	10,000
Long-term notes payable	60,000	70,000
Bonds payable	400,000	400,000
Premium on bonds payable	20,303	25,853
Common stock	240,000	220,000
Paid-in capital in excess of par—common stock	25,000	17,500
Retained earnings	123,297	88,747
Total liabilities and stockholders' equity	$910,600	$871,100

MICHAEL S COMPANY
INCOME STATEMENT AND DIVIDEND INFORMATION
FOR THE YEAR ENDED DECEMBER 31, 2012

Sales revenue		$1,160,000
Cost of goods sold		748,000
Gross margin		412,000
Operating expenses		
Selling expenses	$ 79,200	
Administrative expenses	156,700	
Depreciation/Amortization expense	40,500	
Total operating expenses		276,400
Income from operations		135,600
Other revenues/expenses		
Gain on sale of land	8,000	
Gain on sale of short-term investment	4,000	
Dividend revenue	2,400	
Interest expense	(51,750)	(37,350)
Income before taxes		98,250
Income tax expense		39,400
Net income		58,850
Dividends to common stockholders		(24,300)
To retained earnings		$ 34,550

Instructions

Prepare a statement of cash flows for Michaels Company using the direct method accompanied by a reconciliation schedule. Assume the short-term investments are classified as available-for-sale.

P23-5 (SCF—Indirect Method) You have completed the field work in connection with your audit of Alexander Corporation for the year ended December 31, 2012. The balance sheet accounts at the beginning and end of the year are shown below.

	Dec. 31, 2012	Dec. 31, 2011	Increase or (Decrease)
Cash	$ 277,900	$ 298,000	($20,100)
Accounts receivable	469,424	353,000	116,424
Inventory	741,700	610,000	131,700
Prepaid expenses	12,000	8,000	4,000
Investment in subsidiary	110,500	-0-	110,500
Cash surrender value of life insurance	2,304	1,800	504
Machinery	207,000	190,000	17,000
Buildings	535,200	407,900	127,300
Land	52,500	52,500	-0-
Patents	69,000	64,000	5,000
Copyrights	40,000	50,000	(10,000)
Bond discount and issue cost	4,502	-0-	4,502
	$2,522,030	$2,035,200	$486,830
Accrued taxes payable	$ 90,250	$ 79,600	$ 10,650
Accounts payable	299,280	280,000	19,280
Dividends payable	70,000	-0-	70,000
Bonds payable—8%	125,000	-0-	125,000
Bonds payable—12%	-0-	100,000	(100,000)
Allowance for doubtful accounts	35,300	40,000	(4,700)
Accumulated depreciation—buildings	424,000	400,000	24,000
Accumulated depreciation—machinery	173,000	130,000	43,000
Premium on bonds payable	-0-	2,400	(2,400)
Common stock—no par	1,176,200	1,453,200	(277,000)
Paid-in capital in excess of par—common stock	109,000	-0-	109,000
Retained earnings—unappropriated	20,000	(450,000)	470,000
	$2,522,030	$2,035,2(●)	$486,830

STATEMENT OF RETAINED EARNINGS
FOR THE YEAR ENDED DECEMBER 31, 2012

January	1, 2012	Balance (deficit)	$(450,000)
March	31, 2012	Net income for first quarter of 2012	25,000
April	1, 2012	Transfer from paid-in capital	425,000
		Balance	-0-
December	31, 2012	Net income for last three quarters of 2012	90,000
		Dividend declared—payable January 21, 2013	(70,000)
		Balance	$ 20,000

Your working papers from the audit contain the following information:

1. On April 1, 2012, the existing deficit was written off against paid-in capital created by reducing the stated value of the no-par stock.
2. On November 1, 2012, 29,600 shares of no-par stock were sold for $257,000. The board of directors voted to regard $5 per share as stated capital.
3. A patent was purchased for $15,000.
4. During the year, machinery that had a cost basis of $16,400 and on which there was accumulated depreciation of $5,200 was sold for $9,000. No other plant assets were sold during the year.
5. The 12%, 20-year bonds were dated and issued on January 2, 2000. Interest was payable on June 30 and December 31. They were sold originally at 106. These bonds were retired at 100.9 plus accrued interest on March 31, 2012.
6. The 8%, 40-year bonds were dated January 1, 2012, and were sold on March 31 at 97 plus accrued interest. Interest is payable semiannually on June 30 and December 31. Expense of issuance was $839.
7. Alexander Corporation acquired 70% control in Crimson Company on January 2, 2012, for $100,000. The income statement of Crimson Company for 2012 shows a net income of $15,000.
8. Extraordinary repairs to buildings of $7,200 were charged to Accumulated Depreciation—Buildings.
9. Interest paid in 2012 was $10,500 and income taxes paid were $34,000.

Instructions

From the information given, prepare a statement of cash flows using the indirect method. A worksheet is not necessary, but the principal computations should be supported by schedules or general ledger accounts. The company uses straight-line amortization for bond interest.

 P23-6 (SCF—Indirect Method, and Net Cash Flow from Operating Activities, Direct Method) Comparative balance sheet accounts of Marcus Inc. are presented below.

MARCUS INC.		
COMPARATIVE BALANCE SHEET ACCOUNTS		
AS OF DECEMBER 31, 2012 AND 2011		

	December 31	
Debit Accounts	2012	2011
Cash	$ 42,000	$ 33,750
Accounts Receivable	70,500	60,000
Inventory	30,000	24,000
Investments (available-for-sale)	22,250	38,500
Machinery	30,000	18,750
Buildings	67,500	56,250
Land	7,500	7,500
	$269,750	$238,750
Credit Accounts		
Allowance for Doubtful Accounts	$ 2,250	$ 1,500
Accumulated Depreciation—Machinery	5,625	2,250
Accumulated Depreciation—Buildings	13,500	9,000
Accounts Payable	35,000	24,750
Accrued Payables	3,375	2,625
Long-Term Notes Payable	21,000	31,000
Common Stock, no-par	150,000	125,000
Retained Earnings	39,000	42,625
	$269,750	$238,750

Additional data (ignoring taxes):

1. Net income for the year was $42,500.
2. Cash dividends declared and paid during the year were $21,125.
3. A 20% stock dividend was declared during the year. $25,000 of retained earnings was capitalized.
4. Investments that cost $25,000 were sold during the year for $28,750.
5. Machinery that cost $3,750, on which $750 of depreciation had accumulated, was sold for $2,200.

Marcus's 2012 income statement follows (ignoring taxes).

Sales		$540,000
Less: cost of goods sold		380,000
Gross margin		160,000
Less: Operating expenses (includes $8,625 depreciation and $5,400 bad debts)		120,450
Income from operations		39,550
Other: Gain on sale of investments	$3,750	
Loss on sale of machinery	(800)	2,950
Net income		$ 42,500

Instructions

(a) Compute net cash flow from operating activities using the direct method.
(b) Prepare a statement of cash flows using the indirect method.

 P23-7 (SCF—Direct and Indirect Methods from Comparative Financial Statements) Chapman Company, a major retailer of bicycles and accessories, operates several stores and is a publicly traded company. The comparative balance sheet and income statement for Chapman as of May 31, 2012, are shown on the next page. The company is preparing its statement of cash flows.

CHAPMAN COMPANY
COMPARATIVE BALANCE SHEET
AS OF MAY 31

	2012	2011
Current assets		
Cash	$ 28,250	$ 20,000
Accounts receivable	75,000	58,000
Inventory	220,000	250,000
Prepaid expenses	9,000	7,000
Total current assets	332,250	335,000
Plant assets		
Plant assets	600,000	502,000
Less: Accumulated depreciation—plant assets	150,000	125,000
Net plant assets	450,000	377,000
Total assets	$782,250	$712,000
Current liabilities		
Accounts payable	$123,000	$115,000
Salaries and wages payable	47,250	72,000
Interest payable	27,000	25,000
Total current liabilities	197,250	212,000
Long-term debt		
Bonds payable	70,000	100,000
Total liabilities	267,250	312,000
Stockholders' equity		
Common stock, $10 par	370,000	280,000
Retained earnings	145,000	120,000
Total stockholders' equity	515,000	400,000
Total liabilities and stockholders' equity	$782,250	$712,000

CHAPMAN COMPANY
INCOME STATEMENT
FOR THE YEAR ENDED MAY 31, 2012

Sales	$1,255,250
Cost of goods sold	722,000
Gross profit	533,250
Expenses	
Salaries and wages expense	252,100
Interest expense	75,000
Depreciation expense	25,000
Other expenses	8,150
Total expenses	360,250
Operating income	173,000
Income tax expense	43,000
Net income	$ 130,000

The following is additional information concerning Chapman's transactions during the year ended May 31, 2012.

1. All sales during the year were made on account.
2. All merchandise was purchased on account, comprising the total accounts payable account.
3. Plant assets costing $98,000 were purchased by paying $28,000 in cash and issuing 7,000 shares of stock.
4. The "other expenses" are related to prepaid items.
5. All income taxes incurred during the year were paid during the year.
6. In order to supplement its cash, Chapman issued 2,000 shares of common stock at par value.
7. Cash dividends of $105,000 were declared and paid at the end of the fiscal year.

Instructions

    (a) Compare and contrast the direct method and the indirect method for reporting cash flows from operating activities.

    (b) Prepare a statement of cash flows for Chapman Company for the year ended May 31, 2012, using the direct method. Be sure to support the statement with appropriate calculations. (A reconciliation of net income to net cash provided is not required.)

    (c) Using the indirect method, calculate only the net cash flow from operating activities for Chapman Company for the year ended May 31, 2012.

 P23-8 (SCF—Direct and Indirect Methods) Comparative balance sheet accounts of Sharpe Company are presented below.

SHARPE COMPANY
COMPARATIVE BALANCE SHEET ACCOUNTS
AS OF DECEMBER 31

Debit Balances	2012	2011
Cash	$ 70,000	$ 51,000
Accounts Receivable	155,000	130,000
Inventory	75,000	61,000
Investments (Available-for-sale)	55,000	85,000
Equipment	70,000	48,000
Buildings	145,000	145,000
Land	40,000	25,000
Totals	$610,000	$545,000
Credit Balances		
Allowance for Doubtful Accounts	$ 10,000	$ 8,000
Accumulated Depreciation—Equipment	21,000	14,000
Accumulated Depreciation—Buildings	37,000	28,000
Accounts Payable	66,000	60,000
Income Taxes Payable	12,000	10,000
Long-Term Notes Payable	62,000	70,000
Common Stock	310,000	260,000
Retained Earnings	92,000	95,000
Totals	$610,000	$545,000

Additional data:

    1. Equipment that cost $10,000 and was 60% depreciated was sold in 2012.
    2. Cash dividends were declared and paid during the year.
    3. Common stock was issued in exchange for land.
    4. Investments that cost $35,000 were sold during the year.
    5. There were no write-offs of uncollectible accounts during the year.

Sharpe's 2012 income statement is as follows.

Sales		$950,000
Less: Cost of goods sold		600,000
Gross profit		350,000
Less: Operating expenses (includes depreciation expense and bad debt expense)		250,000
Income from operations		100,000
Other revenues and expenses		
Gain on sale of investments	$15,000	
Loss on sale of equipment	(3,000)	12,000
Income before taxes		112,000
Income taxes		45,000
Net income		$ 67,000

Instructions

    (a) Compute net cash provided by operating activities under the direct method.

    (b) Prepare a statement of cash flows using the indirect method.

P23-9 (Indirect SCF) Dingel Corporation has contracted with you to prepare a statement of cash flows. The controller has provided the following information.

	December 31	
	2012	2011
Cash	$ 38,500	$13,000
Accounts receivable	12,250	10,000
Inventory	12,000	10,000
Investments	–0–	3,000
Buildings	–0–	29,750
Equipment	40,000	20,000
Copyrights	5,000	5,250
Totals	$107,750	$91,000
Allowance for doubtful accounts	$ 3,000	$ 4,500
Accumulated depreciation—equipment	2,000	4,500
Accumulated depreciation—buildings	–0–	6,000
Accounts payable	5,000	4,000
Dividends payable	–0–	5,000
Notes payable, short-term (nontrade)	3,000	4,000
Long-term notes payable	36,000	25,000
Common stock	38,000	33,000
Retained earnings	20,750	5,000
	$107,750	$91,000

Additional data related to 2012 are as follows.

1. Equipment that had cost $11,000 and was 30% depreciated at time of disposal was sold for $2,500.
2. $5,000 of the long-term note payable was paid by issuing common stock.
3. Cash dividends paid were $5,000.
4. On January 1, 2012, the building was completely destroyed by a flood. Insurance proceeds on the building were $33,000 (net of $4,000 taxes).
5. Investments (available-for-sale) were sold at $1,500 above their cost. The company has made similar sales and investments in the past.
6. Cash and long-term note for $16,000 were given for the acquisition of equipment.
7. Interest of $2,000 and income taxes of $5,000 were paid in cash.

Instructions

(a) Use the indirect method to analyze the above information and prepare a statement of cash flows for Dingel. Flood damage is unusual and infrequent in that part of the country.
(b) What would you expect to observe in the operating, investing, and financing sections of a statement of cash flows of:
   (1) A severely financially troubled firm?
   (2) A recently formed firm that is experiencing rapid growth?

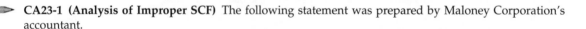

CONCEPTS FOR ANALYSIS

CA23-1 (Analysis of Improper SCF) The following statement was prepared by Maloney Corporation's accountant.

MALONEY CORPORATION
STATEMENT OF SOURCES AND APPLICATION OF CASH
FOR THE YEAR ENDED SEPTEMBER 30, 2012

Sources of cash	
Net income	$111,000
Depreciation and depletion	70,000
Increase in long-term debt	179,000
Changes in current receivables and inventories, less current	
liabilities (excluding current maturities of long-term debt)	14,000
	$374,000

Application of cash	
Cash dividends	$ 60,000
Expenditure for property, plant, and equipment	214,000
Investments and other uses	20,000
Change in cash	80,000
	$374,000

The following additional information relating to Maloney Corporation is available for the year ended September 30, 2012.

1. Wage and salary expense attributable to stock option plans was $25,000 for the year.
2. Expenditures for property, plant, and equipment $250,000
   Proceeds from retirements of property, plant, and equipment   36,000
   Net expenditures $214,000

3. A stock dividend of 10,000 shares of Maloney Corporation common stock was distributed to common stockholders on April 1, 2012, when the per share market price was $7 and par value was $1.
4. On July 1, 2012, when its market price was $6 per share, 16,000 shares of Maloney Corporation common stock were issued in exchange for 4,000 shares of preferred stock.
5. Depreciation expense $ 65,000
   Depletion expense   5,000
   $ 70,000

6. Increase in long-term debt $620,000
   Retirement of debt   441,000
   Net increase $179,000

Instructions

(a) In general, what are the objectives of a statement of the type shown above for Maloney Corporation? Explain.
(b) Identify the weaknesses in the form and format of Maloney Corporation's statement of cash flows without reference to the additional information. (Assume adoption of the indirect method.)
(c) For each of the six items of additional information for the statement of cash flows, indicate the preferable treatment and explain why the suggested treatment is preferable.

(AICPA adapted)

 CA23-2 **(SCF Theory and Analysis of Improper SCF)** Teresa Ramirez and Lenny Traylor are examining the following statement of cash flows for Pacific Clothing Store's first year of operations.

PACIFIC CLOTHING STORE	
STATEMENT OF CASH FLOWS	
FOR THE YEAR ENDED JANUARY 31, 2012	
Sources of cash	
From sales of merchandise	$ 382,000
From sale of capital stock	380,000
From sale of investment	120,000
From depreciation	80,000
From issuance of note for truck	30,000
From interest on investments	8,000
Total sources of cash	1,000,000
Uses of cash	
For purchase of fixtures and equipment	330,000
For merchandise purchased for resale	253,000
For operating expenses (including depreciation)	170,000
For purchase of investment	95,000
For purchase of truck by issuance of note	30,000
For purchase of treasury stock	10,000
For interest on note	3,000
Total uses of cash	891,000
Net increase in cash	$ 109,000

Teresa claims that Pacific's statement of cash flows is an excellent portrayal of a superb first year, with cash increasing $109,000. Lenny replies that it was not a superb first year—that the year was an operating failure, the statement was incorrectly presented, and $109,000 is not the actual increase in cash.

Instructions

    (a) With whom do you agree, Teresa or Lenny? Explain your position.

    (b) Using the data provided, prepare a statement of cash flows in proper indirect method form. The only noncash items in income are depreciation and the gain from the sale of the investment (purchase and sale are related).

CA23-3 (SCF Theory and Analysis of Transactions) Ashley Company is a young and growing producer of electronic measuring instruments and technical equipment. You have been retained by Ashley to advise it in the preparation of a statement of cash flows using the indirect method. For the fiscal year ended October 31, 2012, you have obtained the following information concerning certain events and transactions of Ashley.

    1. The amount of reported earnings for the fiscal year was $700,000, which included a deduction for an extraordinary loss of $110,000 (see item 5 below).

    2. Depreciation expense of $315,000 was included in the income statement.

    3. Uncollectible accounts receivable of $40,000 were written off against the allowance for doubtful accounts. Also, $51,000 of bad debt expense was included in determining income for the fiscal year, and the same amount was added to the allowance for doubtful accounts.

    4. A gain of $6,000 was realized on the sale of a machine. It originally cost $75,000, of which $30,000 was undepreciated on the date of sale.

    5. On April 1, 2012, lightning caused an uninsured building loss of $110,000 ($180,000 loss, less reduction in income taxes of $70,000). This extraordinary loss was included in determining income as indicated in item 1 above.

    6. On July 3, 2012, building and land were purchased for $700,000. Ashley gave in payment $75,000 cash, $200,000 market price of its unissued common stock, and signed a $425,000 mortgage note payable.

    7. On August 3, 2012, $800,000 face value of Ashley's 10% convertible debentures was converted into $150,000 par value of its common stock. The bonds were originally issued at face value.

Instructions

Explain whether each of the seven numbered items above is a cash inflow or outflow, and explain how it should be disclosed in Ashley's statement of cash flows for the fiscal year ended October 31, 2012. If any item is neither an inflow nor an outflow of cash, explain why it is not, and indicate the disclosure, if any, that should be made of the item in Ashley's statement of cash flows for the fiscal year ended October 31, 2012.

CA23-4 (Analysis of Transactions' Effect on SCF) Each of the following items must be considered in preparing a statement of cash flows for Cruz Fashions Inc. for the year ended December 31, 2012.

    1. Fixed assets that had cost $20,000 $6\frac{1}{2}$ years before and were being depreciated on a 10-year basis, with no estimated scrap value, were sold for $4,750.

    2. During the year, goodwill of $15,000 was considered impaired and was completely written off to expense.

    3. During the year, 500 shares of common stock with a stated value of $25 a share were issued for $32 a share.

    4. The company sustained a net loss for the year of $2,100. Depreciation amounted to $2,000 and patent amortization was $400.

    5. Uncollectible accounts receivable in the amount of $2,000 were written off against Allowance for Doubtful Accounts.

    6. Investments (available-for-sale) that cost $12,000 when purchased 4 years earlier were sold for $10,600. The loss was considered ordinary.

    7. Bonds payable with a par value of $24,000 on which there was an unamortized bond premium of $2,000 were redeemed at 101. The gain was credited to ordinary income.

Instructions

For each item, state where it is to be shown in the statement and then how you would present the necessary information, including the amount. Consider each item to be independent of the others. Assume that correct entries were made for all transactions as they took place.

CA23-5 (Purpose and Elements of SCF) GAAP requires the statement of cash flows be presented when financial statements are prepared.

Instructions

    (a) Explain the purposes of the statement of cash flows.

    (b) List and describe the three categories of activities that must be reported in the statement of cash flows.

    (c) Identify and describe the two methods that are allowed for reporting cash flows from operations.

    (d) Describe the financial statement presentation of noncash investing and financing transactions. Include in your description an example of a noncash investing and financing transaction.

CA23-6 (Cash Flow Reporting) Brockman Guitar Company is in the business of manufacturing top-quality, steel-string folk guitars. In recent years, the company has experienced working capital problems resulting from the procurement of factory equipment, the unanticipated buildup of receivables and inventories, and the payoff of a balloon mortgage on a new manufacturing facility. The founder and president of the company, Barbara Brockman, has attempted to raise cash from various financial institutions, but to no avail because of the company's poor performance in recent years. In particular, the company's lead bank, First Financial, is especially concerned about Brockman's inability to maintain a positive cash position. The commercial loan officer from First Financial told Barbara, "I can't even consider your request for capital financing unless I see that your company is able to generate positive cash flows from operations."

Thinking about the banker's comment, Barbara came up with what she believes is a good plan: With a more attractive statement of cash flows, the bank might be willing to provide long-term financing. To "window dress" cash flows, the company can sell its accounts receivables to factors and liquidate its raw materials inventories. These rather costly transactions would generate lots of cash. As the chief accountant for Brockman Guitar, it is your job to tell Barbara what you think of her plan.

Instructions
Answer the following questions.

  (a) What are the ethical issues related to Barbara Brockman's idea?
  (b) What would you tell Barbara Brockman?

USING YOUR JUDGMENT

FINANCIAL REPORTING

Financial Reporting Problem

 The Procter & Gamble Company (P&G)

The financial statements of **P&G** are presented in Appendix 5B or can be accessed at the book's companion website, **www.wiley.com/college/kieso**.

Instructions
Refer to P&G's financial statements and the accompanying notes to answer the following questions.

  (a) Which method of computing net cash provided by operating activities does P&G use? What were the amounts of net cash provided by operating activities for the years 2007, 2008, and 2009? Which two items were most responsible for the increase in net cash provided by operating activities in 2009?

  (b) What was the most significant item in the cash flows used for investing activities section in 2009?

  What was the most significant item in the cash flows used for financing activities section in 2009?

  (c) Where is "deferred income taxes" reported in P&G's statement of cash flows? Why does it appear in that section of the statement of cash flows?

  (d) Where is depreciation reported in P&G's statement of cash flows? Why is depreciation added to net income in the statement of cash flows?

Comparative Analysis Case

The Coca-Cola Company and PepsiCo, Inc.

Instructions
Go to the book's companion website and use information found there to answer the following questions related to **The Coca-Cola Company** and **PepsiCo, Inc.**

  (a) What method of computing net cash provided by operating activities does Coca-Cola use? What method does PepsiCo use? What were the amounts of cash provided by operating activities reported by Coca-Cola and PepsiCo in 2009?

(b) What was the most significant item reported by Coca-Cola and PepsiCo in 2009 in their investing activities sections? What is the most significant item reported by Coca-Cola and PepsiCo in 2009 in their financing activities sections?

(c) What were these two companies' trends in net cash provided by operating activities over the period 2007 to 2009?

(d) Where is "depreciation and amortization" reported by Coca-Cola and PepsiCo in their statements of cash flows? What is the amount and why does it appear in that section of the statement of cash flows?

(e) Based on the information contained in Coca-Cola's and PepsiCo's financial statements, compute the following 2009 ratios for each company. These ratios require the use of statement of cash flows data. (These ratios were covered in Chapter 5.)
   (1) Current cash debt coverage ratio.
   (2) Cash debt coverage ratio.

(f) What conclusions concerning the management of cash can be drawn from the ratios computed in (e)?

Financial Statement Analysis Case

Vermont Teddy Bear Co.

Founded in the early 1980s, the Vermont Teddy Bear Co. designs and manufactures American-made teddy bears and markets them primarily as gifts called Bear-Grams or Teddy Bear-Grams. Bear-Grams are personalized teddy bears delivered directly to the recipient for special occasions such as birthdays and anniversaries. The Shelburne, Vermont, company's primary markets are New York, Boston, and Chicago. Sales have jumped dramatically in recent years. Such dramatic growth has significant implications for cash flows. Provided below are the cash flow statements for two recent years for the company.

	Current Year	Prior Year
Cash flows from operating activities:		
Net income	$ 17,523	$ 838,955
Adjustments to reconcile net income to net cash provided by operating activities		
Deferred income taxes	(69,524)	(146,590)
Depreciation and amortization	316,416	181,348
Changes in assets and liabilities:		
Accounts receivable, trade	(38,267)	(25,947)
Inventories	(1,599,014)	(1,289,293)
Prepaid and other current assets	(444,794)	(113,205)
Deposits and other assets	(24,240)	(83,044)
Accounts payable	2,017,059	(284,567)
Accrued expenses	61,321	170,755
Accrued interest payable, debentures	—	(58,219)
Other	—	(8,960)
Income taxes payable	—	117,810
Net cash provided by (used for) operating activities	236,480	(700,957)
Net cash used for investing activities	(2,102,892)	(4,422,953)
Net cash (used for) provided by financing activities	(315,353)	9,685,435
Net change in cash and cash equivalents	(2,181,765)	4,561,525

Other information:

Current liabilities	$ 4,055,465	$ 1,995,600
Total liabilities	4,620,085	2,184,386
Net sales	20,560,566	17,025,856

Instructions

(a) Note that net income in the current year was only $17,523 compared to prior-year income of $838,955, but cash flow from operations was $236,480 in the current year and a negative $700,957 in the prior year. Explain the causes of this apparent paradox.

(b) Evaluate Vermont Teddy Bear's liquidity, solvency, and profitability for the current year using cash flow-based ratios.

Accounting, Analysis, and Principles

The income statement for the year ended December 31, 2012, for Laskowski Manufacturing Company contains the following condensed information.

LASKOWSKI CO. INCOME STATEMENT		
Revenues		$6,583,000
Operating expenses (excluding depreciation)	$4,920,000	
Depreciation expense	880,000	5,800,000
Income before income tax		783,000
Income tax expense		353,000
Net income		$ 430,000

Included in operating expenses is a $24,000 loss resulting from the sale of machinery for $270,000 cash. The company purchased machinery at a cost of $750,000.

Laskowski reports the following balances on its comparative balance sheets at December 31.

LASKOWSKI CO. COMPARATIVE BALANCE SHEETS (PARTIAL)		
	2012	**2011**
Cash	$672,000	$130,000
Accounts receivable	775,000	610,000
Inventory	834,000	867,000
Accounts payable	521,000	501,000

Income tax expense of $353,000 represents the amount paid in 2012. Dividends declared and paid in 2012 totaled $200,000.

Accounting

Prepare the statement of cash flows using the indirect method.

Analysis

Laskowski has an aggressive growth plan, which will require significant investments in plant and equipment over the next several years. Preliminary plans call for an investment of over $500,000 in the next year. Compute Laskowski's free cash flow (from Chapter 5) and use it to evaluate the investment plans with the use of only internally generated funds.

Principles

How does the statement of cash flows contribute to achieving the objective of financial reporting?

BRIDGE TO THE PROFESSION

Professional Research: FASB Codification

As part of the year-end accounting process for your company, you are preparing the statement of cash flows according to GAAP. One of your team, a finance major, believes the statement should be prepared to report the change in working capital, because analysts many times use working capital in ratio analysis. Your supervisor would like research conducted to verify the basis for preparing the statement of cash flows.

Instructions

If your school has a subscription to the FASB Codification, go to *http://aaahq.org/ascLogin.cfm* to log in and prepare responses to the following. Provide Codification references for your responses.

(a) What is the primary objective for the statement of cash flows? Is working capital the basis for meeting this objective?

(b) What information is provided in a statement of cash flows?

(c) List some of the typical cash inflows and outflows from operations.

Professional Simulation

The professional simulation for this chapter asks you to address questions related to the accounting for the statement of cash flows.

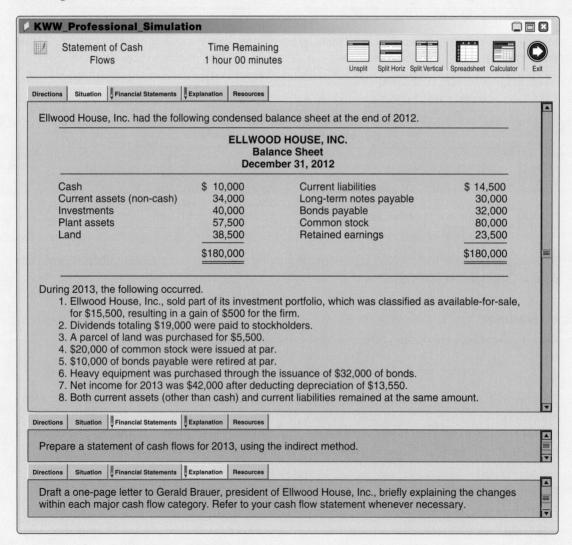

As in GAAP, the statement of cash flows is a required statement for IFRS. In addition, the content and presentation of a U.S. statement of cash flows is similar to one used for IFRS. However, the disclosure requirements related to the statement of cash flows are more extensive under GAAP. *IAS 7* ("Cash Flow Statements") provides the overall IFRS requirements for cash flow information.

RELEVANT FACTS

- Companies preparing financial statements under IFRS must prepare a statement of cash flows as an integral part of the financial statements.
- Both IFRS and GAAP require that the statement of cash flows should have three major sections—operating, investing, and financing—along with changes in cash and cash equivalents.
- Similar to GAAP, the cash flow statement can be prepared using either the indirect or direct method under IFRS. For both IFRS and GAAP, most companies use the indirect method for reporting net cash flow from operating activities.
- The definition of cash equivalents used in IFRS is similar to that used in GAAP. A major difference is that in certain situations, bank overdrafts are considered part of cash and cash equivalents under IFRS (which is not the case in GAAP). Under GAAP, bank overdrafts are classified as financing activities.
- IFRS requires that non-cash investing and financing activities be excluded from the statement of cash flows. Instead, these non-cash activities should be reported elsewhere. This requirement is interpreted to mean that non-cash investing and financing activities should be disclosed in the notes to the financial statements instead of in the financial statements. Under GAAP, companies may present this information in the cash flow statement.
- One area where there can be substantive differences between IFRS and GAAP relates to the classification of interest, dividends, and taxes. IFRS provides more alternatives for disclosing these items, while GAAP requires that except for dividends paid (which are classified as a financing activity), these items are all reported as operating activities.

ABOUT THE NUMBERS

Significant Non-Cash Transactions

Because the statement of cash flows reports only the effects of operating, investing, and financing activities in terms of cash flows, it omits some **significant non-cash transactions** and other events that are investing or financing activities. Among the more common of these non-cash transactions that a company should report or disclose in some manner are the following.

1. Acquisition of assets by assuming liabilities (including finance lease obligations) or by issuing equity securities.
2. Exchanges of non-monetary assets.
3. Refinancing of long-term debt.
4. Conversion of debt or preference shares to ordinary shares.
5. Issuance of equity securities to retire debt.

Investing and financing transactions that do not require the use of cash are excluded from the statement of cash flows. If material in amount, these disclosures may be either narrative or summarized in a separate schedule. This schedule may appear in a separate note or supplementary schedule to the financial statements.

Illustration IFRS23-1 shows the presentation of these significant non-cash transactions or other events in a separate schedule in the notes to the financial statements.

ILLUSTRATION
IFRS23-1
Note Presentation of
Non-Cash Investing and
Financing Activities

Note G: Significant non-cash transactions. During the year, the company engaged in the following significant non-cash investing and financing transactions:	
Issued 250,000 ordinary shares to purchase land and building	$1,750,000
Exchanged land in Steadfast, New York, for land in Bedford, Pennsylvania	$2,000,000
Converted 12% bonds to 50,000 ordinary shares	$ 500,000

Companies do not generally report certain other significant non-cash transactions or other events in conjunction with the statement of cash flows. Examples of these types of transactions are **share dividends, share splits, and restrictions on retained earnings**. Companies generally report these items, neither financing nor investing activities, in conjunction with the statement of changes in equity or schedules and notes pertaining to changes in equity accounts.

Special Disclosures

IAS 7 indicates that cash flows related to interest received and paid, and dividends received and paid, should be separately disclosed in the statement of cash flows. Each item should be classified in a consistent manner from period to period as operating, investing, or financing cash flows. *For homework purposes, classify interest received and paid and dividends received as part of cash flows from operating activities and dividends paid as cash flows from financing activities.* The justification for reporting the first three items in cash flows from operating activities is that each item affects net income. Dividends paid, however, do not affect net income and are often considered a cost of financing.

Companies should also disclose income taxes paid separately in the cash flows from operating activities unless they can be separately identified as part of investing or financing activities. While tax expense may be readily identifiable with investing or financing activities, the related tax cash flows are often impracticable to identify and may arise in a different period from the cash flows of the underlying transaction. Therefore, taxes paid are usually classified as cash flows from operating activities. IFRS requires that the cash paid for taxes, as well as cash flows from interest and dividends received and paid, be disclosed. The category (operating, investing, or financing) that each item was included in must be disclosed as well.

An example of such a disclosure from the notes to **Daimler**'s financial statements is provided in Illustration IFRS23-2.

ILLUSTRATION
IFRS23-2
Note Disclosure of
Interest, Taxes, and
Dividends

Daimler

Cash provided by operating activities includes the following cash flows:

(in millions of €)	2009	2008	2007
Interest paid	(894)	(651)	(1,541)
Interest received	471	765	977
Income taxes paid, net	(358)	(898)	(1,020)
Dividends received	109	67	69

Other companies choose to report these items directly in the statement of cash flows. In many cases, companies start with income before income taxes and then show income taxes paid as a separate item. In addition, they often add back interest expense on an accrual basis and then subtract interest paid. Reporting these items in the operating activities section is shown for Mermel Company in Illustration IFRS23-3.

MERMEL COMPANY STATEMENT OF CASH FLOWS ($000,000) (OPERATING ACTIVITIES SECTION ONLY)		
Income before income tax		$ 4,000
Adjustments to reconcile income before income tax to net cash provided by operating activities:		
Depreciation expense	$1,000	
Interest expense	500	
Investment revenue (dividends)	(650)	
Decrease in inventories	1,050	
Increase in trade receivables	(310)	1,590
Cash generated from operations		5,590
Interest paid	(300)	
Income taxes paid	(760)	(1,060)
Net cash provided by operating activities		$ 4,530

ILLUSTRATION IFRS23-3
Reporting of Interest, Taxes, and Dividends in the Operating Section

Companies often provide a separate section to identify interest and income taxes paid.

ON THE HORIZON

Presently, the IASB and the FASB are involved in a joint project on the presentation and organization of information in the financial statements. With respect to the cash flow statement specifically, the notion of *cash equivalents* will probably not be retained. The definition of cash in the existing literature would be retained, and the statement of cash flows would present information on changes in cash only. In addition, the IASB and FASB favor presentation of operating cash flows using the direct method only. This approach is generally opposed by the preparer community.

IFRS SELF-TEST QUESTIONS

1. Which of the following is true regarding the statement of cash flows under IFRS?
   (a) The statement of cash flows has two major sections—operating and non-operating.
   (b) The statement of cash flows has two major sections—financing and investing.
   (c) The statement of cash flows has three major sections—operating, investing, and financing.
   (d) The statement of cash flows has three major sections—operating, non-operating, and financing.

2. In the case of a bank overdraft:
   (a) GAAP typically includes the amount in cash and cash equivalents.
   (b) IFRS typically includes the amount in cash equivalents but not in cash.
   (c) GAAP typically treats the overdraft as a liability, and reports the amount in the financing section of the statement of cash flows.
   (d) IFRS typically treats the overdraft as a liability, and reports the amount in the investing section of the statement of cash flows.

3. Under IFRS, significant non-cash transactions:
   (a) are classified as operating, if they are related to income items.
   (b) are excluded from the statement of cash flows and disclosed in a narrative form or summarized in a separate schedule.

(c) are classified as an investing or financing activity.

(d) are classified as an operating activity, unless they can be specifically identified with financing or investing activities.

4. For purposes of the statement of cash flows, under IFRS interest paid is treated as:

(a) an operating activity in all cases.

(b) an investing or operating activity, depending on use of the borrowed funds.

(c) either a financing or investing activity.

(d) either an operating or financing activity, but treated consistently from period to period.

5. For purposes of the statement of cash flows, under IFRS income taxes paid are treated as:

(a) cash flows from operating activities unless they can be separately identified as part of investing or financing activities.

(b) an operating activity in all cases.

(c) an investing or operating activity, depending on whether a refund is received.

(d) either operating, financing, or investing activity, but treated consistently to other companies in the same industry.

IFRS CONCEPTS AND APPLICATION

IFRS23-1 Where can authoritative IFRS related to the statement of cash flows be found?

IFRS23-2 Briefly describe some of the similarities and differences between GAAP and IFRS with respect to cash flow reporting.

IFRS23-3 What are some of the key obstacles for the FASB and IASB within its accounting guidance in the area of cash flow reporting? Explain.

IFRS23-4 Stan Conner and Mark Stein were discussing the statement of cash flows of Bombeck Co. In the notes to the statement of cash flows was a schedule entitled "Non-cash investing and financing activities." Give three examples of significant non-cash transactions that would be reported in this schedule.

IFRS23-5 Springsteen Co. had the following activity in its most recent year of operations.

(a) Pension expense exceeds amount funded.   **(g)** Amortization of intangible assets.

(b) Redemption of bonds payable.   **(h)** Purchase of treasury shares.

(c) Sale of building at book value.   **(i)** Issuance of bonds for land.

(d) Depreciation.   **(j)** Payment of dividends.

(e) Exchange of equipment for furniture.   **(k)** Increase in interest receivable on notes receivable.

(f) Issuance of ordinary shares.   **(l)** Purchase of equipment.

Instructions

Classify the items as (1) operating—add to net income; (2) operating—deduct from net income; (3) investing; (4) financing; or (5) significant non-cash investing and financing activities. Use the indirect method.

IFRS23-6 Following are selected statement of financial position accounts of Sander Bros. Corp. at December 31, 2012 and 2011, and the increases or decreases in each account from 2011 to 2012. Also presented is selected income statement information for the year ended December 31, 2012, and additional information.

Selected statement of financial position accounts	2012	2011	Increase (Decrease)
Assets			
Property, plant, and equipment	$277,000	$247,000	$30,000
Accumulated depreciation	(178,000)	(167,000)	(11,000)
Accounts receivable	34,000	24,000	10,000

Selected statement of financial position accounts	2012	2011	Increase (Decrease)
Equity and liabilities			
Share capital—ordinary, $1 par	$ 22,000	$19,000	$ 3,000
Share premium—ordinary	9,000	3,000	6,000
Retained earnings	104,000	91,000	13,000
Bonds payable	49,000	46,000	3,000
Dividends payable	8,000	5,000	3,000

Selected income statement information for the year ended December 31, 2012

Sales revenue	$155,000
Depreciation	38,000
Gain on sale of equipment	14,500
Net income	31,000

Additional information:

1. During 2012, equipment costing $45,000 was sold for cash.

2. Accounts receivable relate to sales of merchandise.

3. During 2012, $25,000 of bonds payable were issued in exchange for property, plant, and equipment.

There was no amortization of bond discount or premium.

Instructions

Determine the category (operating, investing, or financing) and the amount that should be reported in the statement of cash flows for the following items.

(a) Payments for purchase of property, plant, and equipment.
(b) Proceeds from the sale of equipment.
(c) Cash dividends paid.
(d) Redemption of bonds payable.

IFRS23-7 Dingel Corporation has contracted with you to prepare a statement of cash flows. The controller has provided the following information.

	December 31	
	2012	2011
Buildings	$ –0–	$29,750
Equipment	45,000	20,000
Patents	5,000	6,250
Investments	–0–	3,000
Inventory	12,000	9,000
Accounts receivable	12,250	10,000
Cash	33,500	13,000
	$107,750	$91,000
Share capital—ordinary	$ 43,000	$33,000
Retained earnings	20,750	6,000
Allowance for doubtful accounts	3,000	4,500
Accumulated depreciation on equipment	2,000	4,500
Accumulated depreciation on buildings	–0–	6,000
Accounts payable	5,000	3,000
Dividends payable	–0–	5,000
Long-term notes payable	31,000	25,000
Notes payable, short-term (non-trade)	3,000	4,000
	$107,750	$91,000

Additional data related to 2012 are as follows.

1. Equipment that had cost $11,000 and was 40% depreciated at time of disposal was sold for $2,500.

2. $10,000 of the long-term notes payable was paid by issuing ordinary shares.

3. Cash dividends paid were $5,000.

4. On January 1, 2012, the building was completely destroyed by a flood. Insurance proceeds on the building were $32,000.

5. Equity investments (non-trading) were sold at $1,700 above their cost.
6. Cash was paid for the acquisition of equipment.
7. A long-term note for $16,000 was issued for the acquisition of equipment.
8. Interest of $2,000 and income taxes of $6,500 were paid in cash.

Instructions

Prepare a statement of cash flows using the indirect method.

Professional Research

IFRS23-8 As part of the year-end accounting process for your company, you are preparing the statement of cash flows according to IFRS. One of your team, a finance major, believes the statement should be prepared to report the change in working capital because analysts many times use working capital in ratio analysis. Your supervisor would like research conducted to verify the basis for preparing the statement of cash flows.

Instructions

Access the IFRS authoritative literature at the IASB website (*http://eifrs.iasb.org/*). When you have accessed the documents, you can use the search tool in your Internet browser to respond to the following questions. (Provide paragraph citations.)

(a) What is the primary objective for the statement of cash flows? Is working capital the basis for meeting this objective?

(b) What information is provided in a statement of cash flows?

(c) List some of the typical cash inflows and outflows from operations.

International Financial Reporting Problem:
Marks and Spencer plc

IFRS23-9 The financial statements of **Marks and Spencer plc (M&S)** are available at the book's companion website or can be accessed at *http://corporate.marksandspencer. com/documents/publications/2010/Annual_Report_2010*.

Instructions

Refer to M&S's financial statements and the accompanying notes to answer the following questions.

(a) Which method of computing net cash provided by operating activities does M&S use? What were the amounts of net cash provided by operating activities for the years 2009 and 2010? Which two items were most responsible for the increase in net cash provided by operating activities in 2010?

(b) What was the most significant item in the cash flows used for investing activities section in 2010? What was the most significant item in the cash flows used for financing activities section in 2010?

(c) Where is "deferred income taxes" reported in M&S's statement of cash flows? Why does it appear in that section of the statement of cash flows?

(d) Where is depreciation reported in M&S's statement of cash flows? Why is depreciation added to net income in the statement of cash flows?

ANSWERS TO IFRS SELF-TEST QUESTIONS

1. c 2. c 3. b 4. d 5. a

Remember to check the book's companion website to find additional resources for this chapter.

Full Disclosure in Financial Reporting

LEARNING OBJECTIVES

After studying this chapter, you should be able to:

1 Review the full disclosure principle and describe implementation problems.

2 Explain the use of notes in financial statement preparation.

3 Discuss the disclosure requirements for major business segments.

4 Describe the accounting problems associated with interim reporting.

5 Identify the major disclosures in the auditor's report.

6 Understand management's responsibilities for financials.

7 Identify issues related to financial forecasts and projections.

8 Describe the profession's response to fraudulent financial reporting.

High-Quality Financial Reporting—Always in Fashion

Here are excerpts from leading experts regarding the importance of high-quality financial reporting:
Warren E. Buffett, Chairman and Chief Executive Officer, **Berkshire Hathaway Inc.**:

> Financial reporting for Berkshire Hathaway, and for me personally, is the beginning of every decision that we make around here in terms of capital. I'm punching out 10-Ks and 10-Qs every single day. We look at the numbers and try to evaluate the quality of the financial reporting, and then we try to figure out what that means for the bonds and stocks that we're looking at, and thinking of either buying or selling.

Judy Lewent, Executive Vice President and Chief Financial Officer, **Merck & Co., Inc.**:

> . . . Higher standards, when properly implemented, drive excellence. I can make a parallel to the pharmaceutical industry. If you look around the world at where innovations come from, economists have studied and seen that where regulatory standards are the highest is where innovation is also the highest.

Floyd Norris, Chief Financial Correspondent, **New York Times**:

> We are in a situation now in our society where the temptations to provide "bad" financial reporting are probably greater than they used to be. The need to get the stock price up, or to keep it up, is intense. So, the temptation to play games, the temptation to manage earnings—some of which can be legitimate and some of which cannot be—is probably greater than it used to be.

Abby Joseph Cohen, Chair, Investment Policy Committee, **Goldman, Sachs & Co.**:

> High-quality financial reporting is perhaps the most important thing we can expect from companies. For investors to make good decisions—whether those investors are buying stocks or bonds or making private investments—they need to know the truth. And we think that when information is as clear as possible and is reported as frequently as makes sense, investors can do their jobs as best they can.

We can also get insight into the importance of high-quality reporting based on the market assessment of companies perceived to have poor-quality reporting. In a recent quarter, **Coach, Inc.** stopped reporting as separate items sales from regular stores (full price) and factory outlets. As a result, readers of its financial statements have a hard time determining the source of Coach's sales growth. Analysts are especially concerned that the less-transparent reporting may obscure slowing sales at its regular stores, as consumers cut down on luxury goods in the sluggish economy. Did Coach's stock price suffer as a result of this lower-quality reporting? You bet, as shown in the price graph on the next page.

Out of Fashion

DOLLARS

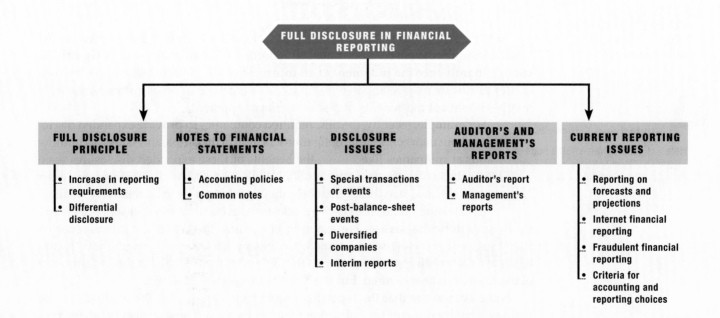

Coach Stock Price

MAY '07 — MAY '08

Data: Bloomberg Financial Markets.

Since the change in reporting in 2007, Coach's stock price has been down 34 percent. As one analyst noted, "It's never a good sign when you reduce transparency . . . It's a sign of weakness."

In short, the analysts' comments above illustrate why high-quality reporting is always in fashion—for companies, investors, and the capital markets. And, as the Coach example illustrates, full disclosure is at the heart of high-quality reporting.

Sources: Excerpts taken from video entitled "Financially Correct with Ben Stein," Financial Accounting Standards Board (Norwalk, Conn.: FASB, 2002). By permission. See also J. Porter, "As Belts Tighten, Coach Feels the Pinch," *BusinessWeek* (May 29, 2008), p. 66.

IFRS IN THIS CHAPTER

▶ See the **International Perspectives** on pages 1515, 1532, and 1548.

▶ Read the **IFRS Insights** on pages 1573–1581 for a discussion of:

—Differential disclosure

—Subsequent events

—Interim reports

PREVIEW OF CHAPTER 24

As the opening story indicates, our markets will not function properly without transparent, complete, and truthful reporting of financial performance. Investors and other interested parties need to read and understand all aspects of financial reporting—the financial statements, the notes, the president's letter, and management's discussion and analysis. In this chapter, we cover the full disclosure principle in more detail and examine disclosures that must accompany financial statements so that they are not misleading. The content and organization of this chapter are as follows.

FULL DISCLOSURE IN FINANCIAL REPORTING

FULL DISCLOSURE PRINCIPLE	NOTES TO FINANCIAL STATEMENTS	DISCLOSURE ISSUES	AUDITOR'S AND MANAGEMENT'S REPORTS	CURRENT REPORTING ISSUES
• Increase in reporting requirements • Differential disclosure	• Accounting policies • Common notes	• Special transactions or events • Post-balance-sheet events • Diversified companies • Interim reports	• Auditor's report • Management's reports	• Reporting on forecasts and projections • Internet financial reporting • Fraudulent financial reporting • Criteria for accounting and reporting choices

FULL DISCLOSURE PRINCIPLE

FASB Concepts Statement No. 1 notes that some useful information is best provided in the financial statements, and some is best provided by means other than in financial statements. For example, earnings and cash flows are readily available in financial statements—but investors might do better to look at comparisons to other companies in the same industry, found in news articles or brokerage house reports.

FASB rules directly affect financial statements, notes to the financial statements, and supplementary information. Other types of information found in the annual report, such as management's discussion and analysis, are not subject to FASB rules. Illustration 24-1 indicates the various types of financial information.

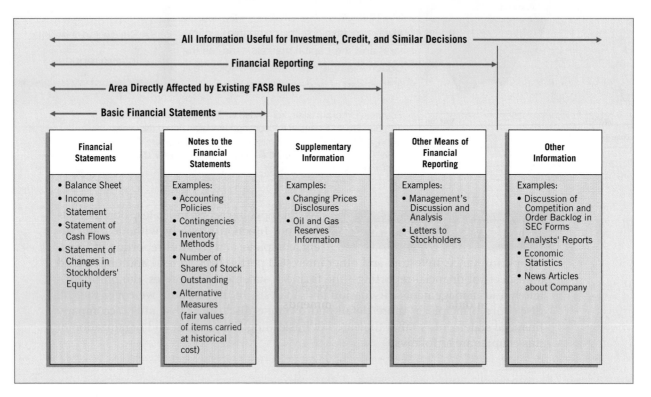

ILLUSTRATION 24-1
Types of Financial Information

As Chapter 2 indicated, the profession has adopted a full disclosure principle. The full disclosure principle calls for financial reporting of **any financial facts significant enough to influence the judgment of an informed reader**. In some situations, the benefits of disclosure may be apparent but the costs uncertain. In other instances, the costs may be certain but the benefits of disclosure not as apparent.

For example, recently, the SEC required companies to provide expanded disclosures about their contractual obligations. In light of the off-balance-sheet accounting frauds at companies like Enron, the benefits of these expanded disclosures seem fairly obvious to the investing public. While no one has documented the exact costs of disclosure in these situations, they would appear to be relatively small.

On the other hand, the cost of disclosure can be substantial in some cases and the benefits difficult to assess. For example, at one time the *Wall Street Journal* reported that if segment reporting were adopted, a company like Fruehauf would have had to increase its accounting staff 50 percent, from 300 to 450 individuals. In this case, the cost of disclosure can be measured, but the benefits are less well defined.

Some even argue that the reporting requirements are so detailed and substantial that users have a difficult time absorbing the information. These critics charge the profession with engaging in **information overload**.

Financial disasters at Microstrategy, PharMor, WorldCom, and AIG highlight the difficulty of implementing the full disclosure principle. They raise the issue of why investors were not aware of potential problems: Was the information these companies presented not comprehensible? Was it buried? Was it too technical? Was it properly presented and fully disclosed as of the financial statement date, but the situation later deteriorated? Or was it simply not there? In the following sections, we describe the elements of high-quality disclosure that will enable companies to avoid these disclosure pitfalls.

Increase in Reporting Requirements

Disclosure requirements have increased substantially. One survey showed that the size of many companies' annual reports is growing in response to demands for increased transparency. For example, annual report page counts ranged from 70 pages for Gateway up to a whopping 244 pages in Eastman Kodak's annual report. Compared to prior years' reports, the percentage increase in pages ranged from 17 percent at IBM to over 80 percent at Siebel Systems.[1] This result is not surprising; as illustrated throughout this textbook, the FASB has issued many pronouncements in the last 10 years that have substantial disclosure provisions.

The reasons for this increase in disclosure requirements are varied. Some of them are:

Complexity of the business environment. The increasing complexity of business operations magnifies the difficulty of distilling economic events into summarized reports. Such areas as derivatives, leasing, business combinations, pensions, financing arrangements, revenue recognition, and deferred taxes are complex. As a result, companies extensively use **notes to the financial statements** to explain these transactions and their future effects.

Necessity for timely information. Today, more than ever before, users are demanding information that is current and predictive. For example, users want more complete **interim data**. Also, the SEC recommends published financial forecasts, long avoided and even feared by management.

Accounting as a control and monitoring device. The government has recently sought public disclosure of such phenomena as management compensation, off-balance-sheet financing arrangements, and related-party transactions. An "Enronitis" concern is expressed in many of these newer disclosure requirements, and the SEC has selected accountants and auditors as the agents to assist in controlling and monitoring these concerns.

Differential Disclosure

A trend toward differential disclosure is also occurring. For example, the SEC requires that companies report to it certain substantive information that is not found in annual reports to stockholders. Likewise, the FASB, recognizing that certain disclosure requirements are costly and unnecessary for certain companies, has eliminated reporting requirements for nonpublic enterprises in such areas as fair value of financial instruments and segment reporting.[2]

Underlying Concepts

The AICPA's Special Committee on Financial Reporting notes that business reporting is not free, and improving it requires considering the relative costs and benefits of information. Undisciplined expansion of mandated reporting could result in large and needless costs.

Underlying Concepts

The AICPA's Special Committee on Financial Reporting states that to meet users' changing needs, business reporting must: (1) Provide more forward-looking information. (2) Focus more on the factors that create longer-term value, including nonfinancial measures. (3) Better align information reported externally with the information reported internally.

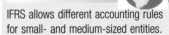

INTERNATIONAL PERSPECTIVE

IFRS allows different accounting rules for small- and medium-sized entities.

---

[1] Aliya Sternstein, "Heavy Lifting Required," *Forbes* (October 13, 2003) p. 58.

[2] The FASB has a disclosure-framework project. The revised pension and postretirement benefit disclosures discussed in Chapter 20 are one example of how disclosures can be streamlined and made more useful. However, as noted by one FASB member, the usefulness of expanded required disclosure also depends on users' ability to distinguish between disclosed versus recognized items in financial statements. Research to date is inconclusive on this matter. See Katherine Schipper, "Required Disclosures in Financial Reports," Presidential Address to the American Accounting Association Annual Meeting; San Francisco, CA (August 2005).

What do the numbers mean?

As we discussed in the opening story, financial disclosure is one of a number of institutional features that contribute to vibrant security markets. In fact, a recent study of disclosure and other mechanisms (such as civil lawsuits and criminal sanctions) found that good disclosure is the most important contributor to a vibrant market.

The study, which compared disclosure and other legal and regulatory elements across 49 countries, found that countries with the best disclosure laws have the biggest stock markets. Countries with more successful market environments also tend to have regulations that make it relatively easy for private investors to sue corporations that provide bad information. That is, while criminal sanctions can be effective in some circumstances, disclosure and other legal and regulatory elements encouraging good disclosure are the most important determinants of highly liquid and deep securities markets.

These findings hold for nations in all stages of economic development, with particular importance for nations that are in the early stages of securities regulation. The lesson: Disclosure is good for your market.

Source: Rebecca Christie, "Study: Disclosure at Heart of Effective Securities Laws," *Wall Street Journal Online* (August 11, 2003).

Underlying Concepts

The AICPA Special Committee on Financial Reporting indicated that users differ in their needs for information and that not all companies should report all elements of information. Rather, companies should report only information that users and preparers agree is needed in the particular circumstances.

LEARNING OBJECTIVE **2**
Explain the use of notes in financial statement preparation.

Some still complain that the FASB has not gone far enough. They note that certain types of companies (small or nonpublic) should not have to follow complex GAAP requirements such as those for deferred income taxes, leases, or pensions. This issue, often referred to as "**big GAAP versus little GAAP**," continues to be controversial. The FASB takes the position that there should be one set of GAAP, except in unusual situations.[3]

NOTES TO THE FINANCIAL STATEMENTS

As you know from your study of this textbook, notes are an integral part of the financial statements of a business enterprise. However, readers of financial statements often overlook them because they are highly technical and often appear in small print. **Notes are the means of amplifying or explaining the items presented in the main body of the statements.** They can explain in qualitative terms information pertinent to specific financial statement items. In addition, they can provide supplementary data of a quantitative nature to expand the information in the financial statements. Notes also can explain restrictions imposed by financial arrangements or basic contractual agreements. Although notes may be technical and difficult to understand, they provide meaningful information for the user of the financial statements.

Accounting Policies

Accounting policies are the specific accounting principles and methods a company currently uses and considers most appropriate to present fairly its financial statements.

---

[3]In response to cost-benefit concerns, the SEC has exempted some small public companies from certain rules implemented in response to the Sarbanes-Oxley Act of 2002. For example, smaller companies have more time to comply with the internal control rules required by the Sarbanes-Oxley law and have more time to file annual and interim reports. Both the FASB and the AICPA are studying the big GAAP/little GAAP issue to ensure that any kind of differential reporting is conceptually sound and meets the needs of users. See Remarks of Robert H. Herz, Chairman, Financial Accounting Standards Board, 2004 AICPA National Conference on Current SEC and PCAOB Reporting Developments (December 7, 2004).

GAAP states that information about the accounting policies adopted by a reporting entity is essential for financial statement users in making economic decisions. It recommended that companies should present **as an integral part of the financial statements a statement identifying the accounting policies adopted and followed by the reporting entity**. Companies should present the disclosure as the first note or in a separate Summary of Significant Accounting Policies section preceding the notes to the financial statements.

The Summary of Significant Accounting Policies answers such questions as: What method of depreciation is used on plant assets? What valuation method is employed on inventories? What amortization policy is followed in regard to intangible assets? How are marketing costs handled for financial reporting purposes?

Refer to Appendix 5B, pages 258–277, for an illustration of note disclosure of accounting policies (Note 1) and other notes accompanying the audited financial statements of The Procter & Gamble Company.

Analysts examine carefully the summary of accounting policies to determine whether a company is using conservative or liberal accounting practices. For example, depreciating plant assets over an unusually long period of time is considered liberal. Using LIFO inventory valuation in a period of inflation is generally viewed as conservative.

Companies that fail to adopt high-quality reporting policies may be heavily penalized by the market. For example, when Microstrategy disclosed that it would restate prior-year results due to use of aggressive revenue recognition policies, its share price dropped over 60 percent in one day. Investors viewed Microstrategy's quality of earnings as low.

Common Notes

We have discussed many of the notes to the financial statements throughout this textbook, and will discuss others more fully in this chapter. The more common are as follows.

MAJOR DISCLOSURES

INVENTORY. Companies should report the basis upon which inventory amounts are stated (lower-of-cost-or-market) and the method used in determining cost (LIFO, FIFO, average cost, etc.). Manufacturers should report, either in the balance sheet or in a separate schedule in the notes, the inventory composition (finished goods, work in process, raw materials). Unusual or significant financing arrangements relating to inventories that may require disclosure include transactions with related parties, product financing arrangements, firm purchase commitments, involuntary liquidation of LIFO inventories, and pledging of inventories as collateral. Chapter 9 (pages 514–515) illustrates these disclosures.

PROPERTY, PLANT, AND EQUIPMENT. Companies should state the basis of valuation for property, plant, and equipment. It is usually historical cost. Companies also should disclose pledges, liens, and other commitments related to these assets. In the presentation of depreciation, companies should disclose the following in the financial statements or in the notes: (1) depreciation expense for the period; (2) balances of major classes of depreciable assets, by nature and function, at the balance sheet date; (3) accumulated depreciation, either by major classes of depreciable assets or in total, at the balance sheet date; and (4) a general description of the method or methods used in computing depreciation with respect to major classes of depreciable assets. Finally, companies should explain any major impairments. Chapter 11 (pages 626–627) illustrates property, plant, and equipment.

CREDITOR CLAIMS. Investors normally find it extremely useful to understand the nature and cost of creditor claims. However, the liabilities section in the balance sheet can provide the major types of liabilities only in the aggregate. Note schedules regarding such obligations provide additional information about how a company is financing its operations, the costs that it will bear in future periods, and the timing of future cash outflows. Financial statements must disclose for each of the five years following the date of the statements the aggregate amount of maturities and sinking fund requirements for all long-term borrowings. Chapter 14 (pages 806–807) illustrates these disclosures.

EQUITYHOLDERS' CLAIMS. Many companies present in the body of the balance sheet information about equity securities: the number of shares authorized, issued, and outstanding and the par value for each type of security. Or, companies may present such data in a note. Beyond that, a common equity note disclosure relates to contracts and senior securities outstanding that might affect the various claims of the residual equityholders. An example would be the existence of outstanding stock options, outstanding convertible debt, redeemable preferred stock, and convertible preferred stock. In addition, it is necessary to disclose certain types of restrictions currently in force. Generally, these types of restrictions involve the amount of earnings available for dividend distribution. Examples of these types of disclosures are illustrated in Chapter 15 (pages 868–869) and Chapter 16 (pages 932–933).

CONTINGENCIES AND COMMITMENTS. A company may have gain or loss contingencies that are not disclosed in the body of the financial statements. These contingencies include litigation, debt and other guarantees, possible tax assessments, renegotiation of government contracts, and sales of receivables with recourse. In addition, companies should disclose in the notes commitments that relate to dividend restrictions, purchase agreements (through-put and take-or-pay), hedge contracts, and employment contracts. Disclosures of such items are illustrated in Chapter 7 (page 392), Chapter 9 (page 503), and Chapter 13 (pages 746–749).

FAIR VALUES. Companies that have assets or liabilities measured at fair value must disclose both the cost and the fair value of all financial instruments in the notes to the financial statements. Fair value measurements may be used for many financial assets and liabilities, investments, impairments of long-lived assets, and some contingencies. Companies also provide disclosure of information that enables users to determine the extent of usage of fair value and the inputs used to implement fair value measurement. This fair value hierarchy identifies three broad levels related to the measurement of fair values (Levels 1, 2, and 3). The levels indicate the reliability of the measurement of fair value information. An appendix to Chapter 17 (pages 1025–1028) discusses in detail fair value disclosures.

DEFERRED TAXES, PENSIONS, AND LEASES. The FASB also requires extensive disclosure in the areas of deferred taxes, pensions, and leases. Chapter 19 (pages 1165–1168), Chapter 20 (pages 1229–1239), and Chapter 21 (pages 1321–1323) discuss in detail each of these disclosures. Users of financial statements should carefully read notes to the financial statements for information about off-balance-sheet commitments, future financing needs, and the quality of a company's earnings.

CHANGES IN ACCOUNTING PRINCIPLES. The profession defines various types of accounting changes and establishes guides for reporting each type. Companies discuss, either in the summary of significant accounting policies or in the other notes, changes in accounting principles (as well as material changes in estimates and corrections of errors). See Chapter 22 (pages 1368–1383).

Underlying Concepts

The AICPA Special Committee on Financial Reporting notes that standard-setters should address disclosures and accounting requirements for off-balance-sheet financial arrangements. The goal should be to report the risks, opportunities, resources, and obligations that result from those arrangements, consistent with users' needs for information.

In earlier chapters we discussed the disclosures listed above. The following sections of this chapter illustrate four additional disclosures of significance—special transactions or events, subsequent events, segment reporting, and interim reporting.

FOOTNOTE SECRETS

What do the numbers mean?

Often, note disclosures are needed to give a complete picture of a company's financial position. A good example of such disclosures is the required disclosure of debt triggers that may be buried in financing arrangements. These triggers can require a company to pay off a loan immediately if the debt rating collapses; they are one of the reasons Enron crumbled so quickly. But few Enron stockholders knew about the debt triggers until the gun had gone off. Companies are also disclosing more about their bank credit lines, liquidity, and any special-purpose entities. (The latter were major villains in the Enron drama.)

How can you get better informed about note disclosures that may contain important information related to your investments? Beyond your study in this class, a good Web resource for understanding the contents of note disclosures is *http://www.footnoted.org/*. This site highlights "the things companies bury in their SEC filings." It notes that company reports are more complete of late, but only the largest companies are preparing documents that are readable. As the editor of the site noted, "[some companies] are being dragged kicking and screaming into plain English."

Source: Gretchen Morgenson, "Annual Reports: More Pages, but Better?" *New York Times* (March 17, 2002); and D. Stead, "The Secrets in SEC Filings," *BusinessWeek* (August 25, 2008), p. 12.

DISCLOSURE ISSUES

Disclosure of Special Transactions or Events

Related-party transactions, errors and fraud, and illegal acts pose especially sensitive and difficult problems. The accountant/auditor who has responsibility for reporting on these types of transactions must take care to properly balance the rights of the reporting company and the needs of users of the financial statements.

Related-party transactions arise when a company engages in transactions in which one of the parties has the ability to significantly influence the policies of the other. They may also occur when a nontransacting party has the ability to influence the policies of the two transacting parties.[4] Competitive, free-market dealings may not exist in related-party transactions, and so an "arm's-length" basis cannot be assumed. Transactions such as borrowing or lending money at abnormally low or high interest rates, real estate sales at amounts that differ significantly from appraised value, exchanges of nonmonetary assets, and transactions involving enterprises that have no economic substance ("shell corporations") suggest that related parties may be involved.

In order to make adequate disclosure, companies should report the economic substance, rather than the legal form, of these transactions. GAAP requires the following disclosures of material related-party transactions. [1]

 See the FASB Codification section (page 1554).

1. The nature of the relationship(s) involved.
2. A description of the transactions (including transactions to which no amounts or nominal amounts were ascribed) for each of the periods for which income statements are presented.

---

[4]Examples of related-party transactions include transactions between (a) a parent company and its subsidiaries; (b) subsidiaries of a common parent; (c) a company and trusts for the benefit of employees (controlled or managed by the enterprise); and (d) a company and its principal owners, management, or members of immediate families, and affiliates. Two classic cases of related-party transactions were Enron, with its misuse of special-purpose entities, and Tyco International, which forgave loans to its management team.

3. The dollar amounts of transactions for each of the periods for which income statements are presented.

4. Amounts due from or to related parties as of the date of each balance sheet presented.

Illustration 24-2, from the annual report of Harley-Davidson, Inc., shows disclosure of related-party transactions.

ILLUSTRATION 24-2
Disclosure of Related-Party Transactions

Harley-Davidson, Inc.

Note 22. Related Party Transactions
The Company has the following material related party transactions. A director of the Company is Chairman and Chief Executive Officer and an equity owner of Fred Deeley Imports Ltd. (Deeley Imports), the exclusive distributor of the Company's motorcycles in Canada. The Company recorded motorcycles and related products revenue and financial services revenue from Deeley Imports during 2009, 2008 and 2007 of $177.2 million, $258.3 million and $231.9 million, respectively, and had accounts receivables balances due from Deeley Imports of $13.9 million and $31.5 million at December 31, 2009 and 2008, respectively. All such products were provided in the ordinary course of business at prices and on terms and conditions that the Company believes are the same as those that would result from arm's-length negotiations between unrelated parties.

Many companies are involved in related-party transactions. Errors, fraud (sometimes referred to as irregularities), and illegal acts, however, are the exception rather than the rule. Accounting errors are **unintentional** mistakes, whereas fraud (misappropriation of assets and fraudulent financial reporting) involves **intentional** distortions of financial statements.[5] As indicated earlier, companies should correct the financial statements when they discover errors. The same treatment should be given fraud. The discovery of fraud, however, gives rise to a different set of procedures and responsibilities for the accountant/auditor.[6]

Illegal acts encompass such items as illegal political contributions, bribes, kickbacks, and other violations of laws and regulations.[7] In these situations, the accountant/auditor must evaluate the adequacy of disclosure in the financial statements. For example, if a company derives revenue from an illegal act that is considered material in relation to the financial statements, this information should be disclosed. The Sarbanes-Oxley Act of 2002 is intended to deter these illegal acts. This law adds significant fines and longer jail time for those who improperly sign off on the correctness of financial statements that include willing and knowing misstatements.

Disclosure plays a very important role in these types of transactions because the events are more qualitative than quantitative and involve more subjective than objective evaluation. Users of the financial statements need some indication of the existence and nature of these transactions, through disclosures, modifications in the auditor's report, or reports of changes in auditors.

---

[5]"Consideration of Fraud in a Financial Statement Audit," *Statement on Auditing Standards No. 99* (New York: AICPA, 2002). We have an expanded discussion of fraudulent financial reporting later in this chapter. Since passage of the Sarbanes-Oxley Act of 2002, auditors of public companies are regulated by the Public Company Accounting Oversight Board (PCAOB). The PCAOB is now the audit standard-setter for auditors of public companies. It has adopted much of the prior auditing standards issued by the Auditing Standards Board of the AICPA.

[6]The profession became so concerned with certain management frauds that affect financial statements that it established a National Commission on Fraudulent Financial Reporting. The major purpose of this organization was to determine how fraudulent reporting practices could be constrained. Fraudulent financial reporting is discussed later in this chapter.

[7]"Illegal Acts by Clients," *Statement on Auditing Standards No. 54* (New York: AICPA, 1988).

Post-Balance-Sheet Events (Subsequent Events)

Notes to the financial statements should explain any significant financial events that took place after the formal balance sheet date, but before the statement is issued. These events are referred to as post-balance-sheet events, or just plain subsequent events. Illustration 24-3 shows a time diagram of the subsequent events period.

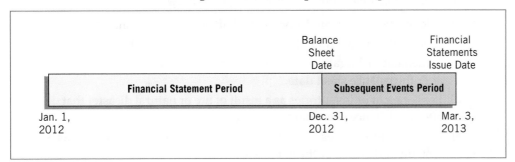

ILLUSTRATION 24-3
Time Periods for
Subsequent Events

A period of several weeks, and sometimes months, may elapse after the end of the fiscal year but before the company issues financial statements. Various activities involved in closing the books for the period and issuing the statements all take time: taking and pricing the inventory, reconciling subsidiary ledgers with controlling accounts, preparing necessary adjusting entries, ensuring that all transactions for the period have been entered, obtaining an audit of the financial statements by independent certified public accountants, and printing the annual report. During the period between the balance sheet date and its distribution to stockholders and creditors, important transactions or other events may occur that materially affect the company's financial position or operating situation.

Many who read a balance sheet believe the balance sheet condition is constant, and they project it into the future. However, readers must be told if the company has experienced a significant change—e.g., sold one of its plants, acquired a subsidiary, suffered extraordinary losses, settled significant litigation, or experienced any other important event in the post-balance-sheet period. Without an explanation in a note, the reader might be misled and draw inappropriate conclusions.

Two types of events or transactions occurring after the balance sheet date may have a material effect on the financial statements or may need disclosure so that readers interpret these statements accurately:

Underlying Concepts

The periodicity or time period assumption implies that economic activities of an enterprise can be divided into artificial time periods for purpose of analysis.

1. Events that provide additional evidence about conditions **that existed** at the balance sheet date, including the estimates inherent in the process of preparing financial statements. These events are referred to as recognized subsequent events and require adjustments to the financial statements. All information available prior to the issuance of the financial statements helps investors and creditors evaluate estimates previously made. To ignore these subsequent events is to pass up an opportunity to improve the accuracy of the financial statements. This first type of event encompasses information that an accountant would have recorded in the accounts had the information been known at the balance sheet date.

   For example, if a loss on an account receivable results from a customer's bankruptcy subsequent to the balance sheet date, the company adjusts the financial statements before their issuance. The bankruptcy stems from the customer's poor financial health existing at the balance sheet date.

   The same criterion applies to settlements of litigation. The company must adjust the financial statements if the events that gave rise to the litigation, such as personal injury or patent infringement, took place prior to the balance sheet date.

2. Events that provide evidence about conditions that **did not exist** at the balance sheet date but arise subsequent to that date. These events are referred as nonrecognized subsequent events and do not require adjustment of the financial statements.

To illustrate, a loss resulting from a customer's fire or flood *after* the balance sheet date does not reflect conditions existing at that date. Thus, adjustment of the financial statements is not necessary. A company should not recognize subsequent events that provide evidence about conditions that did not exist at the date of the balance sheet but that arose after the balance sheet date.

The following are examples of nonrecognized subsequent events:

(a) Sale of a bond or capital stock issued after the balance sheet date.

(b) A business combination that occurs after the balance sheet date.

(c) Settlement of litigation when the event giving rise to the claim took place after the balance sheet date.

(d) Loss of plant or inventories as a result of fire or natural disaster that occurred after the balance sheet date.

(e) Losses on receivables resulting from conditions (such as a customer's major casualty) arising after the balance sheet date.

(f) Changes in the quoted market prices of securities or foreign exchange rates after the balance sheet date.

(g) Entering into significant commitments or contingent liabilities, for example, by issuing significant guarantees after the balance sheet date. [2][8]

Underlying Concepts

A company also should consider supplementing the historical financial statements with pro forma financial data. Occasionally, a nonrecognized subsequent event may be so significant that disclosure can best be made by means of pro forma financial data.

Some nonrecognized subsequent events may have to be disclosed to keep the financial statements from being misleading. For such events, a company discloses the nature of the event and an estimate of its financial effect.

Illustration 24-4 presents an example of subsequent events disclosure, excerpted from the annual report of Xerox.

ILLUSTRATION 24-4
Disclosure of
Subsequent Events

Xerox

Note 1 (in part) Summary of Accounting Policies

Foreign Currency Translation and Re-measurement

We have operations in Venezuela where the U.S. Dollar is the functional currency. At December 31, 2009 our Venezuelan operations had approximately 90 million in net Bolivar-denominated monetary assets that were re-measured to U.S. Dollars at the official exchange rate of 2.15 Bolivars to the Dollar. In January 2010, Venezuela announced a devaluation of the Bolivar to an official rate of 4.30 Bolivars to the Dollar for our products. As a result of this devaluation, we expect to record a loss of approximately $21 million in the first quarter of 2010 for the re-measurement of our net Bolivar-denominated monetary assets.

Many subsequent events or developments do not require adjustment of or disclosure in the financial statements. Typically, these are nonaccounting events or conditions that management normally communicates by other means. These events include legislation, product changes, management changes, strikes, unionization, marketing agreements, and loss of important customers.

LEARNING OBJECTIVE **3**
Discuss the disclosure requirements for major business segments.

Reporting for Diversified (Conglomerate) Companies

In certain business climates, companies have a tendency to diversify their operations. Take the case of conglomerate General Electric (GE), whose products

---

[8]The effects from natural disasters, like hurricanes Katrina and Rita, which occurred after the year-end for companies with August fiscal years, require disclosure in order to keep the statements from being misleading. Some companies may have to consider whether these disasters affect their ability to continue as going concerns. *Accounting Trends and Techniques—2010* listed the following types of subsequent events and their frequency of occurrence among the 500 companies surveyed: business combinations pending or effected, 44; debt incurred, reduced or refinanced, 56; discontinued operations or asset disposals, 33; litigation, 37; restructuring/bankruptcy, 16; capital stock issued or purchased, 17; stock splits or dividends, 4; and employee benefits, 17.

include locomotives and jet engines, credit card services, and water purification systems. Its NBC Universal subsidiary owns NBC TV, Vivendi Universal Entertainment, and Universal Pictures. When businesses are so diversified, investors and investment analysts want more information about the details behind conglomerate financial statements. Particularly, they want income statement, balance sheet, and cash flow information on the **individual segments** that compose the total income figure.

Illustration 24-5 shows **segmented** (disaggregated) financial information of an office equipment and auto parts company.

ILLUSTRATION 24-5
Segmented Income
Statement

OFFICE EQUIPMENT AND AUTO PARTS COMPANY INCOME STATEMENT DATA (IN MILLIONS)			
	Consolidated	Office Equipment	Auto Parts
Net sales	$78.8	$18.0	$60.8
Manufacturing costs			
Inventories, beginning	12.3	4.0	8.3
Materials and services	38.9	10.8	28.1
Wages	12.9	3.8	9.1
Inventories, ending	(13.3)	(3.9)	(9.4)
	50.8	14.7	36.1
Selling and administrative expenses	12.1	1.6	10.5
Total operating expenses	62.9	16.3	46.6
Income before taxes	15.9	1.7	14.2
Income taxes	(9.3)	(1.0)	(8.3)
Net income	$ 6.6	$ 0.7	$ 5.9

Much information is hidden in the aggregated totals. If the analyst has only the consolidated figures, he/she cannot tell the extent to which the differing product lines **contribute to the company's profitability, risk, and growth potential**. For example, in Illustration 24-5, the office equipment segment looks like a risky venture. Segmented reporting would provide useful information about the two business segments and would be useful for making an informed investment decision regarding the whole company.

In addition to the example of Coach, Inc. in the opening story, a classic situation that demonstrates the need for segmented data involved Caterpillar, Inc. The SEC cited Caterpillar because it failed to tell investors that nearly a quarter of its income in one year came from a Brazilian unit and was nonrecurring in nature. The company knew that different economic policies in the next year would probably greatly affect earnings of the Brazilian unit. But Caterpillar presented its financial results on a consolidated basis, not disclosing the Brazilian operations. The SEC found that Caterpillar's failure to include information about Brazil left investors with an incomplete picture of the company's financial results and denied investors the opportunity to see the company "through the eyes of management."

Companies have always been somewhat hesitant to disclose segmented data for various reasons:

1. Without a thorough knowledge of the business and an understanding of such important factors as the competitive environment and capital investment requirements, the investor may find the segmented information meaningless or may even draw improper conclusions about the reported earnings of the segments.

2. Additional disclosure may be helpful to competitors, labor unions, suppliers, and certain government regulatory agencies, and thus harm the reporting company.

3. Additional disclosure may discourage management from taking intelligent business risks because segments reporting losses or unsatisfactory earnings may cause stockholder dissatisfaction with management.

4. The wide variation among companies in the choice of segments, cost allocation, and other accounting problems limits the usefulness of segmented information.

5. The investor is investing in the company as a whole and not in the particular segments, and it should not matter how any single segment is performing if the overall performance is satisfactory.

6. Certain technical problems, such as classification of segments and allocation of segment revenues and costs (especially "common costs"), are formidable.

On the other hand, the advocates of segmented disclosures offer these reasons in support of the practice:

1. Investors need segmented information to make an intelligent investment decision regarding a diversified company.

(a) Sales and earnings of individual segments enable investors to evaluate the differences between segments in growth rate, risk, and profitability, and to forecast consolidated profits.

(b) Segmented reports help investors evaluate the company's investment worth by disclosing the nature of a company's businesses and the relative size of the components.

2. The absence of segmented reporting by a diversified company may put its unsegmented, single product-line competitors at a competitive disadvantage because the conglomerate may obscure information that its competitors must disclose.

The advocates of segmented disclosures appear to have a much stronger case. Many users indicate that segmented data are the most useful financial information provided, aside from the basic financial statements. As a result, the FASB has issued extensive reporting guidelines in this area.

Objective of Reporting Segmented Information
The objective of reporting segmented financial data is to provide information about the **different types of business activities** in which an enterprise engages and the **different economic environments** in which it operates. Meeting this objective will help users of financial statements do the following.

(a) Better understand the enterprise's performance.

(b) Better assess its prospects for future net cash flows.

(c) Make more informed judgments about the enterprise as a whole.

Basic Principles
Financial statements can be disaggregated in several ways. For example, they can be disaggregated by products or services, by geography, by legal entity, or by type of customer. However, it is not feasible to provide all of that information in every set of financial statements. GAAP requires that general-purpose financial statements include selected information on a single basis of segmentation. Thus, a company can meet the segmented reporting objective by providing financial statements segmented based on how the company's operations are managed. The method chosen is referred to as the management approach. [3] **The management approach reflects how management segments the company for making operating decisions.** The segments are evident from the components of the company's organization structure. These components are called **operating segments**.

Identifying Operating Segments
An operating segment is a component of an enterprise:

(a) That engages in business activities from which it earns revenues and incurs expenses.

(b) Whose operating results are regularly reviewed by the company's chief operating decision-maker to assess segment performance and allocate resources to the segment.

(c) For which discrete financial information is available that is generated by or based on the internal financial reporting system.

Companies may aggregate information about two or more operating segments only if the segments have the same basic characteristics in each of the following areas.

(a) The nature of the products and services provided.

(b) The nature of the production process.

(c) The type or class of customer.

(d) The methods of product or service distribution.

(e) If applicable, the nature of the regulatory environment.

After the company decides on the possible segments for disclosure, it makes a quantitative materiality test. This test determines whether the segment is significant enough to warrant actual disclosure. An operating segment is deemed significant, and therefore a reportable segment, if it satisfies **one or more** of the following quantitative thresholds.

1. Its **revenue** (including both sales to external customers and intersegment sales or transfers) is 10 percent or more of the combined revenue of all the company's operating segments.

2. The absolute amount of its **profit or loss** is 10 percent or more of the greater, in absolute amount, of (a) the combined operating profit of all operating segments that did not incur a loss, or (b) the combined loss of all operating segments that did report a loss.

3. Its **identifiable assets** are 10 percent or more of the combined assets of all operating segments.

In applying these tests, the company must consider two additional factors. First, segment data must explain a significant portion of the company's business. Specifically, the segmented results must equal or exceed 75 percent of the combined sales to unaffiliated customers for the entire company. This test prevents a company from providing limited information on only a few segments and lumping all the rest into one category.

Second, the profession recognizes that reporting too many segments may overwhelm users with detailed information. The FASB decided that 10 is a reasonable upper limit for the number of segments that a company must disclose.

To illustrate these requirements, assume a company has identified six possible reporting segments, as shown in Illustration 24-6 (000s omitted).

ILLUSTRATION 24-6
Data for Different Possible Reporting Segments

Segments	Total Revenue (Unaffiliated)	Operating Profit (Loss)	Identifiable Assets
A	$ 100	$10	$ 60
B	50	2	30
C	700	40	390
D	300	20	160
E	900	18	280
F	100	(5)	50
	$2,150	$85	$970

The company would apply the respective tests as follows.

Revenue test: 10% × $2,150 = $215; C, D, and E meet this test.

Operating profit (loss) test: 10% × $90 = $9 (note that the $5 loss is ignored, because the test is based on non-loss segments); A, C, D, and E meet this test.

Identifiable assets tests: 10% × $970 = $97; C, D, and E meet this test.

The reporting segments are therefore A, C, D, and E, assuming that these four segments have enough sales to meet the 75 percent of combined sales test. The 75 percent test is computed as follows.

75% of combined sales test: 75% × $2,150 = $1,612.50. The sales of A, C, D, and E total $2,000 ($100 + $700 + $300 + $900); therefore, the 75 percent test is met.

Measurement Principles

The accounting principles that companies use for segment disclosure need not be the same as the principles they use to prepare the consolidated statements. This flexibility may at first appear inconsistent. But, preparing segment information in accordance with generally accepted accounting principles would be difficult because some principles are not expected to apply at a segment level. Examples are accounting for the cost of company-wide employee benefit plans, accounting for income taxes in a company that files a consolidated tax return, and accounting for inventory on a LIFO basis if the pool includes items in more than one segment.

The FASB does not require allocations of joint, common, or company-wide costs solely for external reporting purposes. Common costs are those incurred for the benefit of more than one segment and whose interrelated nature prevents a completely objective division of costs among segments. For example, the company president's salary is difficult to allocate to various segments. Allocations of common costs are inherently arbitrary and may not be meaningful. There is a presumption that if companies allocate common costs to segments, these allocations are either directly attributable or reasonably allocable.

Segmented Information Reported

The FASB requires that an enterprise report the following.

1. *General information about its operating segments.* This includes factors that management considers most significant in determining the company's operating segments, and the types of products and services from which each operating segment derives its revenues.

2. *Segment profit and loss and related information.* Specifically, companies must report the following information about each operating segment if the amounts are included in determining segment profit or loss.
   (a) Revenues from transactions with external customers.
   (b) Revenues from transactions with other operating segments of the same enterprise.
   (c) Interest revenue.
   (d) Interest expense.
   (e) Depreciation, depletion, and amortization expense.
   (f) Unusual items.
   (g) Equity in the net income of investees accounted for by the equity method.
   (h) Income tax expense or benefit.
   (i) Extraordinary items.
   (j) Significant noncash items other than depreciation, depletion, and amortization expense.

3. *Segment assets.* A company must report each operating segment's total assets.

4. *Reconciliations.* A company must provide a reconciliation of the total of the segments' revenues to total revenues, a reconciliation of the total of the operating segments' profits and losses to its income before income taxes, and a reconciliation of the total of the operating segments' assets to total assets.

5. *Information about products and services and geographic areas.* For each operating segment not based on geography, the company must report (unless it is impracticable):

(1) revenues from external customers, (2) long-lived assets, and (3) expenditures during the period for long-lived assets. This information, if material, must be reported (a) in the enterprise's country of domicile and (b) in each other country.

6. *Major customers.* If 10 percent or more of company revenue is derived from a single customer, the company must disclose the total amount of revenue from each such customer by segment.

Illustration of Disaggregated Information

Illustration 24-7 shows the segment disclosure for Johnson & Johnson.

ILLUSTRATION 24-7
Segment Disclosure

Johnson & Johnson
(notes excluded)

Segments of Business and Geographic Areas

(Dollars in Millions)	Sales to Customers 2009	2008	2007
Consumer—United States	$ 6,837	$ 6,937	$ 6,408
International	8,966	9,117	8,085
Total	15,803	16,054	14,493
Pharmaceutical—United States	13,041	14,831	15,603
International	9,479	9,736	9,263
Total	22,520	24,567	24,866
Medical Devices and Diagnostics—United States	11,011	10,541	10,433
International	12,563	12,585	11,303
Total	23,574	23,126	21,736
Worldwide total	$61,897	$63,747	$ 61,095

(Dollars in Millions)	Operating Profit 2009	2008	2007	Identifiable Assets 2009	2008	2007
Consumer	$ 2,475	$ 2,674	$ 2,277	$24,671	$23,765	$26,550
Pharmaceutical	6,413	7,605	6,540	21,460	19,544	19,780
Medical Devices and Diagnostics	7,694	7,223	4,846	22,853	20,779	19,978
Total	16,582	17,502	13,663	68,984	64,088	66,308
Less: Expense not allocated to segments	827	573	380			
General corporate				25,698	20,824	14,646
Worldwide total	$15,755	$16,929	$13,283	$94,682	$84,912	$80,954

(Dollars in Millions)	Additions to Property, Plant & Equipment 2009	2008	2007	Depreciation and Amortization 2009	2008	2007
Consumer	$ 439	$ 499	$ 504	$ 513	$ 489	$ 472
Pharmaceutical	535	920	1,137	922	986	1,033
Medical Devices and Diagnostics	1,114	1,251	919	1,124	1,146	1,080
Segments total	2,088	2,670	2,560	2,559	2,621	2,585
General corporate	277	396	382	215	211	192
Worldwide total	$2,365	$3,066	$2,942	$2,774	$2,832	$2,777

(Dollars in Millions)	Sales to Customers 2009	2008	2007	Long-Lived Assets 2009	2008	2007
United States	$30,889	$32,309	$32,444	$22,399	$21,674	$21,685
Europe	15,934	16,782	15,644	17,347	14,375	15,578
Western Hemisphere excluding U.S.	5,156	5,173	4,681	3,540	3,328	3,722
Asia-Pacific, Africa	9,918	9,483	8,326	1,868	1,898	1,261
Segments total	61,897	63,747	61,095	45,154	41,275	42,246
General corporate				790	785	702
Other non long-lived assets				48,738	42,852	38,006
Worldwide total	$61,897	$63,747	$61,095	$94,682	$84,912	$80,954

Interim Reports

Another source of information for the investor is interim reports. As noted earlier, **interim reports** cover periods of less than one year. The stock exchanges, the SEC, and the accounting profession have an active interest in the presentation of interim information.

The SEC mandates that certain companies file a **Form 10-Q**, in which a company discloses quarterly data similar to that disclosed in the annual report. It also requires those companies to disclose selected quarterly information in notes to the annual financial statements. Illustration 24-8 presents the selected quarterly disclosure of **Tootsie Roll Industries, Inc.** In addition to Form 10-Q, GAAP narrows the reporting alternatives related to interim reports. [4]

ILLUSTRATION 24-8
Disclosure of Selected
Quarterly Data

Tootsie Roll Industries, Inc.

For the Year Ended December 31, 2009

| | (Thousands of dollars except per share data) | | | | |
	First	Second	Third	Fourth	Total
Net product sales	$94,054	$107,812	$183,408	$110,318	$495,592
Product gross margin	33,335	39,005	65,701	38,906	176,947
Net earnings	8,320	10,338	27,247	7,570	53,475
Net earnings per share	0.15	0.18	0.49	0.14	0.95

| | Stock Prices | | Dividends |
| | 2009 | | 2009 |
	High	Low	
1st Qtr	$25.77	$19.46	$0.08
2nd Qtr	$24.42	$21.82	$0.08
3rd Qtr	$24.64	$22.67	$0.08
4th Qtr	$28.06	$23.60	$0.08

Because of the short-term nature of the information in these reports, there is considerable controversy as to the general approach companies should employ. One group, which favors the **discrete approach**, believes that companies should treat each interim period as a separate accounting period. Using that treatment, companies would follow the principles for deferrals and accruals used for annual reports. In this view, companies should report accounting transactions as they occur, and expense recognition should not change with the period of time covered.

Another group, which favors the **integral approach**, believes that the interim report is an integral part of the annual report and that deferrals and accruals should take into consideration what will happen for the entire year. In this approach, companies should assign estimated expenses to parts of a year on the basis of sales volume or some other activity base.

At present, many companies follow the discrete approach for certain types of expenses and the integral approach for others, because the standards currently employed in practice are vague and lead to differing interpretations.

Interim Reporting Requirements

Generally, companies should use the same accounting principles for interim reports and for annual reports. They should recognize revenues in interim periods on the same basis as they are for annual periods. For example, if Cedars Corp. uses the installment-sales method as the basis for recognizing revenue on an annual basis, then it should use the installment basis for interim reports as well. Also, Cedars should treat costs directly associated with revenues (product costs, such as materials, labor and related fringe benefits, and manufacturing overhead) in the same manner for interim reports as for annual reports.

Companies should use the same inventory pricing methods (FIFO, LIFO, etc.) for interim reports and for annual reports. However, the following exceptions are appropriate at interim reporting periods.

1. Companies may use the gross profit method for interim inventory pricing. But they must disclose the method and adjustments to reconcile with annual inventory.
2. When a company liquidates LIFO inventories at an interim date and expects to replace them by year-end, cost of goods sold should include the expected cost of replacing the liquidated LIFO base, rather than give effect to the interim liquidation.
3. Companies should not defer inventory market declines beyond the interim period unless they are temporary and no loss is expected for the fiscal year.
4. Companies ordinarily should defer planned variances under a standard cost system; such variances are expected to be absorbed by year-end.

Companies often charge to the interim period, as incurred, costs and expenses other than product costs (often referred to as **period costs**). But companies may allocate these costs among interim periods on the basis of an estimate of time expired, benefit received, or activity associated with the periods. Companies display considerable latitude in accounting for these costs in interim periods, and many believe more definitive guidelines are needed.

Regarding disclosure, companies should report the following interim data at a minimum.

1. Sales or gross revenues, provision for income taxes, extraordinary items, and net income.
2. Basic and diluted earnings per share where appropriate.
3. Seasonal revenue, cost, or expenses.
4. Significant changes in estimates or provisions for income taxes.
5. Disposal of a component of a business and extraordinary, unusual, or infrequently occurring items.
6. Contingent items.
7. Changes in accounting principles or estimates.
8. Significant changes in financial position.

The FASB encourages, but does not require, companies to publish an interim balance sheet and statement of cash flows. If a company does not present this information, it should disclose significant changes in such items as liquid assets, net working capital, long-term liabilities, and stockholders' equity.

Unique Problems of Interim Reporting

GAAP reflects a preference for the integral approach. However, within this broad guideline, a number of unique reporting problems develop related to the following items.

Advertising and Similar Costs. The general guidelines are that companies should defer in an interim period costs such as advertising if the benefits extend beyond that period; otherwise the company should expense those costs as incurred. But such a determination is difficult, and even if the company defers the costs, how should it allocate them between quarters?

Because of the vague guidelines in this area, accounting for advertising varies widely. At one time, some companies in the food industry, such as RJR Nabisco and

Pillsbury, charged advertising costs as a percentage of sales and adjusted to actual at year-end, whereas **General Foods** and **Kellogg** expensed these costs as incurred.

The same type of problem relates to such items as Social Security taxes, research and development costs, and major repairs. For example, should the company expense Social Security costs (payroll taxes) on highly paid personnel early in the year, or allocate and spread them to subsequent quarters? Should a major repair that occurs later in the year be anticipated and allocated proportionately to earlier periods?

Expenses Subject to Year-End Adjustment. Companies often do not know with a great deal of certainty amounts of bad debts, executive bonuses, pension costs, and inventory shrinkage until year-end. **They should estimate these costs and allocate them to interim periods as best they can.** Companies use a variety of allocation techniques to accomplish this objective.

Income Taxes. Not every dollar of corporate taxable income is taxed at the same rate; the tax rate is progressive. This aspect of business income taxes poses a problem in preparing interim financial statements. Should the company use the **annualized approach**, which is to annualize income to date and accrue the proportionate income tax for the period to date? Or should it follow the **marginal principle approach,** which is to apply the lower rate of tax to the first amount of income earned? At one time, companies generally followed the latter approach and accrued the tax applicable to each additional dollar of income.

The profession now, however, uses the annualized approach. This requires that "at the end of each interim period the company should make its best estimate of the effective tax rate expected to be applicable for the full fiscal year. The rate so determined should be used in providing for income taxes on income for the quarter." **[5]**[9]

Because businesses did not uniformly apply this guideline in accounting for similar situations, the FASB issued authoritative guidance. GAAP now requires companies, when computing the year-to-date tax, to apply the **estimated annual effective tax rate** to the year-to-date "ordinary" income at the end of each interim period. Further, the **interim period tax** related to "ordinary" income shall be the difference between the amount so computed and the amounts reported for previous interim periods of the fiscal period. **[6]**[10]

Extraordinary Items. Extraordinary items consist of unusual and nonrecurring material gains and losses. In the past, companies handled them in interim reports in one of three ways: (1) absorbed them entirely in the quarter in which they occurred; (2) prorated them over four quarters; or (3) disclosed them only by note. **The required approach now is to charge or credit the loss or gain in the quarter in which it occurs**, instead of attempting some arbitrary multiple-period allocation. This approach is consistent with the way in which companies must handle extraordinary items on an annual basis. No attempt is made to prorate the extraordinary items over several years.

Some favor the omission of extraordinary items from the quarterly net income. They believe that inclusion of extraordinary items that may be large in proportion to interim results distorts the predictive value of interim reports. Many, however, consider such an omission inappropriate because it deviates from actual results.

Earnings per Share. Interim reporting of earnings per share has all the problems inherent in computing and presenting annual earnings per share, and then some. If a company issues shares in the third period, EPS for the first two periods will not reflect year-end EPS.

---

[9]The estimated annual effective tax rate should reflect anticipated tax credits, foreign tax rates, percentage depletion, capital gains rates, and other available tax-planning alternatives.

[10]"Ordinary" income (or loss) refers to "income (or loss) from continuing operations before income taxes (or benefits)" excluding extraordinary items and discontinued operations.

If an extraordinary item is present in one period and the company sells new equity shares in another period, the EPS figure for the extraordinary item will change for the year. On an annual basis, only one EPS figure can be associated with an extraordinary item and that figure does not change; the interim figure is subject to change.

For purposes of computing earnings per share and making the required disclosure determinations, each interim period should stand alone. That is, all applicable tests should be made for that single period.

Seasonality. Seasonality occurs when most of a company's sales occur in one short period of the year while certain costs are fairly evenly spread throughout the year. For example, the natural gas industry has its heavy sales in the winter months. In contrast, the beverage industry has its heavy sales in the summer months.

The problem of seasonality is related to the expense recognition principle in accounting. Generally, expenses are associated with the revenues they create. In a seasonal business, wide fluctuations in profits occur because off-season sales do not absorb the company's fixed costs (for example, manufacturing, selling, and administrative costs that tend to remain fairly constant regardless of sales or production).

To illustrate why seasonality is a problem, assume the following information.

Selling price per unit	$1
Annual sales for the period (projected and actual)	
100,000 units @ $1	$100,000
Manufacturing costs	
Variable	10¢ per unit
Fixed	20¢ per unit or $20,000 for the year
Nonmanufacturing costs	
Variable	10¢ per unit
Fixed	30¢ per unit or $30,000 for the year

ILLUSTRATION 24-9
Data for Seasonality Example

Sales for four quarters and the year (projected and actual) were:

		Percent of Sales
1st Quarter	$ 20,000	20%
2nd Quarter	5,000	5
3rd Quarter	10,000	10
4th Quarter	65,000	65
Total for the year	$100,000	100%

ILLUSTRATION 24-10
Sales Data for Seasonality Example

Under the present accounting framework, the income statements for the quarters might be as shown in Illustration 24-11.

	1st Qtr	2nd Qtr	3rd Qtr	4th Qtr	Year
Sales	$20,000	$ 5,000	$10,000	$65,000	$100,000
Manufacturing costs					
Variable	(2,000)	(500)	(1,000)	(6,500)	(10,000)
Fixed[a]	(4,000)	(1,000)	(2,000)	(13,000)	(20,000)
	14,000	3,500	7,000	45,500	70,000
Nonmanufacturing costs					
Variable	(2,000)	(500)	(1,000)	(6,500)	(10,000)
Fixed[b]	(7,500)	(7,500)	(7,500)	(7,500)	(30,000)
Net income	$ 4,500	$(4,500)	$ (1,500)	$31,500	$ 30,000

ILLUSTRATION 24-11
Interim Net Income for Seasonal Business—Discrete Approach

[a]The fixed manufacturing costs are inventoried, so that equal amounts of fixed costs do not appear during each quarter.
[b]The fixed nonmanufacturing costs are not inventoried, so equal amounts of fixed costs appear during each quarter.

An investor who uses the first quarter's results might be misled. If the first quarter's earnings are $4,500, should this figure be multiplied by four to predict annual earnings of $18,000? Or, if first-quarter sales of $20,000 are 20 percent of the predicted sales for the year, would the net income for the year be $22,500 ($4,500 × 5)? Both figures are obviously wrong, and after the second quarter's results occur, the investor may become even more confused.

The problem with the conventional approach is that the fixed nonmanufacturing costs are not charged in proportion to sales. Some enterprises have adopted a way of avoiding this problem by making all fixed nonmanufacturing costs follow the sales pattern, as shown in Illustration 24-12.

ILLUSTRATION 24-12
Interim Net Income for
Seasonal Business—
Integral Approach

	1st Qtr	2nd Qtr	3rd Qtr	4th Qtr	Year
Sales	$20,000	$ 5,000	$10,000	$65,000	$100,000
Manufacturing costs					
Variable	(2,000)	(500)	(1,000)	(6,500)	(10,000)
Fixed	(4,000)	(1,000)	(2,000)	(13,000)	(20,000)
	14,000	3,500	7,000	45,500	70,000
Nonmanufacturing costs					
Variable	(2,000)	(500)	(1,000)	(6,500)	(10,000)
Fixed	(6,000)	(1,500)	(3,000)	(19,500)	(30,000)
Net income	$ 6,000	$ 1,500	$ 3,000	$19,500	$ 30,000

This approach solves some of the problems of interim reporting: Sales in the first quarter are 20 percent of total sales for the year, and net income in the first quarter is 20 percent of total income. In this case, as in the previous example, the investor cannot rely on multiplying any given quarter by four but can use comparative data or rely on some estimate of sales in relation to income for a given period.

The greater the degree of seasonality experienced by a company, the greater the possibility of distortion. Because there are no definitive guidelines for handling such items as the fixed nonmanufacturing costs, variability in income can be substantial. To alleviate this problem, the profession recommends that companies subject to material seasonal variations disclose the seasonal nature of their business and consider supplementing their interim reports with information for 12-month periods ended at the interim date for the current and preceding years.

The two illustrations highlight the difference between the **discrete** and **integral** approaches. Illustration 24-11 represents the discrete approach, in which the fixed nonmanufacturing expenses are expensed as incurred. Illustration 24-12 shows the integral approach, in which expenses are charged to expense on the basis of some measure of activity.

Continuing Controversy. The profession has developed some rules for interim reporting, but much still has to be done. As yet, it is unclear whether the discrete or the integral method, or some combination of the two, will be settled on.

Discussion also persists about the independent auditor's involvement in interim reports. Many auditors are reluctant to express an opinion on interim financial information, arguing that the data are too tentative and subjective. On the other hand, more people are advocating some examination of interim reports. As a compromise, the SEC currently requires that auditors perform a review of

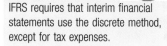

INTERNATIONAL
PERSPECTIVE

IFRS requires that interim financial statements use the discrete method, except for tax expenses.

Underlying Concepts

The AICPA Special Committee on Financial Reporting indicates that users would benefit from separate fourth-quarter reporting, including management's analysis of fourth-quarter activities and events. Also, the Committee recommended quarterly segment reporting, which companies now provide.

interim financial information. Such a review, which is much more limited in its procedures than the annual audit, provides some assurance that the interim information appears to be in accord with GAAP.[11]

Analysts and investors want financial information as soon as possible, before it's old news. We may not be far from a continuous database system in which corporate financial records can be accessed via the Internet. Investors might be able to access a company's financial records whenever they wish and put the information in the format they need. Thus, they could learn about sales slippage, cost increases, or earnings changes as they happen, rather than waiting until after the quarter has ended.[12]

A steady stream of information from the company to the investor could be very positive because it might alleviate management's continual concern with short-run interim numbers. Today, many contend that U.S. management is too oriented to the short-term. The truth of this statement is echoed by the words of the president of a large company who decided to retire early: "I wanted to look forward to a year made up of four seasons rather than four quarters."

"I WANT IT FASTER"

The SEC has decided that timeliness of information is of extreme importance. First, the SEC has said that large public companies will have only 60 days to complete their annual reports, down from 90 days. Quarterly reports must be done within 40 days of the close of the quarter, instead of 45. In addition, corporate executives and shareholders with more than 10 percent of a company's outstanding stock now have two days to disclose their sale or purchase of stock.

Also, in a bid to increase Internet disclosure, the SEC encourages companies to post current, quarterly, and annual reports on their websites—or explain why they don't. The Internet postings would have to be made by the day the company submits the information to the SEC, rather than within 24 hours as current rules allow.

What do the numbers mean?

AUDITOR'S AND MANAGEMENT'S REPORTS

Auditor's Report

Another important source of information, which is often overlooked, is the **auditor's report**. An **auditor** is an accounting professional who conducts an independent examination of a company's accounting data.

If satisfied that the financial statements present the financial position, results of operations, and cash flows fairly in accordance with generally accepted accounting principles, the auditor expresses an **unqualified opinion**. An example is shown in Illustration 24-13 (on page 1534).[13]

> **5 LEARNING OBJECTIVE**
> Identify the major disclosures in the auditor's report.

---

[11]"Interim Financial Information," *Statement on Auditing Standards No. 101* (New York: AICPA, 2002).

[12]A step in this direction is the SEC's mandate for companies to file their financial statements electronically with the SEC. The system, called EDGAR (electronic data gathering and retrieval) provides interested parties with computer access to financial information such as periodic filings, corporate prospectuses, and proxy materials.

[13]This auditor's report is in exact conformance with the specifications contained in "Reports on Audited Financial Statements," *Statement on Auditing Standards No. 58* (New York: AICPA, 1988). The last paragraph refers to the assessment of the company's internal controls, as required by the PCAOB.

ILLUSTRATION 24-13
Auditor's Report

Best Buy Co., Inc.

Report of Independent Registered Public Accounting Firm

To the Board of Directors and Shareholders of Best Buy Co., Inc.:

We have audited the accompanying consolidated balance sheets of Best Buy Co., Inc. and subsidiaries (the "Company") as of February 27, 2010 and February 28, 2009, and the related consolidated statements of earnings, shareholders' equity, and cash flows for the each of the three years in the period ended February 27, 2010. Our audits also included the financial statement schedule listed in the Index at Item 15(a). These financial statements and financial statement schedule are the responsibility of the Company's management. Our responsibility is to express an opinion on the financial statements and financial statement schedule based on our audits.

We conducted our audits in accordance with the standards of the Public Company Accounting Oversight Board (United States). Those standards require that we plan and perform the audit to obtain reasonable assurance about whether the financial statements are free of material misstatement. An audit includes examining, on a test basis, evidence supporting the amounts and disclosures in the financial statements. An audit also includes assessing the accounting principles used and significant estimates made by management, as well as evaluating the overall financial statement presentation. We believe that our audits provide a reasonable basis for our opinion.

In our opinion, such consolidated financial statements present fairly, in all material respects, the financial position of Best Buy Co., Inc. and subsidiaries as of February 27, 2010 and February 28, 2009, and the results of their operations and their cash flows for each of the three years in the period ended February 27, 2010, in conformity with accounting principles generally accepted in the United States of America. Also, in our opinion, such financial statement schedule, when considered in relation to the basic consolidated financial statements taken as a whole, presents fairly, in all material respects, the information set forth therein.

As discussed in Note 1 to the financial statements, the Company changed its method of accounting for noncontrolling interests with the adoption of FASB ASC 810, *Consolidation* (formerly FASB Statement No. 160, *Noncontrolling Interests in Consolidated Financial Statements—an amendment of ARB No. 51*).

We have also audited, in accordance with the standards of the Public Company Accounting Oversight Board (United States), the Company's internal control over financial reporting as of February 27, 2010, based on the criteria established in *Internal Control—Integrated Framework* issued by the Committee of Sponsoring Organizations of the Treadway Commission and our report dated April 28, 2010, expressed an unqualified opinion on the Company's internal control over financial reporting.

Deloitte & Touche LLP

Minneapolis, Minnesota
April 28, 2010

In preparing the report, the auditor follows these reporting standards.

1. The report states whether the financial statements are in accordance with generally accepted accounting principles.

2. The report identifies those circumstances in which the company has not consistently observed such principles in the current period in relation to the preceding period.

3. Users are to regard the informative disclosures in the financial statements as reasonably adequate unless the report states otherwise.

4. The report contains either an expression of opinion regarding the financial statements taken as a whole or an assertion to the effect that an opinion cannot be expressed. When the auditor cannot express an overall opinion, the report should

state the reasons. In all cases where an auditor's name is associated with financial statements, the report should contain a clear-cut indication of the character of the auditor's examination, if any, and the degree of responsibility being taken.

In most cases, the auditor issues a standard unqualified or clean opinion. That is, the auditor expresses the opinion that the financial statements present fairly, in all material respects, the financial position, results of operations, and cash flows of the entity in conformity with generally accepted accounting principles.

Certain circumstances, although they do not affect the auditor's unqualified opinion, may require the auditor to add an explanatory paragraph to the audit report. Some of the more important circumstances are as follows.

1. *Going concern.* The auditor must evaluate whether there is substantial doubt about the entity's **ability to continue as a going concern** for a reasonable period of time, taking into consideration all available information about the future. (The future is at least, but not limited to, 12 months from the end of the reporting period.) If substantial doubt exists about the company continuing as a going concern, the auditor adds to the report an explanatory note describing the potential problem. [7]

2. *Lack of consistency.* If a company has changed accounting principles or the method of their application in a way that has a material effect on the comparability of its financial statements, the auditor should refer to the change in an explanatory paragraph of the report. Such an explanatory paragraph should identify the nature of the change and refer readers to the note in the financial statements that discusses the change in detail. The auditor's concurrence with a change is implicit unless the auditor takes exception to the change in expressing an opinion as to fair presentation in conformity with generally accepted accounting principles.

3. *Emphasis of a matter.* The auditor may wish to emphasize a matter regarding the financial statements but nevertheless intends to express an unqualified opinion. For example, the auditor may wish to emphasize that the entity is a component of a larger business enterprise or that it has had significant transactions with related parties. The auditor presents such explanatory information in a separate paragraph of the report.

In some situations, however, the auditor is required to express (1) a **qualified** opinion or (2) an **adverse** opinion, or (3) to **disclaim** an opinion.

A qualified opinion contains an exception to the standard opinion. Ordinarily, the exception is not of sufficient magnitude to invalidate the statements as a whole; if it were, an adverse opinion would be rendered. The usual circumstances in which the auditor may deviate from the standard unqualified short-form report on financial statements are as follows.

1. The scope of the examination is limited or affected by conditions or restrictions.

2. The statements do not fairly present financial position or results of operations because of:
   (a) Lack of conformity with generally accepted accounting principles and standards.
   (b) Inadequate disclosure.

If confronted with one of the situations noted above, the auditor must offer a qualified opinion. A qualified opinion states that, except for the effects of the matter to which the qualification relates, the financial statements present fairly, in all material respects, the financial position, results of operations, and cash flows in conformity with generally accepted accounting principles.

Illustration 24-14 shows an example of an auditor's report with a qualified opinion. The auditor qualified the opinion because the company used an accounting principle at variance with generally accepted accounting principles.

ILLUSTRATION 24-14
Qualified Auditor's
Report

Helio Company

Independent Auditor's Report

(Same first and second paragraphs as the standard report)

Helio Company has excluded, from property and debt in the accompanying balance sheets, certain lease obligations that, in our opinion, should be capitalized in order to conform with generally accepted accounting principles. If these lease obligations were capitalized, property would be increased by $1,500,000 and $1,300,000, long-term debt by $1,400,000 and $1,200,000, and retained earnings by $100,000 and $50,000 as of December 31, in the current and prior year, respectively. Additionally, net income would be decreased by $40,000 and $30,000 and earnings per share would be decreased by $.06 and $.04, respectively, for the years then ended.

In our opinion, except for the effects of not capitalizing certain lease obligations as discussed in the preceding paragraph, the financial statements referred to above present fairly, in all material respects, the financial position of Helio Company, and the results of its operations and its cash flows for the years then ended in conformity with generally accepted accounting principles.

An **adverse opinion** is required in any report in which the exceptions to fair presentation are so material that in the independent auditor's judgment, a qualified opinion is not justified. In such a case, the financial statements taken as a whole are not presented in accordance with generally accepted accounting principles. Adverse opinions are rare, because most companies change their accounting to conform with GAAP. The SEC will not permit a company listed on an exchange to have an adverse opinion.

A **disclaimer of an opinion** is appropriate when the auditor has gathered so little information on the financial statements that no opinion can be expressed.

The audit report should provide useful information to the investor. One investment banker noted, "Probably the first item to check is the auditor's opinion to see whether or not it is a clean one—'in conformity with generally accepted accounting principles'—or is qualified in regard to differences between the auditor and company management in the accounting treatment of some major item, or in the outcome of some major litigation."

Management's Reports

Management's Discussion and Analysis

The SEC mandates inclusion of **management's discussion and analysis (MD&A)**. This section covers three financial aspects of an enterprise's business—liquidity, capital resources, and results of operations. In it, management highlights favorable or unfavorable trends and identifies significant events and uncertainties that affect these three factors. This approach obviously involves subjective estimates, opinions, and soft data. However, the SEC believes that the relevance of this information exceeds the potential lack of faithful representation.

Illustration 24-15 presents an excerpt from the MD&A section (2009 "Business Risks" only) of **PepsiCo**'s annual report.

PepsiCo, Inc.

MD&A Our business risks (in part)

Risk Management Framework

The achievement of our strategic and operating objectives will necessarily involve taking risks. Our risk management process is intended to ensure that risks are taken knowingly and purposefully. As such, we leverage an integrated risk management framework to identify, assess, prioritize, manage, monitor and communicate risks across the Company. This framework includes:

- The PepsiCo Risk Committee (PRC), comprised of a cross-functional, geographically diverse, senior management group which meets regularly to identify, assess, prioritize and address strategic and reputational risks;
- Division Risk Committees (DRCs), comprised of cross-functional senior management teams which meet regularly to identify, assess, prioritize and address division-specific operating risks;
- PepsiCo's Risk Management Office, which manages the overall risk management process, provides ongoing guidance, tools and analytical support to the PRC and the DRCs, identifies and assesses potential risks, and facilitates ongoing communication between the parties, as well as to PepsiCo's Audit Committee and Board of Directors;
- PepsiCo Corporate Audit, which evaluates the ongoing effectiveness of our key internal controls through periodic audit and review procedures; and
- PepsiCo's Compliance Department, which leads and coordinates our compliance policies and practices.

Market Risks

We are exposed to market risks arising from adverse changes in:

- commodity prices, affecting the cost of our raw materials and energy,
- foreign exchange rates, and
- interest rates.

In the normal course of business, we manage these risks through a variety of strategies, including productivity initiatives, global purchasing programs and hedging strategies. Ongoing productivity initiatives involve the identification and effective implementation of meaningful cost saving opportunities or efficiencies. Our global purchasing programs include fixed-price purchase orders and pricing agreements.

ILLUSTRATION 24-15
Management's Discussion and Analysis

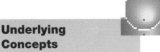

Underlying Concepts

FASB Concepts Statement No. 8 notes that management knows more about the company than users and therefore can increase the usefulness of financial information by identifying significant transactions that affect the company and by explaining their financial impact.

The MD&A section also must provide information about the effects of inflation and changing prices, if they are material to financial statement trends. The SEC has not required specific numerical computations, and companies have provided little analysis on changing prices.

An additional voluntary disclosure provided in the MD&A of many companies is discussion of the company's critical accounting policies. This disclosure identifies accounting policies that require management to make subjective judgments regarding uncertainties, resulting in potentially significant effects on the financial results.[14] For example, in its critical accounting policy disclosure, PepsiCo showed the impact on stock-based compensation expense in response to changes in estimated interest rates and stock return volatility. Through this voluntary disclosure, companies can expand on the information contained in the notes to the financial statements to indicate the sensitivity of the financial results to accounting policy judgments.

Gateway to the Profession

Expanded Discussion of Accounting for Changing Prices

Management's Responsibilities for Financial Statements

The Sarbanes-Oxley Act requires the SEC to develop guidelines for *all* publicly traded companies to report on management's responsibilities for, and assessment

6 LEARNING OBJECTIVE
Understand management's responsibilities for financials.

---

[14]See *Cautionary Advice Regarding Disclosure about Critical Accounting Policies,* Release Nos. 33-8040; 34-45149; FR-60 (Washington, D.C.: SEC); and *Proposed Rule: Disclosure in Management's Discussion and Analysis about the Application of Critical Accounting Policies,* Release Nos. 33-8098; 34-45907; International Series Release No. 1258; File No. S7-16-02 (Washington, D.C.: SEC).

of, the internal control system. An example of the type of disclosure that public companies are now making is shown in Illustration 24-16.[15]

ILLUSTRATION 24-16
Report on Management's
Responsibilities

Home Depot

Management's Responsibility for Financial Statements

The financial statements presented in this Annual Report have been prepared with integrity and objectivity and are the responsibility of the management of The Home Depot, Inc. These financial statements have been prepared in conformity with U.S. generally accepted accounting principles and properly reflect certain estimates and judgments based upon the best available information. The financial statements of the Company have been audited by KPMG LLP, an independent registered public accounting firm. Their accompanying report is based upon an audit conducted in accordance with the standards of the Public Company Accounting Oversight Board (United States).

The Audit Committee of the Board of Directors, consisting solely of independent directors, meets five times a year with the independent registered public accounting firm, the internal auditors and representatives of management to discuss auditing and financial reporting matters. In addition, a telephonic meeting is held prior to each quarterly earnings release. The Audit Committee retains the independent registered public accounting firm and regularly reviews the internal accounting controls, the activities of the independent registered public accounting firm and internal auditors and the financial condition of the Company. Both the Company's independent registered public accounting firm and the internal auditors have free access to the Audit Committee.

Management's Report on Internal Control over Financial Reporting

Our management is responsible for establishing and maintaining adequate internal control over financial reporting, as such term is defined in Rule 13a-15(f) promulgated under the Securities Exchange Act of 1934, as amended (the "Exchange Act"). Under the supervision and with the participation of our management, including our Chief Executive Officer and Chief Financial Officer, we conducted an evaluation of the effectiveness of our internal control over financial reporting as of January 31, 2010 based on the framework in *Internal Control–Integrated Framework* issued by the Committee of Sponsoring Organizations of the Treadway Commission (COSO).

Based on our evaluation, our management concluded that our internal control over financial reporting was effective as of January 31, 2010 in providing reasonable assurance regarding the reliability of financial reporting and the preparation of financial statements for external purposes in accordance with U.S. generally accepted accounting principles. The effectiveness of our internal control over financial reporting as of January 31, 2010 has been audited by KPMG LLP, an independent registered public accounting firm, as stated in their report which is included on page 30 in this Form 10-K.

Francis S. Blake
Chairman & Chief Executive Officer

Carol B. Tomé
Chief Financial Officer &
Executive Vice President—Corporate Services

CURRENT REPORTING ISSUES

LEARNING OBJECTIVE **7**
Identify issues related to financial forecasts and projections.

Reporting on Financial Forecasts and Projections

In recent years, the investing public's demand for more and better information has focused on disclosure of corporate expectations for the future.[16] These disclosures take one of two forms:[17]

[15]As indicated in this disclosure, management is responsible for preparing the financial statements and establishing and maintaining an effective system of internal controls. The auditor provides an independent assessment of whether the financial statements are prepared in accordance with GAAP, and for public companies, whether the internal controls are effective (see the audit opinion in Illustration 24-13 on page 1534).

[16]Some areas in which companies are using financial information about the future are equipment lease-versus-buy analysis, analysis of a company's ability to successfully enter new markets, and examination of merger and acquisition opportunities. In addition, companies also prepare forecasts and projections for use by third parties in public offering documents (requiring financial forecasts), tax-oriented investments, and financial feasibility studies. Use of forward-looking data has been enhanced by the increased capability of microcomputers to analyze, compare, and manipulate large quantities of data.

[17]"Financial Forecasts and Projections," and "Guide for Prospective Financial Information," *Codification of Statements on Standards for Attestation Engagements* (New York: AICPA 2006), paras. 3.04 and 3.05.

Financial forecasts. A financial forecast is a set of prospective financial statements that present, to the best of the responsible party's knowledge and belief, a company's expected financial position, results of operations, and cash flows. The responsible party bases a financial forecast on conditions it expects to exist and the course of action it expects to take.

Financial projections. Financial projections are prospective financial statements that present, to the best of the responsible party's knowledge and belief, given one or more *hypothetical assumptions*, an entity's expected financial position, results of operations, and cash flows. The responsible party bases a financial projection on conditions it expects *would* exist and the course of action it expects *would* be taken, given one or more hypothetical assumptions.

The difference between a financial forecast and a financial projection is clear-cut: A forecast provides information on what is **expected** to happen, whereas a projection provides information on what **might** take place, but is not necessarily expected to happen.

Whether companies should be required to provide financial forecasts is the subject of intensive discussion with journalists, corporate executives, the SEC, financial analysts, accountants, and others. Predictably, there are strong arguments on either side. Listed below are some of the arguments.

Arguments for requiring published forecasts:

1. Investment decisions are based on future expectations. Therefore, information about the future facilitates better decisions.

2. Companies already circulate forecasts informally. This situation should be regulated to ensure that the forecasts are available to all investors.

3. Circumstances now change so rapidly that historical information is no longer adequate for prediction.

Arguments against requiring published forecasts:

1. No one can foretell the future. Therefore, forecasts will inevitably be wrong. Worse, they may mislead, if they convey an impression of precision about the future.

2. Companies may strive only to meet their published forecasts, thereby failing to produce results that are in the stockholders' best interest.

3. If forecasts prove inaccurate, there will be recriminations and probably legal actions.[18]

4. Disclosure of forecasts will be detrimental to organizations, because forecasts will inform competitors (foreign and domestic), as well as investors.

Underlying Concepts

The AICPA's Special Committee on Financial Reporting indicates that the legal environment discourages companies from disclosing forward-looking information. Companies should not have to expand reporting of forward-looking information unless there are more effective deterrents to unwarranted litigation.

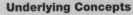

The AICPA has issued a statement on standards for accountants' services on prospective financial information. This statement establishes guidelines for the preparation and presentation of financial forecasts and projections.[19] It requires accountants to provide (1) a summary of significant assumptions used in the forecast or projection and (2) guidelines for minimum presentation.

---

[18]The issue is serious. Over a recent three-year period, 8 percent of the companies on the NYSE were sued because of an alleged lack of financial disclosure. Companies complain that they are subject to lawsuits whenever the stock price drops. And as one executive noted, "You can even be sued if the stock price goes up—because you did not disclose the good news fast enough."

[19]Op cit., par. 1.02.

To encourage management to disclose prospective financial information, the SEC has a **safe harbor rule**. It provides protection to a company that presents an erroneous forecast, as long as the company prepared the forecast on a reasonable basis and disclosed it in good faith.[20] However, many companies note that the safe harbor rule does not work in practice, since it does not cover oral statements, nor has it kept them from investor lawsuits.

Experience in Great Britain

Great Britain permits financial forecasts, and the results have been fairly successful. Some significant differences do exist between the English and the U.S. business and legal environments.[21] But such differences probably could be overcome if influential interests in this country cooperated to produce an atmosphere conducive to quality forecasting. A typical British forecast adapted from a construction company's report to support a public offering of stock is as follows.

ILLUSTRATION 24-17
Financial Forecast of a British Company

> Profits have grown substantially over the past 10 years and directors are confident of being able to continue this expansion . . . . While the rate of expansion will be dependent on the level of economic activity in Ireland and England, the group is well structured to avail itself of opportunities as they arise, particularly in the field of property development, which is expected to play an increasingly important role in the group's future expansion.
>
> Profits before taxation for the half year ended 30th June were 402,000 pounds. On the basis of trading experiences since that date and the present level of sales and completions, the directors expect that in the absence of unforeseen circumstances, the group's profits before taxation for the year to 31st December will be not less than 960,000 pounds.
>
> No dividends will be paid in respect of the current year. In a full financial year, on the basis of above forecasts (not including full year profits) it would be the intention of the board, assuming current rates of tax, to recommend dividends totaling 40% (of after-tax profits), which will be payable in the next two years.

A general narrative-type forecast issued by a U.S. corporation might appear as follows.

ILLUSTRATION 24-18
Financial Forecast of a U.S. Company

> On the basis of promotions planned by the company for the second half of the fiscal year, net earnings for that period are expected to be approximately the same as those for the first half of the fiscal year, with net earnings for the third quarter expected to make the predominant contribution to net earnings for the second half of the year.

Questions of Liability

What happens if a company does not meet its forecasts? Can the company and the auditor be sued? If a company, for example, projects an earnings increase of 15 percent and achieves only 5 percent, should stockholders be permitted to have some judicial recourse against the company?

One court case involving **Monsanto Chemical Corporation** set a precedent. In this case, Monsanto predicted that sales would increase 8 to 9 percent and that earnings

---

[20]"Safe-Harbor Rule for Projections," *Release No. 5993* (Washington, D.C.: SEC, 1979). The Private Securities Litigation Reform Act of 1995 recognizes that some information that is useful to investors is inherently subject to less certainty or reliability than other information. By providing safe harbor for forward-looking statements, Congress has sought to facilitate access to this information by investors.

[21]The British system, for example, does not permit litigation on forecasted information, and the solicitor (lawyer) is not permitted to work on a contingent-fee basis. See "A Case for Forecasting—The British Have Tried It and Find That It Works," *World* (New York: Peat, Marwick, Mitchell & Co., Autumn 1978), pp. 10–13.

would rise 4 to 5 percent. In the last part of the year, the demand for Monsanto's products dropped as a result of a business turndown. Instead of increasing, the company's earnings declined. Investors sued the company because the projected earnings figure was erroneous, but a judge dismissed the suit because the forecasts were the best estimates of qualified people whose intents were honest.

As indicated earlier, the SEC's safe harbor rules are intended to protect companies that provide good-faith projections. However, much concern exists as to how the SEC and the courts will interpret such terms as "good faith" and "reasonable assumptions" when erroneous forecasts mislead users of this information.

Internet Financial Reporting

Most companies now use the power and reach of the Internet to provide more useful information to financial statement readers. All large companies have Internet sites, and a large proportion of companies' websites contain links to their financial statements and other disclosures. The popularity of such reporting is not surprising, since companies can reduce the costs of printing and disseminating paper reports with the use of Internet reporting.

Does Internet financial reporting improve the usefulness of a company's financial reports? Yes, in several ways: First, dissemination of reports via the Web allows firms **to communicate more easily and quickly with users** than do traditional paper reports. In addition, **Internet reporting allows users to take advantage of tools** such as search engines and hyperlinks to quickly find information about the firm and, sometimes, to download the information for analysis, perhaps in computer spreadsheets. Finally, **Internet reporting can help make financial reports more relevant** by allowing companies to report expanded disaggregated data and more timely data than is possible through paper-based reporting. For example, some companies voluntarily report weekly sales data and segment operating data on their websites.

Given the widespread use of the Internet by investors and creditors, it is not surprising that organizations are developing new technologies and standards to further enable and enhance Internet financial reporting. An example is the increasing use of eXtensible Business Reporting Language (XBRL). **XBRL** is a computer language adapted from the code of the Internet. It "tags" accounting data to correspond to financial reporting items that are reported in the balance sheet, income statement, and the cash flow statement. Once tagged, any company's XBRL data can be easily processed using spreadsheets and other computer programs. In fact, the SEC is planning to require all companies and mutual funds to prepare their financial reports using XBRL, thereby allowing users to more easily search a company's reports, extract and analyze data, and perform financial comparisons within industries.[22]

To complement the implementation of XBRL use, the SEC has also announced a major upgrade to its EDGAR database. The new system is called IDEA (short for Interactive Data Electronic Applications). This replacement of EDGAR marks the SEC's transition from collecting forms and documents to making the information itself freely available to investors in a timely form they can readily use. With IDEA, investors will be able to quickly collate information from thousands of companies and forms and create reports and analysis on the fly, in any way they choose. It is hoped that IDEA will open

---

[22]C. Twarowski, "Financial Data 'on Steroids'," *Washington Post* (August 19, 2008), p. D01. See also *www.xbrl.org/us/us/BusinessCaseForXBRL.pdf* for additional information on XBRL. The IASB and the FASB are collaborating to implement XBRL with their standards. See *http://www.ifrs.org/XBRL/XBRL/htm.*

the door for both the SEC and investors to the new world of financial disclosure in interactive data (XBRL) format.[23]

NEW FORMATS, NEW DISCLOSURE

What do the numbers mean?

As indicated earlier in the *IFRS Insights* discussions, the FASB and the IASB are exploring better ways to present information in the financial statements. Recently, these two standard-setters have issued a discussion paper that requests input on a proposed reformatting of the financial statements. The table below provides a "snapshot" of the proposed changes (go to *http://www.fasb.org/ project/financial_statement_presentation.shtml* to learn more about this joint international project).

Statement of Financial Position	Statement of Comprehensive Income	Statement of Cash Flows
Business	Business	Business
• Operating assets and liabilities	• Operating income and expenses	• Operating cash flows
• Investing assets and liabilities	• Investing income and expenses	• Investing cash flows
Financing	Financing	Financing
• Financing assets	• Financing asset income	• Financing asset cash flows
• Financing liabilities	• Financing liability expenses	• Financing liability cash flows
Income Taxes	Income Taxes	Income Taxes

As indicated, each statement will use the same format. While the proposed changes will not affect the measurement of individual financial statement elements, the use of a consistent format (e.g., Business, Financing, Income Taxes), will help users understand the interrelationships in the financial statements. In addition, a new schedule reconciling cash flows to comprehensive income will be provided. As part of this schedule, changes in fair value will be included. It is a good thing the timeline for the project is lengthy, as these changes in presentation are significant.

Fraudulent Financial Reporting

LEARNING OBJECTIVE **8**
Describe the profession's response to fraudulent financial reporting.

Economic crime is on the rise around the world. A recent global survey of over 3,000 executives from 54 countries documented the types of economic crimes, as shown in Illustration 24-19 and Illustration 24-20.

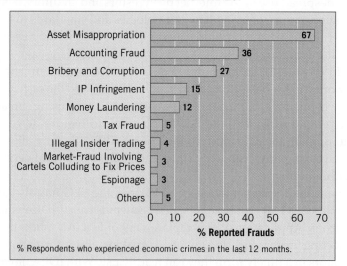

ILLUSTRATION 24-19
Types of Economic Crime

[23]See "SEC Announces Successor to EDGAR Database," *http://www.sec.gov/news/press/2008/2008-179.htm.* The SEC has implemented other regulations to ensure that investors get high-quality disclosures. For example, as discussed in Chapter 4, the SEC was concerned that companies may use pro forma reporting to deflect investor attention from bad news. In response, the SEC issued Regulation G, which requires companies to reconcile non-GAAP financial measures to GAAP. This regulation provides investors with a roadmap to analyze adjustments companies make to their GAAP numbers to arrive at pro forma results. [See SEC Regulation G, "Conditions for Use of Non-GAAP Financial Measures," Release No. 33-8176 (March 28, 2003).] Regulation FD (Release Nos. 33-7881) was issued in 2000 to address the concern that some analysts were receiving information sooner than the general public (e.g., during conference calls with analysts when earnings releases were discussed). Regulation FD requires that when relevant information is released, all have equal access to it.

As indicated, a wide range of economic crimes are reported, and unfortunately for the top three areas, the trend is not good. As shown in Illustration 24-20, there has been a steady upward trend of economic crime, with accounting fraud in the top three.

ILLUSTRATION 24-20
Trends in Reported Fraud

Fraudulent financial reporting is defined as "intentional or reckless conduct, whether act or omission, that results in materially misleading financial statements."[24] Fraudulent reporting can involve gross and deliberate distortion of corporate records (such as inventory count tags), or misapplication of accounting principles (failure to disclose material transactions). Although frauds are unusual, recent events involving such well-known companies as **Enron**, **WorldCom**, **Adelphia**, and **Tyco** indicate that more must be done to address this issue.

Causes of Fraudulent Financial Reporting

Fraudulent financial reporting usually occurs because of conditions in a company's internal or external environment. Influences in the **internal environment** relate to poor internal control systems, management's poor attitude toward ethics, or perhaps a company's liquidity or profitability. Those in the **external environment** may relate to industry conditions, overall business environment, or legal and regulatory considerations.

General incentives for fraudulent financial reporting vary. Common ones are the desire to obtain a higher stock price, to avoid default on a loan covenant, or to make a personal gain of some type (additional compensation, promotion). Situational pressures on the company or an individual manager also may lead to fraudulent financial reporting. Examples of these situational pressures include the following.

- *Sudden decreases in revenue or market share* for a single company or an entire industry.
- *Unrealistic budget pressures* may occur when headquarters arbitrarily determines profit objectives (particularly for short-term results) and budgets without taking actual conditions into account.
- *Financial pressure resulting from bonus plans* that depend on short-term economic performance. This pressure is particularly acute when the bonus is a significant component of the individual's total compensation.

---

[24]"Report of the National Commission on Fraudulent Financial Reporting" (Washington, D.C., 1987), page 2. Unintentional errors as well as corporate improprieties (such as tax fraud, employee embezzlements, and so on) which do not cause the financial statements to be misleading are excluded from the definition of fraudulent financial reporting.

Opportunities for fraudulent financial reporting are present in circumstances when the fraud is easy to commit and when detection is difficult. Frequently, these opportunities arise from:

1. *The absence of a board of directors or audit committee* that vigilantly oversees the financial reporting process.
2. *Weak or nonexistent internal accounting controls.* This situation can occur, for example, when a company's revenue system is overloaded as a result of a rapid expansion of sales, an acquisition of a new division, or the entry into a new, unfamiliar line of business.
3. *Unusual or complex transactions* such as the consolidation of two companies, the divestiture or closing of a specific operation, and the purchase and sale of derivative instruments.
4. *Accounting estimates requiring significant subjective judgment* by company management, such as the allowance for loan losses and the estimated liability for warranty expense.
5. *Ineffective internal audit staffs* resulting from inadequate staff size and severely limited audit scope.

A weak corporate ethical climate contributes to these situations. Opportunities for fraudulent financial reporting also increase dramatically when the accounting principles followed in reporting transactions are nonexistent, evolving, or subject to varying interpretations.[25]

The AICPA has issued numerous auditing standards in response to concerns of the accounting profession, the media, and the public.[26] For example, the recent standard on fraudulent financial reporting "raises the bar" on the performance of financial statement audits by explicitly requiring auditors to assess the risk of material financial misstatement due to fraud.[27] As indicated earlier, the Sarbanes-Oxley Act now raises the penalty substantially for executives who are involved in fraudulent financial reporting.

DISCLOSURE OVERLOAD

What do the numbers mean?

As we discussed in Chapter 1 and throughout the text, IFRS is gaining popularity around the world. And in 2011, the U.S. Securities and Exchange Commission plans to rule on whether publicly traded companies in the United States will be required to adopt IFRS. There is some debate on U.S. readiness to make the switch. For example, there are several areas in which the FASB and the IASB must iron out a number of technical accounting issues before they reach a substantially converged set of accounting standards. Here is a list of six important areas yet to be converged.

1. *Error correction.* According to *IAS 8*, it's not always necessary to retrospectively restate financial results when a company corrects errors, especially if the adjustment is impractical or too costly. GAAP, on the other hand, requires restatements in many error-correction cases.

---

[25]The discussion in this section is based on the Report of the National Commission on Fraudulent Financial Reporting, pp. 23–24. See "2004 Report to the Nation on Occupational Fraud and Abuse, Association of Certified Fraud Examiners," (*www.cfenet.com/pdfs/2004RttN.pdf*) for fraudulent financial reporting causes and consequences.

[26]Because the profession believes that the role of the auditor is not well understood outside the profession, much attention has been focused on the expectation gap. The **expectation gap** is the gap between (1) the expectation of financial statement users concerning the level of assurance they believe the independent auditor provides, and (2) the assurance that the independent auditor actually does provide under generally accepted auditing standards.

[27]"Consideration of Fraud in a Financial Statement Audit," *Statement on Auditing Standards No. 99* (New York: AICPA, 2002).

2. *Death of LIFO.* Last-in, first-out (LIFO) inventory accounting is prohibited under *IAS 2*, so any U.S. company using the method will have to abandon it (and the tax benefits) and move to another methodology. Although LIFO is permitted under GAAP, the repeal of LIFO for tax purposes is an ongoing debate.

3. *Reversal of impairments.* *IAS 36* permits companies to reverse impairment losses up to the amount of the original impairment when the reason for the charge decreases or no longer exists. However, GAAP bans reversal.

4. *PP&E revaluation.* *IAS 16* allows for the revaluation of property, plant, and equipment, but the entire asset class must be revalued. That means a company can choose to use the revaluation model if the asset class's fair value can be measured reliably. But, it must choose to use one model or the other; both cannot be used at the same time. GAAP does not allow revaluation.

5. *Component depreciation.* Also under *IAS 16*, companies must recognize and depreciate equipment components separately if the components can be physically separated from the asset and have different useful life spans. In practical terms, that means controllers will have to rely on the operations side of the business to help assess equipment components. GAAP allows component depreciation, but it is not required.

6. *Development costs.* Based on *IAS 38*, companies are permitted to capitalize development costs as long as they meet six criteria. However, research costs are still expensed. GAAP requires that all R&D costs be charged to expense when incurred.

Some are already debating what will happen if and when U.S. companies adopt these new standards. It is almost certain that expanded disclosure will be needed to help users navigate accounting reports upon adoption of IFRS. As one accounting analyst remarked, "Get ready for an avalanche of footnotes." Since using IFRS requires more judgment than using GAAP, two to three times as many footnotes will be needed to explain the rationales for accounting approaches. So while principles-based standards should promote more comparability, they require investors to dig into the disclosures in the footnotes.

Source: Marie Leone, "GAAP and IFRS: Six Degrees of Separation," *CFO.com* (June 30, 2010).

Criteria for Making Accounting and Reporting Choices

Throughout this textbook, we have stressed the need to provide information that is useful to predict the amounts, timing, and uncertainty of future cash flows. To achieve this objective, companies must make judicious choices between alternative accounting concepts, methods, and means of disclosure. You are probably surprised by the large number of choices that exist among acceptable alternatives.

You should recognize, however, as indicated in Chapter 1, that accounting is greatly influenced by its environment. It does not exist in a vacuum. Therefore, it is unrealistic to assume that the profession can entirely eliminate alternative presentations of certain transactions and events. Nevertheless, we are hopeful that the profession, by adhering to the conceptual framework, will be able to focus on the needs of financial statement users and eliminate diversity where appropriate. The SEC's and FASB's projects on principles-based standards are directed at these very issues. They seek to develop guidance that will result in accounting and financial reporting that reflects the economic substance of the transactions, not the desired financial result of management. The profession must continue its efforts to develop a sound foundation upon which to build financial standards and practice. As Aristotle said, "The correct beginning is more than half the whole."

Underlying Concepts

The FASB concept statements on the objective of financial reporting, elements of financial statements, qualitative characteristics of accounting information, and recognition and measurement are important steps in the right direction.

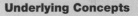
You will want to read
IFRS INSIGHTS
on pages 1573–1581

for discussion of IFRS related to disclosure.

SUMMARY OF LEARNING OBJECTIVES

1 **Review the full disclosure principle and describe implementation problems.** The full disclosure principle calls for financial reporting of any financial facts significant enough to influence the judgment of an informed reader. Implementing the full disclosure principle is difficult, because the cost of disclosure can be substantial and the benefits difficult to assess. Disclosure requirements have increased because of (1) the growing complexity of the business environment, (2) the necessity for timely information, and (3) the use of accounting as a control and monitoring device.

2 **Explain the use of notes in financial statement preparation.** Notes are the accountant's means of amplifying or explaining the items presented in the main body of the statements. Notes can explain in qualitative terms information pertinent to specific financial statement items, and can provide supplementary data of a quantitative nature. Common note disclosures relate to such items as: accounting policies; inventories; property, plant, and equipment; creditor claims; contingencies and commitments; and subsequent events.

3 **Discuss the disclosure requirements for major business segments.** Aggregated figures hide much information about the composition of these consolidated figures. There is no way to tell from the consolidated data the extent to which the differing product lines contribute to the company's profitability, risk, and growth potential. As a result, the profession requires segment information in certain situations.

4 **Describe the accounting problems associated with interim reporting.** Interim reports cover periods of less than one year. Two viewpoints exist regarding interim reports. The discrete approach holds that each interim period should be treated as a separate accounting period. The integral approach is that the interim report is an integral part of the annual report and that deferrals and accruals should take into consideration what will happen for the entire year.

Companies should use the same accounting principles for interim reports that they use for annual reports. A number of unique reporting problems develop related to the following items: (1) advertising and similar costs, (2) expenses subject to year-end adjustment, (3) income taxes, (4) extraordinary items, (5) earnings per share, and (6) seasonality.

5 **Identify the major disclosures in the auditor's report.** The auditor expresses an unqualified opinion if satisfied that the financial statements present the financial position, results of operations, and cash flows fairly in accordance with generally accepted accounting principles. A qualified opinion contains an exception to the standard opinion; ordinarily the exception is not of sufficient magnitude to invalidate the statements as a whole.

An adverse opinion is required when the exceptions to fair presentation are so material that a qualified opinion is not justified. A disclaimer of an opinion is appropriate when the auditor has so little information on the financial statements that no opinion can be expressed.

6 **Understand management's responsibilities for financials.** Management's discussion and analysis (MD&A) section covers three financial aspects of an enterprise's business: liquidity, capital resources, and results of operations. Management's responsibility for the financial statements is often indicated in a letter to stockholders in the annual report.

7 **Identify issues related to financial forecasts and projections.** The SEC has indicated that companies are permitted (not required) to include profit forecasts in their reports. To encourage management to disclose such information, the SEC issued a safe harbor rule. The rule provides protection to a company that presents an erroneous forecast, as long as it prepared the projection on a reasonable basis and disclosed it in good faith. However, the safe harbor rule has not worked well in practice.

8 **Describe the profession's response to fraudulent financial reporting.** Fraudulent financial reporting is intentional or reckless conduct, whether through act or omission, that results in materially misleading financial statements. Fraudulent financial reporting usually occurs because of poor internal control, management's poor attitude toward ethics, poor performance, and so on. The Sarbanes-Oxley Act has numerous provisions intended to help prevent fraudulent financial reporting.

| APPENDIX **24A** | **BASIC FINANCIAL STATEMENT ANALYSIS** |

What would be important to you in studying a company's financial statements? The answer depends on your particular interest—whether you are a creditor, stockholder, potential investor, manager, government agency, or labor leader. For example, **short-term creditors** such as banks are primarily interested in the ability of the firm to pay its currently maturing obligations. In that case, you would examine the current assets and their relation to short-term liabilities to evaluate the short-run solvency of the firm.

Bondholders, on the other hand, look more to long-term indicators, such as the enterprise's capital structure, past and projected earnings, and changes in financial position. **Stockholders**, present or prospective, also are interested in many of the features considered by a long-term creditor. As a stockholder, you would focus on the earnings picture, because changes in it greatly affect the market price of your investment. You also would be concerned with the financial position of the company, because it affects indirectly the stability of earnings.

The **managers** of a company are concerned about the composition of its capital structure and about the changes and trends in earnings. This financial information has a direct influence on the type, amount, and cost of external financing that the company can obtain. In addition, the company managers find financial information useful on a day-to-day operating basis in such areas as capital budgeting, break-even analysis, variance analysis, gross margin analysis, and for internal control purposes.

PERSPECTIVE ON FINANCIAL STATEMENT ANALYSIS

Readers of financial statements can gather information by examining relationships between items on the statements and identifying trends in these relationships. The relationships are expressed numerically in ratios and percentages, and trends are identified through comparative analysis.

A problem with learning how to analyze statements is that the means may become an end in itself. Analysts could identify and calculate thousands of possible relationships and trends. If one knows only how to calculate ratios and trends without understanding how such information can be used, little is accomplished. Therefore, a logical approach to financial statement analysis is necessary, consisting of the following steps.

9 LEARNING OBJECTIVE
Understand the approach to financial statement analysis.

Underlying Concepts

Because financial statements report on the past, they emphasize the *qualitative characteristic of feedback value.* This feedback value is useful because it can be used to better achieve the *qualitative characteristic of predictive value.*

1. *Know the questions for which you want to find answers.* As indicated earlier, various groups have different types of interest in a company.

2. *Know the questions that particular ratios and comparisons are able to help answer.* These will be discussed in this appendix.

3. *Match 1 and 2 above.* By such a matching, the statement analysis will have a logical direction and purpose.

Several caveats must be mentioned. **Financial statements report on the past.** Thus, analysis of these data is an examination of the past. When using such information in a decision-making (future-oriented) process, analysts assume that the past is a reasonable basis for predicting the future. This is usually a reasonable approach, but its limitations should be recognized.

Also, ratio and trend analyses will help identify a company's present strengths and weaknesses. They may serve as "red flags" indicating problem areas. In many cases, however, such analyses will not reveal **why** things are as they are. Finding answers about "why" usually requires an in-depth analysis and an awareness of many factors about a company that are not reported in the financial statements.

Another caveat is that a **single ratio by itself is not likely to be very useful**. For example, analysts may generally view a current ratio of 2 to 1 (current assets are twice current liabilities) as satisfactory. However, if the industry average is 3 to 1, such a conclusion may be invalid. Even given this industry average, one may conclude that the particular company is doing well if one knows the previous year's ratio was 1.5 to 1. Consequently, to derive meaning from ratios, analysts need some standard against which to compare them. Such a standard may come from industry averages, past years' amounts, a particular competitor, or planned levels.

Finally, **awareness of the limitations of accounting numbers used in an analysis** is important. We will discuss some of these limitations and their consequences later in this appendix.

RATIO ANALYSIS

LEARNING OBJECTIVE **10**
Identify major analytic ratios and describe their calculation.

In analyzing financial statement data, analysts use various devices to bring out the comparative and relative significance of the financial information presented. These devices include ratio analysis, comparative analysis, percentage analysis, and examination of related data. No one device is more useful than another. Every situation is different, and analysts often obtain the needed answers only upon close examination of the interrelationships among all the data provided. Ratio analysis is the starting point. Ratios can be classified as follows.

MAJOR TYPES OF RATIOS

LIQUIDITY RATIOS. Measures of the company's short-run ability to pay its maturing obligations.

ACTIVITY RATIOS. Measures of how effectively the company is using the assets employed.

PROFITABILITY RATIOS. Measures of the degree of success or failure of a given company or division for a given period of time.

COVERAGE RATIOS. Measures of the degree of protection for long-term creditors and investors.[28]

We have integrated discussions and illustrations about the computation and use of these financial ratios throughout this book. Illustration 24A-1 summarizes all of the ratios presented in the book and identifies the specific chapters that presented that material.

---

[28]Some analysts use other terms to categorize these ratios. For example, liquidity ratios are sometimes referred to as *solvency* ratios; activity ratios as *turnover* or *efficiency* ratios; and coverage ratios as *leverage* or *capital structure* ratios.

Ratio	Formula for Computation	Reference
SUMMARY OF RATIOS PRESENTED IN EARLIER CHAPTERS		
I. Liquidity		
1. Current ratio	$\dfrac{\text{Current assets}}{\text{Current liabilities}}$	Chapter 13, p. 749
2. Quick or acid-test ratio	$\dfrac{\text{Cash, short-term investments, and net receivables}}{\text{Current liabilities}}$	Chapter 13, p. 750
3. Current cash debt coverage ratio	$\dfrac{\text{Net cash provided by operating activities}}{\text{Average current liabilities}}$	Chapter 5, p. 234
II. Activity		
4. Receivables turnover	$\dfrac{\text{Net sales}}{\text{Average trade receivables (net)}}$	Chapter 7, p. 392
5. Inventory turnover	$\dfrac{\text{Cost of goods sold}}{\text{Average inventory}}$	Chapter 9, p. 516
6. Asset turnover	$\dfrac{\text{Net sales}}{\text{Average total assets}}$	Chapter 11, p. 627
III. Profitability		
7. Profit margin on sales	$\dfrac{\text{Net income}}{\text{Net sales}}$	Chapter 11, p. 628
8. Rate of return on assets	$\dfrac{\text{Net income}}{\text{Average total assets}}$	Chapter 11, p. 628
9. Rate of return on common stock equity	$\dfrac{\text{Net income minus preferred dividends}}{\text{Average common stockholders' equity}}$	Chapter 15, p. 870
10. Earnings per share	$\dfrac{\text{Net income minus preferred dividends}}{\text{Weighted-average shares outstanding}}$	Chapter 16, p. 922
11. Payout ratio	$\dfrac{\text{Cash dividends}}{\text{Net income}}$	Chapter 15, p. 871
IV. Coverage		
12. Debt to total assets ratio	$\dfrac{\text{Total debt}}{\text{Total assets}}$	Chapter 14, p. 808
13. Times interest earned	$\dfrac{\text{Income before income taxes and interest expense}}{\text{Interest expense}}$	Chapter 14, p. 808
14. Cash debt coverage ratio	$\dfrac{\text{Net cash provided by operating activities}}{\text{Average total liabilities}}$	Chapter 5, p. 234
15. Book value per share	$\dfrac{\text{Common stockholders' equity}}{\text{Outstanding shares}}$	Chapter 15, p. 871

ILLUSTRATION 24A-1
Summary of Financial Ratios

You can find additional coverage of these ratios, accompanied by assignment material, at the book's companion website, at **www.wiley.com/college/kieso**. This supplemental coverage takes the form of a comprehensive case adapted from the annual report of a large international chemical company that we have disguised under the name of Anetek Chemical Corporation.

Gateway to the Profession

Financial Analysis Primer

Limitations of Ratio Analysis

The reader of financial statements must understand the basic limitations associated with ratio analysis. As analytical tools, ratios are attractive because they are simple and convenient. But too frequently, decision-makers base their decisions

11 LEARNING OBJECTIVE
Explain the limitations of ratio analysis.

on only these simple computations. The ratios are only as good as the data upon which they are based and the information with which they are compared.

One important limitation of ratios is that they generally are **based on historical cost, which can lead to distortions in measuring performance**. Inaccurate assessments of the enterprise's financial condition and performance can result from failing to incorporate fair value information.

Also, investors must remember that **where estimated items (such as depreciation and amortization) are significant, income ratios lose some of their credibility**. For example, income recognized before the termination of a company's life is an approximation. In analyzing the income statement, users should be aware of the uncertainty surrounding the computation of net income. As one writer aptly noted, "The physicist has long since conceded that the location of an electron is best expressed by a probability curve. Surely an abstraction like earnings per share is even more subject to the rules of probability and risk."[29]

Underlying Concepts

Consistency and comparability are important concepts for financial statement analysis. If the principles and assumptions used to prepare the financial statements are continually changing, accurate assessments of a company's progress become difficult.

Probably the greatest limitation of ratio analysis is the **difficult problem of achieving comparability among firms in a given industry**. Achieving comparability requires that the analyst (1) identify basic differences in companies' accounting principles and procedures, and (2) adjust the balances to achieve comparability. Basic differences in accounting usually involve one of the following areas.

1. Inventory valuation (FIFO, LIFO, average cost).
2. Depreciation methods, particularly the use of straight-line versus accelerated depreciation.
3. Capitalization versus expensing of certain costs.
4. Capitalization of leases versus noncapitalization.
5. Investments in common stock carried at equity versus fair value.
6. Differing treatments of postretirement benefit costs.
7. Questionable practices of defining discontinued operations, impairments, and extraordinary items.

The use of these different alternatives can make a significant difference in the ratios computed. For example, at one time Anheuser-Busch InBev noted that if it had used average cost for inventory valuation instead of LIFO, inventories would have increased approximately $33,000,000. Such an increase would have a substantive impact on the current ratio. Several studies have analyzed the impact of different accounting methods on financial statement analysis. The differences in income that can develop are staggering in some cases. Investors must be aware of the potential pitfalls if they are to be able to make the proper adjustments.[30]

Finally, analysts should recognize that a **substantial amount of important information** is not included in a company's financial statements. Events involving such things as industry changes, management changes, competitors' actions, technological developments, government actions, and union activities are often critical to a company's successful operation. These events occur continuously, and information about them must come from careful analysis of financial reports in the media and other sources. Indeed many argue, in what is known as the **efficient-market hypothesis**, that financial statements contain "no surprises" to those engaged in market activities. They contend that the effect of these events is known in the marketplace—and the price of the company's stock adjusts accordingly—well before the issuance of such reports.

---

[29]Richard E. Cheney, "How Dependable Is the Bottom Line?" *The Financial Executive* (January 1971), p. 12.

[30]See for example, Eugene A. Imhoff, Jr., Robert C. Lipe, and David W. Wright, "Operating Leases: Impact of Constructive Capitalization," *Accounting Horizons* (March 1991).

COMPARATIVE ANALYSIS

Comparative analysis presents the same information for two or more different dates or periods, so that like items may be compared. Ratio analysis provides only a single snapshot, for one given point or period in time. In a comparative analysis, an investment analyst can concentrate on a given item and determine whether it appears to be growing or diminishing year by year and the proportion of such change to related items. Generally, companies present comparative financial statements.[31] They typically include two years of balance sheet information and three years of income statement information.

In addition, many companies include in their annual reports five- or ten-year summaries of pertinent data that permit readers to examine and analyze trends. As indicated in GAAP, "the presentation of comparative financial statements in annual and other reports enhances the usefulness of such reports and brings out more clearly the nature and trends of current changes affecting the enterprise." Illustration 24A-2 presents a five-year condensed statement, with additional supporting data, of Anetek Chemical Corporation.

> **12 LEARNING OBJECTIVE**
> Describe techniques of comparative analysis.

ILLUSTRATION 24A-2
Condensed Comparative
Financial Information

	ANETEK CHEMICAL CORPORATION CONDENSED COMPARATIVE STATEMENTS (000,000 OMITTED)						
	2012	2011	2010	2009	2008	10 Years Ago 2002	20 Years Ago 1992
Sales and other revenue:							
Net sales	$1,600.0	$1,350.0	$1,309.7	$1,176.2	$1,077.5	$636.2	$170.7
Other revenue	75.0	50.0	39.4	34.1	24.6	9.0	3.7
Total	1,675.0	1,400.0	1,349.1	1,210.3	1,102.1	645.2	174.4
Costs and other charges:							
Cost of sales	1,000.0	850.0	827.4	737.6	684.2	386.8	111.0
Depreciation and amortization	150.0	150.0	122.6	115.6	98.7	82.4	14.2
Selling and administrative expenses	225.0	150.0	144.2	133.7	126.7	66.7	10.7
Interest expense	50.0	25.0	28.5	20.7	9.4	8.9	1.8
Income taxes	100.0	75.0	79.5	73.5	68.3	42.4	12.4
Total	1,525.0	1,250.0	1,202.2	1,081.1	987.3	587.2	150.1
Net income for the year	$ 150.0	$ 150.0	$ 146.9	$ 129.2	$ 114.8	$ 58.0	$ 24.3
Other Statistics							
Earnings per share on common stock (in dollars)[a]	$ 5.00	$ 5.00	$ 4.90	$ 3.58	$ 3.11	$ 1.66	$ 1.06
Cash dividends per share on common stock (in dollars)[a]	2.25	2.15	1.95	1.79	1.71	1.11	0.25
Cash dividends declared on common stock	67.5	64.5	58.5	64.6	63.1	38.8	5.7
Stock dividend at approximate market value				46.8		27.3	
Taxes (major)	144.5	125.9	116.5	105.6	97.8	59.8	17.0
Wages paid	389.3	325.6	302.1	279.6	263.2	183.2	48.6
Cost of employee benefits	50.8	36.2	32.9	28.7	27.2	18.4	4.4
Number of employees at year end (thousands)	47.4	36.4	35.0	33.8	33.2	26.6	14.6
Additions to property	306.3	192.3	241.5	248.3	166.1	185.0	49.0

[a]Adjusted for stock splits and stock dividends.

[31]All 500 companies surveyed in *Accounting Trends and Techniques—2010* presented comparative 2009 amounts in their 2008 balance sheets and presented comparative 2006 and 2007 amounts in their 2008 income statements.

PERCENTAGE (COMMON-SIZE) ANALYSIS

LEARNING OBJECTIVE 13
Describe techniques of percentage analysis.

Analysts also use percentage analysis to help them evaluate and compare companies. Percentage analysis consists of reducing a series of related amounts to a series of percentages of a given base. For example, analysts frequently express all items in an income statement as a percentage of sales or sometimes as a percentage of cost of goods sold. They may analyze a balance sheet on the basis of total assets. Percentage analysis facilitates comparison and is helpful in evaluating the relative size of items or the relative change in items. A conversion of absolute dollar amounts to percentages may also facilitate comparison between companies of different size.

Illustration 24A-3 shows a comparative analysis of the expense section of Anetek for the last two years.

ILLUSTRATION 24A-3
Horizontal Percentage Analysis

ANETEK CHEMICAL CORPORATION
HORIZONTAL COMPARATIVE ANALYSIS
(000,000 OMITTED)

	2012	2011	Difference	% Change Inc. (Dec.)
Cost of sales	$1,000.0	$850.0	$150.0	17.6%
Depreciation and amortization	150.0	150.0	0	0
Selling and administrative expenses	225.0	150.0	75.0	50.0
Interest expense	50.0	25.0	25.0	100.0
Income taxes	100.0	75.0	25.0	33.3

This approach, normally called horizontal analysis, indicates the proportionate change over a period of time. It is especially useful in evaluating trends, because absolute changes are often deceiving.

Another comparative approach, called vertical analysis, is the proportional expression of each financial statement item in a given period to a base figure. For example, Anetek Chemical's income statement using this approach appears in Illustration 24A-4.

ILLUSTRATION 24A-4
Vertical Percentage Analysis

ANETEK CHEMICAL CORPORATION
INCOME STATEMENT
(000,000 OMITTED)

	Amount	Percentage of Total Revenue
Net sales	$1,600.0	96%
Other revenue	75.0	4
Total revenue	1,675.0	100
Less:		
Cost of sales	1,000.0	60
Depreciation and amortization	150.0	9
Selling and administrative expenses	225.0	13
Interest expense	50.0	3
Income taxes	100.0	6
Total expenses	1,525.0	91
Net income	$ 150.0	9%

Vertical analysis is frequently called common-size analysis because it reduces all of the statement items to a "common size." That is, all of the elements within each statement are expressed in percentages of some common number and always add up to 100 percent. Common-size (percentage) analysis reveals the composition of each of the financial statements.

In the analysis of the balance sheet, common-size analysis answers such questions as: What percentage of the capital structure is stockholders' equity, current liabilities, and long-term debt? What is the mix of assets (percentage-wise) with which the company has chosen to conduct business? What percentage of current assets is in inventory, receivables, and so forth?

Common-size analysis of the income statement typically relates each item to sales. It is instructive to know what proportion of each sales dollar is absorbed by various costs and expenses incurred by the enterprise.

Analysts may use common-size statements to compare one company's statements from different years, to detect trends not evident from comparing absolute amounts. Also, common-size statements provide intercompany comparisons regardless of size because they recast financial statements into a comparable common-size format.

SUMMARY OF LEARNING OBJECTIVES FOR APPENDIX 24A

9 **Understand the approach to financial statement analysis.** Basic financial statement analysis involves examining relationships between items on the statements (ratio and percentage analysis) and identifying trends in these relationships (comparative analysis). Analysis is used to predict the future, but ratio analysis is limited because the data are from the past. Also, ratio analysis identifies present strengths and weaknesses of a company, but it may not reveal *why* they are as they are. Although single ratios are helpful, they are not conclusive; for maximum usefulness, analysts must compare them with industry averages, past years, planned amounts, and the like.

10 **Identify major analytic ratios and describe their calculation.** Ratios are classified as liquidity ratios, activity ratios, profitability ratios, and coverage ratios: (1) *Liquidity ratio analysis* measures the short-run ability of a company to pay its currently maturing obligations. (2) *Activity ratio analysis* measures how effectively a company is using its assets. (3) *Profitability ratio analysis* measures the degree of success or failure of a company to generate revenues adequate to cover its costs of operation and provide a return to the owners. (4) *Coverage ratio analysis* measures the degree of protection afforded long-term creditors and investors.

11 **Explain the limitations of ratio analysis.** Ratios are based on historical cost, which can lead to distortions in measuring performance. Also, where estimated items are significant, income ratios lose some of their credibility. In addition, comparability problems exist because companies use different accounting principles and procedures. Finally, analysts must recognize that a substantial amount of important information is not included in a company's financial statements.

12 **Describe techniques of comparative analysis.** Companies present comparative data, which generally includes two years of balance sheet information and three years of income statement information. In addition, many companies include in their annual reports five- to ten-year summaries of pertinent data that permit the reader to analyze trends.

13 **Describe techniques of percentage analysis.** Percentage analysis consists of reducing a series of related amounts to a series of percentages of a given base. Analysts use two approaches: *Horizontal analysis* indicates the proportionate change in financial statement items over a period of time; such analysis is most helpful in evaluating trends.

KEY TERMS

acid-test ratio, *1549*

activity ratios, *1548*

asset turnover, *1549*

book value per share, *1549*

cash debt coverage ratio, *1549*

common-size analysis, *1552*

comparative analysis, *1551*

coverage ratios, *1548*

current cash debt coverage ratio, *1549*

current ratio, *1549*

debt to total assets ratio, *1549*

earnings per share, *1549*

horizontal analysis, *1552*

inventory turnover, *1549*

liquidity ratios, *1548*

payout ratio, *1549*

percentage analysis, *1552*

profit margin on sales, *1549*

profitability ratios, *1548*

quick ratio, *1549*

rate of return on assets, *1549*

rate of return on common stock equity, *1549*

receivables turnover, *1549*

times interest earned, *1549*

vertical analysis, *1552*

Vertical analysis (common-size analysis) is a proportional expression of each item on the financial statements in a given period to a base amount. It analyzes the composition of each of the financial statements from different years (a) to detect trends not evident from the comparison of absolute amounts and (b) to make intercompany comparisons of different-sized enterprises.

FASB CODIFICATION

FASB Codification References

[1] FASB ASC 850-10-05 [Predecessor literature: "Related Party Disclosures," *Statement of Financial Accounting Standards No. 57* (Stamford, Conn.: FASB, 1982).]

[2] FASB ASC 855-10-05 [Predecessor literature: "Subsequent Events," *Statement on Auditing Standards No. 1* (New York: AICPA, 1973), pp. 123–124.]

[3] FASB ASC 280-10-05-3. [Predecessor literature: "Disclosures about Segments of an Enterprise and Related Information," *Statement of Financial Accounting Standards No. 131* (Norwalk, Conn.: FASB, 1997).]

[4] FASB ASC 270-10. [Predecessor literature: "Interim Financial Reporting," *Opinions of the Accounting Principles Board No. 28* (New York: AICPA, 1973).]

[5] FASB ASC 740-270-30-2 through 3. [Predecessor literature: "Interim Financial Reporting," *Opinions of the Accounting Principles Board No. 28* (New York: AICPA, 1973), par. 19.]

[6] FASB ASC 740-270-35-4. [Predecessor literature: "Accounting for Income Taxes in Interim Periods," *FASB Interpretation No. 18* (Stamford, Conn.: FASB, March 1977), par. 9.]

[7] FASB ASC 205-30 [Predecessor literature: "The Auditor's Consideration of an Entity's Ability to Continue as a Going Concern," *Statement on Auditing Standards No. 59* (New York: AICPA, 1988).]

Exercises

If your school has a subscription to the FASB Codification, go to *http://aaahq.org/ascLogin.cfm* to log in and prepare responses to the following. Provide Codification references for your responses.

CE24-1 Access the glossary ("Master Glossary") to answer the following.

    (a) What is the definition of "ordinary income" (loss)?
    (b) What is an error in previously issued financial statements?
    (c) What is the definition of "earnings per share"?
    (d) What is a publicly traded company?

CE24-2 What are some examples of related parties?

CE24-3 What are the quantitative thresholds that would require a public company to report separately information about an operating segment?

CE24-4 If an SEC-registered company uses the gross profit method to determine cost of goods sold for interim periods, would it be acceptable for the company to state that it's not practicable to determine components of inventory at interim periods? Why or why not?

An additional Codification case can be found in the Using Your Judgment section, on page 1572.

Be sure to check the book's companion website for a Review and Analysis Exercise, with solution.

Questions, Brief Exercises, Exercises, Problems, and many more resources are available for practice in WileyPLUS.

Note: All asterisked Questions, Exercises, and Problems relate to material in the appendix to the chapter.

QUESTIONS

1. What are the major advantages of notes to the financial statements? What types of items are usually reported in notes?

2. What is the full disclosure principle in accounting? Why has disclosure increased substantially in the last 10 years?

3. The FASB requires a reconciliation between the effective tax rate and the federal government's statutory rate. Of what benefit is such a disclosure requirement?

4. What type of disclosure or accounting do you believe is necessary for the following items?

(a) Because of a general increase in the number of labor disputes and strikes, both within and outside the industry, there is an increased likelihood that a company will suffer a costly strike in the near future.

(b) A company reports an extraordinary item (net of tax) correctly on the income statement. No other mention is made of this item in the annual report.

(c) A company expects to recover a substantial amount in connection with a pending refund claim for a prior year's taxes. Although the claim is being contested, counsel for the company has confirmed the client's expectation of recovery.

5. The following information was described in a note of Canon Packing Co.

"During August, Holland Products Corporation purchased 311,003 shares of the Company's common stock which constitutes approximately 35% of the stock outstanding. Holland has since obtained representation on the Board of Directors."

"An affiliate of Holland Products Corporation acts as a food broker for Canon Packing in the greater New York City marketing area. The commissions for such services after August amounted to approximately $20,000."

Why is this information disclosed?

6. What are the major types of subsequent events? Indicate how each of the following "subsequent events" would be reported.

(a) Collection of a note written off in a prior period.

(b) Issuance of a large preferred stock offering.

(c) Acquisition of a company in a different industry.

(d) Destruction of a major plant in a flood.

(e) Death of the company's chief executive officer (CEO).

(f) Additional wage costs associated with settlement of a four-week strike.

(g) Settlement of a federal income tax case at considerably more tax than anticipated at year-end.

(h) Change in the product mix from consumer goods to industrial goods.

7. What are diversified companies? What accounting problems are related to diversified companies?

8. What quantitative materiality test is applied to determine whether a segment is significant enough to warrant separate disclosure?

9. Identify the segment information that is required to be disclosed by GAAP.

10. What is an operating segment, and when can information about two operating segments be aggregated?

11. The controller for Lafayette Inc. recently commented, "If I have to disclose our segments individually, the only people who will gain are our competitors and the only people that will lose are our present stockholders." Evaluate this comment.

12. An article in the financial press entitled "Important Information in Annual Reports This Year" noted that annual reports include a management's discussion and analysis section. What would this section contain?

13. "The financial statements of a company are management's, not the accountant's." Discuss the implications of this statement.

14. Olga Conrad, a financial writer, noted recently, "There are substantial arguments for including earnings projections in annual reports and the like. The most compelling is that it would give anyone interested something now available to only a relatively select few—like large stockholders, creditors, and attentive bartenders." Identify some arguments against providing earnings projections.

15. The following comment appeared in the financial press: "Inadequate financial disclosure, particularly with respect to how management views the future and its role in the marketplace, has always been a stone in the shoe. After all, if you don't know how a company views the future, how can you judge the worth of its corporate strategy?" What are some arguments for reporting earnings forecasts?

16. What are interim reports? Why are balance sheets often not provided with interim data?

17. What are the accounting problems related to the presentation of interim data?

18. Dierdorf Inc., a closely held corporation, has decided to go public. The controller, Ed Floyd, is concerned with presenting interim data when a LIFO inventory valuation is used. What problems are encountered with LIFO inventories when quarterly data are presented?

19. What approaches have been suggested to overcome the seasonality problem related to interim reporting?

20. What is the difference between a CPA's unqualified opinion or "clean" opinion and a qualified one?

21. Jane Ellerby and Sam Callison are discussing the recent fraud that occurred at LowRental Leasing, Inc. The fraud involved the improper reporting of revenue to ensure that the company would have income in excess of $1 million. What is fraudulent financial reporting, and how does it differ from an embezzlement of company funds?

*22. "The significance of financial statement data is not in the amount alone." Discuss the meaning of this statement.

*23. A close friend of yours, who is a history major and who has not had any college courses or any experience in business, is receiving the financial statements from companies in which he has minor investments (acquired for him by his now-deceased father). He asks you what he needs to know to interpret and to evaluate the financial statement data that he is receiving. What would you tell him?

*24. Distinguish between ratio analysis and percentage analysis relative to the interpretation of financial statements. What is the value of these two types of analyses?

*25. In calculating inventory turnover, why is cost of goods sold used as the numerator? As the inventory turnover increases, what increasing risk does the business assume?

*26. What is the relationship of the asset turnover ratio to the rate of return on assets?

*27. Explain the meaning of the following terms: (a) common-size analysis, (b) vertical analysis, (c) horizontal analysis, (d) percentage analysis.

*28. Presently, the profession requires that earnings per share be disclosed on the face of the income statement. What are some disadvantages of reporting ratios on the financial statements?

BRIEF EXERCISES

2 ▶ **BE24-1** An annual report of Crestwood Industries states, "The company and its subsidiaries have long-term leases expiring on various dates after December 31, 2012. Amounts payable under such commitments, without reduction for related rental income, are expected to average approximately $5,711,000 annually for the next 3 years. Related rental income from certain subleases to others is estimated to average $3,094,000 annually for the next 3 years." What information is provided by this note?

2 ▶ **BE24-2** An annual report of Ford Motor Corporation states, "Net income a share is computed based upon the average number of shares of capital stock of all classes outstanding. Additional shares of common stock may be issued or delivered in the future on conversion of outstanding convertible debentures, exercise of outstanding employee stock options, and for payment of defined supplemental compensation. Had such additional shares been outstanding, net income a share would have been reduced by 10¢ in the current year and 3¢ in the previous year. . . . As a result of capital stock transactions by the company during the current year (primarily the purchase of Class A Stock from Ford Foundation), net income a share was increased by 6¢." What information is provided by this note?

2 ▶ **BE24-3** Morlan Corporation is preparing its December 31, 2012, financial statements. Two events that occurred between December 31, 2012, and March 10, 2013, when the statements were issued, are described below.

  1. A liability, estimated at $160,000 at December 31, 2012, was settled on February 26, 2013, at $170,000.
  2. A flood loss of $80,000 occurred on March 1, 2013.

What effect do these subsequent events have on 2012 net income?

3 ▶ **BE24-4** Tina Bailey, a student of intermediate accounting, was heard to remark after a class discussion on segment reporting, "All this is very confusing to me. First we are told that there is merit in presenting the consolidated results, and now we are told that it is better to show segmental results. I wish they would make up their minds." Evaluate this comment.

3 ▶ **BE24-5** Foley Corporation has seven industry segments with total revenues as follows.

Penley	$600	Cheng	$225
Konami	650	Takuhi	200
KSC	250	Molina	700
Red Moon	275		

Based only on the revenues test, which industry segments are reportable?

3 **BE24-6** Operating profits and losses for the seven industry segments of Foley Corporation are:

Penley	$ 90	Cheng	$ (20)
Konami	(40)	Takuhi	34
KSC	25	Molina	150
Red Moon	50		

Based only on the operating profit (loss) test, which industry segments are reportable?

3 **BE24-7** Identifiable assets for the seven industry segments of Foley Corporation are:

Penley	$500	Cheng	$200
Konami	550	Takuhi	150
KSC	250	Molina	475
Red Moon	400		

Based only on the identifiable assets test, which industry segments are reportable?

10 *BE24-8 Answer each of the questions in the following unrelated situations.

   (a) The current ratio of a company is 5:1 and its acid-test ratio is 1:1. If the inventories and prepaid items amount to $500,000, what is the amount of current liabilities?
   (b) A company had an average inventory last year of $200,000 and its inventory turnover was 5. If sales volume and unit cost remain the same this year as last and inventory turnover is 8 this year, what will average inventory have to be during the current year?
   (c) A company has current assets of $90,000 (of which $40,000 is inventory and prepaid items) and current liabilities of $40,000. What is the current ratio? What is the acid-test ratio? If the company borrows $15,000 cash from a bank on a 120-day loan, what will its current ratio be? What will the acid-test ratio be?
   (d) A company has current assets of $600,000 and current liabilities of $240,000. The board of directors declares a cash dividend of $180,000. What is the current ratio after the declaration but before payment? What is the current ratio after the payment of the dividend?

10 *BE24-9 Heartland Company's budgeted sales and budgeted cost of goods sold for the coming year are $144,000,000 and $99,000,000, respectively. Short-term interest rates are expected to average 10%. If Heartland can increase inventory turnover from its present level of 9 times a year to a level of 12 times per year, compute its expected cost savings for the coming year.

EXERCISES

2 **E24-1 (Post-Balance-Sheet Events)** Keystone Corporation issued its financial statements for the year ended December 31, 2012, on March 10, 2013. The following events took place early in 2013.

   (a) On January 10, 10,000 shares of $5 par value common stock were issued at $66 per share.
   (b) On March 1, Keystone determined after negotiations with the Internal Revenue Service that income taxes payable for 2012 should be $1,320,000. At December 31, 2012, income taxes payable were recorded at $1,100,000.

Instructions
Discuss how the preceding post-balance-sheet events should be reflected in the 2012 financial statements.

2 **E24-2 (Post-Balance-Sheet Events)** For each of the following subsequent (post-balance-sheet) events, indicate whether a company should (a) adjust the financial statements, (b) disclose in notes to the financial statements, or (c) neither adjust nor disclose.

   _____ **1.** Settlement of federal tax case at a cost considerably in excess of the amount expected at year-end.
   _____ **2.** Introduction of a new product line.
   _____ **3.** Loss of assembly plant due to fire.
   _____ **4.** Sale of a significant portion of the company's assets.
   _____ **5.** Retirement of the company president.
   _____ **6.** Issuance of a significant number of shares of common stock.
   _____ **7.** Loss of a significant customer.
   _____ **8.** Prolonged employee strike.
   _____ **9.** Material loss on a year-end receivable because of a customer's bankruptcy.
   _____ **10.** Hiring of a new president.
   _____ **11.** Settlement of prior year's litigation against the company.
   _____ **12.** Merger with another company of comparable size.

3 **E24-3 (Segmented Reporting)** LaGreca Company is involved in four separate industries. The following information is available for each of the four industries.

Operating Segment	Total Revenue	Operating Profit (Loss)	Identifiable Assets
W	$ 60,000	$15,000	$167,000
X	10,000	1,500	83,000
Y	23,000	(2,000)	21,000
Z	9,000	1,000	19,000
	$102,000	$15,500	$290,000

Instructions
Determine which of the operating segments are reportable based on the:

(a) Revenue test.
(b) Operating profit (loss) test.
(c) Identifiable assets test.

10 *E24-4 (Ratio Computation and Analysis; Liquidity)** As loan analyst for Madison Bank, you have been presented the following information.

	Plunkett Co.	Herring Co.
Assets		
Cash	$ 120,000	$ 320,000
Receivables	220,000	302,000
Inventories	570,000	518,000
Total current assets	910,000	1,140,000
Other assets	500,000	612,000
Total assets	$1,410,000	$1,752,000
Liabilities and Stockholders' Equity		
Current liabilities	$ 300,000	$ 350,000
Long-term liabilities	400,000	500,000
Common stock and retained earnings	710,000	902,000
Total liabilities and stockholders' equity	$1,410,000	$1,752,000
Annual sales	$ 930,000	$1,500,000
Rate of gross profit on sales	30%	40%

Each of these companies has requested a loan of $50,000 for 6 months with no collateral offered. In as much as your bank has reached its quota for loans of this type, only one of these requests is to be granted.

Instructions
Which of the two companies, as judged by the information given above, would you recommend as the better risk and why? Assume that the ending account balances are representative of the entire year.

10 *E24-5 (Analysis of Given Ratios)** Robbins Company is a wholesale distributor of professional equipment and supplies. The company's sales have averaged about $900,000 annually for the 3-year period 2011–2013. The firm's total assets at the end of 2013 amounted to $850,000.

The president of Robbins Company has asked the controller to prepare a report that summarizes the financial aspects of the company's operations for the past 3 years. This report will be presented to the board of directors at their next meeting.

In addition to comparative financial statements, the controller has decided to present a number of relevant financial ratios which can assist in the identification and interpretation of trends. At the request of the controller, the accounting staff has calculated the following ratios for the 3-year period 2011–2013.

	2011	2012	2013
Current ratio	1.80	1.89	1.96
Acid-test (quick) ratio	1.04	0.99	0.87
Accounts receivable turnover	8.75	7.71	6.42
Inventory turnover	4.91	4.32	3.72
Total debt to total assets	51.0%	46.0%	41.0%
Long-term debt to total assets	31.0%	27.0%	24.0%
Sales to fixed assets (fixed asset turnover)	1.58	1.69	1.79
Sales as a percent of 2011 sales	1.00	1.03	1.05
Gross margin percentage	36.0%	35.1%	34.6%
Net income to sales	6.9%	7.0%	7.2%
Return on total assets	7.7%	7.7%	7.8%
Return on stockholders' equity	13.6%	13.1%	12.7%

In preparation of the report, the controller has decided first to examine the financial ratios independent of any other data to determine if the ratios themselves reveal any significant trends over the 3-year period.

Instructions

(a) The current ratio is increasing while the acid-test (quick) ratio is decreasing. Using the ratios provided, identify and explain the contributing factor(s) for this apparently divergent trend.

(b) In terms of the ratios provided, what conclusion(s) can be drawn regarding the company's use of financial leverage during the 2011–2013 period?

(c) Using the ratios provided, what conclusion(s) can be drawn regarding the company's net investment in plant and equipment?

10 *E24-6 (Ratio Analysis)** Howser Inc. is a manufacturer of electronic components and accessories with total assets of $20,000,000. Selected financial ratios for Howser and the industry averages for firms of similar size are presented below.

	Howser			2013 Industry
	2011	2012	2013	Average
Current ratio	2.09	2.27	2.51	2.24
Quick ratio	1.15	1.12	1.19	1.22
Inventory turnover	2.40	2.18	2.02	3.50
Net sales to stockholders' equity	2.75	2.80	2.95	2.85
Net income to stockholders' equity	0.14	0.15	0.17	0.11
Total liabilities to stockholders' equity	1.41	1.37	1.44	0.95

Howser is being reviewed by several entities whose interests vary, and the company's financial ratios are a part of the data being considered. Each of the parties listed below must recommend an action based on its evaluation of Howser's financial position.

Citizens National Bank. The bank is processing Howser's application for a new 5-year term note. Citizens National has been Howser's banker for several years but must reevaluate the company's financial position for each major transaction.

Charleston Company. Charleston is a new supplier to Howser and must decide on the appropriate credit terms to extend to the company.

Shannon Financial. A brokerage firm specializing in the stock of electronics firms that are sold over-the-counter, Shannon Financial must decide if it will include Howser in a new fund being established for sale to Shannon Financial's clients.

Working Capital Management Committee. This is a committee of Howser's management personnel chaired by the chief operating officer. The committee is charged with the responsibility of periodically reviewing the company's working capital position, comparing actual data against budgets, and recommending changes in strategy as needed.

Instructions

(a) Describe the analytical use of each of the six ratios presented above.

(b) For each of the four entities described above, identify two financial ratios, from those ratios presented in Illustration 24A-1 (on page 1549), that would be most valuable as a basis for its decision regarding Howser.

(c) Discuss what the financial ratios presented in the question reveal about Howser. Support your answer by citing specific ratio levels and trends as well as the interrelationships between these ratios.

(CMA adapted)

> **See the book's companion website, www.wiley.com/college/kieso, for a set of B Exercises.**

PROBLEMS

2 **P24-1 (Subsequent Events)** Your firm has been engaged to examine the financial statements of Almaden Corporation for the year 2012. The bookkeeper who maintains the financial records has prepared all the unaudited financial statements for the corporation since its organization on January 2, 2007. The client provides you with the information on the next page.

ALMADEN CORPORATION
BALANCE SHEET
DECEMBER 31, 2012

Assets			Liabilities		
Current assets	$1,881,100		Current liabilities	$ 962,400	
Other assets	5,171,400		Long-term liabilities	1,439,500	
			Capital	4,650,600	
	$7,052,500			$7,052,500	

An analysis of current assets discloses the following.

Cash (restricted in the amount of $300,000 for plant expansion)	$ 571,000
Investments in land	185,000
Accounts receivable less allowance of $30,000	480,000
Inventories (LIFO flow assumption)	645,100
	$1,881,100

Other assets include:

Prepaid expenses	$ 62,400
Plant and equipment less accumulated depreciation of $1,430,000	4,130,000
Cash surrender value of life insurance policy	84,000
Unamortized bond discount	34,500
Notes receivable (short-term)	162,300
Goodwill	252,000
Land	446,200
	$5,171,400

Current liabilities include:

Accounts payable	$ 510,000
Notes payable (due 2015)	157,400
Estimated income taxes payable	145,000
Premium on common stock	150,000
	$ 962,400

Long-term liabilities include:

Unearned revenue	$ 489,500
Dividends payable (cash)	200,000
8% bonds payable (due May 1, 2017)	750,000
	$1,439,500

Capital includes:

Retained earnings	$2,810,600
Common stock, par value $10; authorized 200,000 shares, 184,000 shares issued	1,840,000
	$4,650,600

The supplementary information below is also provided.

1. On May 1, 2012, the corporation issued at 95.4, $750,000 of bonds to finance plant expansion. The long-term bond agreement provided for the annual payment of interest every May 1. The existing plant was pledged as security for the loan. Use the straight-line method for discount amortization.
2. The bookkeeper made the following mistakes.
   (a) In 2010, the ending inventory was overstated by $183,000. The ending inventories for 2011 and 2012 were correctly computed.
   (b) In 2012, accrued wages in the amount of $225,000 were omitted from the balance sheet, and these expenses were not charged on the income statement.
   (c) In 2012, a gain of $175,000 (net of tax) on the sale of certain plant assets was credited directly to retained earnings.
3. A major competitor has introduced a line of products that will compete directly with Almaden's primary line, now being produced in a specially designed new plant. Because of manufacturing innovations, the competitor's line will be of comparable quality but priced 50% below Almaden's line. The competitor announced its new line on January 14, 2013. Almaden indicates that the company will meet the lower prices that are high enough to cover variable manufacturing and selling expenses, but permit recovery of only a portion of fixed costs.

4. You learned on January 28, 2013, prior to completion of the audit, of heavy damage because of a recent fire to one of Almaden's two plants; the loss will not be reimbursed by insurance. The newspapers described the event in detail.

Instructions

Analyze the above information to prepare a corrected balance sheet for Almaden in accordance with proper accounting and reporting principles. Prepare a description of any notes that might need to be prepared. The books are closed and adjustments to income are to be made through retained earnings.

3 **P24-2 (Segmented Reporting)** Cineplex Corporation is a diversified company that operates in five different industries: A, B, C, D, and E. The following information relating to each segment is available for 2013.

	A	B	C	D	E
Sales revenue	$40,000	$ 75,000	$580,000	$35,000	$55,000
Cost of goods sold	19,000	50,000	270,000	19,000	30,000
Operating expenses	10,000	40,000	235,000	12,000	18,000
Total expenses	29,000	90,000	505,000	31,000	48,000
Operating profit (loss)	$11,000	$(15,000)	$ 75,000	$ 4,000	$ 7,000
Identifiable assets	$35,000	$ 80,000	$500,000	$65,000	$50,000

Sales of segments B and C included intersegment sales of $20,000 and $100,000, respectively.

Instructions

(a) Determine which of the segments are reportable based on the:

(1) Revenue test.

(2) Operating profit (loss) test.

(3) Identifiable assets test.

(b) Prepare the necessary disclosures required by GAAP.

10 **12** *P24-3 (Ratio Computations and Additional Analysis)** Bradburn Corporation was formed 5 years ago through a public subscription of common stock. Daniel Brown, who owns 15% of the common stock, was one of the organizers of Bradburn and is its current president. The company has been successful, but it currently is experiencing a shortage of funds. On June 10, Daniel Brown approached the Topeka National Bank, asking for a 24-month extension on two $35,000 notes, which are due on June 30, 2013, and September 30, 2013. Another note of $6,000 is due on March 31, 2014, but he expects no difficulty in paying this note on its due date. Brown explained that Bradburn's cash flow problems are due primarily to the company's desire to finance a $300,000 plant expansion over the next 2 fiscal years through internally generated funds.

The commercial loan officer of Topeka National Bank requested financial reports for the last 2 fiscal years. These reports are reproduced below and on page 1562.

BRADBURN CORPORATION
BALANCE SHEET
MARCH 31

Assets	2013	2012
Cash	$ 18,200	$ 12,500
Notes receivable	148,000	132,000
Accounts receivable (net)	131,800	125,500
Inventories (at cost)	105,000	50,000
Plant & equipment (net of depreciation)	1,449,000	1,420,500
Total assets	$1,852,000	$1,740,500

Liabilities and Stockholders' Equity		
Accounts payable	$ 79,000	$ 91,000
Notes payable	76,000	61,500
Accrued liabilities	9,000	6,000
Common stock (130,000 shares, $10 par)	1,300,000	1,300,000
Retained earnings[a]	388,000	282,000
Total liabilities and stockholders' equity	$1,852,000	$1,740,500

[a]Cash dividends were paid at the rate of $1 per share in fiscal year 2012 and $2 per share in fiscal year 2013.

BRADBURN CORPORATION
INCOME STATEMENT
FOR THE FISCAL YEARS ENDED MARCH 31

	2013	2012
Sales revenue	$3,000,000	$2,700,000
Cost of goods sold[a]	1,530,000	1,425,000
Gross margin	1,470,000	1,275,000
Operating expenses	860,000	780,000
Income before income taxes	610,000	495,000
Income taxes (40%)	244,000	198,000
Net income	$ 366,000	$ 297,000

[a]Depreciation charges on the plant and equipment of $100,000 and $102,500 for fiscal years ended March 31, 2012 and 2013, respectively, are included in cost of goods sold.

Instructions

(a) Compute the following items for Bradburn Corporation.
  (1) Current ratio for fiscal years 2012 and 2013.
  (2) Acid-test (quick) ratio for fiscal years 2012 and 2013.
  (3) Inventory turnover for fiscal year 2013.
  (4) Return on assets for fiscal years 2012 and 2013. (Assume total assets were $1,688,500 at 3/31/11.)
  (5) Percentage change in sales, cost of goods sold, gross margin, and net income after taxes from fiscal year 2012 to 2013.
(b) Identify and explain what other financial reports and/or financial analyses might be helpful to the commercial loan officer of Topeka National Bank in evaluating Daniel Brown's request for a time extension on Bradburn's notes.
(c) Assume that the percentage changes experienced in fiscal year 2013 as compared with fiscal year 2012 for sales and cost of goods sold will be repeated in each of the next 2 years. Is Bradburn's desire to finance the plant expansion from internally generated funds realistic? Discuss.
(d) Should Topeka National Bank grant the extension on Bradburn's notes considering Daniel Brown's statement about financing the plant expansion through internally generated funds? Discuss.

13 *P24-4 (Horizontal and Vertical Analysis)** Presented below are comparative balance sheets for the Gilmour Company.

GILMOUR COMPANY
COMPARATIVE BALANCE SHEET
AS OF DECEMBER 31, 2013 AND 2012

	December 31	
	2013	2012
Assets		
Cash	$ 180,000	$ 275,000
Accounts receivable (net)	220,000	155,000
Short-term investments	270,000	150,000
Inventories	1,060,000	980,000
Prepaid expenses	25,000	25,000
Fixed assets	2,585,000	1,950,000
Accumulated depreciation	(1,000,000)	(750,000)
	$3,340,000	$2,785,000
Liabilities and Stockholders' Equity		
Accounts payable	$ 50,000	$ 75,000
Accrued expenses	170,000	200,000
Bonds payable	450,000	190,000
Capital stock	2,100,000	1,770,000
Retained earnings	570,000	550,000
	$3,340,000	$2,785,000

Instructions
(Round to two decimal places.)

(a) Prepare a comparative balance sheet of Gilmour Company showing the percent each item is of the total assets or total liabilities and stockholders' equity.

(b) Prepare a comparative balance sheet of Gilmour Company showing the dollar change and the percent change for each item.

(c) Of what value is the additional information provided in part (a)?

(d) Of what value is the additional information provided in part (b)?

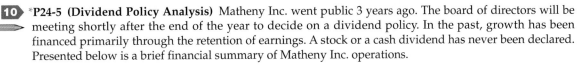

10 *P24-5 (Dividend Policy Analysis)** Matheny Inc. went public 3 years ago. The board of directors will be meeting shortly after the end of the year to decide on a dividend policy. In the past, growth has been financed primarily through the retention of earnings. A stock or a cash dividend has never been declared. Presented below is a brief financial summary of Matheny Inc. operations.

	($000 omitted)				
	2013	2012	2011	2010	2009
Sales revenue	$20,000	$16,000	$14,000	$6,000	$4,000
Net income	2,400	1,400	800	700	250
Average total assets	22,000	19,000	11,500	4,200	3,000
Current assets	8,000	6,000	3,000	1,200	1,000
Working capital	3,600	3,200	1,200	500	400
Common shares:					
Number of shares outstanding (000)	2,000	2,000	2,000	20	20
Average market price	$9	$6	$4	—	—

Instructions

(a) Suggest factors to be considered by the board of directors in establishing a dividend policy.

(b) Compute the rate of return on assets, profit margin on sales, earnings per share, price-earnings ratio, and current ratio for each of the 5 years for Matheny Inc.

(c) Comment on the appropriateness of declaring a cash dividend at this time, using the ratios computed in part (b) as a major factor in your analysis.

CONCEPTS FOR ANALYSIS

CA24-1 (General Disclosures; Inventories; Property, Plant, and Equipment) Koch Corporation is in the process of preparing its annual financial statements for the fiscal year ended April 30, 2013. Because all of Koch's shares are traded intrastate, the company does not have to file any reports with the Securities and Exchange Commission. The company manufactures plastic, glass, and paper containers for sale to food and drink manufacturers and distributors.

Koch Corporation maintains separate control accounts for its raw materials, work in process, and finished goods inventories for each of the three types of containers. The inventories are valued at the lower-of-cost-or-market.

The company's property, plant, and equipment are classified in the following major categories: land, office buildings, furniture and fixtures, manufacturing facilities, manufacturing equipment, and leasehold improvements. All fixed assets are carried at cost. The depreciation methods employed depend on the type of asset (its classification) and when it was acquired.

Koch Corporation plans to present the inventory and fixed asset amounts in its April 30, 2013, balance sheet as shown below.

Inventories	$4,814,200
Property, plant, and equipment (net of depreciation)	6,310,000

Instructions
What information regarding inventories and property, plant, and equipment must be disclosed by Koch Corporation in the audited financial statements issued to stockholders, either in the body or the notes, for the 2012–2013 fiscal year?

(CMA adapted)

CA24-2 (Disclosures Required in Various Situations) Ace Inc. produces electronic components for sale to manufacturers of radios, television sets, and digital sound systems. In connection with her examination of Ace's financial statements for the year ended December 31, 2013, Gloria Rodd, CPA, completed field work 2 weeks ago. Ms. Rodd now is evaluating the significance of the following items prior to preparing her auditor's report. Except as noted, none of these items have been disclosed in the financial statements or notes.

Item 1

A 10-year loan agreement, which the company entered into 3 years ago, provides that dividend payments may not exceed net income earned after taxes subsequent to the date of the agreement. The balance of retained earnings at the date of the loan agreement was $420,000. From that date through December 31, 2013, net income after taxes has totaled $570,000 and cash dividends have totaled $320,000. On the basis of these data, the staff auditor assigned to this review concluded that there was no retained earnings restriction at December 31, 2013.

Item 2

Recently Ace interrupted its policy of paying cash dividends quarterly to its stockholders. Dividends were paid regularly through 2012, discontinued for all of 2013 to finance purchase of equipment for the company's new plant, and resumed in the first quarter of 2014. In the annual report, dividend policy is to be discussed in the president's letter to stockholders.

Item 3

A major electronics firm has introduced a line of products that will compete directly with Ace's primary line, now being produced in the specially designed new plant. Because of manufacturing innovations, the competitor's line will be of comparable quality but priced 50% below Ace's line. The competitor announced its new line during the week following completion of field work. Ms. Rodd read the announcement in the newspaper and discussed the situation by telephone with Ace executives. Ace will meet the lower prices that are high enough to cover variable manufacturing and selling expenses but will permit recovery of only a portion of fixed costs.

Item 4

The company's new manufacturing plant building, which cost $2,400,000 and has an estimated life of 25 years, is leased from Wichita National Bank at an annual rental of $600,000. The company is obligated to pay property taxes, insurance, and maintenance. At the conclusion of its 10-year noncancelable lease, the company has the option of purchasing the property for $1. In Ace's income statement, the rental payment is reported on a separate line.

Instructions

For each of the above items, discuss any additional disclosures in the financial statements and notes that the auditor should recommend to her client. (The cumulative effect of the four items should not be considered.)

CA24-3 (Disclosures, Conditional and Contingent Liabilities) Presented below are three independent situations.

Situation 1

A company offers a one-year warranty for the product that it manufactures. A history of warranty claims has been compiled, and the probable amounts of claims related to sales for a given period can be determined.

Situation 2

Subsequent to the date of a set of financial statements but prior to the issuance of the financial statements, a company enters into a contract that will probably result in a significant loss to the company. The amount of the loss can be reasonably estimated.

Situation 3

A company has adopted a policy of recording self-insurance for any possible losses resulting from injury to others by the company's vehicles. The premium for an insurance policy for the same risk from an independent insurance company would have an annual cost of $4,000. During the period covered by the financial statements, there were no accidents involving the company's vehicles that resulted in injury to others.

Instructions

Discuss the accrual or type of disclosure necessary (if any) and the reason(s) why such disclosure is appropriate for each of the three independent sets of facts above.

(AICPA adapted)

CA24-4 (Post-Balance-Sheet Events) At December 31, 2012, Coburn Corp. has assets of $10,000,000, liabilities of $6,000,000, common stock of $2,000,000 (representing 2,000,000 shares of $1 par common stock), and retained earnings of $2,000,000. Net sales for the year 2012 were $18,000,000, and net income was $800,000. As auditors of this company, you are making a review of subsequent events on February 13, 2013, and you find the following.

1. On February 3, 2013, one of Coburn's customers declared bankruptcy. At December 31, 2012, this company owed Coburn $300,000, of which $60,000 was paid in January 2013.
2. On January 18, 2013, one of the three major plants of the client burned.
3. On January 23, 2013, a strike was called at one of Coburn's largest plants, which halted 30% of its production. As of today (February 13), the strike has not been settled.
4. A major electronics enterprise has introduced a line of products that would compete directly with Coburn's primary line, now being produced in a specially designed new plant. Because of manufacturing innovations, the competitor has been able to achieve quality similar to that of Coburn's products but at a price 50% lower. Coburn officials say they will meet the lower prices, which are high enough to cover variable manufacturing and selling costs but which permit recovery of only a portion of fixed costs.
5. Merchandise traded in the open market is recorded in the company's records at $1.40 per unit on December 31, 2012. This price had prevailed for 2 weeks, after release of an official market report that predicted vastly enlarged supplies; however, no purchases were made at $1.40. The price throughout the preceding year had been about $2, which was the level experienced over several years. On January 18, 2013, the price returned to $2, after public disclosure of an error in the official calculations of the prior December, correction of which destroyed the expectations of excessive supplies. Inventory at December 31, 2012, was on a lower-of-cost-or-market basis.
6. On February 1, 2013, the board of directors adopted a resolution accepting the offer of an investment banker to guarantee the marketing of $1,200,000 of preferred stock.

Instructions
State in each case how the 2012 financial statements would be affected, if at all.

CA24-5 (Segment Reporting) You are compiling the consolidated financial statements for Winsor Corporation International. The corporation's accountant, Anthony Reese, has provided you with the segment information shown below.

Note 7: Major Segments of Business
WCI conducts funeral service and cemetery operations in the United States and Canada. Substantially all revenues of WCI's major segments of business are from unaffiliated customers. Segment information for fiscal 2013, 2012, and 2011 follows.

	Funeral	Floral	Cemetery	(thousands) Real Estate	Dried Whey	Limousine	Consolidated
Revenues							
2013	$302,000	$10,000	$ 73,000	$ 2,000	$7,000	$12,000	$406,000
2012	245,000	6,000	61,000	4,000	4,000	4,000	324,000
2011	208,000	3,000	42,000	3,000	1,000	3,000	260,000
Operating Income							
2013	74,000	1,500	18,000	(36,000)	500	2,000	60,000
2012	64,000	200	12,000	(28,000)	200	400	48,800
2011	54,000	150	6,000	(21,000)	100	350	39,600
Capital Expenditures							
2013	26,000	1,000	9,000	400	300	1,000	37,700
2012	28,000	2,000	60,000	1,500	100	700	92,300
2011	14,000	25	8,000	600	25	50	22,700
Depreciation and Amortization							
2013	13,000	100	2,400	1,400	100	200	17,200
2012	10,000	50	1,400	700	50	100	12,300
2012	8,000	25	1,000	600	25	50	9,700
Identifiable Assets							
2013	334,000	1,500	162,000	114,000	500	8,000	620,000
2012	322,000	1,000	144,000	52,000	1,000	6,000	526,000
2011	223,000	500	78,000	34,000	500	3,500	339,500

Instructions
Determine which of the above segments must be reported separately and which can be combined under the category "Other." Then, write a one-page memo to the company's accountant, Anthony Reese, explaining the following.

(a) What segments must be reported separately and what segments can be combined.
(b) What criteria you used to determine reportable segments.
(c) What major items for each must be disclosed.

CA24-6 (Segment Reporting—Theory) Presented below is an excerpt from the financial statements of H. J. Heinz Company.

Segment and Geographic Data

The company is engaged principally in one line of business—processed food products—which represents over 90% of consolidated sales. Information about the business of the company by geographic area is presented in the table below.

There were no material amounts of sales or transfers between geographic areas or between affiliates, and no material amounts of United States export sales.

(in thousands of U.S. dollars)	Domestic	United Kingdom	Canada	Foreign Western Europe	Other	Total	Worldwide
Sales	$2,381,054	$547,527	$216,726	$383,784	$209,354	$1,357,391	$3,738,445
Operating income	246,780	61,282	34,146	29,146	25,111	149,685	396,465
Identifiable assets	1,362,152	265,218	112,620	294,732	143,971	816,541	2,178,693
Capital expenditures	72,712	12,262	13,790	8,253	4,368	38,673	111,385
Depreciation expense	42,279	8,364	3,592	6,355	3,606	21,917	64,196

Instructions
(a) Why does H. J. Heinz not prepare segment information on its products or services?
(b) What are export sales, and when should they be disclosed?
(c) Why are sales by geographical area important to disclose?

CA24-7 (Segment Reporting—Theory) The following article appeared in the *Wall Street Journal*.

WASHINGTON—The Securities and Exchange Commission staff issued guidelines for companies grappling with the problem of dividing up their business into industry segments for their annual reports.

An industry segment is defined by the Financial Accounting Standards Board as a part of an enterprise engaged in providing a product or service or a group of related products or services primarily to unaffiliated customers for a profit.

Although conceding that the process is a "subjective task" that "to a considerable extent, depends on the judgment of management," the SEC staff said companies should consider . . . various factors . . . to determine whether products and services should be grouped together or reported as segments.

Instructions
(a) What does financial reporting for segments of a business enterprise involve?
(b) Identify the reasons for requiring financial data to be reported by segments.
(c) Identify the possible disadvantages of requiring financial data to be reported by segments.
(d) Identify the accounting difficulties inherent in segment reporting.

CA24-8 (Interim Reporting) Snider Corporation, a publicly traded company, is preparing the interim financial data which it will issue to its stockholders and the Securities and Exchange Commission (SEC) at the end of the first quarter of the 2012–2013 fiscal year. Snider's financial accounting department has compiled the following summarized revenue and expense data for the first quarter of the year.

Sales revenue	$60,000,000
Cost of goods sold	36,000,000
Variable selling expenses	1,000,000
Fixed selling expenses	3,000,000

Included in the fixed selling expenses was the single lump-sum payment of $2,000,000 for television advertisements for the entire year.

Instructions

(a) Snider Corporation must issue its quarterly financial statements in accordance with generally accepted accounting principles regarding interim financial reporting.

    (1) Explain whether Snider should report its operating results for the quarter as if the quarter were a separate reporting period in and of itself, or as if the quarter were an integral part of the annual reporting period.

    (2) State how the sales revenue, cost of goods sold, and fixed selling expenses would be reflected in Snider Corporation's quarterly report prepared for the first quarter of the 2012–2013 fiscal year. Briefly justify your presentation.

(b) What financial information, as a minimum, must Snider Corporation disclose to its stockholders in its quarterly reports?

(CMA adapted)

 CA24-9 (Treatment of Various Interim Reporting Situations) The following statement is an excerpt from the FASB pronouncement related to interim reporting.

Interim financial information is essential to provide investors and others with timely information as to the progress of the enterprise. The usefulness of such information rests on the relationship that it has to the annual results of operations. Accordingly, the Board has concluded that each interim period should be viewed primarily as an integral part of an annual period.

    In general, the results for each interim period should be based on the accounting principles and practices used by an enterprise in the preparation of its latest annual financial statements unless a change in an accounting practice or policy has been adopted in the current year. The Board has concluded, however, that certain accounting principles and practices followed for annual reporting purposes may require modification at interim reporting dates so that the reported results for the interim period may better relate to the results of operations for the annual period.

Instructions

Listed below are six independent cases on how accounting facts might be reported on an individual company's interim financial reports. For each of these cases, state whether the method proposed to be used for interim reporting would be acceptable under generally accepted accounting principles applicable to interim financial data. Support each answer with a brief explanation.

(a) J. D. Long Company takes a physical inventory at year-end for annual financial statement purposes. Inventory and cost of sales reported in the interim quarterly statements are based on estimated gross profit rates, because a physical inventory would result in a cessation of operations. Long Company does have reliable perpetual inventory records.

(b) Rockford Company is planning to report one-fourth of its pension expense each quarter.

(c) Republic Company wrote inventory down to reflect lower-of-cost-or-market in the first quarter. At year-end, the market exceeds the original acquisition cost of this inventory. Consequently, management plans to write the inventory back up to its original cost as a year-end adjustment.

(d) Gansner Company realized a large gain on the sale of investments at the beginning of the second quarter. The company wants to report one-third of the gain in each of the remaining quarters.

(e) Fredonia Company has estimated its annual audit fee. It plans to pro rate this expense equally over all four quarters.

(f) LaBrava Company was reasonably certain it would have an employee strike in the third quarter. As a result, it shipped heavily during the second quarter but plans to defer the recognition of the sales in excess of the normal sales volume. The deferred sales will be recognized as sales in the third quarter when the strike is in progress. LaBrava Company management thinks this is more representative of normal second- and third-quarter operations.

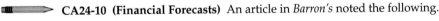 **CA24-10 (Financial Forecasts)** An article in *Barron's* noted the following.

Okay. Last fall, someone with a long memory and an even longer arm reached into that bureau drawer and came out with a moldy cheese sandwich and the equally moldy notion of corporate forecasts. We tried to find out what happened to the cheese sandwich—but, rats!, even recourse to the Freedom of Information Act didn't help. However, the forecast proposal was dusted off, polished up and found quite serviceable. The SEC, indeed, lost no time in running it up the old flagpole—but no one was very eager to salute. Even after some of the more objectionable features—compulsory corrections and detailed explanations of why the estimates went awry—were peeled off the original proposal.

    Seemingly, despite the Commission's smiles and sweet talk, those craven corporations were still afraid that an honest mistake would lead them down the primrose path to consent decrees and class action suits.

To lay to rest such qualms, the Commission last week approved a "Safe Harbor" rule that, providing the forecasts were made on a reasonable basis and in good faith, protected corporations from litigation should the projections prove wide of the mark (as only about 99% are apt to do).

Instructions

(a) What are the arguments for preparing profit forecasts?
(b) What is the purpose of the "safe harbor" rule?
(c) Why are corporations concerned about presenting profit forecasts?

CA24-11 (Disclosure of Estimates) Nancy Tercek, the financial vice president, and Margaret Lilly, the controller, of Romine Manufacturing Company are reviewing the financial ratios of the company for the years 2012 and 2013. The financial vice president notes that the profit margin on sales ratio has increased from 6% to 12%, a hefty gain for the 2-year period. Tercek is in the process of issuing a media release that emphasizes the efficiency of Romine Manufacturing in controlling cost. Margaret Lilly knows that the difference in ratios is due primarily to an earlier company decision to reduce the estimates of warranty and bad debt expense for 2013. The controller, not sure of her supervisor's motives, hesitates to suggest to Tercek that the company's improvement is unrelated to efficiency in controlling cost. To complicate matters, the media release is scheduled in a few days.

Instructions

(a) What, if any, is the ethical dilemma in this situation?
(b) Should Lilly, the controller, remain silent? Give reasons.
(c) What stakeholders might be affected by Tercek's media release?
(d) Give your opinion on the following statement and cite reasons: "Because Tercek, the vice president, is most directly responsible for the media release, Lilly has no real responsibility in this matter."

CA24-12 (Reporting of Subsequent Events) In June 2012, the board of directors for McElroy Enterprises Inc. authorized the sale of $10,000,000 of corporate bonds. Jennifer Grayson, treasurer for McElroy Enterprises Inc., is concerned about the date when the bonds are issued. The company really needs the cash, but she is worried that if the bonds are issued before the company's year-end (December 31, 2012) the additional liability will have an adverse effect on a number of important ratios. In July, she explains to company president William McElroy that if they delay issuing the bonds until after December 31 the bonds will not affect the ratios until December 31, 2013. They will have to report the issuance as a subsequent event which requires only footnote disclosure. Grayson expects that with expected improved financial performance in 2013 ratios should be better.

Instructions

(a) What are the ethical issues involved?
(b) Should McElroy agree to the delay?

*CA24-13 (Effect of Transactions on Financial Statements and Ratios)** The transactions listed below relate to Wainwright Inc. You are to assume that on the date on which each of the transactions occurred, the corporation's accounts showed only common stock ($100 par) outstanding, a current ratio of 2.7:1, and a substantial net income for the year to date (before giving effect to the transaction concerned). On that date, the book value per share of stock was $151.53.

Each numbered transaction is to be considered completely independent of the others, and its related answer should be based on the effect(s) of that transaction alone. Assume that all numbered transactions occurred during 2013 and that the amount involved in each case is sufficiently material to distort reported net income if improperly included in the determination of net income. Assume further that each transaction was recorded in accordance with generally accepted accounting principles and, where applicable, in conformity with the all-inclusive concept of the income statement.

For each of the numbered transactions you are to decide whether it:

(a) Increased the corporation's 2013 net income.
(b) Decreased the corporation's 2013 net income.
(c) Increased the corporation's total retained earnings directly (i.e., not via net income).
(d) Decreased the corporation's total retained earnings directly.
(e) Increased the corporation's current ratio.
(f) Decreased the corporation's current ratio.
(g) Increased each stockholder's proportionate share of total stockholders' equity.
(h) Decreased each stockholder's proportionate share of total stockholders' equity.
(i) Increased each stockholder's equity per share of stock (book value).
(j) Decreased each stockholder's equity per share of stock (book value).
(k) Had none of the foregoing effects.

Instructions

List the numbers 1 through 9. Select as many letters as you deem appropriate to reflect the effect(s) of each transaction as of the date of the transaction by printing beside the transaction number the letter(s) that identifies that transaction's effect(s).

Transactions

_____ 1. In January, the board directed the write-off of certain patent rights that had suddenly and unexpectedly become worthless.

_____ 2. The corporation sold at a profit land and a building that had been idle for some time. Under the terms of the sale, the corporation received a portion of the sales price in cash immediately, the balance maturing at 6-month intervals.

_____ 3. Treasury stock originally repurchased and carried at $127 per share was sold for cash at $153 per share.

_____ 4. The corporation wrote off all of the unamortized discount and issue expense applicable to bonds that it refinanced in 2013.

_____ 5. The corporation called in all its outstanding shares of stock and exchanged them for new shares on a 2-for-1 basis, reducing the par value at the same time to $50 per share.

_____ 6. The corporation paid a cash dividend that had been recorded in the accounts at time of declaration.

_____ 7. Litigation involving Wainwright Inc. as defendant was settled in the corporation's favor, with the plaintiff paying all court costs and legal fees. In 2010, the corporation had appropriately established a special contingency for this court action. (Indicate the effect of reversing the contingency only.)

_____ 8. The corporation received a check for the proceeds of an insurance policy from the company with which it is insured against theft of trucks. No entries concerning the theft had been made previously, and the proceeds reduce but do not cover completely the loss.

_____ 9. Treasury stock, which had been repurchased at and carried at $127 per share, was issued as a stock dividend. In connection with this distribution, the board of directors of Wainwright Inc. had authorized a transfer from retained earnings to permanent capital of an amount equal to the aggregate market value ($153 per share) of the shares issued. No entries relating to this dividend had been made previously.

(AICPA adapted)

Gateway to the Profession

Additional Financial Statement Analysis Problems

USING YOUR JUDGMENT

FINANCIAL REPORTING

Financial Reporting Problem

 The Procter & Gamble Company (P&G)

As stated in the chapter, notes to the financial statements are the means of explaining the items presented in the main body of the statements. Common note disclosures relate to such items as accounting policies, segmented information, and interim reporting. The financial statements of **P&G** are provided in Appendix 5B or can be accessed at the book's companion website, **www.wiley.com/college/kieso**.

Instructions

Refer to P&G's financial statements and the accompanying notes to answer the following questions.

(a) What specific items does P&G discuss in its Note 1—Summary of Significant Accounting Policies? (List the headings only.)

(b) For what segments did P&G report segmented information? Which segment is the largest? Who is P&G's largest customer?

(c) What interim information was reported by P&G?

Comparative Analysis Case

The Coca-Cola Company and PepsiCo, Inc.

PEPSICO

Instructions

Go to the book's companion website and use information found there to answer the following questions related to The Coca-Cola Company and PepsiCo, Inc.

(a) **(1)** What specific items does Coca-Cola discuss in its **Note 1—Accounting Policies**? (Prepare a list of the headings only.)

   (2) What specific items does PepsiCo discuss in its **Note 2—Our Summary of Significant Accounting Policies**? (Prepare a list of the headings only.)

(b) For what lines of business or segments do Coca-Cola and PepsiCo present segmented information?

(c) Note and comment on the similarities and differences between the auditors' reports submitted by the independent auditors of Coca-Cola and PepsiCo for the year 2009.

*Financial Statement Analysis Case

RNA Inc. manufactures a variety of consumer products. The company's founders have run the company for 30 years and are now interested in retiring. Consequently, they are seeking a purchaser who will continue its operations, and a group of investors, Morgan Inc., is looking into the acquisition of RNA. To evaluate its financial stability and operating efficiency, RNA was requested to provide the latest financial statements and selected financial ratios. Summary information provided by RNA is presented below and on the next page.

RNA INC.
INCOME STATEMENT
FOR THE YEAR ENDED NOVEMBER 30, 2013
(IN THOUSANDS)

Sales (net)	$30,500
Interest income	500
Total revenue	31,000
Costs and expenses	
Cost of goods sold	17,600
Selling and administrative expenses	3,550
Depreciation and amortization expense	1,890
Interest expense	900
Total costs and expenses	23,940
Income before taxes	7,060
Income taxes	2,800
Net income	$ 4,260

RNA INC.
BALANCE SHEET
AS OF NOVEMBER 30
(IN THOUSANDS)

	2013	2012
Cash	$ 400	$ 500
Short-term investments (at cost)	300	200
Accounts receivable (net)	3,200	2,900
Inventory	6,000	5,400
Total current assets	9,900	9,000
Property, plant, & equipment (net)	7,100	7,000
Total assets	$17,000	$16,000

	2013	2012
Accounts payable	$ 3,700	$ 3,400
Income taxes payable	900	800
Accrued expenses	1,700	1,400
Total current liabilities	6,300	5,600
Long-term debt	2,000	1,800
Total liabilities	8,300	7,400
Common stock ($1 par value)	2,700	2,700
Paid-in capital in excess of par	1,000	1,000
Retained earnings	5,000	4,900
Total stockholders' equity	8,700	8,600
Total liabilities and stockholders' equity	$17,000	$16,000

SELECTED FINANCIAL RATIOS

	RNA INC. 2012	RNA INC. 2011	Current Industry Average
Current ratio	1.61	1.62	1.63
Acid-test ratio	.64	.63	.68
Times interest earned	8.55	8.50	8.45
Profit margin on sales	13.2%	12.1%	13.0%
Asset turnover	1.84	1.83	1.84
Inventory turnover	3.17	3.21	3.18

Instructions

(a) Calculate a new set of ratios for the fiscal year 2013 for RNA based on the financial statements presented.

(b) Explain the analytical use of each of the six ratios presented, describing what the investors can learn about RNA's financial stability and operating efficiency.

(c) Identify two limitations of ratio analysis.

(CMA adapted)

Accounting, Analysis, and Principles

Savannah, Inc. is a company that manufactures and sells a single product. Unit sales for each of the four quarters of 2012 are projected as follows.

Quarter	Units
First	80,000
Second	150,000
Third	550,000
Fourth	120,000
Annual Total	900,000

Savannah incurs variable manufacturing costs of $0.40 per unit and variable nonmanufacturing costs of $0.35 per unit. Savannah will incur fixed manufacturing costs of $720,000 and fixed nonmanufacturing costs of $1,080,000. Savannah will sell its product for $4.00 per unit.

Accounting

Determine the amount of net income Savannah will report in each of the four quarters of 2012, assuming actual sales are as projected and employing the integral approach to interim financial reporting. (Ignore income taxes.)

Analysis

Compute Savannah's profit margin on sales for each of the four quarters of 2012. What effect does employing the integral approach instead of the discrete approach have on the degree to which Savannah's profit margin on sales varies from quarter to quarter?

Principles

Explain the conceptual rationale behind the integral approach to interim financial reporting.

BRIDGE TO THE PROFESSION

Professional Research: FASB Codification

As part of the year-end audit, you are discussing the disclosure checklist with your client. The checklist identifies the items that must be disclosed in a set of GAAP financial statements. The client is surprised by the disclosure item related to accounting policies. Specifically, since the audit report will attest to the statements being prepared in accordance with GAAP, the client questions the accounting policy checklist item. The client has asked you to conduct some research to verify the accounting policy disclosures.

Instructions

If your school has a subscription to the FASB Codification, go to *http://aaahq.org/ascLogin.cfm* to log in and prepare responses to the following. Provide Codification references for your responses.

(a) In general, what should disclosures of accounting policies encompass?

(b) List some examples of the most commonly required disclosures.

*Professional Simulation

In this simulation, you are asked to evaluate a company's solvency and going-concern potential, by analyzing a set of ratios. You also are asked to indicate possible limitations of ratio analysis. Prepare responses to all parts.

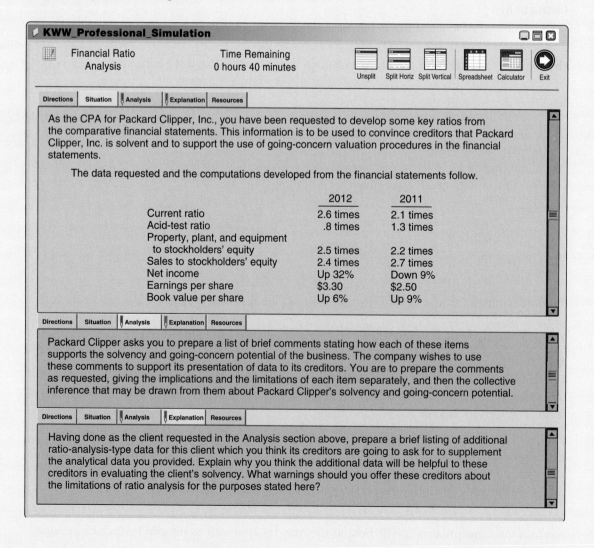

IFRS Insights

IFRS and GAAP disclosure requirements are similar in many regards. The IFRS addressing various disclosure issues are *IAS 24* ("Related Party Disclosures"), disclosure and recognition of post-statement of financial position events in *IAS 10* ("Events after the Balance Sheet Date"), segment reporting IFRS provisions in *IFRS 8* ("Operating Segments"), and interim reporting requirements in *IAS 34* ("Interim Financial Reporting").

RELEVANT FACTS

- Due to the broader range of judgments allowed in more principles-based IFRS, note disclosures generally are more expansive under IFRS compared to GAAP.
- GAAP and IFRS have similar standards on post-statement of financial position (subsequent) events. That is, under both sets of standards, events that occurred after the statement of financial position date, and which provide additional evidence of conditions that existed at the statement of financial position date, are recognized in the financial statements. Subsequent events under IFRS are evaluated through the date that financial instruments are "authorized for issue." GAAP uses the date when financial statements are "issued." Also, for share dividends and splits in the subsequent period, IFRS does not adjust but GAAP does.
- Like GAAP, IFRS requires that for transactions with related parties, companies disclose the amounts involved in a transaction; the amount, terms, and nature of the outstanding balances; and any doubtful amounts related to those outstanding balances for each major category of related parties. There is no specific requirement to disclose the name of the related party.
- Following the recent issuance of *IFRS 8*, "Operating Segments," the requirements under IFRS and GAAP are very similar. That is, both standards use the management approach to identify reportable segments, and similar segment disclosures are required.
- Neither GAAP nor IFRS require interim reports. Rather, the SEC and stock exchanges outside the United States establish the rules. In the United States, interim reports generally are provided on a quarterly basis; outside the United States, six-month interim reports are common.

ABOUT THE NUMBERS

Differential Disclosure

A trend toward **differential disclosure** is occurring. The IASB has developed IFRS for small- and medium-sized entities (SMEs). SMEs are entities that publish general-purpose financial statements for external users but do not issue shares or other securities in a public market. Many believe a simplified set of standards makes sense for these companies because they do not have the resources to implement full IFRS. Simplified IFRS for SMEs is a single standard of fewer than 230 pages. It is designed to meet the needs and capabilities of SMEs, which are estimated to account for over 95 percent of all companies around the world. Compared with full IFRS (and many national accounting standards), simplified IFRS for SMEs is less complex in a number of ways:

- Topics not relevant for SMEs are omitted. Examples are earnings per share, interim financial reporting, and segment reporting.
- Simplified IFRS for SMEs allows fewer accounting policy choices. Examples are no option to revalue property, equipment, or intangibles, and no corridor approach for actuarial gains and losses.

- Many principles for recognizing and measuring assets, liabilities, revenue, and expenses are simplified. For example, goodwill is amortized (as a result, there is no annual impairment test), and all borrowing and R&D costs are expensed.
- Significantly fewer disclosures are required (roughly 300 versus 3,000).
- To further reduce standard overload, revisions to the IFRS for SMEs will be limited to once every three years.

Thus, the option of using simplified IFRS helps SMEs meet the needs of their financial statement users while balancing the costs and benefits from a preparer perspective.[32]

Events after the Reporting Period (Subsequent Events)

Notes to the financial statements should explain any significant financial events that took place after the formal statement of financial position date, but before the statements are authorized for issuance (hereafter referred to as the authorization date). These events are referred to as **events after the reporting date**, or **subsequent events**. Illustration IFRS24-1 shows a time diagram of the subsequent events period.

ILLUSTRATION IFRS24-1
Time Periods for Subsequent Events

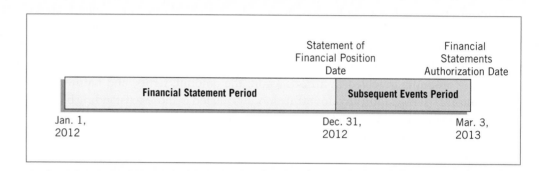

A period of several weeks, and sometimes months, may elapse after the end of the fiscal year but before the management or the board of directors authorizes issuance of the financial statements. Various activities involved in closing the books for the period and issuing the statements all take time: taking and pricing the inventory, reconciling subsidiary ledgers with controlling accounts, preparing necessary adjusting entries, ensuring that all transactions for the period have been entered, obtaining an audit of the financial statements by independent certified public accountants, and printing the annual report. During the period between the statement of financial position date and its authorization date, important transactions or other events may occur that materially affect the company's financial position or operating situation.

Many who read a statement of financial position believe the financial condition is constant, and they project it into the future. However, readers must be told if the company has experienced a significant change—e.g., sold one of its plants, acquired a subsidiary, suffered unusual losses, settled significant litigation, or experienced any other important event in the post-statement of financial position period. Without an explanation in a note, the reader might be misled and draw inappropriate conclusions.

---

[32]In the United States, there has been a preference for one set of GAAP except in unusual situations. With the advent of simplified IFRS for SMEs, this position is under review. Both the FASB and the AICPA are studying the big GAAP/little GAAP issue to ensure that any kind of differential reporting is conceptually sound and meets the needs of users. The FASB has formed a Private Company Financial Reporting Committee, whose primary objectives are to provide recommendations on FASB standard-setting for privately held enterprises (see *http://www.pcfr.org/*).

Two types of events or transactions occurring after the statement of financial position date may have a material effect on the financial statements or may need disclosure so that readers interpret these statements accurately:

1. Events that provide additional evidence about conditions **that existed** at the statement of financial position date, including the estimates inherent in the process of preparing financial statements. These events are referred to as **adjusted subsequent events** and require adjustments to the financial statements. All information available prior to the authorization date of the financial statements helps investors and creditors evaluate estimates previously made. To ignore these subsequent events is to pass up an opportunity to improve the accuracy of the financial statements. This first type of event encompasses information that an accountant would have recorded in the accounts had the information been known at the statement of financial position date.

   For example, if a loss on an account receivable results from a customer's bankruptcy subsequent to the statement of financial position date, the company adjusts the financial statements before their issuance. The bankruptcy stems from the customer's poor financial health existing at the statement of financial position date.

   The same criterion applies to settlements of litigation. The company must adjust the financial statements if the events that gave rise to the litigation, such as personal injury or patent infringement, took place prior to the statement of financial position date.

2. Events that provide evidence about conditions that **did not exist** at the statement of financial position date but arise subsequent to that date. These events are referred to as **non-adjusted subsequent events** and do not require adjustment of the financial statements. To illustrate, a loss resulting from a customer's fire or flood *after* the statement of financial position date does not reflect conditions existing at that date.

   Thus, adjustment of the financial statements is not necessary. A company should not recognize subsequent events that provide evidence about conditions that did not exist at the date of the statement of financial position but that arose after the statement of financial position date.

   The following are examples of non-adjusted subsequent events:

   - A major business combination after the reporting period or disposing of a major subsidiary.
   - Announcing a plan to discontinue an operation or commencing the implementation of a major restructuring.
   - Major purchases of assets, other disposals of assets, or expropriation of major assets by government.
   - The destruction of a major production plant or inventories by a fire or natural disaster after the reporting period.
   - Major ordinary share transactions and potential ordinary share transactions after the reporting period.
   - Abnormally large changes after the reporting period in asset prices, foreign exchange rates, or taxes.
   - Entering into significant commitments or contingent liabilities, for example, by issuing significant guarantees after the statement date.[33]

---

[33]The effects from natural disasters, like the recent eruption of the Icelandic volcano, which occurred after the year-end for companies with March fiscal years, require disclosure in order to keep the statements from being misleading. Some companies may have to consider whether these disasters affect their ability to continue as going concerns.

Some non-adjusted subsequent events may have to be disclosed to keep the financial statements from being misleading. For such events, a company discloses the nature of the event and an estimate of its financial effect. Illustration IFRS24-2 presents an example of subsequent events disclosure, excerpted from the annual report of Cadbury plc.

ILLUSTRATION IFRS24-2
Disclosure of Subsequent Events

Cadbury plc

Note 38. Events After the Balance Sheet Date

On 23 January 2009, the Group obtained committed credit facilities totalling £300 million. This facility expires at the earlier of the disposal of Australia Beverages, capital market debt or equity issuance or 28 February 2010.

On 4 March 2009, the Group issued a £300 million bond that matures in 2014. On issuance of the bond the £300 million committed credit facilities expired.

The Group announced that it had entered into a conditional agreement with Asahi Breweries, Ltd ("Asahi") on 24 December 2008 to sell the Australia Beverages business and, as a result of this agreement, Australia Beverages was treated as a discontinued operation in the presentation of the results for 2008.

Subsequent to the balance sheet date, on 12 March 2009, the Group entered into a definitive sale and purchase agreement for the sale of the Australia Beverages business to Asahi for a total consideration in cash of approximately £550m (AUDI, 185m). The agreement with Asahi is subject to normal closing conditions, which do not include financing or competition authority clearance conditions, and the Group expects that the pre-conditions to closing will have been satisfied by 30 April 2009.

Many subsequent events or developments do not require adjustment of or disclosure in the financial statements. Typically, these are non-accounting events or conditions that management normally communicates by other means. These events include legislation, product changes, management changes, strikes, unionization, marketing agreements, and loss of important customers.

Interim Reports

Another source of information for the investor is interim reports. As noted earlier, **interim reports** cover periods of less than one year. The securities exchanges, market regulators, and the accounting profession have an active interest in the presentation of interim information.

Because of the short-term nature of the information in these reports, there is considerable controversy as to the general approach companies should employ. One group, which favors the **discrete approach**, believes that companies should treat each interim period as a separate accounting period. Using that treatment, companies would follow the principles for deferrals and accruals used for annual reports. In this view, companies should report accounting transactions as they occur, and expense recognition should not change with the period of time covered.

Another group, which favors the **integral approach**, believes that the interim report is an integral part of the annual report and that deferrals and accruals should take into consideration what will happen for the entire year. In this approach, companies should assign estimated expenses to parts of a year on the basis of sales volume or some other activity base. In general, IFRS requires companies to follow the discrete approach.

Interim Reporting Requirements

Under IFRS, companies should use the same accounting policies for interim reports and for annual reports. They should recognize revenues in interim periods on the same basis as they are for annual periods. For example, if Cedars Corp. uses the percentage-of-completion method as the basis for recognizing revenue on an annual basis, it should use the percentage-of-completion method for interim reports as well. Also, Cedars should treat costs directly associated with revenues (product costs, such as materials, labor and related fringe benefits, and manufacturing overhead) in the same manner for interim reports as for annual reports.

Companies should use the same inventory pricing methods (FIFO, average cost, etc.) for interim reports and for annual reports. However, companies may use the gross profit method for interim inventory pricing. But, they must disclose the method and adjustments to reconcile with annual inventory.

Discrete Approach. Following the discrete approach, companies record in interim reports revenues and expenses according to the revenue and expense recognition principles. This includes costs and expenses other than product costs (often referred to as period costs). No accruals or deferrals in anticipation of future events during the year should be reported. For example, the cost of a planned major periodic maintenance or overhaul for a company like Airbus or other seasonal expenditure that is expected to occur late in the year is not anticipated for interim reporting purposes. The mere intention or necessity to incur expenditure related to the future is not sufficient to give rise to an obligation.

Or, a company like Carrefour may budget certain costs expected to be incurred irregularly during the financial year, such as advertising and employee training costs. Those costs generally are discretionary even though they are planned and tend to recur from year to year. However, recognizing an obligation at the end of an interim financial reporting period for such costs that have not yet been incurred generally is not consistent with the definition of a liability.

While year-to-date measurements may involve changes in estimates of amounts reported in prior interim periods of the current financial year, the principles for recognizing assets, liabilities, income, and expenses for interim periods are the same as in annual financial statements. For example, Wm Morrison Supermarkets plc records losses from inventory write-downs, restructurings, or impairments in an interim period similar to how it would treat these items in the annual financial statements (when incurred). However, if an estimate from a prior interim period changes in a subsequent interim period of that year, the original estimate is adjusted in the subsequent interim period.

Interim Disclosures. IFRS does not require a complete set of financial statements at the interim reporting date. Rather, companies may comply with the requirements by providing condensed financial statements and selected explanatory notes. Because users of interim financial reports also have access to the most recent annual financial report, companies only need provide explanation of significant events and transactions since the end of the last annual reporting period. Companies should report the following interim data at a minimum.

1. Statement that the same accounting policies and methods of computation are followed in the interim financial statements as compared with the most recent annual financial statements or, if those policies or methods have been changed, a description of the nature and effect of the change.

2. Explanatory comments about the seasonality or cyclicality of interim operations.

3. The nature and amount of items affecting assets, liabilities, equity, net income, or cash flows that are unusual because of their nature, size, or incidence.

4. The nature and amount of changes in accounting policies and estimates of amounts previously reported.

5. Issuances, repurchases, and repayments of debt and equity securities.

6. Dividends paid (aggregate or per share) separately for ordinary shares and other shares.

7. Segment information, as required by *IFRS 8*, "Operating Segments."

8. Changes in contingent liabilities or contingent assets since the end of the last annual reporting period.

9. Effect of changes in the composition of the company during the interim period, such as business combinations, obtaining or losing control of subsidiaries and long-term investments, restructurings, and discontinued operations.

10. Other material events subsequent to the end of the interim period that have not been reflected in the financial statements for the interim period.

If a complete set of financial statements is provided in the interim report, companies comply with the provisions of *IAS 1*, "Presentation of Financial Statements."

ON THE HORIZON

Sir David Tweedie, chair of the IASB, recently stated, "By 2011–2012, U.S. and international accounting should be pretty much the same." There is no question that IFRS and GAAP are converging quickly. We have provided expanded discussion in the *International Perspectives* and *IFRS Insights* to help you understand the issues surrounding convergence as they relate to intermediate accounting. After reading these discussions, you should realize that IFRS and GAAP are very similar in many areas, with differences in those areas revolving around some minor technical points. In other situations, the differences are major; for example, IFRS does not permit LIFO inventory accounting. Our hope is that the FASB and IASB can quickly complete their convergence efforts, resulting in a single set of high-quality accounting standards for use by companies around the world.

IFRS SELF-TEST QUESTIONS

1. Which of the following is *false*?
   (a) In general, IFRS note disclosures are more expansive compared to GAAP.
   (b) GAAP and IFRS have similar standards on subsequent events.
   (c) Both IFRS and GAAP require interim reports although the reporting frequency varies.
   (d) Segment reporting requirements are very similar under IFRS and GAAP.

2. Differential reporting for small- and medium-sized entities:
   (a) is required for all companies less than a certain size.
   (b) omits accounting topics not relevant for SMEs, such as earnings per share, and interim and segment reporting.
   (c) has different rules for topics such as earnings per share, and interim and segment reporting.
   (d) requires significantly more disclosures, since more items are not recognized in the financial statements.

3. Subsequent events are reviewed through which date under IFRS?
   (a) Statement of financial position date.
   (b) Sixty days after the year-end date.
   (c) Date of independent auditor's opinion.
   (d) Authorization date of the financial statements.

4. Under IFRS, share dividends declared after the statement of financial position date but before the end of the subsequent events period are:
   (a) accounted for similar to errors as a prior period adjustment.
   (b) adjusted subsequent events, because they are paid from prior year earnings.
   (c) not adjusted in the current year's financial statements.
   (d) recognized on a prospective basis from the date of declaration.

5. Interim reporting under IFRS:
   - **(a)** is prepared using the discrete approach.
   - **(b)** is prepared using a combination of the discrete and integral approach.
   - **(c)** requires a complete set of financial statements for each interim period.
   - **(d)** permits companies to omit disclosure of material events subsequent to the interim reporting date.

IFRS CONCEPTS AND APPLICATION

IFRS24-1 Where can authoritative IFRS be found related to the various disclosure issues discussed in the chapter?

IFRS24-2 What are the major types of subsequent events? Indicate how each of the following "subsequent events" would be reported.

   - **(a)** Collection of a note written off in a prior period.
   - **(b)** Issuance of a large preference share offering.
   - **(c)** Acquisition of a company in a different industry.
   - **(d)** Destruction of a major plant in a flood.
   - **(e)** Death of the company's chief executive officer (CEO).
   - **(f)** Additional wage costs associated with settlement of a four-week strike.
   - **(g)** Settlement of an income tax case at considerably more tax than anticipated at year-end.
   - **(h)** Change in the product mix from consumer goods to industrial goods.

IFRS24-3 Morlan Corporation is preparing its December 31, 2012, financial statements. Two events that occurred between December 31, 2012, and March 10, 2013, when the statements were authorized for issue, are described below.

1. A liability, estimated at $160,000 at December 31, 2012, was settled on February 26, 2013, at $170,000.

2. A flood loss of $80,000 occurred on March 1, 2013.

Instructions

What effect do these subsequent events have on 2012 net income?

IFRS24-4 Keystone Corporation's financial statements for the year ended December 31, 2012, were authorized for issue on March 10, 2013. The following events took place early in 2013.

   - **(a)** On January 10, 10,000 ordinary shares of $5 par value were issued at $66 per share.
   - **(b)** On March 1, Keystone determined after negotiations with the taxing authorities that income taxes payable for 2012 should be $1,320,000. At December 31, 2012, income taxes payable were recorded at $1,100,000.

Instructions

Discuss how the preceding subsequent events should be reflected in the 2012 financial statements.

IFRS24-5 (Subsequent Events) For each of the following subsequent events, indicate whether a company should (a) adjust the financial statements, (b) disclose in notes to the financial statements, or (c) neither adjust nor disclose.

_____ **1.** Settlement of a tax case at a cost considerably in excess of the amount expected at year-end.

_____ **2.** Introduction of a new product line.

_____ **3.** Loss of assembly plant due to fire.

_____ **4.** Sale of a significant portion of the company's assets.

_____ **5.** Retirement of the company president.

_____ **6.** Issuance of a significant number of ordinary shares.

_____ **7.** Loss of a significant customer.

_____ **8.** Prolonged employee strike.

_____ **9.** Material loss on a year-end receivable because of a customer's bankruptcy.

_____ **10.** Hiring of a new president.

_____ **11.** Settlement of prior year's litigation against the company.

_____ **12.** Merger with another company of comparable size.

IFRS24-6 What are interim reports? Why is a complete set of financial statements often not provided with interim data? What are the accounting problems related to the presentation of interim data?

IFRS24-7 Dierdorf Inc., a closely held corporation, has decided to go public. The controller, Ed Floyd, is concerned with presenting interim data when an inventory write-down is recorded. What problems are encountered with inventories when quarterly data are presented?

IFRS24-8 Bill Novak is working on an audit of an IFRS client. In his review of the client's interim reports, he notes that the reports are prepared on a discrete basis. That is, each interim report is viewed as a distinct period. Is this acceptable under IFRS? If so, explain how that treatment could affect comparisons to a GAAP company.

IFRS24-9 Snider Corporation, a publicly traded company, is preparing the interim financial data which it will issue to its shareholders at the end of the first quarter of the 2012–2013 fiscal year. Snider's financial accounting department has compiled the following summarized revenue and expense data for the first quarter of the year.

Sales revenue	$60,000,000
Cost of goods sold	36,000,000
Variable selling expenses	1,000,000
Fixed selling expenses	3,000,000

Included in the fixed selling expenses was the single lump-sum payment of $2,000,000 for television advertisements for the entire year.

Instructions

(a) Snider Corporation must issue its quarterly financial statements in accordance with IFRS regarding interim financial reporting.

   (1) Explain whether Snider should report its operating results for the quarter as if the quarter were a separate reporting period in and of itself, or as if the quarter were an integral part of the annual reporting period.

   (2) State how the sales revenue, cost of goods sold, and fixed selling expenses would be reflected in Snider Corporation's quarterly report prepared for the first quarter of the 2012–2013 fiscal year. Briefly justify your presentation.

(b) What financial information, as a minimum, must Snider Corporation disclose to its shareholders in its quarterly reports?

Professional Research

IFRS24-10 As part of the year-end audit, you are discussing the disclosure checklist with your client. The checklist identifies the items that must be disclosed in a set of IFRS financial statements. The client is surprised by the disclosure item related to accounting policies. Specifically, since the audit report will attest to the statements being prepared in accordance with IFRS, the client questions the accounting policy checklist item. The client has asked you to conduct some research to verify the accounting policy disclosures.

Instructions

Access the IFRS authoritative literature at the IASB website (*http://eifrs.iasb.org/*). When you have accessed the documents, you can use the search tool in your Internet browser to respond to the following questions. (Provide paragraph citations.)

- **(a)** In general, what should disclosures of accounting policies encompass?
- **(b)** List some examples of the most commonly required disclosures.

International Financial Reporting Problem:
Marks and Spencer plc

IFRS24-11 The financial statements of **Marks and Spencer plc (M&S)** are available at the book's companion website or can be accessed at *http://corporate.marksandspencer.com/documents/publications/2010/Annual_Report_2010*.

Instructions

Refer to M&S's financial statements and the accompanying notes to answer the following questions.

- **(a)** What specific items does M&S discuss in its Note 1—Summary of Significant Accounting Policies? (List the headings only.)
- **(b)** For what segments did M&S report segmented information? Which segment is the largest? Who is M&S's largest customer?
- **(c)** What interim information was reported by M&S?

ANSWERS TO IFRS SELF-TEST QUESTIONS

1. c **2.** b **3.** d **4.** c **5.** a

NOTES

NOTES

NOTES